Environment on Trial

A GUIDE TO ONTARIO ENVIRONMENTAL LAW AND POLICY

Third Edition

David Estrin and John Swaigen

J John Swaigen

**A Project of the Canadian Institute
for Environmental Law and Policy**

**1993
EMOND MONTGOMERY PUBLICATIONS LIMITED
TORONTO, CANADA**

Printed in Canada.

Edited, designed, and typeset by WordsWorth Communications of Toronto, Canada.

Canadian Cataloguing in Publication Data

Main entry under title:

Environment on trial : a guide to Ontario environmental law and policy

Co-published by the Canadian Institute for Environmental Law and Policy.
3rd ed.
Includes index.
ISBN 0–920722–51–2

1. Environmental law – Ontario.   2. Environmental policy – Ontario.
I. Swaigen, John, 1944 –   .   II. Canadian Institute for Environmental Law and Policy.

KE0717.E58 1993   344.713'046   C93–094619–7
KF3775.E58 1993

Table of Contents

Contributors

Joseph F. Castrilli

Mr. Castrilli specializes in environmental law in Toronto at Morris, Rose, Ledgett and has worked as counsel at the federal and provincial levels on a wide range of environmental issues. A consultant to the International Joint Commission, Law Reform Commission of Canada, and federal Department of the Environment, he has published widely in law journals, texts, and professional publications. He lectures in environmental protection law at Queen's University and the University of Toronto and is a member of the executive of the Environmental Law Section of the Canadian Bar Association, Ontario.

Mark Denhez

Mark Denhez is a lawyer who has worked extensively in the area of Canada's national heritage. A former research director of the Heritage Canada Foundation, he has received a National Heritage Award from Environment Canada, and was delegated by the Canadian Commission for UNESCO to serve on an international joint study on historic buildings. He has lectured at almost every university in Canada, and has published 300 works in five countries and five languages, including the book *Heritage Fights Back*. He is currently on retainer to the heritage agencies of all 10 provincial governments and both territorial governments.

Ian Dick

Ian Dick is a lawyer with experience in all areas of litigation and administrative law, with particular emphasis in the areas of environmental and energy law. He is currently a partner in the Government and Regulatory Law Department at Cassels, Brock & Blackwell.

Brian Gallaugher

Brian Gallaugher is a graduate of the University of Waterloo, School of Urban and Regional Planning, and is a planning and development consultant in Kitchener-Waterloo, Ontario.

Stephen Garrod

Mr. Garrod, the first graduate of the combined programs of law and environmental studies at York University in 1978, has been practising exclusively in the areas of environmental law and municipal and planning law since 1980. As adjunct associate professor at the University of Waterloo, he lectures on environmental and planning law. He co-authored *The Regulation of Toxic and Oxidant Air Pollution in North America*, and has been an associate editor of the *Canadian Environmental Law Reports*. He frequently speaks at environmental and planning conferences and is a member of the Conservation Council of Ontario.

Barbara Heidenreich

Barbara Heidenreich, who holds master's degrees in economic geography and international business, is a member of the Ontario Municipal Board and teaches at Trent University's Environmental and Resource Studies Program. She has been the executive director of the Canadian Institute for Environmental Law and Policy and associate professor and coordinator of the Native Management and Economic Development program at Trent, and was a senior policy adviser with the Department of Indian and Northern Affairs.

Nina Lester

Nina Lester practised corporate law with the Toronto law firm of Osler, Hoskin & Harcourt for three years and is currently a candidate for a master's degree in environmental studies at York University's Faculty of Environmental Studies. Her area of concentration is environmental law and policy.

Richard Lindgren

A staff lawyer with the Canadian Environmental Law Association, Richard Lindgren practices civil, criminal, and administrative law. His casework and law reform activities have involved a variety of environmental issues including wetlands, forestry, land contamination, waste management, and air and water pollution. He teaches environmental assessment law at Trent University and is a member of the Ontario Task Force on the Environmental Bill of Rights, the Attorney General's Advisory Committee on Class Action Reform, the executive of the Environment Law Section – CBAO, and the board of directors of the Canadian Institute for Environmental Law and Policy.

Burkhard Mausberg

Burkhard Mausberg combines a solid scientific background with a wide-ranging interest in environmental law and policy. Initially studying chemistry, in his post-graduate work he has focused on applied environmental issues, particularly the areas of Great Lakes water quality and biotechnology. He has made numerous presentations on these and other topics, and has published a variety of papers. He has been a researcher for Pollution Probe and is a research associate for the Canadian Institute for Environmental Law and Policy.

John P. McGowan

John McGowan was called to the bar in 1986 and joined Cassels, Brock & Blackwell's Government and Regulatory Law Department in 1988. He practises primarily in the environmental law field, with an emphasis on environmental assessment and approvals.

Pamela L. Meneguzzi

Pamela Meneguzzi is an associate in the Government and Regulatory Law Department of Cassels, Brock & Blackwell. She has represented clients before provincial boards and municipal committees and has assisted on environmental assessments and environmental litigation.

Kevin McNamee

Kevin McNamee has spent the last 10 years advocating the preservation of the Canadian wilderness. Director of the Canadian Nature Federation's Protected Areas Program in Ottawa, he was also with the Canadian Parks and Wilderness Society from 1983 to 1986, and taught a wilderness philosophy and management course at Trent University. He played a major role in the creation of the South Moresby, Ellesmere Island, Grasslands, Bruce Peninsula, and Aulavik national parks. He successfully lobbied for amendments to the *National Parks Act*, including the need to maintain the ecological integrity of each park as the primary management goal.

Patricia Mohr

Patricia Mohr has an honours bachelor of science degree from the University of Toronto and 12 years' experience working as an environmental biologist for federal, provincial, and municipal governments, as well as private and non-profit agencies.

Paul Muldoon

Paul Muldoon practises environmental law. He is a research associate of the Canadian Institute for Environmental Law and Policy, holding degrees from Wilfrid Laurier University, the University of Ottawa, McMaster University, and McGill University. He has written three books in the field of environmental and public interest law, prepared over two dozen scholarly articles on these subjects, and presented papers at many conferences in Canada and the United States. He has represented various public interest groups such as Pollution Probe before judicial and administrative tribunals in Ontario.

Rodney Northey

Rodney Northey is an associate lawyer at McCarthy Tétrault in Toronto, specializing in environmental assessment. He has published law journal articles on constitutional law and environmental law and policy, and teaches a course on environmental assessment law at Osgoode Hall Law School. He is on the board of directors of the Canadian Environmental Defence Fund.

Peter Pickfield

Peter Pickfield obtained his law degree from Queen's University in 1984 and a master's degree in constitutional law from Osgoode Hall Law School in 1990. He has practised exclusively in the areas of environmental law and municipal and planning law since 1986. He is counsel to the Ontario Environmental Assessment Advisory Committee, and has represented clients before the Environmental Assessment Board, the Environmental Appeal Board, the Ontario Municipal Board, and a joint board. He has written and spoken extensively on matters relating to this area of practice.

John Swaigen

John Swaigen has practised at the Ontario bar for 19 years in regulatory, administrative, and environmental law. He has taught environmental law at the University of Toronto Institute for Environmental Studies. He has written and edited several books, and his articles have appeared in law journals, newspapers, and magazines. He is currently chair of the Ontario Environmental Appeal Board and a research associate of the Canadian Institute for Environmental Law and Policy.

John Tidball

John Tidball is a partner in the Environmental Law Services Group of Miller Thomson in Markham, Ontario. From his call to the bar in 1983 until 1988, he was a solicitor with the Ontario Ministry of the Environment.

Toby Vigod

Toby Vigod, a graduate of the University of Toronto and Queen's University, has been a commissioner with the Commission on Planning and Development Reform in Ontario since June 1991. She has appeared as counsel at the provincial and federal level, on cases involving a wide range of environmental matters, has written extensively on environmental law, and has taught environmental law courses at Queen's University and the University of Toronto. She has also been a consultant to the Law Reform Commission of Canada, and was appointed to the Ontario Round Table on the Environment and the Economy. She is a member of the Law Society of Upper Canada's Environmental Specialist Certification Committee.

Mark Winfield

Mr. Winfield is director of research for the Canadian Institute for Environmental Law and Policy. He recently completed a PhD in political science at the University of Toronto, and is an instructor in the environmental studies program there.

Acknowledgments

This book is a project of the Canadian Institute for Environmental Law and Policy (CIELAP) and was made possible by grants from individuals, governments, foundations, and corporations, and by the hard work of many individuals. We would like to thank those who provided financial support, carried out research, read chapters and offered helpful comments, provided administrative support, sent information, gave permission to quote their publications, and helped in many other ways.

We would particularly like to thank the following for their generous financial support: the Environmental Partners Fund of Environment Canada; the Research and Technology Branch of the Ontario Ministry of the Environment; the Environmental Youth Corps program of the Ontario Ministry of the Environment; the Ontario Ministry of Natural Resources; the Canadian Studies and Special Projects of the Department of the Secretary of State; the Helen McCrea Peacock Foundation; The Richard and Jean Ivey Fund; The Samuel and Saidye Bronfman Foundation; DuPont Canada; Falconbridge Ltd.; McDonald's Restaurants of Canada; Professor J.G.W. (Ted) Manzig; Christine Lucyk; Gardiner, Roberts; and the Margaret Laurence Fund.

We would also like to thank the Faculty of Law at the University of Windsor and the Law Foundation of Ontario for their support. The Law Foundation gave a grant to the Windsor Faculty of Law for research assistance to its professors, and the faculty, through the auspices of Professor Manzig, kindly allocated some of this research assistance to the preparation of this book.

Many thanks also to our continuing corporate, government, and individual donors, whose ongoing support covers the large portion of CIELAP's operating costs that is not provided by donations earmarked for specific projects.

We would like to offer special thanks to several people. To Ted Manzig, who provided ongoing support to this project and to its editor in many ways, including reading and commenting on the drafts of each chapter as a member of the project's editorial committee. To Alan Potter of McClelland and Stewart, also a member of the editorial committee, both for his comments on chapter drafts and for his ongoing advice about publishing books. To Joyce Young, for ongoing fund-raising and strategic advice, administrative support, editorial assistance, and moral support. And to our "lay" readers. For each edition of *Environment on Trial*, we have had at least one person with no legal training read the chapters and advise us when we were falling into the error of legal jargon or otherwise making things too complicated or unclear. In this case, Kathy Cooper of the Canadian Environmental Law Association and Deborah Curran fulfilled this function. Deborah volunteered her time to do this after spending the summer of 1990 conducting research for the book under the auspices of the Ministry of the Environment's Environmental Youth Corps program. And to Rosemary Gray-Snelgrove, the project coordinator, who brought order out of chaos.

Greg Hiscock, Nina Lester, Michael Mezei, Patricia Mohr, Therese Reilly, Jim Renick, Timm Rochan, Hiroko Sawai, and Marianna Tzabiris carried out research.

Harry Dahme, David Estrin, Harry Poch, and John Willms recruited students and lawyers to assist in carrying out research. We would like to thank them and their law firms—Gowling, Strathy and Henderson, Gardiner, Roberts, and Willms and Shier — for this assistance. Thanks also to Robert Taylor and Jay Josepho for updating the appendix on Small Claims Court; Helena Hu, who helped update the appendix on water sampling and analysis; and Thea Dorsey, who helped update the appendix on searches.

Barbara Heidenreich, CIELAP's former executive director, and Anne Mitchell, its current executive director, made stone soup with limited resources to take this project from a conviction that a third edition of *Environment on Trial* was overdue to a final manuscript, and handled the editor's occasional crankiness with tact and aplomb. CIELAP staff who provided administrative and research assistance include Fé de Leon, Seana Irvine, Helen-Louise Mitchel, Patricia Merriman, and Joanne Rappaport.

The following people generously donated their time to review and comment on individual chapters and appendixes or specific portions of them: Julian Wieder of the Investigations and Enforcement Branch of the Ministry of Environment and Energy; Professor Michael Dickman of Brock University; Jack Gibbons of CIELAP; Doug Hallett; George Howse; Monte Hummell of the World Wildlife Fund (Canada); Professor Robert Gibson of the University of Waterloo; Wanda Michalowicz, Sally Marin, Bob Shaw, and Sharon Suter of the Ontario Ministry of Environment and Energy; Richard Lindgren and Sarah Miller of the Canadian Environmental Law Association; Patricia Mohr; Paul Muldoon; Michael Perley of the Canadian Foundation on Acid Rain; Ian Attridge; Norm Richards and John Riley of the Ontario Ministry of Natural Resources; Howard Samoil of the Environmental Law Centre, Alberta; Hajo Versteeg; Terry McIntyre; Louise Duke; Jane Roots; J.E. Hollebone of Agriculture Canada; and Tim Grant of the Wildlands League.

Among those who also provided needed information and offered comments on parts of the book are: Bob Bossin; Professor Phil Byers; Lyn MacMillan; Leslie Kende of the Ministry of Environment and Energy; H.J.M. Spence of the Atomic Energy Control Commission; and Brian Bellmore, George Rust-D'Eye, and Christine Schmidt of Weir and Foulds.

Thanks also to Professor Paul Emond of Osgoode Hall Law School at York University and the students in his environmental law class, who assisted in our research: Tim Bartkiw, Sol Chrom, Kevin Griener, Jane Keenan, Jana Roth, and Renee van Kessel.

Difficult-to-find reports and documents were often available from the Canadian Environmental Law Association's Public Resource Centre, and its librarians, Mary Vise and Christine Beckerman, were always friendly and helpful.

Jim Lyons and Paula Pike of WordsWorth Communications oversaw the transformation of a manuscript into a final publication with efficiency and good cheer under tight deadlines.

Ian MacFee Rogers kindly gave permission to quote a passage from *Canadian Municipal Law*, and Dianne Saxe gave permission to quote from her article in the *Canadian Environmental Law Reports*, "Application of Provincial Environmental Statutes to the Federal Government."

Because the writing of this book has gone on over a period of three years, we will undoubtedly have left someone out. It seems to happen in every edition of this book. For example, it did not come to our attention until recently that we had forgotten to acknowledge the writing of the appendix on prosecution procedure in 1974 by Angel White, a.k.a. Lloyd Greenspoon. Our apologies to Lloyd and to anyone we have missed in this edition.

As they always say at the end of the acknowledgment sections in books, although we appreciate everyone's help, the editor and the authors of the chapters take full responsibility for any errors as well as for the opinions expressed by them in this book.

Environmental law and policy reforms are moving along at a rapid clip, and since the writing of this edition began in August 1990, there have been numerous new statutes, regulations, and policies. Indeed, much of Canada's environmental law and policy was rewritten during this time or is in the process of change. We have attempted to make this book accurate to at least October 1992, but we may have missed some changes that took place since the earliest chapters were written. We would be pleased if our readers would bring any errors or omissions to our attention.

Dedication

This edition of *Environment on Trial* is dedicated to two of our co-workers in the development of Ontario's environmental law and policy who have passed on.

Before her death in 1976 in an air crash, **Dolores Montgomery** devoted herself to public service through her work with the Canadian Environmental Law Association, the Public Interest Coalition for Energy Planning, the Toronto Distress Centre, the Federation of Information Centres of Metropolitan Toronto, and other public interest organizations. She worked with the elderly, with psychiatric patients, and with neighbourhood groups — the "grass roots."

Patricia Doty Reed was an anomaly, a middle-aged mother of teenage children, when she joined the environmental crusade, which was largely a youth movement in the early 1970s. When Pollution Probe was looking for a volunteer to handle noise complaints, Pat called them up and said, "Here I am." She taught herself the theory of acoustics and learned how to operate a noise meter. In 1972, she was hired by the newly formed Canadian Environment Law Association to handle noise complaints, appear in court as an expert witness, and write briefs to government agencies. That year, *The Toronto Star* called her "Toronto's only full-time campaigner against noise." She wrote the chapter on noise in the first edition of *Environment on Trial*. Pat went on to become a lawyer, returning briefly to the Canadian Environmental Law Association as an articling student. She practised family law until her death in 1991.

About the Canadian Institute for Environmental Law and Policy

Founded in 1970 as the Canadian Environmental Law Research Foundation (CELRF), the Canadian Institute for Environmental Law and Policy (CIELAP) is an independent, not-for-profit professional research and educational institute that provides environmental law and policy analysis. CIELAP is incorporated under the laws of the province of Ontario and registered with Revenue Canada as a charity (registration number 0380584-59).

CIELAP's mission is to provide leadership in the development of environmental law and policy that promotes the public interest and the principles of sustainability, including the protection of the health and well-being of present and future generations and the natural environment.

CIELAP's work includes identifying emerging strategic environmental law and policy issues facing Canada and the world; analyzing current environmental law and policy issues; researching and evaluating policy options for public and private sector responses; and communicating the conclusions of its research results to lay and professional audiences in a clear and non-partisan manner.

CIELAP's financial support comes from governments, foundations, corporations, and individuals, from fees for services, and from the sale of publications. We welcome your support. Tax-creditable donations to support leading edge environmental law and policy research projects may be made by sending your cheque made out to CIELAP or authorizing CIELAP to make a deduction from your Visa or Mastercard.

Further information about CIELAP and a list of its publications can be obtained by contacting CIELAP at 517 College Street, Suite 400, Toronto, Ontario M6G 4A2. Our telephone number is (416) 923-3529 and our fax number is (416) 923-5949. CIELAP can also be reached electronically through the WEB network. Our electronic identification is "cielap."

Foreword to the First Edition

Air and water pollution, noise, lack of parks, incompatible land uses — all of these suddenly became major social and economic issues in the late 1960s.

Citizens concerned about their neighbourhoods, cottage owners, and long-time conservationists, all of whom had been literally crying in the wilderness about these problems, found they had the support of the public and the news media. Pollution horror stories were featured on the front pages of newspapers and in television specials — about DDT, mercury, phosphates in laundry detergents killing off lakes, and a host of other dangers. Demonstrations were held to stop demolition of historic buildings or the destruction of greenspace by developers, or cutting off access to lakeshores, and ratepayers' groups protested increasingly before any forum they could find.

Public pressure on governments and individual politicians to "clean up pollution" and ensure a "healthful and attractive environment" increased dramatically. But government action, though loudly demanded, has seldom seemed more limited. This may have been due in part to the stark contrast caused by such sudden and even violent awakening to the peril. The long-range pattern which usually promotes social change was not present.

For in this process of increasing government control over the environment, the role and desires of the citizen — as to the nature of the control he might wish to have over his environment and the uses to which he might want it put in his lifetime and that of his children — seemed muted at every turn.

At first, many citizens apparently were content to rely entirely on government. They expected prompt and dramatic action. As the author of the American "Environmental Bill of Rights" Act, Professor Joseph L. Sax of the University of Michigan, says:

> We are a peculiar people. Though committed to the idea of democracy, as private citizens we have withdrawn from the governmental process and sent in our place a surrogate to implement the public interest.

This substitute — the bureaucratic agency or department — is charged with looking after that elusive, ever-changing thing called the public interest, but so often the bureaucracy seems to impede desired action.

The agencies' record of enforcement of "their" legislation is perhaps a good example of what we are saying. In Ontario, over a recent two-year period, February 23, 1970 to April 7, 1972, there were only 50 prosecutions for water pollution offences. An incredibly low sum of $19,075 was levied in fines, for an average of $465 per conviction. It is apparent that more effective action will result only from public scrutiny and perhaps even private enforcement.

The administrative agency, whether it is, for example, the Ontario Ministry of the Environment or the Ontario government's Planning Branch, is admittedly an essential element in our society. Someone must take the initiative for planning, must set standards, supervise the granting of permits and see that regulations are enforced. Yet, all too often, the citizen has been left out of the decision-making, rule-setting process. In many cases, the citizen is actually forbidden to take part.

The very fact that you have priority of possession, the fact that there may be no good reason for a new factory next to your cottage or farm, or for a hydro line running through it, or the fact that better sites (less costly, environmentally speaking) are available, are some of the arguments that our citizens are claiming the opportunity to present. New developments are often considered to be strictly a matter between the developer and the government. If the Ministry decides to impose a term on obtaining the certificate of approval, which the applicant does not like, the applicant has the right of appeal — but there is still no opportunity for anyone in the area to be notified about the appeal or appear to argue against the application.

This situation must change — and there are a few signs that change may take place: for example, the announcement in the spring of 1973 that the Ontario government plans an environmental agency to assess the impact of both governmental and private projects prior to their implementation and that the reports and recommendations of the agency, while not binding on the Minister, would at least be public information. If passed, such a law would be a real step in the environmental area towards opening the planning and decision-making process to the people at the earliest possible opportunity. For this process to be effective it must provide for public hearings at an early stage, while a project may still be modified or cancelled without major dislocation of all the elements involved. Public participation is an important feature of the *Planning Act*, and it has served this province well. The administration of the natural environment is also public business and there is no logical reason to deny the public an opportunity not only to protect its own property and neighbourhoods, but also to have a voice in the formulation of plans and policies. The citizen should not be forced to oppose such a project after it is presented as a *fait accompli*.

Citizen participation is fundamental to any sound program to keep Ontario an attractive and healthful place in which to work, live and play. We are still a long way from ensuring public involvement in the environmental planning process and from ensuring that the true costs of projects which will affect the environment are calculated in advance. The process must include a meaningful assessment of the long-term costs to the people of Ontario, both social and economic, and of the impairment of the natural environment by the project, so that the true value of what will take place is recognized when trade-offs are made.

It seems to me that the call by the Canadian Environmental Law Association for an Environmental Bill of Rights for Ontario is worthy of serious consideration. It would seem that such a Bill, as explained by CELA, would provide mechanisms to ensure that proper planning is done, that citizens have a forum and a legal right to criticize environmentally unsound projects, and that a legally recognized right to a healthy and attractive environment can be asserted.

But while that important goal is pursued and achieved, many citizens are suffering real environmental problems or are fighting to stop projects that won't wait for an Environmental Bill of Rights.

This book will for the first time give the citizen an insight into his environmental rights and how he can assert them, legally and politically.

Lawyers have been reluctant, until quite recently, to get involved in the question of environmental rights. However, with the formation of the Canadian Environmental Law Association, important initiatives in environmental protection through the law are being taken. Such remedies as the law now provides (although there are large gaps, there are some remedies), for the first time, are being brought by CELA to the citizen who previously would never think of approaching a lawyer or the courts for assistance. In its relatively short existence CELA has been responsible for the favourable resolution of a number of environmental problems of general concern and problems affecting particular individuals who appeared unable to find effective help elsewhere.

But even the free legal assistance the CELA lawyers provide to those who need such services in environmental areas, although a great step forward, is not sufficient to bring current laws fully to bear on environmental situations.

Most people who have given thought to the subject agree that the cost of resort to our courts, especially our civil courts, has placed this means of obtaining justice beyond the reach of the vast majority of our citizens in far too many cases. The cost of pursuing necessary processes before even administrative tribunals, especially before our courts, must be reviewed to bring this important facet of justice within the reach of those who cannot afford it today. The only relief I see lies in a concerted public demand by the people, who must always have the final say.

There is another problem with our civil courts, where the common law is applied: when a situation affects many persons, and affects them all in the same way, then no one person has "standing" in our courts to call the law-breaker into question. For example, if a factory is pouring out smoke over a wide area, it would be a "public" nuisance, and unless some person can prove he is being harmed in a degree and manner different from his neighbours, none of them can sue, although public nuisance is definitely a wrong for which the courts can give remedies — both money damages and an injunction. Or if a government department is breaking one of its own laws, again our courts say individual citizens have no "standing" unless they can prove special damage.

This glaring defect in our civil court system has historical origins — but it was made by judges in past court cases, and could still be changed by the courts. However, it may now require legislative action. To change the law to get rid of this concept — and allow any citizen to sue another for harm caused to the public generally, or a government agency for breaking public law — would not be that radical a step. This private right in matters of public concern has been recognized before now in many ways.

Under the *Municipal Act*, any ratepayer can use our civil courts to obtain an injunction to restrain the breach of a municipal by-law. This is an exception to the common law rule. Similarly, the *Planning Act* provides that any ratepayer can also ask for an injunction in civil courts to restrain the breach of an official plan or zoning by-law.

The Municipal Board has not applied the strict common law rule and allows any citizen who wishes to take the time and trouble to present an argument before the Board to do so. This has not in any way come close to paralysing the Board, nor has it resulted in, for example, a developer being subject to multiple Board proceedings, each dealing with the same proposal. If there are several persons interested in having the Board rule on a particular issue or project, the Board has developed procedures to ensure fairness to the person or government department whose project is under scrutiny.

All of these precedents show that to remove the problem of "standing" from our civil court system would hardly be a novel or radical move, but one which would be, in view of these precedents, merely giving a long overdue dusting to the closet of legal remedies. We must have changes in the "costs" and "standing" areas so that citizens can utilize fully the civil remedies outlined in this book.

This book then, in my view, shows that basic changes are needed in our planning procedures — indeed in our lifestyles — if a real environmental crisis is going to be avoided; but that even now we have the right to a clean and attractive environment. This book outlines the steps now available to protect these rights, limited though they be. Beyond this, however, is the long-term goal of an Environmental Bill of Rights for Ontario to ensure maximum citizen participation in the achievement of a quality environment.

J.A. Kennedy, Q.C., Chairman of the
Ontario Municipal Board 1960-1972
July 1973

Preface

Environment on Trial was originally intended to help ordinary people, with little understanding of our legal system, to understand how that system works and to enable them to use the existing laws and administrative structures to protect the environment. The purpose was both to explain the existing laws and how ordinary citizens could use them, and to explain how and why our laws and administrative arrangements were failing to protect the environment and to suggest what changes were needed to make them more effective.

Although *Environment on Trial* was aimed at the ordinary citizen, it became a standard textbook, used in university and community college courses on environmental law and policy and other areas of environmental studies. To our surprise, it also became an important reference book for lawyers, planners, consultants, and government officials. Today, dog-eared copies of the first two editions can still be found in many law libraries and government offices, and on the bookshelves of corporate executives, engineers, and others involved in the growing environmental protection industry.

There have been continuing requests for a new edition to reflect the extensive changes in environmental law and policy since the 1978 edition of *Environment on Trial*.

In this third edition, we have made some significant changes. There is more of a balance between "global" and "local" environmental issues. For example, there is much more emphasis on international law, an aspect of the legal framework for environmental protection that was largely ignored in the first two editions. Moreover, as the new subtitle indicates, there is more emphasis on government policies than in previous editions. *Environment on Trial* is now a book about environmental law and policy, not just law.

In addition, as a result of my experience teaching environmental law at the Institute for Environmental Studies of the University of Toronto, I have reorganized the book to make it a more useful teaching tool.

Recognizing that *Environment on Trial* has a much wider audience than the general public for whom it was originally intended, we have also structured it to be more useful to lawyers, environmental protection practitioners, and academics. We have tried to keep the text clear and simple; but it is heavily footnoted with information needed to make the book a useful reference book for the environmentally sophisticated reader.

We hope that this edition of *Environment on Trial* will be as successful in meeting these more ambitious goals as earlier editions were in meeting the needs of their time.

A glance at the table of contents will show that *Environment on Trial* has also been expanded to cover many more topics than past editions. New chapters include biotechnology, wildlife, and wetlands. The scope of chapters that were in previous editions has been expanded to cover many additional topics. For example, the chapter on noise has been expanded to include vibration; the chapter on air pollution now includes a discussion of indoor air quality; and the evidence chapter now also discusses hearing procedures.

Nevertheless, limited resources did not permit us to cover every significant topic. There is no chapter on forest preservation, soil conservation, the preservation of agricultural lands, energy conservation and the regulation of energy, emergency response, or environmental law enforcement. The regulation of toxic substances, and in particular the role of the *Canadian Environmental Protection Act* and the *Transportation of Dangerous Goods Act*, is not discussed extensively, except in the context of specific issues such as air pollution, water pollution, and noise.

However, there is a growing body of literature on individual issues in environmental law and policy. For some of these topics, other books and studies are available, some of them published by the Canadian Institute for Environmental Law and Policy.

Given limited resources, the emphasis in this book is necessarily idiosyncratic, reflecting the interests and knowledge of the editor and the contributors. Despite the omissions, we can say without fear of contradiction that *Environment on Trial* is still by far the most comprehensive text on environmental law and policy in Canada.

Although this edition of *Environment on Trial* is intended to be as much a teaching tool and a useful reference book for environmental practitioners as a handbook and a call to arms for ordinary citizens, it is important that we not forget the legal, policy, and institutional failures that made this book necessary in the first place.

Helping people to understand and apply their democratic rights and encouraging reform of our laws and institutions remain fundamental purposes of this book. Although there are now many more policies, laws, and institutions devoted to the regulation of activities that impair environmental quality than there were in 1974, many of the concerns and criticisms expressed in the foreword and introduction to the first edition are just as valid and pressing today as they were almost two decades ago. Our institutional arrangements for protecting the environment, public health, and the rights of ordinary people to enjoy their homes and surroundings have improved, but these improvements have not kept pace with the destruction of the environment. Planning processes still largely reflect short-term concerns at the expense of long-term considerations. Regulatory institutions still mirror political boundaries rather than ecosystems, making an "ecosystem" approach to planning and regulation difficult, if not impossible.

Nor has the attitude of government agencies toward citizens trying to obtain information and to enlist their help in protecting the environment fundamentally changed. A letter to the editor in *The New York Times* once tried to explain the difference between Canadians' and Americans' relationships with their respective governments: "In the United States, people hate the government. In Canada, the government hates the people." Unfortunately, our institutional arrangements and the behaviour of our public servants all too often suggest that there is a grain of truth in this pronouncement.

There may be many reasons why public servants and politicians have not become more open and responsive to the concerns of ordinary people. The "capture" of regulatory agencies by the industries they are supposed to regulate may be one. A natural reaction to the distrust in them that citizens often exhibit is another. However, one of the most important reasons why government agencies and government officials have locked their doors against involvement by concerned citizens is simply their lack of resources. When the agencies charged with environmental protection have insufficient resources to collect baseline data, carry out needed research, inspect facilities, or enforce the laws, the last thing they may want to do is spend any of their budget or their time listening to the public.

Most of the changes in our laws, policies, and governmental institutions over the past two decades have been designed to enhance the discretionary powers of government officials to take action — if and when they want to. Few of these changes have imposed duties on government or empowered citizens. The effectiveness of freedom of information laws is often thwarted by the civil servants who administer the legislation. Lack of resources is in large part responsible for the frustration and siege mentality of some of our public servants, which fosters their resistance to cooperation with the citizenry.

At the time of writing, Ontario has given first reading to an environmental bill of rights, an initiative advocated in the first edition of this book, back in 1974. However, many of the "rights" in this Act will still be discretionary, and the only right citizens will have to ensure that the environmental bill of rights is implemented is a right to complain to yet another bureaucrat, the environmental commissioner. This approach is understandable. In the end, in a democracy, the elected officials must have the last word on many matters. Moreover, the government intends to apply this bill of rights initially only to a few of its ministries. Once again, government urges us to trust that the bill will eventually be extended to other government agencies. Again, gradual implementation is understandable, given the natural tendency of people and organizations to resist dramatic change in the way they operate and the limited resources available to the government.

It is important, however, that the public monitor closely the implementation of the environmental bill of rights. Experience with broken government promises to extend the *Environmental Assessment Act* to more than a small fraction of the environmentally significant undertakings in Ontario raises questions whether there will be more than token implementation of the environmental bill of rights.

As the plethora of environmental laws, policies, and environmental protection agencies discussed in this book demonstrates, we have come a long way since 1974. But we still have a long way to go before our governments are as responsive to environmental concerns as they are to economic concerns and proponents of development. Therefore, helping ordinary people fight for their rights and encouraging reform of our laws and institutions remain fundamental goals of this book.

John Swaigen
June 1993

Introduction: Sustainable Development, the Law, and Public Policy

CONTENTS

SUSTAINABLE DEVELOPMENT: LINKING THE ENVIRONMENT AND THE ECONOMY

If we are to succeed in preserving both a healthy economy and a healthy environment in Canada, substantial changes in our laws and public policies will be needed. In the past, neither our legal system nor our economic system has been developed to ensure the integration of environmental considerations into economic decisions.

The traditional models of economic development pursued by Canadian governments emphasized the maximization of economic returns from the intensive development and exploitation of natural resources.[1] Pollution and other negative environmental effects resulting from these activities were regarded as externalities.[2] The capacity of the natural environment to absorb this pollution was assumed to be infinite. Pollution and other negative environmental effects, such as the loss of species and the destruction of habitats, were seen as natural and inevitable products of the application of ingenuity and knowledge to serve human wants.[3] As a consequence of this view, environmental protection measures were seen by governments and industry to involve substantial opportunity costs in terms of lost efficiencies in resource use, and to bring only marginal economic returns. Indeed, as described in other parts of this book, the government of Ontario took substantial steps to limit the availability of common law remedies to industrial pollution during the 1940s, 1950s, and 1960s.[4] The government viewed this limiting of remedies as an extension of its role as a facilitator of economic development.[5]

During the 1970s and 1980s, many elements of Canadian society, including producers, consumers, investors, suppliers, and politicians, began to modify their understanding of the relationship between environmental protection and the economy. This change came as a result of the emergence of a substantial body of information regarding environmental damage. As a result, steps to develop means of limiting the environmental effects of new projects began to be undertaken. Environmental protection legislation was enacted for the purpose of abating existing pollution and reducing the emission of contaminants into the air, land, and water. Attempts were made to ensure that pollution control equipment was added to existing facilities that were causing pollution problems and that pollution control considerations were incorporated into the design of new plants. These measures resulted in significant improvements in a few areas, such as phosphate levels in the Great Lakes and the overall levels of lead in the environment. However, successes of this nature were over-whelmed by a growing body of knowledge regarding the pervasiveness of toxic chemicals in the environment and a progressive deterioration in air and water quality.[6]

This increasing evidence of continuing environmental decline suggested that a more fundamental re-examination of traditional models of economic development was required. It was becoming apparent that mitigation efforts, which took established patterns of development as given, were inadequate in the face of such worldwide phenomena as global warming due to carbon dioxide emissions resulting from fossil fuel use.[7] Developments of this character indicated that there were limits to the carrying capacity of the biosphere, and that we might already be exceeding those limits.

In response to this situation, a World Commission on Environment and Development, chaired by Sgro Brundtland, the prime minister of Norway, was established by the United Nations in 1983. The commission delivered its final report, entitled *Our Common Future*, in 1987. The central element of the commission's report was the introduction of the concept of "sustainable development." "Sustainable development" was defined by the commission as:

> development that meets the needs of the present generation without compromising the ability of future generations to meet their own needs.[8]

This principle was embraced by governments throughout the world, including the Canadian federal and provincial governments,[9] following the release of the commission's report.

The sustainable development concept adds an environmental component to what is understood to constitute the "good life." It does not deny a need for rising real incomes, embodied in the terms "development" and "economic growth," especially in the developing world. At the same time, however, it recognizes that the quality of life is determined by more than the amassing of material wealth. Sustainable development also adds a new dimension to the understanding of our economic system — its interdependence with the natural environment. The effects of economic activity on the environment are clearly visible in such phenomena as air and water pollution. The notion that the quality of the environment has direct and indirect effects on the performance of the economy has not yet been as clearly understood.

The linkages between the environment and the economy are straightforward. Every production unit, also known as an economic enterprise or firm, depends on the environment in some way for its material inputs, in the forms of natural raw materials or semiprocessed natural resources. Energy is also required to transform these materials into more useful products. Because of inefficiencies in the processes of using raw materials and transforming them into goods for human consumption, wastes may be generated. In addition, when a product reaches the end of its useful life, it too becomes waste that requires disposal.

The most common ways of dealing with these wastes have been to dissipate them into the atmosphere, discharge them into lakes and rivers, or dump them on the land or into the ocean. If the release of pollutants into the environment in this way exceeds the environment's capacity to assimilate them, the receiving air, water, and land are rendered unfit for further human use. Consequently, the initial waste of resources represented by pollution is compounded by the despoiling of additional resources.

Ultimately, the environment is the source of all the material inputs into an economic activity and a sink for all the material outputs. The goal of sustainable development is the establishment of an economic system that uses ecological resources at a rate that does not exceed the regenerative ability of the renewable resource base. At the same time, wastes cannot be discharged into ecosystems in quantities that exceed the ability of the system to absorb them. The overriding policy objective must be to reduce the amount of waste generated and to transform an increasing amount of the remaining waste into resources for use and re-use.[10]

The concept of sustainable development acknowledges that the ecosystems within which our economic systems operate have limited carrying capacities. It also stresses the importance of the essential biospheric systems, such as nutrient recycling, climate stabilization, and soil building, and the significance of maintaining biodiversity. These things are not generally recognized within the current political-economic system or adequately protected by our laws and regulations. The sustainable development principle is built on the conclusion that activities that damage the productive capacity of the biosphere will ultimately undermine the basis of economic activity as well. The overfishing of northern cod off Newfoundland, for example, has not only drastically reduced the number of fish, but has also devastated the economy of the 400 communities that depend on the cod fishery.

One of the central problems in our economic system is that proper values have not been placed on aspects of the environment that are used in the production process. Many of the resource inputs have been seriously undervalued, while the air, water, and land have been regarded as "free" waste disposal facilities.

The possibility that natural systems could have intrinsic status and value independent of their economic utility has been virtually ignored. Resources with a zero or low value are at serious risk of being overused: when something is provided at no cost, more of it will be demanded than if the good or service has a positive price. The results of the undervaluing of environmental resources in Canada are evident in the overharvesting of our forests, agricultural practices that destroy soil-building processes, and the degradation of our air, water, and land by pollution. In modern industrial societies, increases in material wealth, as measured by annual increases in our gross national product, have been achieved through the consumption of the biological interest generated by the planet and, much more seriously, by depleting its natural capital.[11]

The lasting contribution of the Brundtland commission is that, through the introduction of the sustainable development concept, societal developmental objectives have been broadened to include:

- the assignment of value to environmental health, acknowledging that it is the key to economic performance;
- the recognition of the importance of equity, both through time, with the notion that future generations should not be disadvantaged by the actions of present generations (intergenerational equity), and in the sense that the wants and needs of one group in society should not be met at the expense of the wants and needs of other groups (intragenerational and interregional equity);
- the extension of the time dimension of policy decisions well beyond a five-year electoral horizon and into the long-term future; and
- time as a policy concept, which requires consideration of the likely environmental consequences of decisions before they are made; steps can then be taken to avoid the costs of having to react to and cure unanticipated outcomes in the future.

The adoption of sustainable development as the guiding principle of economic and environmental policy in Canada means that we must ensure that we live off the biological interest created by the biosphere. Above all, we must not deplete the stock of natural capital that sustains life on earth.

ACHIEVING SUSTAINABLE DEVELOPMENT IN CANADA

To achieve sustainable development in Canada, we first need to develop a basic understanding of the ways in which ecosystems function, and how the changes caused by human beings affect them. In many cases, even minimum base-line data regarding the state of the environment, and the effects of human activities on it, are unavailable. Our knowledge of the potential hazards posed, for example, by many of the substances to which people, animals, and plants are exposed is very incomplete. There also is a need to develop a systematic approach to reporting on the state of the environment so that the effectiveness of our efforts to protect the environment can be evaluated. Environment Canada has begun to develop reports on the state of the environment to address this need.[12] Much more, however, needs to be done to ensure that decisions regarding development and environmental protection are made on an intelligent and informed basis.

In addition to gathering information about the state of the environment and the effects of human activities on it, we need to change the ways in which we measure the performance of the economy. Our basic economic indicators and accounting methodologies have typically failed to take into account the depletion or deterioration of natural resources and the long-term implications of these developments in terms of the sustainability of our current economic system.[13] This problem is perhaps best illustrated by the way in which the consequences of the Exxon Valdez disaster were measured in terms of their impact on the US economy. The US gross national product (GNP) rose as a result of the large expenditures on the clean-up of the spill. The event was therefore recorded as having been a net benefit to the American economy. No weight was given to the value of the resources destroyed or the environmental damage caused by the spill in the calculation of GNP. The economic practice of "discounting" the value of future benefits and costs also deserves serious attention. This practice tends to overemphasize the economic importance of short-term profits and to understate the long-term costs of environmental damage and resource depletion.[14]

Beyond the development of an adequate information base and the establishment of more appropriate means of measuring economic and environmental performance, a number of instruments are available to governments to directly influence societal actions and attitudes regarding environmental protection and resource use. The range of options open to members of society can be constrained through the use of *regulatory instruments* (also known as the command-and-control approach). Alternatively, the relevant cost-benefit ratios of various options can be changed through manipulation of the marketplace, employing *economic instruments*. These may be applied to make different courses of action more or less economically attractive. Third, behaviour might be modified through the use of *suasive instruments*. These encourage the internalization of the environment within the preference structure of the individual. The introduction of an environmental bill of rights might also be an important means of moving our economy toward a model that can both sustain development and promote human well-being.

These strategies for bringing about changes in human behaviour need to work, not only to provide incentives to change, but also to remove the disincentives and barriers to change. There is a need for regulations that constrain activities that are hazardous or unsustainable, and a need for an education system that supports and promotes sustainable behaviour. At the same time, policies, financial subsidies, and marketing techniques that encourage unsustainable activities, such as the overconsumption of natural resources and energy, must be phased out.

Regulatory Instruments

Almost all environmental protection statutes in Ontario have employed some form of "command-penalty" or "command-control" regulatory model. Certain activities have been prohibited outright, restricted through standards set down in regulations, or authorized subject to certain conditions through licensing or permit systems. Breaches of established standards or conditions can result in licence suspensions and revocations, or prosecutions.

Several themes are apparent in the following chapters regarding the application of regulatory instruments for environmental protection purposes in Ontario. The regulatory approach requires extensive and costly administrative structures for enforcement to ensure compliance.[15] Consequently, environmental regulators have often taken an "administrative" approach to pollution control, negotiating the contents of abatement strategies for particular plants with their operators, rather than vigorously prosecuting violations of established standards. The resulting pollution-control requirements have been widely regarded as weak, with action occurring only after obvious and serious problems have emerged.[16] The Ministry of the Environment has, however, taken a more aggressive approach toward prosecutions since the formation of an investigations and enforcement branch within the ministry in 1985.[17]

It is clear that our legal system has traditionally lagged behind developments in the environmental field. With the exception of the *Environmental Assessment Act*,[18] environmental protection statutes in Ontario have been fundamentally reactive in nature. They have not been designed to anticipate and prevent environmental damage. Rather, statutes like the *Environmental Protection Act*[19] have taken development patterns as given and have then sought to mitigate their environmental effects. Furthermore, the implementation of environmental protection statutes in Ontario has tended to be approached on a media- or issue-specific basis. The environmental protection issue has rarely been treated as an integrated whole.

Notwithstanding these limitations, tough laws and regulations are essential for the protection of the environment. They are especially important when particular types of activities, such as the discharge of persistent toxic pollutants into the environment, must be prohibited outright. However, regulatory instruments are not, in and of themselves, sufficient to bring about sustainable development. A wider range of policy instruments are needed to address the complex problem of developing an ecologically conscious society such as that envisioned in the sustainable development concept.[20]

Economic Instruments

"Command-and-control" regulations and economic instruments are often discussed as alternative options. Economic instruments, however, are often created through legislative and regulatory measures. They are, in fact, a less direct form of regulation and may be used to complement direct regulatory measures. Economic instruments may be employed by policy makers to affect the costs and benefits of different behavioural options. The price structure of the available options may be modified in such a way that companies produce, and individuals choose, goods and services that are less harmful to the environment. The key idea behind the concept of economic instruments is to bring about an internalization of the previously externalized environmental costs of particular activities and products. The price of a given service or product will then more accurately reflect the true costs associated with its delivery. In the result, the prices of goods and services associated with high environmental costs will rise, and the prices of more sustainable products will fall.

There are five broad categories of market-based pollution abatement mechanisms or environmentally progressive programs. They are:[21]

- taxes and effluent and input charges;
- subsidies;
- deposit-refund systems;
- financial enforcement instruments; and
- the creation of markets through the introduction of tradeable emission permit schemes or the privatization of common property resources.

Taxes and Effluent Charges

These instruments follow the "polluter-pays" principle, first articulated by the Organisation for Economic Co-operation and Development (OECD) in 1972.[22] The intention of effluent charges, in particular, is to bring about a direct internalization of waste management costs, which firms may have previously externalized through pollution. Under a system of effluent charges, a firm is charged for each unit of pollution it emits. Ideally, the tax or effluent charge is set at a level designed to compensate for environmental damage caused by the firm's discharge of pollutants into the environment. The taxes or charges paid by the firm rise and fall as a direct function of the amount of pollution the firm emits. Efforts to reduce pollution will result in a direct economic return to the firm in the form of reduced effluent taxes or charges. To be successful in reducing pollution, however, the system of effluent charges must make the costs of polluting greater than the savings achieved by polluting.

The application of effluent charges in Canada has been limited to the provision of surcharges on discharges of effluent that exceed legislated limits under municipal sewer-use bylaws. Effluent charges have not been employed at either the federal or the provincial level to address direct discharges of pollutants into the air and water. Charges have been widely employed in Western Europe. As has been the case with municipal sewer-use bylaws in Canada, however, they have tended to be directed toward the raising of revenues rather than the express purpose of influencing the behaviour of polluters and their customers. Consequently, they have been set at too low a level to be expected to have a significant effect on the behaviour of the targeted firms. It is therefore difficult to arrive at an accurate assessment of the usefulness of effluent charges in pollution control.[23]

One area in which a form of effluent charge is being applied with increasing frequency is the field of municipal solid waste management. Many jurisdictions in the United States and Western Europe have adopted user-pay systems for household garbage collection.[24] These systems provide direct incentives to households to reduce the amount of waste they produce. Rising tipping fees for the dumping of industrial, commercial, and institutional (ICI) sector wastes have provided similar incentives to waste generators in those sectors. The government of Ontario is currently considering granting Ontario municipalities the powers necessary under the *Municipal Act* to introduce user-pay systems.[25] Full-cost user-pay systems have also been proposed for other public utilities, particularly sewer and water services, as a means of promoting resource conservation and ensuring the proper financing of infrastructure maintenance.

Other forms of taxes or charges that have been employed include taxes or charges on the material inputs of production. The most prominent examples of these instruments are the carbon taxes that have been introduced in the Netherlands, Finland, Norway, and Sweden. These taxes have been imposed on fossil fuels whose use generates carbon dioxide, the major cause of global warming. Charges or taxes might also be based on the potential of a particular product to harm the environment. The best known example of such a scheme in Canada is Ontario's "gas guzzler" tax/"gas sipper" rebate system for new automobile purchases.

A recently introduced instrument for bringing about the direct internalization of the environmental costs of a product is the concept of "product stewardship." Under product stewardship systems, manufacturers are required to take back their products at the end of the products' useful lives, or to pay a tax to cover their disposal costs. This provides a strong incentive to producers to extend the life of their products and to ensure that they can be easily recycled. The best-known example of such a system is the packaging return requirement introduced in the Federal German Republic in 1991.[26] In the spring of 1992 the Waste Reduction Advisory Committee (WRAC) proposed the implementation of a product stewardship system in Ontario.[27]

Subsidies

Subsidies are financial assistance instruments that are used to induce companies and individuals to alter their behaviour. In Canada, they have taken the form of non-repayable grants, soft loans that have interest rates below market rates, flowthrough tax features, and tax deductions, rebates, and credits. Subsidies have usually been employed in the environmental field to induce firms to undertake targeted pollution abatement activities or other environmentally progressive programs. Many observers find the use of public funds to finance pollution control activities on the part of waste-generating industries objectionable, since the practice departs from the "polluter-pays" principle. Nevertheless, subsidies have found widespread use in Canada.

The results of the application of environmental subsidies in Canada have been mixed. The federal pulp and paper modernization program, for example, appears to have been helpful in overcoming industry resistance to the installation of pollution control equipment.[28] The positive impact of the accelerated capital cost allowance for pollution abatement equipment under federal, and some provincial, tax legislation has been less clear. It is widely regarded to have had, at best, a symbolic rather than a practical impact.[29]

Subsidies have also been used in Ontario to support markets for materials collected through the "blue box" recycling program.[30] Similarly, government purchasing policies can play an important role in the development of markets for recycled or otherwise environmentally friendly products. By favouring such goods and services over less benign alternatives, governments can help to strengthen the demand for environmentally appropriate products.

Consideration should be given not only to the granting of subsidies to promote environmentally sound behaviour. The possibility of withdrawing public subsidies to activities that damage the environment should also be explored. It has been suggested, for example, that governments in North America, Western Europe, and Japan could reallocate their agricultural budgets in ways that encourage their farmers to adopt practices that enhance, rather than deplete, the soil and water base.[31] Similar action might also be examined in such fields as energy, transportation, and forestry.

Deposit-Refund Systems

Deposit-refund systems place a surcharge on the price of a potentially polluting product, which is refunded when the item is returned. The deposits paid on refillable containers for beer and soft drinks are well-known examples of such systems in Canada. In Europe and the United States, deposit-refund systems have been successfully used to encourage the organized collection and recycling of batteries, old cars, and "white goods" (stoves, refrigerators, washers, and dryers).[32] The effectiveness of this approach is very much a function of the amount of the deposit charged, and of the convenience of the system for returning used goods for the refund of the deposit.

Financial Enforcement Incentives

Financial enforcement incentives are essentially a legal rather than an economic tool. Under such a system, a firm is automatically charged a non-compliance fee when its emissions exceed the levels permitted by its pollution licence or certificate of approval. A formal prosecution is not required to collect the fee. This provides the firm with a direct economic incentive to stay in compliance with the terms and conditions of its environmental approvals, and greatly reduces the administrative costs of enforcement. To be effective, the fees must be set at a level that exceeds the cost of treating the pollutant; otherwise, there is no incentive to comply. Given the nature of our constitutional requirements regarding procedural justice, a system of this nature could only by implemented with the consent and agreement of the affected firm. In addition, some form of appeal mechanism would have to be provided.

The posting of surety bonds by a potentially polluting firm is another useful instrument in situations where enforcement is difficult or a specific potential offender is to be targeted. The value of these bonds is forfeited to the government if a regulatory infraction occurs or if the firm fails to carry out the terms and conditions of an approval or control order. The use of performance bonds of this nature is particularly common in the waste management field, where there are concerns that firms may abandon sites that require extensive, and expensive, environmental clean-up efforts. As is the case with non-compliance fees, some means of appeal is necessary when instruments of this nature are employed.

Market Creation

Market creation is a widely discussed alternative to command-and-control regulation. Proposals of this nature have taken two principal forms. The first is the creation of *emission-trading* systems. The second is the *privatization of common property resources.*

Emission Trading

It has been proposed that, where there are sufficient participants, and the type of emission is appropriate, governments should establish tradeable emission credit systems. Waste-generating firms would be given emission limits, as under normal pollution control programs. If, however, a discharger released less pollution than allowed by its limit, the enterprise would have the option of "banking" the difference, in case it might need the credit at a later date. Alternatively, it could sell or trade the "unused level of permitted discharge" to another firm. That firm would then have the right to release that amount more than permitted by its initial limit. Because the purchasing firm is only buying unused permits within the same defined region, and assuming that all parts of the region have an equal pollution assimilative capacity, there will be no cumulative effect of the system on the environment.

The appeal of this mechanism is its economic efficiency. Polluters with high abatement costs will prefer to buy permits, and polluters with low abatement costs will sell permits and be encouraged to further reduce pollution in order to generate revenue through the sale of "rights to pollute." The overall standard for environmental quality is determined by the authorities that set the number of permits. Environmental quality can theoretically be improved by reducing the number of permits available, or by reducing the amount of pollution allowed under each permit unit.[33]

Operational experience with emission-trading schemes is extremely limited,[34] although 1990 amendments to the US *Clean Air Act* will introduce an extensive emission-trading system for acid-causing gas emissions in that country. The introduction of emission trading is a highly controversial issue. Many environmental advocates strongly object to the concept of governments selling proprietary rights to pollute the public's air and water.

In addition to these broad concerns, emission-trading systems suffer from a number of specific deficiencies. Clearly they cannot be used to address substances for which it has been determined that the only acceptable level of discharge is zero. Such substances must be subject to direct regulatory bans. In addition, emission-trading systems must be subject to some form of limitation to ensure that local ambient conditions do not fall below an acceptable minimum as a result of a firm's buying and using a large number of permits. The limited availability of permits could also be used by existing firms in a given sector as a barrier to entry by new firms.[35]

The potential complexity of the emission-trading schemes has been raised as a significant concern. Even supporters of emission trading have been known to admit that PhD economists often have trouble explaining the concept to each other, and that the development of secondary markets for rights and credits would add a high degree of complexity to the system.[36] Keeping track of who had what rights to emit and when could become a major challenge to administrators.

Furthermore, improvements in the overall level of environmental quality will be entirely dependent on the willingness of governments to reduce the total number of permits available, or the amount of pollution permitted under each permit, on a regular basis. Such action would almost certainly prompt very strong resistance from the affected firms, since they would either have to give up permits for which they had paid or have the value of their existing permits reduced. It is unlikely that governments will be any more willing to act in the face of such resistance than they have been when confronted with objections to new regulatory standards. Finally, if emission-trading schemes were to be introduced in Canada and then found to be a failure, they could prove to be very difficult, and expensive, to reverse. Firms would be likely to demand compensation if the permits and credits for which they had paid were cancelled.

Privatization of Common Property Resources

The notion of privatizing common property resources, such as the air and water, wildlife, and Crown forests, is an attempt to address the problem of the overexploitation of such resources. It is argued that the private ownership of a resource will ensure that its value will be protected and maximized over the resource stock's life cycle, since such behaviour maximizes the economic return to the owner of the resource.[37] There is little empirical evidence to support these claims, and it is doubtful that the privatization of common property resources will ever be politically acceptable within Canada.

Suasive Instruments

In Chapter 1, the importance of unwritten rules of social conduct, such as traditions and taboos, as tools for improving environmental quality will be discussed. Established customs and norms that individuals must follow, or risk being rejected by others, are often more powerful motivators of behaviour than written laws. Education, information dissemination, training, and peer pressure are all methods of altering the ways in which the advantages or disadvantages of certain products or kinds of behaviour are perceived.

The effectiveness of an environmentally conscious consumer was first felt by manufacturers and retailers in the late 1980s. Virtually overnight consumers stopped buying aerosols that contained CFCs and apples that had been sprayed with Alar. To be really green, however, consumers need assistance. Over the past few years the authors of green consumer guidebooks,[38] companies, and governments attempted to offer guidance to shoppers by providing information on the environmental effects of various products. The green consumerism movement may become dissipated by the confusion created by conflicting information regarding what is actually green. The process of deciding what products and processes are environmentally sound is extremely complex. Such factors as the amounts of energy and materials used, the environmental costs of handling, storage, transportation, and disposal, and use of toxic substances must be taken into account. Governments, backed by sound research, may be the most suitable agents for disseminating information of this nature.[39]

Consumer protection laws also may be required to strengthen the green consumerism movement. These laws would prohibit false claims of product "greenness." Criteria might be established for what can be legally labelled "green" or "environmentally friendly," in the event that industry does not do so voluntarily.

For green consumerism to be truly effective, more than just information needs to be provided. Knowledge about the environmental effects of various products needs to be reinforced by pricing considerations. The market needs to send the right signals. At present, green products are attractive to manufacturers because they can be sold at a premium. In a sense, this is a reversal of the "polluter-pays" principle. It would make more sense if the price of environmentally unsound goods were higher than the price of environmentally "friendly" products. The effective application of the various instruments described earlier in this chapter will be essential to the achievement of this goal, since they will help to ensure that the price of a given good or service reflects its full environmental and economic costs.

Another means by which suasion can become an effective means of affecting corporate decision making is the role that some business leaders can play in attempting to motivate their peers to change their attitudes toward environmental issues. The president of the International Chamber of Commerce, Hugh Faulkner, has observed that the "single most important factor in corporate environmentalism is whether the chairman and board members are convinced that it works."[40] It may be necessary, however, to accept that some business leaders will never be convinced. Others will accept the notion because they see a market opportunity and a chance to boost sales. The fear of being held liable for environmental damage may also be an important factor in changing business attitudes toward environmental issues. An enlightened few have already come to realize that without environmentally responsible companies, there will be no environment and therefore no economy and, ultimately, no life worth living. These individuals have become the leaders of the greening of the corporate sector.[41]

The development of a corporate mandate that reflects environmental responsibility often decreases the company's impact on the environment, and reduces costs, by increasing the efficiency of the company's overall operations.[42] These savings result from the adoption of waste reduction, re-use, and recycling schemes and energy-efficiency strategies in the firm's operations. Such steps have been identified as an important means of improving the competitive position of companies.[43]

THE ROLE OF AN ENVIRONMENTAL BILL OF RIGHTS IN FACILITATING SUSTAINABLE DEVELOPMENT

An environmental bill of rights (EBR) can also be useful in facilitating sustainable development. Such a bill could be an important means of infusing all government decision making with environmental considerations. Environmental bills of rights have been enacted in a number of US states, including Michigan, Minnesota, and Pennsylvania. In Canada, there are environmental bills of rights in the Yukon and the Northwest Territories. The Ontario government introduced a similar measure in May 1993.[44]

The concept of an environmental bill of rights will be discussed in more detail in Chapter 25. Environmental bills of rights were originally conceived as a means of balancing the property and economic development rights of firms and individuals with a right to environmental quality that can be enforced by the individual citizen. In practice, when interpreting the right to environmental quality found in the constitution of the state of Pennsylvania and other US EBRs, the courts have held that such rights are not absolute. Rather, they have been interpreted as requiring the incorporation of environmental considerations into government decision making — the very goal of sustainable development.

One of the best examples of such a law is article 1, section 27 of the Pennsylvania state constitution, which states:

> The People have a right to clean air, pure water and to the preservation of the natural, scenic, historic and aesthetic values of the environment. Pennsylvania's public natural resources are the common property of all the people, including generations yet to come. As trustee of these resources, the Commonwealth shall conserve and maintain them for the benefit of all the people.

Although this sounds like an absolute right to put the environment before development, the courts have not interpreted it that way. Instead, they have held it to require the integration of environmental protection into economic decisions.[45]

In the result, article 1, section 27 has had two major effects:

- it has encouraged government agencies to pass laws incorporating a requirement that their decision making must consider environmental impacts; and
- where there is no such legislated standard, the courts will ensure that the agency has considered environmental impacts before developing a project itself or granting a licence, permit, or approval to the private sector — including permits to carry out activity on private property.

In this way, the Pennsylvania bill has raised the profile of environmental considerations in public policy decision making. Agencies that otherwise might not have examined the environmental aspects of their activities have been encouraged to do so.

THE WORK OF THE ONTARIO ROUND TABLE ON THE ENVIRONMENT AND THE ECONOMY

In 1991, the Ontario Round Table on the Environment and the Economy (ORTEE), a committee of six Cabinet ministers, six major corporate CEOs and representatives from labour, and the environmental and native communities, established a series of sectoral task forces in the areas of energy, mining, agriculture, forestry, urban and commercial development, transportation, and manufacturing. The mandate of each task force was to consult with key stakeholders and to prepare a report outlining the strategic issues and priority actions to move sustainable development objectives forward in its sector. No environmental protection or sustainable development objectives were imposed by the government on the task forces' deliberations. Most of the task forces identified two key objectives that they felt were essential elements of sustainable development. These were the twin goals of protecting the biosphere and maintaining economic viability.[46]

A pragmatic approach was taken to the definition of sustainability. It was seen as a relative term, not an absolute, and was described as a managed process of change in which alternative means, with relatively better environmental performance, of achieving specific objectives are systematically identified and adopted. The result of this task force process was a series of reports for each sector that contained suggestions for more stringent regulations, identified economic incentives to improve performance, and recommended an extensive program of self-regulation. Together with the action agenda for an ecologically sustainable future[47] prepared by members of the Ontario Environmental Network (OEN), there exists a clear picture of the necessary steps that are required to achieve sustainability in Ontario.

The principles that emerged from the ORTEE government-sponsored studies and from the work of the members of the non-profit OEN are similar. They include the conclusions that:

1. economic growth can never be made environmentally benign; however, it can be made greener;
2. without government intervention, the environment cannot be fully protected;
3. self-regulation by industry and individuals can only work within a framework of clear goals established by laws and regulations;
4. regulations can only establish goals and standards; they cannot ensure a sustainable society;
5. the marketplace must reinforce the achievement of societal goals, even if this requires state intervention;
6. the marketplace may fail to give appropriate value to critical life support systems, just as it may fail to reflect the interests of future generations;
7. no society can achieve sustainable development objectives unless environmentalism, through education and suasion, becomes an integral part of its understanding of the world and its place in it and of its political and economic decision-making processes; and
8. leadership is the most critical element in achieving sustainable development objectives.

CONCLUSIONS

Achieving the goal of a sustainable society will require cleaning up the environment, the preservation of nature, and the maintenance and restoration of biodiversity. These measures will require action by governments, industry, and members of the public. Governments may act through regulation, economic interventions, and public education programs. Industry, for its part, must accept that change is necessary if we are to address our environmental problems effectively. Firms need to make the most efficient use of the resources available to them and minimize or eliminate the negative environmental effects of their activities. Members of the public must educate themselves about environmental issues and make environmentally sound decisions about their consumption patterns and lifestyles. They must also continue to press governments and industry to take the steps necessary to ensure that we have an environmentally sustainable society.

Barbara Heidenreich and Mark Winfield

FURTHER READING

Francis Cairncross, *Costing the Earth* (London: Random Century House and The Economist Books Ltd., 1991).

Canadian Bar Association, *Sustainable Development in Canada: Options for Law Reform* (Ottawa: CBA, 1990).

H.E. Daly and J.B. Cobb, *For the Common Good: Redirecting the Economy Toward Community, the Environment, and a Sustainable Future* (Boston: Beacon Press, 1989), especially parts 1 and 2.

International Union for the Conservation of Nature, United Nations Environmental Program, and World Wildlife Fund, *Caring for the Earth: A Strategy for Sustainable Living* (Gland, Switzerland: IUCN/UNEP/WWF, 1991).

D. Macdonald, *The Politics of Pollution: Why Canadians Are Failing Their Environment* (Toronto: McClelland and Stewart, 1991).

Organisation for Economic Co-operation and Development, *Economic Instruments for Environmental Protection* (Paris: OECD, 1989).

D. Pearce, A. Markandya, and E. Barbier, *Blueprint for a Green Economy* (London: Earthscan Publications, 1989).

R. Repetto et al., *Wasting Assets: Natural Resources in the National Income Accounts* (Washington, DC: World Resources Institute, 1989).

J. Owen Saunders, ed., *The Legal Challenge of Sustainable Development* (Calgary: Canadian Institute of Resources Law, 1990).

T. Schrecker, *The Political Economy of Environmental Hazards* (Ottawa: Law Reform Commission of Canada, 1988).

K. Webb, *Pollution Control in Canada: The Regulatory Approach in the 1980's* (Ottawa: Law Reform Commission of Canada, 1988).

ENDNOTES

1   See, for example, H.V. Nelles, *The Politics of Development: Forests, Mines, and Hydro-Electric Power in Ontario 1849-1941* (Toronto: Macmillan Canada, 1974).

2   Externalities are defined by economists as the consequences of transactions that affect persons who did not participate in the transactions.

3   See A.R. Tussing, "Environmental Policy Issues: Market Failure in the Third Phase of Production," in G.B. Doern, ed., *The Environmental Imperative: Market Approaches to the Greening of Canada* (Toronto: C.D. Howe Institute, 1990), 56-57.

4   The most famous example of such behaviour is the 1949 Ontario *McKie et al. v. KVP Co. Ltd.* case and the subsequent *KVP Act* of the Ontario Legislature.

5   For a detailed development of this argument see T. Schrecker, "Of Invisible Beasts and the Public Interest: Environmental Cases and the Judicial System," in R. Boardman, ed., *Canadian Environmental Policy: Ecosystems, Politics, and Process* (Toronto: Oxford University Press, 1992), 83-105.

6   Lester Brown, *State of the World*, annual reports by the World Watch Institute (New York: W.W. Norton).

7   For a detailed discussion of this phenomenon, see C. Flavin, "The Heat Is On," in L.R. Brown, ed., *The World Watch Reader on Global Environmental Issues* (New York: W.W. Norton, 1991), 75-97.

8   World Commission on Environment and Development, *Our Common Future* (New York: Oxford University Press, 1987), 43.

9   See the National Task Force on Environment and Economy, *Report of the National Task Force on Environment and Economy* (Toronto: Canadian Council of Resource and Environment Ministers, 1987).

10 Supra endnote 8, at 227.

11 For an extensive discussion of the relationship between the environment and economy, the meaning of sustainable development, and the challenge to government producers and consumers in greening our economic system, see David Pearce, Anil Markandya, and Edward Barbier, *Blueprint for a Green Economy* (London: Earthscan Publications, 1989) and Francis Cairncross, *Costing the Earth* (London: Random Century House and The Economist Books Ltd., 1991). See also the thought-provoking book by Herman Daly and John Cobb, *For the Common Good* (Boston: Beacon Press, 1989).

12 See Canada, Environment Canada, *The State of Canada's Environment* (Ottawa: Supply and Services, 1991).

13 World Resources Institute, *World Resources: 1992-1993* (Washington, DC: World Resources Institute, 1992), 235. See also J. MacNeill, P. Winsemious, and T. Takushiji, *Beyond Interdependence: The Meshing of the World's Economy and the Earth's Ecology* (New York: Oxford University Press, 1991), especially chapter 2.

14 For a detailed discussion of the practice of "discounting," see *For the Common Good*, supra endnote 11, at 152-58.

15 On the effectiveness of fear of legal reprisal as a motivating force in corporate greening, see Addison and Mack, "Creating an Environmental Ethic in Corporate America: The Big Stick of Jail Time" (1991), Sw. LJ 1427 and Dianne Saxe, "The Impact of Prosecution upon Regulatory Compliance by Corporations" (1990), 1 JELP 91.

16   See, for example, D.P. Emond, "Environmental Law and Policy: A Retrospective Examination of the Canadian Experience," in I. Bernier and A. Lajoie, eds., *Consumer Protection, Environmental Law, and Corporate Power* (Toronto: University of Toronto Press, 1985), 123 and 135.

17   See, for example, Ontario, Ministry of the Environment, *Environmental Prosecutions in Ontario* (Toronto: the ministry, 1992).

18   *Environmental Assessment Act*, RSO 1990, c. E.18.

19   *Environmental Protection Act*, RSO 1990, c. E.19.

20   Canadian Bar Association, *Sustainable Development in Canada: Options for Law Reform* (Ottawa: CBA, 1990).

21   Economic instruments and their use are described more fully in: Organisation for Economic Co-operation and Development, *Economic Instruments for Environmental Protection* (Paris: OECD, 1989); Organisation for Economic Co-operation and Development, *Recent Developments in the Use of Economic Instruments for Environmental Protection in OECD Countries* (Paris: OECD, 1991); Organisation for Economic Co-operation and Development, *Guideline for the Application of Economic Instruments in Environmental Policy* (Paris: OECD, 1991); *The Environmental Imperative*, supra endnote 3; R.N. Stavins, *Project 88 — Round II, Incentives for Action: Designing Market-Based Environmental Strategies*, a public policy study sponsored by Senator Timothy Wirth, Colorado and John Heinz, Pennsylvania (Washington, DC, May 1991); J.A. Cassils, "Opportunities for Economic Instruments," prepared for the Ontario Round Table on the Environment and the Economy (February 1992).

22   See Organisation for Economic Co-operation and Development, "Guiding Principles Concerning International Economic Aspects of Environmental Policies," Council Recommendation C(72)128 (May 26, 1972).

23   See, for example, Tussing, supra endnote 3, at 62-63.

24   See, for example, G. Harder and L. Knox, "Implementing Variable Trash Collection Rates" (April 1992), *Biocycle*.

25   See Ontario, Ministry of Municipal Affairs and Ministry of the Environment, *Municipal Waste Management Powers in Ontario: A Discussion Paper* (Toronto: Queen's Printer, 1992).

26   See F. Cairncross, "Europe's Companies Reposition To Recycle" (March-April 1992), *Harvard Business Review* 34-45.

27   See Ontario, Ministry of the Environment, Waste Reduction Advisory Committee, *The Shared Model: A Stewardship Approach to Waste Management in Ontario* (Toronto: the ministry, 1992).

28   Under this program, the government subsidized the upgrading of production facilities provided that it was accompanied by improved pollution control. The actual costs of new pollution control equipment were also subsidized. See K. Webb, "Between Rocks and Hard Places: Bureaucrats, Law, and Pollution Control," in R. Paehlke and D. Torgerson, eds., *Managing Leviathan: Environmental Politics and the Administrative State* (Peterborough, Ont.: Broadview Press, 1990), 209-11.

29   Ibid.

30   See Ontario, Ministry of the Environment, *Towards a Sustainable Waste Management System* (Toronto: the ministry, 1990).

31 See *Beyond Interdependence*, supra endnote 13, at 34.

32 See, for example, J. Glenn, "The State of Garbage in America" (March-April 1992),
    Biocycle and Cairncross, supra endnote 26.

33 See *Blueprint for a Green Economy*, supra endnote 11, at 165.

34 *Recent Developments in the Use of Economic Instruments for Environmental Protec-*
    tion in OECD Countries, supra endnote 21.

35 See Canada, Environment Canada, *Economic Instruments of Environmental Protec-*
    tion (Ottawa: Supply and Services, 1992), 26-27.

36 See, for example, Tussing, supra endnote 3, at 76.

37 For examples of such proposals, see W.E. Block, ed., *Economics and the Environment:*
    A Reconciliation (Vancouver: The Fraser Institute, 1990).

38 Pollution Probe, *The Canadian Green Consumer Guide* (Toronto: McClelland and
    Stewart, 1989; rev. ed., 1991); Marjorie Lamb, *Two Minutes a Day for a Greener*
    Planet (Scarborough, Ont.: HarperCollins, 1991); Annie Berthold-Bond, *Clean and*
    Green: The Complete Guide to Environmentally Safe Housekeeping (Toronto: Ceres
    Press, 1990).

39 Francis Cairncross, "The Consumer, Green But Fickle," in *Costing the Earth*, supra
    endnote 11.

40 Quoted in "Brundtland's Legacy: Can Corporations Really Practice Environmental-
    ism While Fattening Their Profit Margins?" (September-October 1990), *Garbage* 60.

41 George Winter, *Business and the Environment* (Toronto: McGraw-Hill, 1988), a
    handbook of industrial ecology with 22 checklists for practical use.

42 Monica Campbell and William Glenn, *Profit from Pollution Prevention: A Guide to*
    Industrial Waste Reduction and Recycling (Toronto: Pollution Probe, 1982); Munroe,
    Glenn, et al., *Profit from Pollution Prevention* (Toronto: Pollution Probe, 1990).

43 See, for example, Michael E. Porter, "America's Green Strategy" (April 1991),
    Scientific American 168.

44 Ontario, Legislative Assembly, Bill 26, *Environmental Bill of Rights Act, 1993*, first
    reading May 31, 1993.

45 *Payne v. Kassab*, 312 A.2d 86, 11 Pa. Cmwlth. 14 (1973), aff'd. 323 A.2d 407, aff'd.
    361 A.2d 263, 468 Pa. Cmwlth. 226; *Borough of Moosic v. Pennsylvania Public Utility*
    Commn., 429 A.2d 1237, 59 Pa. Cmwlth. 338 (1981); *Com. Dept. of Environmental*
    Resources v. Precision Tube Co., Inc., 358 A.2d 137, 24 Pa. Cmwlth. 647 (1976).

46 Ontario Round Table on the Environment and the Economy, *Manufacturing Task*
    Force Report (Toronto: ORTEE, 1991).

47 Ontario Environmental Network, *Sustainability As If We Mean It* (Guelph, Ont.: OEN,
    1991).

PART I

Understanding Your Rights

1

How the Legal System Works

CONTENTS

If you like laws and sausages, you should never watch either one being made.

Otto von Bismarck

This book has two purposes:

1. to help you to understand what laws and policies exist to protect the environment, and how to use them effectively; and
2. to help you to understand where the legal framework for environmental protection is absent, incomplete, or otherwise inadequate so that you can work to obtain stronger laws and policies.

We hope to explain the law in clear and simple language, to "demystify" it and make it more accessible: to the ordinary citizen trying to persuade government officials to take action; to citizens trying to use the courts and environmental tribunals themselves; to environmental professionals such as engineers, biologists, and planners; and to lawyers who have limited familiarity with the rapidly expanding field of environmental law. Readers of past editions of this book have used it successfully to cut through bureaucratic red tape and solve environmental problems. By laying out the law as clearly as we can, and focusing on practical strategies for achieving results, we hope to reinforce your understanding that you can make a difference. If it was ever true that "you can't fight city hall," it isn't anymore. In fact, many of the citizens who became environmental activists 10 or 15 years ago by organizing their communities to fight polluting garbage dumps or destruction of farmland are now *in* city hall as elected officials and public servants.

Before we describe and analyze the specific laws and policies that affect our environmental quality, however, we want to introduce you to the political and legal context in which they are made. This introduction is mainly for people who have limited training in law or political science. Some readers may want to skip directly to the chapter or chapters that address specific environmental problems. For others, it may be useful to know what laws and policies are, how they are made, who makes them, and how they are administered or enforced.

To understand your environmental rights and the opportunities available to participate in government decisions that affect the environment, it is helpful to understand the general scheme of laws, policies, and government agencies that regulate Canada's environmental quality. Environmental laws are enforced by a complicated network of "departments," "ministries," "boards," "commissions," "agencies," and "tribunals" — generally referred to throughout this book as "departments," "agencies," or "tribunals." They span three levels and three branches of government, and administer or enforce a bewildering array of "laws," "regulations," "standards," "criteria," "objectives," "guidelines," and "policies."

Knowing something about the principles underlying this complex system will help you to find out whether there are laws or policies that apply to your concern, what tools they contain that are useful to you, who administers them, and how. It is much easier to participate in the decision-making process once you have figured out who the decision makers are, what decisions must be made on the way to a final decision on the development of environmentally harmful projects, and the legal and policy* constraints on those decision makers.

What Is a Law?

Most dictionaries will have a definition of law similar to the one in *Webster's New Collegiate Dictionary*, which defines law as a "rule of conduct or action prescribed or formally recognized as binding or enforced by a controlling authority." In a democracy, such as Canada, the only controlling authority that can validly make a binding rule that will be considered a "law" is a group of elected public officials, such as a legislature, Cabinet, or municipal council, or an agency to which the federal government or a provincial legislature has passed a law delegating law-making powers. For example, conservation authorities are agencies established by the Ontario government to protect the quality of water, provide parkland, and prevent flooding within a watershed. Each conservation authority consists of representatives of the provincial government and of each of the municipalities within a watershed. The *Conservation Authorities Act*[1] gives each of these agencies the power to make regulations governing the protection of the watershed.

Other authorities such as schools, universities, or employers can also make and enforce binding rules. For example, a university may have a rule against plagiarism, and its governing body may expel a student who cheats. This rule may be referred to as a "rule" or "regulation," but we usually reserve the term "law" for rules and regulations that are made by elected governments and enforced by agencies delegated by governments to make binding rules.

Making and enforcing strong environmental laws is only part of the fight to change our attitudes and conduct toward the environment. Such formal rules of conduct are not the only important tools to improve environmental quality. There are unwritten rules of social conduct that are just as important as laws, and often more important. These are often called "traditions," "customs," or "norms." These are patterns of conduct that you must follow, or risk rejection by others (the opposite is a "taboo" — something you dare not do for fear of rejection). Many traditions and taboos are even more effective in controlling conduct than formal laws. That is why it is so important to educate people about the importance of the environment and to change public attitudes toward consumption. Obviously, if reducing or recycling waste becomes second nature to people, or if it becomes socially unacceptable to smoke in confined areas where others are forced to inhale the fumes, this is better than having a law that says you must recycle or you must not smoke.

How Laws Regulate Conduct

Laws regulate our conduct in several ways: by taking away or restricting people's rights and freedoms, by creating new rights or expanding existing ones, by giving government the power to take action, by setting out the conditions under which government agencies can

---

* Policies are the internal rules and guidelines used by government agencies to guide their application and enforcement of the law. We discuss policies in more detail below.

carry out these activities and the procedures that must be followed, and by imposing duties, responsibilities, and obligations on people.

WHERE OUR RIGHTS AND FREEDOMS COME FROM

You may have been surprised that the first function of laws that we mentioned was to take away rights rather than confer them. We did this to emphasize that in a democratic society, the basic rule is that every individual has the right to do whatever he or she wants unless and until a valid law is passed restricting this conduct, even if the conduct interferes with others, destroys parts of the natural environment, or depletes non-renewable resources. Because we start from the premise that people have freedom, it is important that the government have the power to make laws that will create responsibilities and rights that balance the freedoms of individuals against the needs of society as a whole, regulate how these freedoms are used, and impose obligations that go with the freedoms. It is also important, however, to confine government powers to those granted by validly enacted laws,* and to make laws that limit how the government uses its powers, in order to prevent any erosion of our basic freedoms beyond what is necessary to protect the public welfare.

The government can restrict our freedoms, therefore, only by passing laws, not by arbitrary decisions that have not been approved by our elected representatives. However, except for certain fundamental freedoms described below, which can only be restricted to a limited degree, the elected representatives of the public can pass any laws within their authority to restrict these personal freedoms.

It is important to understand that laws are not the only source of rights and freedoms. In fact, laws may more often restrict rights and freedoms than create them. People are often shocked to learn that there is a right to pollute or, to turn this idea around, that there is no law absolutely prohibiting all pollution. If this seems unfair or ineffective, think of the alternatives. Would we be better off if we had no rights or freedoms except those granted by the government? Or if we had extensive rights and freedoms, but they could be taken away arbitrarily without the safeguards of a democratically elected body passing a law?

It is precisely because we have such freedom that we must work for laws that regulate our freedom, to prevent unwarranted or excessive interference with the rights and freedoms of others to enjoy a clean, attractive, healthy, and sustained environment.

WHAT ARE THE DIFFERENT KINDS OF LAWS, AND HOW ARE THEY MADE?

In Canada, we have two main bodies of law: the common law and statute law. There are substantial, and sometimes confusing, differences between the purpose and scope of these two bodies of law and how they are administered and enforced. Although this is an oversimplification, the common law can be described primarily as "private law" and statutes as "public law." Private law is intended primarily to be a tool for resolving disputes between

---

* That is, laws that have been enacted by the agency that has the jurisdiction to do so, following the correct procedures, and conforming with our constitution. The requirements for validity and constitutionality of laws are described below.

individuals (or companies) where the outcome is of concern primarily to them and not to society as a whole. Public law is made to address problems that have been recognized to have wider dimensions — for example, laws regulating the wholesomeness of food and drugs or consumer protection.

In reality, there is significant overlap between common law and statute law. Much of our common law has a public interest aspect, and a lot of our statutes are most often applied in the context of resolving disputes between individuals that are of little concern to society as a whole. However, the concepts of "public" and "private" law are useful because they help us understand differences in how the law is applied that don't make much sense otherwise.

For example, using common law I can sue someone for compensation for harming my health by discharging a pollutant. If I lose my law suit, I will have to pay him or her a substantial part of their legal costs. However, instead of suing the person for compensation, I can launch a prosecution for violation of a statute prohibiting the same pollution. If I win the case, I get no compensation, but the polluter must pay a fine to the government, and in some cases the court may also order him or her to stop polluting. If I lose, I do not have to pay any of that person's legal expenses.

Why is there a difference in the remedies available and in the financial consequences of losing? In the first case, I am considered to be enforcing my own private rights. In the second, I am deemed to be defending the rights of the public as a whole for the benefit of the public rather than my own self-interest.

Up to 20 years ago, most of the rights of citizens to prevent harm to the environment were found in common law. Today, most of the rights and responsibilities that were found in the common law, and many new ones, are enshrined in statutes. This shift from "private law" to "public law" reflects a fundamental change in society's values — a recognition of the importance of environmental protection to the public as a whole, not only to individuals who suffer direct harm to their health or their economic and property interests.

Common Law

Common law is the body of rules established by judges over the past centuries in the course of making decisions in disputes between people. The common law embodies important rights and principles relating to, among other things, environmental quality. These include principles such as: you may use your property in any way you please, as long as the use does not unduly interfere with your neighbours' use and enjoyment of their property or harm your neighbours' health.* These old rights and principles serve as "precedents" for future decision making. Judges are not free to make any reasonable decision, but must apply these established rights and principles to the cases they decide. Thus, present-day judicial decisions can modify these old principles only to a limited extent. When new principles to govern our conduct are needed, they must usually spring from laws made by our provincial legislatures or the federal Parliament. These bodies make laws called statutes, or acts. These statutes provide the authority for making and administering regulations, municipal bylaws, policies, guidelines, criteria, and objectives.

The most important areas of common law are *torts*, *contracts*, and *administrative law*.

---

* These common law rights and principles are discussed in greater detail in Chapter 6.

Torts

A tort is a civil injury or wrong that is recognized by the courts as falling within a category of improper conduct that warrants stopping the conduct from continuing or requiring the wrongdoer to pay compensation to the person who has been harmed, but does not warrant punishing the wrongdoer. The word "civil" is used to refer to private rights and remedies rather than criminal law, which is intended to reflect fundamental values held by the public as a whole and to protect the public from violent or dishonest conduct. Civil wrongs are different from criminal conduct in that a person who has had a tort inflicted upon him or her must initiate legal action to obtain compensation and sometimes an order (injunction) prohibiting the conduct from continuing, while the government will take legal action against criminal conduct and criminal proceedings result in punishment (although in recent years, the courts have been given more powers to impose other consequences of conviction for a criminal offence, such as ordering compensation or injunctions).

The torts that are most useful to protect you against environmental harm are described in Chapter 6.

Contracts

A contract is a written or oral promise by one person to provide goods or services to another, in return for a promise by the second person to provide something of value (usually money, but sometimes giving the first person some good or service). Once both have made their respective promises, they have an agreement called a "contract," which is legally binding. If either person fails to carry out his or her end of the bargain, the other can sue for compensation (called "damages" in legal jargon), and in some limited circumstances for an order to carry out the promise.

The difference between tort and contract is that in tort, the courts have decided what rights people have, while in contract, the parties to the contract determine what rights each of them has in the agreement itself. The law of contracts consists largely of determining when an agreement will be considered a contract, and rules for interpreting the contents of contracts where the words of the contract are subject to different interpretations.

The only people who can enforce a contract are the parties to the contract. If you are a citizen opposing the construction of a project, contract law will be less important to you than other areas of law, since you cannot require the developer to enter into a contract with others, such as his or her engineers and contractors, nor can you participate in the negotiation of the terms of their agreement or enforce the contract they have signed.

Contract law has, however, become a major part of environmental law in the past few years, for developers and those whom they hire to construct facilities, and for people who buy and sell land or businesses or loan money to companies that pollute. As the law has imposed much greater obligations and liabilities to prevent and clean up contamination of land, soil, and water, buyers and sellers of land and businesses, landlords and tenants, and borrowers and lenders of money are becoming much more careful about specifying in great detail in their contracts who will have responsibility for investigating whether soil and groundwater have been polluted and for preventing or paying for any environmental harm that occurs. Urea formaldehyde foam insulation (UFFI) is an example we are all familiar with. The standard real estate offer of purchase now contains a clause stating that the seller guarantees that the house is not insulated with urea formaldehyde. Similarly, purchasers and lenders now routinely require landowners to sign contracts guaranteeing that the land is not contaminated or that they will be responsible for removing all contaminated soil and treating contaminated groundwater. Such contracts provide a powerful incentive to prevent future contamination and to ensure that existing pollution is cleaned up.

Although most of the law governing contracts is common law, many statutes (see below) have been passed that modify and codify the common law rules. For example, to protect consumers, insurance laws and consumer protection laws often contain provisions that require that certain kinds of insurance policies and other contracts contain certain provisions, and that prohibit the inclusion of other kinds of provisions in the contract.

Administrative Law

The courts also have the power to supervise the actions of government departments and agencies. Administrative law is a body of law that requires these departments and agencies to act only within their "jurisdiction" (the powers conferred on them by law), and to exercise their powers in accordance with certain minimal rules of procedural fairness. The courts exercise their supervision through what is called "judicial review" of the actions taken by government officials, or their failure or refusal to act where the law requires them to. In a judicial review, the court decides whether a government agency is acting within its powers, according to law, and with fairness, reasonableness, or impartiality.

Upon receiving an application for judicial review, the court may grant orders:

- to compel a public official or tribunal to perform a duty that he, she, or it is required by statute to perform;
- to prohibit an official or tribunal whose decision may affect someone's rights from proceeding with a hearing unless he, she, or it has a clear right in law to make such a decision, and unless all procedures specified by relevant statutes and by the common law rules of "natural justice" or "fairness" are followed;
- to quash a decision or order already made by an official or tribunal if the decision was not arrived at properly; or
- to declare the conduct of the government or of officials to be contrary to the law; this "declaration" is an opinion given by the court and is not an order to do or cease to do any specific action; however, a declaration carries great moral weight, especially to governments, and is difficult to ignore.

Statutes or Acts, Regulations, and Bylaws

Although the common law is relatively frozen in time, our elected representatives in the provincial legislatures and federal Parliament are constantly passing new laws that add to, modify, or replace the common law, called "statutes" or "acts." The government leaves the enforcement of common law rights up to aggrieved individuals and simply provides them with a court system and a set of rules for using the courts. However, statutes, as public laws intended to regulate conduct in the public interest, are usually administered by the government. There are two basic types of statute: criminal laws and regulatory or public welfare statutes. Criminal laws *prohibit* conduct that is wrong or evil in and of itself, such as theft or murder. Regulatory or public welfare statutes *regulate* conduct that is socially acceptable and useful, but that must be regulated because of the risks it entails; this conduct includes various business activities such as banking, manufacturing, and buying and selling land. There is considerable debate about where pollution stands. Is it an inherently evil practice that should be governed by criminal laws? Or is it an unfortunate, but partly unavoidable, byproduct of legitimate business activities that should be regulated, rather than prohibited, under public welfare legislation?

Statutes set out the powers of government agencies and the rights and responsibilities of people in general terms. They provide the skeleton that often needs to be fleshed out through more detailed rules and procedures. Statutes generally contain provisions that authorize Cabinet to make "regulations," which will contain these detailed rules and specify the subject matter of these regulations. Any regulation that goes beyond what the statute authorizes is invalid.

Statutes also provide the basis for all bylaws passed by municipalities. Municipalities have no power to govern activities within their boundaries except by the authority given to them by the provincial government in statutes such as the *Municipal Act*.[2] This statute consists largely of a series of provisions that set out the kinds and scope of bylaws that municipalities may pass. Again, any municipal bylaw that is not provided for in a provincial statute will be invalid.

Regulations and municipal bylaws are often referred to as "subordinate legislation" since they owe their existence to statutes made by the two senior levels of government.

How Statutes, Regulations, and Bylaws Are Made and Come Into Effect

Statutes

When the Cabinet minister responsible for an area of public concern such as education, labour relations, or environmental protection decides that a new statute or an amendment to an existing statute is needed, the staff of his or her department and the staff of the Ministry of Justice or Attorney General, or both, draft the new law. After consideration by internal committees within the department and various committees of Cabinet, the minister will receive approval from Cabinet to introduce these provisions in the legislature or Parliament in the form of a "bill." The bill must receive three "readings" in the House and receive "royal assent." After the second "reading," there is an opportunity for all members of the House to debate the contents of the bill, to propose and vote on amendments, and possibly even to defeat all or parts of it. The bill may or may not be sent to a committee of legislators who will hear submissions from the public and propose amendments. The real opportunities to amend a bill are after first and second readings. Third reading consists of putting the bill before the House with any amendments made at the earlier stages of debate, with no further discussion. When it is read the third time, it is automatically given "royal assent," and is then considered "passed." It is now an "act."

Now it is law, but it still may not be binding on anyone. The law takes effect only when it is "proclaimed in force."* Unless the act stipulates otherwise, it comes into force upon

---

* An act is "proclaimed in force" nominally by the governor general of Canada, but actually by the federal Cabinet, if it is a law passed by Parliament, or by the lieutenant governor of the province (actually the provincial Cabinet) if it is a provincial law.

receiving royal assent, but Cabinet often leaves itself an escape hatch by inserting into the bill a provision that it will come into effect at a specific date set out in the bill, or "upon proclamation."

After a law is passed, it may not be proclaimed for years if it proves difficult or costly to implement, if government priorities change, or if it is unpopular with some powerful segment of society. For environmentalists, this means that the fight to get a law passed must be looked at as only the first battle in a long war. Just as the affected industries will continue to lobby against proclamation of an act, environmentalists must be prepared to continue to press for proclamation.

Long delays in implementing new environmental laws are not uncommon. Canada's *Nuclear Liability Act*[3] was passed in 1970 but not proclaimed until 1976. It took six years and a change of government for Ontario's "spills bill" (part X of the *Environmental Protection Act*[4]) to be proclaimed.

Regulations

Governments have other methods of delaying the implementation of statutes even after they are proclaimed. One way is to fail to make any regulations. As mentioned above, regulations are the flesh to the skeletal statutes. Many statutes consist largely of a list of powers to make regulations, and are useless without them. For instance, Ontario's *Endangered Species Act*[5] makes it an offence to kill any animal, bird, fish, or plant of a species that the regulations designate as endangered. It took the government 2 years to designate any species as endangered, and after 21 years only 20 species of animals and plants had been designated by the regulations, although many others were in danger of extinction. The *Canadian Environmental Protection Act*[6] imposes strict limits on the importation, manufacture, distribution, and disposal of chemicals designated by regulation as toxic. However, of the thousands of substances known to be hazardous, only a handful are designated by the regulations.

Like statutes, regulations are prepared by civil servants, often in closed-door consultation with the regulated industry, and rarely in consultation with the affected public or public interest groups that represent them. Regulations are approved by Cabinet. Unlike statutes, they do not pass through Parliament or the provincial legislature, where MPs and MPPs* can criticize them and propose amendments. So the final version reflects only the views of the party in power, not the views of the opposition parties or the general population. Only occasionally does a statute provide that the government must give the public notice of a proposed regulation, and an opportunity to comment on it, before making it law. Even more rarely, a government agency will adopt a policy of giving public notice of particularly significant proposed regulations even though the law does not require this.

Municipal Bylaws

Municipal councils may authorize actions in only two ways: by passing bylaws and by passing resolutions. Bylaws authorize action generally. Resolutions instruct municipal staff to carry out specific actions that have been generally authorized. For example, a bylaw may

---

* Members of provincial Parliament, known in some provinces as MLAs (members of the Legislative Assembly), and in Quebec as members of the National Assembly.

authorize the municipal council to give names to new roads. The naming of each new road may be done by passing a resolution.

Municipal bylaws are passed in a manner that is similar to the way statutes are passed. Municipal civil servants draft a bill that is introduced and debated, and possibly amended, by the council at a council meeting. These meetings are open to the public to give them an opportunity to observe and sometimes to make submissions. Before reaching the council meeting, the bill may also be debated by committees of the council members, particularly in larger cities, and members of the public sometimes also have a chance to make submissions at those committees.

Policies, Guidelines, Criteria, Objectives, Etc.

To make matters even more confusing, many of the rules that industries, government agency staff, and ordinary people are expected to follow are not found in statutes, regulations, or bylaws that are passed by legislators, accessible to the public, and legally binding. They are located in government policies, guidelines, objectives, and criteria, which we will refer to collectively as "policies."

These policies are the very backbone of our regulatory system, because they govern how agencies will interpret, administer, and enforce the laws, and determine how agencies will exercise the broad discretion often granted to them by the law. Policies are necessary to provide the flexibility that rules often lack when they are cast in concrete, as laws are, and to guide the exercise of administrative discretion. Yet they often receive no consent from any elected official. They are often secret — there is no requirement that the politicians or bureaucrats tell the public, or even each other, what their policies are. These policies are not always collected, even within a large agency, in one place — sometimes the agency does not even have a list of all its policies.

It is not uncommon to find that agencies have policies that conflict with each other, or that civil servants responsible for administering laws are unaware of the policies they are supposed to follow. One of the dangers of such policies, because they are not binding, and especially when they are kept secret, is that they will be applied inconsistently, and that they will be easily changed or ignored when an official finds them inconvenient. The opposite problem occurs when officials approve or refuse to approve projects on the basis of draft policies that have no formal approval and may be based on incomplete or inaccurate information. This is a problem particularly because it is not unusual for government agencies to take several years to finalize policies. Ontario's Ministry of Agriculture and Food, for example, has been working on amendments to its Code of Agricultural Practice for about a decade, and at any time during that period, ministry officials would always advise the public that amendments were expected "any time now."

It is difficult to determine government policy because there is no one way to indicate that something is policy, and no single place to look for policy.

Although some policies are expressed in regulations, such as Ontario's ambient air quality criteria, more often they are found in pamphlets published by the government agency and disseminated to the public. Sometimes they are announced in press releases. Other times they are found only in a speech by a Cabinet minister. Often, the policies are found only in internal directives. Although these directives are not publicized, sometimes it is the agency's practice or policy to give out the document to anyone lucky or expert enough to find out about it. Sometimes, however, the agency will not give out policy documents.

One way of avoiding the release of policy documents to the public is to call them "procedures" or "practices" rather than "policies." In Ontario, for example, the government passed a statute in 1989 that takes away the right of residents bothered by noise, dust, and odours to sue neighbouring farmers. These residents must now either rely on the Ministry of Environment and Energy (MEE) to prosecute for violation of the *Environmental Protection Act*,[7] or take their concerns before a tribunal of farmers appointed by the minister of agriculture, aptly named the Farm Practices Protection Board. As a result, it is particularly important for such neighbours to know how the MEE will treat requests to prosecute farmers for polluting, and how it coordinates its investigation with the Ministry of Agriculture, which has often refused to cooperate with MEE in the past. However, in preparing this book, when we requested the government to provide us with a copy of the protocol governing how the two ministries would cooperate in such investigations, the government refused to provide it, because "it is an internal set of practices."

DISCRETION

Many laws deliberately leave officials with wide latitude in how to administer the law, and whether to enforce it at all. This latitude is called "discretion." Of even greater concern than vague, contradictory, or unfollowed policies, therefore, is the failure to make policies at all. Because broad discretion is such a common characteristic of environmental laws, it is important that there be policies to guide the exercise of that discretion. Thus, in evaluating the effectiveness of environmental laws, one of the questions you will ask is: "How much discretion does the law leave to officials?" If the answer is: "A great deal," you must try to uncover the policies that govern how this discretion should be exercised or press for the development of such policies.

WHO MAKES THE IMPORTANT DECISIONS?

The Three Branches of Government

As we have seen, there are effectively three levels of government: federal, provincial, and municipal. Each of these levels has "branches." The federal and provincial governments have three branches: the "legislative," the "executive," and the "judicial."

Municipal governments have only a legislative and an executive branch. Municipal bylaws are interpreted and enforced by judges of the judicial branches of the two senior levels of government.

The Legislative Branch

Elected representatives, whether in the federal Parliament, the provincial legislatures, or the municipal councils, make up the *legislative* branch. As we have seen, this branch passes statutes or, at the municipal level, bylaws.

The Executive Branch

The second branch of government is the *executive*, which consists of the federal or provincial Cabinet, the executive committees or boards of control of municipal councils,* and the staff of many thousands of civil servants that report to them. This branch administers the laws that the legislative branch passes (and in the case of the federal and provincial Cabinets, also makes the regulations that implement the statutes, a function that seems more logically to be legislative). The executive is the branch of government that is most intimately responsible for the implementation and observance of our laws.

You will note that Cabinets and executive committees are chosen from among elected representatives. In theory, this keeps the people who carry out the laws, as well as the people who make them, responsible to *you*. However, these executive groups are merely the tip of the iceberg. They are assisted by thousands of civil servants and members of appointed agencies, boards, and tribunals — one of the country's largest work forces — who are *not* directly responsible to the citizen. The "real" executive branch is the civil service, a vast system of bureaucracy over which the small executive groups have only nominal control.

The executive branch is divided into two major groups: the departments and "ABCs." At the core of the civil service are the departments (in the Ontario government called "ministries") that report to a Cabinet minister or, in the case of municipal governments, directly to the municipal council. The "ABCs" — agencies, boards, and commissions — report through a Cabinet minister to the Legislature as a whole. (We will generally call these ABCs "agencies." Agencies that hold court-like hearings we will call "tribunals.")

Until the 1950s and 1960s, most of the work of the executive branch was carried out by the government departments. As society became more complex, however, the business of legislating, administering, and enforcing laws and policies did as well. Therefore, agencies proliferated, supplementing the work of the departments.

In 1989, there were at least 1,500 agencies in Canada, of which at least 580 were agencies of the Ontario government.[8] Some agencies give advice to Cabinet, to individual Cabinet ministers, or to the Legislature as a whole. Others operate a business or program, and still others make decisions (the Ontario government refers to the latter as regulatory or administrative agencies). Of the 580-plus agencies of the Ontario government, the government has categorized 91 of them as regulatory.[9] As Robert Macauley points out, however, in his report analyzing the functions and effectiveness of these agencies, even the term "regulatory" is an oversimplification: the functions of the agencies may include administering, legislating, adjudicating, and regulating.[10]

Depending on the nature of the agency and the terms of the statute that creates it, agency members and staff may be part of the regular civil service or they may be political appointees. The members of quasi-judicial tribunals are often political appointees and are often not subject to any rigorous method of "quality control" or performance appraisal.

The existence of these agencies is important to environmental advocates, since they tend to be somewhat more visible and open than government departments. They often provide opportunities for public involvement in government decision making that are not available

---

* Members of this group, the actual title of which varies from city to city, are a select few of the municipal councillors. Boards of control are elected directly, whereas executive committees are chosen by all the councillors from among themselves. The two bodies have the same executive functions.

through departments, particularly when their role includes holding public hearings or adjudicating disputes. They often have a greater degree of independence from politicians and political considerations than do department staff, and operate to a greater or lesser degree at arm's length from the departments and the politicians.

The adjudicative function of such agencies is particularly important to environmental advocates. Tribunals such as the Environmental Assessment Board and the Ontario Municipal Board provide an opportunity for extensive public hearings before significant projects are approved. Robert Macauley lists 17 advantages of regulating through agencies. Two of them are particularly important in the environmental context: "Agencies offer an inexpensive alternative to the very high cost of gaining access to the courts to enforce rights that fall within the administrative area," and agencies are "a very manageable forum for public participation, which is one of the corner-stones of open government."[11]

As Macauley warns, however, and as experienced environmental activists found out long ago, although some agencies are more independent and receptive to the public than the departments, this varies greatly, and there are continual pressures on agencies that mitigate against their full independence and impartiality: "A high degree of ambivalence exists because on the one hand, the agencies are fed, financed, supported and appointed through the Ministries, while on the other hand, they are perceived by some to be 'independent' of the Ministries. Still others see agencies as extensions of Ministries."[12]

The Judicial Branch

The third branch of government is the judiciary. The judiciary consists of the courts and judges that decide whether someone has broken the law and, if so, what punishment to impose, what compensation must be paid, or what other action the violator must take. As we mentioned earlier, the judiciary in some cases can even decide whether the government itself has broken its own laws. The judiciary therefore provides an important protection for the citizen. In addition, since the passage of the *Canadian Charter Rights and Freedoms*[13] in 1983, the courts can strike down any law that offends people's fundamental rights and freedoms as set out in the *Charter*, and grant a wide range of remedies for infringement of those rights.

In making these decisions, the courts often have occasion to interpret what the law means and whether it applies to a particular situation. This gives judges great power: they can interpret the law broadly and cover a wide variety of situations, or they can apply the law so narrowly that it abridges our rights.

The most important characteristic of the judiciary is its independence. The courts are independent and impartial. Judges have "tenure." They can be removed from their office only for flagrant misbehaviour, such as imprisoning a lawyer or witness because they disapprove of something he or she said (as happened twice in Ontario in 1989), but not because the government or some other powerful segment of society dislikes the way they decided a case. It has often been said that the courts are the only place where the little guy and big government or big business can meet as equals.

In this sense, courts are different from the tribunals in the executive branch that perform functions similar to courts. Most of the members of these quasi-judicial tribunals are appointed for a relatively brief fixed term (often two or three years) or "at pleasure" (which means that if a tribunal member's decision displeases the minister, he or she can be fired at the stroke of a pen). This lack of tenure reduces the independence of members of tribunals, because they may feel that they must please the government to keep their jobs. (On the other hand, the security of tenure of judges is notorious for contributing to "judge-itis": some judges become lazy, rude, arrogant, and tyrannical).

Apart from the question of security of tenure, another important factor that affects the quality of both judges and agency members is the method of choosing them. The public has been very concerned for many years about the possibility that judges and agency members may be selected primarily on the basis of political patronage rather than merit. Indeed, there is ample evidence that to a greater or lesser extent the pork barrel has always been deep and full throughout Canada.

Both judges and agency members have been largely selected in the past from a relatively narrow segment of society: the WASP business community and its professional advisers. In the past, many judges and agency appointees, before being appointed to the bench or a tribunal, had spent their careers protecting the interests of corporations and government rather than the victims of corporate or government action (or inaction). Their collective objectivity may be impaired by the kind of constraints that familiarity and close dealing tend to breed. Although this background may not destroy all objectivity, it can give the bench and administrative tribunals a tendency to exhibit what might be described as a curious neutrality-in-favour-of-the-establishment-interests.[14]

We are extremely pleased to be able to say in this edition of *Environment on Trial* that both the Liberal and the NDP governments of Ontario have gone to great lengths to open up the appointment of agency members and provincially appointed judges to people of a much wider range of backgrounds than in past. In the environmental field, for example, environmental activists have been appointed members of the Environmental Compensation Corporation, the Environmental Assessment Board, the Environmental Assessment Advisory Committee, and the Environmental Appeal Board. A broadly representative public advisory committee has been established to recommend judicial appointments to the provincial attorney general. The results of this process have been dramatic. "Storefront" lawyers and other lawyers whose careers have been devoted to defending the rights of minorities and the poor have been made judges. However, a federal change in the method of selecting judges, touted by the government as opening up the selection of federally appointed judges, has created only an appearance of change.

THE DIVISION OF POWERS: THE CONSTITUTIONAL FRAMEWORK

For a law to be valid, it must conform to Canada's constitution. The constitution is the supreme law of the land that sets out the most fundamental principles of government, and it can be changed only with a high degree of consensus among the 10 provincial governments and the federal government. Because the constitution gives each level of government the exclusive right to pass certain kinds of laws, any law passed by the "wrong" level of government is invalid and will be struck down. The distribution of powers between the federal government and the provincial governments, therefore, is crucial in determining whether laws will be passed and upheld as valid. A second restraint that the constitution places on the power to make laws is that the laws must not infringe certain basic personal rights and freedoms. Any law that interferes with these "civil liberties" to a greater extent than is necessary to protect the public may be struck down as unconstitutional. We discuss these two aspects of "constitutionality" below.

The Levels of Government and Their Jurisdiction Under the Constitution

Canada was established in 1867 by the *British North America Act* (renamed the *Constitution Act, 1867* in 1981 when a "charter of rights" was added to it and ownership of natural resources was clarified).[15] The *Constitution Act, 1867* created a "Confederation" — a union of individual political communities, each of which had its own government prior to Confederation. The *Constitution Act, 1867* established a central or "federal" government and a Supreme Court of Canada, which could decide appeals from the courts of all provinces and whose rulings would be binding on all courts throughout Canada. However, each of the original partners in Confederation, the provinces, kept its own government and its own courts, whose rulings were binding only within the province.

The Fathers of Confederation made a list of the powers they thought would be required to run a country, and, through negotiations, they divided these powers between the federal government and the provincial governments. The *Constitution Act, 1867* apportions the power to make, enforce, and administer laws for Canada between these two levels of government.

The federal government and the provincial governments each are granted exclusive control over specific matters. Broadly speaking, the federal government has the legal authority to make laws concerning matters that were considered to be national in scope at the time of Confederation, such as navigation and shipping, interprovincial and international trade and commerce, banking, and seacoast and inland fisheries. Matters that were thought to be of a merely local or private nature, such as the control of natural resources, the regulation of property, and most business activities, were placed within provincial legislative competence.

As we indicated above, a municipality is a specialized type of corporation that is granted power by the government of the province in which it is located to pass legislation known as bylaws, which deal with local matters within its own boundaries. Created by the province, municipalities have no jurisdiction, responsibilities, or powers except those that are granted expressly by provincial statutes or that can be implied from them. Municipal powers, such as the power to pass bylaws, are not set out in the *Constitution Act, 1867*. They are *delegated* to the municipalities by the province. This means that these powers can be expanded or contracted at the will of the province.

In the environmental field, for example, for many years the *Municipal Act*[16] gave Ontario municipalities the primary responsibility and authority for providing sewage treatment and garbage collection and for regulating noise and air pollution, and responsibility for many land-use planning matters within their own boundaries. However, as it became apparent that many municipalities were unable or unwilling to carry out these responsibilities effectively and as public demand for stricter standards grew, the provincial government, which originally granted these powers, took many of them back in the late 1960s and early 1970s. Now the provincial government's role in controlling air and noise pollution, noise control, regulating waste disposal, and providing sewage treatment facilities has expanded, while the role of the municipalities has contracted. However, since the provincial departments have found that they have bitten off more than they can chew, there are now numerous initiatives to give back some of these responsibilities to the municipalities, who have no choice but to accept them if the province demands it, even if they have insufficient resources to carry out these responsibilities.

The role of municipalities will be described in greater detail in Chapter 2 and Chapter 15.

The Canadian Charter of Rights and Freedoms

Until 1981, the Canadian constitution, unlike the American constitution, did not contain a "bill of rights." When Canadian courts considered whether a law was constitutional, they did not decide whether it infringed people's fundamental rights and freedoms, such as freedom of speech, religion, and association. A law could not be ruled invalid solely because it violated these traditional rights. The courts were solely concerned with whether the law was passed by the "right" level of government. If they decided that a statute passed by a province could only be passed by the federal government, they would strike it down, no matter how useful it might be. Conversely, if the law was passed by the right level of government, the courts would uphold it no matter how oppressive it was. Most often, it was not one level of government complaining to the court that the other level's law should be struck down, but the person being sued or prosecuted. This person's real interest was not to determine the law's validity, but to protect his or her operations from obligations imposed by the law, or to prevent punishment for activities that everyone might agree were wrong.

The *Canadian Charter of Rights and Freedoms* guarantees all Canadians certain fundamental freedoms, democratic rights, mobility rights, legal rights, equality rights, and language rights.

1. The *fundamental freedoms* are:

    (a) freedom of conscience and religion; and
    (b) freedom of thought, belief, opinion, and expression (what we commonly think of as "freedom of speech"), including:

        (i) freedom of the press,
        (ii) freedom of peaceful assembly, and
        (iii) freedom of association.

2. The *democratic rights* ensure that the federal Parliament and provincial legislatures will sit at least once a year and will call an election at least once every five years, and guarantee all citizens the right to vote and to run for election.
3. The *mobility rights* guarantee all citizens the right to live and work in the province or territory of their choice.
4. The *legal rights* guarantee:

    (a) the right to life, liberty, and security of the person, and the right not to be deprived of these rights except in accordance with the principles of "fundamental justice";
    (b) security against unreasonable search and seizure by police, government inspectors and investigators, and other government officials;

(c) the right not to be arbitrarily detained or imprisoned;

(d) the right of anyone detained or arrested to be informed promptly of the reasons for the arrest or detention and to talk to a lawyer without delay; and

(e) the right of anyone charged with an offence to be informed of the nature of the alleged offence, to a trial within a reasonable time, not to testify against himself or herself, to be presumed innocent until proven guilty, to a fair trial before an independent and impartial court, not to be subjected to any cruel and unusual treatment or punishment, and to have an interpreter at the trial.

5. *Equality rights* guarantee everyone equal protection and equal benefit of the law and prohibit discrimination on the basis of race, national or ethnic origin, colour, religion, sex, age, mental or physical disabilities, or characteristics that are analogous to these relatively fixed and immutable personal qualities.

The *Charter* also provides that the guarantee of these rights and freedoms is not to be interpreted to restrict the aboriginal, treaty, and other rights of Canada's native peoples.

The rights guaranteed by the *Charter* are not absolute, however. The *Charter* allows the courts to balance these individual civil liberties against the collective rights of the public as a whole. If a law, or the way the government is applying the law, offends these fundamental rights, it may still be upheld, but only if the government can demonstrate that the intrusion is justified in a free and democratic society. This puts the onus on the government to demonstrate that the purpose of the restrictions on liberty is important for the benefit of the community, and that this intrusion is no greater than is necessary to achieve this social benefit.

How the legal principles discussed throughout this chapter apply to the environment is discussed in Chapter 2.

John Swaigen

FURTHER READING

G. Bruce Doern and Richard B. Phidd, eds., *Canadian Public Policy: Ideas, Structure, Process* (Scarborough, Ont.: Nelson Canada, 1992).

Patrick Fitzgerald, *This Law of Ours* (Toronto: Prentice-Hall, 1977).

Michael Howelett and M. Ramesh, *The Political Economy of Canada* (Toronto: McClelland and Stewart, 1992).

Winfield Holmes Jennings and Thomas G. Zuber, *Canadian Law*, 5th ed. (Toronto: McGraw-Hill Ryerson, 1991).

Kenneth Kernaghan and David Siegel, eds., *Public Administration in Canada: A Text* (Scarborough, Ont.: Nelson Canada, 1991).

A. Paul Pross, *Group Politics and Public Policy* (Toronto: Oxford University Press, 1992).

Steven N. Spetz, *Take Notice: An Introduction to Canadian Law*, 3d ed. (Toronto: Copp Clark Pitman, 1989).

C.R. Tindal, *You and Your Local Government* (Toronto: Ontario Municipal Management Development Board, 1982).

G. White, ed., *Government and Politics of Ontario* (Scarborough, Ont.: Nelson Canada, 1990).

Michael Whittington and Glen Williams, eds., *Canadian Politics in the 1990s* (Scarborough, Ont.: Nelson Canada, 1990).

ENDNOTES

1   *Conservation Authorities Act*, RSO 1990, c. C.27.
2   *Municipal Act*, RSO 1990, c. M.45.
3   *Nuclear Liability Act*, RSC 1985, c. N-28.
4   *Environmental Protection Act*, RSO 1990, c. E.19.
5   *Endangered Species Act*, RSO 1990, c. E.15.
6   *Canadian Environmental Protection Act*, RSC 1985, c. 16 (4th Supp.), first enacted as SC 1988, c. 22.
7   *Environmental Protection Act*, supra endnote 4.
8   Robert J. Macauley, *Directions: Review of Ontario's Regulatory Agencies Report* (Toronto: Queen's Printer, September 1989), 1–1.
9   Ibid., at 1–2 and 2–6.
10 Ibid., at 2–6.
11 Ibid., at 2–10.
12 Ibid., at 8–50.
13 *Canadian Charter of Rights and Freedoms*, Part I of the *Constitution Act, 1982*, RSC 1985, app. II, no. 44.
14 We have paraphrased former American Chief Justice Warren Berger when he criticized the bias of an administrative agency. See Joseph L. Sax, *Defending the Environment: A Strategy for Citizen Action* (New York: Knopf, 1971), 134.
15 *British North America Act*, 30 & 31 Vict., c. 3 (UK), since renamed the *Constitution Act, 1867*.
16 *Municipal Act*, supra endnote 2.

2

The Framework for Protecting Ontario's Environment

CONTENTS

All right!! Confederation through at six o'clock this evening — constitution adopted — a creditable document — a complete reform to the abuses and injustices we've complained of.

George Brown, 1867, in a note to his wife

The consequence of these federal-provincial and interdepartmental divisions in responsibility for environmental matters is a patchwork that makes it almost impossible to assign public accountability for safeguarding Canada's environment. There is no focal point of responsibility or accountability to the Canadian people in respect of this crucial issue.

Auditor general of Canada, 1990

In this chapter, we will try to apply the general information from Chapter 1 to the process of regulating activities harmful to the environment. We will give you an overview of the laws and agencies involved in environmental protection in Ontario.

THE DIVISION OF POWER TO MAKE LAWS TO PROTECT THE ENVIRONMENT

Here, we will try to give you a general picture of which level of government is responsible for dealing with which environmental problem, although the answer is not always clear. You will find that there is a great deal of confusion and buck-passing in the enforcement of environmental laws as a result of the division of powers between the federal and provincial governments in the *Constitution Act, 1867*,[1] between the province and its municipalities in provincial legislation, and between different departments of the same government, where they have overlapping mandates.

The constitution, based as it is on political negotiations reflecting the problems and concerns of government leaders in 1867, obviously makes no reference to the environment. Nowhere is pollution mentioned. And of course there is no reference to such modern developments as nuclear energy, automobiles, aircraft, and biotechnology, or to many other concerns of environmentalists today.

Accordingly, when a government decides whether it has the power to pass a law regulating these kinds of activities, and when a court looks at that law to decide whether it is valid, they look at the list of powers given to both levels of government, and see which subject matter the environmental concern fits into most neatly — a process that often resembles trying to fit square pegs into round holes.

Federal Powers

Some of the exclusive federal powers that provide a basis for the federal government to pass environmental protection laws are the power:

- to regulate international and interprovincial trade and commerce;
- to regulate navigation and shipping;
- to regulate seacoast and inland fisheries;
- to impose taxes and to spend money raised by taxation in any way the federal government chooses, as long as the spending does not interfere with provincial jurisdiction;
- to make criminal laws (which has been interpreted as a power to protect public health); and
- to regulate works or undertakings that are interprovincial or international in nature (for example, shipping, railways, telegraphs, and interprovincial pipelines) and works that, although they are wholly situated in one province, are declared by Parliament to be for the general advantage of Canada (for example, grain elevators in the prairies and nuclear power plants throughout Canada).

In addition to these specific powers, the federal government has the general power to make laws for the "peace, order, and good government of Canada." This has been interpreted as a power to make laws that would otherwise be within the exclusive realm of the provincial governments when a problem usually considered to be local in nature has become so severe that it has achieved a "national dimension." (Examples include legislation to prohibit drinking alcohol in the 1920s and anti-inflation legislation in the 1970s.) This doctrine has been used once to uphold a federal environmental law that would normally be within the exclusive jurisdiction of a province.[2]

Provincial Powers

Exclusive powers of the province that have been used to support provincial environmental laws include:

- control of natural resources (except uranium, which is under federal control);
- the management and sale of public lands belonging to the province and timber and wood on these lands;
- the establishment and control of municipal institutions in the province;
- power over property and civil rights within the province (civil rights in this context include the right to make contracts and carry on businesses — obviously a far-reaching power); and
- generally, power over all matters of a merely local or private nature in the province.

Joint Powers

There are other matters that are within the competence of *both* levels of government under the *Constitution Act, 1867* — agriculture, for example. The treaty power gives Ottawa the right to sign treaties with other countries; but legislation that would make the treaty effective within the province must be passed by the provincial legislature if the subject matter of the treaty is otherwise within provincial jurisdiction.

SLICING UP THE ENVIRONMENTAL PIE

The constitutional division of powers has created many problems for environmentalists. For example, deciding whether a matter of environmental concern is exclusively within the power of the federal government, exclusively within the power of the provinces, or shared by both, is often very difficult. There has been no agreement on who has the constitutional jurisdiction to control pollution in the country as a whole. All who have written on the subject agree that both governments have significant powers to prevent and limit activities harmful to the environment, but there is considerable variance in opinion as to the scope of the federal and provincial roles.[3]

Thus, when constitutional problems of an environmental nature arise, ways have to be found to apply the wording of our 126-year-old constitution to the new situation. It is not always an easy task, nor is the result always satisfactory.[4] It is not possible simply to take the two lists, federal and provincial, and then to place every government function relating to environmental management in one list or the other. In reality, there is an interdependence of federal and provincial functions, which can be used by both levels of government to cooperate in controlling pollution and other harm to the environment. It can also be used by one level or the other to avoid taking responsibility. Or, as mentioned, it can be used by polluters to try to prevent either level of government from acting. Some of the ways in which this interdependence works are described below.

Overlapping Jurisdictions

The generality of some of the language used in the *Constitution Act, 1867* to describe federal and provincial powers has meant that many problems fall within both federal and provincial competence. In fact, most problems that arise from 20th-century conditions are likely to involve both jurisdictions. The general rule is that where overlapping jurisdictions exist, both levels of government are free to deal with the matter. If, however, federal and provincial laws dealing with the same problem conflict with each other, the federal law takes priority, and the provincial law is regarded as invalid to the extent of the conflict.[5]

Thus, if both levels of government have jurisdiction to deal with a problem and the federal government does not act, the provincial government may pass a law that will be valid until the federal government passes a law that is inconsistent with it.

Another aspect of overlapping jurisdictions is that there may well be overlapping — and different — sets of standards. Some judges have said that in a situation where *both* jurisdictions can make laws, provincial laws may validly require stricter standards for environmental protection than those found in the federal legislation.[6]

Provincial legislation and municipal bylaws covering the same subject matter may also coexist. The general rule is the same as the one governing conflicts between federal and provincial laws: as long as a provincial statute such as the *Planning Act*[7] or the *Municipal Act*[8] has given the municipality the power to pass bylaws governing an area of concern, municipal bylaws that overlap provincial responsibilities will generally be valid as long as they provide for standards of environmental quality that are as high as the provincial acts or higher. To the extent that they provide lower standards, they will be invalid.[9]

However, the levels of government will often use the overlap to shift responsibility for action to each other. Sometimes they will deny there is any overlap, claiming that the matter is solely the responsibility of the other. When the fish in the English-Wabigoon river system were discovered to be contaminated with mercury in 1969, for example, the natives of the White Dog and Grassy Narrows reserves demanded that the rivers be closed to all fishing. For years, however, the federal government continued to claim that this was the responsibility of the province, while the Ontario government claimed that this was up to the federal government.

A similar problem occurs when both levels of government claim jurisdiction. Often, rather than cause a confrontation with the other level, the government seeking to regulate will withdraw its regulation under pressure from the other level of government. For example, when the federal government introduced new legislation in 1977 to replace the outmoded *Atomic Energy Control Act*,[10] the provinces argued that the legislation impinged on aspects of provincial jurisdiction. Rather than reduce the scope of the legislation to keep it within areas that were clearly federal, the government withdrew the entire statute, leaving the public more than a decade later with an act the government had admitted was no longer adequate. (See Chapter 21, "Radiation.")

Delegation of Power

It is possible in some circumstances for the federal and provincial governments to delegate their functions to each other. The courts have held that although one level of government may not make a direct, formal delegation of its powers to make laws to the Parliament or legislature of the other,[11] one government may delegate other powers to the subordinate agencies of the other.[12] For example, the federal government cannot give Ontario the power to pass legislation regulating fisheries, but it can, and does, validly delegate its power to enforce the federal *Fisheries Act*[13] to the Ontario Ministry of Natural Resources.

This kind of delegation makes it possible, with federal-provincial cooperation, to overcome many of the constitutional obstacles to the creation of sound environmental management programs.

The Spending Power

As stated above, although the federal government may not directly regulate many matters under provincial responsibility, there is nothing to stop it from spending the money it raises through taxation on research, pilot projects, and other assistance to provincial environmental management programs. For instance, although the federal government has no jurisdiction to regulate the installation, maintenance, inspection, and removal of underground tanks containing petroleum products that may spill or leak into the ground, Environment Canada has taken a leadership role in preventing such leaks by commissioning research into methods of preventing leaks and by drafting an "environmental code of practice" — a model law that can be passed by provincial governments.[14] The federal spending power has been described as "a genteel form of blackmail,"[15] because the federal government can persuade the provinces to implement new programs within provincial jurisdiction or modify how they carry out provincial programs by offering money to support those programs, subject to terms and conditions set by the federal government.

The provincial governments have similarly broad spending powers, which they can use to tackle problems under federal jurisdiction.

Interjurisdictional Immunity

Probably the least satisfactory feature of the present constitutional arrangement, according to one authority on constitutional aspects of environmental law,[16] is the immunity from provincial legislation that the courts have accorded to the federal government and to enterprises under its jurisdiction. If provincial environmental laws cannot be enforced against federal polluters, it is crucial that the federal government pass equally stringent laws that can validly regulate its own officials and enterprises such as aircraft, airports, and interprovincial trucking companies. Otherwise, there is a huge gap in protection of the public.

But as one author noted:

> There are many areas of environmental law in which the federal government has no adequate controls. For example, the federal government, its agents and servants, own thousands of properties across the country, many of which may be contaminated. Yet there is no effective federal legislation with which such properties may be identified and cleaned up. No federal legislation requires the federal Crown, its agents or servants, to report or to clean up spills which contaminate soil, nor to compensate those who suffer damages as a result, except in a few very limited cases.
>
> Nor is there effective federal legislation to require federal agents and servants to practise proper waste disposal. No Act requires federal agents and servants to deposit their wastes in licensed sites, to use licensed carriers when disposing of them, nor to use special sites for hazardous wastes or manifests to track them. Some, like the armed forces base in Trenton, are reported to use primitive methods long forbidden to industry and municipalities, such as burning garbage, generating noxious smoke. On Indian lands, the maximum fine for the most reckless disposal is only $100.
>
> Although these gaps have been frequently brought to the attention of federal officials, little has been done.[17]

The general rule has been that private businesses regulated by the federal government must also obey the laws of the provinces in which they choose to operate, but they may ignore any local law that would unduly interfere with any essential feature of their operation.[18] For example, the courts have held that an ocean freighter that emitted black smoke in a harbour of a municipality was immune from the municipality's anti-smoke bylaw because the federal government has jurisdiction over this activity under the shipping and navigable waters section of the *Constitution Act, 1867*;[19] and a railway was allowed to dump fill into Hamilton Harbour to create a bed for a railway track contrary to regulations made under Ontario's *Conservation Authorities Act*.[20]

Although provincial laws may restrict the activities of federally regulated businesses to a degree, the federal government and its agencies and employees have even broader immunity. There is some doubt whether provincial laws can ever bind these entities[21] unless they are acting outside their authority.[22] At best, they can be bound only where the provincial legislation expressly names them, they are covered by necessary implication, or they have sought the benefits of the provincial law.[23] Thus, for example, a federal Crown corporation that discharged radioactive material into Lake Ontario could not be convicted of polluting under the *Ontario Water Resources Act*,[24] and several departments, agencies, and employees of the federal government who released hazardous materials to an unlicensed waste hauler who dumped them down the nearest sewer were immune from Ontario legislation requiring waste generators to use only licensed waste haulers and to use waybills to record all shipments of liquid industrial waste.[25]

Furthermore, only the federal government can legislate with regard to interprovincial pollution problems. Many environmental problems cross geographical as well as legal borders. Air and water flow between provinces, carrying contaminants from one province to another. Yet the Supreme Court of Canada has decided that legislation of one province, which is otherwise constitutionally valid, cannot be applied to activities in an adjoining province that contaminates the rivers of the first province.[26] In the *Interprovincial Cooperatives* case, chemical manufacturing plants in Ontario and Saskatchewan deposited wastes into rivers that flowed into Manitoba, creating mercury pollution in that province. The Manitoba government passed the *Fishermen's Assistance and Polluters Liability Act*[27] to remove some of the barriers to suing for compensation. The Supreme Court declared the legislation invalid on the grounds that the victim province could not pass laws governing activities in a different province. Four of the judges ruled that only the federal government could pass such a law, while three ruled that only the province that harboured the polluter could pass the law.

The problem could be simply solved if the federal government passed legislation making provincial environmental protection laws applicable to federal establishments and to private businesses under federal jurisdiction, or made standards and rules for these federal operators similar to those passed by the provinces to control all other establishments. But the federal government has frequently preferred to create its own "pollution havens" by failing to legislate.

THE IMPACT OF THE CHARTER OF RIGHTS ON THE ENVIRONMENT

It is too early to predict the effect that the *Charter of Rights and Freedoms*[28] will have on environmental protection. It may be an environmentalist's dream come true[29] or his worst nightmare, depending on how the courts interpret it. The *Charter* elevates the importance of individual liberties considered "fundamental" by restricting the right of government to interfere with those liberties, except to the extent that the government can demonstrate that this interference is justified for the good of the public as a whole. The extent to which this will create new rights to environmental quality or restrict the right of government to pass and enforce legislation to protect the environment will depend largely on what rights are defined as "fundamental" and who has such rights. The courts have already decided that corporations can take advantage of some of the rights guaranteed by the *Charter* to individuals,[30] and that some rights, such as freedom of expression, include commercial activities.[31] These decisions may restrict the right of government to pass strong environmental protection legislation restricting the development of land and natural resources and business activities that pollute the environment.

Corporations and individuals prosecuted for environmental offences have made several attempts to strike down legislation that give inspectors the right to enter and inspect business premises and to collect information without a search warrant.[32] They claim that these powers infringe the right to be free from unreasonable search and seizure and to be presumed innocent until proven guilty. So far, however, the courts have been prepared to follow the American example. They have distinguished between the power to inspect business premises for compliance with regulatory laws and to require businesses to provide information about discharges and spills of pollutants on the one hand, and the power to search premises, seize evidence, and require people to give information as part of a criminal investigation on the other.[33]

The business community's lobbying efforts to have the constitution amended to include a right to the enjoyment of property have so far been unsuccessful,[34] as have their efforts to convince the courts to interpret section 7, which recognizes a right to "life, liberty and security of the person," as preserving the sanctity of property and commercial and industrial activities.[35] However, the efforts of the Canadian Environmental Law Association (CELA) to convince the government to include a right to a clean and healthy environment also failed, and it is too soon to tell whether section 7 may be interpreted to encompass a right to environmental quality.[36]

Energy Probe has launched an important test case against the attorney general of Canada, claiming that the *Nuclear Liability Act* infringes section 7 of the *Charter*, as well as section 15, which guarantees equal treatment under the law.[37] On its face, it is clear that the Act jeopardizes people's traditional right to sue for full compensation for harm to their health and the health of their children.

The Act provides rights and advantages that victims of a nuclear accident would not have at common law. If a meltdown occurred at a nuclear power plant, people could obtain compensation for harm to their health from a fund established under the Act without the need to go to court or prove negligence. However, the Act bars victims of the incident from any other right of action against those who may be responsible, and limits the liability of the nuclear power plant operator to $75 million, an amount far less than the damage that such an incident is likely to cause. The Act also requires all victims to make their claims within 10 years of the incident, even though cancer and genetic mutation that might be caused by the incident might not be detectable within 10 years, and therefore such victims would go uncompensated. The obvious question for the court in this case is whether the advantages conferred on some victims by this statute justify depriving others of their traditional right to full compensation for harm. This case is likely to have a profound impact on the interpretation of the *Charter* and its applicability to the protection of the environment and human health.

FEDERAL DEPARTMENTS, AGENCIES, AND LAWS

There are several federal departments and agencies that administer environmental protection statutes, regulate activities that may harm the environment, or carry on environmentally harmful activities that require regulation. Some of them are described below.

Environment Canada

The federal government department primarily responsible for environmental matters is the Department of the Environment, commonly known as Environment Canada. It gets its powers from the *Department of the Environment Act*,[38] which gives the minister of the environment the power to carry out all duties and functions of the federal government relating to the preservation and enhancement of the natural environment, renewable resources, water, meteorology, national parks, and national battlefields, historic sites, and monuments that are not assigned to any other department or agency.[39]

The environment minister not only regulates pollution from some private business activities, but he or she also has limited power to act as a "watchdog" over the polluting activities of other federal departments. This is particularly important, since development-oriented departments like Public Works and National Defence may be reluctant to introduce strong laws that will limit their own pollution and, as mentioned above, they often are beyond the reach of provincial laws.

The environment minister may prepare only non-binding "guidelines" for the control of the activities of other federal departments and of the businesses that those departments regulate, and then only with Cabinet's consent, and he or she may make binding regulations curtailing those activities only with the concurrence of the minister responsible for that department. (An exception is limits on the release of air and water pollutants by federal departments and agencies, and their waste disposal practices. Here, Cabinet can make regulations on the recommendation of the environment minister even if the responsible minister does not agree.)

In 1992, Environment Canada had five divisions: the Atmospheric Environment Service, the Conservation and Protection Service (formerly the Environmental Protection Service), the Canadian Parks Service, Finance and Administration Program, and a State of the Environment Reporting group. The Atmospheric Environment Service (AES) collects information about weather and provides it to the public. As well as being the "weatherperson" whose forecasts we love to criticize, AES collects data on climate, sea conditions, ice conditions, and air quality. Its activities include research into the impacts of pollution on the atmospheric ozone layer and climate changes that might result from global warming (the "greenhouse effect"). The Conservation and Protection Service has the front-line responsibility for pollution control and clean-up, as well as monitoring water quantity and quality, reducing flood damage, river-basin planning, land resources development, the management of migratory birds, the protection of threatened and endangered species, and other national and international water and wildlife issues. The Parks Service develops and manages national parks, national historic parks and sites, heritage canals, and cooperative heritage areas. In addition, several advisory and regulatory agencies report to the minister of the environment, or through the minister to the federal Cabinet. These include the Round Table on the Environment and the Economy, the National Battlefields Commission, the Historic Sites and Monuments Board, and the Federal Environmental Assessment and Review Office (FEARO), which administers the federal environmental assessment review process (EARP), including setting up panels to hold public hearings into whether projects should proceed.

The Canadian Environmental Advisory Council, which served as a watchdog agency, reporting on many gaps and problems in Canada's environmental protection regime, was disbanded in 1992 as a cost-cutting measure.[40]

Environment Canada administers the *Canadian Environmental Protection Act*,[41] the *Canada Water Act*,[42] the *International Boundary Waters Treaty Act*,[43] the *National Wildlife Week Act*,[44] the *Migratory Birds Convention Act*,[45] the *Canada Wildlife Act*,[46] the *Game Export Act*,[47] the *National Parks Act*,[48] the *Mingan Archipelago National Park Act*,[49] the *National Battlefields at Quebec Act*,[50] the *Historic Sites and Monuments Act*,[51] the *Interna-*

tional Rivers Improvements Act,[52] the *Heritage Railways Stations Protection Act*,[53] the *Weather Modification Information Act*,[54] the *Canadian Environment Week Act*,[55] the *Resources and Technical Surveys Act*,[56] and the pollution-control provisions of the *Fisheries Act*.[57]

The most far-reaching of these statutes for pollution control is the *Canadian Environmental Protection Act (CEPA)*,[58] which incorporates the former *Clean Air Act*,[59] the *Environmental Contaminants Act*,[60] the *Ocean Dumping Control Act*,[61] and parts of the *Canada Water Act*[62] and the *Department of the Environment Act*.[63] The *Canadian Environmental Protection Act* is particularly important because it attempts to impose "cradle-to-grave" control of toxic substances manufactured in Canada or imported, from their creation or introduction into the country, through distribution and sale, to ultimate disposal. It creates a framework for the establishment of nationwide environmental standards for toxic substances used in Canada and exported to other countries, and for setting in motion cooperative ventures between the federal and provincial governments. It also provides a framework for the federal environment minister to suggest standards and practices to fellow Cabinet ministers to govern pollution from the activities of their departments.

The *Canadian Environmental Protection Act*, together with the *Fisheries Act*,[64] has great potential for controlling water pollution. The *Fisheries Act*, in fact, has been the main tool for prosecuting water polluters outside Ontario. The Ontario government prefers to use its own *Ontario Water Resources Act*.[65]

Environment Canada is also responsible for ensuring that the federal government minimizes adverse effects from its own existing and future works, undertakings, and businesses, and those that take place on federal lands or that involve the expenditure of federal funds. It does this by negotiating with other government agencies to abate their pollution, since it has no power to make regulations that will bind them, without consent of Cabinet, and by encouraging them to plan future projects through an environmental impact assessment process. The federal environmental impact assessment process has been carried out in the past under the supervision of the Federal Environmental Assessment and Review Office under an order in council made by the federal Cabinet. However, the *Canadian Environmental Assessment Act*[66] was passed in 1992, and will provide a new framework for future environmental assessments. For more information about environmental assessment, see Chapter 9.

The Department of Transport (Transport Canada) administers several statutes that contain environmental protection provisions relating to various modes of transportation on air, land, and water. Among them are the *Transportation of Dangerous Goods Act*,[67] the *Motor Vehicle Safety Act*,[68] the *Canada Shipping Act*,[69] the *Arctic Waters Pollution Prevention Act*,[70] the *Northern Pipeline Act*,[71] the *Navigable Waters Protection Act*,[72] the *National Transportation Act*,[73] the *Railway Act*,[74] and the *Aeronautics Act*.[75] The department also operates several airports and harbours, where pollution such as noise and oil spills result from its activities.

The Department of Indian Affairs and Northern Development administers statutes such as the *Oil and Gas Production and Conservation Act*,[76] the *Northern Inland Waters Act*,[77] the *Arctic Waters Pollution Prevention Act*,[78] the *Canada Oil and Gas Act*,[79] and *The Lake of the Woods Control Board Act*[80] (under this Act, representatives of Canada, Ontario, Manitoba, and Michigan regulate water levels in the lake).

The Department of Energy, Mines and Resources administers the *Nuclear Liability Act*[81] and the *Energy Supplies Emergency Act*.[82] The *Atomic Energy Control Act*[83] is administered by an independent Atomic Energy Control Board, answering to Parliament through the minister of energy, mines, and resources.

The minister of agriculture administers a key environmental statute, the *Pest Control Products Act*,[84] which determines which pesticides will be licensed for use in Canada, as well as the *Pesticide Residue Compensation Act*,[85] which provides for compensation to farmers whose crops are contaminated by drifting pesticides sprayed by others.

The Criminal Code of Canada

The federal government has exclusive authority to pass laws making conduct a crime. "Crimes" are usually those actions considered to be the most serious transgressions against people and property, and usually carry the heaviest penalties, including imprisonment. With a few exceptions, unlawful activity is a crime only if it is done deliberately, or with willful blindness to its potential consequences. The same activity may be a violation of the *Criminal Code*[86] if it is done deliberately, but only a violation of a provincial statute if it is done inadvertently. For example, a person who dumps a toxic chemical into a watercourse, thinking it is harmless, may be guilty only of a violation of Ontario's environmental laws; but if he or she knew the chemical was harmful, the same activity might be a crime.

The *Criminal Code* is not administered by a regulatory department like Environment Canada or Transport Canada. Federal, provincial, and municipal police forces investigate crimes and lay charges. The provincial Crown attorneys, who report to the attorney general of the province, prosecute the charges.

Code provisions are divided into the more serious offences (indictable offences), relatively minor offences (summary conviction offences), and those offences that can be very serious or relatively minor, depending on the circumstances (hybrid offences). The Crown attorney decides whether a hybrid offence should be prosecuted by indictment, leading to a heavier penalty, or by summary conviction procedure, leading to a lighter penalty. In general, the police and Crown attorneys do not have a monopoly on the enforcement of criminal laws. Any person may lay a charge for a summary conviction offence, and prosecute it himself or herself if the Crown attorney does not do so. However, only the Crown attorney may prosecute a hybrid or an indictable offence.

Although the *Criminal Code* has several provisions that could make it a powerful tool to protect the environment, it has seldom been used to prosecute polluters. There are probably at least three reasons for this. First, it is only in recent years that the public has begun to view pollution as one of the most serious and immoral acts of humankind. More important, most polluting activities result from carelessness rather than deliberate attempts to cause harm. Even where the polluter does foresee the consequences of his or her actions, it is seldom possible to prove this beyond a reasonable doubt (the standard of proof required to convict someone of a crime). In addition, the courts would probably interpret provisions of the *Criminal Code* as limited to activities that seriously threaten human health, and in some cases to noise and other nuisances. The *Code* would probably not be available to protect aesthetic values alone, which are generally considered beyond the scope of criminal law.

Finally, government agencies have an unwritten rule that they will enforce only their own legislation and, indeed, their staff seldom have the expertise, experience, or time to competently enforce the legislation of other departments. As a result, the legal staff of an environment department would be likely to prosecute only pollution offences under statutes the department administers, such as the *Fisheries Act*[87] and the *Environmental Protection Act*,[88] even if they were serious enough to deserve prosecution as crimes. Police and Crown attorneys, who are accustomed to using the *Criminal Code* to prosecute only traditional crimes like theft and drunk driving, would be unlikely to lay or proceed with charges under the *Criminal Code* for environmental crimes. Although the obvious answer to this problem is cooperation between these officials, such a coordinated approach to law enforcement is rare.

There are several *Criminal Code* provisions that may be available to punish deliberate or reckless pollution or other forms of damage to the environment:

Criminal negligence. Section 219 provides that "Everyone is criminally negligent who ... shows wanton or reckless disregard for the lives or safety of others."[89] Court decisions have left it unclear whether this includes inadvertent negligence (which would make this an exception to the general rule that actions will not be a crime unless the person acted deliberately, or at least put his or her mind to the possible consequences of carelessness) or whether the provision applies only to someone who has *consciously* taken serious and unjustified risks.

Mischief. Section 430 provides that a person commits mischief who willfully:

- destroys or damages property;
- renders property dangerous, useless, inoperative, or ineffective;
- obstructs, interrupts, or interferes with the lawful use, enjoyment, or operation of property; or
- obstructs, interrupts, or interferes with any person in the lawful use, enjoyment, or operation of property.

The punishment is imprisonment for up to 2 years, or 10 years if the property damaged by the mischief is worth more than $1,000. If the mischief also causes danger to life, the penalty can be life imprisonment.

Common nuisance. Section 180 defines common nuisance as doing an unlawful act or failing to discharge a legal duty, which (1) endangers the lives, safety, health, property, or comfort of the public, or (2) obstructs the public in the exercise or enjoyment of any right that is common to all members of the public.

Disturbing the peace. Section 175 may have application to noise pollution. (See Chapter 19 for a description of this offence.)

Dangerous substances and offensive volatile substances. Sections 79 to 81 require everyone to use reasonable care in dealing with explosive substances, and section 178 makes it an offence in a public place to deposit, throw, or inject an offensive volatile substance that is likely to alarm, inconvenience, discommode, or cause discomfort to any person or cause damage to property.

Under the *Criminal Code*, one does not actually have to cause a disturbance, create a nuisance, or cause mischief to be punished. The mere attempt to commit an offence is illegal. In addition, anyone who is a party to someone else's offence by aiding or conspiring with the person to commit the offence is also guilty of the same offence.[90]

In 1985, the Law Reform Commission of Canada concluded that these and other existing provisions of the *Criminal Code* are not adequate to address serious harm to the environment. "Environmental quality," the commission said, "is a value so fundamental, unique and threatened, that very seriously to harm or endanger it merits express prohibition in a new and distinct offence we have labelled a 'crime against the environment.'"[91] The commission concluded that this crime against the environment should include not only intentional or reckless pollution, but also inadvertent negligence that causes or risks death or bodily injury, and harmful or endangering omissions. Everyone who has created a danger of grave environmental damage or who has control over it would have a specific duty to take reasonable care to prevent or mitigate the harm to the environment.[92]

The commission followed this report with another report that recommended the creation of a crime of "endangerment." At common law, there is generally no duty to remove a danger that you did not create, or even to warn of such a danger. Even when a person creates or is in control of a dangerous situation, his or her failure to remove the danger usually only gives rise to civil liability and is not a crime. The commission proposed to make it a crime to fail to take reasonable steps to remove a danger to life a crime, whether or not the person created the danger, and even if the failure to act was not deliberate or reckless, but merely negligent.[93]

Clearly, if these recommendations were incorporated into the *Criminal Code*, they would strengthen the usefulness of the *Code* to punish serious pollution. However, it is unlikely that a specific "crime against the environment" will be created in the near future, since an offence very similar to the proposed crime was incorporated in 1988 into the *Canadian Environmental Protection Act*.[94]

PROVINCIAL DEPARTMENTS, AGENCIES, AND LAWS

The most important Ontario government departments in the areas of conservation and protection of the environment are the Ministry of the Environment and Energy (MEE) and the Ministry of Natural Resources (MNR).

The ministries of energy and environment were amalgamated in February 1993. MEE administers the *Environmental Protection Act*,[95] the *Ontario Water Resources Act*,[96] the *Pesticides Act*,[97] the *Environmental Assessment Act*,[98] the *Consolidated Hearings Act*,[99] the *Ontario Waste Management Corporation Act*,[100] the *Waste Management Act*,[101] and the *Niagara Escarpment Planning and Development Act*.[102] Its name suggests that the ministry has broad jurisdiction to protect the environment against the squandering of natural resources and the destruction of environmentally sensitive areas. In fact, however, the ministry's jurisdiction is limited largely to pollution control, except for its power under the *Environmental Assessment Act*[103] to refuse approval to projects that may have adverse cultural, economic, or social impacts and its recent acquisition of jurisdiction over the Niagara Escarpment.

The Ministry of Environment and Energy controls pollution through its powers to refuse approval or impose conditions on the approval of any facility that may cause pollution, by issuing pollution abatement orders and by issuing or refusing to issue licences and permits to businesses such as well drillers, pesticide sprayers and vendors, waste disposal site operators, waste haulers, sewage haulers, and septic tank installers.

Historically, the former Ministry of the Environment has suffered from insufficient powers, too few staff, too little in-house expertise, and internal role conflicts. In recent years, the ability of the ministry to carry out its functions effectively has improved. The laws it administers have been substantially rewritten to give officials greater preventive and corrective powers and to impose substantial penalties on law breakers; its budget and staff have increased; and one of the most obvious role conflicts may be eliminated. The ministry designs, constructs, and operates most of the municipal sewage treatment plants in Ontario. However, the ministry also regulates the operation of these plants, and is required to impose tough conditions on the operation of the plants through the contents of certificates of approval or control orders, and to prosecute ministry employees running the plants if they polluted. The Liberal government proposed to establish a separate agency to design, construct, and operate the sewage treatment plants. In February 1993, the NDP government announced that it would proceed to establish a new Clean Water Agency, which would be responsible for building both sewage and water treatment plants. However, the agency would report to the minister of environment and energy, not the minister of municipal affairs as the Liberal government had contemplated.

Other conflicts still remain, however. For example, the ministry regulates waste disposal facilities. It should refuse to approve any new facility that may cause excessive pollution and it has the power to shut down existing facilities that cannot meet today's rigorous standards of design and operation. Yet the ministry is aware of the shortage of waste disposal facilities in Ontario, and many officials feel that their mandate is to ensure that sufficient waste disposal facilities are available. The "garbage crisis" creates pressure on the ministry to approve inadequate facilities or allow the operation of existing polluting ones to continue. In 1990, the ministry took over from several municipalities in the Metropolitan Toronto area the role of establishing waste disposal facilities, by creating an Interim Waste Authority, reporting to the minister, to select the waste disposal sites.

The ministry is divided into several "regions" and "branches." The regions are the front-line troops who recommend whether to approve new facilities or grant licences to businesses such as pesticide sprayers and waste haulers, and who inspect factories, garbage dumps, and sewage treatment plants and monitor the quality of air and water. The six regions have regional and district offices throughout the province. These are the offices to which you will go initially to make a complaint about existing pollution, to obtain information about local air and water quality, to oppose the establishment of a new facility, or, if you are a business person, to apply for a licence or permit or approval for a new facility.

In addition, members of the Investigations and Enforcement Branch are found in many of the regional and district offices. These "pollution police" are responsible for carrying out lengthy or difficult investigations of violations of the legislation administered by the ministry. They assist the inspectors in collecting evidence, and bring to bear their specialized training in investigative techniques. If local inspectors are unresponsive to your pollution complaints, you can sometimes enlist the help of the Investigations and Enforcement Branch.

The regions are supported by several "head office" branches of scientific and legal specialists. These branches provide expertise not always available in the regions, carry out extensive scientific research, develop policy, and grant approvals to new facilities. They include the Environmental Assessment Branch, which coordinates the response of various government agencies to environmental impact assessments; the Laboratory Services Branch, which runs several ministry labs that carry out analyses of air, soil, water, and waste samples; the Hazardous Contaminants Branch, which decides which substances should be designated as hazardous; and the Air Resources Branch, the Water Resources Branch, and the Waste Management Branch.

Among the advisory and regulatory agencies that report to the environment minister, or through the minister to the Legislature, are the Farm Pollution Advisory Committee, the Hazardous Waste Advisory Committee, the Advisory Committee on Environmental Standards, the Environmental Assessment Advisory Committee, the MISA Advisory Committee, the Waste Reduction Advisory Committee, the Pesticides Advisory Committee, the Environmental Assessment Board, the Environmental Appeal Board, the Niagara Escarpment Commission, the Environmental Compensation Corporation, and the Ontario Waste Management Corporation.

The purpose of the former Ministry of Energy, now amalgamated with the Ministry of the Environment, is to ensure that Ontario has "an adequate and secure supply of energy that meets the needs of Ontario residents and industry, at reasonable prices, in a manner consistent with environmental protection."[104] Both the Ontario Energy Board and Ontario Hydro report to the Legislature through the minister of energy. The ministry has an Energy Conservation and Renewable Energy Group.

Clearly, the policies of this ministry will have a great impact on whether Ontario's energy needs are met through energy conservation and renewable sources of energy, or through the use of non-renewable energy sources, and whether more-polluting or less-polluting sources of energy are used.

The Ministry of Natural Resources is responsible for regulating Ontario's resource extraction industries, including mining, the operation of gravel pits and sand and stone quarries, commercial hunting and fishing, and logging. MNR also administers all the Crown lands (lands still owned by the provincial government, which are not within areas organized into municipalities). This includes most of the land in northern Ontario. MNR is responsible for land-use planning on these public lands, and activities such as farming and resource extraction on these lands are subject to permits from MNR.

For well over a decade, the unfairness of the manner in which MNR carries out its land-use planning functions and the lack of any appeals from its decisions have been criticized by, among others, the Royal Commission on the Northern Environment, the ombudsman, and participants in the Timber Management Class Environmental Assessment hearings. Finally, in December 1992, MNR agreed to consider a more open and responsive process.[105]

MNR administers the *Provincial Parks Act*,[106] the *Public Lands Act*,[107] the *Aggregate Resources Act*,[108] the *Conservation Authorities Act*,[109] the *Endangered Species Act*,[110] the *Lakes and Rivers Improvement Act*,[111] and the *Beds of Navigable Waters Act*,[112] among others. All have great potential for protecting the environment and its resources.

This ministry, however, has two conflicting responsibilities. On the one hand, it is responsible for the conservation of the natural environment, including the establishment and management of provincial parks and financial support of the programs of the conservation authorities throughout the province and the preservation of wetlands, the protection of fisheries, and the preservation of endangered species of plants and animals. On the other hand, it is also responsible for regulating the commercial and recreational exploitation of public lands and natural resources. In practice, these responsibilities frequently clash head-on.

Among the agencies that report to this department, or through it to the Legislature, are Ontario's conservation authorities, which are responsible for watershed management, including forestation, flood control, and the establishment and management of regional parks, and the Algonquin Forestry Authority (which regulates logging in Ontario's oldest provincial park). The mining and lands commissioner reports both to the minister of natural resources and to the minister of northern development and mines.

Other government departments and legislation that play major roles in regulating the environment include the Ministry of Agriculture and Food, the Ministry of Health, the Ministry of Labour, the Ministry of Municipal Affairs, the Ministry of Northern Development and Mines, and the Ministry of Transportation.

The Ministry of Agriculture and Food (OMAF) has numerous programs designed to assist or encourage farmers to conserve soil, use pesticides carefully, and prevent water pollution from spills and runoff of manure and fertilizers. For example, the Land Stewardship Program is designed to encourage farmers to adopt "conservation farming practices," including planting trees, crop rotation, and erosion control. Food Systems 2002 is a program to reduce farmers' reliance on pesticides by 50 per cent by the year 2002. However, OMAF also administers programs that encourage the creation of new farmland at the cost of destruction of wetlands. For example, OMAF administers the *Drainage Act*,[113] which is the instrument of much of the destruction of wetlands, and gives farmers millions of dollars in grants and loans to encourage drainage projects. The ministry's efforts are directed primarily at preserving the viability of agriculture, sometimes even when this involves practices that cause substantial pollution.

The Ministry of Health and the local boards of health that report to the ministry are responsible for safeguarding public health. Together, they administer the *Health Protection and Promotion Act*.[114] The ministry operates laboratories throughout the province for testing the quality of drinking water for conventional contaminants such as bacteria. When other ministries or members of the public need advice on the toxicity of a contaminant, or expert evidence to present in court, they turn to the local medical officer of health or to the doctors and toxicologists employed by the Health Ministry or the Ministry of Labour for assistance. The Ministry of Labour, which is responsible for the health and safety of workers, administers the *Occupational Health and Safety Act*.[115]

The Ministry of Transportation is responsible for building and maintaining provincial highways, an obvious source of noise, dust, and destruction of natural habitats, and for regulating a variety of forms of transportation within the province, including trucks and other vehicles on public roads, off-road vehicles such as snowmobiles and all-terrain vehicles, ferries, and some railways. The ministry carries out environmental impact assessments of highway expansion, and administers the *Dangerous Goods Transportation Act*,[116] which implements the federal *Transportation of Dangerous Goods Act*[117] in Ontario.

The Ministry of Municipal Affairs (MMA) supervises the operation and expansion of municipalities and coordinates the development of land-use policy. This ministry can have a major impact on whether Ontario municipalities remain livable or turn into Detroits, Washingtons, and New Yorks, and whether municipal boundaries and services continue to spill over onto environmentally sensitive areas and prime farmland. MMA administers the *Municipal Act*,[118] which sets out the powers of municipalities, and the *Planning Act*,[119] which regulates all land-use planning, except on public lands administered by MNR (see above). The Ontario Municipal Board, probably the most powerful tribunal in Ontario, reports to this ministry.

Finally, the Ministry of Northern Development and Mines is responsible for promoting economic development in northern Ontario. The ministry administers government grant programs and oversees the administration of the *Mining Act*.[120] Until 1991, this Act contained no provisions to require rehabilitation of abandoned mines.

The two most important provincial tribunals that deal with environmental issues are the Environmental Assessment Board (EAB) and the Ontario Municipal Board (OMB). Both provide citizens with an opportunity to challenge major projects and significant land-use planning decisions. As will be discussed in greater detail in Chapter 9, any citizen may request a hearing before the EAB before the environment minister approves any project subject to environmental impact assessment under the *Environmental Assessment Act*.[121] This includes many public undertakings and a few private ones, such as the establishment or expansion of major waste disposal sites, highway expansion, and the construction of new government buildings. The Ontario Municipal Board provides public hearings into proposed changes in zoning, land severances, minor variances, subdivision plans, the establishment of municipal official plans, and amendments to them. The OMB has several other responsibilities, including hearing tax-assessment appeals, deciding disputes over compensation for expropriation of or injurious affection to land, and approving certain expenditures of local governments and public school boards.

Government structure and the allocation of responsibilities change frequently. For more complete and up-to-date information about the structure and functions of Ontario government departments and agencies, and the names, addresses, and phone numbers of government offices and officials, see two Ontario government directories that are updated each year — the *Government of Ontario KWIC Index to Services* and the *Government of Ontario Telephone Directory* — as well as the "blue pages" of your telephone directory.

MUNICIPAL DEPARTMENTS, AGENCIES, AND LAWS

If anything, the structure of local government is even more complex than that of federal and provincial government departments and agencies. There are over 800 municipalities in Ontario, each of which has power under provincial legislation to pass bylaws regulating certain matters within its boundaries.

These municipalities range in size from small rural villages and townships to gigantic city-states, like Metropolitan Toronto, whose geographic territory and population are larger than those of some nations. The categories of municipalities include towns, separated towns, townships, improvement districts, villages, counties, regional municipalities, cities, and the last remaining borough in Ontario, East York. Each kind of municipality has different powers, intended to be suited to its needs. In northern Ontario, most cities, towns, townships, villages, and improvement districts are not part of a larger municipality, but are surrounded by "unorganized territory" — that is, public lands administered by MNR. In southern

Ontario, however, most such municipalities are part of a two-tier system of government. These "lower-tier" municipalities are situated within larger "upper-tier" municipalities known as counties and district or regional municipalities. In general, the lower-tier munici-palities have the authority to pass bylaws dealing with matters of concern mainly within their own boundaries, and upper-tier municipalities have the authority to regulate matters that require a coordinated approach throughout the entire area. For example, the city of Toronto and the other four cities and one borough within the municipality of Metropolitan Toronto each has jurisdiction to establish and maintain local roads, but the major "arterial" roads that connect the six "area" or "local" municipalities to each other and to the provincial highway system are under the jurisdiction of the senior level of municipal government, "Metro."

The important functions of municipal governments for environmental protection include: land-use planning; the establishment and maintenance of roads; the establishment and maintenance of parks; garbage collection and disposal; sewers and sewage treatment; the provision of drinking water; the operation of public transit systems; the licensing of about 100 kinds of businesses; and, sometimes, the provision of "utilities" such as electricity and telephone service (often through "public utilities commissions").

Most of these functions are carried out through "departments" whose names, structures, and responsibilities vary from municipality to municipality. There is usually a roads or traffic department responsible for the streets, a public works department or public utilities commis-sion responsible for sewage, water, and electricity, and a planning department responsible for administering the *Building Code Act*[122] and the *Planning Act*.[123] There is often a parks department. The fire department may be a valuable resource in acting on complaints about excessive smoke from open fires, and in monitoring the operation of factories with flammable and explosive chemicals, and other facilities, such as garbage dumps and tire dumps, that can catch fire. The police department may respond to noise complaints.

Some large municipalities, such as the city of Toronto, have a noise control section with its own staff. Many municipalities have a public health department. The city of Toronto is the first municipality in the province to have an environmental protection office within its Public Health Department. Some municipalities have a department, or an official within a depart-ment, whose job it is to attract new industry (for example, London's development commis-sioner). His or her efforts may conflict with the attempts of other municipal departments to control pollution and encourage environmentally sound planning.

There are also "local boards" that are analogous to the "ABCs" of the federal and provincial governments. These are agencies that carry out specialized functions. They may include boards of education, public utility commissions, library boards, police commissions, and licensing commissions. Like the agencies of the senior levels of government, these local boards have a degree of autonomy from the elected council and departments.

Many of these local boards are made up of a combination of elected councillors, department heads, and ordinary people appointed to represent the community as a whole. The quality of these appointments will be important in determining the extent to which the boards are sensitive to environmental issues. Some municipalities, such as the regional municipality of Waterloo and the city of Toronto, have appointed environmental advisory committees, consisting of knowledgeable members of the public.

Many of these departments and agencies have inspectors and bylaw enforcement officers who will investigate complaints about environmental concerns such as excessive noise, littering, illegal waste disposal, zoning violations, or unlawful cutting of trees, and who may prosecute offenders or issue orders to rectify problems.

The coordination among these various departments and boards and their skills and commitment to environmental protection vary greatly from municipality to municipality. A study in the late 1970s, for example, found that only about one-third of Ontario municipalities surveyed had a tree protection bylaw, and in those municipalities that did, many of the officials responsible for streets and buildings were not aware of its existence. Many municipalities have no one on staff who is trained to ensure that trees are properly pruned instead of lopped haphazardly, or that they are protected during the construction of buildings or maintenance of roads or utilities. A follow-up study several years later found that although the *Trees Act*[124] was strengthened in 1978 to give municipalities more power to protect trees, there was still little enforcement of tree protection bylaws.[125] Other studies have found that there is inadequate and inconsistent enforcement of municipal sewer use bylaws, which limit the pollutants that can be discharged from factories into sewers.[126]

The sources of most municipal powers to prevent environmental impairment are the *Planning Act*[127] and the *Municipal Act*.[128] These statutes are supplemented in the case of the regional municipalities by specific statutes, such as the *Regional Municipality of Ottawa-Carleton Act*[129] and the *Municipality of Metropolitan Toronto Act*,[130] that give each of these mega-municipalities additional powers.

Municipal councils pass bylaws regulating the use of land under the *Planning Act*.[131] Such bylaws regulate zoning, urban renewal, construction, repair, and demolition of buildings, heating plants, and equipment. The municipal council may prohibit the erection of buildings on marshy land and the use of land or buildings for hazardous purposes. It may permit or prohibit a gravel or sand pit or stone quarry.[132]

The *Municipal Act*,[133] which contains over 500 sections, is one of Ontario's oldest and longest statutes. Because it has been amended many times since the 1890s, it no longer bears much resemblance to modern reality. It is confusing and often antiquated. For example, nowhere in the *Municipal Act* will you find a municipality's power to license restaurants and inspect them for sanitation. Instead, the Act gives municipalities the power to pass bylaws to regulate "victualling houses, ordinaries, and houses where fruit, fish, oysters, clams or victuals are sold to be eaten therein, and places for the lodging, reception, refreshment or entertainment of the public ... [and] places where food stuffs intended for human consumption are made for sale, offered for sale, stored or sold."[134] To determine what powers a municipality has, it is often necessary to read several sections of the Act in conjunction with the provisions of other statutes and court cases interpreting these provisions.

The Act also permits municipal councils to make bylaws "as may be deemed expedient" for the "health, safety, morality and welfare of the inhabitants of the municipality in matters not specifically provided for" in the Act.[135] Although this section appears to give broad powers, the courts have held that this section standing alone is so general that it can give no additional powers to a municipality beyond the specific powers set out in the Act.[136]

These specific powers enable municipalities to pass bylaws covering such diverse matters as the supply of water, the operation of sewage works, street cleaning, aircraft landing grounds, the control of drainage and floods, the regulation of harbours, wharves, highways, sidewalks, bridges, and fences, the acquisition of parks, the keeping of animals and explosives, fire fighting and prevention, and the inspection of food.

Bylaws for *health, sanitation, and safety* may be passed to regulate cesspools, indoor and outdoor toilets, the repair of private drains, and the cleaning up and draining of yards.[137] Bylaws passed under this heading could also cover the collection and disposal of garbage[138] and the control of slaughterhouses and trailer camps.[139]

Under a power to *prevent nuisances*, the municipality may regulate or prohibit gas works, tanneries, distilleries, and other noxious industrial activities. It may regulate, among other things, pits and quarries, the location of stables, barns, outhouses, and manure pits, signs and billboards, and material that may be discharged into sewers.[140]

The municipal council also has wide powers to regulate many trades and businesses through *licensing*.[141] This is an important power for preventing the establishment or continuation of polluting businesses. Licensing commissions often hear complaints from the public about excessive noise, odours, traffic congestion, and other nuisances caused by restaurants, taverns, public garages, and other businesses that require a municipal licence. On occasion, a licence has been refused or revoked because of such nuisances (see also Chapter 3).

This by no means exhausts the list of bylaws dealing with environmental quality that municipalities can pass. The *Trees Act*,[142] the *Public Transportation and Highway Improvement Act*,[143] the *Woodlands Improvement Act*,[144] and the *Forestry Act*[145] also give municipalities added powers and provincial subsidies to encourage them to plant and maintain trees and forests within their boundaries. The *Topsoil Preservation Act*[146] gives them the power to prevent stripping land of topsoil. The *Conservation Authorities Act*[147] gives municipalities wider powers to control land erosion and flooding and access to provincial funds to create parks if they join together to form a conservation authority.

This brief overview cannot do justice to the complexity of the network of departments, agencies, and laws that affect environmental quality negatively or positively. You will find more detailed information on many of these matters in the chapters dealing with individual areas of environmental concern.

John Swaigen

FURTHER READING

David Estrin, *Environmental Law* (Scarborough, Ont.: Carswell, 1984).

Doug Macdonald, *The Politics of Pollution* (Toronto: McClelland and Stewart, 1991).

ENDNOTES

1 *Constitution Act, 1867*, 30 & 31 Vict., c. 3 (UK).
2 *R. v. Crown Zellerbach* (1988), 3 CELR (NS) 1, 84 NR 1 (SCC). The Supreme Court of Canada upheld the anti-dumping provision of the *Ocean Dumping Control Act* to an area of the ocean under the jurisdiction of the province of British Columbia. The court characterized the legislation as being "for the prevention of marine pollution," and said that this was a matter of national concern.

3   See, for example, Dale Gibson, "The Environment and the Constitution: New Wine in Old Bottles," in O.P. Dwivedi, ed., *Protecting the Environment* (Toronto: Copp Clark, 1974); B. Laskin, "Jurisdictional Framework for Water Management," in (1961), I *Resources for Tomorrow: Background Papers* 211, at 218; B. Stamp, "The Constitutional Aspects of Water Pollution and the Need for Governmental Co-operation," in Dale Gibson, ed., I *Constitutional Aspects of Water Management* (1968); Dianne Saxe, "Application of Provincial Environmental Statutes to the Federal Government, Its Servants, and Agents" (1990), 4 CELR (NS) 115; Paul Emond, "The Case for a Greater Federal Role in the Environmental Protection Field" (1972), 10 *Osgoode Hall LJ* 647.

4   For example, the result of the *National Research Council* case, which left the public unprotected against civil servants who hire unlicensed haulers to transport hazardous waste. This case is discussed in Saxe, supra endnote 3.

5   *R. v. Lake Ontario Cement Ltd. et al.* (1973), 2 OR 247 (HCJ).

6   *Interprovincial Cooperatives Ltd. and Dryden Chemicals Ltd. v. The Queen* (1975), 53 DLR (3d) 321 (SCC). This is an *obiter dictum*.

7   *Planning Act*, RSO 1990, c. P.13.

8   *Municipal Act*, RSO 1990, c. M.45.

9   *Township of Uxbridge v. Timbers Bros. Sand & Gravel Limited* (1973), 2 CELN 3, at 44 (Ont. HCJ), aff'd. (1975), 7 OR (2d) 484, 55 DLR (3d) 516 (CA), leave to appeal to SCC refused (1975), 7 OR (2d) 484n. See also *Raes v. Township of Plympton* (1971), 3 OR 445, 20 DLR (3d) 645 (CA).

10 *Atomic Energy Control Act*, RSC 1985, c. A-16.

11 *Attorney General of Nova Scotia v. Attorney General of Canada (Nova Scotia Interdelegation Case)*, [1951] SCR 31.

12 *Prince Edward Island Potato Marketing Board v. Willis*, [1952] 2 SCR 392.

13 *Fisheries Act*, RSC 1985, c. F-14.

14 Canadian Council of Resource and Environment Ministers, *Environmental Code of Practice for Underground Storage Systems Containing Petroleum Products*, rev. ed. (1988).

15 *The Globe and Mail*, October 4, 1992.

16 Gibson, in *Protecting the Environment*, supra endnote 3.

17 Saxe, supra endnote 3.

18 *TNT Canada Inc. v. Ontario* (1986), 1 CELR (NS) 109, 58 OR (2d) 410, leave to appeal to SCC refused (1987), 61 OR (2d) 480n.

19 *R. v. Canada Steamship Lines* (1960), OWN 277, 127 CCC 205 (Cty. Ct.).

20 *R. v. Canadian National Railways Co.* (summary) (1975), 4 CELN 78 (Ont. Prov. Ct.).

21 *The Queen in Right of Alberta v. Canadian Transport Commission*, [1978] 1 SCR 61, at 62.

22 *R. v. Canadian Broadcasting Corp.* (1980), 30 OR (2d) 239 (CA), aff'd. [1983] 1 SCR 339; *R. v. Stradiotto* (1973), 2 OR 375 (CA).

23 *R. v. Eldorado Nuclear Ltd.* (1981), 34 OR (2d) 243 (Div. Ct.).

24 Ibid.

25 Saxe, supra endnote 3.

26 *Interprovincial Cooperatives*, supra endnote 6; and see (1975), 4 CELN 109 for excerpts of the Supreme Court of Canada decision and a comment on it.

27 *Fishermen's Assistance and Polluters Liability Act*, RSM 1987, c. F100.

28 *Canadian Charter of Rights and Freedoms, Constitution Act, 1982*, RSC 1985, app. II, no. 44.

29 The potential of the *Charter* to support procedural safeguards for the environment was so described in Colin P. Stevenson, "A New Perspective on Environmental Rights After the Charter" (1983), 21 *Osgoode Hall LJ* 390, at 417.

30 For example, even though corporations cannot use section 7 of the *Charter* for some purposes, such as civil or administrative actions, they can rely on this section in defence of prosecutions. See *R. v. Wholesale Travel Group Inc.*, [1991] 3 SCR 154, 84 DLR (4th) 161 and *R. v. Big M Drug Mart Ltd.*, [1985] 1 SCR 295, (1985), 18 DLR (4th) 321.

31 *Ford v. Quebec (Attorney General)* (1988), 54 DLR (4th) 577; *Irwin Toy Ltd. v. Quebec (Attorney General)*, [1989] 1 SCR 927, 58 DLR (4th) 577. However, the trend has been to deny the protection of section 7 to economic activities: *Institute of Edible Oil Foods v. Ontario* (1987), 63 OR (2d) 436 (HCJ), aff'd. (1989), 71 OR (2d) 158 (CA). In *Re Aluminium Co. of Canada Ltd. and the Queen in Right of Ontario* (1986), 55 OR (2d) 522, the Ontario Divisional Court rejected the argument that a regulation under the *Environmental Protection Act* delaying the introduction of aluminum pop cans into Ontario infringed section 7. The court doubted that the right to market aluminum pop cans was envisioned by "security of the person."

32 For example, *R. v. Island Farm and Fishmeal Ltd.* (1992), 8 CELR (NS) 234 (PEISC—App. Div.); *R. v. Weil's Food Processing Ltd.* (1990), 6 CELR (NS) 249 and 259 (Ont. Gen. Div.); and *R. v. Vandervoet* (1986), 26 CRR 173 (Ont. Prov. Ct.).

33 *R. v. McKinlay Transport Ltd.*, [1990] 1 SCR 627, 76 CR (3d) 129, 54 CCC (3d) 417; *Thomson Newspapers Ltd. v. Canada (Director of Investigation and Research)*, [1990] 1 SCR 425, 76 CR (3d) 129, 54 CCC (3d) 417; *Re Belgoma Transportation Ltd. and Director of Employment Standards* (1985), 51 OR (2d) 509 (CA); *R. v. Rao* (1984), 46 OR (2d) 80 (CA); *R. v Quesnel* (1985), 53 OR (2d) 338 (CA); *Re Eagle Disposal Systems Ltd. and Minister of the Environment* (1983), 5 DLR (4th) 70 (Ont. HCJ); and *Canada Cement Lafarge Ltd. v. Municipality of Metropolitan Toronto* (1989), 4 CELR (NS) 29 (Ont. Prov. Off. App. Ct.). However, in *R. v. Texaco Canada Inc.* (1986), 1 CELR (NS) 100 (Ont. Dist. Ct.), the court held that the power of an MOE investigator to inspect for leakage of gasoline from an underground storage tank at a service station did not include the right to seize the records of a third party, and in *Re Allen and City of Hamilton* (1986), 55 OR (2d) 387 (HCJ), the court ruled that the removal of material from someone's property pursuant to an invalid bylaw authorizing the removal of debris was an infringement of the landowner's right to be secure against unreasonable seizure. However, this decision was overturned by the Court of Appeal: *Re Allen and City of Hamilton* (1987), 59 OR (2d) 498 (CA).

34 For a description of "the rush to entrench property rights," see Harry Poch, *Corporate and Municipal Environmental Law* (Agincourt, Ont.: Carswell, 1989), 449-52.

35 See cases referred to at endnote 31. However, the *Manicom* case is an example of how the *Charter* cuts both ways. Although the courts have so far been reluctant to assist businesses in resisting government regulation by extending section 7 to economic rights, including the right to use property for economic gain, they have also refused to apply section 7 to protect property owners who argued that an Ontario Cabinet decision

to approve a waste disposal site would result in water pollution, traffic hazards, noise, litter, and changed topography that would diminish their use and enjoyment of their property and make their community a less desirable place to live: *Manicom v. County of Oxford* (1985), 21 DLR (4th) 611 (Ont. HCJ).

36 See Stevenson, supra endnote 29, for a description of CELA's lobbying efforts, and for a discussion of the likelihood that the courts will interpret section 7 to include a right to a reasonably clean and safe environment.

37 *Energy Probe v. Attorney General of Canada* (1989), 3 CELR (NS) 262 (Ont. CA).

38 *Department of the Environment Act*, RSC 1985, c. E-10.

39 Ibid., section 4.

40 In 1992, the federal government announced that it would disband the Canadian Environmental Advisory Council, which had published numerous reports calling for stronger federal environmental laws and criticizing some federal initiatives. The government also announced the abolition of several other agencies that have promoted strong environmental laws and policies, including the Law Reform Commission of Canada and the Economic Council of Canada. The reason given was to save money.

41 *Canadian Environmental Protection Act*, RSC 1985, c. 16 (4th Supp.).

42 *Canada Water Act*, RSC 1985, c. C-11.

43 *International Boundary Waters Treaty Act*, RSC 1985, c. I-17.

44 *National Wildlife Week Act*, RSC 1985, c. W-10.

45 *Migratory Birds Convention Act*, RSC 1985, c. M-7.

46 *Canada Wildlife Act*, RSC 1985, c. W-9.

47 *Game Export Act*, RSC 1985, c. G-1.

48 *National Parks Act*, RSC 1985, c. N-14, as amended by SC 1988, c. 48.

49 *Mingan Archipelago National Park Act*, SC 1984, c. 34.

50 *National Battlefields at Quebec Act*, SC 1907-8, c. 57, 58.

51 *Historic Sites and Monuments Act*, RSC 1985, c. H-4.

52 *International River Improvements Act*, RSC 1985, c. I-20.

53 *Heritage Railways Stations Protection Act*, SC 1988, c. 62.

54 *Weather Modification Information Act*, RSC 1985, c. W-5.

55 *Canadian Environment Week Act*, RSC 1985, c. E-11.

56 *Resources and Technical Surveys Act*, RSC 1985, c. R-7.

57 *Fisheries Act*, supra endnote 13.

58 *Canadian Environmental Protection Act*, supra endnote 41.

59 *Clean Air Act*, RSC 1985, c. C-32.

60 *Environmental Contaminants Act*, RSC 1985, c. E-12.

61 *Ocean Dumping Control Act*, RSC 1985, c. O-2.

62 *Canada Water Act*, supra endnote 42.

63 *Department of the Environment Act*, RSC 1985, c. E-10.

64 *Fisheries Act*, supra endnote 13.

65 *Ontario Water Resources Act*, RSO 1990, c. O.40.

66 *Canadian Environmental Assessment Act*, SC 1992, c. 37.

67 *Transportation of Dangerous Goods Act*, RSC 1985, c. T-19.

68 *Motor Vehicle Safety Act*, RSC 1985, c. M-10.

69 *Canada Shipping Act*, RSC 1985, c. S-9.

70 *Arctic Waters Pollution Prevention Act*, RSC 1985, c. A-12. The administration of this Act is divided among three departments: Transport Canada; Energy, Mines and Resources; and Indian Affairs and Northern Development.

71 *Northern Pipeline Act*, RSC 1985, c. N-26.

72 *Navigable Waters Protection Act*, RSC 1985, c. N-22.

73 *National Transportation Act*, RSC 1985, c. N-20.01.

74 *Railway Act*, RSC 1985, c. R-3.

75 *Aeronautics Act*, RSC 1985, c. A-2.

76 *Oil and Gas Production and Conservation Act*, RSC 1985, c. O-7.

77 *Northern Inland Waters Act*, RSC 1985, c. N-25.

78 *Arctic Waters Pollution Prevention Act*, supra endnote 70.

79 *Canada Oil and Gas Act*, RSC 1985, c. O-6.

80 *The Lake of the Woods Control Board Act*, RSM 1987, c. L30.

81 *Nuclear Liability Act*, RSC 1985, c. N-28.

82 *Energy Supplies Emergency Act*, RSC 1985, c. E-9.

83 *Atomic Energy Control Act*, supra endnote 10.

84 *Pest Control Products Act*, RSC 1985, c. P-9.

85 *Pesticide Residue Compensation Act*, RSC 1985, c. P-10.

86 *Criminal Code*, RSC 1985, c. C-46, as amended.

87 *Fisheries Act*, supra endnote 13.

88 *Environmental Protection Act*, RSO 1990, c. E.19.

89 *Criminal Code*, supra endnote 86.

90 For further discussion of the potential effectiveness of these and other *Criminal Code* provisions in relation to harm to the environment, see Law Reform Commission of Canada, *Crimes Against the Environment*, Working Paper no. 44 (Ottawa: LRCC, 1985), as well as the studies referred to in endnote 3, above. For a similar discussion in the context of occupational health and safety, see Harry Glasbeek and Susan Rowland, "Are Injuring and Killing at Work Crimes?" (1979), 17 *Osgoode Hall LJ* 506.

91 *Crimes Against the Environment*, supra endnote 90, at 65. For a critique of Working Paper no. 44, see Rod McLeod, "The Provincial Perspective," in Environmental Law Centre (Alberta) Society, *Environmental Protection and the Canadian Constitution*, 13-17.

92 *Crimes Against the Environment*, supra endnote 90, at 69.

93 Law Reform Commission of Canada, *Omissions, Negligence, and Endangering*, Working Paper no. 46 (Ottawa: LRCC, 1985).

94 *Canadian Environmental Protection Act*, supra endnote 41, section 115.

95 *Environmental Protection Act*, supra endnote 88.

96 *Ontario Water Resources Act*, supra endnote 65.

97 *Pesticides Act*, RSO 1990, c. P.11.

98 *Environmental Assessment Act*, RSO 1990, c. E.18.

99 *Consolidated Hearings Act*, RSO 1990, c. C.29.

100 *Ontario Waste Management Corporation Act*, RSO 1990, c. O.39.

101 *Waste Management Act*, SO 1992, c. 1.

102 *Niagara Escarpment Planning and Development Act*, RSQ 1990, c. N.2.

103 *Environmental Protection Act*, supra endnote 88.
104 Ontario, *Government of Ontario KWIC Index to Services, 1989-90* (Toronto: Queen's Printer, 1990), 203.
105 Ontario, Ministry of Natural Resources, *Discussion Paper: Improving Planning for Ontario's Natural Resources* (Toronto: the ministry, December 1992).
106 *Provincial Parks Act*, RSO 1990, c. P.34.
107 *Public Lands Act*, RSO 1990, c. P.43.
108 *Aggregate Resources Act*, RSO 1990, c. A.8.
109 *Conservation Authorities Act*, RSO 1990, c. C.27.
110 *Endangered Species Act*, RSO 1990, c. E.15.
111 *Lakes and Rivers Improvement Act*, RSO 1990, c. L.3.
112 *Beds of Navigable Waters Act*, RSO 1990, c. B.4.
113 *Drainage Act*, RSO 1990, c. D.17.
114 *Health Protection and Promotion Act*, RSO 1990, c. H.7.
115 *Occupational Health and Safety Act*, RSO 1990, c. O.1.
116 *Dangerous Goods Transportation Act*, RSO 1990, c. D.1.
117 *Transportation of Dangerous Goods Act*, supra endnote 67.
118 *Municipal Act*, supra endnote 8.
119 *Planning Act*, supra endnote 7.
120 *Mining Act*, RSO 1990, c. M.14.
121 *Environmental Assessment Act*, supra endnote 98.
122 *Building Code Act*, RSO 1990, c. B.13.
123 *Planning Act*, supra endnote 7.
124 *Trees Act*, RSO 1990, c. T.20.
125 M.J. Puddister, *The Response of Ontario Municipalities to Tree Conservation* (Guelph, Ont.: University of Guelph, 1982).
126 See, for example, Ontario, Office of the Provincial Auditor, *1992 Annual Report* (Toronto: Queen's Printer, December 1992), 64.
127 *Planning Act*, supra endnote 7.
128 *Municipal Act*, supra endnote 8.
129 *Regional Municipality of Ottawa-Carleton Act*, RSO 1990, c. R.14.
130 *Municipality of Metropolitan Toronto Act*, RSO 1990, c. M.62.
131 *Planning Act*, supra endnote 7.
132 Ibid., sections 36 and 39.
133 *Municipal Act*, supra endnote 8.
134 Ibid., sections 234(1).5 and 234(1).6.
135 Ibid., section 102.
136 *Morrison v. City of Kingston*, [1938] OR 21, (1937), 4 DLR 740 (CA).
137 *Municipal Act*, supra endnote 8, sections 210.79-80.
138 Ibid., sections 210.89-92.
139 Ibid., sections 210.100-102.
140 Ibid., sections 210.134-150.
141 Ibid., sections 207.26, 210.152, 210.154, 210.163, 233, and 234.6.
142 *Trees Act*, supra endnote 124.
143 *Public Transportation and Highway Improvement Act*, RSO 1990, c. P.50.

144 *Woodlands Improvement Act*, RSO 1990, c. W.10.
145 *Forestry Act*, RSO 1990, c. F.26.
146 *Topsoil Preservation Act*, RSO 1990, c. T.12.
147 *Conservation Authorities Act*, supra endnote 109.

3

Choosing Your Remedies

CONTENTS

The most effective way to cope with change is to help create it.

Far East Fortune Cookies Co. Ltd.

INTRODUCTION

As you read this book, you may recognize a situation that requires you to take action to protect the environment. The situation may fall into one of these categories:

1. Someone is about to take an action that is *legal* as long as he or she follows the laws that set out where, when, how, and under what conditions this kind of activity can be carried on. No law is being broken, but the activity may be harmful to the environment — for example, the construction of a road, a dam, or a power plant, the subdivision of land for development, or the expansion of a building.
2. Someone is doing something *illegal*. For example:

   (a) a statute, a regulation, or a bylaw is being broken;
   (b) one of your common law rights is being violated; or
   (c) a government official is not performing a duty imposed by statute or by the requirements of "fairness" or "natural justice." He or she may be about to make an order affecting people's rights without consulting those likely to be affected, or to take some action that is not authorized by a statute; or he or she may already have made a decision without following proper procedures or taken an action that is not authorized by a statute.

In the first part of this chapter, we will point out different forums for your activity, such as courts and tribunals, and the advantages and disadvantages of each. *It is important to understand that using one approach does not necessarily prevent you from using the others.* In some cases you may use two or more approaches at the same time. In other cases, one approach excludes another. Obviously, in addition to other strategic considerations, you should consider whether using a particular approach will prevent you from using others.

In the second part of the chapter, we will discuss several general laws that do not deal specifically with the environment but that are useful to combat a variety of environmental problems such as noise, traffic congestion, litter, and other nuisances. We will also discuss where you can get help to finance the costly process of protecting your rights.

WHAT WILL THE LAW DO FOR YOU?

Agencies, Boards, and Tribunals

If an activity is legal as long as a prior approval is obtained from some government agency, you cannot go to a court to stop it. However, there is often a right to oppose the development before a specialized agency, board, or tribunal, such as a licensing commission, planning board, or environmental board. These agencies are set up to apply government policies to the decision-making process, to determine whether the proposal represents sound planning, and to listen to objectors.

In addition, once a potentially harmful project or business has been licensed or approved, if it does not comply with the law, there are two approaches to ensure compliance: (1) to prosecute for violations of statutes or to sue for breach of one's common law rights; or (2) to ask the licensing or approving agency to suspend or revoke the licence or approval or to impose conditions of operation on the licence or approval. In such cases, there is often a tribunal that will hear public complaints and can take these actions.

Advantages

1. One judge has eloquently summarized the advantages of administrative tribunals over courts:

   > The traditional rationale for the establishment of administrative tribunals is cheapness, expedition, and expertise. The objectives are freedom from what is popularly seen as the undue delay and cost of court proceedings and the inexpertise of judges trained in the law but not in matters of social improvement.[1]

In addition:

2. Tribunals rarely award costs against citizen intervenors.
3. Occasionally, intervenor funding is available to citizen groups.
4. Citizens can often appear before tribunals without the assistance of lawyers or expert witnesses. Sometimes, the tribunal will have its own lawyer, who may assist you in bringing forward the evidence you wish to put before the tribunal. Some tribunals have their own investigative staff, who will collect the evidence needed to show wrongdoing, and experts on the type of business or activity being carried on, who can testify whether the applicant or licensee is acting properly.
5. The procedure of such tribunals is often less formal than that of the courts, and the tribunal may have the right to hear evidence that would not be admissible in court.

Disadvantages

1. The range of remedies may be limited. Although the tribunal may impose conditions or suspend or revoke a licence, most tribunals cannot compensate you for harm that a regulated business has caused. The scope of their authority is also limited. For example, licensing authorities can look at the conduct of an applicant, but they have limited power to look at problems that will be caused by the location of a business, rather than its operation (such as customers taking up all the parking spots in the area, or how far a building is from the neighbour's property line), since these are land-use planning matters and must be considered by the planning authorities and the Ontario Municipal Board.[2] Sometimes, you may have to go before two or three tribunals to deal with different aspects of the problem.
2. Such agencies are subject to "capture" by the regulated industry. The members of the agency often come from the regulated industry or from the government department that regulates the industry. From constantly listening to the industry point of view, they

can become sympathetic to the problems the industry faces. Certain lawyers special-
ize in appearing before specific tribunals to represent these industries. They become
very familiar with the kinds of evidence and arguments that will sway the agency, and
the agency gets used to seeing these lawyers. A citizen or a group that makes an
isolated appearance or that is represented by a lawyer who is not familiar with the
tribunal may be at a disadvantage.

3. These tribunals do not have the same degree of independence as courts. They
sometimes blindly follow what they perceive to be government policies, whether or not
these policies apply to the situation at hand. They may be concerned to please the
minister they report to.

4. The informality of these tribunals is a two-edged sword. Sometimes they tromp all over
the rights of people who appear before them. Not all tribunals are sympathetic to the
ordinary citizen. If you happen to appear before a board that has no use for citizen
participation, there is little you can do to overturn its decision unless it grossly
oversteps its jurisdiction or the rules of procedural fairness. The judge who spelled out
the advantages of such tribunals also said: "Courts are generally reluctant to intervene
in the business of tribunals, and with their decisions, and the fact that they can is no
guarantee that they will."[3]

The Courts

Prosecutions

The breach of a statute, a regulation, or a bylaw is cause to prosecute the offenders. If the
defendant (the person accused of committing the offence) continues or repeats the illegal
conduct, he or she can often be charged and convicted of an offence for each day the conduct
occurs. In addition, people who authorize, assist in, encourage, participate in, or cover up the
conduct may also be charged. In some cases, they can be convicted only if they had *mens rea*
(a guilty mind); in others, it is sufficient to show that their involvement was negligent. If a
corporation is convicted, this does not prevent the officers, directors, employees, and agents
of the company from being convicted as well.

Charges for criminal offences and breaches of federal environmental laws are laid and
pursued using procedures set out in the *Criminal Code*.[4] Violations of provincial statutes and
municipal bylaws are pursued using simplified procedures set out in Ontario's *Provincial
Offences Act*.[5]

Which Court?

If the charge is laid under the *Criminal Code* or a federal environmental statute, the court that
has jurisdiction to hear the case will depend on whether the offence is indictable, a summary
conviction offence, or a hybrid. In some cases, the defendant has a choice of courts. In such
cases, the case may be heard before a judge alone or before a judge and jury in the Ontario
Court of Justice (General Division), or by a judge or a justice of the peace in the Ontario Court
of Justice (Provincial Division).

If there is a violation of a provincial statute or a municipal bylaw, the case will be heard
by a justice of the peace or by a judge of the Ontario Court of Justice (Provincial Division).

Judges are always lawyers; justices of the peace are not. They are often former police officers or municipal officials who have picked up some knowledge of the law in their past career. They receive some legal training, but many of them never do grasp the basic principles of the law, despite years of on-the-job training. In most parts of Ontario, environmental cases will automatically go before a justice of the peace unless one of the parties requests that it be heard by a judge and convinces the court that there are important legal or constitutional issues that warrant the attention of a judge.

The advantage of a trial before a justice of the peace is that it is available relatively quickly, and many justices of the peace intuitively reach the right result through common sense, even if they don't understand the law. However, if important legal issues are involved, there is a serious drawback to a trial before a justice of the peace. Under the *Provincial Offences Act*, the only appeal from a justice of the peace is to a judge of the Provincial Division, while a judgment made by a judge of the Provincial Division may be appealed to the General Division. A decision of the General Division carries much greater weight than a decision of a Provincial Division judge. (In either case, there may be an appeal to the Court of Appeal only if that court feels that it raises legal issues of provincial significance.)

It is important to understand that anyone can lay a charge for any provincial offence and for summary conviction criminal and federal offences, and prosecute the offence himself or herself, with or without the assistance of a lawyer. You may wish to consider this approach if law enforcement officials will not act, or if you want to retain control of how the prosecution unfolds. For this reason, we set out the procedures for conducting prosecutions, collecting evidence, and obtaining search warrants in Chapter 4 and appendixes II, III, and V.

Prosecutions have some advantages over civil actions, and some disadvantages.

Advantages

1. *Cost.* Initiating and pursuing a prosecution is much cheaper than suing in civil courts. Unlike civil courts, there is no fee for laying charges, subpoenaing witnesses, and other steps in the process. If you lose the case, the court usually cannot order you to pay the expenses of the defendant. In the few cases in which costs can be awarded against the prosecutor, they are restricted to small sums.
2. *Standing.* Except for indictable offences, and a few offences for which the law prohibits private prosecutions, anyone can prosecute for violation of a statute or a bylaw. When Shirley Strathy was angered by the destruction of trees on a city street by a contractor who was renovating a public school, she successfully prosecuted for violation of the *Trees Act*, even though she didn't own the trees. Usually, however, the only person who can sue for violation of common law rights is a person who suffers harm from the offending activity. Even then, there are standing barriers that may prevent legal action if the harm is no greater than that suffered by many others.
3. *Speed.* From the time you lay a charge until the date the trial begins is often six months or less. Civil actions are much slower. Because of all the procedural steps involved, it may take several years from the time a civil suit is launched to the start of the trial.
4. *Procedure.* Prosecution procedure is less complicated in many ways than civil procedure. For example, to draft a charge, setting out what the offender did that was illegal, you just follow the wording of the section of the statute or bylaw that creates the

offence and fill in the details of the time and place. Drafting a statement of claim for damages in a civil suit, in contrast, is an art.

5. *Deterrence.* Prosecution, or even fear of prosecution, is a very potent deterrent to continuing harmful conduct. In some ways, the fear of prosecution may have a greater deterrent value than the fear of civil suits, for several reasons:

  (a) Conviction of an offence carries a greater stigma than being sued successfully.
  (b) The publicity that a prosecution will attract is often greater than the publicity that a civil suit would attract.
  (c) Well-heeled defendants know that they can usually settle a civil suit out of court for a fraction of the damages claimed, and that the delays and costs will usually wear down all but the most determined plaintiffs. If you are using a civil suit not just to obtain compensation but also to set a legal precedent, you may have to settle rather than proceed to trial. If you proceed to trial and obtain a judgment for less than the settlement offer, you will have to pay the defendants' costs even though you won the case.
  (d) People charged with offences know that if they are convicted, the conviction will make it difficult to defend the civil suits that may follow. Conviction of an offence is often treated as evidence of negligence in a civil suit. If your prosecution is successful, the defendant knows you probably have the evidence to obtain an injunction or damages in a civil suit and is much more likely to stop the conduct. You have succeeded in stopping the offending activity without the cost of seeking an injunction.
  (e) As mentioned above, at relatively little cost, you can lay charges not only against the principal offender, but against everyone else working on the project who knows or should know that the principal offender's conduct is illegal.

Once you have warned employees, contractors, subcontractors, and suppliers of equipment and materials that the activity is illegal, you may have grounds to show that they were parties to the offence if they continue to participate.

Once others have been warned that they are breaking the law, or charged with the same offence as the principal offender, the principal offender will have many anxious people on his or her hands. This may sometimes be enough to stop work on the project until the case comes to court. In some cases, to keep the proceedings manageable, you may later withdraw charges against everyone but the main offenders. There is nothing wrong with doing this provided that you had reasonable grounds to lay the charge initially and were not doing so only for the purpose of intimidating the defendants.

Disadvantages

1. *The standard of proof.* In a prosecution, you must prove guilt beyond a reasonable doubt. In addition, a person usually cannot be convicted unless he or she was negligent or, in some cases, did the act deliberately. This can be very difficult to establish, especially for the private prosecutor, who has little access to information about the offender's business practices and procedures. In a civil action, it is

necessary only to prove the wrongdoing on the balance of probabilities. In some cases, you may succeed in a civil suit without showing negligence.

2. *Access to evidence*. In a civil suit, each party must disclose all relevant documents to the other and make the most knowledgeable people available for an "examination for discovery" in which they must reveal under oath everything they know about the events. In a prosecution, the prosecutor has a duty to reveal his or her evidence to the defendant, but the defendant generally has no duty to provide any information to the prosecutor.[6] Although the prosecutor may obtain a search warrant, it is difficult for public officials to persuade justices of the peace to issue a search warrant, and even more difficult for the private citizen to get one.

3. *Remedies available*. Traditionally, the main remedy in a prosecution was a fine, kept by the government rather than the person who conducted the prosecution. These fines were usually so low that many polluters would choose to pay a series of fines while continuing to pollute, because it was less expensive than installing new equipment. Because criminal courts could not make the orders that civil courts could — for example, injunctions and damages awards — these low fines often became nothing more than licences to pollute.

However, these disadvantages have been greatly reduced by amendments to many environmental statutes in recent years that have dramatically increased fine levels and allowed the courts to make many of the same kinds of orders as the civil courts, including, in some cases, awarding compensation to victims of the offence. In particular, it is noteworthy that under the *Planning Act*[7] and the *Municipal Act*,[8] the court that convicts an offender can issue an injunction that prohibits further breaches as well as impose a fine. Anyone who violates such an order deliberately or negligently may be found in contempt of court and fined or imprisoned.[9] Imprisonment is more frequently an option under environmental statutes than in the past, and the courts are becoming more willing to imprison environmental scoff-laws.

4. *Cost*. Although prosecutions are less costly than civil suits, successful prosecution can still be very expensive. The fact that costs cannot be awarded against the unsuccessful prosecutor is extremely important, but a potential disadvantage is that the successful prosecutor cannot recover any costs from the defendant.

5. *Limitation periods*. Except for indictable offences, which can often be prosecuted at any time, most environmental offences have a relatively short "limitation period." That is, charges must be laid within a time specified by statute, normally six months. However, as discussed below, a few environmental statutes have longer limitation periods. In addition, under the *Charter of Rights and Freedoms*,[10] any delay in proceeding to trial after charges are laid that is caused by the prosecutor or his or her witnesses not being ready to go or that is caused by inefficiency or overloaded court dockets can result in the dismissal of the charges. For most civil suits, there is a six-year limitation period,[11] and delays must be very lengthy and prejudicial to the defendant before they will result in the dismissal of a suit.

6. *Reverse onus*. In a prosecution, the prosecutor must prove *every* element of an offence beyond a reasonable doubt. This rule has been interpreted by the courts to mean that if the law puts the onus of proving any aspect of an offence on the defendant, this "reverse onus" may offend the *Charter*.[12]

This rule does not apply to civil suits, and in some cases where it is impractical in a civil suit for the plaintiff to prove something that is exclusively within the defendant's knowledge, the Legislature or the courts have required the defendant rather than the plaintiff to bring forward the evidence. For example, where harm occurs in a manner that is highly unlikely without negligence, the courts have said that negligence will be assumed unless the defendant proves otherwise.

Civil Remedies

Common Law Rights

Common law rights and remedies will be explained in some detail in Chapter 6. When should you use a civil suit for damages or an injunction instead of, or in addition to, a prosecution?

Advantages

1. *Remedies.* As mentioned above, compensation for losses and injunctions to prevent further misbehaviour is available in civil suits but sometimes not in a prosecution.
2. *Discovery.* The defendant must provide full disclosure of all relevant evidence in a civil suit. This provides the plaintiff with evidence not readily available to the private prosecutor.
3. *Settlement.* Because the extensive discovery process leads to the important information coming forward before the trial begins, and because of the cost, delay, and uncertainty of victory associated with civil litigation, the defendant may offer an acceptable amount of compensation to settle your claim without the need for a trial. If your only purpose in suing is to stop the conduct or obtain compensation and you are not interested in setting a precedent, settlement is an advantage.
4. *Costs.* If you are relatively sure of winning, civil suits are attractive because you may recover "costs" from the defendant as well as interest on the money that you are eventually awarded from the date you instituted the lawsuit. These costs usually cover one-half to two-thirds of your actual expenditures.
5. *Control over proceedings.* You may sue on your own or with the assistance of your lawyer. No government participation is necessary; there is no need to wait for the government to act, except in the case of a public nuisance (and if recommendations of the Ontario Law Reform Commission are implemented, not even then). Nor can the government step in and take over or stop a civil suit, as it can a prosecution.
6. *Immediate relief.* In some cases, a court will issue an immediate injunction against offending conduct, which remains in effect until the rights of the parties are decided by a trial. You must have a strong case to convince a court to issue this kind of injunction. So, if you succeed in getting one, you may need to go no further with your lawsuit. The defendant might decide it is better to switch than fight.
7. *Lower standard of proof than in prosecutions.*
8. *Availability of reverse onuses.*
9. *Longer limitation periods.* Although limitation periods are usually much longer for civil suits than for prosecutions, this advantage is dwindling as environmental statutes are being amended to lengthen the limitation periods.

For example, the *Environmental Protection Act*,[13] the *Ontario Water Resources Act*,[14] the *Pesticides Act*,[15] and the *Canadian Environmental Protection Act*[16] all provide that the limitation period does not begin to run until an environmental inspector discovers the offence. This reduces the problem, for example, of prosecuting offenders who illegally buried toxic waste many years ago. Even with longer limitation periods in civil suits, there is still a problem in suing for harm in such circumstances, or for environmental diseases that have long latency periods.

Disadvantages

The disadvantages of civil litigation are largely the same factors that have been listed above as advantages of prosecution: cost, delay, greater procedural and substantive complexity, standing barriers, and in many cases less certainty of success.

The Small Claims Court, discussed below, has many of the advantages of prosecution, without its disadvantages. It is designed to be accessible to ordinary citizens without the need for lawyers (the judge will often assist both parties in putting forward all the relevant evidence); quick (the trial will usually take place within a few months of starting the action); and inexpensive (fees charged by the court are minimal and the costs that can be awarded against you if you lose are limited); and it has fairly simple procedures.

Civil Suits To Prohibit Further Violations of Certain Statutes

Some statutes now provide that the court that convicts someone of an offence can make an order prohibiting further offences. In those cases, a private prosecutor can use the prosecution to obtain an injunction. Sometimes, however, it is necessary to go to a different court to get this remedy. In that case, only the attorney general or the minister responsible for administering the statute can obtain a restraining order. At common law, the ordinary citizen has no right to launch a civil action to restrain breaches of statutes and bylaws, unless those violations also happen to be violations of his or her personal common law rights. However, many statutes, such as the *Environmental Protection Act*, the *Ontario Water Resources Act*, the *Pesticides Act*, and the *Canadian Environmental Protection Act*, now give the minister or the attorney general the right to go to court to obtain an injunction against violations of statutes and bylaws. In addition, the attorney general has the right to take such action even in the absence of a statutory provision authorizing this.

Judicial Review of Government Action

Judicial review of government action is a special type of civil remedy, described in Chapter 1. The advantages and disadvantages are largely similar to those of other civil actions. There are some differences, however. First, there may be a shorter limitation period, or no limitation period. It is necessary to check a variety of statutes to be sure of the limitation period, which varies according to the remedy sought and the nature of the proceedings. Second, the evidence in many judicial review applications is limited to affidavits, and if proceedings of a quasi-judicial tribunal are being challenged, the transcripts of the proceedings of the tribunal may be the only evidence. Without the need for lengthy discoveries or examination and cross-examination of witnesses in court, most judicial review applications take less time to prepare and less time before the court. The cost of proceeding is therefore generally lower and much more predictable than that of other forms of civil action. One disadvantage, however, is that if the government has erred, often all the court can do is require the government to do it over again in a fair way. Often, the court cannot substitute its own decision for that of the government agency. In many cases, therefore, it is necessary to decide whether victory in a judicial review will accomplish anything.

Which Court?

Different branches of the Ontario Court (General Division) handle civil suits depending on the amount of money you are seeking. You can claim up to $6,000 in the Small Claims Court. You cannot, however, obtain an injunction in the Small Claims Court. An award of costs in this court cannot exceed 15 per cent of the amount claimed or the value of the property you are seeking to recover. The court may, however, award higher costs in those rare circumstances in which it "considers it necessary in the interests of justice to penalize a party, counsel or agent for unreasonable behaviour in the proceedings."[17] If the amount involved is more than $500, the losing party may appeal to the Divisional Court. Otherwise, there is no appeal. Claims for an injunction or for more than the Small Claims Court limits are heard by the General Division. Appeals are to the Court of Appeal.

All applications for judicial review of the actions of Ontario government and municipal officials are brought in the Divisional Court, a branch of the Ontario Court (General Division). This court was set up to provide expertise and consistency in this specialized area of law. Appeals from Divisional Court are to the Court of Appeal. Actions of federal departments and agencies are reviewed by the Federal Court of Canada. Decisions of this court are appealed to the Federal Court of Appeal.

Other Remedies

Intervention in Proceedings

Courts and tribunals play different roles in the legal system. These differences are reflected in the ease with which "outsiders" can participate in their proceedings. Courts usually resolve disputes between a small number of parties. Tribunals exist to explore public policy options and to decide which option best represents the public interest. As a result, it is often relatively easy for individuals, community groups, and public interest groups to intervene in proceedings launched by others before boards such as the Ontario Municipal Board (OMB), the Environmental Assessment Board (EAB), and the Ontario Energy Board. For example, in the 1970s, Pollution Probe used to intervene in hearings held to determine whether a specific site would be approved for waste disposal. The group tried to show that approving more landfill sites was not the answer to waste problems, by leading evidence of options for waste reduction and recycling that would reduce the need for large waste disposal sites.

Because courts deal primarily with private disputes or prosecutions by the government, they are not as welcoming of intervention by "outsiders" as tribunals are. The traditional attitude of the courts toward public interest intervenors was summed up by a justice of the

House of Lords: "A suit is not like an omnibus in which anyone is entitled to find a place who hails it from the pavement in the course of its journey."[18]

The courts do recognize, however, the possibility that their decisions may occasionally raise broader issues of public policy. The rules of various courts often allow people to intervene in two ways: (1) as an "added party," when the person's rights and liabilities are directly and substantially affected by the outcome of the suit, and (2) as a "friend of the court," when the person wants the court to be aware of the broader implications of its decision and its potential effect on the public or groups within the public. A person who is recognized as an added party has all the rights of other parties to lead evidence, cross-examine, etc., as well as the same liability as other parties to pay costs to the winner and collect from the loser. A friend of the court has a more limited role and less exposure to financial liability. The rules governing proceedings in the Ontario courts allow any person, with the court's permission, to intervene as a "friend of the court" to assist the court by way of argument.[19] Usually, there will be no costs awarded against a person who is accepted as a friend of the court. You may wish to intervene in a court case if you are concerned that the parties may not bring forward a public interest perspective or raise issues that affect the broader public interest. There is no specific intervention rule in the Federal Court, which uses other rules to authorize interventions when it sees fit. The Supreme Court of Canada has its own set of rules, which include a rule allowing the court to entertain interventions.[20]

The Ontario Court of Appeal has recognized the importance of interventions in *Charter*[21] cases, where a judgment will have a great impact on others who are not immediate parties to the proceeding, and has recognized the wisdom of a "relaxation of the rules" and the increased desirability of permitting interventions in *Charter* cases. The court has said that in deciding whether to grant an application, the matters to be considered are the nature of the case; the issues that arise; and the likelihood that the applicant will be able to make a useful contribution to the resolution of the case without causing injustice to the immediate parties.[22] Environmental groups have intervened in several important cases, including a challenge to decisions of Ontario environmental tribunals to award interim costs and costs in advance of a hearing to intervenors,[23] a pesticide company's challenge to a federal advisory committee's recommendation to ban the pesticide Alachlor,[24] and a test of whether the federal government's environmental assessment and review process (EARP) guidelines applied to a dam in Alberta.[25] Although costs can be awarded against such intervenors, it is very unlikely.[26]

The Reference[27]

Another way to bring important matters before the courts is to ask the government to refer important legal questions to the Court of Appeal, such as the correct interpretation of a statute or whether the government has the power to pass the statute. This is called a reference. To initiate a reference, it is not necessary to have a special property or financial interest, or to wait for someone else to launch a suit. You need only convince the government that the law is unclear, that important issues are at stake, and that it would be better for the government to ask the court for a ruling than to deprive someone of justice or to wait for private disputes to arise. If a reference is held, the court will often welcome intervention by knowledgeable public interest groups.

The Ombudsman: A "Court of Last Resort" when All Other Remedies Fail

The Office of the Ombudsman

Since 1975, Ontario has had an ombudsman — that is, a person to whom anyone can take complaints about unfair treatment by government, without going through the expensive, time-consuming, and worrisome process of hiring lawyers and using courts. This person is meant to be a watchdog, to keep government administrators from abusing the wide powers given them to make countless decisions that affect our daily lives.

In principle, the ombudsman is an impartial investigator who is above politics and independent of the bureaucracy. To insulate the ombudsman from political pressure, he or she has a 10-year term of office and cannot be removed except for misconduct.

Although the ombudsman started with a single office in Toronto in 1975, by 1992 complaints could also be made to and investigated from eight regional offices, located in Sudbury, Kenora, London, North Bay, Ottawa, Sault Ste. Marie, Thunder Bay, Timmins, and Windsor.

What Complaints Can the Ombudsman Deal with?

Under the *Ombudsman Act*,[28] the ombudsman may investigate any decision, recommenda-tion, act, or omission by a "governmental organization" that affects any person or body of people in their personal capacity. "Governmental organizations" include branches and ministries of the Ontario government, as well as its agencies, boards and commissions.[29] This includes tribunals such as the Environmental Assessment Board and the Environmental Appeal Board that adjudicate disputes.[30]

There are some matters the ombudsman cannot investigate. The ombudsman cannot look into the actions of a private business. If, however, a private business is harming the environment with the assistance of a government agency (which has given it an approval or licence or a grant or subsidy, or has refused to enforce the law when the business is breaking it), the ombudsman can sometimes investigate the government's part in it. The ombudsman also cannot investigate the activities or decisions of municipalities, the federal government, the courts,[31] or any deliberations or proceedings of Cabinet or a Cabinet committee. Thus, in one case, the ombudsman had to advise a concerned citizens' group that he had no jurisdiction to investigate a Cabinet decision on the location of a hydro transmission line corridor through environmentally sensitive areas. The citizens had questioned whether the government had acted fairly in approving the location against the recommendations of its own Environmental Hearing Board (now the Environmental Assessment Board).[32]

The ombudsman may not investigate any decision, recommendation, act, or omission if the complainant still has a right to appeal or to apply for a rehearing or review by another government agency, such as the Environmental Assessment Board or the Ontario Municipal Board, under any provincial statute. The ombudsman can investigate only after the right has been exercised or the time for exercising it has expired.

The ombudsman does not have to investigate a complaint if he or she feels that there is another remedy available, that the complaint is frivolous, vexatious, or in bad faith, or that the complainant does not have a sufficient personal interest in the matter. In one case, the ombudsman's staff refused to investigate a complaint made by the Canadian Environmental

Law Association (CELA) on behalf of a client because a staff member decided that CELA was using the ombudsman's office to further its own agenda of reforming systemic unfairness within the Ministry of Natural Resources (MNR). It took a meeting with the ombudsman himself to compel the staff to do their job. (The ombudsman ultimately found the complaint — that MNR had acted unfairly in allowing Crown land to be used as a fishing resort without any notice to neighbours who might be affected by noise, traffic, and other nuisances — to be justified.) If the ombudsman refuses to investigate a complaint or abandons an investigation, he or she must notify the complainant of this decision, but has no duty to give any reasons for refusing help.[33]

The ombudsman is not limited to individual cases and individual remedies. He or she can investigate systemic wrongs, and can launch an investigation in his or her own name to take preventive action against government policies before they cause harm to individuals.

How Does the Ombudsman Deal with a Complaint?

A lawyer in the legal services branch of the office of the ombudsman will give an opinion on whether the matter is within the ombudsman's jurisdiction. If the lawyer states that the complaint is outside the ombudsman's jurisdiction, the ombudsman will inform the complainant of this in writing, giving reasons for his or her decision. The ombudsman's staff will often refer the complainant to the appropriate agency to help.

One of the reasons that government officials refuse to help people is their belief — often mistaken — that a matter is outside their jurisdiction. Although decisions of the ombudsman are not generally open to judicial review, a refusal to help because a matter is outside his or her jurisdiction is probably an exception. If the ombudsman has interpreted his or her powers too narrowly, the Divisional Court would probably order the ombudsman to carry out an investigation.

If the ombudsman does decide that he or she can investigate, the head of the governmental organization to be investigated will then be informed of this intention. The ombudsman may require any officer, employee, or member of any governmental organization to furnish him or her with information pertinent to the matter despite the oath of secrecy taken by civil servants. Government employees often refuse to assist individuals because they are afraid of losing their jobs if they give out information. The *Ombudsman Act* provides, however, that giving information to the ombudsman is not a breach of the oath of secrecy that government employees must take under the *Public Service Act*.[34] The ombudsman's staff also have the right to enter government offices, seize files, hold hearings, and summon anyone who may have relevant information to appear before the ombudsman and tell what he or she knows about the complaint.

What Can the Ombudsman Do After Investigating?

If the ombudsman concludes that a decision, a recommendation, an act, or an omission was illegal, unreasonable, unjust, oppressive, improperly discriminatory, or just plain *wrong*; if it was done in accordance with an unfair or an unreasonable law or practice; if it was based on a mistake; or if a discretionary power was exercised for an improper purpose or on irrelevant grounds, the ombudsman must report his or her opinion to the responsible governmental organization, and to the Cabinet minister to whom that governmental organization reports. The ombudsman may make any recommendation he or she sees fit to rectify the problem for the complainant and to prevent others from being harmed by the offending practice. The recommendations may be to change a statute, a regulation, a policy, or a practice, to administer them in a different manner, or to compensate people for financial losses that result from the offending practice.

The ombudsman may give the organization a time limit to report on the steps it has taken to implement his or her recommendations. If the ombudsman is not satisfied that appropriate action is being taken, he or she may send her report to the premier. If the premier does not order the organization to take the recommended action, the ombudsman's ultimate power is to report to the Legislature, through its Standing Committee on the Ombudsman. If the committee agrees with the ombudsman, it can call officials before it to justify their refusal to implement the recommendations, and it may report to the Legislature its support for the ombudsman's recommendations. This recourse to the Legislature and its committee allows the opposition parties, the media, and the public to become aware of the situation.

How Do You Bring a Matter to the Ombudsman's Attention?

The *Ombudsman Act* requires that all complaints be made in writing. A letter to the ombudsman should include all the facts of the case, including a reason for the complaint. However, the ombudsman's office is not rigid about the statutory requirement. If someone phones or goes to the office, he or she will be interviewed in a way that will enable the ombudsman's staff to put the complaint into writing.

How Does the Ombudsman Treat Environmental Complaints?

Ironically, although several ombudsmen have announced their intention to "reach out" to the public to make them more aware of the ombudsman's services, the ombudsman's staff refused our request for information about how the ombudsman handles environmental complainants on the grounds of secrecy. The experience of the Canadian Environmental Law Association has been that when it refers complainants to the ombudsman, their complaints "disappear into a black hole."[35] However, a few examples do appear in the ombudsman's annual reports, which show a concern with environmental protection both when upholding complaints and when upholding the actions of government officials. For example:

1. A complainant who held a licence to harvest wild rice from lakes in northern Ontario complained that the Ministry of Natural Resources (MNR) was unreasonable in prohibiting him from applying fertilizers to the lakes to increase their production of wild rice. The ombudsman accepted the view of the Ministry of the Environment, which was providing advice to MNR on this issue that adding nutrients to lakes may result in algal blooms, oxygen depletion, and fish kills.[36]

2. A complainant living near the site of a proposed subway station was concerned about the environmental impact of the site and the associated development it would attract. The Environmental Assessment Advisory Committee (see Chapter 9) had recommended to the minister of the environment that the project be subject to an environmental impact

assessment under the *Environmental Assessment Act*; but the ministry rejected the recommendation. The ombudsman rejected the minister's conclusion that the impact would be minor. He felt that the residents would be significantly affected by the development that would follow construction of the station, and found the minister's decision to be unreasonable.[37]

3. The ombudsman concluded that MNR was not unreasonable in requesting that a privately owned cottage be removed from public land. The complainant's grandfather had built a cabin on an island in the North Channel of Lake Huron in the 1930s. Although the ombudsman recognized the complainant's strong emotional ties to the land, he felt that the public interest in preserving the land in its natural state for all to enjoy was paramount.[38]

4. An owner of a secluded lakefront cabin was concerned that MNR's sale of the adjacent land to a tourist outfitter would result in disturbance of his enjoyment of his cabin. The ombudsman's suggestions led to the cabin owner giving up his property to the Crown and receiving a secluded lot in return.[39]

5. Information provided by the ombudsman led to the Ministry of the Environment's insurer to agree to compensate homeowners for damage when sewage backed up in a sewage collection system operated by the ministry.[40]

Who Watches the Watchdog?

The ombudsman is supposed to act as a watchdog over citizens' rights to help humanize the process of dealing with government. What if the ombudsman sets up another unresponsive government bureaucracy in turn? The ombudsman's office is insulated from public account-ability in the same way as most other government departments: the staff work in secret, they have to give very little information, even to the person initiating the complaint (in fact, if the investigator agrees with the complainant and recommends action but more senior officials in the ombudsman's office overrule this recommendation, the ombudsman and the ombuds-man's staff will not reveal this to the complainant), and their decisions and actions are largely immune from judicial review or scrutiny by other government agencies. In addition, the very independence of the ombudsman can be a barrier to accountability. The ombudsman has objected to a committee of the Legislature looking into allegations of excessive delay in resolving cases on the grounds that this investigation would threaten the ombudsman's independence.[41]

Complainants have, in fact, had difficulties getting attention from the ombudsman, for such reasons as incompetent investigators and lengthy delays in completing investigations, particularly in the early years of the office. If you have complaints about the ombudsman, you should bring them first to his or her attention. If you are still not satisfied, you might send them in writing to the premier, the leaders of the opposition parties, and your local MPP, or to the Standing Committee on the Ombudsman at Queen's Park. Although the committee has stated that it will not act as a "court of appeal" on decisions by the ombudsman or an "ombudsman on the ombudsman," it will occasionally review the decisions and practices of the ombuds-man at the request of members of the public, at its discretion. The committee set out the circumstances under which it will do this and the procedure it will follow in its 1989 report.[42]

A Federal Ombudsman?

Although 9 of Canada's 10 provinces now have an ombudsman, the federal government does not, even though in October 1977 it announced its intention to appoint one. The government does have several ombudsman-like offices for special areas of concern: a commissioner of official languages to handle complaints about implementation of the *Official Languages Act*,[43] a correctional investigator or "prisoners' ombudsman" to investigate inmates' complaints of mistreatment by prison officials, a human rights commissioner, a privacy commissioner to ensure that the government does not divulge personal information in its files, and an access to information commissioner to ensure that the government does give out other information. Canada's first information commissioner, Inger Hansen, resigned in 1990, after releasing a report that was highly critical of government stonewalling of citizens' attempts to get information.[44] When Hansen left, the government combined the information commissioner and privacy commissioner positions, creating an institutional arrangement less likely to champion public access to information.

The Provincial Auditor and the Federal Auditor General

Both Ontario and the federal government have auditors who annually scrutinize the spending of government departments. Their role has evolved from ensuring proper financial management to evaluating programs to determine whether the public is getting good value for their money. Both officials have at times made scathing comments about the competence of the respective environment departments. Although these auditors do not accept and investigate complaints from individuals, there is nothing to stop individuals or groups from bringing systemic incompetence or inefficiency to their attention. When they are carrying out their annual reviews of agencies, they may decide to investigate areas of concern brought to their attention by the public.

GENERAL LAWS THAT CAN BE USED TO PROTECT THE ENVIRONMENT

Licensing Bylaws

Municipalities have the power[45] to license, regulate, and in some cases to prohibit about 70 specific callings or activities, from auctioneers and bankruptcy sales to waxworks and wheeled vehicles. In some cases the municipal council itself licenses and regulates these trades, but council is often given power to delegate this role to various commissions or boards. (In Metropolitan Toronto, the Metropolitan Toronto Licensing Commission is responsible for issuing business licences.) In many cases these powers are to be exercised subject to specific statutes such as the *Bread Sales Act*,[46] the *Milk Act*,[47] the *Theatres Act*,[48] the *Planning Act*,[49] or the *Health Protection and Promotion Act*.[50]

Business licences must be renewed annually. Many possibilities for the control of nuisances lie buried in the licensing bylaws. Much more use could be made, for example, of Metropolitan Toronto bylaw no. 20-85,[51] which states in part that

> No person licensed under this Part shall use or permit his automobile service station to be used for the purpose of wrecking, parking, storing or selling motor vehicles, or *except in an enclosed*

building for ... vulcanizing tires or tubes, or performing therein any repairs to motor vehicles other than minor or running repairs [emphasis added];[52]

and that ice cream vending vehicles shall

refrain from ringing bells or chimes or making any other recognizable sounds more frequently than at five-minute intervals or for more than five seconds at a time in one place, or after sunset;

No amplification of any sounds of recognition used on such vehicle shall be used so as to constitute a nuisance.[53]

Citizens have been successful in having licences refused, suspended, or revoked when the business activities do not comply with a licensing law or otherwise cause a nuisance.

Property Tax Reductions as a Remedy for Environmental Impacts

What can you do if your once peaceful home is now on the flight path of noisy aircraft? Or if the new mill or mine upstream from your property has polluted your water? Pollution and other environmental impacts may interfere with your enjoyment of your property. They may also lower the market value of your home. Since the amount of property tax you pay is based on the value of your property, if the assessment of your property value is reduced, your taxes are also reduced.

The rules for assessing property values are set out in the *Assessment Act*.[54] Based on this assessment, the municipality collects taxes. To appeal the assessment, you initially present your arguments to the Assessment Review Board. This is a permanent body set up under the *Assessment Review Board Act* by the Ontario government to hear such appeals.[55] It can sit anywhere in the province that the chair decides. If you and your neighbours get together to have the assessments lowered, it is likely that the board will come to your area.[56] This is an informal tribunal, in which you may not need the services of a lawyer to present your case.

If this body does not alter your assessment, or does not reduce it as much as you think it should, you may appeal its decision to the Ontario Municipal Board.

Perhaps the most famous example of a property tax reduction due to pollution is the case of the Malvern subdivision in Toronto. Homes were built on land where low-level radioactive waste had been disposed of. As a result, they were unsalable, and their assessment was reduced to one dollar. Other examples of assessment reductions include homes close to a waste disposal site,[57] lands subject to flooding,[58] homes insulated with urea formaldehyde foam,[59] homes on a busy street with heavy traffic,[60] an area of Sudbury where ice falls from the Inco superstack onto homes and streets, and where there is noise, odours, shaking from underground blasting, interference to TV reception from the Inco railway, and oxygen lines and 130,000 volt electrical lines running overtop the buildings,[61] a condominium unit that had a less attractive view than others in an apartment building, lack of privacy, lack of security, and interference by lights and fumes from cars,[62] and industrial property consisting of lagoons filled with pulp mill waste.[63]

Early Closing and Holiday Closing Laws

Nuisances from the operation of businesses can be reduced by controlling their hours of operation.

Sunday Shopping

Sunday closing laws could be an important tool for reducing traffic and other nuisances at least one day a week. There is a law limiting Sunday shopping, but in the face of a recession, high consumer prices, cross-border shopping hurting the economy of Canadian border towns, retailers consistently defying the law, and public opinion polls showing that many people favour Sunday shopping, the Ontario government announced on June 3, 1992 that it will no longer enforce this law. We get the kinds of laws we deserve, and Ontarians have made it clear that the chance to buy a stereo on Sunday is a more important value than a common day of rest.

The *Retail Business Holidays Act*[64] prohibits everyone who carries on a retail business in a retail business establishment from offering any goods or services for sale or admitting members of the public to the premises on Sundays and on eight statutory holidays, with a limited number of exceptions. One such exception, to protect the freedom of religion, is that a person whose religion requires him or her to close on another day of the week may stay open on Sunday.[65] Carrying on business on these days is an offence punishable by a fine of the greater of $50,000 and the gross sales on the day of the offence.[66] In addition, a municipality or the attorney general can apply to the Ontario Court (General Division) for an order forcing the offender to close.[67]

On June 3, 1992, the government introduced an amendment that would redefine "holiday" so as to *not* include Sundays (except Easter Sunday) to allow shopping on Sundays. This would be retroactive to June 3, 1992, when the government announced it would stop enforcing the *Retail Business Holidays Act*.[68]

The *Retail Business Holidays Act*, however, controls only Sunday shopping. Since the repeal of the federal and provincial *Lord's Day Acts*, which prohibited a wider variety of business activities, there is no law that generally prohibits the carrying on of other business activities that may cause a nuisance on Sundays, such as operating a factory. The only other laws that can assist in ensuring at least one day of relative peace are two statutes aimed at protecting workers. The *One Day's Rest in Seven Act*[69] provides that hotels, restaurants, and cafés must give employees at least one day off a week, and "wherever possible" that day must be Sunday. The *Employment Standards Act*[70] prohibits all employers from forcing workers to work more than 8 hours a day or 48 hours a week. By hiring additional workers, though, the business or industry can stay open 24 hours a day, seven days a week.

Early Closing Bylaws

The *Municipal Act* gives the councils of cities, towns, and villages the power to order shops[71] and gas stations[72] to be closed at certain times. "Shops" are defined to include a building or part of a building, booth, stall, or place where goods are exposed for sale by retail; and barber shops, beauty parlours, shoe repair shops, and hat cleaning and blocking businesses, but not licensed hotels or taverns, restaurants, or banquet halls.

Council may pass bylaws ordering shops and gas stations to be closed from 6 PM until 5 AM of the following day, and on holidays. In addition, council may order shops to shut down for the whole of one day of the council's choosing and for the afternoon of another day each week. For instance, a council that wanted to slow the pace of life could order all shops to close all day Sunday and every Wednesday afternoon, as used to be the normal business practice in some areas of Canada.

Council may order one class of shop (beauty parlours, for example) to close at a certain hour, or on a certain day, while allowing another class (such as barber shops) to remain open. However, council may not discriminate between two beauty parlours by ordering one to close and allowing the other to remain open.

Because council may not discriminate between shops within the same class, it is questionable whether early closing bylaws could be used to lessen noise and traffic in residential areas that are close to shopping centres and large stores. Council probably could not, for example, pass a bylaw that required all department stores adjacent to residential areas to close early. To prevent nuisance from such stores may require recourse to land-use planning, licensing, or environmental protection laws on a case-by-case basis. In contrast, the *Municipal Act* explicitly gives municipalities the power to regulate the hours of operation of gas stations on an area-by-area basis.[73]

Misleading Advertising

In recent years, several companies have taken advantage of a groundswell of public concern about the environment by dubbing their products "green" or "environmentally friendly." Containers have been given names like "Envirocan" and "Enviropac." Other companies have taken out full-page ads in newspapers and magazines touting how much they are doing for the environment. These companies have included mining and forest products companies, which are among the worst polluters and exploiters of both renewable and non-renewable resources. Still others try to associate their products with nature in the public mind, no matter how wasteful of energy or resources those products may be, by filling their ads with scenes of howling wolves and verdant forests.

Is this kind of advertising legal? Only if it is accurate. It is not legal if it is false or misleading.

What Does the Law Say?

False and misleading advertising is an offence under both federal and provincial law. Section 52(1) of the federal *Competition Act*[74] states:

> No person shall, for the purpose of promoting, directly or indirectly, the supply or use of a product or for the purpose of promoting, directly or indirectly, any business interest, *by any means whatsoever, (a) make a representation to the public that is false or misleading in a material respect* [emphasis added].

The *Competition Act* also prohibits:

- any statement regarding the performance, efficacy, or length of life of a product that is not based on a proper test;
- any warranty or guarantee or promise to repair a product that is unlikely to be carried out;
- any misleading representation as to the price at which the product is ordinarily sold;[75]
- any representation that a test of the performance or efficacy of a product has been made and any publishing of a testimonial for a product, unless the test or testimonial is accurate and has either been published previously or is published with the permission of the person who made the test or gave the testimonial.[76]

These misleading statements are prohibited not only in the media but also on the product itself, its wrapper or container, and on anything accompanying the product, in the store, over the telephone, or at the homeowner's door.[77]

Violations of these provisions are offences. If the prosecutor proceeds by the summary conviction route, fines of up to $25,000 and imprisonment for up to one year are possible. If the prosecutor considers the offence to be particularly serious, he or she may proceed by indictment, allowing the court to impose a fine as high as it wishes and up to five years in prison.[78]

Ontario's *Business Practices Act*[79] also prohibits false and misleading advertising. The Act prohibits "unfair practices,"[80] and deems any "false, misleading or deceptive" consumer representation to be an unfair practice.[81] If such a representation is made *knowingly*, the person who made it is committing an offence. If this person is an individual, the penalty is a fine of up to $25,000 or imprisonment of up to one year, or both.[82] A corporation may be fined up to $100,000.[83] Whether the misrepresentation was deliberate or accidental, the Ministry of Consumer and Commercial Relations may order the person to stop making these representations.[84]

How Is the Law Enforced?

At his or her discretion, the director of investigation and research of the *Competition Act* in the federal Department of Consumer and Corporate Affairs may undertake an investigation as a result of complaints from the public or studies by the director's staff.[85] If any six adults apply for an inquiry, the director *must* investigate their complaint. They must submit a "statutory declaration" stating that they believe an offence has been or is about to be committed. The director must also investigate if he or she has reason to believe that the offence has been or is about to be committed.[86]

Unless six people sign a statutory declaration, however, the director has no obligation to investigate a complaint, and in fact most complaints are not investigated. Because staff resources are limited, the director will investigate only those cases that he or she believes are "likely to bring about an overall improvement in the quality of market information."[87]

In fact, the director will not even tell a complainant whether his or her complaint is one that will be investigated or one that will be ignored. Even if the director does investigate, the complainant will not be advised of the progress or the final result of the investigation. The department takes the position that a provision in the Act that requires the investigation to be carried on in private prevents officials from extending even the common courtesy of telling citizens whether any action has been taken on their complaints.

The *Business Practices Act*[88] is administered by the Ontario Ministry of Consumer and Commercial Relations (MCCR). Complaints may be addressed to the branch. MCCR officials say that, unlike their federal counterparts, they are willing to reveal whether they are pursuing your complaint and the results of their investigation.

The advertising industry also has a self-policing group. The Canadian Advertising Foundation has developed several codes of standards for different kinds of advertisement.

Complaints about false and misleading advertising that violates these codes can be made to the Canadian Advertising Standards Council. Compliance with these codes is voluntary, but if the council rules that an ad violates a code, many newspapers and broadcasters will not carry it.[89]

A prosecution for misleading advertising will not solve anyone's individual environmental problem. However, proceedings in the courts and before tribunals such as the Commercial Registration Appeal Tribunal and publicity arising out of the case can impress upon unprincipled segments of the business community that they cannot go on indefinitely misleading the public about the state of the environment and manipulating public opinion for profit.

FINANCING YOUR PARTICIPATION IN THE LEGAL SYSTEM

Environmental hearings before tribunals and litigation in the courts are often so expensive that only the very poor who obtain legal aid and the very rich can afford to exercise their rights. Enforcing your rights or participating in the decision-making processes of boards and tribunals can be extremely costly. There are three kinds of expenses you may incur in using courts and tribunals: legal fees, disbursements, and "costs."

Legal fees are the fees you must pay your own lawyer. These vary according to the complexity of the case, the time involved, the forum in which you bring your action, your lawyer's experience, and the location of his or her practice. *Disbursements* are the out-of-pocket expenses your lawyer incurs in setting the court or tribunal system in motion and collecting evidence. They include amounts paid to the court or board to purchase subpoenas, file documents, and obtain copies of documents, and witness fees. If you need expert witnesses such as doctors or scientists, you may have to pay them substantial fees. Again, the cost of disbursements will vary greatly with the complexity of the case, the forum chosen, and the time involved. *Costs* are awards made by the court (or, in rare cases, by a tribunal) to compensate the winner of a lawsuit for some of his or her legal expenses.

The expense is sometimes so great that it is impossible for the ordinary person to participate without help.

Where To Get Help

Pro Bono Assistance

Lawyers have a tradition of providing service for free to those who cannot afford to enforce their rights. When a serious issue of public importance is involved, lawyers may donate their services. Some young lawyers will do this to establish a reputation. However, lawyers' overhead is high, and few lawyers can afford to conduct a lengthy trial or hearing without substantial payment. Occasionally, a law professor will donate his or her services because a case raises important issues. The professor does not have the same overhead and may have a little more time than a busy practitioner.

Universities are also the best places to find experts such as scientists and economists for the same reasons. There is an additional reason. Most consultants cannot afford to alienate their potential clientele — industry and government — while academics are less dependent on these sectors for their livelihood.

For a lengthy case, however, it may be necessary to turn to other sources for help.

Legal Aid

The purpose of the *Legal Aid Act*[90] is to ensure that no one is deprived of the opportunity to protect *certain* legal rights merely because he or she lacks money. Unlike the Ontario health insurance plan, which covers most medical problems, the legal aid plan does not cover many problems for which one needs a lawyer. The plan is intended to provide a lawyer to defend you against criminal charges or provincial offences charges that carry severe penalties such as imprisonment. The plan will also defend you when you are sued. However, if you want to initiate legal action yourself, the plan is restricted to cases that a person of modest means would take to court. The availability of legal aid to hire a lawyer to represent you before a board or tribunal is very limited. Cases that a person of modest means would take to court are considered to be those in which a person has substantial financial or property interests at stake, rather than cases of general public interest.

There are two branches of the legal aid plan. The first assists you in obtaining the services of a lawyer in private practice. The second establishes community legal clinics, staffed with lawyers.

Two factors will determine whether an application for legal aid for funds to hire a "private lawyer" or a request for the help of a legal aid clinic will be successful:

1. the financial position of the applicant, and
2. legal and policy restrictions.

Obtaining Legal Aid To Retain a Lawyer in Private Practice

When you apply for a legal aid "certificate," you must undergo a financial assessment and a legal assessment (an assessment of the strength of your case and whether it is the kind of case the plan will fund, and whether a person of modest means would pursue it using his or her own money).

1. The Financial Position of the Applicant

The philosophy behind the legal aid plan is that you pay what you can afford and still have the right to retain the lawyer of your choice. In practice, legal aid is provided on two bases, depending on your assets and income:

- You may be granted an unconditional certificate, under which legal aid will pay for the lawyer's services and disbursements and, in exceptional cases, the costs awarded against you if you lose. If you cannot afford to, you will not have to repay any of the money.
- In some instances, legal aid is granted on a repayment basis. In effect, you are given an interest-free loan that covers the lawyer's services and disbursements and, again in exceptional cases, costs. You agree to repay a certain amount of the money, usually less than the original grant. The amount varies with your ability to repay, not the amount of time the lawyer actually puts into the case. You enter into a contract with legal aid to repay the amount, usually in installments over the next several months or years. You are not charged interest. Failure to make any of the payments might result in the loss of the legal aid certificate.

There is some flexibility. If your financial circumstances change after you enter the agreement, your ability to pay might be reassessed and the repayment agreement altered.

Court costs are not covered by the legal aid certificate. Since the costs that can be awarded against the loser in a civil suit are so high, they remain a serious deterrent to the enforcement of common law rights, even if your own lawyer's fees are being paid. The regulation provides for an application to the provincial director to pay your court costs if you lose.[91] As a matter of practice, legal aid will not pay your costs if you lose to a corporation, only if you lose a case against another individual.[92]

In determining your financial position, legal aid will look at both your income and your assets. For example, you may have little income, but own valuable property. If you must agree to repay but cannot make installment payments, legal aid may take a lien on any real estate you may own that has sufficient value to cover the amount you owe them. For example, if you own a house or a farm, legal aid could put a lien on it and would recover the amount paid out for legal expenses if you sold the property, or refinanced, or you died and the property was left to someone in your will.

As a rule of thumb, if you are on welfare, or if you have only a small income and have dependants to support, are not leading an expensive lifestyle, and own few assets, you will probably receive free legal assistance if your case is one that fits within the kinds that legal aid covers.

If you have an income, own a house or a farm or an expensive car or other property, do not have any dependants or have an expensive lifestyle, you may be expected to repay or may be refused legal aid.

2. Legal and Policy Restrictions

The *Legal Aid Act* itself is very broad. It provides that if a person is otherwise entitled (that is, meets the financial eligibility requirements), the administrators must provide legal aid in some situations, and may provide assistance in most other situations, including hearings before quasi-judicial or administrative boards or commissions (where most environmental issues are resolved).[93]

However, the scope of the Act has been drastically narrowed by the regulations made under it. Legal aid may not be granted if the action only benefits the applicant as "a member of the public."[94] Generally, if the legal aid applicant is one of a number of people who have a problem, the administrators of the plan would deny legal aid if the group together could afford to pay a lawyer. For example, if a group of 200 people were all interested in attacking the same problem and each of them could raise $100, and if the cost of a lawyer and disbursements would not be over $20,000, legal aid would probably be denied. In all probability, legal aid would also be denied if the applicant or group of applicants is affected by the problem in the same manner as many other people (for example, smog over a city). The regulation under the *Legal Aid Act* authorizes, but does not require, the administrators to refuse to fund any action in which the applicant seeks to sue on behalf of others as well as himself or herself (class actions).[95]

Another restriction is that the administrators must consider it "reasonable" to initiate the case, and at any point in the case they may reconsider the reasonableness of continuing with it. Whether the case is reasonable will depend on the view the administrators take of the possibilities of success, the cost of success, and the benefits to be gained. Thus, the administrators may consider cases unreasonable if they are novel, in the sense that people traditionally have not gone to court over the issues involved; if the costs of litigation are likely

to be disproportionately high compared with the damages that are likely to be recovered; or
if the damage is being done to the general public rather than to one specific individual. These
criteria for refusing help form a classic description of many environmental cases.

Group Applications and Test Cases

For several years, the harshness of these criteria was mitigated by the existence of a Group
Applications and Test Cases Sub-Committee of the Legal Aid Committee. The Law Society
of Upper Canada had recognized that there must be exceptions to these restrictions. Many
cases affecting large numbers of people, such as long hearings before environmental and
planning tribunals, are so expensive that ordinary people cannot afford to participate, even
if they band together to raise money. In addition, novel cases or cases that raise broad public
concerns, which would not normally be eligible for funding, may be funded as test cases if
they raise important legal issues. In 1991, however, this subcommittee recommended to the
Law Society that certain environmental cases no longer be funded, because "the cost of
environmental cases coming before the Sub-Committee is extraordinary, and is vastly
beyond the cost of other cases that it considers." Of course, this is precisely the reason citizens
need legal aid in environmental cases more than in other cases. Nevertheless, the Law Society
adopted this recommendation and, once again, citizens can get no legal aid for cases before
the Environmental Assessment Board, a Joint Board, or the Environmental Appeal Board.
The subcommittee recommended that the *Intervenor Funding Project Act*[96] (see Chapter 9)
be extended to cover these cases, but the Ontario government has not done this. Therefore,
we suggest that you apply to this subcommittee for funding and point out that the premise on
which it discontinued funding environmental cases — that the *Intervenor Funding Project
Act* should cover them — is no longer applicable.[97] Moreover, the decision not to fund
environmental cases may not apply to tribunals other than the ones mentioned above.

Community Legal Aid Clinics

In 1992, there were about 70 community legal aid clinics[98] throughout Ontario. Most clinics
are "general" clinics found in the community in storefront and highrise offices, with a board
of directors from the community itself, or in university law faculties, where law students
assist the public under the direction of law professors. These clinics handle a variety of cases
that fall within the area often referred to as "poverty law" — that is, areas of law in which poor
people are most affected and lawyers in private practice often have little experience. These
include landlord and tenant law, social assistance law, workers' compensation law, employment law, and immigration law. There are several "specialty" clinics that provide legal
assistance, public education, and law reform activities in specific areas of law. Among them
are clinics for children, the handicapped, the elderly, and injured workers. One such clinic,
the Canadian Environmental Law Association, provides legal advice and assistance to
victims of environmental harm, and often assists other environmental groups.

The legal aid plan requires these clinics to restrict their services to people who cannot
afford private lawyers.[99] However, the groups have some discretion to take cases for
wealthier clients when to do so will help develop law and policy and be beneficial to the
community. These clinics play an important role in developing stronger laws to protect
individuals and the environment. As a former Ontario attorney general said: "While clinics

may frequently disturb the complacent and powerful, including many in government, the resulting unpopularity in those circles must not be allowed to inhibit their work."[100]

The Canadian Environmental Defence Fund

The Canadian Environmental Defence Fund[101] (CEDF), whose offices are in Toronto, raises funds from individuals, corporations, charitable foundations, and government to support environmental cases before courts and tribunals. CEDF will give grants to support litigation and will help groups in their fundraising efforts. It can sometimes help citizens' groups find lawyers, scientists, and planners who are willing to provide their services for free or for a reduced fee. Because its resources are limited, CEDF restricts its assistance to cases that are likely to set a legal precedent or that are of national significance. CEDF has assisted New Brunswick sprayers of dioxin who sued Dow Chemicals to obtain compensation for alleged death and illness caused by the banned herbicide 2,4,5-T; Kingston, Ontario residents who opposed the establishment of a waste disposal site on a significant wetland; and Innu people in Labrador who opposed NATO low-level flying exercises involving bombers and jet fighters over Innu hunting grounds.

A PARTING WORD

Those who contemplate using the law to deal with environmental degradation should bear in mind that strategy and public relations are as important in solving a problem as winning a particular legal action. In some cases, it may be advantageous to take legal action even if there is a good possibility that it will fail. A lost legal action may demonstrate grave deficiencies in the laws that supposedly "protect" the environment, thus highlighting the need for immediate legislative reform.

However, litigation is costly, adversarial, and lengthy. In some cases, the choice of litigation will restrict what you can say about the issues publicly without fear of being in contempt for trying to influence the court or tribunal through the media.

The decision whether to litigate and, if so, in what forum should always be part of a larger, long-term strategy. The question should be: are there other means of influencing government and industry? If so, how does litigation fit within the overall strategy? Will it enhance or impede our other efforts?

As the former dean of the University of Calgary Law School has pointed out:

> Litigation is not going to solve the total pollution problems of, for example, a large city or an extensive river system. It is, however, one instrument which can be used in the absence of effective solutions from more appropriate sources in situations where there is a clearly definable local pollution problem. Moreover, if enough environmental lawsuits are launched against polluters and succeed, a beneficial psychological effect on polluters in general may accrue. A new spectre will be created, the possibility of being forced into a public forum and asked to explain their conduct and lack of concern for environmental values. Thus the stimulus for redemption may be broader than the cases in which compulsion is actually applied.[102]

John Swaigen

ENDNOTES

1   *Re Roosma and Ford Motor Co.* (1988), 66 OR (2d) 18 at 24 (Div. Ct.) *per* Reid J.

2   In *Re Tenenbaum and the Local Board of Health for the City of Toronto*, [1955] OR 622 (CA), the court ruled that the Board of Health could take into account in considering an application for a permit for a slaughterhouse not only health effects but also whether the operation would be a nuisance or offensive because of its proximity to a residential area. However, in *Re Texaco Ltd. and the City of Vanier* (1981), 120 DLR (3d) 184 (SCC), the court ruled that a licensing bylaw could not control the external appearance of property since this had nothing to do with the character of the business or its conduct.

3   Supra endnote 1, at 27c-d.

4   *Canadian Charter of Rights and Freedoms*, Part I of the *Constitution Act, 1982*, RSC 1985, app. II, no. 44.

5   *Provincial Offences Act*, RSO 1990, c. P.33.

6   The attorney general has published a directive requiring prosecutors to disclose their cases to the defendants. There is no reason in principle why these rules would not apply to private prosecutors as well as the Crown. See Ontario, Attorney General, Criminal Laws Division, Directive no. 02, October 1, 1989.

7   *Planning Act*, RSO 1990, c. P.13.

8   *Municipal Act*, RSO 1990, c. M.45.

9   *Metropolitan Toronto (Municipality) v. Siapas* (1989), 3 CELR (NS) 122, sentencing reported at 151; 44 CRR 153 (Ont. HCJ).

10 *Charter of Rights*, supra endnote 4.

11 Legislation has been proposed that will replace this six-year limitation with a two-year limit. However, this legislation is likely to include a longer limitation period for environmental damage that is not discovered until a later date.

12 *R. v. Oakes*, [1986] 1 SCR 103, 53 OR (2d) 719n, 26 DLR (4th) 260.

13 *Environmental Protection Act*, RSO 1990, c. E.19.

14 *Ontario Water Resources Act*, RSO 1990, c. O.40.

15 *Pesticides Act*, RSO 1990, c. P.11.

16 *Canadian Environmental Protection Act*, RSC 1985, c. 16 (4th Supp.).

17 *Courts of Justice Act*, RSO 1990, c. C.43, section 29.

18 Lord Bowen, quoted in *Life of Lord Bowen*, 185.

19 Rules of Civil Procedure, O. reg. 560/84, rule 13.

20 Rules of the Supreme Court of Canada, SOR/83-74, as amended by SOR/83-930, SOR/ 87-292.

21 *Charter of Rights*, supra endnote 4.

22 *Peel v. A & P Ltd.* (1989), 74 OR (2d) 165 (CA).

23 Energy Probe and the Canadian Environmental Law Association intervened in *Re Ontario Energy Board* (1985), 19 DLR (4th) 753, 51 OR (2d) 333 (Div. Ct.) and in *Re Regional Municipality of Hamilton-Wentworth and Hamilton-Wentworth Save the Valley, Inc.* (1985), 51 OR (2d) 23 (Div. Ct.).

24 *Monsanto Canada Inc. v. Min. of Agriculture* (1986), 18 Admin. LR 161 (FCTD).

25 *Friends of the Oldman River Society v. Canada (Minister of Transport)* (1992), 7 CELR (NS) 1 (SCC).

26 The most comprehensive source of information about interventions is Paul R. Muldoon, *Law of Intervention: Status and Practice* (Aurora, Ont.: Canada Law Book, 1989). This book contains references to most of the other literature on the subject. See also John Swaigen, *How To Fight for What's Right* (Toronto: James Lorimer and Company, 1981), chapter 2.

27 The information on references is taken from *How To Fight for What's Right*, supra endnote 26, chapter 2. The power of the Ontario Cabinet to refer questions to the Court of Appeal and the powers of the court on a reference are found in section 19 of the *Courts of Justice Act*, RSO 1990, c. C.43.

28 *Ombudsman Act*, RSO 1990, c. O.6.

29 Ibid., section 15.

30 *Ontario (Ombudsman) v. Ontario (Board of Radiological Technicians)* (1990), 72 OR (2d) 632, 114 DLR (3d) 638 (HCJ); aff'd. 29 OR (2d) 696n, 114 DLR (3d) 576n (CA); *Re Ombudsman of Ontario and Ontario Labour Relations Board* (1985), 52 OR (2d) 237, 21 DLR (4th) 63 (Div. Ct.).

31 Complaints regarding a provincially appointed judge's misbehaviour or neglect of duty, or his or her inability to perform his or her duties may be made to the Ontario Judicial Council, at Osgoode Hall, 130 Queen Street West, Toronto, Ontario M5H 2N5. The council, which consists of senior judges, lawyers, and others appointed by the Ontario Cabinet, can take steps ranging from a reprimand to a dismissal. There is also a Justices of the Peace Review Council, which has a similar mandate to investigate the conduct of justices of the peace, at Room 207, 60 Queen Street West, Toronto, Ontario M5H 2M4. For complaints about federally appointed judges (any judge of the Ontario Court (General Division) or of the Federal Court), contact the Canadian Judicial Council, Place de Ville, Tower B, Suite 450, 112 Kent Street, Ottawa, Ontario K1A 0W8.

32 The group, called the Interested Citizens Group, was advised by the ombudsman, in a letter dated April 6, 1976, that he did not have jurisdiction to investigate the location of the proposed Bradley-Georgetown transmission line.

33 *Ombudsman Act*, supra endnote 28, section 17(3).

34 *Public Service Act*, RSO 1990, c. P.47.

35 Conversation with Toby Vigod, director, CELA community legal clinic, January 1991.

36 Ombudsman of Ontario, *Annual Report*, 1987-88 (Toronto: Queen's Printer, 1988), 18.

37 Ombudsman of Ontario, *Annual Report*, 1985-86 (Toronto: Queen's Printer, 1986), 18.

38 Ombudsman of Ontario, *Annual Report*, 1988-89 (Toronto: Queen's Printer, 1989), 18.

39 Ombudsman of Ontario, *Annual Report*, 1989-90 (Toronto: Queen's Printer, 1990), 7.

40 Ibid.

41 Ombudsman of Ontario, "Special Report to the Legislature," August 17, 1992.

42 Standing Committee on the Ombudsman, Seventeenth Annual Report, 1989, appendixes A and B.

43 *Official Languages Act*, RSC 1985, c. 31 (4th Supp.).

44 Information Commissioner of Canada, *Annual Report*, 1989-90 (Ottawa: Supply and Services, 1990).

45   Under the *Municipal Act*, RSO 1990, c. M.45, sections 377, 378, and 382-385.

46   *Bread Sales Act*, RSO 1990, c. B.11.

47   *Milk Act*, RSO 1990, c. M.12.

48   *Theatres Act*, RSO 1990, c. T.6.

49   *Planning Act*, RSO 1990, c. P.13.

50   *Health Protection and Promotion Act*, RSO 1990, c. H.7.

51   Metropolitan Toronto bylaw no. 20-85.

52   Ibid., schedule 24, part 4, section 2.

53   Ibid., schedule 26, part 2, sections 4(4) and 5.

54   *Assessment Act*, RSO 1990, c. A.31, section 30.

55   The right of appeal to the Assessment Review Board, the powers of the board, and the procedure to be followed are established by section 38 of the *Assessment Act*. The board itself is established by the *Assessment Review Board Act*, SO 1982, c. 40. This statute simply renames the former Assessment Review Court, established in 1972 under the *Assessment Review Court Act*, SO 1972, c. 111. In 1991, the board had nine regional registrars to whom an appeal could be addressed, located in North York, Toronto, Newmarket, Ottawa, Peterborough, London, North Bay, and Sault Ste. Marie.

56   *Assessment Review Board Act*, supra endnote 55, section 9.

57   *Regional Assessment Commissioner, Region 27 v. Meloche et al.* (1988), 21 OMBR 463.

58   *Regional Assessment Commissioner, Region 26 v. Lorne Avenue, Dresden* (1987), 20 OMBR 490.

59   *Erzar v. Regional Assessment Commissioner, Region 19* (1984), 17 OMBR 175. In this case, the provincial government established a policy of reducing the assessment of all buildings insulated with urea formaldehyde. The assessment commissioner reduced the assessment of certain buildings by 35 per cent. The building owner sought a further reduction, but his appeal to the Ontario Municipal Board was unsuccessful.

60   *Re City of Gloucester Forest Valley Drive Assessment Appeals* (1989), 23 OMBR 496.

61   *Regional Assessment Commissioner, Region 30 v. Bertulli* (1987), 21 OMBR 224.

62   *Reigate v. Regional Assessment Commissioner, Region 11* (1989), 23 OMBR 359.

63   *Re Assessment Appeal, Hawkesbury River Front Estates Inc.* (1989), 23 OMBR 492.

64   *Retail Business Holidays Act*, RSO 1990, c. R.30, as amended by SO 1991, c. 43.

65   Ibid., section 5. Retailers argued before the courts that this statute infringed their rights under the *Charter of Rights*, but the validity of the Act was upheld by the Supreme Court of Canada: *R. v. Edwards Books and Art Ltd.*, [1988] 2 SCR 713, 28 CRR 1.

66   *Retail Business Holidays Act*, supra endnote 64, section 8.

67   Ibid., section 9.

68   *Retail Business Holidays Amendment Act (Sunday Shopping)*, 1992, Bill 38, first reading June 3, 1992. As of February 1993, the bill had not received second reading.

69   *One Day's Rest in Seven Act*, RSO 1990, c. O.7.

70   *Employment Standards Act*, RSO 1990, c. E.14.

71   *Municipal Act*, supra endnote 45, section 214.

72   Ibid., section 215.

73   Ibid., section 215(a).

74   *Competition Act*, RSC 1985, c. C-34, as amended by RSC 1985, c. 27 (1st Supp.), c. 19 (2d Supp.), c. 34 (3d Supp.), and cc. 1 and 10 (4th Supp.).

75   Ibid., section 52.

76   Ibid., section 53(1).

77   Ibid., section 52(2).

78   Ibid., sections 52(5) and 53(2).

79   *Business Practices Act*, RSO 1990, c. B.18.

80   Ibid., section 3.

81   Ibid., section 2(1).

82   Ibid., section 17(2).

83   Ibid., section 17(3).

84   Ibid., section 6.

85   Some of the information in this section is taken from Canada, Department of Consumer and Corporate Affairs, "Misleading Advertising, Promotions and Deceptive Marketing Practices," April 1, 1984, available on request. Other information is based on the author's efforts to persuade the director to investigate a complaint and to inform him of the results of the investigation.

86   *Competition Act*, supra endnote 74, sections 9 and 10.

87   "Misleading Advertising," supra endnote 85.

88   *Business Practices Act*, supra endnote 79.

89   The Canadian Advertising Foundation is a trade association that represents advertisers and advertising agencies and media. It has developed the Canadian Code of Advertising Standards, the Broadcast Code for Advertising to Children, the Code of Consumer Advertising Practices for Non-Prescription Medicines, and the Television Code of Standards for the advertising of feminine sanitary protection products. The Advertising Standards Council enforces these codes. The council consists of representatives from the advertiser, media, and agency sectors, as well as the public (for example, the Consumers Association of Canada). It investigates complaints from the public about false and misleading advertising. If the complaints are found to be justified, the advertiser is expected to withdraw the ad voluntarily. If this is not done, many media associations have agreed not to publish or broadcast the ad.

90   *Legal Aid Act*, RSO 1990, c. L.9.

91   Ibid., RRO 1990, reg. 710, section 118, as amended. The provincial director has delegated this role to the staff solicitor.

92   Conversation with Lee David, legal aid staff solicitor, January 17, 1991. Mr. David interpreted the *Legal Aid Act* as prohibiting this. In fact, the regulation says that if a legal aid client has had costs awarded against him or her, he or she may apply for payment of these costs. However, the costs would then be paid to the winner of the case. If the client does not apply for these costs, a corporation that won the case may not apply, because under section 118(2) of the regulation, only a "person" may apply to legal aid for this relief, and the Act defines "person" as an individual. Thus, the reasoning seems to be that Legal Aid would refuse the client, and this would deprive the corporation of costs, since it cannot apply.

      The assumption seems to be that this does not leave the client in a difficult position, since he or she has no money for the corporation to get or he or she would not have been granted legal aid.

93   *Legal Aid Act*, supra endnote 90, sections 12-14.

94   Reg. 710, supra endnote 91, section 44(1)(b)(iii).

95   Ibid., sections 44(b)(i) and (ii).

96   *Intervenor Funding Project Act*, RSO 1990, c. I.13.

97   Law Society of Upper Canada, Group Applications and Test Cases Sub-Committee of the Legal Aid Committee, "Guidelines To Be Considered on Applications for Group Certificates or in Test Cases Adopted by the Sub-Committee of the Legal Aid Committee re Group Applications and Test Cases — June 10, 1985," approved by convocation (the governing body) of the Law Society, October 25, 1985. The subcommittee followed written guidelines in deciding whether to fund such a case. They include: consideration of other efforts the applicants have made to raise funds; the significance or importance of the issue to the applicant or others; if it is a test case, whether the benefits of success will flow to many others.

98   Community legal clinics are established under part IV of reg. 710, supra endnote 91, "Clinic Funding," and their operation is described in that regulation. The Ontario legal aid plan publishes an annual report on the operation of community legal clinics, available from the Law Society of Upper Canada, 130 Queen Street West, Toronto, Ontario M5H 2N6. This report gives the name, address, and telephone number of every legal aid clinic.

99   See Clinic Funding Committee Policy Guidelines on Financial Eligibility, April 1, 1988.

100   Ian Scott, attorney general of Ontario, in remarks before the Justice Committee of the Legislature of Ontario, November 6, 1985.

101   In 1993, the Canadian Environmental Defence Fund was located at 347 College Street, Suite 301, Toronto, Ontario M5T 2V8, (416) 323-9521.

102   John P.S. McLaren, "The Common Law Nuisance Actions and the Environmental Battle — Well-Tempered Swords or Broken Reeds?" (December 1972), vol. 10, no. 3 *Osgoode Hall LJ* 505-61, at 560.

4

Evidence, Hearing Procedures, and Environmental Litigation

CONTENTS

If you are considering launching legal proceedings or intervening before an administrative board,* one of the first questions you must consider is whether you have the "evidence" to support your case. "Evidence" is simply information that tends to prove or disprove any matter in question, or that can reasonably and fairly influence the judge or board member's belief about such a matter. Evidence may consist of oral statements, usually under oath ("testimony"), objects, such as a bottle containing a sample of effluent or waste ("real evidence"), or documents. The rules that determine what will be considered evidence, and therefore may be put before the tribunal, and what will not, are complicated. They are designed to "weed out" any information that might unfairly influence the court or board's decision, because it is not reliable.

A set of rules governing what a court or board may hear could err on the side of overinclusiveness or underinclusiveness; that is, since it is impossible to design a set of rules that will always allow all the reliable information to come forward but never let any unreliable information slip in, rules must be designed to allow either too much information or too little. The rules of evidence err on the side of underinclusiveness.

Proving an environmental case can be very difficult for many reasons. Evidence of past or future environmental damage is often difficult and expensive to obtain. The relevant facts are often known only to the offender; information may be difficult to obtain from the offender or from the government; the causes and effects of environmentally harmful activities may be uncertain, or may be ascertainable only through sophisticated studies and measurements; the meaning of data and events may not be apparent unless interpreted by experts; and the rules of evidence themselves may exclude much of the information you have collected, unless it falls into categories of evidence considered admissible by the tribunal and is presented in a manner that complies with the complicated rules of evidence.

We cannot hope in this brief chapter to tell you how to find all the evidence you will need, to explain all the rules of evidence and procedure, or even to deal with all the intricacies of the ones we do discuss. However, you may take some heart from the fact that the rules that delineate what is useful evidence and the procedures for bringing this evidence before the tribunal are largely the same in civil suits, prosecutions, before administrative boards, and in applications for judicial review. The difference from an evidence viewpoint is not primarily the kind of evidence that will be accepted, but the amount of evidence that will be required before a tribunal can act. In addition, the rules of evidence are more liberal in proceedings

---

* For the rest of this chapter we will use the term "tribunal" to refer to both courts and administrative boards that hold hearings.

before administrative tribunals. Evidence that a court would not listen to may sometimes be put before an administrative tribunal.

THE BURDEN OF PROOF

The term "burden of proof" refers to the issue of who has the obligation to bring evidence before a tribunal. Generally, the person who alleges a fact has the burden (or "onus") of proving it. In a prosecution, the burden of proving the guilt of the accused is on the prosecutor. (This is what we mean when we say someone is "innocent until proved guilty.") In a civil suit, the burden is on the plaintiff. Before administrative boards, it is often unclear where the burden lies, and it may be necessary to obtain information about this from the board itself.

Occasionally, when a fact is well known to the accused or defendant but the prosecutor or plaintiff would have great difficulty obtaining the information, the onus will be reversed; that is, the accused or defendant will have the burden of bringing out the evidence. Because of the great difficulty of proving the causes and effects of environmental damage, environmentalists have argued for decades that there should be more "reverse onuses" in environmental cases. Chemicals, they argue, should be guilty until proved innocent.

THE STANDARD OF PROOF

The standard of proof is the level of certainty that is required for a tribunal to accept the case of the person who has the burden of proof. Unless the correct degree of proof is presented, a court or board is powerless to act. In any *prosecution* for breach of a statute, regulation, or bylaw, the accused must be shown on the evidence presented in court to have committed the offence "beyond a reasonable doubt." This means that while the judge need not be absolutely certain of guilt, since absolute certainty is rarely achievable, she must have a *moral* certainty of guilt. This is a very high standard.

In a *civil action* for damages or for an injunction, in an application for judicial review, or in a case before an administrative tribunal, the usual standard of proof is "the balance of probabilities." That is, the tribunal need only be satisfied that it is more likely than not that the defendant or respondent did the act complained of, that the actions required by a pollution control order must be carried out to protect the environment, or that a licence should be refused, suspended, or revoked.

"Balance of probabilities" is a much lower standard of proof than the one required in prosecutions, but this standard can still be difficult to achieve. For example, critics of the current regulatory system often recommend that polluters should not be prosecuted but brought before an administrative tribunal instead. They assume that because of the lower standard of proof required, an administrative tribunal could more easily take strong action to protect the environment than the courts. However, the courts have held that even where a tribunal may decide a case on the balance of probabilities, this means that "the proof must be clear and convincing and based upon cogent evidence," and nothing less will justify an administrative tribunal in revoking a licence to practise a profession or gain a livelihood in business.[1]

WHERE DO I FIND THE RULES OF EVIDENCE AND HEARINGS PROCEDURES?

Originally, the rules of evidence were developed by the courts themselves. The rules were not written down in statutes, but were passed on through court judgments. Many of these rules are still not codified, and may be found only in textbooks.

There are, however, statutory codes of evidence that govern prosecutions under federal statutes (the *Canada Evidence Act*),[2] a code that governs prosecutions under Ontario statutes and municipal bylaws and in civil suits (the *Ontario Evidence Act*),[3] and a code that governs evidence and procedure before Ontario boards (the *Statutory Powers Procedure Act*).[4] There is no code of evidence or procedure like Ontario's *Statutory Powers Procedure Act* that covers federal tribunals, although the federal government has been thinking about creating one. Before you appear before a federal board, it is wise to contact the board to find out what rules of evidence it follows.

In addition to these general statutes, the courts and many tribunals have sets of rules of procedure that add further rules of evidence applicable only to those tribunals. For example, the rules of evidence and procedure that govern the Ontario Municipal Board and the Environmental Assessment Board are found in regulations made under the *Ontario Municipal Board Act*[5] and the *Environmental Assessment Act*.[6]

Many statutes that regulate specific activities also contain provisions that make documents that are generated during the regulation of the activities that they govern admissible in courts or boards. For example, under the common law rules of evidence, a document that sets out the results of testing at a laboratory of the Ministry of Environment and Energy (MEE) would normally not be accepted by the court as evidence without calling as a witness everyone who handled the sample or participated in its analysis. Under section 175 of the *Environmental Protection Act*,[7] however, the court is allowed to accept such "certificates of analysis" and "certificates of custody."

WHAT IS ADMISSIBLE EVIDENCE?

The judge or board members may take notice only of "admissible" evidence — that is, facts or opinions that the rules of evidence allow because they are considered to be "material," "relevant," and "reliable." All evidence, whether it be what a witness says or what a document or object shows, must help the tribunal decide the issues before it. Evidence that cannot help the judge or board member on these questions is not admissible.

Materiality and Relevance

Evidence is "material" if it refers to the *act or omission* that is being judged, the *identity* of the person whose conduct is being judged, or that person's *intent or diligence*.

Material evidence is "relevant" if it refers to the person's act or omission, identity, and fault or lack of fault, *and* has a logical connection with the points in issue between the parties to the proceeding.

For instance, Mr. Sluggem is charged with assault. Evidence is brought forward that he has six fingers on his left hand. This evidence is *material* because it concerns his identity. But it may or may not be relevant. If Mr. Sluggem's defence is that someone else, not he, committed the act, then the identity of the assailant is "in issue." That is, it is a question that must be answered before the court can make its decision. This evidence would then be relevant to identify Mr. Sluggem as the person who did this act, or to prove that he was not the person. If, however, Mr. Sluggem admits that he did the act but claims that he is not guilty because he was defending himself, his identity is not in issue. Therefore, this evidence is probably irrelevant.

In an environmental context, suppose you obtain statistics that show an increasing rate of lung disease among the residents of Kapuskasing, and statistics that show a corresponding increase in the number of motor vehicles being used in that city. If you are a resident of Kapuskasing suing the Killer Kar Kompany because you have developed emphysema or lung cancer, this evidence may be material, since it relates to the time and place and the health effects in issue, but it may not be relevant. The fact that there is a rising incidence of lung disease and also an increase in the number of cars may not mean that there is a cause-and-effect relationship between these facts. Even if there is such a cause-and-effect relationship, it may not show a cause-and-effect relationship between your particular illness and the design of the Killer Kar Kompany's car. The court therefore may not consider this evidence to be relevant to your case. The evidence must be logically important to prove the points in issue; otherwise, it will be inadmissible.

Reliability

The rules of admissible evidence do not seem strictly logical. What an ordinary person would consider relevant evidence is often excluded as inadmissible. The reason for these exclusions is a concern for the reliability of evidence brought before the court.

The rules of evidence are an attempt to ensure that only the "best" — that is, the most reliable — evidence is used to decide important questions.

This concern for reliability means that witnesses will rarely be allowed to put other people's statements (known as "hearsay")* before the court. Thus, you can seldom state what another person told you, or put forward documents prepared by others as proof of statements made in the document. It is necessary to call as a witness the person who made the statement or who made the observations recorded in the document. Reliability also underlies the reluctance of the court to accept a photocopy of a document rather than the original, or evidence given in writing rather than in person. Similarly, when a person relies on an analysis of a sample as evidence of its properties, the court tries to ensure that the analysis was accurate by applying rules that limit the weight of the evidence unless there is proof that no one tampered with the sample between the time it was collected and the time it was analyzed. (See the discussion under the heading "'Continuity' of Evidence," below.)

The key rules to ensure reliability are: (1) personal knowledge and (2) personal attendance before the tribunal.

---

* The term "hearsay" is often used to refer only to oral statements made to a witness by a third party. However, we use it in this chapter to refer also to statements made by a third party in a document that the witness seeks to rely on, since the reasons for excluding oral third-party statements and the reasons for excluding documents prepared by third parties are the same.

Personal Knowledge

What a person observed with her own five senses is generally more reliable than what that person has been told someone else observed. If a neighbour of a waste disposal site comes before the tribunal and says that she saw a truck dumping a foul-smelling liquid at the site at 3 AM, her sincerity, memory, powers of observation, and the accuracy of her observations can be tested by cross-examining her about where she was located, the acuity of her vision and sense of smell, and any positive or negative feelings she might have toward the dump site operator or, indeed, about pollution in general, that might have influenced her perception of what happened.

If, however, the neighbour comes to court and says that another neighbour told her that he had seen this, there is no way to cross-examine the witness about the accuracy of the second neighbour's statement. This evidence is inherently unreliable.

Any evidence of what someone else observed is hearsay. The hearsay rule is that if Bob is testifying before a court or board, he cannot say what Mary Jo told him. What Mary Jo told Bob is hearsay evidence and is inadmissible. However, Mary Jo could come to the tribunal and testify as to what she saw, and that would be admissible evidence. The hearsay rule does not only prohibit *A* from saying what he was told by *B*, but also stops *A* from bringing to the court documents prepared by someone else to prove the truth of statements made in them. That is just another way of *A* saying what he has learned from *B* (the person who prepared the document).

Personal Attendance Before the Tribunal

A second safeguard of the reliability of evidence is that the person giving it must attend personally and testify before the tribunal. This gives an opportunity for cross-examination, as well as an opportunity for tribunal members and other parties to assess the witness's credibility by observing his or her demeanour. A person's non-verbal communication and the manner in which evidence is given may be as important in deciding whether to accept evidence as the words themselves.

Oral Versus Written Evidence

There are three basic ways to prove a fact in court: by calling a witness to swear to it, by producing a document that records it, and by bringing an object to court. Generally, in a court proceeding, evidence must be given orally. Unless a person is dead, seriously ill, or out of the country, the general rule of evidence is that she must come to court to testify personally and orally as to what she saw, heard, smelled, or felt. A written statement from a witness is not sufficient if he or she is able to attend court in person.

Of course, photographs, tape recordings, measurements, samples of dust and chemicals that were taken or collected, and notes that were made at the time an act took place are all matters that might be helpful to a judge. Being helpful, they are relevant; but even all these kinds of "documentary" and "real" evidence are generally admissible only if a person in court will testify orally that on a certain day at a certain time and place, he took the pictures, samples, measurements, etc. or personally saw the photographer or scientist taking the pictures, measurements, or samples.

These rules are somewhat relaxed before tribunals. Tribunals have the right to accept written reports and other documents, particularly where the tribunal has its own staff that collects the evidence and prepares the reports and documents. However, this may be done only if all parties to the proceedings are given the opportunity to see the reports and to rebut them. If a party presents (or "leads") any credible evidence that the contents of reports or documents are untrue or inaccurate, the tribunal cannot rely on them. The reports must be disregarded or the people who made the observations recorded in the reports must testify.

Exceptions to the Rules Safeguarding Reliability

There are numerous exceptions to the rule that a person must testify orally before the tribunal and to the hearsay rule.

Documents

Although documents are generally not admissible to prove the truth of statements made in them, it may be important, apart from whether its contents are true, to prove the very existence of the document, or that it was in someone's possession at a particular time. The document is generally admissible for this purpose. However, certain documents can also be used to prove the truth of their contents.

Government Documents

Copies of certain government documents, when they have been "certified" — that is, when they have been marked with an official seal or stamp proclaiming their accuracy — are admissible as evidence of what is contained in them without calling as a witness the person who made the statements in them and often without calling the person in whose custody they are kept.[8]

These documents provide easily obtainable evidence of many essential facts, such as:

- that a municipal bylaw has been properly passed and is in force (something that must be proved in every prosecution for breach of a bylaw);
- the ownership of a motor vehicle (found by tracing the licence number);
- that a corporation legally existed on a certain date (again, an essential fact to prove in a court case against a corporation); or
- the identity of the owner of a piece of land.*

Routine Business Records

Copies of certain routine business records are admissible to prove the truth of the information in them without calling as a witness the person who made the observations recorded in the documents or the person who prepared the records, as long as a company official in charge of the records can testify that it was company practice to make and keep such records.

---

* See Appendix V for a description of how to obtain such documents and have them certified for use as evidence.

Results of Scientific Analysis

Under certain statutes, a written statement that contains the results of a scientific analysis of some material will be admitted into evidence without calling the analyst to the witness stand. If the analysis of the material — perhaps water from a lake in which fish are dying, or a blood sample from someone exposed to high levels of lead in the air around her home — has been made by a qualified government technician appointed under a statute, the statute may provide for the introduction of the results in a "certificate of analysis," and sometimes even for some hearsay statements as to how the sample was obtained and how it was handled.

Affidavits

In certain legal proceedings — for example, in an application for a temporary injunction or a judicial review — the court does not require spoken evidence at all. In these cases, the evidence on which each party relies must be given in the form of affidavits (written statements under oath). Parties are usually given an opportunity to cross-examine each other's witnesses on the accuracy of their affidavits before an official examiner, and the transcript of this cross-examination is also used by the court. Thus, the reliability of the written testimony is protected by cross-examination, although the court loses the opportunity to observe the demeanour of the witness.

It is, of course, much more convenient to obtain evidence in affidavits than to have the witness attend court, where she might have to wait for hours or days until it is her turn to testify. For example, expert witnesses (see below) are often reluctant to come to court unless they are paid a large fee. Instead, a written statement may be prepared stating the expert's knowledge and opinions and given to him to sign. A lawyer or other person appointed as a notary public or commissioner for taking oaths can administer an oath to him anywhere. When the expert takes the oath and signs his name to the document, it becomes an affidavit, which is admissible evidence in such proceedings.

Other Exceptions to the Hearsay Rule

We have used the term "hearsay" to refer to all statements of what others have said, whether orally or contained in documents. Hearsay is not admissible unless it is both reliable — that is, the statement was made under circumstances in which it could not have been a lie or a mistake[9] — and it is necessary to prove a fact in issue. The term "hearsay" is most often used to refer to oral statements. In this sense of "hearsay," there are several specific and very limited situations that give a witness the right to testify to what someone else told her, despite the hearsay rule.

1. *Res gestae*: *Res gestae* is Latin for "the thing itself." If a statement was made spontaneously during the actual progress of the act that is the subject of the judicial proceedings and this statement sheds some light on the nature of the act, the identity of the perpetrator, or his motives, the statement will be admissible. The spontaneity of the utterance and the lack of opportunity to concoct a fabrication are considered to provide some assurance of the reliability of the evidence.

   For example, the Dirty Oil Company is charged under the *Fisheries Act* with letting oil flow into Vancouver Harbour. The oil spill occurred because an employee of the company — a delivery man delivering fuel to the bus depot — filled the wrong tank. The pipe he pumped the oil into led to an abandoned tank on the floor below. The oil spilled out of this tank and into sewers that emptied into the harbour.

The company's defence is that it is not responsible for the acts of its employee because the offence was committed without its knowledge or consent and the company had given clear instructions as to which tank should be filled. At the time of the trial, the delivery man is unable to testify, because he slipped on some of the spilled oil a few minutes later and suffered a concussion, which resulted in amnesia.

A worker in the bus terminal tells the court that he saw the delivery man struggling to open the valve to the abandoned tank. As he was struggling, the delivery man said, "This valve is damned hard to loosen, but I just phoned head office and they told me it was this one, not the one over there." Even though the worker's testimony is hearsay, it may be admissible as part of the *res gestae*.

2. Statements made by a person who has since died are admissible in certain circumstances.

3. Perhaps most important, a witness can testify to confessions or admissions made to him by a party to the proceedings, or made by a third party in the presence of a party to the proceedings and accepted by that party. Such admissions are accepted more readily in civil proceedings than in prosecutions. In a prosecution, if the admission or confession was made to a person in authority, such as a police officer or an MOE inspector, the statement will be admissible only if the prosecutor proves that it was not made as a result of any threats, promises, or other inducements.

An illustration of an "admission" would be found in the Dirty Oil Company example above if the facts were changed slightly. If an Environment Department inspector arrived at the scene of the spill and phoned the company, and an official said, "The delivery man phoned a few minutes ago and told me he was having trouble opening the valve. He wanted to know if he had the wrong valve. I told him he had the right valve, keep trying. I guess I was wrong," the inspector could testify to this conversation. It would not be necessary to call the company official to testify that he had made this statement.

Much of the current environmental legislation — for example, sections 165 to 167 of the *Environmental Protection Act* — imposes a legal duty to provide information needed to administer the statutes. Such information may later be used by a prosecutor as admissions in legal proceedings instituted against the person or company that provided the information. However, the *Freedom of Information and Protection of Privacy Act*[10] and the *Charter of Rights and Freedoms*[11] may limit the use of such information as evidence. The extent to which such limitations exist has not yet been determined.[12]

Opinion Evidence: Expert Witness or Ordinary Citizen?

One of the basic rules of evidence is that a witness may testify only as to facts within his or her own knowledge. In general, "facts within his or her own knowledge" means what the witness has done or observed. Evidence of an opinion, as opposed to a fact, is generally admissible only when it is given by an expert witness — that is, a person who, because of education or experience in a field, is an authority on a particular subject.

For example, in a prosecution of a company for polluting a pond with oil that may harm fish, Barbara may tell the court that she observed a thin film on the surface of the pond, and that the fish were swimming to the surface and "gulping" for air. Unless she is an aquatic biologist, however, she cannot say that in her opinion this meant the oil was stressing the fish and causing them to have trouble breathing. It is up to the court to draw conclusions from Barbara's observations, and there might be other rational explanations for the behaviour of the fish. If anyone could speculate about the cause of such behaviour without the proper training to interpret the meaning of the phenomena, this could seriously mislead the court.

However, Barbara can state *facts*. She might be able to testify that she has seen this pond on many occasions at the same time of day in the same month, and in similar weather conditions, and she has never observed the fish gulping for air before. This factual information is useful to the court in drawing the conclusion that the cause of the gulping was the oil, but it involves no expression of Barbara's opinion.

In many environmental cases, expert witnesses are critical to success; nevertheless, it is sometimes possible for an ordinary witness to give an opinion. Ordinary people are allowed to state their opinions in court as to sensations within the range of everyday experience — for example, whether there was an odour at a given time and place, or what kind of odour they thought they smelled. Similarly, a person ordinarily experiences many kinds of sounds and therefore is entitled to testify whether a particular sound was disturbing or annoying and whether it was made by a human voice or by a machine. On the subject of aesthetic pollution, an ordinary person would obviously be able to testify whether a given sight was obnoxious. What is a "nuisance" or "impairment" of a stream is a question on which the court will usually listen to the opinions of ordinary people as well as those of experts. In fact, when these views conflict, the court will sometimes accept the common-sense testimony of the ordinary citizen over the tortured attempts of the expert to twist the facts to suit the needs of his or her client.[13]

Expert evidence is also an exception to the hearsay rule. Unlike ordinary citizens, expert witnesses are entitled to base their opinions on studies, reports, and textbooks prepared by others. It is unrealistic to expect the expert to duplicate every study or the observations made in the field by others. Thus, the expert may rely on a variety of information, including her own studies and observations, those of other witnesses, and a variety of documents. One way to bring forward government documents when government scientists refuse to cooperate is to have an expert witness use them in preparing his or her opinion.

Similar Fact Evidence

If someone is charged with or sued for harming a particular environment on a specific date, the court will usually be reluctant to allow evidence that the person did a similar act at some other location or at the same location at some other time. The fact that the person did the same thing before does not mean he did it this time. Therefore, similar fact evidence will rarely be admissible to prove the identity of the person who committed the act. If the person before the court denies being responsible for the harm, the court will usually consider it unfair to that person to try to prove that he or she did it by bringing in evidence of similar acts on other occasions.[14]

There are, however, situations in which you may be allowed to show that the accused or defendant committed similar acts at other times or in other areas. Similar fact evidence is frequently admissible to rebut a defence. The accused may admit that he did the harmful act, but he may lead evidence that he was not aware the act would cause damage, that he exercised all reasonable care to avoid the harm, or that the conduct was an isolated event and not his usual way of carrying on business. In some circumstances, these excuses, if believed, will avoid liability. In such circumstances, the court will sometimes listen to evidence of similar acts done by the accused if the acts are sufficiently similar to the one before the court and not too remote in time from it. The admissibility of the evidence is largely a question of the degree of similarity.

For example, you lay charges against the Anti-Arbour Construction Company for damaging the roots and trunk of a tree with a bulldozer. Neither you nor any of your witnesses actually saw the damage occur but you saw bulldozers and trucks with the name Anti-Arbour Construction on them in the vicinity of the tree immediately before and immediately after the damage was done. Your witnesses have actually seen the company's employees damage a number of other trees near this one, and damage the same tree on other occasions. The evidence of other damage may be admissible to prove the identity of the person who committed the offence if the company denies that its employees did the damage this time, but only if the manner in which the damage was done this time is strikingly similar to the manner in which they caused harm on other occasions. If, however, the company admits that it did the damage but that the damage occurred mistakenly or accidentally and without any negligence, the other incidents will probably be admissible to show otherwise, even if the manner of causing the harm was somewhat dissimilar.[15]

Even if the similar fact evidence is admissible only to rebut a defence, you should try to put this evidence before the tribunal *before* the accused or defendant takes the stand and calls her witnesses. If there is any possibility that the person will claim ignorance, mistake, accident, or innocent intent or motive, that the incident was an isolated incident, that someone else caused the harm, or any other defence on which the similar fact evidence will cause doubt, you should call your witnesses before the accused or defendant calls hers. The courts require you to *anticipate* defences and call evidence to rebut them even before they are raised. If you do not put forward the evidence in advance, you may not be allowed to do so later.

If the tribunal refuses to hear the evidence on the grounds that it is premature until the defence is actually raised, you may introduce it again in your "reply" (see the discussion under the heading "Hearing Procedure: Getting Evidence Admitted," below), after the accused and her witnesses have testified, if they have raised a defence that can be rebutted by this kind of evidence.

COLLECTING AND PRESERVING EVIDENCE

Some kinds of evidence are particularly useful in environmental cases. Some sources of such evidence, such as weather data, are discussed in Appendix V. We set out here some suggestions for collecting and preserving the evidence needed to prove a case.

Notes and the Pollution Journal

Memories fade with time, and it may take years before an environmental case comes to court. However, as long as you make notes of what you observe at the time of your observations or shortly afterward, you may use these notes to refresh your memory both before a hearing and while you are on the witness stand. Many people make notes on a wall or desk calendar and preserve the calendar. That way, they can glance at the calendar to confirm the date on which an event occurred. Others open a file or start a diary in which they keep notes of events as they unfold.

Unfortunately, if you are complaining about pollution episodes, the government inspector will often arrive after the incident is over and will not observe the pollution. By the time the inspector finally manages to arrive during an incident and is prepared to believe you and take action, months or even years may have passed. If you have failed to keep notes or have thrown them away in despair, the government may use this as an excuse — "insufficient evidence" — not to take action on past occurrences.

It would seem to be merely basic competence for inspectors to provide complainants with a "pollution journal" such as the one shown on the facing page, and to inform them to fill it in whenever an incident occurs, but we know of no regulatory agency that provides citizens with such basic assistance. In fact, many inspectors feel it would be improper to "stir people up" by assisting them in collecting evidence of wrongdoing.

It is wise not only to make a personal record in your own handwriting of daily occurrences, but also to encourage your neighbours to keep similar "pollution journals" or diaries.

Upwind, Downwind; Upstream, Downstream

"Upwind, Downwind; Upstream, Downstream" may sound like the name of a former TV soap opera, but it is a basic rule of collecting evidence of air and water pollution (a rule, incidentally, that many environmental inspectors have never learned). To determine the source of water pollution in a stream, it is important to observe the appearance of the water and take a sample immediately downstream of the suspected source, and as soon as possible thereafter to make observations and take a sample upstream for comparison. If the pollutant is in the downstream sample but is missing from the upstream sample, this is strong evidence that the suspected source is the only source. If possible, observations should also be made and samples taken at the outfall of the suspected source and at any other watercourses that enter the watercourse where the pollution was observed.

Similarly, when trying to isolate a source of air pollution, one should make observations and take samples both upwind and downwind of the suspected source, and between the suspected source and any other possible sources in the area. This is particularly important when tracing the source of an odour. This is usually done by the human nose, since it is much more sensitive and better able to distinguish different kinds of odours than most instruments. When you smell an odour downwind of a suspected source, you should follow it to the suspected source. If you smell it at the suspected source, go upwind of the source to see whether there is an odour. Then, position yourself between the suspected source and each of the other potential sources in the area, noting the estimated wind speed and direction at each observation point. Ideally, you should cover all four points of the compass in this manner. Weather data available from Environment Canada can then be obtained to corroborate your observations.

Photographs

If you can see the pollution or other forms of destruction, you should photograph it, being careful to note in your own handwriting the date and time when you took the pictures. As you

The Pollution Journal

*NB: This journal is intended to be kept as a detailed record of ONE POLLUTION SOURCE ONLY, especially for regularly repeated offences from the same source. If you are reporting several different sources, use one journal for each.

INSTRUCTIONS: Make each entry in your own handwriting and on the day which the incident occurred or you were affected by it. Only your own personal observations are to be recorded, not those you are told by others.

YOUR CELA INVESTIGATOR IS:
Dudley Duright
Phone: 555-2166

NAME   John Gasp
ADDRESS
221 Sulphur St., Sudbury
Journal From   May 16/93
          To   May 30/93

Type of Pollution
          Air

Date	Time Began	Ended	My Location	Pollution Description	Effects	Appropriate Meter Reading (if available)	Wind Direction
May 16	9:00 am	3:06 pm	221 Sulphur	Black dust + acrid fumes	Choking, eye irritation	—	SW
May 18	8:00 am	11:00 am	"	Dust + fumes	Same, black deposit on sills	—	SW
May 21	9:30 am	4:15 pm	"	Dust + fumes	Choking, dust film on car + laundry	—	SW
May 23	9:00 am	12:15 pm	"	Fumes	Eye irritation	—	SW
May 27	9:20 am	2:30 pm	"	Dust + fumes	Choking, dust on sills, etc.	—	SW
May 30	9:15 am	2:15 pm	"	Dust + acrid fumes	Black deposit, eye irritation	—	SW

take each picture, it is useful to make a note of what will be shown in the picture, where you were standing, the direction in which you were shooting, and the distance from the point where you took the picture to the important objects in the picture. To show scale, it is sometimes useful to put a ruler, book, bottle, or some other common object beside the object you are photographing. If possible, have someone witness your taking the pictures. Be sure to date each picture and make a note of what it shows on the back or in the margin of the print when you receive it.

Tape Recordings

You might also make a tape recording of noise, but be very careful to use a clean tape, observe and note the volume level at which you are recording, and be able to swear that you did not change the level of volume at any time while the recording was being made. Again, it would be helpful to have someone besides you to testify, corroborating your evidence as to the manner in which the sound was recorded.

Water, Soil, and Air Pollution Samples

For water, soil, and air pollution, you may be able to get samples of the contaminants. You could collect a sample on each day a contaminant is deposited. Again, label the samples properly with the date, time, and location, and seal them (see the discussion below under the heading "'Continuity' of Evidence"). In the case of water samples being analyzed for biological contamination, and many other contaminants whose physical or chemical properties change over time, it may also be important to prove that you collected them in an appropriate manner, placed them in a clean container made of an appropriate material, preserved them in an acceptable manner, and had them analyzed within a specified number of hours after the samples were taken. Although the collection, preservation, and analysis of samples in a manner that will be acceptable to a tribunal is often difficult for the ordinary person, it may still be important to attempt to collect, preserve, and analyze samples where officials are slow or reluctant to investigate and the evidence will disappear before they can collect it.

For further information about sampling and the analysis of water pollution, see Appendix VI.

GETTING THE EVIDENCE TO THE TRIBUNAL

As we mentioned earlier, if the evidence you need is in the possession of others, you may have difficulty obtaining it and ensuring that it is brought before the tribunal. In addition, there are special steps that must be taken to get some scientific evidence before the tribunal. Here, we will discuss some of these issues.

Subpoenas

The subpoena — a summons to a witness to appear before the tribunal — is used to ensure that witnesses will attend and bring all relevant things and documents, even if they are reluctant to do so. If a person has personal knowledge of facts or has possession of things or documents that will assist you in making your point in a case, you may summons or "subpoena" her to appear before the tribunal to testify on your behalf and to bring any relevant things or documents.

A subpoena is a written order issued under the authority of a tribunal that orders the person named in it to appear at a given time and place and to testify and bring the things or documents listed in the subpoena (sometimes called a "summons to witness"). If the witness is reluctant to assist you, it is particularly important to list all specific documents and all classes of documents that you would expect her to have (for example, "all inspection reports, laboratory analysis results, maintenance and operation logs, invoices, purchase orders, and receipts"). As long as a document is specifically named or falls into a class of documents listed in the subpoena, the witness is required to produce it before the tribunal. (The procedure to obtain and use subpoenas is described in Appendix III.)

Before you can obtain a subpoena, some tribunal proceeding must already have been initiated, and usually a trial or hearing date must have been set. To obtain evidence or necessary facts *before the commencement of a judicial proceeding*, you may be able to obtain a search warrant (see below), or use freedom of information laws to compel the government to disclose the information.

Subpoenas and the Reluctant Witness

A subpoena requires government and company officials who have relevant evidence to attend before the tribunal, but it does not require them to give you the documents or discuss their evidence with you in advance. Company officials may refuse to cooperate out of loyalty to the company or out of fear of retribution. Government officials will sometimes refuse to cooperate as a matter of policy or will reveal their evidence to you only in the presence of your opponent (a practice that is often unacceptable). Therefore, although they can be subpoenaed to testify, you often cannot be sure what these officials will say on the witness stand.

However, prior knowledge of what your witness will say and the contents of documents in her possession, and rehearsal of the testimony beforehand, are essential to a competent examination. Unless you have carefully gone through the questions and answers in advance with your witness, her testimony will not be given in the most meaningful and effective way. She needs rehearsal just as an actor preparing to go on stage does — to refresh her memory, to put her recollections into the best order, and to avoid surprises. Unless you have had an opportunity to talk with your witness and find out what her answers to your questions will be, you cannot know whether she will be a "friendly" witness or a "hostile" one (see below). Because you called her as your witness, you will not be allowed to cross-examine her or ask leading questions, even if she is a hostile witness.

The problem of not knowing what an official will say on the stand can be partly overcome in the following way. Subpoena the official and his or her records for a tribunal hearing on a specific date. Before that date, request that the person meet with you and provide his information so that you can prepare your case properly. If your request is refused, tell the judge or board member that the information was not previously available and that you are therefore asking for an adjournment (of half an hour, half a day, or however long you need) to study the subpoenaed documents so that you can properly examine the official who has brought the documents to the tribunal. Under those circumstances, the government official may also agree to talk with you, or the company's lawyer may agree to let you interview the company official in the lawyer's presence before calling him as a witness.

The tribunal may not always permit an adjournment (although an unreasonable refusal of a reasonable request for an adjournment may be successfully challenged by judicial review), but an adjournment is one of the few methods by which government and corporate evidence can be used by private citizens if the government or corporation is unwilling to divulge evidence in advance of the hearing.

Search Warrants

As we noted earlier, it is not possible to use a subpoena to obtain evidence before a legal proceeding has been commenced. If, however, you have reason to believe the law is being or has been broken, you may be able to obtain a search warrant to seize documents and things that will provide evidence of these violations. The documents and things obtained can then be used both to support the laying of charges and as evidence at the trial. (Although some legislation may allow search warrants to obtain evidence in support of administrative proceedings, search warrants are generally available only to support prosecution for offences and not proceedings before an administrative tribunal to suspend a licence or decide whether a project will be approved.) Under the authority of a search warrant, you may enter private property, seize anything relevant, and take pictures.[16]

A search warrant is an order signed by a justice of the peace (JP) or a judge that authorizes the persons named in the warrant to search premises, seize property, and use the documents or things obtained for the purpose of prosecuting an offence. To obtain a warrant, you must already have substantial evidence that things or documents that provide evidence of an offence will be found at a particular time and place, and you must swear an "information" that sets out your grounds for believing this is true.

To obtain a warrant, it is not necessary to first start a prosecution. The warrant may be issued before a charge is laid, or to obtain additional evidence after the charge has been laid. If no charge is laid after the warrant has been obtained and "executed" (the search has been carried out), or if charges are laid but are not successful, the search and seizure remain lawful if they were carried out in accordance with the terms of the warrant.

The warrant will specify how long you may keep the material seized. If you do not lay charges within the time limits set out in the warrant, you must return the material to the person from whom it was seized. It is illegal to use the material seized for any purpose other than the prosecution for which it was obtained.

Because searches and seizures invade the privacy of people who often have not yet been charged with any offence, the requirements for obtaining a search warrant are becoming more and more stringent. In the past, JPs and judges almost automatically granted search warrants to police officers, with few questions asked. Today, however, it is difficult even for police officers to satisfy the court officials that they have sufficient evidence to support a search warrant.

It is very unusual for a private citizen to request a search warrant, and if you do so, you can expect close and careful scrutiny of your documentation and great resistance to your request, no matter how well founded it is. However, if you are properly prepared with the reasonable and probable grounds required, have set out your grounds clearly in the information, and have consulted your lawyer (and perhaps brought him or her along to assist), it is possible, and not without precedent, for a private citizen to obtain a search warrant.

The procedure for preparing, obtaining, and executing a search warrant is set out in Appendix III.

The Usefulness of Search Warrants in Environmental Cases

Search warrants may be useful where a government agency declines to go onto private property to obtain a sample of pollution or waste. If it is necessary to go onto private property to take an effluent sample, a search warrant gives you the legal authority to do so yourself. The warrant may also be useful where the government refuses to enforce the law, and you have substantial evidence to use in a private prosecution, but lack a few specific documents or things that you know can be obtained at the offender's premises.

If you have a search warrant but are afraid to exercise it, you may, if necessary, call on the police to provide protection. (In fact, search warrants may be drafted to include a clause that specifically authorizes the police to accompany the person who is authorized to search.)

Search warrants may not be used to obtain evidence for a civil suit or an application for judicial review. There is, however, a system for obtaining extensive evidence in civil suits (see Chapter 3).

"Continuity" of Evidence

Any samples, recordings, or photographs (at least when they are in the form of negatives) should be kept in your possession or under your control (for example, in a locked box or room) at all times until you show them to the tribunal so that you will be able to swear under oath that there was no opportunity for anyone to interfere with them by adding anything to them, taking anything from them, adulterating them, erasing them, or tampering with them in any other manner. This is a strict rule that must be followed carefully, particularly in court proceedings. The courts wish to ensure that when a person is convicted or found responsible for a harmful act, the result is founded on evidence that is credible.

The "Locked Box" and Pollution Samples

It is important that pollution samples can be proven to be in the same condition when they reach the courtroom as when they were taken. You can prove that the evidence has not been tampered with by showing "continuity of possession." It is relatively easy to show continuity of possession of evidence if you can keep the evidence in your possession from the time you obtain it until you go before the tribunal. You just keep it under lock and key, transport it personally, and testify that no one else had access to it. Some kinds of pollution evidence, however, must leave your possession for days or weeks to be analyzed. For example, you collect a sample by brushing dust into a container or collecting a vial of contaminated water, and then have it analyzed in a laboratory to determine what pollutants are present and in what quantities. The tribunal will want to be sure that no one had any opportunity to replace this sample with a different one or to change its properties in any way (such as by adding a chemical to it or by heating it) before it was analyzed. In some cases — for example, where the physical appearance of the sample is important — the tribunal may also be concerned about whether it was tampered with between the time it was analyzed and the time it came before the tribunal.

You must account for the security of the sample while it was in your hands, while it was in transit from you to the lab, while it went through the hands of various people at the lab, while it was being returned to you, while you kept it for use at the tribunal, and while it was in transit from your home or office to the tribunal. To establish an unbroken chain of possession, place the sample in a sealed container (the "locked box") as soon as you collect it, preferably in the presence of witnesses. Ensure that this container is not opened until it reaches the analyst. If you do this, one person can take the sample and another can do the analysis without losing continuity of possession.

The best way to prove continuity of possession is to take the sample to the lab yourself. If you must mail it, send it by courier or registered mail and arrange for a receipt showing that it was received by the lab.

If you inform the lab that the analysis results are to be used as evidence in legal proceedings, the lab will usually follow special procedures that are designed to minimize the opportunity for tampering and to record all steps that are taken at the lab. These procedures are designed to facilitate proof of continuity of possession while the sample was at the lab. (Sometimes a sample will be handled by several people at the lab.)

When the analysis is completed, the sample should be placed in the same container, resealed, and not opened again until it reaches court. Again, the best way to prove continuity of possession is to pick up the sample yourself.

When government officials take samples to be analyzed for use in legal proceedings, they often rely on numbered seals instead of the "locked box" for proof of continuity. The person who takes the sample seals the bottle or container with a uniquely numbered seal. The person who receives the sample at the lab notes that the numbered seal was intact at the time of receipt. The analyst notes that the numbered seal remained intact until the bottle or container was opened to analyze its contents. After the analysis is completed, the container is resealed with another numbered seal, this procedure is recorded, and the bottle is returned to the sender, who in turn notes that the seal is intact when he receives it. The seal remains intact until the bottle is shown to the tribunal.

It is important to follow these procedures carefully. Cases have been lost because the person who took the sample did not deliver it personally or send it by registered mail to the analyst, or produce it in court.[17]

If a government laboratory will carry out the analysis for you, this is better than taking it to a private lab. Not only do you avoid the expense of paying a private lab, but the government often has authority to submit a document that states how continuity was preserved at the lab, while a private lab must send its technicians to testify — at your expense.

Certificates of Analysis as Evidence

Sometimes, you may not have to subpoena the analyst to testify. Some statutes provide for the tribunal to accept a document that states the method of analysis and the result, if the analysis was done by an accredited government laboratory and by analysts designated by the government. A few statutes, such as the *Environmental Protection Act*,[18] the *Ontario Water Resources Act*,[19] and the *Pesticides Act*,[20] also provide for continuity of possession to be proven through documents.

If a statute provides for the admissibility of such documents, the court will accept the contents of the report, the competence of the analyst, and the steps taken to maintain continuity, without requiring the analyst and others who handled the sample to testify, unless the defendant brings forward some evidence to the contrary. Thus, if the certificate of analysis shows that the sample of water contained 320 parts per million of zinc or copper, the court must accept this evidence unless the defendant produces some evidence to the contrary.

Note, however, that the person who took the sample will still have to testify as to where, when, and how he took it, how he delivered it to the government lab, and the fact that he received from the lab the certificate of analysis of the sample.

HEARING PROCEDURE: GETTING EVIDENCE ADMITTED

Getting the witnesses and the relevant documents and things to the tribunal door is one thing; putting them before the tribunal is another. Most tribunals have a procedure for putting forward evidence. Usually, the person who has the primary responsibility for proving his case calls his witnesses, followed by others who have the same interest. Then the opposite parties call their witnesses. Finally, the parties who have led the evidence have an opportunity to lead evidence to rebut any evidence that arose unexpectedly after they had closed their case ("rebuttal" or "reply").

Each witness will be asked questions by the person who called her as a witness ("examination-in-chief"); cross-examined by all other parties; then asked more questions by the party who called her as a witness if any new and unexpected evidence comes out during her cross-examination ("re-examination").

If any party who hears a question feels that the answer will elicit evidence that is inadmissible, the court procedure is to stand up quickly and say "I object!" or "Objection!" before the witness can give her answer. You then explain why the evidence should not be given. If your objection is well founded, the tribunal member will instruct the witness not to answer the question.

Examination-in-Chief, Cross-Examination, and Re-Examination

When a witness testifies in a legal proceeding, he is first "examined" by the person who called him to testify; that is, he is asked questions that allow him to tell his story in his own words ("examination-in-chief"). He may then be cross-examined by the person on the other side and by any other parties. For example, the plaintiff's witnesses may be cross-examined by the defendant (or her lawyer), and vice versa. Following the cross-examination, the witness may be "re-examined" by the party who called him as a witness, but only to clarify new facts that came out during the cross-examination.

During examination-in-chief or re-examination, the person who presents a witness in court must not use questions that suggest an answer, or that contain all the information the witness is intended to give, so that the witness need only say "yes" or "no." These are called "leading questions." Only a person who is cross-examining may ask leading questions. Leading questions are discouraged because they put words in the witness's mouth and the court does not find out what the witness really knows or thinks about the matters in question.

Here is an example of a leading question asked to one's own witness (and thus improper):

Question: Mr. Keenose, you are a government air pollution inspector who on Thursday, January 6, 1992 at 4:00 PM attended at the premises of the Black Coal Company, and there saw a cloud of black, oily smoke being emitted from chimney number 5. Is that correct?

This is a leading question because all the information the court needs is in the question itself, and all the witness has to do is answer "yes" or "no."

Here is how the examination-in-chief should be conducted:

Question: Mr. Keenose, you are a government inspector. Do you recall the day of January 6, 1992?

Answer: Yes, I attended at the premises of the Black Coal Company.

Question: And will you tell the court what you observed on January 6 at those premises?

Answer: Yes, I observed a cloud of black, oily smoke coming from chimney number 5 at 4:00 PM.

The Hostile Witness

The rule against leading questions in examination-in-chief is designed to prevent dishonesty. However, the rule can be very restrictive when you subpoena a person who is not willing to testify. Although a person who is subpoenaed must attend and answer questions, if he is reluctant to testify, he can simply say he does not remember or he can state facts in a way that distorts them. Because you can only ask him what happened and cannot fashion the question in a manner to which he can only answer "yes" or "no," you are stuck with the answer he gives.

For example, if the witness is the example above were hostile, in answer to the question, "Do you remember the day of January 6?" he could simply say, "No." That would be the end of his testimony.

That is why it is important to call only "friendly" witnesses — people who are prepared to be objective and, at best, sympathetic to your case. If you call as your witness someone unsympathetic, he may choose not to remember what he saw or choose to state facts inaccurately, yet you may have no other witnesses to contradict him.

If you can convince a judge that your witness is "hostile" or "adverse," you may ask leading questions and cross-examine your own witness as if she were called by the opposite party. Cross-examination, of course, allows a person to ask a question any way she wishes, short of badgering a witness or otherwise acting unreasonably.

However, a tribunal will rarely declare a witness hostile. Usually, a witness will be declared hostile only if he clearly contradicts a statement previously made in his own handwriting or written down and signed by him, or tape recorded with the witness's knowledge and consent. That is why it is so important to obtain written or recorded statements from potential witnesses who may later become reluctant to assist, and to otherwise ascertain in advance exactly what your witness will say when called to testify.

A CHECKLIST OF IMPORTANT EVIDENCE

The following checklist comprises some important evidence that should be presented to a court in an anti-pollution prosecution or civil suit.

1. *The correct name of the accused or defendant.* If the defendant is an individual, use at least one full given name plus the family name. If it is a corporation, do a corporate search. If it is a partnership or sole proprietorship (a one-owner unincorporated business), do a search and charge the individuals involved by setting out their full names and then adding "carrying on business as" and insert the business name. (For search procedures, see Appendix V.)

2. *The correct name of the municipality,* county, or other legally described area or place where the alleged offence was committed, and the name of the owner of the land on which the pollution source is located. (See Appendix V.)

3. *If a watercourse or other body of water has been impaired, its correct name should be given.* Local residents may have a name for a creek, lake, or river that is not the official or legal name. The local office of the Ministry of Natural Resources (MNR) can often assist in determining the correct name for a watercourse, usually from maps prepared by MNR. If necessary, the correct name can be obtained from the Secretary of the Ontario Geographic Names Board, part of the Surveys, Mapping, and Remote Sensing Branch of MNR.

   If the watercourse is a storm ditch or a small creek with no name, or if the waste is discharged to a point of land, such as a sewer, then a general description of the location of the creek and its direction of flow, or of the location of the point of discharge (sewer), that is sufficient to enable it to be identified is required.

4. *Dates on which the offence occurred.* Such dates should be clear in the minds of witnesses, and obviously must correspond to the dates charged in the information or the statement of claim.

5. *The type and amount of contaminant discharged or deposited* and testimony concerning continuity of sampling and analysis. (See above.)

6. *The effects of the contaminant on people,* vegetation, animals, or property, or on all four.

7. *What efforts the complainant has made to have the problem rectified,* short of taking legal action.

8. If the prosecution or suit is for the breach of a municipal bylaw, *enter as an exhibit at the hearing a copy of the bylaw* that is "certified" as a true copy by the clerk of the municipality. If the bylaw is effective only after approval by some government agency, supply a certified copy of the approval as well. Many bylaws are not "consolidated" — that is, when they are amended, they are not reprinted with all the amendments included. Therefore, it is often necessary to file certified copies of all amendments to the bylaw, whether or not they affect the section that is allegedly being violated.

John Swaigen

FURTHER READING

Rupert Cross and Colin Tapper, *Cross on Evidence*, 7th ed. (London: Butterworths, 1990).

Rupert Cross and Nancy Wilkins, *An Outline of the Law of Evidence*, 6th ed. (London: Butterworths, 1986).

Douglas Drinkwalter and J. Douglas Ewart, *Ontario Provincial Offences Procedures* (Toronto: Carswell, 1980).

E.G. Ewaschuk, *Criminal Pleadings and Practice in Canada*, 2d ed. (Aurora, Ont.: Canada Law Book, 1993).

M.N. Howard, Peter Crane, and Daniel A. Hochberg, *Phipson on Evidence*, 14th ed. (London: Sweet & Maxwell, 1990).

Peter K. McWilliams, *Canadian Criminal Evidence*, 3d ed. (Aurora, Ont.: Canada Law Book, 1992).

Andrew J. Roman, *Effective Advocacy Before Administrative Tribunals* (Toronto: Carswell, 1989).

R.E. Salhany, *Canadian Crminal Procedure*, 5th ed. (Aurora, Ont.: Canada Law Book, 1989).

John Sopinka, *The Trial of an Action* (Toronto: Butterworths, 1981).

John Sopinka, William Lederman, and Alan Bryant, *The Law of Evidence in Canada* (Toronto: Butterworths, 1992).

ENDNOTES

1   *Re Bernstein and College of Physicians and Surgeons of Ontario* (1977), 15 OR (2d) 447, 76 DLR (3d) 38 (Div. Ct.); *Coates v. Registrar Motor Vehicle Dealers* (1988), 65 OR (2d) 526 (Div. Ct.). See also *Re Beckon* (1992), 9 OR (3d) 256 (CA).

2   *Canada Evidence Act*, RSC 1985, c. C-5, sections 19, 20, and 31.

3   *Ontario Evidence Act*, RSO 1990, c. E.23, section 53.

4   *Statutory Powers Procedure Act*, RSO 1990, c. S.22.

5   *Ontario Municipal Board Act*, RSO 1990, c. O.28, Rules of Procedure, RRO 1990, reg. 889.

6   *Environmental Assessment Act*, RSO 1990, c. E.18, Rules of Practice — Environmental Assessment Board, RRO 1990, reg. 335.

7   *Environmental Protection Act*, RSO 1990, c. E.19.

8   Statutory provisions that authorize the admission of specific documents include the *Highway Traffic Act*, RSO 1990, c. H.8, section 210(7); the *Corporations Information Act*, RSO 1990, c. C.39, sections 19 and 20; the *Business Corporations Act*, RSO 1990, c. B.16, sections 257-259; the *Assessment Act*, RSO 1990, c. A.31, section 42; the *Ontario Evidence Act*, supra endnote 3, section 53; the *Municipal Act*, RSO 1990, c.

M.45, section 127(4); the *Municipality of Metropolitan Toronto Act*, RSO 1990, c. M.62, section 19(2); the *Canada Evidence Act*, supra endnote 2, sections 19-36; the *Land Titles Act*, RSO 1990, c. L.5, section 117(2); and the *Regulations Act*, RSO 1990, c. C.21, sections 5(4) and 5(2).

Some significant court decisions interpreting such statutory provisions include *R. v. Anthes Business Forms Ltd.* (1975), 26 CCC (2d) 348 (Ont. CA); *R. v. Mullen* (1979), 47 CCC (2d) 499 (Ont. CA); *Setak Computer Services Corporation Ltd. v. Burroughs Business Machines Ltd.* (1977), 15 OR (2d) 750 (HCJ); *MSM Construction Ltd. v. Deiluiis* (1985), 49 OR (2d) 633 (Div. Ct.); and *Tecoglas, Inc. v. Domglas, Inc.* (1985), 51 OR (2d) 196 (HCJ).

9   *R. v. Khan*, [1990] 2 SCR 531; *R. v. Smith* (1992), 75 CCC (3d) 257 (SCC).

10   *Freedom of Information and Protection of Privacy Act*, RSO 1990, c. F.31.

11   *Canadian Charter of Rights and Freedoms*, Part I of the *Constitution Act, 1982*, RSC 1985, app. II, no. 44.

12   *R.v. Weil's Food Processing Ltd.* (1991), 6 CELR (NS) 249 (OCGD).

13   For example, *McKie v. KVP*, [1948] 3 OLR 401 (HCJ).

14   Traditionally, the courts have limited similar fact evidence to events that are "strikingly similar" to the one before the court. The probative value of the evidence must outweigh its prejudice to the accused or defendant.

15   For an example of the admissibility of similar fact evidence in an environmental case, see *R. v. Chinook Chemicals Corp. Ltd.* (1974), 3 CELN 208, 3 OR (2d) 768 (Prov. Ct.).

16   *Criminal Code*, RSC 1985, c. C-46, section 489, as amended by RSC 1985, c. 42 (4th Supp.), section 3. The wording is: "may seize, in addition to the things mentioned in the warrant, any thing that the person believes on reasonable and probable grounds has been obtained by or has been used in the commission of an offence." Photographs are authorized by RSC 1985, c. 23 (4th Supp.), section 2; the *Provincial Offences Act*, RSO 1990, c. P.33, section 15. Officers may seize "(a) anything upon or in respect of which an offence has been or is suspected of being committed," or "(b) anything that there is reasonable ground to believe will afford evidence as to the commission of an offence."

17   *R. v. British Columbia Forestry Products Ltd.* (1977), 6 CELN 7 (BC Co. Ct.). Ewaschuk states that proof of continuity goes to weight rather than admissibility. As long as at least one witness is able to identify the exhibit at the tribunal, the failure to prove an unbroken chain of possession will not make the exhibit inadmissible, but will affect the weight to be given to the evidence. See Ewaschuk, *Criminal Pleadings and Practice in Canada*, 2d ed. (Aurora, Ont.: Canada Law Book, 1987), 16–29 and 16–81. Similarly, if the important issue is the accuracy of the analysis, the failure to produce the sample at the tribunal should not be crucial. The important question is how tampering was prohibited before analysis, not what happened to the sample afterward. In many cases, the sample is not even brought to court where the accuracy of the analysis is the issue. Nevertheless, to avoid any problems, the best practice is to retain the sample after analysis, maintain its security, and be prepared to bring it before the tribunal if necessary.

18   *Environmental Protection Act*, supra endnote 7.

19   *Ontario Water Resources Act*, RSO 1990, c. O.40.

20   *Pesticides Act*, RSO 1990, c. P.11.

5

How To Wage a Campaign: Organizing To Protect Your Environment

Contents

My mother used to say, "The Lord helps those who help themselves." Others have said, "There's safety in numbers," and "Governments don't lead, they follow." All of these sayings seem to be true when it comes to protecting the environment. It's often up to ordinary citizens to protect their immediate environment and to create the pressure necessary to convince government and industry to protect the global environment. In past editions of this book, we had chapters that described ways other than legal action to protect the environment, and that explained how to organize a citizens' group, raise funds, gain allies, publicize your cause, and make effective representations to government agencies.

Today, however, there are many excellent publications available to help citizens organize a successful campaign to protect the environment. Rather than try to reinvent the wheel, we commend these books to our readers.*

Organizing

Saul D. Alinsky, *Rules for Radicals: A Practical Primer for Realistic Radicals* (New York: Random House, 1971).

---

* Some of these books are out of print, but are still available at libraries.

101

Elizabeth Amer, *Yes We Can! How To Organize Citizen Action* (Ottawa: Synergistics Consulting Limited, 1980).

John Fisher, *Handbook for Cooperating Associations* (Ottawa: Parks and Environment Canada, 1986).
  Available from Environment Canada or Department of Secretary of State.

Stuart Hilts, Malcolm Kirk, and Ron Reid, eds., *Islands of Green: Natural Heritage Protection in Ontario* (Toronto: Ontario Heritage Foundation, 1986).
  Available from Ontario Heritage Foundation, 77 Bloor St. W., Toronto, Ontario.

Christine Holloway and Shirley Otto, *Getting Organized* (London: Bedford Square Press).
  To purchase, contact Bedford Square Press, 26 Bedford Square, London WC1B 3HU, England.

Anthony Jay, *The Householder's Guide to Community Defence Against Bureaucratic Aggression* (London: Jonathon Cape Limited, 1972).

Donald R. Keating, *The Power To Make It Happen: Mass-Based Community Organizing — What It Is and How It Works* (Toronto: Green Tree Publishing Company, 1975).

Fred Wilcox, *Grass Roots: An Anti-Nuke Source Book* (Trumansburg, NY: The Crossing Press, 1980).

EFFECTIVE PUBLIC PARTICIPATION

Sherry R. Arnstein, "A Ladder of Citizen Participation" (July 1969), *American Institute of Planning Journal.*

Desmond Connor, ed., *Constructive Citizen Participation* (Victoria, BC: Development Press).
  This is a quarterly newsletter.

Desmond Connor, ed., *Constructive Citizen Participation: A Resource Book* (Victoria, BC: Development Press).
  This is a binder with materials from back issues of the Constructive Citizen Participation *newsletter. Both it and the newsletter are available from Development Press, 5096 Catalina Terrace, Victoria, British Columbia V8Y 2A5.*

Clifford Maynes and the Ontario Environmental Network, *Public Consultation: A Citizens' Handbook* (Toronto: Ontario Environmental Network, 1987).
  This deals with what we want from public consultation, when to say no, and how to consult effectively. Available from the Ontario Environmental Network, Box 125, Station P, Toronto, Ontario M5T 2Z7.

Ontario, Ministry of the Environment, *Public Consultation: A Resource Kit for Ministry Staff* (Toronto: the ministry, 1989).

Praxis, *Manual on Public Involvement in Environmental Assessment: Planning and Implementing of Public Involvement Programs*. Prepared for the Federal Environmental Assessment Review Office.

> *Available from Praxis, 2215 – 19 St. S.W., Calgary, Alberta T2T 4X1*

Barbara Wallace and Maureen Turner, *Citizens' Guide to Waste Management in Ontario in the 1990s* (Toronto: Canadian Environmental Law Association [undated]).

> *Available from Canadian Environmental Law Association, 517 College Street, Suite 401, Toronto, Ontario M6G 4A2.*

Waterloo Public Interest Research Group, *Waste Management Master Plans: What You Should Know* (Waterloo, Ont.: WPIRG, May 1987).

> *Available from Waterloo Public Interest Research Group, University of Waterloo, Waterloo, Ontario N2L 3G1.*

Phil Weller and John Jackson, *Managing Wastes: A Guide to Citizen's Involvement* (Waterloo, Ont.: WPIRG, January 1984).

FUND RAISING

Alan Arlett and N. McClintock, *Canadian Directory to Foundations* (Toronto: The Canadian Centre for Philanthropy).

> *Updated each year. Available from The Canadian Centre for Philanthropy, 74 Victoria Street, Suite 920, Toronto, Ontario M5C 2A5.*

Joan Flanagan, *The Grass Roots Fundraising Book: How To Raise Money in Your Community* (Chicago: Contemporary Books Inc.).

> *To purchase, contact Contemporary Books Inc., 180 North Michigan Ave., Chicago, Illinois 60606.*

Joyce Young, *Fundraising for Non-Profit Groups*, 3d ed. (North Vancouver, BC: Self-Counsel Press, 1989).

OBTAINING INFORMATION FROM GOVERNMENT AND INDUSTRY

Heather Mitchell and Murray Rankin, *Using the Access to Information Act* (Toronto: International Self-Counsel Press Limited, 1984).

Ken Rubin, *Using Canadian Freedom of Information Legislation, 1990.*

> *Available from Ken Rubin, 212 Third Avenue, Ottawa, Ontario K1S 2K3.*

P.L.S. Simon, *Hazardous Products: Canada's Right To Know Laws* (Toronto: CCH Canadian, 1987).

RESOURCE BOOKS

Gerald F.M. Dawe, *The Urban Environment: A Sourcebook for the 1990s* (Birmingham, Eng.: Centre for Urban Ecology, 1990).

> *Available from Centre for Urban Ecology, The Birmingham Settlement, 318 Summer Lane, Birmingham B19 3RL, England.*

Federation of Ontario Naturalists and Ontario Waste Management Corporation, *Hazardous Waste Educational Resource Kit.*

Ontario Environmental Network, *Environmental Resource Book: A Directory of Ontario's Environmental Groups and Their Printed and Audio-Visual Resources* (Toronto: Ontario Environmental Network, 1991).

> *Available from the Ontario Environmental Network, 2 Quebec Street, Suite 201C, Guelph, Ontario N1H 2T3.*

CASE STUDIES OF ENVIRONMENTAL CAMPAIGNS

Peter Lewington, *No Right-of-Way: How Democracy Came to the Oil Patch* (Toronto: Fitzhenry and Whiteside, 1991).

Elizabeth May, *Budworm Battles* (Tantallon, NS: Four East Publications Limited, 1982).

Elizabeth May, *Paradise Won: The Struggle for South Moresby* (Toronto: McClelland and Stewart, 1990).

Walter Robbins, *Getting the Shaft: The Radioactive Waste Controversy in Manitoba* (Winnipeg: Queenston House Publishing Co. Ltd., 1984).

APPEARING BEFORE BOARDS AND TRIBUNALS

Andrew J. Roman, *Effective Advocacy Before Administrative Tribunals* (Toronto: Carswell, 1989).

LEGAL STRATEGY

Linda F. Duncan, *Enforcing Environmental Law: A Guide to Private Prosecution* (Edmonton: Environmental Law Centre, 1990).

> *Available from the Environmental Law Centre (Alberta) Society, 202, 10110 124th Street, Edmonton, Alberta T5N 1P6.*

John Swaigen, *How To Fight for What's Right* (Toronto: James Lorimer and Company, 1982).

John Swaigen

PART II

Common Law and Statutory Remedies

6

Common Law Rights and Remedies

CONTENTS

Some evidence was given on behalf of the defendant to show the importance of its business in the community, and that it carried it on in a proper manner. Neither of these elements is to be taken into consideration in a case of this character, nor are the economic necessities of the defendant relevant to be considered.

In my view, if I were to consider and give effect to an argument based on the defendant's economic position in the community, or its financial interests, I would in effect be giving to it a veritable power of expropriation of the common law rights of the riparian owners, without compensation.

Chief Justice McRuer in McKie v. The KVP Co. Ltd.

The common law is a body of legal principles that has evolved through decisions made by judges of our civil courts over hundreds of years.

Historically, common law rights and remedies were developed to protect individuals against harm to their person or property. A person with interests in land — whether as a landowner or as a tenant — may use the common law to prevent other people from harming or interfering with his or her ordinary and peaceful enjoyment of that land. Such harm or interference may take the form of unpleasant fumes; noise and vibrations; dust that settles in the house; sewage that escapes from a neighbouring property; or flooding or erosion of land. In some cases, people also have rights to fair treatment in their business dealings and other rights that are not based on ownership of land, but on a more general duty to anticipate and prevent harm to others.

In many instances, these principles have been replaced or supplemented by statute law (see Chapter 1). In such cases, an injured person may have a choice of statutory or common law remedies. In Chapter 3 we discussed the advantages and disadvantages of different types of remedies, and how to decide whether to exercise your common law rights, launch a prosecution, appear before a tribunal, or choose a different legal remedy. However, statutes have by no means replaced all of the common law. There are still many common law rights that are not available in statutes, or that are more difficult to enforce through prosecutions or public participation in statutory decision-making processes. Many of these statutes only provide for a fine or allow the government to restrain harmful activity, but provide no remedy to the individual. More and more frequently, these statutes incorporate the possibility of clean-up orders, injunctions, and compensation to victims of offences in the range of sentences that can be imposed when an offender is convicted. Despite all the new statutes, however, the common law civil suit is still often the only method of obtaining compensation for injury to your health or damage to your property, or an injunction to prevent further harm.

REMEDIES: DAMAGES AND INJUNCTIONS

"Damages" is the term used for an award of money the court grants to compensate a person who has suffered a loss or injury caused by the act complained of. Normally, damages will be awarded to compensate a person for actual financial losses (for example, loss of income from reduced crops or devaluation of property) and out-of-pocket expenses ("special damages"); and also for less tangible losses, such as annoyance, inconvenience, pain and suffering, and loss of enjoyment of property ("general damages"). Rarely, if the defendant's* conduct was high-handed, malicious, or contemptuous of the plaintiff's** rights, the court may order him or her to pay an additional sum above and beyond the plaintiff's actual loss, to punish the defendant and make an example of him or her to deter others from committing such wrongs ("punitive" or "exemplary" damages).[1]

An injunction is an order made by the court prohibiting the defendant from doing something he or she intends to do, such as building an addition to a factory; prohibiting him or her from continuing to do something he or she is already doing, such as dumping sewage from the factory into a stream; or ordering him or her to do something he or she does not want to do, such as installing pollution abatement equipment in the factory or pulling down a building in a flood-prone area. An injunction may be temporary or permanent. A temporary injunction is intended to protect the plaintiff from harm until his or her rights can be determined by the court. A permanent or "perpetual" injunction may be issued after the court reaches its final decision at trial. An offender who ignores the order is in contempt of court and may be fined or jailed until the order is carried out.

If you are asking for a permanent injunction — for example, an order that the defendant stop discharging pollutants — you may request the court to order the defendant to stop this activity until the trial is over. In deciding whether to grant this temporary injunction, the court will consider whether you have a reasonably strong case, whether the injunction is necessary to protect you from harm until the trial or whether damages will adequately compensate you for any harm that occurs before trial, and whether stopping the activities or carrying out costly work will cause the defendant irreparable damage (for example, putting a company out of business).

Sometimes a temporary injunction can send a message to the defendant, and it is unnecessary to proceed to trial. In 1970, a group of landowners around Ramsay Lake in Sudbury went to court seeking a permanent injunction against powerboat races that the local Rotary Club planned to hold on the lake.[2] Because the trial could not be held before the date scheduled for the races, the plaintiffs asked for a temporary injunction to postpone the races until after the trial. Once the court granted the temporary injunction, they did not have to proceed to trial for their permanent injunction. The Rotary Club agreed to abandon its plans.

The court may impose conditions on the granting of a temporary injunction. For example, the judge may order the plaintiff to bring the matter to trial as quickly as possible. The plaintiff will probably be required to give an undertaking to pay any damages suffered by the defendant as a result of the injunction if the plaintiff ultimately loses at trial.

The court may refuse to award an injunction, particularly a temporary one, if the plaintiff has unnecessarily delayed instituting the action or if, in the opinion of the court, an injunction would be too harsh on the defendant. Although there was a time in Ontario when the courts believed that once it was shown that a person's common law rights had been infringed, the person was entitled to an order eliminating the hardship, no matter how much harm the order might do to the defendant or to the community,[3] the current rule is that an injunction will never be granted where damages will afford an adequate remedy.[4] For instance, in Ontario, if the economic loss can be measured and if it is relatively slight, the usual practice is to award only

---

*   The person against whom a lawsuit (legal action) is launched.
** The person who initiates the civil action (roughly equivalent to the "complainant" or "informant" in a prosecution).

damages. In one case,[5] a brick-making plant emitted sulphur dioxide that damaged the crop in part of the plaintiff's orchards each year. The relief granted by the court was damages, since the economic loss to the plaintiff could be measured and compensated in money.

COMMON LAW RIGHTS AND THE ENVIRONMENT

There are many common law rights that may occasionally be useful to prevent or obtain damages for environmental wrongs. For example, generally when someone buys property, the rule is "buyer beware." What you see — or don't see — is what you get. If the soil is contaminated, or the walls of the house contain asbestos or urea formaldehyde, the purchaser cannot sue the vendor. In some cases, however, if the vendor or real estate agent knows about hidden contamination and conceals it or lies about it to the purchaser or to someone else, and as a result the purchaser buys the land, the vendor or agent may be committing the torts of fraud (which is also a criminal offence), deceit, or injurious falsehood.[6] Even if the conduct falls short of fraud, failure to disclose a dangerous condition may be another form of civil wrong, a breach of a fundamental condition of the contract.[7]

There are, however, three "environmental torts" and two torts of more general application that are frequently useful in environmental cases. These five "causes of action" (rights to sue) are: nuisance, riparian rights, strict liability, trespass, and negligence.

The same harm may give rise to more than one cause of action. The fouling of a river that causes your drinking water to become polluted would probably be a nuisance. Depending on the circumstances, it might also be negligence, trespass, a breach of riparian rights, and a case of strict liability. If they appear to apply, all these rights can be claimed in one action. It is not necessary to start a separate law suit for each cause of action.

Nuisance

Nuisance is the most useful common law tool in environmental cases. It can provide a remedy for air and water pollution, noise, vibration, smells, soil contamination, flooding, and many other intrusions upon your peaceful use and enjoyment of your property.

There are two kinds of nuisance recognized by the common law: private and public.

Private Nuisance

A private nuisance consists of the unreasonable interference with another's use or enjoyment of land that he or she owns or occupies.[8] The reasonableness of the interference depends largely on the degree of impact that it has on a neighbour's enjoyment of his or her property, rather than on how useful, necessary, or diligent the offending activity is.[9] The activity may be reasonable from the viewpoint of the person carrying it out or of society generally. The negative impacts on neighbours may be unavoidable except at great cost. However, the activity may still be considered "unreasonable" in the context of nuisance if it interferes substantially with others' use and enjoyment of their property.

Whether the impact will be considered unreasonable by a court is somewhat unpredictable in cases where the activity is of great social importance and economic benefit and the negative effects are impossible or extremely difficult to avoid. Determining the "reasonableness" of the impact always involves balancing several factors, including the severity of the harm, the character of the locale, any abnormal sensitivity of the person suffering the harm or of his or her use of the property, and the utility of the defendant's conduct.[10] In determining liability, however, the courts distinguish between activities that cause actual and substantial physical harm to human health or damage to property and activities that result only in a loss of the use or enjoyment of property.[11]

If an activity results in actual physical damage to health or property, or results in economic losses flowing from the injury, it will generally be found to be a nuisance even if the defendant's activity was reasonable and valuable to the community, was carried on without negligence and no reasonable alternatives were available to the defendant, and the activity occurred in a location where such nuisances might be expected, such as a factory area.[12]

If, however, the activity results only in personal inconvenience and annoyance, the interference must be more substantial to be actionable; it must cause recurring or continuous inconvenience to a person of "ordinary" sensitivity.[13] If the person complaining is using his or her property in an unusual or abnormal way that makes him or her exceptionally vulnerable to the neighbour's activity (carrying on a business of growing rare orchids in one's home might be an example), the person may not be entitled to recover damages.[14] In such cases, the court will take into account the character of the neighbourhood. What would be a nuisance in a quiet residential neighbourhood might not be a nuisance in a factory district.[15] Even if an industry is located in an industrial area, however, it must still operate its plant with as little annoyance to neighbours as possible.[16] Moreover, even if a person moved to an industrial area and could not successfully sue for existing levels of noise, dust, odour, or other contaminants, any substantial increase in the level of contamination will give rise to a nuisance action.[17]

The person suffering the annoyance or inconvenience is not the only person entitled to sue for the nuisance. If the person suffering is a customer of a store who takes his business elsewhere or a tenant who moves to get away from the nuisance, the operator of the business or the owner of the premises may sue for lost revenues.[18]

Nor is the person causing the nuisance the only one who can be sued. If a landlord rents to a tenant knowing that the use he intends to make of the property may result in a nuisance, the landlord may also be liable.[19] If the nuisance is carried on by a corporation, officers and directors who knew or should have known of the nuisance may be liable as well as the company.[20] Although the person responsible for a nuisance will usually be the owner or occupant of nearby land, others may also be sued — for example, a construction contractor paving nearby public land, a hydro repairman working on a line, or an airplane pilot spraying nearby land with herbicides.[21]

Historically, some of the more colourful successful nuisance suits have involved such matters as early and persistent ringing of church bells, hammering and beating trays against a common wall to interrupt a neighbour's occupation of teaching music, and spiteful firing of guns near a neighbour's breeding pens to cause his silver foxes to miscarry.[22]

Other nuisances include annoyance by noxious fumes,[23] particulate matter,[24] pesticides,[25] vibration,[26] and noise.[27] So are smoke and fumes from a tobacco factory that saturated neighbours' clothing and furniture and made them ill,[28] odours from a pulp and paper mill that interfered with a resident's comfort and enjoyment of his home,[29] vibrations from engines that damaged a house,[30] noise and dust from demolition and construction of buildings,[31] and junkyard noise.[32]

Nuisances also encompass physical changes to the landscape as well as pollution — for example, flooding,[33] depriving land of support so that it subsides into a hole that has been dug,[34] and lowering the watertable under farmland.[35] Whether a nuisance causes actual damage or merely loss of enjoyment of property, the complainant must show that the person causing the nuisance knew about it or ought to have foreseen the harm that the activity could cause and did not act upon that knowledge to prevent the injury.[36]

Public Nuisance

Public nuisances are activities that unreasonably interfere with the public's use of public lands and waters, obstruct the access of occupants of neighbouring lands to the public land, or interfere with people's access to premises adjacent to public land. Most often these nuisances involve the use of highways and navigable waters.[37] However, the term also has a second, and less clear, meaning: wrongs against the public at large. Thus, private nuisances can become public nuisances when they affect more than one or two people or affect whole neighbourhoods. When something affects many people, however, the common law may deny any one person the right ("standing") to sue, unless he or she can show damage to his or her property or show that any obstruction or inconvenience suffered is much different from or much greater than that suffered by his or her neighbours. Otherwise, the action may only be brought by the provincial attorney general or someone who has the written consent of the attorney general.[38]

Some nuisances cause damage that can have both public and private aspects. For instance, a factory might emit smoke and smells that disturb everyone for miles around, and cause the walls of everyone's apartment or house to turn grey. Despite the "public" aspect, you can sue for damage done to your own property, or interference with your enjoyment of it, even if this is not substantially different from the damage done to other people's property. If, however, you do not own or rent property, you cannot sue for relief from smells that disturb the neighbourhood unless your discomfort is substantially greater than or different from that of your neighbours.

Unfortunately, the public nuisance concept restricts the opportunities for private citizens to take legal action, not only for the common good, but also to protect their own livelihood. The theory that the attorney general will sue is often a meaningless fiction. The Ontario Law Reform Commission has endorsed the concern that the attorney general's power may be influenced by "partisan or improper political motives."[39] The commission questioned whether the attorney general should be considered the sole protector of the public interest:

> It is important to recall that the early public nuisance cases involved relatively minor interferences, such as obstructing a public highway or blocking the passage of vessels in a river, and it is in this context that the governing principles were articulated. Today, the nature and extent of harm that may constitute a public nuisance might conceivably be of an entirely different order — for example, threatening the destruction of fish in a lake or the pollution of a water supply. The consequences for the public of a failure of the Attorney General to act, whether by bringing proceedings or consenting to a relator action, are potentially much more serious today than in the era when these principles were first developed.[40]

The commission recommended that any person should have the right to sue in public nuisance without any personal, proprietary, or pecuniary interest or injury different in kind or degree from that of others.

Defences

In any law suit, the defendant may raise a variety of defences. Some of them work and some do not. In a nuisance action, most of the defences usually raised will not serve to justify the defendant's activity.

Defences That Work

In public nuisance actions, the main defence is usually that the plaintiff has no standing to sue. If the plaintiff is trying to protect a right he or she has in common with others, such as fishing or boating in lakes and rivers, or using the highway or breathing the air, this defence is likely to succeed, unless the plaintiff can show that the public nuisance is also a private nuisance, substantially affecting his or her property or health.*

The defences of "statutory authority," "prescription," and "acquiescence" are often encountered. The common law holds that a public authority has "statutory authority" to commit a nuisance, and therefore no remedies are available for harm caused by this nuisance, if and *only if* the law imposes a duty on the authority to carry out an activity and nuisance is an unavoidable result of the activity. If the law merely permits, but does not require, the agency to carry on the harmful activity, the defence of statutory authority will not prevail. In recent years, some courts had ruled that if the Legislature gives an agency the power to carry out an activity, this authority is enough to deprive others of their right to compensation, unless the activity is carried out negligently. In 1989, the Supreme Court of Canada rejected this broadening of the scope of the defence.[41] Three of the justices ruled that the defence is available only if there is a duty to cause the nuisance.[42] Two others ruled that people should be compensated even where the agency is acting under a duty,[43] and the sixth justice would have broadened the defence to bar redress any time a statute authorizes activity that can only be carried out by causing a nuisance.[44] Thus, five of the six justices ruled in favour of making this defence available only under very narrow circumstances.

Statutory authority is often given for operations like electricity generating stations and sewage treatment plants (see below). For example, section 30 of the *Ontario Water Resources Act* (*OWRA*), discussed below, deems all sewage works that are constructed, maintained, and operated in accordance with the Act and in accordance with any order or approval issued under the Act to have statutory authority. It is important to note, however, that the certificates of approval and licences that may be granted to some industries under the *Environmental Protection Act* (*EPA*) and other statutes do not provide immunity from a nuisance action, unless the licence expressly orders the polluter to carry on the activities in a specific manner and the obvious and necessary effect of carrying on in this manner is to create a nuisance. Only the *Ontario Water Resources Act* purports to restrict the common law rights of environmental damage victims.

---

* However, 1977 amendments to the *Fisheries Act* removed this defence against commercial fishers suing for damages for pollution causing loss of income. See chapters 7 and 18.

The defence of "prescription" refers to a right to pollute acquired by a polluter because he or she has caused a private nuisance to the neighbours continuously for 20 years with the neighbours' knowledge and acquiescence.[45] When a right of prescription has been acquired, and the circumstances permit its assertion, the courts will not act; but no prescriptive right may be acquired to create or continue a *public* nuisance.

A plaintiff who acquiesces in the offending activity is also barred from suing. But acquiescence requires express consent or active encouragement of the activity. As Linden says: "Merely standing idly by is not enough."[46]

Occasionally, a new "defence" is created by the passage of a statute that is desgined specifically to take away the right to sue for nuisances. For example, the *Farm Practices Protection Act*, passed in 1988, abolished neighbours' rights to sue farmers in nuisance for any odour, noise, or dust arising from "normal" farm practices.[47] Similarly, the Ontario Legislature took away the right to sue to prevent neighbours from obstructing sunlight and the flow of fresh air, after the courts complained that the right to fresh air and sunlight was interfering with development.[48]

Defences That Do Not Work

In a nuisance suit, defendant after defendant will rely on several other defences that do not justify a nuisance.[49] The list is lengthy. If there is actual harm to property, rather than just inconvenience, it is no defence that the defendant is making a reasonable use of the land or that the activities are carried on without negligence. Nor can the defendant rely on the fact that the best technology has been used to control the nuisance or that other people contributed to the nuisance. The defendant may be responsible for some kinds of injury even if the cost of abating the nuisance is disproportionately high compared with the damage to the plaintiff, the activities are beneficial to the general public, or the defendant was creating the nuisance before the plaintiff came to live or carry on business in the area.

Riparian Rights

Rights to the use of water in a stream, river, or lake stem from a person's property interest in, or possession of, the land bordering on the water. An interest in the land gives him or her, according to this traditional English doctrine, a right to the continued flow of the water in its natural quantity and quality, undiminished and unpolluted. A person with these rights is called a "riparian owner" and the rights are called "riparian rights."* If a person upstream changes the quality or level of the water flowing past his or her land to the detriment of people downstream, he or she may be liable to a suit in civil court.

Riparian rights may also be used to stop the channelling of streams (a favourite pastime of highway and parks planners) or the damming and diversion of waters upstream from your property. The law not only prevents upstream owners from *decreasing* the flow to the downstream owner, but also from unreasonably *increasing* the flow so that water entering the stream exceeds the stream's capacity, causing flooding and erosion of the bed and banks downstream.[50]

---

* From *ripa*, a Latin word meaning the shore or bank of a body of water. See also Chapter 8.

Similarly, although perhaps less clearly but no less logically, a downstream owner may not interfere with the water passing through the land of upstream owners. For example, a downstream owner may not cause flooding of the upstream owner's land by damming the stream or by refusing to accept water that naturally flows onto the downstream land so that it backs up into the stream above and causes it to exceed its capacity on the upstream land.[51]

There are certain exceptions. Other riparian owners are entitled to make reasonable use of their portions of the water. Diverting water for household purposes is a reasonable use that can be made without fear of liability. Draining one's land into the stream is also reasonable, as long as the drainage is not excessive.

As a riparian owner, you may sue for damages or for an injunction to restrain the offender from polluting the water or significantly altering the flow regime. Unlike most common law causes of action, the riparian rights doctrine does not require you to show any actual injury to succeed in court. If you do not show actual injury, however, you must at least demonstrate to the court that the activity is likely to continue and to cause further alteration of water quality and quantity; that the water has been made less suitable for some purpose that it might be used for; and that there is a causal connection between the alteration and the defendant's activities.

If there are several people taking or polluting the water, none of them may escape liability by blaming the others. You need only show that each is discharging pollutants or diverting water and that in combination they affect the quantity or quality of water flowing beside or through your land. Injunctions and damages can be obtained against each of them.

A person cannot raise the defence that he or she was taking water or discharging pollutants into the river before the plaintiff became a riparian landowner. Thus, for example, if you move into a wilderness area only to find the water already despoiled by an upstream pulp mill, you might still validly assert your right to unpolluted water.

There are no riparian rights to undiminished groundwater flow, since groundwater saturates the soil and does not flow in a visible, defined channel like surface water.[52] Therefore, a person who pumps out the groundwater and thereby dries up a neighbour's well cannot be sued in riparian rights. Nevertheless, there is some protection for groundwater quality and quantity. Any pollution of groundwater is a nuisance.[53] Moreover, it is illegal to pump out substantial quantities of groundwater without a permit from the Ministry of the Environment.[54] These water-taking permits usually contain conditions intended to prevent depletion of the groundwater. Anyone who takes groundwater without a permit or in contravention of conditions in the permit is not only subject to prosecution for violation of the *Ontario Water Resources Act*, but may also be sued for nuisance or negligence.[55]

Statutory authority is also available as a defence to a riparian rights action. This is particularly a problem where public authorities have a right or duty to construct drains, water lines, or sewers. When these conduits back up into basements, leak, or flood land, courts have often been reluctant to award compensation.[56]

As mentioned above, sewage works approved under the *Ontario Water Resources Act* are specifically given a statutory authority defence. Since these approvals authorize a degree of pollution with no assurance that they have been drafted to minimize the pollution, this provision appears to take away the right to sue even where the amount of pollution authorized by the approval is greater than is necessary to operate the plant properly.

Although the defence of statutory authority is usually available only to public agencies, the poor draftsmanship of the *Ontario Water Resources Act* appears to extend the defence to industrial polluters, since the term "sewage works" includes both municipal sewage treatment plants and any industrial facility that handles waste from factories before discharging it into a lake or river.[57] Moreover, although it is unlikely that the drafters of the Act contemplated this possibility, this immunity has also been held to extend to flooding and the erosion of stream banks caused by storm sewers carrying runoff from city streets.[58] However, all is not lost. Section 29 of the Act gives the right to sue for "injurious affection" (see Chapter 15) if a *municipal* (but not a private) sewage works interferes with the use of your land. Although the damages you can get for injurious affection may be lower than in nuisance or riparian rights, the Legislature has to some extent given back with one hand what it took with the other.[59]

Trespass

Common Law Trespass

The common law of trespass refers to the physical intrusion of people or objects onto one's land, or even over it (for example, a bullet passing over someone's land is a trespass onto the land)[60] without the consent of the owner or occupant. If the intrusion is intentional, the intruder is liable for any harm that results *directly* from the intrusion even if the harm was unintentional. An intentional trespass creates liability for damages for the mere fact of intruding even if no tangible, ascertainable damage is done. Moreover, the intentional trespasser is liable for any damage done while on the land even if his or her motives were good. One advantage of the trespass action is that once the plaintiff proves the physical intrusion on or over his or her land, the defendant must prove that the intrusion was both unintentional and not negligent, or the plaintiff's claim will succeed.[61]

The mere fact of trespassing, however, does not result in compensation for harm that is "consequential" rather than direct. For example, when herbicide sprayers accidentally allowed the herbicide to drift from their airplanes onto land other than the forests they intended to spray, the intrusion of the herbicide into the air above the land was a trespass. But the sprayers were not liable for the loss of blueberry crops caused by this drift. The reason? The drifting poison did not kill the blueberries; it killed the bees that pollinated the blueberries. Thus, the harm was "consequential" rather than direct.[62] (The farmer did, however, recover damages on the basis of nuisance.)

There is still some doubt about how far above and below the ground property rights extend. Modern technology has greatly increased the ability of strangers to physically intrude both above and below the surface of the land, as well as the capacity of landowners to make use of the airspace above and the ground below the surface. This capability increases the likelihood of conflicts. Whether the courts give priority to the privacy of landowners or the business requirements of pilots, construction companies, mining companies, and others will provide insights into society's values and priorities.

Land rights extend both above and below the surface, but how far above and below is not yet precisely defined. Above, they extend to the air space occupied by buildings on the land. It is also fairly clear that you own the air space above the property as high as is necessary for the proper enjoyment of the surface. But can you sue the pilots or owners of aircraft that disturb you by flying over your land for trespass, hovercraft that zoom across your land, or construction cranes that swing across your property? The Ontario Supreme Court has resolved at least one of these issues. In Ontario, a swinging crane is a nuisance but not a trespass.[63]

Although the scope of trespass is narrow, in some cases air pollutants that land on your property, water pollution that despoils your beaches or water banks, and anything washed up, propelled, dropped, or otherwise placed on your land may give rise to this ancient remedy, as would trespass by hunters, snowmobilers, canoeists who intrude farther than necessary to portage, or trail users who leave the trail. People have been successful in using trespass to sue neighbours who removed soil from their property,[64] dumped fill on the property,[65] or cut down their trees.[66]

Trespass Statutes: The Trespass to Property Act, the Motorized Snow Vehicles Act, and the Off-Road Vehicles Act

Some of the procedural difficulties of using the common law trespass action can be overcome by using statutes such as the *Trespass to Property Act*,[67] the *Motorized Snow Vehicles Act*,[68] and the *Off-Road Vehicles Act*[69] to prosecute trespassers and to recover damages for harm they cause. The *Trespass to Property Act* puts penal sanctions on what used to be only a common law cause of action; that is, a person can be fined for trespassing in a car, truck, by snowmobile, dirt bike, all-terrain vehicle (ATV), or on foot. The *Off-Road Vehicles Act* and *Motorized Snow Vehicles Act* do not specifically make it an offence to trespass on a snowmobile, dirt bike, or ATV, but the *Trespass to Property Act* probably also covers these vehicles.[70] Although the *Off-Road Vehicles Act* does not deal directly with trespass, it does require that any driver found driving on someone else's land must produce proof within 72 hours if requested by a peace officer that the vehicle was insured.[71]

All three statutes make owners of vehicles liable for damages awarded in a civil suit for any harm done by the drivers, unless the vehicle was being driven without the owner's consent.[72] In addition, the *Motorized Snow Vehicles Act* and the *Off-Road Vehicles Act* facilitate identification of the trespasser by requiring clearly visible identification of the vehicle. The *Motorized Snow Vehicles Act* requires that all snowmobiles have a registration number printed in large letters on both sides.[73] The *Off-Road Vehicles Act* requires the driver to carry a permit and the vehicle to have a licence plate on it.[74]

The *Trespass to Property Act* makes it an offence to enter land, do anything on the land that is prohibited by the Act, or remain on the land when asked to leave, without the *express* permission of the occupant.[75] Trespassing is an offence even if there is no notice to keep out, if the land is fenced or otherwise enclosed in a manner that shows the occupant's intention to keep people or animals off the premises, or if the land is cultivated.[76] Occupants can allow limited access to their land — for example, for bird watching only. The occupant can post notices that all activities are prohibited on the land, that certain activities are prohibited, or that certain activities are allowed. If the notice specifies that certain activities are allowed, entry for the purpose of any other activity is deemed to be prohibited.[77]

All three statutes carry substantial fines. Under the *Trespass to Property Act*, the maximum fine is $2,000.[78] Failure to show the registration number clearly on a snowmobile carries a maximum fine of $1,000.[79] A person caught driving an off-road vehicle on someone else's land who fails to produce proof of insurance within 72 hours is subject to a fine of not less than $200 and not more than $1,000.[80]

The *Trespass to Property Act* is one of the few statutes that allows the court that convicts the offender to award compensation as well as impose a fine. The trial judge can order the trespasser to pay up to $1,000 in compensation for damage done to the property.[81] This statute is also a rarity in encouraging private prosecution by authorizing the court to order the trespasser to pay the landowner who conducts his or her own case the costs of prosecuting.[82] If the landowner hires a lawyer to conduct the prosecution, the lawyer's fees can be recovered, as long as the court considers the fees to be reasonable.

Strict Liability*

The notion of strict liability for harm caused by the escape of dangerous substances arises from an English decision of the 19th century, *Rylands v. Fletcher*.[83] This case established the principle that people who bring onto their land for their own use anything likely to do harm if it escapes do so at their own peril. They may be held fully accountable for all damages that result from its escape even if they have taken the utmost care to prevent it from escaping. They are responsible even if the escape was unintended and was not negligent (see "Negligence," below). For this reason, liability is often referred to as "absolute," even though there are actually numerous exceptions to the rule.

This unusual principle can have broad application to environmental actions. It is not reserved for persons who develop a fetish for half-starved tigers. Rather, it applies to any abnormal use of land. That is, as long as the thing that escapes or the activity that results in the escape is not normally found in that area, and its existence in that location creates a substantial risk of harm to neighbours, the landowner may automatically be liable for any injury that results from its escape.[84]

The material need not be one that is inherently dangerous, like poisons or explosives. In the *Rylands* case, the "dangerous" material was nothing more frightening than water, but the landowner was held strictly liable for damage caused when this water escaped from a reservoir on his land and flooded his neighbour's mine. Nevertheless, some courts have looked at strict liability as if it were based on the use of abnormally dangerous substances or the carrying on of abnormally hazardous activities, rather than how unusual the land use is. If this additional basis for liability also becomes accepted by the courts, the *Rylands* doctrine will become even more useful in environmental cases.[85]

Noxious gases, effluent discharges, mercury, radioactivity, lead, and the like might, under some circumstances, be caught by this rule. Saskatchewan farmers used the *Rylands* principle to recover compensation for crop damage from pesticide drift in the 1960s. The court decided that the spraying of herbicides from the air was a "non-natural" rather than a "natural" use of property because it was an unusual method at that time and involved more risk to others than tractor-drawn spray machines.[86] Biotechnological escapes would also logically fall within the category events covered by this doctrine (see Chapter 10).

---

*   Here, it is necessary to warn you not to confuse "strict liability" in the common law context with "strict liability" in the context of violations of statutes. Before the Supreme Court decision in *R. v. Sault Ste. Marie*, certain offences were referred to as "strict liability" offences, meaning that one would be convicted even if he or she were not at fault at all. In both the statutory and common law context, "strict liability" was used to mean absolute liability. Since *Sault Ste. Marie*, however, "strict liability offences" are offences based on negligence, and the term "absolute liability offences" refers to offences for which a person will be punished even if he or she was not at fault. Strict liability in the common law context continues to mean liability that is not based on fault.

There are defences and exceptions to the rule, however. As it is with nuisance and riparian rights, statutory authority is a defence. If the harm occurs as a result of actions completely beyond the control of the landowner — for example, an "act of God" (an unforeseeable and unavoidable natural phenomenon such as a flood, tornado, or earthquake) or sabotage by an outsider — this will be a defence, as will the plaintiff's consent to the dangerous activity.

Negligence

Negligence is conduct that falls below the standard regarded as normal or reasonable in a given community. This standard of conduct (called the "standard of care") is the steps or precautions that a reasonable person would be expected to take under the circumstances to avoid foreseeable harm to people who might be expected to suffer harm if care were not taken. If conduct falls below that standard, the person or company responsible for the conduct will be liable for the damage caused. Sometimes the standard that must be met is obvious. For example, suppose a tank holds a toxic substance, the contents are clearly stated on the tank, and the valve for emptying the contents is clearly marked to show when it is open and when it is shut. A person who leaves the valve open and thereby causes a spill is obviously negligent. The standard of care in such a situation is, obviously, to read the signs so that you know that the tank contains a dangerous substance and to look at the markings on the valve to ensure that you have left it closed, rather than in the open position.

In many cases involving environmental harm, however, the standard of care is less obvious. Industrial operations often involve physical and communications systems of great complexity. It is difficult to foresee and guard against everything that can go wrong. The standard of conduct to be expected of a business operator is usually the precautions that others in the same business take; however, if a situation is particularly hazardous, the court may impose a higher standard. This complexity causes many problems. First, every industrial operation and its surrounding environment are unique, so it is difficult to establish that the systems in place in one company should also apply to other operators. Second, it is extremely difficult for a plaintiff to find out what other companies do and to obtain their cooperation in testifying against their fellow operators. Most important, our understanding of the risks to the environment involved in various activities, the ability to measure trace amounts of contamination, the technology available to control pollution and other forms of environmental damage, the sophistication of systems employed by companies to prevent harm, the requirements imposed by government, and the expectations of society are constantly changing. Many companies are in a position to argue that the conduct that has caused harm was normal and acceptable at the time it occurred, and has only become unacceptable in the light of recent developments.

To succeed in proving negligence, the plaintiff must not only prove that the conduct under attack was below the standard of reasonable care in the community; he or she must also show that the defendant should have foreseen the damage that resulted, and that he or she was in a class of people whom the defendant should have foreseen would be hurt if such damage did result.

Negligence will sometimes also be available to obtain redress from government agencies that approved the harmful conduct or failed to take steps to prevent it when they knew or should have known it would cause harm. Many dangerous activities cannot be carried out without a licence, permit, or other form of approval from the government, and are subject to government scrutiny. If the government knows that an activity that requires a permit is being carried on without the permit and does nothing, or condones potential harm in other ways, you can sometimes sue the regulator for damage caused by the regulated industry. This ability is important since the companies that cause harm are often empty shells. They have no assets or income with which to pay your damages, and even if you win, you lose. The circumstances under which the government will be liable for negligent regulation and enforcement have traditionally been very limited, but recent decisions of the Supreme Court of Canada have expanded this liability.[87]

Although it is difficult to prove negligence, defendants are sometimes liable for negligence when they would not be liable in any of the other causes of action mentioned in this chapter. For example, the defence of statutory authority is not available. Furthermore, if you are making an unusual or abnormal use of your property, the nuisance doctrine may not be available to you, but the negligent defendant must take the plaintiff as he finds him or her. Unusual uses of land have a right to freedom from the harmful effects of negligence, as long as those uses are known to the defendant, or reasonably foreseeable. Moreover, you need not be an owner or occupant of land to sue for nuisance, as you do to use riparian rights, trespass, or nuisance.

CONCLUSION

As we said at the beginning of this chapter, despite all the advances in statutes, the common law continues to be important because it is still often the only way to stop harm from continuing or to obtain compensation for it. Nevertheless, the common law has many drawbacks. The advantages and disadvantages of different remedies will be discussed in more detail in Chapter 3. You should know, however, that exercising your common law rights is expensive and often takes several years, and because it is difficult to predict what a court will consider reasonable or unreasonable, the outcome is often uncertain. In addition, even if you succeed, your legal bills may be so high that the litigation is not worthwhile, or the defendant may not have the money to pay the damages awarded to you. Recognizing the limitations in the common law, the federal and provincial governments have enacted several compensation schemes that allow you to collect damages for environmental harm without going to court, or make it easier to succeed in court. In the next chapter, we will alert you to this hodgepodge of statutory compensation schemes.

John Swaigen

FURTHER READING

Beth Bilsen, *The Canadian Law of Nuisance* (Toronto and Vancouver: Butterworths, 1991).

Allen M. Linden, *Canadian Tort Law*, 4th ed. (Toronto and Vancouver: Butterworths, 1988).

John P.S. MacLaren, "The Common Law Nuisance Actions and the Environmental Battle: Well-Tempered Swords or Broken Reeds?" (1972), 3 *Osgoode Hall LJ* 505.

John Swaigen, "The Role of the Civil Courts in Resolving Risk and Uncertainty in Environmental Law" (1990), 1 JELP 199.

ENDNOTES

1   For example, a trespasser who removed topsoil from a neighbour's land was required to pay punitive damages: *Popoff v. Kalmikoff* (1982), 12 CELR 53 (Sask. QB). However, where the owner of land and a real estate agent failed to tell a purchaser that the soil contained radioactive waste, a court said that this fell "far short of the kind of evil, wanton or grossly fraudulent behaviour required to support a claim for exemplary or punitive damages": *Sevidal v. Chopra et al.*, (1987), 64 OR (2d) 169 (HCJ). Our description of punitive or exemplary damages is a paraphrase of Justice Linden's explanation in Allen M. Linden, *Canadian Tort Law*, 4th ed. (Toronto and Vancouver: Butterworths, 1988), 55. Note that, as Linden points out, not all Canadian courts agree that punitive or exemplary damages are appropriate in tort cases, and even those that do support their availability restrict them primarily to intentional torts. They are rarely available in cases of negligence. Until the Supreme Court of Canada rules on the availability of these remedies, this issue will remain in doubt.

2   *Gauthier v. Naneff*, [1971] 1 OR 97 (HCJ).

3   See, for example, *Gauthier v. Naneff*, ibid.; *McKie v. The KVP Co. Ltd.*, [1948] OR 398 (HCJ); *Stephens v. Village of Richmond Hill*, [1955] 4 DLR 572 (Ont. HCJ).

4   *Canada Paper Co. v. Brown*, [1922] 63 SCR 752, 66 DLR 287.

5   *McNiven v. Crawford*, [1940] OWN 323 (CA).

6   See, for example, *Sevidal v. Chopra*, supra endnote 1; *CRF Holdings Ltd. v. Fundy Chemical International Ltd.* (1980), 10 CELR 10, 21 BCLR 345, aff'd. (1983), 39 BCLR 43 (CA); *Tuttahs v. Maciak* (1980), 6 Man. R. (2d) 52 (QB).

7   For further discussion of civil liability for selling contaminated land, see Waldemar Braul, *Toxic Real Estate in British Columbia: Liability* (Vancouver: West Coast Environmental Law Research Foundation, 1990) and Dianne Saxe, *Contaminated Land* (Ottawa: Law Reform Commission of Canada, 1990).

8   See, for example, *Scarborough Golf and Country Club v. City of Scarborough* (1986), 55 OR (2d) 193, at 231; aff'd. (1988), 66 OR (2d) 257 (CA).

9   *Russell Transport Ltd. v. Ontario Malleable Iron Co. Ltd.*, [1952] 4 DLR 719 (Ont. HCJ). One commentator has said that "[r]easonableness in this context is a two-sided affair" in which what is reasonable must be looked at from the viewpoint of both the defendant and the neighbours: Fleming, *The Law of Torts*, 3d ed. (Sydney: Law Book Co., 1971), cited in *340909 Ontario Ltd. v. Huron Steel Products (Windsor) Ltd.* (1990), 73 OR (2d) 641 (HCJ), aff'd. (1992), 10 OR (3d) 95 (CA).

10 *Scarborough,* supra endnote 8, at 232.

11 *Walker v. McKinnon Industries Ltd.,* [1949] 4 DLR 739 (Ont. HCJ), aff'd. with a variation [1950] 3 DLR 159 (Ont. CA), aff'd. [1951] 3 DLR 577 (PC). The line between devaluation of property and physical injury to property is a fine one. See *Salmond on the Law of Torts,* 14th ed. (London: Sweet & Maxwell, 1965), 89-94. See also Philip Anisman, "Water Pollution Control in Ontario" (1972), *Ottawa Law Review* 342, at 358.

12 See, for example, *Scarborough,* supra endnote 8; *Schenk v. Ontario; Rokeby v. Ontario* (1981), 34 OR (2d) 595, additional reasons (1982), 40 OR (2d) 410, aff'd. (1984), 49 OR (2d) 556n (CA), aff'd. [1987] 2 SCR 289.

13 *Walter v. Selfe* (1851), 4 De G. & Sm. 315, at 322.

14 *Robinson v. Kilvert* (1889), 41 Ch. D. 88, at 97; *Nor-Video Services Ltd. v. Ontario Hydro* (1978), 19 OR (2d) 107, at 118 (Ont. HCJ).

15 *St. Helen's Smelting Co. v. Tipping* (1865), 11 HLC 642, at 650.

16 *Russell Transport Ltd.,* supra endnote 9.

17 *340909 Ontario Ltd.,* supra endnote 9.

18 *Ibid.*

19 *Banfai v. Formula Fun Centre Inc.* (1984), 51 OR (2d) 361, at 376 (HCJ).

20 *Ibid.*

21 See, for example, *Esso Petroleum Co. v. Southport Corp.* (1956), AC 218, at 224-25 (HL); *Gertsen v. Municipality of Metropolitan Toronto* (1973), 41 DLR (3d) 646 (Ont. HCJ); *Halsey v. Esso Petroleum Co.,* [1961] 2 All ER 145 (QB); *Newman v. Conair Aviation Ltd.* (1972), 33 DLR (3d) 474 (BC SC); *Bridges Brothers Ltd. v. Forest Protection Ltd.* (1976), 72 DLR (3d) 335 (NB SC).

22 Fleming, *The Law of Torts,* supra endnote 9, at 374 and 376.

23 *Walker,* supra endnote 11.

24 *Russell Transport Ltd.,* supra endnote 9.

25 *Bridges* and *Newman,* supra endnote 21.

26 *340909 Ontario Ltd.,* supra endnote 9.

27 *Muirhead v. Timbers Brothers Sand and Gravel Ltd.* (1977), 3 CCLT 1 (Ont. HCJ); *Epstein v. Reymes* (1972), 29 DLR (3d) 1 (SCC); *Walker v. Pioneer Construction Co. (1967) Ltd.* (1975), 8 OR (2d) 35 (HCJ).

28 *Bottom v. Ontario Leaf Tobacco Co. Ltd.,* [1935] OR 205 (CA).

29 *Canada Paper Co.,* supra endnote 4.

30 *Grosvenor Hotel Co. v. Hamilton* (1894), 2 QB 836, at 841.

31 *Andreae v. Selfridge* (1938), 1 Ch. 1.

32 *Savage v. Mackenzie* (1961), 25 DLR (2d) 175 (NB SC).

33 *Scarborough,* supra endnote 8.

34 *Muirhead,* supra endnote 27; *Dye and Durham v. Redfern Construction Co.,* [1962] OR 1025, 35 DLR (2d) 102 (HCJ).

35 *Penno v. Government of Manitoba* (1974), 49 DLR (3d) 104 (Man. QB).

36 *Nor-Video,* supra endnote 14.

37 See, for example, *Pollock and Pizel v. Link Mfg. Co.* [1955], OWN 463 (Co. Ct.); *Newell v. Smith* (1971), 20 DLR (2d) 598 (NS SC); *Schenk,* supra endnote 12.

38 The latter action is called a "relator" action. For example, "The Attorney General of Ontario *on the relation of* John Smith v. The Deadly Smoke Company."

39 Ontario Law Reform Commission, *Report on the Law of Standing* (Toronto: Ministry of the Attorney General, 1989), 42.

40 Ibid., at 40.

41 *Tock v. St. John's Metropolitan Area Board*, [1989] 2 SCR 1181.

42 Ibid., per Wilson J, with whom Lamer J and L'Heureux-Dubé J concurred.

43 Ibid., per La Forest J, with whom Dickson CJC concurred.

44 Ibid., per Sopinka J.

45 *Russell Transport Ltd.*, supra endnote 9; *Sturges v. Bridgman* (1879), 11 Ch. D. 852.

46 Linden, *Canadian Tort Law*, supra endnote 1, at 516.

47 *Farm Practices Protection Act*, RSO 1990, c. F.6. "Normal farm practice" is defined in the Act as "a practice that is conducted in a manner consistent with proper and accepted customs and standards as established and followed by similar agricultural operations under similar circumstances and includes the use of innovative technology used with advanced management practices." For a critique of this legislation, see John Swaigen, "Right To Farm Movement and Environmental Protection" (1990), 4 CELR (NS) 121.

48 *Hall v. Evans* (1877), 43 UCQB 190; *Limitations Act*, RSO 1990, c. L.15, section 33.

49 See *Salmond on the Law of Torts*, supra endnote 11, at 94-99 for a fuller description of ineffectual defences to a nuisance action. These defences were recognized as ineffectual in the Ontario Supreme Court in *Russell Transport Ltd.*, supra endnote 9, at 726.

50 *Scarborough*, supra endnote 8.

51 For example, this appears to be the ruling in *Krohnert v. Regional Municipality of Halton* (1989), 70 OR (2d) 430, at 434 (Dist. Ct.). Although the facts are not entirely clear, it appears that the defendant was a downstream riparian owner and the blockage in its storm sewer that caused flooding of the plaintiff's property was downstream from that property.

52 See *Pugliese v. National Capital Commission* (1978), 8 CELR 68 (SCC) and *Epstein v. Reymes*, supra endnote 27, for cases setting out this proposition.

53 *Groat v. City of Edmonton*, [1928] 3 DLR 725, at 730-31, [1928] SCR 522, at 532-33; *Jackson v. Drury Construction Co. Ltd.* (summary) (1974), 4 OR (2d) 735, 3 CELN 43 (CA).

54 *Ontario Water Resources Act*, RSO 1990, c. O.40, section 34.

55 *Pugliese*, supra endnote 52.

56 For example, *Vergamini v. Regional Municipality of Hamilton-Wentworth* (1986), 54 OR (2d) 494 (Dist. Ct.); *Lee v. City of North York* (1986), 32 MPLR 136 (Ont. HCJ).

57 This legal loophole for industry appeared in the 1957 *Ontario Water Resources Commission Act*, which was passed to remedy the problem of inadequate municipal sewage treatment throughout Ontario. Some of the history behind this Act is explained in Chapter 18.

The loophole resulted from the combination of two provisions of the new Act. The first provision was that any "sewage works" would be granted statutory authority, provided that its operators had a certificate of approval and provided that the works were constructed and operated in accordance with the terms of the certificate.

The second provision was a broadening of the definition of "sewage" to include industrial wastes so that private sewage works as well as public ones would require a certificate of approval. The intent was excellent — to ensure that all the controls that applied to domestic sewage would also be available to control these industrial wastes. However, the result of this wording, probably unforeseen, was that the provision deeming a sewage works to be carried on by statutory authority if it has a certificate of approval, also applies to private sewage works.

Section 30 of the *Ontario Water Resources Act*, supra endnote 54, which currently contains this immunity, was amended in 1988. It is difficult to tell whether the amendment narrows or broadens the immunity from nuisance and riparian rights suits. The amendment provides that the immunity will apply not only where, as before, the sewage works is constructed, maintained, and operated in accordance with the Act, and with *OWRA* approvals and orders, but also in compliance with the *Environmental Protection Act*. Thus, it might be argued that any violation of the *EPA* pollution offences will permit a civil suit even if there is compliance with the *Ontario Water Resources Act* (a situation that is difficult to envision). However, this raises the possibility that the immunity is extended to private sewage works, which are issued under part VII of the *Environmental Protection Act*, rather than the *Ontario Water Resources Act*, and to certificates of approval and orders issued under section 8 of the *Environmental Protection Act* for air pollution from sewage works approved under the *Ontario Water Resources Act*.

58 *Krohnert*, supra endnote 51.

59 This provision highlights what an anomaly the legislature has created. While statutory authority is usually only available to protect public agencies, in this case it gives limited protection to public agencies, but total protection to private polluters. Moreover, the action for injurious affection under the *Expropriations Act*, RSO 1990, c. E.26, usually provides only for damages for the construction of public works, not their operation. Section 29, however, states that compensation will be available for harm suffered from the operation and maintenance of sewage works as well as from their construction. The Court of Appeal made some comments about the relationship between the *Expropriations Act* and section 58 of the *Ontario Water Resources Act* (supra endnote 54) in *Scarborough*, supra endnote 8, at 267.

60 *Dahlberg v. Nadiuk* (1969), 10 DLR (3d) 319 (Man. CA).

61 *Tillander v. Gosselin*, [1967] 1 OR 203, (1966), 60 DLR (2d) 18, aff'd. (1967), 61 DLR (2d) 192n (Ont. CA); *Bell Canada v. Cope (Sarnia) Ltd.* (1980), 11 CCLT 170, at 180 (Ont. HCJ); *Trespass to Property Act*, RSO 1990, c. T.21.

62 *Bridges Brothers Ltd.*, supra endnote 21.

63 *Kingsbridge Development Inc. v. Hanson Needler Corp.* (1990), 71 OR (2d) 636 (HCJ). In cases referred to in the *Kingsbridge* decision, courts in Newfoundland, Britain, and Australia have ruled, however, that swinging cranes are a trespass, while the Alberta Court of Appeal has ruled that they merely constitute a nuisance.

64 *Popoff*, supra endnote 1.

65 *Athwal v. Pania* (1981), 11 CELR 17 (BC SC).

66 *Scarborough v. R.E.F. Homes Ltd.* (1979), 10 CELR 40 (Ont. CA).

67 *Trespass to Property Act*, supra endnote 61.

68 *Motorized Snow Vehicles Act*, RSO 1990, c. M.44

69 *Off-Road Vehicles Act*, RSO 1990, c. O.4.

70 Section 23 of the *Motorized Snow Vehicles Act*, supra endnote 68, which was passed in 1974, made trespassing by snowmobile an offence. When the badly out-dated *Petty Trespass Act* was replaced by the *Trespass to Property Act*, supra endnote 61, in 1980, this provision was repealed, by SO 1981, c. 42, section 8, presumably because it had become superfluous. The effect of the repeal of this offence, however, seems to be that owners of snowmobiles that trespass are not liable for the drivers' offence. The reason for this is that the *Trespass to Property Act* provides that owners of motor vehicles as defined in the *Highway Traffic Act* (RSO 1990, c. H.8, section 1(1)) are liable to conviction for trespass by the driver; but the definition of "motor vehicle" in the *Highway Traffic Act* excludes snowmobiles. However, although the *Off-Road Vehicles Act*, supra endnote 69, does not make trespass an offence, it appears that many of these vehicles would be included in the *Highway Traffic Act* definition of "motor vehicle," so the owners of these vehicles would be subject to conviction for trespass by the drivers.

71 *Off-Road Vehicles Act*, supra endnote 69, section 15(4).

72 *Trespass to Property Act*, supra endnote 61, section 12; *Motorized Snow Vehicles Act*, supra endnote 68, section 23; *Off-Road Vehicles Act*, supra endnote 69, section 12.

73 *Motorized Snow Vehicles Act*, supra endnote 68, section 2(7)

74 *Off-Road Vehicles Act*, supra endnote 69, section 3.

75 *Trespass to Property Act*, supra endnote 61, section 2

76 Ibid., section 3.

77 Ibid., sections 3-8.

78 Ibid., section 2(1).

79 *Motorized Snow Vehicles Act*, supra endnote 68, section 25.

80 *Off-Road Vehicles Act*, supra endnote 69, section 15(8).

81 *Trespass to Property Act*, supra endnote 61, section 12(1).

82 Ibid., section 12(2).

83 *Rylands v. Fletcher* (1866), LR 1 Ex. 265, aff'd. (1868), LR 3 HL 330, 37 LJ Ex. 161.

84 *Rickards v. Lothian*, [1913] AC 263; *Gertsen*, supra endnote 21: filling a ravine with garbage known to be capable of generating explosive methane gas in a residential neighbourhood was also treated as a non-natural use of land.

85 For a discussion of this alternative basis for strict liability, see Linden, *Canadian Tort Law*, supra endnote 1.

86 *Mihalchuk v. Ratke* (1966), 55 WWR 555 (Sask. QB).

87 For example, *Kamloops (City) v. Nielsen* (1984), 10 DLR (4th) 641, [1984] 2 SCR 2; *Just v. The Queen in Right of British Columbia* (1989), 64 DLR (4th) 689 (SCC); *City of Vernon v. Manolakos*, [1989] 2 SCR 1259.

7

Statutory Compensation, Clean-Up, and Environmental Restoration Schemes

As yet there have not been any major environmental catastrophes documented in the northern region under study which could be attributed to mining activities. However, I have heard members of the mining community admit that some adverse environmental impacts have been associated with the industry in the past. However, from the evidence received by this Commission, the mining sector can be generally applauded for its efforts of the past 20 years to avert adverse environmental impacts. It is most assuring when senior mining executives demonstrate their awareness of the needs to protect the environment and waterways by their preparedness to make the expenditures necessary to do so.

The Royal Commission on the Northern Environment, June 1985

The long history of mining in Ontario has left behind scars ranging from unsightliness to "abandoned mine hazards." These include sites with no landscaping, revegetation or other visual reclamation; old mill buildings in danger of falling down; unconfined sulphide tailings that may contaminate waterways with silt and acid; and excavations which may cave in unexpectedly. Roads and parking lots have been built over old workings that have collapsed. Hazards also exist after surface explorations; dangers could arise from trenches left in dangerous condition or from uncapped exploration pits and shafts. This legacy of potential hazards must be addressed and eliminated.

Ontario Ministry of Northern Development and Mines, December 1988[1]

A spill of toxic gold mine tailings that contaminated the water supply for about 180 residents of a nearby town isn't the mine's fault, says the president of the company.

"I don't feel responsible at all," said Richard McCloskey, president of Matachewan Consolidated Mines. "You'd have to be an idiot to be liable for rain." ...

"I'm somewhat ticked off because we lost a couple hundred thousand tonnes of tails and there's probably anywhere from two to five thousand ounces of gold that we've lost," he said.

On Thursday, Environment [sic] Minister Bud Wildman visited the site and said the government already has spent up to $150,000 on the spill and the clean-up cost could exceed $1 million.

The Toronto Star, *October 28, 1990*

There are three components of any plan for rectifying the results of pollution. The first aspect is cleaning up the mess — what has come to be known as "remediation." The first aspect of remediation is the removal of contamination. This could involve, for example, soaking up oil from the surface of water bodies and beaches and cleaning the bodies of oil-soaked birds and animals; dredging contaminated sediments from the beds of water bodies; removing contaminated soil; or taking other steps to arrest the movement of the contaminant, contain it, and remove it from the environment.

The second aspect is often the most difficult and costly — restoring the environment to its previous condition. Restoration is needed not only when pollution has occurred, but also to heal the scars on the earth from mining, forest clearcutting, the draining of wetlands, and other physical changes to the land. Restoration can range from simple and cheap procedures like replacing contaminated soil and planting grass, to attempts to recreate complex ecosystems.[2] Restoration may include revegetating devastated farms and forests, restocking contaminated rivers with fish, and taking other steps to restore the environment or people's property to their previous condition.

The third aspect is called compensation or, sometimes, restitution.[3] It consists of providing money to the victims of environmental harm. To be fair, any compensation scheme should provide this money quickly and at little cost to the pollution victim, and should provide it in an amount that fairly reflects the loss that has been suffered.

It is convenient to deal with these issues together, because the faster and more complete the clean-up and restoration of the environment is, the less harm there will be for which victims need to be compensated. Both remediation and compensation are dealt with by a hodgepodge of statutory schemes that supplement or replace the common law remedies. Until recently, the law has focused on compensation and clean-up. There have been few efforts to require restoration. In general, apart from common law rights, the laws requiring compensation and clean-up — and particularly restoration — are still in their infancy.

In this chapter, we will describe some of the statutory remedies that have become available to assist in solving these problems. This is by no means an exhaustive list — other statutory schemes are mentioned in other chapters — but it will give you an idea what to look for if you have a specific problem.

COMPENSATION

On April 19, 1986, a series of explosions rocked downtown Saint John, New Brunswick. At first, observers thought this must be the work of terrorists. About 2,000 people were evacuated from the area. Some of them couldn't return to their homes for three days. An investigation determined that the explosions had been caused by a leak in an underground pipe at a gas bar.

Gasoline fumes travelled through the city's sewer system. When they surfaced inside buildings, all it took to cause an explosion was a spark, such as a light switch or a furnace being turned on. According to media reports, three buildings in different parts of the downtown area were destroyed, and several others caught fire.

Nine businesses, a church, and the city of Saint John sued the owner of the gas bar for their losses. Six years later, the legal battles were still raging and the case was still before the courts.

This case is only one of many that have demonstrated the need for a more efficient and less expensive and uncertain method of providing timely compensation to victims of pollution. If justice delayed is justice denied, it is clear that the delays and uncertainty faced by victims of pollution in obtaining compensation for harm from pollution and other damage to the environment cry out for reform of the law.

To date, this law reform has consisted of a patchwork quilt of statutory schemes, and a few voluntary programs established by high-risk industries, each limited to a narrow subject matter. Whether you are entitled to compensation, and under what conditions, depends on whether you fit into a particular "pigeon hole." For example, if you are a farmer whose crops are so contaminated by a pesticide that they cannot legally be sold, you may be entitled to compensation for up to 80 per cent of the market value under the *Pesticide Residue Compensation Act*.[4] If you suffer from leukemia as a result of an accident at a nuclear power plant, you may obtain compensation from the operator or the federal government under the *Nuclear Liability Act*.[5] If you suffer economic loss from pollution damage to vegetation or livestock, Ontario's Board of Negotiation will assist you in negotiating with the alleged polluter.[6] If there is a spill from a ship carrying a "pollutant in bulk" (usually oil), there is a federal fund under the *Canada Shipping Act* that may compensate you.[7] If pollution seeps out of a well used for waste disposal into your water supply, you may obtain compensation from the Waste Well Disposal Security Fund established under the *Environmental Protection Act*.[8] If a trespasser has damaged your property, the court that convicts him or her of the offence can order compensation of up to $1,000, in addition to fining the offender.[9] If you are harmed by a spill of a pollutant from a structure, vehicle, or other container in a quantity or having a quality that is "abnormal," Ontario's Environmental Compensation Corporation can reimburse you for your losses.

However, if you are the victim of the accumulated impacts of routine discharges of pollutants to the air or water,[10] the unwitting purchaser of property whose soil is contaminated,[11] live downwind from a fire at a salvage yard or used tire dump, or your well dries up because of the operation of an irrigation system, a gravel pit, or dewatering a construction site,[12] there is no statutory scheme to compensate you. If a spill causes gasoline fumes to build up in sewers and emerge in your basement where they cause your house to catch fire, this is an offence under the *Environmental Protection Act*, and the polluter may be fined, but this is not classified as a "spill" under the Act, so you can't get compensation from the

Environmental Compensation Corporation. Under all these circumstances, you must fall back on your common law rights. If you are harmed by radiation from a nuclear power plant, you may be compensated under the *Nuclear Liability Act*, but if a truck carrying radioactive materials spills them, that Act will not cover this harm. Nor will the Environmental Compensation Corporation, since radiation is not defined as a "pollutant" under the *Environmental Protection Act*. Clearly, there is little coherence or logic to this collection of compensation laws.

Other laws do not actually provide for a streamlined method of obtaining compensation, but they do ensure that if you are successful in court, there will be some money available to pay your damages. Most insurance policies cover only sudden and accidental pollution (spills), unless some law requires the insurer to cover pollution. But there are very few laws that require insurers to cover pollution or that require persons who may harm the environment to carry insurance to pay the successful claims of victims of their activities. And those laws that do require insurance as a condition of carrying on hazardous activities generally require too little coverage. For example, the regulations under Ontario's *Pesticides Act* require the operators of extermination businesses to carry at least $25,000 worth of insurance for each employee to cover injury to them.[13] Structural exterminators (that is, those who spray or fumigate buildings) must carry at least $300,000 in liability insurance to cover the death or bodily injury of others, and at least $200,000 to cover property damage.[14] Land exterminators, who spray lawns, farms, and forests, must carry at least $200,000 in coverage for personal injury and $10,000 to compensate for property damage.[15] Under the *Nuclear Liability Act*, operators of nuclear reactors must carry $75 million in liability insurance provided through a combination of private insurers and the federal government.[16] In neither case is the required coverage sufficient to provide compensation for the most serious accidents, nor have the amounts been raised over the years to reflect the effects of inflation. Instead, the levels required have been dictated by the amounts of coverage the insurance industry is prepared to provide, rather than the amount of harm to be compensated. The Ministry of Environment and Energy can include a condition in the certificates of approval issued to pollution sources, requiring them to carry liability insurance or put up other security for harm they might cause, but it seldom does.[17]

Many other hazardous businesses can be carried on without obtaining any insurance coverage. The *Gasoline Handling Act*,[18] for example, does not require operators of service stations, bulk plants, refineries, and other facilities where petroleum products are stored to have any insurance coverage, despite the fact that thousands of leaks and spills from such facilities have contaminated soil and groundwater, polluted wells, and caused fires and explosions.

CLEAN-UP AND RESTORATION

Like compensation, whether harm will be rectified depends largely on whether a problem falls within a particular pigeon hole. If damage to property or the environment results from a "spill" as defined in part X of the *Environmental Protection Act*, both the owner of the pollutant and the person in control of it when it spilled have a duty to clean up the spill and to make reasonable efforts to restore the environment to its previous condition. If, however, the harm results from the cumulative effects of routine industrial discharges, clean-up is required only if the Ministry of Environment and Energy issues an order specifying what must be done (See Chapter 16). If a person operates a gravel pit or a quarry, the *Aggregate Resources Act*[19] provides for payments into a fund. If the pit or quarry is not rehabilitated when it is worked out, the money is forfeited and the Ministry of Natural Resources can use it for clean-up. The *Mining Act* also contains provisions that can be used to require the decontamination and restoration of mining sites. These include requirements for progressive rehabilitation,[20] site closure plans,[21] and financial assurance requirements,[22] and public consultation in developing rehabilitation and site closure plans.[23] How effective these requirements will be in requiring the remediation of abandoned mining sites depends on how they are administered. These provisions became effective on June 3, 1991, and shortly thereafter the Ministry of Northern Development issued guidelines for public notice and consultation and some regulations governing the criteria for public notice, the preparation of site closure plans, the carrying out of public information sessions, the ingredients of closure plans, and financial requirements.[24]

In a few cases, when an offence is committed the court that convicts the offender can order remediation as well as fines and other punishments. For example, under the *Environmental Protection Act*, offenders can be ordered by the court to clean up environmental damage and restore the environment.[25] One of the potentially most far-reaching but little used remedial provisions is found in the *Trees Act*. It provides that when anyone is convicted of cutting down trees in contravention of a municipal tree protection bylaw, in addition to penalties that may be imposed, the court may order the offender to replant and maintain the trees "in such manner as the court considers proper."[26] In contrast, no similar provision is found in the *Topsoil Preservation Act*,[27] which authorizes municipalities to pass bylaws to prohibit or regulate the removal of topsoil.[28] These bylaws may also require the rehabilitation of lands from which topsoil has been removed, to standards prescribed by the bylaw. However, there is no requirement that such a bylaw require any rehabilitation. Therefore, if the bylaw is silent on the question of rehabilitation, a person who strips topsoil illegally can be fined, but the court cannot order him or her to rehabilitate the land.[29]

One problem with the approach taken by the *Trees Act* and the *Topsoil Preservation Act* is that environmental protection depends on action by individual municipalities. In 1993, only 51 of Ontario's 500 rural municipalities had passed topsoil protection bylaws.[30]

In other cases, remediation depends on whether a requirement is put into licences or permits issued by government authorities. Under the *Public Lands Act*,[31] for example, the Ontario Ministry of Natural Resources issues permits for mining exploration and other activities on public lands. These permits may contain conditions requiring clean-up of the site before the mining company leaves it.

However, there is no general provision requiring clean-up and restoration of damaged environments. The existing provisions leave many gaps in the regulatory framework. For example, one of the favourite tricks of developers who want to eliminate opposition to their projects for environmental reasons is to bulldoze the environment before applying for approval. There is nothing in the *Planning Act*[32] to prevent this. Indeed, the Ontario Municipal Board has ruled that it has no jurisdiction in an application under the *Planning Act* for approval of a subdivision to order restoration of a disturbed wetland.[33]

CONCLUSION

Canada and the province of Ontario both pay lip service to the "polluter-pays" principle. This principle, which was espoused in 1974 by the Organisation for Economic Co-operation and Development, holds that the costs of pollution should be internalized by the companies that create the pollution, not passed on to the public at large or the innocent victims of pollution. As you will see in reading other chapters, however, many businesses leave a legacy of environmental damage to be rectified by others; and this is the way it will continue until our laws uniformly require those who cause the harm to clean it up, compensate the victims, and restore the environment and ensure that they cannot operate unless they have the resources to do this. Companies will avoid damaging the environment only if they believe that if they don't, they will have to pay for the results of their activity. Without financial assurance requirements for all businesses that can harm the environment, and without an environmental clean-up fund to which polluters must contribute, polluting companies will continue to escape liability and the taxpayers and victims of pollution will pay to rectify their damage.

John Swaigen

FURTHER READING

John Swaigen, *Compensation of Pollution Victims in Canada* (Ottawa: Economic Council of Canada, 1980).

ENDNOTES

1   Ontario, Ministry of Northern Development and Mines, *Ontario's Mines and Minerals — Policy and Legislation: A Green Paper* (Toronto: the ministry, December 1988).
2   See Dianne Saxe, "Reflections on Environmental Restoration" (1991), 2 JELP 75.
3   The terms "compensation" and "restitution" are often used interchangeably. For a discussion of the meaning of the two terms, see John Swaigen and Gail Bunt, *Sentencing in Environmental Cases* (Ottawa: Law Reform Commission of Canada, 1985), 66ff.
4   *Pesticide Residue Compensation Act*, RSC 1985, c. P-10, section 3. An 80 per cent ceiling is set in the regulations under this Act. Pesticide Residue Compensation Regulations, CRC, 1978, c. 1254, section 4.
5   *Nuclear Liability Act*, RSC 1985, c. N-28.
6   *Environmental Protection Act*, RSO 1990, c. E.19, section 172. Since December 1985, the functions of the Board of Negotiation have been carried out by the Environmental Assessment Board (EAB). When these functions were carried out by a separate board of negotiation, the proceedings and their outcome were secret. However, the EAB has carried out these functions in public and has published reports of the proceedings and their outcome.

7   *Canada Shipping Act*, RSC 1985, c. S-9, part XVI.

8   *Environmental Protection Act*, supra endnote 6, section 47.

9   *Trespass to Property Act*, RSO 1990, c. T.21, section 12.

10 In *McCann v. Environmental Compensation Corp.* (1990), 5 CELR (NS) 247, the Court of Appeal required an "identifiable spill" before the corporation can compensate.

11 *419212 Ontario Ltd. and Sygounas v. Environmental Compensation Corp.*, Ontario Court (General Division), October 26, 1990, Matlow J, Court File Re 1439/90.

12 However, unlike many other permits issued by various authorities, water-taking permits issued under the *Ontario Water Resources Act* contain a standardized clause making it a condition of the permit that if the taking of water interferes with the water supply of others, the permittee must replace the water supply or compensate the victim for the cost of obtaining an alternate water supply.

13 *Pesticides Act*, RRO 1990, reg. 914, section 20(2).

14 Ibid., section 20(4)(a).

15 Ibid., section 20(4)(b).

16 *Nuclear Liability Act*, supra endnote 5, section 15.

17 Mario Faieta, "Liability Insurance for Environmental Contamination" (April 1991), vol. 2, no. 2 *Canadian Insurance Law Review* 125, at 127.

18 *Gasoline Handling Act*, RSO 1990, c. G.4. Gasoline Handling Code, RRO 1990, reg. 532.

19 *Aggregate Resources Act*, RSO 1990, c. A.8.

20 *Mining Act*, RSO 1990, c. M.14, section 143.

21 Ibid., section 144.

22 Ibid., section 145.

23 Ibid., sections 141-142.

24 O. regs. 114/91, 116/91, and 113/91, as amended by O. reg. 253/91. For more information about mine closure and rehabilitation, see Heather A. Frawley, "Environmental Law Developments Affecting Ontario's Mining Industry" (1991), 2 JELP 107.

25 *Environmental Protection Act*, supra endnote 6, section 190.

26 *Trees Act*, RSO 1990, c. T.20, section 6(2).

27 *Topsoil Preservation Act*, RSO 1990, c. T.12.

28 Joe Castrilli, "Legislation — Ontario Moves To Protect Topsoil" (1978), 7 CELR 133.

29 If the bylaw does require rehabilitation and the rehabilitation requirements are drafted in such a manner that it is an offence not to comply with them, the court that convicts the offender can order rehabilitation. If it is not carried out, the municipality can then rehabilitate the land and recover the cost from the offender under section 326 of the *Municipal Act*.

30 Information provided by the Soil and Water Management Branch of the Ontario Ministry of Agriculture and Food, March 1993. This was 20 more than had passed bylaws as of June 1990, according to the same source.

31 *Public Lands Act*, RSO 1990, c. P.43.

32 *Planning Act*, RSO 1990, c. P.13.

33 *Wallace v. West Carlton (Twp.)* (August 29, 1990), Ontario Municipal Board file nos. R890345, R890639, S900003, cited in Saxe, supra endnote 2.

PART III
The Planning Process

8

Land-Use Planning

Contents

... there will always be sufficient green space among the gray.

> *William Davis, premier of Ontario, reassures the public,*
> *quoted in* The Globe and Mail, *June 5, 1973*

We're going to cut the approvals process in half.

> *Premier David Peterson, June 8, 1988 meeting of regional chairmen*
> *of the Greater Toronto Area municipalities,*
> *quoted on the cover of "Project X"*

We made a commitment to cut out red tape and all the things that make it hard for builders to build things quickly.

> *John Sweeney, minister of housing, on Global TV, May 2, 1989,*
> *quoted on the cover of "Project X"*

... this government is committed to ensuring that we have an efficient and effective land use approvals process and that environmental considerations are an integral part of that system.

> *Premier David Peterson, letter to Toby Vigod, Canadian Environmental*
> *Law Association, October 17, 1989*

Let me be clear: accelerating the decision-making process does not mean that projects will be approved that would not have been in the past. What it does mean, however, is that a decision will be made sooner.

> *Municipal Affairs Minister Dave Cooke, April 19, 1992,*
> *announcing that the Ontario government would speed up*
> *the decision-making process for development proposals*

So, although the ecosystem approach to planning could and should be a revolution in planning practice, there is a real danger that it may become instead a descriptive veneer shallowly applied to doing things in the old way, just as such terms as "environmentally friendly" and "green" are sometimes used in advertising.

Regeneration, *the final report of the Royal Commission on the Future of the Toronto Waterfront*

INTRODUCTION

The use that is made of any particular area of land is fundamental to the environmental integrity of that area of land and adjacent areas of land. The physical destruction of the natural environment, the consumption of agricultural land, the loss of potential habitat for natural species, and the contamination of air, land, and water can all result from the inappropriate use of land or inadequate control over the way in which an area of land is used.

Land-use planning is the process that is intended to regulate the private and public use of land and buildings in order to resolve conflicts between private and public interests and between present and future needs. In the absence of land-use planning controls, an owner of land may use that land for whatever purposes he or she wishes, as long as other laws or the common law rights of others are not infringed. Restrictions that are imposed by planning controls on individual rights are justified on the basis that the public has a legitimate interest in land-use decisions, to the extent that those decisions might otherwise result in negative implications for society at large.

Because of the very large financial gains that can result from the development or redevelopment of the land either by obtaining permission to change the use of a particular piece of land or by obtaining permission to intensify its existing use, very strong vested interests are active in the land-use planning process.

Development and redevelopment of land are essential activities in our society and contribute to our economic and social well-being in many ways. The creation of housing, economic opportunities, and many other facilities and amenities to service our expanding population and economy is, in our society, largely dependent on private initiatives for the development or redevelopment of land. However, such changes can also have significant negative impacts on the nature or character of an established neighbourhood; impose unacceptable burdens on services such as sewers, roads, parks, schools, and recreational facilities; seriously damage significant natural areas; or consume significant natural resources.

Under the constitution, the task of establishing a planning process to regulate the use of land in Canada is largely the responsibility of the provincial governments. The federal government does have a limited role in land-use planning, which will be discussed later in this chapter; however, the provincial governments have most of the responsibility. Provincial legislatures across Canada have enacted statutes that typically provide for the creation of master plans to guide development, establish policies for particular planning areas, and give municipalities the power to pass zoning bylaws to limit the uses to which land and buildings can be put. In Ontario, the central piece of legislation is the *Planning Act*.[1]

The most recent substantial amendments to the Ontario *Planning Act* were made in 1983. Despite those reforms, many concerns have been raised by all involved in the planning process. Environmental concerns have been particularly serious and have been well documented in two reports by the Environmental Assessment Advisory Committee regarding the adequacy of the planning process for protecting the environment in the Ganaraska Watershed, in Grey County, and in the province generally. Those two reports are the subject of two case studies at the end of this chapter.

From June 1991 to June 1993, the *Planning Act* was reviewed by a commission of inquiry known as the Commission on Planning and Development Reform. The commission was given a two-year mandate to examine the relationship between the public and private interests in land use and development. It was to recommend changes to the legislation or other actions needed to restore confidence in the integrity of the land-use planning system.[2]

In its final report, the commission recommended sweeping changes to the existing legislation, including provisions to significantly strengthen the ways in which the legislation may be used to enhance and protect the environment. Its recommendations included amending the *Planning Act* to provide more opportunities for public involvement in the planning process. It also made recommendations for streamlining the planning process to reduce the length of time that is currently taken to process and decide on development applications.

The overall approach of the commission is to set out common goals for the planning process that it considers should be incorporated into the legislation. The commission also recommends that the province should ensure that these goals are implemented through the establishment of provincial policy direction to planning authorities.

Incorporating explicit goals into the *Planning Act* will be a significant departure from the current approach in Ontario. At present, the *Planning Act* establishes a largely value-free planning process that is designed to facilitate the expression of local planning priorities while providing opportunities for public input and government agency review. However, the Act provides opportunities for provincial priorities to override local priorities. This overriding provincial interest is provided for in a variety of ways including: the opportunity for the province to specifically declare a provincial interest in a particular area, as has been done for the Oak Ridges Moraine; the ability to establish provincial policy statements that municipalities and others "must have regard to"; and by providing that many municipal decisions may be appealed or referred to the Ontario Municipal Board, which in most cases would then make the final decision. Since the Ontario Municipal Board is made up of members who are appointed by the provincial Cabinet and has the responsibility for protecting the integrity of planning decisions throughout Ontario, the combination of these mechanisms, at least in theory, provides a substantial opportunity for the province to control the significant land-use decisions throughout Ontario.

In fact, provincial control over local decisions, particularly as they relate to environmental protection, is less comprehensive than these opportunities suggest. It is obvious that the provincial government that established the commission, and the commissioners themselves, do not consider that the planning process gives sufficient weight to environmental concerns. This criticism of the existing planning process is widely held and was one of the major motivating factors for the establishment of the commission.

The commission's solution to this problem would be to enshrine goals in the legislation to ensure that environmental protection will receive the degree of consideration that it deserves in future planning decisions. It is difficult to determine whether the existing structure of the legislation was inadequate to accomplish this purpose, because the province failed to take advantage of the opportunity that the legislation provided to establish strong provincial policies to guide municipalities and the Ontario Municipal Board. There is no provincial policy statement that would establish the priority of environmental protection in the planning process.

Provincial policy statements that have been established include one relating to mineral aggregate resources (pits and quarries), one relating to floodplain planning, and one relating to housing policy. After 10 years of discussion papers, drafts, and considerable controversy, a wetlands policy statement was issued in the summer of 1992. An agricultural land protection policy statement has gone through a similarly lengthy and tortuous evolution and is still only in draft form.

Even if the *Planning Act* is amended to incorporate goals such as environmental protection, the protection of wetlands and other natural areas, and the protection of agricultural land, it will still be necessary for the details of those goals to be set out in policy statements. Unless the government is prepared to move forward on these initiatives in a meaningful way, the planning process under the new legislation is not likely to function any more effectively than it has under the old legislation.

THE PLANNING PROCESS IN ONTARIO

Legislation

In exercising their power to carry out land-use planning, most provincial governments have passed statutes that prescribe procedures to be followed through either a planning act or a municipal act. There are often additional statutes that pertain to specific geographic areas or planning functions. In Ontario, for example, specific pieces of legislation address subjects such as transportation (*Public Transportation and Highway Improvement Act*),[3] significant physical features (*Niagara Escarpment Planning and Development Act*),[4] specific natural resources (*Aggregate Resources Act*),[5] particular municipalities (*Regional Municipality of Waterloo Act*),[6] and building permits and construction standards (*Building Code Act*).[7]

Provincial legislation generally assigns the administration of land-use planning to municipalities, including the power to make decisions on the current and long-range use of land. Appeal and supervisory roles are reserved to the provincial government or sometimes to the regional levels of government.

Instruments of Planning

Municipalities are given the power to use a number of tools for controlling the use of land, including official plans, zoning bylaws, subdivision control, site plan control, demolition control, and expropriation powers. Provincial governments typically retain a significant degree of control over the exercise of these powers, including the right to issue general policy statements that must be taken into account in planning decisions. The purpose, usefulness, and limitations of each of the main instruments of planning are described below.[8]

Official Plan

An official plan usually encompasses the whole of the municipality or region that has formulated it. It is a formal set of principles and policies concerning the nature, pattern, extent, and scheduling of future growth and change within the municipality for a specified period of time, typically about 20 years. A plan will normally set out a series of policies on matters such as housing, industrial and commercial development, health, transportation, environmental protection, economic development, heritage preservation, utilities, municipal finance, public participation, agriculture, floodplain protection, the management of environmentally sensitive areas, aggregate extraction, and land severance and subdivision. These policies set out the aspirations and objectives of the municipality in each of these subject areas.

An official plan will almost always include a land-use map, to indicate the areas where urban growth and redevelopment are intended to occur and to designate the ultimate land use or function that the municipality considers to be appropriate for each area. Official plans do not have to conform to existing land-use patterns; they are intended to guide the future of the municipality. Common designations are residential, settlement, industrial, commercial/core, agricultural/rural, and open space. Plans also typically include details on planned infrastructure, including major roads and public transportation facilities, watermains, sanitary sewers, and stormwater management facilities. The availability of these public works often controls the rate and direction of development, since development normally will be considered premature until the necessary physical services are available.

Secondary Plans

Many municipalities also employ secondary or community plans, which are more detailed plans of specific parts of the area covered by the official plan. Where the official plan may designate an area as being residential, the secondary plan may show this area as high-, medium-, or low-density or estate residential, and might specify the housing types to be permitted. In some municipalities, secondary plans form a part of the official plan, go through the same approval process, and have the same legal effect as that of the official plan. In other municipalities, the secondary plan is more of a guideline, approved by resolution of council but without the legal status and the appeal opportunities provided under the *Planning Act*.

Open Space Designation

The designation given a parcel of land in a plan generally determines its ultimate development potential, at least within the time-frame of the plan. However, the designation "open space" may not mean that the land is to remain undeveloped forever. An area may be designated "open space" for a positive reason, meaning that the municipality has decided to prohibit most building on the area designated in order to protect a significant feature (for example, a woodlot) or to reserve it for public use, generally for parkland purposes. Alternatively, an area may be designated "open space" because it is not suitable for development due to a physical constraint; the land may be wetland, hazard lands, or below the floodline of local rivers and streams. The environmental value of this land is often incidental to the "open space" designation.

Land designated as "open space" need not be in public ownership. However, if the municipality does not eventually acquire it, an affected landowner is likely to succeed in having the designation changed, unless the land is physically unsuitable for any development.

"Open space" designations may also be used by a municipality to *hold* lands that are not yet serviced but that are expected to be developed at some time in the future. This practice can be misleading to those who may interpret an "open space" designation to have a positive meaning, since the municipality may be prepared to entertain amendment proposals once the constraints to development are cleared.

Environmentally Sensitive Designation

The official plan may also provide for the application of special policies regarding environmentally significant or sensitive areas, sometimes freestanding and sometimes in conjunction with another designation — for example, residential or industrial — thereby modifying the usual policies that apply to the base designation. A variation on this measure is the inclusion of a policy regarding environmentally sensitive protection areas (ESPAs). Such a policy will allow the application of an ESPA designation to a significant natural feature that is owned privately, in conjunction with a voluntary agreement with the landowner to protect the area from development or other forms of environmental degradation.

The use of designations such as "open space" or "environmentally sensitive" obviously can offer potential protection to the natural environment. Nevertheless, the extent of environmental protection afforded even by these designations may be slight and may require strengthening by amendment to the official plan. An "open space" designation will not generally prevent the conversion of a natural area into an active park, for example, or the use of land for certain public works such as reservoirs or hydro transmission corridors. Similarly, "environmentally sensitive" designations, if used in conjunction with another designation, will usually permit some development in conformity with the base designation. This development could be substantial enough to lead to the eventual loss of or damage to the natural feature that originally prompted the "environmentally sensitive" designation. For example, limited residential construction may be permitted in a woodlot that is residentially designated and subject to the environmentally sensitive policies. The removal of some trees for construction, the necessary grading and drainage changes, and the subsequent activities of the residents may combine to result in the eventual loss of the whole woodlot, or at least the loss of its natural significance.

The overall approach of such designations is problematic as well. It suffers from an "islands of green" or confetti approach to natural area protection. There is an increasingly recognized need for a systems approach that would identify, maintain, and restore not only particular natural areas but also high-quality corridors linking such areas.

Implementation

An official plan in Ontario does not, by itself, restrict anyone in the actual use of land. It is a statement of intention.[9] The plan is implemented through the zoning bylaw that may, and often does, restrict individuals. The *Planning Act* does, however, provide that no bylaw (including a zoning bylaw) may be passed by a municipality unless the bylaw conforms with the official plan.[10] For example, a bylaw to spend public money for a road project through an area that has been designated as "environmentally sensitive" could be challenged in court if it did not meet the requirements of the policies laid down in the plan to protect these areas.[11] Conversely, no restriction may be applied to the use of land that is not supported by a policy in the official plan.

In areas of two-tier municipal government (for example, counties and regional, district, or metropolitan municipalities composed of a number of area municipalities), lower-tier (area municipality) plans are required to conform with the upper-tier plan.[12] In case of conflict between the plans, the regional plan will have precedence.[13] Because of this provision, it may be possible to influence environmental issues throughout a wide area by pursuing changes in regional official plan policies.[14]

Official plans, like all planning tools, may be — and are — amended frequently and are subject to interpretation. The legislation that authorizes the creation of official plans (for example, the *Planning Act* in Ontario) may require a review of official plans at regular intervals; in Ontario, plans must be reviewed at least once every five years. In addition to such regular reviews, proposed amendments may be initiated at any time to permit specific development projects that are not in conformity with the existing plan.

Ideally, a plan should clearly set out the policy choices that the municipal council is making and the rationale for those choices, because the plan is, in effect, a political document, almost quasi-constitutional.[15] The generality of many policies and absence of others can be serious weaknesses in the degree of environmental protection provided by a plan. Policies that are too general allow decisions to be made on an *ad hoc* basis.

The public participation aspects of the creation and amendment of a plan and the appeal rights of citizens, as explained in the section entitled "The Approval and Amendment Process," below, can provide opportunities for protecting and improving the environmental integrity of the policies incorporated in the plan and preserving the environmental resources of the community.

Zoning Bylaws

Zoning bylaws regulate the use of land and the use, siting, and many other aspects of the buildings erected on the land, including, in Ontario, density, height, bulk, setbacks, and parking. Zoning bylaws do not lay out any policies or rationale for the development of the municipality; that is the function of the plan. However, zoning bylaws may not permit anything that does not conform to the general purpose and intent of the plan.

The zoning bylaw is a legal document, passed by council, and is specific in its provisions. For example, there may be six or seven residential zones (R1, R2, etc.), any of which would be permitted in an area designated in the plan as "residential." However, each one would permit a different size, siting, type, density, or combination of residential lot and dwelling unit and may also specify certain other uses that are permitted in the zone. It is important to realize that bylaw standards are not carved in stone. Approval bodies (committees of adjustment in Ontario) may grant minor variances from the standards of the bylaw in appropriate circumstances. Moreover, additional uses (extensions of use) and exemptions from setbacks or any other provision of the general zoning bylaw may be authorized by *site-specific* zoning amendments, usually to accommodate a particular development.

There are only a few circumstances in which zoning bylaws may be used to prevent *any* development from taking place, rather than restricting the kinds and intensity of development. The *Planning Act* specifically authorizes municipalities to pass zoning bylaws that prohibit the development of land that is subject to flooding, or marshy areas,[16] which are sometimes of environmental significance. Such areas are generally unsuitable for building in any case, but this provision may be useful in protecting sensitive areas even though the protection is incidental. In addition, development may be prohibited specifically because municipal services are not available.[17] Other than in these circumstances, municipalities may not prohibit all uses of land in private ownership. For example, the preservation of a significant environmental feature through zoning has been viewed as the reservation of private land for public purposes and has been seen as confiscation without compensation. Planning acts generally do not authorize this type of zoning bylaw, although municipalities are certainly permitted to purchase or expropriate land for public purposes.[18] However, simply reducing the value of land through the zoning process by, for example, a reduction in densities (downzoning) or the application of land-use restrictions that are less lucrative than those desired by the landowner is a valid use of the zoning power. The shifting of financial benefits and burdens among property owners and the public is implicit in every land-use decision. The courts will interfere only if it is obvious that the zoning is being applied to reduce the value of the property so that it can be acquired by the municipality more economically *and* expropriation of the property is in progress or imminent or, as mentioned above, if no reasonable land use is available under the zoning applied to the property.[19]

The zoning of a parcel of land may be changed as circumstances change. Land is often rezoned from an agricultural or a rural zone to permit new development on urban fringes, if that is in accordance with the plan. Such rezoning is usually granted only when the municipality is satisfied that services are available and a need for development has been demonstrated. Proposals to rezone for uses other than a use that conforms to the official plan will not be approved, unless, of course, the applicant also proposes a concurrent amendment to the official plan that is approved.

Zones generally reflect the use of the land when the bylaw was prepared and they may not be in conformity with the plan if the use was in place before the adoption of the plan. In such cases, it is normally the municipality's intent that, during the life of the plan, proposals for rezoning will be considered that will bring the use of land into conformity with the official plan designation for the area. Only area (lower-tier) municipalities have zoning bylaws. The official plans of upper-tier municipalities are implemented through the lower-tier plans and their zoning bylaws.

Legal Non-Conforming Uses

It is also common, in older areas, to find land or buildings being used for purposes other than the ones permitted by the zone in which they are situated, or buildings that do not conform to the regulations of that zone. If those uses existed when the zoning bylaw was passed, they have a legal right to continue indefinitely and are known as *legal non-conforming uses*.[20] They may even be expanded if special permission is granted. Many legal non-conforming uses are innocuous operations, such as corner stores in residential zones. However, some uses can create serious environmental problems — for example, a lead smelter surrounded by residential neighbourhoods. These uses cannot be controlled through the tools of land-use planning unless the operation shuts down for a significant period of time, thereby losing its legal non-conforming use status. Over time, economic pressures tend to sort out such anomalies, but the impacts in the meantime can be severe.

The provisions of zoning bylaws have important legal implications. A building permit will not be issued for any structure that does not meet the specifications of the zone in which it is proposed. In addition, landowners may be prosecuted for using land or buildings in contravention of the zoning bylaw. As the result of a conviction, the offending buildings may be ordered demolished or the land use stopped.

Municipalities have often taken this regulatory power to great lengths, including specifying the relationships required among those living together in a house (for example, a property zoned single-family may not have more than five unrelated occupants), although in Ontario the provincial government has stepped in to prohibit this type of regulation.[21]

Zoning provides a form of stability to neighbourhoods, because the uses and forms of development permitted within a zone are generally quite narrow. Landowners, businesses, and residents can know how their neighbourhoods and districts will develop over time, protecting the value of their property and, incidentally, the quality of the environment. Unfortunately, the emphasis on physical form (setbacks, lot size, etc.) and restricted uses can lead to monotonous tracts of similar buildings, interspersed with islands of different uses. Look at any urban area to see how many visually interesting and socially viable residential and commercial areas (with uses often mixed together) in older sections were built without the benefit of zoning or planning as we know it. In contrast, newer sections built under current procedures often can lack vitality and diversity.

The zoning bylaw, like the official plan, is subject to amendment. This is a continuous process, because almost any form of development or redevelopment will require a zone change. New development on the edge of an expanding urban area will require rezoning from agricultural or rural to various residential, commercial, open space, and industrial zones. Redevelopment of already developed lands may require rezoning to increase density or to change the use or form of a building. If the desired zoning is not in conformity with the official plan, an amendment to the official plan will also be required.

Holding, Temporary Use, Bonusing, and Interim Control Bylaws

In addition to the standard zoning bylaw described above, the Ontario *Planning Act* provides for four specialized zoning bylaws for specific purposes: holding bylaws, temporary use bylaws, "bonusing" bylaws, and interim control bylaws.

Councils may create *holding* zones, which indicate the *intended* use of land so zoned once the constraint attached to the holding provision is removed. Constraints are usually technical — for example, a lack of capacity at the sewage treatment plant serving the area. Such zones are identified in Ontario by the prefix "H."[22] *Temporary use* zones may also be assigned[23] in circumstances where a short-term use is to be permitted and then phased out. Legal non-conforming status does not result from this type of situation — that is, the right to use the land temporarily does not create a right to continue the use once the temporary zoning runs out. The maximum term of a temporary use bylaw in Ontario is three years.

A zoning bylaw may also allow greater density or higher buildings than ordinarily permitted in a zone *in return for* "facilities, services or matters"[24] from the applicant. This can be a useful provision for trading a more valuable zoning to a developer in return for the conveyance of environmentally significant features to public ownership, for example. This is commonly referred to as *bonusing*.

Interim control bylaws[25] are another form of zoning bylaw that can be particularly useful for environmental protection. These bylaws can restrict the use of land to a specified purpose for a period of up to two years while studies are undertaken to determine the most appropriate future use of the land. The value of these bylaws lies in the fact that no notice need be given until after the bylaw is passed, and they come into force as soon as they are passed, even if they are appealed.

Normally, a municipality has no choice but to issue a building permit if the proposal conforms with the zoning bylaw, if other requirements (for example, the requirement to obtain approval from the Ministry of Environment and Energy for the sewage system) are met, and if the permit application is filled out correctly. In appropriate cases, however, where a development is under consideration in an area that is under study by the municipality, a municipality can freeze development using this technique, even if the proposed development would otherwise comply with the existing zoning bylaw.

Implementation

As with the official plan, to ensure that environmental concerns are taken into account, care is required to ensure that environmentally significant areas and surrounding lands carry a zone (commonly "park" or "natural area") that will afford sufficient protection, and that the policies of the official plan are being reflected in the zoning bylaw and its many amendments. Once a building permit is issued, it is too late to change the zoning of a site, even if environmental degradation may result, since a legal non-conforming use will have been established.

In the final analysis, regardless of how a property is zoned, the property owner decides whether to propose that it be developed. The municipality may set out the uses and structures that it feels are appropriate for the proper and orderly development of the municipality, but the owner may decide not to proceed, generally for economic reasons, and allow existing buildings or vacant lots to continue in existence. For example, many vacant lots in otherwise fully developed areas are zoned for development, but the buildings have not been erected because the owners do not see the potential for an acceptable return on investment in the economic environment of the day. This inability to realize the level of development envisaged in the official plan and permitted by the zoning bylaw may create situations in which there is increased demand for housing or industrial land at the expense of agricultural or environmentally significant land in other parts of the municipality.[26] Such a limitation may be partially overcome by the increased activity of municipal housing authorities and others in *infilling* (the process of creating additional housing in currently developed areas) on properties that are not being developed by private initiative.

Subdivision Control and Consent To Sever

No subdivision of land (the creation of new lots) is permitted under the *Planning Act* without approval.[27] Because most new development and some redevelopment involve the creation of a number of new lots from larger parcels, the power to control this process of subdivision can offer a means of controlling development. In areas where no zoning exists or no zone change is required, the subdivision approval process will be the only opportunity for public input into the development process.

Implementation

An owner of land who wishes to subdivide the land for any purpose is required to apply to the proper authority. Generally, the owner will apply for *consent to sever*[28] if the proposal is to create only one or two new lots. In all other cases, the owner will apply for approval of a *plan of subdivision*.[29] The applicant will provide information about the proposed subdivision and the approving authority will consider it with regard to many criteria, including the health, safety, convenience, and welfare of present and future inhabitants of the municipality, matters of provincial interest, the public interest, the conservation of natural resources, and general conformity with the official plan.[30] It is also necessary to show that the proposed subdivision is not premature; in other words, that the infrastructure required to service the development adequately is or will be in place.[31]

The approving authority may attach any reasonable conditions to the approval of the subdivision that it feels necessary, a potentially important tool for environmental protection. Conditions are routinely attached to subdivision approvals regarding saving trees, groundwater recharge, and environmental impact analysis, to protect wetlands, streams, and woodlots. In addition, developers are normally required to *dedicate* (donate) 5 per cent of the land area of residential subdivisions to the municipality for park purposes, or cash equal to the value of 5 per cent of the land, to be used for park purposes elsewhere.[32] In fact, parkland dedication can be made a condition of all development and redevelopment plans, even those that require no approval other than the issuance of a building permit, if the municipality passes a bylaw requiring it.[33] This parkland dedication is one means of gaining public ownership of environmental features.

Interested parties have the right to object to and be heard regarding the merits of any proposed subdivision, although the *Planning Act* does not require notice to be given of pending plans of subdivision, as explained below.[34] Since almost all new development goes through the subdivision process, the hearing provides an opportunity to air concerns about environmental impacts and to argue for positive changes.

In the case of the subdivision of agricultural land, both the provincial *Food Land Guidelines* and most official plans stipulate that the conversion of good farmland (including land that could be productive but is currently not farmed or may currently be a significant environmental resource, such as a woodlot) to other non-farm purposes must be justified according to a number of criteria. These criteria include the need for development and the lack of other less agriculturally favourable locations for the proposed development. In most cases, the need is difficult to justify, since the basic reason a certain property is proposed for subdivision is its owner's desire to make a profit, rather than any inherent qualities of the site. If conversion cannot be *justified*, it can sometimes be *rationalized* — that is, other benefits may be offered for the agricultural community in return for the conversion of some farmland. The need to justify or rationalize land conversion may create a useful opportunity for intervention[35] in the planning process.

Site Plan Control

The *Planning Act*[36] allows a municipality to designate by law all or part of its territory as a site plan control area as defined in the official plan or to designate lands within certain zones as being subject to site plan control. Within such an area, no development may proceed until a site plan — and, in some cases, building plans — has been approved by the municipality. By passing a site plan control bylaw, the municipality may regulate many aspects of a development, including landscaping, fencing, lighting, grading, the massing of the buildings, the layout of the site, the amount and location of parking, and the design and location of access points to the site.

Site plan control may be used to protect certain features of the environment, such as trees and woodlots, to improve the aesthetics of a project, and to provide for adequate and environmentally sound landscaping within new developments or redevelopments.

There is no provision in the *Planning Act* for public notice, no formal opportunity for the public to become involved in the approval process, and no right of appeal of the municipality's approvals for the general public. Public input is limited to informal discussions with municipal staff and the applicant (in the event that the application happens to come to the attention of a member of the public), if they are willing to engage in discussion. If the applicant and the municipality are unable to reach an agreement, the applicant may appeal to the Ontario Municipal Board (OMB), in which case other interested persons may be granted party status by the board to participate in the hearing.

Demolition Control and Heritage Designation

Municipalities may also pass bylaws that designate an area of the municipality as a demolition control area. Within a demolition control area, it is necessary to obtain a permit before any residential building may be demolished.[37] (If the applicant for a demolition permit possesses a valid building permit for the same property, council must issue the demolition permit.)[38] The demolition permit system prevents the creation of unsightly and potentially dangerous vacant lots while the approval process is pending for redevelopment of the land, and may protect housing stock if property standards are enforced.

A council may delay demolition by designating a building, a feature of a building, or an entire district as architecturally or historically significant and worthy of preservation. Currently, in Ontario, such a designation may prevent demolition of a property for only a maximum of 270 days, but this will provide some time for negotiation with the owner to attempt to preserve the heritage structure.[39] Such designations are rarely applied against the owner's will but can provide a worthwhile forum for those concerned about the preservation of our built environment (see Chapter 14).

Again, no formal opportunity exists for concerned citizens to have input into the decision-making process on regular demolition permit applications, although heritage designations do receive a hearing before council. No right of appeal is provided, except for the applicant.

Expropriation and Injurious Affection

Expropriation is the taking of land by a public authority, or by a private corporation that has been so authorized in the public interest — for example, utility and transmission companies

— against the will of the landowner, with fair compensation. Injurious affection refers to harmful effects suffered by an owner of land as a result of public works undertaken nearby, even though the land itself is not taken. These proceedings generally occur in connection with the construction of significant public works, often roads and highways.

Expropriation is an essential tool and can be beneficial. For example, one uncooperative owner could otherwise jeopardize the construction of a badly needed light rapid transit line designed to curb the demand for expressway expansion. Expropriation could also be used to force private owners to convey important environmental resources to the municipality for protection,[40] especially if they are not being adequately managed.

However, expropriation is usually seen in a negative light by landowners. For example, land may be taken for environmentally unsound road construction projects; for an airport that will destroy an important wetland that is being managed well in private hands; or for a regional landfill site on an environmentally sensitive area. Hearings may be conducted at an objector's insistence under the federal or provincial expropriations legislation to determine the necessity and fairness of the proposed expropriation. These hearings can serve as a convenient forum for increasing awareness and garnering publicity.

However, the inquiry officer may not rule on the validity of the objectives of the expropriating authority. He or she may rule only on whether the expropriation is "fair, sound and reasonably necessary" to achieve those objectives.

Policy Statements and Provincial Interest

The minister of municipal affairs, in carrying out his or her duties under the *Planning Act*, is required to have regard for matters of *provincial interest*. Ten such matters are listed in the Ontario *Planning Act*, including the protection of the natural environment, the protection of features of significant natural interest, and the supply, efficient use, and conservation of energy.[41] The minister carries out this duty in two ways: by declaring provincial interest in individual land-use planning decisions, and by formulating provincial policy statements.

When a planning matter is appealed to the Ontario Municipal Board by an objector, the Ontario *Planning Act* generally gives the board the authority to make a binding decision. However, the Act reserves the right of final determination of planning decisions relating to the creation and amendment of official plans and zoning bylaws to the lieutenant governor-in-council (that is, Cabinet), *if* the minister has informed the OMB, *at least 30 days before the start of the hearing*, that he or she considers the matter to be of *provincial interest*.

In a highly publicized situation involving environmental resources that could be considered of provincial interest, it may be advantageous to encourage the minister to take the steps needed to permit Cabinet to make the final decision. If the political mood is right, politicians may rule in favour of the environment. This power can be a double-edged sword, however, since Cabinet may also overrule an environmentally sound decision by the OMB. The mood of Cabinet must be carefully judged before an attempt is made to use this political tactic.

It seems that the utility of this provision is limited, however. The minister has seen fit to inform the OMB of a matter of provincial interest in only two cases in the last seven years.[42] In the first case, through interpretation of the issues by the OMB, Cabinet did not have the opportunity to review the OMB's decision. The second case is still under consideration.

The minister may also issue *policy statements*.[43] These are formal policy documents, approved by Cabinet, on matters related to land-use planning that are of provincial interest. Every municipality and ministry or agency of the province, including Ontario Hydro and the OMB, must have regard for provincial policy as enunciated in these policy statements. Approved policy statements as of August 1992, issued jointly by the Ministry of Natural Resources and Ministry of Municipal Affairs were as follows: the *Mineral Aggregate Resources Policy Statement*,[44] regarding gravel resources; the *Flood Plain Planning Policy Statement*;[45] the *Wetlands Policy Statement*;[46] and the *Land Use for Housing Policy Statement*,[47] which is designed to increase the supply of affordable housing in Ontario. The Ministry of Agriculture and Food still uses the *Food Land Guidelines* (1978),[48] which address the need for agricultural resource protection, although this policy document predates the *Planning Act* provisions for policy statements and has never been formally endorsed as a policy statement under the *Planning Act*. A draft policy statement dealing with agricultural land preservation was released in the mid-1980s, but as of September 1992 it had still not been finalized.

Building Code

The Building Code is a province-wide standard for the structural and safety aspects of building construction. It is administered by the Building Code Branch of the Ministry of Consumer and Commercial Relations, although building permits that allow the construction of buildings are issued by municipalities. The building permit system is an integral part of the control of land use since no permit that contravenes the planning controls in place for the property will be issued.

HOW CITIZENS CAN USE THE PLANNING PROCESS TO PROTECT THE ENVIRONMENT

quote

The planning process is a system of procedures and organizations that, in theory, is designed to ensure that all decisions related to the formulation of plans and the approval of development proposals are made in an open, public process, after consideration of all available relevant information. The process includes opportunities for interested parties to obtain information, to be given notice, to be given a hearing before some decisions are made (this right is specifically mentioned in the *Planning Act*),[49] and the right to appeal some kinds of decisions to the Ontario Municipal Board for a formal, impartial, public hearing.

When an individual, corporation, municipality, or other body makes a proposal for a new policy or land use, the law requires that the process prescribed by the *Planning Act* be followed before that policy can be incorporated into the municipality's official plan or before the proposed development can be built or uses commenced. Throughout that process, there are opportunities for citizens to influence the final decision. Proposals may be defeated or changed at many stages in the process — as a result of negotiation with planners and proponents, by effective lobbying of municipal councillors and their advisers, or by a convincing presentation to the Ontario Municipal Board.

Applicants for development approvals are usually expert at using the planning process to maximize their chances of obtaining the approvals they require. It is up to the individual or organization concerned with environmental protection to know and to make the best use of these same opportunities. The sections below outline the procedural and political systems involved and ways to make your voice effective.

Most development and planning proposals and plans go through a series of approvals, interspersed with negotiations, revisions, and sometimes rejections. This process can be very lengthy and time-consuming and can wear down intervenors. The financial and human costs of organizing, raising money, preparing presentations and written material, and attending hearings are substantial.

To use the land-use planning process for environmental protection, it is necessary to know when, and by whom, decisions are made and what statutory requirements are involved. Set out below is a summary of the approval processes for the three most important planning tools: official plans, zoning bylaws, and plans of subdivision, as laid out in the Ontario *Planning Act*. Requirements for other forms of planning control may be also found in the *Planning Act* and you should consult experienced professionals and become familiar with the legislation at the beginning of any intervention process. Many of the detailed requirements are not described here. It is important to be able to take advantage of every opportunity provided by the legislation. The most important strategy in any intervention process is *to start early*.

Official Plans

The preparation and approval of an official plan in an Ontario municipality is governed by section 17 of the *Planning Act*. (Areas not organized into municipalities also follow the procedures laid out in section 17, except that the municipal council is replaced by a planning board appointed by the minister of municipal affairs.)[50] Municipalities may also voluntarily combine into planning areas; if they do, they will appoint members to a planning board as constituted by the minister.[51]

Since most municipalities are currently covered by official plans, amendments and revisions to plans are now more common than the adoption of an entire plan. However, an amendment or a revision to an official plan must go through the same steps as those for a new plan. These steps are as follows:

1. *Preparation of the amendment, public meeting, agency circulation, and notice.* The *Planning Act* states that the municipal council is responsible for initiating amendments to the official plan. Individuals who have an interest in a matter may also apply to council for an amendment. Council may either immediately refuse such amendment requests or process them as if they were initiated by council. If council initiates the amendment or supports an individual's proposed amendment, the municipality's planning department, a consultant hired for the purpose by the municipality, or the planning department of a district or regional municipality or county, depending on the arrangement in place in the municipality, will prepare the proposed plan or amendment. During this process, at least one public meeting must be held before council decides whether to adopt the amendment. If the creation of a new plan or a major revision is contemplated, it is common for a series of informal public information and input meetings to be held. For a minor amendment, however, the only public meeting may take place at the council meeting where approval is being considered.

Anyone may attend these meetings and make representations. Concerned citizens should attend as many meetings as possible, and make both written and oral presentations. At least one meeting must be advertised by public notice, usually in a local newspaper of general circulation, at least 30 days before the meeting, unless the existing official plan specifies other provisions for public notice and participation. In the case of a site-specific amendment, a sign is usually placed on the subject property notifying the public of the application.

All other agencies, including municipal departments, provincial ministries, and even federal agencies, that are considered to have an interest in the plan or amendment will be *circulated* — that is, they will be provided with information relating to the proposal and their comments will be solicited.[52] The role of these agencies is discussed below under the heading "The Provincial Role: The Actors."

2. *Consideration by council.* Once all comments have been received, a report will be prepared for council that contains all the relevant information. This report, if prepared by the planning department or a consulting planner, will usually contain a recommendation for approval or rejection. Often, a last chance is available to speak to council when this report is considered. If council approves, it will adopt the plan or amendment by passing a bylaw. Sometimes council only passes a resolution of support. In that case, a bylaw must be passed (and usually is, at the following council meeting) before the next step can be taken.

If council does not deal with an amendment proposed by any person within 30 days of an application, or if council refuses to process it or refuses to adopt it, the applicant can request the minister of municipal affairs to *refer* the amendment to the Ontario Municipal Board. Since official plan amendments may take many months to come before council, depending on their complexity and controversiality, this ability to refer the decision directly to the OMB can be useful to the person who proposes the amendment if he or she feels that the municipality will not approve or will even refuse to consider the amendment and undue delay could be harmful. This procedure is not often used without giving council time to process an application according to its normal procedures, since council's support is a large advantage before the OMB.

If the plan or amendment is adopted by council, the clerk of the municipality must notify, within 15 days of the adoption, the minister and each person or agency that has requested, *in writing,* notification of the plan's approval.[53]

3. *Approval.* Once the plan or amendment is adopted by council, it is forwarded to the minister of municipal affairs or to the regional council, which exercises the minister's approval power in certain regional municipalities where the minister has delegated that power. This delegation has taken place in almost every regional municipality except the regional municipality of York, immediately north of Metropolitan Toronto, because the region of York has no official plan itself. (A regional official plan or amendment must still be forwarded to the minister for approval.)

The minister or the regional council will consult with whichever agencies or persons are considered appropriate and may then approve the plan or amendment in whole or in part, refuse to approve the plan, or make modifications to it after consultation with the municipality *(minister's modification).* This stage provides an additional opportunity for input. Letters may be written to the minister or the regional council suggesting modifications or commenting on modifications proposed by others. If the minister or the regional council approves and there are no referral requests, the plan becomes official.

4. *Referral requests.* Any person or agency that is dissatisfied with the plan or amendment or any part of it as adopted by council, or an applicant who is dissatisfied with council's delay or refusal of a proposed amendment, may request the minister or the regional council to *refer* the matter to the Ontario Municipal Board. The minister or the regional council, or the council that produced the amendment or plan, may also make a referral request. Written reasons must be supplied along with the request. There is no time limit for requesting referral although delay is not recommended, because a referral may not be made after the minister or the delegated regional council has given approval. Anyone contemplating such an appeal should inform the minister or the regional council in writing and determine when approval is expected so that this critical deadline will not be missed.[54]

The minister or the regional council will generally try to resolve referral requests through negotiation before referring the matter to the OMB, but he or she must accede to the request unless he or she feels that the request is frivolous, vexatious, or made for the purposes of delay. If the minister or the regional council refuses to refer the plan or amendment to the OMB, he or she must supply written reasons.[55]

In the case of an amendment, if the minister or the regional council is satisfied that no matter of provincial interest is affected and if no request for referral was received, he or she can waive, in writing, the requirement for the minister's or the regional council's approval.[56]

5. *Ontario Municipal Board.* The OMB will hold a public hearing, after requiring that notice be given to persons or bodies as the board directs. The lack of intervenor funding for citizens' groups making representations before the OMB can place them at a significant disadvantage, particularly when they are dealing with issues of a highly complex nature for which both legal counsel and expert witnesses are required (the issue of intervenor funding is considered in greater detail in Chapter 9). The OMB's decision is final unless the minister declares the issue to be of *provincial interest.*

6. *Provincial interest.* If the minister is of the opinion that a matter of provincial interest is, or is likely to be, affected by the plan or amendment, he or she may so notify the OMB at least 30 days before the hearing date. In this case, the OMB will still hold a hearing and make a decision, but that decision is not final. It must be confirmed, varied, or rescinded by Cabinet.[57] In cases where such a review might be advantageous because of the political nature of an environmental issue, it is important to lobby the minister to notify the OMB of the provincial interest.

In addition, if the minister is of the opinion that a matter of provincial interest *as set out in a provincial policy statement* — for example, the Mineral Aggregate Resource Planning Policy Statement — is affected by a plan, he or she may unilaterally amend the plan. Any person or municipality can request the minister to refer such a unilateral amendment to the OMB. The OMB shall decide the issue, but its decision is not final and must be confirmed, varied, or rescinded by Cabinet.[58]

Cabinet, therefore, could be an important last resort for those battling an environmental issue to the extent that matters of provincial interest are recognized by the provincial government to include the protection of natural resources and the environment.

Zoning Bylaws

Under section 34 of the *Planning Act*, zoning bylaws follow an approval format similar to that for the official plan or amendments, although the minister or the regional council is not involved in the process, except under exceptional circumstances. Again, the main avenues for participation by those concerned with the environment are informal discussions with planners and politicians, formal public meetings, and the right to appeal. Since most Ontario municipalities are covered by a comprehensive zoning bylaw, the approval process outlined below is the process that is followed by an amendment. (The creation of a new zoning bylaw generally follows the same steps.)

1. *Application, circulation, public meeting.* An individual who wishes to change the zoning of land (one need not be the owner of land to submit a rezoning application, although an applicant would need a strong case to achieve a zone change on land owned by someone else) submits an application to the municipality outlining the zone and special provisions desired and the desired use of the land. The application will be circulated for comment to provincial, federal, and municipal agencies that may have an interest, at least 20 days before council considers the application. These agencies may ask for a brief extension. In practice, circulation periods last anywhere from 30 to 90 days or more if an important agency is slow in submitting comments.

   Alternatively, an amendment may be initiated by the municipality, in which case the same procedure is followed, except that no application need be submitted.

   Whether the amendment is initiated by the municipality or by an application, the municipality is required to make information about the amendment available to the public. The minimum requirement for public participation is one public meeting with at least 20 days' notice, at which interested parties may and should speak on the issue. (If there are policies in the official plan regarding notice and public participation, these procedures will apply.) In many site-specific cases, a sign will be posted on the subject property informing the public of the application.

   Council will then consider the application, agency comments, and the planners' report and recommendation, and approve or reject the application. The application may also be deferred for further revision, or even revised right at the meeting. There is no requirement for further public notice if the proposal is revised after a public meeting but before council makes its final decision, unless council feels that such a step is necessary. In controversial cases, it is important to be present at all stages of the approval process so that last-minute changes are not made without input from concerned citizens.

   If the proposal is approved by *resolution,* council will confirm its decision at a later meeting formally, by passing a bylaw to amend the existing zoning bylaw. Council's decision is not final until this new bylaw has been passed. Once the bylaw has been passed, a notice is placed in the newspaper and sent to the owners of property that abuts the subject property, informing them of council's approval and indicating the last day to appeal the bylaw to the Ontario Municipal Board. Any person or agency or the minister of municipal affairs may launch an appeal within 20 days of the giving of notice. If no appeal is lodged, the bylaw becomes effective as of the day it was passed, unless it is dependent on a concurrent official plan amendment. In that case, the bylaw does not take effect until the plan amendment receives final approval.

If the proposed bylaw is rejected by council, notice is given only to the applicant, who may appeal to the OMB without regard to time limits.[59] In that case, neighbours find out about their rights to participate in the OMB hearing through notice by the applicant, who is required by the OMB to notify them of the hearing once a date has been set.

2. *Appeal.* If an appeal is launched, the Ontario Municipal Board will hold a hearing at which the appellant, the municipality, the applicant, and others whom the OMB feels should be included are able to argue the merits of their position. The OMB will make a final decision that may confirm, amend, or rescind council's bylaw.[60]

3. *Provincial interest.* As is the case with official plans and amendments, if the minister of municipal affairs notifies the OMB 30 days before the hearing that a matter of provincial interest is affected by the zoning bylaw being appealed, the OMB's ruling in the case will not be final. It will be subject to review by Cabinet, which must confirm, vary, or rescind the OMB's decision.[61]

4. *Interim control, holding, temporary use, and bonusing bylaws.* These special types of zoning bylaws are approved in the same manner as standard zone changes, except for the *interim control bylaw,* which does not require any previous notice or hearing and may be passed as long as council has directed the planning department to undertake a study of the area in question. After the bylaw is passed, notice must be given and an appeal may be launched, but during the hearing of an appeal the interim control bylaw remains in effect. Such interim control bylaws have a maximum life of two years; however, this should allow enough time to complete the study and amend the regular zoning bylaw in cases where environmental resources are under immediate threat from development permitted by the existing zoning.[62]

The minister may also, by order, impose zoning controls, including temporary zones and interim control bylaws, on land in any part of the province. These orders override municipal bylaws, if there are any, and go into effect without any notice or public hearing. Objectors may ask the minister to refer such a *zoning order* to the Ontario Municipal Board, and the OMB will make a final decision unless the minister has notified the OMB that a matter of provincial interest is involved, in which case Cabinet will make the final determination.[63]

Plans of Subdivision

In many cases, applications for subdivision also require a zone change and sometimes an amendment to the official plan. In such cases, all the approval processes and hearings required are carried out concurrently and changes in one will affect the others. If no zone change or official plan amendment is required, however, the subdivision approval process will afford the only opportunity for interested citizens to influence the development. The lack of requirement for public notice makes informed comment difficult and requires extra care on the part of the intervenor.

1. *Application, circulation.* A landowner may apply to the minister of municipal affairs (or, in some regional municipalities, to the regional council, as is the case with official plans) for approval of a draft plan of subdivision. A plan is submitted that shows the layout of the proposed subdivision, including lots, types of housing or other uses, roads, parks, existing watercourses, swamps, woodlots, etc. The minister or the regional council will circulate this draft plan to other ministries, agencies, and the local municipality involved, but there is no requirement for public or abutting landowner notice.[64]

   If amendments are also required to the official plan or the zoning bylaw, these applications will normally be processed concurrently with the draft plan of subdivision.

   Through the notice requirements for zone changes, interested parties may become aware of the draft plan. Since a municipality must hold at least one public meeting with regard to any zone change, these meetings present opportunities where concerned individuals may make their case regarding not only the zoning but also the subdivision. If the municipality is opposed to the proposed draft plan, the minister or the regional council will be hesitant to approve it.

2. *Draft approval.* After comments have been received, the minister or the regional council is required to consider the draft plan with regard to the "health, safety, convenience, and welfare of the present and future inhabitants of the municipality" and, among other things, matters of provincial interest, the public interest, the suitability of the land, the conservation of natural resources and flood control, energy conservation, and the dedication of land for public purposes.[65] *Reasonable* conditions may be attached to the draft approval, including agreements between the municipality and the minister or the regional council and agreements between the municipality and the applicant, which are registered on title and may be enforced against subsequent purchasers of the land. These agreements or conditions could contain provisions for the protection of environmental resources, including groundwater, trees, and wetlands (see section 2.2.3). The minister or the regional council then gives or refuses to give approval to the draft plan (this is known as draft plan approval).[66]

3. *Appeal.* At any time *before* the minister or the regional council grants draft plan approval, any person, agency, or municipality may ask the minister or the regional council to *refer* the draft plan to the Ontario Municipal Board. The minister or the regional council may refer the draft plan himself or herself if he or she feels that this would be appropriate. There is no requirement, however, for the minister or the regional council to notify the public or interested individuals that draft plan approval is imminent.[67] Once draft plan approval is granted, only the applicant, local municipality, or county or region may appeal the conditions to the OMB. The applicant may also ask for a referral to the OMB if the minister or the regional council refuses to approve his or her draft plan.[68] Concerned citizens have no right of appeal after draft plan approval is granted unless a zone change is involved.

   In case of an appeal, the OMB will hear the case and make a final decision.

4. *Final approval and registration.* The minister or the regional council may change the terms of draft plan approval, or even withdraw draft plan approval, at any time before *final approval*. Usually, if the applicant proceeds to lay out the subdivision and fulfils

the conditions imposed in the draft plan approval, the minister or the regional council will issue final approval. The plan may then be registered and the subdivision is a reality.[69] The newly created lots may now be sold and building may start if all other necessary approvals are in place.

THE ACTORS

Municipal Role

The municipality is the basic level for decision making in most planning matters. It is also the level of government that is most accessible to the public and the level that is most susceptible to both citizen and development pressure. For these reasons, it is important to be aware of the workings and characteristics of the approval-giving bodies at the municipal level so that opportunities to influence these bodies are fully exploited.

Area Municipality Council and Committees

The councils of municipalities are elected bodies that are chosen, in Ontario, by the citizens on a fixed date every three years. Their composition varies from municipality to municipality, but they generally consist of aldermen or councillors, elected on a ward basis in most urban municipalities or at large in most rural municipalities, and are usually headed by a mayor or reeve who is elected by the whole municipal electorate.

In Ontario, political parties, whether they are the well-known federal and provincial parties or those formed specifically for the municipal arena, are ostensibly not involved in local politics as they are in other provinces, although this situation is changing in some of the largest cities. Many councillors are members of political parties, however, and a consistent voting pattern on matters of land use can often be discerned in their council record. Informal groups of like-minded councillors will often form. These loose coalitions are often based on their members' approach to land-use issues.

Councils in larger municipalities and regional municipalities will establish committees, one of which is usually a planning committee. It will deal with all planning-related matters, hear all delegations, and recommend, or refuse to recommend, proposals to the full council. Because the councillors on the planning committee also sit on the full council, proposals that pass the planning committee will usually pass council. The converse is also true.

If a council does not divide its members into committees, it will generally meet from time to time as a committee of the whole to hear planning matters. Discussion is more informal in this type of meeting than in a council session. This is the forum at which concerned members of the public are expected to make their representations. Council may pass proposals by resolution in committee of the whole, to be confirmed later by passing a bylaw at a regular council meeting.

Council is an intensely political entity, subject to all the pressures of electoral politics. It can be influenced by many forces, including promises of financial or economic benefits to the municipality, the hope of re-election, loyalties to ideologies, and the endless compromising that is part of any democratic process. How influence can be exerted is discussed below in the section concerning directions for reform.

Organizational Chart for Municipal Planning Decisions

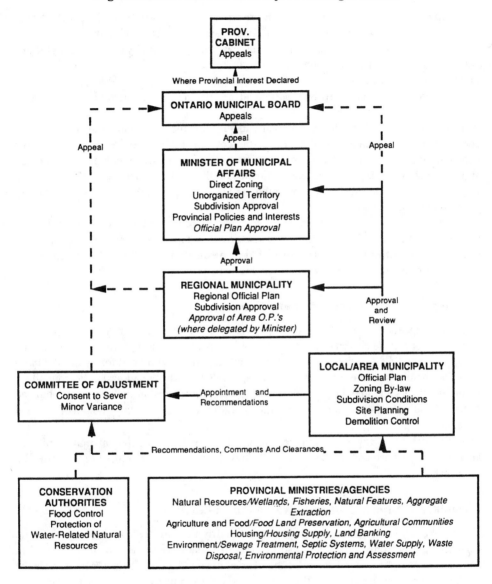

Regional Municipality/County Council

Local (lower-tier) municipalities in Ontario are organized into district or regional municipalities or counties (upper-tier municipalities). District and regional municipalities include all of the area municipalities within their limits, whereas counties generally exclude cities located within their boundaries, and therefore are usually composed of rural and smaller urban municipalities. In a county situation, it is often more difficult for land-use planning to be coordinated between the large urban centres and the surrounding rural municipalities because of the exclusion of the cities.

Depending on the upper-tier municipality in question, the council that governs it may be composed of certain members of the lower-tier councils or may be directly elected by the voters during municipal elections. Some regional councils will select their own chairperson and this person can have a significant influence on the work and decisions of the council. Regional councillors, especially those who are also members of local councils, are often preoccupied with local issues.

The upper-tier municipal council will also generally be divided into committees, including a planning committee. Groupings will also be evident in this council and its committee, based on approaches to land-use issues, and also sometimes on the different needs and aspirations of urban and rural lower-tier municipalities.

Planning and Environmental Advisory Committees

The *Planning Act* provides for planning advisory committees that may be composed of councillors or private citizens, or both.[70] An environmental advisory committee may also be set up at council's discretion, although this is not specifically provided for by the *Planning Act*. The members of these committees are appointed to advise and assist the council on planning matters and may be paid. They have no effective decision-making power, but can be useful bodies for publicizing issues, taking initiatives, and persuading council of the need for action.

Individuals who express an interest in planning or the environment may apply for appointment to these committees, and well-known figures in the community will often be members.

Committee of Adjustment/Land Division Committee

Variances to zoning requirements may be authorized by a committee of adjustment where the variances are not only minor but also desirable for the development of the area and in conformity with the general intent of the official plan and zoning bylaw. Minor variance applications may be used to avoid the need to amend the zoning bylaw in appropriate cases.[71] Decisions of the committee may be appealed to the Ontario Municipal Board by either an applicant or another interested party.[72]

Council may delegate its power to approve or not approve land severances and minor variances to the zoning bylaw to a committee of adjustment or a land division committee, or both. The members of these bodies are appointed by council but act independently of it. The municipal planners will provide a report to the committee in advance as to whether the proposal conforms with the relevant plans and zoning bylaw. The committee will generally follow the advice of the planners but is not required to do so. The committee's decisions are not subject to council review. Its decisions may only be appealed to the Ontario Municipal Board.

Municipal Staff

Most larger municipalities have a planning department composed of one or more professional planners, technicians, and cartographers. If it is large enough, the department will be divided into a planning division, which is responsible for the formulation of official plans and amendments and planning policy for the municipality, and a development division, which prepares reports and recommendations to council on proposed zone changes and subdivisions. Most input to the planning process will be made to, and information about proposals will be received from, the planning department and its members.

The engineering department is also intimately involved with decisions relating to land-use planning, because it is responsible for the physical infrastructure of the municipality, including sewers, water, and roads. Important information may be available from this department. The parks department will be a player in decisions made regarding environmental resources. The clerk's department ensures that the proper procedure is followed regarding notice and record keeping, and is also a potential source of information. Keep in mind, however, that in looking at many planning documents available at the clerk's office, you may need the help of the planning staff to interpret the documents and to give advice on where you should look to get the information you want. The planning process generates tremendous amounts of paperwork in itself, for which you may need a guide. If you have reason to believe that the municipal staff will not give you the help you need, it may be necessary to go to private practitioners such as planning and engineering consultants or lawyers.

In many smaller municipalities, several responsibilities may be handled by one person, or an upper-tier municipal government may provide staff services. This is especially common in counties and regions where the upper-tier municipality will provide planning services to rural townships and small towns. Alternatively, a small municipality may engage a private consultant to perform these functions.

Staff members are generally university-educated professionals who sometimes see themselves as having a monopoly on knowledge and experience as to what is best for the municipality. It is sometimes difficult for planning departments to accept public comment, especially if an atmosphere of confrontation has grown up around an issue. Council makes the final decision in all cases, and planners can become discouraged by seeing their recommendations, based on planning principles, rejected on the basis of political considerations. Planners can be effective allies in an environmentally oriented issue, but they will often take the role of a mediator, and they may not effectively defend proposals before council. Concerned members of the public must never leave the job entirely to the professionals, because council is most responsive to effective *public* involvement.

Provincial Role

The provincial government exercises a supervisory and appeal function in the planning process, as noted above, primarily through the Ministry of Municipal Affairs and the Ontario Municipal Board. Other ministries are involved through the circulation and comment procedures that are followed when proposals and policies are being approved at the municipal level. These other ministries and agencies have no formal approval function and are considered to be advisory only.[73] Commenting agencies that are unsatisfied with municipal decisions have the right, under the *Planning Act*, to appeal or ask for referral of decisions to the Ontario Municipal Board, but may be unwilling to take this step for political or resource reasons.

The nature of the input from these commenting agencies and ministries is a serious flaw in the protection that the planning process can give to the environment. Municipal councils have the right to approve development proposals even over the strenuous objections of commenters. Additional problems arise when there is lack of expertise or resources in the commenting agencies and from an overall lack of coordination between commenters in different ministries. To exacerbate the problem, if commenters are slow in submitting their concerns, the municipality may go on to consider the matter and grant approval without the benefit of all the necessary information.

The provincial government apparatus is both intensely political, concerned with image and electoral success, and bureaucratic, moving slowly and cautiously in addressing concerns. Parliamentary organization allows control of the government by parties and party discipline is enforced, unlike municipal politics. Cabinet and the governing party can be quick to respond to public and opposition pressure that is applied effectively, especially on a case-by-case basis. Conversely, the day-to-day operation of the government is the responsibility of the public service, which may be slow to respond to an increased awareness of the need for environmental protection by society at large. The interests of the key ministries and agencies are presented below.

Ministry of Municipal Affairs

The Ministry of Municipal Affairs is the primary provincial government agency involved in land-use planning. The minister is given power by the *Planning Act* to make final decisions on many approvals. He or she must have regard to items of *provincial interest* in carrying out his or her responsibilities and may issue policy statements that are binding on planning decisions made by all other approval bodies. The minister may reserve final decisions to Cabinet by appealing or referring decisions to the Ontario Municipal Board and then notifying the OMB that a matter of provincial interest is involved. Where an issue covered by a provincial policy statement is affected by an official plan, the minister may make amendments to the plan unilaterally.[74] All of these provisions allow the ministry to take a very active role in the planning process. In reality, the ministry has been content to allow municipalities and the Ontario Municipal Board to make the decisions with minimal involvement of the provincial government.

Ministry of Natural Resources

The Ministry of Natural Resources is responsible for many environmentally significant features throughout the province. Recently, it has become more active in its efforts to protect class 1 to 3 wetlands, forests, fish habitat streams, and other elements of the natural environment that are of provincial significance.[75] One method of accomplishing this has been to work with municipalities and local conservation authorities to create master watershed studies for rivers and streams in areas where development is imminent. These studies delineate wetlands, fish habitat, and groundwater recharge areas, and propose plans for stormwater management designed to reduce the risk of flooding. Once approved by the municipality, the conservation authority, and the ministry, the watershed studies require developers to prepare environmental reports that show how the environmental resources identified will be protected. This work must be done before a draft plan of subdivision is submitted, and the draft plan must reflect the findings of the environmental reports. The ministry will not provide its comments or indicate its clearance of any proposal in a watershed subject to a master watershed study until this information has been provided and the ministry is satisfied that the resources will be adequately protected.

The ministry is also responsible for the aggregate (sand and gravel) resources of the province. It has issued a provincial policy statement covering this area, the Mineral Aggregate Resources Planning Policy Statement. Because it is a policy statement, all municipalities and other approval-granting bodies are required to take its provisions into account, and the Ontario Municipal Board will rely heavily on it in its decisions.

The policy statement indicates that aggregate resources are important and should be used whenever possible without unreasonable interference with neighbouring land uses. The ministry will generally encourage the exploitation of this resource before the development of land is permitted. This policy statement, the environmental significance of aggregate extraction, and the relationship between the *Aggregate Resources Act* and the land-use planning process are discussed further in Chapter 23.

The mandate of the Ministry of Natural Resources — both to protect and to facilitate the exploitation of the natural resources of the province — may lead to conflicting priorities. Decisions of the ministry and how it exercises its review function in land-use planning matters should be monitored by citizens to ensure that the environment comes first.

Ministry of Agriculture and Food

Many urban areas started as agricultural service centres often surrounded by fertile farmland, which has been converted to urban uses as desired. It is now recognized that the rate of this conversion is a matter of concern. The Ministry of Agriculture and Food is concerned with the needs of agriculture. It promotes the preservation of good farmland and the perpetuation of the agricultural community. To address this problem, it has formulated the *Food Land Guidelines*, a document similar to a provincial policy statement covering, among other things, the conversion of fertile agricultural land to other uses and the introduction of non-farm uses into farming areas. The document encourages the use of less fertile farmland for non-farm uses and may be useful in protecting some environmental resources.

Development applications that propose to convert good quality farmland to other uses, ranging from large subdivisions to a single new residential building to be located on farmland, even if for the use of the farmer, will be scrutinized by the Ministry of Agriculture and Food and will generally result in a negative comment.

Ministry of Housing

The Ministry of Housing is primarily involved in the provision of low-cost and low-rental housing and financing. As part of its mandate, it has accumulated significant holdings of land around existing urban areas. The ministry is also responsible for the development of "new towns." Approval of any development on government land is not subject to the same process as that for private proposals. However, since the Crown is not bound by municipal bylaws, the magnitude of the developments involved can have a significant impact on environmental resources on provincially owned land without the checks and balances provided by the *Planning Act*. Large provincial initiatives may be subject to the *Environmental Assessment Act*[76] (see Chapter 9) or may be made subject to an *ad hoc* approval process. The opportunities for public input that are provided will often depend on the political sensitivity of the issues.

Ministry of Environment and Energy

The Ministry of Environment and Energy becomes directly involved in land-use issues through its responsibility for both public sewage disposal (sewage treatment plants) and private sewage treatment systems (generally septic systems) in many areas of the province, especially rural areas. The ministry has two functions: it reviews applications under the *Planning Act* and it issues certificates of approval for sewage facilities. The ministry will examine development proposals and offer comments on the suitability of the soils and groundwater conditions to support private sewage disposal systems or the capacity of public treatment facilities and their receiving bodies (that is, the watercourses to which they discharge). Where the land is not suitable for a septic system, many development proposals are considered premature because of inadequate capacity in a sewage treatment plant. Similarly, standards for septic system installation are under renewed scrutiny because of widespread contamination of groundwater from this source.[77] Comments provided by the ministry will generally be followed by the municipal council in the planning process, although in the past councils have not always done so.

This responsibility for approving private sewage systems is carried out by health units rather than the ministry in some parts of the province. In these areas, land-use applications will usually be circulated to the health unit for comment.

Proper monitoring by the ministry or health units can go a long way toward protecting the integrity of ground and surface water resources.

As discussed in Chapter 19, the Ministry of Environment and Energy will also comment on potential noise impacts of development. The ministry also administers the *Environmental Protection Act*[78] and the *Environmental Assessment Act*,[79] both of which can have an impact on land use, especially with respect to solid waste disposal (see Chapter 24).

Ministry of Transportation

The Ministry of Transportation constructs new highways and administers the existing highway network in Ontario and also subsidizes municipal road construction. Studies are often conducted for new highways or revised routes of existing major highways to reduce congestion and facilitate the movement of traffic. The integrity of environmental resources should be a prime consideration in the planning of these routes, and concerned citizens should become involved in the planning process associated with them. Major routes will also be shown in the official plan of the municipalities through which they pass.

The Ministry of Transportation generally comments on development applications that are circulated to it. Its primary concerns usually relate to access points to the provincial highway system. Access permits may be refused by the ministry where access is considered to be undesirable or unsafe. Thus, the ministry can play an important role in the land-use planning process, since lack of access to a highway can be fatal to a proposed development.

Conservation Authorities

Conservation authorities and their mandate are described in chapters 11 and 18. Conservation authorities have become active in a number of environmentally significant roles, including flood control and the protection of wetlands, forests, and other elements of nature that help regulate the flow of water.

Conservation authorities comment on proposed land-use approvals and developments with regard to their effect on the ability of watercourses to pass flood flows and the contributions that a particular development will make to flood runoff. Development activity of any kind in the *floodway* (areas that will be inundated in the event of a flood) is strictly regulated and for the most part prohibited. In some cases, the conservation authority may purchase property necessary for flood control or for the abatement of flood damage, both upland (generally forest) or in the floodplain. Since many environmentally significant features are located on this type of land, the power of the conservation authority to prohibit development and purchase land may afford useful protection.

However, conservation authorities sometimes develop land under their control for recreational purposes that may not be environmentally sound. Environmentalists in Toronto have long opposed the Metro Toronto and Region Conservation Authority's proposed conversion of the Leslie Street Spit, a man-made protrusion into Lake Ontario that has become habitat for many wildlife species, into a site for an aquarium and marina.

Conservation authorities are headed by an executive committee composed of representatives of constituent municipalities and provincial appointees. They generally have professional staff who review applications and make recommendations to the committee for decisions. They are less susceptible to public pressure than are directly elected councils, but they may be influenced by sound technical arguments.

Ontario Hydro

Undertakings of Ontario Hydro approved under the *Environmental Assessment Act* are not subject to the provisions of the *Planning Act*.[80] The hearing and appeal processes provided by the *Environmental Assessment Act* become particularly important as a result of this limitation, since the issues of compatible and appropriate land use for major transmission and generating facilities must be addressed through that process rather than through the planning process.

Ontario Hydro is a Crown corporation that has not been known for public responsiveness. The monolithic nature of this organization and its seeming lack of public accountability make the task of influencing Hydro's plans difficult. However, proceedings under the *Environmental Assessment Act* can provide a forum, and pressure applied through the provincial government may have some effect.

Ontario Municipal Board/Joint Boards

Proceedings before the Ontario Municipal Board are similar to those in a courtroom although they are less formal. Lawyers are generally engaged by the parties to an appeal, and testimony is given under oath by planners and others through the question-and-answer method. Except in the most important cases, the hearing will be conducted by a single board member, who may take an active part in the proceedings as well by ask questions the parties have not asked. After the conclusion of the hearing, the board will give its decision, usually in writing, and notify all the interested parties.

Members of the Ontario Municipal Board serve full time and are appointed by the provincial Cabinet. They have sometimes been offered positions on the board for service to the political party in power, but members are usually appointed in recognition of their expertise and service to a planning-related profession. Many are former municipal or provincial politicians, planners, engineers, or lawyers. The quality and independence of the members of the OMB are extremely important, since a single member of the board may overrule a unanimous decision of an elected municipal council, and except in certain matters involving a provincial interest, there is no further appeal available. Board members are not bound by precedent, but patterns may be determined from an analysis of board decisions. In the past, the OMB has tended to rule fairly conservatively, in favour of the owners of property and their right to use land for profit, although all decisions are ostensibly made on the basis of *good planning*. Recently, environmental considerations have played a more significant part in board decisions. The power held by board members is significant, because their rulings may not be challenged except on a point of law, and this rarely provides an opportunity to overturn a board decision, since most decisions do not turn on legal issues. It is impossible to influence the rulings of the OMB except through effective presentations at hearings and the much slower process of Cabinet appointments of environmentally aware members to the board.

The OMB may award costs, although this is not a common occurrence. This power has both positive and negative implications for the intervenor in that, in the event of a poorly argued or unfounded case, the board could award costs against an intervenor. The board has published guidelines setting out when an award of costs would be appropriate. Generally, costs will only be awarded against a party that has abused the process.

In cases where multiple appeals relating to the same development are launched — that is, a zone change, a draft plan of subdivision, and an official plan amendment — the OMB will hear all the issues at one time and make a comprehensive ruling. If hearings under other acts before other boards are required — for example, the Environmental Assessment Board — the hearings may be combined and held before a *joint board*, described in greater detail in Chapter 9.

Provincial Cabinet

The provincial Cabinet makes the final decision on matters declared to be of provincial significance, approves policy statements, appoints members of the Ontario Municipal Board, and sets the tone for the policy initiatives and work of all provincial ministries. Because it is composed of members of the governing party, Cabinet can be responsive to public pressure, especially in highly politicized areas such as the environment, but it is unlikely to overturn an OMB decision on a matter it perceives to be only of local interest, unless there is widespread opposition to the decision. Always concerned about image, electoral success, and party politics, Cabinet is sensitive to movements in public opinion and occasionally can be prevailed upon to make bold moves, especially as elections grow nearer. For example, the

Progressive Conservative government stopped the Spadina expressway in the 1970s over the objections of the municipality of Metropolitan Toronto due to an intense lobbying campaign mounted by residents living in the area through which the expressway was to run, after the expressway had been approved by the OMB.

The Federal Role

Airports

The federal government has constitutional authority over almost all aspects of air transportation in Canada, including ground installations such as airports. To promote safety, the Department of Transport implements height restrictions around airports through *zoning regulations*. It also publishes data regarding noise expected from aircraft taking off and landing. Municipalities often impose zoning bylaws that restrict development within high noise-level zones or at least require noise abatement measures for buildings constructed in these zones.

Significantly, federal powers regarding air transportation take precedence over provincial (and municipal) regulation. The priority given federal regulation will render ineffective any safeguards regarding the environment that have been incorporated into municipal official plans and zoning bylaws. For example, the federal government need not comply with any provincial or municipal law, bylaw, policy, or regulation when contemplating the location of a new airport. The consequences for environmental features worthy of protection are obvious.

This is not to say that the federal government is insensitive to the needs of the environment or that it does not observe its own environmental guidelines and the rules of the applicable province whenever possible. In addition, provinces may have other methods at their disposal to discourage locations that they do not favour. They may, for example, refuse to build access roads or other necessary facilities. This was the tactic used by the Ontario government to stop the proposed Pickering airport for Toronto. Nevertheless, the federal level may be more difficult to influence than the local level, and it must be remembered that environmental protection won at the provincial and local levels has limited effect on federal agencies and industries regulated by the federal government, including railroads, telecommunication, and shipping.

Initiatives

From time to time the federal government will involve itself in issues of land-use planning although it has no direct constitutional authority to do so. Such initiatives have involved the funding of research and projects to find innovative or more efficient housing types, speed the development-approval process, and promote better urban design.

Various programs developed under the mantle of regional development have been useful in protecting environmental resources in the agricultural area, particularly soil conservation. These programs are administered under a junior Cabinet portfolio relating to urban affairs or housing, regional development, or the Canada Mortgage and Housing Corporation, which, in addition to its primary function of helping finance housing, produces large amounts of useful statistical information on the housing and development industry in Canada.

The federal government is a useful source for information regarding the rate and effect of development on the environment. It may also be a source for funding to develop responses to environmental problems stemming from development. The ability to implement any action in relation to these issues, however, is governed by the financial resources available or by provincial cooperation, both of which seem to be scarce commodities.

PLANNING AND THE ENVIRONMENT: DIRECTIONS FOR REFORM

Over the past 10 years the level of dissatisfaction with Ontario's land-use planning regime has been increasing. This dissatisfaction is shared by developers, environmentalists, municipal and provincial politicians, and planning and environmental experts. In short, the adequacy of the existing land-use planning process to serve the various functions for which it was designed is a matter of concern among the full range of stakeholders who participate in and preside over the land-use planning process in the province. There is a growing recognition that there is a need for major reform.

Impetus for Reform

The main source of the dissatisfaction of environmentalists and citizens who want to protect their neighbourhoods from development that may degrade the quality of life in their communities is a perception that the existing land-use planning process is outdated and does not ensure the protection of environmental values. It fails to ensure that planning decisions will not have adverse long-term environmental consequences. At the same time, the lengthy, complex, and seemingly circuitous approval processes for land-use changes are seen by developers, administrators, and politicians as a barrier to growth and development. Of particular concern to developers is the length of time required by government agencies to review and provide input on development proposals.

The government agencies that review development proposals are frustrated too. Increasing awareness of environmental issues has translated into an increasing need to scrutinize and study the potential environmental impacts of land-use proposals. The government agencies charged with the responsibility of reviewing these proposals have found themselves without adequate staff and resources to give each development proposal proper scrutiny. This has led not only to delays but, in many cases, to an inability to provide a meaningful assessment of the long-term or cumulative environmental impacts of a development proposal.

Finally, there is considerable dissatisfaction among members of the public who have participated in the planning process. The only way to participate meaningfully appears to be by retaining lawyers and consultants to appear at Ontario Municipal Board hearings. These hearings, however, do not provide participants either with up-front funding or with "costs." As a result, participation often translates into an expensive, time-consuming, and energy-draining experience.

The visible strains on the existing land-use planning process can be illustrated by two case studies from which a number of common themes emerge. These two cases illustrate not only a number of significant deficiencies in the existing land-use planning regime, but also provide valuable insight into the challenges that lie ahead.

Case Study 1: The Ganaraska Watershed

In early 1989, a ratepayers' group wrote to the Ontario minister of the environment about a proposed 13-lot subdivision in the town of Newcastle. The residents were concerned that the existing land-use planning process was not adequate to ensure that the proposed subdivision would receive adequate environmental scrutiny. The local residents felt that they would only play a "token role in the planning process because they did not have the expertise, time and resources to compete with developers who have financial incentive to pursue the proposal through the planning process."[81] The residents were therefore requesting that the proposal be subject to the *Environmental Assessment Act*, a parallel environmental planning process that is discussed in Chapter 9. Land-use planning matters are not generally subject to this Act. The *Environmental Assessment Act* would apply to a private initiative such as a proposed subdivision only if the minister of the environment specifically designated this project by special regulation. This occurs rarely, and usually in cases of major undertakings such as dam projects or waste management facilities. There is no precedent for designating a subdivision under the *Environmental Assessment Act*.

The residents believed that the minister should make an exception in this case for a number of reasons. First, the proposed subdivision was to be located on the Oak Ridges Moraine, an area both environmentally significant and vulnerable to development impacts. The area in which the proposed development was to take place is located at the headwaters of the Ganaraska River and was therefore thought to be of primary environmental significance because of its influence on groundwater and surface water quantity and quality in the area. The headwaters of the Ganaraska are an important source of water supply to local residents, and the area is regionally significant as a major forest resource, fishery, and wildlife habitat, and as an important "residual green space in a rapidly urbanizing area of Southern Ontario." The residents were concerned that a decision on this subdivision could set a precedent for future development in the area. They were concerned that there did not appear to be any clear set of planning rules to protect a significant environmental resource, left unprotected from growing development pressure.

The minister decided not to apply the *Environmental Assessment Act* in this case. He did, however, respond to the larger issues raised by the residents' concerns. Recognizing that "long-term effects of development in the Ganaraska Watershed are important" and suspecting that the existing land-use planning process in the area of the Ganaraska may not provide the protection that is needed, the minister referred the matter to the Environmental Assessment Advisory Committee, a special committee that advises the minister on environmental planning issues.[82] This action by the minister began a series of events that would place Ontario's existing land-use planning regime under considerable public scrutiny.

The committee conducted public meetings in the headwaters area of the Ganaraska and received written and oral submissions from government agencies, environmental groups, and individuals. It then produced a report entitled *The Adequacy of the Existing Environmental Planning and Approval Process for the Ganaraska Watershed* that included 14 specific recommendations on how to address problems that the committee had identified in planning on the Ganaraska Watershed.[83]

The committee reported a surprising degree of consensus among environmental groups, residents, and government agencies regarding the situation on the Ganaraska Watershed. It was generally agreed that:

- the headwaters of the Ganaraska River represented a highly significant set of environmental values that merit long-term protection and conservation;
- this area is vulnerable to environmental impacts, and increasingly subject to development pressures arising from sought-after residential housing in the Greater Toronto Area, signalled by the commencement of large-scale assembly of lands in the headwaters area; and
- there is significant question whether the long-term protection of the headwaters area could be achieved through existing planning policy.

The committee identified a number of deficiencies in the planning process for the headwater area. First, it observed that there was a lack of existing baseline information on the nature and extent of existing environmental resources in the headwaters area and their vulnerability to land-use impacts. The committee noted submissions that indicated a need for a better understanding of surface water and groundwater movement, fisheries, wildlife habitat, forest resources, and other environmental resources, and the potential impact of increased development on these resources.

Second, the committee noted that existing land-use planning policies were general in nature, and not based on the environmental information described above.

Third, even if the needed environmental studies and official plan policy revisions were completed, the committee was skeptical that this would result in adequate protection of the headwaters area.

The committee had some more general concerns about the existing approvals process. First, the planning process is not well designed to consider the cumulative environmental impacts of a particular development together with other existing development and potential future development in the area. The committee noted that "the case-by-case consideration of official plan amendments militates against the consideration of overall cumulative environmental impacts." Furthermore, the committee noted that government agencies that review development applications do not have the resources or expertise to look beyond the individual application before them. For example, the Ministry of the Environment made a submission to the committee that it "does not generally consider cumulative impacts in its review of 'development' applications during the planning process." Other commenting agencies also noted that they focus on specific technical aspects of individual proposal and do not address the cumulative impacts.[84]

Finally, the committee noted that the planning process is hamstrung because planning jurisdictions are based on political rather than ecosystem boundaries. The committee concluded that "if adequate attention is to be given to the cumulative impacts of land-use planning decisions, planning will have to be done, or at least coordinated, on an ecosystem basis."[85]

The committee's report included two kinds of recommendations. The first set of recommendations dealt with the establishment of a planning process to protect the headwaters area. These recommendations built on the fortuitous circumstance that the region of Durham was conducting an official plan review. The committee provided specific suggestions on how to build environmental values into that planning process through the collection of data on environmental resources and the development of planning policies based on this information.

More significantly, the committee also developed a set of more general conclusions and recommendations arising from the case. The committee felt that the Ganaraska case raised general questions about the ability of the existing planning process to protect the environment adequately. It identified four "basic requirements" that an "environmentally enlightened land-use planning process" must meet:

- it must ensure the collection of adequate baseline information on environmental resources, their importance, and their vulnerability;
- it must ensure that land-use plans and planning policies recognize resource preservation and environmental protection goals and needs, identify the cumulative as well as the specific impacts to be avoided, and set appropriate development objectives and limitations;
- it must ensure consistent and effective adherence to the identified goals, requirements, and limitations in all decision making on official plan amendments and on individual development proposals; and
- it must be sufficiently broad, or at least well coordinated enough, to ensure that interregional environmental resources (for example, watersheds, extensive natural features such as the Oak Ridges Moraine, etc.) are recognized and given comprehensive and consistent protection.[86]

The committee concluded that none of these prerequisites was currently being met in planning under Ontario's current planning regime.

Case Study 2: Land Severance Activity in Grey County

Shortly after the Environmental Assessment Advisory Committee reported to the minister with regard to land-use planning in the Ganaraska Watershed, the minister of the environment referred a second matter to the committee, land severance activity in Grey County. At issue were many of the same concerns about the adequacy of the planning process in Ontario. The Grey County case also pointed to a number of other stresses that were challenging the existing planning regime.

Grey County is located on the southwest shore of Georgian Bay. Until recently, the county has been largely rural in character, with an agricultural economic base combined with significant environmental resources. These resources include a majority of the significant wetlands in southern Ontario and over 70 per cent of southern Ontario's cold water streams. The Niagara Escarpment is the prominent land form in the county and covers about 15 per cent of the county's lands. In the past 5 to 10 years, however, the natural beauty of the area has begun to attract rural residents from the Greater Toronto Area. As a result, Grey County has been facing unprecedented growth pressures.

The task of trying to cope with these new pressures has fallen to a number of planning jurisdictions, including the county's Planning Approvals Committee, which deals with severance applications, the county's 27 local municipalities, and the Niagara Escarpment Commission. In addition, three conservation authorities have responsibility for watersheds in the county. The jurisdictions of these various planning authorities are overlapping, leading to conflict and uncertainty over planning decisions.

Once again, the minister asked the committee to review whether the existing planning and approvals process was adequate to ensure environmental protection, this time across an entire county. In this case the referral arose out of a continuing conflict in the county between residents and the county's Planning Approvals Committee over the way the county was responding to increased development pressure. The number of severances granted by the Planning Approvals Committee had increased from 281 in 1984 to a record 1,887 in 1989. This rapid increase had also caught the attention of the Ministry of Municipal Affairs. In 1986, that ministry reviewed severance activity in the county and concluded that the Planning Approvals Committee, composed of municipal politicians, was approving the vast majority of severance applications that it received. Of these approvals, 78 per cent were granted even though objections or concerns were raised by commenting agencies, including the county's own planning department.[87]

The level of controversy over land-use planning was reflected in the two public meetings that the committee held in the county, both of which were attended by over 400 residents. The committee received over 140 written submissions from individuals, groups, and agencies. One important issue that arose during the public meetings was the future of agriculture in the county. Many farmers relied on their "right" to sever their lands in order to finance agricultural operations. Others viewed increased residential development and its economic spinoffs as the county's only economic hope in the face of the increasing decline of the agricultural industry. However, a number of environmental groups and residents were frustrated by the actions of the county's Planning Approvals Committee and feared that the absence of sound environmental planning would lead to severe long-term environmental consequences.[88]

Building on its conclusions in the Ganaraska referral, the committee identified four underlying issues arising from the Grey County case.[89]

First, the committee observed that the existing planning system relies on government agencies with fragmented responsibilities, which are ill coordinated and focus on case-by-case decision making. This makes it difficult, if not impossible, to make comprehensive and integrated planning decisions that consider the interrelated and cumulative effects on the environment.

Second, the committee recognized the problem of reconciling the rights of property owners to the reasonable enjoyment and use of their land with the public goals of overall environmental protection. For example, an individual may own lands that are environmentally significant and merit special protections but have no economic incentive to protect these lands, and, on the other hand, have a strong economic incentive to pursue land development opportunities.

Third, the Grey County case brought out the potential conflicts that exist between demand for local control and accountability, participation by individuals in the planning process, and the role of the provincial government in protecting provincial interests and using provincial expertise. A number of presentations argued strongly that local politicians should be able to make planning decisions without interference from local residents or provincial government agencies, such as the Niagara Escarpment Commission and the Ministry of the Environment.

Finally, the Grey County case illustrated the difficulty of making planning decisions in the face of economic pressures and uncertainties. Clearly, the planning decisions in Grey County were influenced by concerns about the future viability of agriculture in the county, and the perception among many residents of the need to diversify the county's economic base.

Once again, the committee put forward extensive recommendations dealing both with the specific concerns in Grey County and the broader concerns about Ontario's land-use planning process. The committee's major recommendation was that the provincial government establish a "comprehensive public review of the process and context for land-use planning and approvals in the province, in order to develop a package of reforms to ensure long-term environmental protection and wise management of environmental resources."[90]

In proposing this review, the committee also suggested changes that must be made to address existing deficiencies including:[91]

- integrated collection of environmental data on environmental resources and their interrelationships, importance, and vulnerability;
- consideration of planning options and of individual development proposals in the light of this information;
- preparing land-use plans and planning policies that protect environmental resources and ecosystem integrity;
- developing a process that looks at cumulative as well as specific impacts of developments, articulates specific development objectives and limitations, and provides certainty for participants in land-use decision making;
- clarifying the provincial role, including spelling out provincial guidelines and priorities, interests, and concerns;
- addressing the problem of ensuring adherence to goals, requirements, and limitations;
- coordination among planning jurisdictions to protect natural features that cross jurisdictional boundaries;
- finding more effective means of involving the public in land-use decision making and lowering the financial burden for intervenors;
- increasing the incentives and obligations of property owners to preserve natural areas;
- finding new ways for public acquisition and maintenance of environmentally sensitive or significant areas; and
- incorporating the strengths of the *Environmental Assessment Act*,[92] including public evaluation of alternatives and their environmental implications, into the land-use planning and approvals process.[93]

Government Response

The government's response to the problems in the land-use planning process has been rather like the man who jumped on his horse and rode off in all directions at once. On the one hand, the government talks about *greening* the process — that is, integrating environmental concerns into the land-use planning process. On the other hand, the government keeps announcing its intention to "streamline" the various approvals processes. Streamlining often boils down to giving civil servants tighter deadlines for reviewing applications for environmental and land-use approvals and requiring them to create guidelines to guide applicants and to channel the exercise of discretion in their review functions. Streamling also involves allowing some activities without any approvals that formerly needed approval, doing away with provincial government reviews of applications, and delegating provincial review and approval powers to municipalities, which have the fewest resources and experience the most pressure from local developers. Although streamlining the approvals process is a worthy objective, the fact that the ministries responsible for reviewing applications are also receiving fewer resources to carry out their responsibilities means that reviews may become less comprehensive. Consequently, there is a serious risk that streamlining the approvals process and "greening" the approvals process may be initiatives that are contradictory in their effect on ensuring that environmental planning is comprehensive.

Streamlining Initiatives

Perhaps the most infamous streamlining initiative was Project X, in which the treasurer of Ontario presided over a secret review of Ontario's land-use planning process, which began soon after the premier promised the regional chairmen of the Greater Toronto Area that Queen's Park would cut in half the amount of time needed to approve lands for residential development. The Project X documents leaked to the press advised the government to take environmental assessment from the Ministry of the Environment, give it to the Ministry of Municipal Affairs, then delegate most of the administration to municipal governments.

A proposal announced in May 1990 also raised concerns about whether its intention was to speed up the development process. One of the major constraints to new land-use development is the lack of capacity in existing sewage treatment plants and water treatment facilities to handle new development. In May 1990, the government announced its intention to take the process of building such facilities and give it to a new Crown corporation that would report to the minister of municipal affairs, rather than to the minister of the environment. The money used for the design and construction of such facilities — $246 million — would be taken from the budget of the Ministry of the Environment and given to this new Crown corporation. This made sense in theory because it would eliminate a conflict of interest, since the Ministry of the Environment is responsible for approving and regulating projects that its staff designs and operates. However, the proposal, which was put on hold when the NDP formed the government, raised concerns that the hidden agenda was to prevent environmental considerations from slowing down development. According to *The Toronto Star*:

> Sources have said that [provincial treasurer] Nixon is concerned that the province's environmental protection system is inhibiting growth and making it hard on developers. Sources say that in cabinet, Nixon has launched a full-scale attack on the environment ministry, its minister Jim Bradley and many of its programs.[94]

More recently, the government's 1992 throne speech made reference to its intention to speed up approvals processes. In April 1992, Municipal Affairs Minister Dave Cooke announced plans "to speed up the provincial decision-making process for development proposals." The minister's press release stated that "[s]peeding up the planning process could create thousands of jobs in the construction industry"; however, the press release emphasized that "the principles of good planning, including environmental safeguards, will continue to be the foundation of every land use decision."[95] The guidelines for implementing this streamlining process consisted primarily of setting deadlines for screening applications, consultation with review agencies and the public, and decision making.[96] These guidelines assume that municipal bureaucrats and reviewing agencies are simply inefficient, and that the review and approval process can be speeded up by improving efficiency, without any additional resources, and with no less consideration of environmental concerns. The minister of the environment has also stated her intention to set time limits and reduce the time required to issue approvals under the *Environmental Protection Act*[97] and the *Environmental Assessment Act*[98] and to exempt some projects from the approvals system.[99]

Greening the Land-Use Planning Process

As the two case studies discussed above indicate, the need for reform poses daunting problems. The economic and environmental stakes are high. There is no clear consensus or common vision among the stakeholders, aside from the shared view that change is needed.

The need to reform the existing land-use planning process is slowly translating itself into government action. Change needs to take place at three levels. First, there is a need to redefine the way land-use planning takes place. The strategies and tools for land-use planning must be revisited to incorporate a new understanding of the interrelationship between the environment and land-use planning decisions. Relatively new concepts such as cumulative effects and ecosystem planning must be translated into practical, workable planning techniques. Land-use planning must be based on a better understanding of environmental resources and features, their interrelationship, and their capacity to sustain new land uses. This information must be translated into clear policies, guidelines, and directives — clear rules that are fair and provide certainty for all participants in the land-use planning process.

Second, the institutions that preside over the land-use planning process must also be reformed. Government agencies must be better coordinated and provide a more thorough, integrated, and efficient review of environmental issues associated with land-use planning. One key defect that has come to light in recent cases is the fragmented nature of government participation in the land-use planning process. Different government agencies, each with narrow, sometimes overlapping, sometimes conflicting mandates, are simply not designed or properly funded to address key components of a new planning framework such as cumulative impacts and ecosystem-based planning.

Third, the way that environmental decisions are made — the land-use planning process itself — must be rethought, including its relationship to, and its overlap with, the planning process governed by the *Environmental Assessment Act*. Members of the public are demanding access to the decision-making process. They are insisting that their involvement be both affordable and meaningful. Land developers and others seeking approval under the existing process are frustrated by the waiting period and uncertainty associated with land-use planning decisions. New conflict resolution and mediation approaches must be considered. To what extent can up-front public involvement and planning avoid costly and divisive hearings at the end of the process? What opportunities are there for a compromise among various stakeholders that will serve both the interests of growth and development on the one hand and long-term preservation and conservation of environmental values on the other?

The government response to these challenges has taken a number of forms, which are outlined below.

Ministry of Municipal Affairs

The Ministry of Municipal Affairs, the government department charged with administering the land-use planning process in Ontario, has responded to the call for change by developing a report entitled *The Green Report: Policy Framework for Ecological Considerations in the Municipal Planning Process*.[100] This report includes:

- a statement of principles to be used by both the province and municipalities in doing "more environmentally sensitive planning";
- a summary of provincial policy direction that would provide leadership for this new kind of planning;
- a general description of how more environmentally sensitive planning principles could be implemented by municipalities; and
- a list of possible amendments to the *Planning Act* to encourage "green" planning.

The environmental principles listed are very general in nature but do include the principle of an "ecosystem approach" and the need to account for cumulative effects of land-use decisions over time and space rather than only on a site-specific basis. The suggested framework for incorporating environmentally sensitive planning into the existing land-use planning process includes the following steps. First, the municipality must develop goals and objectives and establish "ecosystem benchmarks" as indicators of environmental quality. Second, the municipality must determine information requirements and develop an inventory of environmental resources within the municipality; the suggestion is that each municipality develop a "state of the environment report." Third, the municipality would carry out an analysis to understand how the ecosystem functions, to set specific environmental targets, and to understand the carrying capacity and thresholds of the environment. Fourth, the municipality would consider alternative land-use options consistent with its goals and objectives and evaluate these options on the basis of environmental impacts. On the basis of this analysis, a preferred alternative or alternatives would be selected that would form the basis for the official plan. Fifth, official planning policies would be developed on the basis of these alternatives. Sixth, there would be ongoing policy development and monitoring and feedback. Based on new information, environmental and land-use policies would be continually updated and revised.

"Growth and Settlement: Policy Guidelines"

In September 1992, the Ministry of Municipal Affairs released a set of guidelines on how and where new provincial growth and settlement should occur.[101] The report tells municipalities that when considering official plan amendments and development proposals, they should integrate environmental, economic, and social considerations; ensure that land-use planning contributes to the protection of the natural environment and cultural heritage; and promote energy and water efficiency and the conservation of natural resources. Development is to be directed away from significant environmental features and areas, prime agricultural land, and other resource lands; land-use planning is to be coordinated with watershed plans and remedial action plans (see Chapter 18); and potentially contaminated sites are to be identified and evaluated for their remediation and redevelopment potential.

Special Commissions

Both the federal and provincial governments have set up special commissions to begin to address some of the issues and concerns described above. Perhaps the most important initiative is the establishment of the Commission on Planning and Development Reform in Ontario (the Sewell commission). Starting from the premise that "almost everyone is unhappy about planning in Ontario," this commission set out to define land-use planning goals for the province and to "broaden the traditional scope of planning and more strongly integrate environment, energy, agriculture, and heritage concerns into land-use considerations."[102] Some of the questions raised by the commission reflect and echo the concerns identified above:

- how to make public participation more meaningful;
- how to integrate the *Planning Act*[103] and the *Environmental Assessment Act*;[104]
- how to address the question of protecting agricultural land in the face of a declining agricultural economy and development pressures;
- how to contain urban sprawl while developing affordable and environmentally sound housing; and
- how to address cumulative effects and the need to plan on a land-form or ecosystem basis when our planning system is structured around political boundaries.[105]

The commission's final report, released in June 1993, contained proposals that set out a picture of comprehensive reform for the planning process in Ontario, including: provincial roles, municipal roles, environmental planning, and development controls and standards.[106]

The commission's recommendations to protect the natural environment include: provincial policies would require the protection of significant natural features from development; municipalities must assess the environmental impacts of options when preparing land-use plans; municipalities must map or describe environmental resources, monitor environmental indicators, and plan on a watershed basis; municipal infrastructure should be subject to an environmental review process; and private septic systems should be better regulated. Planning decisions would have to be consistent with provincial policies designed to protect the environment, promote housing, protect agricultural land, conserve energy and water, and protect non-renewable resources. Public involvement would be encouraged by requiring that all information in relation to plans and land development applications be available to the public at a nominal charge, opening meetings of municipal councils, committees of adjustment, and land division committees to the public, and giving the public earlier and clearer notice of planning matters. Streamlining would be accomplished by setting time limits for various steps in the planning process, including decisions by municipalities and the province, and requiring the Ontario Municipal Board to hold a procedural meeting of all parties within 30 days of receiving an appeal and making mediation available.

Whether those reforms will be implemented remains to be seen. Whether they will resolve the problems with the existing system, even if implemented, will take some time to assess.

Two other commissions have greatly influenced the debate about land-use planning reform. The Royal Commission on the Future of the Toronto Waterfront, headed by David Crombie, has actively pursued specific methods and mechanisms for carrying out cumulative impact- and ecosystem-based planning. The commission's August 1990 report, *Watershed*,[107] included background papers on scientific, legal, and planning issues, all pursuing the question of how one could implement an ecosystem-based approach to waterfront planning.

The commission's final report, *Regeneration*,[108] was released in December 1991. This report recommends: that the province prepare a comprehensive, integrated set of ecosystem-based policy statements under section 3 of the *Planning Act*; that guidelines be prepared for ecosystem planning practices to be used in the preparation of official plans and other planning instruments, such as watershed plans; that environmental performance requirements be established, dealing with matters such as greenspace protection, buffers between natural areas and other land uses, habitat restoration, energy efficiency, stormwater management, dust control, and other environmental matters; that the *Trees Act*,[109] the *Topsoil Preservation Act*,[110] and the *Planning Act* be amended to require municipalities to regulate such activities as the removal of trees and other vegetation, grading, the removal of topsoil, filling, and drainage.

The Report on the Greater Toronto Area Greenlands Strategy (the Kanter report)[111] explored strategies for protecting environmental resources and open space areas in an urban setting. This report included, among others, a background paper[112] describing land stewardship options that explores the role of the public and private sector in conserving and maintaining environmentally significant areas and features.

In spite of all these initiatives, Ontario's land-use planning process continues to operate much as it always has. Some recent Ontario Municipal Board decisions have shown a heightened sensitivity to the environmental implications of land-use decisions.[113] Many municipalities across the province are looking carefully at their existing environmental resources and developing strategies for their long-term protection. Although these changing attitudes among decision makers within the existing system are an important part of the needed change, there continues to be a growing recognition that new demands and stresses on the existing land-use planning regime signal the need for significant reform, including legislative change.

Stephen Garrod, Peter Pickfield, and Brian Gallaugher

FURTHER READING

Canada, Royal Commission on the Future of the Toronto Waterfront, *Regeneration: Toronto's Waterfront and the Sustainable City — Final Report* (Ottawa: Supply and Services, May 1992).

Ron Kanter, *Space for All: Options for a Greater Toronto Area Green Land Strategy* (Toronto: Queen's Printer, 1990).

Ontario Environmental Assessment Advisory Committee, *Report No. 38: The Adequacy of the Existing Environmental Planning and Approvals Process for the Ganaraska Watershed* (Toronto: the committee, November 1989).

Ontario Environmental Assessment Advisory Committee, *Report No. 41: Environmental Planning and Approvals in Grey County* (Toronto: the committee, December 1990).

Ontario, Ministry of Municipal Affairs, *The Green Report: Policy Framework for Ecological Considerations in the Municipal Planning Process* (Toronto: the ministry, January 1991).

ENDNOTES

1 *Planning Act*, RSO 1990, c. P.13.

2 The commission's terms of reference were established by order in council no. 1355/ 91 and include a number of specific matters that fall within the general mandate.

3 *Public Transportation and Highway Improvement Act*, RSO 1990, c. P.50

4 *Niagara Escarpment Planning and Development Act*, RSO 1990, c. N.2.

5 *Aggregate Resources Act*, RSO 1990, c. A.8.

6 *Regional Municipality of Waterloo Act*, RSO 1990, c. R.17.

7 *Building Code Act*, RSO 1990, c. B.13.

8 The province of Ontario has issued a series of general but informative pamphlets covering aspects of the instruments of planning under the name "A Citizen's Guide." They are usually available at municipal planning departments or the Community Planning Advisory Branch, Ministry of Municipal Affairs. Check the telephone book for toll-free numbers. Topics include the *Planning Act*, northern Ontario, official plans and amendments, zoning bylaws and minor variances, subdivisions, land severances, building permits, and the Ontario Municipal Board.

    The Ontario Ministry of Municipal Affairs also put out a series of guidelines in 1983 to inform those involved in land-use planning of some of the provisions of the *Planning Act*, which was amended in that year. These guidelines are more detailed and cover the following topics, among others: local planning in northern Ontario; delegation of minister's authority; official plan policies on public notice; zoning and other land-use controls; official plans and the use of site plan control; official plan documents: preparation, adoption, submission, and lodging; committees of adjustment; minor variances; and non-conforming uses. These should be available from the Local Planning Policy Branch, 13th Floor, 777 Bay Street, Toronto, Ontario M5G 2E5.

9 See *Re Township of Southwold and Caplice* (1979), 22 OR (2d) 804, 94 DLR (3d) 134, 8 CELR 11 (Div. Ct.).

10 *Planning Act*, supra endnote 1, section 24.

11 See *Holmes v. Regional Municipality of Halton* (1977), 2 MPLR 153, 16 OR (2d) 263 (HCJ), in which a bylaw authorizing a landfill site was struck down because the official plan designation for the subject area did not permit this use.

    See also *Re Cadillac Development Corp. and City of Toronto* (1974), 1 OR (2d) 20, 39 DLR (3d) 188 (HCJ), in which the court held that official plan designations were *permissive*, not mandatory, and although no zoning bylaw could be passed that exceeded the density permitted in the official plan, the city could pass zoning bylaws permitting much lower density than that contemplated in the plan.

12 *Planning Act*, supra endnote 1, section 27(1).

13 Ibid., section 27(4).

14 See *Campeau Corporation v. Township of Gloucester et al.* (1979), 6 MPLR 290, 21 OR (2d) 4 (HCJ), appeal dismissed 8 MPLR 147 (Ont. CA). In this case, a local municipality was restrained from issuing a building permit for a shopping centre because the regional official plan in effect did not designate the land for commercial use. A competing commercial developer asked the court to issue the injunction restraining the issuance of a building permit even though the application was in conformity with local zoning bylaws because the local official plan and zoning bylaw

were not in conformity with the regional official plan. This is an example of an official plan directly affecting land use.

See also *LeRoy v. Regional Municipality of Halton* (1986), 19 OMBR 383, in which a severance granted by the Regional Land Division Committee was disallowed because it was not in conformity with the regional official plan although it did conform to the area municipality plan and zoning bylaw.

15 Stanley Makuch, *Canadian Municipal and Planning Law* (Toronto: Carswell, 1983), 187. This is an excellent work for general reference on the legal aspects of land-use planning.

16 *Planning Act*, supra endnote 1, section 34(1).3.

17 Ibid., section 34(5).

18 See *Rodenbush v. District of North Cowichan* (1978), 3 MPLR 121, 76 DLR (3d) 731 (BC SC), in which the court struck down the municipality's bylaw because it left the owner with no proper use for his land. This amounted to acquiring the land by zoning bylaw, rather than by purchase or expropriation.

19 See *City of Vancouver v. Simpson*, [1977] 1 SCR 71, (1976), 3 WWR 97, 7 NR 550, 65 DLR (3d) 669. In this case, a development proposal was refused because it was judged not to be in the public interest and the development would make the land more costly for the municipality to acquire in the future, although the court recognized that this was not a case of an expropriating authority specifically attempting to contain the value of the land. See also Makuch, supra endnote 15, at 219-22 for a good discussion on the limitations to use that can be legally applied to land.

20 In any legal action, the onus is on the defendant to prove any claimed legal non-conforming status.

21 *Planning Act*, supra endnote 1, section 35.

22 Ibid., section 36.

23 Ibid., section 39.

24 Ibid., section 37.

25 Ibid., section 38.

26 See the Ontario Municipal Board decision in *Jean Grandoni v. City of Niagara Falls* (1986), OMB file nos. S840029 and R850373, in which a farmer objected to a subdivision proposed for property abutting her farm because the proximity of urban development was making her ability to continue farming uneconomical. She argued that land was available for development in areas of the city that were less detrimental to agriculture and that the official plan called for these areas to be fully developed first. The board ruled, however, that the municipality cannot force landowners to develop their property and therefore development in a second phase should not be arrested until all available land in a first phase is used. The development was allowed to proceed.

27 *Planning Act*, supra endnote 1, section 50(3).

28 Ibid., section 53(1).

29 Ibid., section 50(3).

30 Ibid., section 51(4).

31 Ibid., section 51(4).

32 Ibid., section 51(5).

33 Ibid., section 42.

34   Ibid., section 51(15).
35   See two Ontario Municipal Board decisions, *Piercey v. Regional Municipality of Peel*
     (1985), 17 OMBR 351 and *Tkalec v. Regional Municipality of Peel* (1987), 20 OMBR
     473, in which the rejection of applications for consent to sever building lots from
     agricultural land, even when not in production, were upheld by the board on the basis
     of official plan policies and reference to the *Food Land Guidelines*.
36   *Planning Act*, supra endnote 1, section 41.
37   Ibid., section 33.
38   Ibid., section 33(6).
39   *Ontario Heritage Act*, RSO 1990, c. O.18.
40   Expropriation was the method used by the Ontario government to prevent the
     destruction of sand dunes on the border by Sandbanks Provincial Park in the late 1970s.
     The province had leased the sand dunes to a cement company, and agreed to expropriate
     the lease after a campaign by Pollution Probe and the Canadian Environmental Law
     Association.
41   *Planning Act*, supra endnote 1, section 2.
42   See the OMB decision in *Minister of Municipal Affairs v. City of Thunder Bay* (1989),
     OMB file nos. O870057, C840055, and C840056. These appeals concerned severance
     applications in a subdivision near the Thunder Bay airport that were appealed by the
     Ministry of Municipal Affairs because they were not in conformity with the official
     plan. The city proceeded to amend the official plan to create conformity. The ministry
     referred this official plan amendment to the OMB and declared the issue of housing
     located in noise zones around airports to be of provincial interest.
         An unusual situation developed due to a court decision (*Brennan v. Minister of
     Municipal Affairs* (1988), 63 OR (2d) 236 (Div. Ct.)) that came down before the OMB
     hearing. The court decided that only those issues for which an approved policy
     statement had been issued under section 3 of the *Planning Act* (supra endnote 1) could
     be declared to be of provincial interest. The provincial government then proceeded to
     pass retroactive legislation amending the *Planning Act* (section 3(6)) to allow the
     minister to declare any issue to be of provincial interest and to ensure that the present
     official plan amendment would be included.
         The board appeared to find this action somewhat distasteful and used very
     convoluted arguments to discount the minister's ability to declare a provincial
     interest in this case. It also approved the official plan amendment. To ensure that the
     board's decision would not be varied, it also declared that the official plan amend-
     ment was not really required because the zoning bylaw would allow for the
     severances and was conclusively in conformity with the official plan under section
     24(4) of the *Planning Act*. In the board's opinion, the severances could be granted
     whether or not the official plan was amended. The minister of municipal affairs did
     not take the case further.
         Only one other case has been subject to a declaration of provincial interest and it is
     currently under consideration (OMB file no. O880125, City of Etobicoke).
43   *Planning Act*, supra endnote 1, section 3.
44   Ontario, Ministry of Natural Resources and Ministry of Municipal Affairs, *Mineral
     Aggregate Resources Policy Statement*, order in council no. 1249/86, 1986.

45   Ontario, Ministry of Natural Resources and Ministry of Municipal Affairs, *Flood Plain Planning Policy Statement*, order in council no. 1946/88, 1988.

46   Ontario, Ministry of Natural Resources and Ministry of Municipal Affairs, *Wetlands Policy Statement*, order in council no. 1448/92, 1992.

47   Ontario, Ministry of Natural Resources and Ministry of Municipal Affairs, *Land-Use Planning for Housing Policy Statement*, order in council no. 1812/89, 1989.

48   Ontario, Ministry of Agriculture and Food, *Food Land Guidelines*, 1978.

49   *Planning Act*, supra endnote 1, section 61.

50   Ibid., section 10.

51   Ibid., section 9.

52   Ibid., sections 17(1) to (5) and 21(1).

53   Ibid., section 8.

54   Ibid., sections 17(11) and (12).

55   Ibid., section 17(13).

56   Ibid., section 21(2).

57   Ibid., sections 17(19) to (21).

58   Ibid., section 23.

59   Ibid., sections 34(11) to (21).

60   Ibid., sections 34(21), (22), (26), and (27).

61   Ibid., sections 34(28) to (30).

62   Ibid., section 38.

63   Ibid., section 47.

64   Ibid., sections 51(1) to (3).

65   Ibid., section 51(4).

66   Ibid., sections 51(5), (6), and (13).

67   Ibid., sections 51(15) and (16).

68   Ibid., sections 51(14) and (17).

69   Ibid., sections 51(18) to (21).

70   Ibid., section 8.

71   Ibid., section 45(1).

72   Ibid., section 45(12).

73   See a recent Ontario Municipal Board decision, *Nichol Construction and the Ministry of Natural Resources et al. v. Township of West Carleton and Regional Municipality of Ottawa-Carleton* (August 29, 1990), OMB file nos. R890345, R890639, and S900003. This case concerned a Ministry of Natural Resources appeal against a zoning bylaw and subdivision that had the effect of permitting a golf course development on a portion of a class 1 wetland. Although the board accepted the ministry's position and disallowed the golf course on the wetland, it reaffirmed the principle that commenting agencies like the Ministry of Natural Resources are advisory only and do not have veto powers.

74   *Planning Act*, supra endnote 1, section 23.

75   The OMB case referred to in endnote 73, above, is an example of the ministry becoming more active in protecting wetlands.

76   *Environmental Assessment Act*, RSO 1990, c. E.18.

77   The region of Waterloo is considering an amendment to its official plan that will prohibit all development on septic tanks in areas that could be serviced with sanitary

sewers. Developments that must proceed on private services would be subject to much more thorough investigation to determine the effects on groundwater. This action is being sparked by evidence that virtually all shallow wells and some deeper ones are contaminated by improperly purified effluent entering the groundwater from inefficient septic systems, among other sources. Needless to say, landowners who had expected to develop their property on private services have protested loudly at this proposed reduction in their property value.

78 *Environmental Protection Act*, RSO 1990, c. E.19.

79 *Environmental Assessment Act*, supra endnote 76.

80 *Planning Act*, supra endnote 1, section 62.

81 Ontario Environmental Assessment Advisory Committee, *Report No. 38: The Adequacy of the Existing Environmental Planning and Approvals Process at the Ganaraska Watershed* (Toronto: the committee, November 1989), 13.

82 Ibid., at 2.

83 Ibid., at 30-41.

84 Ibid., at 34.

85 Ibid., at 36-37.

86 Ibid., at 35-36.

87 Ontario Environmental Assessment Advisory Committee, *Report No. 41 (Part 2): Environmental Planning and Approvals in Grey County* (Toronto: the committee, December 1990), 12-13.

88 Ibid., at 14-15.

89 Ibid., at 15.

90 Ibid., at 48 (recommendations 16-18).

91 Ibid., at 28-45 (recommendations 1-15).

92 *Environmental Assessment Act*, supra endnote 76.

93 *Report No. 41*, supra endnote 87.

94 David Israelson, "Environmentalists Alarmed by Nixon Plan," *Toronto Star*, May 1, 1990.

95 Ontario, Ministry of Municipal Affairs, *News Release*, "Government To Improve Development Process," April 9, 1992.

96 Ontario, Ministry of Municipal Affairs, *Streamlining Guidelines: The Development Review Process* (Toronto: the ministry, 1992).

97 *Environmental Protection Act*, supra endnote 78.

98 *Environmental Assessment Act*, supra endnote 76.

99 See, for example, Ontario, Ministry of the Environment, *Environmental Assessment Update* (Toronto: the ministry, Summer 1992), 4; Ontario, Ministry of the Environment, *Backgrounder: Streamlining Approvals Process for Certificates of Approval and Permits* (Toronto: the ministry, Spring 1992).

100 Ontario, Ministry of Municipal Affairs, Municipal Planning Policy Branch, *The Green Report: Policy Framework for Ecological Considerations in the Municipal Planning Process* (Toronto: the ministry, January 1991).

101 Ontario, Ministry of Municipal Affairs, *Growth and Settlement: Policy Guidelines* (Toronto: the ministry, September 14, 1992).

102 Commission on Planning and Development Reform in Ontario, *New Planning News*, vol. 1, no. 1, September-October 1991.

103   *Planning Act*, supra endnote 1.
104   *Environmental Assessment Act*, supra endnote 76.
105   Ibid.
106   Commission on Planning and Development Reform in Ontario, *New Planning for Ontario* (Toronto: the commission, June 1993).
107   Canada, Royal Commission on the Future of the Toronto Waterfront, *Watershed* (Ottawa: Supply and Services, August 1990).
108   Canada, Royal Commission on the Future of the Toronto Waterfront, *Regeneration* (Ottawa: Supply and Services, December 1991).
109   *Trees Act*, RSO 1990, c. T.20.
110   *Topsoil Preservation Act*, RSO, c. T.12.
111   Ron Kanter, *Space for All: Options for a Greater Toronto Greenlands Strategy* (Toronto: Queen's Printer, 1990).
112   Ronald Reid and Stuart Hilts, *Land Stewardship Options: Greater Toronto Greenlands Strategy* (Toronto: Queen's Printer, 1990).
113   For example, see the Ontario Municipal Board decision on the Sydenham Mills subdivision in Grey County, OMB file nos. R900179 and S890057, October 19, 1990 [unreported].

9

Environmental Assessment

CONTENTS

In the West Patricia area [of northwestern Ontario], 40 technical and 27 background information reports were distributed between 1978 and 1981. This was followed by the *West Patricia Land Use Plan: Proposed Policy and Optional Plans in June, 1982*. It stated that, "The approved District Land Use Plan will then provide, for the District, overall guidance for the operation of the resource management programs of the Ministry of Natural Resources." ...

In response to questions submitted by the Commission November 24, 1982, the Minister of Natural Resources stated ... "The land use plans then are *guidelines* for resource management by MNR and will be implemented under appropriate existing legislation and the approved programs and activities of the Ministry." (Emphasis added) ...

At his appearance before me in the Thunder Bay hearing on April 11, 1983, the Minister of Natural Resources explained further:

> **Mr. Pope:** Well first of all the use of the word plan is one of the issues that Cabinet's examining in the total review of this issue. It's been one of the contentious issues that has arisen during the course of public forums and open houses. And the whole purpose of the exercise that the Ministry undertook was one of information gathering and information dissemination. And I have indicated on many occasions that there will be a number of pieces of information and documentation that I would look at when I make an allocation decision under the laws of the Province of Ontario.

> **Mr. Surdykowski** (Solicitor representing the Kayahna Area Tribal Council): Well, my question really boils down to this, if this is not, by this I mean the West Patricia land use document, this document here, which when I look at it says land use plan. That's not designed to give an outline for what's going to happen. I mean, why was the term land use plan used?

> **Mr. Pope:** Well, obviously because there's such a disagreement over what it means, it probably shouldn't have been used ...

In questioning by the Kayahna Area Tribal Council, the Ministry of the Environment added ... :

> **Mr. Surdykowski:** Were these guidelines at one time plans, and they changed to guidelines? ...

Mr. Rennick (Director, Environmental Assessment Branch, Ministry of the Environment): I would say the answer to that is yes. That would be my understanding.

Mr. Surdykowski: And at the time that they were plans, the environmental assessment process would have been applicable to these documents?

Mr. Rennick: If those plans were with respect to specific activities and enterprises, as the Act indicates, then yes, it would apply to them ...

I must, however, speculate on a number of important questions — first, was the change in status from "*plans*" to "*guidelines*" merely one of terminology or were other factors at work? With all due respect, it is not difficult to conclude that there were at least two related reasons for this tardy revision. First, the Ministry may have realized that the creation of something akin to official plans created a more binding authority for their contents that [*sic*] would then be desirable, i.e., "*flexibility*" would be a more acceptable goal for the Ministry. Second, the Ministry may recognize that such plans created expectations by interested parties that there would be predictable, clearly defined rules to live by and therefore, public challenge would be possible, leading to an erosion of the Ministry's discretionary powers.

The Ministry, despite the eager acceptance of its policy as expressed by the Ministry of the Environment, may have recognized that a characterization of the plans as undertakings under the *Environmental Assessment Act* would result in an unfavorable assessment of the documents themselves, i.e., the Ministry must assess "*alternatives*" to the undertaking. As well, in sharing a perception that the environmental assessment process would entail added delay and expense, it was to be avoided.

Excerpts from the Final Report and Recommendations of Ontario's Royal Commission on the Northern Environment, June 1985

INTRODUCTION

Environmental assessment, or, as it is called in the United States,[1] environmental impact assessment,* is one of the first environmental reforms to address what has come to be known as "sustainable development." The idea of sustainable development is that environmental and economic considerations are to be integrated with each other — and that is precisely what environmental impact assessment was supposed to ensure.

Considering the close relationship of environmental assessment to sustainable development, a concept embraced by both governments and industries throughout Canada, it is unclear why both of these sectors continue to oppose full and consistent implementation of EA laws.

Most environmental protection measures have met initial resistance from those who were subject to them, but were soon accepted. Predictions that these measures would lead to loss

---

* In this chapter, we will use the term "environmental assessment." The abbreviation "EA" will also be used.

of jobs and hinder the international competitiveness of Canadian industry have been shown to be exaggerated, if not inaccurate.

Environmental assessment, however, has turned out to be an exception. Seventeen years after Ontario introduced Canada's first environmental impact assessment law, environmental assessments of projects, plans, and programs that may harm the environment are still very much the exception, rather than the rule. The EA process continues to be attacked not only by government and industry, who feel it is too time-consuming and expensive, but also by environmentalists, who feel that the implementation of environmental assessment legislation has been too little and too late.

The Ontario *Environmental Assessment Act*[2] in particular has been the focus of ongoing criticism since its inception. Environmentalists have criticized the government's failure to apply the Act to the private sector, its exemption of many significant public undertakings, the lack of requirements for information sharing and public involvement, and the failure to provide intervenor funding at the planning stages of assessment.

Government agencies and industry have been critical of the cost and complexity of the process, the delays in obtaining approval, the adversarial nature of hearings before the Environmental Assessment Board, and the lack of clarity about how much and what kind of information in an environmental assessment will lead to approval from the Ministry of Environment and Energy and the Environmental Assessment Board. In particular, the private sector has been frustrated by the Act's requirements that projects *and* the alternatives to them be assessed in terms of need. To a company that owns a gravel pit where it wants to *dump* garbage, a requirement that appears to mean that the company must consider methods of *reducing* waste and evaluate the suitability of other parcels of land that it does not own makes no sense.

The implementation of the federal EA process has bogged down for different reasons. Although approvals do not involve adversarial hearings and the minister carrying out or regulating the project has broad authority, the process has bogged down because court challenges have overturned several project approvals and raise the risk of overturning an approval at any stage of its implementation.

WHAT IS ENVIRONMENTAL ASSESSMENT?

An environmental impact assessment is a planning process designed to identify and assess the effects that a program, plan, project, or other undertaking might have on the natural and human environment. For an assessment process to be acceptable, the assessment must be used to determine whether the undertaking should proceed and, if so, what steps should be taken to reduce or mitigate the negative impacts.

This planning process usually consists of carrying out a study of the program, plan, or project. The study should be comprehensive. It should identify the direct and indirect costs of an undertaking in terms of such things as environmental degradation, the use of energy and resources, and social and economic disruption, and weigh these costs against the benefits from the undertaking. Its purpose is to discover the problems an undertaking might cause before a final decision is made to go ahead with it.

How much of our dwindling energy, agricultural land, forests, wetlands, and other resources will a policy, plan, or project use up? Will it direct resources away from more innovative and environmentally sound approaches to addressing the problem? Do the advantages outweigh its disadvantages? Who will benefit and who will suffer? Will the beneficiary compensate those who must pay the price of "progress"? Are there better alternatives? Is the project really needed? And if so, what steps can be taken to reduce the negative impacts or distribute them fairly? These are some of the questions an environmental impact assessment can address.

Once completed, the study is required to undergo some form of public scrutiny. Thus, environmental assessment, unlike many traditional planning and decision-making processes, is designed to be an open and public process.

As environmentalists pointed out long before the idea became popular in the concept of sustainable development, a full integration of economic and environmental concerns requires environmental assessment to go beyond considering impacts on the natural environment. It must also evaluate positive and negative impacts on the cultural, economic, and social environment as does the Ontario process. In addition, environmental assessment can also address society's needs — whether society, not just the proponent of the project, needs yet another garbage dump, pulp and paper plant, or car factory, or whether feasible alternatives to the project are more environmentally and socially benign.

To achieve the goal of sustainable development, environmental assessment should not simply focus on individual projects. The overall purpose of environmental assessment is to ensure that environmental concerns are considered throughout the planning process, from a general evaluation of needs and alternative responses to detailed design of the preferred alternative. Environmental assessment may be more effective as a planning tool by scrutinizing not only individual projects but also the larger framework of plans, programs, and policies into which the individual projects fit.

Why Do We Need Environmental Impact Assessments?

Promoters of public works such as airports, roads, pipelines, and power plants and of commercial and industrial enterprises such as factories, mines, and mills usually communicate effectively their advantages, which include jobs, more consumer goods, and faster transportation and communications. These "proponents," as they are called in EA jargon, frequently have a staff and an advertising, promotion, and lobbying budget devoted to extolling the virtues of their product or project. Moreover, these projects are often the product of an overall policy, plan, or program that leads inexorably to the development of this particular kind of project.

However, there is often no similar system in place to analyze the environmental or societal costs or risks involved in these projects or the policies that support them. Equally, groups who may be harmed by these developments, such as neighbourhoods and native bands, seldom have similar resources to study and communicate the costs or negative effects of development. Nor, until the advent of environmental assessment, did such groups have any right to know about intended programs and projects, much less discover and oppose the harm they may cause.

To make a rational, informed decision about development, the benefits of programs, policies, and projects must be weighed against the costs. Usually, it is in the proponent's interest to ensure that the economic benefits of its proposal are carefully examined. However, environmental and social costs are more difficult to quantify, and in the absence of an EA process these costs have rarely been given the same consideration. The indirect or hidden costs that are paid by the public, such as the loss of biodiversity and greenspace, the costs of medical care for victims of air or water pollution, and the emotional stress resulting from the disruption of established social patterns, have generally not been assessed. Equally, the effects contributing to these costs have escaped notice until the plan or project is in operation, so all that can be done is alleviate them where it is possible and live with them where it isn't.

Since it is usually much more expensive to solve an environmental problem than to prevent it, this lack of anticipatory and preventive action is extremely costly to society. Think of the billions of dollars now being spent to clean up contaminated soil and groundwater as a result of past industrial processes and waste disposal practices that were once legal, normal, and acceptable. In addition, the failure to analyze the alternatives to government policies and programs can foreclose more environmentally benign projects in the future, as society becomes "locked in" to technologies and methodologies that harm the environment. For example, in the past, Ontario tried to keep up with ever-increasing demands for electricity by simply expanding nuclear power and coal- or oil-fired electrical generating plants. Full consideration was not given to the alternative of reducing demand through energy conservation. Now, it is difficult to change direction, even though the expansion of these power plants has proved to be costly and polluting.

As is discussed in Chapter 18, traditional environmental legislation was aimed at abating existing pollution and cutting down on environmental degradation by controlling and reducing emissions of contaminants to air, land, and water. This was accomplished in the early years by identifying existing polluting facilities and requiring them — and often subsidizing them — to install pollution equipment.[3] Later, governments decided to adopt a more preventive strategy, by requiring pollution-control equipment to be incorporated into *new* plant design. Nevertheless, such an approach often ignored aspects of environmental concern other than pollution, such as the impacts of production on the sustainability of non-renewable energy and natural resources, or what to do with the waste generated at the end of the production process. Solutions to these pollution concerns were poorly integrated (or not integrated at all) with responses to other concerns, such as land-use planning, energy conservation, and traffic concerns. Moreover, such laws and policies did not question the underlying political and economic assumptions that promoted the continuous development of new facilities and technologies that provide short-term benefits but cause long-term economic and environmental harm.

Environmental assessment encourages pollution prevention, and at the same time shifts from the technological emphasis of pollution control approvals under acts such as the *Environmental Protection Act* to a wider concern for the social, economic, cultural, and environmental implications of development. It also provides those who may suffer from development with an opportunity to bring their knowledge to bear on the decision. Instead of leaving the analysis solely to industrial experts and government bureaucrats and politicians, environmental assessment asks the public about their concerns and gives them a chance to make their own evaluation of the effects of a project. Thus, environmental assessment shifts power away from proponents, bureaucrats, and experts toward the affected public. This loss of authority explains one aspect of the ongoing opposition to environmental assessment.[4]

Environmental assessment may also facilitate a significant change in responsibility for paying the costs of health problems, social disruption, and environmental degradation. As discussed above, projects may cause significant social costs. In the past, these costs have been "externalized"; that is, they have not been borne by the proponent, but by others. One of the questions raised by environmental assessment is, "Who will pay for the adverse effects?" Environmental assessment forces this question to be asked and answered *before* the program or project is approved.[5]

In the end, the effectiveness of an environmental impact assessment depends on whether the goal of the process is merely to assess the impacts, or to ensure protection of the environment. The significance of public involvement, the adequacy of the safeguards to ensure that the ultimate decision is based on the evidence rather than political considerations, the implementation of the project, and the monitoring of its effects may all vary considerably, depending on the goal of the assessment system chosen by the government.

JURISDICTION: THE RELATIONSHIP BETWEEN ONTARIO AND FEDERAL ENVIRONMENTAL ASSESSMENT

Whether the federal government or a province is primarily responsible for carrying out an environmental assessment depends on whether the program or project falls under federal or provincial jurisdiction. For projects carried out by a federal or a provincial government agency or department, the answer is usually simple. The construction of a military base by the federal Department of National Defence would obviously be assessed under federal EA laws; the construction of a coal-fired power plant by Ontario Hydro, a provincial government agency, would be assessed under Ontario's *Environmental Assessment Act*.[6] For most private business activities, environmental control is a provincial responsibility. Therefore, a car maker that is building a factory could be asked to submit to Ontario's EA process. However, a diversion of a navigable river would require federal assessment under federal laws since the regulation of navigation and shipping is solely a federal government responsibility.

The problem becomes more complex when a project impinges on both federal and provincial jurisdiction. A project that is normally within provincial jurisdiction — such as a dam or generating station built by Ontario Hydro — may have impacts on matters within federal jurisdiction, such as fisheries, navigable waters, or nuclear power. In these circumstances, will the project require a federal environmental assessment, a provincial one, or both?

One cannot be sure a project will be considered wholly "provincial" even where the proponent is a provincial government or a provincial Crown corporation.[7] The most significant example of an area of provincial responsibility that has a federal aspect to it is activity involving water resource management such as dam construction, watercourse diversion, dredging, or filling. This activity may require permits or approvals under the *Fisheries Act*[8] or the *Navigable Waters Protection Act*.[9] Businesses conducted largely across provincial or international borders, and facilities located close to federal lands, native reserves, or provincial or international borders, may have potential for transboundary effects. The regulation of such *effects* may largely be the domain of the federal government, and the regulation of the *projects* themselves may be a provincial responsibility.

Because of overlapping jurisdiction over the environment, there is also potential for a project to "fall between the cracks" so that no environmental assessment is done, or for an incomplete assessment to be carried out — one that focuses on concerns regulated by one level of government while largely ignoring aspects of the proposal regulated by the other. The failure of provincial environmental assessments of certain major projects to adequately address environmental concerns was instrumental in several court challenges by environmentalists in the late 1980s and early 1990s.[10] Some of these challenges resulted in the courts ordering the federal government to carry out an additional environmental assessment under federal laws. Indeed, in the *Oldman River* case, the Supreme Court of Canada confirmed that projects will often require assessment under both federal and provincial EA processes.[11]

The question of the scope of the federal EA process and the ability of the federal government to assess projects that might appear to be primarily within provincial jurisdiction became a battleground between the provincial governments and the federal Department of the Environment during consideration of the *Canadian Environmental Assessment Act (CEAA)*,[12] in 1991 and 1992. In fact, even after the Act had been passed in the House of Commons, Progressive Conservative senators from Quebec threatened to break ranks with the rest of their party, and try to block the passage of the Act in the Senate, on the grounds that it infringed on provincial jurisdiction and therefore threatened the autonomy or "sovereignty" of Quebec.

The *Canadian Environmental Assessment Act* contains several provisions to permit its application to projects that appear to be primarily local. For example, a federal environmental assessment may be undertaken where the project relies on any federal funding, or where it requires any federal licence or approval (for example, a permit under the *Navigable Waters Protection Act*).[13] Moreover, in considering the scope of the Act, it may be noted that the environmental assessment process mandated by the EARP guidelines order, which preceded the *Canadian Environmental Assessment Act*, led to courts requiring federal assessments in cases involving irrigation dams in Alberta and Saskatchewan. These court decisions may lead to broad application of the Act to projects under provincial jurisdiction.[14]

An environmental assessment that evaluates only some kinds of impact and not others will not adequately protect the environment. However, an environmental assessment by one level of government that assesses matters within the jurisdiction of the other may be open to attack in the courts because the assessment body is exceeding its jurisdiction. Obviously, the solution to this dilemma is federal-provincial cooperation to ensure that federal and provincial environmental assessments are coordinated. There is no reason in principle why federal and provincial EA processes cannot be jointly administered.[15] In fact, the *Canadian Environmental Assessment Act* makes explicit provision for joint environmental assessments, accommodating several joint formats to address the potential for interprovincial or international impacts, impacts on Indian reserves, and impacts on areas of federal jurisdiction.[16] The Act also contains "equivalency" provisions; that is, the federal government may forgo a federal assessment where the provincial EA process is equivalent to the study that would be carried out federally. Unlike the environmental assessment statutes of some other provinces,[17] the Ontario *Environmental Assessment Act* makes no explicit provision for joint environmental assessments, but the regulation-making powers granted to the Ontario Cabinet appear to be broad enough to allow the government to make regulations exempting a particular project or class of projects from the standard EA process, and negotiating a joint federal-provincial environmental assessment for such undertakings.

In this chapter we will discuss both the federal and provincial environmental impact assessment processes, since both may apply in Ontario. However, since the vast majority of projects that you may encounter will be subject to the Ontario law, we will discuss the Ontario process first.

ONTARIO ENVIRONMENTAL ASSESSMENT

Background to the Ontario EA Process

The Ontario government passed Canada's first environmental impact assessment law, the *Environmental Assessment Act (EAA)*,[18] in July 1975. However, it was not proclaimed in force until October 1976, and even then it had limited application. Although the Act applies to all public sector undertakings unless they are exempted, and to private sector undertakings designated as "major," the Act was initially applied only to undertakings of the Ontario government departments and agencies. Even then, proclamation was accompanied by the publication of 200 pages of orders exempting individual undertakings, such as the Darlington Nuclear Generating Station, and whole classes of significant undertakings, such as all projects by conservation authorities and municipalities.

The first public sector expansion of the Act was to conservation authorities in 1977.[19] Municipal undertakings were made subject to the Act in 1980, following years of successful lobbying by municipalities to delay implementation.[20] Even then, municipal projects budgeted to cost less than $2 million were exempt from assessment,[21] an exemption that has no logical relationship to the amount of harm a project may cause. (This exemption was later increased to $3.5 million[22] to take inflation into account.)

The Act is still rarely applied to the private sector, even though private undertakings are less harmful to the environment than government activities.[23] Despite repeated promises by both the Liberal government and the NDP to extend the Act to the private sector, the only classes of private projects that are subject to the Act are major energy-from-waste undertakings and the establishment or expansion of facilities for landfilling, incineration, processing, or transfer of wastes, where the facility exceeds a certain size. The Act was extended to these projects, whether public or private, in May 1987.[24] Previously, private waste management facilities had been subject only to the *Environmental Protection Act*, under which the matters requiring consideration before approval are much narrower.

The most significant impacts of this increased scope have occurred in solid waste management, where decisions of the Environmental Assessment Board and joint boards on both private and public applications have resulted in improvements in the quality of study and investigation associated with assessment waste disposal sites. Major EA hearings on landfill proposals have occurred in Halton Region, Peel Region, Simcoe County, and Meaford/St. Vincent Township; and in the latter two hearings, the joint board rejected the environmental assessments as inadequate and refused to approve the undertakings.[25]

In addition to waste facilities, a few other high-profile private projects have been individually designated for assessment. These include a power dam proposed by Inco on the

Spanish River and a paper mill proposed by Reed Pulp and Paper at Ear Falls, in northwestern Ontario.

To What and Whom Does the Act Apply?

The *Environmental Assessment Act* does not apply only to "projects," which would limit its ambit to physical structures and their operation, but also to "enterprises," "activities," "programs," "proposals," and "plans," all of which are defined as "undertakings" under the Act.[26] Thus, the Act can potentially apply not just to "things" but also to concepts or ideas. The Act defines the "environment" very broadly to include not only the natural environment but also cultural, economic, and social factors. Thus, the Act potentially applies to a wide variety of planning processes. As some of the Act's detractors have jokingly said, environment as defined in the *Environmental Assessment Act* means "the universe as we know it, and everything in it."

The persons whose undertakings are subject to assessment include the Ontario government and its departments, all "public bodies," and municipalities. Public body is defined to mean any public body other than a municipality that is so defined in the regulations. These regulations have designated as "public bodies," among others, Ontario Hydro, the Toronto Area Transit Operating Authority, and all colleges, universities, and conservation authorities.[27] For the purposes of the Act, municipalities are broadly defined to include counties, regions, and districts, as well as local boards (which includes a variety of municipal agencies such as school boards). Other municipal agencies such as the Toronto Transit Commission are also included.[28]

In addition, the Act applies to any *major* business or commercial undertakings that are designated by regulation, and to *any* private activity, whether "major" or not, if it is carried out on behalf of the Ontario government. Exactly when an activity is "on behalf of" the government or is "major" is unclear. If the government were to apply the Act fully to the private sector, there would undoubtedly be grey areas, in which proponents of projects subject to the Act would use the courts to challenge the designation of their projects on the grounds that they are not "major" or that the activities are not being carried out "on behalf of" the government. This would lead to judicial interpretation of what these terms mean. However, this has not been an issue, since the Act has rarely been applied to private projects, and then only to a few that clearly would have severe effects on the environment.

Exemptions

When the Ontario government first proposed an environmental impact assessment process, it envisioned an amendment to the *Environmental Protection Act* that would authorize the government, in its absolute discretion, to designate individual projects that it considered significant. Environmentalists feared — with justification, as it turns out — that such a process would result in the vast majority of harmful projects escaping assessment. Led by the Canadian Environmental Law Association (CELA), public pressure caused the government to reverse its earlier position and enact a statute that required *all* public sector projects to be assessed. A more logical approach would have been a statute such as the US *National Environmental Policy Act*, specifying that undertakings having *significant* environmental impact would be subject to assessment; but looking at the successful efforts made in the courts by US environmentalists to litigate the meaning of "significant," the Ontario government tried to avoid using terms that would allow the courts to fetter its discretion to avoid assessments. Instead, the government made the *Environmental Assessment Act* apply to the entire public sector, but included a provision allowing it to exempt any undertaking, without any criteria for deciding which undertakings should be exempted.[29]

Obviously, such a provision was subject to abuse, and potentially undermined the purpose of the Act. In response to this concern, the premier appointed a steering committee, reporting directly to him, to scrutinize the development of the regulations through which the Act would be implemented. The Environmental Assessment Act Steering Committee was composed of the chair and vice-chair of the Environmental Assessment Board and a representative of the concerned public, Dr. Donald Chant, who was at that time the chairman of the Pollution Probe Foundation.[30]

One of the committee's main functions was to back up the former Ministry of the Environment (now the Ministry of Environment and Energy) when it ran into trouble with other ministries that would be affected by the Act — many of which were determined to avoid having their programs and projects undergo environmental assessment, and which resented the new power their sister ministry had over them.

In response to lobbying by CELA, the government continued the existence of the steering committee as a "watchdog" over exemptions of public projects and the requests from the public to designate significant private projects.[31] Soon, however, the committee lost all its members, leaving no mechanism to ensure effective implementation of the Act. First, the chair and vice-chair of the committee recognized that their participation represented a potential conflict of interest and resigned from the committee, leaving Dr. Chant as a one-person committee. Environmentalists and members of the public continued to bring their concerns to him, and he was successful on occasion in persuading the government to apply the Act to projects that were about to escape assessment. However, when Dr. Chant also resigned as a result of a conflict of interest arising from his chairmanship of Pollution Probe, he was not replaced.

It took two years of lobbying by the Conservation Council of Ontario and other environmental groups before the government formed another group to carry out similar functions. In 1983, the government appointed the Environmental Assessment Advisory Committee (EAAC), consisting of three members from outside government, to advise the Minister of the Environment on matters such as exemptions and designation requests, EA procedures, and any other matter relating to environmental assessment about which the minister seeks the committee's advice.

EAAC has proven time and time again to be a useful watchdog, notifying the public of cases it is considering, consulting the public, and even holding informal public hearings into requests for designation of projects and removal of exemptions. The committee has often put forward useful compromises or well-reasoned recommendations for partial or full environmental assessment. However, its effectiveness is hampered by the fact that EAAC can review a case only on the request of the minister. Thus, individuals or groups cannot directly request the EAAC to look into an exemption or refusal of the government to apply the Act. They must go through the minister, who, on the advice of the ministry's Environmental Assessment Branch, often refuses to refer these requests to the Committee. Moreover, although EAAC makes its reports and recommendations available to the public, it may not do so until the minister makes a decision on the case. Thus, public access to EAAC's recommendations may be delayed for months, or even years, after it submits its report to the minister.

What Does an Adequate Environmental Assessment Consist of?

Section 5 of the *Environmental Assessment Act* sets out the minimum contents of an environmental assessment:

5(3) An environmental assessment ... shall consist of,

(a) a description of the purpose of the undertaking;

(b) a description of and a statement of the rationale for,

(i) the undertaking,

(ii) the alternative methods of carrying out the undertaking, and

(iii) the alternatives to the undertaking;

(c) a description of,

(i) the environment that will be affected or that might reasonably be expected to be affected, directly or indirectly,

(ii) the effects that will be caused or that might reasonably be expected to be caused to the environment, and

(iii) the actions necessary or that may reasonably be expected to be necessary to prevent, change, mitigate or remedy the effects upon or the effects that might reasonably be expected upon the environment, by the undertaking, the alternative methods of carrying out the undertaking and the alternatives to the undertaking; and

(d) an evaluation of the advantages and disadvantages to the environment of the undertaking, the alternative methods of carrying out the undertaking and the alternatives to the undertaking.

It has been suggested that implicit in these explicit requirements is a further requirement — that the environmental assessment address the *need* for the undertaking. This requirement flows from the need to assess advantages and disadvantages of undertakings and their alternatives, and from the requirement to assess alternatives. One alternative that must always be assessed, for example, is the "do-nothing" or "null" alternative. To address the issue whether it is necessary to carry out the undertaking at all, one must address the need for such an undertaking.[32]

Regulations have also expanded or elaborated on the requirements for documentation. Under the regulations, the environmental assessment must include a summary of the assessment, a list of studies and reports done in connection with the assessment, whether or not these documents are in the proponent's possession, and a map of the proposed location.[33]

In the light of the broad definition of environment in the Act and the lengthy list of matters that must be considered in an environmental assessment, it is not surprising that proponents have expressed frustration with the EA process. A proponent may carry out an environmental impact study, only to be told by the minister or the Environmental Assessment Board that it did not study a sufficient number of alternatives to its undertaking, or did not study certain alternative sites in sufficient depth or give them enough importance even though the proponent may not have any practical ability to implementing alternative other than the one it proposes. This is particularly a problem for private sector proponents, who may own a specific parcel of land, carry on a specific kind of business, and propose to carry on that business at that location. Why should they assess alternative sites if they have no power to expropriate other land? Why should they examine alternative processes or facilities if they have no desire to conduct a different business?

The breadth of the Act's requirements can make it difficult even to determine what is the undertaking. The Act states that an undertaking may encompass more than one activity, as long as there is a common element to the activities grouped together.[34] This can assist the proponent, but it can also add to the confusion, since the minister or the board can overrule the proponent, and determine that the undertaking is actually something other than the proponent decided. Under the Act, the proponent defines the undertaking and its purpose and thus the range of relevant alternatives; nevertheless, the Environmental Assessment Board has held that proponents are subject to some limitations of reasonableness in defining the undertaking.[35] Thus, a proponent that describes its undertaking in a way that unduly limits public discussion of reasonable alternatives or inhibits good overall planning, may find that it faces difficulties in obtaining the cooperation of the staff of the Environmental Assessment Branch and the board.

It is particularly important to determine the scope of the undertaking because this will influence many other decisions during the course of the environmental impact study. For example, the scope of the undertaking will determine the "study area" (the geographic area throughout which alternative sites must be systematically studied and evaluated), which in turn will determine the area in which people could be affected by the project or its alternatives. This in turn will determine how many communities the proponent must notify and involve in each stage of the planning process.[36]

Similarly, in an area of the province where there is a shortage of waste disposal capacity, the proponent may describe its proposed undertaking as a landfill site, a waste disposal facility, or a waste management facility. Since each of these terms can encompass a different range of facilities, which term is used can be very significant. If the undertaking is described in terms of a landfill site, it could be described as merely locating a landfill, or as locating, designing, constructing, operating, and closing a landfill. Alternatively, instead of describing the undertaking in terms of facilities, the proponent could describe it as a plan or program for waste management for the area.

Similarly, if Ontario Hydro wants to transmit power from a generating station in one part of the province to communities in another part of the province, its "undertaking" might be narrowly described as the construction of a specific power line of a specific size through a specific corridor; alternatively, the undertaking may be described more broadly as a plan or program for serving the electricity supply needs of a part of the province.

Alternatives and Alternative Methods

Ministry guidelines, board decisions, and decisions of the courts have gradually reduced the uncertainty surrounding the scope and depth of study required by the Act for alternatives to the undertaking and alternative methods of carrying out the undertaking. The proponent must present a "reasonable" range of alternatives to the undertaking that are "both practical and feasible."[37] It has been suggested that the alternatives studied may be limited to "functional alternatives."[38] For example, where the undertaking is a landfill site, the Ministry of Environment and Energy has stated that functional alternatives that must be considered include reduction, re-use, and recycling.[39] Thus, the ministry requires study of exact alternatives, as well as approximate alternatives. For example, for waste disposal, none of the three alternatives mentioned above can wholly replace the function of a landfill; each of them simply reduces the amount of waste requiring disposal in a landfill. Yet a proponent proposing a landfill would still be expected to study the feasibility of implementing 3R programs to achieve acceptance of the environmental assessment. In addition, as mentioned above, proponents are always expected to address the "do-nothing" alternative, since this establishes the extent of the need for the undertaking.

In considering proposed alternative *methods* of carrying out the undertaking, proponents have been expected to address the questions "how," "what," and "where," although specific legislation and policies or the nature of the undertaking itself may expand or restrict the scope of this analysis. For example, the *Waste Management Act* (1992)[40] relieved the proponent of a waste management facility to serve the Greater Toronto Area (GTA) from the need to consider alternative locations beyond the borders of the GTA. Similarly, Ontario Hydro's environmental assessment of its 25-year plan for regulating supply and demand for electricity, submitted to the Environmental Assessment Board in 1989, did not address location of facilities. The location of facilities was to be dealt with by individual assessments once the 25-year plan was finalized.[41]

The following is a rough guide for considering the role that each aspect of the issue of alternative methods plays in an environmental assessment:

1. *How: Alternative technologies or activities.* Technology, in the preparation of environmental assessments, may be generic or specific. The analysis of alternative technologies will sometimes involve the comparison of general approaches, and other times the comparison of specific types of equipment. An examination of general alternative technologies or activities may encompass the same alternatives as "functional alternatives." For example, in a waste disposal case, a consideration of alternatives to a landfill may include a discussion of centralized and local composting facilities, source separation, sorting facilities, recycling ventures, and disposal facilities such as landfill and incinerators. On the other hand, discussion may be focused on alternative kinds of incineration technologies, as it was in the board's hearing on the environmental assessment for the Peel energy-from-waste incinerator.[42] Technologies that fit into this category of assessment are often ones whose potential impacts require site-specific testing and evaluation.

2. *What: Alternative designs.* A proponent may also consider alternative designs for the undertaking. In the waste management example, the assessment of alternative designs might involve, for example, deciding whether the preferred approach requires one site or many. Should there be one landfill or two? It may also involve linking facilities. For example, should a waste composting site be located within a landfill? This step should also identify the amount of land required for the undertaking.

3. *Where: Alternative locations.* Several decisions of joint boards and the Environmental Assessment Board have laid out general principles governing how the location of facilities is to be assessed.[43] In assessing waste management facilities, an alternative

location is considered to mean an alternative site. In relation to energy transmission, an alternative location means an alternative transmission line route. In either case, the evaluation of alternative locations should move from the general to the specific. The process for identifying the preferred location for an undertaking typically involves a sophisticated process of narrowing down the options. This process has at least three steps:

- step 1: eliminate areas having unacceptable qualities for locating the undertaking;
- step 2: identify locations from the remaining areas that would be acceptable for the undertaking; and
- step 3: compare the advantages and disadvantages of identified locations to select the preferred location.

Preserving the Integrity of the Environmental Assessment Process

The purpose of the EA process is to ensure that decisions are made following a rational and objective planning process. The EA process should make visible, and hopefully limit, purely political considerations that interfere with such a process. To ensure that the EA process fulfils this function, the courts and boards have rejected environmental assessments for following improper processes,[44] and in one case refused to approve an undertaking that appeared to be marginally acceptable using established criteria of acceptability, because the assessment process was tainted.[45] The boards have insisted that proponents establish criteria for acceptability of their undertaking at the beginning of the study process, and follow these criteria in good faith in coming to their final conclusions on the advantages and disadvantages of the project.

The ministry and the boards have said that to be acceptable, an environmental assessment must be rational, consistent, traceable, reproducible, and fair.[46] These requirements mean that the environmental assessment must show continuity in the development of the assessment process; provide sufficient information for any member of the public to trace the decision-making process; show rational decision making at each stage of the process; and show an open process — that is, a process without a predetermined result.[47] To satisfy this last requirement, proponents may be expected to follow three steps: devise the methodology and criteria before beginning the study; gather data in accordance with the methodology and criteria; and assess alternatives using the proposed methodology and criteria. All three steps should receive scrutiny from the public and from commenting and regulatory agencies.

When Must an Assessment of an Undertaking Be Done?

In the past, developers have often tried to build first and seek approval later, gambling that they would not be prosecuted for violating the law and that regulators would feel compelled to issue an after-the-fact approval rather than leave perpetual evidence of their failure to enforce the law.[48] Another approach to development that traditionally put government agencies under pressure to issue approvals was the "shopping bag" approach to obtaining approvals. A developer would obtain approvals from as many agencies as possible, and then, with its "bagful" of approvals, would demonstrate to the last "holdout" agency that the project must be sound, because everyone else had issued an approval. In addition, before the formal EA process under the *Environmental Assessment Act*, many environmental studies were carried out only as a result of a public outcry. This meant that the study was done after months or years of planning and after much money had been spent on the project, and everyone but the people affected by it had decided the project should go ahead. Under such circumstances, the possibility of an objective and fair assessment of the project was greatly reduced. As a newspaper editorial said of one such belated environmental study: "When minds close, inquiry is futile."[49]

The *Environmental Assessment Act* contains provisions intended to prevent this approach to environmental assessment. With the exception of feasibility studies,[50] the Act prohibits the proponent from taking any steps toward implementation of the project before approval has been granted, including purchasing land for the project.[51] No municipal or provincial government agency may issue any licence or grant any approval, and no provincial agency may make a loan, a loan guarantee, a grant, or a subsidy to an undertaking subject to the Act until approval has been issued.[52]

The Act also allows the Minister of the Environment and Energy to apply to the Divisional Court for an order enjoining anyone from proceeding with an undertaking without carrying out an environmental assessment or for an order invalidating any licence, permit, or approval issued by any agency contrary to the Act.

Moreover, it is an offence to proceed with an undertaking without first obtaining the approval of the Environmental Assessment Board or the minister, or without complying with any terms and conditions imposed on approval. As a matter of interest, the only prosecution ever undertaken for evasion of the environmental assessment process was a prosecution of Ontario's minister and deputy minister of transport, undertaken by environmentalists. These officials had proceeded with construction of a provincial highway without carrying out an environmental assessment as required by the Act.[53]

How Is an Ontario Environmental Assessment Administered?

In this section, we briefly describe the process a proponent must follow under the Act and under the guidelines and practices that have evolved over the years, once it has been determined that the *Environmental Assessment Act* applies to an undertaking. In summary, if an undertaking is subject to the Act, its proponent must prepare an assessment of its potential environmental impact, and submit this assessment to the Ministry of Environment and Energy. This assessment is in addition to the requirements of any other laws, such as obtaining the approval of a municipality if a zoning change is needed or a municipal business licence is required. The minister must then make two decisions: whether to accept the assessment document and whether to approve the project.

When an assessment is received the minister will have ministry staff and other relevant government agencies review it.[54] The ministry's Environmental Assessment Branch is responsible for circulating the document to other agencies for their comments. In practice, the review has three stages. First, the Environmental Assessment Branch will obtain comments from other branches within the ministry that are responsible for concerns about the natural environment, such as potential air and water pollution, noise, and vibration. Second, the Environmental Assessment Branch will seek the comments of other public agencies. The comments received are coordinated by the branch into an overall government review of the assessment. Third, at the end of this review, the Environmental Assessment Branch will comment on whether the environmental assessment contains the components required by section 5(3) of the Act. In the eyes of the branch, merely addressing each of the issues covered by section 5(3) will not constitute compliance. If need, alternatives, impacts, etc. are addressed, but not in sufficient detail or quality of study to satisfy the review agencies, this may lead the branch to make a finding that the environmental assessment does not meet the requirements of section 5(3).[55]

Once this government review has been done, the Act requires the ministry to notify the public and tell them where the environmental assessment, the government review, and any supporting documents may be inspected — usually at the offices of the ministry and at the municipal offices of the area where the undertaking would be carried out.

In practice, interested members of the public have often been provided with the draft EA documents throughout the planning process and interested people are sometimes sent a copy of the EA document when it is submitted to the Environmental Assessment Branch for review. Once the public notice has been issued on completion of the government review, for a minimum of 30 days, or longer if the ministry decides this is required and specifies a longer comment period in the notice, the minister will consider written submissions from the public. Then the minister will notify the proponent and anyone who made written submissions that he or she intends to accept the assessment; or, if ministry staff are not satisfied that the assessment complies with the requirements of the Act, that he or she intends to amend it. The minister does not appear to have the power to reject an assessment if it continues to be inadequate.[56] The minister can only order the proponent to do further studies.[57]

Any person who makes a written submission can request a public hearing on the adequacy of the assessment document and also on whether the undertaking should be approved. The proponent can also request a public hearing to challenge a decision by the minister that the assessment is inadequate. In either case, the minister must then order a hearing unless he or she considers the request to be frivolous or vexatious, or believes a hearing is unnecessary or may cause undue delay in carrying out the undertaking.[58]

If no one requests a hearing or the minister refuses a request for a hearing, the ministry will then notify the proponent and anyone who has made written submissions or requested a hearing that the minister has accepted the assessment or that he or she intends to amend it before acceptance.

The second decision is project approval. Any person can request a hearing before the Environmental Assessment Board on project approval as well as document acceptance. Following such a request, the minister will decide whether to order a public hearing or approve the undertaking, with or without conditions of approval, on the same grounds as the decision on document acceptance.

The way the Act is written, it appears as though there could be two separate public hearings — one on document acceptance and one on whether to approve the undertaking itself in the light of its potential impacts. In practice, both decisions are made together and dealt with in a single public hearing. The boards and ministry staff have struggled with how to coordinate these different aspects of the process. Obviously, an EA documént may be acceptable in the sense that it covers all the topics required by the Act, such as need and alternatives, but the quality of the study may be inadequate in the ministry's view. Should the ministry then accept the assessment document but turn down the undertaking? Or should the assessment document itself be rejected? Similarly, the minister or the boards may find that the undertaking appears

Three Routes to Decision

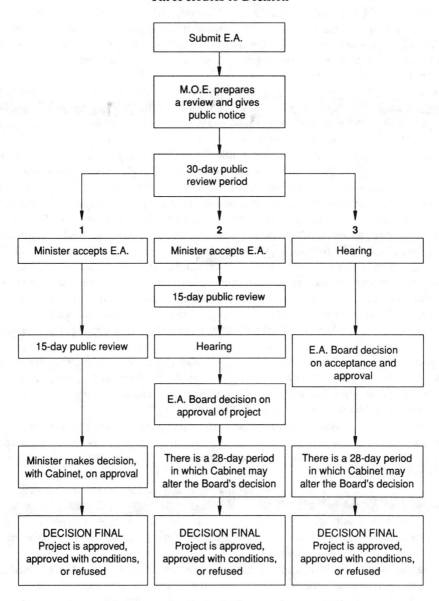

Note: E.A. refers to Environmental Assessment
M.O.E. refers to Ministry of the Environment

Courtesy of the Ontario Ministry of the Environment, *A Proponent's Guide to the Environmental Assessment Act.*

to be acceptable even though the study was flawed. Should an otherwise marginally acceptable project be approved even though the assessment process was seriously flawed, or should this be enough to justify turning down the project? The boards have ruled that under these circumstances they can not only reject the assessment, but turn down the project as well.[59]

A hearing on document acceptance or project approval will be held before the Environmental Assessment Board; however, if the consideration of the project involves more than one hearing because of approval requirements under other statutes such as the *Planning Act*[60] or *Environmental Protection Act*,[61] a joint board composed of members of the Environmental Assessment Board and the Ontario Municipal Board will hold the hearing and make a binding decision. (The role of the joint board is discussed further below, under the heading "The Consolidated Hearings Act.") At the hearing, either board must follow the procedures set out in the *Statutory Powers Procedure Act*[62] (see Chapter 4). The Environmental Assessment Board has also developed a set of rules governing its practice and procedure, which have been promulgated as a regulation under the *Environmental Assessment Act*.[63] To assist the public in appearing before it,[64] the board has published a *Citizens' Guide*. The procedures followed by the board in holding a hearing under the *Environmental Assessment Act* are substantially the same as those it follows in waste management hearings under the *Environmental Protection Act*. These procedures and how the public can participate are described in more detail in Chapter 24.

The board must give notice of its hearing to the proponent, the minister, any person who made a written submission to the minister, and the public. Hearings are generally open to the public.[65]

After the hearing, the board will make two decisions. It may accept or amend an assessment. It may also give unqualified approval to the undertaking, approve it subject to terms and conditions, or reject it. Where a board appears likely to accept an environmental assessment, much hearing time may still be required to consider appropriate terms and conditions of approval to prevent and mitigate adverse impacts of projects. Parties are often required to draft conditions they would like to see imposed if approval is granted, and to circulate these conditions to other parties for discussion. Outside the hearing room there may be considerable negotiation among the parties in an attempt to reach agreement on suitable terms and conditions to assist the board in making its decision. The Environmental Assessment Board has ruled that even if the ministry and the proponent reach a settlement and agree on approval of an undertaking, the board still has the power to review this arrangement to ensure that it is in the public interest. That is, the board can override the settlement if it feels the environment is not adequately protected or the arrangement does not deal adequately with the concerns of other parties to the hearing.[66]

Within 28 days of receiving the board's decision, the minister may still vary it, reject it, substitute his or her own decision, or require the board to hold another hearing and reconsider its decision;[67] however, the minister may not intervene in this way without the approval of Cabinet. Questions of legal jurisdiction may be dealt with by the courts, but otherwise the Act prohibits anyone from using the courts to question or review any of the decisions or rulings of the board. There is no such restriction on the right of the courts to review the ministry's actions; however, in most matters the minister's discretion is almost limitless, so ministry actions are often immune from successful review.

The Assessment Process in Practice

The brief overview above summarizes the main provisions of the *Environmental Assessment Act*. However, the actual administration of the process has evolved over the years, and many additional practices have been developed to streamline and clarify the process and enhance public involvement. Some of these developments include the invention and use of the "class assessment," the "environmental assessment design document" and "pre-submission consultation," and the passage of the *Consolidated Hearings Act*[68] and the *Intervenor Funding Project Act*.[69] These developments are discussed below.

Class Assessments

From 1972, when Premier William Davis first announced his intention to consider an EA process for Ontario, until 1975, when the *Environmental Assessment Act* was finally passed, everyone involved in the discussion treated the process as if it would require an individual environmental assessment for each environmentally significant undertaking. The Act made no mention of "class assessments,"[70] and it came as a surprise to everyone concerned when the ministry, with little or no public discussion, soon began to substitute "generic" assessments of whole classes of undertakings for assessments of individual undertakings.

Ministry guidelines authorize a proponent to carry out an assessment of an entire class of undertakings where the activity in question occurs frequently, has a predictable range of effects, and is likely to have only minor impacts on the environment.[71] Where the government feels that a class of undertakings meets these requirements, it may authorize an agency that frequently carries out this kind of undertaking to carry out a generic assessment of the impacts of the entire class of projects.

Because a class assessment is an environmental assessment, it must comply with all the requirements of the Act, just like an individual assessment. Thus, like an individual assessment, the class assessment must consider the need for the entire class of undertakings, alternatives to this kind of undertaking, alternative ways of carrying out this kind of undertaking, potential negative impacts, and ways of preventing or mitigating such impacts. In addition, the assessment is subject to government review and public comments, and any person who is dissatisfied with the quality of the assessment can require an Environmental Assessment Board hearing on whether the minister should accept the class assessment. In fact, one such hearing, to determine whether the minister should approve the timber management plan of the Ministry of Natural Resources (MNR) for administering logging on all Crown lands in Ontario, has been underway for about four years. As a result of extensive participation by other government agencies, the forest industry, native groups, and environmentalists, the hearing process has resulted in numerous improvements to how MNR intends to administer public forests. For example, the cross-examination of MNR's officials and experts and evidence led by those who felt the plan was inadequate has led MNR to make many beneficial modifications to its plan.

The use of a class environmental assessment provides for streamlined planning and approval of individual projects within the class. Once the government has approved the class environmental assessment, Cabinet will generally make a regulation exempting all individual projects from compliance with the full EA process, and requiring instead that the approved procedures to prevent or mitigate damage to the environment and procedures for public consultation found in the class environmental assessment be followed when each individual project is carried out.

Perhaps the chief concern of environmentalists about the substitution of class environmental assessments for individual ones is that every undertaking is different, and generalized environmental protection measures that are adequate in one case may be completely inadequate in others. Generally, proponents carrying out class environmental assessments have recognized this concern by further grouping undertakings into subclasses, according to their potential for causing adverse environmental effects. Each of these subclasses of undertaking will require a specific degree of individual assessment and specific kinds of mitigation measures tailored to the kind and degree of environmental impact to be expected from that kind of project.

For example, for two of the most important class environmental assessments carried out by municipalities, those covering roads and sewage and water works, there is a common classification scheme:

- Small undertakings that raise *no environmental concerns*, or that are subject to sufficient environmental review through other processes outside the environmental assessment process, are listed as "pre-approved." They will require no further environmental assessment, and no study of their effects or documentation of their design and implementation is required.

- For projects identified in the class environmental assessment as having *minimal potential for adverse impacts*, an "environmental screening" will be required for each individual project. This screening consists of the proponent describing the expected effects of the project, evaluating the advantages and disadvantages of each alternative, and providing public notice and opportunity for public comment, including comment by other public agencies. The proponent must then assess each option and select the preferred option.

- Projects with *more significant impacts*, as defined in the class assessment, are subject to a requirement to carry out "environmental study reports" (ESRs). This includes the environmental screening process described above, but also includes several additional steps, such as describing alternative designs for the undertaking, detailing potential environmental impacts, and determining whether further assessment is necessary. Unlike the undertakings subject only to environmental screening, this process must result in documentation of all the findings of the study in a formal ESR.

- Finally, the class environmental assessment provides for circumstances in which a full individual environmental assessment under the *Environmental Assessment Act* will be required in addition to the class environmental assessment. For example, the municipal road and sewage and water class environmental assessments provide for a "bump-up" to a full environmental assessment where the project may have severe environmental effects or significant public controversy surrounds the project.

Therefore, the class EA process provides for the possibility that each level of undertaking may be "bumped up" to a higher level of study within the range of subclasses if the scrutiny shows this is necessary. For example, if the environmental screening of a project thought to have minimal adverse impact reveals that the impacts may be substantial, this project may be "bumped up" to the third category, where it will receive more intensive evaluation. If this evaluation in turn reveals even greater potential for harm, any concerned member of the public may petition the minister of the environment to designate the project as subject to the full requirements of the *Environmental Assessment Act*, including a hearing before the Environmental Assessment Board. At least, this is the theory; in practice, "bump-ups" to the full EA process are rarely granted. However, in several cases, the minister has asked the Environmental Assessment Advisory Committee to review requests for bump-ups. In cases where EAAC has recommended a bump-up, the minister has followed its recommendation.[72]

Monitoring the Undertaking

One of the concerns often expressed by environmentalists is the lack of requirements in the *Environmental Assessment Act* for monitoring of the impacts of projects approved by the minister once they are under way. If a proposal comes before the board, monitoring requirements are frequently made conditions of approval. However, if the minister approves an undertaking without a hearing, there may be no monitoring program. One potential advantage of class environmental assessments is the opportunity they provide for including in the assessment a program for monitoring undertakings following approval.

However, the class EA process does not require monitoring, even though monitoring is particularly important in relation to projects that have not had a full assessment. Monitoring is the only way to determine whether the assumption on which the class EA system is based — that such projects have minimal impact — is sound. At present, several class environmental assessments require monitoring only where an ESR has been required.[73] The task force studying improvements to the EA process has recommended that monitoring be required for all future class environmental assessments.[74]

The Consolidated Hearings Act

Another innovation that has substantially changed the environmental assessment process was the passage of a statute designed to streamline the approval process by consolidating two or more hearings. The *Consolidated Hearings Act* creates a new tribunal, the joint board, consisting of members of both the Environmental Assessment Board and the Ontario Municipal Board. The intention of the Act is to "eliminate a multiplicity of hearings before different tribunals concerning matters relating to the same application."[75]

In many instances, undertakings that are subject to the *Environmental Assessment Act* also require hearings by other tribunals before other agencies grant needed approvals. For example, a waste disposal site may require hearings by the Environmental Assessment Board and the Ontario Municipal Board under the *Environmental Protection Act*, the *Ontario Water Resources Act*,[76] the *Planning Act*,[77] the *Municipal Act*,[78] and the *Expropriations Act*,[79] as well as the hearing by the Environmental Assessment Board under the *Environmental Assessment Act*. To reduce the time and expense involved in multiple hearings, the proponent (but no one else involved in the environmental assessment process)[80] may require that a joint board be set up. The joint board may consider all the matters dealt with in 12 statutes listed in a schedule to the Act, and may issue all the approvals that can be granted after hearings by other tribunals under those statutes. In addition, Cabinet can make regulations to have approvals required under other statutes heard by a joint board. For example, when Metro Toronto was undergoing assessment of certain aspects of its landfill site in Maple, involving rezoning, it became apparent that in addition to any other approvals, Metro would need a licence under the *Aggregate Resources Act*[81] to operate a clay pit to supply clay to the landfill site. Accordingly, a regulation was made giving the joint board jurisdiction to decide whether to issue this licence.[82]

In practice, joint hearings under the *Consolidated Hearings Act* have become more common than hearings under the *Environmental Assessment Act* alone. Nevertheless, this streamlining mechanism has done little to mute the continuing opposition of proponents to the EA process, on the grounds of duplication and cost. Nor has it satisfied the concerns of environmentalists and others that there is a continuing lack of coordination between environmental assessment and the land-use planning process, and that environmental considerations are still often ignored in approvals under the *Planning Act* and other government approval processes. (See Chapter 8 for further discussion.)

Financing Public Participation in the Environmental Assessment Process

One of the earliest concerns about the effectiveness of the process under the *Environmental Assessment Act* was the lack of funding to assist ordinary people in understanding and evaluating the complex scientific and planning studies submitted by proponents, and in hiring experts and lawyers to represent their interests.[83]

The complexity of the EA process can easily overwhelm part-time or casual participants. Effective opposition to an undertaking often requires access to expertise and legal representation, which requires financial resources beyond the means of most individuals, community groups, and environmental organizations. Public funding is necessary for a fair and effective process. Where used, public funding and public participation have been shown to significantly improve the quality of the EA process.[84]

The battle for intervenor funding in Ontario was led by two tribunals dealing with environmental issues, the Environmental Assessment Board and the Ontario Energy Board. In the absence of any explicit power to grant intervenor funding, these boards interpreted their power to award "costs" (see Chapter 3) as authorizing them to award costs in advance of a hearing, instead of at the end, when these costs are usually awarded.[85] Thus, the boards ordered the proponents of projects to fund their citizen-group opponents by ordering the proponents to pay "costs" to these groups in advance. However, the courts refused to stretch the normal meaning of costs to include advance funding, and struck down these orders.[86]

In 1984, a coalition of environmental groups submitted a brief to then Environment Minister Andrew Brandt, making the case for intervenor funding.[87] Brandt agreed, and the Ontario government responded to the problem by issuing orders-in-council authorizing intervenor funding on a hearing-by-hearing basis.[88] In 1988, the government took a large step toward permanent acceptance of intervenor funding by passing the *Intervenor Funding Project Act*[89] to provide funding to public interest intervenors at three boards: the joint board, the Environmental Assessment Board, and the Ontario Energy Board.[90]

As its name suggests, this "project" was to be an experiment, which would end in three years. At that time, the Act would expire and the government would decide whether to continue intervenor funding and, if so, whether to expand it to other tribunals. Despite its status as a pilot project, the government established no criteria for evaluating its success, and made no ongoing efforts to collect statistics or otherwise monitor the process on an ongoing basis. When the time came for the Act to expire, the government hurriedly commissioned a few studies of its effectiveness. Unfortunately for the cause of intervenor funding, the Act expired in the midst of one of the worst economic recessions since the Great Depression. In 1991, a time of massive cutbacks in government spending, there was no possibility of an extension of intervenor funding to citizens appearing before other tribunals. Nevertheless, although many social programs were threatened, the government extended the Act for a further four years.

Under the *Intervenor Funding Project Act*, once an application for intervenor funding is submitted to the tribunal holding the hearing, a funding panel is set up, consisting of members of that tribunal who will not participate in the hearing itself.[91] To qualify for funding under the Act, intervenors must show that the issues they intend to address at the hearing affect a significant segment of the public and affect the public interest, and not just private interests.[92] If the proposed intervention meets these threshold criteria, the funding panel must consider whether the application meets several other criteria. These criteria include:

- whether the intervenor represents a clearly ascertainable interest that should be represented at the hearing;
- whether the intervention would assist the board and contribute substantially to the hearing;
- whether the intervenor could afford to represent the interest adequately without funding and whether it has made reasonable efforts to raise funds from other sources;
- whether the intervenor has a record of concern and interest in the issue;
- whether efforts have been made to form an umbrella group to deal with the issues the intervenor intends to address; and
- whether the intervenor has a clear proposal for the use of the funds and appropriate financial controls to prevent misuse of the funds.[93]

Given these criteria, considerable care must be taken in filling out funding applications to ensure that each of these considerations is addressed. To assist applicants for funding and to ensure that successful applicants use the funds for their intended purpose and account for their expenditures, the Environmental Assessment Board and the joint board have published a set of rules of practice and procedure governing intervenor funding hearings,[94] as well as an application form designed to ensure that applicants address the criteria set out in the statute, and a set of general principles for the submission of claims.[95] This material is available from the Environmental Assessment Board.

The Act does not require all the funding to come from the public purse. Under the Act, the proponent of the undertaking, or any other party to the hearing who stands to substantially benefit financially from approval of the project, can be named by the funding panel as a "funding proponent." This means that such a proponent can be required to repay to the government some of the funding granted to intervenors. The proponent can also be required, through a costs award at the end of the hearing, to "top up" the amounts granted from the public purse, to give the intervenors more resources.

The *Intervenor Funding Project Act* has played a significant role in opening up the EA process and improving the quality of citizen participation. From the time it was proclaimed until December 15, 1991, $25 million was awarded to 71 intervenors in 22 cases.[96] The Act, however, requires improvement. Some of the problems that have been identified include the lack of funding for appearances before other environmental tribunals such as the Ontario Municipal Board[97] and the Environmental Appeal Board, the perception of some parties that they have been forced into uncomfortable alliances with other intervenors who did not share their interests, the need for a more flexible funding process for aboriginal groups, lack of coverage of some legitimate expenses, the need for clarification of the extent to which groups must meet each of the eligibility criteria before they can get funding, the need to adapt a staged approach to funding, and the need for better financial controls to monitor the spending of intervenors.[98]

Even more significantly, there is no provision in the environmental assessment process for funding in the early stages of the assessment process. Studies of the effectiveness of the environmental assessment process[99] and of the *Intervenor Funding Project Act* have identified a need for what is being called "participant funding" — that is, funding of participation not only at the hearing stage but also early in the environmental assessment process.[100] In addition, the Interim Waste Authority, set up by the provincial government to find and construct several waste disposal facilities in the Greater Toronto Area, granted a form of participant funding as part of its environmental assessment process in August 1992. The funding was to be given to three "technical committees" made up of members of the public to retain independent experts to audit the authority's technical studies.

In its press release announcing this process, the Interim Waste Authority said: "Participant funding is a new approach to encouraging public participation and the IWA is one of the first proponents in Ontario to offer it. We see it as a benefit to both the public and the IWA. It will give the public an independent perspective on the search process and it will give us a second, expert opinion on the data we gather."[101]

THE ROLE OF THE PUBLIC: HOW YOU CAN PARTICIPATE EFFECTIVELY IN THE ENVIRONMENTAL ASSESSMENT PROCESS

Under the *Environmental Assessment Act*, the only formal mechanisms to participate in the EA process are the opportunities to comment on the environmental assessment and to appear at a hearing before the Environmental Assessment Board or joint board, should one be held. Indeed, the Act does not even make it clear at what stage an environmental assessment must be made available, and in the past, it was not released until after the government review was complete. Thus, citizens were deprived of any opportunity to influence the design of the study itself or the quality of the government review.

Nevertheless, although the Act has not yet been amended to provide more opportunities for public involvement, the ministry and the boards have actively encouraged proponents to involve the public earlier and more frequently in the process. Although the wording of the Act focuses on three stages of the EA process — the submission of the EA document to the minister of environment and energy, the government review of the environmental assessment, and the decisions by the minister or the boards as to the adequacy of the environmental assessment and approval of the undertaking — there is actually an earlier stage, the quality of which is crucial to everything that happens afterward. This may conveniently be called the planning stage — the stage at which the EA study is designed and prepared by the proponent, often with advice and assistance from the ministry's Environmental Assessment Branch. This is also the stage at which the proponent should design its public participation program.

Pre-Submission Consultation

Although there is no statutory requirement for either the proponent or the government to give out information or consult the public until the completion of the government review, the ministry has encouraged early information sharing and consultation since 1981 through a policy and guidelines on public consultation[102] and the publication of guidelines on pre-submission consultation.[103] The guidelines recommend that even before the environmental assessment is done, proponents make technical information and information and decisions regarding proposed planning activities available. The guidelines suggest that this material be disseminated to government ministries and agencies; individuals and groups with a record of involvement in similar undertakings; known experts in aspects of the study; and people likely to be directly or indirectly affected by the undertaking and its alternatives. In addition, the Environmental Assessment Branch assigns an adviser to each undertaking, who will give the proponent advice as to the kind and degree of information and consultation that will facilitate the assessment process.

The pre-submission consultation guidelines, together with decisions of the boards that make it clear that adequate public consultation is a factor in determining the integrity of the assessment,[104] have encouraged many proponents to establish public consultation procedures early in the planning process. Proponents — particularly proponents of large projects — now often establish committees of members of the public (often called liaison committees or stakeholder committees), which meet on a regular basis and are consulted on a variety of issues relevant to the EA process.[105] In some cases, the proponent will also make independent experts, facilitators, or mediators available to these committees at its own expense and will sometimes reimburse participants in these committees for some of their expenses.

Thus, the ministry's guidelines and board decisions have done a great deal to open up the process to the public at an early stage. Nevertheless, in the absence of any statutory framework or guidelines as to what will constitute adequate public participation, the process is still open to manipulation by proponents. Public participation "consultants" hired by proponents can be used to turn public consultation into a public relations exercise instead of real consultation. The boards, however, have shown increasing interest in examining public consultation activities, and have been particularly critical of proponents who attempt to hide information or manipulate the public, although this hasn't stopped some proponents from trying!

Environmental Assessment Proposals

A more recent attempt to clarify what is required in an adequate environmental assessment, and to involve the public in the process, is the assessment design document (ADD) or environmental assessment proposal (EAP). In 1991, the EA task force proposed a substantial reform to the EA planning process by suggesting that before carrying out an environmental assessment, proponents prepare and release to the public for their comment an ADD, which outlines a proposed planning process. This proposal would describe the methodology for carrying out the study, the criteria that will be employed in assessing alternatives and their possible impacts, a schedule for development of the environmental assessment, and a public consultation plan.[106] The ADD may still appear if the proposed package of legislative and regulatory reforms is implemented. In 1992, the ministry renamed this document an environmental assessment proposal. [107] The EAP is intended to be a blueprint for the entire EA process, and offers an opportunity to improve the quality of environmental assessments and reduce conflict at later stages of the process. Proponents have already begun to prepare similar documents and release them for comment by government agencies and the public before finalizing the study design.[108]

Reform of the Ontario Environmental Assessment Process

There are many shortcomings in the current *Environmental Assessment Act* and in the way it is administered. The time taken to complete the EA process is sometimes extremely lengthy and capable of exhausting both proponents and the affected public. At present, there are no legislated time limits on any of the phases of the review and decision-making process, although the Environmental Assessment Branch has announced a target of a six-month review period. (Past reviews have often taken a year or more.) How much of the cost and delay associated with the EA process is caused by the need to assess impacts thoroughly and objectively and how much of it is unnecessary and can be avoided through more efficient administration of the Act is a key question that must be answered to have effective reform that reduces cost and delay without resulting in superficial or manipulated assessment. Two substantive weaknesses of the Act are the absence of requirements to assess either cumulative and synergistic impacts or the sustainability of the undertaking. Other problems include the weak application of the Act to the private sector, the questionable use of class environmental assessments, inconsistent application of the Act to plans and programs, the lack of assessment of government policies and programs,[109] a weak process for screening exemptions, designations, and bump-ups, and lack of mandatory monitoring of the results of approving undertakings.[110]

As we indicated at the outset of this chapter, the Ontario EA process has been under attack since its inception. The constant criticisms of the Act have led to an unsuccessful takeover attempt by other government departments in the mid-1970s, efforts by senior ministry officials in the mid-1980s to apply the Act only to a few major projects, and the infamous "Project X" in 1989, when leaked documents revealed that the provincial treasurer sought to dismantle the EA process in the name of "sustainable development." According to Project X documents, the EA process tries to conserve the environment, which is incompatible with encouraging development; and therefore environmental assessment is incompatible with "sustainable development."

Apart from stimulating such covert action, dissatisfaction with the administration of Ontario's EA process has led to a series of studies aimed at reforming it. After the Environmental Assessment Branch prepared internal reports aimed at reducing the scope of the EA process, the Ministry of the Environment and several major public companies funded a study by the Canadian Environmental Law Research Foundation (now the Canadian Institute for Environmental Law and Policy). Published in December 1986, this study made numerous recommendations to streamline the process and make it fairer to all concerned.[111]

The ministry responded by initiating a further review by the ministry staff, the Environmental Assessment Program Improvement Project (EAPIP) in 1988. EAPIP completed the first phase of its review, dealing with supposedly minor, non-controversial "housekeeping" aspects of the process. Its first report, dealing with these "housekeeping" matters — among which was enshrining class assessments in the Act — was released in 1989. In phase two, EAPIP was to report on more substantive matters. Instead, in response to concerns about the two-phase approach and, in particular, in response to the public outcry over Project X, the minister changed the process. An in-house EA task force took over the review to deal with both housekeeping and substantive matters (EAPIP phases one and two). In December 1990, the task force produced a discussion paper, "Toward Improving the EA Program in Ontario," which was released by the new minister, Ruth Grier. This report recommended:

- that a planning and consultation phase become a mandatory part of the EA process;
- provision for "scoping" (focusing, resolving, and eliminating issues);
- clarification of the roles and responsibilities of those involved in the EA process and the development of criteria to assist in decision making;
- placing time limits on steps in the review and decision-making process;
- clarification of the administrative process, including class environmental assessments, designations, and exemptions; and
- that the Environmental Assessment Board revise its rules of practice and procedure to improve the hearing process.[112]

Instead of accepting these recommendations, the minister asked the Environmental Assessment Advisory Committee to hold public consultations on the task force report and report back to her. EAAC submitted its final recommendations for reform of the EA process to the minister of the environment in two parts, in October 1991 and January 1992. As of July 1993, the minister had not released this two-part report.

FEDERAL ENVIRONMENTAL ASSESSMENT

Background to the Canadian EA Process

The federal government's environmental impact assessment process has evolved in a very different manner from Ontario's EA process. Instead of a legislated, formal approach to environmental assessment, the federal government initially chose a process with no statutory basis and no requirements for formal, adversarial hearings. In contrast to the Ontario approach, which requires the assessment of all public projects unless they were specifically exempted from the process, the federal government chose a more discretionary procedure: proponents themselves could choose whether to submit their projects to assessment, and the government and proponents retained much more discretion as to how comprehensive an environmental assessment would be and the extent of public involvement. Moreover, instead of incorporating the possibility of hearings by an independent tribunal leading to a binding approval with terms and conditions that were enforceable in law, the federal government provided for public meetings held by a federal environmental assessment panel. The panel could only make recommendations, which the minister of the environment and proponent could ignore.

The criticisms levied against the federal process, which were met with decades of resistance and delay, have recently led the federal government to create a legislated process that is closer to Ontario's process than its original environmental assessment and review process (EARP).

EARP was born in December 1973 as a Cabinet directive authorizing the minister of the environment to establish a process to ensure that:

- environmental effects are taken into account early in the planning of new federal projects, programs, and activities;
- an environmental assessment is carried out for all projects that may have an adverse effect on the environment, before commitments or irrevocable decisions are made, and that projects with potentially significant environmental effects are submitted to the Department of the Environment; and
- the results of these assessments are used in planning, decision making, and implementation.

EARP was described in an Environment Canada document, the *Guide to the Federal Environmental Assessment and Review Process*.[113] Although the wording of the guide left an impression that proponents were subject to specific requirements, a careful reading revealed that the requirements were actually quite vague and ambiguous, and that the guide was capable of many interpretations.[114] In reality, lacking any statutory authority to compel an environmental assessment in any individual case, the environment minister had to rely on the cooperation of the project initiator, cooperation from his or her Cabinet colleagues, or a public outcry to ensure that projects were assessed and that the findings of the assessment were implemented. After observing the process in action for its first few years, Paul Emond, in his book on environmental assessment, concluded that, initially, "EARP seems to have been as bad as its critics suggested," but that "the experience of almost five years under EARP has led to substantial, even dramatic, improvements in the way in which the Process is being administered."[115] Not dramatic enough, however, to quell the tide of criticism from academics, environmentalists, and the courts. In 1979, the ministry began an internal review of EARP with a view to improving it.

In 1979, the *Government Organization Act* provided the first statutory recognition of a federal EA process: the minister of the environment was granted the power to establish, by order, environmental guidelines for use by federal departments, boards, and agencies.[116] However, the Act did not address the central weaknesses of EARP: the lack of any power in the minister of the environment to compel an assessment, the lack of clear procedures for carrying out assessments, and the lack of assurance that the findings of an assessment would be implemented.

In 1984, the guidelines were formalized by issuing them as an order under the *Department of the Environment Act*.[117] Under the EARP guidelines order, proposals by federal government departments, boards, and agencies were subject to an environmental screening or initial assessment to determine whether they might have any adverse environmental effects. Where this initial screening revealed that the proposal may cause significant adverse impacts, the guidelines order stated that it must be referred for public review by an EA panel. At the time, the federal government considered this order to be nothing more than a unenforceable guideline.

In the late 1980s, however, when several environmental groups asked the courts to order the federal government to carry out environmental assessments, the courts ruled that the guidelines order was more than a guideline. It was a binding law requiring an assessment of any federal proposal that might have significant environmental impacts. Moreover, the courts interpreted the guidelines order to require assessment of proposals when any federal licence was needed from any federal department, and even if there had already been a provincial environmental assessment.[118]

However, problems remained, such as the federal government overriding a strong recommendation by a Federal Environmental Assessment Review Office (FEARO) panel not to build three new runways at Pearson International Airport near Toronto in 1992 and the Federal Court condemning the inadequacy of the "environmental assessment" of the proposed bridge to Prince Edward Island in March 1993. Having lost the flexibility of a totally discretionary process, the federal government had little choice but finally to introduce the binding legislation it had talked about for years. At the time this legislation was initiated, the government most likely saw the *Canadian Environmental Assessment Act* as an opportunity to narrow the guidelines order, as interpreted by the courts. At one time, the courts had turned compliance with that order into a planning requirement for almost every proposal in every area of federal jurisdiction.[119] In the course of drafting the new *Canadian Environmental Assessment Act*,[120] the federal government also clearly provided itself with the power to exempt projects.[121]

The environment minister introduced the *Canadian Environmental Assessment Act* in the House of Commons on June 18, 1990, but it was not finally given royal assent until more than two years later, amid angry accusations by environmentalists that it was weaker than the EARP guidelines order, and by Progressive Conservative senators from Quebec that it infringed provincial jurisdiction.

As of July 1993 we are in a twilight zone. The *Canadian Environmental Assessment Act* is not yet in force, and will not be proclaimed until all the regulations setting out what projects are to be assessed have been finalized, and EARP still applies. However, in the expectation that the *Canadian Environmental Assessment Act* will soon govern the process, we will focus our discussion on that statute, rather than EARP. Like EARP, the process under the Act involves discretion, and its scope remains to be determined by regulations, guidelines, and procedures that have not yet been developed. Thus, our discussion is rather tentative.

To Whom and What Does the Canadian Environmental Assessment Apply?

In general, the *Canadian Environmental Assessment Act* applies to projects involving federal authorities as proponents, as vendors of land or landlords, as donors of financial aid to the project, and, in designated cases, as a licensing or regulatory authority.[122] The federal authorities who are subject to the Act are federal Cabinet ministers, federal government agencies, certain Crown corporations, and any other body so designated by regulations.[123] The Toronto harbour commissioners, the Hamilton harbour commissioners, and band councils under the *Indian Act*[124] have been excluded from the definition of federal authorities, but they can be made subject to the EA process by regulations. The Act provides that if the harbour commissioners are proponents, provide aid for projects, or allow the use of land they administer, they can be required by regulation to ensure that an environmental assessment of the project is carried out.[125] Under similar circumstances, band councils can be required by regulation to ensure that projects carried out on reserves are assessed.[126]

It is important to understand that if a project falls under the *Canadian Environmental Assessment Act* only because it requires some form of federal licence or is seeking funding from a federal agency, it need not undergo a federal environmental assessment if the proponent can find some way of carrying it out without receiving federal funding or without the need for a federal licence.

A project does not require assessment if it is being carried out in response to an emergency or is on an exclusion list.[127] The *CEAA* exclusion list will be created in the form of a regulation and will contain projects and classes of projects for which an environmental assessment is not required. Projects will be allowed on the exclusion list where, in the Cabinet's opinion, an environmental assessment would interfere with national security, the environmental impacts are minor, or the environmental impacts are significant, but the contribution of the federal agency to the project is minimal (for example, presumably, where a federal department gives a small grant to a private sector proponent).[128] Opportunities to challenge such a list will be limited.[129] However, the government has promised that there will be some form of public input into the development of the exclusion list.[130] The government has suggested that examples of projects with minimal impact that may go on this list are "simple renovations, routine operations, purchasing supplies, minor construction, engineering studies, and controlled scientific studies."[131]

All other projects will be subject to some form of environmental assessment. However, "project" is defined as a physical work or activity. Although the terms "physical," "work," and "activity" are not defined, the actions that are subject to assessment appear to be narrower than under EARP, which covered "proposals," and under the Ontario *Environmental Assessment Act*, which governs plans and programs as well as projects. However, when the government introduced the Act, it also announced that an assessment of new government policies and programs would be carried out through a separate process. New policies and programs will be accompanied by a statement of their expected environmental impact when they are announced, and the House of Commons Standing Committee on the Environment will be able to question the environment minister on the environmental implications of the policy or program.[132] This is an improvement over the current situation; however, it is fraught with difficulties — among them, that many policies and programs are never formally announced to the public, and that policies and programs can be given other names, such as "plans" or "guidelines," to avoid public scrutiny. (See the example of such word games at the beginning of this chapter.)

Once it has been determined that a project is not on the exclusion list or is not otherwise excluded by a regulation, it will undergo *some* degree of environmental assessment. The extent of the assessment will range from a comprehensive study of all aspects of construction, operation, modification, and abandonment of the project, to a more cursory evaluation of these aspects through a "screening" or a "class screening."

The *Canadian Environmental Assessment Act* does accommodate other types of federal environmental assessment. For example, the National Energy Board (NEB) has exercised a discretionary power to require an environmental assessment since 1975. Since that time, the board's rules of practice and procedure have required applicants for a certificate to construct an oil or gas pipeline to file an assessment of the impact of the pipeline on the environment,

Canadian Environmental Assessment Act

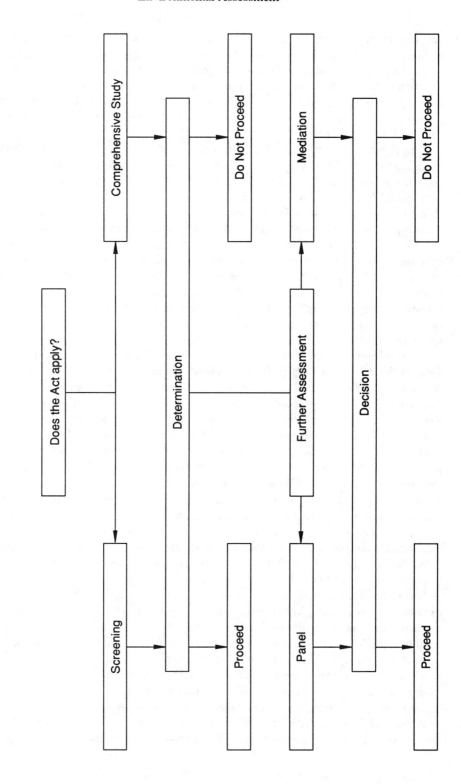

and a statement of the measures proposed to mitigate the impact.[133] More recently, the NEB has started to apply the requirements of EARP to its processes.[134] Under the *Canadian Environmental Assessment Act*, provision is made for joint panels where an EA hearing is required of a project that is also subject to the jurisdiction of another federal agency like the NEB. [135]

The Scope of the Environmental Assessment

The scope of any environmental assessment under the *Canadian Environmental Assessment Act* is limited to environmental effects, as defined in the Act. The Act's definitions of "environment" and "environmental effects" severely limit the extent to which the Act can apply to social, economic, and cultural impacts. Environment is defined in terms of air, land, and water — that is, the natural environment. Environmental effects go beyond the natural environment to include impacts on health, cultural, and socioeconomic conditions, land uses and resources, but only where the effect is a result of changes to the natural environment.[136]

Within these constraints, projects will undergo different degrees of scrutiny depending on how they are classified by federal regulations. The three levels of environmental assessment, and which projects they will cover, are described below.

Comprehensive Study

The fullest study is the "comprehensive study." If Cabinet believes that an individual project or a class of projects will have significant adverse environmental effects, the project or projects will be placed on a "comprehensive study list" promulgated as a regulation.[137] Any project on this list must undergo a comprehensive study. It would appear from the Act that the "responsible authority" (that is, the federal authority that is the proponent of the project, the landowner or landlord, or a funder) must either supervise the EA process itself and carry out the study, ensure that the proponent carries the study out in accordance with the Act, or refer the study to the minister of the environment, who then sends it to a review panel or mediator.[138] How a review panel or mediator can supervise the carrying out of a complex EA process and still carry out the functions of mediating or, in the case of panels, holding public hearings on the adequacy of the environmental assessment is less than clear.

A comprehensive study must consider two groups of matters. The first group of matters includes:

- the environmental effects of the project, including the environmental effects of malfunctions or accidents, and any cumulative effects of the project in combination with other projects and activities;
- the significance of these environmental effects;
- comments from the public;
- measures that would mitigate any significant adverse environmental effects, provided that the measures are technically and economically feasible; and
- any other matter that is relevant to the study, such as the need for the project and alternatives to the project, that the responsible authority or the minister, as the case may be, determines should be studied.

The second group of matters includes:

- the purpose of the project;
- alternative means of carrying out the project that are technically and economically feasible, and the environmental effects of any such alternative means;
- the need for a follow-up program and how it should be carried out; and
- the capacity of renewable resources that are likely to be affected by the project to meet the needs of the present and the future (sustainability).

The government has suggested that the classes of projects that will be placed on the comprehensive study list will include: major projects for national parks; water management projects; projects involving the development of oil, gas, and mineral resources; pulp and paper mills; smelters; defence works; projects affecting navigable waterways; and waste management projects.[139]

Screening

For projects that are not on the comprehensive study list, a less rigorous assessment must be carried out. Called a "screening," this study must only look at the first group of matters listed above, and need not take into account the matters in the second group.

In preparing a screening report, the responsible authority need not carry out a study if it feels existing information is adequate for an assessment of the project's impacts.[140] Thus, a screening may consist merely of compiling existing information about the project or the class of projects into which it falls. Only if the responsible authority is of the opinion that it does not have enough information to determine the impacts of the project is it required to do any independent study or obtain any further information.

Moreover, the requirement to screen projects that are not on the exclusion list or the comprehensive study list does not mean that each project will be individually screened. Such projects may be subject instead to "class screening," as described below.

Class Screening

Class screening is the federal counterpart to the class assessment used under Ontario's *Environmental Assessment Act*. FEARO has said that class screenings will be used "where a type of project is routine and repetitive in nature and is known not to cause significant or unmitigable effects."[141] FEARO has suggested that such projects would include dredging, culvert installations, highway maintenance, rail and tie replacement, and rebuilding of facilities on the same site.[142]

The responsible agency may avoid individual screenings by asking the Canadian Environmental Assessment Agency — the body that will replace FEARO in overseeing the administration of the Act — to designate a report of a screening of an individual project as a class screening report. Before the agency declares a report to be a class screening report, which can be used as a model for all future screenings of projects within the same class, it must notify the public of the authority's request and provide an opportunity for comment.

Once the Canadian Environmental Assessment Agency has declared a screening report to be a class screening report, the responsible authority can use it, or permit proponents to use it "to whatever extent the responsible authority considers appropriate" in carrying out future screenings.[143] However, the authority must still ensure that any adjustments are made that are necessary to take into account local circumstances and cumulative environmental effects when applying such class assessments to future projects.[144] Moreover, if the agency decides that a class screening report is no longer adequate for use as a model in conducting screenings, it can declare it not to be a class screening report.[145]

When Must an Environmental Assessment Be Carried out?

The responsible authority must ensure that the environmental assessment is done as early as possible in the planning stages of the project, and before any irrevocable decisions have been made.[146] Where any form of federal environmental assessment is required, the responsible authority is forbidden to perform its duty or function in relation to that project (for example, constructing the project if it is the proponent, or otherwise, granting approval, giving financial assistance, disposing of land, etc.) until the environmental assessment has been completed.[147] This is a significant improvement over the EARP guidelines order. Under that order, courts had ruled that a proponent could proceed with a project even though the public review of the project was not complete. This allowed government agencies to carry out, for example, a military program testing low-level flying over Innu lands and the construction of irrigation dams in Alberta and Saskatchewan before the EA process was complete.[148]

The Act states that proof that assessment has been completed may be provided by a certificate signed by the responsible authority.[149] However, unlike Ontario's *Environmental Assessment Act*, the *Canadian Environmental Assessment Act* does not make it an offence to proceed to fund or construct a project before the environmental assessment has been done. Only the minister can issue a stop order to prevent this, although citizens must succeed in an application for judicial review to stop a project from proceeding under these circumstances.[150]

Mediation and Panel Review

In addition to the opportunities for public comment that must be provided by the responsible authority when preparing a comprehensive study or screening study, there may be an opportunity for the public to participate in a mediation process or a hearing before an independent panel of experts, or both.

The independent panel mode of public participation resembles the public participation regime under EARP. As with EARP, the minister responsible for the project has broad discretion whether to require further assessment. Under the *Canadian Environmental Assessment Act*, if the responsible authority feels that a project may cause significant adverse effects or there is sufficient public concern, the authority may ask the minister of the environment to refer the project to a mediator or a panel.[151] However, even if the responsible authority does not wish to refer the project to a mediator or a panel, the minister of the environment may do so at any time if he or she feels that the project may have significant negative environmental impacts, or if public concerns warrant such action.[152] A mediator or panel is required to take into consideration all the factors dealt with in a comprehensive study.[153]

Environmental Mediation

In their efforts to find more efficient ways of resolving environmental and other disputes, many commentators have begun to look to alternative dispute resolution mechanisms (often referred to as ADR).[154] Until recently, there has been a lot more talk about ADR than action.

However, the *Canadian Environmental Assessment Act* is one of the few attempts to formally integrate a form of ADR — mediation — into the environmental decision-making process. Mediation is a process designed to facilitate parties to a dispute voluntarily reaching a consensus on how to resolve the dispute. Unlike litigation, there is no single decision maker. The mediator plays the role of consensus builder. For environmental assessments, mediation has the greatest prospect for success when all parties agree on the legitimacy of the project and the disagreement is mainly on how it will be implemented, such as the measures needed to mitigate significant effects, the benefits objectors will get (such as jobs), or the compensation that will be available to redress negative impacts. If any of the parties do not accept the need for the project, mediation is less likely to succeed.

Mediation is a voluntary and consensual process. The minister cannot appoint a mediator unless all interested parties have been identified and are willing to participate in the mediation.[155] The Act provides that the mediator must be unbiased, free from any conflict of interest, and have training or experience in mediation.[156] Before appointing a mediator, the minister must consult with the responsible authority and all the parties who are to participate in the mediation, to ensure that the mediator is satisfactory to everyone concerned.[157] If the mediation efforts break down, the minister must refer the environmental assessment to a panel for a public hearing.[158]

Mediation may also be used in conjunction with a panel hearing. At any time during its deliberations, a panel may recommend to the minister that a mediator be appointed to try to resolve one or more of the issues before the panel, and if all the parties agree, portions of the environmental assessment may be dealt with by the mediator.[159]

Panel Review

Alternatively, the minister may establish a panel to hold a hearing. The Act provides no clear role for the public in selecting the panel members or in establishing the terms of reference for the hearing. However, there are safeguards to ensure a fair and impartial hearing. The minister of the environment is required to appoint a panel of people who are unbiased, free from conflicts of interest, and have expertise that is relevant to the anticipated environmental effects of the project.[160]

The panel is required to hold its hearings in public, unless it is satisfied that certain documents or evidence must be kept confidential;[161] and it must conduct its hearings in a manner that offers the public an opportunity to participate.[162] Unlike the panels appointed under EARP, a panel will have the power to subpoena witnesses and compel them to attend the hearings and give evidence.[163] It is unclear, however, whether panel hearings will require sworn testimony or permit the cross-examination of witnesses and experts.

The Act also appears to contemplate that a panel may not only review an environmental assessment carried out by a proponent, but may actually design and carry out the assessment itself.

The Outcome of Mediation or Panel Review

The mediator or panel is required to prepare a report, which is submitted to the minister of the environment and to the responsible authority.[164] In the case of a panel, its report must set out the panel's reasoning, conclusions, and recommendations relating to the environmental assessment, including any mitigation measures and follow-up program that should be implemented.[165]

However, neither a mediator nor a panel has any decision-making authority. How the decision is made whether to proceed with a project and whether to implement mitigation measures or a follow-up program is described below. However, first a word about the funding available to participate in a panel review or mediation.

Intervenor Funding

Section 58(1)(i) of the *Canadian Environmental Assessment Act* authorizes the minister of the environment to "establish a participant funding* program to facilitate the participation of the public in mediations and assessments by review panels." Although there is no requirement to establish such a program, and the Act does not provide for any possibility of funding at earlier stages of the EA process, this is an improvement over the EARP guidelines order, which made no mention of funding.[166] FEARO has suggested that the following criteria will be used to decide whether to grant funding to an applicant:

- whether the participant is directly affected by the project or has a special interest in the potential environmental effects and related health and socioeconomic effects of the project;
- whether the applicant can demonstrate a connection between his or her interests and a "public interest";
- the participant's need for resources and commitment to contribute his or her own time and resources to the process;
- quality of presentation, with emphasis on the degree of originality and uniqueness of the application;
- cooperation with other participants and avoidance of duplication of the efforts of other participants; and
- preparation of a clearly defined plan of activity that is consistent with the terms of reference for the review.[167]

At this point, funding may not be used for legal assistance at a public review or panel review hearing.

The Decision-Making Process

Unlike Ontario's *Environmental Assessment Act*, under which the minister of the environment or an independent board makes the final decision whether a project should proceed and may attach binding conditions of approval, the *Canadian Environmental Assessment Act* leaves the final decision to the responsible authority, which may be a regulatory or financial assistance agency or the proponent itself. However, the Act contains limited safeguards to ensure that the responsible agency cannot ignore the findings of an environmental assessment. First, the responsible authority can proceed with or support the project only if the screening comprehensive study report or the report of the mediator or review panel shows

---

*   What the Act refers to as "participant funding" is usually called "intervenor funding." See the section of this chapter dealing with financing public participation in the Ontario process for an explanation of the distinction.

either that the project is unlikely to cause significant adverse impacts, or that there will be negative effects, but they "can be justified in the circumstances."[168] Second, if the authority concludes that there will be negative effects, but they are justifiable, and therefore proceeds with the project, it must ensure that mitigation measures are implemented — but only those measures that the authority has decided are reasonable.[169] Third, the authority must design and implement a follow-up program to verify the accuracy of the environmental assessment and to determine the effectiveness of any mitigation measures that are implemented.[170] However, the follow-up program may consist of whatever the agency considers appropriate, in accordance with the regulations governing such programs, which have not yet been made.

In the end result, public scrutiny is the only real limit on the considerable discretion of federal agencies whether to implement the findings of an environmental assessment. All environmental assessments as well as the decisions of responsible authorities on the course of action pursued, the mitigation measures to be implemented, the extent to which the authority has adopted the recommendations of mediation or review panel reports, and the follow-up program are public documents.[171]

Enforcement

One of the major weaknesses of the Act is its lack of enforceability. Contrary to what the term might seem to imply, the "follow-up" program required by the Act does not necessarily refer to monitoring of compliance with enforceable terms and conditions of approval, since a project may be approved without formal terms and conditions. This appears likely where the responsible agency is also the proponent of the project. The follow-up program simply verifies the information contained in the environmental assessment and scrutinizes the effectiveness of any mitigation measures that *are* implemented. Only where the proponent is subject to some other form of approval, such as a permit under the *Navigable Waters Protection Act*, does it appear likely that enforceable conditions may be attached requiring specific mitigation and follow-up measures.

The Limitations of the Canadian Environmental Assessment Act

The *Canadian Environmental Assessment Act* will encourage greater use of environmental assessment as a planning tool by federal agencies and those private sector proponents who are subject to federal regulation, who use federal lands, or who seek financial assistance from the federal government. Nevertheless, the Act does not encompass all environmental impacts on areas under federal jurisdiction. Many areas of federal activity will be assessed only if they are designated by regulation. There continues to be significant potential for projects to escape federal assessment, yet be exempt from provincial assessment because of constitutional limits.

Moreover, the Act provides insufficient opportunity for independent assessment of projects. Whether a project will be subject to mediation or panel review is up to the minister of the environment or the responsible authority, who also have substantial control over the terms of reference of such study, whether to provide intervenor funding, and whether to apply the findings and recommendations of the environmental assessment. This lack of independent decision making affects the vigour of the entire assessment process, since proponents are not required to prove the comprehensiveness of their assessment or the rationality of their consideration of alternatives.

The quality of public participation is also unclear. Unlike the Ontario process, which has evolved to include extensive public consultation from the earliest stages in the EA process, and may require formal hearings with clearly defined rules, subject to the minimum fairness requirements of the *Statutory Powers Procedure Act*,[172] EARP has favoured informality throughout the assessment process. Since the process under the *Canadian Environmental Assessment Act* remains to be determined by regulations, it is unclear how the desire for informality and the wish to expedite the process will be balanced against the procedural safeguards provided through the requirements of the Ontario *Environmental Assessment Act* and the *Statutory Powers Procedure Act*, which give affected members of the public standing to participate, allow them to be represented by lawyers and agents, and permit cross-examination.

Robert Gibson, an authority on environmental assessment, has identified several weaknesses in the *Canadian Environmental Assessment Act*:

- the lack of clear criteria for deciding whether a project should be assessed and in what manner, for determining the acceptability of proposed projects, and for determining whether mitigation measures are appropriate;
- the lack of application of environmental assessment to the plans and programs that facilitate individual projects, and the lack of coverage of related groups of activities, or plans and programs that generate such activities, that are likely to have significant cumulative effects;[173]
- the lack of adequate assessment of need for a project, alternatives to the project, and socioeconomic and cultural effects of projects;
- the lack of any effective commitment to achieving sustainability or any mechanism to ensure that projects are consistent with sustainability;
- too many discretionary powers, including excessive discretion and inefficiency in the methods of determining when assessment will be required;
- the right to approve projects with significant adverse environmental effects, if a government agency feels these effects are justifiable (even if the projects may compromise sustainability); and
- the lack of a clear, effective and equitable means of specifying and enforcing conditions of approval, or follow-up programs.

CONCLUSIONS

Long as this chapter has been, it cannot begin to do justice to the importance and complexity of the EA process. Adequate environmental assessment is central to ensuring that all government and private decisions that affect the sustainability of the environment or that have the potential to harm the environment or communities are infused with an environmental ethic. It is a crucial component of any effort to integrate environmental, cultural, social, and economic effects into one rational and coordinated planning process. This was recognized by the Brundtland commission, when it recommended that EA processes would be more effective if they were mandatory and entrenched in legislation. As we said at the beginning of this chapter, continued resistance to the EA process is a significant measure of our lack of commitment to environmental sustainability. Our failure to implement an EA process at either the federal or provincial level that covers all environmentally significant decisions and prevents powerful interests from escaping the process limits our ability as a society to attain sustainable development.

Rodney Northey and John Swaigen

FURTHER READING

William J. Couch, ed., *Environmental Assessment in Canada: 1988 Summary of Current Practice* (Ottawa: Federal Environmental Assessment and Review Office, 1988).

P.S.B. Duffy, ed., *Initial Assessment Guide: Federal Environmental Assessment and Review Process* (Ottawa: Federal Environmental Assessment and Review Office, 1986).

Paul Emond, *Environmental Assessment Law* (Toronto: Emond Montgomery, 1978).

R.B. Gibson and B. Savan, *Environmental Assessment in Ontario* (Toronto: Canadian Institute for Environmental Law and Policy, 1986).

Ontario, Ministry of the Environment, *Towards Improving the Environmental Assessment Program in Ontario* (Toronto: Queen's Printer, 1990).

ENDNOTES

1   Environmental impact assessment was first made a legal requirement in the United States. In 1969, the United States Congress passed the *National Environmental Policy Act*, 42 USCA ¶ 4321 *et seq.* Its purpose was "to declare a national policy which will encourage productive and enjoyable harmony between man and his environment." Its cornerstone was the environmental impact study.

2   *Environmental Assessment Act*, RSO 1990, c. E.18.

3   See, for example, the *Pollution Abatement Incentive Act*, RSO 1970, c. 352.

4   Another reason for the continuing resistance of government agencies in Ontario to the environmental assessment process is the power that it gives one minister over his or her other Cabinet colleagues. This opposition culminated in an unsuccessful attempt by these other ministries shortly after the *Environmental Assessment Act* was proclaimed to have control of the process taken from the Ministry of the Environment. See "Ontario Environmental Assessment Act Proclaimed for Public Sector" (October 1976), *CELA Newsletter* 59, at 60.

5   For example, in a ground-breaking decision, the Ontario Environmental Assessment Board ordered a municipality applying for expansion of its waste disposal site to use the "tipping fees" — that is, the fees charged for dumping garbage — only for the development of an adequate waste management and waste reduction system, and not to divert this money to other municipal programs, such as maintaining roads. *Re Orillia*

Landfill Enlargement Application, February 24, 1992, EAB, file no. EP-90-03. The decision was immediately appealed to the provincial Cabinet, with the support of the Association of Ontario Municipalities.

6   *Environmental Assessment Act*, supra endnote 2.

7   For example, in *Friends of the Oldman River Society v. Canada (Minister of Transport)* (1992), 7 CELR (NS) 1 (SCC) (the *"Oldman River"* decision), the Supreme Court of Canada affirmed that the federal EA process applied to a project of the Alberta government, even though no extraprovincial environmental impacts were expected.

8   *Fisheries Act*, RSC 1985, c. F-14.

9   *Navigable Waters Protection Act*, RSC 1985, c. N-22.

10 For example, *Canadian Wildlife Federation Inc. v. Minister of the Environment* (1989), 3 CELR (NS) 287 (FCTD), aff'd. (1989), 4 CELR (NS) 1, 37 Admin. LR 39 (FCA) (the *"Rafferty-Alameda Dam"* decision).

11 *Oldman River*, supra endnote 7.

12 *Canadian Environmental Assessment Act*, SC 1992, c. 37.

13 Ibid., section 5. This permit was the critical approval involved in *Oldman River*, supra endnote 7.

14 See *Canadian Wildlife Federation*, supra endnote 10; *Oldman River*, supra endnote 7.

15 The Canadian Council of Ministers of the Environment, a coordinating body of the federal environment minister and the environment ministers of the provinces, has begun to establish a framework for federal-provincial cooperation in coordinating environmental assessments: see Canadian Council of Ministers of the Environment, *Communique*, March 19, 1992; Canadian Council of Ministers of the Environment, "Cooperative Principles for Environmental Assessment," May 6-7, 1991. For an excellent discussion of federal-provincial cooperation and joint environmental assessments, see Steven A. Kennett, "Issues and Options for Intergovernmental Cooperation in Environmental Impact Assessment" (Summer 1992), 39 *Resources* 1 (*Resources* is the newsletter of the Canadian Institute of Resources Law).

16 *Canadian Environmental Assessment Act*, supra endnote 12, sections 12(4), 17, 40, and 46-48.

17 For example, Manitoba's *Environment Act*, SM 1987-88, c. 26, section 13.1(2), as amended; Saskatchewan's *Environmental Assessment Act*, SS 1979-80, c. E-10.1, section 5(f).

18 *Environmental Assessment Act*, supra endnote 2.

19 O. reg. 636/77.

20 This was done through O. reg. 468/80, which revoked O. reg. 836/76, which had exempted municipal undertakings.

21 *Environmental Assessment Act*, supra endnote 2, RRO 1990, reg. 293, section 3(a).

22 Ibid., RRO 1990, reg. 334, section 1(2)(a). This regulation provides that projects are exempt from assessment if their "estimated cost" is less than $3.5 million. However, the proponent is responsible for estimating the cost, and can avoid assessment by underestimating it, or sometimes by dividing the project into different components or phases, each of which is estimated to cost less than $3.5 million. In addition, the definition of estimated cost excludes many types of costs from the calculation to determine whether a project falls within the exemption.

23 Between 1977, when the parts of the Act applying to the private sector were proclaimed in force, and 1980, only three private projects were subjected to the Act. However, as of June 1992, at least 10 private sector undertakings were undergoing environmental assessment. These were: Kam 1 Hydro-Electric Project, designated by O. reg. 335/88; Reclamation Systems Inc., O. reg. 17/89; Steetley Quarry Products Inc. (application for approval of a landfill site), O. reg. 283/89; mining at Stevens, Cameron and Shoal Islands, O. reg. 486/89; Browning-Ferris Industries Limited, O. reg. 576/89; Tricil Limited (expansion of a hazardous waste disposal site), O. reg. 640/89; Unitech Disposal Inc., O. reg. 641/89; Morton Terminal, O. reg. 244/90; St. Lawrence Cement Limited, O. reg. 418/90; Lake Ontario Steel Limited, O. reg. 13/91; and Laidlaw Waste Systems Inc., O. reg. 457/91.

24 See Ontario, Ministry of the Environment, *News Release*, March 13, 1987.

25 See, respectively, the decisions and reasons for the decision of the board in *Re Regional Municipality of Halton Landfill Application* (CH-86-02), February 29, 1989 (Joint Board); *Re Petro-Sun/SNC Inc. Proposed Construction of a Resource Recovery Facility and Associated Energy Distribution System* (CH-87-01) October 24, 1988 (Joint Board), *Re North Simcoe Waste Management Association Landfill Application* (CH-87-03), November 17, 1989 (Joint Board), *Re Town of Meaford/ Township of St. Vincent Disposal Site Application* (CH-88-03), December 13, 1990 (Joint Board).

26 *Environmental Assessment Act*, supra endnote 2, sections 1 and 3.

27 Ibid., reg. 334, section 3. However, for conservation authorities, see the exemption in section 8 of the regulation.

28 Although the *Environmental Assessment Act* does not explicitly address agents acting for municipalities, a recent board hearing involving a private energy-from-waste facility discussed this matter and found that SNC Inc., the private proponent, was implementing the regional municipality of Peel's waste management master plan and was, therefore, in effect the agent for the municipality. The underlying concern of the board was that municipalities might be encouraged to contract out their contentious projects to avoid the requirements of the environmental assessment process if the Act was interpreted not to include private companies carrying out work for municipalities. See *Re Petro-Sun/SNC*, supra endnote 25, at 30.

29 *Environmental Assessment Act*, supra endnote 2, section 29.

30 For further information about the implementation of the Act in its early years and the establishment and role of the steering committee, see the second edition of this book, as well as a very interesting and informative paper by one of the key civil servants involved in the development and implementation of the Act: David R. Young, "The Environmental Assessment Act's Regulations for Municipalities: A Case Study in Environmental Regulation-Making," presented to the 1982 Canadian Environmental Law Research Foundation Conference, *Boardrooms, Backrooms and Backyards: Environmental Regulation-Making in the '80s*. This paper also contains a frank discussion of the lack of cooperation from municipalities that the Ministry of the Environment encountered in attempting to implement the Act.

31 See "Committee Will Review Environmental Assessment Act Exemptions" (1978), 3 *CELA Newsletter* 81.

32 See Ontario, Ministry of the Environment, *Interim Guidelines on EA Planning* (Toronto: the ministry, 1988), 28. In its decision on the environmental assessment for *Highway 416*, the Environmental Assessment Board commented that the requirement to assess need derives from the requirement to assess the advantages and disadvantages of their undertaking and alternatives to it. The board concluded: "If there is no need [for the undertaking], the Board cannot accept that the wise management and conservation of the environment [which are the purposes of the Act] would in fact be accomplished." *Highway 416* decision, EA-86-01, July 31, 1987, 24.

33 *Environmental Assessment Act*, supra endnote 2, reg. 334, section 2.

34 Ibid., section 41.

35 See, for example, the joint board's decision under the *Consolidated Hearings Act* in the Peel SNC (Brampton) EFW case, CH-87-01, October 24, 1988.

36 The definition of the study area is tied to public notice requirements. A proponent must give adequate notice of the environmental assessment to all persons potentially affected by the undertaking; otherwise, the assessment may be rejected: *Re Central Ontario Coalition and Ontario Hydro* (1984), 46 OR (2d) 715, 16 OMBR 172; (1985), 17 OMBR 389 (CA); 13 CELR 113 (Div. Ct.); *Re Joint Board and Regional Municipality of Ottawa-Carleton* (1985), 17 OMBR 389 (CA); *Re Ontario Hydro Eastern Ontario Bulk Electricity System Facilities* (1985), 14 CELR 45 (Div. Ct.).

37 For discussion for what constitutes a reasonable range of alternatives, see Ontario, Ministry of the Environment, "Minister's Statement on the Application of the *Environmental Assessment Act* to Private Sector Energy from Waste Proponents." This statement accompanied the designation of private sector energy from waste projects under the Act. See also *Re Proposed Transmission Plan of Ontario Hydro for Southwestern Ontario* (1987), 1 CELR (NS) 261, and the Environmental Assessment Board's decision, May 27, 1986 (EA-85-01), on the application by the Ministry of Transportation and Communications for approval of the realignment of a portion of highway 69 near Parry Sound.

38 *Re Proposed Transmission Plan*, supra endnote 37, at 287.

39 *Interim Guidelines on EA Planning*, supra endnote 32, at 16.

40 *Waste Management Act*, SO 1992, c. 1 (Bill 143).

41 Hydro withdrew its plan from the board in January 1993, ending the hearing prematurely. Its forecasts of demand for electricity had proved to be so inaccurate that it could no longer defend the plan. It is likely that Hydro will submit proposed facilities to individual environmental assessments, but not in the context of an overall demand-supply plan.

42 See *Re Petro-Sun/SNC*, supra endnote 25, at 40-43.

43 *Re Regional Municipality of Halton, Re North Simcoe*, and *Re Town of Meaford* decisions, supra endnote 25.

44 *Re North Simcoe* and *Re Town of Meaford* cases, supra endnote 25, and *Re Central Ontario Coalition and Ontario Hydro*, supra endnote 36.

45 *Re North Simcoe*, supra endnote 25. The proponent appealed the board's decision to Cabinet, which overturned the board's outright rejection of the undertaking (order in council no. 1529/90, June 14, 1990) and remitted the case to the board, giving the proponent an opportunity to lead further evidence to satisfy the concerns raised by the board.

46   See, in particular, *Re North Simcoe*, supra endnote 25, at 30-32, and *Re Town of Meaford*, supra endnote 25, at 30-33.

47   *Re Town of Meaford*, supra endnote 25, at 30-32.

48   This approach is still possible for federal approvals under the *Navigable Waters Protection Act*, supra endnote 9: see *Oldman River*, supra endnote 7.

49   This was said in relation to the environmental impact study of the proposed Pickering Airport near Toronto. See the second edition of this book at 48. Also see the Environmental Assessment Report of the Panel Respecting the Oldman River Dam, released August 1992 when the panel, recognizing that the dam was complete, recommended that it be decommissioned.

50   *Environmental Assessment Act*, supra endnote 2, section 6(2).

51   Ibid., section 5.

52   Ibid., section 6.

53   *R. v. Snow* (1981), 11 CELR 13 (Ont. Prov. Ct.).

54   *Environmental Assessment Act*, supra endnote 2, section 7(1) says only that "the Minister shall cause a review of the assessment to be prepared." It doesn't say by whom. But the practice is to circulate the assessment to other provincial government agencies, as well as other public bodies whose interests may be affected, such as municipalities and conservation authorities.

55   *Interim Guidelines on EA Planning*, supra endnote 32, at 32. See, for example, Ontario, Ministry of the Environment, Environmental Assessment Branch, *Government Review of the Ministry of Natural Resources Class Environmental Assessment for Timber Management on Crown Lands in Ontario* (Toronto: the ministry, 1987), 93-94.

56   *Environmental Assessment Act*, supra endnote 2, section 8.

57   Ibid., section 11.

58   Ibid., section 12(2).

59   See *Re North Simcoe*, supra endnote 25.

60   *Planning Act*, RSO 1990, c. P.13.

61   *Environmental Protection Act*, RSO 1990, c. E.19.

62   *Statutory Powers Procedure Act*, RSO 1990, c. S.22.

63   Ibid., RRO 1990, reg. 35.

64   *Citizens' Guide to the Environmental Assessment Board*, published in English and French in 1988, and available from the board.

65   *Environmental Assessment Act*, supra endnote 2, section 19. Although the board may order part of a hearing closed if it decides that the importance of keeping some information secret (for example, trade secrets) outweighs the desirability of public access to the hearing.

66   *Re County of Oxford Holbrook Waste Disposal Expansion* (1983), 15 OMBR 68, at 72. The courts have not yet ruled on whether the board does in fact have this power, which is not set out explicitly in the *Environmental Assessment Act*, supra endnote 2, or the *Statutory Powers Procedure Act*, supra endnote 62.

67   *Environmental Assessment Act*, supra endnote 2, section 24.

68   *Consolidated Hearings Act*, RSO 1990, c. C.29.

69   *Intervenor Funding Project Act*, RSO 1990, c. I.13.

70 Ibid. Sections 40 and 41 of the Act authorize Cabinet to group undertakings together and thus create classes of undertakings, but this power is found in the context of making regulations. It was presumably intended to facilitate designating classes of undertakings as being subject to individual assessments, and exempting other kinds of undertakings from individual assessment. There is no explicit authority to carry out a class assessment.

71 See Ontario, Ministry of the Environment, *General Guidelines for the Preparation of Environmental Assessments* (Toronto: the ministry, 1985), 16. An earlier version of these guidelines was published in 1981, which also made provision for class assessments under these circumstances. Current recommendations arising out of the process of reviewing the environmental assessment process call for a general MOE guideline on class environmental assessments and suggest that any extension of the conditions under which a class environmental assessment will be done should include responsiveness of the class of undertakings to mitigation as a criterion for using class assessment. See Ontario, Ministry of the Environment, Environmental Assessment Branch, Environmental Assessment Improvement Project, *Towards Improving the Environmental Assessment Program in Ontario* (Toronto: Queen's Printer, December 1990), recommendation 6.12 (herein referred to as "*TIEAP*").

72 See Ontario Environmental Assessment Advisory Committee, sixth and seventh annual reports, 1988-89 and 1989-90; Environmental Assessment Advisory Committee, "List of Environmental Assessment Exemption, Designation, Bump-Up Requests — From January 1988," available from EAAC. As of June 1993, five bump-up requests had been referred to EAAC. In two cases, EAAC recommended a bump-up and the minister concurred. (These figures do not include timber management.) Telephone contact with Philip Byer, chair, Environmental Assessment Advisory Committee, June 15, 1993.

73 For example, the class environmental assessment for municipal road projects, Municipal Engineers Association, approved April 9, 1987, order in council no.837/87, 45.

74 *Environmental Assessment Act*, supra endnote 2; *TIEAP*, supra endnote 71, 51-56.

75 Michael Jeffery, *Environmental Approvals in Canada* (Toronto: Butterworths) (looseleaf), paragraph 1.78.

76 *Ontario Water Resources Act*, RSO 1990, c. O.40.

77 *Planning Act*, RSO 1990, c. P.13.

78 *Municipal Act*, RSO 1990, c. M.45.

79 *Expropriations Act*, RSO 1990, c. E.26.

80 Section 3(3) of the *Environmental Assessment Act*, supra endnote 2, allows parties other than the proponent to request a joint board hearing, but this section has never been proclaimed.

81 *Aggregate Resources Act*, RSO 1990, c. A.8.

82 O. reg. 201/90. See also similar regulations made respecting the *Lakes and Rivers Improvement Act*, RSO 1990, c. L.3, O. reg. 174/89.

83 An extensive bibliography on the subject of intervenor funding is found in Canadian Environmental Defence Fund, *Intervenor Funding and the Intervenor Funding Project Act in Ontario* (Toronto: CEDF, May 1991). One of the first comprehensive discussions of the need for intervenor funding in environmental decision making in Canada

was co-authored by Ian Scott. A lawyer in private practice when the article was written, Scott later became the attorney general of Ontario and was responsible for the introduction of the *Intervenor Funding Project Act*, supra endnote 69, discussed below. The article was R. Anand and I. Scott, "Financing Public Participation in Environmental Decision-Making" (1982), 60 *Canadian Bar Review* 81.

84 Canadian Environmental Defence Fund, supra endnote 83, at 119-20.

85 For the EAB decision on this issue, see *Re Regional Municipality of Hamilton-Wentworth East-West North-South Transportation Facility Application (Redhill Creek Expressway)*, EAB Registrar's file no. CH 82-08; orders and reasons for orders dated October 16, 1984 and November 5, 1984.

86 *Re Regional Municipality of Hamilton-Wentworth and Hamilton-Wentworth Save the Valley Committee, Inc.* (1985), 51 OR (2d) 23 (Div. Ct.).

87 F. Giorno, "A Brief to Ontario's Minister of the Environment on Intervenor Funding," Canadian Environmental Law Association, on behalf of the Citizens Network Concerned about Waste Management, July 17, 1984.

88 For example, intervenor funding for two lengthy and complex hearings, the Ministry of Natural Resources Timber Management Class Environmental Assessment and the Ontario Waste Management Corporation application for approval of a hazardous waste treatment and disposal facility, was provided pursuant to such orders in council. The implementation of those orders in council by the Environmental Assessment Board and the joint board is discussed in four decisions of those boards dated December 15, 1988, January 16, 1990, April 19, 1991, and June 17, 1991.

89 *Intervenor Funding Project Act*, supra endnote 69.

90 It is interesting to note in passing that until the Brandt breakthrough, although the government had always refused requests by citizen groups for intervenor funding, it had no hesitation in funding the participation of private sector proponents before environmental boards. The government was so desperate to find a way of dealing with hazardous waste that it agreed to fund the hearing costs of some private sector proponents if they would apply to the Ministry of the Environment for approval to operate a hazardous waste facility. None of these ill-conceived projects was approved, and ultimately the government established its own Crown corporation, the Ontario Waste Management Corporation, to develop such a facility.

91 *Intervenor Funding Project Act*, supra endnote 69, section 4.

92 Ibid., section 7(1).

93 Ibid., section 7(2).

94 "Environmental Assessment Board and Joint Board Rules of Practice and Procedure," under the *Intervenor Funding Project Act*, 1988, revised March 1991.

95 "Intervenor Funding Program — General Principles for the Submission of Claims," revised, January 10, 1991.

96 W.A. Bogart and Marcia Valiante, *Access and Impact: An Evaluation of the Intervenor Project Funding Act*, February 1992, study prepared for the Ministry of the Attorney General, the Ministry of Energy, and the Ministry of the Environment.

97 When the intervenor funding program was being prepared, the government was prepared to consider providing funding to intervenors at the Ontario Municipal Board, but the chair of the board made it clear that the board did not want intervenors to have

funding: see Michael Jeffrey, "Ontario's Intervenor Funding Project Act" (1990), 3 CJALP 69.

98   Ibid.; Canadian Environmental Defence Fund, supra endnote 83.

99   *TIEAP* (supra endnote 71) has recommended providing funding during the planning stages of an environmental assessment (at 17-18), and the EAB supported this recommendation: See Environmental Assessment Board, "Recommendations on the Environmental Assessment Task Force Report: Towards Improving the Environmental Assessment Program in Ontario," presented to the Environmental Assessment Advisory Committee March 25, 1991, 7. One of the first efforts to provide participant funding was the Ontario Waste Management Corporation's allocation of some funds to outside parties for review purposes in advance of submission of its environmental assessment to the ministry.

100 See Bogart and Valiante, supra endnote 96, and Canadian Environmental Defence Fund, supra endnote 83.

101 Interim Waste Authority Limited, *News Release*, "Participant Funding Available To Audit Landfill Site Searches," August 17, 1992. Earlier, the authority had commissioned the Canadian Institute for Environmental Law and Policy (CIELAP) to prepare a discussion paper on options for participant funding: See Deborah Curran, *Participant Funding — A Discussion Paper* (Toronto: CIELAP, July 1991). The CIELAP study became a rallying point for citizen groups, who immediately criticized the authority's participant funding program as less satisfactory than the one proposed by CIELAP: See letter, R. Paul Middleton, director, Pickering Ajax Citizens Together for the Environment (PACT), to C.E. McIntyre, general manager, Interim Waste Authority, August 26, 1992.

102 Ontario, Ministry of the Environment, *Policy Manual*, policy no. 03-03, "Pre-Submission Consultation in the EA Process"; General Guidelines for the Preparation of Environmental Assessments," May 1985, appendix E; *Policy Manual*, policy no. 03-04, "Environmental Assessment Planning and Approvals," effective date June 20, 1989; Ontario, Ministry of the Environment, Environmental Assessment Branch, "Interim Guidelines on Environmental Assessment Planning and Approvals," July 1989, 7.

103 *Re Town of Meaford*, supra endnote 25, at 35 refers to 1981 PSC Guidelines; Ontario, Ministry of the Environment, "Guidelines on Pre-Submission Consultation in the EA Process," February 1987; see also *Interim Guidelines*, supra endnote 32.

104 For example, see *Re Town of Meaford*, supra endnote 25, at 38, where the board indicated that a flawed EA process might have been improved by the proponent engaging in more substantial public consultation at an earlier stage.

105 For example, the Interim Waste Authority has facilitated the establishment of such groups, which it calls regional consultation networks, in areas being considered for landfill sites.

106 *Environmental Assessment Act*, supra endnote 2; *TIEAP*, supra endnote 71, at 13.

107 See Ontario, Ministry of the Environment, Environmental Assessment Branch, *EA Update*, Summer 1992, 5.

108 See, for example, the *Design and Criteria Documents* issued by the Interim Waste Authority in August 1990 for the environmental assessment for landfill studies in

Durham region, Peel region, and the combined area of Metropolitan Toronto and York region. Some proponents have privately expressed frustration in dealing with ministry officials in relation to such ADDs. Having agreed that it makes sense to prepare such a document, they have done so and submitted it to the ministry; but when they asked for the ministry's comments on the adequacy of the design, they were told that since it is not yet ministry policy to require such a document, the ministry has no criteria against which to evaluate an ADD, and therefore the ministry will not offer any comments on the document. This, however, does not render the document useless, since it can still be released to the public for its comments, which will assist the proponent in addressing the issues of concern to the public.

109   This problem may be addressed by Ontario's proposed environmental bill of rights. See Chapter 25.

110   For a critique of the *Environmental Assessment Act* and its administration and a discussion of the reform process initiated by the Ministry of the Environment, see Robert B. Gibson, "Lessons of a Legislated Process: Twelve Years of Experience with Ontario's Environmental Assessment Act" (1990), vol. 8, no. 3 *Impact Assessment Bulletin* 63.

111   Robert B. Gibson and Beth Savan, *Environmental Assessment in Ontario* (Toronto: Canadian Institute for Environmental Law and Policy, 1986).

112   In 1990, the Environmental Assessment Board released for public discussion "The Hearing Process: Discussion Papers on Procedural and Legislative Change," September 1990, in which it discussed potential streamlining procedures such as requiring expert witnesses for all the parties to meet together to seek common ground without any lawyers being present, meetings of parties to agree on uncontroversial facts and list outstanding issues, pre-hearing mediation and conciliation, the use of pre-filed evidence, motions for early dismissal, and imposing time limits on presentations.

113   Environment Canada, Office of the Chairman of the Environmental Assessment Panel (later renamed the Federal Environmental Assessment and Review Office), *Guide to the Environmental Assessment and Review Process* (Ottawa: Environment Canada, February 1977). A revised version of the guide was published by FEARO in 1979.

114   For a discussion of the ambiguity of the guide, ibid., see the previous edition of this book, at 53-60.

115   Paul Emond, *Environmental Assessment Law in Canada* (Toronto: Emond Montgomery, 1978), 236.

116   *Government Organization Act*, 1979, SC 1979, c. 13, section 6 (proclaimed in force April 2, 1979).

117   Cabinet approved the guidelines order on June 21, 1983. It was formulated under section 6 of the *Department of the Environment Act*, RSC 1985, c. E-10, which had formerly been the *Government Organization Act*, and was promulgated as SOR/84-467.

118   For example, *Canadian Wildlife Federation*, supra endnote 10; *Oldman River*, supra endnote 7.

119   See *Oldman River*, supra endnote 7.

120   *Canadian Environmental Assessment Act*, supra endnote 12.

121   Under the guidelines order, there was no explicit power of exemption, but the federal government was able to pass valid exemption orders under the *Department of the*

Environment Act, supra endnote 117. See *Carrier-Sekani Tribal Council v. Canada (Minister of the Environment)* (1991), 6 CELR (NS) 265 (FCTD), (1992), 8 CELR (NS) 157 (FCA).

122 *Department of the Environment Act*, supra endnote 117, section 5.

123 Ibid., section 2.

124 *Indian Act*, RSC 1985, c. I-5.

125 *Canadian Environmental Assessment Act*, supra endnote 12, section 9.

126 Ibid., section 10.

127 Ibid., sections 2 and 59(c).

128 Ibid., section 59(c).

129 If the government does use a regulation under section 55 to create the exclusion list, it will be very difficult to challenge the government's decision to exclude projects from environmental assessment. For example, under the former EARP guidelines order, the Federal Court of Appeal overturned a Trial Division judgment that had nullified an order exempting a project from the EARP process: *Carrier-Sekani Tribal Council*, supra endnote 121. The appeal judgment sets out the limited basis for overturning an order in council.

130 Federal Environmental Assessment and Review Office, *Fact Sheets — Federal Environmental Assessment Reform*, fact sheet 5, June 18, 1990.

131 Ibid.

132 Ibid., fact sheet 7.

133 SOR 75/41.

134 See, for example, National Energy Board, *Environmental Screening Document*, re GHW — 2-90, June 1992.

135 *Canadian Environmental Assessment Act*, supra endnote 12, section 41.

136 Ibid., definitions in section 2.

137 Ibid., sections 2 and 55(d).

138 Ibid., sections 15 and 29.

139 See the draft regulations issued by FEARO on September 20, 1991. The fact sheets issued earlier by FEARO suggested that a "mandatory study list" would include: large oil and gas developments, uranium mines, major hydroelectric developments, large military installations, major transboundary linear facilities (for example, highways, pipelines, and high-voltage transmissions lines), and large industrial plants. An updated draft list issued February 5, 1993 suggests that the comprehensive study list will include projects in national parks and protected areas, uranium mines, hazardous waste facilities, large military installations, oil and gas developments, mines, quarries, industrial plants (for example, pulp and paper mills, smelters), and transportation or energy plants.

140 *Canadian Environmental Assessment Act*, supra endnote 12, section 18(1).

141 *Fact Sheets*, supra endnote 130, fact sheet 5.

142 Ibid.

143 *Canadian Environmental Assessment Act*, supra endnote 12, section 19(4).

144 Ibid., section 19(5).

145 Ibid., section 19(6).

146 Ibid., section 11(1).

147   Ibid., sections 5, 11, 13, and 15.

148   *Naskapi-Montagnais Innu. Assn. v. Canada (Minister of Natural Defence)* (1990), 5 CELR (NS) 287, 35 FTR 161, additional reasons at (1990), 5 CELR (NS) 313 (FCTD); *Canada (Attorney General) v. Saskatchewan* (1990), 5 CELR (NS) 252, at 285 (Sask. QB); *Canadian Wildlife Federation v. Canada (Minister of the Environment)* (1990), 6 CELR (NS) 89 (FCA) (or the *"Tetzlaff"* decision because of additional applicants with family name of Tetzlaff). Note that in *Tetzlaff* the Federal Court ruled that under the EARP guidelines order "moderate" impacts are to be interpreted as significant. Presumably the same interpretation of significance will apply to the *Canadian Environmental Assessment Act.*

149   *Canadian Environmental Assessment Act,* supra endnote 12, section 39.

150   Ibid., sections 50 and 51.

151   Ibid., section 25.

152   Ibid., section 28.

153   Ibid., section 16.

154   An extensive bibliography of writings on the subject of environmental mediation and other forms of ADR can be found in Steven Shrybman, *Environmental Mediation: From Theory to Practice* (Toronto: Canadian Institute for Environmental Law and Policy, 1984). See also Alan R. Talbot, *Settling Things: Six Case Studies in Environmental Mediation* (Washington, DC: The Conservation Foundation and the Ford Foundation, 1983).

155   *Canadian Environmental Assessment Act,* supra endnote 12, section 29.

156   Ibid., section 30.

157   Ibid., section 30.

158   Ibid., section 29(4).

159   Ibid., section 29(3).

160   Ibid., section 33(1).

161   Ibid., sections 35(3) and (4).

162   Ibid., section 34.

163   Ibid., section 35.

164   Ibid., sections 32(1) and 34(c).

165   Ibid., section 34(c).

166   Funding was provided for a number of public reviews by a panel: see, for example, Environmental Assessment Report 19 Respecting the Beaufort Sea Hydrocarbon Production and Transportation Proposal.

167   *Fact Sheets,* supra endnote 130, fact sheet 10.

168   *Canadian Environmental Assessment Act,* supra endnote 12, section 37.

169   Ibid., section 37(2).

170   Ibid., section 38(1) and the definition of "follow-up" program in section 2.

171   Ibid., sections 19, 20, 22, 23, 36, 37, 38, and 55.

172   *Statutory Powers Procedure Act,* supra endnote 62.

173   Robert B. Gibson, "The New Canadian Environmental Assessment Act: Possible Responses to Its Main Deficiencies" (1992), 2 JELP 223.

10

The Regulation of Biotechnology

CONTENTS

Gene-jockeys ... get a thrill out of creating life. I know a man in California who talks about building potatoes. He's going to build potatoes by adding genes. What arrogance! Man, you've already got a potato.

Jane Rissler, biotechnology specialist with the US National Wildlife Federation, as quoted in P. Weintraub, "The Coming of the High-Tech Harvest" (August 1992), Audubon

Every introduction is a hit-or-miss ecological roulette.

Jeremy Rifkin, as quoted in P. Weintraub, "The Coming of the High-Tech Harvest" (August 1992), Audubon

---

INTRODUCTION: "ASLEEP AT THE SWITCH"[1]

For the past two decades, the biotechnology industry has grown rapidly, almost without notice by the Canadian public.[2] For the 1990s, the biotechnology industry is hoping its investment in research and development will pay off with the introduction of a wide array of commercially viable products. While the industry is growing significantly, the question is whether the government and the public have been "asleep at the switch." The development of a regulatory framework to ensure environmental protection and occupational health and safety seems to have lagged behind the explosion of this new industry.

About This Chapter

With the range of applications being developed or contemplated, there is virtually no aspect of human endeavour that in some direct or indirect way will not be affected by the modern age of biotechnology. This chapter will not attempt to review all regulatory aspects of this new industry. Instead, it will focus on deliberate "open environment" releases where genetically engineered organisms are purposely released into the environment. Deliberate releases raise crucial regulatory issues, since control of the genetically engineered organisms is virtually lost and mitigation of ecological problems is potentially costly and often impossible.

There are certainly risks associated with "contained" biotechnology applications, such as accidental releases of new species or effects of exposure on workers' health.[3] At present, there is a body of law and policy pertaining to contained applications and releases. The research guidelines of the Medical Research Council (MRC), and the work conducted by the

Biohazards Committee of the MRC, outline some minimum standards for human safety and environmental protection in the context of recombinant DNA and virus research.[4] Moreover, there are occupational health and safety laws in most provinces that would take into account contained applications, such as the Ontario *Occupational Health and Safety Act*.[5] This is an important area of law that deserves more specific treatment on its own, and thus is beyond the scope of this chapter.

The first section will examine the applications of biotechnology and its risks. In exploring the existing and emerging regulatory framework for biotechnology, the next section will examine the constitutional framework governing biotechnology. With this framework in mind, the laws and policies of the federal and provincial governments will be examined. The last section will provide some guidelines toward improving the regulation of biotechnology.

What Is Biotechnology?[6]

There is no universally accepted definition of biotechnology, but essentially any process or method in which biology is used to make a product or service is called biotechnology. The National Biotechnology Advisory Committee states:

> Biotechnology is the use of living organisms, or parts thereof, for the production of goods and services.[7]

This definition is similar to the one used by the Organisation for Economic Co-operation and Development,[8] the National Research Council,[9] and the federal[10] and Ontario governments.[11]

Such a broad definition includes a range of activities, many of which are hardly new or revolutionary. For example, fermentation in the making of beer or the biological processes in sewage treatment plants could be considered biotechnology activities. Most agricultural practices can also be considered biotechnology.

Modern biotechnology, however, is different from these traditional practices. All living things have the same genetic material called DNA (deoxyribonucleic acid), the hereditary information code that determines life. What makes each species, and each member of a species, unique, is the distinctive arrangement of its DNA. Since the early 1970s, scientists have been able to take this genetic material from one species and implant it into an unrelated one. By doing so, they can add very specific characteristics to plants, animals, and microorganisms, resulting in genetic combinations that otherwise would not naturally occur. This is called genetic engineering and it is fundamentally different from traditional genetics in which scientists could only breed closely related species. According to one commentator:

> the principal significance of the new technology was that it made possible the transfer of genes between species with considerable specificity and ease. It, therefore, removed the specific barriers of conventional genetics.[12]

Genetic engineering means that the desirable characteristics or attributes of one organism or species, whether a plant, animal, or bacterium, can be transferred to another to create new life forms or "genotypes." These new life forms, in turn, can pass on the new characteristics to their offspring.

With the discovery of genetic engineering techniques, the development of a biotechnology industry soon followed, hoping to translate the scientifically novel techniques into commercial products and services.

The Biotechnology Industry and Its Applications

Over the last two decades, the main focus of the biotechnology industry has been research and development, while products have been somewhat slow to reach the market. However, this is expected to change throughout the 1990s, although it is difficult to predict with any certainty which new products or applications of biotechnology will be available. Some of the genetic engineering products currently available include human insulin, coloured cotton fibres, and milk-curdling enzymes for cheese production.

Canadian and US biotechnology companies have enjoyed large investments in the early 1980s and again in the early 1990s. This success in obtaining financing led the Toronto Stock Exchange to initiate a separate biotechnology index in February 1992 to monitor the stock prices of biotechnology firms. There is an unlimited horizon for biotechnology.

Modern biotechnology applications can be categorized under the following subject headings: human health, agriculture, mining and petrochemicals, and environmental protection.

Human Health

Human insulin, produced by genetically engineered microorganisms, was one of the first products to reach the market in the early 1980s. Since then, a tremendous amount of product development has occurred, especially since large pharmaceutical companies and entrepreneurial biotechnology firms have merged their operations. "Never have so many revolutionary therapies come into the marketplace in so short a time," notes an industry observer.[13] Applications in the health field aim at disease treatment, vaccines, diagnostic products, and disease prevention for hemophilia, hepatitis C, diabetes, AIDS, cancer, and other diseases.

Agriculture

The potential applications of biotechnology in the agriculture area are vast. They include genetically engineered (transgenic) crops, genetically engineered microorganisms (GEMs), and animal health and production products.

Transgenic Crops

With a variety of techniques, scientists are now able to breed crops with specific characteristics or traits. For example, new crop strains are developed to improve crop nutritional and growth characteristics. Others, and perhaps the most controversial at the present time, are those developed to increase resistance to pesticides and herbicides. Such applications would continue, and even increase, the application of synthetic chemicals on our food. For example, Monsanto is developing canola (a plant used to make vegetable oil) to be resistant to its herbicide Glyphosate. Hence, this herbicide can be used without affecting that specific strain of canola, but killing all other weeds around it.

Genetically Engineered Microorganisms

One of the earlier applications of GEMs is the use of microbes that can be sprayed on temperature-sensitive plants and crops to help protect them from frost damage. This so-called ice-minus bacterium allows longer growing seasons and a reduction in crop loss due to late frosts. Other agricultural applications include genetically engineered growth hormones that are given to farm animals to increase their productivity.

Animal Products

In addition to the applications noted, there is a whole array of other applications. Products are being developed or used to induce growth in animals. For example, the controversial hormone BST, produced by genetic engineering techniques, can be injected into cows to substantially increase milk production. Animal vaccines can now be made cheaper and more efficiently to fight chronic cattle diseases such as shipping fever and bovine virus diarrhoea.

Mining and Petrochemicals

There are a variety of biotechnology applications that, although still in the developmental stages, hold considerable potential to make a number of industrial sectors more efficient and more environmentally benign. For example, genetically altered microbes may be able to leach minerals such as copper, nickel, and gold from ores and tailings in concentrations that could not be extracted economically by traditional means.

With respect to petrochemicals, biotechnology will allow the production of specialty chemicals that previously were more expensive, or even impossible, to produce by traditional practices.

Environmental Protection

Many applications of biotechnology are being developed for environmental protection purposes. According to the National Biotechnology Advisory Committee, waste treatment will be the largest market for biotechnology applications.[14] Through the use of new biotechnology products, for example, it may be possible to accelerate processes of degrading inoculated sludges from waste water facilities. The Canada Centre for Inland Waters in Burlington, Ontario and the National Research Council's Biotechnology Research Institute in Montreal, Quebec have research programs oriented toward the use of biotechnology for the treatment of municipal and industrial waste water.[15]

Other uses that may further environmental protection goals include the creation of microorganisms capable of detoxifying hazardous waste or rendering organic pollutants such as polychlorinated biphenyls (PCBs) less toxic. Similarly, new life forms will be able to clean up oil and other chemical spills, and will form the foundation for new waste management technologies.

Almost invariably, the proponents of biotechnology have repeated its potential benefits with an almost evangelical zeal. What is usually overlooked, however, are the risks of these new products and services to the integrity of local, regional, and, indeed, global ecosystems. Although the benefits are better known, the risks should not and cannot be overlooked, even if the state of knowledge of those risks remains woefully inadequate.

The Risks of Biotechnology

Certainly, it is not possible to outline in any detail all the real or potential risks of biotechnology. However, three overall issues can be identified in this regard.

The Lack of Knowledge

One of the difficulties in identifying the "risk" side of genetic engineering is simply the lack of knowledge and information about how new life forms will interact in the environment.[16] In effect, the database to make informed decisions is incomplete at best and, more realistically, virtually absent. As two microbiologists have noted:

Unfortunately, when dealing with the potential risks to biological systems, the existing data base is meagre and the predictive ability of the ecological sciences is almost nil.[17]

According to the US Congressional Subcommittee on Science and Technology, there is at present

[n]o historical and scientific data base concerning the behavioral characteristics of genetically-engineered organisms in the environment and no standard ecological methodology for predicting the outcome of exotic introduction.[18]

The Inability To Evaluate the New Technologies

Because of the absence of data, the ability to predict the consequences of the deliberate introduction of new life forms in the environment is not great. Comprehensive prediction methodologies cannot be developed when the nature of the organism, the nature of the ecosystem, and the interrelationship between the two have major information gaps. Such questions led the US Congressional Subcommittee on Science and Technology to state:

Predicting the specific type, magnitude, or the probability of environmental effects associated with the deliberate release of genetically engineered organisms will be extremely difficult, if not impossible, at the present time.[19]

The potential risk is most often stated to be of a "low probability, high consequence risk."[20] In other words, although the chances of something going wrong may be very slight, if something does go wrong, the ecological consequences may be tremendous. Hence, what must be asked is *not* only whether something may go wrong but, if it does, what is the present capability to address the consequences.

Thus, it is clear that identifying the risks in the absence of a sound information base makes informed decision making a perplexing, often impossible, task. In a very generic fashion, however, there are a number of potential risks that can occur by introducing genetically altered life forms into the environment. Some of these are:[21]

- genetically modified microorganisms may transmit, promote, or carry diseases that are infectious to humans, plants, or animals;
- genetically altered organisms can expand beyond their niche or prove destructive to non-target organisms;
- genetically engineered organisms may have a resistance to certain diseases and thus establish a competitive advantage over natural species;
- genetically modified organisms may survive and reproduce after their intended function is completed, since they can move and reproduce;
- genetically engineered organisms may be accidentally released from laboratories; and

- transgenic crops that are pesticide-resistant may transfer this resistance to weeds and other plants.[22]

These specific risks sometimes overshadow the more general risk of reducing biological diversity in any given ecosystem.[23] Biotechnology can threaten the biodiversity by the drive to breed uniformity in plants and animals, and by furthering and encouraging monocultures. Furthermore, genetically engineered species may disturb food chains or habitats, which in turn will affect biodiversity. Indeed, the analogy to introducing exotic species is often used when examining ecological impacts of biotechnology. In both cases, a new species is introduced into an ecosystem with detrimental results, even though the anticipated introduction was thought to be quite harmless in some cases. There are many examples in which the introduction of exotic species has led to significant ecological disruption in North America; such species include the common sparrow, the gypsy moth, Dutch elm disease, starlings, zebra mussels, and various species of plants.[24]

Are All New Applications Appropriate?

Finally, there is a broader and perhaps more philosophical question. Are all biotechnology products legitimate? If not, how does society distinguish between legitimate applications and applications that ought not to be developed? Clearly, some products can be said to address the symptoms and not the causes of our problems. In forestry, for example, one of the areas in which research is vigorously pursued is the development of genetically improved trees for quicker reforestation.[25] These trees are supposed be grown on clearcuts. But are the slow-growing trees the problem, or is the real problem the practice of clearcutting? In the agricultural field, crops are being developed that will be resistant to pesticides and herbicides. Does this practice not reinforce the legitimacy of spraying synthetic chemicals on food products?

There is little doubt that there are benefits and risks to biotechnology. The question now is whether the regulatory framework is adequate to identify and address the environmental implications of this technological revolution.

THE REGULATORY FRAMEWORK FOR BIOTECHNOLOGY

While industrial activity forges ahead, the regulatory framework governing biotechnology remains embryonic. Countries such as Germany, the Netherlands, and Denmark, and a number of US states such as North Carolina and Minnesota have enacted specific biotechnology legislation.[26] Canada and Ontario have failed to do so.

This section examines the federal and provincial regulatory regimes, although it should be recognized that local authorities may also have a role in the regulation of biotechnology, a subject that has been discussed elsewhere.[27]

Constitutional Issues

The regulatory framework governing biotechnology is divided between federal and provincial levels of government in accordance with specifically allocated legislative powers under sections 91 and 92 of the *Constitution Act, 1867*.[28]

The federal government can use a number of its constitutional powers to govern biotechnology products. For example, it can regulate the importation of biotechnology products through its jurisdiction over interprovincial trade and commerce.[29] Other areas of federal jurisdiction that could be used for the basis for legislative authority include "sea coast and inland fisheries"[30] and the criminal law.[31] Perhaps one of the most important federal powers is the "residual power" to make laws for the peace, order, and good government of Canada (POGG), found in section 91 of the *Constitution Act, 1867*.[32] An analogy is nuclear power, a matter given a federal legislative mandate under the POGG section of the constitution. This power could authorize the federal government to regulate aspects of biotechnology on a number of grounds. First, biotechnology was a matter not apparent in 1867. Second, biotechnology may be seen as having a "national dimension" since it is of concern to the whole country and cannot be effectively regulated by cooperative provincial action.

Provincial authority to regulate biotechnology activities is based on the powers over "property and civil rights,"[33] "local works and undertakings,"[34] and "matters of a merely local or private nature."[35] Other provincial powers that relate to biotechnology include the provincial rights of ownership of public lands and natural resources, and the authority over the exploitation, development, conservation, and management of non-renewable natural resources, forestry resources, and electric energy production.[36]

In reality, the regulatory framework governing biotechnology will probably involve a considerable federal-provincial overlap and require coordination. If regulation of biotechnology follows the lines of division of legislative powers that the courts have upheld in other areas of law, the federal government's authority will probably be limited to the *control and licensing* of biotechnology products, and the provincial focus will be on the safe *application and use* of such products. Hence, the federal government would decide whether biotechnology products could be registered for sale in Canada, and the provincial government could regulate for worker safety, appropriate use of biotechnology products and their waste disposal, and other environment-related matters. The federal *Pest Control Products Act*[37] and the Ontario *Pesticides Act*[38] provide a general analogy as to how the jurisdiction can be shared. The federal Act controls the pesticide *products* (importation and registration), and the provincial law regulates the *users* of pesticides.

The legal and constitutional complexity of the field is amplified by the fact that there are also jurisdictional issues among agencies within a level government. For example, there are about 17 federal and 46 provincial agencies that have some regulatory mandate pertaining to biotechnology.[39] As a result of this fragmented regulatory framework,

[t]he extent to which these regulatory mandates embrace various aspects of the new biotechnologies is unclear in many instances, particularly regarding intentional environmental release of biological wastes and introduction of some biological products.[40]

Even though the provincial government has limited authority to address the environmental aspects of biotechnology, the federal government is undertaking essentially all of the regulatory activity. Perhaps this is not too surprising, since the federal government has to face these issues first because many biotechnology products are just now approaching the feasibility of commercial use and because the federal government has been the catalyst in furthering the technology.

Federal Law and Policy

The History of Federal Biotechnology Regulations

The economic potential of biotechnology has been recognized at least since the 1970s.[41] By 1983, the National Biotechnology Strategy had been introduced by the Ministry of State for Science and Technology.[42] This industrial development strategy for biotechnology targeted its commercial applications for health care, mining and mineral leaching, plant strain development, nitrogen fixation, cellulose utilization, and waste treatment. Under the strategy, the National Biotechnology Advisory Committee was formed to advise the minister of state for science and technology on issues related to the subject. As the strategy evolved, it focused more on the economic development aspects of biotechnology than on the development of a regulatory oversight for the industry.

As the strategy was being implemented, so was the research infrastructure for Canada. In 1984, the National Research Council launched its biotechnology program, which coordinates the work of four institutes: the Biotechnology Research Institute in Montreal for industrial applications, the Plant Biotechnology Institute in Saskatoon for plant technologies, the Institute for Biological Sciences in Ottawa for studies pertaining to mammalian research, and the Institute for Marine Biosciences in Halifax, Nova Scotia.[43]

While the industry was steadily growing in Canada, regulatory concerns continued to surface. The National Biotechnology Advisory Committee identified several issues that need to be addressed in private sector decision making and public policy.[44] The advisory committee recommended that new products be regulated based on the *uses* of biological organisms and their category of risk, rather than on an assumption that every biologically based product or process forms a risk. The advisory committee further noted that an increase in staff and expertise to evaluate and process new products and processes was required, as well as the need to harmonize the regulatory requirements and approval systems with those in Europe and the United States.[45]

As part of the National Biotechnology Strategy, the Federal Interdepartmental Committee on Biotechnology was formed, in part to further examine these problems. This committee, in turn, established the Working Group on Safety and Regulations, which has been associated with a number of initiatives:

- It examined the adequacy of the current regulatory system by sponsoring a number of studies concerning the development of a regulatory framework for biotechnology.[46]
- It created the Ad Hoc Committee on Environmental Release in 1987, which is composed of regulators from the three key regulatory departments — Health and Welfare, Environment, and Agriculture.[47] The ad hoc committee spearheaded the federal guidance document to the regulation of biotechnology, *Bio-Tech Regulations — A User's Guide to Federal Regulation on Biotechnology.*[48]
- It uses the National Biotechnology Coordination Office as a secretariat. The coordination office was established through the Department of Industry, Science and Technology in 1988.[49] Its task is to coordinate regulatory information at international, national, and provincial levels between public and private sectors.

It was not until the development of the *Canadian Environmental Protection Act*[50] that the question of the legislation of biotechnology had to be faced head-on. During the consultations on the draft bill, environmentalists called for a new biotechnology statute or even a specific biotechnology part in the Act to provide an overall legislative framework.[51] By that time, however, the federal government had decided that biotechnology would not be regulated by some omnibus approach. Instead, it was decided that biotechnology would be regulated through existing law, most of which is administered by two federal departments — Agriculture Canada and Health and Welfare Canada. One of the problems with regulating biotechnology through existing legislation is that the drafters of the legislation did not envision such products, so the legislation may be ill-suited to this use and the courts may be reluctant to interpret it to include biotechnology. Moreover, agency staff who administer the legislation will often be reluctant to apply it to biotechnology unless the legislation explicitly states that biotechnology products are covered. In effect, by the time the *Canadian Environmental Protection Act* was promulgated in 1988, it became a backstop, empowering Environment Canada only to regulate those products of biotechnology that are not covered by other legislation. Thus, Environment Canada does not have regulatory oversight over most of the agricultural, forestry, and health-related products.

In December 1990, the government of Canada released its "Green Plan," which outlined its environmental agenda for upcoming years.[52] In this plan, the federal government committed itself to a national regulatory regime to address the environmental risks of the biotechnology industry. This national regulatory regime is to include national standards and codes of practice to prevent problems arising from accidental or deliberate releases of genetically engineered microorganisms, and regulations under the *Canadian Environmental Protection Act* requiring notification to Environment Canada and Health and Welfare Canada of new products of biotechnology before they are introduced to the market or released into the environment.[53] The federal government set 1995 as the deadline to fulfil these obligations.

Despite the Green Plan commitments, many have been critical of the continued delay of federal regulations. This problem has been recently recognized by the National Biotechnology Advisory Committee. In 1991 it noted:

> Federal regulations are a critical determinant of the cost and time required to bring a new biotechnology product to market. Current delays and regulatory uncertainties are discouraging new research and investments in commercial facilities, driving up the costs of innovation and undermining public confidence.[54]

Because the federal government deals with biotechnology products through the existing laws and agencies, it is difficult to generalize as to how each and every product is dealt with under federal law. Table 1 gives an overview of biotechnology products and the applicable laws.

When reviewing the federal regulatory framework in this chapter, it is convenient to ask the following questions: Is it a biotechnology product? If so, what statute regulates it? Under those statutes, what are the requirements for: field-tests? commercial use? importation?

Although there are other categories, the biotechnology products examined in this chapter include: pest control, transgenic crops, microbes, and other agricultural- and animal-related products.

Table 1: An Overview of Federal Laws and Agencies for Biotechnology

Biotechnology Products/Organisms	Relevant Laws and Regulations	Applicable Agencies
Animal pathogens, veterinary biologics, animal products and byproducts	*Health of Animals Act* and regulations	Agriculture Canada
Feeds and feed additives	*Feeds Act* and regulations	Agriculture Canada
Fertilizers/ supplements	*Fertilizers Act* and regulations	Agriculture Canada
Foods and food additives	*Food and Drugs Act* and regulations	Health and Welfare Canada
Medical devices	*Food and Drugs Act* and regulations	Health and Welfare Canada
Pest control agents	*Pest Control Products Act* and regulations	Agriculture Canada; Health and Welfare Canada
Food and drugs	*Foods and Drugs Act* and regulations	Health and Welfare Canada
Plant pests	*Plant Protection Act* and regulations	Agriculture Canada
Plants/seeds	*Seeds Act* and regulations	Agriculture Canada
Consumer products	*Hazardous Products Act* and regulations; *Consumer Protection Act*	Health and Welfare Canada; Consumer and Corporate Affairs
Chemical products	*Canadian Environmental Protection Act* and regulations	Environment Canada; Health and Welfare Canada
Other products (pollution control, mineral leaching, chemical residue destruction, waste disposal, novel uses not elsewhere covered)	*Canadian Environmental Protection Act* and regulations	Environment Canada; Health and Welfare Canada

Source: Adapted from Canada, *Bio-Tech Regulations—A User's Guide to Federal Regulation on Biotechnology* (Ottawa: Agriculture Canada, Environment Canada, Health and Welfare Canada, Ministry of State for Science and Technology, Labour Canada, and Consumer and Corporate Affairs Canada, 1991).

Legislation for Pest Controls: Pest Control Products Act

The Pesticides Directorate of Agriculture Canada regulates the manufacture, sale, and use of pest controls under the *Pest Control Products Act*.[55] A "control product" is defined as "any device, organism, substance or thing that is manufactured, represented, sold or used as a means of directly controlling, preventing, destroying, mitigating, attracting or repelling any pest."[56] The Act defines a pest as "any injurious, noxious or troublesome insect, fungus, bacterial organism, virus, weed, rodent or other plant or animal pest, and includes any injurious, noxious or troublesome organic function of a plant or animal."[57] The broad definition of pest and pest control products could catch a broad range of biotechnology products. For example, microorganisms produced by genetic engineering techniques (that is, bacteria, viruses, fungi, and protozoa) could be included.[58]

The Act and regulations[59] require anyone who intends to import, field-test, or sell pest control products in Canada, to apply to the Pesticides Directorate for research permits and registration.[60] Research permits are required for importing pest control products and prior to field-testing them (that is, experimental environmental releases). These permits are granted on a case-by-case basis. The Pest Control Products Regulations under the Act include exemptions, such as research being conducted on premises owned or operated by the researcher.[61]

The Act suffers from several problems, such as limited public participation in the decision-making process pertaining to pesticide registration, very limited public access to health and safety tests relied on for registration purposes, and the lack of a review process for pesticides already registered.[62] These problems have been recognized and the *Pest Control Products Act* has been reviewed by a multi-stakeholder task force. If the task force recommendations are implemented by the federal government, the Act will undergo some significant changes.[63]

Legislation for Transgenic Crops

The first wave of deliberate releases of genetically engineered products into the environment is transgenic crops. Put simply, these are plants like canola, potatoes, or alfalfa that have been engineered for a desired trait, such as herbicide resistance, pest resistance, or virus resistance. These applications are regulated through the *Pest Control Products Act*, the *Plant Protection Act*,[64] the *Seeds Act*,[65] and other statutes. In many cases, attempting to regulate agricultural products of biotechnology through existing legislation is a difficult task since the drafters of the legislation did not contemplate such products. Furthermore, different regulations for biotechnology products do not exist for the variety of stages of application, such as research and development, small-scale field-testing, large-scale field-testing, and commercialization. This sketchy patchwork of legislation has been recognized in an Agriculture Canada report, which states:

> there are a number of legislative acts in Canada that could be applied to biotechnology control. However, most of these are not clear cut and would require modifications for them to be applicable to biotechnology. Plant biotechnology currently has very little regulation both federally and provincially.[66]

To guide agricultural applications through the regulatory process, the federal government has designated Agriculture Canada, and specifically the Food Production and Inspection

Branch, as the lead federal agency.[67] For plant material, including genetically altered agricultural crops, other than seed potatoes, the Seed Section of the Plant Products Division has been made the lead regulatory agency. For seed potatoes, the Plant Protection Division of Agriculture Canada is the lead regulatory agency. The Seed Section receives and reviews applications for field-tests, and coordinates responses to the applicant and the issuance of approvals. By and large, the intent of the federal government is to develop a "one-stop" regulatory approach by employing a product-based regulatory system for biotechnology.[68] That is, Agriculture Canada is expected to coordinate all necessary approvals with other regulatory agencies for the applicant. This way, applicants have to deal with only one government department.

As noted above, the *Pest Control Products Act*[69] regulates pest products such as microbial pest control products. Moreover, genetically engineered plant material, containing novel pest-resistant properties and pesticide-tolerant properties also falls under the jurisdiction of this Act. For these applications, the field-testing requirements and registration regimes under the Act also apply.

The Plant Protection Act

The purpose of the *Plant Protection Act*[70] is to "protect plant life and the agricultural and forestry sectors of the Canadian economy by preventing the importation, exportation and spread of pests and by controlling or eradicating pests in Canada."[71] The Act regulates products being imported or developed in Canada that are or could be plant pests, including genetically altered plants and organisms. The Act defines a pest as any thing that is injurious or could be injurious to plants or plant products, and includes any plant named by the government as a pest itself.[72]

Transgenic plants are regulated under the Act to the extent that they are considered "pests." For example, transgenic plants could be "pests" when:

- the plants develop into weeds and affect other plants in a negative way;
- the plants supply the genetic material to create more virulent weeds from plants that have received the engineered trait; and
- the plant contains a vector, used to transport a foreign gene into a transgenic plant, that could cause an infectious plant disease.[73]

The Act prohibits any person from moving, growing, raising, culturing or producing any thing when there are *reasonable grounds* to believe it could be a pest.[74] If an inspector believes a thing may be a pest, written authorization is needed from an inspector to move it,[75] or to import or export it, except in accordance with the statute and regulations.[76] Permits are issued by the Import Section of the Plant Protection Division, after considering the recommendations of the Seed Division, which conducts an assessment of risks *to the plant health only*.

The *Plant Protection Act* could regulate field-tests and the movement of transgenic crops because Agriculture Canada requires information before the tests to assess the status of the plant as a pest. If it is deemed to be a pest, controls could be imposed. However, this framework is not without some pitfalls. First, the requirement under section 6 that there must be "reasonable grounds" to predict a plant to be a pest sets a formidable threshold, since there is generally little empirical information as to the behaviour of engineered plants in the open environment. Second, because the scope of the Act is limited to the protection of agricultural and forestry ecosystems,[77] the Act could ignore the broader impacts on other natural ecosystems "such as the loss of genetic diversity in wild plant relatives due to the transfer of an engineered trait."[78]

The Seeds Act

The *Seeds Act*[79] regulates the designation, sale, and importation of seeds. A "seed" is defined as "any plant part or any species belonging to the plant kingdom represented, sold or used to grow a plant."[80] Before a variety of an agricultural crop may be marketed, it must proceed through the variety registration process. This process is based on minimum standards such as agronomic and processing merit, genetic purity, varietal identity, and, for some crops, food safety, which must be satisfied before they can be sold in Canada. The requirements for variety registration are found in part III of the Seeds Regulations.[81] Genetically altered plant material is required to undergo the same registration process as conventionally developed varieties.

The *Seeds Act* has a number of limitations for the effective assessment and control of transgenic crops. As one commentator noted, the "emphasis is on the quality and health of the crop which will be grown from the seed, not the potential interactions of the plant ecosystem."[82] Second, although the *Seeds Act* provides authority for all seeds, the Seeds Regulations exempt some species from some requirements. Hence, some variety registration requirements do not apply to all species. For example, horticultural crop varieties need not be registered and, therefore, neither are genetically altered horticultural crop varieties.[83] The regulations also do not cover vegetables, herbs, and trees.[84] Thus, the *Seeds Act* does not provide a complete regime to control production, testing, or environmental releases of biotechnology products.[85] This issue is discussed further under the heading "Environmental Assessments of Field-Tests," below.

Legislation for Other Agricultural and Animal-Related Products

Apart from the statutes described above, there are a host of other statutes that regulate, in some fashion, biotechnology products that affect agriculture and animal-related products. For example, the *Health of Animals Act*[86] and its regulations give authority to Agriculture Canada to regulate the production, evaluation, importation, and registration of veterinary biologics, animal products, and animal pathogens in Canada. The term "veterinary biologics" is given a broad meaning, including those that restore, correct, or modify organic functions in animals.[87] For example, the Act would cover BGH (bovine growth hormone), a controversial product that dramatically enhances the production of milk in cows.

Under the regulations to the *Health of Animals Act*, tests must be carried out to establish the purity, safety, potency, and efficacy of a veterinary biologic. Agriculture Canada also grants permits to qualified importers after completing inspection and approval requirements. Hence, this provision could be used to assess the impacts of new products, and to assess the appropriateness of field-tests and registration for commercial use. However, it has been noted that

> [a]n amendment in the regulations will be needed to determine that the vaccines containing genetically manipulated living organisms are safe not only to animals but also for humans and the environment.[88]

Agriculture Canada also regulates the manufacture, sale, and importation of livestock feeds and feed ingredients, including those produced by biotechnology, under the *Feeds Act*[89] and regulations. The exercise of regulatory authority includes pre-sale registration and post-sale inspection. Research permits are not needed for livestock feeds used for experimental purposes,[90] although Agriculture Canada requires information to assess whether a product is in fact exempt. Before a product can be sold, it must be registered with Agriculture Canada. Similarly, approval is needed before livestock feeds or their ingredients can be imported.

As with feeds, Agriculture Canada regulates the sale and distribution of fertilizers and fertilizer supplements through a pre-sale registration and a post-sale inspection under the *Fertilizers Act*.[91] A fertilizer is defined as "any substance or mixture of substances containing nitrogen, phosphorus, potassium or other plant food, manufactured ... for use as a plant nutrient." A fertilizer supplement is defined as "any substance ... for use in the improvement of the physical condition of soils, or to aid plant growth or crop yields."

The *Fertilizers Act*, then, potentially regulates a broad array of biotechnology products, including products that provide nutrients to the soil, promote plant growth, or otherwise improve the condition of the soil. Under the Act, field-tests are approved on a case-by-case basis on submission of information regarding the fertilizer product. For commercialization purposes, all products must be registered before sale and use in Canada, following an evaluation of specific information required under the regulations of the *Fertilizers Act*.

Legislation for Microorganisms

The *Canadian Environmental Protection Act*[92] provides the key regulatory instrument for Environment Canada for products that are not caught under other acts. Biotechnology is addressed under part II of the Act, which pertains to toxic substances. Biotechnology products are caught as a result of the definition of "substance" under section 3, which means "any distinguishable kind of organic or inorganic matter, *whether animate or inanimate*" [emphasis added].

More specifically, biotechnology products are covered under the "new substances" provisions of the *Canadian Environmental Protection Act*. These provisions set out information requirements for new substances that must be provided before their manufacture or importation into Canada. These requirements enable the pertinent departments to assess the potential environmental or health effects of these new substances. Section 25 of the Act defines a new substance as one that is not on the domestic substances list (DSL).[93] If it is a new substance, section 26 authorizes the minister to prescribe information requirements for assessing it. To date, the DSL does not contain any biotechnology products, but a biotechnology component to the DSL is currently under development.[94] In this process, manufacturers or importers can provide satisfactory evidence to substantiate that specific products were in commerce in Canada within the timeframe defined in the Act.

As of November 1992, Environment Canada and Health and Welfare Canada had yet to exercise their authority to promulgate regulations outlining notification and information requirements. A third draft of the new substances notification regulation for biotechnology products, however, was released in October 1992. This draft regulation is geared to microorganisms and biochemicals and thus would be relevant to new biotechnological products pertaining to: bioremediation, mineral leaching, degradation of chemicals, mining, waste treatment, waste disposal, chemical production, lignin degradation, microbial enhanced oil recovery, and energy production.

The draft regulation defines a series of notification requirements based on how close the product is to commercial application.[95] Several development phases have been defined, each of which has prescribed notification and assessment periods, as well as a corresponding schedule, defining the information to be submitted. More particularly:

1. For contained use, notification is required 45 days before the manufacture of a biotechnology product commences or the importation of a biotechnology product takes place.
2. For environmental introduction, notification is required:

    (a) before small-scale field-trials (60-day assessment period);
    (b) before large-scale field-trials (90-day assessment period); and
    (c) before uses other than small-scale or large-scale field-tests (120-day assessment period).

3. Each of the four information schedules specifies the applicable information requirements. Categories of information to be submitted include:

    (a) identification and characterization of the microorganisms;
    (b) data on environmental fate and effects on non-target substances in the environment;
    (c) human health safety testing data;
    (d) description of intended uses, manufacturing methods, and quality control and quality assurance procedures; and
    (e) specifics on field-tests including location and procedures to be used during the trial, where applicable.

The draft regulation proposes a number of possible exemptions from informational requirements and assessments. First, a schedule of organisms is proposed that will be exempt from the assessment process on the basis that there is a sufficient history of safe use. Second, waiver provisions will exist for specific products, where the progression through the stages is not required. Finally, provisions pertaining to confidential business information are also proposed.

It is expected that these regulations under the *Canadian Environmental Protection Act*, with certain modifications, will become law in 1993.

Other Potentially Applicable Federal Legislation

Because biotechnology product regulation is "piggy-backed" on other relevant statutes, there are a number of other laws that could be applicable to biotechnology. To name a few, the *Forestry Development and Research Act*,[96] the *Hazardous Products Act*,[97] and the *Transportation of Dangerous Goods Act*[98] may have express or indirect relevance to biotechnology products. In addition, the *Food and Drugs Act*, the *Department of National Health and Welfare Act*, and the *Plant Breeders' Rights Act* can be used to regulate biotechnology products.[99]

Provincial Law and Policy

The History of Ontario Biotechnology Regulation

The history of the provincial regulatory development governing biotechnology is a relatively short one. For over a decade now, the Ontario government has had an interest in biotechnology. However, this interest has been more in promoting the technology as an industrial development strategy than in developing a comprehensive environmental protection regime. In 1982, the Ontario government made substantial investments in one of Canada's largest biotechnology companies, Allelix Inc., by taking a 20 per cent equity interest with over $30 million in loan guarantees and contributions to operations.[100] The province has since sold its interests in Allelix.

For 1992, Ontario biotechnology firms forecast that sales will total some $5 billion, representing an annual growth rate of 46 per cent.[101] Biotechnology firms have an average of six products in production and another seven in development. One-third of Ontario's biotechnology industry is dedicated to health care.[102]

By 1989, the government of Ontario had decided to convene a multi-agency advisory committee to produce a green paper on biotechnology. (A green paper is a discussion document that precedes a formal government policy.) The discussion paper, *Biotechnology in Ontario — Growing Safely*, was released in September 1989 and submissions were received well into 1990. As of September 1992, the government has not responded to the public comments received in response to the discussion paper. In 1990, the Ministry of the Environment established a biotechnology unit within the Hazardous Contaminants Branch, consisting of two full-time staff. The purpose of the unit is to provide in-house expertise on biotechnology and to develop a regulatory strategy for the ministry. As of September 1992, details of such a strategy had not been announced by the ministry.[103]

Provincial Regulation of Biotechnology

There are a number of provincial statutes that are potentially applicable to some aspects of biotechnology. However, none of these statutes provides for a comprehensive framework, and none of them has yet to be applied to biotechnology products.

The Environmental Protection Act and the Ontario Water Resources Act

The *Environmental Protection Act*[104] prohibits the release or discharge of any contaminant into the natural environment in an amount likely to cause adverse effects.[105] A similar prohibition, applicable to water discharges, is found in the *Ontario Water Resources Act*.[106] Any person intending to release or discharge a contaminant must obtain a certificate of approval for the facility from the Ministry of the Environment.[107] Authority is also given to issue "control orders," "stop orders," and other preventive and remedial orders governing the release of contaminants in specified circumstances.[108]

The extent to which these statutes could be used to regulate the release of genetically engineered organisms into the environment is questionable. First, a biotechnology product might not be deemed to be a "contaminant" since the definition, on its face, does not seem to include living organisms.[109] Second, most of these provisions are really geared to regulating more known risks to the environment, as opposed to the biotechnology products, whose risks are highly uncertain.

The Pesticides Act

Under the *Pesticides Act*,[110] the Ministry of the Environment regulates the sale, use, transport, and disposal of all pesticide products in Ontario. The provincial law complements the federal pesticide registration process under the *Pest Control Products Act*. Definitions under the *Pesticides Act* seem to be broad enough to include biological agents and biotechnology products used for pest control purposes. Hazard assessment protocols and guidelines concerning all aspects of these products have yet to be developed.[111] Moreover, there are a number of exemptions under the Act, most notably for farmers, who will be significant users of biotechnological products.

Other Relevant Provincial Statutes

There are a number of provincial statutes that may have some relevance to products of genetic engineering. Some of these statutes are: the *Animals for Research Act*,[112] the *Artificial Insemination of Livestock Act*,[113] the *Plant Diseases Act*,[114] and the *Milk Act*.[115] However, the applicability and effectiveness of these statutes to biotechnology products depend both on the nature of the issue (for example, field-tests, approvals, etc.) and the nature of the application.

REGULATORY ISSUES IN BIOTECHNOLOGY

Owing to its novelty, there are many issues in regulating biotechnology that need to be researched, discussed, and resolved. This section outlines three of the major issues.

Environmental Assessments of Field-Tests

As the industry enters the 1990s, the commercial use of new biotechnology products will dramatically increase. However, quite often products must go through some type of field-test before their commercial application is possible. A field-test is generally the first open environmental release, raising ecological concerns and opening the window for the environmental assessment process. What, then, is the basis in law for the federal or provincial governments to undertake environmental assessments before genetically engineered organisms are field-tested? It depends, to put it simply.

At first glance, it could be expected that the *Canadian Environmental Assessment Act*,[116] passed in July 1992, would be applicable. However, the Act only governs "projects," which is defined as a "physical work." Is testing an organism in the field a "physical work"? Assuming that field-tests will be interpreted to fall within these definitions, assessments may be required under section 5 — namely, where the federal government is a proponent, or when a federal authority issues some type of approval.

In 1991, Agriculture Canada conducted one-tenth of all field-tests of transgenic crops, making the federal government an obvious proponent. However, these field-tests may not be included under the federal environmental assessment process for two reasons. First, under section 6 of the *Canadian Environmental Assessment Act*, any project can be automatically excluded if it appears on the "exclusion list," which has yet to be published. Thus, the federal government could avoid undertaking environmental assessments for its own tests. Second, the type of environmental assessment undertaken can be very limited. Under section 13, the responsible authority, or the department carrying out the field-test, undertakes an initial screening process. Following this screening, the authority may decide to carry on with a more comprehensive assessment, or finish the assessment by declaring that there are no significant environmental effects. Given the weak environmental assessments undertaken with the over 300 field-tests under the old environmental assessment and review process, comprehensive assessments cannot be expected under the new *Canadian Environmental Assessment Act*. For example, none of the environmental assessments to date has addressed the first two questions of a proper environmental assessment: the purpose of and need for the new life-form, and what other alternatives exist to fulfil a similar purpose.

Field-tests proposed by companies and universities may also be subject to the new federal environmental assessment regime when some sort of federal approval is needed to conduct the tests. However, whether or not such tests are included under the Act will be based on provisions that have yet to be developed in regulations under section 55(f). Furthermore, it is currently unclear what types of approvals would trigger the Act, since federal approvals for biotechnology products are not uniform in nature and formal permits are often not needed.

Apart from the *Canadian Environmental Assessment Act*, the extent and nature of environmental assessments for field-tests of transgenic crops will depend on whether a specific statute authorizes some type of assessment. There are a number of applications where present laws could be used to include an assessment. For example, if the field-test falls within the *Pest Control Products Act*,[117] the authority to require information to assess the products is clear.[118]

However, the situation is much less clear under the *Seeds Act*,[119] where there is no provision to allow for the control of field-testing outside of the varietal testing for registration purposes.[120] Moreover, under the varietal-testing regime, the rules are different for seeds that are imported and for those developed in Canada. Section 39 of the Seeds Regulations[121] provides the ability to regulate the importation of seeds of an unregistered variety. Through this section, Agriculture Canada is able to set terms and conditions governing the field-test.[122]

When genetically altered plant material originates in Canada — that is, when it is produced domestically — the field-tests may be regulated under section 78 of the Seeds Regulations. This section prohibits a change in the genetic constitution of a variety without the written approval of the registrar. Hence, there may be authority for the registrar to give or withhold permission for scientists to conduct research that alters a variety genetically to such an extent that it becomes a different variety from the one registered under the Act. However, Agriculture Canada puts forth the view that section 78 of the Seeds Regulations would not be used to regulate the field-testing of genetically altered seeds.[123] In effect, there is questionable legal authority to regulate the field-testing of domestic materials under the *Seeds Act*. As such, legal authority must be found in other statutes, such as the *Plant Protection Act*.[124] As noted, though, the *Plant Protection Act* regulates material that is or has the potential to be a pest and does not provide general authority to regulate field-tests.

The piecemeal approach to field-tests has led many to question the adequacy of the regulatory framework.[125] Indeed, one commentator concluded:

> the current regulatory framework under which Agriculture Canada conducts environmental assessments for transgenic plant field-tests inspires little confidence that potential environmental impacts are being minimized and that the new technologies will not leave a legacy of environmental degradation and economic disruption.[126]

Liability and Compensation

Other chapters in this book deal with the questions of common law and statutory liability regimes. However, it is important to note the particular problems that arise when these traditional regimes are applied to biotechnology. It is clear that there are various limits of traditional common law doctrines to environmental lawsuits and, when the doctrines are applied to the field of biotechnology, these problems are amplified.

Perhaps the most obvious problem pertains to causation — the requirement that the victim establish the causative link between the victim's injury and the defendant's conduct. As noted:

> For new life forms released into the environment, it may be decades after the release before any impact on the ecosystem and humans is detected or fully understood. Moreover, the release of genetically-engineered organisms may start a chain reaction of disturbances or consequences.[127]

Apart from liability, there are also issues pertaining to compensation for harm resulting from the release of biotechnology products. At present, there is no general fund, or biotechnology-specific fund, to remediate the environment and compensate victims from environmental damage or contamination. Creating specific environment-related funds is not uncommon, though. For example, under the *Pesticide Residue Compensation Act*,[128] compensation is available to farmers for the loss of crops that have become so contaminated by a registered pesticide that its sale would be contrary to the *Food and Drugs Act*.[129] Other schemes include the protection of fisherman for loss of income under the *Fisheries Act*[130] and the Maritime Pollution Claims Fund under part XVI of the *Canada Shipping Act*,[131] which deals with damage caused by oil pollution. There are also certain compensation and cost recovery provisions under the *Plant Protection Act*.[132] All of these regimes, though, have limited application, if any, to harm incurred as a result of the release of genetically engineered organisms.

At the provincial level, it is an interesting question whether part X of Ontario's *Environmental Protection Act*[133] ("the spills bill"), which deals with liability and compensation issues for harm by spills of pollutants, would cover the release of a genetically engineered organism. The question remains whether or not a new life form is a "pollutant" under part X of the *Environmental Protection Act*.[134]

Patent Laws and the Plant Breeders' Rights Act

One of the most controversial issues in the biotechnology field pertains to the issue whether new life forms can be patented.[135] The issue is so controversial because of the range of questions it invokes:

- Can someone actually own or appropriate a blueprint of life?[136]
- Is genetic material a public or private resource?
- How does one define what a "new" life is under the appropriate legislation?

In 1982, the Patent Appeal Board granted the first Canadian patent of life to Abitibi-Price for a culture of specified fungal species adopted to metabolize chemical waste.[137] The decision was thought to be of major significance and broad applicability. Indeed, the ruling itself noted:

This decision will extend to all micro-organisms, yeasts, moulds, fungi, bacteria, actinomycetes, unicellular algae, cell lines, viruses or protozoa.[138]

However, while the Patent Appeal Board dealt with single-cell organisms, it omitted the patentability of higher life forms, like plants and animals, in its ruling.

In 1989, the Supreme Court of Canada was asked to address higher life forms in *Pioneer Hi-Bred Ltd. v. Commissioner of Patents.*[139] In that case, the applicant sought to have a new strain of soybean patented, which was developed through intense cross-breeding. Lower court rulings decided that the new variety, which was developed by cross-breeding, was not an "invention"[140] within the meaning of section 2 of the *Patent Act*. The Supreme Court of Canada, however, based its decision not to grant the patent on the failure of the applicant to meet other specific requirements in the *Patent Act*. Thus, the Supreme Court did not address the issue whether new life forms are "inventions." Other relevant parts of the decision are thought to be *obiter*.[141]

Although the court did not expressly rule on the patentability of all multi-cellular life forms, it did give some indication as to the outcome of the issue.[142] New life forms that result from such techniques as cross-breeding are probably not patentable since new strains that result from cross-breeding are more of a "chance transformation." In other techniques, such as those used for certain genetic engineering activities, the results are more predictable. Thus, new strains that result from genetic engineering seem to stand a better chance of meeting the definition of "invention."

Although a degree of uncertainty remains as to whether patent laws protect multi-cellular life forms, limited proprietary protection exists under the *Plant Breeders' Rights Act*.[143] Proclaimed in force on August 1, 1990, the Act provides a framework to protect the propriety interests of only *new* plant varieties. The meaning of "new" variety is defined and, in effect, establishes a standard of absolute novelty. In addition, only new varieties of species prescribed by regulation can be protected. The regulations identifying the prescribed species to be included in the patent regime have yet to be enacted.

Once holders of patents for new varieties have satisfied the conditions of the Act, they are granted exclusive rights to produce the new variety for the purpose of selling propagating material, to sell it, and to make repeated use of the variety to produce another plant varieties commercially. The patent protection lasts for 18 years from the date of registration.

Seventeen months after the enactment of the *Plant Breeders' Rights Act*, Canada gained the opportunity to be a member of the International Convention for the Protection of New Varieties of Plants (UPOV).[144] The goal of the convention, now ratified by about 20 countries, is the standardization of the member countries' practices by adopting UPOV's standards and scope as national law.

Overall, the protection of intellectual property for biotechnology is quite complicated at this point. For single-cell life forms, patent laws are available. Certain plant life forms will be protected once regulations under the *Plant Breeders' Rights Act* are enacted. In general, protection of new plant varieties is to be undertaken either by patent or by breeders' rights, but not both. There are, however, significant differences between the protection afforded by plant breeders legislation and patent laws. Apparently, there are

quite different implications with regard to breadth of coverage and utilization of the protected material in subsequent research and production of propagating material and of crops for sale.[145]

Toward a Comprehensive Biotechnology Regime

The Need for a Comprehensive Regime

One curious observation about the law and policy governing biotechnology is that, even though the industry is still in its early stages, given its promised potential, the regulatory framework is complex at best, if not disparate. Although the federal and provincial governments still maintain the view that the existing regulatory schemes are sufficient to address biotechnology, there are a number of arguments that support a comprehensive regime solely for the biotechnology industry.

Some of these arguments are:

- Biotechnology products need to be regulated because they pose an environmental risk. This risk may be of low probability, but can have significant ecological consequences.[146]
- The industry is still in its early stages of development and needs certainty and predictability of the regulatory framework, which can be better achieved through a clear and comprehensive law.
- The industry is at a point where a new law would not cause massive transition problems.
- The uncertainty and complexity of the present regime would suggest that there are probably gaps for some new biotechnology products while other products may receive inconsistent application.
- The present regulatory approach is simply not up to the tasks of dealing with the multiplicity and diversity of biotechnology products approaching commercialization.
- There is a need to make the federal and provincial laws consistent with each other, as well as to streamline the laws between the provinces.
- It seems fair and reasonable that a constructive public debate take place on the benefits and risks of biotechnology and its limits, a debate that could take place during the development of a comprehensive regime.
- The public has the right to participate in decisions that will affect them, and certainly various applications of biotechnology will not only have environmental impacts, but social and economic impacts as well.

These arguments suggest that a comprehensive biotechnology law for the federal and provincial governments is needed and appropriate. Certainly, the recognition of the need for a comprehensive regime is not new.[147] However, what would this broad regime look like?

Components of a Biotechnology Legal Framework

Throughout this chapter, a number of issues were raised that could be dealt with in the context of a national and a provincial biotechnology legal framework.[148] Some of the components of this framework could include:

1. *Biotechnology and Sustainable Development.* Over the past few years, there has been much discussion on how to integrate environmental protection into economic decision making. Biotechnology provides an excellent case study, and one that could be carried out in a legislative context.

2. *Methodology and Protocols.* Certainly, one of the weakest links in the current scheme is the inadequacy of the protocols and methodologies for adjudging the environmental

consequences of given applications of biotechnology. The legal framework could promote the establishment of a comprehensive and effective set of measures to determine the appropriateness of releases of biotechnology products.

3. *Assessments*. As noted, one of the very unclear aspects of biotechnology pertains to what is assessed, by whom, when, and for what reasons. The present approach, thus, could give rise to inconsistency or gaps.

4. *Field-Tests*. At present, not all information concerning field-tests is available. Hence, not only should there be a clear and consistent process to approve field-tests, but there should be a registry for all biotechnology field-test applications to ensure that the public has access to all information, except to the extent that privacy is necessary to protect interests like trade secrets or national security.

5. *Regulatory Controls*. At this point, there is a potential for a whole host of regulatory controls. The question remaining is what type of controls should be used for what type of applications. Furthermore, controls should deal with notice and comment provisions for all important decisions affecting product approvals.

6. *Liability and Compensation*. The basic problems associated with liability and compensation have already been described (under the heading "Liability and Compensation"). It seems that some special rules could be enacted to deal with the peculiarities of biotechnology.

7. *Public Participation*. As discussed below, the role of the public is essential in the regulation of this industry, especially during the various decision-making processes.

8. *Institutional Reform*. At present, there are so many government departments with jurisdiction over the field that it is very difficult to further the goal of government accountability. One of the options that should be considered is the establishment of an independent body to assess the environmental appropriateness of biotechnology products and to provide a formal forum for public participation. This body could also be responsible in part for information sharing and coordination of governmental activities in this regard.

Under the national biotechnology legal framework proposed here, the federal government would implement sections under its legislative powers. Part of the statute would be a model law for the provinces to adapt and enact. As more provinces enact this law, the goal of harmonization of a regulatory framework across Canada could be realized.

The Role of the Citizen

At present, there remains considerable debate about the necessity and shape of the biotechnology legal framework. In the meantime, the public should have an effective role in the decision-making processes affecting these new products. The right to participate in biotechnology decisions is justified for at least three reasons. First, the public's tax dollars support the development of biotechnology under the national biotechnology strategy. Second, the public will be the consumers of biotechnology products. Finally, the public will bear the risk associated with biotechnology products.

It is, at present, very difficult for the public to participate in the approval processes for products of biotechnology. Moreover, there appears to be no way for citizens to stop a field-test or the first deliberate release of a biotechnology product, or to influence the design of a field-test. This exclusion can be attributed to three main factors:

1. there is a lack of a comprehensive regime for public participation in the *existing* legislation governing the applications of biotechnology;
2. much of the regulatory framework that will govern certain biotechnology products is still under development, and thus the public participation scheme is not yet in place; and
3. there is a general hesitancy by government officials to allow public input into the biotechnology decision-making processes — for example, citizens have no access to environmental assessment data.

Nevertheless, it is important that the public be involved in the decision-making processes affecting biotechnology. There are some opportunities. For example, those interested in field-tests can contact the appropriate federal government ministry and request information pertaining to the approval of field-tests. However, certain information regarding field-tests is not available to the public. For example, the exact location of the tests, the vector of the genetic code transferred, and the risk-assessment forms are withheld by the federal government. Whatever information is available regarding field-tests of transgenic crops, for example, is available on a product-basis and includes the following:

- the names of the testers and their associated university, company, or government department;
- the general location of the field-test, such as the closest town;
- the type of plant and test such as herbicide-resistant canola or virus-resistant potatoes; and
- the cover sheet of the risk-assessment document.

Public involvement with biotechnology should not simply stop at field-tests. But it is a good place to start. Below are addresses of agencies dealing with biotechnology. These are good places to ask for more information as well as to voice your concerns over the present status of biotechnology initiatives to protect the environment.

There is no doubt that biotechnology will emerge as an important environmental issue in coming years. The challenge is to prevent the types of environmental problems we have seen with previous technological revolutions. For example, regulators showed little foresight during the 1940s and 1950s when the synthetic chemical and nuclear industries began to grow rapidly. Consequently, toxic chemicals and nuclear products have contaminated the environment and have endangered human health.[149] A similar mistake with biotechnology products will be more devastating, since these products are generally alive and thus can reproduce, mutate, and spread. This history makes it imperative that the Canadian and provincial governments establish the rules governing this industry sooner rather than later.

Paul Muldoon and Burkhard Mausberg

FEDERAL AGENCIES DEALING WITH BIOTECHNOLOGY

Agriculture Canada

Veterinary Biologics:	Associate Director Veterinary Biologics and Biotechnology Animal Health Division Health of Animals Directorate Agriculture Canada 3851 Fallowfield Road Nepean, Ontario K2H 8P9
Livestock Feeds and Fertilizers:	Feed or Fertilizer Section Plant Products Division Animal and Plant Health Directorate Agriculture Canada 960 Carling Avenue Ottawa, Ontario K1A 0C6
Pest Control Products:	Pesticide Directorate Agriculture Canada 2323 Riverside Drive SBI Building Ottawa, Ontario K1A 0C6
Plants and Crops:	Seed Section/Plant Products Division Animal and Plant Health Directorate Agriculture Canada 960 Carling Avenue Ottawa, Ontario K1A 0C6

Health and Welfare Canada

Drugs and Cosmetics:	Chief, Drug Regulatory Affairs Division Drugs Directorate Room 139, Health Protection Building Health and Welfare Canada Ottawa, Ontario K1A 0L2
Food and Food Additives:	Chief, Food Regulatory, International and Interagency Affairs Division Food Directorate Health Protection Building Health and Welfare Canada Ottawa, Ontario K1A 0L2

Medical Devices: Chief, Legislative and Regulatory Processes
                              Environmental Health Directorate
                              Environmental Health Centre
                              Health and Welfare Canada
                              Ottawa, Ontario K1A 0L2

Environment Canada

All products not covered   Chief, Biotechnology Centre
by other departments: Commercial Chemicals Division
                              Environment Canada
                              351 St. Joseph Blvd.
                              Ottawa, Ontario K1A 0H3

                              Chief, New Substances Division
                              Commercial Chemicals Branch
                              Environment Canada
                              351 St. Joseph Blvd.
                              Ottawa, Ontario K1A 0H3

FURTHER READING

Cary Fowler, Eva Lachkovics, Pat Mooney, and Hope Shand, "The Laws of Life: Another
Development and the New Biotechnologies" (1988), *Development Dialogue* 1-2.

Calestous Juma, *The Gene Hunters: Biotechnology and the Scramble for Seeds*
(Princeton, NJ: Princeton University Press, 1989).

June Fessendon Macdonald, ed., *Agricultural Biotechnology at the Crossroads*
(Ithaca, NY: NABC Report 3, National Agricultural Biotechnology Council, 1991).

Steve Olson, *Biotechnology: An Industry Comes of Age* (Washington, DC: National
Academy Press, 1986).

ENDNOTES

1 This expression is taken from the PhD thesis of Terry McIntyre, Faculty of Environmental Studies, University of Waterloo.
2 Some of the material in this chapter is an update and an expansion of the material used
   in Marcia A. Valiante and Paul R. Muldoon, "Biotechnology and the Environment: A
   Regulatory Proposal" (Summer 1985), 23 *Osgoode Hall LJ* 359-94.
3 Ibid., at 360.
4 Medical Research Council, "Guidelines for Handling Recombinant DNA Molecules
   and Animal Viruses and Cells," catalogue no. MR 21-1/1980 (December) and
   catalogue no. MR 21-1/1979 (June), revised catalogue no. MR 21-1/1977 (February).

5 *Occupational Health and Safety Act*, RSO 1990, c. O.1. There is no doubt that there are many issues here that should be explored elsewhere. For example, contained laboratory and greenhouse plant research is not regulated in Canada. What is in place for researchers are the Medical Research Council guidelines. Such research may be regulated by provincial labour laws that govern human health and safety in the workplace. See M.J. Kalous and L.H. Duke, *The Regulation of Plant Biotechnology in Canada: Part 2 — The Environmental Release of Genetically Altered Plant Material* (Ottawa: Seed Division, Agriculture Canada, 1989), 13. See also Ontario, *Biotechnology in Ontario — Growing Safely* (Toronto: Queen's Printer, 1989), 16-17.

6 For an easy-to-understand overview of the science behind biotechnology, see S. Witt, *Biotechnology and Genetic Diversity* (San Francisco: California Agriculture Land Project, 1985) and S. Witt, *Genetic Engineering of Plants* (Washington, DC: National Academy Press, 1984).

7 National Biotechnology Advisory Committee, *National Biotechnology Business Strategy: Capturing Competitive Advantage for Canada* (Ottawa: Department of Industry, Science and Technology, 1991), 11.

8 The Organisation for Economic Co-operation and Development defines biotechnology as the "application of scientific and engineering principles to the processing of materials by biological agents to produce goods and services." From United States, Environmental Protection Agency, Chemical Control Division, Office of Toxic Substances, "Regulation of Genetically Engineered Substances under TSCA," in United States, House of Representatives, Committee on Science and Technology, *The Environmental Implications of Genetic Engineering* (Washington, DC: US Government Printing Office, February 1984), 1, at 112.

9 The National Research Council of Canada uses the following definition: "The application of science and engineering to the direct or indirect use of cells from plants or animals, or micro-organisms, in their natural or modified forms, for the production of goods or the provisions of services." From A. Albagli, "The Current State of Biotechnology in Canada," in Canadian Environmental Law Research Foundation, *The Regulation of Biotechnology* (Toronto: CELRF, 1984), 1, at 3.

10 Section 3 of the *Canadian Environmental Protection Act* defines "biotechnology" as "the application of science and engineering in the direct or indirect use of living organisms or parts of products of living organisms in their natural or modified forms." A similar definition has also been adopted in: Canada, *Bio-Tech Regulations — A User's Guide to Federal Regulation on Biotechnology* (Ottawa: Agriculture Canada, Environment Canada, Health and Welfare Canada, Ministry of State for Science and Technology, Labour Canada, and Consumer and Corporate Affairs Canada, 1991), iii.

11 See *Biotechnology in Ontario*, supra endnote 5, at 4, where biotechnology is defined as "the application of science and engineering to the direct and indirect use of living organisms and parts of products of organism to provide goods and services."

12 Sheldon Krimsky, *Regulatory Policies on Biotechnology in Canada* (October 1984), 19.

13 G.S. Burrill and K.B. Lee Jr., *Biotech '92: Promise to Reality — An Industry Annual Report* (San Francisco: Ernst & Young, 1991), 14.

14 *National Biotechnology Business Strategy*, supra endnote 7, at 31.

15 Ibid., at 32.

16   M. Alexander, "Ecological Consequences: Reducing the Uncertainties" (1985), vol. 1, no. 3 *Issues in Science and Technology* 57-68.

17   J.J. Pasternak and B.R. Glick, "Assessing the Environmental Consequences of Genetically-Engineered Organisms" (1987), vol. 14, no. 3 *Alternatives* 39.

18   US Environmental Protection Agency, supra endnote 8, at 20.

19   Ibid., at 20.

20   Ibid., at 13.

21   See also Penny Chan, "Environment and Health: Potential Risks and Benefits," in *Law in the Age of Biotechnology* (Edmonton: Environmental Law Centre, 1992), 37-58.

22   Summarized from Krimsky, supra endnote 12, at 16, and Valiante and Muldoon, supra endnote 3, at 376.

23   D. Pimentel, M.S. Hunter, J.A. LaGro, R.A. Efroymson, J.C. Landers, F.T. Mervis, C.A. McCarthy, and A.E. Boyd, "Benefits and Risks of Genetic Engineering in Agriculture" (1989), vol. 39, no. 9 *Bioscience* 606-14, at 609.

24   US Environmental Protection Agency, supra endnote 18, at 18 and 19.

25   *National Biotechnology Business Strategy*, supra endnote 7, at 30.

26   See S. Shackley and J. Hodgson, "Biotechnology Regulation in Europe" (1991), 9 *Bio/Technology* 1056-61.

27   See Larry A. Reynolds, "Local Public Authorities and the Regulation of Biotechnology in Canada," in *Law in the Age of Biotechnology*, supra endnote 21, 101-31.

28   *Constitution Act, 1867*, 30 & 31 Vict., c. 3 (UK).

29   Ibid., section 91(2).

30   Ibid., section 91(12).

31   Ibid., section 91(27).

32   See *Labatt's Breweries v. Attorney General of Canada, et al.* (1979), 110 DLR (3d) 594 (SCC).

33   *Constitution Act, 1867*, supra endnote 28, section 92(13).

34   Ibid., section 92(10).

35   Ibid., section 92(16).

36   Ibid., section 92A(1).

37   *Pest Products Control Act*, RSC 1985, c. P-9.

38   *Pesticides Act*, RSO 1990, c. P.11.

39   Beak Consultants Ltd., *Regulatory Issues Concerning Biotechnology in Canada*, a report for the Biotechnology Unit, Ministry of Science, State and Technology (Toronto: the ministry, 1986), 1.

40   Ibid., at i.

41   Terry C. McIntyre, "The Development of New Substances Regulations for Biotechnology Products Under the *Canadian Environmental Protection Act*: An Overview," in *Law in the Age of Biotechnology*, supra endnote 21, 61-75.

42   Canadian Environmental Law Research Foundation [now Canadian Institute for Environmental Law and Policy], *Biotechnology Policy Development*, vol. 1, prepared for the Ontario Ministry of the Environment (Toronto: the ministry, 1988), 4-4 and 4-5.

43   For a full description of the NRC program, see National Research Council, *The National Research Council Biotechnology Program* (Ottawa: NRC, 1991).

44   *National Biotechnology Business Strategy*, supra endnote 7, at 21.

45 Ibid., at 6 and 7.

46 For example, see Beak Consultants Ltd., supra endnote 39; Canada, *Co-ordinated Study on Government Processes in Safety and Regulation of Modern Biotechnology* (Ottawa: Ministry of State for Science and Technology, 1986); and National Biotechnology Advisory Committee, *Annual Report 1987-1988 — The Regulation of Biotechnology: A Critical Issue for Canadian Research and Industrial Development* (Ottawa: Department of Industry, Trade and Technology, 1989).

47 For a more detailed description, see B.S. Samagh, *Guidelines for the Regulation of Veterinary Biologics by Biotechnology* (Ottawa: Agriculture Canada, August 1989), 84-88.

48 *Bio-Tech Regulations*, supra endnote 10.

49 This office was recommended in a report by a consultant to the Ministry of State for Science and Technology in 1986: see Beak Consultants Ltd., supra endnote 39. For other recommended reforms with respect to institutional reform, see National Biotechnology Advisory Committee, supra endnote 46.

50 *Canadian Environmental Protection Act*, RSC 1985, c. 16 (4th Supp.).

51 Letter from Doug Macdonald, Executive Director, Canadian Environmental Law Research Foundation, to Barry Turner, Chairman, Legislative Committee on Bill C-74, House of Commons, February 15, 1988.

52 Environment Canada, *Canada's Green Plan for a Healthy Environment* (Ottawa: Supply and Services, 1990), 50.

53 Ibid.

54 *National Biotechnology Business Strategy*, supra endnote 7, at 2.

55 *Pest Control Products Act*, supra endnote 37.

56 Ibid., section 2.

57 Ibid.

58 Guidelines used to field-test genetically modified microorganisms are based on Agriculture Canada, "Requirements for Field Trials of Naturally Occurring Microbial Pest Control Agents," no. R-90-02. Research permit guidelines specifically for genetically modified microbial pest control products are being prepared by Agriculture Canada.

59 Pest Control Products Regulations, CRC 1978, c. 1253.

60 *Pest Control Products Act*, supra endnote 37, section 5. For naturally occurring and genetically altered microbial products, the requirements are outlined in Agriculture Canada, "Guidelines for Registration of Microbial Pesticides," no. R-90-03.

61 *Pest Control Products Act*, supra endnote 37, section 5(b).

62 See J.F. Castrilli and T. Vigod, *Pesticides in Canada: An Examination of Federal Law and Policy* (Ottawa: Law Reform Commission of Canada, 1987).

63 See Canada, *Recommendations for a Revised Federal Pest Management Regulatory System—Final Report of the Pesticide Registration Review Team* (Ottawa: Supply and Services, December 1990).

64 *Plant Protection Act*, SC 1990, c. 22.

65 *Seeds Act*, RSC 1985, c. S-8.

66 R.B. Caldwell and L.H. Duke, *The Regulation of Plant Biotechnology in Canada* (Ottawa: Seed Division, Agriculture Canada, 1988), 16.

67 Agriculture Canada is the lead agency under more than six statutes: *Health of Animals Act*, RSC 1985, c. H-3.3; *Feeds Act*, RSC 1985, c. F-9; *Fertilizers Act*, RSC 1985, c. F-10; *Pest Control Products Act*, supra endnote 37; *Plant Protection Act*, supra endnote 64; *Seeds Act*, supra endnote 65; and *Food and Drugs Act*, RSC 1985, c. F-27.

68 Samagh, supra endnote 47, at 89.

69 *Pest Control Products Act*, supra endnote 37.

70 *Plant Protection Act*, supra endnote 64.

71 Ibid., section 2.

72 Ibid., section 3.

73 G.M. Lewis, "Federal Environmental Assessment of Transgenic Plant Field Tests" (1991), 1 JELP 169.

74 *Plant Protection Act*, supra endnote 64, section 6.

75 Ibid., section 6(2).

76 Ibid., section 7. The Regulations under the *Plant Protection Act* were the regulations that were enacted under its predecessor statute, the *Plant Quarantine Act*. These regulations, among other provisions, provide a permit system for the importation of plants. There are provisions pertaining to exemptions, labelling, inspection, compensation, among other such provisions. See Plant Quarantine Regulations, CRC 1978, c. 1273; as amended by SOR/91-241, March 27, 1991; SOR/91-345, May 27, 1991; SOR/91-606, October 25, 1991.

77 *Plant Protection Act*, supra endnote 64, section 2.

78 Lewis, supra endnote 73, at 170. In addition, the federal government introduced an act in November 1991 designed to protect wild animals and plants. Although the *Wild Animal and Plant Protection Act* is designed to protect wild animals and plants from poaching and smuggling, it may be helpful as a legal tool to control the import of designated species or their genetic material. See: Environment Canada, *Wild Animal and Plant Protection Act—Highlights and Steps to Implementation* (Ottawa: Environment Canada, 1991).

79 *Seeds Act*, supra endnote 65.

80 Ibid., section 2.

81 Correspondence from L.H. Duke, chief, Variety Registration Office, Animal and Plant Products Division, Ottawa, to Burkhard Mausberg and Paul Muldoon, Pollution Probe, Toronto, May 12, 1992.

82 Valiante and Muldoon, supra endnote 2, at 376.

83 Kalous and Duke, supra endnote 5, at 11.

84 CRC 1978, c. 1400, section 65, enacted in SOR/86-849.

85 Caldwell and Duke, supra endnote 66, at 17.

86 *Health of Animals Act*, supra endnote 67.

87 Ibid., section 2.

88 Samagh, supra endnote 47, at 102.

89 *Feeds Act*, supra endnote 67.

90 Experimental feeds are exempt from the regulations, provided they meet the requirements of sections 3(C) and 3(F) of the Feeds Regulations.

91 *Feeds Act*, supra endnote 67.

92 *Canadian Environmental Protection Act*, supra endnote 50.

93 Under section 25 of the *Canadian Environmental Protection Act*, ibid., a new substance is one that is not on the domestic substances list (DSL). The DSL refers to chemicals that were, between January 1, 1984 and December 31, 1986, (1) manufactured or imported in Canada in quantities more than 100 kilograms within one calendar year; (2) in Canadian commerce or used for commercial manufacturing purposes in Canada. Environment Canada is also developing a DSL for biotechnology products that will include microbial products that were in Canadian commerce between January 1, 1984 and December 31, 1986.

94 *Canada Gazette Part I*, June 13, 1992, 1606-9.

95 McIntyre, supra endnote 41.

96 *Forestry Development and Research Act*, RSC 1985, c. F-30, as amended by *Department of Forestry Act*, SC 1989, c. 27.

97 *Hazardous Products Act*, RSC 1985, c. H-3.

98 *Transportation of Dangerous Goods Act*, RSC 1985, c. T-19.

99 For a review of the regulatory framework for genetically engineered food products, see Keith Bailey, "Regulatory Process for Food and Pharmaceuticals" and Frank W. Welsh, "Regulatory Process for Novel Foods and Novel Food Processes," in *Law in the Age of Biotechnology*, supra endnote 21; *Food and Drugs Act*, supra endnote 67; *Department of National Health and Welfare Act*, RSC 1985, c. N-10; *Plant Breeders' Rights Act*, SC 1990, c. 20.

100 *Biotechnology in Ontario*, supra endnote 5, at 13.

101 Winter House Scientific Publications, Industrial Biotechnology Association of Canada, and the Canadian Biotechnology Institute, *The Canadian Biotechnology Directory— 1990/91* (Ottawa: Winter House Scientific Publications, 1990), editorial section, 8.

102 Ibid.

103 Personal communication with Dr. J. Stuart Bailey, supervisor, Biotechnology Unit, Ontario Ministry of the Environment, Toronto, Ontario, July 1992.

104 *Environmental Protection Act*, RSO 1990, c. E.19.

105 Ibid., section 13.

106 For example, see *Ontario Water Resources Act*, RSO 1990, c. O.40, sections 16 and 23.

107 *Environmental Protection Act*, supra endnote 104, sections 5 and 8.

108 Ibid., sections 6, 7, and 11.

109 A "contaminant" is defined as "any solid, liquid, gas, odour, heat, sound, vibration, radiation or any combination of any of them resulting directly or indirectly from human activities that may cause an adverse effect." Ibid., section 1(c).

110 *Pesticides Act*, supra endnote 38.

111 *Biotechnology in Ontario*, supra endnote 5, at 18.

112 *Animals for Research Act*, RSO 1990, c. A.28.

113 *Artificial Insemination of Livestock Act*, RSO 1990, c. A.29.

114 *Plant Diseases Act*, RSO 1990, c. P.14.

115 *Milk Act*, RSO 1990, c. M.12.

116 *Canadian Environmental Assessment Act*, SC 1992, c. 37.

117 *Pest Products Control Act*, supra endnote 37.

118 However, one commentator does not think the situation is always clear, especially for products like herbicide resistant crops. See Lewis, supra endnote 73, at 168.

119 *Seeds Act*, supra endnote 65.

120 New agricultural products must go through a registration process whereby they are tested for a number of attributes. This is called the variety registration process. The focus of this existing process is to test the new variety for its agronomic merit (that is, its economic worth) against existing varieties before allowing it to go to commercial production.

121 Seeds Act Regulations, CRC 1978, c. 1400, enacted in SOR/86-849; SOR/86-850, *Canada Gazette*, September 3, 1986, 3576; SOR/87-62, *Canada Gazette*, February 18, 1987, 421; SOR/88-242, *Canada Gazette*, May 11, 1988, 2356; SOR/88-297, *Canada Gazette*, June 8, 1988, 2681; SOR/89-368, *Canada Gazette*, August 16, 1989, 3569.

122 Section 39 states that the importer of an unregistered variety of seed that is to be used for research purposes must provide a statutory declaration to the collector of customs stating the purpose for which the seed is being imported and that the seed and any seed progeny or grain will disposed of as authorized, in writing, by the director of the seed division. This allows the director to set the terms and conditions of the field-test and the disposal of the progeny before the importation authorization. See Kalous and Duke, supra endnote 5, at 12.

123 With the variety registration process, plant breeders perform trials of their own on a small scale to see which experimental varieties warrant a registration attempt. In effect, Agriculture Canada has interpreted the regulation to mean that permission is required only when the plant material is moved from the laboratory to the greenhouse or elsewhere. See Kalous and Duke, supra endnote 5, at 13. See also Lewis, supra endnote 73, at 173. See also correspondence from L.H. Duke, chief, Variety Registration Office, Animal and Plant Products Division, Ottawa, to Burkhard Mausberg and Paul Muldoon, Pollution Probe, Toronto, May 12, 1992.

124 *Plant Protection Act*, supra endnote 64.

125 Caldwell and Duke, supra endnote 66, at 7.

126 Lewis, supra endnote 73, at 175.

127 Valiante and Muldoon, supra endnote 2, at 381.

128 *Pesticide Residue Compensation Act*, RSC 1985, c. P-10.

129 *Food and Drugs Act*, supra endnote 67.

130 *Fisheries Act*, RSC 1985, c. F-14.

131 *Canada Shipping Act*, RSC 1985, c. S-9.

132 *Plant Protection Act*, supra endnote 64, sections 39-46.

133 *Environmental Protection Act*, supra endnote 104.

134 According to section 79(1)(f) of the *Environmental Protection Act*, a "pollutant" means "a contaminant other than heat, sound, vibration or radiation, and includes any substance from which a pollutant is derived." Given that definition, the question whether a "pollutant" can be a new life form is similar to the question whether a "contaminant" can be a new life form. See above for that discussion.

135 For a further discussion of the legal complexities of this topic, see Mary Jane McKay-Carey, "Patenting and Intellectual Property Rights for Biotechnical Inventions," in *Law in the Age of Biotechnology*, supra endnote 21, at 157-90.

136 See Brian Belcher and Geoffrey Hawtin, *A Patent on Life: Ownership of Plant and Animal Research* (Ottawa: International Development Research Centre, 1990), 17-25.

137 *Re: Application of Abitibi Co.* (1982), 62 CPR (2d) 81 (PAB).

138 Ibid., at 89.

139 *Pioneer Hi-Bred Ltd. v. Commissioner of Patents* (1989), 25 CPR (3d) 257 (SCC).

140 "Invention" means "any new and useful art, process, machine, manufacture or composition of matter, or any new and useful improvement in any art, process machine, manufacture or composition of matter": section 2 of the *Patent Act*, RSC 1985, c. P-4. In particular, section 12.03.01(a) of the *Manual of Patent Office Practice* interprets section 2 in this way:

> Subject matter for a process for producing a new genetic strain or variety of plant or animal, or the product thereof, is not patentable. This exclusion does not include a microbiological process or product thereof.

141 C.J. Ledgley and M.I. Steward, "Patent Protection for Plants and Animals in the Wake of Pioneer Hi-Bred" (1990), 7 CIPR 291.

142 R.W. Maruskyk, "The Patentability of New Plant Life Forms in Canada" (May 1990), 16 *Canadian Business Law Journal* 333-40, at 338.

143 *Plant Breeders' Rights Act*, supra endnote 99.

144 Geneva, 1961, as revised in 1991.

145 Belcher and Hawtin, supra endnote 138, at 8. See also Ledgley and Steward, supra endnote 141, at 296.

146 For a good discussion on the environmental risks, see L.M. Tiedje, R.K. Colwell, Y.L. Grossman, R.E. Hodson, R.E. Lenski, R.N. Mack, and P.J. Regal, "The Planned Introduction of Genetically Engineered Organisms: Ecological Considerations and Recommendations" (1989), vol. 70, no. 2 *Ecology* 298-315.

147 See, for example, Valiante and Muldoon, supra endnote 2, at 359.

148 For a description of other reform suggestions in Alberta, see Glennis M. Lewis, "The Alberta Environmental Protection and Enhancement Act: Establishing a Provincial Regulatory Framework for Biotechnological Products" in *Law in the Age of Biotechnology*, supra endnote 21, 133-55.

149 See, for example, International Joint Commission, *Sixth Biennial Report on Great Lakes Water Quality* (Ottawa: IJC, 1992). The events around Chernobyl and Love Canal in New York have certainly demonstrated this concern.

PART IV

Preserving and Protecting Our Resources

11

Preserving Ontario's Natural Legacy

CONTENTS

- A tropical rainforest the size of Austria is lost every year to agricultural and urban development.
- More than 3,000 animal species are endangered.
- Every day, more than 100 plant and animal species disappear.

United Nations Environment Program, December 1992

I regret the views of ecologists who want to put a giant condom over our forest.

Gilberto Mestrinho, governor of Brazil's largest state, 1992

INTRODUCTION

Over the past century, Ontario has established parks to preserve natural areas for the benefit of present and future generations. Decisions by the Ontario government to preserve large tracts of wilderness lands have produced a legacy of parks such as Algonquin, Quetico, and Killarney. Each year, eight million visitors experience the beauty and raw inspirational power of Ontario's wilderness parks, nature reserves, and other protected areas.

The establishment of provincial parks is a political act. In creating new parks, politicians make conscious decisions to limit or prohibit the commercial exploitation of natural resources within a specific geographical area, emphasizing the need to preserve its ecological and recreational values. Politicians can make such a decision because legislation allows them to do so. The permanency of such decisions depends on the ability of that legislation to provide lasting protection. This chapter examines how effective Ontario's legislative and policy frameworks are in preserving the province's natural legacy.

Ontario is a leader in the establishment and management of provincial parks. In 1893, it became the first province to establish a provincial park, Algonquin. It has preserved more lands in a natural or wilderness state than any other province: 61,015 square kilometres.[1] In 1978, it became one of the first governments in Canada to adopt a comprehensive provincial parks policy. And in 1983, Ontario established 155 new provincial parks covering two million hectares, an unprecedented accomplishment in Canadian conservation history.

The rationale for creating parks and protected areas both in Ontario and elsewhere has evolved over the decades. Early parks were established to conserve natural resources, such as forests and lakes, to guarantee both timber and scenery for human consumption and recreation. The emphasis was on their economic value to society. For example, Algonquin park was established as a "public park and forest reservation, fish and game preserve, health resort and pleasure ground for the benefit, advantage and enjoyment of the people of the Province."[2]

Today, parks and protected areas are essential elements in national and global conservation strategies. The underlying philosophy of protected areas has evolved from the "romantic" concept of protecting land for spiritual and intangible reasons on the one hand, and recreational opportunities on the other, to a greater concern for the protection of biological diversity. Protected areas preserve geological and physical features, ecosystems, and wildlife habitats such as forests, wetlands, and lake systems that are unique or representative examples of the diversity of species and landscapes that make up Ontario and, ultimately, the planet.

The important contribution of parks and protected areas to protecting ecological values, and to sustaining human societies, was emphasized by the World Commission on Environment and Development (the Brundtland commission). It called on all nations to represent their major ecosystems within a network of strictly protected areas as part of a national commitment to implementing sustainable development. A century's experience in identifying and protecting natural areas within a provincial protected areas network should enable Ontario to respond to this challenge.

Unfortunately, Ontario's protected areas legislation, particularly the *Provincial Parks Act*,[3] has not kept pace with the emerging international emphasis on the ecological value of protected areas. The *Provincial Parks Act* continues to reflect the century-old notion that governments can protect and exploit parks at the same time. It places no onus on the government as trustee of the parks to preserve their natural resources. Thus, any conservation gains made over the past century remain at risk because the existing Act has yet to enshrine in the law the emphasis on preserving parks from exploitation.

In a society where the exploitation of natural areas remains a dominant economic policy, Ontario's unprotected wilderness areas and existing parks are increasingly threatened. There is no provincial legislation that compels the Ontario government to protect additional natural areas, or to promote a preservation ethic within existing parks. In addition, existing legislation does not provide any permanent protection to Ontario's network of about 260 provincial parks. Nor does it provide the government with the necessary powers to eliminate the threats from logging and other industrial activities on lands adjacent to the parks.

If Ontario is to respond successfully to the Brundtland commission, it must represent the full diversity of its landscape within a network of protected areas on both Crown and private land. And it must enhance its ability to maintain the ecological integrity and intrinsic wilderness values of the existing parks. Ontario's legal and policy frameworks must be updated to reflect the emerging international and national consensus on the need to expand protected area networks around the world.

In the following sections we will examine existing legislation and policies and analyze their ability to preserve Ontario's natural heritage. The focus is on the establishment and management of national and provincial parks, since they remain the major mechanisms that governments can use to preserve Crown lands, which cover 88 per cent of the province. Other mechanisms that can be used to protect lands will also be discussed, with less emphasis on how such areas are managed. The chapter concludes with suggestions on how the current *Provincial Parks Act* can be improved.

THE FEDERAL SYSTEM OF PROTECTED AREAS IN ONTARIO

The federal government contributes to the protection of Ontario's landscape through several protected area designations. Although the *Constitution Act, 1982*[4] confirms the control of provincial governments over natural resources, the federal government does play a role in protecting nationally significant landscapes and important wildlife habitat. This role can be fulfilled when: (1) the federal government identifies natural areas of national significance in terrestrial and aquatic environments; (2) the governments of Canada and Ontario agree to manage specific areas under federal conservation policies; and (3) international agreements requiring the protection of migratory birds and other wildlife require joint action by both governments.

National Parks in Ontario

Five of Canada's 36 national parks are located in Ontario. Although they protect less than 0.1 per cent of Ontario, the legislation and policy under which the national parks are administered provide some valuable insights into the management of protected areas. Three of the parks are Canada's smallest national parks and the first established in Eastern Canada: St. Lawrence Islands (5 square kilometres); Point Pelee (16 square kilometres); and Georgian Bay Islands National Park (25 square kilometres). In addition, the governments of Ontario and Canada acted in 1978 to protect 1,878 square kilometres of wilderness along Lake Superior in Pukaskwa National Park, and they agreed to the establishment of the Bruce Peninsula National Park in 1987. Although the lands comprising Pukaskwa and the Bruce Peninsula are managed as national parks, neither is currently protected under the *National Parks Act*.[5]

Pukaskwa cannot be protected under the *National Parks Act*, or its boundaries described or gazetted within the Act, until two steps are completed. First, the Act was amended in 1988 to conform with the provisions of the Robinson-Superior Treaty, which confirmed the right of the Ojibway Indians to hunt, trap, and fish within Pukaskwa National Park. Second, the province has to complete the transfer of land for the park to the federal government. The land transfer process has been slow because the province had to acquire some mineral rights and private property before transferring the land to Canada, and because new legislation regarding land transfers was enacted by the Ontario Legislature. However, by using a number of provincial acts, such as the *Game and Fish Act*,[6] the Canadian Parks Service has the authority it requires to administer Pukaskwa to national park standards.

The Bruce Peninsula is not listed under the *National Parks Act* for several reasons. A large portion of the proposed park is held by private owners. It is unlikely that the park will be gazetted until the government has purchased a large amount of the land required for the park. Of the 35,000 acres required for the park, 17,000 acres have been acquired from the province, and a further 7,000 acres have been purchased from private landowners.[7]

The park will also not be gazetted until the Ontario government has resolved a number of outstanding treaty obligations with the Ojibway Indians who reside at the nearby Cape Croker Indian Reserve. Until the park is gazetted, the federal government is using several provincial acts, such as the *Trespass to Property Act*,[8] to enforce the protection of the Bruce Peninsula National Park. Part of the Fathom Five National Marine Park, including Flowerpot Island, is gazetted under the Act as part of the existing Georgian Bay Islands National Park.

The area that will be eventually protected under the Act is less than what the federal government had originally hoped to protect. The government's parks policy compels it to seek the support of local communities prior to acquiring and administering a proposed national park. In the case of the Bruce Peninsula, the southern portion of the proposed park, which was located in Lindsay Township, was deleted when the citizens of that township voted against the park in a November 1985 referendum. A lesser form of protection is provided under the Niagara Escarpment Plan.

The Bruce Peninsula National Park also continues a trend that has characterized park establishment in Canada and the United States: the exclusion of areas from parks that are of economic value. The Ontario government insisted that the proposed park be further reduced on the western side to compensate for the loss of hunting opportunities. This position was taken because of the opposition of the provincial hunting lobby to the national parks policy statement that prohibits hunting in parks such as the Bruce Peninsula.

Administration of the National Parks

National parks are established and administered under the *National Parks Act*[9] by the Canadian Parks Service, formerly Parks Canada. The boundaries of national parks are described in the Act, and unlike Ontario's provincial parks, a national park cannot be eliminated, or its boundary reduced, without the approval of Parliament. However, the governor in council can add lands to national parks after the Standing Committee on Environment has heard witnesses and approved the additions, and the House of Commons has approved the committee's report without debate.[10] Thus, any attempt to increase, reduce, or delete national parks is subject to a political and public review. The Act requires that the federal government own all surface and subsurface rights to national parklands; thus, if new parks are to be established within the provinces, the provincial governments must agree to transfer such rights to the federal Crown.

The Act states that the national parks are "dedicated to the people of Canada for their benefit, education and enjoyment" and "shall be maintained and made use of so as to leave them unimpaired for the enjoyment of future generations."[11] Although the courts have not provided a legal interpretation of the term "unimpaired," it has been generally assumed that it means no industrial development within the national parks. And although the Act itself does not explicitly prohibit industrial development within national parks, regulations established under the Act prohibit logging, mining, and hunting in national parks.

The government only recently put an end to some activities that were permitted in the parks that were considered contrary to the Act. Hunting in Ontario's Point Pelee National Park was finally terminated by the federal government in 1988. Until then, it was the only national park in Canada that permitted recreational hunting. The original 1918 order in council establishing the park compelled the government to hold an annual hunt in the park. However, although a 1942 order in council revoked the compulsory nature of the hunt, and made it a discretionary matter, several members of Parliament lobbied against an end to the hunt for years. The Ontario government also opposed an end to the hunt unless the federal government made sufficient other land available for hunting outside Point Pelee and agreed to make up for any loss of hunting opportunities in the park.[12]

And in 1992 the Federal Court of Canada declared a 1983 agreement between the federal government and Canadian Forest Products Limited that permitted logging within Wood Buffalo National Park in Alberta as "invalid and unauthorized by the provisions of the National Parks Act or any regulations thereunder."[13] The case was filed by the Canadian Parks and Wilderness Society and the Sierra Legal Defence Fund, which sought an end to the only commercial logging operation in Canada's national parks. Interestingly, the government did not defend itself against the action. It agreed that the *National Parks Act* did not give the federal Cabinet the power to allow logging in Wood Buffalo National Park. For example, section 6(1) authorizes the governor in council to sell, lease, or dispose of public lands within the parks, but only for rights of ways and other related purposes.

Although the prohibitions against logging, mining, and hunting are clear, the extent to which the Act requires restrictions on tourism development is less obvious. The *National Parks Act* permits the federal Cabinet to make a range of regulations that facilitate the recreational use of the parks and permit the construction of roads and tourism facilities. Thus, for many years the government stated that national parks had a dual mandate: to facilitate both the use and the preservation of park resources.

In 1979 the federal Cabinet approved the Parks Canada Policy, establishing the protection of natural resources as a fundamental prerequisite to use. And in 1988, the Canadian Parks and Wilderness Society successfully lobbied the federal government to amend the *National Parks Act* to reflect this priority. The Act now states that the "maintenance of ecological integrity through the protection of natural resources shall be the first priority when considering park zoning and visitor use in a management plan."[14] However, the expansion of downhill ski facilities and golf courses, the development of hotels and backcountry accommodation, and further construction of roads in national parks continue to erode their ecological integrity.

The 1988 amendments to the Act strengthened the government's ability to stop the incremental loss of parklands and its resident wildlife populations to development and poaching. For example, no new downhill ski facilities are permitted within the parks except through an amendment to the Act,[15] and a boundary is placed around existing downhill ski areas.[16] Poachers can receive up to $150,000 in fines and six months in jail for the illegal hunting and possession of certain wildlife species.[17]

The location of new national parks is guided by the federal government's 1990 National Parks System Plan.[18] The objective is to establish in each of 39 federally recognized terrestrial natural regions a national park that is characteristic of the physical, biological, and geographic features of that region. In Ontario, the terrestrial national parks system is deemed to be complete. However, given the very small size of Ontario's national parks, a fuller examination of their ability to represent these natural regions is required.

Despite the power of the *National Parks Act*, none of Canada's national parks is immune to environmental degradation. This is particularly true of Ontario's parks because of their very small size and the level of commercial and industrial development in southern Ontario. For example: Point Pelee has lost almost half of the wildlife species found there when Europeans first settled the area. St. Lawrence Islands National Park is being degraded by air, water, and noise pollution from industrial and agricultural practices on adjacent lands. Acid rain is reducing water quality and species reproduction in Georgian Bay Islands National Park. Industrial developments outside Pukaskwa National Park could degrade the park's wildlife populations and water quality.[19]

Because lands surrounding national parks are either privately owned or provincial Crown lands, the federal Crown has no power to stop unrestricted development on them. Greater cooperation from the provincial government and municipalities in controlling development, and using provincial powers to prosecute polluters and vandals on adjacent lands, is important to their survival, which in turn is necessary to preserve the parklands themselves. Indeed, the federal government must secure such cooperation if it is to meet the spirit of the

National Parks Act and its emphasis on ecological integrity and leaving national parklands unimpaired.

Over the next decade, priority must be placed on gazetting Pukaskwa and the Bruce Peninsula national parks under the *National Parks Act*; assessing the ability of the five existing national parks to represent Ontario's natural regions; and ensuring that activities on adjacent lands are monitored and are corrected when it is confirmed that they are degrading the national parks. It is hoped that the Ontario government and municipal councils will work with the federal government to ensure the future viability of national parks within the province.

National Marine Parks

In 1986, the federal government approved its long-awaited national marine parks policy,[20] thereby establishing a framework aimed at representing each of Canada's 29 marine regions within a system of national marine parks. The objective is to establish marine parks along the Atlantic, Pacific, and Arctic coastlines and in the Great Lakes to protect and conserve for all time those places which are significant examples of Canada's marine heritage. Canada's first national marine park was established in 1987 at Fathom Five at the tip of the Bruce Peninsula.

The *National Parks Act* was amended in 1988 to permit the establishment of marine parks. This is an interim measure, however, as the government intends to adopt a separate National Marine Parks Act by 1994.[21] The government hopes by then to have developed enough expertise in managing several national marine parks that it will be able to present to Parliament a credible legislative package.

Separate legislation is required because, unlike terrestrial national parks, national marine parks do not prohibit the commercial exploitation of natural resources. For example, commercial fishing continues in marine parks under the provisions of the federal *Fisheries Act*,[22] and oil tankers are not prohibited from travelling through marine parks. Aquaculture is permitted. Transportation, navigation, and the operation of pleasure craft are to be regulated under the *Canada Shipping Act*.[23] Thus, control of national marine parks will require strong cooperation between a number of federal departments and a regulatory framework that is much stronger than and different from the one provided under the *National Parks Act*.

Five of the 29 marine regions that constitute the proposed national marine parks system are found within the Great Lakes. Ontario also touches on two additional marine regions to the north: Hudson Bay and James Bay. The Georgian Bay region is represented through the Fathom Five National Marine Park. Studies to identify future marine parks have been completed for Lake Ontario, and are progressing in several other areas. However, as long as the federal government limits itself to the goals for marine parks set under the Green Plan (three by 1996 and three more by 2000), action on future marine parks within Ontario is likely to result only if there is public pressure for new national marine parks.

In addition, because the management of all fisheries in the Great Lakes is delegated to provincial agencies, the federal government will require cooperative working agreements with the Ontario government to fully implement a national marine parks program in Ontario. National marine parks could make a significant contribution to the protection of Ontario's aquatic ecosystems because the Ontario government has not adopted legislation or any plans for protecting Great Lake ecosystems within its provincial parks network.

National Wildlife Areas and Migratory Bird Sanctuaries

The federal government administers two types of wildlife reserves: national wildlife areas and migratory bird sanctuaries. To date, there are 23 such areas in Ontario, but in total they protect only 443 square kilometres. Although the two designations have not been widely used, they remain an opportunity for federal-provincial cooperation in the protection of natural areas and wildlife habitat of national and international significance.

In 1916, Canada and the United States signed the Treaty for International Protection of Migratory Birds to protect certain migratory birds. Parliament passed the *Migratory Birds Convention Act*[24] in 1917, to implement the treaty in Canada. Section 4(2)(f) of the Act provides the federal government with the authority to establish migratory bird sanctuaries. In Ontario, 13 sanctuaries cover a total of 391 square kilometres. Under the Act, the government can make regulations that protect migratory birds from hunting, or prohibit the taking of eggs or nests or the pollution of habitat. However, the government can also still grant permits for mineral exploration and development.

Habitat that is important for migratory birds can be protected under the Act only with the consent of the landowner, and only as long as the area remains essential to the protection of migratory birds. Landowners whose consent might be needed include provincial governments, private landowners, the Department of Indian Affairs and Northern Development in northern Canada, as well as aboriginal people in areas where land claim settlements have been ratified. Because some birds migrate to the United States and Central and South America, migratory bird sanctuaries will play an increasingly important role in global conservation.

The *Canada Wildlife Act*[25] was passed by Parliament in 1973 to promote wildlife research, interpretation, and the conservation of wildlife habitat. It provides the federal minister of the environment with the authority to purchase, lease, or accept through donation lands for research, conservation, and interpretation of wildlife. The minister may enter into agreements with provincial and municipal governments, as well as non-government organizations, to achieve these goals. Unlike under the *National Parks Act*, the minister can make changes to the boundaries of national wildlife areas and permit the extraction of natural resources without having the approval of Parliament. Thus, the minister is not accountable for decisions that may jeopardize the integrity of national wildlife areas.

Ten national wildlife areas protect 52 square kilometres of Ontario. Part of Long Point, for example, protects native vegetation in a natural condition in the Great Lakes' most extensive sand dunes complex. Unlike under the *National Parks Act*, the federal government does not have to own the land outright to establish migratory bird sanctuaries or national wildlife areas. It can lease, dispose of, buy, and sell such lands or enter into agreements with other governments or private landowners — agreements that can be revoked through mutual consent. The minister may also sell off such lands, provided that disposition is compatible with wildlife research, conservation, and interpretation activities.

In addition, resource extraction activities are not prohibited; thus, a conservation philosophy rather than a preservation philosophy of management predominates in that while the lands are to be conserved, human manipulation of wildlife habitat can be permitted if it does not harm wildlife. Under the *Canada Wildlife Act*, the minister can permit any activity as long as the use is compatible with wildlife research, conservation, and interpretation. Although the types of activities that are permitted are extensive, provisions under the *Canada Wildlife Act* do limit ministerial discretion to a greater extent than a *carte blanche*.

[handwritten margin notes:] 100 × 100 m² / 10,000 m² / 100 km²

It is permissible to alter national wildlife areas by such activities as blasting out new ponds to create breeding sites for waterfowl, and to plant trees and shrubs as cover for birds and deer. The natural plant cover may be altered to increase food and shelter, and grain may be planted to draw migrating birds away from farmers' fields. However, the minister may also prohibit entry onto such lands, make regulations for the preservation, control, and management of these lands, and close the lands to persons who endanger the wildlife in the area.

It is surprising that the *Canada Wildlife Act* has not been more widely used to protect important wildlife habitats. For example, it could be used to protect lands adjacent to national and provincial parks that are important to park wildlife while not requiring a transfer of land to the federal government. It could be used to facilitate greater federal involvement in public education and research into wildlife issues. Perhaps once the federal and provincial governments agree on how to implement the National Wildlife Habitat Strategy promised under Canada's Green Plan,[26] Ontario may agree to the expansion of the national wildlife areas and migratory bird sanctuaries within the province.

Canadian Heritage Rivers

In response to growing public concern and political interest in Canada's diminishing wild rivers, the federal, provincial, and territorial parks ministers established the Canadian Heritage Rivers System in 1984. The objectives of the system are: (1) to give national recognition to important Canadian rivers; and (2) to ensure that they are managed to conserve and interpret the natural and cultural heritage they represent. Participation in the system by governments is voluntary. To date, only Alberta and British Columbia have not joined the program, but both have commissioned studies to determine under what conditions they may join the program.

The system is administered by representatives from the governments that choose to participate in the program and they comprise the Canadian Heritage Rivers Board. Each jurisdiction can nominate rivers to be heritage rivers. Nominations are submitted to the board for review and the nominating jurisdiction must demonstrate to the board that the river is of outstanding natural significance. Once the river is accepted, the government that nominated the river has three years to submit a management plan. On receipt of a plan, the river is officially designated by the board as a heritage river.

The conferring of Canadian heritage river status has no legal standing or power. It is a cooperative program; participation by the provinces and territories is voluntary. The provinces retain their jurisdictional power over heritage rivers, including ownership, the choice to recommend a river for heritage status, and the right to manage such areas as they see fit. The contents of a management plan are the prerogative of the managing agencies alone. The board has no power to approve or reject submitted management plans.

The power in the designation rests solely on the profile such status gives rivers. Designation conveys a message to the public that these are significant rivers. The program also gives the river's management authorities a formal route to access river management expertise across Canada and draw more resources to the project than they could if it were "just another river." In addition, the board has the right to terminate the designation if rivers are affected to the point that they lose their heritage values. The chair of the board can convey any concerns regarding loss of Canadian heritage river values to the minister(s) responsible.

The Canadian Heritage Rivers policy states that the boundaries of designated heritage rivers should contain those ecosystem components required for the continuity of species, features, and objects protected by the river. The areas within the boundaries must be of sufficient size to protect the river, and the maintenance of water quality is critical. The board will review the status of each heritage river and its management plan at least once every 10 years, with the power to undertake an independent assessment.

In Ontario, both the French and Mattawa rivers are designated as Canadian heritage rivers. In addition, the board has approved nomination of four additional rivers to the system: Bloodvein, Missinaibi, Boundary Waters, and the Grand.[27] Once management plans have been approved for these rivers, they will then be declared Canadian heritage rivers. Except for the Grand River, the designated and nominated rivers are wholly within existing provincial parks. Thus, the program has generally failed to increase the amount of land and waters protected from development. However, the Canadian Heritage Rivers Board hopes that such status will encourage landowners and governments to manage water resources so as to protect values; otherwise, the status will be lost.

The stipulation that a management plan must be produced has resulted in the Ontario government allocating a higher level of financing to the management of Canada heritage rivers. In the absence of such a designation, no funding would have been allocated to the Grand River, for example.

Some of the potential benefits of the program include more effective management of some rivers, a greater commitment to management planning for heritage rivers, and an opportunity to promote to the public the need to support the conservation of Canadian rivers. However, if the program is to continue to improve, the governments will soon have to allow non-government representatives to be members of the Canadian Heritage Rivers Board in order to make the process more publicly accountable. In addition, greater protection could be placed on Canadian heritage rivers if jurisdictions were to enshrine their commitments to these rivers in legislation.

THE PROVINCIAL SYSTEM OF PARKS AND PROTECTED AREAS

Ontario has developed an impressive array of mechanisms to preserve critical natural areas. Provincial parks and wilderness areas are created and administered under the *Provincial Parks Act*[28] and the *Wilderness Areas Act*.[29] The identification and protection of areas of natural and scientific interest (ANSIs), wetlands, and other types of natural areas on both Crown and private lands is encouraged by the *Conservation Land Act*,[30] the *Ontario Heritage Act*,[31] and the *Conservation Authorities Act*.[32] The *Niagara Escarpment Planning and Development Act*[33] resulted in the development of a regional plan to preserve the escarpment's natural values, and to create a series of provincial parks linked by the Bruce Trail.

After a century of provincial action, 6.5 per cent of Ontario is preserved within 4,045 protected areas conserving over 69,000 square kilometres. Lands protected in a wilderness state where logging, mining, and hunting are prohibited total only 2.2 per cent of the province.[34] Although it is in southern Ontario that fully one-third of Canada's endangered species are found, opportunities to protect large wilderness areas greater than 50,000 hectares, roughly the size of Killarney Provincial Park, no longer exist in this region.[35] These numbers alone underscore the need to protect additional areas and to preserve the substantial gains already made through enhanced legislation.

In 1989, the World Wildlife Fund (Canada) and the Canadian Parks and Wilderness Society launched the Endangered Spaces Campaign to promote greater political action across Canada to preserve the nation's disappearing wilderness. The two groups called on all major governments to commit themselves to completing their networks of parks and protected areas by the year 2000. The objective is to get each jurisdiction to establish a protected area that would represent each of the nation's almost 350 distinct natural regions. Ontario gave its commitment to achieve this target when the New Democratic Party was elected in 1990. To date, 32 of Ontario's 65 natural regions are represented within the parks system while an additional 18 are partially represented, and 15 are unrepresented.

Responding to the Endangered Spaces challenge, the Ontario Ministry of Natural Resources released in 1992 a proposed Natural Heritage Areas Strategy for Ontario. It proposes "a strategy that maximizes efforts to protect natural heritage areas," including actions to improve legislation.[36] It states that the *Provincial Parks Act*, the *Conservation Land Act*,[37] and a proposed *Ecological Reserves Act* could provide the cornerstones for the identification, protection, and stewardship of a system of natural heritage areas. A strength of the strategy is that it provides a focus for a number of protected area statutes, and seeks to use them to achieve global, national, and provincial protected area goals.

The Provincial Parks System

The Ontario government manages the province's 260 individual provincial parks through the Ministry of Natural Resources (MNR). Each park makes its own unique contribution to the preservation of Ontario's natural and cultural heritage, while offering a variety of recreational opportunities. Park visitors can canoe in a wilderness setting, or hike in a relatively natural but human-altered landscape. They can visit large unaltered northern tracts of wilderness, or small but nationally significant stands of Carolinian forest and wetlands across southern Ontario.

Through legislation, regulations, and policy, the Ontario government manages the system to meet four objectives: (1) protection; (2) recreation; (3) appreciation; and (4) tourism. However, inconsistencies between legislation and policy, and inconsistencies in both the interpretation and application of these policies, have sometimes undermined the ability of parks to preserve natural areas in perpetuity, and to meet provincial and international conservation goals. The inconsistencies also reflect the fact that the enactment of legislation invariably trails the formulation of policy.

The Purpose of Provincial Parks

Ontario passed its first *Parks Act* in 1913, giving the government the power to create parks on Crown lands not suitable for agriculture or settlement. The Ontario government currently draws its power to establish and administer provincial parks from the *Provincial Parks Act*.[38] The current Act was passed in 1954 by the Ontario Legislature to bring the parks system under the administration of one branch of government, the Parks Branch of the Department of Lands and Forests (now the Ministry of Natural Resources), and to give the government the power to administer the parks. The government had earlier established eight parks, including

Ontario Provincial Parks -- A Treasured Legacy

> Provincial parks in Ontario have 100 years of history.

In May 1893, an "Act to Create the Algonquin National Park of Ontario" was approved and passed by the Ontario Legislature. As a *Toronto Telegram* headline declared at the time, "Ontario's Own Park" became a reality.

Over the years, provincial parks have evolved from the "public park and forest reservation, fish and game preserve, health resort and pleasure ground" as Algonquin was described in 1893, to the diverse system of parks we have today.

1893	Algonquin became Ontario's first provincial park.
1894	Rondeau became a provincial park.
1913	The first *Parks Act* was passed. It gave the government the power to set aside Crown lands not suitable for settlement or agriculture for park purposes. Quetico Provincial Park was created.
1921	Long Point became Ontario's fourth provincial park.
1922	Presqu'ile became a provincial park.
1938	Ipperwash joined the list of provincial parks.
1944	Sibley (now called Sleeping Giant) and Lake Superior Provincial Parks were created. The first interpretive programs were offered in Algonquin.
1954	A stronger *Provincial Parks Act* was passed and a separate Division of Parks was established in the Department of Lands and Forests.
1956	Administration of 30 roadside parks was transferred from the Department of Highways (10 were later returned).
1959	First park policy statement was read in the Legislature and the *Wilderness Areas Act* was passed.
1960	Ontario had 72 parks with five million visitors a year.
1961	Nature Reserves Committee produced a list of candidate areas for protection.
1965	Special funding through Agricultural Rural Development Agreement (ARDA) led to 10 new parks.
1967	A new policy was adopted requiring all parks to have master plans (later called park management plans). A park classification system was developed.
1973	The Department of Lands and Forests became the Ministry of Natural Resources.
1974	The Ontario Provincial Parks Council, a citizens' advisory committee, was established.

Rondeau - 1908

1978	Cabinet approved a new parks policy. It outlined park philosophy, system rationale, program targets and management policies. It refined the classification system and introduced zoning.
	The *Ontario Provincial Parks: Planning and Management Policies* binder was issued to staff to act as a guide for delivering the parks policy.
1983	155 candidate parks were designated through province wide land-use planning. The first co-operating association agreement was signed (Friends of Algonquin).
1988	Cabinet gave additional policy direction for provincial parks with a renewed emphasis on environmental protection, particularly in the wilderness and nature reserve class parks and zones.
1989	The regulation of the 155 new parks was completed.
1992	The Ministry of Natural Resources released a draft *Natural Heritage Areas Strategy from Ontario: Responding to the Endangered Spaces Challenge* as part of the government's commitment to completing a system of parks and protected areas by the year 2000.
1993	Ontario will commemorate the provincial parks Centennial.

Legislation

More than 50 Ontario Acts and the regulations under those Acts, apply to activities in provincial parks. Some examples are:

Provincial Parks Act
Game and Fish Act
Environmental Assessment Act
Highway Traffic Act
Liquor Licence Act
Aggregates Resources Act
Environmental Protection Act

Federal legislation also applies, including the *Fisheries Act*, *Migratory Birds Convention Act* and the *Criminal Code*.

Provincial parks are created by the Lieutenant Governor in Council through regulations under the *Provincial Parks Act*. The first *Parks Act* was passed in 1913 and gave the government the power to set aside Crown lands not suitable for settlement or agriculture for park purposes.

In the 1950s, increased population growth, a rising standard of living and a better educated, more mobile public caused an explosion in the demand for outdoor recreation opportunities. To meet the pressures of this increased demand, the Ontario Government passed a stronger *Provincial Parks Act* (1954).

That Act, revised over the years, is still in use today.

Although not part of the Parks Class EA process, the *Provincial Parks Act* is being reviewed to ensure that it meets today's needs. Complementary ecological reserves legislation is being considered at the same time.

A separate public consultation process is being set up to give you a chance to participate in the review of the legislation. For more information, please contact **John Simpson**, Manager, Legislation Review, Parks and Natural Heritage Policy Branch, 90 Sheppard Avenue East, North York, Ontario M2N 3A1.

From *Class Environmental Assessment for Provincial Park Management.*

Algonquin in 1893, Quetico in 1913, and Lake Superior in 1944, under a different type of legislative and administrative arrangement.

A general statement of purpose for provincial parks is provided in the dedication clause, which is section 2 of the Act. It states:

> All provincial parks are dedicated to the people of the Province of Ontario and others who may use them for their healthful enjoyment and education, and the provincial parks shall be maintained for the benefit of future generations.

Unlike the *National Parks Act*,[39] it provides no direction to manage parklands so as to leave them "unimpaired." Rather, the emphasis is on resource use, allowing for the possible exploitation of provincial parks in a variety of ways. The Act places no environmental responsibility on the government. It does not provide decision makers with any mandate to preserve a park's natural values, to exclude resource extraction, or to prevent the overdevelopment of tourism facilities.

In 1978, the provincial Cabinet approved a new Provincial Parks Policy statement,[40] which rules out industrial resource extraction in most classes of park, sets the development of recreational opportunities within an environmental context, and places a heavy emphasis on preserving natural values. However, the *Provincial Parks Act* was never updated to reflect this more preservationist attitude.

In short, the policy describes provincial parks as a distinctive land use classification where resource extraction is generally prohibited and the natural, scientific, and educational values of parklands are given priority. Most often, the use and the management of these parklands are consistent with a preservation ethic as enshrined in the *National Parks Act* and subsequent national park policy statements. The *Provincial Parks Act*, in sharp contrast, is very permissive in that it does not prohibit the extraction of timber, ore bodies, or wildlife. Although the Act does little to distinguish parks from other forms of land use, the associated regulations, policies, and practices do make a substantial distinction between parks and other Crown lands.

Administration and Management

A provincial park is simply an area of land designated as such by the Ontario Cabinet under the *Provincial Parks Act*. In theory, the bulk of power relating to the establishment, administration, and management of provincial parks rests with Cabinet. It can set aside, or acquire, any area of Ontario as a provincial park. Unlike under the *National Parks Act*, Cabinet may subsequently eliminate a park by an order in council, without the permission of the Ontario Legislature and any public consultation or legislative review. In October 1986, the government exercised this authority and dropped Holiday Beach Provincial Park from the park system. It was only two months later that the Federation of Ontario Naturalists discovered this decision.[41] Formerly a recreation class park, it is a site well known for migrating hawks and used by birders. Holiday Beach is now managed by the Essex Region Conservation Authority under the *Conservation Authorities Act* as conservation land.

Cabinet has the power to make regulations to control or prohibit any activity carried on in a provincial park. Because there are no legislative caveats on its action, Cabinet can approve virtually any activity including the licensing of trades, businesses, amusements, sports, boat and air traffic, and, most significant, exploration and development by logging and mining companies, and the granting, renewing, and transferring licences of occupation to tourism and recreational operations and businesses.

A critical weakness is section 18(1) of the Act,[42] which states that prospecting, the staking of mining claims, and the development of mineral interests or the working of mines in provincial parks is prohibited, subject to the regulations. But under section 19(1), Cabinet has the power to make regulations that can nonetheless permit prospecting, staking, and development of mineral interests and the working of mines. Cabinet did exercise its right to permit mining in parks in 1983 when it allowed mineral exploration and development in some of the province's 155 new parks. The regulations currently list 23 provincial parks, including 5 wilderness parks, where mining could occur if a licence of occupation or a lease was issued under subsection 190(2) of the *Mining Act*.[43] Although current policy prohibits it, legally the government can issue an exploration or development permit in these parks until such time as it amends the regulations and drops the 23 parks from the regulations and prohibits the issuance of any mining permit.

However, the government can make regulations under the *Provincial Parks Act* to preserve park values. For example, under section 21(1)(a), Cabinet can make regulations "for the care, preservation, improvement, control and management of the provincial parks." Generally such regulations have focused on the limiting of recreational activities so as to preserve parklands. To protect wilderness campsites, there are regulations that: prohibit food containers in Algonquin, Killarney, Lake Superior, and Quetico parks; limit to six persons the occupation of interior campsites in specific parks; and prohibit the operation of power boats in specific parks or portions of them.

Under the Act, the power to control activities in provincial parks is usually delegated by Cabinet to the minister of natural resources. For example, the Minister may permit the construction and operation of golf courses or other facilities for sport or amusement, accommodation, or transportation, and other facilities for the convenience of the public. The regulations allow the landing of aircraft in over 30 provincial parks, under the authority of an aircraft landing permit.

The minister appoints a superintendent or supervisor to manage each park, who has wide-ranging powers that may be exercised with the minister's approval. Under the Act, the superintendent is in charge of constructing recreational facilities, shops, and restaurants, buying boats and other vehicles, and making contracts with people to establish or operate facilities or services. Although a 1985 review of the ministry's contracting policies [44] recommended that no further parks be contracted out to private operators for management, the government will continue to use individual service contracts and concessions in provincial parks, except in those areas involving information, education, and interpretation.

The internal structure of government departments and Cabinet appointments also serve to undermine park values. The minister of natural resources, in addition to a parks mandate, is responsible for other programs for public lands: aggregate extraction, forestry, and management of fish and wildlife. All these conflicting responsibilities can cause negative impacts on parks. In addition, several natural resources ministers have had dual portfolios, creating potential conflicts of interest. Former Natural Resources Minister Vince Kerrio lobbied for the development of hydroelectric sites in provincial parks when he was also the minister of energy.[45] Thus, in the absence of guiding legislation, ministers can promote compromises that result in the incremental loss of park values.

[handwritten marginalia: Public Trust Doctrine]

The Public Trust Doctrine

The dedication clause of the *Provincial Parks Act* seems to constitute a trust between the government and the people of Ontario that the provincial parks will be protected. The common idea behind a public trust is that elected officials, rather than civil servants, are given responsibility for maintaining provincial parklands and cannot permit activities that damage the parks, which are essentially a property held in trust. Under this notion, the public has enforceable legal rights that are designed to protect the parklands, and that can prevent the government from allowing activities within the parks that are in the self-interest of private parties.

In 1972, however, an Ontario court concluded that the *Provincial Parks Act* imposes no such public trust on the government after researcher Larry Green and the Canadian Environmental Law Association tried to test the public trust doctrine. The case involved the allocation of a lease by the Ontario government to Lake Ontario Cement Limited in 1968 for the excavation of sand in Prince Edward County. Two years later Sandbanks Provincial Park was established pursuant to the *Provincial Parks Act*, in an area immediately adjacent to the land leased to the cement company. In *Green v. The Queen in Right of the Province of Ontario*,[46] the plaintiff asserted that the lease constituted a breach of the public trust because the sand dunes, located both in the park and on the adjacent leasehold property, were a unique ecological, geological, and recreational resource that the province had a duty to maintain for the benefit of the Ontario people.

Mr. Justice Lerner rejected Green's assertion of a public trust. He concluded that the discretion of the government in administering provincial parklands under the Act is "so complete as to make the power of the Province in the whole concept of park lands absolute." Hence, there was no public trust. For example, the Act empowers the government to increase, decrease, or even to terminate the existence of a park. The justice concluded that because the government is not compelled to hold park property for the advantage of the public for any certain period of time, it did not meet a critical condition necessary to assert a trust.

Furthermore, Mr. Justice Lerner found that section 19 of the Act[47] gave the government wide-ranging and unfettered powers in issuing permits to private business interests, amusement operators, tourist operators, and all manner of trades and businesses to operate in the park. Thus, for the justice, the issue was not about public trust, but whether the government followed correct procedures in issuing permits for the exploitation of provincial parks.

Finally, Mr. Justice Lerner found that members of the public do not have standing to sue where a park is being exploited, because even if this were illegal, it would be a public nuisance in which everyone was equally affected. Therefore, only the attorney general of the province could sue.

Critics of the decision argue that Mr. Justice Lerner did not understand the concept of a public trust and, as a result, his decision was "clearly erroneous." The purpose of this chapter is not to debate the decision; however, *Green v. Ontario* clearly points out the weaknesses inherent in the *Provincial Parks Act*, and how it must be improved in order to assert a stronger public trust doctrine.

In *Canadian Parks and Wilderness Society v. Her Majesty the Queen in Right of Canada*,[48] while the court found that logging in Wood Buffalo National Park was illegal under the *National Parks Act*,[49] it did not rule on the existence of a public trust under the Act. However, in its written submission to the court, the federal government outlined how the regulations under the Act, and the activities permitted in the national parks, are restrictive. Thus, unlike under the *Provincial Parks Act*, the federal government does not have absolute power to allow activities such as commercial logging within the parks; hence, the notion of a public trust is inherent in the provisions of the *National Parks Act*.

For example, section 6(1) of the *National Parks Act* states that "public lands within the parks shall not be disposed of or located or settled upon and no person shall use or occupy any part of such lands, except under the authority of this Act or the regulations." Under the regulations, clearcut logging is not permitted. And although under section 6(2) the government "may authorize the sale, lease or other disposition of public lands within a park," that authority is restricted to rights of ways and the installation and operation of radio and television repeater stations. In effect, the present *National Parks Act* does not authorize the disposition of public lands in the park or of the natural resources found within them to industrial development. The extent to which this applies to tourism development remains unclear.

Ontario Provincial Parks Policy and Classification System

The Ontario Cabinet approved the Ontario Provincial Parks Policy in 1978.[50] It provides a general statement of principles as well as specific goals and objectives for the provincial parks system, and establishes direction to the government in the planning of new parks, and the management of existing and future provincial parks. Unlike the Act, it allows the public to point to government failures in meeting targets for creating new parks, or in preserving provincial parklands from development.

The policy states that the goal is to provide the people of Ontario with a provincial parks system that offers a variety of outdoor recreation opportunities, and to protect provincially significant natural, cultural, and recreational environments. The parks system has four basic objectives in the areas of protection, heritage appreciation, recreation, and tourism:

- To *protect* provincially significant elements of the natural and cultural landscape of Ontario.
- To provide opportunities for exploration and *appreciation* of the outdoor natural and cultural heritage of Ontario.
- To provide provincial park outdoor *recreation* opportunities ranging from high-intensity day use to low-intensity wilderness experiences.
- To provide Ontario residents and out-of-province visitors with opportunities to discover and *experience* the distinctive regions of the Province [emphasis added].

The policy includes a statement of principles to guide management of the parks system. For example, parks are established to secure representative features of Ontario's natural heritage. This principle reflects the goals of both the Brundtland commission and the Endangered Spaces campaign. Another principle is that individual parks contribute to the overall objectives of the provincial parks system in that all objectives cannot be met in each park. Cabinet was unequivocal on this point: "No individual park can be all things to all people."

Cabinet also approved a zoning system for the parks. Zoning recognizes that every park includes a particular combination of significant resources, features, and visitor experiences that relate to the overall purpose of the park. Zoning allocates areas of parkland on the basis of their significance for protection and their potential for recreation. Within the parks, there are the following zones: wilderness; nature reserve; access; historical; natural environment; and development. Although Algonquin is classified as a natural environment park in which commercial logging is permitted, a portion of the park is zoned wilderness in recognition of both its ecological and recreational values, and logging is prohibited in this zone.

When Cabinet approved the Ontario Provincial Parks Policy, it also decided "that the appropriate legislative changes should be undertaken to reflect this policy."[51] Unfortunately, the Act was never updated to reflect this policy, thus allowing future political decisions to undermine this policy statement.

The Provincial Park Classification System

Cabinet also approved a park classification scheme, which is the backbone of the park system. It organizes the system into broad park categories. Each category has a particular purpose and characteristic, and distinctive planning, management, and visitor service policies. The classification system is described in detail in a document entitled *Ontario Provincial Parks: Planning and Management Policies*, or the "blue book" for short. The blue book provides excellent direction to field managers on the park classification scheme, park objectives, permissible activities including habitat manipulation, control of species, facility develop-ment, recreational objectives, and many other issues and activities. The Ministry of Natural Resources has reviewed the document to reflect changes in parks policy approved over the last 15 years.[52]

The purpose of the classification system is threefold: (1) to express the role of individual parks in achieving the objectives for the park system as a whole; (2) to enable managers to ensure that each park visitor has the opportunity to participate in the diverse opportunities provided by the parks system; and (3) to promote the best management of the diverse resources of the system, through public understanding and appreciation of the characteristics of each park and the system as a whole.

To date, of the 260 provincial parks, there are 8 wilderness parks, 83 nature reserves, 63 natural environment parks, 29 waterway parks, 4 historical parks, and 73 recreation parks. The parks classification system is outlined below:

1. *Wilderness parks* are substantial areas where the forces of nature are permitted to function freely and where visitors travel by non-mechanized means and experience expansive solitude, challenge, and personal integration with nature. They are large enough to allow natural processes to continue on a large scale, relatively unaffected by human action, and for visitors to experience a wilderness trip. Commercial mineral development and forest operations, agricultural practices, and sport hunting are prohib-ited. Wilderness parks should average not less than 100,000 hectares in size, and should be not less than 50,000 hectares as an absolute minimum. Wilderness parks include Polar Bear, Killarney, and Quetico.

2. *Nature reserves* represent the distinctive natural habitats and landforms of the province, and are protected for educational purposes and as gene pools for research. The priority

is on the achievement of protection and heritage appreciation objectives, with recreation being a much lesser objective. They are similar to the ecological reserves category used by other jurisdictions because they protect natural features primarily for their aesthetic, interpretive, educational, and scientific value. Activities are strictly managed to further scientific and visitor understanding.

Two types of management philosophies can be used in managing nature reserves: (a) natural features and conditions will remain undisturbed, or (b) they may be altered to provide suitable habitat for a species in order to perpetuate it. Logging, mining, commercial trapping, and sport hunting and are not permitted. Fishing is allowed in nature reserves unless prohibited through sanctuary provisions. Motorized land vehicles and watercraft are prohibited.

3. *Natural environment parks* combine outstanding recreational landscapes with representative natural features and historical resources to provide high quality recreational and educational experiences. These parks incorporate natural, cultural, and recreational features within a natural area that has been developed over time. Many of the oldest parks such as Algonquin, Rondeau, Presqu'île, Sibley, and Lake Superior are within this category, primarily because of the level of development.

These parks are to meet all the park system objectives of protection, recreation, tourism, and heritage appreciation. The impact of our technological society is clearly in evidence — logging in Algonquin and Lake Superior, cottages in Rondeau. They are typically more accessible, contain buildings, and generally reflect an earlier vision for protected areas as multiple-use areas. Commercial mineral exploration and forest operations are prohibited, except for commercial forest operations in Algonquin. The manipulation of habitat, sport hunting, and certain other activities are permitted.

4. *Waterway parks* incorporate outstanding recreational water routes with representative natural features and historical resources to provide high-quality recreational and educational experiences. The policy recognizes watersheds as ecological units and river systems as their arteries. They range from wild rivers to highly developed river corridors, and permitted activities range from motorboat travel to wilderness canoeing. Park boundaries are not to be less than 200 metres from shoreline, and should be ecologically defensible and aesthetically pleasing. Waterway parks can include lands that are either Crown lands or privately owned. Logging and mining are prohibited, and hunting is permitted only in natural environment zones under certain conditions.

In some cases, waterway parks may not provide sufficient protection for natural values. Waterway parks may be limited to the minimum 200-metre boundary. They may not encompass complete watersheds and are thus subject to significant external impacts. Or protection-oriented zones may be scaled down or eliminated to accommodate the many uses on the waterway.

5. *Historical parks* are areas selected to represent the distinctive historical resources of the province in open-space settings, and are protected for interpretive, educational, and research purposes. They incorporate outstanding recreational land and water routes with representative natural features and historical resources to provide high quality recreational and educational experiences.

6. *Recreation parks* are areas that support a wide variety of outdoor recreation opportunities for large numbers of people in attractive surroundings, such as Bronte Creek Provincial Park near Hamilton. These parks do not have a protection objective, but play an important role in heritage appreciation and outdoor recreation. Established in areas where there are significant recreational environments such as large beaches or landscapes of outstanding potential for recreational development, they guarantee to the people of Ontario places where they can enjoy themselves in outdoor surroundings. Targets are based on recreational and tourism needs of surrounding areas.

Representing Ontario's Natural Regions

In the 1970s the Ministry of Natural Resources developed a classification scheme that called for the protection of a system of earth and life science features that represent Ontario's diversity of natural landscapes. Studies to identify such features are conducted within a framework that divides the province into 13 site regions defined by a different combination of vegetation, soil, and climate characteristics. These regions are further subdivided into 65 site districts that represent more locally definable landform characteristics.

The blue book establishes the following targets for each category of park defined within the classification system:

- one wilderness park for 11 of the 13 site regions (two site regions in southern Ontario do not have a wilderness area left that meets the policy's minimum size criteria of 50,000 hectares for wilderness parks);
- nature reserves wherever provincially significant natural features exist, with a focus on the representation of 150 vegetation types;
- one natural environment park in each of the 65 site districts;
- one waterway park in each of the 65 site districts; and
- recreation parks wherever they are required to satisfy outdoor recreation requirements.

To achieve its goal of representing each of the province's natural regions, the government recognizes the contribution of other protected areas. For example, Pukaskwa National Park represents the Lake Abitibi Site Region of the provincial parks system. Under the proposed Natural Heritage Areas Strategy, the province is prepared to recognize the protection or co-management of First Nation Reserves that protect aboriginal lands.

To date, 9 of the site regions are represented by 8 provincial wilderness parks and 1 national park; 62 natural environment parks and equivalent-size natural environment zones have been established in 55 of 65 site districts; and 29 waterway parks, or their equivalent, have been established in 31 of 65 site districts. The Ontario government estimates that 49 per cent of the province's geological features and 46 per cent of its biological features are currently represented within the parks system.[53]

It also estimates that to complete the provincial parks system it requires an additional 2 wilderness parks, 10 natural environment parks, and about 15 waterway parks.

Provincial Park Establishment

These targets remain policy commitments, which are not necessarily adhered to by successive governments and the different political parties. This is in part because governments are not compelled by the *Provincial Parks Act* either to achieve the targets or to ensure that the blue book policies for the park classification scheme are implemented. The creation of the 155 new parks in 1983 illustrates this point.

In 1982 the government identified 245 candidate provincial parks, including 7 wilderness parks, 34 natural environment parks, 35 waterway parks, and 147 nature reserves.[54] The candidate parks were then assessed within the context of the government's Strategic Land Use Planning program and reviewed by the public through a series of open houses across the province. Cabinet then sat down in 1983 to make a decision on the candidate parks.

In June 1983, the government announced the establishment of 155 new provincial parks, including 6 wilderness parks, 35 natural environment parks, 25 waterway parks, and 74 nature reserves. However, several aspects of the government's announcement underscore the failure of the political and regulatory system to establish all 245 candidate parks, and to produce a parks system that matches the goals of Ontario's provincial parks policy.

Ninety of the 245 candidate parks were dropped because of the strong opposition expressed against these parks by local people and other resource users. The total area protected by the 155 new parks, about 2,100,000 hectares, was only 60 per cent of the total size of the 245 candidates identified for protection. For example, 36 per cent of the area proposed as wilderness park was deleted and over half the area suggested for waterway parks was dropped. Finally, non-conforming or commercial exploitation activities such as mining, hunting, and trapping were permitted in the new parks despite the prohibitions placed on such activities by the 1978 parks policy.

Thus, on June 2, 1983, Ontario inherited a two-tier provincial parks system: parks established before that date were managed in accordance with the blue book; and parks established on that date would be subject to a range of commercial developments that would permit the exploitation of natural resources. Logging was permitted in 2 parks, hunting in 82 parks, trapping in 79 parks, mining in 48 parks (or 80 per cent of the total area), and commercial tourism in 23 parks. In reality, the new parks differed little from the management of surrounding Crown lands.

Cabinet's decision to allow non-conforming uses in the parks was meant as a positive response to the concerns expressed by local residents against the proposed parks, to minimize socioeconomic dislocation, and to compensate for the loss of income from some activities that would be prohibited, such as commercial logging.

Cabinet also believed that park values would not be jeopardized by some of the non-conforming uses if they were carefully managed. The park management planning process would be used to decide how, where, and to what extent such uses would be incorporated into, and managed in, individual parks.[55]

Cabinet was able to delete or reduce the size of proposed candidate parks, and to permit resource development activities within the approved parks, partly because of the lack of a strong and preservation-oriented *Provincial Parks Act*. Cabinet was not bound by any legal restraints on what activities could be permitted within the parks, or required to demonstrate that the reduced size would not compromise the ecological integrity of a candidate park. In contrast, national park candidates are reviewed to ensure they meet the legislative requirement to maintain their ecological integrity.

Cabinet's decision to allow non-conforming uses in wilderness parks brought the planning process to a halt. When the government started to develop a management plan for the new Woodland Caribou Wilderness Park, the process quickly bogged down as participants in the public consultation process sought clarification of the government's parks policy.[56] On the one hand, the policy stated that nature was to function free of human manipulation in wilderness parks, and visitors were entitled to experience solitude. On the other hand, hunting, trapping, mineral exploration, and increased tourism were now proposed. It was an impossible dilemma that the public servants of the time could not resolve, and a dilemma, as we discuss below, that environmental groups spent the next five years trying to resolve.

Park Reserve Status

The government can designate lands as park reserves under the *Public Lands Act*[57] or the *Mining Act*[58] to give interim protection to areas that may be designated as provincial parks in the future. This designation ensures that the Crown maintains control over the area, and that no new long-term leases or licences of occupation are issued that may compromise the area's value as provincial parkland. A park reserve is established by a minister's order under one of the acts, and by filing a boundary description and a map of the area.

Different degrees of protection are afforded to an area, depending on which Act is used. Designation under the *Mining Act* restricts mineral exploration or exploitation. One type of reservation prohibits both surface and subsurface mining, while another prohibits surface activities but not underground mining. Unfortunately, neither the *Public Lands Act* nor the *Mining Act* provides for the protection of forests in a reserved area.

The use of the park reserve status provides a good alternative to giving lands provincial park status during periods of fiscal restraint. In addition, park reserve status allows the government to review the ecological, recreational, and socioeconomic impacts and benefits of park establishment for a specific area while ensuring the area is not lost to development in the interim. The federal government used federal legislation to designate the northern Yukon and Ellesmere Island areas as park reserves while negotiations were completed with territorial governments and native organizations.

In Saskatchewan, *The Parks Act*[59] gives Cabinet the power to establish a parkland reserve on Crown land to protect park candidates "while a determination is made as to whether or not the lands should be established as a provincial park or protected area." A parkland reserve designation expires after five years.[60]

Exploitation of Provincial Parks

Resource extraction, intensive recreational development, and tourism have been evident in many of Canada's park systems.

The *Provincial Parks Act* does not prohibit any activity in the parks, but subjects certain ones, such as mining, to regulations. The 1978 classification system curtails many uses allowed under the Act, particularly logging, mining, hunting, and hydroelectric dams. In all the parks types, the classification system also directs the government to remove human-constructed structures and physical improvements unless they are of value for park management or visitor services, significant to the park's history, or complementary to its cultural landscapes. Uses designated as non-conforming will be permitted in the park until the lands are acquired, the uses disappear, or equal opportunities are provided elsewhere.

Cottages are permitted in Algonquin and Rondeau provincial parks because at the time they were allowed, few saw the contradiction between cottages and the preservation of wilderness areas. Cottages were permitted in the two parks before July 1954. In 1986, the government attempted to terminate the leases in Algonquin and Rondeau, but failed because of strong opposition from the cottage owners, and from the Algonquin Wildlands League, which felt the government should move first on terminating the logging leases in Algonquin, because they posed a greater threat to the park's natural environment. Because of the lack of public support for removal of the cottages, parks policy now permits the existing cottages to remain in Algonquin and Rondeau until December 31, 2017.

It is the lack of legislated guidelines on permitted uses that allows for a continual erosion of the public trust in maintaining the natural values of protected areas. This is best exemplified by the debate that ensued after the 1983 decision. By January 1986, 104 of the proposed 155 new parks were set in regulations. The Liberal government of David Peterson had promised during the 1987 campaign to complete the task. However, when Natural Resources Minister Vince Kerrio attempted to put the remaining parks into regulation, allowing the non-conforming uses in the parks, other ministers balked. Some accused the minister of trying to get the new Liberal government to put a stamp of approval on the old Tory policy.[61] For the next two years, various departments, including the premier's office, argued over the permissible uses in the parks, as they tried to forge a new policy.

The new twist to Kerrio's direction was that he also wanted to allow hydroelectric power generation in a number of existing and proposed provincial parks that have potential for small-scale hydro power generation. For example, Cabinet was informed that two recommended parks, the Lower Madawaska and the Missinaibi, were potential sites for hydro development. Thus, the Liberal government sought to further weaken the parks policy, and this was possible because of the lack of legislated protection. Regulation of these 51 parks was deferred until the resolution of the issue.

Finally, in May 1988, the Liberal government resolved the policy issue in favour of ecological protection. The announcement,[62] focusing on the values of wilderness and nature reserve parks and zones, now prohibits logging, mining, hunting, trapping, mineral exploration, and hydroelectric development in these areas. In addition, commercial trapping and wild rice harvesting will be phased out by 2010 (except for Status Indians with treaty rights), existing tourism operations will remain, and expansion of tourism operation will be decided following consultations during the park management process. In addition, trapping, mining, and hydroelectric development will be prohibited in all parks, and logging will be permitted only in Algonquin. This decision permitted the regulation of the remaining 51 provincial parks plus several new parks in the Temagami area and fulfilled an outstanding Liberal election promise.

The ban on mineral development does not extend to aggregate extraction. Thus, under the 1988 policy revisions, sand, gravel, crushed stone, peat, and coal and other petroleum resources can still be extracted from parklands. A permit to remove aggregates from parklands can be issued under the *Aggregate Resources Act*.[63] Although legal, this clearly violates the protection mandate of parks.

The government's announcement did nothing, however, to remove commercial logging from Algonquin Park. Only 14 per cent of the park is protected from logging within wilderness and nature reserve zones. About 75 per cent of the park is open to logging. For example, between 1985 and 1990, over 700 square kilometres of Algonquin was logged, and there are now over 2,000 kilometres of logging roads within the park. The Wildlands League has called on the government to phase out logging in the park and to immediately end road construction.[64] Unfortunately, the Ontario Provincial Parks Council, in its review of Algonquin's management plan, supported continued logging in the park. However, the council also recommended an increase in the nature reserve zones and a ban on logging within the proposed areas.[65]

Examples of other attempts by government to exploit park resources are numerous. Hunting is permitted in 68 provincial parks. Past breaches of park policy and law are highlighted in Paul Eagles's 1984 report entitled "A study of the Ontario Provincial Parks Act." In 1988, Natural Resources Minister Vince Kerrio announced his plan to make Sibley Provincial Park near Thunder Bay a regional tourist attraction. Plans included the development of a lodge and a seminar centre, the widening of a scenic drive within the park, and the construction of equestrian stables, a store, and a marina. The 1988 management plan for the Mattawa River Park allows hunting and motorboating within areas that were originally proposed as nature reserve zones because they contain rare plants and unique cliff habitat for plants and birds.[66] On the positive side, the government announced in July 1992 that timber harvesting will be discontinued in Lake Superior Provincial Park.

The Wilderness Areas Act

The title of the *Wilderness Areas Act*[67] is misleading because it cannot preserve wilderness areas larger than one square mile (260 hectares or 640 acres), an area too small to protect a self-sustaining wilderness. However, it reflects a 1959 vision of a need to preserve wilderness areas that predated the passage of the monumental US *Wilderness Act*[68] in 1964. The Act states that Cabinet "may set apart any public lands as a wilderness area for the preservation of the area as nearly as may be in its natural state in which research and educational activities may be carried on, for the protection of the flora and fauna, [or] for the improvement of the area, having regard for its historical, aesthetic, scientific, and recreational value."[69]

However, section 2 of the Act destroys its ability to preserve wilderness areas because the Act's regulations cannot limit the exploitation of the natural resources in any wilderness area outside the 640-acre limit. This size is far too small to allow the area to be ecologically self-regulating, or to allow visitors to enjoy a wilderness experience. The current provincial park policy clearly states that a wilderness area should not be any smaller than 50,000 hectares.

Under the *Wilderness Areas Act*, the Ministry of Natural Resources currently preserves 37 areas that have natural or cultural values or both, protecting a total of 618 square kilometres. However, with the adoption of the Ontario Provincial Parks Policy in 1978, wilderness areas have been identified and protected within the provincial parks system.

The concept of regulating specific zones within a provincial park could be accomplished by designating the boundaries of special sites under the *Wilderness Act*. This precedent was set through amendments to the *National Parks Act* that permit the government to regulate wilderness zones in national parks. This also provides Ontario with the precedent for enabling the regulation of zones under new provincial parks legislation.

The ministry is reviewing the existing wilderness areas to determine which ones might be more appropriately regulated as historical parks or nature reserves. As a result, no new areas have been established under this legislation, and it has outlived its usefulness. The government has not defined how the *Wilderness Areas Act* will contribute to its Natural Heritage Areas Strategy. However, the spirit of the Act in promoting the need to preserve wilderness areas, and flora and fauna, should be captured in any further revisions to this and the parks legislation.

Areas of Natural and Scientific Interest

Cabinet approved the Areas of Natural and Scientific Interest (ANSI) program in 1983 to identify, protect, and manage natural features that are of provincial, regional, and local significance. The ministry has nominated 564 ANSIs in its *District Land Use Guidelines*, and an additional 230 plus sites, totalling about one million hectares of land and water. The protection of ANSIs is encouraged through a number of statutes, particularly the *Conservation Land Act*, the *Public Lands Act*, and the *Planning Act*.[70] In 1987, the government promised to spend $25 million on the program. However, little money has flowed to the program; yet its potential remains great.

The ANSI program enables the Ministry of Natural Resources to identify both Crown and private lands containing natural ecosystems and geological features that represent a variety of landscapes. Once identified, either the ministry or private landowners attempt to protect them so that they contribute to some of the earth science and life science targets defined in the blue book,[71] and in the government's *Strategic Land Use Plan* and *District Land Use Guidelines*. The ANSI program is a government initiative that is complementary to, but separate from, the provincial parks program.

The ANSI program differs from the provincial parks program in several ways. ANSIs protect representative natural features not found in the provincial parks system. Although parks are Crown lands protected by regulations under the *Provincial Parks Act*,[72] ANSIs may be located on private, public, or Crown land; the boundaries of such areas are generally not protected by regulations; and they may be managed either by the government or by corporate or private landowners to achieve a variety of objectives.

There are two ANSI categories:

- *Earth science ANSIs* are areas that are either natural or modified by human activities that contain Ontario's best examples of rock, fossil, and landform features produced by thousands of years of geological processes. For example, the sides of a worked-out quarry might be significant because of the fossils and geological formations that are exposed.
- *Life science ANSIs* are natural areas that represent the best examples of the vegetation-landform features found within the 13 site regions of the province.

Together, the two categories capture representative natural landscapes of Ontario, as well as unique communities of plant species and special areas that support rare, threatened, and endangered species. Thus, the ANSI program augments the province's contribution to the Endangered Spaces campaign goals and to the achievement of sustainable development.

ANSIs can be given total protection through provincial nature reserves or partial protection through conservation easements, formal and informal landowner agreements, and designations in land-use plans on private land. On Crown land, ANSIs are identified in district land-use guidelines[73] and integrated into Crown management units and forest management agreements[74] as areas of concern. They can be administered to protect natural and scientific values under section 12 of the *Public Lands Act*,[75] or for research and management under section 11 of the *Public Lands Act*; or withdrawn from staking and prospecting under section 36 of the *Mining Act*.[76]

There is no legislative basis for the ANSI program itself. There are, however, a number of legislative initiatives by the government that contribute to the protection of ANSIs and other natural areas on private land and will be examined below. Thus, the ministry's job is to identify ANSIs and promote their recognition and protection. The legislation enables their protection once identified. However, because the implementation of this program rests with district offices of the MNR that have few, if any, district ecologists and little money for inventory work, groups such as the Federation of Ontario Naturalists fear the program is doomed.

The Conservation Land Act[77]

About 500[78] natural areas required to meet the government's conservation objectives to represent natural features and protect biodiversity are located on private land. However, these areas are continually being lost to development because of the lack of economic incentives to motivate landowners to protect important natural areas. Regulatory, taxation, and planning systems continue to reward their development. For example, the *Planning Act* allows a request for a building permit to lead to rezoning that will allow adverse developments to occur. High and rising property taxes forced landowners to sell or convert their land to other uses — land they might have preferred to protect. In the past, their choices were limited: either pay high taxes or achieve tax relief through sale or development.

Organizations such as the Federation of Ontario Naturalists, the Nature Conservancy of Canada, and the Natural Heritage League lobbied for legislation that would encourage landowners to commit land to conservation. In particular, they sought legislation that would assist landowners who wanted to protect their land, but who wanted to retain private ownership and did not wish to sell their land to the government or non-government conservation groups such as the Nature Conservancy. Then Premier David Peterson responded to their lobby by promising legislation that would "ease the property tax burden that threatens the preservation of land that is vital to Ontario's natural heritage."[79]

The *Conservation Land Act* was passed in 1988 to promote and assist in the stewardship of natural areas on private lands. The Act encourages private landowners to act as stewards of natural areas of provincial and regional significance through the payment of grants. Until the Act was passed, such incentives were only available for managed forest lands and agricultural areas. For example, the Ministry of Natural Resources provides planting and management services under agreements with landowners that prohibit them from cutting trees without the minister's permission for a minimum of 15 years under the *Woodlands Improvement Act*[80] and 20 years under the *Forestry Act*;[81] but there was no similar assistance to preserve or create other natural areas such as wetlands.

The *Conservation Land Act* is only enabling legislation that allows the minister of natural resources to establish programs that recognize, encourage, and support the stewardship of conservation lands, and provide for the payment of grants to the owners of identified conservation lands. To implement the Act, Cabinet approved the Conservation Land Tax

LAND OWNERS BEWARE!

M.N.R. PROPOSALS FOR PRIVATE LAND COULD SERIOUSLY AFFECT YOUR PROPERTY RIGHTS

The M.N.R. is proposing to extend a revamped "TREES ACT" to cover all North and Northwestern Ontario. Under the Act municipalities would set out by-laws to control cutting or removal of trees on PRIVATE LANDS.

PRIVATE LANDS IN UNORGANIZED TOWNSHIPS would be controlled directly by M.N.R.

PROVISIONS FOR TREE CUTTING APPLICATIONS, STOP WORK ORDERS and FINES of up to $500,000.00 for infractions are proposed for tree by-laws passed under the proposed Act.

TIMBER HARVESTING, LAND DEVELOPMENT, and LAND CLEARING for homes, farms, pits, etc., would all be affected.

AS PROPERTY OWNERS, WE CANNOT SUPPORT THE M.N.R. PROPOSALS BECAUSE:

PROPERTY RIGHTS now enjoyed by owners would be replaced with a giant bureaucrative nightmare of fear and confusion.

PROPERTY TAXES would have to increase substantially to cover the heavy administrative and policing requirements of the Act.

LAND VALUES will decrease due to new government controls on private land use.

INCREASED RESTRICTIONS on development of land, pits, roads, sub-divisions, etc., would become a side effect of the Act.

THE NORTH should not be penalized for the problems stemming from Southern Ontario's massive urban over-expansion program of the 1980's

WE NEED YOUR SUPPORT NOW TO WORK EFFECTIVELY WITH OTHER GROUPS ACROSS THE NORTH, TO PRESERVE OUR PROPERTY RIGHTS.

TO PRESERVE OUR PROPERTY RIGHTS CAMPAIGN

Name: _____

Address: _____

City: _____

Postal Code: _____

☐ YES, I SUPPORT NORTH SHORE LOGGERS & TRUCKERS ASSOC. CAMPAIGN TO PRESERVE PROPERTY RIGHTS

Additional comments:

_____

_____

_____

These comments clippings will be forwarded to M.N.R. in Sault St. Marie, Ont.

Please clip and send to:

NORTHSHORE LOGGING & TRUCKING ASSOCIATION
P.O. Box 622
Elliot Lake, Ontario
P5A 2R5
Phone: (705) 843-2216
Fax: (705) 843-2072
      (705) 848-2884

Advertisement in northern Ontario newspapers, summer of 1992, opposing amendments to the *Trees Act* allowing small rural municipalities to control cutting of trees on private land.

Reduction Program in 1988[82] through an order in council as the first program established under the Act. The order, which is currently reviewed every three years, defines the terms and conditions under which the government will pay up to 100 per cent of the amount of property tax assessed on eligible conservation lands to a maximum of $25,000 a year per landowner. The requirement to periodically renew the order in council, and hence the program itself, makes it politically vulnerable. For example, a new order in council could reduce the rebate level to 75 or 50 per cent.

Lands eligible for such grants include:

- class 1, 2, and 3 wetlands that are provincially or regionally significant;
- provincially significant ANSIs;
- conservation authority lands that are not managed to produce revenue for the authority, such as wetlands, forested areas, valley lands, flood plains, and areas of environmental significance;
- natural areas within the Niagara Escarpment Planning Area; and
- other conservation lands owned by non-profit charitable organizations that contribute to provincial conservation and heritage program objectives — for example, land owned by the Bruce Trail Association or the Federation of Ontario Naturalists.

Owners must agree to retain their land as conservation lands and not carry out any activities that would have a negative effect on the natural heritage values of the land. The Act does not prohibit development that is inconsistent with the conservation of the area's values, but the order in council defines criteria under which the conservation land ceases to be eligible for tax rebates. If development does occur, the government can conduct a review of the area and conclude that its natural values no longer exist or are not adequately protected. The minister can then serve notice that the land is excluded from the program, and the owner may appeal within 30 days to the mining and lands commissioner. If the conservation land ceases to be recognized as such within 10 years from the date the grant was first approved, the owner must repay all the grant received, plus 10 per cent per annum interest. [83]

The government has identified some 372,000 hectares of land that are eligible for tax relief under the Conservation Land Tax Reduction Program.[84] About 23,000 landowners, primarily in southern Ontario, where most of the land is private, are eligible for a grant and can assist the province in meeting its objectives for protected areas, as well as contributing to national and international conservation programs. As of June 1992, the Act had facilitated the participation of 4,295 private landowners in protecting 49,500 hectares of land. About $1.4 million was rebated to private landowners in 1990.[85]

Consideration should be given to making the *Conservation Land Act* part of a three-pronged approach to private stewardship that includes a landowner contact program to encourage people to participate, and an education program to inform people of the values of natural areas and the need to protect and maintain these heritage values. Evaluations of landowner contact programs on the Niagara Escarpment and in the Carolinian Canada forest zone reveal that although there was a high level of interest on the part of landowners, there was little or no government follow-up with individuals to maintain their interest or to offer assistance when required.[86] Perhaps the *Conservation Land Act* should be amended to permit a permanently funded landowner contact program given its importance to the long-term success of land conservation.

To date, the government has not completed an audit of the Conservation Land Tax Reduction Program to evaluate its effectiveness. Thus, although the program has honourable intentions, it is not clear whether it is meeting its original objectives, and there is no assurance that the land is being afforded a high level of protection and meeting the province's standards. Periodic reviews are critical to ensure that the government is spending money in a manner that ensures the long-term conservation of significant natural areas on private lands.

Under its draft Natural Heritage Areas Strategy, the government proposes to amend the Act by 1995 in order to provide better protection for ANSIs. The strategy also suggests that the definition of conservation lands under the Act be expanded to include old growth forests, and land containing rare, threatened, and endangered species. Under section 2(1) of the Act, the government would also like to create programs to fund inventories, standard conservation agreements, stewardship awards, a conservation land fund, and a more effective landowner contact program.

The objective of the *Conservation Land Act* could also be met through amendments to related acts. For example, a new conservation assessment category under the *Assessment Act* could reduce taxes or exempt specified lands from paying property tax.

The Ontario Heritage Act

The *Ontario Heritage Act*,[87] passed in 1980, can also assist in the protection of private lands. The act created the Ontario Heritage Foundation to assist and encourage the preservation of heritage and culture. Section 10 of the Act allows the foundation to receive, acquire by purchase or donation, or lease property of recreational, aesthetic, and scenic interest for the use, enjoyment, and benefit of the people of Ontario.

Clearly, the language of the Act directs the foundation to acquire land and hold it in trust for the people of Ontario. The foundation can also enter into agreements or use conservation easements to conserve, protect, and preserve natural areas. For example, the foundation, the Ministry of Natural Resources, and a private landowner negotiated an easement for part of the Workman Creek ANSI in the Owen Sound area. The easement affords legal protection to a provincially significant bedrock and fossil area by prohibiting activities that might endanger its features. Thus, the government has created an arm's-length agency that can assist in the achievement of conservation objectives on private land.

The foundation has established a revolving fund to assist in the immediate purchase of threatened property of heritage value. It works in cooperation with the Natural Heritage League, a coalition of 38 conservation groups and government agencies dedicated to the protection and management of Ontario's natural heritage. For example, the foundation and the Federation of Ontario Naturalists, Nature Conservancy of Canada, and Wildlife Habitat Canada joined forces to acquire properties on the Bruce Peninsula and Pelee Island. The foundation, with help from other government and non-profit groups, also acquired a 320-hectare property near the Oak Ridges Moraine, west of Peterborough, that was classified by the Ministry of Natural Resources as an area of natural and scientific interest. Thus, provincial conservation objectives can be met on private land through the donation of private lands or conservation easements as facilitated by the *Ontario Heritage Act* and the creation of the Ontario Heritage Foundation. For more information about this Act and foundation see chapters 14 and 15.

A New Ecological Reserves Act

Former Natural Resources Minister Vince Kerrio announced the government's intention to pass an Ecological Reserves Act in 1987 at the annual meeting of the Federation of Ontario Naturalists. The purpose of the Act would be to protect natural areas for research, education, and nature appreciation. Although the commitment has been reiterated many times, no bill has been introduced into the Legislature for debate. Thus, we can only speculate about what the Act will include.

Across Ontario there are many sites of outstanding, representative, or rare ecological, scientific, and educational value that merit protection as ecological reserves, and that require the force of law to ensure their long-term protection. Ecological reserves across Canada tend to be smaller than the larger national and provincial parks, and the extraction of natural resources is prohibited. Although the focus is on providing opportunities for scientific and educational use, such activities may be prohibited or strictly limited where sensitive natural features are threatened by even non-consumptive uses. However, human manipulation of some ecological reserves through fire control or tree removal may be required to ensure the perpetuation of natural processes and communities that have either been altered or eliminated by prior human developments, or to preserve a succession stage in a natural area.

The ANSI program provides a good beginning for an ecological reserves program. However, field and regional staff, alerted to the existence of over 500 sites, have to resort to a range of tools under various pieces of legislation to pursue protection of these areas through municipal planning documents, land-use guidelines, provincial park designations, and the *Planning Act* and the *Public Lands Act*. The Ecological Reserves Act should consolidate these tools so that government staff and the public can consult a single piece of legislation for a range of protective mechanisms.

The Act should clearly set out a purpose statement that specifies that ecological reserves are natural areas held in trust both for their inherent value and for the benefit of future generations. It should compel the government either to prohibit resource extraction activities or to allow the manipulation of such areas only where such activities are required to ensure the perpetuation of the area's natural features.

The Newfoundland *Wilderness and Ecological Reserves Act*[88] provides Cabinet with a comprehensive set of reasons why the government may create ecological reserves: (1) to provide for scientific research and educational purposes; (2) to preserve the habitat of rare and endangered plants and animals; (3) to act as scientific benchmarks; (4) to study the recovery of ecosystems that have been modified by humans; (5) to preserve rare botanical, zoological, geological, or geographical characteristics; (6) to preserve representative ecosystems of the province; and (7) to preserve gene pools.

In 1988 the Federation of Ontario Naturalists recommended that an Ecological Reserves Council be established to advise on matters relating to the implementation of an Ecological Reserves Act. Again, the Newfoundland *Wilderness and Ecological Reserves Act* provides an interesting model. It established the Wilderness and Ecological Reserves Advisory Council to advise the government "on all matters in relation to the establishment, management, and termination of reserves and for the better administration of this Act."[89] Membership includes both government and non-government representatives. It has a more expansive role than the present Ontario Provincial Parks Council in that it can recommend areas for protection and review the suitability of proposed areas.

The Newfoundland council can examine any area of the province to determine if it is suitable for protection as a wilderness or ecological reserve, hold public hearings to examine the boundary description of a management plan for a proposed reserve, and report to the minister its conclusions on a proposed reserve and on issues raised in public hearings. Once the council has completed its initial review and determined that an area may be suitable as an ecological reserve, the government can establish a provisional reserve to ensure that the area is protected while it prepares a proposed management plan and the council holds public hearings.

The Act is particularly interesting because it compels the government to produce, and the council to review, a boundary description of the area, a management plan outline, and a detailed statement of the management plan and proposed regulations. Thus, the public review is focused on specific management details rather than just on a "go/no go" park decision, promoting a more informed public debate. In addition, the Act allows the public to recommend to the council the establishment of, or a change in, a reserve.

An Ecological Reserves Act for Ontario should provide a strong regulatory structure to promote a conservation ethic in such areas, consolidate the government's power to protect ANSIs on Crown, public, and private land under one piece of legislation, establish an advisory council to identify candidate sites and hold public hearings, and compel and assist the owners of ecological reserves to produce and implement a management plan to guide the area's long-term protection. It should also seek to use the programs already established under existing legislation, such as the *Conservation Land Act*, to promote private stewardship. Finally, it should provide the government with sufficient incentives and enforcement powers to ensure the protection of ecological reserves, and the appropriate management of adjacent lands.

The Conservation Authorities Act

The conservation authorities of Ontario play a large role in protecting natural areas and green spaces. Under the *Conservation Authorities Act*,[90] first passed in 1946, groups of municipalities sharing a watershed may form a conservation authority. The Act encourages each conservation authority "to establish and undertake, in the area over which it has jurisdiction, a program designed to further the conservation, restoration, development, and management of natural resources other than gas, oil, coal, and minerals."[91] The Act envisioned integrated resource management at the local level. Found primarily in southern Ontario, conservation authorities cover only 10 per cent of the province, but almost 95 per cent of Ontario's residents live within the boundaries of the province's 38 conservation authorities.[92]

Conservation authorities play a major role in identifying and protecting forests, wetlands, shorelines, marshes, wildlife habitat, and other natural areas within their jurisdiction. They can work with other organizations such as the Natural Heritage League and the Ontario Heritage Foundation to acquire and protect land. They are consulted by ratepayers, municipal politicians, provincial government ministries, and other public authorities whenever development threatens natural areas. Applications for subdivision approval are circulated to the conservation authorities, and if they comment publicly or privately on the ecological importance of natural lands where development is proposed, they may have a significant effect on the outcome of such applications for development.

After the Act was passed in 1946, many of the authorities were actively acquiring hazardous valley lands, headwaters, and flood-prone areas and other natural areas, providing land- and water-based recreation opportunities, managing forests on private lands, and promoting reforestation. However, once the authorities were placed under the administration of the Ministry of Natural Resources in the early 1970s, the government moved to limit their role to water management, dam construction, and flood control.[93] However, they remain a major player in the acquisition of natural areas in southern Ontario. By 1992, they protected almost 110,000 hectares of natural area, half of it being wetland and natural forests.[94]

Fiscal restraint has curtailed the conservation authorities' major role in land acquisition, and this has worked to the detriment of natural areas under their control. Authorities are reluctant to accept land donations because of the tax burden and management costs inherent in such acquisitions; for example, the tax on conservation authority land along the Niagara Escarpment increased by over 360 per cent between 1978 and 1984.[95] At present, the Conservation Land Tax Reduction Program relieves some of this burden. About 44 per cent of conservation authority lands are eligible for tax rebates. The authorities generate almost a quarter of their revenues from recreational and other resource uses. Backus Woods, an area of natural and scientific interest, was threatened by a conservation authority's plans to log the site to generate revenue. The site is now protected and has become an education and information centre for the authority.

The *Conservation Authorities Act* requires Cabinet approval of any disposition of land by a conservation authority. However, it appears to be toothless in preventing conservation authorities from degrading natural areas under their stewardship. When the Grand River Conservation Authority permitted the construction of a bridge over the spectacular Elora Gorge, the centrepiece of the Elora Gorge Conservation Area, a coalition of conservation groups challenged the legality of this decision in court. They claimed the conservation authority was acting outside its jurisdiction by permitting the use of greenspace for a bridge to solve local traffic problems when the authority's responsibility is to conserve natural resources. However, the courts held that the two members of the conservation authority who brought the law suit on behalf of the conservation groups had no standing to challenge the decisions made by the conservation authority.[96]

A strength of the Act is that the government can enforce its provisions if there is a violation of the Act or its regulations. It provides a model for other Acts, many of which do not provide the government with powers of enforcement, incentives, or investigatory powers. If protected area legislation is to include a public trust, that trust must both be enforceable and provide citizens with standing before the courts so that they can promote government action to preserve natural areas.

MANAGEMENT PLANNING AND PUBLIC PARTICIPATION

The establishment of parks and protected areas is no guarantee that an area's natural features will be preserved. Hence, it is critical that protected area administrators develop a plan to ensure that the area is managed to protect its natural features. These plans could serve as a social contract between the government and the public by defining how the government intends to protect and manage these areas for the benefit and enjoyment of present and future generations. However, until the public can challenge the validity of such plans in court, management plans will remain a legally unenforceable bureaucratic document.

The Ontario government generally seeks public input on draft management plans, and attempts to incorporate such input where possible. This gives the public a voice in how they want their provincial parks managed. It also allows the government planners to identify a range of sensitive political and resource management issues that must be resolved. To solicit such input, the Ontario government uses a variety of forums including advisory councils, public hearings, open houses, and opportunities for written comments. However, it is under no legal obligation either to produce management plans or to seek public comments on its park policies and management plans.

Management Plans

At the federal level, amendments to the *National Parks Act* in 1988 strengthened the government's commitment to develop park management plans, and are presented here only as a model for amendments to the *Provincial Parks Act*. The federal Act now states that the minister of the environment shall, within five years of the proclamation of a park, table in the House of Commons a management plan for that park in respect of resource protection, zoning, visitor use, and any other matter the minister deems appropriate.[97] Thus, it becomes a public document, and can be reviewed by the Parliamentary Standing Committee on Environment, who can also call for witnesses to discuss the strengths and weaknesses of the plan.

The minister must review such plans every five years and retable each plan, with amendments, in the House of Commons. If a park is not proclaimed for a number of years, the Canadian Parks Service is recommending that management plans be tabled in the House of Commons within five years of the transfer of proposed national parklands to the federal government.

The *National Parks Act* now states that the "maintenance of ecological integrity shall be the first priority when considering park zoning and visitor use in a management plan." Although the Act does not define the concept of ecological integrity, the civil service is now working to define the term and to identify actions required to measure and implement the concept. This is critical because section 5(1.5) now directs the minister to report to Parliament every two years on the state of the national parks and progress toward the establishment of new parks. The tabling of management plans and a state of the parks report every two years gives national parks a higher public and political profile, which is necessary for the parks program to survive.

Thus, members of Parliament and the public can now evaluate the ability of the government to meet the provisions of the *National Parks Act* and parks policy, and to maintain the national parks "unimpaired." The first state of the parks report, tabled in 1990, confirmed that none of the national parks are immune to internal and external threats to their natural resources.[98] Armed with a list of threats for each national park, such as the threats from tourism development within the parks and logging on adjacent lands, the public can now raise these issues when they comment on specific management plans, or proposed revisions.

In 1967, the Ontario government began to develop master plans, now called management plans, to describe official policies for resource protection, use and development of all existing and new provincial parks. To date, only 97 of 260 provincial parks have management plans; 18 of these plans are under review; and plans for other parks are in preparation.[99] Thus, many of the province's parks are managed, or neglected, with little direction from an approved plan. In addition, the Ministry of Natural Resources has only completed 11 resource management plans, which are more specific attempts to protect a park's vegetation, wildlife, fisheries, and landforms. This complete lack of resource management plans is symptomatic of the government's declining parks management budget.

The *Provincial Parks Act* was amended in 1976 to define the term "master plan" so as to give the concept some legislative authority. The amendment authorized the minister of natural resources to prepare and approve a master plan (herein referred to as a management plan) for any existing or proposed provincial park, and to carry out periodic reviews and make necessary amendments to an approved management plan.

However, under section 8,[100] the minister has no duty to prepare a plan; rather, the minister *may* prepare a plan and *may* review existing plans. Nor does the minister have a duty to consult with the public on the preparation of the plan. Nor is the minister or parks staff legally bound to follow the plan. But parks policy is clear: the government must prepare a plan for each park. Cabinet direction is that each park is to have a particular purpose, as well as a distinctive management and visitor services policy. For example, there is to be no further expansion of non-conforming uses within wilderness parks.

In 1983 the Ministry of Natural Resources adopted guidelines for the preparation of management plans.[101] The park management plan is to provide:

- a definition of the role, significance, and classification of a park within the provincial park system;
- a statement of policy for the protection, planning, development, and management of the resources and attributes of a park, including zoning;
- guidance for the preparation of required natural resource, client services, site, and development and operations plans required to implement park policies and achieve park objectives;
- a rationale and priorities for the funding of capital development and park operations;
- a record of public consultation and input to the planning process; and
- a basis for auditing the development and management of a park.

The *Provincial Parks Act* has several shortcomings that weaken the government's responsibility to produce such management plans. There is:

1. no legal requirement for the government to produce a management plan;
2. no guideline on the components of a management plan;
3. no deadline for the production of management plans;
4. no requirement for public consultation;
5. no direction on what ecological and recreational priorities the plans are to assign to the protection and use of natural resources;
6. no requirement for updating the plans and monitoring their effectiveness; and
7. no right for the public to appeal management decisions or otherwise ensure ecological integrity in the planning and implementation of a management plan.

Environmental Assessment

The *Environmental Assessment Act* compels the proponents of any activities defined under the Act to complete an environmental assessment. Both the Ontario government and any activity carried out as part of its provincial parks program are subject to the Act. However, regulations made under the Act exempt projects started or constructed before the Act came in force in 1975. Thus, major developments within parks constructed before the Act's passage are exempt, but the expansion of such developments is not exempt.

However, the *Environmental Assessment Act* has not been applied to the parks program because it has been operating under a series of "temporary" exemption orders since 1980, which is permissible under section 29 of the Act. Since 1980, Cabinet and the minister of environment have approved a number of exemption orders for the parks program because the Ministry of Natural Resources is preparing a class environmental assessment.

When it comes to environmental assessments and the provincial parks program, the government has two options: (1) conduct individual environmental assessments on all projects and activities in all 260 parks, which could prove to be an exhausting process; or (2) conduct a class environmental assessment for the parks program. (See Chapter 9 for a description of what class environmental assessments are and how they are administered.) The government has chosen the latter course.

The class environmental assessment for provincial park management will describe what is involved in park management, the potential environmental impacts of visitor centre developments such as trails and road construction, and how they are to be mitigated through a common environmental planning procedure. The government continues to slowly develop its class environmental assessment for parks, and had planned to submit it by December 1993 to the minister of environment, who will then conduct a public review of the document. A hearing before the Environmental Assessment Board may follow.

It is likely that by the time this process is complete, 20 years or more will have passed, by the time the parks system is subjected to a proper assessment of park developments as required by the 1975 Act. In the meantime, exemption orders made under the *Environmental Assessment Act* continue to provide the Ministry of Natural Resources with some operational guidelines with respect to environmental assessment and the parks program.

The current exemption order, referred to as MNR-59, and approved by order in council 2014/92, was approved on June 24, 1992 and expires on December 31, 1993. It can be amended and renewed after December 31, 1993. The order exempts a number of activities from an environmental assessment including: parks management plans, resource management strategies, sewage and water works within provincial parks, amending and rescinding boundary regulations, site plans, capital construction, and lease purchase projects. Activities related to protecting park values, managing uses and activities, and developing new facilities in provincial parks or areas recommended as provincial parks on an interim basis are also exempt.

The Ministry of Natural Resources argues in the exemption order that if these exemptions are not provided, the following injury, damage, or interference will occur:

- environmental and recreational features in the park could be damaged in the absence of provincial park projects that address park management issues;

- the public will be damaged by the loss of anticipated benefits associated with resource protection and the provision of outdoor recreation opportunities, associated benefits, and economic benefits to local communities; and
- consultations and completion of the class environmental assessment will be hampered by having to prepare separate exemption orders or environmental assessments for all provincial park projects at the same time.

In the exemption order, the minister of the environment supports this perspective for two major reasons. First, the provincial parks program is carried out within a context of conservation, protection, and wise management of the environment with an emphasis on the preservation of significant natural and cultural features in Ontario. More important, the exemption order includes a number of conditions under which a plan or project is not exempt. For example, the exemption order does not apply "where the undertaking is likely to affect the known habitat of a species designated under the *Endangered Species Act*" or "where the estimated completion costs of a sewage or water works or a capital construction or lease purchase project is in excess of $2 million, not including land acquisition costs."

The exemption order also gives the Ontario Provincial Parks Policy and the Ontario Provincial Parks Planning and Management Policies legal status. They are listed in the exemption order along with a number of other policies, and the government is obliged to plan, implement, and manage provincial parks according to these policies to retain the exemption from the *Environmental Assessment Act*. The order also compels the government to notify and to consult with the public when proposing to amend park boundaries or eliminate them entirely. Failure by the government to live up to the standards set in the exemption order for the provincial parks program could place the Ministry of Natural Resources in violation of the *Environmental Assessment Act*.

Until the completion of the class environmental assessment, the terms and conditions in the exemption orders approved under the *Environmental Assessment Act* are an important instrument in the management of Ontario's provincial parks. Thus, members of the public who are interested in park management issues should ensure that they have a copy not only of the parks policy and management policy, but also of the most recent exemption order. All these documents can be obtained from the Ministry of Natural Resources. When an exemption order is up for renewal, it is published in the Ontario *Gazette* and the public has an opportunity to comment on the proposed exemption order.

Before completing the provincial parks class environmental assessment, the Ministry of Natural Resources wants to confirm its overall program strategy for parks and protected areas so as to provide a firm foundation for an environmental assessment process.[102] This includes updating the blue book to reflect anouncements on parks policy in 1983 and 1988, developing a Natural Heritage Areas Strategy, revising the *Provincial Parks Act*, and introducing an *Ecological Reserves Act* or other appropriate legislation. However, the class environmental assessment may well be completed in advance of new legislation and government acceptance of a Natural Heritage Areas Strategy.

It is hoped that the class environmental assessment will confirm the need for a cumulative impact assessment of all developments within a particular park. The true impact of a particular development can only be assessed in combination with all the other developments permitted in a park. Thus, we need to conduct cumulative assessments of current developments in the parks to determine their current impact on park ecosystems, to identify developments that should be terminated, and to establish base line data against which to measure the impact of additional developments within parks.

Finally, the class environmental assessment should confirm a process that ensures that developments on lands adjacent to provincial parks are both assessed and monitored for their impact on park resources. The greatest threat to protected areas is their growing isolation as islands of nature within a sea of development. Logging and mining operations outside parks can have a tremendous negative impact on park resources, such as the loss of wildlife and wildlife habitat, the destruction of air and water quality, and the loss of aesthetic values. The impact of such developments must be accounted for within the context of protected area management.

Public Consultation

The government is under no legal obligation to consult with the public on any aspect of its parks and protected area program. It does not have to discuss either its procedures or its policies with the public, which is clearly not in keeping with the notion of parks being a "public trust." Through various announcements, the government has made "a commitment to an open planning process with public participation."[103] However, Paul Eagles from the University of Waterloo concluded on the basis of a number of case studies that "this intent is not always carried out in field situations."[104] And this situation is exacerbated by the lack of a legal requirement that the government involve the public.

The government uses a variety of means to involve the public. The Ontario Provincial Parks Council was established in 1974 as a citizens' committee to advise the minister about the planning, management, and development of provincial parks. The council generally holds public meetings throughout the province and receives both oral presentations and written comments on subjects ranging from the privatization of park services to the management of wilderness parks.

In recent years, the council has held extensive public hearings and reported to the minister on the privatization of provincial parks and park services, the termination of cottage leases in Algonquin and Rondeau provincial parks, and the development of management plans for Algonquin and Quetico provincial parks. This third-party review of park issues forces a focused and in-depth review and reporting on issues.

For example, in reviewing the cottage issue, the council found that (1) the Ministry of Natural Resources lacked a strong conservation rationale for their removal; (2) the government was not prepared to compensate the cottage owners for the substantial investment some of them had made in these areas; and (3) there was a lack of public support for the plan to terminate their leases.

The government is not required to respond to, implement, or even publicly release the recommendations of the council. For example, the council recommended in 1978 that the *Provincial Parks Act* be rewritten, but over a decade has passed and this has not been done. The council is not guided by a legislated set of procedures as the Wilderness and Ecological Reserves Council is in Newfoundland. Despite this, the council has, to date, played an influential and positive role in shaping the management of Ontario's provincial parks. However, it is losing its public role because it no longer produces annual reports that detail its activities. The new Act should outline the role of the council and compel it to release annual reports and to detail issues.

Public hearings and written submissions made directly to government officials are more the norm for public consultation by the Ministry of Natural Resources. Heather Cook, former president of the Wildlands League, completed an analysis of 10,000 submissions made during public hearings conducted by the ministry across the province in 1982 on the 245 candidate provincial parks.[105] Cook concluded that the manner in which the ministry conducted its hearings failed to obtain valuable and useful comments from a broad spectrum of participants. As a result, the hearings broke down into a "parks/no parks" debate and failed to promote a rational resolution of some of the issues posed by some of the candidates for park status. The government's decision to delete some parks, reduce the size of others, and ignore its own park policies reflected the simplicity of both the debate and the way in which government made decisions based on compromise.

Cook cited examples where the government failed to notify people of the public hearings, provided too short a period for public response, provided inadequate background information, and was not prepared to handle the public response. Thus, in the future, early and adequate public notification of public hearings is required; relevant information must be provided prior to the consultation; and there must be a reasonable time-frame to respond. Amendments to the *Provincial Parks Act* outlining some of these criteria could be easily made, and could contribute to a more effective process.

Public hearings are often attended mainly by local residents expressing local concerns. They often favour the deletion of a park, or the commercial exploitation of parks to improve the local employment situation, particularly because many parks are located in areas experiencing short- and long-term economic hardship. For example, local opposition forced a significant reduction in the original size of the Madawaska River Waterway Park.[106] In the absence of a coherent legislative framework that emphasizes the preservation values of parks and broader economic development strategies, regional, provincial, national, and international conservation priorities can be lost to such local considerations.

The government is now involving aboriginal people in the identification of new parks and decisions regarding the management of existing parks. This is extending the concept of public consultation to participation; however, in the case of native people, the government and native people view this as negotiations between governments, not just discussions with one specific interest group. The government has invited aboriginal people to join working groups that will recommend a long-term strategy for completing the province's protected areas network by the year 2000, and to identify and recommend new candidate areas for protection. Native people also sit on a park management committee that is preparing a management plan for Polar Bear Provincial Park. Other agreements with Golden Lake Algonquins and Ojibway in Quetico provide opportunities for active negotiations on future plan amendments and specific activities within parks.

The *National Parks Act* directs the minister of the environment to provide opportunities for public participation at the national, regional, and local levels in the development of parks policy, management plans and other relevant matters. However, the Act states the minister shall, "as appropriate," provide such opportunities;[107] thus, there is no mandatory direction on the nature of the consultation, the need for prior notification (except in the area of park establishment), or any duty on the minister to take into account or respond to public input.

Unlike the Ontario government, the federal government also has a policy of conducting a public review of proposed regulations that are developed pursuant to the *National Parks Act*.[108] In the coming years, the federal government will be seeking public input on regulations to protect wilderness zones within national parks, and for protection of the flora, soil, waters, natural features, and air quality of the national parks. Again, the government is not legally bound by such input.

The process can also be used by the government to back out of previous commitments. For example, public hearings on a draft management plan for Banff National Park confirmed support for the closing down of the airstrips in Banff and Jasper national parks. However, a strong lobby by pilots who used the airstrip and by federal members of Parliament from Alberta forced the government to withdraw the amendment, putting off the decision to the next review of the park's management plan. The government's press release announcing the decision stated that the regulatory review was not an appropriate way to resolve park issues, when in fact the issue had already been resolved during public hearings.[109]

In 1984, the Ontario Region of Parks Canada released an amendment to the zoning plan for Pukaskwa National Park as a *fait accompli*. Parks Canada had changed a wilderness zone within the park to an outdoor recreation zone to permit the construction of a road in the Hattie Cove area of the park. They had violated their own policy, which calls for a public review of such amendments. A coalition of environmental groups met with then Minister of the Environment Charles Caccia, and the minister cancelled the zoning change.

OTHER TYPES OF PROTECTED AREAS IN ONTARIO

In addition to parks and protected areas, there are other programs that contribute to the protection of significant landscapes and natural areas. Two such programs are discussed here: the Niagara Escarpment Plan and the Ontario trails program.

Niagara Escarpment Plan

The Niagara Escarpment is a mosaic of cliffs, waterfalls, fertile agricultural lands, wildlife habitats, recreational areas, mineral resources, urban centres, and an increasingly populated rural landscape resulting from urban sprawl and recreation housing. It is a unique geological and historical asset that lends itself to hiking, nature study, and cross-country skiing; but it also lends itself to more profitable uses such as residential and commercial development and gravel pits and quarries, which have threatened to destroy the landscape. Stretching from Niagara Falls to the Bruce Peninsula National Park, it supports many impressive natural areas and wildlife species. At one time, it was a natural obstacle to development; now the escarpment is a destination for people seeking both temporary and permanent refuge from the city.

Efforts to protect the Niagara Escarpment provide an important example of how a number of mechanisms can be used to protect a mixture of natural areas and a cultural landscape that sustains local communities and protects natural habitats and wildlife. Such landscapes could not be protected within a single large park; rather a combination of parks, special land use zones, and planning development policies is required. Such an approach has been activated through the *Niagara Escarpment Planning and Development Act*.[110]

The Act was passed in 1973 to assure the public that the escarpment would be preserved for the future. The objective of the Act is to maintain the Niagara Escarpment as a "continuous natural environment" and to ensure that only such development occurs as is compatible with that natural environment. A key word here is the recognition that this continuous strip of nature cannot be dismembered — it must be maintained as a natural corridor. However, for over three decades, the debate has raged over what lands constitute the escarpment and how "natural" the escarpment should remain.

The Act created the Niagara Escarpment Commission (NEC) and placed it in the midst of the storm. Made up of appointed members from municipalities along the escarpment and from the public at large, the commission was responsible for preparing a land-use plan for a 5,200 square kilometre area designated by the government as the Niagara Escarpment Planning Area. The Act directs the commission to accomplish seven objectives, including the protection of unique ecological and historic areas, the protection of streams, and the provision of opportunities for outdoor recreation.

In July 1985 an escarpment plan was approved by the Conservative government, two days before leaving office after a crushing defeat at the polls by the Liberals. All three parties in the Legislature gave their approval and the Liberals publicly committed their government to the protection of the escarpment and the plan. Environmentalists were delighted; this was Ontario's first environmental land-use plan and exemplified the concept of sustainable development in action. It struck a balance between development, preservation, and the enjoyment of this important natural landscape.

The commission is responsible for implementing the plan. All applications for building developments, alterations, road construction, the removal of top soil, and mineral extractions have to get a development permit from the commission before proceeding. The land-use plan states quite clearly the seven land-use designations, the policies associated with each designation, and the way land is to be used through the area of the plan.

However, a plan is only as good as its implementation. Unfortunately, and unforgivably, the government forgot about its commitments and appointed a commission that, far from being a bastion, was a broken reed. Many of the commissioners were openly opposed to the plan, and some were even opposed to the Act. Development is allowed to occur that is in conflict with the plan. The Ministry of Municipal Affairs, which was responsible for the escarpment plan, did little monitoring of these wayward decisions. It cut back on funding for the planning staff of the commission, even though its workload had increased by 70 per cent. After strong lobbying by opposition parties and the Coalition on the Niagara Escarpment, new appointments were made to the commission and the administration of the plan was transferred from the Ministry of Municipal Affairs to the Ministry of Environment and Energy.[111]

Development continues. Applications for development have risen from 700 a year in 1975 to about 1,500 in 1990-91.[112] A 1990-91 review of the plan provided for a proposal to monitor the implementation of the plan, which was not being done.[113] A program was to be designed to track NEC decisions for consistency of application of development criteria and conformity with plan policies. An enforcement program to deal with non-compliance was also discussed. There was discussion of a monitoring system to establish baseline data and a process to monitor how well the NEC policies are maintaining the natural environment. All this was seen as necessary to ensure that the legislative requirement to maintain and enhance the quality of the natural environment was being met.

Critics see the plan as one that largely regulates development rather than protects the essential features of the escarpment, which continue to be treated as constraints to development rather than values worthy of preservation. The original idea was to monitor the plan's effectiveness and comment to the government on a regular basis, because the plan is to be reviewed every five years under the Act.

Improvements that could be made to the *Niagara Escarpment Planning and Development Act* include: better enforcement measures including clarified administrative orders; permanent recognition of the plan boundaries in the Act; recognition of the role of Bruce Trail and the Bruce Trail Association; improved development permit processes, including a recognition of ecological integrity beyond the purpose and objective sections; and clarified plan amendment and review procedures.

The plan itself is a good one. It can work, but it requires a continuing government commitment to protect this special and unique area. Ruth Grier, minister of the environment from 1990 to February 1992, reiterated that "the time is ripe to push government to live up to or even increase its commitment to preserving the Escarpment."[114] In the meantime, the Niagara Escarpment was designated a biosphere reserve under the UNESCO Man and the Biosphere Program in recognition of its world-class values and integrated human and natural systems landscape.[115] However, if it is truly to earn this designation, it must be managed as an integrated whole. Unfortunately, development continues to whittle away a landscape whose owners are more interested in profiting from it than passing it on to future generations.

Ontario's Trails

There is a plethora of recreational trails crisscrossing the province, located on both public and private land. In 1977, it was estimated that over 80,000 kilometres of trails were maintained for canoeing, cross country skiing, horseback riding, hiking, snowmobiling, and bicycling.[116] The crown jewel of the trails network is the Bruce Trail, which extends for 720 kilometres along the Niagara Escarpment from Tobermory to Niagara Falls.

Many of these trails have been developed by voluntary organizations, who have approached landowners for permission to maintain trails across their lands. With little government assistance, they have identified, developed, and maintained trails across the province. They seek a variety of agreements with landowners for permission to develop and maintain the trails. These trails provide an important recreational resource and an important alternative to government-operated parks and recreational facilities.

However, there is little protection for this important resource. In 1971, the Conservation Council of Ontario called on the premier to pass a Trails Act to guide the development of an Ontario trails system. The Parks Planning Branch of the Ministry of Natural Resources developed a trails policy that was subsequently rejected.[117] In 1974 a new policy suggested a four-point action program: (1) the ministry should be responsible for an inter-ministerial trails program; (2) an Ontario trails council should be established to report to the minister on trail issues; (3) a foundation should be established to raise funds; and (4) a 10-year funding program of $3 million should fund trail development.[118]

Only the recommendation for a trails council was implemented. The Ontario Trails Council, a 17-member body that held public hearings across the province, issued a final report with over 100 recommendations in 1977. The council listed several problems facing trail associations: the loss of permission from current landowners; the lack of permission from landowners for potential new trails; the legal liability of landowners for injury to people using the trail on their land; and the spread of urban development leading to the loss of trail routes and length and, ultimately, the natural values that make for an attractive trail corridor.

Liability was a major issue. In 1974, the Supreme Court of Canada awarded damages to a snowmobiler who struck his head on a mining company's fence while trespassing on the company's property at night. The Supreme Court ruled that the landowner had a duty to trespassing snowmobilers to construct fences in such a way that they would not hurt trespassers. This put the principle of self-help of trail development in jeopardy because landowners, once burned, were twice shy. They were reluctant to let people use their lands for trails if they would be legally responsible every time trail users hurt themselves through their own carelessness.

The Ontario government responded with an amendment to the *Motorized Snow Vehicles Act* for the relief of occupiers' (landowners' and tenants') liability with respect to snowmobiles.[119] The Act makes it clear that the occupier of the land owes no duty of care toward a snowmobiler who is either trespassing or using the land with permission. Owners can be liable for snowmobile accidents only if they charge snowmobilers a fee or maliciously set traps for snowmobiles.

The Ontario Trails Council concluded that "the relief of landowner liability is so important to the success of a system of public trails in Ontario that the council has requested the minister of natural resources to take immediate legislative action."[120] This was done in short order. In 1980, the *Occupiers' Liability Act*[121] established that the landowner owes a duty to take such care as to see that persons entering an area are reasonably safe while on the premises. However, the basic duty of care does not apply to entrants who willingly assume the risk of entry, such as "non-paying recreational entrants on most rural land."[122] Although landowners must not create a danger with deliberate intent to injure, they are not liable for injuries incurred by the above types of entrants.

The *Trespass to Property Act*[123] was also passed to give occupiers greater control over entry and use of their premises and to clearly define when trespass occurs. The law shifted the onus of proof, making it the responsibility of individual recreationists or groups such as the Bruce Trail Association to prove that entry to private lands is permitted. The landowner does not have to prove or show by signs that entry is forbidden.

Other recommendations of the Ontario Trail Council were rejected, and the trails issue faded from view for almost a decade. The Ontario Trails Council was reconstituted in 1988 as a non-government organization to promote the creation, development, management, and use of an integrated recreational trail network for the public. Its focus has been on the conversion of abandoned railway lines into recreational greenways, and to influence plans that affect the historic use of trails being eroded by land development.[124] For example, the Georgian Trail, a 32-kilometre corridor along the southern shore of Georgian Bay from Collingwood to Meaford, was officially designated a recreational greenway in 1989.[125]

In the field of conservation biology, increasing emphasis is being placed on the need to prevent landscape fragmentation. The development and maintenance of natural corridors to enable the movement of species between natural areas, to escape both natural and exotic predators, and to adjust to potential impacts of global warming on flora and fauna is part of this effort. The development of recreational corridors should be repositioned within this context. Amendments to the *Public Lands Act*[126] should be made to provide greater protection to corridors in these areas developed by voluntary associations, and between large wilderness parks and other natural areas. Citizens' groups could become forces of public support for a network of natural corridors that promote both species movement and recreation.

A NEW PROVINCIAL PARKS ACT

The provincial parks system is the centrepiece of Ontario's protected areas network. However, the *Provincial Parks Act*[127] needs a total overhaul if the areas preserved within the provincial parks system are to meet the province's conservation objectives for years to come. This section outlines some of the changes required.

The central weakness of the *Provincial Parks Act* is that it does not provide a framework that compels Cabinet and the civil service to resolve park issues in favour of wilderness protection or the preservation of ecological reserves. Instead, issues are often resolved in favour of intensive recreation or industrial exploitation. An effective Act is one that would: (1) promote a preservation ethic so that park issues are resolved in favour of park values; (2) provide checks and balances against which to measure proposed uses; and (3) provide the government with enforcement powers and establish fines for actions that are in contravention of the Act.

The Act is weak in the area of enforcement powers. Although the government does have some enforcement powers, they fall short of the range of powers available for enforcement under Ontario's pollution statutes. There are no public enforcement provisions, and certain powers are scattered in other Acts rather than consolidated in the *Provincial Parks Act*.

The fines for offences under the Act, to a maximum of $5,000, are virtually worthless to deter any major damage or serious poaching. They fall far short of the maximum fine of $150,000 under the *National Parks Act* for the taking of certain wildlife species.

The following principles are suggested as a foundation for a revision of the *Provincial Parks Act*:[128]

- the principles to which the managers of parkland are committed must be clearly articulated and available to the public;
- to be effective in creating effective countervailing pressure to destructive pressures, these principles must be reduced to a form that will have a high degree of moral persuasion and permanence;
- decisions affecting the planning and management of parkland or its loss must be subjected as a matter of right to public participation and scrutiny;
- the onus of proving the necessity of their actions must be shifted from those who wish to preserve parkland to those who wish to destroy it; and
- those public bodies charged with holding and managing parkland must have a duty to preserve it, and this duty must be enforceable by any member of the public.

The Act should place a public trust on the government to preserve the wilderness values and natural resources within the parks for the benefit of present and future generations. To enforce a public trust, the boundaries of the wilderness, nature reserve, natural environment, and waterway parks should be set in legislation. Cabinet should no longer have the power to reduce the size of or delete provincial parks; park boundaries should only be changed through an amendment approved by the Legislature.

Furthermore, the Act should prohibit commercial logging, mineral exploration and development, the construction of hydroelectric dams, and sport hunting in parks. Other activities could be defined and controlled through a regulatory framework that emphasizes conservation. However, the Act should stipulate that no leases or licences of occupation and use should be approved until a park management plan is developed and approved. And the legislation should require the government to develop a management plan and table it in the Legislature within a specific period of time, and to undertake periodic reviews of such plans.

Like the *National Parks Act*, the *Provincial Parks Act* should direct the government to make the maintenance of ecological integrity through the protection of natural resources a first priority in management plans, zoning programs, visitor services, and the allocation of parklands to recreational use. Eagles suggested that the Act should contain a statement that "the provision of programs and facilities for outdoor recreation should not be allowed to destroy the significant natural, cultural, and recreational environments that are found in provincial parks."[129]

To ensure some accountability, the Act should compel the government to table a periodic Ontario state of the parks and protected areas report in the Legislature. The Act should direct the government to develop a report that: (1) includes a list of no fewer than 10 candidate areas that are being examined for parks and protected area status; (2) provides an update on government action to meet its protected area objectives as outlined in the blue book; (3) outlines the ecological health of the provincial parks by listing the internal and external threats to such areas; (4) identifies where improvements in the system could be made, or where additional resources and personnel are required to achieve management plan targets; and (5) provides information on investigations, charges, and convictions.

The Act should give the government the power to establish park reserves.[130] The legislation should clearly define that park reserves are established in areas of aboriginal land-claim negotiations, or in areas where further study is required. During the park reserve stage, the minister should not be allowed to issue permits for the taking of commercial timber or mineral exploration or extraction activities, or permits for the construction or expansion of existing facilities including roads and other utility corridors.

Eagles's examination of the effectiveness of the park planning process and the effectiveness of the *Provincial Parks Act* suggests that the following is required: a legislative framework that provides clear and enforceable rules on what activities are permissible and that compels a high level of protection for significant ecological sites; the timely production of a park management plan to avoid the incremental loss of parkland to development; and adequate notice to the public of the government's parks planning program and the scheduling of meetings to receive public input.

Finally, the Act should give the Ministry of Natural Resources the mandate to secure cooperative agreements with other government agencies and private landowners to ensure that lands adjacent to parks are managed to ensure the protection of park values. Legislation that permits the allocation of Crown land to development could be amended to compel the government to identify natural areas for protection that are required to meet the needs of the Ontario provincial parks and protected areas system. This would require an assessment of natural area values prior to development.

In its proposed Natural Heritage Areas Strategy, the government suggested several actions that should be taken in strengthening the Act:

- the goal, objectives, and principles of the Ontario Provincial Park Policy should be enshrined in the Act;
- the Act should define system planning standards and commit to the completion of the provincial park system;
- the preparation of management plans should be mandatory and subject to a class environmental assessment under the *Environmental Assessment Act*;
- park boundaries should be legislated rather than regulated, and park zones should be regulated rather than established by management plan policies;
- the public should be allowed to participate in making decisions and be given the right to appeal under the Act; and
- penalties for abusing, defacing, removing, or other inappropriate uses of natural and scientific features should be increased and reasonably enforced.

Considerable thought and consistent written commentary since 1978 have recommended changes to and the strengthening of the *Provincial Parks Act*. It is now time to translate those opinions into draft legislation for tabling and debate within the Ontario Legislature to ensure a more prosperous future for Ontario's park system in its second century.

CONCLUSION

Ontario's wilderness landscapes continue to diminish. After almost a century of park establishment, very little of the province is protected against industrial and commercial development. And none of the province's parks, save for several national parks, are legally protected against the incursion of natural resource extraction activities.

Thus, in Ontario, politicians and civil servants have a great effect on the expansion and preservation of the province's parks and protected areas network. In the absence of strong legislation, the public must play an even greater role in holding the government, the minister of natural resources, and the civil service responsible for the preservation of park values. In addition, the Ontario government must be persuaded to strengthen the *Provincial Parks Act*, pass an Ecological Reserves Act, and implement its Natural Heritage Areas Strategy.

The New Democratic Party, which came to power in 1990, has made commitments to both expand and strengthen the provincial parks system. The government announced in 1992 that it intends to add five new parks and protected areas to the system during the 1993 centennial year celebrations.[131] In addition, the NDP's environmental platform supported the passage of legislation that would set down park boundaries and the classification system into law: "The government should pass legislation that, by setting down park boundaries and classification in law, firmly establishes the parks system for future generations to enjoy."[132] The strengthening of the *Provincial Parks Act*, the *Conservation Land Act*, and the *Niagara Escarpment Planning and Development Act* would serve to both consolidate the achievements of the past 100 years and provide a strong foundation for future decisions on the preservation of Ontario's natural heritage.

Kevin McNamee

FURTHER READING

James K. Agee and Darryll R. Johnson, *Ecosystem Management for Parks and Wilderness* (Seattle: University of Washington Press, 1988).

Matt Bray and Ashley Thomson, eds., *Temagami: A Debate on Wilderness* (Toronto: Dundurn Press, 1990).

Canadian Environmental Advisory Council, *A Protected Areas Vision for Canada* (Ottawa: Supply and Services Canada, 1991).

Stuart Hilts, M. Kirk, and R. Reid, eds., *Islands of Green: Natural Heritage Protection in Ontario* (Toronto: Ontario Heritage Foundation, 1986).

Monte Hummel, ed., *Endangered Spaces: The Future for Canada's Wilderness* (Toronto: Key Porter Books, 1989).

Lori Labatt and Bruce Littlejohn, eds., *Islands of Hope: Ontario's Parks and Wilderness* (Willowdale, Ontario: Firefly Books, 1992).

H. Ian Rounthwaite, "The National Parks of Canada: An Endangered Species" (1981-82), 46 *Sask. Law Review* 43.

David J. Simon, ed., *Our Common Lands: Defending the National Parks* (Washington, DC: Island Press, 1988).

ENDNOTES

1 The greatest amount of protected wilderness is found in the Northwest Territories, almost 132,000 square kilometres, but this land has been reserved by the federal government in national parks and the Thelon Game Sanctuary. The province with the most protected wilderness is Alberta. However, of its 62,683 square kilometres of wilderness, the federal government protects over 54,000 square kilometres in the national parks. See World Wildlife Fund (Canada), *Endangered Spaces Progress Report No. 3* (Toronto: WWF, 1992).

2 Ontario, Ministry of Natural Resources, *Ontario Provincial Park Planning and Management Policies* (Toronto: Queen's Printer, 1978), Wi-I-2.

3 *Provincial Parks Act*, RSO 1990, c. P.34.

4 *Constitution Act, 1982*, RSC 1985, app. II, no. 44.

5 *National Parks Act*, RSC 1985, c. N-14, as amended by SC 1988, c. 48.

6 *Game and Fish Act*, RSO 1990, c. G.1.

7 Personal communication with Robert Day, superintendent, Bruce Peninsula National Park, August 20, 1992.

8 *Trespass to Property Act*, RSO 1990, c. T.21.

9 *National Parks Act*, supra endnote 5.

10 Ibid., section 3.

11 Ibid., section 4.

12   Ontario had opposed the end to the hunt on the grounds that it had provided some of the land within the park and therefore was entitled to have the federal government provide alternative land for hunting. An investigation by the Canadian Environmental Law Association (CELA) revealed that there was no evidence that the province had ever transferred any land: "Minister Says Pelee Hunt To End" (June 1977), *CELA Newsletter* 25; "Attempt To End Pelee Hunt Fails" (October 1977), *CELA Newsletter* 53; "Ontario Opposition to Banning Pelee Buck Hunt Is Based on Incorrect Information, CELA Learns," ibid., at 54.

13   *Canadian Parks and Wilderness Society v. Her Majesty the Queen in Right of Canada*, Federal Court — Trial Division, June 12, 1992 [unreported]. Court file T-272-92

14   *National Parks Act*, supra endnote 5, section 5(1.2).

15   Ibid., section 8.3(2), regarding downhill ski facilities.

16   Ibid., section 8.1, regarding townsite boundaries.

17   Ibid., section 8(1.1), regarding poaching fines.

18   Environment Canada — Parks, *National Parks System Plan* (Ottawa: Supply and Services, 1990).

19   Environment Canada — Parks, *State of the Parks: 1990 Profiles* (Ottawa: Supply and Services, 1991).

20   Environment Canada — Parks, *National Marine Parks Policy* (Ottawa: Supply and Services, 1986).

21   Environment Canada, Canadian Parks Service, *CPS Response to Recommendations of Canadian Environmental Advisory Council — A Protected Areas of Canada* (Ottawa: Supply and Services, 1981), 11.

22   *Fisheries Act*, RSC 1985, c. F-14.

23   *Canada Shipping Act*, RSC 1985, c. S-9.

24   *Migratory Birds Convention Act*, RSC 1985, c. M-7.

25   *Canada Wildlife Act*, RSC 1985, c. W-9.

26   Environment Canada, *Canada's Green Plan* (Ottawa: Supply and Services, 1991).

27   Personal communication, Don Gibson, secretariat, Canadian Heritage Rivers Board, Ottawa, August 20, 1992.

28   *Provincial Parks Act*, supra endnote 3.

29   *Wilderness Areas Act*, RSO 1990, c. W.8.

30   *Conservation Land Act*, RSO 1990, c. C.28.

31   *Ontario Heritage Act*, RSO 1990, c. O.18.

32   *Conservation Authorities Act*, RSO 1990, c. C.27.

33   Ibid.

34   Monte Hummel, ed., *Endangered Spaces: The Future for Canada's Wilderness* (Toronto: Key Porter Books, 1989), 279.

35   World Wildlife Fund (Canada), *Endangered Spaces Progress Report No. 2* (Toronto: WWF, 1991), 4.

36   Ontario, Ministry of Natural Resources, Provincial Parks and Natural Heritage Policy Branch, *A Natural Heritage Areas Strategy for Ontario*, draft for discussion (Toronto: the ministry, 1992).

37   *Conservation Land Act*, supra endnote 30.

38   *Provincial Parks Act*, supra endnote 3.

39 *National Parks Act*, supra endnote 5.
40 Ontario, Ministry of Natural Resources, Provincial Parks Branch, *Ontario Provincial Parks Policy*, pamphlet no. 5739/1978 (Toronto: the ministry, 1978).
41 Don Huff, "Holiday Beach: A Provincial Park Disappears, Unannounced and Almost Unnoticed" (Spring 1987), vol. 27, no.1 *Seasons* 4.
42 *Provincial Parks Act*, supra endnote 3.
43 *Mining Act*, RSO 1990, c. M.14.
44 Ontario Provincial Parks Council, *Report on Contracting in Provincial Parks* (Toronto: Queen's Printer, February 6, 1986).
45 Rosemary Speirs, "Cabinet Wrestles with Provincial Parks," *The Toronto Star*, April 1, 1987.
46 *Green v. Province of Ontario* (1972), 34 DLR (3d) 20 (Ont. HCJ).
47 *Provincial Parks Act*, supra endnote 3.
48 *Canadian Parks and Wilderness Society*, supra endnote 13.
49 *National Parks Act*, supra endnote 5.
50 *Ontario Provincial Park Planning and Management Policies*, supra endnote 2.
51 Memorandum from A.J. Herridge, assistant deputy minister, Policy and Priorities Office, Ontario Ministry of Natural Resources to Mr L.H. Eckel, executive coordinator, Outdoor Recreation, subject: Cabinet minute no. 2-28/78, May 9, 1978, Provincial Parks Policy, May 18, 1978.
52 Ontario, Ministry of Natural Resources, *Ontario Provincial Parks: Planning and Management Policies*, 1991 update, draft for discussion (Toronto: Queen's Printer, 1991).
53 *A Natural Heritage Areas Strategy for Ontario*, supra endnote 36, at 13.
54 Ontario, Ministry of Natural Resources, *Report of the Task Force on Parks System Planning*, 2 vols. (Toronto: Queen's Printer, 1982).
55 Ontario, Ministry of Natural Resources, "Recommended Uses in Provincial Parks," Cabinet submission, March 12, 1986, Toronto.
56 Federation of Ontario Naturalists, "How Will This Wilderness Be Managed?" (Fall 1986), vol. 26, no.3 *Seasons* 36.
57 *Public Lands Act*, RSO 1990, c. P.43.
58 *Mining Act*, supra endnote 43.
59 *The Parks Act*, SS, c. P-1.1.
60 *National Parks Act*, supra endnote 5, sections 9-12.
61 Speirs, supra endnote 45.
62 Marion Strebig, "Ontario Government Severely Limits Non-Conforming Uses in Parks" (Summer 1988), vol. 28, no. 2 *Seasons* 4.
63 Correspondence from James E. Jackson, parks and planning coordinator, North Central Region, Ontario Ministry of Natural Resources to Marion Strebig, environmental director, Federation of Ontario Naturalists, June 1, 1990.
64 Wildlands League, "Algonquin Park Threatened" (tabloid published by Wildlands League Chapter of the Canadian Parks and Wilderness Society, Toronto, 1992).
65 Ontario, Ministry of Natural Resources, *Algonquin Provincial Park Master Plan Review 1989-1990: Provincial Parks Council Recommendation and Minister's Response* (Toronto: Queen's Printer, 1991).

66   See Mike Bryan, "Plans for High-Impact Tourism Threaten Sibley and Other Parks" (Spring 1989), vol. 29, no. 1 *Seasons* 8, and Marion Strebig, "Park Protection: Now You See It, Now You Don't" (Fall 1989), vol. 29, no. 3 *Seasons* 46.

67   *Wilderness Areas Act*, supra endnote 29.

68   *Wilderness Act*, Pub. L. no. 88-577, 16 USC 1131-1136, 88th Cong., 2d Sess., September 3, 1964.

69   Ibid., section 1.

70   *Conservation Land Act*, supra endnote 30.

71   *Ontario Provincial Parks: Planning and Management Policies*, 1991, supra endnote 52.

72   *Provincial Parks Act*, supra endnote 3.

73   In 1983 the Ontario government approved a strategic land-use plan for all Crown land. In addition, 42 district land-use guidelines were produced for the Ministry of Natural Resource's various districts. They provide goals, objectives, and guidelines for the integrated use and protection of a specific parcel of Crown land.

74   There are several types of forest management units established by the *Crown Timber Act*, RSO 1990, c. C.51. (1) *Crown management units*: the Ministry of Natural Resources prepares timber management plans for these areas and carries out timber operations itself. The ministry may also contract companies or individuals to carry operations according to the approved plan prepared by the ministry. (2) *Forest management agreement forests* (FMAs): these management units are licensed to large companies, who are required through negotiated agreements with the ministry to carry out the planning and all operational aspects of timber management, except insect and disease pest control.

75   *Public Lands Act*, supra endnote 57.

76   *Mining Act*, supra endnote 43.

77   *Conservation Land Act*, supra endnote 30.

78   Ontario, Ministry of Natural Resources, Parks and Recreational Areas Branch, *The Conservation Land Tax Reduction Program—Internal Fact Sheet* (Toronto: Queen's Printer, October 1988), 10.

79   Ontario, Ministry of Natural Resources, Provincial Parks and Recreational Areas Branch, *Untaxing Nature: Ontario's New Conservation Land Tax Reduction Program* (Toronto: Queen's Printer, November 6, 1989) (monograph).

80   *Woodlands Improvement Act*, RSO 1990, c. W.10.

81   *Forestry Act*, RSO 1990, c. F.26.

82   Ontario, Conservation Land Tax Reduction Program, 1987, 1988, and 1989, order in council 365/90.

83   Ontario, Ministry of Natural Resources, Parks and Recreational Areas Branch. *The Conservation Land Tax Reduction Program—Internal Fact Sheet* (Toronto: Queen's Printer, October 1989), 12.

84   Ibid., at 1.

85   Memorandum to the Natural Heritage League from Norm R. Richards, director, Provincial Parks and Natural Heritage Policy Branch, Ontario Ministry of Natural Resources, subject: Conservation Land Tax Reduction Program, June 10, 1992.

86   Personal communication, Jane Roots, Parks and Natural Heritage Policy Branch, Ontario Ministry of Natural Resources, Toronto, April 3, 1992.

87 *Ontario Heritage Act*, RSO 1990, c. O.18.

88 *Wilderness and Ecological Reserves Act*, RSN 1990, c. W-9.

89 Ibid.

90 *Conservation Authorities Act*, supra endnote 32.

91 Ibid., section 20.

92 Ron Reid, "Ontario's Conservation Authorities: Coming of Age at 40" (Summer 1986), vol. 26, no. 2 *Seasons* 41.

93 Ibid., at 42.

94 Supra endnote 85.

95 Reid, supra endnote 92, at 43.

96 *Rosenberg v. Grand River Conservation Authority* (1976), 12 OR (2d) 496 (CA).

97 *National Parks Act*, supra endnote 5, section 5(1.1).

98 Environment Canada, Parks Service, *State of the Parks 1990 Report* (Ottawa: Supply and Services, 1990).

99 Ontario, Ministry of Natural Resources, Provincial Parks and National Heritage Policy Branch, *Ontario Provincial Parks — Management Planning* (Toronto: Queen's Printer, May 1, 1992) (3 pages).

100 *Provincial Parks Act*, supra endnote 3.

101 Paul Eagles, *A Study of the Ontario Provincial Parks Act* (Waterloo, Ont.: University of Waterloo, Department of Recreation, 1984), 23.

102 Personal communication with Norm Richards, director, Provincial Parks and Natural Heritage Branch, Ontario Ministry of Natural Resources, April 22, 1991.

103 Eagles, supra endnote 101, at 25.

104 Ibid.

105 Heather Cook, "Public Consultation and the Ontario Ministry of Natural Resources Land Use Planning Program," in *Heritage for Tomorrow — Canadian Assembly on National Parks and Protected Areas* (Ottawa: Supply and Services, 1987).

106 Personal communication, Marion Strebig, Federation of Ontario Naturalists, October 23, 1992.

107 *National Parks Act*, supra endnote 5, section 5(1.4).

108 Kevin McNamee, *Strengthening the National Parks Act: A Review of Legislative Changes to the National Parks Act Resulting from Passage of Bill C-30* (Toronto: Canadian Parks and Wilderness Society, December 1988).

109 Environment Canada, *News Release*, "Status of Banff/Jasper Airstrips To Be Part of 1993 Management Plans Reviews," February 11, 1992. PR-HQ-092-06.

110 *Niagara Escarpment Planning and Development Act*, RSO 1990, c. N.2.

111 Correspondence from Lyn MacMillan to John Swaigen, July 1990.

112 Ontario, Ministry of the Environment, "Niagara Escarpment Program Areas — Background Information," September 1990, 1.

113 Ibid., at 2.

114 Rick Lindgren, "On the Edge: The Niagara Escarpment Plan Review" (1991), vol. 16, no. 4 *Intervenor* (published by the Canadian Environmental Law Association, Toronto).

115 Canada/MAB Committee, "Inauguration of the Niagara Escarpment Biosphere Reserve" (May 1990), newsletter no. 2 *Biosphere Reserves in Canada*.

116 Ontario Trails Council, *Final Report* (Toronto: Queen's Printer, 1977), 25.

117   Kevin McNamee, "Institutional Arrangements To Protect Long Distance Trails: An Evaluation of the Appalachian and Bruce Trail Experiences" (MA thesis, University of Waterloo, 1983), 93.

118   Ibid., at 90.

119   *Motorized Snow Vehicles Act*, RSO 1990, c. M.44, section 22.

120   Ontario Trails Council, supra endnote 116.

121   *Occupiers' Liability Act*, RSO 1990, c. O.2.

122   Ibid.

123   *Trespass to Property Act*, supra endnote 8.

124   See Ontario Trails Council, *Trails for Today and Tomorrow: Converting Ontario's Abandoned Rail Lines to Recreational Trails* (Stouffville, Ont.: OTC, May 1990).

125   *Strengthening the National Parks Act*, supra endnote 108, at 13 and 14.

126   *Public Lands Act*, supra endnote 57.

127   *Provincial Parks Act*, supra endnote 3.

128   John Swaigen, "Does Ontario Need a New Provincial Parks Act?" (1982), vol. 14, no. 1 *Environments* 57-59.

129   Eagles, supra endnote 101, at 28.

130   Ibid.

131   Ontario, Ministry of Natural Resources, *News Release*, "Minister Announces Commitment To Protect Endangered Spaces," January 23, 1992.

132   Ontario New Democratic Party, *Greening the Party, Greening the Province: A Vision for the Ontario NDP* (Toronto: Ontario NDP, 1990).

12

Wetlands

CONTENTS

Even now, wetlands are still being filled for agricultural use, paved over as mall sites, and destroyed to make room for housing subdivisions, marinas or golf courses. Losses due to development have been staggering: in southern Ontario an estimated 80 per cent of original wetland areas have been lost. In Michigan the figure is 71 per cent, and in Illinois it is 90 per cent!

Regeneration, *Royal Commission on the Future of the Toronto Waterfront*

INTRODUCTION

Wetlands have traditionally been regarded as mosquito-infested wastelands that possess little or no value unless they are dredged, drained, filled, and converted by man to an urban or agricultural use. As a result, most of the original wetlands within southern Ontario and throughout Canada have been permanently lost, damaged, or converted to non-wetland uses, and many of the remaining wetlands are now at risk from various kinds of unsustainable development. Recently, however, there has been a growing public recognition that wetlands are essential ecosystems that must be protected against further loss or degradation. Accordingly, the purpose of this chapter is to provide an overview of the statutes, policies, and strategies that may be used by citizens who are seeking to protect and conserve wetlands. In some cases, common law rights, particularly riparian rights, may also be relied on to protect wetlands; however, the circumstances in which common law rights may be applicable are limited in the context of wetlands protection, and hence the common law is not discussed in this chapter.

What Is a Wetland?

The term "wetland" has been defined in a variety of ways, but most definitions refer to lands that are periodically or permanently inundated with surface water or groundwater, and that are characterized by the presence of saturated soils and hydrophytic plant communities. For example, Ontario's *Conservation Land Act* defines wetland in the following manner:

"Wetland" means land, (a) that is seasonally or permanently covered by shallow water, or (b) in respect of which the water table is close to or at the surface, so that the presence of abundant water has caused the formation of hydric soils and has favoured the dominance of either hydrophytic or water-tolerant plants.[1]

The same wetland definition is used in the Environment Canada and Ontario Ministry of Natural Resources *Evaluation System for Wetlands of Ontario South of the Precambrian Shield*. As the evaluation system points out, however, "lands under active agricultural uses that are periodically 'soaked' or 'wet' are not considered to be wetlands" under this definition.[2]

Many persons use terms such as "swamp" or "marsh" interchangeably to describe wetland areas. In fact, however, these terms describe very different wetland types and ecosystems. In Ontario, the major wetland types are *bogs*, *fens*, *swamps*, and *marshes*, and any particular wetland may contain one or more of these distinct types. The evaluation system has described these wetland types on the basis of the following characteristics:

1. *Bogs* are peat-covered areas or peat-filled depressions with a high water table and a surface carpet of mosses, chiefly *Sphagnum* ... [T]he surface bog waters and peat are strongly acid and upper peat layers are extremely deficient in mineral nutrients. Peat is usually formed *in situ* under closed drainage and oxygen saturation is very low. Although bogs are covered with *Sphagnum*, sedges may grow on them. ...

2. *Fens* are peatlands characterized by surface layers of poorly to moderately decomposed peat, often with well-decomposed peat near the base. They are covered by a dominant component of sedges, although grasses and reeds may be associated in local pools. *Sphagnum* is usually subordinate or absent, with other more exacting mosses being common. Often there is much low to medium height shrub cover and sometimes a sparse layer of trees. The waters and peats are less acid than in bogs of the same areas, and sometimes show somewhat alkaline reactions. ...

3. *Swamps* are wooded wetlands where standing to gently flowing waters occur seasonally or persist for long periods on the surface. Frequently there is an abundance of pools and channels indicating subsurface water flow. The substrate is usually continually waterlogged. Waters are circumneutral to moderately acid in reaction, and show little deficiency in oxygen or in mineral nutrients. The vegetation cover may consist of coniferous or deciduous trees, tall shrubs, herbs, and mosses. ...

4. *Marshes* include wet areas periodically inundated with standing or slowly moving water, and/ or permanently inundated areas characterized by robust emergents, and to a lesser extent, anchored floating plants and submergents. ... [T]he substratum usually consists of mineral or organic soils with a high mineral content, but in some marshes there may be as much as two metres of peat accumulation. Waters are usually circumneutral to slightly alkaline, and there is a relatively high oxygen saturation. Marshes characteristically show zones or mosaics of vegetation, frequently interspersed with channels or pools of deep or shallow open water. Marshes may be bordered by peripheral bands of trees and shrubs but the predominant vegetation consists of a variety of emergent non-woody plants such as rushes, reeds, reedgrasses, and sedges. ...[3]

These various wetland types occur within different physiographic locations throughout the landscape, which can greatly affect the biological productivity of the wetland. For example, wetlands located at rivermouths are generally more productive and diverse than ponds with no surface water flow entering or exiting the wetland. In Ontario, there are four major kinds of wetland site locations: *lacustrine wetlands, riverine wetlands, palustrine wetlands*, and *isolated wetlands*. Again, the evaluation system has described wetland site locations on the basis of the following characteristics:

1. *Lacustrine wetlands* are associated with lakes, that is, large bodies of standing water that are usually larger than eight hectares and deeper than two metres. Lacustrine wetlands include areas normally covered by the seasonally high water level as well as contiguous areas of wetland vegetation. ...

2. *Riverine wetlands* include the channels of continuously moving water to 2 m depth as well as adjacent wetlands and normal floodplains of rivers and permanent streams. ... The "upland" edge of Riverine wetlands is located at the interface between wetland and upland vegetation. ...

3. *Palustrine wetlands* are generally areas that occur in lands positioned physiographically above Lacustrine and Riverine wetlands ... [and] are defined either by absent or intermittent stream inflow and either intermittent or permanent stream outflow. They are often headwater areas. ...

4. *Isolated wetlands* are defined as wetlands that have no surface runoff. The source of nutrients is precipitation, diffuse overland flow, and occasionally groundwater. ...[4]

These differences in wetland type and site location are significant because they can affect the nature and extent of the *values* that may be associated with a particular wetland (see "Why Protect Wetlands?" below). Accordingly, these differences are important for the purposes of assessing the vulnerability of a wetland to a particular development proposal, and for the purposes of formulating an appropriate strategy to protect and conserve specific wetlands against various disturbances.

Wetland Loss

Wetlands occur throughout the world, particularly in the temperate and equatorial regions, but it has been estimated that wetland ecosystems represent only 6 per cent of the global landbase.[5] Until recently, most of these wetlands were protected by reason of their remote location, vast size, and marginal utility for agricultural and other economic activities. Within the last 30 years, however, there has been a rapid increase in the rate of wetland loss and degradation on all continents because of agricultural activities, urban development, hydrological disruption, and pollution impacts. Accordingly, wetlands may be properly regarded as "among the most threatened of all environmental resources."[6]

In Canada, it has been estimated that over 127 million hectares (14 per cent) of the landbase is covered by wetlands.[7] This area represents about 24 per cent of the world's total wetland stock,[8] which emphasizes the national and international importance of protecting Canada's remaining wetlands. Across Canada, there is increasing pressure on the remaining wetlands, and many activities, including agricultural drainage, urban expansion, industrial development, energy development, and peat harvesting continue to be undertaken within wetlands. In the result, the loss or conversion of original wetlands has been severe in many regions of Canada; for example, there has been a loss of 65 per cent of Atlantic tidal and salt marshes, 71 per cent of prairie potholes and sloughs, and 80 per cent of Pacific estuarine wetlands.[9] In the Great Lakes region, it has been estimated that less than 30 per cent of original wetlands remain intact.[10]

In Ontario, wetland loss has been particularly acute throughout the southern portion of the province. Before European settlement, wetlands covered over 2.4 million hectares of southern Ontario; however, by the 1980s, this area was reduced to 1.4 million hectares, representing about 60 per cent of the pre-settlement total. In many areas, the losses have been even greater; for example, some counties in eastern and south-central Ontario have experienced a 60-80 per cent loss of original wetlands, while several counties in southwestern Ontario have experienced an 80-100 per cent loss of original wetlands. Agricultural conversion accounts for the majority of the province's wetland losses, although urban growth is now occurring on better agricultural land in southern Ontario and is expected to contribute to further wetland losses in rural areas.[11] It has been estimated that wetland loss is continuing to occur within southern Ontario at a rate of 1-2 per cent per year.[12] These trends clearly point to the need for landowners, citizens' groups, and all levels of government to develop and implement a coordinated and comprehensive strategy to protect and conserve the remaining wetlands and to rehabilitate previously lost or degraded wetlands.

Why Protect Wetlands?

Historically, wetlands have been regarded as unproductive areas that harboured insects, diseases, and other forms of pestilence. Accordingly, wetland drainage and filling was actively encouraged to eliminate these nuisances, as well as to increase the amount of land available for agricultural activities and urban expansion. In recent decades, though, conservationists, scientists, wetland specialists, and the public have acquired a greater understanding of the ecological, hydrological, and socioeconomic value of wetlands. Today, there is an increasing awareness that wetlands are critically linked to many global environmental issues, including climate change, soil and water conservation, the maintenance of biological diversity, and the protection of rare, threatened, or endangered species.

In general, wetland values may be summarized as follows:

1. *Ecological Values.* Wetlands are highly fertile areas of primary biological production, as biomass energy is created through photosynthesis by bacteria, algae, lichen, and plants. In fact, marshes and swamps have greater primary productivity than other ecosystems such as grasslands, lakes, or boreal forests.[13] Wetlands also contribute to the maintenance of biological diversity since they support extremely diverse plant and animal communities and provide feeding and breeding habitat with considerable structural and functional diversity. Accordingly, wetlands supply food and habitat for a variety of fish, waterfowl, non-game birds, mammals, herpetiles, and invertebrates. In addition, wetlands provide critical habitat for many rare, threatened, or endangered plant and animal species. In short, wetlands are diverse and productive ecosystems that perform essential biological functions and greatly contribute to the ecological richness of the natural landscape.

2. *Hydrological Values.* Wetlands play a critical role in the water cycle by maintaining and protecting water quality and quantity within watersheds. In particular, wetlands can perform a variety of important hydrological functions, such as floodwater storage and shoreline stabilization. Wetlands can also trap and retain nutrients and sediment in runoff, thereby protecting downstream watercourses from excessive algal growth and sedimentation. Similarly, wetlands can retain and detoxify chemicals, heavy metals, and pathogens in runoff, particularly within highly developed watersheds. Wetlands can also serve as important groundwater discharge/recharge areas, particularly where wetlands are located along river floodplains or other areas that are hydrologically connected to the local groundwater regime.[14]

3. *Socioeconomic Values.* It has been estimated that Canadians annually derive over $10 billion in economic benefits from wetlands.[15] For example, wetlands provide renewable natural resources such as fish, timber, and wild rice, which can be harvested commercially. As "green space," wetlands can also offer significant aesthetic enjoyment, particularly when they are present within or near urban areas. In addition, wetlands can provide excellent recreational opportunities for both consumptive uses (that is, fishing

and hunting) and non-consumptive uses (such as hiking, canoeing, bird watching, and photography). Important scientific and educational activities may also be undertaken within wetlands. The socioeconomic values of wetlands are only now being appreciated and quantified, and they provide a further justification for wetlands protection and conservation in Ontario and elsewhere.

Despite the clear need to protect wetland values, there are no comprehensive wetland protection statutes or regulatory regimes in Canada. Although certain laws, policies, and programs relating to wetlands exist at both the federal and provincial levels, these initiatives have generally proven to be ineffective in stopping or reversing the loss of wetlands across the country. Accordingly, many governmental authorities and agencies are continuing to authorize or encourage activities that result in further loss loss and degradation of wetlands. It is therefore incumbent on concerned individuals and citizens' groups to become knowledgeable about the jurisdictional framework for wetlands protection, and to become actively involved in the planning and approvals processes in which decisions concerning wetlands are being made.

WETLANDS PROTECTION: THE REGULATORY FRAMEWORK

There are a number of statutes, policies, and programs related to wetlands that have been developed or proposed by federal, provincial, and territorial governments in Canada. Many of these initiatives are of recent origin, while several others still exist only in draft form. Significantly, these initiatives have not been coordinated with other governmental programs that provide incentives for wetland conversion, as described below.

Federal Jurisdiction

International Wetlands Initiatives

The federal government has frequently espoused the value of wetlands, and has systematically identified and mapped the wetlands of Canada. The federal government has also been involved in several international wetland conservation initiatives. For example, Canada is a signatory to the RAMSAR Convention on Wetlands of International Importance, which obligates participants to promote the conservation of critically important wetlands. Sponsored by the International Union of Conservation of Nature (IUCN), the convention directs signatory countries to designate wetlands that are outstanding examples of a region, highly productive communities, valuable for educational or scientific purposes, or valuable as critical wildlife habitat.[16] Thirty RAMSAR-designated wetlands exist across Canada, including three in southern Ontario: the Long Point wetlands, the Lake St. Clair marshes, and the Point Pelee marshes. It must be noted that a RAMSAR designation does not, in and of itself, provide any substantive protection for a wetland. For example, the Long Point wetlands continue to be at risk from encroaching residential and marina development despite their designation.

Similarly, the federal government has participated in the development of the 1986 North American Waterfowl Management Plan (NAWMP) in conjunction with numerous participants, including provincial, territorial, state, and American federal governments as well as non-governmental organizations and the private sector in both countries. The plan is intended to protect 2 million hectares of wetlands within Canada in order to enhance international waterfowl populations and to assist in various soil and water conservation programs. A number of major regional projects, such as the Eastern Habitat Joint Venture, have been initiated in Canada pursuant to the NAWMP, and the Canadian Wetland Council was established in 1990 as a funding and coordinating agency for the plan.

Federal Wetland Policies and Programs

It has been estimated that over 29 per cent of Canada's wetlands are located on land or water under federal control or jurisdiction.[17] About 7.3 million hectares of federal wetlands have received some form of protected status as national parks, migratory bird sanctuaries, or national wildlife areas. For example, some of the Long Point wetlands and Lake St. Clair marshes are within national wildlife areas, and part of the Point Pelee marshes are within a national park.

To assist in the management of federal wetlands, as well as to provide guidance to provincial and territorial wetland managers, the federal government developed a draft federal policy on wetland conservation in 1987. Following consultation with interested parties, a revised draft policy was prepared in 1989 together with a draft implementation plan. After further consultation, the *Federal Policy on Wetland Conservation* was finalized and issued in 1991 pursuant to the federal Green Plan.[18]

The objective of the federal wetlands policy is to "promote the conservation of Canada's wetlands to sustain their ecological and socio-economic functions, now and in the future." The policy also commits the federal government to several important wetland goals, including:

- no net loss of wetland functions on all federal lands and waters;
- the enhancement and rehabilitation of wetlands where wetland losses or degradation have reached critical levels;
- the securement of significant wetlands; and
- the use of wetlands in a manner that enhances prospects for their sustained and productive use by future generations.[19]

The federal wetlands policy also contains seven strategies to protect and conserve Canada's wetlands. They are:

1. to develop public awareness of wetland resources and encourage public participation in wetland conservation;
2. to develop and implement exemplary management practices and sustainable uses of federal wetlands;
3. to promote wetland protection in federally protected areas;
4. to develop partnerships with other governmental agencies and non-governmental organizations;
5. to develop a systematic network of secured wetlands with significance to Canadians;
6. to support wetlands research and monitor wetland trends; and
7. to promote wetlands conservation through international initiatives.[20]

There are a number of other federal policies that are relevant to wetlands and that should be consulted by citizens' groups when wetlands under federal responsibility may be at risk. For example, the 1987 Federal Water Policy identifies wetlands as a specific area of concern and commits the federal government to enhancing and protecting Canadian wetlands through various short- and long-term measures. Similarly, the 1986 Management of Fish Habitat Policy, administered by the Department of Fisheries and Oceans, can be used for wetlands protection purposes since the policy calls for: "no net loss" of existing fish habitat, the rehabilitation of damaged fish habitat, and the enhancement of fish habitat in selected areas. Other key policy documents include the Environmental Quality Policy Framework, the Arctic Marine Conservation Strategy, and the Federal Policy on Land Use.[21]

Federal Statutes Related to Wetlands

There is no comprehensive federal legislation that specifically protects or conserves wetlands. Instead, limited wetland protection may be indirectly achieved through other non-wetland statutes, such as the *Migratory Birds Convention Act*[22] or the *Canada Wildlife Act*,[23] which can be used by Environment Canada to establish wetland sanctuaries for migratory birds. Similarly, the *National Parks Act*[24] confers some measure of protection for wetlands within national park boundaries. Hence, federal statutory protection for wetlands is largely indirect or implied under certain statutes, but it is open to citizens to request that a particular wetland be placed within the protective programs that do exist at the federal level.

It must be noted, however, that the federal *Fisheries Act*, in theory, provides a potent weapon against activities that threaten or impair wetlands. Although the Act is not specifically geared to wetlands, many wetlands constitute "fish habitat" as defined by the Act, and hence the statute's prohibition against the destruction or degradation of fish habitat may be relied on by citizens' groups or the government.[25] For example, an Ontario developer was recently charged by the Ministry of Natural Resources under the *Fisheries Act* after a portion of the provincially significant Constance Creek wetland near Ottawa was filled, dredged, and bulldozed without any statutory approvals.[26] As noted in Chapter 18, fines and imprisonment may be imposed for offences under the *Fisheries Act*, and prosecutors may also seek an order requiring the restoration of damaged fish habitat.[27]

The *Fisheries Act* is also helpful in the context of wetlands protection since the Act empowers the federal minister to require the submission of detailed plans before the alteration of fish habitat. The Ontario Ministry of Natural Resources (MNR) and the federal Department of Fisheries and Oceans (DFO) have signed a memorandum of intent on the management of fish habitat that has been used to establish a joint notification, referral, and approval process for developments or projects that require authorization under the *Fisheries Act*. To date, several wetland developments in Ontario, such as a proposed residential development within the provincially significant Leitrim wetlands near Ottawa, have been reviewed under this process, even though other statutory approvals (that is, under the provincial *Planning Act*[28]) may also be required.

Because a primary objective of the federal Management of Fish Habitat Policy (discussed above) is the "net gain of habitat," the MNR and the DFO can withhold *Fisheries Act* approval of projects that are inconsistent with the policy, or can ensure that the proponent redesigns the development, selects an alternative site, or mitigates the impacts on fish habitat. If the alteration of fish habitat is unavoidable, the proponent may be required to compensate for the loss of productive habitat (that is, by replacing natural habitat near the site or off-site). The policy recognizes that there is a need to provide opportunities for public review and comment on proposed alterations of fish habitat; therefore, depending on the scale of the development or the amount of public concern, there may be either formal or informal opportunities for interested members of the public to participate in the review process.

In the light of recent case law regarding the federal environmental assessment process, the federal Department of Justice has indicated that projects requiring DFO authorization under the *Fisheries Act* may be also subject to the environmental assessment and review process (EARP). Thus, EARP may apply to the proposed development of privately owned wetlands where there are potential impacts on areas of federal decision-making responsibility. For example, a proposed residential development within a provincially significant wetland on Lake Simcoe has resulted in the application of EARP by the DFO because of the potential destruction of fish habitat. In such cases, the DFO will generally require the proponent to produce environmental impact data, which are then circulated to federal departments as part of the "environmental screening" required by EARP. If significant adverse environmental impacts are likely to be caused by the project, the matter may be subject to a public hearing pursuant to EARP (see Chapter 9 for a fuller description of EARP). In the future, the use of certain *Fisheries Act* powers may trigger the application of the new *Canadian Environmental Assessment Act*,[29] as described in Chapter 9, when it comes into force.

Provincial Jurisdiction

It has been estimated that about 50 million hectares of wetlands originally existed throughout Ontario, including over 2 million hectares of wetlands that were located in southern Ontario. As noted above, however, most of the southern Ontario wetlands have been permanently lost, and many northern Ontario wetlands are experiencing pressure as a result of urbanization, shoreline disturbance, and resource extraction and development activities (for example, the impoundment of water in hydroelectric reservoirs).

Wetland Evaluation/Classification

In the past 20 years, considerable public concern has been expressed about the continued loss and degradation of Ontario's wetlands. In 1981, the provincial government responded to this increasing concern by publishing a discussion paper entitled *Towards a Wetlands Policy for Ontario*.[30] This document identified the need to develop a provincial wetlands strategy, and designated the MNR as the lead government agency with respect to wetlands. In particular, the document charged the MNR with developing a wetland inventory/evaluation system and administering wetland programs. In addition, the document called for the development of "planning guidelines" to ensure that land-use planning and land management decisions recognized wetland benefits.

In accordance with this document, from 1981 to 1984 Environment Canada and the MNR developed and field-tested a *wetland evaluation system* intended to identify and evaluate the relative values of wetlands. The system was developed to quantify wetland values so that particularly significant wetlands could be identified and informed land-use decisions could be made in a relatively objective manner. Currently, there is a wetland evaluation system for wetlands south of the Precambrian shield, and a similar system has recently been developed and field-tested for northern Ontario wetlands.[31] The evaluation system itself does not prohibit or circumscribe potential uses of wetlands; however, "in many cases, the potential uses are *clearly implied* by the evaluation for each component."[32] Accordingly, it is important for concerned individuals and citizens' groups to understand how the evaluation system works and how to interpret the resulting wetlands classification.

Essentially, there are three components to the MNR evaluation system: the *wetland data record*, the *wetland evaluation*, and the *wetland classification system*.

The *data record* is a form that is completed by MNR staff or consultants for a particular wetland on the basis of field work, photo-interpretation, map work, and other research. The data record is broken down into four main components (that is, biological component; social component; hydrological component; and "special features" component), and it essentially serves as a checklist of the wetland values found or measured by the investigators.

The *wetland evaluation* is a separate form that simply assigns numerical "scores" for each of the values identified in the data record, depending on their significance. The maximum score for each component of the evaluation is 250, and therefore the highest possible total score for a wetland is 1,000 points.

The *wetland classification system* categorizes wetlands into seven classes based on the point score under the evaluation system:

- *class 1*: 700 or more total points or 3 out of 4 components that score more than 200 points each;
- *class 2*: 650 or more total points or 2 out of 4 components that score more than 200 points each;
- *class 3*: 600 or more total points or 1 out of 4 components that score more than 200 points;
- *class 4*: 550 or more total points or all components that score more than 100 points each;
- *class 5*: 500 or more total points or 3 out of 4 components that score more than 100 points each;
- *class 6*: 450 or more total points or 2 out of 4 components that score more than 100 points each; and
- *class 7*: all other evaluated wetlands.

As described below, wetlands in the Great Lakes – St. Lawrence region that have been scored and classified as class 1, 2, or 3 wetlands are considered to be "provincially significant" because of their particularly valuable features and functions. Many of southern Ontario's wetlands have been evaluated by the MNR, and it has been estimated that only a small percentage of these wetlands are classified as "provincially significant."[33]

Wetland data records and evaluations are public documents, and it is important for concerned citizens to obtain copies of this documentation from the MNR for wetlands that are at risk from development. If a particular wetland has not yet been evaluated by the MNR, concerned citizens should request the MNR to carry out the evaluation. For example, the MNR had not evaluated the Leitrim wetland near Ottawa and had no objections to a proposed residential development beside and within the wetland. Local conservation groups objected and requested that the MNR evaluate the wetland. An evaluation was then undertaken by the MNR, and it revealed that the wetland was a class 1 wetland containing about 150 rare and significant species of flora and fauna. The results of the evaluation caused the MNR to reverse its position on the proposed development, and the MNR proceeded to object to the development.[34]

It is also possible that a wetland evaluation for a particular wetland may become outdated by reason of the passage of time or the discovery of fresh information. When this occurs, concerned citizens should request the MNR to update the evaluation. The new information obtained during the re-evaluation can increase the wetlands' total score and thus elevate the wetlands' classification, which may, in turn, result in better protection for the wetland. For example, the Creditview bog in Mississauga was originally evaluated as a class 6 wetland, and the local municipality approved the construction of subdivisions within the wetland since it was not provincially or regionally significant. As a result of lobbying and research by local naturalists, however, the wetland classification was eventually increased to class 3, which prompted provincially sponsored negotiations intended to preserve part of the bog.[35]

Provincial Wetland Policies and Programs

In 1984, the MNR released *Guidelines for Wetlands Management in Ontario* to "ensure that wetlands are managed in keeping with both present and long-term needs of the people of Ontario."[36] The guidelines set out general planning principles intended to assist municipalities in protecting "significant wetlands" from "incompatible activities" through appropriate land-use designations in official plans and zoning bylaws. However, wetlands advocates within Ontario strongly criticized the guidelines for being too vague and for permitting development of provincially significant wetlands.[37] Moreover, the guidelines were not issued under the *Planning Act*,[38] and hence municipalities were not actually required to incorporate the document's planning principles into their land-use planning and approvals process.

To address this latter problem, the MNR and the Ministry of Municipal Affairs (MMA) jointly released a draft wetlands policy statement in 1989 under section 3 of the *Planning Act*. This policy statement, together with accompanying implementation guidelines, primarily applied to class 1 and 2 (provincially significant) wetlands and directed municipalities to allow either no development or only "compatible" development within provincially significant wetlands.[39] This draft wetlands policy statement was extensively reviewed by government agencies and public interest groups, and a number of serious deficiencies were identified.[40] To address the problems with the 1989 draft policy statement, the MNR and MMA released a revised draft in 1991, which was again extensively criticized by wetlands advocates.[41] In 1992, the wetlands policy statement was further revised, approved by Cabinet, and released by the minister of municipal affairs, thereby ending a decade of inertia by the provincial government on this issue.

The approved wetlands policy statement became effective in June 1992, and its stated objective is to ensure no loss of wetland function or area of provincially significant wetlands in the Great Lakes – St. Lawrence region, and no loss of wetland function of provincially significant wetlands in the boreal region. The policy statement specifically requires all planning jurisdictions, including municipalities and resource management agencies, to protect provincially significant wetlands. These planning authorities are also "encouraged" to protect other wetlands that are not provincially significant.[42] Curiously, the policy statement treats southern Ontario wetlands differently from northern Ontario wetlands, ostensibly because of the greater abundance of northern wetlands and the different development pressures upon southern wetlands.

In particular, within the Great Lakes – St. Lawrence region, the policy provides that "development shall not be permitted within provincially significant wetlands."[43] "Development" is broadly defined as:

- the construction, erection, or placing of a building or structure;
- activities such as site grading, excavation, removal of topsoil or peat, and the placing or dumping of fill; and
- drainage works, except for the maintenance of existing municipal and agricultural drains.[44]

Within land adjacent to provincially significant wetlands (that is, land within 120 metres or connecting lands within a wetland complex) in the Great Lakes – St. Lawrence region, development may be permitted if an environmental impact study (EIS) by the proponent demonstrates that the proposal does not result in:

- a loss of wetland functions;
- a subsequent demand for future development that will impair wetland functions;
- a conflict with site-specific wetland management practices; and
- a loss of contiguous wetland area.[45]

In contrast, within the boreal region, development may be permitted within provincially significant wetlands and adjacent lands if the EIS demonstrates that the proposal does not result in:

- a loss of wetland functions;
- a subsequent demand for future development that will impair wetland functions; and
- a conflict with existing site-specific wetland management practices.[46]

In both the boreal and Great Lake – St. Lawrence regions, established agricultural activities are permitted on adjacent lands without an EIS.[47] The policy statement further provides that proposals for new utilities or facilities (that is, for transportation, communication, or sanitation) must be located outside provincially significant wetlands whenever possible.[48]

Implementation guidelines for the wetlands policy statement were released by the MNR and MMA in November 1992.[49] These guidelines should be read in conjunction with the policy statement, since they provide specific directions on how the policy statement is to be interpreted. In particular, the implementation guidelines explain the content requirements for EISs and provide various options and approaches for incorporating wetlands protection into the land-use planning process. Depending on the use and interpretation of the guidelines, the wetlands policy statement should provide another important tool for environmentalists to protect and conserve wetlands at risk from development. In fact, in one of the first decisions concerning the wetlands policy statement, the Ontario Municipal Board used the policy statement to protect a small unclassified wetland on Stoney Lake after a member of the public appealed a zoning bylaw that would have permitted residential development within and beside the wetland.[50]

In addition to the initiatives described above, the provincial government has made certain policy and program commitments intended to promote wetlands protection. For example, the MNR has established a limited acquisition fund to purchase privately owned wetlands of particular importance. Similarly, the Carolinian Canada Program, administered by the MNR, has a major wetland component. In addition, the province has established the Conservation Land Tax Reduction Program, which permits owners of class 1, 2, or 3 wetlands to obtain up to a 100 per cent rebate of certain property taxes, provided that the landowner agrees to the long-term maintenance of the wetland in its natural state.[51] The province's revised Strategic Plan for Ontario Fisheries (SPOF II) also contains several provisions and recommendations relating to wetlands protection.[52] In addition, the Niagara Escarpment Commission has recently proposed a number of revisions to the existing Niagara Escarpment plan in order to strengthen the protection of wetlands within the Niagara Escarpment area. As described below, the MNR has also formed a partnership in 1992 with Wildlife Habitat Canada and Ducks Unlimited to implement a three-year, $3 million program to enhance private land stewardship of provincially significant wetlands and areas of natural or scientific interest (ANSIs). ANSIs and the Conservation Land Tax Reduction Program are discussed more fully in Chapter 11.

Provincial Statutes Relating to Wetlands

Like the federal government, Ontario lacks a single statute that specifically requires the protection or conservation of wetlands within the province. Accordingly, wetlands protection may be indirectly achieved through various non-wetland statutes, particularly those relating to water quality and public lands. At the same time, however, there are certain provincial statutes still in effect that serve to encourage wetlands loss and degradation. Accordingly, many public interest groups have called upon the provincial government to remove all statutory incentives to drain or fill wetlands, and to enact comprehensive wetlands protection legislation.

The following is a brief overview of the provincial statutes that are relevant to wetlands in Ontario.

Aggregate Resources Act

Administered by the MNR, the *Aggregate Resources Act*[53] prohibits persons from operating pits or quarries without a licence from the minister. Although this statute does not usually apply in the wetland context, there have been instances in which companies or municipalities have proposed to extract gravel within or beside significant wetlands.[54] Before a licence may be issued, the minister must have regard for the impact of the proposed activities on the natural environment, and terms and conditions may be attached to the licence if it is granted. A public hearing before the Ontario Municipal Board is possible under this statute, which is discussed in Chapter 23.

Beds of Navigable Waters Act

In effect, the *Beds of Navigable Waters Act*[55] provides that the bed of any navigable water within Ontario is Crown land. Accordingly, if a wetland is on or within a navigable waterway, the bed of the wetland may be publicly owned, and the placement of fill on the bed may be prohibited by virtue of the *Public Lands Act* (see below).

Conservation Authorities Act

Administered by the MNR, the *Conservation Authorities Act*[56] permits the creation of conservation authorities, which are semi-autonomous agencies established at the request of municipalities and are responsible for the conservation and management of natural resources within a given watershed. Conservation authorities undertake a variety of activities that may directly affect wetlands, such as dam construction, floodwater control, shoreline stabilization, and watercourse diversion. In some instances, conservation authorities have proposed to sell or lease wetlands under their control to permit the construction of golf courses or residential development. In addition, conservation authorities may develop "watershed management plans," and may pass regulations restricting or regulating activities within floodplains (that is, "cut and fill" regulations). Conservation authorities often review and comment upon proposed zoning bylaws and official plan amendments that touch on issues within their mandate. For further discussion, see chapters 11 and 18.

Conservation Land Act

Administered by the MNR, the *Conservation Land Act*[57] permits the establishment of programs designed to encourage the stewardship of "conservation land," which is defined as including class 1, 2, and 3 wetlands. As discussed in Chapter 11, this Act provides the statutory basis for Ontario's Conservation Land Tax Rebate Program described above.

Drainage Act

Administered by the Ontario Ministry of Agriculture and Food (OMAF), the *Drainage Act*[58] provides for the construction of municipal drainage works and the provision of grants for such projects (see also the *Tile Drainage Act*[59]). This Act has been frequently used to undertake and finance the drainage of many wetlands in southern Ontario.[60] It is, however, possible for landowners who are affected by proposed drainage works to appeal the matter to the Ontario Drainage Tribunal and to request that the proposal be altered or abandoned. In addition, it is possible under the Act for a municipality, a conservation authority, or the MNR to request an environmental appraisal of the proposed drainage works, and to appeal the appraisal to the tribunal if it is unsatisfactory. In the light of the definition of "development" in the wetlands policy statement, which includes drainage, the tribunal should be expected to give substantial weight to wetlands preservation concerns.

Endangered Species Act

Administered by the MNR, the *Endangered Species Act*[61] prohibits the interference or destruction of any species of flora or fauna, or its habitat, that is listed as endangered. The present list of endangered species under Ontario regulation 328 includes several species that require wetlands habitat, and thus this legislation may be invoked where such species are found within a particular wetland. More information about this statute can be found in Chapter 13.

Environmental Assessment Act

Administered by the Ministry of Environment and Energy (MEE), the *Environmental Assessment Act*[62] establishes a process for assessing the environmental impacts of undertakings subject to the Act. For example, public sector undertakings that might affect a wetland will require an environmental assessment unless the undertaking has been specifically exempted from the Act. Private sector development, however, is not subject to the Act unless the development is designated as an undertaking to which the Act applies. Interested individuals or groups can request the minister to designate private development, such as subdivisions or golf courses, if wetlands are at risk from the development. In addition, individuals or groups can request that municipal infrastructure projects (that is, waterworks, sewer works, or municipal roads) be "bumped up" to individual environmental assessment when the projects may put wetlands at risk. This bump-up mechanism was successfully invoked by groups opposing proposed development within provincially significant wetland on Lake Simcoe, since the minister ordered the township to prepare an individual environmental assessment of sewage and water works proposed within the wetlands. It is noteworthy that municipal drainage works under the *Drainage Act* are specifically exempted from the Act by Ontario regulation 334.[63] If a development is subject to the Act, environmental assessment documentation must be prepared by the proponent, and there is a possibility of a public hearing before the Environmental Assessment Board or the joint board (see Chapter 9 for a fuller description of the environmental assessment process).

Environmental Protection Act

Administered by the MEE, the *Environmental Protection Act*[64] prohibits the discharge of a contaminant into the natural environment that causes or is likely to cause an adverse effect. Thus, this Act may be applicable if the emission of a contaminant may adversely affect a wetland. Similarly, this Act establishes a regulatory regime for the licensing of waste disposal sites, and there have been instances in which landfills or incinerators have been proposed within or beside significant wetlands within Ontario (see Chapter 16 for a fuller description of this Act).

Lakes and Rivers Improvement Act

Administered by the MNR, the *Lakes and Rivers Improvement Act*[65] regulates potential uses or "improvements" (that is, dams) of lakes and rivers within Ontario to protect aquatic species and habitat and to safeguard public and private rights in such waterbodies. Thus, an "improvement" involving a riverine wetland may require approval under the Act, which can result in a public inquiry by a hearing officer who reports to the minister. For example, in 1989 a private landowner near Welland sought approval under the Act to construct a bridge across a class 1 wetland; however, the hearing officer accepted the position of the MNR and public interest groups and refused to grant the approval on environmental grounds.[66]

Ministry of Government Services Act

The *Ministry of Government Services Act*[67] empowers the provincial government to acquire the whole, part of, or an easement in respect of, property within the province. In particular, this Act permits the creation of statutory easements that may be registered against the land, and thus may be used to create "conservation easements" (see below) to constrain the landowner from undertaking certain activities within the property.

Municipal Act

Administered by the MMA, *Municipal Act*[68] authorizes municipalities to enact bylaws regulating various matters related to wetlands, such as the acquisition and drainage of wetlands, the alteration of watercourses, the regulation of construction on or over watercourses along municipal highways, the preservation of shorelines and streambanks, and other related matters. Municipalities may also enact sewer-use bylaws to regulate stormwater or effluent discharge that may deleteriously affect receiving waterbodies such as wetlands.

Ontario Heritage Act

Administered by the Ministry of Culture and Communications, the *Ontario Heritage Act*[69] empowers the Ontario Heritage Foundation to acquire property of historical, recreational, aesthetic, or scenic interest in trust for the people of Ontario. The Act also authorizes the foundation to enter into and enforce agreements, covenants, and easements with landowners for the conservation, protection, and preservation of Ontario's heritage. Although the Act has not been widely used to date to conserve and protect wetlands, the statute potentially provides important mechanisms, such as conservation easements, that may be used with respect to wetlands. For further discussion, see Chapter 14.

Ontario Water Resources Act

The *Ontario Water Resources Act*[70] confers supervisory jurisdiction over all surface water and groundwater in Ontario to the MEE, and thus can be used to protect the hydrological values of wetlands. For example, the Act prohibits the discharge of any material into any water or onto shores or banks that may impair water quality. Similarly, the Act prohibits the taking of water without a permit, and permits MEE directors to restrict or prohibit activities that interfere with private or public interests in water. New sewage treatment facilities and the expansion of existing ones must obtain approval under this Act. This is significant because sewage treatment plants and sewage lagoons sometimes discharge effluent into wetlands. In the 1970s, environmentalists fought such a facility at Cootes Paradise, a marsh near Hamilton, and in 1992 conservationists were objecting to the construction of a sewage facility that would discharge effluent into the Mindemoya marsh, on Manitoulin Island.

Planning Act

Administered by the MMA, the *Planning Act*[71] empowers municipalities to regulate land use through a variety of measures, including the passage of official plans, the enactment of zoning bylaws, site-plan control, and subdivision and severance approval. As described above, the government also used its powers under section 3 of the *Planning Act* to pass the new wetlands policy statement, which must be considered by all planning jurisdictions within the province. It is noteworthy that proposed official plan amendments, plans of subdivision, and other planning instruments are normally circulated to the MNR, MEE, MMA, local conservation authorities, and other interested agencies for review and comment. In theory, these commenting powers can be used by municipalities and reviewing agencies to protect wetlands through appropriate land-use designations, land-use restrictions, and conditional approvals. As described below, however, the land-use planning process to date has generally failed to protect wetlands against further loss or degradation. (See also Chapter 8 for a fuller description of the land-use planning process.)

Provincial Parks Act

Administered by the MNR, the *Provincial Parks Act*[72] confers limited protection on natural resources, such as wetlands, that are found within Ontario's provincial park system. For more information, see Chapter 11.

Public Lands Act

Administered by the MNR, the *Public Lands Act*[73] regulates various uses and development of Crown land. As noted above, beds of navigable waterways are deemed to be public land pursuant to the *Beds of Navigable Waters Act*,[74] even if the watercourse flows through private property, and the *Public Lands Act* prohibits the clearing or filling of public lands, or the dredging or filling of "shorelands," without approval. In addition, this Act empowers the courts to order persons to rehabilitate damaged public lands or shorelands by replacing dredged material or removing fill material. Thus, this Act may be used to protect wetlands that form part of a navigable waterway. For example, the Ottawa developer (discussed above) who filled a portion of the class 1 Constance Creek wetland without approval was charged by the MNR under this Act.[75] On Crown lands, of course, the wetlands are owned by the Crown even if they are not part of a navigable waterway, and are automatically covered by the *Public Lands Act*.

• • •

The preceding review of wetlands-related legislation clearly indicates the lead role played by the MNR in terms of wetlands protection and conservation. Accordingly, if a particular wetland is being threatened, interested citizens should immediately contact the local MNR office and request that the ministry take action. The MNR also plays a key role in managing wetlands located on Crown land, most of which are found in northern Ontario. Land-use planning decisions for Crown land wetlands are generally made in the context of the MNR's regional strategic land-use plans, district land-use guidelines, and other resource management policies and procedures (see Chapter 11).

Municipal Jurisdiction

It has been estimated that over 80 per cent of Ontario municipalities have wetlands within their jurisdiction. Accordingly, municipalities can play an integral role in protecting and conserving wetlands, particularly through the judicious exercise of *Planning Act* powers.

Traditionally, under zoning bylaws and official plans, municipalities have mapped and designated wetlands as "hazard lands," "environmental constraints," "organic soils," or "marginal resource." Frequently, these designations are primarily concerned about the physical hazards associated with building within wetlands, rather than about protecting the ecological, hydrological, and socioeconomic values of wetlands.

In a few instances, wetlands have been placed in more restrictive categories, such as "natural environment," "environmental protection," or "environmentally sensitive area."

However, municipalities are often reluctant to use these categories because of concerns over the potential loss of tax assessment base, the potential loss of jobs or prestige, and the "sterilization" of private property. There is also concern that placing wetlands in restrictive categories may amount to a form of expropriation. On this latter point, the Ontario Municipal Board has often held that municipalities should purchase private property that is placed within a category that denies landowners the reasonable use of the property in accordance with proper planning principles.[76] More recently, however, the board has ruled that a municipal reclassification of a wetland into a more restrictive official plan designation does not constitute a "taking" under the *Expropriations Act*[77] and does not entitle the landowner to compensation for loss of business opportunity.[78]

It should be noted, however, that even if a wetland is initially placed in a restrictive category, the long-term protection of the wetland is not ensured since landowners can apply for official plan amendments or rezoning bylaws that permit the development of the wetland.[79] Accordingly, it is important for interested citizens to ensure that municipal planning authorities develop and comply with official plans that contain clear goals and policies relating to wetland protection and conservation. Similarly, citizens should exercise their right to participate in decisions under the *Planning Act* to ensure that planning authorities have adequate wetland information during the decision-making process. This may be accomplished by participating during official plan preparation or revision, initiating or responding to proposed official plan amendments, responding to proposed rezoning of wetlands, seeking governmental declarations of provincial interest in significant wetlands, and appealing bylaws or having official plan amendments referred to the Ontario Municipal Board where necessary.

In recent years, several citizens' groups have been successful in persuading the Ontario Municipal Board to disallow the development of significant wetlands in Ontario. In 1989, for example, private citizens successfully opposed the proposed construction of a marina complex within the class 3 Point Comfort marsh on the St. Lawrence River near Lansdowne.[80] Similarly, in 1989 the Ontario Municipal Board refused to permit the proposed development of a recreational resort within a class 1 wetland in Eramosa Township.[81] In addition, in 1990 the board turned down a proposal to build a golf course within the class 1 Constance Creek wetland near Ottawa.[82] These and other examples clearly demonstrate that concerned individuals and public interest groups can successfully use the public participatory rights under the *Planning Act* to protect and conserve wetlands in Ontario.

WETLANDS PROTECTION: NON-REGULATORY INITIATIVES

In addition to the governmental policies and programs described above, there are a number of wetland protection initiatives carried out by individuals and private organizations within Ontario and across Canada. Many of these initiatives have been undertaken through partnerships with governmental agencies. These tools are particularly useful in southern Ontario because many wetlands that are at risk are privately owned, and because public acquisition is not always feasible due to prohibitive costs. These non-regulatory initiatives, such as private stewardship, conservation easements, and restrictive covenants, have resulted in the protection of over 1 million hectares of Canadian wetlands.[83] Thus, individuals and groups such as the Federation of Cntario Naturalists, Ducks Unlimited, Natural Heritage League, Nature Conservancy of Canada, and Wildlife Habitat Canada play an important role in wetland protection by facilitating private acquisition, management, and stewardship of wetlands.

The major private tools[84] for wetlands protection include stewardship, conservation easements, restrictive covenants, and gifts and trusts.

Stewardship

Stewardship generally refers to a landowner's voluntary decision to maintain and manage his or her land in its natural state for an extended period of time. This decision may be either formal or informal, and may be the subject of an agreement between the landowner and a sponsoring agency such as Ontario's Natural Heritage League. Ontario and several other provinces have established "stewardship programs" to contact owners of significant natural areas such as wetlands, and to provide the owners with educational information, technical assistance, or monetary incentives for the long-term preservation of their property. Landowners who participate in such programs may also receive formal recognition or awards for their conservation efforts. In 1992, the MNR, Wildlife Habitat Canada, and Ducks Unlimited developed a three-year, $3 million wetland habitat agreement to enhance private land stewardship for provincially significant wetlands and ANSIs, largely in southern Ontario. The agreement will be used to implement a variety of securement techniques such as management agreements, leases, and acquisitions.

Conservation Easements

Conservation easements refer to common law or statutory mechanisms that place partial or complete restrictions on a landowner's ability to use or develop his or her land. The easement is typically created when the landowner agrees to let a named party carry out certain activities (for example, build a duck pond or manage a wetland) on the property without interference from the landowner. The easement holder may be a government agency, an incorporated body, a private individual, or a non-governmental environmental organization. The easement may be donated or purchased from the landowner, who retains title to the property; however, the easement may be registered against the land title, and is thus enforceable against present and future landowners. Easements created for conservation purposes have been widely used throughout Britain and the United States to protect wetlands, but to date the tool has been underused in Canada. These easements are discussed in detail in Chapter 15, as are the covenants, gifts, and trusts below.

Restrictive Covenants

Like conservation easements, restrictive covenants may be used to place partial or complete restrictions on a landowner's ability to use or develop his or her land. The restrictive covenant is usually created when the landowner agrees not to carry out certain activities (for example, drain a wetland or pollute a wetland) on the property. Provided that the necessary legal conditions are met, restrictive covenants may be registered against title and "run with the land," and can be enforced by the covenant holder against present and future landowners.

Restrictive covenants have been long established in Canadian law, but to date few covenants have been expressly created for the conservation of wetlands.

Gifts, Trusts, and Other Tools

Landowners may choose to donate wetland property to private individuals, charitable organizations, or public agencies, keeping in mind that such dispositions often have significant income tax implications. Similarly, landowners may establish trusts (for example, by will), and may convey property to the trust or to trusts already in existence. It is also possible for landowners to sell their land to private individuals, conservation organizations, or governmental agencies, and vendors may negotiate a "leaseback" from the buyer if they wish to continue to use the land in some manner. Loans and mortgage assistance may also be used to achieve conservation land objectives through the imposition of appropriate restrictions by the lender or mortgagee.[85]

THE FUTURE OF ONTARIO'S WETLANDS

Although there is a widespread recognition that wetlands are essential ecosystems containing valuable natural resources, wetlands are still threatened by further loss and degradation within Ontario and across Canada. The federal, provincial, territorial, and municipal governments have jurisdiction in relation to wetlands, but to date the exercise of this jurisdiction has resulted in a convoluted mix of generally ineffective laws, policies, and programs. Accordingly, there is a growing consensus that governments must undertake a much more aggressive and comprehensive approach to wetlands protection. In particular, a number of public interest groups have called for the development of specific wetlands protection legislation based on the principle of "no loss of wetland area or function."[86]

Other reforms are also necessary to ensure the long-term protection and sustainability of Canadian wetlands. For example, all levels of government must remove all incentives and subsidies for wetlands drainage, and must expand public acquisition budgets for wetlands purchases. Similarly, governments must require the restoration and rehabilitation of significant wetlands that have been previously altered, degraded, or destroyed. In addition, the land-use planning process must be revised to ensure that planning is carried out on an ecosystem basis (that is, watersheds or bioregions), and that the environmental impacts associated with proposed development, including cumulative effects, are properly identified and considered by decision makers.[87] Thus, concerned citizens and public interest groups must continue to press governments to implement these long overdue reforms in order to halt and reverse the alarming rate of wetland loss that has occurred to date.

Richard D. Lindgren

FURTHER READING

Environment Canada et al., *Sustaining Wetlands: International Challenge for the 90s* (Ottawa: Canadian Wildlife Service, Environment Canada, 1988).

Federation of Ontario Naturalists, *Wetlands: Inertia or Momentum?* (Toronto: FON, 1989).

Great Lakes Wetlands Policy Consortium, *Final Report: Preserving Great Lakes Wetlands — An Environmental Agenda* (Conway, Mich.: Tip of the Mitt Watershed Council [PO Box 300, Conway, Mich. 49722], 1990).

National Wetlands Working Group, *Wetlands of Canada* (Ottawa: Environment Canada, 1988).

ENDNOTES

1 *Conservation Land Act*, RSO 1990, c. C.28, section 1.
2 Canada, Environment Canada and Ontario, Ministry of Natural Resources, *An Evaluation System for Wetlands of Ontario South of the Precambrian Shield*, 2d ed. (Toronto: the ministry, 1984), 7.
3 Ibid., at 26-27.
4 Ibid., at 32-33.
5 Kerry Turner, "Economics and Wetland Management" (April 1991), vol. 20, no. 2 *Ambio* 59.
6 Ibid. Note that Ontario wetlands are also under threat from non-native plant species such as purple loosestrife: see Jack Hanna, "Purple Invader" (Summer 1989), vol. 29, no. 2 *Seasons* 20.
7 National Wetlands Working Group, *Wetlands of Canada* (Ottawa: Environment Canada, 1988), 4.
8 Environment Canada et al., *Sustaining Wetlands: International Challenge for the 90s* (Ottawa: Sustaining Wetlands Forum, 1990), 3.
9 Ibid. See also National Wetlands Working Group, supra endnote 7, chapter 10, "Wetland Utilization in Canada."
10 Great Lakes Wetlands Policy Consortium, *Final Report: Preserving Great Lakes Wetlands — An Environmental Agenda* (Conway, Mich.: Tip of the Mitt Watershed Council, 1990), 3.
11 Elizabeth A. Snell, *Wetland Distribution and Conversion in Southern Ontario*, Working Paper no.48 (Ottawa: Environment Canada, 1987), 32-33.
12 Ron Reid, "A Critic's View of Wetland Policies," in *Proceedings of the Ontario Wetlands Conference* (Toronto: Federation of Ontario Naturalists, 1981).
13 National Wetlands Working Group, supra endnote 7, at 384.
14 Gerald A. Paulson, *Wetlands and Water Quality: A Citizen's Handbook for Protecting Wetlands* (Chicago: Lake Michigan Federation, 1990), 30.
15 National Wetlands Working Group, supra endnote 7, at 382.
16 Ibid., at 192. See also D.I. Gillespie et al., *Wetlands for the World: Canada's RAMSAR Sites* (Ottawa: Supply and Services, 1991).

17 Environment Canada, *The Federal Policy on Wetland Conservation* (Ottawa: Supply and Services, 1991), 4.
18 Ibid., at 2.
19 Ibid., at 7.
20 Ibid., at 9-12.
21 Ibid., at 10.
22 *Migratory Birds Convention Act*, RSC 1985, c. M-7.
23 *Canada Wildlife Act*, RSC 1985, c. W-9.
24 *National Parks Act*, RSC 1985, c. N-14.
25 *Fisheries Act*, RSC 1985, c. F-14, section 35.
26 These charges were subsequently stayed by the trial judge on the basis of unreasonable delay; however, this decision is under appeal.
27 See Canada, Department of Fisheries and Oceans, *Policy for the Management of Fish Habitat* (Ottawa: the department, 1986), 20.
28 *Planning Act*, RSO 1990, c. P.13.
29 *Canadian Environmental Assessment Act*, SC 1992, c. 37.
30 Ontario, Ministry of Natural Resources, *Towards a Wetland Policy for Ontario: Discussion Paper* (Toronto: the ministry, 1981).
31 However, some public interest groups question the efficacy and accuracy of the current wetland evaluation system.
32 *An Evaluation System for Wetlands*, supra endnote 2, at 3.
33 See Ontario, Ministry of Natural Resources, *Provincially and Regionally Significant Wetlands in Southern Ontario: Interim Report, 1987* (Toronto: the ministry, 1988), 6.
34 Unfortunately, the MNR subsequently reversed itself again and withdrew its formal objection to the development, thereby leaving local environmental groups to continue the opposition to the development.
35 See Ontario, Environmental Assessment Advisory Committee, *Report No. 37: Creditview Wetland* (Toronto: the committee, 1989), which recommended negotiation as a means to resolve the wetlands dispute.
36 Ontario, Ministry of Natural Resources, *Guidelines for Wetlands Management in Ontario* (Toronto: the ministry, 1984).
37 See, for example, Federation of Ontario Naturalists, "Brief of the Federation of Ontario Naturalists to the Minister of Natural Resources Regarding Guidelines for Wetlands Management in Ontario," 1984.
38 *Planning Act*, supra endnote 28.
39 Ontario, Ministry of Natural Resources, *Wetlands Policy Statement: Implementation Guidelines* (Toronto: the ministry, 1989), 15-17.
40 See, for example, Federation of Ontario Naturalists and Ontario Federation of Anglers and Hunters, "Response to Government of Ontario: Wetlands Policy Statement and Implementation Guidelines," 1989.
41 See, for example, Canadian Environmental Law Association, "Submissions of the Canadian Environmental Law Association to the MNR on the Draft Wetlands Policy Statement," 1991.
42 Ontario, Ministry of Natural Resources and Ministry of Municipal Affairs, *Wetlands Policy Statement* (Toronto: Queen's Printer, 1992), 10.

43 Ibid.

44 Ibid., at 8.

45 Ibid., at 10.

46 Ibid., at 11.

47 Ibid., at 10-11.

48 Ibid., at 11.

49 Ontario, Ministry of Natural Resources and Ministry of Municipal Affairs, *Manual of Implementation Guidelines for the Wetlands Policy Statement* (Toronto: Queen's Printer, November 1992).

50 OMB file no. R920103 (October 20, 1992).

51 Ontario, Ministry of Natural Resources, *1990 Ontario Conservation Land Tax Reduction Program* (Toronto: the ministry, 1990).

52 See, for example, SPOF II Working Group, "Summary of Tactics To Implement a Revised Strategic Plan for Ontario Fisheries," SPOF II Forum, 1990. The working group recommends that wetlands destruction be prevented through education programs, improved law enforcement, and development of wetlands legislation.

53 *Aggregate Resources Act*, RSO 1990, c. A.8.

54 For example, a private company is currently seeking approval to establish a gravel pit beside a class 1 wetland in Smith Township near Peterborough.

55 *Beds of Navigable Waters Act*, RSO 1990, c. B.4.

56 *Conservation Authorities Act*, RSO 1990, c. C.27.

57 *Conservation Land Act*, RSO 1990, c. C.28.

58 *Drainage Act*, RSO 1990, c. D.17.

59 *Tile Drainage Act*, RSO 1990, c. T.8.

60 M.J. Bardecki, *Institutional Arrangements and How They Affect Wetlands: Agricultural Land Drainage* (Waterloo, Ont.: Heritage Resources Centre, University of Waterloo, 1991).

61 *Endangered Species Act*, RSO 1990, c. E.15.

62 *Environmental Assessment Act*, RSO 1990, c. E.18.

63 RRO 1990, reg. 334, section 5(2)(c).

64 *Environmental Protection Act*, RSO 1990, c. E.19.

65 *Lakes and Rivers Improvement Act*, RSO 1990, c. L.3.

66 "Report to Minister of Natural Resources Regarding A. Mete Application," September 25, 1989.

67 *Ministry of Government Services Act*, RSO 1990, c. M.25.

68 *Municipal Act*, RSO 1990, c. M.45.

69 *Ontario Heritage Act*, RSO 1990, c. O.18.

70 *Ontario Water Resources Act*, RSO 1990, c. O.40.

71 *Planning Act*, supra endnote 28.

72 *Provincial Parks Act*, RSO 1990, c. P.34.

73 *Public Lands Act*, RSO 1990, c. P.43.

74 *Beds of Navigable Waters Act*, supra endnote 55.

75 The Ontario Court (Provincial Division) subsequently dismissed these charges on the grounds that Constance Creek was not proven to be "navigable." This dismissal was unsuccessfully appealed by the Crown.

76   Harry Dahme, "Wetlands Protection in Canada," in *Wetlands: Inertia or Momentum?*
     (Toronto: Federation of Ontario Naturalists, 1989). For example, see the Ontario
     Municipal Board's decision in *Re Township of Nepean Restricted Area By-law 73-76*
     (1978), 9 OMBR 36, at 55: "This Board has always maintained that if lands in private
     ownership are to be zoned for conservation or recreational purposes for the benefit of
     the public as a whole, then the appropriate authority must be prepared to acquire the
     lands within a reasonable time otherwise the zoning will not be approved." See also *Re
     South Nation Planning Area Official Plan Amendment 5: Re the Alfred Bog* (1983), 16
     OMBR 262.

77   *Expropriations Act*, RSO 1990, c. E.26.

78   OMB file no. L910042 (March 25, 1992).

79   See Ontario, Environmental Assessment Advisory Committee, *Report No. 38:
     Ganaraska Watershed* (Toronto: the committee, 1989) and Ontario, Environmental
     Assessment Committee, *Report No. 44: Eagle Creek Golf Course* (Toronto: the
     committee, 1991).

80   OMB file nos. 0870039 and R-880461 (August 9, 1989).

81   OMB file nos. 0-890034 and R-880358 (October 11, 1989).

82   OMB file nos. R-890345, R-890639, and 5900003 (August 29, 1990).

83   Environment Canada et al., supra endnote 8, at 3.

84   See Chapter 15 for a fuller discussion of this subject. See also O. Trombetti and K. Cox,
     Land, Law and Wildlife Conservation: Reference Paper No. 3 (Ottawa: Wildlife
     Habitat Canada, 1990), and Wildlife Habitat Canada, *Wildlife Conservation on Private
     Lands* (Ottawa: Wildlife Habitat Canada, 1987).

85   See Simon Valleau, *Loan and Mortgage Assistance in the Prairie: A Conservation
     Perspective.* (Ottawa: Wildlife Habitat Canada, 1989).

86   Great Lakes Wetlands Policy Consortium, supra endnote 10. See also Pauline Lynch-
     Stewart, *No Net Loss: Implementing "No Net Loss" Goals To Conserve Wetlands in
     Canada — Issue Paper No. 1992-2* (Ottawa: North American Wetlands Conservation
     Council, 1992).

87   *Report No. 38*, supra endnote 79. See also Canada, Royal Commission on the Future
     of the Toronto Waterfront, *Planning for Sustainability: Towards Integrating Environ-
     mental Protection into Land Use Planning* (Ottawa: Supply and Services, 1991).

13

Wildlife

CONTENTS

Like wind and sunsets wild things were taken for granted until progress began to
do away with them.

Aldo Leopold

Once, the sky used to be black with ducks everywhere you looked. There
appeared to be no end to their numbers. What a shame to see them go.

Market gunner, with an estimated lifetime kill of 500,000 ducks

---

In 1987, the federal government carried out a survey of the importance of wildlife to
Canadians. Of Ontarians surveyed, over 85 per cent regarded maintaining wildlife in
abundance and protecting endangered species as important. About 85 per cent expressed an
interest in participating in non-consumptive wildlife-related activities compared with 24 per
cent for consumptive activities. Only about 6 per cent of the respondents hunted wildlife, 28
per cent participated in recreational fishing, and less than 1 per cent trapped in that year.[1]
However, existing wildlife legislation primarily addresses traditional harvesting practices
and reflects hunting, fishing, and trapping interests. These laws not only discriminate against
select species; they obstruct protection efforts.

Although this chapter encompasses all wild living species, "wildlife" in the traditional
definition includes only birds and land mammals, while marine mammals are lumped with
fish to reflect their commercial value. This is the manner in which species are treated in the
statutes and regulations.

FEDERAL LEGISLATION

The federal government is responsible for the protection and management of migratory birds
and nationally significant wildlife habitat, for some aspects of endangered species and the
control of international trade in these species, for research on wildlife issues of national
importance, and for educating the public about wildlife.

The Canadian Wildlife Service, a branch of Environment Canada, assumes responsibility
for these concerns under the authority of the *Migratory Birds Convention Act*, the *Canada
Wildlife Act*, and the *Game Export Act*.

Migratory Birds Convention Act

Under the Migratory Birds Convention Treaty of 1916, Canada and the United States agreed
to establish legislation to protect birds migrating through their countries that "are of great
value as a source of food or in destroying insects which are injurious to forests and forage
plants on the public domain, as well as to agricultural crops." The *Migratory Birds
Convention Act*, which was created the following year to fulfil Canada's obligation, contains
specifications agreed upon by both countries.

Species protected under the Act are listed as migratory game birds, migratory insectivorous birds, or other migratory non-game birds, and are confined to those that "are either useful

to man or harmless."[2] Other migratory birds such as raptors, upland game birds, jays, crows, blackbirds, kingfishers, pelicans, cormorants, and introduced species receive no protection.[3] The failure of the Act to protect raptors is of particular concern in the light of evidence that they are picking up high loadings of pesticides in Central America.

The Act prohibits the hunting of non-game and insectivorous migratory birds, but makes provision for some hunting by native people and for scientific study.[4] Migratory game birds can be hunted during the open seasons established in the regulations under the Act. Nests and eggs of all three categories of birds cannot be taken unless the removal is authorized for scientific or propagation purposes.

The number of game birds that can be taken during the open season is specified in the regulations. So is the manner of hunting allowed, not just for the three defined groups of birds but for all migratory birds, including the ones that are either not "useful" or "harmless." The Act is enforced primarily by the Ontario Ministry of Natural Resources.

Permits may be issued that authorize exceptions to the regulations. For example, farmers may be allowed to shoot birds to protect their crops, as long as they do not ship or sell them. However, such permits should only be issued to kill birds that "under extraordinary conditions, may become seriously injurious to the agricultural or other interests in any particular community."[5] Individuals may also obtain a permit to keep species for avicultural purposes, as long as they submit reports and do not release them into the wild.

The Act also allows the minister to make regulations that prescribe areas for the management of migratory birds.[6] There are 13 sanctuaries in Ontario, consisting of land and water mostly under Crown ownership.[7] Migratory bird sanctuaries were established to protect migratory birds. Hunting, the possession of firearms or other hunting devices, and the disturbance of migratory birds or their nests or eggs are prohibited within sanctuary boundaries. Permits may be issued to allow the use of firearms for predator control.

People caught buying, selling, shipping, or possessing any of the birds defined under the Act or any of their parts, eggs, or nest during the closed season without a permit are committing an offence.[8] The fine for contravening the Act or its regulations ranges from $10 to $300 or imprisonment for a maximum of six months or both.[9] Although most other fines for environmental offences under federal and provincial laws have been raised dramatically in recent years, the fines under this Act remain at levels that have long been rendered meaningless by decades of inflation. The reason for the inadequate fines lies in the failure of longstanding efforts by the federal government, in cooperation with the provinces, to update this Act. Revisions to the Act have been under consideration for at least a decade, but the stumbling block has been the resolution of native issues. Progress is unlikely until native hunting and fishing rights, which may conflict with wildlife preservation programs, are clarified.

The *Migratory Birds Convention Act* was designed to protect birds and not habitat. Accordingly, the *Canada Wildlife Act* was enacted to allow the acquisition of land for this purpose.[10]

Canada Wildlife Act

The *Canada Wildlife Act* was passed in 1973, giving the minister of the environment responsibility to undertake public education and research programs on wildlife conservation and interpretation, and to coordinate and implement wildlife policies.[11]

In the Act, provisions respecting wildlife apply to wildlife habitat as well.[12] The Act defines wildlife as "any non-domestic animal."[13] The minister has the authority to acquire and manage habitats for migratory birds or, with the approval of the provinces or territories, for "other wildlife."[14] The minister may enter into agreements with provinces, municipalities, organizations, or individuals to carry out its programs or manage land.[15]

In 1966 the National Wildlife Area Program was initiated to allow the acquisition of areas either used by large concentrations of migratory birds or with critical or unique habitat. The primary objective of the program is to preserve or increase the value of these areas to wildlife. Ontario has 10 national wildlife areas.[16] Combined with migratory bird sanctuaries, they cover 44,300 hectares of the province.[17] Permitted activities, such as hunting and fishing, are specified in the regulations.

Under the *Canada Wildlife Act*, the minister, in cooperation with the province, may also "take such measures as the Minister deems necessary for the protection of any species of wildlife in danger of extinction." There is no federal endangered species statute to address these concerns. However, the federal Green Plan suggested that such an act should be considered for Canada. Given the limited jurisdiction of the federal government in this area, such a statute would have to be drafted very carefully to avoid overlap with provincial statutes and subsequent confusion. Conservative members of Parliament introduced a private member's bill, the *Endangered Species and Biological Diversity Act*, as Bill C-303 on October 2, 1991.

Those who contravene the Act or regulations are guilty of an offence punishable on summary conviction.[18] Under the *Criminal Code*, any summary conviction offence for which a statute does not specify a penalty is subject to a fine of up to $2,000 and six months' imprisonment.[19]

In fulfilling its role, the Canadian Wildlife Service carries out a number of scientific projects such as conducting environmental impact studies, researching the effects of pollutants on wildlife, cooperating with Latin America on migratory bird programs, developing more humane trapping systems, and coordinating volunteers in the Breeding Bird Atlas Program. Over half of the service's budget goes to non-game programs. The Canadian Wildlife Service is also responsible for the *Game Export Act*.

Game Export Act and Wild Animal and Plant Protection Act

The *Game Export Act*, first enacted in 1941, prohibits persons from knowingly taking or shipping game across provincial boundaries, or possessing or receiving game for this purpose, without an export permit issued under the laws of that province.[20] The Act gives provincial governments the power to issue such permits, but the provinces are under no obligation to use the Act. Those that do use the Act must accept responsibility for issuing permits and providing enforcement. In Ontario, the Ministry of Natural Resources assumes this role.[21]

Under the Act, "game" includes the carcass or part of the carcass of a wild animal or bird, or a domestically raised fur-bearing animal.[22] Those who contravene the Act are liable to a fine ranging between $10 and $1,000 or, in default of payment, maximum imprisonment of one year. The fine may be computed for each article of game involved.[23]

The *Game Export Act* was replaced by a new federal *Wild Animal and Plant Protection and Regulation of International and Interprovincial Trade Act* of 1992,[24] but as of May 1993 the new Act had not been proclaimed in force. The new Act will prohibit the export or interprovincial transport of listed plants and animals or their products without a permit. It will also prohibit the importation of plants and animals into Canada if their export violates the laws of the country from which they came. Penalties will be increased to fines of up to $150,000 and up to five years in jail.

Customs Tariff Act

The *Customs Tariff Act* was enacted in 1867 and is administered by Revenue Canada. It deals with the imposition of duties of customs and other charges. Among the goods that may not be imported into Canada are "live specimens of the mongoose family," "any non-game bird," and the parts and skins "of wild birds, either raw or manufactured."

There are exceptions, however. Dead birds of the starling family and a few live species, domestic birds used for food, and birds used solely for a public zoo or public entertainment may be imported. Also allowed are the feathers of ostriches, English pheasants, Indian peacocks, birds imported alive, and wild game birds that have an open season in Canada. Wild birds may also be imported as museum specimens or for scientific or educational purposes, in accordance with regulations made by the minister.[25]

Export and Import Permits Act

The *Export and Import Permits Act*, enacted in 1947, authorizes the federal Cabinet to establish lists of goods that may not be imported or exported without a permit issued under the Act.[26] Among the prohibited goods on the export control list are the species, or derivatives thereof, covered by the Convention on International Trade in Endangered Species (discussed below).[27]

The maximum penalty for exporting or attempting to export a prohibited good is $25,000 or five years in jail or both.[28] Since the maximum fine is too low to protect species such as falcons that may be worth $80,000 to a poacher, the courts may impose jail terms to compensate.[29]

National Parks Act

The *National Parks Act* was created in 1930. Under the Act, the first priority when drawing up a park management plan is the "maintenance of ecological integrity through the protection of natural resources."[30] According to the Act, the minister should allow opportunities for public participation in the development of parks policy and management plans.[31] There are five national parks in Ontario, which together comprise 217,080 hectares.

The governor in council may make regulations for "the preservation, control and management of the parks" and the protection of such features as fauna, flora, soil, waters, and air quality; but may also allow the harvesting of resources or the "destruction or removal of dangerous or superabundant fauna."[32]

Parks may be declared wilderness areas where activities "likely to impair the wilderness character of the area" are prohibited. Nonetheless, this does not stop the minister from authorizing such activities for the purposes of administration, public safety and facilities such as trails or campsites, or traditional renewable resource harvesting activities.[33]

It is an offence to hunt, disturb, confine, or possess threatened or protected species in national parks.[34] Under the Act, threatened species are specifically listed and include bighorn sheep, Dall's sheep, grizzly bear, gyrfalcon, mountain goat, peregrine falcon, piping plover, polar bear, and whooping crane. Protected species include American bison, American elk, Atlantic salmon, black bear, caribou, cougar, moose, mule deer, white-tailed deer, and wolf.[35] A number of these species are certainly not rare, and many species that are recognized as endangered, threatened, or rare by the Committee on the Status of Endangered Wildlife in Canada (discussed below) are absent from the list.

As the wildlife occurring in legal hunting areas dwindle through overharvesting and habitat destruction, national parks have become the last easily accessible strongholds for exceptional animals. For example, Rocky Mountain bighorn sheep, elk, and grizzlies rank high on poachers' lists and the Canadian West is one of the last areas where all three species can be found in abundance.

Until recently, the fines for poaching in national parks were ludicrous — a maximum of $500. The shortage of staff to patrol the parks and a lack of arms or aircraft to assist them provided further incentive for poachers. To compensate for ineffective legislation, park officials in Jasper National Park began marking bighorn sheep of trophy status near highways with identification brands to discourage poaching.[36]

In 1988, the fines were increased. A maximum fine of $150,000 or six months' imprisonment, or both, can be imposed in the case of a threatened species.[37] This is a more reasonable fine, considering that poachers may get as much as $20,000 for a bighorn sheep.[38] In the case of a protected species, the possible prison sentence is the same but the maximum fine is only $10,000.[39]

Fisheries Act

The federal government's powers to protect fish species come under the authority of the *Fisheries Act*. The Department of Fisheries and Oceans is responsible for all Canadian fisheries through the administration of the Act, which was first enacted in 1868. The department manages the fisheries of not only transboundary and international locations, but also the whole or part of provinces with marine waters. The provincial Ministry of Natural Resources administers the federal legislation in Ontario, although regulations must still be promulgated by the federal government.[40]

Under the Act, fish are defined as "shellfish, crustaceans, marine animals and the eggs, spawn, spat, and juvenile stages of fish, shellfish, crustaceans and marine animals," and include fish parts. Fishing is any method of "catching or attempting to catch fish," and "fishery" describes the area in which fish are being caught.[41]

The Act prohibits fishing without a licence, and makes regulations that allow for the issuance of fish licences and that establish open seasons for angling and commercial fishing.[42]

Also prohibited is "any work or undertaking that results in the harmful alteration, disruption or destruction of fish habitat" except under the authority of the minister or under regulations made by the governor in council.[43] Included as fish habitat are "spawning grounds and nursery, rearing, food supply and migration areas."[44] In a case brought before a court in 1990, a Prince Edward Island Provincial Court judge actually dismissed charges of harmful alteration of fish habitat on the grounds that the site did not contain all five elements of fish habitat. In a subsequent trial, it was held that one element was sufficient to constitute fish habitat.[45] The interpretation of the definition of fish habitat is, as a result, extremely broad, and provides one of the most powerful available tools in Ontario for the protection of aquatic ecosystems.

It is also illegal to discharge any substance into water where it is likely to be deleterious to fish or fish habitat or to human use of fish, without authorization in regulations made by Cabinet.[46] Fish may not be left to decay in nets or on the shore.[47]

The minister can request plans describing work that may alter, disrupt or destroy fish or fish habitat that include prevention or mitigation proposals; and may approve the work under certain conditions, or restrict the operation of the work.[48] Mitigation proposals that may be accepted by the ministry are currently considered to include the creation of potential, new fish habitat as compensation for the destruction or modification of actual, existing fish habitat. This type of negotiable flexibility, while administratively desirable, has the potential for abuse.

Penalties for contravening the Act are high. The maximum penalty for general fishing offences is $500,000, with a possible two years' imprisonment for subsequent offences.[49] Penalties for damaging fish habitat can run up to $1 million, with up to three years' imprisonment for subsequent offences.[50] These penalties reflect major increases in fine levels made law in 1991. Each day an offence continues constitutes a separate offence.[51]

FEDERAL POLICIES AND SELECT PROGRAMS

Wildlife Policy for Canada

In 1990, the Wildlife Ministers' Council of Canada adopted a wildlife policy for Canada. This policy was developed from the 1982 guidelines for a wildlife policy, using recommendations from federal, provincial, and territorial governments, as well as aboriginal organizations, wildlife professionals, non-governmental groups, and the general public. It provides a framework to assist in the development of policies, programs and legislation affecting wildlife. It is a statement of intent or philosophy that is supposed to guide actions. However, there are no mechanisms to ensure compliance with it, other than public pressures.

The policy takes an ecosystem approach, broadening its scope beyond that of existing policies. It defines wildlife as "all wild organisms and their habitats — including wild plants, invertebrates, and microorganisms, as well as fishes, amphibians, reptiles, and the birds and mammals traditionally regarded as wildlife."

The goal of the policy is to maintain or enhance wildlife "for its own sake," as well as for people. The maintenance and restoration of ecological processes and biodiversity (number of species and number of animals within a species), and the sustainable use of wildlife are the prerequisites to achieving this goal.[52]

Fish Habitat Management Policy

The Department of Fisheries and Oceans adopted a fish management policy in 1986. It has been described as "the first national example of a workable environmentally sustainable approach to resource management in Canada" that "helps to fulfill Canada's commitment to the United Nations' World Conservation Strategy."

The Department of Fisheries and Oceans concentrates its application of the policy on sites where habitat damage has already occurred or has the greatest risk of occurring. It does not actively do so in areas like Ontario that it does not directly manage, but encourages the application of the policy by provincial agencies through agreements and protocols.

The objective of this policy is to achieve an overall *net gain* in the productive capacity of fish habitats through the conservation of the existing productive capacity of habitats, the restoration of damaged habitats, and the development of habitats. The policy sets out strategies for achieving its goals.[53]

North American Waterfowl Management Plan and RAMSAR Convention

In 1986, Canada and the United States signed a North American waterfowl management plan agreement to address the serious decline in numbers of ducks, swans, and geese. Conservation groups and government agencies of both countries are sharing the cost of wetland protection and enhancement ($1.5 billion).[54] However, Ducks Unlimited, a non-government organization, played a central role in conceiving this plan and pushing government to implement it, and has committed over $300 million to carrying it out. Over 90 per cent of the funding comes from the United States.

The RAMSAR Convention is an international program that came about in 1975 with the objective of designating and protecting globally important wetlands, especially those important to waterfowl. Canada became involved in 1981, and by 1988 had designated 30 sites, with 5 in Ontario — the largest total area (2,449,528 hectares) committed out of the 60 member countries. The Canadian Wildlife Service is responsible for selecting the sites and ensuring that adequate legislative protection is provided. The convention places one restriction on these areas: "Permitted activities should not alter or destroy the ecological character of the wetland."[55] This convention merely gives a higher profile to wetlands that are already protected by giving them international recognition. It does not protect any additional areas, and it is questionable whether existing protected areas are given any additional protection.

Wildlife Habitat Canada

In 1985, the federal government created Wildlife Habitat Canada, an autonomous body, to assist non-governmental organizations in habitat conservation activities such as habitat acquisition and research on topics such as federal subsidies that tend to promote destruction of wildlife habitat — for example, drainage programs. This agency also produces periodic reports on the status of wildlife habitat in Canada. Much of the funding is generated through the sale of wildlife habitat stamps. These stamps are required to hunt migratory game birds, but they are also purchased by non-hunters to support conservation.[56]

COSEWIC, RENEW, and CITES

The Federal-Provincial Wildlife Conference coordinates national wildlife conservation efforts and is composed of federal, provincial, and territorial governments as well as several non-governmental organizations. In 1976, a standing committee of this body was formed called the Committee on the Status of Endangered Wildlife in Canada (COSEWIC) to assume responsibility for determining the status of species for all of Canada.

When a species is suspected of being in danger, and if funding permits, COSEWIC commissions a status report by an expert. The committee uses this report to decide whether to assign the species to one of five categories: vulnerable, threatened, endangered, extirpated, or extinct.[57] Among the types of species considered are mammals, birds, reptiles, amphibians, fish, and plants. By 1991, there were 211 species on the list, including 45 with endangered status. In fact, the list is missing many species that are widely recognized as being at risk, primarily because of the stringent technical requirements for individual status reports. Habitat destruction is the main reason for the growing list.[58]

COSEWIC has no regulatory powers and no authority to make recommendations regarding wildlife conservation. Furthermore, provincial agencies are not required to adopt the status designations, or to regulate such species under provincial legislation. However, species that are listed by COSEWIC as endangered become the focus of conservation efforts by both government, and non-governmental organizations such as World Wildlife Fund Canada, a member of COSEWIC and RENEW (discussed below) that has provided funds for most of the status reports.

Recovery of Nationally Endangered Wildlife (RENEW) is a joint federal-provincial government program that involves government and non-government agencies in the development of recovery plans for species on COSEWIC's list. Responsibilities include not only raising individuals in captivity and introducing them into the wild, but also controlling human impact on the species' natural habitat. The goal is to complete recovery plans for 28 species by 1992, using the coordinated efforts of government, non-government organizations, corporations, and private individuals.[59]

The Convention on International Trade in Endangered Species of Wild Flora and Fauna (CITES) regulates international trade in over 15,000 species of plants and animals and their raw or manufactured parts worldwide. It is directed at species that are actually endangered through world trade. Illegal trade has almost eliminated some species and is threatening others. The Canadian Wildlife Service is responsible for implementing CITES in Canada and has a lead role in RENEW as well as COSEWIC.[60]

PROVINCIAL LEGISLATION

Game and Fish Act

The *Game and Fish Act* was re-enacted in 1907, consolidated from two statutes dating back to 1885. It is administered by the Ontario Ministry of Natural Resources to provide "for the management, perpetuation and rehabilitation of the wildlife resources in Ontario, and to establish and maintain a maximum wildlife population consistent with all other proper uses of lands and waters."[61] The Act authorizes the provincial government to acquire land or enter into agreements with landowners to create wildlife management areas to carry out this responsibility.[62]

The stated purpose is broad, but the main role of the *Game and Fish Act* is the control of hunting, trapping, and fishing, which were the concerns during the period when it was formulated. Species that are "protected" by the Act are the ones that are targeted in these activities, and no discrimination among common or rare species is made. Land acquired under the Act is generally intended for harvesting purposes. All but 15 (809,120 hectares) of the 121 Crown game preserves have now been rescinded because they never really served as preserves, and almost all 34 wildlife management areas (36,950 hectares) provide hunting opportunities.[63]

The Act includes game animals, fur-bearers, game birds, and any part of them in the definition of the species it regulates. Large game animals with an open season in Ontario are white-tailed deer, moose, and black bear. Licences are also available to hunt smaller game like native rabbit, hare, and non-native squirrel.

Fur-bearers include wolf, coyote, fox, opossum, raccoon, skunk and weasel, which can be hunted with a small game licence to hunt; and badger, beaver, bobcat, fisher, lynx, marten, mink, muskrat, otter, red squirrel, and wolverine, which require a licence to trap. The trapping licence allows both hunting and trapping of fur-bearers. The distinction between fur-bearers merely reflects traditional practices.

Wild turkey, pheasant, ruffed grouse, sharp-tailed grouse, spruce grouse, ptarmigan, Hungarian partridge, and bobwhite quail are non-migratory birds that can be hunted with a small game licence. Also included in the definition of game birds are those protected under the *Migratory Birds Convention Act*. Migratory game bird hunting requires, in addition to the small game licence, a migratory game bird hunting permit and a wildlife habitat conservation stamp, to comply with the *Migratory Birds Convention Act*.

Licences are also required to hunt, possess, sell, or buy some reptiles and amphibians, but only those species defined under the Act. Included are 10 species of snakes, all native turtles, and one species each of toad, frog, and salamander. Only bullfrogs and snapping turtles have an open season.[64]

The *Game and Fish Act* does not include domestic animals and birds, which are defined as "any non-native species kept in captivity, except pheasants, and any fur-bearing animals kept on a fur farm, as defined in the *Fur Farms Act*." The *Game and Fish Act* states, however, that it does include "native species otherwise kept in captivity or non-native species present in the wild state."[65]

The Act defines hunting not only as capturing, injuring, or killing but also as "chasing, pursuing, following after or on the trail of, searching for, shooting, shooting at, stalking or lying in wait for, worrying, molesting."[66] This means that a licence is required to subject a species defined under the Act to any of these activities.

Hunting is controlled through the use of site-specific licences that restrict the kind of species, quota, date, time, and mode of hunting. The designated hunting area may be Crown land, or private land where permission is granted.[67] Regulations may be made to provide for hunting in provincial parks.[68]

The use of aircraft in hunting, even for spotting wildlife, is prohibited, unless provided for in the regulations.[69] It is illegal to hunt at night or with the use of beams of light.[70] Revolvers, pistols, and fully automatic weapons are prohibited, as is the use of poison.[71] Body-gripping or leg-hold traps can be used to trap fur-bearers, but are otherwise illegal unless they are designated by the minister as a humane trap.[72]

The Act makes it an offence to allow the pelt of any fur-bearer or the flesh of an animal, bird, or fish that is suitable for food to be destroyed or spoiled.[73] The holder of a licence is entitled to sell the meat of bear, beaver, muskrat, and raccoon, if the animal was legally acquired.[74]

The minister can issue a permit to allow the transport in Ontario or export of any game, dead or alive, that has been lawfully taken.[75] The Act also allows the importation of a game species into Ontario if it was legally captured, but prohibits the release of any imported birds or animals, or their offspring without written permission from the minister.[76] Once released under these terms, such birds, other than pheasants and Hungarian partridge, can be hunted at any time of the year.[77]

Licences are required to keep live game or a wolf in captivity for more than 10 days, except in the case of a zoo operated by a municipality or for scientific or educational purposes in a public institution.[78]

Most legislation directed at fish is covered by the federal *Fisheries Act*. Under the Act, the sale, purchase, or possession of fish or fish parts or eggs taken from Ontario waters during the closed season is prohibited. Licences are issued to allow the ownership or operation of a fishing preserve, and the sale and rearing of certain species of fish. Some species require a commercial fishing licence. The Act also controls the possession and sale of fish nets.[79]

The general penalty for any offence committed against the *Game and Fish Act* was increased in 1989 from $5,000 to $25,000.[80] Careless use of a firearm carries the same fine or a maximum prison term of one year, or both.[81] The Act also gives conservation officers extensive powers to search vehicles and vessels, and to confiscate guns, boots, cars, trucks, and other vehicles used in the course of violating the Act.

Although few statistics are available on poaching, it is believed to be a significant problem in Ontario. In 1986, an investigation revealed an operation that sold 60 deer in a single season. The cargo of the Air India jet that crashed in 1985 after leaving Toronto included gall bladders from about 1,000 black bears valued at $1 million. It is highly unlikely that the animals were legally taken.[82]

The Act contains insufficient penalties, a flaw that is enhanced by inadequate enforcement. Another fault lies in the exceptions. For example, any landowner has the right to take or destroy an animal if it is damaging or destroying his or her property, provided that the animal is not a caribou, deer, elk, moose, or a species protected under the *Endangered Species Act* and that no unnecessary suffering is inflicted.[83] Farmers are entitled to hunt and trap on their lands during the open season without a licence.[84] They are allowed to use body-gripping or leg-hold traps, and can also use vehicles or vessels to harass, chase, injure, or kill the animal or bird.[85]

The Act discriminates against unpopular species. For example, no licence is needed to hunt crows, cowbirds, blackbirds, starlings, or house sparrows, or to destroy the den of a fox or a skunk. At night, a licence holder can hunt raccoons with a licensed dog using non-vehicular lights; or chase fox, coyote, or wolf, as long as they do not capture or kill the animal.[86] Black bears can be hunted in the spring as well as the fall, provided that cubs or females with them are not killed.[87]

Skunk, coyote, and timber wolf have no closed season and there is no limit to the number of kills.[88] Ontario is one of the few provinces with no closed season on wolves. It may have the highest rate of kills each year, estimated at one in five wolves.[89] They are also being killed through the predator control program of the Ministry of Natural Resources.

The provincial bounty on wolves in Ontario existed from 1793 to 1972. The municipal bounty was not removed until 1980 with the passing of regulation 242/80, which declared wolves and coyotes "fur-bearing animals," giving them protected status under the *Game and Fish Act*.[90] Bounties are now known to be generally ineffective at controlling population numbers.[91]

Although the payment of bounties became illegal, some municipalities continued the practice unimpeded until nine years later when the ministers of natural resources and municipal affairs declared a termination date after which legal action would be taken.[92] One county still pays a bounty on coyotes and two pay bounties on foxes. Several others are attempting to reinstate bounties.[93]

Attempts at updating the *Game and Fish Act* in a piecemeal fashion can prove grossly ineffective. For example, concern was raised regarding the use of leg-hold traps on predatory birds attacking wildlife in farms or sanctuaries. In 1989, regulation 136/89 was made, prohibiting the practice without permission of the minister. However, the regulation does little to protect the birds when the legal alternative under the Act is to shoot them.[94]

The Act also suffers from confusing and contradictory statements that stem from the combined effects of its pre-Confederation roots and frequent amendments. In a case decided by the Ontario Supreme Court in 1987, such deficiencies were put to the test and an important legal precedent was set.

The case involved the African Lion Safari and Game Farm Limited, accused by the Ministry of Natural Resources of keeping live game without a licence. Confusion arose over whether the raptors kept by the organization were actually "game birds" under the *Game and Fish Act*. The Act prohibits the hunting of raptors,[95] which leaves them "protected by this Act," thereby fulfilling the definition of a game bird.[96] However, a subsequent section of the Act implies that all game birds have a hunting season. Historical analysis led the court to decide in favour of the second interpretation, that birds with no hunting season are not game birds. A licence was not required to keep the raptors.

However, even if they were considered game, no licence was needed. The raptors had originated from outside Ontario and the Act states that nothing can prevent the possession of imported game if it was legally taken.[97] The case set a harmful precedent that led to the legal possession of indigenous species without a licence. This opened the door to the captivity of wild native species in zoos, where there is no legislation to protect them.

Practically anyone can open a zoo, and there is virtually no restriction on the type or source of the species or the conditions of confinement, and no minimum qualification for the zoo keeper. There is currently no licensing system controlling the operation of zoos. The Canadian Association of Zoological Parks and Aquariums has recommended standards but, without legislative backing, zoo operators have little incentive to meet these guidelines.[98]

The rationale behind the existence of zoos is being questioned, and some countries have in place or are considering legislation that will greatly reduce or eliminate zoos and aquariums.[99] There are organizations that disagree with spending extensive funds on operating a zoo when the species' habitat is being destroyed, while others believe that zoos are needed to generate public interest in habitat preservation.

Although there are few restrictions when it comes to running zoos, strong legislation can be used against citizens who rescue wildlife in distress. Rehabilitators of species defined in the *Migratory Birds Convention Act* and the *Game and Fish Act* are committing an offence if they lack a permit issued under the authority of these Acts.

Existing laws are out of date and no new legislation has been passed to cover wildlife rehabilitation. In response, the Canadian Wildlife Service issues scientific migratory bird permits and the Ministry of Natural Resources turns a blind eye; but this does not remedy the situation. Lack of legislation means an absence of standards for the care and release of wildlife. A licensing system is vital to ensure proper feeding and minimal imprinting. Legalization of this activity will also remove the barrier to government funding.[100]

Bill 162, *An Act To Amend the Game and Fish Act*, received first reading in November 1991, but as of May 1993 it had not yet received second reading. The proposed Act applies to all mammals, birds, reptiles, amphibians, fish, and invertebrates found in the province, regardless of their place of origin. Non-game animals are generally protected, although taking or killing is still permitted in defence of property. Provisions are made for regulations that declare a non-native species "undesirable." Also proposed are regulations for the use of captive wildlife in game farming, falconry, sporting dog training and trialing, zoos and displays, and wildlife rehabilitation. Once the bill is passed, the Act will be renamed the *Wildlife and Fish Act*.[101]

Fur Farms Act

The Ministry of Agriculture and Food administers the *Fur Farms Act*, enacted in 1971. Under the Act, licences are issued for the raising of fur-bearers.[102] Over 99 per cent of the animals bred on fur farms are mink and fox.[103] Fur farm animals are excluded from the *Game and Fish Act*. Hunting or trapping of fur-bearers for the purposes of transfer to a fur farm requires written authority from the minister under the *Game and Fish Act*.[104]

To comply with the conditions of the licence, operators must ensure that the animal's premises are kept clean, that measures are taken to prevent cruelty or neglect, and that the enclosures are properly constructed and maintained to prevent escape or entry.[105] Fines for contravening the Act or regulations were increased in 1990 to a maximum of $2,000 for a first offence and $5,000 for subsequent offences.[106]

The farming of indigenous species other than fur-bearers defined under the *Fur Farms Act* was illegal until the *African Lion Safari* case. The decision not only broadened the scope of farming indigenous species, but also increased associated threats. Such farms can transmit disease or genetic variation to wild populations,[107] and may also lead to decreased appreciation of wildlife in its natural habitat. Furthermore, if the meat is sold and becomes popular, increased poaching follows. The farming of non-indigenous species carries its own hazards. The ecological and economic disasters that result when escapees outcompete native species have been well documented all over the world. There are more than 100 game farms in Ontario, and interest in game farming is growing.[108]

Endangered Species Act

The *Endangered Species Act*, which was also enacted in 1971, is administered by the Ministry of Natural Resources. Under the Act's regulations species are declared to be endangered (threatened with extinction). The Act prohibits persons from wilfully killing, injuring, taking, or interfering with any of these species or their habitat.[109]

To determine the status of species in Ontario, the province considers relevant sections of COSEWIC reports and commissions its own studies. As of 1992, there were 19 species regulated under the Act, including 1 mammal, 7 birds, 4 reptiles, 2 insects, and 6 plants.[110] Of these, at least 2 species are already extirpated from Ontario. The Act does not require that endangered species be identified or that recovery plans be established.[111]

Species that may be approaching endangered status are classed as threatened (likely to become endangered) or rare (small, but relatively stable populations); there are also lists of species of concern. No protection exists for these species or their habitat, either under authority of the Act or in policies or guidelines. This is a serious flaw, considering the slow process involved in declaring a species as endangered.

Updating the regulations has proven to be a very slow process, creating a list of questionable accuracy and unquestionable incompleteness. Because non-statutory procedures have been adopted that require extremely detailed status reports and acceptance of the regulation by affected landowners, very few species are even considered for regulation. As a result, non-government lists of rare, threatened, and endangered species are often considered by professionals and the interested public to have more credibility.

Even species declared as endangered under the Act are not assured of protection. The maximum penalty increased in 1989 to $50,000 or imprisonment of up to two years or both.[112] It is still unlikely to provide sufficient deterrence to land developers, for example, who can reap profits much larger than the maximum fine by destroying habitat — that is, if the prosecution stage is ever reached. The Act is seldom used because of the need to demonstrate wilful intent. It has also failed to prevent the use of the endangered peregrine falcon in falconry, because the activity is interpreted as possession rather than "taking." In fact, only four cases have been brought to court under the Act since it was proclaimed, and one of these was thrown out.[113]

The latter case involved a golden eagle that was captured in a leg-hold trap within the Jack Miner Bird Sanctuary. It was brought to court in 1987 by the Ontario Ministry of Natural Resources, but the charge was later dropped because the provincial *Jack Miner Act* of 1936 predated the *Endangered Species Act* and therefore took precedence. Under the *Jack Miner Act*, the trappers were allowed to "feed, shelter, protect and defend migratory ducks and geese," and the eagle had been attacking geese in the sanctuary. The Act was written at a time when Canada geese were a threatened species.[114] This case is a good example of the potential conflicts that can result from outdated wildlife legislation.

Provincial Parks Act

The *Provincial Parks Act* provides for the establishment and management of provincial parks and is administered by the Ministry of Natural Resources. It is discussed in detail in Chapter 11. Ontario has 261 regulated provincial parks (covering 6,328,407 hectares) and the degree of protection provided by the parks system varies, depending on its classification. Regulations permitting hunting in provincial parks are made under the *Game and Fish Act*.[115] The penalty for contravening the Act was increased from $500 to $5,000 in 1989.

Wilderness Areas Act

Under the *Wilderness Areas Act*, which was enacted in 1959 and is administered by the Ministry of Natural Resources, the lieutenant governor in council can establish wilderness areas to preserve land "as nearly as may be in its natural state." There are 37 such areas in Ontario (covering 61,800 hectares). The minister can take measures to protect the fish, animals, and birds, and regulations may be made respecting management and use. However, the Act or regulations cannot "limit or affect the development or utilization of the natural resources" for areas larger than 260 hectares. Contravention of the Act carries a maximum fine of $500.[116]

Legislation for Plants

Unlike adjacent US jurisdictions, Ontario has no wildflower protection legislation. Even the provincial flower, the white trillium, lacks official protection through legislation. Laws regarding plant life came about for the same reason as those for animal life. Accordingly, the existing statutes focus primarily on the forest industry and the economic management of trees. These Acts are administered by the Ministry of Natural Resources.

The *Forestry Act* and the *Woodlands Improvement Act* allow the minister to enter into agreements with landowners to manage forest lands or establish private forest reserves. The *Crown Timber Act* enables the minister to grant licences to cut Crown timber and to enter into agreements with the forest industry to ensure a sustained yield basis of management, or to form Crown management units that have agreements for the supply of Crown timber. The *Forest Tree Pest Control Act* provides for the control of outbreaks of forest tree pests and disease. Finally, the *Trees Act* and the *Municipal Act* enable the passing of bylaws that control the destruction of trees.[117]

The *Trees Act* was originally passed in 1946 to address concerns regarding extensive clearcutting. Counties, regional municipalities, and municipalities separated from counties were given authority to pass bylaws. When this chapter was written, the Act was undergoing changes to address such deficiencies as the limited focus, inadequate fines, and the exclusion of local municipalities. The proposed amendments would enable lower-tier municipalities to pass bylaws to control tree cutting on lands ranging from individual properties to development sites and areas bought for clearcutting. However, passing these bylaws remains optional.[118]

The Class Environmental Assessment for Timber Management began in 1988 and was still proceeding at the time of writing this chapter. It is expected to result in the restoration of degraded ecosystems and increased integration of wildlife and habitat needs with forest management practices.[119]

Another species that has received legislative attention is wild rice. The *Wild Rice Harvesting Act* prohibits the harvesting of wild rice on Crown land without a licence.[120]

Plants and other species may be protected through park legislation or a designation under the *Endangered Species Act*. Protection may also be provided through statutes or policies that are directed at habitat such as fish habitat or wetlands. (See Chapter 12 on wetlands.)

Conservation Land Act

The *Conservation Land Act*, enacted in 1987, enables programs "to recognize, encourage and support the stewardship of conservation land." The only program implemented to date is the Conservation Land Tax Reduction Program, which offers 100 per cent rebates of property taxes for defined conservation lands: provincially significant areas of natural and scientific interest, class 1, 2, and 3 wetlands, Niagara Escarpment natural lands, non-revenue-producing conservation authority lands; and other conservation lands owned by non-profit organizations.

In 1990, over $1,400,000 in rebates were provided for 4,300 properties. This innovative program has attracted considerable international attention.

PROVINCIAL PROGRAMS AND NON-GOVERNMENTAL INVOLVEMENT

A "Wild Life" Strategy for Ontario

As yet, there is no provincial wildlife policy. In 1991, the Ontario Wildlife Working Group, appointed by the Ministry of Natural Resources, released "A Wild Life Strategy," containing input from ministry staff and various interest groups.

The goal of the strategy is "a diversity of healthy ecosystems and associated wild life populations and habitats that provide sustained social, cultural and economic benefits for all people." The objectives are to maintain biodiversity, to rehabilitate degraded ecosystems, and to treat "wild life" responsibly with an appreciation of healthy ecosystems.

The guiding concepts used in developing the strategy refer to limiting the use of "wild life" to species with self-sustaining populations; including humans as part of the ecosystem; prohibiting the placing of "wild life" in artificial environments, with few exceptions; and controlling the conditions of "wild life" in captivity.

A fundamental breakthrough of the strategy is its adoption of a new definition for wildlife that includes all wild organisms. This is consistent with the federal wildlife policy. The province has gone so far as to change the spelling to "wild life" (two words), to emphasize the new definition. More important, it has included a definition for native wildlife, as species indigenous to Ontario, as well as their progeny, and any individuals brought in from outside the province.

Bill 162, *An Act To Amend the Game and Fish Act*, discussed earlier, is a step in this direction, incorporating many of the recommendations in the strategy. But certain key elements, such as plant and habitat protection, have not been resolved at this stage in the Act's amendments.

The Ministry of Natural Resources, like the federal government, is involved in COSEWIC, RENEW, and CITES. The ministry has non-game programs such as rare and endangered species mapping, rabies research, habitat inventories, species recovery plans, and population monitoring. It supports community participation through the Breeding Bird Atlas Program, the Ontario Rare Breeding Bird Program, the Stewardship Program, the Community Wildlife Involvement Program (CWIP), and the Community Fisheries Involvement Program (CFIP). Ministry programs may also involve cooperation with industry, for example, in the modification of forest policy to accommodate wildlife.

The Ministry of Natural Resources has also identified areas of natural and scientific interest (ANSIs) to protect significant natural heritage areas outside the park system. Although the lack of consistent funding or a policy statement hinders this program, significant achievements have been made in protecting the present state of 600 ANSIs.

To date, most of the ANSIs have been identified on private lands across southern Ontario. The ministry has been very slow in identifying ANSIs on Crown lands, where their identification may logically lead to constraints on resource extraction activities on public lands. Most of the progress has been made through inventory and communication of ANSI values, the incorporation of ANSIs into municipal official plans, and private landowner stewardship awards and tax rebates. The identification of ANSIs has also focused conservation efforts on many of the most significant natural areas across Ontario and conserved extensive areas of wildlife habitat.

Municipal Involvement

Municipal animal control centres respond to public complaints concerning wild animals and birds. The practices adopted to deal with this problem vary considerably. Even within the boundaries of Metropolitan Toronto, municipal governments have widely divergent policies. One offers a comprehensive program of trapping, sheltering (for deworming and rabies shots), and release outside the city. Another simply kills the animals.

The *Planning Act* has profound effects on wildlife habitat in Ontario. Land-use planning is the largest "ecological experiment" going on in Ontario today — and it is an experiment without "controls" or "conclusions." A municipal official plan may include "nature" as part of the preservation of open space. Many municipalities now have environmentally sensitive areas, environmental policies, and environmental and ecological advisory committees incorporated into their official plans.[121]

In 1991, a commission was appointed to reform planning and development in Ontario and produce a final report after two years. A new outlook was adopted that would consider environmental impacts on future generations, and would promote stewardship of natural resources and a harmony between human activity and natural systems. (See Chapter 8.)

CONCLUSION

Wildlife legislation is outdated, and most laws are narrowly focused on species that represent a consumptive benefit to humans. Even this legislation, which is plagued with inconsistencies, vague definitions, and unsuitable penalties, is inadequate to protect these species. Furthermore, except in the case of fish, this legislation is almost entirely ineffective in dealing with the loss of habitat critical to wildlife.

The statute enacted to protect endangered species has limited effect. In addition, the concept of waiting until a species is threatened with extinction before action is taken makes little sense, especially when the process of designating species is so slow and cumbersome. By the time a species is on the list, its habitat may be completely destroyed. Habitat destruction is the reason most species make it on to the list in the first place.

Wildlife protection should extend to all types of organisms and be directed at habitat protection and the overall health of the ecosystem. This should involve not only the maintenance of thriving habitats but the restoration of others. Legislation must be introduced that will ensure that these goals are met.

Cooperation between government agencies and non-governmental organizations should continue to grow. Local implementation efforts, such as through the identification of environmentally sensitive areas and the empowerment of environmental advisory committees, are critical to "acting locally." Revision and strengthening of the *Planning Act*'s treatment of provincial policies on wildlife, habitat, and the natural heritage in general is critical.

Current government policy statements and strategies are developed with input from non-governmental organizations and private citizens. They reflect today's values and represent an important step toward preserving wildlife. Environmental groups can contribute by ensuring that the principles are incorporated into strong legislation before species and habitat preservation becomes all restorative with nothing to maintain.

Patricia Mohr

FURTHER READING

David S. Favre, *Wildlife: Cases, Laws and Policy* (Tarrytown, NY: Associated Faculty Press, 1983).

David S. Favre, *International Trade in Endangered Species: A Guide to CITES* (Boston: M. Nijhoff Publishers, 1989).

Frederick F. Gilbert and Donald G. Dodds, *The Philosophy and Practice of Wildlife Management* (Malabar, Fla.: Robert E. Krieger, 1987).

James M. Peek, *A Review of Wildlife Management* (Englewood Cliffs, NJ: Prentice-Hall, 1986).

Marc Reisner, *The Undercover Pursuit of Wildlife Poachers* (Toronto: Douglas & McIntyre, 1991).

ENDNOTES

1   Environment Canada, *The Importance of Wildlife to Canadians: Highlights of a National Survey* (Ottawa: Environment Canada, 1989), 20, 27, and 28.
2   *Migratory Birds Convention Act*, RSC 1985, c. M-7, section 2, schedule.
3   Personal communication with the Canadian Wildlife Service.
4   *Migratory Birds Convention Act*, supra endnote 2, article II.
5   Ibid., article VII.
6   Ibid., section 4(2)(f).
7   H. Levesque, G.B. McCullough, and P. Mohr, *Migratory Bird Sanctuaries in Ontario* (Ottawa: Canadian Wildlife Service, Environment Canada, 1984).
8   *Migratory Birds Convention Act*, supra endnote 2, section 5.
9   Ibid., section 12.
10 D.I. Gillespie, H. Boyd, and P. Logan, *Wetlands for the World: Canada's RAMSAR Sites* (Ottawa: Canadian Wildlife Service, Environment Canada, 1991), 7.
11 *Canada Wildlife Act*, RSC 1985, c. W-9, section 3.

12 Ibid., section 2(2).

13 Ibid., section 2(1).

14 Ibid., section 9.

15 Ibid., section 5.

16 P. Mohr and L. Maltby, *A Summary of Background Information on National Wildlife Areas in the Ontario Region* (Ottawa: Canadian Wildlife Service, Environment Canada, 1982).

17 Monte Hummel, *Endangered Spaces* (Toronto: Key Porter Books Ltd., 1989), 279.

18 *Canada Wildlife Act*, supra endnote 11, section 13.

19 *Criminal Code*, RSC 1985, c. C-46, as amended, section 787(1).

20 *Game Export Act*, RSC 1985, c. G-1, section 3.

21 Personal communication, Canadian Wildlife Service, 1992.

22 *Game Export Act*, supra endnote 20, section 2.

23 Ibid., section 9.

24 *Wild Animal and Plant Protection and Regulation of International and Interprovincial Trade Act*, SC 1992, c. 52.

25 *Customs Tariff Act*, RSC 1985, c. C-54, section 114, schedule VII.

26 *Export and Import Permits Act*, RSC 1985, c. E-19, section 3.

27 *Canada Gazette Part II*, vol. 123, no. 9, April 26, 1989, 2260.

28 *Export and Import Permits Act,* supra endnote 26, section 19.

29 *R. v. Krey* (1982), 12 CELR 105, sentence modified, [1983] NWTR 379, 14 CELR 20 (NWTSC).

30 *National Parks Act*, RSC 1985, c. N-14, section 5(1.2).

31 Ibid., section 5(1.4).

32 Ibid., sections 7(1)(a), 7(1)(b), 7(1)(c), and 7(1)(ee).

33 Ibid., section 5(10).

34 Ibid., section 8.

35 Ibid., schedule II.

36 Mark Hume, "The Head Hunters" (May-June 1986), *Equinox* 43.

37 *National Parks Act*, supra endnote 30, section 8.

38 Hume, supra endnote 36, at 43.

39 *National Parks Act*, supra endnote 30, section 8.

40 Canada, Department of Fisheries and Oceans, *Policy for the Management of Fish Habitat* (Ottawa: the department, 1986).

41 *Fisheries Act*, RSC 1985, c. F-14, section 1.

42 Ibid., section 23.

43 Ibid., section 35(1).

44 Ibid., section 34(1).

45 *R. v. Maritime Electric Co.* (1990), 4 CELR (NS) 289 (PEI Prov. Ct.).

46 *Fisheries Act*, supra endnote 41, section 36(3).

47 Ibid., sections 36(1)(b) and 36(1)(c).

48 Ibid., section 37(1).

49 *Fisheries Act*, as amended by SC 1991, c. 1, section 24.

50 Ibid., section 40.

51 Ibid., section 78.1.

52 Wildlife Ministers' Council of Canada, *A Wildlife Policy for Canada* (Ottawa: Supply and Services, 1990), 5, 6, and 8.

53 *Policy for the Management of Fish Habitat*, supra endnote 40, at 8 and 10.

54 Ontario, Ministry of Natural Resources, *Matchedash Bay Provincial Wildlife Area News* (Toronto: the ministry, 1989).

55 Gillespie, Boyd, and Logan, supra endnote 10, at 5-6.

56 Ibid., at 7.

57 Mike Cadman, "What Is Rare?" (Spring 1989), vol. 29, no. 1 *Seasons* 24.

58 World Wildlife Fund (Canada), *Canadian Endangered Species* (Toronto: WWF, 1991).

59 Canadian Wildlife Service, *Focus on the Canadian Wildlife Service* (Ottawa: Canadian Wildlife Service, Environment Canada, 1991).

60 Ibid.

61 *Game and Fish Act*, RSO 1990, c. G.1, section 3.

62 Ibid., section 6(1).

63 Ontario, Ministry of Natural Resources, *Looking Ahead: A Wild Life Strategy for Ontario* (Toronto: the ministry, 1990), 68-69.

64 Ontario, Ministry of Natural Resources, "Hunting Regulations: Summary, Fall '91 – Spring '92."

65 *Game and Fish Act*, supra endnote 61, section 1(6).

66 Ibid., section 1(17).

67 Hunting Regulations, supra endnote 64.

68 *Game and Fish Act*, supra endnote 61, section 26(1).

69 Ibid., section 20(1).

70 Ibid., section 20(2) and (3).

71 Hunting Regulations, supra endnote 64

72 *Game and Fish Act*, supra endnote 61, section 30(2).

73 Ibid., section 31.

74 Ibid., section 71.

75 Ibid., section 83(3).

76 Ibid., sections 32 and 33.

77 Ibid., section 55.

78 Ibid., section 82.

79 Ibid., sections 72-74.

80 *Provincial Penalties Adjustment Act*, SO 1989, c. 72, section 73. Now contained in *Game and Fish Act*, supra endnote 61, section 91.

81 *Game and Fish Act*, supra endnote 61, section 19.

82 *Looking Ahead*, supra endnote 63, at 122.

83 *Game and Fish Act*, supra endnote 61, section 2(b).

84 Ibid., section 62(7).

85 Ibid., sections 30(3)(b) and 20(2).

86 Ibid., sections 23, 24, and 55.

87 Hunting Regulations, supra endnote 64.

88 Ontario, Ministry of Natural Resources, "Summary of the Fur Management Regulations: Fall '90 – Spring '91."

89   John T. Theberge, "The Future of the Wolf: Biology or Bioethics?" (Spring 1989), vol. 29, no. 1 *Seasons*.

90   R.D. Lawrence, "Cracking Down on Bounties" (Autumn 1988), vol. 28, no. 3 *Seasons* 14.

91   *Looking Ahead*, supra endnote 63, at 98.

92   "Updates: Ontario Cracks Down on Bounties" (Spring 1989), vol. 29, no. 1 *Seasons* 13.

93   *Looking Ahead*, supra endnote 63, at 97-98.

94   "Updates: Wolf Bounties" (Spring 1990), vol. 30, no. 1 *Seasons* 11.

95   *Game and Fish Act*, supra endnote 61, section 55.

96   Ibid., sections 1-14.

97   *African Lion Safari and Game Farm Ltd. v. Kerrio et al.* (1987), 1 CELR (NS) 197 (Ont. SC).

98   Barry Kent MacKay, "Wild But Not Free" (Spring 1991), vol. 31, no. 1 *Seasons* 18.

99   Patricia Orwen, "Do Zoos Protect Rare Species or Just Entertain Humans?" *The Toronto Star*, February 23, 1991.

100 MacKay, supra endnote 98.

101 Ontario, Bill 162, *An Act To Amend the Game and Fish Act*, 35th Legislature, 1st Sess., 1991.

102 *Fur Farms Act*, RSO 1990, c. F.37, section 3.

103 *Looking Ahead*, supra endnote 63, at 133.

104 *Game and Fish Act*, supra endnote 61, section 67(a).

105 *Fur Farms Act*, supra endnote 102, section 5.

106 *Provincial Penalties Adjustment Act*, SO 1989, c. 72, section 6; proclaimed in force March 31, 1990. Now contained in *Fur Farms Act*, supra endnote 102, section 10.

107 *Looking Ahead*, supra endnote 63, at 133.

108 Ibid., at 131.

109 *Endangered Species Act*, RSO 1990, c. E.15, section 5.

110 Ontario, Ministry of Natural Resources, *Rare, Threatened, Endangered, Extirpated or Extinct Species of Ontario* (Toronto: the ministry, May 1991).

111 *Looking Ahead*, supra endnote 63, at 52-53.

112 *Provincial Penalties Adjustment Act*, supra endnote 106, section 72. Now contained in *Endangered Species Act*, RSO 1990, c. E.15, section 6.

113 Personal communication, Ontario Ministry of Natural Resources, 1992.

114 "Earthwatch: Eagles Beware: Jack Miner Act Given Priority Over Endangered Act" (Winter 1988), vol. 28, no. 4 *Seasons* 7.

115 *Game and Fish Act*, supra endnote 61, section 92(32).

116 *Wilderness Areas Act*, RSO 1990, c. W.8.

117 Ontario, Ministry of Natural Resources, *Statistics 1989-1990* (Toronto: the ministry, 1990), 90-92.

118 *Tweed News*, August 12, 1992.

119 *Looking Ahead*, supra endnote 63, at 81.

120 *Statistics 1989-1990*, supra endnote 117, at 94.

121 Examples of municipalities that have established environmental advisory committees and incorporated environmental policies into their official plans and developed environmentally sensitive area designations include Halton, Waterloo, Niagara, Durham, Toronto, Scarborough, King City, Richmond Hill, and Whitchurch-Stouffville.

14

Conserving and Upgrading the Built Environment

Contents

369

Environ: To extend around; encircle; surround.

Funk & Wagnall's Canadian Dictionary

Canada: The place of houses.

The Canadian Encyclopaedia

INTRODUCTION

At any given time, the overwhelming majority of Canadians are inside buildings; and the majority of those buildings are in cities, towns, and villages. In short, at most times of the day or night, Canadians' immediate environment is a built environment.

The administration of this built environment has some idiosyncratic features. Canada's population is mostly urbanized; consequently, when the Brundtland commission[1] called for "sustainable development," one might have expected at least some attention to be devoted to "sustainable urban development." Similarly, when the Government of Canada's Green Plan[2] emphasized the principle of "re-use, recycle and recover," one might have expected some allusion to the built environment, if only for purely pragmatic reasons. Canada's level of re-use of older buildings is substantially lower than that of most other western countries: in fact, about one-sixth of all Canadian landfill materials is composed of "used construction material."[3] In the case of two buildings proposed for demolition by the city of Ottawa, the waste concrete and flooring alone (which would have to be deposited at the local landfill site) would have the volume of more than 10 million crushed pop bottles.

Furthermore, the built environment represents perhaps the largest inventory of assets on which Canada has no policy whatever pertaining to use or re-use, even though this environment has a substantial value. It is estimated to include some eight million buildings,[4] among which the pre-World War II stock alone was tentatively appraised in 1986 at $114.9 billion.[5] Normally, one would expect that with an inventory of that economic magnitude, there would be a public policy on whether to upgrade it, replace it, or whatever; one would not expect that kind of inventory to be merely ignored, any more than one would expect Canada to disregard how it would deal with other major inventories such as its oil reserves, fish stocks, forestry reserves, or other collections of assets. "It is like having an elephant in your garage: sooner or later you have to decide what to do with it."[6]

Until relatively recently, however, conventional wisdom postulated that the built environment was unlikely to be placed on the public agenda. Although both officialdom and average citizens could allegedly become concerned about the re-use and recycling of items as small as pop bottles and tin cans, there appeared to be no commensurate level of interest in the re-use or recycling of items as large as entire buildings, neighbourhoods, and cities.[7]

However, declarations within the past three years appear to be reversing this position, and auguring a policy that could more accurately be called "sustainable urban development." Those statements are found at three governmental levels. At the federal level, the merger of natural environment issues with building conservation issues is reflected in symposium proceedings published by the Department of Environment and the Department of Communications in October 1990, entitled *Heritage in the 1990s — Towards a Government of Canada Strategy*.[8] At the provincial level, the same process is clearly evident in documents such as *A Strategy for Conserving Ontario's Heritage*.[9] At the municipal level, it is clearly enunciated in *Capitalizing on Heritage, Arts and Culture* published by the Federation of Canadian Municipalities.[10] In the case of each of these documents, one should not be misled by the word "heritage" in the title: these policy positions clearly disclose that the subject matter is not confined to properties of "outstanding architectural and historic significance," but extends to the built environment generally; in fact, the phrase "built environment" as a whole is used repeatedly throughout these publications.

Legal Intervention in the Built Environment

Clearly one way to conserve, upgrade, and recycle such buildings is through their purchase by persons dedicated to their retention; but since it is impossible to acquire all such buildings, this chapter will examine alternate approaches. The legal mechanisms that govern the protection of the built environment operate at five levels: international, federal, provincial, municipal, and private.

The legal structure connected with the built environment seems to be narrow in its application: about 0.15 per cent of Canada's building stock is subject to specific controls and inducements under the rubric of "heritage."[11] The other 99.85 per cent of Canada's estimated eight million buildings is not. Not even the federal government's Green Plan addressed this component of the environment.[12] In other words, there is no comprehensive screening mechanism to address whether destruction of the built environment is necessary or desirable. For that matter, subject to minor exceptions, there are no screening mechanisms that apply generically to sub-categories of the built environment (for example, buildings of a certain age or character); instead, virtually all regulatory control operates on an *ad hoc* basis triggered by a "heritage" designation that is confined to a tiny fraction of the built environment.

There are exceptions, which provide some level of screening for generic sub-categories. For example, there are certain rules that are applicable to all federal departmental buildings over 40 years old (described later). However, although generic legislation is not common on the regulatory side of protecting the built environment, it is far more common on the economic side — that is, legislation that directly intervenes in the economic or structural viability of that building stock. For example, certain legislation that applies to repairs and renovations affect all the existing building stock; and since that legislation can affect decisions whether the built environment is upgraded, preserved, or destroyed, it will be summarized in this chapter.

That point raises an important series of distinctions. As with any other area of legislative activity, legislation pertaining to the built environment can be divided into two main categories: regulation and inducements. In turn, each of these categories can apply to either the public sector or the private sector. Expressed another way:

- the public sector can control itself;
- the public sector can assess how its own activities can be an inducement to positive action in the built environment;
- the public sector can impose controls on the private sector;
- the public sector can introduce inducements for the private sector;
- private individuals can sign contracts with one another (contracts bear features that control behaviour and that provide a "consideration" — that is, a *quid pro quo* or inducement).

Finally, legislative intervention can take place at any of several possible levels: the international level, the federal level, the provincial level, and the regional/municipal level. This chapter will summarize some of the basic approaches.

THE INTERNATIONAL LEVEL

Treaties

There are two principal international treaties dealing with that component of the built environment that can be considered "heritage." The first is the Hague Convention[13] of 1954, which focuses on the protection of historic monuments in times of armed conflict. Canada is one of the few NATO countries to have failed to adhere to the convention. The reasons have not been disclosed.

The second convention is one that Canada accepted.[14] It is the World Heritage Convention of 1972.[15] The "heritage" referred to includes both the natural heritage and the immoveable cultural heritage: examples that have been cited in Canada include Dinosaur Provincial Park in Alberta, the L'Anse aux Meadows Viking archaeological site in Newfoundland, and the old city of Quebec. The convention imposes on each signatory to the convention a "duty ... of ensuring the identification, protection, conservation, presentation, and transmission to future generations of the cultural and natural heritage. ... It will do all it can to this end, to the utmost of its own resources."[16] This includes the obligation "to take the appropriate legal, scientific, technical, administrative, and financial measures for the identification, protection, conservation, presentation and rehabilitation of this heritage."[17] Although the convention confines this duty to sites of "outstanding universal value,"[18] it is up to each member state to determine how those properties will be defined.[19]

International treaties such as the Hague Convention and the World Heritage Convention were drafted to promote the protection of outstanding landscapes, architecture, and historic sites. When Canada adhered to the latter treaty, it formally committed itself to a number of objectives concerning heritage conservation, including the integration of conservation principles into national policy. These obligations have not been translated into legislation for buildings in any generic sense.

Responsibility for Canada's liaison (pertaining to the international developments) has been vested in the same agency as the one involved with federal policy pertaining to older buildings: the Canadian Parks Service of the Department of Environment.

Official Recommendations

International treaties on the subject have been supplemented by international recommendations.[20] These recommendations were drafted from time to time at international meetings of experts convened by the United Nations Educational Scientific and Cultural Organization (UNESCO) over a period of some 20 years, and covered topics as diverse as archaeological licensing and the loan structures that would be desirable in historic districts. Each set of recommendations was then submitted to the General Conference of UNESCO for ratification and was typically adopted unanimously. The standard protocol is then for the recommendations to be distributed to the member states of UNESCO for comment on proposed implementation. Although Canada voted for these recommendations, which outline the contents of appropriate heritage legislation, the recommendations (unlike the treaties) are not binding on Canada, and Canada has not lodged any formal comments on them.

Certain non-governmental organizations such as the International Council of Monuments and Sites (ICOMOS)[21] have disseminated their opinion of standards of good behaviour pertaining to heritage properties, under legal-sounding names. For example, ICOMOS has publicized its document called the Venice Charter.[22] However, these documents have no intrinsic legal status, nor do they have a semi-official status comparable to the UNESCO recommendations.

THE FEDERAL GOVERNMENT AND REGULATORY CONTROLS

Federal Controls on the Public Sector

The federal government is the largest entrepreneur in Canada, and its own projects can have significant impact on the built environment. The question therefore arises whether the environmental impact assessment procedures of the federal government will have an impact on federally funded projects that could have negative effects on that built environment. Although those procedures are clearly designed to screen effects on the natural environment, their role pertaining to the built environment is less clear. In countries such as the United States[23] and Australia,[24] the central government is under a statutory obligation to protect at least heritage properties, if not the built environment generally.[25]

The Canadian initiatives on new federal legislation focus on the new *Canadian Environmental Assessment Act*.[26] It evolved in marked contrast with that of the United States,[27] whose *National Historic Preservation Act*[28] (1966) originally targeted only properties that were on the US "national register": impact assessments were required when those registered properties were threatened by any initiative that was federally funded. By the same token, injunctions could be applied for (for example, by citizen's groups) when a national register property was threatened but the assessment procedure had been circumvented or overlooked. In 1976, the US legislation was amended to include properties that were not on the national register, but on a supplementary list of properties "eligible" for the national register. This approach became fully operational when implementing regulations were passed in 1979. Between 1981 and 1985, a web of new regulations was systematically introduced, creating a new cumulative effect: federal officials now had a positive legal duty to inventory all sites that met a specified list of criteria for eligibility, published in another regulation When a community group had evidence that a totally unlisted property objectively met those criteria, it could apply for an injunction compelling its inclusion in the list of "eligible" property and (collaterally) blocking any destruction until the consequential assessment procedures (which flow from inclusion on the list) had been complied with. The effect of this legislation and the cases interpreting it today is therefore to create a screening procedure that can be invoked for all properties that intrinsically meet the historical and architectural standards laid out in the criteria for eligibility. It is now the view of the senior counsel of the Advisory Council on Historic Preservation that the procedure under the *National Historic Preservation Act* functions more methodically and predictably than the US environmental impact procedures for the natural environment.[29]

The *Canadian Environmental Assessment Act* goes some distance in bringing Canada up to date with its foreign counterparts in a single step. In the definition section of the new Act,[30] an environmental assessment is designed to take into account "environmental effects," which are defined as:

> any change that the project may cause in the environment, including any effect of any such change on health and socio-economic conditions, on the *current use of lands and resources for traditional purposes by aboriginal persons, or on any structure*, site or thing that is of historical, archaeological, palaeontological or architectural significance [emphasis added].

This initiative should go some distance in mitigating concerns about the federal government's ability to destroy heritage property in its own hands.

The federal government also has an existing non-statutory procedure for screening decisions affecting buildings under its own ownership. The federal government is the largest owner of buildings in Canada. The federal government's screening process is administered through a document called the "Policy on Federal Heritage Buildings."[31] The policy outlines objectives, including one "to provide federal heritage buildings with the degree of protection required" and to encourage "continuity of use and function for federally owned heritage buildings." It also aims "to recognize local, regional and provincial policies and priorities and explore all reasonable alternatives before making decisions about federal heritage buildings." In terms of protection for federally owned heritage buildings, a screening mechanism is established pertaining to all buildings that are owned by government departments and that are 40 years old or more. Proposals pertaining to the alteration, demolition, or disposition of these properties must be routed by other departments to an interdepartmental committee called the Federal Heritage Buildings Review Office (FHBRO), which is operated with the support of the Canadian Parks Service. The committee reviews the historical or architectural merits of the property, attaches a numerical level of significance,[32] and ultimately makes a recommendation as to what should occur. However, Crown corporations are not bound by the policy unless they voluntarily choose to be bound. One of Canada's most notable owners of important properties, Canada Post, has so far declined to do so.

Federal Controls on the Private Sector

The closest the federal government comes to a regulatory instrument that is applicable generically to the built environment is the *National Building Code*. Despite its title, the *Code* is not intended primarily as a statutory instrument; instead, it is a document that has been prepared and updated by the National Research Council of Canada (NRC) since 1937 as a model for provincial and municipal building codes.[33] The *Ontario Building Code*,[34] for example, is generally modelled on the *National Building Code*.

The *National Building Code* affects the built environment because any major renovation work usually must bring the building into line with applicable municipal or provincial building code standards, which are in turn usually modelled on the standards of the *Code*. That gives rise to an important parenthetical observation. One crucial difference between the natural environment and the built environment is the need for human intervention. The natural environment can exist quite adequately (in the view of some, optimally) without human intervention, and still avoid degradation; the built environment, on the contrary, requires constant human intervention in the form of ongoing maintenance and periodic upgrading in order to avoid degradation.

The *National Building Code* treats major renovations as if they were new construction, and the two must meet the same specifications. However, what happens when an existing building does not coincide with the mathematical dimensions specified in the *Code*? Does that mean that no renovation can proceed unless the walls are torn out? The answer is that chapter 6 of the *Code* provides for "equivalents" — that is, measures that render a building as safe as a *Code* building but that use alternative methodologies. For example, stairwells with incorrect dimensions may have sprinklers installed in them to provide an equivalent degree of fire safety to wider stairwells without sprinklers.

However, the *National Building Code* does not codify these alternative approaches. Instead, "equivalents" are usually left to the discretion of the local building inspector on an *ad hoc* basis. At the provincial level, Ontario has taken the initiative of providing statutory guidance in part II of the *Ontario Building Code* (as described later), but at the national level, the *National Building Code* is a different matter. This silence has been accused of (at best) lengthening the time required for approval of renovation plans, and (at worst) sometimes prompting building inspectors to refuse exercising their discretion on principle.[35] The officials responsible for the *National Building Code*[36] had received overtures[37] pertaining to a codification of proper renovation practice. Initially, the committee responsible for the *Code* issued a "direction to the standing committees that a separate code for existing buildings was not to be developed,"[38] purportedly "because the requirements of the [*Code*] are considered to be minimum levels to ensure safety." However, there now appears to be recognition that the codification[39] of acceptable alternative measures is *also* supposed to produce identical "minimum levels to ensure safety" (albeit by different means), and NRC research for that purpose is expected to be launched soon.[40]

In the meantime, some provinces undertook research independently of the National Research Council. Ontario is the most notable case in point, as described later.

In other respects, federal regulation affecting built environment is the very opposite of the *National Building Code*: whereas the *Code* is accused of being too generic (by assimilating existing construction to new construction), the rest of federal legislation is sometimes accused of not being sweeping enough.[41] As alluded to earlier, the components of the built environment mentioned in the Green Plan would represent less than 1/200 of 1 per cent of Canada's inventory in buildings.[42] In fairness, most authority for the protection of heritage belongs to the provinces. Although the federal government has entrusted a large heritage program to the Canadian Parks Service, the extent to which it can actually protect buildings against demolition is severely limited by constitutional factors. For example, the federal *Historic Sites and Monuments Act*[43] does not protect buildings against demolition.[44] For that matter, even among the federal buildings, the FHBRO recommendations are (strictly speaking) merely that: recommendations. They are not binding in a statutory sense.

In the absence of statutory controls on federal heritage property, the question has arisen whether federal property could be subjected to provincial heritage laws. Most authorities, however, contend that federal property is exempt from such provincial legislation.[45]

There is some property that, without being federally owned, is under direct federal control: railway property and harbours are examples. Although in the past it was often assumed that such property shared the same immunity from provincial laws (including heritage laws) as federal property, that assumption has been shaken by litigation: such property can probably be subject to provincial and municipal heritage controls.[46]

Railway stations that are on abandoned railway lines have usually been considered to be under provincial and municipal jurisdiction.[47] In those cases where the railway station still remains under federal jurisdiction, however, Parliament has passed the *Heritage Railway Stations Protection Act*.[48] This should address the fate of railway stations on property that is still in railway use — that is, on property that has not been abandoned.[49]

Under the peculiar wording of section 6 of the Act, the government reserves jurisdiction to rule on the appropriateness of any works that alter the heritage station *per se*, and (under a separate head of power) on any works that affect the "heritage features" of a heritage railway station. This wording suggests the possibility that the government could control works that may "affect heritage features" but that are not works in the vicinity of the station premises themselves (that is, works that are not immediately adjacent to the station, but that are aesthetically or architecturally incompatible with the ambience of the station).

Federal Encouragement for the Public Sector

In other jurisdictions such as the United States, there is a statutory commitment by the federal government to occupy and, if necessary, to recycle existing buildings of historic interest for governmental use.[50] This statutory commitment is intended to ensure that the public sector does its utmost to provide its own market for its own heritage buildings. Various non-governmental organizations (NGOs) have called on the Canadian federal government to move in a similar direction as a matter of policy, if not of statute.[51] Although the Policy on Federal Heritage Buildings[52] includes a commitment to "manage [federal] property to promote ... continued use of heritage buildings" and to "encourage continuity of use and function for federally owned heritage buildings," the NGOs expressed the view that this policy was not reflective of actual practice.[53]

Federal Economic Treatment of the Private Sector

Through the *Income Tax Act*[54] and the *Excise Tax Act*,[55] the government of Canada can intervene directly in every decision pertaining to the use and re-use of the built environment.

Most decisions that bear on the maintenance and upgrading of that environment are affected by the income tax system; and virtually all of them are affected by the goods and services tax. These instruments can change for better or for worse what "normally" would have occurred to this environment if it had been governed by the laws of economics alone.

The Income Tax Treatment for Maintaining and Fixing the Built Environment

As with other areas of law pertaining to the built environment, the tax legislation of the government of Canada reflects no clear or comprehensive policy pertaining to the importance of maintenance, repair, and periodic upgrading of the built environment. Instead, the applicable tax rules represent a web of components that emerged over time for a variety of reasons, none of which was necessarily intended to promote "sustainable development" in an urban context.

Some properties are affected by those rules more than others:

- The properties that are least affected are lands that are held for a taxpayer's personal enjoyment — namely, principal and secondary residences. Broadly speaking, those properties are usually outside the orbit of the tax system: purchase and operating costs of these residences do not normally give rise to significant tax benefits or liabilities.

- The situation is quite different for properties that are held not for enjoyment but for investment. Broadly speaking (and at the risk of some oversimplification of the *Income Tax Act*), properties that are held for short-term production of rental income, commerce, or industry or longer-term speculation are referred to as "capital properties." If the property produces ongoing income (for example, a farm, a woodlot, a commercial building, a rental residential building, etc.), the net income from the property is taxable. If the property is sold for a profit, the profit may be considered a "capital gain," and 75 per cent of that capital gain is added to taxable income. In the computation of the net ongoing profits of the property, routine expenses may be deducted from gross income — that is, may be considered "expensable." A tax deduction is also allowed by the *Income Tax Act* for depreciation on certain kinds of property classified in the Act: this tax-deductible depreciation is called "capital cost allowance."

The interplay of these provisions can be so complex as to create employment for thousands of professionals, working both for governments and for taxpayers. However, that does not mean that the Canadian tax system is beyond analysis, particularly from an environmental perspective. Even if one confines oneself to the broad strokes, certain clear patterns emerge as to the tax system's treatment of:

- the maintenance of the built environment;
- the deterioration of the built environment; and
- the destruction of the built environment.

Those patterns will be discussed in turn.

Income Tax Policies Pertaining to the Maintenance of the Built Environment

As mentioned above, Canadian income tax policy has minimal impact on properties that are not held for investment purposes, such as a principal residence. Those properties are therefore excluded from the following discussion.

How does the *Income Tax Act* react to the maintenance of investment property? The maintenance of the built environment usually implies ongoing cleaning, periodic repainting and refinishing, cyclic rehabilitation work of a more substantial nature (for example, roofs), and even occasional upgrading of certain components whose original materials no longer meet legal construction requirements (for example, outmoded wiring and plumbing).[56]

When a person owns investment property (that is, capital property), the *Income Tax Act* recognizes two main kinds of expenses that can be incurred on that property:

1. "capital expenses," and
2. expenses that are usually called "business expenses" or "expenses on current account."

The distinction is crucial, because capital expenses are not tax-deductible: they are merely depreciable (for example, in the case of most buildings, a 4 per cent capital cost allowance can be deducted annually from taxable income). In contrast, business expenses on current account are 100 per cent deductible from taxable income.

The maintenance of the built environment is in the hands of what is loosely called the "reno industry" ("reno" being short for "renovation"). This is a euphemism for all the industries in Canada that conduct or cater to not only the maintenance and repair of buildings, but also their remodelling (that is, change of physical appearance), rehabilitation or "rehab" (that is, renovation without the connotation of "remodelling"), restoration (that is, return to a previous condition), and even additions:[57]

- Routine maintenance is seldom questioned as a legitimate tax-deductible item.
- However, remodelling and additions are difficult to treat as tax-deductible since they usually imply a conscious and overt departure from the existing state of affairs.
- The problematic grey area is therefore that of repair, rehabilitation, and restoration. For the sake of brevity alone, these will be assimilated under the name of "rehab" in this chapter.

For rehab expenses to be deductible on current account, Revenue Canada insists that they meet a web of at least six criteria. These criteria, which the department call "guidelines," are outlined in the department's paper entitled *Interpretation Bulletin* IT-128R. IT-128R says that the decision whether rehab work is capital or expensable depends, in part, on:

- whether the work confers "enduring benefit";[58]
- whether it confers a "betterment";[59]
- whether it is "stand-alone," as opposed to being an "integral part" of the structure;[60]
- whether its "relative value" is large in comparison with the overall value of the property;[61]
- whether it is on newly acquired "used property";[62] and
- whether it is "in anticipation of sale."[63]

If the answer to any of the above questions is affirmative, the department tends to disallow the tax deductions on the work and to treat the work as capital.[64] However, none of these factors was considered fully conclusive on its own; the expression used by the department was that "each case is judged on its own merits." As reasonable as this may sound, the practical effect was to leave substantial discretion in the hands of departmental officials. Nonetheless, work like new plumbing, etc.[65] would usually have been classified as capital.[66]

In 1987, the Supreme Court of Canada cast new light on the issue. On review, it declined leave to appeal *SMRQ v. Goyer*, a decision of the Quebec Court of Appeal.[67] The latter court's unanimous decision, based on careful review of the jurisprudence,[68] was that the "enduring benefit" test and the "relative value" test are "perhaps in certain cases ... elements of the solution," but were inconclusive *per se*. The "essential question" was instead the following: the work constituted deductible "repairs and maintenance" if it met this three-pronged test:

- a new capital asset is not created,
- the normal value of the capital asset is not increased, and
- an asset that had ceased to exist is not replaced by a new one.[69]

The result was to allow new plumbing, wiring, doors, windows, and balconies to be deductible on current account. The court ignored the other criteria in IT-128R and its Quebec counterpart.[70]

Essentially the same result had been reached independently by Justice Jerome of the Federal Court in *Gold Bar Developments Ltd. v. R.*[71] for the replacement of an entire *façade* that was suffering from a material defect. The Tax Court of Canada, for its part, said in *Bergeron v. MNR* that in order for rehab work to be non-deductible on the grounds of "betterment" (as expressed in IT-128R), the real question is whether the "work involves *such* degree of improvement to an asset that it becomes a new one."[72]

Revenue Quebec promptly issued a new interpretation bulletin to bring itself into line with the *Goyer* judgment.[73] However, Revenue Quebec interpolated an extra condition: it would refuse to allow the use of *Goyer* in the case of work conducted shortly after or before purchase of the property.[74] Nowhere is this condition to be found in the judgment itself. That condition was invoked by Revenue Canada in the subsequent case of *McLaughlin v. MNR*[75] — not surprisingly, since it coincides with one of the "guidelines" of IT-128R. The Tax Court of Canada responded that the department's assessment is "wholly unreasonable and indeed arbitrary. ... Had the Minister applied common sense in making the assessment here, the appellant would not be before the Court." However, Revenue Canada has so far decided to withdraw IT-128R. There is no indication from the department whether this jurisprudence (*Goyer*, *Gold Bar*, *Bergeron*, and *McLaughlin*) will receive any acknowledgment in the information that the department distributes to the public, or whether the department will continue invoking the "guidelines" of IT-128R as if those cases had never occurred.

If the *Goyer* approach were maintained (without interpolations), the broad effect would be to guarantee the deductibility of work on investment property that does not necessarily improve the quality of the built environment, but at least keeps it at its current position (its "normal" value), or that brings buildings into line with the condition they were supposed to have.[76] Although that is not necessarily "progress" or even "positive" tax treatment for the maintenance of the built environment, it appears to be consistent with an element of equilibrium. At the time of writing, however, it is not clear that Revenue Canada intends to comply.

Tax Institutionalization of the Degradation of the Built Environment

For decades, there has been a basic tax assumption that just as the universe moves toward entropy, buildings must deteriorate. This assumption about the degradation of the built environment was the original rationale for depreciation: with each passing year, the market value of buildings supposedly declines numerically, and this deterioration should be reflected in both generally accepted accounting principles and the *Income Tax Act*. Accordingly, the *Income Tax Act* identifies a wide variety of "classes" of capital property, and gives the owner the option of claiming a tax deduction for depreciation, called capital cost allowance (CCA). In the case of most investment buildings, this CCA is 4 per cent per year.

This approach is also founded on a second rationale. Generally accepted accounting principles usually allow investors to write off their investments on their books.[77]

However, when these principles are applied to real estate, a dichotomy occurs: depreciation (for accounting purposes and CCA) is accepted for buildings, but not for land. As a result:

- land itself is not depreciable;
- it is not subject to CCA; and
- and its purchase is not written off over time for tax purposes.

This compels real estate investors to enter purchases of land and buildings separately in their books, with ensuing complications.

Some observers have argued that CCA on buildings has outlived its economic and philosophical usefulness.[78] Economically, for buildings undergoing routine maintenance and repair, the true decline in value should rarely exceed the rate of inflation. If there is enough parity between inflation and the decline in value, then the two figures will cancel each other out, and numerically the figure listed in the books will continue to be reasonably accurate. For example:

- if a building is listed at $100,000 in a given year,
- and 4 per cent inflation drives its value up to $104,000,
- but 4 per cent deterioration drives its value back down again,
- then its value according to the books should logically stay at $100,000 where it started.

However, CCA ignores inflation, so:

- if the value of money declines by 4 per cent annually and CCA allows the value of a building to be written down by a further 4 per cent,
- the cumulative effect is to say that the value of that real estate has declined by 8 per cent in constant dollars.

For example, the current system would allow buildings to be devalued by 63 per cent (in constant dollars) during the decade of the 1980s.[79] In Ontario real estate, that objectively makes no sense.[80]

From a philosophical perspective, why should Canadian tax legislation codify and endorse the deterioration of any component of the environment? For a building to lose more value than the rate of inflation usually implies a failure to repair;[81] but leaving that aside, is it any more responsible for a government to allow inflated writeoffs for the deterioration of the built environment than for any other part of the environment? Why should the tax system automatically provide deductions to acknowledge bad stewardship? Are automatic tax deductions (which would only be explainable on failure to repair) more justifiable than, say, the case in Alberta in which a company reduced its taxes[82] because it had allowed its own property to be contaminated?[83] Do we provide automatic deductions to ranchers who deplete their herds by starving their cattle? Or is the fiscal assumption that buildings must wither away again inconsistent with the premise of "re-use, recycle and recover"?

These objectives cannot be considered nationally meaningful if they are undermined by the tax system. As long as the *Income Tax Act* endorses the notion that the built environment shall wither away, the government's resolve to entrench the three Rs can be called into question.

Tax Treatment of the Destruction of the Built Environment

Demolition is the consummate refusal to "re-use" a component of the built environment; and the voluminous materials from the wreckage can strain waste disposal sites. Nonetheless, this waste enjoys positive treatment from the taxman. Before 1981, demolition enjoyed favourable tax treatment.[84] One could get a better tax deduction by tearing a building down than by donating it to charity.[85] That was because of the size of the terminal loss claimable. A "terminal loss" is a tax deduction that occurs under the *Income Tax Act*:

- when the last item in a given class of capital property is disposed of;
- when this last item in the class disappears from inventory, special rules apply.

Until 1981, demolition was treated as a disposition at zero dollars, or nil (that is, a better tax treatment than donations, as described at Chapter 15), so if depreciable property had been depreciated down to a certain figure (called the undepreciated capital cost or UCC), what happened to that entry in the books? The *Income Tax Act* replied that when this item on inventory disappeared, the remaining value listed on the owner's books (that is, its depreciated value) should be removed from the books by treating that entire figure as a "loss."

Since this "loss" was the last item in that class of property, it was called a "terminal loss." The amount of that loss was the difference between:

- the depreciated value at the time (UCC) and
- the "proceeds of disposition," which, in the case of demolition, were nil.

In other words, the entire book value (UCC) became a tax deduction.

Since 1981, the Act no longer treats demolition as a disposition for nil proceeds.[86] However, the amendment did not produce a simpler tax system (for example, by treating this form of disposition in the same way as donations).[87] Instead, it produced a more complicated formula. The Act now distinguishes between two scenarios:

1. where demolition occurs in anticipation of sale, or
2. where demolition occurs but the owner keeps the land.

Where the land is also disposed of in the same year, the Act "will treat the vendor as if he had sold the building for its fair market value."[88] It follows that a tax deduction arises if fair market value (FMV) is lower than UCC (that is, depreciated cost, as it appears on the books); the tax deduction would be equal to the difference.

The case of buildings whose land is retained by the owner is more complicated. Until 1988, when the building was demolished the Act allowed a terminal loss equal to half the difference between FMV and UCC; but for 1988 and 1989, this was increased to two-thirds; and for 1990 and onward, this has been increased again to three-quarters.[89]

The question is whether any tax deduction should remain at all. Why does the tax system reward people for destroying their own property?

An argument in its favour is that the deduction of "terminal losses" on demolition is a question of entitlement: it is consistent with generally acceptable accounting principles, and is fully anticipated by the property owner throughout the time that the property-owner owned and amortized the building. By that reasoning, the property owner factored in the terminal loss as part of his equation pertaining to amortization and salability of the property; to deprive him of that tax treatment constitutes the imposition of an unanticipated hardship.

The counterargument is that a given tax treatment is never a "right" and that it is the Act that dictates generally accepted accounting principles, and not vice versa.[90] Furthermore, tax deductions associated with destruction of property arguably constitute:

- a reward for an activity that is self-inflicted; and
- a reward for an activity that is inconsistent with the re-use and recycling of property promoted by the "sustainable development" concept and the Green Plan.

In short, if an asset still has a market value at all, the reasoning of the Green Plan suggests that the value should be used. If the taxpayer chooses to wipe out that value, that is his or her decision — but it is not normally up to the tax system to assist him or her in that purpose. That is not, however, the position currently taken by the *Income Tax Act*.

The Built Environment and the Goods and Services Tax

Predictably, the main area in which the goods and services tax (GST) has an effect on the fate of the built environment is in its treatment of the maintenance, repair, and periodic upgrading of that environment. As in the case of the *Income Tax Act*, the resulting rules stem more from non-policy considerations than from any federal strategy pertaining to the built environment.

As in the case of the *Income Tax Act*, the simplest scenario is the renovation or upgrading of the taxpayer's personal residence(s): the owner pays the 7 per cent GST on goods and services, and the matter basically ends there. The situation is more complex in relation to investment properties that are maintained, repaired, or renovated. The basic structure of the GST anticipates that the tax payable is on the difference between the entrepreneur's purchases and sales. Accordingly, the entrepreneur is expected to charge the GST on his output, and can deduct (in his return to Revenue Canada) the GST that he has paid on his input. This series of deductions for GST paid on inputs is logically called the "input tax credit."

One area in which the GST is maximized is that of "substantial renovations." A substantial renovation is normally one that involves the gutting of a residential building: in that kind of "renovation," GST is triggered not only on the services and the building, but also on the land underneath. That is, extra GST is added, as if the land had been bought and sold. For example, an owner who guts an apartment building sitting on land worth $100,000 must pay GST not only on the work, but also an extra $7,000 in GST on the land, which, according to the legislation, the owner is deemed to have sold, then reacquired.

There is another situation that deals with "deemed" substantial renovations: those can occur when a non-residential building is converted to residential use. For example, attempts to preserve the historic districts of many Canadian cities have relied on the conversion of warehouses to condominiums (for example, in Quebec, Montreal, Winnipeg, and Toronto). If those activities had taken place after the GST was introduced on January 1, 1991, it is not immediately clear how the impact of such "deemed substantial renovations" would have affected the outcome of these projects. Furthermore, even though the impact may (in some cases) be more apparent than real because of the effect of various input tax credits, the perception in the development community of these maximum GST impacts could be a deterrent to the renovation of older buildings. If this perception continues, the negative effects on the recycling of built environment could be significant.

At first glance, this appears to run squarely contrary to the notion of "re-using or recycling" otherwise redundant non-residential buildings.

Summary of the Federal Position

When reviewing federal measures in the light of any checklist for policies pertaining to the built environment, it becomes clear that a policy is largely non-existent at the federal level. The controls on the public sector do not compare with those in the United States, although Bill C-13 may provide for some catching up. Measures to encourage the federal government itself to create inducements to positive action (for example, providing a market for its own heritage buildings) similarly do not compare with those in the United States. Federal regulation in the private sector (under federal jurisdiction) has made some progress, at least in the area of railway property (although not that of Crown corporations). However, in the area where the federal government can make its presence most keenly felt (that is, the tax system, which influences every taxpayer in the country), there is no evidence whatever of any policy orientation toward the built environment. One may argue that this should not be surprising: the Green Plan, for its part, made no significant mention of the tax system either. However, the tax system not only fails to introduce any positive policies but actually perpetuates negative ones in a variety of key areas. Even fiscal neutrality would be an improvement.

THE PROVINCIAL LEVEL

Overall Policy

The government of Ontario, like the government of Canada, does not currently have an overall policy for the built environment. However, the Ministry of Culture and Communications' Heritage Legislation Project has proposed to correct that.

In the meantime, the following is a profile of the existing Ontario framework. Its primary focus is on that small percentage of the built environment that is of unusual architectural or historical importance under the rubric of "heritage."

One exception, in the sense of representing legislation that affects all of the built environment, is the *Ontario Building Code*.[91] To bring more order to the question of equivalents than the *National Building Code* had done, Ontario developed its own set of rules entitled the Table of Compliance Alternatives.[92] Although much work remains to be done on codes, Ontario's position has resulted in more progress than its national counterpart.

Regulating Threats to the Built Environment

In the United States and Australia,[93] the environmental impact assessment procedure requires that careful inventory and investigation precede major works that are likely to affect the environment (including the built environment) and that are financed, at least in part, by the government. Ontario, like some other Canadian jurisdictions,[94] has adopted a variant of this system. It is described elsewhere in detail. The *Environmental Assessment Act* gives a progressively broad definition of "environment" including the built environment: "The social, economic and cultural conditions that influence the life or man or a community,"[95] as well as "any building, structure, machine or other device or thing made by man."[96] Furthermore, an assessment must also make "an evaluation of the advantages and disadvantages to the environment of the undertaking and the alternatives to the undertaking."[97]

Let us suppose that a public works project threatens worthwhile 19th-century buildings, or that a hospital wishes to use provincial funds to replace a building by a famous architect. Can the mechanism of environmental assessments ensure that the decision is reached at least fairly, and not capriciously? The pattern that has emerged in some jurisdictions (for example, Alberta, Manitoba, and the United States, though not in Australia) is that heritage-oriented environmental impact assessments deal initially with archaeological resources, not with buildings. Although Ontario has entered the field relatively recently, the same pattern appears in this province: the Ministry of Environment and Energy regards the destruction of the built environment by demolition as outside the ambit of the Act because it is labelled a "retirement" of buildings, which has been exempted from the legislation.[98] No other jurisdiction that uses environmental assessment has a comparable provision. As long as this provision is in effect, it will be possible to use the *Environmental Assessment Act* to investigate the threat to the built environment only when that threat is part of a larger project that is itself subject to the Act (for example, certain major redevelopment schemes).

As a result of this emasculation of an across-the-board policy, advocates for the built environment have had to negotiate on a piecemeal basis to reintroduce the notion of environmental assessments on certain specific kinds of public works. For example, there is now an arrangement in place for the screening of projects that affect bridges of heritage interest.[99] There have been calls[100] for comparable screening mechanisms pertaining to provincial grant policies that subsidize, for example, the demolition of hospital buildings or educational buildings, but although these arrangements exist elsewhere,[101] they do not exist in Ontario. The Ministry of Culture and Communications' Heritage Legislation Project has opened this question up for discussion, without specifying how it will be resolved.[102]

Provincial regulation of the private sector is not appreciably advanced over that of the public sector. Until 1974, it was possible for a provincial minister to at least designate "historic sites"[103] that could not be "altered or excavated" without ministerial approval.[104] This power was repealed in 1974,[105] leaving Ontario as the only province in Canada without a provincial mechanism to protect even historical sites.[106] Thus, the responsibility for preserving the built environment has been put solely on municipalities — a situation that, it has been suggested by conservationists for many years, is in need of remedy.[107] As the Act now stands, the only buildings or structures eligible for provincial protection are "ruins, burial mounds, petroglyphs and earthworks."[108] That is proposed for correction in the new legislation, when it is presented and passed.[109]

Provincial Inducements

Although Ontario, like the federal government, has no equivalent to the American federal statutory commitment to using and re-using space in heritage buildings, this prospect has been broached by the Ministry of Culture and Communications in the course of its Heritage Legislation Project.[110]

A broad range of inducements for the private sector is currently under consideration in the context of the ministry's Heritage Legislation Project. These measures are described in further detail in the Ontario Heritage Policy Review, *Technical Paper No. 2*.[111]

THE MUNICIPAL LEVEL

Overall Policy

Publications such as the Federation of Canadian Municipalities' *Capitalizing on Heritage, Arts and Culture*[112] suggest a slow but steady increase in municipal attention to the built environment. The subject matter dovetails with existing municipal preoccupations pertaining to land-use controls. In fact, some municipalities have already drafted their official plans and ensuing bylaws (under existing legislation) to protect buildings against demolition and unsympathetic alteration, and to maintain the integrity of the scene by discouraging unsympathetic redevelopment or infill construction. The latter purpose is particularly relevant to the preservation of streetscapes and areas.

Three statutes empower municipalities to exercise limited protective powers for buildings and streetscapes: the *Ontario Heritage Act*, the *Planning Act*, and the *Municipal Act*.[113] These will be described later in this chapter.

It would undoubtedly be desirable for every community to consider the built environment (or at least the "heritage" components of it) in its planning process. Unlike other jurisdictions in Canada[114] and elsewhere,[115] there is no obligation for Ontario municipalities to do so, although section 2 of the *Planning Act* opens the door for them to do so if they wish.[116] The further entrenchment of heritage in the planning process is a high priority of the Ministry of Culture and Communications' Heritage Legislation Project.[117] It is not clear, at this stage, to what extent the Ontario Heritage Policy Review's efforts will also succeed in raising the profile of the built environment generally, in the planning process.

Controls on the Public Sector

The extent to which the municipalities are covered by province-wide environmental impact assessment legislation has been described elsewhere in this book; in any event, as mentioned earlier in this chapter, the "retirement" of buildings has usually been exempted from this screening process. However, a kind of screening mechanism does exist when it results from the municipality's official plan. That process can be described as follows.

The legal effect of official plans on public works (of the municipality) and private property is summarized by I.M. Rogers:

> Once a plan takes effect, all by-laws are to conform and no public work is to be undertaken unless it accords with the plan. The Planning Act does not say a private owner cannot undertake work in conflict with the official plan. Therefore, s. 19 of the Act has a one-sided effect only. The statute contemplates that official plans will be implemented by zoning by-laws, but there is no provision to force a council to enact one, although an individual can compel the enactment of an

amendment [section 35(22)]. A plan is a recommendation and must be implemented by-law to be effective. The council, however, does not have to implement it. Obviously a plan that is not in effect, i.e., has not been approved, cannot serve as a legislative impediment. It is clear that an official plan, even after adoption and approval, is not effective to prevent development at variance with the plan in the absence of a zoning by-law giving effect to the use proposals. An Ontario plan has been held no more than a statement of intention of what at the moment the municipality plans to do in the future and is not an effective instrument restricting land use.[118]

There are provisions to compel a municipality to amend a zoning bylaw but there are none to compel original enactment.[119] It follows that an Ontario plan, unlike plans in other jurisdictions,[120] would not necessarily commit the municipality to a certain course of legislative action. In other words, the municipality is not compelled to enact bylaws to put all the provisions of the plan into effect, but when it does enact bylaws, these bylaws must conform with the plan. Thus, the plan does impede municipal courses of action contrary to the plan. Consequently, if the official plan contains provisions that are incompatible with heritage conservation (for example, by proposing the redevelopment of picturesque areas for highrises), an amendment would be desirable.

It also follows, in theory at least, that if the plan specified heritage conservation in an area, it would be hazardous for the municipal council to vote for municipal public works projects that detract from the purposes of heritage conservation. That theory, however, encountered a reversal from Judge Forget of the Ontario Supreme Court,[121] in the case of a nationally recognized heritage building[122] that was covered by a municipality's official plan commitment to "take the necessary steps to preserve and enhance the heritage resources listed in the inventory."[123] Ratepayers argued that municipal demolition of the building would be contrary to section 24(1) of the *Planning Act*, which prohibits any "public work" that is contrary to the plan, where "public work" includes "any improvement of a structural nature or other undertaking."[124] The judge ruled, however, that:

- the plan's obligation "to preserve and enhance" does not preclude destruction: "If demolition was to have been prohibited, it should have been specifically mentioned. It was not, and accordingly the act of demolition as it applies to heritage resources is not a field of land use activity covered by the Official Plan";[125] and
- in his view,[126] a demolition project is not an "undertaking" and hence is outside the purview of the *Planning Act* anyway.[127]

The Ministry of Culture and Communications' Heritage Legislation Project is expected to result in a different arrangement.

Controls on the Private Sector

A municipality can use three mechanisms to control the demolition and alteration of specified properties. The first is in the *Planning Act*; the other two are exercised under the *Ontario Heritage Act*. One applies to individual heritage sites, and the other to sites in heritage areas. These will be addressed in turn.

As mentioned earlier, there is no overall policy (from the provincial level on down) pertaining to the built environment *per se*. The closest that Ontario comes to such a policy, in terms of generically applicable controls, is in its treatment of residential districts.

Demolition Control Areas

Municipalities can by bylaw declare "demolition control areas."[128] The prerequisites for such a designation are:

- that a bylaw exist that prescribes standards of maintenance in that area;[129] and
- that such a bylaw, in turn, presuppose a plan that foresees maintenance bylaws.

The effect of such a designation is to prohibit the demolition of residential dwellings in the area unless new construction on the site is substantially completed within two years after the demolition.[130] This designation obviously does not protect properties from the demolition that accompanies redevelopment. However, it does protect properties from demolition that is carried out for parking lots or for purely speculative or tax purposes.

Individual Sites

Of the three mechanisms that municipalities can use to control demolition and alteration, the control of individual landmarks is the simplest: the municipality simply passes a bylaw to "designate" the property under the *Ontario Heritage Act*.[131] Such a bylaw does not require, as a precondition, a change in the official plan. However, it does require consultation with the local architectural conservation advisory committee (LACAC), if such a committee has been set up.[132] Almost 20 years after the introduction of the *Ontario Heritage Act*, there are still many municipalities in Ontario that have no LACAC.[133]

There is no established procedure under the *Ontario Heritage Act* for the citizenry at large to launch an initiative for designation.

The next step in designation is a "notice of intent" passed by the local council and served on the owner.[134] As soon as notice is given, controls on alteration and demolition come into effect.[135] The owner can object to the Conservation Review Board,[136] but the board's decision is not binding. Rather, it simply makes a recommendation back to the council, which has the discretion to decide whether or not to proceed with the designation.[137] If a municipality decides in the affirmative, it passes a bylaw to designate the structure.

What kinds of reasons are sufficient to sustain a designation? If governmental authorities were to designate a property for reasons that were overtly extraneous to the *Ontario Heritage Act*, the designation would be open to challenge in court.[138] If, however, the designation were enacted for the *bona fide* purpose of protecting heritage, the reasons are not open to attack even if the heritage value of the property is slight.[139] The Supreme Court of Canada has referred to the authorities' selection of properties for protection as "indefeasible."[140]

All alterations to a designated site must be approved by council and council may refuse such permission indefinitely.[141] However, Ontario municipalities (other than Toronto and London), unlike their counterparts in most other jurisdictions,[142] cannot refuse demolition permits indefinitely. Instead, the municipal council is given 90 days in which to decide whether it favours demolition.[143] If it decides against demolition, it can refuse to issue a demolition permit for a further period of 180 days.[144] At the end of that delay, the building may be demolished notwithstanding the council's opposition.[145] The right to demolish is, then, easier to obtain than the right to alter, since it appears that the maximum delay on demolition is 270 days. Ontario is the only province in Canada to withhold, even from its major municipalities, the right to confer permanent protection on any buildings.

It has frequently been said that the Act's preference for temporary demolition control over permanent demolition control constitutes the gravest weakness of the Act; that, in fact, temporary demolition control makes protection meaningless.[146] This is expected to be resolved at the outcome of the Ministry of Culture and Communications' Heritage Legislation Project.

There are two notable exceptions to the above rule. Toronto's legislation[147] is more complex, but is broadly similar in spirit. London's legislation[148] also differs from the norm.

Heritage Conservation Districts

All buildings that are located in designated "heritage conservation districts" are subject to roughly the same controls as are on buildings that are designated individually. However, the required procedure to set up such a district is much more cumbersome than the procedure to designate an individual building. Moreover, the *Ontario Heritage Act* imposes more formal preconditions on the creation of heritage areas than the statute of any other Canadian province.[149] The result has been that district designation is used much less frequently than individual designation.

These preconditions are not fully explained in the Act: some are simply recommendations of the Ontario Ministry of Culture and Communications (MCC). The practical effect, however, is the same. Since all designations of heritage conservation districts must be approved by the Ontario Municipal Board[150] (OMB), it is unlikely that the OMB would approve a designation unless the procedure recommended by the MCC had been followed.

The procedure is that, first, the MCC recommends that the municipality pass a bylaw appointing a LACAC.[151] Second, official plan provisions are a prerequisite to the designation of a heritage conservation district. Consequently, if a municipality has no official plan, it must bring one into existence. This official plan must include general heritage policy statements that indicate the municipal council's "acceptance of heritage conservation in principle and its commitment to act in order to protect the heritage of the municipality."[152] If the municipality already has an official plan that does not mention heritage, the official plan must be amended accordingly. Third, the municipality's planning advisory committee[153] must be involved at certain stages of this process — specifically, in the preparation of the official plan statement. Under the provisions of the *Planning Act*, the planning advisory committee will be required to call public meetings and elicit public participation.[154] Fourth, the official plan or official plan amendment is submitted for the review and approval of the minister of municipal affairs in consultation with the MCC.[155]

Finally, one might infer from a strict reading of the Act that a council could then proceed immediately to the passage of a bylaw designating a heritage conservation district.[156] It is unlikely, however, that the Ontario Municipal Board would approve such a designating bylaw unless even more planning had been done, since the MCC recommends a second plan studying a specific area. This secondary plan or heritage conservation district plan would go into much greater detail than the official plan.[157] The preparation of such a plan requires that two preconditions be met. In the first place, the LACAC would have to be consulted.[158] Second, the municipal council would have to pass a bylaw authorizing the study.[159] In this case, however, there is no further review of the bylaw itself at the provincial level.[160]

This new plan must be referred to the MCC. No review or approval by the minister of municipal affairs is necessary.[161] Once such approval is given, the plan, adopted by the council, is implemented by bylaw designating the area as a heritage conservation district.[162] The bylaw itself does not come into force without the prior approval of the OMB and it is therefore subject to standard procedures for bylaw review by the OMB.[163]

To handle these various steps without mistake, and to produce a heritage conservation district plan that is acceptable to the OMB, it is, in the words of the ministry itself, "advisable that the staff of the MCC and the Ministry of Municipal Affairs be consulted in the early stages of the planning."[164]

Once the area has been designated, the owners of all buildings in the heritage conservation district must apply for municipal permission for external alteration, construction, and demolition.[165] As is the case for individually designated buildings, permission for alterations can be refused indefinitely, but refusal to permit demolition cannot exceed 180 days.[166]

It is important to note that a building cannot be treated as having been designated both individually[167] and as part of the heritage conservation district: it must be either one or the other.[168] A designated building that happens to be in a designated district is subject to the rules applicable to individually designated buildings, and not to the rules of heritage conservation districts, since the consequences of these two forms of designation are slightly different.

First, the interior of a building can be protected if the building was designated individually, but not if it was designated as part of a district.[169] Second, a person who applies unsuccessfully for alteration or demolition of a building can appeal to the Conservation Review Board if the building was individually designated,[170] whereas the person must appeal to the OMB if the building was designated as part of a district.[171] The OMB's ruling carries more weight, since it is binding on the municipality. Third, an individually designated site whose building has been legally demolished[172] is henceforth free of the controls of the *Ontario Heritage Act*,[173] but a site within a heritage conservation district remains subject to the rules of infill construction under the Act even after the building has been demolished. These controls are discussed below.

Measures to simplify and rationalize this highly complex situation are obviously a priority of the MCC's Heritage Legislation Project.

Controlling Infill and Replacement Construction

As mentioned earlier, when a property has been designated under section 29 of the *Ontario Heritage Act*, all alterations must be approved by the municipal council.[174] It has been suggested in this context that the definition of "alteration" is too limited and should be expanded.[175] It does not, for instance, specifically include construction on property,[176] although it does state that anything that "disturbs" or "changes" property is an alteration. Construction, presumably, falls into that category. Consequently, any new construction on a property designated under the Act appears to require municipal approval.

Although it may be politically and socially desirable for the municipality to spell out guidelines for change on heritage sites, it is under no legal obligation to do so and can treat every case individually. A dissatisfied owner can appeal the municipality's decision to the Conservation Review Board.[177] That body, however, does not render a binding decision, but instead submits a report containing recommendations to the municipality.[178] Since the council is free to reject the report in whole or in part,[179] it is this decision of council that is final.[180]

Similarly, when an area has been designated as a heritage conservation district, all construction or change in the area must be approved by the local council,[181] and the council again appears to have wide discretion in rendering its decision. This discretion is seen to be narrower, however, when one considers the appeal procedure that exists for dissatisfied applicants who seek permission to alter or construct. Whereas the dissatisfied owner of an individually designated heritage building applies to the Conservation Review Board,[182] whose decision is not binding on the municipality concerned, the dissatisfied applicant in a heritage conservation district appeals to the OMB, whose decision is binding.[183] Municipal discretion has thus been limited by the supervisory presence of the OMB.

This supervisory power of the OMB is expected to have the following effect on municipal discretion. As in the case of individually designated buildings, guidelines are deemed advisable but are not stated to be a prerequisite. Nevertheless, a municipality may find that it may be incapable, for practical purposes, of refusing applications for construction unless it has already promulgated clear guidelines by which the application can be judged to be unacceptable. It is generally felt that the OMB will be inclined to overrule the municipality and grant the application for construction unless clear municipal guidelines indicate that the owner should do otherwise. Although this hypothesis is still untested, it is recommended that instead of relying on its discretionary powers in a heritage conservation district, a municipality should promulgate clear guidelines for acceptable changes in the area and enunciate those guidelines in municipal bylaws whenever possible.

There are, however, cases in which a municipality may prefer to operate under other enabling legislation. For example, it may wish to protect a neighbourhood without attaching to it the label of "heritage conservation district." Furthermore, certain provisions in municipal enabling legislation can be used to supplement the *Ontario Heritage Act*. As explained earlier, some of the discretionary aspects of that statute may need reinforcing. Similarly, there exist other aspects of heritage conservation for which regulation is required and that are ignored by the *Ontario Heritage Act*. Standards of maintenance and occupancy (provided for in the *Planning Act*) constitute probably the most noteworthy example, since the *Ontario Heritage Act*, unlike some of its counterparts,[184] does not require the maintenance of heritage structures.

Municipal land-use powers are usually exercised over a wide area rather than over a single lot. If a municipality tries to pass a bylaw affecting a single lot (often called "spot zoning"), this effort, although not necessarily illegal, is nevertheless regarded by the courts with suspicion. In the field of heritage preservation, there have been indications that if there is any hint of discriminatory treatment, the courts may invalidate the bylaw; this can occur even when the bylaw ostensibly applies to a wider area.[185]

There are two reasons why size and height controls may be found in almost any attempt to preserve the character of neighbourhoods. First and foremost, the size of a building has a definite impact on its environment, since an oversized building will appear incompatible with its environment regardless of its architectural style. Second, a restrictive size and height bylaw can indirectly discourage unwanted redevelopment. Ontario municipalities are empowered to control the height and bulk of buildings.[186]

Until 1983, the *Planning Act* specifically authorized municipalities to control "the external design and character of buildings."[187] Amendments to the Act in 1983, however, deleted the right to regulate "external design." This change appears to leave Ontario as the only province in Canada, aside from Saskatchewan, that does not normally empower municipalities to regulate design.

Municipalities are empowered to regulate the uses to which property can be put.[188] The decision to preserve an area does not usually imply a change of use. It is customary to retain the existing zoning designation and simply add extra conditions to protect the special features of the area. Some care must be exercised, however, to ensure that the zoning is not so loose as to encourage displacement of the population. For example, residential heritage areas are sometimes vulnerable to an invasion of bars, restaurants, etc., which can have an unsettling effect on the neighbourhood. If the neighbourhood character is to be maintained, use zoning must take account of this effect.[189]

It is unlikely that the regulation of use can be extended to the point of freezing certain lands altogether. For example, the zoning of land as "recreational" or "historical" probably cannot impede other kinds of construction. Despite the fact that several communities attempt to use this "zoning" to freeze land, the practice has run into trouble in the courts.[190]

Setback rules are rules that dictate the proper distance between a building and the street. They are important for the harmonious appearance of a streetscape. The location of buildings can be regulated by municipalities in Ontario.[191]

The regulation of signs by Ontario municipalities[192] is essential to the maintenance of a heritage area, since any outdoor advertising has a significant impact on the area's appearance.[193] Fences and walls can also have an effect on the appearance of a streetscape.[194]

Maintenance is obviously essential to retain the quality of an area and the built environment generally. Under section 31 of the *Planning Act*, municipalities in Ontario can enact bylaws to enforce standards for the maintenance and occupancy of property. The enabling legislation does not distinguish between building interiors and exteriors, nor between residential and non-residential buildings. In the absence of any indication to the contrary, it appears that all these categories can be regulated. The *Planning Act* even foresees the regulation of vacant lots.[195]

One prerequisite for such a bylaw is the existence of an official plan that contains provisions relating to property conditions.[196] If no such statement exists in the plan, the plan must be amended. If there is as yet no plan in the municipality, the municipality may substitute a "policy statement" (approved by the minister), containing provisions relating to property conditions.[197]

It should be noted, however, that maintenance and occupancy standards must be approached with caution. Sometimes, standards have been so strict that owners of older buildings could not meet them without making costly renovations.[198]

Interim Control

Some sites face an immediate threat. If the designation process is long and complicated, there is a chance that the site will not be saved. Statutes in some other provinces have thus made provision for the issuance of a "stop order,"[199] for a delay until an assessment of and a report on the proposed alteration are done, and for the ordering of whatever "protective measures" are considered necessary.[200]

The *Ontario Heritage Act* provides for the issuance of a stop order only under part VI, which deals with the conservation of resources of archaeological value.[201] However, a form of interim protection does take place when a notice of intention to designate a building of historic or architectural value is served. The designation provisions then apply as if the property were already designated under the Act. In addition, any permit for alteration or demolition that is issued by the municipality before the notice becomes void.[202]

Adjustments and Compensation

Even the most stringent land-use controls will not necessarily cause hardship to owners of property, if the controls are inappropriate under the circumstances. For example, in Ontario, committees of adjustment[203] are empowered to grant exemptions or "minor variances" to relieve owners from strict compliance with zoning bylaws, as long as the general intent and purpose of the bylaw and the official plan are respected.[204] The committee's decision can be appealed to the Ontario Municipal Board.[205]

More than one province has had to deal with the thorny question whether an owner or occupier or another person who has an interest in real property that is the object of heritage designation can claim compensation from the municipality that made the designation, downzoned the property, or took other such measures.[206] The fear is, of course, that a municipality will not designate at all if it has to pay compensation for such designations.

In Ontario this issue arises less directly. The only statute that could entitle an owner to compensation is the *Expropriations Act*.[207] The owner has to argue that designation is tantamount to expropriation or, alternatively, that designation has resulted in "injurious affection." Injurious affection is the expression for damage caused by governmental acts to the value of private property. Both expropriation and injurious affection give an owner the right to demand compensation.[208] As far as expropriation is concerned, the *Expropriation Act* defines it as "the taking of land without the consent of the owner";[209] since designation does not involve any taking of land, it would be virtually impossible for a court to equate designation with expropriation.

The question of injurious affection is slightly more complex. If no land has been expropriated, the *Expropriations Act* defines injurious affection as "such reduction in the market value of the land of the owner and such personal and business damages resulting from the construction of the works by the statutory authority."[210] Since no "work" is under "construction," it appears that no claim for injurious affection can result from a heritage designation. In summary, then, there is no provision for compensation for the loss of property value caused by designation under the *Ontario Heritage Act*.

The same rule applies to action taken by a municipality under the *Planning Act*, unless the zoning is being used for improper purposes, such as a municipal attempt to reduce property values prior to an expropriation.[211] Nevertheless, a real problem of financial loss resulting from designation may sometimes exist. Since individual property owners are being called on to subsidize conservation, which benefits the community generally, a number of ways that the community could assume the burden have been suggested. The *Ontario Heritage Act* already provides in sections 39 and 45 that a municipal council "may" make grants or loans to the owner of designated property. Other proposals have been discussed, and are outlined at some length in the Ontario Heritage Policy Review's *Technical Paper No. 2*.[212]

Enforcement

In Ontario, the right of municipal authorities to inspect sites for compliance with bylaws raises problems since this right is not clearly set out and "it is well settled that without a statutory right of entry on property, it does not exist."[213] The *Ontario Heritage Act* authorizes municipal representatives to inspect buildings that have been individually designated or that have been proposed for designation.[214] The same inspection powers exist for buildings in heritage conservation districts.[215] I.M. Rogers points out that there is also a right to inspect for offences against fire and maintenance standards.[216]

Three kinds of penalties are possible for offences. The first penalty is the obligation to restore a site to its appearance before the infraction occurred. Municipalities in Ontario are empowered to order a proprietor to restore a designated building that has been illegally altered or demolished.[217] They can also order that a structure that was illegally erected be made to comply with the bylaws[218] or be torn down.[219] Finally, the municipality can do what the owner failed to do for a designated heritage building, at the owner's expense.[220] A second form of penalty is a fine. The maximum fine that can be imposed for offences against the *Ontario Heritage Act* is $50,000 ($250,000 for corporations).[221] In contrast, offences against the *Planning Act* (and the bylaws thereunder) may invoke maximum fines of $25,000 ($50,000 for corporations).[222] A third form of penalty is imprisonment. Offenders against the *Ontario Heritage Act* face a maximum term of one year as an alternative to or in addition to a fine.[223] Offenders against the *Planning Act* (and the bylaws thereunder), however, do not face imprisonment except on failure to pay the fine, or for repeated violations in the face of a court order to cease violating the law.

As mentioned earlier, the applicability of non-federal regulations (including municipal bylaws) to federal and federally regulated works has been the object of considerable jurisprudence. These regulations may be applicable in certain limited circumstances. Furthermore, unlike their counterparts elsewhere,[224] Ontario municipalities are not empowered to subject provincial works to municipal bylaws. In the absence of any statutory authority to the contrary, municipal bylaws do not apply to the Crown.[225] There have been longstanding calls on the provincial government to extend the authority of municipal councils to designate properties, buildings, or structures owned by the province or any of its agencies.[226]

Municipal Inducements

Municipal inducements for the public or private sectors to take better advantage of the built environment have been the subject of study in the Ministry of Culture and Communications' Heritage Legislation Project's *Technical Paper No. 2*.[227] In addition, the Federation of Canadian Municipalities has provided a brief overview in *Capitalizing on Heritage, Arts and Culture*.[228]

PROTECTION OF THE BUILT ENVIRONMENT BY PRIVATE AGREEMENT

In addition to the regulatory measures that can be imposed on the built environment by the public sector, the built environment can also be protected by private contractual agreement. These agreements, usually entitled "covenants" or "easements," are described at Chapter 15.

These agreements may have a big inducement factor in the form of tax relief. These aspects are also discussed in Chapter 15.

An important feature of these tax advantages has a direct bearing on the question of regulations for the built environment in their entirety. There may be cases in which the public authorities would rather enter into a contractual arrangement (with accompanying benefits possible from Revenue Canada) than impose a legislated solution. That prospect remains to be fully explored.

THE CONFLICT OF POLICIES

The foregoing profile of government policies affecting the built environment leaves open one unsettling prospect: that the various levels of government can work entirely at cross-purposes to one another. For example:

- There are several instances of municipal councils voting to destroy, and actually demolishing, national historic sites that were federally commemorated under the *Historic Sites and Monuments Act*.[229]
- There are innumerable instances of the federal *Income Tax Act* providing significant tax deductions (by means of "terminal losses") that helped subsidize the destruction of buildings that were purportedly targeted for protection under provincial housing policies or municipal heritage designations.
- Within a single tier of government such as the federal government, it is entirely possible for the policies of one department (for example, Finance or Revenue) to undo the stated policies of another (for example, Environment).[230]
- Within the provincial government as well, it is possible for some ministries (for example, Culture and Communications) to extol the virtues of the built environment, at the same time as other provincial legislation (for example, the *Assessment Act*)[231] provides preferential treatment to parking lots.[232]
- Within the province's own funding programs (for example, for schools), there is no clear preference for "re-use, recovery and recycling" of buildings over their waste and destruction.[233]

Projects such as the Ministry of Culture and Communications' Heritage Legislation Project have therefore had to be undertaken in a context in which systemic thinking at the governmental level on the subject of the built environment had been largely non-existent. Some might argue that with certain exceptions such as the Ontario Heritage Policy Review, it is still non-existent.

For example, during the winter of 1991-92, there were briefs submitted to the House of Commons Standing Committee on Communications and Culture that listed the specific areas in which federal tax measures and other policies can run at cross-purposes to provincial policies.[234] It was also observed that this contradiction did nothing to foster public confidence in the ability of governments to work together for common goals, or to throw complementary support behind broad national initiatives. Although the committee responded by recommending a "comprehensive federal strategy,"[235] various other observers remarked that such a systemic vision has already been awaited for years.[236]

In short, it is not clear when (if ever) the built environment will cease being the "poor cousin" of the environmental family of issues, in terms of analytical thinking at the government level.

CONCLUSION

Canada's built environment is difficult to protect. This environment, which determines the quality of life of a large part of our population, is also *our* habitat, with all the complications that that entails. Planning for it is as complex as dealing with the subject of human habitat itself. There are no simple solutions. By the same token, there is no single legal mechanism that is sufficient to deal effectively with the problems facing our built environment.

The proper protection of that environment demands a variety of legal techniques, as well as initiative and imagination in their application. First and foremost, however, it requires an acknowledgment that the habitat of people is as important, in terms of the objectives of "re-use, recycle and recover," as the habitat of moose or birds. Those objectives have not been translated into legal or administrative policy, because there have been large gaps in systemic reasoning at the government level, and an absence of political will pertaining to the built environment. It is hoped that a more consistent system will emerge when Canadian officials discover that environmental commitments do not logically begin beyond their doorstep, but within their offices, homes, and other buildings as well.

Marc Denhez

FURTHER READING

Marc Denhez, *Capitalizing on Heritage, Arts and Culture* (Ottawa: Federation of Canadian Municipalities, 1992).

Marc Denhez, *Heritage Fights Back* (Toronto and Ottawa: Fitzhenry & Whiteside and Heritage Canada, 1978).

Deryck Holdsworth, ed., *Reviving Main Street* (Toronto: University of Toronto Press, 1985).

Ontario Heritage Policy Review, *Heritage: Giving Our Past a Future*, a discussion paper (Toronto: Ministry of Citizenship and Culture, 1987).

Ontario Heritage Policy Review, *Technical Paper No. 2: Background Study on Economic Measures for Historic and Heritage Building Conservation and Restoration in Ontario* (Toronto: Ministry of Culture and Communications, 1990).

E. Neville Ward, *Heritage Conservation — The Built Environment*, Lands Directorate Working Paper No. 44 (Ottawa: Environment Canada, April 1986).

ENDNOTES

1   World Commission on Environment and Development, *Our Common Future* (New York: Oxford University Press, 1987).

2   Canada, Environment Canada, *Canada's Green Plan for a Healthy Environment* (Ottawa: Supply and Services, 1990).

3   These "used construction materials" are partly made up of surplus materials from new construction sites (for example, excess wrapping and waste materials) and partly materials resulting from demolition work. For a full breakdown, see Toronto Homebuilders' Association, *Making a Molehill out of a Mountain* (Toronto: the association, 1990).

4   There is no census of Canadian buildings. Academic research in the United States has suggested that there are some 80 million buildings in that country, and the figure of 8 million buildings for Canada is an extrapolation.

5   Study commissioned from Statistics Canada by the Buildings Revival Coalition and documented in *For Economic Renewal* (Ottawa: Buildings Revival Coalition, 1986) [unpublished].

6   Ibid.

7   The fact that renovating existing buildings uses less energy than tearing them down and building new ones has been established for over a decade. The costs have been documented even to the extent of calculating the number of BTUs required to manufacture each brick. See Advisory Council on Historic Preservation, *Assessing the Energy Conservation Benefits of Historic Preservation: Methods and Examples* (Washington, DC: ACHP, 1979).

8   Canada, Department of Communications, *Heritage in the 1990s — Towards a Government of Canada Strategy* (Ottawa: Supply and Services, 1990) (summary report of proceedings of a conference held in Edmonton October 25-27, 1990).

9   Ontario, Ministry of Culture and Communications, *A Strategy for Conserving Ontario's Heritage* (Toronto: the ministry, 1990).

10   See endnote 112, infra. The document is part of a Federation of Canadian Municipalities "kit" entitled *Heritage, Arts and Culture.*

11   *For Economic Renewal,* supra endnote 5. There are about 12,000 buildings in Canada (out of a total stock of some 8 million) that have been the subject of statutory intervention under the label of "heritage"; the overwhelming majority of these are not individually designated as "heritage," but rather are located within "heritage" districts that have been collectively designated.

12   The Green Plan, supra endnote 2, confines its discussion of buildings to an even smaller scope: it addresses only a few hundred buildings that are part of Canada's "historical heritage."

13   The full title is the Convention for the Protection of Cultural Property in the Event of Armed Conflict, The Hague, 1954. These conventions and related documents are reproduced in *Conventions and Recommendations of UNESCO Concerning the Protection of the Cultural Heritage* (Paris: UNESCO, 1984). The Hague Convention of 1954 is, in several key respects, merely a successor to another convention (also signed at The Hague and called Hague IV) entitled Convention on Laws and Customs of War on Land (1907); article 56 of the 1907 convention states that "all seizure of, destruction or wilful damage done to ... historic monuments ... is forbidden." (This was in turn the direct successor to article 56 of a previous convention called Hague II of 1899.) These principles, of which the Hague convention of 1954 is the latest articulation, were also enforced at the Nuremburg trials. The destruction of "cultural monuments" was part of the indictment (section 8) read at the trials as being "contrary

to international conventions ... the laws and customs of war, the general principles of criminal law ... the internal penal laws of the countries in which such crimes are committed." The principal defendant, pertaining to policies of systematic destruction and looting of heritage property, was the Nazi official Alfred Rosenberg. For these and other offences against humanity, Rosenberg was convicted, sentenced, and hanged. See Merryman and Elsen, *Law, Ethics and the Visual Arts* (Philadelphia: University of Pennsylvania Press, 1987).

14   In July 1976.

15   The full title is the Convention Concerning the Protection of the World Cultural and Natural Heritage.

16   Ibid., article 4.

17   Ibid., article 5(b).

18   Ibid., article 1.

19   The convention also establishes a committee, which has the further mandate of compiling a "world heritage list." This list does not, of itself, have intrinsic legal binding effect, but can serve useful educational purposes, and render certain properties eligible for international financial aid. The list, however, does not (contrary to some lay opinion) constitute the only properties of "outstanding universal value" targeted by the convention: see Marc Denhez, "Pacta Sunt Servanda," in *Old Cultures in New Worlds*, ICOMOS Eighth General Assembly, Symposium Papers (Washington, DC: ICOMOS, 1987), vol. 2, 869. The treaty obligations were also addressed in summary fashion by Marc Denhez in *Protecting the Built Environment*, part 1 (Ottawa: Heritage Canada, 1978).

20   A summary of those recommendations was prepared by Marc Denhez in "La formation en gestion," *ICOMOS 1990 Symposium Papers* (Lausanne: ICOMOS, 1990). The verbatim version of the recommendations is found in the compilation, *Conventions and Recommendations of UNESCO*, supra endnote 13.

21   ICOMOS is a non-governmental organization based in Paris, with a close working relationship with UNESCO pertaining to advice on the drafting of the world heritage list referred to in endnote 19, supra.

22   See Federal Heritage Buildings Review Office, *Charters and Conventions*, Working Group Guidelines for Significant Interventions, 2d ed. (Ottawa: Canadian Parks Service, June 1986). The Venice Charter spawned a host of imitators, such as the so-called Declaration of Deschambault in Quebec, the Appleton Charter for the Protection and Enhancement of the Built Environment in Ontario (1983), and a so-called Charter for Heritage Conservation — Province of Ontario (1985), reproduced in the aforementioned compilation. These should not, however, be confused with legal documents.

23   See, for example, the *National Historic Preservation Act*, 1966, 16 USC, c. 470(f), particularly at section 106.

24   See, for example, the *Environment Protection (Impact of Proposals) Act* (Australia), 1974, c. 164, or the *Australian Heritage Commission Act* of 1975, c. 30.

25   This point was alluded to in *Heritage in the 1990s*, supra endnote 8. It is treated in more detail in "Federal Environmental Impact Assessment and Heritage" (March 1991), *Impact: The Voice of the Canadian Heritage Network* 2.

26   *Canadian Environmental Assessment Act*, SC 1992, c. 37.

27 There are several relevant publications that discuss the impact of the US legislation; see: *Section 4(f) US Federal Highway Administration* (Washington, DC: September 24, 1987); National Trust for Historic Preservation, *Section 4(f) Litigation in Which the National Trust Has Participated* (Washington, DC: NTHP, 1990); National Trust for Historic Preservation, *Highway Litigation Under Section 4(f) of the Department of Transportation Act* (Washington, DC: NTHP, 1990); Advisory Council on Historic Preservation, *Section 106 Participation by Local Governments* (Washington, DC: ACHP, 1988); Advisory Council on Historic Preservation, *Section 106 Participation by State Historic Preservation Officers* (Washington, DC: ACHP, 1988); Advisory Council on Historic Preservation, *Working with Section 106* (Washington, DC: ACHP, 1986); Advisory Council On Historic Preservation, *A Five-Minute Look at Section 106 Review* (Washington, DC: ACHP, 1989); Advisory Council on Historic Preservation, *Identification of Historic Properties* (Washington, DC: ACHP, 1988).

28 *National Historic Preservation Act*, supra endnote 23.

29 John Fowler, telephone interview with Marc Denhez, August 1991.

30 *Canadian Environmental Assessment Act*, supra endnote 26. See the amendments referred to by the Jean Charest in his speech of October 10, 1991.

31 See Canadian Parks Service, *Implementation of the Federal Heritage Buildings Policy*, Ottawa, 1988 [manuscript]. The actual Treasury Board document is entitled "Policy on Heritage Conservation of Federal Buildings," *Treasury Board of Canada Circular* no. 1987-13, and is now incorporated as chapter 9 of the *Treasury Board Manual* (volume on real property management).

32 This is reflected, in part, by the language used by the committee. High-ranking buildings may be referred to as "classified," whereas lower-ranking buildings (which nonetheless maintain some interest) may be referred to as "recognized."

33 It is these provincial and municipal codes that have the binding legal effect on the private sector. When provinces and municipalities translate the *National Building Code* into locally applicable statutory documents, they are free to make adjustments for local conditions, etc. Nonetheless, because of the stature of the National Research Council and the decades of work invested, the *Code* remains a highly influential document in setting the course for legislation.

34 *Ontario Building Code*, RRO 1990, reg. 61.

35 The building inspector's use of discretion can, in certain circumstances, lead to exposure to lawsuit in the event that something untoward later occurs in the building that does not coincide verbatim with the *National Building Code*. See Chapter 6 for a brief discussion of the tort liability of government officials.

36 The *National Building Code* is drafted by a committee entitled the Canadian Commission on Building and Fire Codes. The commission, in turn, is under the supervision of the National Research Council.

37 For example, see Marc Denhez, "Codes and Quakes" (November 1990), *Canadian Association of Municipal Administrators Bulletin* 1. See also "Reno Code Hits Roadblock" (September 1991), *Canadian Home Builders Association National* 4. A detailed set of proposals on amending the *National Building Code* to facilitate residential renovation was submitted by the Association for Preservation Technology

to the Affordability and Choice Today program: see Association for Preservation Technology, *Technical Code Update for Residential Renovation* (unpublished, 1991, available from Marc Denhez).

38 See Alistair J.M. Aikman, *Background Discussion to the Committee Paper of the ACNBC* (Ottawa: Associate Committee of the National Building Code, National Research Council, February 1991).

39 The officials had initially accepted, as a sort of compromise, the notion of drafting "guidelines" to assist building inspectors in "interpreting" the existing sections of the *National Building Code* as they apply to renovation projects. These "guidelines," however, are still subject to discretion by the local building inspector, who would be free to continue refusing all approvals on projects that are not verbatim identical to the *Code*. Furthermore, many of the problematic *Code* provisions affecting renovation (for example, the mathematical specifications for exits, halls, etc.) are black-and-white, and leave no room for "interpretation" anyway.

40 See "Now a Go for Reno Code" (March 1993), *CHBA Renovator Report* 1.

41 See *Heritage in the 1990s*, supra endnote 8.

42 As mentioned at endnote 12, the Green Plan refers only to "historical heritage"; at present, the buildings covered (that is, those commemorated under the *Historic Sites and Monuments Act*, RSC 1985, c. H-4, represent fewer than 400 buildings out of a total estimated inventory of 8 million.

43 *Historic Sites and Monuments Act*, ibid.

44 A description of these limitations, particularly those found in the *Constitution Act, 1867*, now *Constitution Act, 1982*, RSC 1985, app. II, no. 44, is found in *Protecting the Built Environment*, supra endnote 19, at 11-17.

45 Ibid., at 14.

46 See *Hamilton Harbour Com'rs v. City of Hamilton*, Ontario High Court of Justice, 1978 [unreported], appealed unsuccessfully to the Ontario Court of Appeal, *loc. cit.* (1978), 21 OR (2d) 459, 91 DLR (3d) 353, appeal to the Supreme Court of Canada abandoned. See also *Bevark Holdings Ltd. v. Toronto Harbour Com'rs* (1987), 58 OR (2d) 87 (HCJ).

47 "It may be that, while a municipality cannot prohibit the use of land for railway purposes, its authority to restrict the use of such lands once they have been abandoned for purposes connected with the railway undertaking or devoted to a use unconnected with it would be upheld." I.M. Rogers, *Canadian Law of Planning and Zoning* (Toronto: Carswell) (looseleaf), 143.

48 *Heritage Railway Stations Protection Act*, RSC 1985, c. 52 (4th Supp.), first enacted as SC 1988, c. 62.

49 This legislation is far more specific than the previous legislation, which referred to a prohibition on the "removal" of stations without the approval of the Canadian Transport Commission. This prohibition was found at sections 119 and 120 of the *Railway Act*, RSC 1985, c. R-3. Nonetheless, a railway company that proceeded with the demolition of a station (on an active line) without having sought and obtained such approval was open to prosecution and conviction under the *Railway Act*. See, for example, *Canadian Pacific Limited v. R.*, Quebec Sup, Ct., file no. 36-000750-870 (January 27, 1989).

50 *Public Buildings Cooperative Uses Act*, 1974, 40 USC section 606 *et seq*. Major US states have comparable legislation. See C.J. Duerken, ed., *Handbook on Historic Preservation Law* (Washington, DC: National Trust and Historic Preservation, 1983), 165.

51 *Heritage in the 1990s*, supra endnote 8.

52 "Policy on Federal Heritage Conservation of Buildings," supra endnote 31.

53 For example, Ottawa's Daly Building represented some 200,000 square feet of centrally located but unused office space, which the federal government had left in a virtually abandoned state for some 16 years. Normally, no private property owner in Canada would risk leaving his building vacant for even a few days, without risking lapse of insurance policies and mortgage conditions appended to conserve the structural integrity of the property. Various NGOs have argued that the federal government is virtually the only institution in Canada that dares undertake such behaviour.

54 *Income Tax Act*, RSC 1952, c. 148, as amended by SC 1970-71-72, c. 63, and as subsequently amended.

55 *Excise Tax Act*, RSC 1985, c. E-15, as amended.

56 These requirements are typified in the *Ontario Building Code*, supra endnote 34, under the *Ontario Building Code Act*, RSO 1990, c. B.13. This code, which is legally binding on most new construction projects and on most significant major rehabilitation projects, is in turn modelled on the *National Building Code*, prepared by the National Research Council.

57 The affairs of "the reno industry" are the subject matter of a number of current periodicals, including *Canadian Building, Renew*, and *Aluminews*.

58 Revenue Canada, *Interpretation Bulletin* IT-128R, paragraph 4(a). This is sometimes called the "once-and-for-all test." Compare this opinion to Justice Estey's comment in *R. v. Johns-Manville Canada Inc.*, [1985] 2 CTC 111 (SCC): "The regular recurrence of the acquisition is in no way decisive." Compare also the comment by Chief Justice Jacket, speaking to the Corporate Management Trust Conference (1981) and cited in *Healey v. MNR*, [1984] CTC 2001, at 2003: "There is no test that I find less helpful for general application than the 'Once and for All' or enduring asset or advantage test."

59 IT-128R, supra endnote 58, at paragraph 4(b). Compare this opinion with the comment of Judge Proulx in *Bergeron v. MNR*, 90 DTC 1513 (TCC), who says that in order for work to be capital, the test is not just a question of betterment, but whether "the purpose ... is to replace an asset by a new one and work that involves *such* degree of improvement to an asset that it *becomes a new one*" [emphasis added].

60 IT-128R, supra endnote 58, at paragraph 4(c).

61 Ibid., at paragraph 4(d). Compare this test with what Justice Jerome said in *Gold Bar Developments v. R.*, [1987] 1 CTC 262, 87 DTC 5152 (FCTD): "The more substantial the repair, the less likely it is to recur (certainly the fervent hope of the building's owner) but it remains a repair expenditure nonetheless." See also the comment by Judge Jacket in *Canada Steamship Lines v. MNR*, [1966] CTC 255, at 257 (Ex. Ct.): "I cannot accept the view that the cost of repairs ceases to be current expenses and becomes outlays of capital merely because the repairs required are very extensive or because their cost is substantial."

62 IT-128R, supra endnote 58, at paragraph 4(e). Compare this opinion with the comment of Judge Bowman in *McLaughlin v. MNR*, 92 DTC 1030 (TCC), where the department treated as capital all the repair expenses on a recently acquired century home: "I find the premise of the assessment to be wholly unreasonable and indeed arbitrary. No basis for this extraordinary conclusion was given" and "Had the Minister applied common sense in making the assessment here the appellant would not be before the Court."

63 IT-128R, supra endnote 58, at paragraph 4(f).

64 For example, if rehab work conferred an "enduring benefit," this created a presumption that the expenditure was capital, and not deductible; a similar presumption was created when the work improved the property. If the work tended to created a stand-alone item (as opposed to one that was an integral part of the structure), this created a presumption that the work was capital as opposed to deductible; a similar presumption would occur when the value of the rehab work was large in relation to the original acquisition cost of the property. Furthermore, when rehab work was conducted shortly after acquisition of the property (for example, in the first year) or shortly before the property was sold, these factors would also create a presumption that the expense was capital and not deductible.

65 This reasoning would also apply to new wiring, new windows and doors, and new balconies.

66 This would be the likely result under the "enduring benefit" test, the "betterment" test, and in some cases the "relative value" test.

67 The Supreme Court of Canada refused leave to appeal of the *Goyer* decision on October 21, 1987. The Quebec Court of Appeal decision is reported at *SMRQ v. Goyer*, [1987] RJQ 988.

68 Ibid. The jurisprudence included the early British cases and later decisions of the Federal Court.

69 Ibid., at 992 (translation by the Heritage Canada Foundation).

70 Revenue Quebec had issued an interpretation bulletin of its own, which corresponded in most substantial areas with IT-128R. It was called IMP 128-4 (1984). Within weeks of the *Goyer* decision, Revenue Quebec had issued a new interpretation bulletin called IMP 124-4/R1 (1987), December 21, 1987.

71 *Gold Bar*, supra endnote 61.

72 *Bergeron*, supra endnote 59 [emphasis added].

73 IMP 128-4/R1, supra endnote 70.

74 In other words, despite the unambiguous wording of the judgment quoted above, Revenue Quebec wished to maintain the disqualifications on "newly-acquired used property" and work "in anticipation of sale." The practical effect would be to confine *Goyer* to longstanding landlords and to exclude developers who may wish to rehab for profit before or after sale.

75 *McLaughlin*, supra endnote 62.

76 Marc Denhez expands on possible interpretations to be given to the *Goyer* decision in Ontario Heritage Policy Review, *Technical Paper No. 2* (Toronto: Ministry of Culture and Communications, 1990).

77 For example, these same principles allow capital equipment to be written off over a certain number of years.

78 First, the existing practice does nothing to advance the cause of tax simplification, as the following will show. It has been the standard practice for property owners to claim depreciation on what (broadly speaking) could be called the initial cost of a building, called its adjusted cost base (ACB). The practice has been to assume that with each passing year, that value at acquisition declines (numerically) by a set amount: for most buildings, this was assumed to be at a rate of 5 per cent (later changed to 4 per cent). This claim of depreciation on one's initial cost was called "claiming CCA on one's ACB." However, the different tax treatment of building and land has created the necessity for highly complex accounting practices and calculations, not the least of which occur in every purchase or sale of investment buildings in Canada, as the buyer and seller must jockey for position concerning the buyer's desired ACB, the prospective CCA to be claimed, and the vendor's level of capital gain or other tax problems to be encountered. For example, if the seller sells a building at a price that is higher than the point to which he had depreciated the building (called its undepreciated capital cost), the *Income Tax Act* will treat that excess depreciation as constituting entirely taxable income. This is predictable, since the depreciation claimed on the building was tax-deductible. Logically, Revenue Canada takes the view that if CCA was claimed on property that did not in fact depreciate by that amount, this amount should be paid back. This is called "recapture."

79 If a building with an ACB of $100,000 in 1980 merely kept pace with the consumer price index, it would have a value of $178,000 in 1990. Consequently, if it maintained a value of only $100,000 (that is, its ACB), that would mean that its actual value (in constant dollars) had actually depreciated by 44 per cent. However, what CCA does is to hypothesize an even larger decline in real-dollar actual value: the tax system posits that the building would have a 1990 tax value of $66,000 — that is, a constant-dollar decline in actual value of 63 per cent over a decade. Even if a drop in inflation shaved an annual 2 per cent off that figure, the result would still be economically improbable for most of Ontario, and out of the question in the Golden Horseshoe.

80 Even positive in inflation at 3 per cent, the cumulative effect of the decrease in the value of money added to the CCA is this: it postulates that in constant dollars, a building loses 7 per cent of its value annually. This simply fails to correspond to reality in the majority of Canadian markets. Admittedly, CCA is likely to be "recaptured" on disposition; in other words, where property owners have claimed the maximum of tax-deductible depreciation (which is claimable under the Act) and eventually resell the property, the sale price usually reflects this overdepreciation, and that overdepreciation comes back into taxable income. In other words, the effect of this overdepreciation is temporary. However, in the meantime CCA on real estate arguably tends to serve merely as systemic tax deferral, at substantial cost to the treasury, because years may have elapsed and the value of the tax dollars used to repay is substantially lower (in constant-dollar terms) than the value of the taxes that would have been collected if no overdepreciation had been claimed in the first place.

81 For example, in the case of slumlords.

82 In that case, property taxes.

83 The case of the Uniroyal/Domtar property in Alberta, on which chemical leaks had occurred, was reported by several newspapers in October 1991. Domtar had argued that

the chemical leakage had devalued its land, and hence that the assessment (for property tax purposes) should be lowered. The argument was accepted by Alberta provincial authorities. See Randy Ray, "Tax Breaks for Polluters Spark Row in Alberta" (March 1992), *Canadian Bar Association National* 16.

84　The situation was sufficiently unusual that it gave rise to one of the rare negative editorial comments in the *CCH Canadian Master Tax Guide* (Don Mills, Ont.: CCH Canadian Ltd., 1990), paragraph 4155.

85　See Marc Denhez, *Heritage Fights Back* (Toronto and Ottawa: Fitzhenry & Whiteside and Heritage Canada, 1978).

86　The following discussion assumes the exhaustion of buildings in that class. Otherwise, there is a series of complex mathematical calculations of UCC that are less generous than the approach before 1981.

87　That is, a presumption of disposition at fair market value, with or without elections.

88　*CCH Canadian Master Tax Guide 1990*, supra endnote 84, at paragraph 4155.

89　The calculation of the tax deduction can be illustrated by the following equations. Let us suppose that a building had a fair market value (FMV) of $150,000 and a depreciated cost (UCC) of $250,000.

Year	*Equation*	*Illustration*
1981-1987	deduction = $\dfrac{\text{UCC} - \text{FMV}}{2}$	$\dfrac{\$250,000 - \$150,000}{2}$ = \$50,000
1988-1989	deduction = $\dfrac{2(\text{UCC} - \text{FMV})}{3}$	$\dfrac{2(\$250,000 - 150,000)}{3}$ = \$66,666
1990-	deduction = $\dfrac{3(\text{UCC} - \text{FMV})}{4}$	$\dfrac{3(\$250,000 - 150,000)}{4}$ = \$75,000

90　This argument tends to be reflected in actual Finance Canada practice: the department has seen fit to change the terminal loss provisions three times within the last decade.

91　*Ontario Building Code*, RRO 1990, reg. 61. Enacted under the authority of the *Ontario Building Code Act*, supra endnote 56.

92　Table A is used when it can be demonstrated to the chief official that compliance with requirement part 3 of the building code is impractical (1) because of structural or construction difficulties or (2) because it is a threat to the preservation of heritage building. Table B can be used for the requirements of part 9 of the building code (without having to demonstrate the impracticalities noted above). In addition, alternate measures can be substituted for the above conditions. See *Technical Code Update for Residential Renovation*, supra endnote 37.

93　See *National Historic Preservation Act*, supra endnote 23, and *Environment Protection (Impact of Proposals) Act (Australia)*, supra endnote 24.

94　For example, *Alberta Land Surface Conservation and Reclamation Act*, RSA 1980, c. L-3, section 8, and *Alberta Historical Resources Act*, RSA 1980, c. H-8, section 22.

95　*Environmental Assessment Act*, RSO 1990, c. E.18, section 1.

96　Ibid., section 1(c)(iv).

97　Ibid., section 5(3)(d).

98　By virtue of section 4 of O. reg. 836/76, now RRO 1990, reg. 334, section 4. The regulation, proclaimed in October 1976, substantially limits the scope of the Act passed in 1975. Reg. 836/76 states that when a building was started before 1975 (the date of the Act) its "retirement" is exempt from the relevant provision of the Act. According to the Environmental Approvals Branch of the Environmental Assessment and Planning Division of the Ministry of the Environment, the demolition of a public building built before 1975 is really the retirement of the building and the demolition of it may disregard the procedures set forth in the Act.

99   For details on the Ontario Heritage Bridges Policy, contact the Ontario Ministry of Culture and Communications, 77 Bloor Street, Toronto, Ontario M7A 2R9.

100 For example, by Marc Denhez in "We Must Require Debate Before Heritage Is Trashed," *The Ottawa Citizen*, December 19, 1987.

101 For example, New York state.

102 "The legislation should provide general authority for *all* provincial ministries and agencies (not just the Ministry of Culture and Communications) to establish policies and programs for carrying out the purposes of the Act" [emphasis added]. Ontario, Ministry of Culture and Communications, *Proposals for Legislation: The Ontario Heritage Policy Review* (Toronto: the ministry, May 1990), C4.

103 *Archaeological and Historic Sites Protection Act*, RSO 1970, c. 26, section 2.

104 Ibid., section 3.

105 *Ontario Heritage Act*, SO 1974, c. 122, section 71(2), now RSO 1990, c. O.18.

106 For examples of such powers in other provincial statutes see Alberta, *Historical Resources Act*, RSA 1980, c. H-8; British Columbia, *Heritage Conservation Act*, RSBC 1979, c. 165; Manitoba, *The Heritage Manitoba Act*, RSM 1987, c. H39; New Brunswick, *Historic Sites Protection Act*, RSNB 1973, c. H-6; Newfoundland, *Historic Resources Act*, RSN 1990, c. H-4; Prince Edward Island, *Recreation Development Act*, RSPEI 1988, c. R-8; Quebec, *Cultural Property Act*, RSQ 1977, c. B-4; and Saskatchewan, *Heritage Property Act*, RSS 1978, c. 2.2.

107 See Ontario Historical Society, *The Ontario Heritage Act—Present Problems, Future Prospects* (Toronto: OHS, 1977), 3, 9, and 17.

108 *Ontario Heritage Act*, supra endnote 105, section 47(b); see also part VI of the Act generally.

109 *Proposals for Legislation*, supra endnote 102, at C4-C8, discusses "the provincial interest in heritage conservation" and outlines a substantial list of specific statutory proposals.

110 *Technical Paper No. 2*, supra endnote 76.

111 Ibid.

112 Marc Denhez, *Capitalizing on Heritage, Arts and Culture* (Ottawa: Federation of Canadian Municipalities, 1992).

113 *Ontario Heritage Act*, supra endnote 105; *Planning Act*, RSO 1990, c. P.13; *Municipal Act*, RSO 1990, c. M.45.

114 For example, Manitoba, *Planning Act*, RSM 1987, c. P80; *City of Winnipeg Act*, SM 1971, c. 105; New Brunswick, *Community Planning Act*, RSNB 1973, c. C-12.

115 United Kingdom, *Civic Amenities Act*, 1967, c. 69, section 1(1).

116 Section 2(b) of the *Planning Act*, supra endnote 113, even directs the minister, in his surpervision of the overall planning process, to have regard to "the protection of features of significant architectural, historical or archaeological interest." This distin-

guishes Ontario from the predicament which occurred in an Alberta municipality. In *Tegon Developments Ltd. et al. v. Council of the City of Edmonton et al.* (Appellate Division of the Supreme Court of Alberta, December 12, 1977; appeal to the Supreme Court of Canada dismissed November 30, 1978), the Supreme Court of Alberta held (among other things) that preservation of historic sites was not a "planning purpose." In the words of Justice Moir, speaking for the Supreme Court of Alberta (Appellate Division), "it is not a valid exercise of the [planning] power to use it to preserve historical sites and to induce others to advance money to protect historical sites ... It was not a planning purpose." That point was not, however, the deciding issue in the case; the deciding issue was as follows. Alberta municipalities had been empowered (under old legislation that is now amended) to regulate "use of land" and "special aspects of specific kinds of development." Efforts to protect a historic district were invalid because they fell outside these municipal powers: according to the courts, these efforts did not regulate "use" because they tried to protect buildings regardless of use; and they did not regulate "specific kinds of development" because they regulated all development. The Supreme Court of Canada could have decided the issue when *Tegon* was appealed, but instead the court confined its decision to semantic issues, thereby leaving open the question whether conservation of the built environment (or even its heritage components) is a legitimate planning purpose.

117 "Heritage planning and protection should be an integral part of 'mainstream' planning and management at all levels." *Proposals for Legislation*, supra endnote 102, at 7.

118 *Canadian Law of Planning and Zoning*, supra endnote 47, at 69.

119 In the case of regional municipalities, "their area municipalities must amend their zoning by-laws to bring them into line with the plan." Ibid., at 197.

120 For example, the Nova Scotia *Planning Act*, RSNS 1989, c. 346, section 33.

121 *Bredin et al. v. City of Cornwall*, unreported judgment of the Ontario Court, General Division, Cornwall, file no. 294/90.

122 The building was one of fewer than 400 buildings in Canada commemorated under the *Historic Sites and Monuments Act*, supra endnote 42.

123 City of Cornwall Official Plan, section 10.3.3.

124 *Planning Act*, supra endnote 113, section 1(j). "Undertaking" is defined by *Black's Law Dictionary* (St. Paul, Minn.: West Publishing, 1979) as "a promise, engagement or stipulation," and by Canadian jurisprudence as "an arrangement under which physical things are used" (in *Re Regulation and Control of Radio Communication*, [1932] AC 304, at 315 (PC)).

125 *Bredin*, supra endnote 121, at 12-13.

126 This statement was *obiter*.

127 *Bredin*, supra endnote 121, at 14.

128 *Planning Act*, supra endnote 113, section 33(2).

129 Ibid.

130 Ibid., sections 33(3), 33(6), and 33(7).

131 Part IV of the *Ontario Heritage Act*, supra endnote 105.

132 Ibid., section 29(2).

133 As of July 1992, there were 200 LACACs; that is, only 25 per cent of Ontario's municipalities had one. However, those municipalities represent most of the major

communities and 80 per cent of the populated areas. A few large municipalities still had no LACAC — for example, Oshawa.

134 *Ontario Heritage Act*, supra endnote 105, sections 29(1) and 29(3). Notice can be given by registered mail: section 67.

135 Ibid., section 30.

136 Ibid., sections 29(5), 29(7)-(13).

137 Ibid., section 29(14).

138 It is settled that even ministerial discretion is subject to the purposes for which it was granted to the minister: see *Roncarelli v. Duplessis*, [1959] SCR 121.

139 "If there is some evidence [of heritage value] ... this Court cannot substitute its own opinion for that of the [authorities] ... as to whether that evidence was sufficient or good enough, or both, to make the declaration under the Act": *Murray v. Richmond* (1978), 7 CELR 145 (BC SC), *per* Gould J.

140 *St. Peter's Evangelical Lutheran Church v. City of Ottawa* (1983), 140 DLR (3d) 577, at 593 (SCC).

141 *Ontario Heritage Act*, supra endnote 105, section 33.

142 For example: British Columbia, *Heritage Conservation Act*, supra endnote 106; Prince Edward Island, *City of Charlottetown Act*; Newfoundland, *Historic Resources Act*, supra endnote 106; Nova Scotia, *Heritage Property Act*, RSNS 1989, c. 199; Quebec, *Cultural Property Act*, supra endnote 106; Manitoba, *The Heritage Manitoba Act*, supra endnote 106; Saskatchewan, *Heritage Property Act*, supra endnote 106; Alberta, *Historical Resources Act*, supra endnote 106.

143 *Ontario Heritage Act*, supra endnote 105, section 34(2).

144 Ibid.

145 Ibid., section 34(4); see also Ontario, Ministry of Culture and Recreation, *Guidelines on the Designation of Heritage Conservation Districts* (Toronto: the ministry, 1977), 7 and Ontario, Ministry of Culture and Recreation, *Guidelines for Designation of Buildings of Architectural and Historic Importance* (Toronto: the ministry, [1977]), 5.

146 Supra endnote 98. See also C.L. Sandiford, *An Analysis of Ontario's Preservation Legislation* (unpublished), 51 and 56. There may, however, be a way to extend the protective period beyond 270 days. Designation renders void all previous demolition permits, and there is nothing to say that a building cannot be designated more than once. A council could thus spend time deliberating, grant permits, revoke them immediately by designation, then wait for a new application to be submitted and "studied." Although this process could conceivably go on forever, litigation would presumably intervene, in which case the following points should be remembered. Jurisprudence is still divided on the interpretation of land-use controls. Some decisions still hold that the power to restrict private property rights must be interpreted restrictively. Under this interpretation, the mechanism described above would probably be treated as an abuse of the municipal legislative process. However, an increasing volume of jurisprudence now holds that land use controls deserve liberal interpretation and should be supported unless they are clearly beyond the power of the authorities.

The clearest example of this approach is found in the case of *E.J. Murphy et al. v. City of Victoria* (1976), 1 MPLR 166 (BC SC), in which extraordinary demolition controls were upheld because the court refused to challenge the city's assertion that the threat to its heritage constituted an "emergency." In that case, the city was empowered to designate buildings for protection as heritage buildings, but nothing in the city's ordinary powers prevented the owner from demolishing the building between the time he received notice of the impending designation and the time the designation became effective (a period of several months). The city therefore declared a "state of emergency" and invoked the extraordinary powers that it may use in "emergencies." The bylaw stated that because of the emergency no person shall demolish a building mentioned in the schedule to the bylaw except in accordance with the bylaw and no person shall construct a building or structure on the lands designated. Furthermore, all demolition permits then in force were revoked. The court refused to overrule this "state of emergency." An Ontario court could conceivably reach the same decision. However, the case has been described as running "counter to traditional interpretations of municipal powers." (S.M. Makuch, "Annotation," *E.J. Murphy*, ibid., at 167.) The author, nevertheless, balances the statement with a number of cases both pro and con. A similar judicial approach could perhaps uphold attempts to protract a freeze on demolition beyond 270 days. It is important to note, however, that any attempt to use this procedure to protract the freeze on demolition beyond 270 days is unprecedented in Ontario, and one cannot firmly predict a judicial response as positive as the one in the *E.J. Murphy* case. Consequently, any attempt to extend controls beyond 270 days should be viewed as relatively hazardous. This hazard factor is reinforced by the Supreme Court of Canada's severity on the subject of the need for strict observance of all procedural requirements under the *Ontario Heritage Act* (supra endnote 105) (see *St. Peter's Evangelical Lutheran Church*, supra endnote 140).

147 *City of Toronto Act*, SO 1987, c. 19.

148 Ibid., as amended by SO 1990, c. 29.

149 For example, the Quebec *Cultural Property Act*, supra endnote 106, article 45 *et seq.* Gastown and Chinatown in Vancouver were designated under the British Columbia *Archaeological and Historic Sites Protection Act*, SBC 1972, c. 4 (now the BC *Heritage Conservation Act*, SBC 1977, c. 37).

150 *Ontario Heritage Act*, supra endnote 105, section 41(3).

151 See *Guidelines on the Designation of Heritage Conservation Districts*, supra endnote 145, at 3.

152 Ontario, Ministry of Culture and Recreation, *Heritage Conservation Districts and the Ontario Heritage Act* (Toronto: the ministry, 1977) [no pagination]. This recommendation is based on section 41(1) of the Act.

153 The reference here is to the local planning advisory committee of a planning area, appointed by the municipal council, under the *Planning Act*, supra endnote 113. See section 8 and following sections.

154 Ontario Historical Society, supra endnote 107, at 4.

155 Ibid.

156 *Ontario Heritage Act*, supra endnote 105, section 41(1); the "plan" provisions of section 41(1) are not to be confused with those of section 40(1), because the former relate to statements of principle, whereas the latter refer to much more specific plans.

157 "An extensive analysis of the chosen area should be undertaken, examining physical, social and economic conditions." Ibid.

158   Ibid., section 40(1).
159   Ibid.
160   Ibid., section 34(2).
161   Ibid.
162   Ibid.
163   Ibid.
164   Ibid.
165   Ibid., section 42.
166   Ibid., section 42(c).
167   That is, under section 29, ibid.
168   Ibid., section 41(2).
169   The municipality can, under section 33(1) of the *Ontario Heritage Act*, control all alterations of individually designated buildings. In the case of districts, only external alterations of buildings can be controlled: see section 42 of the Act.
170   Ibid., section 33(6).
171   Ibid., section 44(1).
172   Ibid., section 34(5).
173   Ibid., section 42.
174   Ibid., section 33(1).
175   Ontario Historical Society, supra endnote 107, at 12.
176   *Ontario Heritage Act*, supra endnote 105, section 1(a).
177   Ibid., section 33(6).
178   Ibid., section 33(11).
179   Ibid., section 33(13).
180   Ibid.
181   Ibid., section 42.
182   Ibid., section 29.
183   Ibid., section 44(1)(b).
184   For example, the Quebec *Cultural Property Act*, supra endnote 106, article 30; and the Alberta *Historical Resources Act*, supra endnote 106, section 19.
185   See *Re H.G. Winton Ltd. and Borough of North York* (1978), 20 OR (2d) 737 (Div. Ct.).
186   *Planning Act*, supra endnote 113, section 34 (1)(4).
187   Ibid.
188   Ibid., sections 34(1)(2) and 34(1)(4).
189   In other jurisdictions, it is customary to make only minor modifications in the use zoning bylaw applicable to valuable areas. For example, one may see a prohibition on service stations, wholesale outlets, or the like. It should be remembered, however, that no such bylaw can have a retroactive effect. Consequently, any regulation to exclude such uses from the area would have the effect of "freezing" such installations at the number that existed at the time of the passing of the bylaw.
190   See *R. v. Gibson; Ex parte Cromiller*, [1959] OWN 254; also *Canadian Law of Planning and Zoning*, supra endnote 47, at 123-24.
191   *Planning Act*, supra endnote 113, section 34(1) (4). Some cities are currently considering adapting the 80-120 per cent formula to setbacks — that is, by stating that the setback cannot be less than 80 per cent or more than 120 per cent of the average setback

of other buildings on certain streets. This approach is suitable for streets where setback is already irregular. The formula is still untested in Ontario.

192 *Municipal Act*, supra endnote 113, section 354(126).

193 Again, precision is required — see, for example, the Gastown Sign Guidelines, available from the Central Area Division of the Vancouver City Planning Department.

194 Theoretically, fences and walls might fall within the definition of "buildings" and be regulated in the same manner as buildings. However, certain special provisions are usually made for fences: *Municipal Act*, supra endnote 113, section 355(1), paragraph 19. Furthermore, urban municipalities can order any owner to enclose a "vacant lot"; it is not clear whether parking lots fall into this category: *Municipal Act*, section 364, para 12.

195 *Planning Act*, supra endnote 113, section 31(1)(e).

196 Ibid., section 31(3).

197 Ibid., section 31(2).

198 For example, one case, *George Sebok Real Estate Ltd. and David E. Marlow v. The Corporation of the City of Woodstock* (1978), 21 OR (2d) 761, the Court of Appeal held that a bylaw passed under section 36 of the *Planning Act* and prescribing standards for the maintenance of physical conditions and for the occupancy of property could call for thicker walls, new walls in the attic, more exits, and an improved basement floor — that is, for extensive alterations entailing substantial expenditure of money. The court held that such provisions fell within the ambit of standards for the occupancy of property because such standards are higher than those for the maintenance of property. From the point of view of heritage conservation, however, such a high standard may prove to be an incentive for the owner to demolish the building concerned.

199 Alberta *Historical Resources Act*, supra endnote 106, section 35.

200 Ibid., section 22(2).

201 *Ontario Heritage Act*, supra endnote 105, section 62.

202 Ibid., section 30.

203 *Planning Act*, supra endnote 113, section 43(1).

204 Ibid.

205 Ibid., section 43(13).

206 In Alberta the problem arose in connection with section 24 of the *Historical Resources Act*, supra endnote 106. Section 24(1) provides that if a bylaw under section 22 or 23 (allowing for designations) decreases the economic value of a building, structure or land that is within the area designated by the bylaw, the council shall by bylaw provide the owner of that building, structure, or land with compensation for the decrease in economic value. In British Columbia the problem arose in connection with section 478(1) of the *Municipal Act*, RSBC 1979, c. 290, which provides: "The council shall make to owners, occupiers or other persons interested in real property … injuriously affected by the exercise of any of its powers, due compensation for any damages … necessarily resulting from the exercise of such powers beyond any advantage which the claimant may derive from the contemplated work."

207 *Expropriations Act*, RSO 1990, c. E.26.

208 Ibid., sections 13 and 21.

209 Ibid., section 1(1).

210 Ibid.

211 An extensive discussion of such purposes is found in *Canadian Law of Planning and Zoning*, supra endnote 47, at 122-26.

212 *Technical Paper No. 2*, supra endnote 76.

213 *Canadian Law of Planning and Zoning*, supra endnote 47, at 253.

214 *Ontario Heritage Act*, supra endnote 105, section 38.

215 Ibid., section 45.

216 *Canadian Law of Planning and Zoning*, supra endnote 47, at 254.

217 *Ontario Heritage Act*, supra endnote 105, section 69.

218 *Canadian Law of Planning and Zoning*, supra endnote 47, at 259.

219 Ibid., at 265-66.

220 *Ontario Heritage Act*, supra endnote 105, section 69(5).

221 Ibid., sections 69(1)-(2).

222 Ibid., section 66.

223 Ibid.

224 For example, New Brunswick's *Community Planning Act*, RSNB 1973, c. C-12, sections 18(2) and 27; *Municipal Heritage Preservation Act*, RSNB 1973, c. M-21.1, section 2(2).

225 *Canadian Law of Planning and Zoning*, supra endnote 47, at 143.

226 Ontario Historical Society, supra endnote 107, at 3 and 18.

227 *Technical Paper No. 2*, supra endnote 76.

228 *Capitalizing on Heritage, Arts and Culture*, supra endnote 112.

229 *Historic Sites and Monuments Act*, supra endnote 42.

230 For example, the policy declarations of the Green Plan on the importance of re-using historic sites — as compared with the policy of Revenue Canada pertaining to the deductibility (or otherwise) of work to enable such re-use.

231 See the *Assessment Act*, RSO 1990, c. A.31, section 7, particularly section 7(1)(i).

232 Parking lots, for example, have among the most preferential positions in terms of assessment for business tax. See Stanley Makuch, *Canadian Municipal and Planning Law* (Toronto: Carswell, 1983), 97-98:

> The business assessment is based on a percentage of the assessment of real property used and occupied for business purposes. ... In Ontario, the rate of assessment is set in the legislation and is different for different types of businesses. Every person carrying on a business of a car park, for example, will be assessed at an amount equal to 25% of the assessed value of the land occupied and used for that purpose, while a manufacturer will be assessed at 60% of the assessed value of the land used or occupied for that purpose. ... The result is that, in Ontario at least, manufacturing is taxed more heavily than parking lots under the business tax. There is no opportunity for municipalities to alter this burden although it may be argued that parking lots should be taxed more heavily in order to reduce commuting by motor vehicles and because such commuting places a heavy burden on municipalities in terms of road construction and maintenance.

233 The Ottawa Board of Education (OBE), for example, referred to "the province's tendency to favour construction of new schools over the renovation of existing buildings": see *Rebuilding for the Future*, conference hosted by the OBE, March 31-

April 1, 1989, 1. In practice, however, the argument appears overstated. Although the Ministry of Education provides no subsidy preference for re-use (over replacement) in "non-growth areas" (for example, older neighbourhoods where most older schools are located), it does in "growth areas" (for example, suburbs), and does not knowingly subsidize demolitions. The question remains, however, whether this approach goes far enough.

234 For example, the briefs by the Heritage Canada Foundation and Marc Denhez.

235 See Canada, House of Commons, Standing Committee on Communications and Culture, *The Ties That Bind*, report of the Standing Committee on Communications and Culture (Ottawa: Supply and Services, April 1992), xxi, recommendation 13(iv).

236 *Assessing the Energy Conservation Benefits of Historic Preservation*, supra endnote 7.

15

Conservation Covenants, Easements, and Gifts

CONTENTS

If you want to preserve the historical, architectural, archaeological, or natural qualities of your property for the benefit of future generations, you have two options. One is to donate the land to a government agency or a charitable organization that will protect it. But if you don't want to give your land away, there is also a way to have the property permanently protected without actually relinquishing title to it. In this chapter, we will discuss both ways of ensuring long-term protection of land — conservation covenants and easements, and gifts.

COVENANTS AND EASEMENTS

Individuals who want their property to remain in private hands, but are disposed to having a conservation organization or institution exercise protective controls, can enter into special contracts that provide for the protective measures to be registered on title. This kind of contract has been used frequently in North America, for fishing areas and duck ponds; more recently, there has been a growing tendency to apply it to certain cherished buildings. The Ontario Heritage Foundation has negotiated protective contracts over many such properties, and these registered contracts should ensure the future of some 150 properties in Ontario. These properties include sites of geological importance, botanical importance, and a variety of architectural and historic landmarks. Wildlife Habitat Canada has produced an admirable profile of this device.[1]

Most agreements are simple contracts: they bind the signatories, but they do not bind anyone else.[2] If an owner agrees to protect the property against destruction and later sells it or dies, the agreement would usually not be binding on the future owner. Conservationists would usually find this situation unsatisfactory.

Fortunately, two special forms of agreement are available to deal with that problem; called "easements" and "restrictive covenants," they bind future owners as well as the present owner. The situation is summarized in the accompanying chart.

Contract	Purpose	Condition	Applicable Property
Common law restrictive covenant	To stop the owner from doing something on his or her land	• Must own land nearby that is "benefited" • Must not require the owner to spend money	Any
Common law easement	To allow someone else to do something on the owner's land	Same two conditions as above	Any
Statutory covenant/ easement	Either or both of the conditions above	• Neither of the conditions above applies • Available only if the co-signatory is OHF[3] or a municipality	• For OHF: property of historical and archaeological, recreational, aesthetic, or scenic interest • For municipalities: only property of historical or architectural interest

Restrictive covenants and easements are specific kinds of contracts in Anglo-Canadian common law that have been recognized as distinct from other contracts since the Middle Ages:

- technically, an "easement" refers to an agreement that allows someone else to do something on one's own land (for example, a right of passage),
- while a "restrictive covenant" restricts a person's own ability to do something on his or her own land (for example, agrees not to knock down his or her buildings).[4]

Conservation agreements are therefore usually "restrictive covenants."[5] In the United States, however, both kinds of protective agreements are usually lumped together under the name "conservation easements." The Ontario government has also taken to calling them easements,[6] but the recent documentation published by the Ontario Heritage Policy Review carefully refers to both covenants and easements.

The land that is the subject of the agreement is called the "servient tenement." For example, where land is subject to a right of way, the owner of the land (the servient tenement) agrees not to interfere with the passage of someone else over his or her land. Similarly, an owner of land can enter into restrictive covenants not to cut wood, backfill or pollute wetland, damage an archaeological site, alter or demolish a building, and so on.

Although most agreements do not bind future owners, easements and restrictive covenants have a crucial distinguishing characteristic: as mentioned earlier, they can bind future owners. Valid easements and covenants are "registrable interests" — that is, they are contracts that can be registered at the local land titles office. That registration constitutes "notice to the world" and binds future owners (whether they have acquired title by purchase, inheritance, or otherwise).

However, a contract does not become a registrable easement or restrictive covenant merely by its being called one: it may have the words "easement" or "restrictive covenant" typed all over it, and still not constitute a "registrable interest." If an agreement is to be classed as an easement or a covenant binding on future owners, it must at common law meet two standards:[7]

- The first is an obligation for the person benefiting from the easement or covenant to own real estate in the vicinity. At common law, in order for an easement or a covenant to be binding on future owners, it must spell out that the agreement is for the benefit of other land. This other land is called the "dominant tenement."[8] Consequently, at common law conservationists cannot obtain registrable covenants upon property unless they own something in the area. Even then, there would have to be some indication that their own property benefited from the covenant (for example, that it retained its value as part of a heritage district, although even this "benefit" may not be concrete enough to satisfy the demands of the common law in this area).[9]

- There is a second question: what happens if the easement or covenant not only obliges the owner to tolerate something (a right of way, a building, etc.) but also to do something positive (for example, landscaping, maintenance)? At common law, such an agreement is not a registrable covenant because a covenant must be negative in nature. It can only prevent people from taking some action, not require positive action. Historically, the test whether a covenant was positive or negative was whether the covenant required expenditure of money for its performance. If it did, the covenant was "positive" and would fail to be binding on future owners.[10] Consequently, a covenant to landscape or repair would not be binding upon future owners.[11] The same principle applies to easements at common law.[12]

Statutory Reform

Some provinces have introduced specific legislation to clear the way for conservation easements and covenants by removing the common law hurdles. In Ontario, the *Ontario Heritage Act*[13] creates species of statutory covenants and easements, above and beyond the common law variety for the purpose of preserving, maintaining, reconstructing, restoring, or managing significant built and natural features of land.

In Ontario, the legislation provides for three classes of signatory who can enter into such special statutory agreements with the property owner:

- the Ontario Heritage Foundation (OHF);[14]
- the Ontario minister of culture and communications (who can do anything the OHF can do);[15] and
- a municipality.[16]

Once one of these parties has executed the agreement, it can "assign" it to someone else;[17] in other words, in theory the OHF or a municipality could "front" such an agreement for another conservation organization. The OHF is an agent of the Crown,[18] and works closely with the Ministry of Culture and Communications. In the future, it is expected that a much larger range of organizations will be entitled to enter directly into such agreements: this has been proposed by the Ministry of Culture and Communications in its official proposals for legislation.[19]

The OHF appears to have broader powers than municipalities. Although the relevant legislation provides no definition of the kinds of "heritage" property on which the OHF may negotiate easements or covenants,[20] it is possible to infer that the intent of such agreements must relate to property of historical, architectural, archaeological, recreational, aesthetic, or scenic interest.[21] Municipalities, however, can only use such statutory agreements for properties of historical or architectural interest.[22]

Contents of Easements and Covenants

What do such agreements contain? In practice, the OHF has developed fairly lengthy agreements that specify the protective provisions in considerable detail. That specificity has been necessary because in the case of easements and covenants, the courts have been particularly strict on this point, perhaps because these contracts are intended to bind the future owners who never signed the original agreement and hence had little idea of the intent. An easement, for example, must be fairly precise in its effects.[23] The necessity for precision also applies to covenants.[24] The necessity for care also extends to the description of the property,[25] in order to avoid triggering the necessity of a severance.[26] One can expect the usual legal studies of the property, for example, whether there are mortgages. [27]

The literature on "conservation easements" has often discussed the advantages that such agreements have over other arrangements. For example, Ronald Reid summarizes them as follows:

- the initial costs of purchasing an easement may be less than the cost of purchasing the entire property;
- management of the land is provided by the landowner;
- the land remains on the municipal tax roll;
- the land remains in production or use; and
- social disruption is minimized.[28]

Reid also outlines the factors that put a damper on the use of these agreements:

- ignorance by local authorities (for example, rural municipalities);
- fear of outsiders;
- the motives of government agencies seeking easements may be questioned; and
- municipalities may fear the erosion of their tax base by easements, or believe that it is unfair for a present landowner to dictate the future use of a parcel of land.[29]

Nancy Weeks also outlines cases in which easement programs have not performed according to expectations. She cites a study by Coughlin and Plaut[30] that outlines possible pitfalls:

- the effects of the easements were not fully explained to the landowner;
- restricted lands were sold to second and third landowners who did not understand the restrictions;
- development regulations were not fully understood by the landowners;
- the easement agreements were technically faulty; and
- the recipient of the easement failed to specify conditions under which he or she would approve various kinds of development on the subject property.

Precedents

The Ontario Heritage Foundation has signed some 150 of these agreements under the *Ontario Heritage Act*. Other organizations that were able to circumvent the common law hurdles (for example, by having nearby land, and by phrasing the obligations in the negative) have even been able to use common law easements: the Hamilton and Sauble conservation authorities acquired right-of-way easements for the Bruce Trail; the Otonabee and Essex region conservation authorities have used easements concerning water levels; and the Bruce Trail Association has purchased land with the intention of reselling it with easements attached.[31] The OHF agreements include "protective provisions [that] are written relatively loosely, requiring OHF approval for, rather than prohibiting outright, many activities. These approval provisions are used often, with an average of 1 to 2 requests received per week."[32]

Public authorities in the United States have had a longstanding policy of purchasing easements and covenants from landowners for various conservation purposes. The US Fish and Wildlife Service, for example, has bought over 21,000 easements covering 1.2 million acres of prairie pothole wetlands.[33] The traditional rationale is that this allows the protection of property at a much lower cost than purchasing the whole property and all property rights.[34] However, in areas that were undergoing development pressure, US public authorities had indeed been required to spend considerable amounts of money on these acquisitions.[35]

Among non-governmental organizations, one of the most eminent bodies of experience in this area is the National Trust in Great Britain. By 1979, it had already acquired protective covenants on 71,000 acres.[36] Enabling legislation for such restrictive covenants and easements is to be found in a variety of British statutes.[37] New Zealand's *Reserves Act* also provides for such agreements; and comparable agreements are in place in Switzerland, France, the Netherlands, and Sweden.[38]

On the whole, easements and covenants have worked well where they have been used. Reid notes that, "Extensive experience in the U.S. has shown a low violation rate, in the order of 2 percent, and enforcement has not been a major problem there."[39]

Tax Implications

The Basic Principle

In civil law (for example, Quebec), ownership is viewed as a whole[40] from which carefully defined parts can be removed. The common law, on the contrary, almost never refers to ownership as a "whole" from which component parts are removed, but rather as a loose (and ill-defined) composite of a spectrum of various rights or, less charitably, what Oliver Cromwell described as "an ungodly jumble."[41]

One may say that the civil law looks on ownership as a single forest, but ignores the trees, whereas the common law looks on it as a number of trees, but disregards the forest. The significance of calling ownership a "bundle of rights" is simple. If part of those rights are removed (for example, by restrictive covenant or easement), one has, by definition, lost part of one's ownership.

The economic value of this loss can be appraised. This is done routinely in property tax assessment: assessors are indeed directed to take easements and covenants into account in computing the municipal tax base.[42] This has great significance for the creation of easements, because in theory the granting of an easement or a restrictive covenant should give rise to a tax deduction.

If the disposal of a part of one's property rights can have a certifiable value for other legal purposes, why can't it receive comparable treatment under the *Income Tax Act*? In other words, if an altruistic individual enters into a registered restrictive covenant or easement with a government or a registered charity, why can't the value of that transaction be professionally appraised, and give rise to a tax receipt accordingly?

Virtually every writer on the subject in Canada has assumed that it would. As early as 1974, Silverstone[43] postulated with total confidence that "a landowner can donate a conservation easement ... to either a conservation organization with charitable status under the Act or the municipality in which the property is located. ... In either situation, the donor (servient tenement) is entitled to deduct the value of the gift for income tax purposes. ... Similarly, the donation can be made to the Crown with even greater deductions permitted on the part of the donor."[44] For his part, Reid[45] observed that in the case of donations of property, "normal [Ontario Heritage] Foundation practice ... is to commission an independent appraisal (the cost of which may be shared, depending on circumstances), and to issue a tax receipt based on that appraisal."[46] Reid said that "the procedure for donated easements would be identical."

The Environmental Law Centre of Alberta issued its own summary of the situation:

> In donating an easement, the taxpayer gives a charity or the Crown a partial interest in his property, while at the same time retaining legal title and the right to use the property subject only to the easement. With such gifts, the major issue becomes the value of the interest of the property donated by the taxpayer. While a gift of less than fee simple would have certain value, it would not have a value equal to the fair market value of the taxpayer's entire interest in the real property. In this case, the initial difficulty for the taxpayer will be determining the value of the gift made and hence the amount of the donation and the proceeds of disposition.
>
> It would appear that the value of the donation would be the difference between the fair market value of the land unencumbered by the easement and its value subject to the easement. Proper real estate appraisals would be essential to establish such values.[47]

The tax deduction pursuant to a heritage covenant or easement, however, shared this with black holes: although it has been extensively described in theory, until recently no one claimed to have actually seen one.[48]

The OHF helped set precedent with two persons, each of whom, in its terminology, "donated a natural heritage easement."[49] In consultation with the OHF, the donors proceeded to have professional appraisals done before and after registration of the agreement. The OHF issued charitable receipts equivalent to the difference in market value. In both those cases, the receipts were not challenged by Revenue Canada. This was consistent with established legal opinion in the United States:[50]

> A valuable property right having passed to the United States, it was ruled that the taxpayer was entitled to a deduction. ... The central premise of the ruling...asked and answered the question of whether a valuable property right had been given. Assuming that, under local law, the rights transferred were a valuable "something," the 1984 ruling rested comfortably on familiar foundations. In the case of a charitable contribution, the questions to be asked, under general principles are (1) Is there a transfer of something of value? (2) Is the transfer a gift with the requisite donative intent? Is the transfer to an organization contributions to which qualify for the deduction?[51]

If the answer to all three questions was affirmative, the IRS concluded that tax deductibility was unavoidable on legal principle.

Revenue Canada has now committed its position to writing in correspondence with the Island Nature Trust of Prince Edward Island on July 13, 1990:

> A restrictive covenant ... is a mechanism for the legal long term or permanent protection of ... sites. A private landowner may register a restrictive covenant against his land. ... The rights forfeited generally include the right to subdivide or to develop the property for any commercial activities. ... The restriction of land use normally devalues the property. The restrictive covenant could therefore be assigned a value equal to the difference between the property's value before the restrictive covenant is registered against the land and the property's value after the restrictive covenant is registered against the land. Our comments regarding your questions are as follows: Subsection 248(1) of the *Income Tax Act* defines property to include a right of any kind whatever. Since a restrictive covenant registered against land is a right it would be considered a property. Consequently a donation of a restrictive covenant registered against the land to Her Majesty or to a registered charity could be considered a gift for purposes of section 118.1 or 110.1 of the *Income Tax Act.* ... A registered charity may issue receipts respecting donated restrictive covenants providing the donation qualifies as a gift. For example if the donor were to receive services or any valuable consideration in exchange for the restrictive covenant there would be no gift for purposes of the *Income Tax Act.* The individual would have a disposition equal to the value of the gift. The value must be determined by a person competent and qualified to evaluate the restrictive covenant.

Municipal Taxation

As a general rule, the Crown is exempt from municipal taxation. It follows that if the Crown owns property in a municipality, the municipality is in no position to levy property taxes against that property. If, however, the fee simple belongs to a private taxpayer, the fact that a covenant or easement is registered against the property by the Crown will not affect the taxable status of that property for municipal purposes.

A carefully prepared appraisal, which documents any decline in value for income tax purposes, may also come in handy if the property-owner next wants to be reassessed for property tax purposes.

Future Action

The use of covenants and easements for conservation purposes has been a significant success in the United States, and is attracting much interest in Canada. Various charitable organizations are gearing up to become signatories of such agreements, in the hope that property owners can be persuaded to enter into such agreements with them.

If the charity owns nearby lands that can "benefit" from such an agreement, the charity can consider using a classic common law covenant or easement. If, however, the charity does not own such land, it can still consider an agreement within the context of the *Ontario Heritage Act*. If the property is of architectural or historical significance, the covenant or easement could be signed by the owner with either the OHF or a municipality; if the property is of scientific, scenic, or related ecological importance, the overture should logically be made to the OHF. Arrangements may be considered to sign the agreement over from the OHF to another registered charity; however, there has not been a profusion of experience in such assignments.

When a new *Ontario Heritage Act* comes forward, it is expected that property owners will be able to sign such agreements directly with eligible registered charities. If tax consequences are being explored, the relevant recommendations from Revenue Canada should be followed to the letter.

Since the OHF has by far the most experience in such agreements (including their detailed legal contents), close cooperation with that agency would be most advisable.

GIFTS

General Principles

Charitable donations fall into two main categories:

- donations to the Crown (that is, the federal or provincial government), and
- donations to municipalities and registered charitable organizations.[52]

Obviously, a Canadian who is committed to protecting his or her property is free to donate it to the public sector or to a charity. Unfortunately, Canada's tax laws complicate and sometimes even discourage the simple act of giving. In this section we discuss the impact of tax laws on donation of property to government agencies and charitable organizations, and how to avoid some of the tax pitfalls created by such donations.

The two categories of donations, and the distinction between the two, will be discussed later in this chapter. In addition, the *Income Tax Act* distinguishes between:

- donations made by individuals, and
- donations made by corporations.

Donations by individuals give rise to a tax credit, whereas those by corporations give rise to a deduction from taxable income. The relevant sections of the *Income Tax Act* are sections 110 and 118.1; detailed explanations of these positions can be found in several publications, notably *Canadian Taxation of Charities and Donations*.[53] The specific concerns pertaining to donations of environmentally important lands have been described by the author in *You Can't Give It Away*.[54]

The philanthropic tendencies of Canadians (and the occasional lack thereof) have been monitored in a number of studies. Donations of cultural property (for example, art or archival material) are more prevalent than donations of real estate. Part of the reason is that in addition to the sections referred to above, the *Income Tax Act* also provides for a distinct tax treatment of donations of "certified cultural property." As explained later, cultural donations are exempt from capital gains. That feature can be important, particularly in any donation of investment property (such as woodlots, farm property, rental buildings, or real estate held for speculative purposes), as will be seen below.

Capital Gains on Donated Property

The *Income Tax Act* provides for a legal fiction whereby any donation is considered a disposition at fair market value. In other words, when a person donates a million-dollar property, the donor is deemed to receive $1 million in proceeds,[55] even though he or she received nothing. The consequences of this legal fiction can be substantial:

- This deemed income has no tax consequences as long as the property in question was not investment property. For example, if it was property that was not intended to produce income (for example, all or part of one's personal residence), the fictitious proceeds of disposition do not normally enter one's taxable income.

- The situation is different if the donated property was "capital property" — that is, if it was property that was used or potentially intended to produce income. This would be the case of farm property, rental buildings, real estate held for speculative purposes, etc. When property held for investment purposes is disposed of, the deemed profit on disposition can be construed as *"capital gains."*[56]

This deemed "capital gain" is, of course, entirely fictitious: the property has not been disposed of at a profit (on the contrary, the absence of remuneration is a *sine qua non* of a charitable gift). That is not how the government treats it, however. For example, take the case of some wooded land held for speculative purposes since 1971 (when the taxation of capital gains came into existence). Further suppose that the land was then valued at $100,000, and would today be valued at $1,000,000. Broadly speaking, the donation of this land would trigger a $900,000 deemed capital gain. Three-quarters (75 per cent) of capital gains are assimilated to normal taxable income, and are taxed as such.

In an alternative scenario, suppose that a building (with appurtenant land) was purchased for investment purposes in 1980 for $200,000, and had a value split equally between land and building. Over the following years, the land was not depreciated (because the *Income Tax Act* does not allow for the depreciation of land), but the building was the subject of $35,000 in claimed depreciation. Today, the owner proposes to donate the entire real estate, whose fair market value would be appraised at $500,000, divided equally between land and building ($250,000 for each). In that scenario, the donation of land would trigger a capital gain of $150,000 (75 per cent of which is taxable); the building would also give rise to a capital gain of $150,000, with similar consequences; and finally, the claimed depreciation would be entirely turned into taxable income. In the latter scenario, therefore, the donation of this investment real estate would trigger an addition of $260,000 to the donor's taxable income.[57]

Receipts for Donations

As a *quid pro quo* for *bona fide* donations to governments or charities, the donor can receive a receipt from the donee, and this receipt can be used to offset taxable income, either in the form of a tax credit (for individuals) or a deduction (for corporations). However, there are ceilings on the extent to which these receipts can be used, and taxpayers are treated better if they donate to the Crown than if they give their property to municipalities or charities.

In the case of a donation to the Crown (federal or provincial), the usable portion of a receipt cannot exceed the donor's taxable income in any one year; in other words, unlike business expenditures, the donor cannot use his receipt to put himself in a loss position. Any unused portion of the receipt can be carried forward for up to five subsequent years; but in each of these years, the usable portion of the receipt is again limited to the taxpayer's taxable income in that year. In short, a donation to the Crown can be used to offset up to 100 per cent of the donor's taxable income for a maximum period of six years, so if the value of the gift were larger than the donor's income over those six years, the balance would "go to waste." For a farmer who was making $50,000 in the year of his or her retirement and anticipated making $20,000 per year in the subsequent years, the limit of his or her usable tax receipt would be as follows. If the farmer wished to donate a farm to the Ministry of Agriculture, leaving aside the capital gains factor for a moment, the tax receipt would cover $50,000 for the year of the donation, and $20,000 for each of the five subsequent years, for a maximum $110,000. If the farm were worth more than $110,000 at the time the farmer made the donation, the extra amount would be unusable for tax deduction purposes.

In the case of donations to charity or to a municipality, the ceilings are substantially lower. The donor's receipt cannot offset more than 20 per cent of his or her taxable income in the year of the donation; the unused portion can be carried forward for five subsequent years, but in each subsequent year the usable portion is again limited to 20 per cent of the taxpayer's income in that year. For example, in the scenario of the retiring farmer who earns $50,000 in the year of the donation and $20,000 per year thereafter, his or her usable tax receipt (leaving aside capital gains) would be limited to $10,000 in the year of the donation, and $4,000 for each of the five subsequent years; in the other words, the total usable receipt would be $30,000 — for a gift potentially many times that value.

It may be noted in passing that business expenditures incurred for the purposes of operating a business are subject to no such limitation. In other words, the policy of the *Income Tax Act* is to treat charitable expenditures more restrictively and less favourably than business expenditures. These ceilings are another fiction that is added, idiosyncratically, to the tax treatment of philanthropy.

Capital Gains and Receipt Ceilings in Tandem

The above scenario illustrates that in the case of investment property, substantial taxes can be triggered by a donation, but there are limits on the extent to which these extra taxes can be offset by the tax receipts involved.

This leads to some unusual scenarios. In the case of property that is not held for investment purposes, the donor can use his or her tax receipt subject to the applicable ceilings; but for donations of investment property (including most potential donations of significant real estate holdings in Ontario), the donor could actually find himself or herself with a prospective tax liability (resulting from capital gains), which may actually exceed the receipts claimable.

In other words, the taxable capital gains that result from donations may not only erode the value of the receipts, but may even exceed them. As a result, the philanthropist would be fiscally penalized for his or her gift.

However, the *Income Tax Act* has introduced a further legal fiction to mitigate this effect. The donor may "elect" to downvalue the gift so that the deemed proceeds of disposition do not give rise to so high a deemed capital gain.[58] In other words, the *Income Tax Act* legalizes the conscious misrepresentation of the value of a gift to ensure that the donor will not be penalized for making the donation to the government or to charity. The result is an elaborate accounting process whereby the donor's advisers attempt to determine an optimal figure that will produce the maximum usable receipt in relation to the lowest capital gain. That calculation will also be affected by the extent to which the donor can still use his or her capital gains exemptions, which are usually $100,000 for individuals and $500,000 for farm operations.

In many cases, nonetheless, the donor's prospective tax benefit will not represent a mathematical equivalent or *quid pro quo* for the value of the donation.

Predictably, this situation has led to various attempts to define ways in which donors could get a tax treatment more closely related to the actual value of their donations. Some of those measures are described below.

Some Alternative Scenarios

The most obvious way to obtain a different tax treatment is to persuade Parliament to consider amendments to the *Income Tax Act*, on their own merits. That has been the object of vigorous representations by several conservation organizations.

Another technique exists at the Heritage Canada Foundation. The Heritage Canada Foundation has a specific contract with the government of Canada that entitles it to receive property "in trust for the Crown." It follows that when a gift of real property is made to the Heritage Canada Foundation "in trust for the Crown," this gift can receive the same tax treatment as a gift to the Crown (that is, a higher ceiling on deductibility), despite the fact that the Heritage Canada Foundation is a non-governmental registered charity.[59] The Nature Conservancy of Canada has a comparable agreement for donations of land that abut national parks. Other organizations have sought to do likewise; however, unless they can produce an actual contract indicating that they can receive property in trust for or as an agent of the Crown, this tax treatment will be unavailable. That is what one organization learned when it thought that it had received property in the capacity of an agent of the Crown. When Revenue Canada learned of the sizable donation of forested land in British Columbia intended for conservation by a land trust, the department sought to roll back the usable portion of the receipt by challenging the charitable organization's documentation[60] showing its agency for the Crown. The court agreed with the department that the organization had insufficient documentation showing its agency relationship, and the donor lost most of the usable portion of his receipt.[61]

A more unusual tax approach exists by means of the *Cultural Property Export and Import Act*.[62] That federal statute provides for certain property to be designated as "certified cultural property" by the Cultural Property Export and Import Commission; it also provides for certain institutions in Canada (including some registered charities) to be designated as "certified cultural institutions."[63] When a donor makes a gift of "certified cultural property" to a "certified cultural institution," the *Income Tax Act* not only provides a 100 per cent deductibility ceiling on the gift (instead of the 20 per cent usually allowed for charities), but also waives the prospect of deemed capital gains.

Naturally, this has led to some speculation as to the kind of real estate that could be treated in this way. Initially, the intent of the *Cultural Property Export and Import Act* was to deal with property that was potentially exportable; but when that reasoning was raised in the context of a proposed donation of a building in Montreal, it was argued that even buildings are potentially exportable stone by stone and hence should be eligible for this treatment.[64] In fact, there are heritage buildings in three provinces that have been donated to "certified cultural institutions" and whose tax treatment under this heading has been approved first by the Cultural Property Export and Import Commission, and then by Revenue Canada.

In the three cases mentioned above, Revenue Canada also allowed the land under the buildings to receive this tax treatment. The amount of land so treated was the space reasonably required to "seat and serve" the buildings.

However, when Revenue Canada was asked to comment on whether pure natural landscape could receive the same tax treatment, the answer was negative. Revenue Canada returned to the original rationale: although buildings could theoretically be exported and reassembled, a natural landscape or habitat could not.

The Current Controversy

The foregoing should establish that no Canadian should dare to make a significant gift of investment property (whether to government or to a charity) without retaining significant (and expensive) professional advice. The professional fees for advising an altruistic Canadian on how to give away property, may amount to $20,000. Canadians have the federal Department of Finance to thank for this. The layers upon layers of legal fictions that have been introduced to this segment of the *Income Tax Act*:

- complicate this area of the law in the extreme;
- roll back the usable portion of charitable receipts to artificially low levels that may be substantially lower than the actual value of the gift; and
- artificially introduce deemed capital gains (and capital gains tax) to encroach on the value of gifts, even though no profit has been incurred, and therefore drastically lower the incentive for giving.

This is no accident: it has been known to both the department and to the affected charities for years.[65] This position by tax authorities is particularly difficult to reconcile with national priorities, now that Canada is supposedly committed to the Green Plan[66] and its commitment toward "partnership" in the assembly of lands for conservation purposes. In striving toward the objectives of the Green Plan, the tax man must be considered either part of the solution or part of the problem; under the *status quo*, there is no question where he now stands. It is impossible to call the Green Plan a broad national objective when perhaps the two most influential federal departments, the Department of Finance and Revenue Canada, refuse to take part.

It has been suggested[67] that the government of Canada should endorse certain specific measures, as was done in the United States in the case of land trusts. Those measures would

Gifts of Real Estate

Donee	Kind of Gift	Deemed Capital Gain	Capital Gains Exemption		Limit on Usable Receipt	Probability that Capital Gains Tax Will Eliminate Value of Receipt	Solution If Capital Gains Tax Exceeds Value of Receipt
			Individual	*Corp.*			
Federal/ provincial government	All	Possible	$100,000-$500,000	0	100% income	Modest	Legally misrepresent value of gift (downward) to optimize receipt in relation to capital gains tax
Municipality	All	Possible	$100,000-$500,000	0	20% income	Serious	Same as above
Charity	In trust for Crown	Possible	$100,000-$500,000	0	100% income	Modest	Same as above
	Other gift	Possible	$100,000-$500,000	0	20% income	Serious	Same as above
	Certified cultural property	Impossible	Irrelevant	N/A	100% income	None	Irrelevant

dramatically simplify the treatment of donations under the *Income Tax Act*, and return gifts to a more level playing field. The government could:

1. abolish the fiction of deemed capital gains on gifts of real estate to governments and charities; and
2. abolish the artificial 20 per cent limitation on the usability of receipts for such gifts; and in so doing, put donations of Canada's natural heritage on exactly the same footing as donations of Canada's cultural heritage.

Only time will tell, however, whether the government of the day will be disposed to taking such measures. In the meantime, prospective donors may wish to consider other measures. Donations of buildings may (in certain cases of historic or architectural interest) be eligible for treatment as "certified cultural property." Important donations of land may be feasible through the Nature Conservancy of Canada or the Heritage Canada Foundation. With the help of professional advice, the donor may find ways of staggering a gift over a number of years, to attempt to obtain as much tax benefit as possible; alternatively, the donor may choose to donate restrictive covenants instead, in anticipation of other donations at a later date. Unfortunately, there is no substitute for close consultation with one's own lawyers and those of the prospective donee.

Marc Denhez

FURTHER READING

Marc Denhez, *You Can't Give It Away: Tax Treatment of Ecologically-Sensitive Lands* (Ottawa: National Round Table on the Environment and the Economy, 1992).

Arthur Drache, ed., *Canadian Taxation of Charities and Donations* (Toronto: De Boo) (looseleaf).

Oriana Trombetti and Kenneth W. Cox, *Land, Law and Wildlife Conservation*, Wildlife Habitat Canada Reference Paper no. 3 (Ottawa: Wildlife Habitat Canada, November 1990).

ENDNOTES

1   Oriana Trombetti and Kenneth W. Cox, *Land, Law and Wildlife Conservation*, Reference Paper no. 3 (Ottawa: Wildlife Habitat Canada, November 1990).

2   The basic rule, at common law, is that contracts are private agreements that affect only the signatories. This principle is called "privity of contract."

3   Ontario Heritage Foundation, or the minister of culture and communications acting in its stead.

4   This point of distinction, along with others, is further explained in *Megarry's Manual of the Law of Real Property*, 5th ed. (London: Stevens, 1975), 425-26. See, alternatively, E.H. Burn, *Cheshire and Burn's Modern Law of Real Property*, 13th ed. (London: Butterworths, 1982), 488. The technical difference between an "easement" and a "covenant" is sometimes confusing. For example, some organizations (such as the Ontario Heritage Foundation) working with these agreements refer to an "easement" as the interest in the "servient" land that the agreement gives rise to, whereas a "covenant" is the contract that outlines the mutual obligations of the parties. It is not clear where the OHF picked up this terminology. Most texts prefer to define an easement as a proprietor's commitment not to interfere with someone else's activity on the proprietor's land (for example, a right of way), whereas a restrictive covenant is a commitment that the proprietor himself will not do something on his own land. In any event, since both easements and restrictive covenants share the same characteristics for conservation purposes, they are treated together in this description.

5   At least in Anglo-Canadian law. The term "covenant" is also preferable to the term "easement" when one remembers that to some people "easement" connotes the right of strangers to cross one's property (as in the case of Ontario Hydro), when that may have nothing to do with the proprietor's wishes.

6   For example, the practice of the Ontario Heritage Foundation.

7   A third ancient condition, which had been applied, for example, to easements now appears to be superseded. It was that easements would not be binding on future owners if they were merely matters "of recreation and amusement," as opposed to "utility and benefit." See *Aldred's Case* (1611), 9 Rep. 57B. For discussion, see Albert McLean, "The Nature of an Easement" (1966), *Western Law Review* 47 and 56. The issue was also addressed in *Re Ellenborough Park*, [1956] Ch.131 (CA), where the court

suggested (*obiter*) that in any event, the common law rule pertaining to "recreation and amusement" referred only to horse-racing and gaming (at 179). In view of the unmistakable legislative intent of the various statutes that provide for easements and covenants, it appears inconceivable that a court today could view a heritage easement or covenant as being incapable of providing "utility and benefit": on the contrary, the legislation appears to have foreclosed such a negative scenario. In any event, that ancient condition appears to have been circumscribed by modern jurisprudence.

8   See *Megarry's Manual of the Law of Real Property*, supra endnote 4, at 374. For example, an easement or a restrictive covenant for a right of passage is for the benefit of occupants of the neighbouring land. Similarly, an easement or covenant not to demolish will not be binding on future owners unless it specifies a property (a "dominant" land) that will benefit from the agreement aside from the property being protected. On occasion, courts have even insisted that the "dominant" property must not only be specified, but must be shown really to benefit from the agreement (that is, not just nominally): for example, a restrictive covenant allegedly for the benefit of land in another community is not binding upon future purchasers because the other land is not really benefitted. Where, for example, an easement is attempted without the presence of a "dominant tenement," the resulting agreement is called an "easement in gross" and may run into problems of enforceability against subsequent owners accordingly.

9   The jurisprudence refers sometimes to the need for a "direct nexus" between the enjoyment of the right and the user of the dominant tenement: see *Re Ellenborough Park*, supra endnote 7.

10   See *Kelly v. Barrett* (1924), 2 Ch. 379, at 404.

11   *Megarry's Manual of the Law of Real Property*, supra endnote 4, at 375.

12   Ibid., at 394.

13   *Ontario Heritage Act*, RSO 1990, c. O.18, particularly sections 10, 22, and 37.

14   Ibid., sections 10 and 22.

15   Ibid., section 10.

16   Ibid., section 37.

17   Ibid., section 22(3) for the OHF; section 37(4) for municipalities.

18   Ibid., section 11.

19   Ontario, Ministry of Culture and Communications, *Proposals for Legislation: The Ontario Heritage Policy Review* (Toronto: the ministry, May 1990). This document declares (at C29): "The legislation should enable public and private conservation agencies and organizations concerned with natural or cultural property to acquire heritage easements on such property."

20   The *Ontario Heritage Act* is one of the few such statutes to provide no definition of the word "heritage," which appears in almost every line of the statute.

21   That is because that is as close to a definition of "heritage" as the statute gets, in terms of its definition of the OHF's mandate: see *Ontario Heritage Act*, supra endnote 13, section 7(d).

22   Ibid., section 37.

23   The traditional rule is that the formulation of an easement should be sufficiently precise that it could, in another context, have been "capable of forming the subject-matter of a grant." This is addressed, for example, in the classic case of *Re Ellenborough Park*,

supra endnote 7, at 164. See also *Cheshire and Burn's Modern Law of Real Property*, supra endnote 4; this is sometimes called Cheshire's fourth rule on easements. (See also McLean, supra endnote 7, at 46). In *Re Ellenborough Park*, the question was the use of a park as a garden. The court held that this was sufficiently precise to avoid attack on grounds of vagueness. The court went on, however, to address the scenario that would have occurred if the use in question had merely been a right to wander at will over the property (a *jus spatiandi*); the court held that this too would be sufficiently precise to exist as an easement.

24	In *National Trust v. Midlands Electricity Board*, [1952] 1 Ch. 380, at 384-85, the following covenant was held to be void for vagueness: "No act or thing shall be done or placed or permitted to remain upon the land, which shall injure, prejudice, effect or destroy the natural aspect and condition of the land except as hereinafter provided."

25	The optimal way of drafting an easement or restrictive covenant would be to have it worded so as to apply to the entirety of the lot described at the local land titles office, even if the obligations outlined apply only to a part of the property. For example, suppose that the property that one wishes to conserve is A, which is part of a larger property B. Assume further that A has not been surveyed, severed, and laid out in metes and bounds at the local land titles office, but that B has been. The optimal scenario would be to describe A precisely in the covenant or agreement, but deposit the covenant or agreement at the land titles office against the entirety of property B.

26	The reason is that if the covenant or easement is worded so as to be registrable against only a part of a property (as described at the local land titles office), it may be necessary to survey and sever that part before the document becomes registrable. The necessary procedures depend on the land titles legislation of the province or territory. In the case of Ontario, for example, "if an easement is registered on part of a property, a survey and a legal severance are necessary. However, as a provincial agency, OHF is exempt from the normal approval procedures for severances." Ronald Reid, *Conservation Easements*, Report to the Ontario Heritage Foundation (Washaga, Ont.: OHF, April 1987), 10. That merely means, however, that the OHF must go through less red tape than others; it does not dispense the OHF from severances altogether.

27	Ibid., at 10. Reid has summarized the effect of covenants and easements on mortgages as follows:

> If a mortgage is registered on the property, approval of the mortgage holder is not required for an easement. This is because the easement is registered on title after the mortgage, and so has no legal force in the event of a default. The risk of losing an easement due to default can be reduced by using a legal instrument known as a postponement agreement, or by having the [mortgagee] also sign the easement. In practice, these measures are seldom used unless there are strong indications of financial uncertainty.

28	Ibid., at 4. "Landowners who donate conservation easements tend to share several common characteristics. Typically, they are over 50, comfortably well-off, with an income from a source other than the land in question. 'Love for the land' is the primary motivation for donating an easement — 67% of the respondents to the easement survey listed that as the most important factor. Donors are also able to use the tax advantages of their donation, which is listed as the only other significant motivating factor. Donors often are not resident on the land under easement; participation by landowners who depend on their land for their income is very low." Ibid., at 13-14.

29 Ibid., at 13.

30 See Nancy Weeks, *Conservation Easements and the Niagara Escarpment* (Toronto: Sierra Club of Ontario Foundation, 1979), 17.

31 Reid., supra endnote 26, at 6.

32 Ibid., at 10.

33 Ibid., at 14. "The service prefers easements because of the scattered nature of these wetlands, and because easements offer little disruption to the farming pattern, tax structure, and local economy. However, there has been some criticism of the program because it fails to protect sufficient buffer areas."

34 Samuel Silverstone, "Open Space Preservation through Conservation Easements" (1984), 12 *Osgoode Hall LJ* 105.

35 "The National Park Service, for example, found that relatively few land owners along the Appalachian Trail preferred easements to outright acquisition, and that easements averaged 75 percent of the cost of the fee [simple] (within a range of 25-29 percent)." Reid, supra endnote 26, at 15. Reid goes on to state that easements over wetlands in the Otonabee region cost 25 per cent of fee simple; at Hillman Creek marsh in Essex, they cost 90 per cent of fee simple; trail easements along the Bruce Trail tended to be evaluated at 45 per cent of fee simple in one area, and 15 to 25 per cent in another. "Cost of [natural] conservation easements in the U.S. vary widely, but figures in the range of 30-60 percent are common where public access is not included." Ibid., at 20-21.

36 Weeks, supra endnote 30.

37 For example, the *Ancient Monuments in Archaeological Areas Act*, 1979 UK, c. 46, section 16.

38 Weeks, supra endnote 30, at 14.

39 Reid, supra endnote 26, at 20.

40 "Ownership is the right of enjoying and disposing of things in the most absolute manner": article 406 of the Quebec *Civil Code*. Those predetermined components, which can be hived out of the basic principle called "ownership," are defined in Book Second of the Quebec *Civil Code*. Although attempts have occurred to undermine the rigidity of this system, such as the controversial case of *Matamajaw Salmon Club v. Duchaine*, [1921] 2 AC 426 (PC), these have tended to be resisted as an encroachment on the logic of the system.

41 *Megarry's Manual of the Law of Real Property*, supra endnote 4, at 1.

42 For example, the Ontario *Assessment Act*, RSO 1990, c. A.31: "Where an easement is appurtenant to any land, it shall be assessed in connection with and as part of the land at the added value it gives to the land as the dominant tenement, and the assessment of the land that, as the servient tenement, is subject to the easement shall be reduced accordingly": section 9(1). Furthermore," a restrictive covenant running with the land shall be deemed to be an easement within the meaning of this section": section 9(3). The *Municipal Act*, RSO 1990, c. M.45, section 612(3), has similar results. The challenge with this wording, of course, is that it assumes that there is a dominant tenement whose values will increase because of the agreement, and hence counterbalance the decrease affecting the servient tenement.

43   Silverstone, supra endnote 34, at 121-24.

44   Ibid., at 122.

45   Weeks, supra endnote 30.

46   Ibid., at 11.

47   Donna Tingley, F.P. Kirby, and R.D. Hupfer, *Conservation Kit: A Legal Guide to Private Conservancy* (Edmonton: Environmental Law Centre, 1986), 50. The authors continue: "As an example: assume that the taxpayer's entire interest in the property has a current fair market value of $500,000, and that the value of the property subject to an easement is $200,000. By placing an easement on the property, the taxpayer would have made a gift of $300,000. The deductibility of such a gift for income tax purposes (whether to a registered charity or the Crown) is the same as [donations of land]."

48   Silverstone, supra endnote 34, at 123 admitted the following: "It is necessary to point out that the Department of National Revenue, Taxation has never been confronted with the above scheme and refuses to acknowledge it for income tax purposes until this scheme is actually attempted by a landowner." It is equally important to note that this observation is based on an opinion that Silverstone solicited from the department; that opinion was delivered by letter from W.I. Linton, Technical Interpretations Division, Department of National Revenue Taxation, July 25, 1973. Reid, supra endnote 26, admitted that the "evaluation of donated easements has not been addressed." The Environmental Law Centre of Alberta added: "Difficulties may be encountered with the Department of [National] Revenue, Taxation over the valuation of a property gift of less than fee simple."

49   The OHF was not at liberty to disclose the identity of this individual.

50   The Internal Revenue Service first ruled on the deductibility of an open space easement in gross in Rev. rul. 64-205, 1964-2 CB 62. This state of affairs was ultimately entrenched (with various modifications) in subsequent legislation. According to Stefan Nagel of the National Trust for Historic Preservation in Washington (letter to Marc Denhez, February 26, 1990):

> This was followed in 1972 by Treas. Reg. 1.170A-7(b)(ii), which simply restated and interpreted language in the committee report accompanying the *Tax Reform Act* of 1969 to the effect that Congress intended that the limitations on gifts of partial interests in property incorporated in I.R.C. 170(f) were not intended to apply to gifts of open space easements in gross. Rather, such interests were to be treated as gifts of "an undivided portion of the taxpayer's entire interest in property" allowable under I.R.C. 170(f)(3)(B)(iii).
>
> Section 2124(e) of the *Tax Reform Act* of 1976 authorized a charitable contribution deduction for the gift of a 'lease on, option to purchase or easement with respect to real property of not less than 30 years' duration granted to an organization described in subsection (b)(1)(A) exclusively for conservation purposes. The phrase "conservation purpose" was defined to include "the preservation of historically important land areas or structures."
>
> Because of a drafting error, the 1976 conservation purpose easement authority contained a 1977 expiration date. In Section 309 of the *Tax Reduction and Simplification Act* of 1977 Congress repealed the authority to make tax deductible gifts of easements of less than perpetual duration and imposed a June 14, 1981 expiration date for gifts of easements for conservation purposes.

Section 6 of the *Tax Treatment Extension Act* of 1980 (P.L. 96-541) revised, codified and made permanent authority for Federal income, estate, and gift tax charitable contribution deductions for gifts of preservation easements as "a Qualified Conservation Contribution" under I.R.C. 170(f)(3)(B)(iii).

Effective December 17, 1980 only gifts that meet the requirements of Code 170(f)(3)(B)(iii) and (h) qualify as charitable contributions. Regulations implementing the legislation were promulgated in 1986 at Treas. Reg. 1.170A-14.

51 R.L. Brenneman and S.M. Bates, eds., *Land Saving Action* (Covelo, Calif.: Island Press, 1984), 166.

52 Only charitable organizations officially registered by Revenue Canada are discussed in this chapter, under the heading "Charities."

53 Arthur Drache, ed., *Canadian Taxation of Charities and Donations* (Toronto: De Boo) (looseleaf), particularly at chapter 12.

54 Marc Denhez, *You Can't Give It Away: Tax Treatment of Ecologically-Sensitive Lands* (Ottawa: National Round Table on the Environment and the Economy, 1992).

55 Ibid.

56 The amount of the capital gain is subject to some complex mathematics, depending on the improvements that may have been made to the property, the depreciation claimed (called capital cost allowance), etc.

57 Three-quarters (75 per cent) of the capital gain on the land would be taxable income (that is, 75 per cent of $150,000 or $112,500); 75 per cent of the capital gain on the land would be treated identically (75 per cent of $150,000 — that is, another $112,500); and the $35,000 claimed in depreciation would entirely return to taxable income. The resulting total is $260,000.

58 *Income Tax Act*, RSC 1952, c. 148, as amended by SC 1970-71-72, c. 63, and as subsequently amended, section 118.1(6).

59 "It would appear that a registered charity could be specially empowered to receive gifts in trust for Her Majesty, and such gifts would then be exempt from the 20% limitation. It is understood that this is the case with Heritage Canada Foundation which is a registered charity." *CCH Canadian Master Tax Guide 1991* (Toronto: CCH Canadian Ltd.) (looseleaf), paragraph 9185.

60 The organization's primary evidence was a speech given by the then prime minister indicating an agency relationship.

61 *Murdoch v. MNR* (1978), Tax Review Board file no. 77-804.

62 *Cultural Property Export and Import Act*, RSC 1985, c. C-51.

63 There are, at present, some 230 such institutions in Canada.

64 This has been the case of some important heritage structures, notably London Bridge, which is now in Lake Havasu City, Arizona.

65 The chronology of events is described in Denhez, supra endnote 54.

66 Canada, Environment Canada, *Canada's Green Plan for a Healthy Environment* (Ottawa: Supply and Services, 1990).

67 See ibid., and also Marc Denhez's submission to the Parliamentary Committee on the Environment, April 1992.

PART V

Pollution and Resource Management Problems

16

The Environmental Protection Act

CONTENTS

Premier Davis has euphemistically referred to the Environmental Protection Bill as the "Environmental Bill of Rights." It may be called a lot of things with justification, but it is an incredible fantasy to herald this Bill as a Bill of Rights.

Canadian Environmental Law Research Foundation, July 1971

———————————

The *Environmental Protection Act*[1] is administered by Ontario's Ministry of Environment and Energy. Its stated purpose is "to provide for the protection and conservation of the natural environment."[2] However, the actual scope of the Act is much narrower than this. It regulates contaminants and actual and potential sources of contaminants. It is useful primarily to protect the natural environment against pollution. Other aspects of environmental protection, such as energy conservation, land-use planning, the preservation of natural areas, the creation and maintenance of parkland, the regulation of damming and diversion of water bodies, the prevention of soil erosion, the manufacture and sale of toxic chemicals, and environmentally damaging technology, are dealt with by other statutes, usually administered by other government departments.

As a tool for preventing and controlling pollution, the *Environmental Protection Act* has evolved over the past two decades from a relatively short and ineffective statute to a much longer and more comprehensive statute that provides most of the tools needed to control individual sources of pollution.

The provisions of the *Environmental Protection Act* fall into two broad categories. The first category is a group of general provisions that set out a framework for dealing with sources of pollution generally. Parts II, X, XI, XII, XII, XIV, and XV fall into this category.

The second category consists of individual parts of the *Environmental Protection Act* devoted to specific pollutants, sources of pollution, and particular activities and businesses that have potential to cause pollution. These parts include part III (motors and motor vehicles), part IV (ice shelters), part V (waste management), part VI (ozone-depleting substances), part VII (abandoned motor vehicles), part VIII (private sewage systems), and part IX (litter, packaging, and containers).

The provisions of the *Environmental Protection Act* dealing with specific sources of pollution are discussed in other chapters, such as waste management (part V), visual pollution (part IX), air pollution (parts III and VI), and water (part VIII). In this chapter, we will discuss only the parts of the *Environmental Protection Act* that apply to pollution sources generally.

THE GENERAL PARTS

The *Environmental Protection Act* is designed to prevent, control, and provide for the clean-up of discharges of "contaminants" into "the natural environment." The Act also makes provision for the restoration of the environment when it is damaged by "spills," which are discharges of pollutants from structures, vehicles, or other containers in quantities or with qualities that are abnormal,[3] and for the compensation of victims of spills.

"Contaminant" is defined as:

Any solid, liquid, gas, odour, heat, sound, vibration, radiation, or combination of any of them resulting directly or indirectly from human activities that may cause an adverse effect.[4]

"Adverse effect" means one or more of:

- impairment of the quality of the natural environment for any use that can be made of it;
- injury or damage to property or to plant of animal life;
- harm or material discomfort to any person;
- an adverse effect on the health of any person;
- impairment of the safety of any person;
- rendering any property or plant or animal life unfit for use by man;
- loss of enjoyment of normal use of property; and
- interference with the normal conduct of business.[5]

The "natural environment" is defined as "the air, land and water or any combination or part thereof, of the Province of Ontario."[6]

The centrepiece of the *Environmental Protection Act* is section 14, which prohibits the discharge of any contaminant to an extent or degree that may cause an adverse effect. It is one of the strongest anti-pollution provisions in Canadian legislation for two reasons. First, it applies not only to individuals and corporations, but also to government agencies. Second, unlike provisions in other provinces that prohibit pollution only where there is no other statutory provision or regulation that overrides them, section 14 overrides other provisions in the *Environmental Protection Act* that allow pollution, and the Act itself overrides other provincial statutes and municipal bylaws that may conflict with it and allow greater amounts of pollution. Section 14(1) states:

> Notwithstanding any other provisions of this Act or the regulations, no person shall discharge a contaminant or cause or permit the discharge of a contaminant into the natural environment that causes or is likely to cause an adverse effect.

When used as a verb, "discharge" includes add, deposit, leak, or emit, and when used as a noun, it includes addition, deposit, leak, or emission. To "cause or permit" the discharge of the contaminant means not only to discharge it, but also includes taking an action that results in the discharge or failing to take action that would have prevented the discharge.[7]

It is also an offence to discharge or permit the discharge of contaminants at levels that exceed those prescribed by the regulations. Section 6(1) provides:

> No person shall discharge into the natural environment any contaminant, and no person responsible for a source of contaminant shall permit the discharge into the natural environment of any contaminant from the source of contaminant, in an amount, concentration or level in excess of that prescribed by the regulations.

This provision is rarely used, since it is much easier to prove that a contaminant caused or was likely to cause an adverse effect than to prove that it was emitted in an amount greater than allowed by the regulations. No measuring devices but the human senses are needed to prove that a contaminant was likely to cause material discomfort or interfere with the normal use of one's property.

Not only the polluting company and the employees who discharged the contaminants may be convicted of these offences. Officers and directors of corporations that carry on activities that result in the discharge of contaminants may also be convicted if the company causes or permits pollution, if they failed to take all reasonable steps to set up an adequate system of pollution prevention within the company.[8]

Collectively, these provisions make it an offence, punishable by substantial fines and imprisonment, to allow the discharge of any pollutant deliberately or negligently. There are few exceptions. One exception created by the courts is that a person will not be convicted of polluting if the pollution resulted from causes beyond that person's control. For example, the polluter will not be convicted if the pollution resulted from an "act of God" — that is, a natural event such as a storm so severe that it was unforeseeable and that no steps could be taken to prevent its effects. Nor will there be a conviction if the discharge occurred as a result of a reasonable mistake of fact, or despite the fact that the person in control of the source of pollution had taken all reasonable steps to prevent the pollution.

The other exception set out in sections 6 and 14 of the *Environmental Protection Act* is for discharges of animal wastes disposed of in accordance with normal farming practices. Until the 1980s, the Ministry of the Environment was unwilling to prosecute farmers for pollution. However, the ministry has established a Farm Pollution Advisory Committee consisting of some respected and responsible farmers, who advise the ministry on whether a farm practice leading to a discharge of a contaminant was "normal." In the 1970s, no farmer would be prosecuted without the blessing of the committee. However, today the ministry frequently prosecutes farmers as a result of practices that are obviously negligent without consulting the committee. Today, this provision serves primarily to prevent the prosecution of farmers for discomfort to their neighbours resulting from odours from the spreading of manure on fields in the spring and fall and from the storage of manure where the odours are difficult or impossible to prevent.

THE SCOPE OF SECTION 14

To prove a violation of section 14, you must prove:

- that the substance that entered the natural environment was a "contaminant";
- that someone "discharged" it or "caused or permitted" the discharge;
- that, as a result, it ended up in the natural environment; and
- that this caused or was likely to cause one of the kinds of harm, injury, discomfort, or impairment defined as "adverse effects."

Proving that the Substance Was a Contaminant

The definition of "contaminant" is broad enough to include almost all pollution, as long as it results directly or indirectly from human activities. Sand blowing onto neighbouring properties from a construction site, for example, has been held to be a contaminant, even though the sand is a natural material, where its movement resulted from human activities.[9]

In another case, a trucking company that was carrying out a clean-up at an asphalt shingle manufacturing plant where a spill of asphalt had occurred was found guilty of depositing a contaminant in the natural environment, despite the fact that the "pollution" did not occur until weeks after the material was deposited. When the clean-up occurred, the asphalt was hard lumps of solid frozen material. Weeks after it was dumped onto a construction site, as the weather warmed and the sun melted the asphalt, it began to flow, causing animals to get stuck in it. The company argued that the frozen asphalt it had transported was not a contaminant, because it was incapable of flowing and harming animal life in the condition they had handled it. The court ruled that this was too narrow a definition of contaminant; that even if the material was not capable of causing adverse effects at the time it was dumped, as long as it was capable of changing into something that could cause adverse effects as a result of exposure to the sun without any human intervention, it was still a contaminant.[10]

The courts have also held the following to be contaminants: a piece of flying rock, flame and particulate, food odours, gasoline, heat or fire, smoke, lead, mercury, styrene gas, and sulphur dioxide.[11] However, a company that filled a marsh on its own property with clean fill for development purposes was held not to be depositing a contaminant.[12]

Not every physical object is a contaminant, even if it is a nuisance. It is unlikely, for example, that the visual pollution caused by billboards or similar eyesores would be considered contamination, or that the physical objects causing them would be treated as contaminants. "Contaminant" is also not defined to include light. This means that unless light is covered by the words "radiation" or "heat," someone could shine a spotlight in your bedroom window every night — while constructing buildings, for example — without breaching the *Environmental Protection Act*.

Proving that the Contaminant Was "Discharged"

As mentioned above, the Act prohibits not only the "discharge" of a contaminant, but also its "deposit." The courts have held that the word "discharge" has an active connotation, such as something being moved under force or quickly, while the word "deposit" has a more passive connotation, such as a gradual leak or seepage.[13]

"Causing" or "Permitting" the Discharge

In an offence of polluting, the "discharging," "adding," or "emitting" aspect of the offence centres on direct acts of pollution. The "causing" aspect centres on the defendant's active undertaking of something that it is in a position to control that results in pollution. The "permitting" aspect of the offence centres on the defendant's passive lack of interference or, in other words, its failure to prevent an occurrence that it ought to have foreseen.[14] Therefore, a phrase such as "permitting the deposit of" may catch a wide variety of situations. When the word "deposit" is used as a noun in a phrase such as "permitting the deposit of," this can have the connotation of material remaining in place or seeping into or migrating gradually through the environment. By using such a phrase, the Crown can catch not only the person who initially released the material into the environment, but others who "permitted" the release by failing to take steps to prevent the release and those who failed to clean it up. The word "deposit" can refer not only to the activity of polluting, but also to the result or to a resulting condition — for example, the material remaining in place when it should have been cleaned up. For example, when the owner of a sand pit buried drums of liquid industrial waste in the pit, he was found guilty of "permitting the deposit" of the waste when the drums started to rust out and the waste began to migrate through the soil several years after the drums were buried.[15]

Until 1985, although it was an offence to discharge a pollutant, it was not an offence to fail to clean up the contamination and restore the environment, unless the failure to clean up and restore the environment could be said to be "permitting the deposit" of the contaminant. Thus, the *Environmental Protection Act* sometimes indirectly created a duty to clean up the contamination by the use of such words, where there was no direct statutory obligation to clean up.

In 1985, part X of the *Environmental Protection Act* was brought into force. Known as the "spills bill," this part required both the owner of a contaminant and the person in control of the contaminant immediately before a spill to clean up the spill and restore the environment to its previous condition, even if the spill did not result from negligence. Failure to do so became an offence. Previously, it was unclear whether this was an offence, and there was a duty to clean up spills only when they were caused by negligence. This resulted in long delays before spills were cleaned up, allowing the contamination to soak further into the soil or spread through surface water or groundwater. This complicated the clean-up and made it even more expensive. Part X of the *Environmental Protection Act* requires immediate clean-up by everyone concerned, but only where the spill is from a "container." This illogical distinction means that leakage from an underground tank would require immediate clean-up, but leachate seeping through the bottom of a waste disposal site may not. Spills from trucks, tanks, drums, and other enclosed facilities must be cleaned up immediately, but soil and groundwater contaminated by oil from melting tires that have caught fire need not be.

Proving that the "Natural Environment" Was Affected

The environment protected by the *Environmental Protection Act* is limited to the "natural environment," which appears to exclude pollution of the indoor environment. For example, exhaust fumes from vehicles in an enclosed garage, or auditoriums blanketed with tobacco smoke, are probably not covered by the Act. Similarly, where workers are exposed to contaminants while working outdoors at a factory, a question might arise whether they can be prosecuted under the *Environmental Protection Act*, or whether the *Occupational Health and Safety Act* must be used.[16] One loophole was plugged in 1981. The previous year, chemicals were poured down a drain at a paint factory in Toronto. As they flowed through the city's sewers, they emitted vapours that came up through the floor drains and into a school, causing its evacuation. Since the liquids had never entered the "natural environment," it was questionable whether the company had committed an offence under section 14. As a result, the Act was amended. Now, a contaminant that is discharged into the air within a building or structure, as a result of the discharge of the same contaminant or another one into a different building or structure, is deemed to be discharged into the natural environment.

Proving the Likelihood of an "Adverse Impact"

Finally, the concept of harm is implicit in both the definition of contaminant and the elements that must be proved in a section 14 prosecution before there is an offence. No matter how dangerous or obnoxious the substance is, it is not a contaminant unless some harm may result from its discharge, and it is not an offence to discharge it unless some harm is likely.

The easiest way to prove that a discharge is likely to cause one of the adverse effects is to show that the adverse effect actually did occur. However, if one had to prove that the harm actually occurred to convince the court that harm from a discharge would be likely, this would make the words "likely to cause an adverse effect" meaningless. Therefore, a court would probably accept expert evidence of the probability of harm from such a discharge as adequate proof of the likelihood of harm. Nevertheless, to prove a likelihood of harm, it is necessary to prove more than the mere fact that a discharge is capable of causing harm. There must be a probability that someone would actually suffer harm in the circumstances in which the particular discharge occurred.[17]

REPORTING DISCHARGES AND SPILLS

Discharges and spills must be reported to the Ministry of Environment and Energy. Sections 13 and 15 of the *Environmental Protection Act* require everyone who discharges a contaminant into the natural environment, or who is a person responsible for a source of contaminant that discharges into the natural environment, in an amount that exceeds the limits in the regulations or in an amount that is likely to cause an adverse effect, to report the discharge "forthwith" to the ministry.

These sections raise interesting questions whether a company that does not know that it has caused a discharge is still guilty of the offence of not reporting the discharge because it should have had a system to ensure that it would know about the discharge. This problem is addressed in part X of the *Environmental Protection Act*. In section 92 of the Act, the duty to report spills is imposed on everyone who spilled, caused, or permitted a spill that is likely to cause an adverse effect, as soon as that person knows or *ought to know* that the pollutant is spilled and is causing or is likely to cause an adverse effect. Under section 92, the person must report the spill not only to the ministry, but also to the municipality in which the pollutant spilled, and to the owner of the pollutant or the person having control of the pollutant immediately before the spill, if the person spilling it is not the owner or the person in control. It is likely that a person who gives a substantially incomplete or misleading report would be deemed not to have reported the spill, and would be guilty of the offence of failing to report.

THE TOOLS FOR ADMINISTERING THE ACT

Prosecution for polluting or for failing to report pollution is only one of the tools available to the Ministry of Environment and Energy under the *Environmental Protection Act*. The other tools consist primarily of various business licences, permits for activities, and other approvals, as well as a variety of preventive and remedial administrative orders. The ministry has many such tools to ensure that substantial pollution does not occur, or is cleaned up if it does. However, the Act provides no such tools to the ordinary citizen — which is why the Canadian Environmental Law Research Foundation objected so strongly to the premier of the day calling it an "environmental bill of rights" when it was introduced. A bill of rights suggests a statute that makes the government more accountable to the public and provides the public with rights and opportunities to participate in the decision-making process. Most of the amendments to the *Environmental Protection Act* over the years have strengthened the powers of government to take action, but have provided ordinary people with few remedies or rights to participate in decision making.

For example, if a person who has been issued a licence, permit, or other approval fails to comply with the terms or conditions of the approval, or if a person subject to a preventive or remedial order fails to comply with the order, the Act generally gives the ministry the power to carry out the action at the polluter's expense.[18] In addition, the ministry can ask the court for a "restraint order," something that is much like a common law injunction (see Chapter 6), as well as prosecute the polluter for violation of the approval or order. The private citizen can do none of these things, except prosecute for a violation of the Act or the regulations, or a violation of the terms and conditions of an approval or order.

In this section, we will briefly discuss some of the tools available to the ministry.

Certificates of Approval

Under the parts of the *Environmental Protection Act* that deal with specific businesses such as the construction of private sewage works, the hauling of sewage, the transportation of waste, and the operation of waste disposal sites and waste treatment facilities, and the portions of the Act that deal with specific events such as the drilling of a water well, certain activities are prohibited unless formal permission is obtained from the Ministry of Environment and Energy. In some cases this permission is called a licence; in others it is called a permit or a certificate of approval.

The general provisions of the *Environmental Protection Act* , however, do not speak of licences and permits, but require anyone who intends to construct or operate a potential source of pollution to obtain a "certificate of approval" for the equipment, and for the aspects of the operation that have the potential to discharge the contaminants. Thus, a large petrochemical plant may require hundreds of certificates of approval for various sewers, pipelines, reactors, smokestacks, baghouses, holding tanks, and other pieces of equipment or facilities that either are intended to control pollution or may discharge pollutants.

Before issuing a certificate of approval, the ministry may require an applicant to submit plans, specifications, and other information and to carry out tests or experiments to prove that the equipment, facilities, or methods or rates of production will not cause pollution.

Before issuing each of these certificates of approval, the Approvals Branch of the ministry or the regional office, as the case may be, is supposed to carefully scrutinize the plans and specifications and form an opinion as to whether they will result in unacceptable discharges of pollutants to the air, land, or water if they are potential pollution sources, or whether they will achieve adequate reductions in pollution if they are pollution control systems.

This requirement has resulted in a lengthy backlog of applications for certificates of approval and constant complaints from industry and other proponents about delays, unnecessary roadblocks, and inconsistent and arbitrary treatment of applications. As a result of these concerns, the ministry has been considering for several years ways to streamline the approvals process and reduce delays. There is a danger that the ministry will attempt to resolve this problem by delegating its approval functions to municipalities or to the private sector without adequate monitoring to ensure accountability, or that the ministry will revert to an after-the-fact strategy (often referred to in ministry reports as "permit-by-rule"). This would involve the ministry determining the levels of pollution that a facility is to meet, and issuing an approval without forming its own opinion as to whether the proposed pollution controls will work. The applicant or its consultants will be required to certify that the facilities will meet the standards, and will be responsible for replacing or upgrading them if they fail to do so. Unfortunately, this failure will be discovered only after the pollution has occurred. Since it is far more expensive to retrofit or reconstruct polluting facilities than to design them correctly at the outset, many polluters will be unwilling or unable to correct these problems. Thus, environmentalists should be monitoring these ministry initiatives closely to ensure that we do not trade environmental protection for faster approvals.

In addition to requiring a certificate of approval before sources of pollution are constructed or operated, nobody is allowed to make a change in the source of pollution, other than shutting it down, without a certificate of approval.

Section 9 provides:

No person shall, except under and in accordance with a certificate of approval issued by the Director,

(a) construct, alter, extend or replace any plant, structure, equipment, apparatus, mechanism or thing that may discharge or from which may be discharged a contaminant into any part of the natural environment other than water; or

(b) alter a process or rate of production with the result that a contaminant may be discharged into any part of the natural environment other than water or the rate or manner of discharge of a contaminant into any part of the natural environment other than water may be altered.

This provision used to provide that these steps could not be taken unless somebody *first* obtained a certificate of approval. This prevented people from flouting the law by ignoring the certificate of approval requirement, then putting pressure on the ministry to approve what had already been done. However, it was also inflexible, since the ministry could not later approve activities or works that had been carried out or constructed illegally, even if they did not create pollution or the risk of pollution. Therefore, the Act was amended to give the ministry authority to approve works after the fact.

The teeth in certificates of approval are found in the terms and conditions that may be attached to a certificate of approval.

After many years of issuing certificates of approval for the construction and the method of installation of specific pieces of equipment, without any requirements as to how the equipment would be operated or maintained, in the late 1980s the ministry finally began to accept the fact that many pollution incidents occur not because of inadequate equipment but as a result of the improper operation or maintenance of the equipment. Accordingly, the ministry began to draft "generic" terms and conditions for various kinds of facilities. These terms and conditions were designed to anticipate and prevent the kinds of problems that the ministry had learned through experience frequently result in the breakdown or malfunction of pollution control systems. These clauses were designed to be incorporated into individual certificates of approval by the Approvals Branch. However, by 1993 the ministry had managed to produce only one set of draft generic terms and conditions. Those draft terms and conditions cover municipal and industrial sewage works.

Since the utility of certificates of approval in protecting the public will arise largely from the terms and conditions imposed, it is important that the public have some involvement in establishing those terms and conditions. In February 1989, the ministry approved a policy that acknowledges the value of public consultation.[19] This policy provided for public consultation before certificates of approval are issued, but only after criteria that were then under development were approved.[20] As of March 3, 1993, no criteria had been approved, and thus the ministry could and did continue to refuse requests by neighbours to be consulted before certificates of approval were issued. In 1991, a court decision required the ministry to notify neighbours who might be adversely affected by applications for certificates of approval and to give them an opportunity to comment before the approval was issued.[21] As of March 3, 1993, however, this decision had not caused the ministry to implement its policy on public consultation, even though the court's decision required it.

Program Approvals

A person who is responsible for a source of contaminant may submit to the director a program to prevent or to reduce and control the discharge of contaminants. If the director is satisfied with the plan of action, he or she may issue a "program approval."

As we have indicated, the requirements of section 14 appear to apply whether or not higher levels of contamination are permitted by regulations. Section 14 appears to override other provisions of the *Environmental Protection Act* that would permit pollution. However, polluters who are carrying out a pollution abatement program under a program approval cannot be prosecuted for an offence in respect of any of the matters dealt with in the approval that occur during the period covered by the approval, as long as they comply fully with the terms of the approval.[22]

The original purpose of having such an exemption was to recognize that pollution from sources that existed before 1971, when the *Environmental Protection Act* took effect, might be difficult to control immediately without causing severe economic hardship. The purpose of the program approval was to allow a reasonable amount of time for polluters to bring their facilities into compliance. However, the program approval continued to be used for more than a decade after the Act came into effect. From the polluter's point of view, it was better to submit voluntarily to a program approval than to be issued a binding control order. If a control order was violated, the polluter would be committing an offence. However, if the polluter did not comply with a program approval, the only consequence would be the loss of immunity from prosecution for polluting. From the ministry's point of view, this provision gave the directors leverage to negotiate voluntary compliance. If a director issued an order, as we will discuss below, the polluter could appeal the order, and the director would then have to justify the order before the Environmental Appeal Board and commit ministry resources to fighting the appeal. If the promise of a program approval could encourage the polluter to carry out a program without an order, this unpleasant prospect could be avoided.

However, program approvals were subject to abuse, since they gave directors an opportunity to approve unacceptable levels of pollution for an indefinite length of time, rather than enforce section 14 of the Act. As a result, the ministry's policy now allows directors to issue program approvals only where preventive measures are needed, and not for the abatement of pollution that is actually occurring.[23] In addition, the *Environmental Protection Act* has been amended to allow directors to amend or revoke a program approval that was issued in error or that no longer adequately provides for the protection of the environment.[24]

Control Orders

If the ministry is not satisfied that efforts to obtain pollution abatement voluntarily are succeeding, it may issue a control order.[25] The original intent of the legislation was that a control order would set out a pollution abatement program that the ministry believed would be sufficient to prevent substantial pollution, and would order the polluter to comply with it. Such an order can be issued only after a provincial officer prepares a report containing a finding that a contaminant has been discharged into the natural environment in contravention of section 14 of the regulations, or that a contaminant whose use is totally prohibited has been discharged. Thus, control orders are not intended to anticipate and prevent future pollution, but to stop or reduce existing pollution.

Before issuing the order, the director must serve the polluter with notice of his or her intention to issue the order, together with written reasons for issuing it and a copy of the provincial officer's report.[26] The polluter then has 15 days to make submissions to the director to convince him or her not to issue the order, or to change it before it is issued.[27]

The order may be issued to an owner or a previous owner of the source of contaminant, a person who is in occupation of the source of contaminant or was previously in occupation of the source, or a person who has or in past has had the charge, management, or control of the source of contaminant.[28] "Source of contaminant" is defined as anything that discharges any contaminant into the natural environment.[29] The courts have yet to decide the scope of this sweeping definition. In one case, soil and groundwater were contaminated with pollutants from a creosote plant that had accumulated over several decades. The plant went through several changes of ownership and occupancy. In 1987, the ministry issued a control order to the operator of the plant, the former operator, and the owner of the land, which had never operated the polluting facility. The ministry argued that the owner of the land was the owner of a "source of contaminant" since it owned the creosote-soaked soil from which pollutants were continuing to seep into the groundwater, and from the groundwater into Lake Superior. The ministry claimed that the soil through which the contaminants were migrating was a "source of contaminant," and thus the owner of the soil could be ordered to carry out the clean-up. The Ontario Court of Appeal held, however, that although the creosote production facility was a source of contaminant, the contaminated soil itself could not be considered a source of contaminant,[30] so the landowner was not responsible for the clean-up.

Contents of Control Orders

Control orders may direct the persons to whom they are directed: to limit or control the rate of discharge of a contaminant; to stop the discharge permanently or for a specified time; to comply with directions relating to the procedures to be followed in controlling or eliminating the discharge; or to install or replace or alter any pollution control equipment. They may also require the person to monitor and record the discharge, to report to the director in respect of fuel, materials, and methods of production used at the facility or intended to be used or the waste that may be generated, and to study measures to control the discharge, the effects of the discharge on the environment, and the environment itself, and to report the results of the study to the director.[31]

In practice, control orders often do not require anyone to control anything. They are often nothing more than "a plan to make a plan." Because the cost and effectiveness of pollution control systems are often so uncertain, many control orders simply require that a study be done to determine the best solution to the problem. The control order often contains a clause requiring that if the director agrees with the pollution control measures proposed by the study, the polluter must apply for a certificate of approval to carry out the proposal as soon as the director approves it. Many companies subject to such control orders complain that it is unfair to require them, subject to stringent penalties if they fail to do so, to comply immediately with proposals recommended by their consultants, before they can know what those proposals will be or determine their cost or effectiveness.

If the study required by the control order sets out alternative proposals and the director and the polluter disagree as to which proposal is preferable, the outcome of their dispute may depend on the wording of the control order. In some cases, the control order requires the polluter to apply for a certificate of approval to implement the proposal of the director's choice. In other cases, the director may have to issue a further control order requiring the implementation of the proposal of his or her choice. Or the study required by the control order may indicate the need for further studies. The director may then have to issue a further order requiring more studies.

Ultimately, the director and the polluter may agree on the specific action to be taken. The polluter may then apply for a certificate of approval to implement that action, without the need for any further control order. On other occasions, the director may have to issue a further control order, requiring the polluter to apply for a certificate of approval and then to construct and operate the pollution control system applied for.

Public Participation

This system is frustrating to the victims of pollution. First, they see that many control orders merely require a study, and do not remove a single molecule of pollution from the air, soil, or water. Second, they are concerned about the delays that result from this process, and question whether the action stage will ever be reached. Third, as indicated above, victims of pollution have no right to be consulted on the terms of a control order or the timetable for implementation before it is issued.

Ministry policy on whether the public will be consulted before control orders are finalized is vague, ambiguous, and possibly contradictory. A 1985 ministry policy required the director to hold a public information session for "significant pollution problems or for pollution problems that generate high public interest" before issuing control orders.[32] However, when this policy was amended in 1992, under a government that claimed to be more open and accessible than previous governments, this requirement was deleted. The policy now states only that "the Director *may* notify the public during the development of control documents and program approvals" [emphasis added], and the extent of pollution or public concerns are now merely factors the director must consider in determining the extent of public notification and consultation, if any.[33] To confuse matters further, the ministry's policy on public consultation says that notwithstanding the compliance policy, "where a program approval or a legally enforceable abatement tool (such as a control order) is utilized, notification will be given to the public by providing copies of the document to the clerks of the local municipality and upper tier municipality where the undertaking of concern is located and to the appropriate MPP."[34] The policy does not say whether this information will be provided before the control order has been issued, or after, when it is too late to influence its contents. Presumably, this policy simply reflects the 1988 amendments to the *Environmental Protection Act* that require the ministry to notify the municipality of control orders.[35] These amendments do not appear to require any notification before the control order is finalized. We were unable to obtain from the ministry any information as to how often the director initiates public consultation and how often he or she issues a control order with no public consultation. Moreover, as we have indicated, the "teeth" of a control order are often found only in the certificates of approval issued to implement the control orders. Here, there is no policy requiring any public consultation.

Stop Orders

Stop orders may be issued by the ministry when a director has reasonable and probable grounds to believe that contaminant emissions may cause an immediate danger to life, health, or property. The stop order can be issued to the same class of persons as a control order.[36]

A stop order will do exactly that — shut down a polluting activity. It takes effect immediately. However, pollution rarely has an immediate, measurable impact. Because it is so difficult to obtain evidence that there will be an *immediate* danger to health or property, stop orders are rarely used. The ministry's first attempt to impose a stop order — on a Toronto lead smelter — was overruled by the court, because the director had insufficient evidence to support the order. The court ruled that the director who issues a stop order must act "judicially."[37] The court said that acting "judicially" means that "the test that [the director] must apply in order to reach a decision based upon reasonable and probable grounds, is not a subjective test but an objective one." In the case of a stop order, this means that the director must have evidence of an immediate danger. The affidavit of the director in the lead smelter case said only that the lead levels were "considerably in excess of those found in a normal urban environment." Clearly, that did not address the issue whether there was an immediate danger. The court felt that, "whatever that means, [it] is absolutely worthless. ... There is no evidence as to what the lead levels are in a normal environment, let alone what the deponent [the person swearing an affidavit] regards as a normal urban environment." Furthermore, although there was evidence of high lead levels in the blood of three residents of the area, the director's affidavit contained no evidence that it was caused by the lead smelter.

Since then, the ministry has issued a few stop orders. In one case, the stop order prohibited the use of a wood-burning stove in someone's home. A neighbour, who had a pre-existing respiratory problem, was hospitalized and put in intensive care as a result of illness brought on by inhaling the smoke from his neighbour's chimney. Before issuing the stop order, the ministry collected evidence of smoke and smoke odours emanating from the chimney of the wood stove, evidence that there was no smoke from any other source, evidence of complaints from other neighbours, and evidence from two doctors stating that there was a direct correlation between the need to hospitalize the complainant and the fumes from the stove, or that at least it was reasonable to assume the existence of a cause-and-effect relationship. As a result of the order, the neighbour made alterations to the chimney that were designed to reduce the amount of smoke; the ministry then revoked the stop order.[38]

The ministry also issued a stop order against blasting operations in the Thunder Bay area. Blasting at a quarry was sending a shower of rocks flying onto a highway and across the highway onto the land of a nearby resident. The company carrying out the blasting appealed the stop order to the Environmental Appeal Board, but the ministry revoked the order when the operator took steps to prevent this problem from continuing.

Remedial Orders

Section 17 provides:

> Where any person causes or permits the discharge of a contaminant into the natural environment, so that land, water, property, animal life, plant life or human health or safety is injured, damaged or endangered, or is likely to be injured, damaged or endangered, the Director may order the person(s) to:
>
>   (a) repair the injury or damage;
>   (b) prevent the injury or damage; or
>   (c) where the discharge has damaged or endangered or is likely to damage or endanger existing water supplies, provide alternate water supplies.

This section is both preventive and remedial. It can clearly be used both to prevent harm and to rectify it. However, the director's power to make an order is not triggered until a discharge has actually occurred. This section has been substantially broadened since 1971. Originally, this order could be issued only by the minister, and then only when there was actual damage. Thus, it was purely remedial. The preventive aspects have been added. The courts have treated section 17 as an emergency provision that would be frustrated if the director had to give the person subject to the order an opportunity to make submissions before the order took effect. In one case, when a gasoline tank at a service station leaked into the soil and groundwater, the court upheld an order to clean up the gasoline-soaked soil against the owner of the shopping plaza where the service station was located, the operator of the service station, and the oil company that supplied gasoline to the service station. The court held that the companies served with the order could fight it by refusing to comply with it and then defending charges of violating the order, if and when they were prosecuted.[39]

At the time, the arguments of these companies that they should have had an opportunity to comment before the order was issued were strengthened by the fact that there was no right to appeal the order after it took effect. The *Environmental Protection Act* allows anyone to whom a director issues an order to appeal it, but there was no appeal from an order issued by the minister. The section was later changed to give the authority to the director, so these orders may now be appealed to the Environmental Appeal Board.

Preventive Orders

Even if there has been no pollution, the director may make orders that are intended to anticipate and prevent pollution whenever the nature of an undertaking, or of anything on the property where an undertaking is being carried on, is such that if a contaminant were discharged from the undertaking or from the property, it would be likely to result in an adverse effect.[40] Under those circumstances, the director may order the owner or any previous owner of the property or the undertaking and anyone who has management or control of the undertaking or property, or who previously managed or controlled them, to take preventive measures. Such an order can be made whenever the director is of the opinion, based on reasonable and probable grounds, that the requirements specified in the order are necessary to prevent or reduce the risk of a discharge or to prevent, decrease, or eliminate an adverse effect that is likely to result from a discharge.

The measures that the director may require include: keeping equipment and material available; obtaining, constructing, installing, or modifying devices, equipment, and facilities; taking all steps necessary to ensure that procedures specified in the order will be implemented if a contaminant is discharged; monitoring and recording discharges; and studying measures to control a discharge, the effects of a discharge, and the natural environment itself, and reporting the results of the study to the director. The director may even specify the personnel that a company must hire to prevent discharging contaminants. For example, if a company produces waste water that requires treatment, the director could order the company to hire a trained and experienced sewage treatment plant operator to operate the facility. In one case, the director ordered the owners and operators of a used tire dump to hire security guards to patrol the premises to prevent arson.[41]

This provision has been greatly expanded from its origins as an "equipment order," which merely allowed the director to order people to have on hand equipment and material to alleviate the effects of contaminants that might be discharged as a result of their activities. These orders are extremely important, because they allow the director to order anyone who engages in activities that might cause pollution to monitor the quality of discharges as well as the background quality of the surrounding environment, even without any evidence of actual pollution. Ideally, such monitoring should be required as a condition of every certificate of approval that is issued so that operators of businesses or facilities that may cause pollution know at the outset what the public's expectations will be. However, if the ministry does not incorporate appropriate terms and conditions into licences, permits, and certificates of approval needed to prevent harm, it can rectify this omission either by later amending the certificate of approval to add additional terms and conditions, or by issuing a section 18 order.

Spill Clean-Up Orders

Under part X of the *Environmental Protection Act*, everyone who owns a pollutant that spills, or who was in control of it immediately before the spill, has a duty to clean up the spill and restore the environment to its previous condition, even without any formal order to do so.[42] However, the minister may issue spill clean-up orders if he or she is not satisfied with the speed or adequacy of the clean-up being undertaken, or if the person responsible for the spill or in charge of the contaminant cannot be found.

Under section 94, if a pollutant has been spilled and the minister is of the opinion that there are likely to be adverse effects, the minister may instruct employees and agents of the ministry to take action to prevent, eliminate, or ameliorate the adverse effects and to restore the natural environment. The minister may give these directions whenever he or she believes that it is in the best interest of the public to do so, and that the person in control of the pollutant and the owner will not promptly carry out their clean-up duties, cannot be readily identified, or have requested the assistance of the minister in carrying out their clean-up duties.

Under section 97, if the minister believes a spill is likely to cause an adverse effect and it is in the best interest of the public to make an order, the minister may order the owner of the pollutant, the person having control of the pollutant, the person in charge of any property that has been affected or may be affected by the pollutant, the municipality where the spill occurred, any adjacent municipality, any other municipality that may reasonably be expected to be affected by the spill, any public authority, or any person who may be affected by the pollutant or whose assistance is necessary to take the same actions that the polluter would be required to take.

The minister has no duty to give prior notice or to provide an opportunity for a hearing before issuing these directives or orders, nor does there appear to be an appeal from such an order.

PUBLIC CONSULTATION

We have already discussed the ministry's public consultation policies in relation to the issuance of certificates of approval and control orders. The policies regarding control orders generally apply as well to the other kinds of orders discussed above. To determine specifically how public consultation will be implemented with regard to each kind of order, you should look at the ministry's policies on pollution abatement and public consultation. It is interesting to note that the *Environmental Protection Act* was amended in 1988 to require that municipalities be informed of control orders and stop orders[43] (even if only after the fact), but there is no similar requirement for program approvals or any of the other approvals or orders that the director or the minister may issue.

The Appeal Process

In the 1960s, the chief justice of Ontario, Robert McRuer, undertook an inquiry into civil rights in Ontario. Mr. Justice McRuer's report resulted in numerous changes in the way government treats the citizens of Ontario. One of his recommendations was that nobody should be subject to an administrative decision without having a right of appeal.[44] Under many statutes, a staff person issues an order and his or her supervisor hears the appeal. For example, an inspector may issue an order, but the order can be appealed to a senior ministry official or the minister. In the municipal setting, an inspector's order may be appealed to the municipal council or a committee of the council. Under these circumstances, it would not be surprising if the person subject to the order felt that the game was "fixed." Under the *Environmental Protection Act*, most decisions of directors may be appealed to an independent Environmental Appeal Board.

Whenever a director:

- refuses to issue a licence, a permit, or an approval,
- imposes conditions on a licence, a permit, or an approval,
- amends a licence, a permit, or an approval,
- suspends, revokes, or refuses to renew a licence, a permit, or a certificate of approval, or
- issues an administrative order,

the director's decision or order may be appealed to the Environmental Appeal Board.

Only the person who is subject to the director's action may appeal the decision. Thus, if a person subject to the director's decision or order feels that this action is too stringent, he or she can appeal the action. A person who has been refused an approval can appeal the approval. A person who has been granted an approval subject to terms and conditions can appeal those terms and conditions. A person to whom a preventive or remedial order has been issued can appeal the order. The possibility of an appeal acts as a strong incentive to ministry staff to issue approvals that may result in pollution, to forgo or weaken terms and conditions in those approvals, or to issue weak orders, rather than defend their actions before the Environmental Appeal Board.

However, there is nothing in the system to counterbalance this pressure on directors to allow pollution. If neighbours fear that the issuance of an approval may result in contamination or are concerned that the conditions of the approval or an order are too weak to protect the environment, they have no similar right to appeal. Not only are they often not informed of the director's intention to take action, but even if the potential polluter appeals the director's action, they have no right to participate in the appeal, unless the Environmental Appeal Board grants them party status.

Even then, if the director and the person who is subject to the director's action strike a deal before the board hearing starts, the director may revoke an order, reverse his or her decision to refuse an approval, or weaken the terms or conditions of an order or an approval before the hearing begins, and the neighbours may have limited opportunity to make their voices heard.

Even after a hearing begins and neighbours have been made parties to the hearing, the director and the person who is subject to the director's action can strike a private deal without consulting the other parties to the hearing. This happened in the case of an appeal of a groundwater and soil clean-up order in the town of Elmira. A chemical company was ordered to carry out the clean-up when NDMA, a carcinogen, was found in the municipal drinking water supply. The board gave party status to the Town of Elmira, the Regional Municipality of Waterloo, which was responsible for providing a safe water supply, and a local citizens group. After these "intervenors" had participated in over 40 days in hearings lasting over a 13-month period, the ministry and Uniroyal reached a settlement. As a result, the company withdrew its appeal and the ministry then withdrew the order that was being appealed. Both the ministry and the company then argued that the subject matter of the appeal had disappeared, and thus the board had no further jurisdiction. The intervenors, however, were unhappy with the settlement. They felt that this settlement would not protect the municipal water supply or the local creek, and argued that the ministry and the company had no right to settle the case without involving them. The board ruled, however, that it had power to intervene in the settlement reached by the ministry and the chemical company to protect the public interest, including the rights of the intervenors.[45]

When the Director's Decision or Order Takes Effect

Until 1990, a person who was ordered to abate pollution or required to comply with the terms and conditions of an approval could delay the implementation of the terms and conditions or the order simply by launching an appeal to the Environmental Appeal Board. Originally, the *Environmental Protection Act* provided that these director's actions did not take effect until all appeals were exhausted. Thus, the person could appeal the director's order or decision to the board; and from the board to the minister and to the courts. Meanwhile, the action was not effective.

To prevent the misuse of appeals, and to protect the environment, the *Environmental Protection Act* was amended in 1983[46] to provide that the director's decision or order would not be stayed until appeals were finished if the director successfully applied to the board for an order that brought the decision or order into effect notwithstanding the appeal. However, the lawyers representing the directors rarely made such applications. In one case, an application to remove the stay was made, but the board found that the lawyer for the director had not addressed the issues that the statute required him to address before the board could require an order to take effect.[47]

Then came the Hagersville tire fire. At 1:00 AM on February 12, 1990, a pile of several million tires was set on fire by a teenager. The fire raged for 17 days. An area of several kilometres in all directions from the site had to be evacuated. The tires melted, leaving a pool of oily waste that contaminated the surrounding soil and groundwater. In addition to the police department, the fire department, and water bombers supplied by the Ministry of Natural Resources, over 200 Ministry of Environment staff members were involved in controlling the fire and in the subsequent clean-up. Within two months, the Ontario government had spent $6 million on putting out the fire and cleaning up the contamination. It spent an additional $5 or $6 million the following year.

In February 1987, the ministry had ordered the operator of the site, Tyre King Tyre Recycling Inc., to take steps to prevent a fire. Tyre King had appealed the order to the board, which had upheld the order in part. However, Tyre King then appealed the board's decision to the Divisional Court, but took no steps to proceed with its appeal. While the matter was sitting dormant before the court, the fire broke out. During all this time the order was not in effect.

As a result, the *Environmental Protection Act* was amended in June 1990 to provide that the orders and decisions of directors take effect immediately unless the person appealing them persuades the board to stay the operation of the order or decision.[48] Moreover, the board has no jurisdiction to stay the order or decision if the stay might result in harm to the environment.[49] There is also no jurisdiction to stay an order to monitor the condition of the environment and report the results to the ministry.[50]

The Powers of the Environmental Appeal Board

The Environmental Appeal Board has very broad powers. Section 144(1) of the *Environmental Protection Act* provides:

the Board may confirm, alter or revoke the action of the Director that is the subject-matter of the hearing and may by order direct the Director to take such action as the Board considers the Director should take in accordance with this Act and the Regulations, and, for such purposes, the Board may substitute its opinion for that of the Director.

Although these powers appear very broad, the courts have given them a narrower interpretation than the provision appears to support. In the *Lewis* case, the Divisional Court ruled that the board's powers are limited to the subject matter of the appeal, which is the actual order or decision under appeal, and that the board cannot substantially change or enlarge the order or decision of the director.[51] In *Lewis*, the director had added restrictive conditions to the certificate of approval for a polluting landfill site. The operator of the site appealed these conditions. Neighbours of the landfill site were given party status by the board, and were represented by a lawyer from the Canadian Environmental Law Association. Their evidence and their lawyer's submissions convinced the board that the new conditions would not prevent harm to the neighbours from operation of the landfill site. As a result, the board decided that the only action that would prevent nuisance from this site would be to revoke the certificate of approval to operate the site. It did so.

The Divisional Court ruled that the board had no power to revoke the certificate of approval. However, as a result of either the inadequacy of the director's certificate of approval conditions or the ministry's failure to enforce the law, the Ontario Court (General Division) in 1991 issued an immediate and permanent injunction against further operation of the site, which had continued for seven more years to cause a serious nuisance to the neighbours, notwithstanding the terms of the certificate of approval. In shutting down the site, the court said, "there was virtually no defence. ... I found it difficult to understand how one could have so many complaints and receive so little assistance from the government authority." After recounting the evidence that the board had heard in 1984, the court commented, "deja-vu, we have heard it all again — the same music with the same words."[52]

FINANCIAL ASSURANCE

In 1986, the *Environmental Protection Act* was amended to include a new part XII dealing with financial assurance. This part authorizes the director to include financial assurance requirements in an "approval," which is defined to include a program approval, a certificate of approval or permit, or an order in respect of a "works." The order or approval may require that the person to whom it has been directed must provide financial assurance to the provincial government to ensure the performance of any action specified in the order or approval, the provision of alternative water supplies to replace any that have been contaminated by the works to which the approval or order is related, and appropriate measures to prevent adverse effects when the works are closed.[53] "Works" is defined to mean, "an activity, facility, thing, undertaking or site."[54]

The ministry has published a policy and a set of guidelines for financial assurance that list out the circumstances under which financial assurance will be required, the kinds of security that will be considered acceptable, and the method of calculating or estimating the costs associated with different activities.[55] For example, the ministry will determine the worst-case scenario if the facility is abandoned, leaving behind contaminated soil, and it will base the amount of financial assurance on the cost of dealing with that scenario.[56]

The director's power to require financial assurance is extremely important, since it is so simple for anybody to incorporate a shell corporation to carry on hazardous activities. When pollution occurs, the government finds nothing but an empty shell, with no assets or income to be seized to pay for the clean-up of the pollution, and little or no insurance coverage. For example, when a waste transportation company spilled PCBs on the Trans-Canada Highway in 1985, resulting in the closure of the highway and local businesses, and the replacement of miles of highway at a cost of several million dollars, the taxpayers footed the bill since the company had insufficient assets and insufficient insurance coverage to pay for it. Moreover, some entrepreneurs create a tangle of shell companies that is difficult or impossible to unravel.

Unfortunately, part XII does nothing to solve one serious problem: companies that avoid paying fines for pollution offences by hiding behind a barricade of shell corporations. A cement company in Toronto's Junction Triangle was convicted several times during the 1980s of numerous air pollution offences, and chalked up over $40,000 in fines. Whenever the government attempted to collect the fines, it found that the operation was being carried on by yet another corporation, all of them connected in some way to the same family of individuals.

This is a problem in the enforcement of most environmental statutes, not just the *Environmental Protection Act*. For example, Sam Siapas, whose B.E.S.T Plating Shoppe Limited chalked up $63,000 in fines for discharging pollutants into the Toronto sewer system, also used several corporations to shield him and his operations from paying the fines levied under a municipal sewage control bylaw. When prosecutors attempted to have Mr. Siapas jailed for failing to comply with court orders to stop polluting, they discovered the existence of several other corporations. In addition to B.E.S.T Plating, which had been attracting all the pollution convictions, they found Siapas Holdings Limited, 547457 Ontario Limited, and 703048 Ontario Limited. B.E.S.T itself was an empty shell, from which none of the fines could be collected.

A consultant retained by Mr. Siapas to prepare a business plan and to raise funds for an expansion of his plating business testified as follows:

Question: Did Mr. Siapas advise you why he had set up this corporate structure?

Answer: Yes, he told me the reason for creation of the numbered company.

Question: What was it for any of the reasons that you have just described in the course of other small businesses?

Answer: Yes, it was for the purpose of getting the assets, or major assets and operations out of B.E.S.T Plating and into another vehicle.

Question: Did he tell you why?

Answer: Yes, he told me that he had been fined for pollution problems in the past, and that while he wanted to "come clean," I think are his words, in terms of paying his fines in due course, he was not presently in a position to do so, and therefore wanted to give the impression to those who might be in a position to impose the fines, that the company was not as profitable as the financial statements would indicate; thereby maybe buying himself some time to pay those fines.

Mr. Siapas told his loans officer at the bank that he had "structured" yet another company to show that he had no involvement in the plating operation and to protect himself from any further action against him. He told her that "with this particular restructuring he felt comfortable [that the courts and Metropolitan Toronto] were not going to be able to touch him financially." The loans officer recorded her understanding of her discussions with Mr. Siapas in a memorandum: "The reason for setting up the new company with complete new officers, is a direct result of the Municipality of Metropolitan Toronto's action against Mr. Sam Siapas and one of his former companies, B.E.S.T Plating Shoppe Limited."

REMEDIES

When anybody discharges a contaminant that is likely to cause adverse effects or in an amount that exceeds the limits in the regulations, or violates any order issued by the minister or a director, or violates any certificate of approval, licence, or permit, the ministry has available to it a wide range of remedies.

Prosecutions

Violation of any of the provisions of the *Environmental Protection Act* or the regulations or of any order, licence, permit, or approval is an offence. The Ministry of Environment and Energy or any member of the public may prosecute. The ministry has a Legal Services Branch with about 30 lawyers, as well as a specialized Investigations and Enforcement Branch consisting in 1991 of 117 people, 64 of whom were trained investigators. In 1991, the Investigations and Enforcement Branch had a budget of $7.1 million.[57]

Penalties on conviction are substantial. For offences that involve the actual discharge of a contaminant that is likely to cause adverse effects or that involve hazardous waste or liquid industrial waste that may cause adverse effects, individuals are subject to a fine of up to $25,000 per day and up to one year in jail.[58] For the same offences, corporations may be fined up to $200,000 per day.[59] For many other offences, individuals may be fined up to $10,000 per day[60] and corporations up to $100,000 per day.[61] These maximum fines may be increased by the amount of monetary benefit that the individual or corporation obtained by committing the offence.

If the fines are not paid, the court may suspend licences issued by the ministry until they have been paid.[62]

When an individual or a corporation is convicted of an offence, the court may also issue orders to prevent the recurrence or continuation of the offence and to rectify the harm from the offence.[63] The licence plates of vehicles used in offences involving hazardous or liquid industrial waste may be seized to discourage the continuation of the offence.[64]

In the past, when the ministry was reluctant to enforce the law, private prosecution, or even a threat of a private prosecution, was sometimes very effective in getting the ministry to take action when repeated requests by the public had failed to make the ministry move. Today, the pendulum may have swung too far the other way. There are frequent complaints from industry that the ministry's "pollution police" sometimes prosecute trivial offences or initiate prosecution when other less drastic means of obtaining compliance would be just as effective.

Licence Revocations or Suspensions

Because certificates of approval are often issued to construct and operate pollution control devices or facilities, it would be pointless to suspend or revoke this type of approval. However, in the case of certificates of approval, permits, and licences that are issued to authorize people to carry out an activity that may pollute or to conduct a business that may cause pollution, such as the operation of a waste disposal site or waste hauling, the ministry may suspend or revoke the certificate of approval, licence, or permit, or refuse to renew it. Since this suspension, revocation, or refusal to renew takes effect immediately, notwithstanding an appeal to the Environmental Appeal Board, this is a very effective way of achieving compliance.

Restraint Orders

In addition to any other remedy the minister may have and any other penalty that may be imposed, the minister may launch an action for a court order to restrain a polluter from breaching any provision of the *Environmental Protection Act* or regulations, or any direction, order, approval, notice, or permit under the Act.[65] The ministry has rarely attempted to seek such a restraint order. In one case, the ministry sought such an injunction, alleging that the operator of a waste disposal site was depositing more waste on its property than its certificate of approval permitted. The court refused to grant an injunction, suggesting that it would be necessary to show one or more convictions before it would do so. However, that decision was coloured by the fact that the court was presented with conflicting statements from ministry officials as to how much waste was permissible.[66]

Unlike many of the US environmental statutes, which provide for "citizens' suits" to enforce their provisions, the power to restrain violations of the *Environmental Protection Act* is available only to the minister. One might well ask why, if the law is being broken, the public may not also ask a court to prevent further breaches.

CONCLUSION

The problems in relation to the *Environmental Protection Act* fall into three main categories. The first is its emphasis on pollution and its lack of any vision of environmental sustainability, which contributes to the lack of a holistic approach to environmental protection. The second category of shortcoming is the broad discretion given to the ministry and the lack of adequate provisions for government accountability, public participation, and remedies available to the public. The third is the failure to plug obvious loopholes in the law.

We started this chapter with a passage from a critique of the *Environmental Protection Act* by the Canadian Environmental Law Research Foundation (now the Canadian Institute for Environmental Law and Policy). The Act, as one finds it in early 1993, gives the ministry sweeping powers to control pollution. Apart from a right to compensation for harm from spills, however, it does not create a single new remedy for the ordinary citizen. Public participation is completely at the whim of ministry officials. There is no duty even to investigate public complaints, provide information, or respond to letters, much less take action on environmental problems. Many of these problems of participation and accountability may be addressed by the environmental bill of rights introduced by the government; but the task force report on this bill of rights, issued in July 1992, makes it apparent that even this is unlikely to fully address these problems. For example, the task force recommended against giving neighbours the right to notice applications for septic systems on adjacent lands, even though these sewage systems are known to be one of the most frequent causes of groundwater, well, and surface water contamination.

The Act may also be criticized for its narrow focus on pollution. Environmental protection means much more than controlling pollution. This approach reinforces a fragmented approach to environmental issues. The environment continues to be viewed as the natural environment, and artificial distinctions are drawn between the poisoning of indoor and outdoor air, and between the destruction of plant and animal life on the one hand and heritage buildings, on the other.

In addition, there are still many provisions in the *Environmental Protection Act* that need to be clarified or strengthened. For example, section 40 of the Act, in the part dealing with waste management, states:

> No use shall be made of land or land covered by water which has been used for the disposal of waste within a period of 25 years from the year in which such land ceased to be so used, unless the approval of the minister for the proposed use has been given.

Leachate, the toxic liquid that percolates through garbage into the soil and groundwater, does not stay beneath the land that was actually used for the disposal of waste, nor does methane gas, which can migrate through the soil to nearby buildings and cause them to explode. Does this provision only govern the part of a landfill site where the waste was actually deposited, or does it also allow the minister to "freeze" the use of surrounding lands that may be contaminated with leachate or methane gas, to create a "buffer zone"?

Dianne Saxe has pointed out another such anomaly. Section 17 gives the director the power to order polluters to prevent or repair injury or damage to land, water, property, animal life, plant life, or human health. But Saxe states:

> The wording of this section is rather odd and betrays the fact that the reference to humans and to animal life was added in 1990 without a corresponding adjustment to its verbs. One can "repair" property or the physical landscape, for example, an eroded bank can be reconstructed and buttressed with rip rap; a car whose paint has been pitted by air emissions can be repainted. However, the word "repair" is wholly unsuitable for people and animals. One cannot "repair" a living creature as one does a machine; there is no known "repair" for death.[67]

There are many questions like this that the ministry is well aware of, which need to be resolved through amendments to strengthen or clarify the Act.[68] One of the biggest concerns remains the failure to provide a fund, like the United States' Superfund, that can be used for the clean-up of pollution. Much of the contamination of Ontario's environment is still being done by shell corporations or by corporations that may have assets now, but will have none by the time their pollution is discovered. In those cases, the taxpayers of Ontario pay for the clean-up, and will continue to do so unless legislation like the *Environmental Protection Act* is amended to ensure that such companies pay for their pollution.

John Swaigen

FURTHER READING

John W. Adams and Daniel G. Shand, "The Other EAB: A Practitioner's Perspective on Appeals to the Environmental Appeal Board," in *Environmental Law — A Program for the Specialist*, Proceedings of the Canadian Bar Association — Ontario, Institute of Continuing Legal Education, February 1, 1992 (Toronto: CBAO, 1992).

Ian Blue and Robert D. Kligman, *The Ontario Spills Spill: Analysis, Law & Regulations* (Toronto: CCH Canadian Ltd., 1985).

David Estrin, *Handle with Caution* (Scarborough, Ont.: Carswell, 1986).

S.M. Makuch, ed., *The Spills Bill: Duties, Rights and Compensation* (Toronto: Butterworths, 1986).

Grace Patterson, "Practice and Procedure before the Ontario Environmental Appeal Board" (1981-82), 3 *Advocates' Quarterly* 181.

Harry Poch, *Corporate and Municipal Environmental Law* (Scarborough, Ont.: Carswell, 1989), chapter 5.

Dianne Saxe, *Environmental Offences* (Aurora, Ont.: Canada Law Book, 1990).

Dianne Saxe, "Fines Go Up Dramatically in Environmental Cases" (1989), 3 CELR (NS) 104.

Dianne Saxe, *Ontario Environmental Protection Act Annotated* (Aurora, Ont.: Canada Law Book) (looseleaf).

John Swaigen, "The Environmental Appeal Board," in *Environmental Law — A Program for the Specialist*, Proceedings of the Canadian Bar Association — Ontario, Institute of Continuing Legal Education, February 1, 1992 (Toronto: CBAO, 1992).

John Swaigen, "Ontario's Environment Enforcement Statute Law Amendment Act, 1986" (1987-88), 2 CELR (NS) 14.

ENDNOTES

1 *Environmental Protection Act*, RSO 1990, c. E.19.
2 Ibid., section 3.
3 Ibid., section 91(1).
4 Ibid., section 1(1)(c).
5 Ibid., section 1(1)(a).
6 Ibid., section 1(1)(k).
7 *R. v. City of Sault Ste. Marie* (1978), 40 CCC (2d) 353, at 376, 85 DLR (3d) 161 (SCC).
8 Ibid. In *Sault Ste. Marie*, the Supreme Court of Canada ruled that when corporations are charged with offences as a result of acts or omissions of their employees or contractors, they, as well as the employees or contractors, may be guilty of the offence if they failed to establish and implement a system to prevent such violations. Subsequent cases have ruled that such a system must include hiring practices, adequate training and supervision of employees, modern equipment and facilities, maintenance, timely repair and replacement of such equipment, and efficient communications systems. See Dianne Saxe, *Environmental Offences* (Aurora, Ont.: Canada Law Book, 1990) and John Swaigen, *Regulatory Offences in Canada* (Scarborough, Ont.: Carswell, 1992). To eliminate any doubt about whether officers and directors have a duty to prevent offences, the *Environmental Protection Act* and *Ontario Water Resources Act* were both amended in 1986 by adding section 194, which provides for such a duty.
9 *R. v. Glen Leven Properties Limited* (1977), 15 OR (2d) 501, 34 CCC (2d) 349, 6 CELN 2 (HCJ). However, in *R. v. Springbank Sand & Gravel Ltd.* (1976), 25 CCC (2d) 535 (Ont. Cty. Ct.), another judge held that the sand blowing from the same construction site on a different occasion was not an offence under the *Environmental Protection Act* because it was caused by an act of God. In that case, a strong wind had come up, and there was no evidence before the judge that the construction contractor could have taken any action to prevent the sand from blowing.
10 *R. v. Del Chute & Son Limited*, Ontario Provincial Offences Appeal Court, Brantford, May 4, 1987, Macdonald J. [unreported].
11 For cases, see Dianne Saxe, *Ontario Environmental Protection Act Annotated* (Aurora, Ont.: Canada Law Book) (looseleaf).

12 *Rockcliffe Park Realty Ltd. v. Director of the Ministry of the Environment* (1976), 62 DLR (3d) 17, 10 OR (2d) 1 (CA).

13 *R. v. Mac's Convenience Stores Inc.* (1985), 14 CELR 120, at 128 (Prov. Off. Ct.) (see corrigendum (1987), 1 CELR (NS) xxxiv); *R. v. Texaco Canada Inc.* (1984), 13 CELR 124 (Ont. Prov. Ct.); *R. v. Toronto Electric Commissioners* (1991), 6 CELR (NS) 304 (Ont. CJ, Gen. Div.).

14 *R. v. City of Sault Ste. Marie*, supra endnote 7, DLR at 184.

15 *R. v. Liverence* (1986), 1 CELR (NS) 97 (Ont. Prov. Off. Ap. Ct.).

16 This situation arose when contractors constructing a structure at the Cyanamid plant in Welland, Ontario were exposed to buried waste while digging up the ground. In that case, charges were laid under the *Occupational Health and Safety Act* against Cyanamid for exposing the workers to a potentially harmful material and charges were laid under the *Environmental Protection Act* for having an unlawful waste disposal site.

17 *R. v. Toronto Refiners and Smelters Ltd.* (1978), 20 OR (2d) 772, 42 CCC (2d) 76 (Div. Ct.), rev'g. (1977), 17 OR (2d) 38, 37 CCC (2d) 561 (HCJ). See also *R.v. Commander Business Furniture Inc.* (1992), 9 CELR (NS) 185 (Ont. Prov. Div.).

18 *Environmental Protection Act*, supra endnote 1, part 14.

19 Ontario, Ministry of the Environment, "Public Consultation," Policy no. 16-09, February 16, 1989. See the ministry's *Manual of Environmental Policies and Guidelines*.

20 *Environmental Protection Act*, supra endnote 1, section 6.

21 *795833 Ontario Inc. v. Attorney General of Ontario et al.*, Ontario Court of Justice, General Division, file no. 2369/90, Corbett J., December 4, 1990 (the "*Mangialardi*" case) [unreported].

22 *Environmental Protection Act*, supra endnote 1, section 186(4).

23 The ministry began to tighten up the use of program approvals in 1981, when it issued policy no. 05-02, "Pollution Abatement Program: Development, Compliance and Enforcement," setting out a list of items that should be contained in any program approval. This policy was revised and reissued under the name "Compliance" in July 1991. Section 5.2 of the revised policy restricts the use of program approvals to preventive measures.

24 *Environmental Protection Act*, supra endnote 1, section 11(2).

25 Ibid., section 7.

26 Ibid., section 127(1).

27 Ibid., section 116(2).

28 Ibid., section 7(1).

29 Ibid., section 1(1)(p).

30 *Canadian National Railway Co. v. Ontario (Director under the Environmental Protection Act)* (1991), 3 OR (3d) 609 (Div. Ct.), aff'd. (1992), 7 OR (3d) 97 (CA).

31 *Environmental Protection Act*, supra endnote 1, section 124.

32 "Pollution Abatement Program," supra endnote 23, effective date June 15, 1985, section 1.9.

33 "Compliance," supra endnote 23, July 1991, sections 9.0 and 9.1. This revised policy had not yet been incorporated into the ministry's *Manual of Environmental Policies and Guidelines* as of March 3, 1993.

34	"Public Consultation," supra endnote 19, section 8.

35	*Environmental Protection Act,* supra endnote 1, section 7(2).

36	Ibid., section 8(1).

37	*Re: Canada Metal Company Limited and MacFarlane* (1973), 1 OR (2d) 577 (Ont. HCJ).

38	Harry Dahme, "Perspectives on the Regulatory Scheme of the *Environmental Protection Act* (1971)," paper prepared for Osgoode Hall Law School course on administrative law, 1980 [unpublished].

39	*Mac's Convenience Stores Inc. v. Minister of the Environment* (1984), 12 DLR (4d) 443, 48 OR (2d) 9 (Div. Ct.).

40	*Environmental Protection Act,* supra endnote 1, section 18.

41	See *P & L Tire Recycling Ltd. v. Director, Ministry of the Environment,* decision of the Environmental Appeal Board, released May 13, 1992, EAB file no. EPA.001.90.

42	*Environmental Protection Act,* supra endnote 1, section 93.

43	*Environmental Protection Act,* supra endnote 1, section 8(2).

44	Ontario, *Report of the Royal Commission Inquiry into Civil Rights* (Toronto: Queen's Printer, 1969), 234 and 1097 (the McRuer report).

45	*Re Uniroyal Chemical Ltd.* (1992), 9 CELR (NS) 151 (Ont. EAB).

46	*Environmental Protection Act,* supra endnote 1, section 122b, as amended by SO 1983, c. 52.

47	*Re: Domtar Application with Respect to an Amending Control Order,* Ontario Environmental Appeal Board, EAB file no. 18.87, July 17, 1989.

48	*Environmental Protection Act,* supra endnote 1, sections 143(1)-(2).

49	Ibid., section 143(3).

50	Ibid., section 143(20).

51	*Re C.H. Lewis (Lucan) Limited and Director of Environmental Approvals and Project Engineering for Ministry of the Environment et al.* (1985), 50 OR (2d) 23 (HCJ).

52	*Nippa v. C.H. Lewis (Lucan) Limited* (1991), 7 CELR (NS) 149 (Ont. CJ, Gen. Div.); (1991), 7 CELR (NS) 163 (CA).

53	*Environmental Protection Act,* supra endnote 1, section 132.

54	Ibid., section 131.

55	Ontario, Ministry of the Environment, "Financial Assurance," Policy no. 02-03, November 30, 1988, guidelines, part XA (now part XII).

56	Ontario, Ministry of the Environment, "Financial Assurance," Policy no. 02-03-01, November 30, 1988, guidelines, available from the ministry. See also Ontario, Ministry of the Environment, "Guidelines for Economic Analyses of Private Sector Pollution Abatement and Environmental Protection Measures," Policy no. 02-01-01, March 18, 1988.

57	Telephone conversation with Patricia Hollett, assistant director, Investigations and Enforcement Branch, Ontario Ministry of the Environment, October 19, 1991.

58	*Environmental Protection Act,* supra endnote 1, sections 186(5) to 193.

59	Ibid., sections 187 and 193.

60	Ibid., section 186(5).

61	Ibid., section 186(6).

62	Ibid., section 191.

63 Ibid., sections 183(2) and 188.
64 Ibid., section 49.
65 Ibid., section 183.
66 *R. v. Hale* (1983), 13 CELR 19 (Ont. HCJ).
67 Dianne Saxe, "Reflections on Environmental Restoration" (1991), 2 JELP 77.
68 At the beginning of Chapter 24, for example, you will find a series of quotations that make it clear that the government has recognized since at least 1983 the lack of adequate authority in the *Environmental Protection Act* or the *Municipal Act* for municipalities to carry out comprehensive planning for waste management, and in particular to carry out or require "reduce, re-use and recycle" (3Rs) programs.

17

Air Quality

CONTENTS

My throat was burned and my eyes got red and sore. It was aggravating my throat to the point that I said to my pilot enough of this, "Let's get down."

Henry Shannon, a traffic reporter for a radio station, explains why he cut his flight short on the morning of July 12, 1991, when he encountered "a solid smear of filth" in the air above Toronto

---

INTRODUCTION

By the 1970s, increased crowding in Canada's cities, more automobiles, increased industrialization and energy use, and poor land-use planning had all combined to make air pollution a serious concern, particularly in urban areas, where foul odours, smoke, dust, and fumes had little room to dissipate before they landed on people's property or entered their lungs. At best, air pollution had become a serious nuisance, disrupting people's enjoyment of their property and conduct of business, and at worst it was a health hazard. On a few occasions, under adverse weather conditions, pollutants had caused a "killer fog." The best-known incident was the four-day fog in London, England that caused 4,000 deaths in 1952.

By the 1980s, however, we were beginning to understand that air pollutants travelled much further and persisted much longer than scientists realized, as chemicals manufactured in the industrial world were found in the organs of animals in the Arctic and Antarctic, thousands of kilometres from the nearest source of their production or use. Air pollution was no longer merely a local problem, but an international one. We began to realize that some persistent toxic chemicals could travel thousands of miles through the air. In some cases, chemicals such as CFCs that were relatively benign at ground level were found to have persistent and devastating impacts on the upper atmosphere. In other cases, individual chemicals would combine in the air to form more harmful substances such as acid rain. Building taller smoke stacks to carry pollutants farther afield and higher into the atmosphere had alleviated local pollution, but sometimes at the price of creating long-range transport of pollutants that built up in the soil and in lakes and rivers far from their source.

As long as the only victims of this long-range transport were polar bears and penguins, there was not a great deal of public pressure for improvement. In the last few years, however, we have learned that air pollution not only harms people and animals, but can change the world's climate and even alter the chemistry of the earth's atmosphere itself. Therefore, action is urgently needed on an international scale to combat some forms of air pollution. As the federal House of Commons Standing Committee on the Environment noted in relation to chemicals damaging the earth's protective ozone layer and contributing to global warming, "Even if all use of CFCs was halted immediately, the atmospheric concentration of ozone would not return to normal for more than a century."[1]

The Effects of Air Pollution

Wherever we take a breath — indoors or outdoors, at home, in the workplace, and in places of recreation — we inhale air pollutants. Yet much is still unknown about the transportation of pollutants through the air, the pathways they follow, where they will eventually land, and the chemical transformations that may take place along the way. We have learned much about the effects of some air contaminants on human health, but we know almost nothing about others, and we know even less about their effects on the environment. The level of our ignorance can be summed up in a single sentence from a 1992 report by the International Joint Commission: "A lack of ambient air monitoring data, emission inventories, and health-related studies on potentially important toxic substances make it difficult to analyze the potential human health and environmental effects of many toxic chemicals."[2]

We know that many airborne contaminants eventually return to the land and water in one form or another. In fact, the largest source of water pollution is air pollution. Therefore, people can be affected by air pollution not only by breathing polluted air, but also by drinking polluted water or eating food contaminated by pollutants deposited onto the crop or the soil in which it is grown. We also know that two or more pollutants released separately into the air will sometimes combine to form new substances whose harmful effects are greater than the effects of each of the individual components. An example of this "synergism" is the formation of carcinogenic nitrosamines in the air when other substances are emitted into the air. In other cases, even though two pollutants do not undergo a change in chemistry to form a third substance, they may be more harmful in combination than alone. Sulphur oxides and particulate matter are one such harmful combination.

Human reactions to air pollution range from minor skin rashes and irritation of the eyes, ears, and throat to lung diseases. Exposure to pollutants may cause acute or short-term effects such as asthma attacks, respiratory infections, and temporary reduction in the ability of the lungs to take in and force out air. Chronic or long-term effects include bronchitis, emphysema, and lung cancer. Children, the elderly, and people who have existing respiratory disease are often the most susceptible to pollution. In extreme cases, such as Bhopal, India and the 1952 London fog, death may result.

Air pollution has also been shown to affect crops and natural vegetation. In fact, some plants may be even more sensitive than people to some forms of air pollution. Air pollution appears to have contributed to forest "dieback" or decline in both Europe and North America, harm to animals, and the deterioration of our buildings, monuments, statues, and other works of art, as well as changes in the global climate.[3]

Air pollution also has significant social and economic consequences. The consequences of pulmonary disease, for example, include lower productivity in the workplace and higher medicare costs. Damage to forests and crops also has an economic impact. For example, damage caused to crops by ground-level ozone was estimated at $23 million in Ontario in 1980 and up to $2 billion in the United States.[4] By 1988, the damage to Ontario's crops had risen to $50 million,[5] and to $70 million by 1990.[6]

Some Common Air Pollutants: Their Causes and Effects[7]

Oxidants

Various oxidants, such as nitrogen dioxide and peroxyacetyl nitrate, are known to cause harm such as injury to vegetation. The oxidant of most concern, however, is ozone. Ozone occurs naturally, but higher levels of ozone result from other air pollutants, such as nitrogen oxides (NO_x) and volatile organic compounds (described below), upsetting the normal balance between natural oxides of nitrogen in the air and ozone. The concern about ozone may be confusing because we all know that having a layer of ozone in the stratosphere is important to shield us from cancer-causing rays of the sun. At ground level, however, too much ozone causes substantial damage to trees and crops. High short-term levels of ozone can damage the health of animals and humans, particularly the developing lungs of infants and young children. More than half of all Canadians are routinely exposed to ozone in concentrations that can adversely affect health.[8] High levels of ozone resulting from automobile emissions, combustion processes, and industrial emissions are often found as far as several hundred kilometres downwind of highly populated areas.

Sulphur Oxides

Sulphur oxides, particularly sulphur dioxide, have been found in large enough quantities in residential, commercial, and industrial areas within cities to make them one of the earliest pollutants monitored and controlled by the government. In the concentrations normally found in urban air, sulphur dioxide alone does not seem to cause or seriously aggravate illness. However, the pungent, suffocating quality of air polluted by sulphur dioxide made it an early focus of concern even in the absence of harm to health. Moreover, as we mentioned above, high levels of sulphur dioxide combined with exposure to high levels of particulate during severe pollution episodes have resulted in deaths; and there is some evidence of reductions in lung function and mild respiratory symptoms and diseases, such as coughing and bronchitis, from sulphur dioxide alone, even at lower levels. Sulphur dioxide also causes damage to the foliage of plants, and is most notorious in recent years for its contribution to acid rain.

Power plants, smelters, refineries, and other industrial processes have been major sources of emissions. Sulphur oxides in the air come from production of copper, nickel, lead, zinc, gold, and aluminum; pulp and paper plants; oil and natural gas recovery; and the burning of fuels such as coal and oil.

Particulate Matter

"Particulate" is not a precisely defined term, and it means different things to different people. For example, in Ontario's air pollution regulation, particulate and dust are listed as different things, and neither is defined; yet particulate is usually considered to include dust. The term "particulates" usually refers to particles of solid matter or liquid that remain suspended in the air. Thus, particulates may include not only dust but also aerosols. Particulates may have different effects on human health and well-being depending on the size and physical and chemical composition of the particles, how deeply they penetrate the lung, and how long they are retained there. However, our laws generally lump these different kinds of particulates together.

Some particulates may simply cause eye, nose, and throat irritation. However, when they penetrate beyond the natural protective mechanisms of the nose and throat into the respiratory system, some particulates may harm the pulmonary function and contribute to existing pulmonary and cardiovascular disease. For example, sulphur dioxide and nitrogen oxide emissions can lead to the formation of fine particles of sulphates and nitrates, which can affect lung function.

Particulates are also of concern because they soil buildings, cars, and clothing, and because they contribute to a haze that interferes with the transmission of light through the air and reduces visibility. Dust landing on plants can injure them physically and chemically, and it can affect the health of animals that breathe it or eat forage on which it has settled.

Particulates come from many sources, ranging from naturally occurring wind-blown dust to agricultural activities, construction and demolition of buildings, heavy vehicle traffic on roads, the operation of garbage dumps, and the mining, crushing, and milling of sand, gravel, and other minerals. Metal-smelting operations can emit dust containing harmful substances such as beryllium, cadmium, zinc, lead, mercury, and fluorides. Electric power-generating plants, home heating, particularly with wood, and the incineration of garbage can contribute particulates to the air. Forest fires are also a major source of particulates, and may affect thousands of square kilometres of area. For sheer magnitude of effect, though, nothing can match volcanoes, which may have global effects lasting for more than a year.

Carbon Monoxide

Any combustion process that uses organic material such as wood, coal, oil, or gasoline will produce carbon monoxide if this material is burned without sufficient oxygen. Thus, automobiles are a major source of this pollutant. According to Environment Canada, 66 per cent of the carbon monoxide emitted in Canada in 1985 was from the engines of cars, trains, airplanes, and boats.[9] The remainder came largely from heating buildings, burning fossil fuels to generate electricity, and burning wood waste and debris from logging operations, saw mills, and similar industries.

Concentrations of this gas are highest on heavily travelled streets during rush hours, causing drivers to become drowsy. It is such a heavy gas that it may not dissipate completely overnight. Because it is so heavy, its highest concentrations are often found three or four feet from the ground, where children and pets will breathe them. Accidental exposure to high levels of carbon dioxide has caused nausea, headaches, lethargy, and even death, because it is absorbed into the blood and reduces its capacity to carry oxygen to the organs.

In recent years, concern about carbon monoxide has focused on its contribution to global warming. The 5.8 million tonnes of carbon monoxide emitted in 1985 from more than 10 million gasoline-powered cars and trucks[10] is contributing to the "greenhouse effect," which scientist fear may turn wetlands into deserts and deserts into oceans, as the ice of the Arctic and Antarctic melts and raises the level of the seas.

Nitrogen Oxides

Oxides of nitrogen are formed naturally, through bacteriological action in the soil, lightning, and volcanic action. Forest fires also contribute to their production. However, the large amount of nitrogen oxides created through human activities is of great concern. Of almost 2 million tonnes of nitrogen oxides emitted to the air in 1985, Environment Canada has estimated that almost 64 per cent came from burning fuel for transportation, and more than 30 per cent resulted from heating buildings.

The oxide of most concern is nitrogen dioxide, which forms quickly in the air from the nitric oxide created by combustion. This chemical can reduce the resistance of animals to bacterial and viral infection and affect their pulmonary functioning. In humans, exposure can affect odour perception and the ability of vision to adapt to darkness. Children are most susceptible to effects such as bronchitis and changes in pulmonary functions caused by chronic exposure. Like other contaminants mentioned, nitrogen dioxide slows plant growth and can damage materials; for example, it corrodes metals, causes fabric dyes to fade, and breaks down textile fibres. Nitrous oxide is also of concern, since it may contribute to global warming.

Hydrocarbons

Hydrocarbons are ubiquitous in our environment, since they are used as fuels, feedstock, solvents, cleansers, and for many other uses. Hydrocarbons are emitted from fuel combustion, leaks and spills of petroleum products, and from the lighter hydrocarbons "volatilizing" (what we might commonly refer to as "evaporating") into the air during the storage and use of petroleum products. Of particular concern are:

- the volatile organic compounds, because they turn from a liquid to a gas without any human intervention and often cause cancer as well as promoting ground-level ozone formation;
- benzene, toluene, ethylbenzene, and xylene (BTEXs) because they are volatile and cause cancer and other serious diseases;
- methane, because it contributes to global warming; and
- polycyclic aromatic hydrocarbons (described below).

VOCs and PAHs

Two groups of chemicals of particular concern are the volatile organic compounds (VOCs) and the polycyclic aromatic hydrocarbons (PAHs). Although many components of highly refined petroleum products are VOCs, not all VOCs are hydrocarbons. This category includes other volatile organic chemicals as well. Environment Canada has estimated that thousands of VOCs may be in the air at any time. When the air above 13 urban areas was tested in 1988, about 100 of these compounds were found.[11] VOCs come largely from car engines, but also from solvents, paint, glue, dry-cleaning fluid, and many other products.

PAHs are hundreds of semi-volatile organic hydrocarbons that are widely distributed throughout the environment. They have been found in animal and plant tissue, sediments, soils, air, and surface water. Forest fires may be the largest natural source of PAHs, but burning wood for home heating, motor vehicle emissions, and some industrial operations (such as coke ovens and aluminum smelting plants) may also contribute substantially. Over 100 PAHs have been detected in tobacco smoke.[12] PAHs are of concern primarily because some of them, such as benzo(a)pyrene, are highly carcinogenic.

Heavy Metals

Some metals, such as lead and mercury, are also emitted to the air from smelting processes, the burning of fuels, and other industrial processes. These metals are, of course, highly persistent, and some of them are very toxic. Lead, for example, was added to gasoline for decades to boost the octane. However, this poison, which interferes with the functions of the central and peripheral nervous systems, the kidneys, and the blood system, was emitted from the exhaust systems of motor vehicles when leaded gasoline was burned. The air-borne lead not only was breathed in the air, but also accumulated in the soil. One of the difficulties in

Chronology of Some Past Events of Significance for Air Pollution

1872	Term "acid rain" first used in England
1920s	Chlorofluorocarbons developed
1952	First report of Arctic air pollution
1952	4000 excess premature deaths from air pollution in London, England
1958	First clean air legislation in Canada (Ontario)
1962	Acid rain issue raised by Sweden at United Nations conference (Stockholm)
1971	Environment Canada formed
1971	Clean Air Act passed
1973	First world oil crisis
1974	Lead-free gasoline introduced
1975	Light-duty vehicle emissions standards introduced
1976	Lead content of leaded gasoline lowered
1978	Second world oil crisis
1980	Canada-US Memorandum of Understanding on Transboundary Air Pollution
1982	Sulphate deposition target of 20 kg per hectare established
1984	Federal-provincial commitments to reduce sulphur dioxide emissions in eastern Canada
1985	International sulphur dioxide abatement protocol signed
1986	Vienna Convention for the Protection of the Ozone Layer
1987	Montreal Protocol on Substances that Deplete the Ozone Layer
1987	More stringent light-duty motor vehicle standards imposed
1987	Lead content of leaded gasoline lowered
1988	Canadian Environmental Protection Act passed
1988	Heavy-duty motor vehicle emissions standards in effect
1988	Toronto International Conference on the Changing Atmosphere
1988	International oxides of nitrogen protocol signed

From Environment Canada, *Canadian Perspectives on Air Pollution.*

trying to assign responsibility for decontaminating the soil around secondary lead smelters (which emitted lead while recycling materials that contained it) was the problem of determining how much of the lead came from the smelters, and how much was deposited by passing cars and trucks. As a result, the Ontario government has had to absorb much of the cost of cleaning up the contaminated soil around these smelters.

AIR POLLUTION FROM AN INTERNATIONAL PERSPECTIVE

Acid rain, the hole in the atmospheric ozone layer, and the greenhouse effect are international air pollution problems. This reality makes efforts on an international scale to combat these problems vital. When cooperation is required among different countries, agreements generally assume the form of treaties. One method of creating international law is through formal treaties. In some countries, such as the United States, international law immediately becomes the law of the country. This is not the case in Canada, however, because our constitution does not bind us to international law. International obligations become our laws and affect our private rights as Canadians, only when they are implemented by either federal or provincial legislative enactments.[13]

Some of the problems discussed in this chapter require international cooperation. They will be solved only if many countries reduce their emissions of pollutants. Three of these problems — global warming, acid rain, and ozone depletion — are discussed below. Each section will begin with a general explanation of a particular problem, followed by the action taken by Canada and by other countries.

Global Warming: The Greenhouse Effect

Introduction

The importance of climate and climate change to the environment cannot be overstated. Over the past decade, the world has become increasingly aware that a growing human population and accelerating development are changing our global climate. Concern focuses on man-made emissions of so-called greenhouse gases, such as carbon dioxide, nitrous oxide, methane, and chlorofluorocarbons (CFCs).

Greenhouse gases are both natural and manufactured.[14] Decaying vegetation, for example, generates methane gas naturally; CFCs, though, were first created in a laboratory and are not found in nature. The bacterial decomposition of these greenhouse gases is vital to our survival, since — in normal concentrations — they "trap" warmth released by the earth. However, we are producing these gases faster than they can break down.

Global Warming and Canada

In global terms, Canada is not a major contributor to climate change. We produce about 2 per cent of the world's carbon dioxide, 2 per cent of nitric oxide, 1 per cent of methane, and 2 per cent of CFCs. This would suggest that we cannot solve the problem ourselves; accordingly, a global solution is imperative. The amount of greenhouse gases produced throughout the world continues to grow, and most industrialized countries have agreed in principle that the first step is to stabilize the level of greenhouse gas generation. There have been international conferences since the late 1970s on the subject of controlling climate change, gradually working toward a worldwide consensus on what to do. One significant milestone was a meeting in Bergen, Norway in 1979, at which the environment ministers of the countries of the United Nations Economic Commission for Europe, which includes Canada, committed their governments to develop domestic greenhouse strategies or actual targets and schedules to reduce greenhouse gases. At Bergen, Canada urged these nations to work toward a global agreement on climate change, tentatively referred to as the Climate Change Convention. In the fall of 1990, the United Nations General Assembly passed a resolution to establish a negotiating process leading to the passage of such a convention.

Canada has stated consistently since 1988 its desire to achieve a global framework convention on climate change, in time to be signed at the United Nations Conference on Environment and Development (UNCED) held in Brazil in 1992 to promote sustainable and environmentally sound development throughout the globe. This convention was planned to seek an overall agreement of all nations to reduce effects on our global climate, along with appropriate protocols with binding commitments to specific action needed to achieve the objectives of the convention. The convention was in fact signed by more than 150 nations at UNCED in May 1992; however, it contained no specific timetable or numerical target for reductions, largely because the United States refused to sign an agreement that would contain such concrete commitments. The convention establishes a UN watchdog agency to monitor its implementation.

Federal-Provincial Cooperation: The National Action Strategy on Global Warming

The federal government has cooperated with the provincial governments to develop the National Action Strategy on Global Warming, which constitutes a comprehensive framework for addressing the global warming issue within Canada. The strategy contemplates a three-part approach. The first aims to limit net emissions of greenhouse gases by embracing a comprehensive response to climate change, taking into consideration the wider international context, emphasizing flexibility in recognition of the fact that scientific and economic understanding of the problem is not yet complete, and giving due recognition to the importance of regional differences. The second strategy is to help Canadians anticipate and prepare for the potential effects of any warming that might occur. Federal government efforts will include adopting guidelines to ensure that the potential changes in the Canadian environment as a result of climate change are considered in major projects by 1994, assessing the socioeconomic repercussions of climate change in the Great Lakes – St. Lawrence River basin, the prairies, and the Mackenzie River basin by 1996, and assessing policy changes that might be needed to deal with rising sea levels along both the east and the west coasts of Canada by 1996. The third strategy is to improve our understanding of global warming. Through the National Action Strategy on Global Warming, as well as through the Green Plan, the federal government will increase its commitment to scientific research in climate change. The goal of Canada's research effort is significant improvement, by 1994, in our understanding of the rate in climate change and, by 1995, of the distribution of regional repercussions.[15]

The steps Ontario is considering to reduce greenhouse gas emissions include CFC bans and phaseouts, 3Rs initiatives, energy efficiency programs for buildings and energy-use standards for products, tax exemptions for alternative fuel, land-use planning that reduces reliance on automobiles and encourages the use of public transit, and automobile inspection and maintenance programs.[16]

Acid Rain

Introduction

The term "acid rain" was first used in 1872 in a publication entitled "Air and Rain: The Beginnings of a Chemical Climatology," written by Angus Smith, an English scientist. Acid rain is an environmental pollutant that is derived primarily from the burning of fossil fuels in electrical generation plants, industrial activities such as production of nickel and steel, and motor vehicles. The oxides of sulphur and nitrogen emitted from vehicle exhausts, chimneys, and smoke stacks mix with the moisture in the atmosphere to form acids and acid precursors.

The most important of these oxides in the formation of acid rain are sulphur dioxide (SO_2), nitric oxide (NO), and nitrogen dioxide (NO_2). The two oxides of nitrogen together form NO_x.

The efforts to control acid rain can be divided into two separate sets of initiatives: efforts to control SO_2 and attempts to control NO_x. Efforts to control SO_2 have focused on provincial regulations to control a few large stationary sources of emissions in Canada and efforts by the governments of Canada and Ontario to persuade the United States and individual state governments to pass legislation to reduce emissions from similar sources in the United States. However, because the contribution of NO_x to the harm caused by acid rain is less clear, and because NO_x comes not only from a few large generating plant stacks but also from millions of motor vehicles, efforts to control this pollutant have focused on developing more stringent motor vehicle emission standards and gasoline content rules. This aspect of the acid rain control program is discussed below in the sections dealing with the *Motor Vehicle Safety Act* and the *Canadian Environmental Protection Act*. (The control of gasoline is also important because gasoline vapours that escape during the fueling cycle can, in combination with NO_x, produce ozone, which is a key component of smog, but not of acid rain.)

Acid rain is responsible for major damage to lakes and fish populations, forests, historic buildings, and monuments. Acid rain "precursors" (the substances that combine to form acid rain) are also known to affect respiratory health. By the late 1970s, many lakes and rivers in Ontario, the maritime provinces, and the northeastern United States were becoming acidified, and losing their ability to support fish. Similar problems had already been discovered in northern Europe. As a result, the members of the United Nations Economic Commission for Europe (ECE), which includes Canada and the United States, signed a Long-Range Transboundary Air Pollution Convention in 1979. This was an agreement to cooperate with each other to deal with acid rain. The ECE members followed up this agreement with a 1985 protocol in which they agreed to a 30 per cent reduction in their SO_2 emissions, and a 1988 protocol in which they agreed to freeze nitrous oxide emissions.

Canada and the United States signed an agreement similar to the 1979 ECE convention in 1980. This Canada-US memorandum of intent committed both countries to negotiate a transboundary air pollution treaty that would bind them to mutual reductions in emissions causing acid rain. Under the agreement, the two countries set up joint committees of scientists to compile scientific data on the long-range transport of air-borne pollutants. These teams of scientists produced their final reports in 1983. The Canadian scientists concluded that acid rain was causing harm, and the solution was reduction of sulphur emissions. The US scientists, however, were unable to agree that action was required. Perhaps this was an example of politics influencing science under the anti-environment Reagan administration, since two years earlier, in contrast, the US National Academy of Science had found acid rain to be a very serious problem. The United States rejected a joint pollution control program. The reluctance of the United States to make a firm commitment to substantial emissions reductions probably stemmed from the need to keep coal miners employed in the mid-west, where coal with a high sulphur content was being mined.

A Canadian federal government subcommittee on acid rain was first created in 1980. It reported to the House of Commons through the Standing Committee on Fisheries and Forestry. Its first report, entitled *Still Waters*, in 1981, made 38 recommendations to the federal government. The second report, in 1984, *Time Lost*, added another 16 recommendations. In June 1985, a Special Committee on Acid Rain was created to continue the effort of the subcommittee. The committee reported in September 1988. The report summarized the progress made so far and submitted 17 new recommendations to the government.

The total Canadian emissions of SO_2 in 1980 amounted to about 4.6 million tonnes. The total emissions of SO_2 from the United States in 1980 amounted to 24 million tonnes. Although the acid-forming emissions from each country were crossing the borders of the other, Canada was getting more than it was giving. Moreover, Canada found itself with allies in the northeastern United States. States such as New York, Michigan, and Pennsylvania were receiving harmful acid emissions from states such as Ohio and Indiana.

Although half of the emissions that were affecting eastern Canada's lakes were coming from sources in the United States, the Canadian government decided, in the face of unsuccessful efforts to persuade the United States to sign a treaty requiring mutual emissions reductions, to proceed unilaterally. The federal government set a goal of reducing emissions to 50 per cent of the 1980 levels by 1994. Since the power to pass to pass laws controlling air emissions is primarily given to the provinces under our constitution, to meet this goal the federal government had to persuade the seven eastern provinces that were receiving the most damaging levels of acid deposition from sources within their own provinces and from other provinces and the United States — Manitoba, Ontario, Quebec, and each of the maritime provinces — to enact laws requiring their major sources of sulphur emissions to reduce these emissions. This could be accomplished through strategies such as redesigning industrial processes to produce less acid gas, burning cleaner coal, or the installation of pollution control devices such as expensive "scrubbers" that would remove thousands of tonnes of sulphur from the smoke coming out of their stacks. In March 1985, the seven eastern Canadian provinces committed themselves to make regulations requiring sources of emissions within their boundaries to accomplish the emissions reductions recommended by the federal government.

Federal-Provincial Cooperation on Acid Rain

Quebec and Ontario took unilateral action to reduce emissions, even without a formal federal-provincial agreement. However, federal-provincial negotiations bore fruit, and are an excellent example of the results that can be achieved through federal-provincial cooperation. The federal government and the seven eastern provinces reached an agreement in principle on reduction targets in Montreal in early February 1985. Between 1985 and 1988, the federal government signed agreements with Canada's acid rain-producing provinces. In these agreements, the federal government promised to contribute up to $150 million for smelter modernization that would include pollution controls, in return for the provincial legislation on pollution controls.[17] In the Canada-Ontario agreement, signed between Environment Canada and the Ontario Ministry of the Environment on March 10, 1987, each side indicated its intention to assign up to $85 million for Ontario pollution control. Some of the remaining federal funds are being used in Quebec and some in Manitoba. Ontario, Manitoba, and Quebec made regulations requiring their main sources of emissions to achieve specific reductions; New Brunswick is using existing laws to meet its target; Nova Scotia, though, has yet to pass any law or regulation targeted at emissions that cause acid rain.

Ontario did not wait until it had an agreement with the federal government to make regulations requiring reductions in acid gas emissions. In December 1985, the government of Ontario announced a program designed to control emissions of acid rain-causing pollutants in the province. The program, known as Countdown Acid Rain, came into effect on January 4, 1986. The program encompassed five regulations, one for each major source of acid rain-causing emissions, requiring specific reductions by specified deadlines. (The federal-provincial agreement, made on March 10, 1987 was signed long after cooperation had begun, pursuant to Countdown Acid Rain, between Ontario and Canada.)

The purpose of Countdown Acid Rain was to reduce total Ontario SO_2 emissions from the 1980 level of 1,772 kilotonnes (kt) per year to 885 kt per year by 1994 and to 795 kt per year after that. To achieve this goal, one regulation was made for each of the four major corporate SO_2 sources in Ontario and one for industry boilers.

Algoma Steel

Ontario regulation 663/85 limits emissions from Algoma Steel's iron ore sintering plant to 180 kt per year until 1993 and 125 kt per year by 1994. The Special Committee on Acid Rain reported that the capacity of the sintering plant was reduced by 55 per cent between 1985 and 1988, but that the reduction was mostly due to lower production as a result of weak demand for Algoma's product. Countdown Acid Rain requires Algoma to file reports with the Ministry of Environment and Energy every six months and to inspect emissions projections. In 1985 Algoma was sold to Dofasco. The committee noted: "If this merger results in greater use of Algoma's production capacity, then the sintering plant at Wawa might require means other than production cutbacks to meet its SO_2 limits."[18]

Inco

Ontario regulation 660/85 limits the emissions of the Inco smelter at Coppercliff, Ontario, to 685 kt in 1986 and 265 kt in 1994. Inco must also report on the possibility of meeting even stricter limits, such as 525 kt in 1990 and 175 kt at some time in the future. At the time of the special committee's report, the company stated that the 265 kt limit did appear to be feasible,[19] and as of the fall of 1992, Inco was on schedule.[20]

Falconbridge Limited

Ontario regulation 661/85 reduces the legal limit for SO_2 emissions from the Falconbridge nickel-copper smelter to 100 kt per year starting in 1994. Although the plant was allowed to emit 154 kt prior to the regulation, its actual SO_2 emissions in 1986 amounted to about 90 kt. One method of reducing future emissions that was contemplated by Falconbridge was to increase pyrrhotite rejection. The company was also considering a method of increasing the capture of SO_2 during the roasting process and producing sulphuric acid from the gas.

Ontario Hydro

Ontario Hydro is the largest provincial electrical utility in Canada. It operates three coal-fired generating plants in southern Ontario and two smaller plants in the northwestern part of the province. Ontario regulation 662/85 limits the acid rain-causing emissions of Ontario Hydro to 370 kt per year as of 1986, 240 kt per year as of 1990, and 175 kt per year by 1994. Ontario Hydro's strategy to achieve the initial reductions was mainly reliance on the replacement of coal-fired generating capacity with new nuclear capacity. Hydro expected nuclear power-based reductions to continue until about 1992 when the last of the nuclear units was to come into production at the Darlington plant, after which time coal consumption was expected to be half of the 1988 levels. The utility has also started a program to install low-NO_x burners at the Nanticoke generating facility.[21] Hydro had also intended to install scrubbers at its Lambton generating station, but it has been meeting required limits merely by generating less electricity, since demand has been lower than anticipated, so the scrubber may be "scrubbed" as part of a program of financial cutbacks.[22]

The Boiler Regulation

In 1986, a further regulation was made,[23] prohibiting anyone from using oil or coal with a sulphur content of more than 1 per cent as a fuel in any new boiler or a boiler that has been physically modified in a way that changes its ability to use fuel. Certain boilers were exempted from this requirement, such as those at Ontario Hydro generating stations and boilers used only to heat homes housing up to three families. Fuel with a higher sulphur content can be used if the boiler has been equipped with pollution-control devices that would ensure that it emitted no more sulphur dioxide than if the 1 per cent sulphur fuel had been used.

The US Clean Air Act Amendments and the Air Quality Accord

After years of dispute concerning acid rain in eastern North America, the US Congress amended the US *Clean Air Act*[24] in 1990, to require a 10 million ton reduction in SO_2 emissions and has permanently capped these emissions at the reduced level. It is expected that by the year 2000, the *Clean Air Act* program will reduce the transboundary flow of acid rain into eastern Canada by more than 50 per cent.[25]

Formal negotiations to ensure continued protection from acid rain and to provide means for dealing with other transboundary air pollutants, by Canada-US agreement, began in the summer of 1990. Canada and the United States signed an agreement on air quality (the air quality accord) in 1991.[26] This agreement was simply a political reaffirmation of the targets already accepted and the amendments to the US *Clean Air Act* and Canadian federal and provincial regulations already enacted.[27]

Protecting the Ozone Layer

Ozone-Depleting Substances

We now know that CFCs, hydrofluorocarbons (HFCs), halons, methyl chloroform, and carbon tetrachloride are all ozone-depleting substances. Halons were developed after World War II and have grown in popularity as fire-extinguishing agents. Carbon tetrachloride is used primarily as a feedstock in producing CFCs; but it is also used as a pesticide, a dry-cleaning agent, a solvent in synthetic rubbers and dyes, and a grain fumigant.

Since the 1930s, we have emitted millions of kilograms of CFCs and related chemicals, which have slowly migrated to the upper atmosphere. CFCs became widely used in a variety of industrial processes because of their non-toxic and non-flammable nature. They are used as coolants in refrigerators and freezers, and in air conditioners for automobiles and large buildings, in the manufacture of soft foam for cushions and solid foam for packaging and insulation, and as a cleaning solvent for micro-electronic circuitry.[28]

Through a series of chemical reactions, the earth's protective ozone layer has progressively been depleted. This has resulted in a worldwide erosion of the ozone layer and a pronounced seasonal reduction in ozone concentration over a large area of the southern polar region, known as the Antarctic "ozone hole."[29] Scientists fear that the thinning ozone could lead to an epidemic of skin cancers, increased incidences of cataracts, suppression of human immune systems, and crop damage.[30]

International Efforts: The Montreal Protocol

Much effort has been made in the last few years to reduce the amount of CFCs in the atmosphere on a global scale. An international treaty, the 1987 Montreal Protocol on Substances that Deplete the Ozone Layer,[31] committed Canada and 24 other signatories to reduce their production and consumption of CFCs and halons by 50 per cent by 1998. However, since it was clear that this would not stop depletion of the ozone layer, the protocol was revised in June 1990. The London amendments, so called because they were signed at a meeting in London, England, accelerated the phaseout of CFCs and halons, and added a phaseout of methyl chloroform to the agreement. Most of the signatories agreed to eliminate all CFCs and halons by the year 2000. Thirteen nations, including Canada, agreed to an even faster schedule: they would try to eliminate these chemicals by 1997. Canada later decided to phase out halons by January 1, 1995.

In March 1990, federal and provincial environment ministers agreed to further accelerate the planned dates of phasing out of the importation and production of CFCs, halons, and hydrochlorofluorocarbons (HCFCs).[32] Canada pushed for international acceptance of this accelerated phaseout schedule in Copenhagen, and at the Copenhagen meeting 86 other countries agreed to move their CFC phaseout dates up to the end of 1995 and their halon phaseout dates to the beginning of 1994. These countries also agreed to a phased reduction of HCFCs beginning in 2004 and ending in 2030. The use of methyl chloroform is to be reduced by 70 per cent by the year 2000 and completely phased out by 2005. However, methyl bromide, an ozone-depleting pesticide, was not included in the new phaseout dates. The United Nations has also established a fund to transfer CFC reduction technology to developing countries, to which Canada is expected to contribute $10 million.[33]

A panel within the United Nations Environmental Program (UNEP) originally indicated that it would be possible to reduce the use of the five controlled CFCs by 95 per cent by the year 2000. This projection has since been increased to 100 per cent. In Canada's case, the program is working. According to a June 1992 report, between 1986 and June 1992 there has been a 58 per cent decrease in CFC use in Canada.[34]

Efforts in Canada

Canada's contribution to global ozone depletion is less than 2 per cent, but its per capita contribution to CFC emissions is about 0.8 kilograms per year, the second highest in the world, after the United States.[35]

Canada is ahead of its own CFC reduction target date and is a world leader in the progress that has been made to date. A June 1990 report from a federal government committee[36] recommended a faster phaseout than the timetable found within the Montreal protocol.[37] Recommendations include the development of a domestic recovery and recycling system, exhorting the international community to act decisively in combatting ozone depletion, and assisting developing countries to prosper without replicating the harm that the industrialized world has done to the earth's atmosphere.

Two public policies are essential to this program. First, all ozone-depleting substances must be eliminated from further use. Then, all such substances must be recovered from equipment such as air conditioners and refrigerators and destroyed. The report states that if all CFCs that are currently dispersed in refrigeration systems throughout the world were released, the ozone layer would probably be destroyed. CFCs also contribute to global warming, since each molecule has up to 20,000 times the greenhouse effect of carbon dioxide. Therefore, two benefits to these policies are that they will allow the ozone layer to replenish itself gradually and that they will decrease the rate of global warming.[38]

Federal and Provincial Laws

Canada's commitment to reduce the manufacture, import, export, and use of ozone-depleting substances is being implemented in part through federal regulations under the *Canadian Environmental Protection Act (CEPA)* and provincial regulations under Ontario's *Environmental Protection Act (EPA)*.

Regulations Under the Canadian Environmental Protection Act

Canada signed the Montreal protocol in 1987. Canada's international obligations under the Montreal protocol include a total phaseout of CFCs by January 1, 2000. Canada has self-imposed a shorter timetable for phaseout than the current requirements under the protocol: Canada's self-imposed deadline is January 1, 1996.

The federal government's response to the commitments in the protocol has been regulations under the *Canadian Environmental Protection Act*. Two regulations under the Act deal with the control of bulk CFCs and halons respectively.[39] A third regulation bans CFCs in certain applications, such as aerosols, small refill cans, and plastic from food packaging.[40] This regulation was amended to include a ban of hand-held fire extinguishers, with certain exceptions for halon portable extinguishers for use in any tactical military vehicle or vessel; for use on any aircraft; and in training programs related to military or aircraft uses only.[41]

In addition to regulation, the federal Department of the Environment has also undertaken education programs and consultation with provincial governments and industry.

Regulations Under Ontario's Environmental Protection Act

Ontario added a new part to its *Environmental Protection Act* to deal with ozone-depleting substances. Regulations under this part dovetail with the federal regulations under the *Canadian Environmental Protection Act*.

Part VI of Ontario's *Environmental Protection Act* deals specifically with "ozone-depleting substances." As discussed previously, these substances, such as CFCs and halons, react with other chemicals found in the stratosphere and destroy the ozone in our atmosphere that protects us from harmful ultraviolet rays. Part VI prohibits the manufacture, use, transfer, display, storage or disposal of products that:

- use certain designated ozone-depleting substances as propellants;
- contain these substances;
- are made with these substances;
- are packaging, wrapping, or containers made with the use of these substances.[42]

Part VI of the Act applies only to eight types of CFCs and halons, but other substances can be added by regulations designating them as ozone-depleting substances.

The Ozone Depleting Substances General Regulation[43] has been made pursuant to part VI. This regulation is designed to reduce or eliminate the use of "ozone-depleting substances" in three primary applications: the manufacture of pressurized containers, the manufacture of flexible plastic foams, and the manufacture of rigid insulation foams. The regulation attempts to accomplish this by eliminating the use of ozone-depleting substances in the manufacture of pressurized containers for all practical reasons and fixing a schedule for reducing the use of ozone-depleting substances in the manufacture of flexible foams and rigid insulation foams by certain fixed percentages by the year 1993 in accordance with Canada's international treaty obligations.

In early 1993, to the chagrin of the automotive industry, Ontario and several other provinces were also considering a ban on the use of CFCs in automobile air conditioners.[44]

In May 1993, the Ontario Ministry of Environment and Energy released for public comment a draft regulation to prevent the release of CFCs, HCFCs, and HFCs used in refrigerators, freezers, and air-conditioning systems. If enacted in its current form, this regulation will:

- prohibit the venting of these refrigerant fluorocarbons;
- require anyone who services refrigeration equipment to be certified and to drain these substances and dispose of them at approved facilities; and
- prohibit new model cars from being fitted with air conditioners that use CFCs and HCFCs after December 31, 1995.

DIVISION OF POWERS BETWEEN THE FEDERAL AND PROVINCIAL GOVERNMENTS

In the field of air pollution, the division of powers between the federal and provincial governments mirrors the division in other areas discussed in this book, such as noise and vibration. In general, apart from the federal government's role in carrying out research, entering into treaties, and controlling transboundary pollution, its role in controlling air pollution involves setting standards that will protect public health and safety. Air pollution at levels that will not actually harm health or create a safety risk but merely cause discomfort and loss of enjoyment of property — no matter how serious — is generally a provincial responsibility. In addition, as in other fields, the federal government is generally responsible for establishing design standards for polluting equipment that can be manufactured or sold in Canada, while the provinces are responsible for ensuring that such equipment is maintained and operated in a way that minimizes pollution. For example, manufacturers' performance standards are not always maintained by the owners of the vehicles. Studies have shown that two-thirds of vehicles in use had excessive emissions, even though they were designed not to.[45] Setting up an inspection program to ensure proper maintenance would be a provincial responsibility.

FEDERAL LAWS

Canadian Environmental Protection Act

Federal air quality objectives, emissions guidelines, and emissions standards are found in the *Canadian Environmental Protection Act*, which was passed in 1988. This statute amalgamated the *Clean Air Act*, which was passed in 1971, the *Environmental Contaminants Act*, and other environmental statutes, and incorporated all the existing air quality regulations that had been made under the *Clean Air Act*. Apart from specific air quality provisions, the *Canadian Environmental Protection Act* takes a multimedia approach to the control of all toxic chemicals, whether they affect air, land, or water. It attempts to establish a framework for "cradle-to-grave" regulation of toxics, from their manufacture to their sale, distribution, release into the environment, and disposal — to the extent that these operational and use aspects of regulation are not within provincial responsibility.

The *Canadian Environmental Protection Act* requires manufacturers and importers of new chemicals that may be toxic to inform the federal government of the introduction of these chemicals into the market and allows the government to require information about, and testing of, both new and existing chemicals. As well as providing authority to regulate substances known to be toxic, the Act requires the government to compile a list of substances that are to receive priority in assessing whether they are toxic, or capable of becoming toxic (the priority substances list). The Act also allows any member of the public to request that a substance be added to the priority substances list for assessment, and the minister of the environment must consider such a request and respond within 30 days. Once a substance has been assessed and found to be toxic, the government will place it on a schedule of substances to be regulated, and may make regulations governing its manufacture, sale, release, and disposal.

To recognize the provincial role in the regulation of some aspects of the use, release, and disposal of contaminants, the Act requires that before regulations are made, the federal government must consult with the provinces, and its regulations will be effective only if (1) a provincial government has not made an "equivalent" regulation, or (2) the regulation is equivalent but the province lacks provisions for administering the regulation that are "similar" to those of the federal government. As one can readily imagine, the question whether provincial regulations are "equivalent" to the regulation under the *Canadian Environmental Protection Act*, or whether their administration is "similar," raises interesting issues.[46]

Thus, in addition to the specific air regulations under the *Canadian Environmental Protection Act*, other aspects of the Act also apply to air quality regulation, and will be discussed briefly.

Air Quality Regulations

National Air Quality Objectives

National air quality objectives[47] relate to *ambient* air quality. That is, they do not represent the maximum amount of a contaminant that a specific source of pollution may emit, but the amount or concentration of such a contaminant in the air at any particular time as a result of the combined emissions from all the sources in the area.

The regulations establish levels of air quality for major pollutants that are "tolerable," "acceptable," and "desirable." The desirable level is a long-term goal for improvement of existing air quality. The acceptable level is one at which there is "adequate protection" against effects on the environment, personal comfort, and well-being. If air quality falls below the tolerable level, quick action is needed to protect the public's health. In other words, a level of pollution may be considered unacceptable, but still tolerable, or it may be acceptable, but better air quality would be desirable. For example, a concentration of pollution may be considered acceptable because at this level there will be no harm to human health. However, this level of air quality may still be less than desirable because the pollution may still cause discomfort or annoyance.

Different objectives are set for different periods of time. For each pollutant for which there is an objective, there will be a maximum tolerable, acceptable, and desirable average over a year. Over shorter periods, higher exposures might be considered tolerable or acceptable. For example, there is also a 1-hour objective, an 8-hour objective, and a 24-hour objective for each pollutant.

Pollutants for which such objectives have been established include sulphur dioxide, nitrogen oxide, carbon monoxide, ozone, and total suspended particulate. The good news is that air quality has dramatically improved over the past two decades, with the exception of ozone, and the air over most major cities meets these objectives most of the time.[48] The bad news is that even when these objectives are met, the air over many cities is still smoggy and unpleasant.

Although these guidelines do not directly control the amount of air pollution that any individual source may emit, they can be useful in determining whether facilities will be licensed to operate and whether existing facilities will be ordered to reduce their emissions, provided that they are adopted by agencies that regulate pollution. In areas where air quality does not meet these objectives, this should be taken into account in making such decisions, and may result in a refusal to approve new sources of pollution.

National Emission Guidelines

Unlike the national air quality objectives, the national emission guidelines and standards can be used to directly regulate individual pollution sources. The guidelines are suggestions by the federal government as to maximum levels of emissions of various pollutants that should not be exceeded by individual facilities. These guidelines are generally developed by government-industry task forces. They are intended to reflect the best practically achievable technology, and are based on levels that can be achieved using this technology. Thus, the guidelines will vary from industry to industry, since the types and concentrations of pollutants and the available pollution-control technologies will often be industry-specific. Although the ambient air quality objectives are established on the basis of scientific evidence about effects on health and well-being, and are not "watered down" because technology does not exist to meet these objectives or is considered to be too expensive or unreliable, the site-specific guidelines do take these technical and economic factors into account. Thus, these objectives, which are intended to be adopted by the provinces as binding standards, can legalize emissions that exceed the levels of pollution that are considered tolerable, acceptable, or desirable under the objectives.

Existing guidelines cover air emissions of particulate matter and sulphur dioxide from arctic mining and coke ovens, particulate matter from asphalt paving plants and cement plants, particulate matter, hydrogen chloride, and sulphur dioxide from packaged incinerators,* particulate matter, total reduced sulphur compounds, and sulphur dioxide from new wood pulping facilities, and nitrogen oxides, SO_2, and particulate matter from new thermal power electrical generating facilities.

National Emission Standards

The federal government has also established maximum permissible levels of pollution emissions for certain facilities that are binding, enforceable standards under federal legislation. These standards are developed in the same way as the guidelines are, and are subject to the same considerations of practicality. In these cases, the federal government has not waited for the provincial governments to set their own binding emissions limits, although a province could establish even more stringent limits. The emission of a contaminant in a concentration that exceeds the permitted levels is an offence subject to high fines under the *Canadian Environmental Protection Act*.

Emission standards have been promulgated for lead from secondary lead smelters,[49] mercury from mercury-cell chlor-alkali plants,[50] asbestos from mines and mills,[51] and vinyl chloride from the manufacture of vinyl chloride and polyvinyl chloride.[52]

Other Air Pollution Control Regulations Under the Canadian Environmental Protection Act

As discussed above under the heading "The Ozone Layer," there are four regulations under the *Canadian Environmental Protection Act* that are designed specifically to achieve the phaseout of ozone-depleting substances. In addition, there are several regulations that are designed to deal with other specific air pollution sources.

Regulation of Fuels

The *Canadian Environmental Protection Act* also deals with restrictions on fuel content. Pursuant to section 46, the Act prohibits the domestic production or importation of fuels if Canadian standards are not met. Section 47 allows the federal government to create fuel regulations.

1.   Gasoline Regulation[53]
Specific regulations under the Act include those limiting lead and phosphorus in gasoline. Lead is well recognized as a potential toxin in most, if not all, of its chemical and physical forms. In

---

* A packaged incinerator is a furnace for burning solid waste at a rate of less than 90 kilograms per hour.

some urbanized areas, lead additives in gasoline have been the largest single source of lead in the atmosphere. Canada's gasoline regulations are intended to significantly reduce the level of lead particles in the air. These regulations were published in May 1990 and came into force on December 1, 1990, replacing earlier regulations made under the *Clean Air Act*.[54] The regulations prohibit the use of leaded gasoline in most vehicles, and dramatically reduce the lead concentrations allowed in gasoline sold to power boats, heavy trucks, and some farming equipment. All cars and light trucks sold in Canada since the 1970s have been designed to use unleaded gasoline, so leaded gasoline is no longer needed for these vehicles. But some heavy-duty equipment still needs leaded gasoline to prevent premature engine failure, so small quantities of lead will continue to be available in gasoline used for these vehicles.

However, this is not the end of the story. To replace lead as an octane booster, some refineries have begun to add MMT, a manganese compound, or MBTE, made from methanol and isobutylene, to their gasoline. MMT has been described as "extremely toxic," while the effects of inhaling, ingesting or absorbing MTBE through the skin are thought to be "no worse than gasoline," although no comprehensive study of the toxicology of this compound or its combustion products has been done.[55]

2. Contaminated Fuel Regulations[56]

The federal government has also recognized that there is a lot of money to be made by mixing toxic wastes with fuels, and selling the fuel to unsuspecting or unscrupulous customers. Several years ago, *The Globe and Mail* reported that hazardous wastes were being exported into Canada mixed with fuel, but investigators were unable to catch anyone. More recently, several gasoline stations in the Metro Toronto area purchased truckloads of gasoline that had been laced with toxic chemicals. Probably as a result of such highly publicized incidents, the Contaminated Fuel Regulations were issued for public comment in March 1991, and brought into force in August of that year.[57] They prohibit the import and export of fuels containing toxic substances, except for the purpose of destruction, disposal, or recycling of the fuel at an approved facility. "Contaminated fuel," which is defined as fuel that contains substances that are dangerous goods within the meaning of section 2 of the *Transportation of Dangerous Goods Act*,[58] has also been added to the list of toxic substances to be regulated under the Act.

Regulation of PCBs

Because of their persistence, their tendency to bioaccumulate in the food chain, and the suspicion that they may be carcinogens, PCBs have concerned the public and regulators for many years. Their production has been banned, and their use phased out, since the 1970s. However, since few facilities have been available to destroy PCBs, large quantities of oil containing PCBs, from discarded transformers and other electrical equipment, have been stored for many years, awaiting approval of facilities for the destruction of the PCBs. Meanwhile, there have been problems. A facility set up under the auspices of the Ontario government at Smithville contaminated the soil around it with PCBs, resulting in a multi-million dollar clean-up at public expense; a truck transporting a transformer full of oil containing PCBs spilled the oil on the Trans-Canada Highway in the spring of 1985, resulting in closure of the highway for several days; the so-called death ship exporting unwanted PCBs from Canada to Great Britain was refused entry there and had to return to Canada. Most significantly from an air quality standpoint, a fire at a PCB storage facility at St. Basile-le-Grand, Quebec in 1988 released PCBs into the air, resulting in the evacuation of 3,000 residents and arousing public demand that something be done about the large quantities of PCB-laden oil still in storage.

Several regulations have been introduced under the *Canadian Environmental Protection Act* relating to PCBs. The Federal Mobile PCB Treatment and Destruction Regulations[59] govern performance standards for incinerators and treatment facilities and establish maximum levels for air emissions and the release of solids and liquids from these systems. In 1989, there were about 7,500 tonnes of PCB wastes at federal facilities. The PCB Waste Export Regulations ban the overseas export of PCB waste.[60] Finally, the Storage of PCB Wastes Interim Order[61] was introduced after the St. Basile fire to tighten up safety requirements at facilities where these wastes are stored. The interim order was replaced in 1992 by a permanent regulation.[62] This regulation covers all provinces, but the federal government intends eventually to exempt provinces that have an equivalent provincial regulation. Ontario, for example, has a regulation governing PCB storage, which it considers to be just as stringent as the federal one.

CEPA Part V: International Air Pollution

Pursuant to part V of the *Canadian Environmental Protection Act*, the federal government governs domestic sources of international air pollution. The minister of the environment may regulate sources of pollution that violate international agreements or create air pollution in other countries. Before exercising this authority, the minister must have been unsuccessful in persuading the provinces in which the pollution sources are situated to implement the necessary measures to control the pollution.

This is the part of the Act that will be used to make regulations designed to implement the reductions that Canada has agreed to by signing various international agreements. Canada has obtained the provinces' commitment to meet the obligations of the United Nations' Economic Commission for Europe's sulphur dioxide protocol. The federal government anticipates that bilateral agreements with each of the seven easternmost provinces should lead to a 30 per cent reduction of national sulphur dioxide emissions by 1993. To reduce urban smog, Canada will have to persuade the provinces to make regulations or will have to make regulations itself under the *Canadian Environmental Protection Act* to implement the 1988 nitrogen oxides protocol and the 1991 volatile organic compounds protocol, reached under the United Nations' Economic Commission for Europe protocol and the Canada-US air quality accord. The ECE VOC protocol commits most of the countries that signed it to reduce VOC emissions by 30 per cent by the year 1990.

Other Aspects of the Canadian Environmental Protection Act and How They Are Used To Enhance Air Quality

Research, Monitoring, Planning, and Providing Information

The *Canadian Environmental Protection Act* gives the government extensive powers to carry out research, conduct monitoring programs, require companies to provide information, and engage in planning activities in relation to toxic substances, including the ones that pollute the air.

One of the most significant initiatives in this area in relation to air quality is a network of air monitoring stations across Canada operated by Environment Canada — the National Air Pollution Surveillance Network (NAPS). In the network, there are about 117 stations in over 50 urban areas across Canada that regularly measure concentrations of SO_2, NO_2, carbon monoxide, ozone, suspended particulate, and lead in the ambient air. They also record the "soiling index," which is not a pollutant but a measure of the soiling or darkening potential of fine particulate in the air. This is measured in coefficient of haze (COH) units. The system was established as a joint project of the federal and provincial governments in 1969, and it is coordinated by the Pollution Measurement Division of Environment Canada.

Among the publications relating to air quality produced by Environment Canada in carrying out its research and information dissemination functions under the Act are: the Canadian Emissions Inventory of Contaminants, Canadian Perspectives on Air Pollution, an annual National Air Pollution Surveillance (NAPS) summary, and NAPS monthly summaries setting out the results of monitoring under the NAPS program, National Inventory of Sources and Emissions of Benzene, the National Inventory of Sources and Emissions of Carbon Dioxide, National Urban Air Quality Trends (1978-1987), Ozone Concentrations and Trends in Southern Ontario and Southern Quebec (1983-1989), and two Reference Methods for Source Testing: one for measuring releases of carbon monoxide from stationary sources, and one for monitoring of gaseous emissions from fuel-fired boilers.

The Federal-Provincial Advisory Committee

Section 6 of the *Canadian Environmental Protection Act* establishes a Federal-Provincial Advisory Committee, which consists of representatives from Environment Canada, Health and Welfare Canada, and each of the provinces and territories. The group ensures that the governments consult each other on management initiatives, and facilitates coordinated action to protect the environment from toxic substances and to achieve nationally consistent levels of environmental quality throughout Canada by establishing nationally consistent objectives.

Under the auspices of the Federal-Provincial Advisory Committee, the federal government established a working group on controls for ozone layer depleting substances. Its mandate is to develop a national strategy to eliminate these substances and to assist information exchange among all levels of government. The group reports to the Canadian Council of Ministers of the Environment, which consists of the federal and provincial environment ministers.

Guidelines and Codes of Practice

The *Canadian Environmental Protection Act* provides, in section 8, that the minister of the environment has the authority to formulate non-regulatory instruments, such as release guidelines and codes of practice, that provide environmental quality guidance to industries and regulators. These initiatives are very important, since there are often standards that must be met, but little guidance to industry on how to meet them and what precautions to take to prevent accidental spills or emissions of pollutants. Codes and pollutant release guidelines relating to air quality that had been published, or that were under development at the time of printing this book, included: the Thermal Power Generation Emission: National Guidelines for New Stationary Sources (Revised), and the Code of Practice for the Reduction of Chlorofluorocarbon Emissions from Refrigeration and Air Conditioning Systems.

The code of practice for the reduction of chlorofluorocarbons provides guidelines for the reduction of CFCs and to the extent possible, for HFCs and HCFCs. It covers all refrigeration systems within residential, commercial and industrial facilities.

Administrative and Equivalency Agreements

The *Canadian Environmental Protection Act* gives the minister of the environment the authority to conclude with the approval of the governor-in-council two types of agreements with provincial and territorial governments: "administrative agreements," under section 98 of the Act, and "equivalency agreements," under section 34. Administrative agreements make it possible to share the work involved in administering federal regulations. Under an administrative agreement, a provincial government agrees to administer a program or enforce a law, but the federal government remains accountable for the results under such an arrangement by subjecting the agreement to terms and conditions that will ensure that administration or enforcement is properly conducted. As of November 1992, no adminis-trative agreements or equivalency agreements had been signed. However, the federal government was negotiating an equivalency agreement with the Ontario government that would accept provincial PCB waste storage regulations as equivalent to the regulation under the Act.

CEPA Part IV: Controls on Federal Departments, Crown Corporations, and Agencies

Part IV of the *Canadian Environmental Protection Act* gives the minister of the environment the authority to regulate emissions from activities of federal departments, Crown corpora-tions, and federal agencies. This part provides the Minister with the authority to make regulations that apply to federal lands, works, and undertakings where no other Act of parliament applies. Regulations were planned for the summer of 1992 to reduce air emissions at federal boilers; however, by January 1993, they had not materialized.

Opportunities for Public Participation

Under the *Canadian Environmental Protection Act*, any individual may file a "notice of objection" to a proposed order or regulation, a decision not to place an allegedly toxic substance on a list of substances to be regulated, the issuance of a permit, or a decision to change the terms and conditions of an existing permit. In addition, if an applicant has been refused a permit or is dissatisfied with the terms and conditions in a permit, or if a permit is suspended or revoked or its terms and conditions are changed, the applicant or permit holder can file an objection to the decision. This gives interested parties the opportunity to formally appeal a decision or proposed regulation and to have the complaint duly registered. In some circumstances, the Act provides that on receiving a notice of objection, the minister of the environment (and the minister of health and welfare, as the case may be) must establish a board of review to examine the complaint, and in other circumstances the decision whether to carry out such a formal hearing is discretionary.[63] If a board of review is established, it will report its findings and recommendations to the minister(s), and with the exception of some confidential information such as trade secrets, the minister(s) must make the report available to the public as soon as it is received.

Other Acts and Regulations

Although the *Canadian Environmental Protection Act* is the main federal environmental legislation, other federal legislation also has some impact. The following is a sample of federal laws that touch on issues related to the management of air.

Motor Vehicle Safety Act

Next to the *Canadian Environmental Protection Act*, the single most important federal law relating to air quality is the *Motor Vehicle Safety Act*,[64] under which the federal government can make regulations establishing emission limits for vehicles imported into or manufactured in Canada. The legislation could also be used to require importers or manufacturers to install specific pollution control equipment required to meet those standards, but the approach used has been to set emissions based on the capacity of the available equipment to meet the standards, and to allow the manufacturers to choose what equipment or other methods they will use to meet the standards. Manufacturers must build vehicles that meet these standards if they want them sold in Canada. The importance of this legislation is clear when one considers that cars and trucks have been called "public enemy number 1" in relation to air pollution. The main pollutants they produce are hydrocarbons, nitrogen oxides, particulates, and carbon monoxide — pollutants that contribute to global warming, acid rain, smog, and the creation of ground-level ozone.

The regulations[65] prescribe permissible emission levels of hydrocarbons, carbon monoxide, and oxides of nitrogen in exhaust emissions from any vehicle powered by gasoline-fueled or diesel-fueled engines and the particulate content of the exhaust emissions from a vehicle powered by a diesel-fueled engine.[66] The regulations also limit the acceptable opacity of smoke emissions from diesel-fueled heavy-duty vehicles[67] and evaporative emissions from gasoline-fueled motor vehicles.[68]

For many years, Canadian emissions standards lagged behind those in the United States. Until the end of 1988, when more stringent standards came into effect,[69] new Canadian cars were allowed to emit up to 3.1 grams of NO_x per mile, while cars in the United States had been required to meet a standard of 1 gram per mile since 1981.

The 1990 amendments to the US *Clean Air Act*,[70] described above in the section on acid rain, also contained stricter vehicle emissions standards. NO_x emissions were reduced in the United States to 0.4 grams per mile, effective in 1994.

In October 1989, the federal environment minister of the day, Lucien Bouchard, promised that Canadian cars would be also be required to meet this standard by 1994.[71] However, on February 20, 1992, the federal government signed a memorandum of understanding with Canadian car manufacturers in which the commitment to meet the 0.4 gram standard became a *voluntary* agreement, rather than a government commitment to a binding regulation.[72] Taken together, the anticipated federal regulations and this agreement are expected to reduce nitrogen oxide emissions by 60 per cent and hydrocarbons by 29 per cent for new vehicles by 1996.

However, proposed amendments to the *Motor Vehicle Safety Act* being considered in 1992 would allow emissions averaging and emissions credits. Environmentalists have interpreted these provisions to mean that instead of each vehicle having to meet the emissions standards, some models could emit more pollution as long as others emitted less; and, moreover, instead of meeting the overall limits, some manufacturers could continue to exceed the emissions limits by paying a "pollution tax" to the government, while others obtain a "pollution credit"; that is, they could allow some of their vehicles to exceed emissions standards if the emissions of other models fall below the limits.[73]

Criminal Code

There is one brief mention of air management within the *Criminal Code*.[74] Section 178 provides:

> Every one other than a peace officer engaged in the discharge of his duty who has in his possession in a public place or who deposits, throws or injects or causes to be deposited, thrown or injected in, into or near any place,
>
>> (a) an offensive volatile substance that is likely to alarm, inconvenience, discommode or cause discomfort to any person or to cause damage to property, or
>> (b) a stink or stench bomb or device from which any substance mentioned in paragraph (a) is or capable of being liberated, is guilty of an offence punishable on summary conviction.

Canada Shipping Act

Unlike the standards for motor vehicles, there are no legally binding design standards governing air emissions from engines and boilers on ships. However, air pollution regulations[75] under the *Canada Shipping Act*[76] restrict emissions of smoke and soot from the operation of any fuel-burning installation on a ship. Using the old-fashioned smoke density chart, inspectors appointed under the Act compare the density of smoke they see coming from a stack with the various shades of gray on the chart. If the smoke being emitted appears to the inspector to be darker than the maximum density authorized by the regulation, this is an offence, punishable by a fine of up to $500 or up to six months in jail. Different densities of smoke may be legally emitted under different circumstances. The regulation provides for exceptions. The smoke may exceed the permitted density when new fires are being lit; fires are being cleaned or soot is being blown and the ship is not under way; the ship is being laid up or there has been a breakdown; or if it is necessary because of navigational difficulties. But under all these circumstances, excessive smoke is permissible only if all practicable precautions are taken to minimize the emission of smoke.

Railway Act and National Transportation Act

The Air Pollution and Smoke Control Regulations,[77] made jointly under the *Railway Act*[78] and the *National Transportation Act*,[79] limit the amount of smoke that railway companies are permitted to emit from their buildings, incinerators, open fires, and fuel-burning equipment, including locomotives. Municipal bylaw officers and provincial environment ministry inspectors are authorized to enforce the regulations, using a smoke density chart.

Weather Modification Information Act

The *Weather Modification Information Act*[80] was passed in December 1971. It came into effect on June 21, 1974 and it has remained substantially unchanged since then. It is administered by the Atmospheric Environment Service of the Department of the Environment. The Act and the regulations made under it are aimed at collecting information on weather-changing activities.

At the time the Act came into force, there was probably greater concern about weather-modifying activities than there currently appears to be. Indeed, since it came into force there has been little activity reported under the Act. Since 1980, the only activity report to the government has been a series of experiments in Alberta aimed at increasing rain and suppressing hail. The purpose of the Alberta Hail Project, which ceased operation around 1985, was to suppress hail by creating smaller hail stones producing more ice spots in clouds. Similar projects are still ongoing in Europe. There have also been some fog dissipation projects, which have had some success.

The Act requires anyone who intends to engage in any weather-modification activity to notify Environment Canada at least 10 days in advance, and to provide a monthly summary of activities and a report at the end of the project, as well as considerable other information. Failure to provide all the information required by the Act and regulations is punishable by a fine of up to $1,000 or imprisonment for up to six months.

Canada and the United States entered into a formal agreement in 1975 to share the information they receive under their respective weather modification reporting statutes.[81] Recognizing that weather modification carried out on one side of the border may affect the weather on the other side, the two countries have agreed that when any weather modification is to be carried out within 200 miles of the international boundary, the proponent country will inform the other country beforehand, except when extreme emergencies, such as forest fires, require immediate action. Even under these circumstances, the two countries agreed that they will inform each other of the activity as early as possible, and to consult with each other at the request of either country.

ONTARIO LEGISLATION

In addition to the international and federal initiatives already discussed, provincial legislation plays the key role in protecting air quality. In fact, provincial legislation is the principal means of controlling the quality of air in Ontario and many other provinces.

Environmental Assessment Act

The *Environmental Assessment Act*[82] (*EAA*) and how the environmental assessment process is administered are discussed in Chapter 9. Suffice it to say here that when an environmental assessment of an undertaking or a class of undertakings must be done, impacts on air quality will be considered as part of the assessment process. For example, when the potential environmental impact of a waste incinerator or other waste disposal or treatment system is assessed, this will provide an opportunity for a thorough assessment of possible air emissions, and for public participation in the making of the decision. Although the *Environmental Assessment Act* provides a process for the careful review and assessment of an undertaking and allows for the imposition of terms and conditions to ensure that the environmental impacts associated with the undertaking are minimized, its limited application and the sheer magnitude of the time and costs involved in the exercise make it of limited use for policing air quality in Ontario in general.

Environmental Protection Act

In Ontario, the *Environmental Protection Act*[83] (*EPA*) and the regulations made under it are the chief safeguards of provincial air quality. Of the regulations under the Act, regulation 308 is the principal regulation dealing with general air quality, although a host of other regulations relate to various other aspects of air quality, ranging from the operation of motor vehicles to the making of asphalt. This is in addition to a number of other statutes that regulate our quality of air in a less direct way.

The provisions of the *Environmental Protection Act* are the source of virtually all provincial efforts to control the quality of air. Because so much of our knowledge of what affects our atmosphere has resulted from recent scientific developments (as evidenced by the current debates raging as to the significance and cause of ozone depletion and global warming), it is not surprising that the legislation attempting to redress these problems is often sadly out of date. Ontario is no exception.

Under the *Environmental Protection Act*, air is part of the natural environment and all substances that may contaminate air, whether solid, liquid, or gas, are contaminants. Thus, the general provisions of the Act apply to air pollutants. As described in much greater detail in Chapter 16, these general provisions allow the Ministry of Environment and Energy to require all potential sources of air pollution to obtain permits to operate (certificates of approval), and the ministry can issue a variety of orders to prevent, reduce, or eliminate air pollution from these specific sources. Emitting air pollution that may cause various adverse effects is also an offence. However, in addition to these general provisions, there are specific parts of the Act that deal with specific sources of air pollution, and specific regulations. In this chapter, we will restrict our discussion to these aspects of the Act.

The regulatory approach under the *Environmental Protection Act* is similar to the tools found in the federal legislation. There are ambient air quality standards, which describe the concentrations of individual contaminants that may be permissible in the air at any time, and emissions standards governing the amount of each contaminant that an individual source may emit. Exceeding these emissions standards is an offence.

In addition, there are often more stringent standards for specific kinds of facilities, such as iron foundries and asphalt paving plants, and regulations governing specific substances, such as ozone-depleting substances and fuels.

EPA Part III: Motors and Motor Vehicles

Part III of the *Environmental Protection Act* is intended to dovetail with the federal government's motor vehicle emission standards under the *Motor Vehicle Safety Act*. That statute prevents the sale of motor vehicles in Canada unless they meet the federal air emissions standards, but it generally does not tell the manufacturers how to meet those standards. They can build smaller or lighter cars, improve their shape to reduce "drag," install more efficient engines, or install pollution-control devices.

In contrast, the provincial legislation provides that if the manufacturer has installed a pollution-control device or system, it is illegal for the seller or the owner to remove the device, bypass it, or otherwise prevent it from functioning, or to permit the operation of the vehicle without using the device or system.

The regulation[84] under part III spells out additional requirements:

- This regulation prohibits certain practices designed to hinder or defeat the operation of that mystical device that appeared in the bottom of all of our motor vehicles in the 1970s: the "catalytic converter." Since this device requires the use of unleaded gas to function, this regulation requires that the gasoline tank filler inlet of the vehicle must be too small to allow the gas pump nozzle for a leaded gas pump to be inserted into it. For several years, there were instances of gas station operators illegally equipping their leaded gas pumps with the smaller nozzles so that cars with catalytic converters could continue to use less expensive leaded gas. There were also cases of car owners removing the catalytic converters so that they could use leaded gas because it was cheaper, or because they believed the pollution control devices reduced the car's performance. The fact that all cars and light trucks sold in Canada since the 1970s are designed to use unleaded gas and that the federal law bans leaded gas has eliminated these forms of law breaking and has rendered this part of the regulation moot.

- Pollution-control devices must be maintained and kept in repair.

- Cars must be maintained so that there are no visible emissions for more than 15 seconds (usually on starting up a "cold" car).

- The regulation also sets out maximum levels of hydrocarbons, carbon monoxide, and visible emissions during the operation of a car and establishes a testing procedure for determining whether the car meets these emission limits. Ministry inspectors may require drivers and owners of cars to submit their vehicles for testing. Although there have been recommendations that all motor vehicles should be tested every year for emissions, and even though motor vehicles are widely recognized as one of the most significant sources of air pollution, the ministry has cut back its inspection and testing program and may soon phase it out completely. In the 1970s, the ministry had an Automotive Emissions Section, which operated mobile test laboratories and did spot checks on cars to ensure that their pollution control devices were functioning efficiently and had not been tampered with. However, by the fall of 1992, the ministry had only one motor vehicle inspector, carried out no routine testing, and was planning to shut down its testing facility in Etobicoke. The only testing being done was when police officers — primarily the OPP — spotted a smoky vehicle and required it to attend the test centre. About 600 to 800 tests a year were being carried out, leaving the test centre virtually unused most of the time.[85]

Part VI, "Ozone-Depleting Substances," has been described above, under the heading "The Ozone Layer."

The Ambient Air Quality Criteria

The Ambient Air Quality Criteria[86] set out the desirable ambient air quality criteria for each of 23 designated contaminants, ranging alphabetically from arsenic to vanadium. For each contaminant, the maximum amount that should be found in the air in a given length of time — for example, over 1 hour, over 8 hours, over 24 hours, over 30 days, or over one year — is set out.

Regulation 346

Although subsection 6(1) of the *Environmental Protection Act* sets out a general prohibition against contaminating the natural environment, beyond the limits set out in any regulation under the Act, regulation 346,[87] the "General Air Pollution Regulation," deals specifically with controlling the release of air contaminants. This regulation addresses the problem of air pollution through the adoption of three separate standards designed to limit the emission of contaminants to the air, and a number of other provisions to deal with specific areas of concern.

The three general standards relating to air emissions can be characterized as: the nuisance standard, the black smoke standard, and the contaminant level standard.

The Nuisance Standard

Section 6 of regulation 346 contains a prohibition against the emission of any air contaminant that may cause discomfort to persons; cause loss of enjoyment and normal use of property; interfere with normal conduct of business; or cause damage to property. This section basically embraces the concept of "nuisance" as it exists in the common law (see Chapter 6 for a discussion of common law nuisance) and makes such a nuisance an offence, for which a prosecution is available, instead of just a tort, for which an individual must sue in the civil courts. This section was useful until the early 1980s, when section 14 of the *Environmental Protection Act* was expanded to cover everything in it. Since then, it has been a "dead letter," but the ministry has not had it repealed because it is a prerequisite to the use of section 9, which requires reporting violations of section 6.

The Black Smoke Standard

Section 7 of regulation 346 provides for the Ministry of the Environment (MOE) to prepare a "Visible Emission Chart of the Province of Ontario," consisting of a series of shaded squares to provide a background to allow for the measurement of the opacity, or density, of smoke emissions. This is basically a measurement of the amount of particulates contained in the emission. Section 8 of regulation 346 goes on to provide prohibitions against certain "visible emissions" when the opacity of those emissions exceeds certain levels in relation to the visible emission chart.

Initially, the chart was the traditional "Ringelmann" chart described above in the section dealing with smoke from ships and trains. This chart measures opacity in shades of gray. However, because smoke sometimes comes in colours, the government tried to replace this chart with one that would deal with coloured smoke as well.

In theory, this chart was to provide a basis for measuring when an emission was too dense. In reality, the new visible emission chart has never been adopted because of a number of practical problems. In fact, because no simple chart is available, the ministry has been forced to use trained observers to make assessments of the opacity of emissions. With the continuing development of opacity meters and similar devices for measuring particulate emissions, it may soon be possible to regulate visible emissions through stack-monitoring devices that can instantaneously measure the smoke being emitted from a source. Such state-of-the-art devices are already a reality in facilities such as modern incineration units.

Emission Standards

Section 5 of regulation 346 provides that no person shall cause or permit a concentration of a contaminant, at a point of impingement from the source of contaminant (other than from a motor vehicle), that exceeds the concentration listed for that contaminant in schedule 1 to regulation 346. Schedule 1 sets out about 100 contaminants of concern.

Section 5 represents the only regulation in effect in Ontario that attempts to directly control the concentration of contaminants being released to the air. Although its very existence should provide the average resident of Ontario with some degree of comfort, this comfort level might well be increased if that average resident had some comprehension of just what a "point of impingement" was and, more important, how to avoid it. To put it simply, a point of impingement is a hypothetical point where contaminants from a given source (for example, a smokestack) are expected to come into contact with the ground. This point is calculated through the use of mathematical models.

Although regulations that impose limits on allowable emissions are clearly the most effective means for protecting the environment, there are at least three obvious shortfalls in the existing regulations. First, the list of contaminants is far from exhaustive. Second, there is no distinction made between the contaminants listed on the basis of their relative level of concern. Third, the regulated concentrations are based on "point of impingement" measurements rather than pre-stack, or source, measurement of contaminants. This type of logic leads to the construction of those ever-heightening stacks that are becoming a familiar part of the skylines across Ontario. Since it is far cheaper and easier to disperse contaminants over a greater area by using a taller stack (thereby reducing the concentration of contaminants at a given point of impingement in relation to that stack) than to reduce the level of contaminants being emitted at source, there can be little doubt what solution will be most appealing to the producers of contaminants. This is one of the most blatant examples of the so-called solution to pollution through dilution. The contaminants are not reduced, just spread over a greater area to reduce their effect. Such solutions may be effective for pollutants that break down into harmless components in the air, but they are inappropriate for persistent pollutants that do not break down but instead accumulate in soil or water or react in the air to create other pollutants or damage the atmosphere itself.

Other Provisions of Regulation 346

In addition to this three-pronged approach to the general regulation of the release of air contaminants, regulation 346 also contains a number of provisions to deal with specific areas of concern. These include:

- making specific exemptions from the need for approvals under section 8 of the *Environmental Protection Act* for such sources as domestic furnaces, domestic stoves, highway construction equipment, and light emitted by signs and billboards;[88]

- establishing an air pollution index for Ontario and providing for the minister to make certain orders when prescribed index levels are exceeded;[89]
- requiring owners and operators of sources of contaminants to notify the ministry when shutdowns or upsets occur that might result in the emission of air contaminants in excess of the concentrations allowed by regulation 346;[90]
- regulating the fuel to be used in fuel-burning equipment and incinerators;[91]
- requiring that "every step necessary" be taken to control the emission of contaminants from construction, demolition, blasting, sand blasting, and other procedures;[92]
- regulating the general use and operation of incinerators;[93] and
- prohibiting the storage, handling, or transportation of any material in a manner that may release a contaminant to the atmosphere.[94]

In the light of the growing significance we attach to air quality problems, the complexity of the sources that cause these problems, and the variety of technologies currently being put forward as potential solutions to these problems, the provisions of the *Environmental Protection Act* risk becoming rapidly outdated. With this in mind, the Ministry of the Environment began addressing the perceived shortcomings of the Act and regulation 346 by releasing a discussion paper in 1987 entitled "Stopping Air Pollution At Its Source ... The Clean Air Program." This initiative, better known as "CAP," will be addressed later in this chapter.

Specific Sources

In addition to legislation of general application such as the *Environmental Protection Act* and the *Environmental Assessment Act*, there are a number of statutes and regulations dealing with specific sources of air emissions. The following are some of these specific provisions.

Air Contaminants from Ferrous Foundries[95]

This regulation sets limits on allowable emissions of particulate and water plumes from facilities for casting iron and iron alloys in moulds. It requires these foundries to be designed and operated in a manner that will ensure compliance with these limits, as well as the limits for other pollutants found in the general air regulation.

The Hot Mix Asphalt Facilities Regulation[96]

Ontario has had a specific regulation governing particulate emissions and water vapour and droplets from asphalt paving plants since 1972.[97] In 1987, this regulation was updated. The current regulation prohibits the impingement of any visible material, including water, on any area beyond the boundaries of the property where a hot mix asphalt facility is located and establishes an emission limit for suspended particulate matter. However, facilities approved before the end of 1985 need not meet these emission limits. Operators of portable facilities must keep a copy of the certificate of approval available for inspection and must inform the ministry when the facility is relocated. If an asphalt facility malfunctions, resulting in excessive emissions, immediate steps must be taken to rectify the problem and the ministry must be notified.

Waste Incinerators

In addition to regulating the fuels used in waste incinerators under regulation 346, the Ontario government has been gradually reducing the availability of incineration as an option for disposing of waste. Apartment building incinerators have been banned, and in 1992 the government made a regulation prohibiting the construction of any new incinerators for municipal waste.[98] The incineration of hazardous wastes remains controversial. Proponents of this process claim that incineration of wastes at high temperatures ensures almost total destruction of all pollutants, but opponents question this. A study by the US Environmental Protection Agency found higher-than-expected levels of heavy metals, dioxin, furans, and benzine in waste dust from such incinerators.[99]

Sulphur Content of Fuels Regulation[100]

In addition to regulations restricting the sulphur content of fuel designed specifically to combat acid rain, which have been discussed earlier, the provincial government has had a regulation limiting the sulphur content of oil and coal used for fuel within Metropolitan Toronto for over 20 years. No fuel with a sulphur content in excess of the maximum allowable limits prescribed may be used, sold, or offered for sale, unless a certificate has been obtained under section 7 of the *Environmental Protection Act*, stating that the actual sulphur dioxide emissions will be no greater than if the fuel contained the prescribed sulphur content.

The Gasoline Volatility Regulation[101]

As mentioned above, VOCs found in gasoline and other petroleum products can cause cancer and react with nitrogen oxides to produce crop-killing ground-level ozone and smog. Because this reaction is affected by the amount of sunlight, it is more severe during the summer months. Moreover, in hot weather, more gasoline evaporates during refuelling and at other times when gasoline is handled. Therefore, starting in the summer of 1989, the Ministry of the Environment required Ontario refineries to deliver "summer grade gasoline" with reduced volatility from May to September.[102] The ministry estimated that this measure reduced gasoline evaporation from tanks and pumps by 15 per cent and cut smog by 8 to 10 per cent.[103] The ministry intended to require such VOC limits each summer and to make them even lower.[104] This regulation was made permanent in 1991.[105]

In addition to reformulating gasoline to reduce its volatility, special equipment can be added to fuel terminals and delivery trucks to capture emissions before they escape into the air and recycle them. The ministry has also been considering issuing a regulation requiring the oil industry to install devices to reduce the evaporation of gasoline during bulk storage and transportation operations.[106] A draft of this regulation was prepared in August 1990, but as of February 1993 it had not been finalized,[107] even though the federal and provincial environment ministers had jointly agreed in 1990 that such an initiative (known as stage 1 vapour recovery) should be taken as part of the first phase of a national plan to reduce VOCs.[108]

Motor Vehicles: The Highway Traffic Act

In addition to the provisions contained in regulation 346, section 75 of the *Highway Traffic Act*[109] requires every motor vehicle or motor-assisted bicycle to be equipped with a muffler in good working order and in constant operation to prevent excessive or unusual noise and excessive smoke. The engine and power mechanism of the motor vehicle must also be so equipped and adjusted as to prevent the escape of excessive fumes or smoke.

The Air Pollution Index and the Air Quality Index

The Ministry of the Environment operates an air quality monitoring system that monitors the concentration of six pollutants on an hour-by-hour basis at 33 locations in 26 Ontario cities. The six pollutants measured are carbon monoxide, nitrogen oxide, ozone, sulphur dioxide, suspended particles (particulate), and total reduced sulphur (sulphur-containing compounds that cause unpleasant odours). Using these measurements, the ministry advises the public of the quality of the air. To describe air quality, the ministry has devised an air quality index (AQI). In this index, the lower the number, the better the air quality. Zero to 15 indicates very good air quality; 16 to 31 indicates good air quality; 32 to 49 indicates moderate air quality; 50 to 99 indicates poor air quality; and 100 or more indicates very poor air quality. None of these levels, however, indicates that the air quality is "unacceptable," implying that something must be done about it.

The only measurements that actually trigger a requirement to take action are the measurements of sulphur dioxide and suspended particulate, which are part of the overall AQI. The reason for this is that these pollutants come primarily from industries that can be shut down quickly, unlike many other pollutants that come from numerous sources like motor vehicles that are harder to control. In addition, unlike other contaminants, the ministry had scientific evidence of the specific levels at which these two pollutants combined affect human health.

The index developed to measure the impact of these two substances is the air pollution index (API). The index is a numerical scale starting at zero. Readings below 32 are considered acceptable, indicating concentrations of the two pollutants that should have little or no effect on human health. At a reading of 58, people with chronic respiratory diseases may be affected. At a reading of 100, prolonged conditions could have mild effects on healthy people and serious effects on those with severe cardiac and respiratory diseases.

The API functions as an alert system when a combination of industrial pollution and adverse weather conditions creates an air quality that might affect human health. The alert system functions at four index levels: 32 (advisory level), 50 (first alert), 75 (second alert), and 100 (air pollution episode threshold level).

At a reading of 32, if meteorological conditions are expected to remain unfavourable for another six hours, owners of major sources of SO_2 and particulate emissions may be advised to prepare to curtail their operations. At a reading of 50, if weather conditions are expected to remain adverse for another six hours, the owners can be ordered to curtail their operations. If the index reaches 75 despite any curtailment of operations, and weather conditions with a high potential to hold pollution in the air are forecast for another six hours, the ministry may order further reductions in operations that cause air pollution. At a reading of 100, the minister may order all polluting operations not essential to public health to cease.

Since the API began, levels of sulphur dioxide and particulate matter in Ontario's major cities have been reduced. Nevertheless, in 1990, the most recent year for which a report is available, the advisory level of 32 was reached 10 times, at seven sites across Ontario,

The Air Quality Index System

INDEX	CATEGORY	CARBON MONOXIDE CO	NITROGEN DIOXIDE NO_2	OZONE O_3	SULPHUR DIOXIDE SO_2	SUSPENDED PARTICLES SP	SO_2 + SP (as measured by the API)	TOTAL REDUCED SULPHUR TRS
100-OVER	VERY POOR	INCREASING CARDIOVASCULAR SYMPTOMS IN NON-SMOKERS WITH HEART DISEASE. SOME VISUAL IMPAIRMENT	INCREASING SENSITIVITY OF PATIENTS WITH ASTHMA AND BRONCHITIS	LIGHT EXERCISE PRODUCES RESPIRATORY EFFECTS IN PATIENTS WITH CHRONIC PULMONARY DISEASE	INCREASING SENSITIVITY IN PATIENTS WITH ASTHMA AND BRONCHITIS	INCREASING SENSITIVITY IN PATIENTS WITH ASTHMA AND BRONCHITIS	SIGNIFICANT RESPIRATORY EFFECTS IN PATIENTS WITH ASTHMA AND BRONCHITIS	SENSITIVE INDIVIDUALS MAY SUFFER NAUSEA AND HEADACHES DUE TO SEVERE ODOR
50-99	POOR	INCREASED CARDIOVASCULAR SYMPTOMS IN SMOKERS WITH HEART DISEASE	ODOR AND DISCOLORATION. SOME INCREASE IN BRONCHIAL REACTIVITY IN ASTHMATICS	DECREASING PERFORMANCE BY ATHLETES EXERCISING HEAVILY	ODOROUS. INCREASING VEGETATION DAMAGE	VISIBILITY DECREASED. SOILING EVIDENT	INCREASED SYMPTOMS IN PATIENTS WITH CHRONIC RESPIRATORY DISEASE	EXTREMELY ODOROUS
32-49	MODERATE	BLOOD CHEMISTRY CHANGES BUT NO DETECTABLE IMPAIRMENT	ODOROUS	INJURIOUS TO MANY VEGETATION SPECIES E.G. WHITE BEANS, TOMATOES, ETC.	INJURIOUS TO SOME SPECIES OF VEGETATION	SOME DECREASE IN VISIBILITY	INJURIOUS TO VEGETATION DUE TO SULPHUR DIOXIDE	ODOROUS
16-31	GOOD	NO EFFECTS	SLIGHT ODOR	INJURIOUS TO SOME VEGETATION SPECIES IN COMBINATION WITH SO_2 (4 HRS)	INJURIOUS TO SOME VEGETATION SPECIES IN COMBINATION WITH OZONE (4 HRS)	NO EFFECTS	NO EFFECTS	SLIGHT ODORS
0-15	VERY GOOD	NO EFFECTS	NO EFFECTS	NO EFFECTS	NO EFFECTS	NO EFFECTS	NO EFFECTS	NO EFFECTS

Courtesy of the Ontario Ministry of Environment and Energy.

including Hamilton and Sudbury.[110] In Lambton County, a centre of petrochemical production that includes Sarnia, the Lambton Industrial Meteorological Alert, which is used instead
of the API in that area, was called on nine occasions.[111]

MUNICIPAL JURISDICTION

Historically, air pollution was regulated through municipal bylaws enforced by municipal air
pollution inspectors. The provincial *Environmental Protection Act* has largely superseded
these municipal bylaws. Nevertheless, there may still be some residual jurisdiction for
municipalities to pass bylaws regulating air pollution where the provincial government has
not occupied the field, or has explicitly provided for municipal law making (for example,
smoking in the workplace). Under the *Municipal Act*, cities have the power to pass bylaws
controlling industrial nuisances, regulating sandblasters, and prohibiting incinerators for
burning garbage and refuse.[112]

Many of the general powers that municipalities have to pass licensing bylaws and nuisance
bylaws, to control vehicle routes, and to regulate land-use planning, described elsewhere in
this book, may be useful in controlling air pollution. In addition, some adventurous
municipalities have passed bylaws even where they may not have jurisdiction. Such bylaws
sometimes point to a gap in provincial legislation and stimulate discussion and government
action.

In addition, municipal governments can establish many policies and practices that
indirectly determine how much air pollution their residents are subject to, and how much the
municipality contributes to acid rain, global warming, and ozone depletion, even if they
cannot regulate these matters directly. For example, municipal tree-planting programs can
help control air pollution; adequate public transit can encourage less frequent use of cars in
the municipality; bicycle paths can be established and bicycle lanes can be set aside on
roadways; and various energy efficiency and energy conservation programs can be implemented to reduce carbon emissions.[113]

In keeping with recent concerns about global warming, the city of Toronto, at a council
meeting held in January 1990, made an official commitment to reduce carbon emissions into
the atmosphere within the city by 20 per cent of the 1988 levels by the year 2005. Toronto
reinforced its commitment to this policy on February 4, 1992, by passing a bylaw[114] that
provided for the prohibition and abatement of the emission of exhaust fumes from buses
where the services were previously provided by trolley cars. This bylaw was aimed directly
at the Toronto Transit Commission's decision to switch certain routes from trolley cars to
more energy efficient fossil fuels, such as diesel and natural gas.

The city of Toronto also passed an extremely important bylaw in October 1990 regulating
the use, recovery, and disposal of certain products, material, and equipment containing or
manufactured with chlorofluorocarbons, halons, or other ozone-depleting substances.[115] The
bylaw attempts to stem the release of ozone-depleting substances into the air from this
equipment. It requires every person in the city of Toronto to dispose of products or equipment
that contain CFCs or halons in a form in which these chemicals can be drained or recovered
from the product or equipment by prescribed methods. The product or equipment must be
delivered to certain sites established within the city and care must be taken to ensure that the

CFCs are drained and recovered from the product before disposal. Instructions are also given respecting the servicing and repair of air conditioners and fire extinguishers.

OTHER AIR QUALITY CONCERNS

Indoor Air Quality

Although most Canadians spend a lot more time indoors than outdoors, the quality of indoor air has been given relatively little consideration by law makers, despite the fact that pollution levels indoors, especially inside buildings that have been "tightened" for energy conservation, are frequently far higher than those outdoors.[116] Apart from occupational health and safety legislation, which regulates relatively high levels of certain highly hazardous air pollutants in the workplace, there is little legislation that addresses the quality of indoor air. This is a particularly important issue for people who have exceptional sensitivity to exposure to chemicals — what is often referred to as "20th-century disease." Although the precise nature of the problem has defied scientific diagnosis, there is no doubt that some people are affected much more than others by traces of chemical substances in the indoor air. For these people, the "sick building syndrome" is a very serious concern.

Sick Building Syndrome[117]

In recent years, complaints that children in schools, workers in office buildings, and even people in their own homes are suffering headaches, difficulty in breathing, eye irritation, sore throats, lethargy, and other forms of discomfort have become increasingly common. Often, measurements of air quality inside these buildings reveal no source of these symptoms, yet the symptoms persist.[118]

Although scientists have had great difficulty in pinpointing the causes and effects of the sick building syndrome, there appears to be general agreement about two common factors. The first problem results from our efforts to create more energy-efficient buildings and sometimes to save money. We have constructed buildings in which the windows cannot open, so artificial means are required to bring fresh air into the building and remove stale air. Moreover, even if the windows open, buildings are constructed to be much more airtight than in past. As a result, ventilation may be inadequate. Second, many of the materials used in constructing and furnishing modern buildings, as well as chemicals used in the home, such as solvents and various cleansers and polishes, contain chemicals, and these materials give off small quantities of gases inside the building itself. For example, window caulking, carpets, furniture, plywood, and some foam insulation emit gases such as formaldehyde, acrylate, and styrene. Dry-cleaning fluids, disinfectants, paints, and pesticides give off vapours as well.

Pollutants commonly found indoors include carbon monoxide, nitrogen oxides, radon gas (often coming from the soil below the house), ozone, tobacco smoke, asbestos, dust and moulds, bacteria and viruses, and "a host of organic chemical vapours, some of which are known or suspected carcinogens."[119]

There are no legally enforceable standards for air quality in homes and offices for many of these pollutants, although guidelines have been established for some pollutants.[120] These guidelines represent the maximum concentration it would be prudent to accept if one were exposed for any substantial amount of time, taking into account that some groups are particularly sensitive to these substances.[121] When standards do exist for a few pollutants, they are often occupational health standards, which are based on the tolerance of adult workers to pollution, and not the lower tolerance levels of children, pregnant women, the sick, and the elderly, who spend their time in houses, schools, nursing homes, and hospitals. Moreover, occupational health and safety inspectors, used to dealing with gross pollution in factories, have been reluctant to carry out tests in other buildings such as office buildings and schools.[122] When they do carry out such tests, there have been claims that they use antiquated equipment that is not capable of detecting some contaminants at the levels at which they occur indoors.[123]

Because this problem involves so many pollutants from so many sources, action, including policies and laws, will be needed on many fronts to solve it. Among the laws and policies that may be required are amendments to building codes dealing with ventilation; restrictions on building materials that may be used and other aspects of building design; warning systems to notify the chemically sensitive when they are entering a building that has just been painted, sprayed with insecticides, cleaned, or in other ways had chemicals used in it or applied to it that may affect them; restricting the use of some chemicals in furniture, carpets, cleaners, paints, and other consumer goods; and providing low-pollution housing to those who are particularly sensitive to such pollutants.

In the meantime, workers must rely largely on occupational health and safety laws that are not designed for this problem, and those who are so sensitive that they can be considered "disabled" may be able to use workers' compensation laws to obtain compensation and the federal and provincial human rights codes to obtain better working conditions. Human rights codes prohibit discrimination on the basis of disabilities, and require employers to "reasonably accommodate" workers who suffer such disabilities. Reasonable accommodation may include reasonable efforts to provide a workplace that is more free of chemicals than the one where the worker does his or her job.

Second-Hand Smoke[124]

The days of the smoke-filled room are slowly drawing to a close. Smoking is now prohibited or restricted on many forms of public transportation such as airplanes, trains, taxis, and buses. In addition, smoking is restricted in many public places and workplaces.

Perhaps no bylaw has attracted as much attention, or been the topic of as much debate, as Toronto's municipal bylaw respecting smoking in public places, passed May 14, 1979.[125] The bylaw notes in its preamble that, since it has been determined that second-hand tobacco smoke is a health hazard or discomfort for many inhabitants of the city, and it is desirable for the health, safety, and welfare of the inhabitants to prohibit or regulate smoking, this bylaw prohibits smoking in certain establishments. These areas include child care facilities, health care facilities, places of public assembly, hospitals, and elevators. Store owners and other persons in charge of these facilities are required to post notices that smoking is prohibited on the premises in areas where they are clearly visible. Any person who smokes in contravention of the bylaw is considered guilty of an offence.

In other public places such as restaurants, there must be non-smoking areas and they must be clearly marked. If the restaurant contains an area where smoking is allowed, it must display

Warning!

This area contains tobacco smoke, which is known to cause **cancer, heart disease, lung disease,** and may **harm your baby.**

City of Toronto bylaw no. 406-79. Courtesy of the Medical Officer of Health, City of Toronto.

a sign in the smoking section that reads: "This area contains tobacco smoke, which is known to cause cancer, heart disease, and may harm your baby." The city of Toronto further entrenched its anti-smoking policy by passing a bylaw respecting smoking in the workplace on December 14, 1987.[126] The goal of this bylaw is to have every employer adopt and implement a smoking policy in the workplace. Businesses already in existence at that time were given a certain amount of time to create a policy and hand it into the responsible government authority. Employers of businesses created after the implementation of the bylaw were required to implement and create a smoking policy within seven days of commencing business. Although every business must have a plan and a system of implementation, no employer is required under this bylaw to make any expenditures or structural alterations to the workplace to accommodate the preferences of non-smoking employees. The penalty for non-compliance with the bylaw was a fine of $2,000, exclusive of costs for each offence. Fines could be imposed on employers for permitting smoking and failing or neglecting to perform the duties set out in the bylaw.

Eventually, both the federal and provincial governments followed suit — at least in the workplace. In 1988, the federal government passed the *Non-Smokers' Health Act*.[127] This Act requires employers subject to the *Canada Labour Code*[128] (that is, in federal government agencies and private industries subject to federal jurisdiction) to ensure that there is no smoking in the workplace. Certain areas may be designated as smoking areas, but in buildings constructed after January 1, 1990 smoking rooms must have separate ventilation from the rest of the building.

The Act also limits smoking onboard transportation services and in terminals and stations. Smoking is prohibited on all intercity buses and on all flights except charters and private planes. Ships and trains must have non-smoking areas, and at least 70 per cent of the area of stations and terminals must be smoke-free.

In 1989, Ontario passed the *Smoking in the Workplace Act*.[129] This Act prohibits anyone from smoking in any enclosed workplace, except in designated smoking areas and public areas (like the lobby of a building), and requires employers to make every reasonable effort to prevent smoking in the work areas of the building. It covers all workplaces under provincial jurisdiction.

Anyone who smokes can be fined up to $500, and an employer who doesn't make all reasonable efforts to prevent smoking can be fined up to $25,000. The Act specifically recognizes the rights of employers to ban smoking completely and the rights of municipalities to pass even tougher municipal bylaws.

Not to be outdone, the city of Toronto amended its bylaws in 1992 to require that as of January 1, 1993, the smoke-free space in restaurants would have to be increased from 30 per cent of the area to 50 per cent; smoking in workplaces would be allowed only in fully enclosed designated areas that are fully ventilated to the outside; and any employer, proprietor of a public place, or restaurant operator who sees anyone smoking in a non-smoking area would be required to tell the person that smoking is prohibited. The maximum fine for violating the smoking bylaws was raised from $1,000 to $5,000.[130]

Municipal licensing bylaws may also regulate smoking. For example, Metro Toronto's licensing bylaw gives the municipality power to prohibit stores from selling tobacco unless they are licensed to do so.[131] In addition, the bylaw prohibits both taxi drivers and passengers from smoking in taxis without each other's consent.[132]

Other tobacco-related legislation that creates some pressure to reduce smoking, and therefore exposure to second-hand smoke, is legislation that imposes high taxes on tobacco products, such as the *Tobacco Tax Act*,[133] the *Tobacco Restraint Act*,[134] which prohibits sales to minors, but is rarely enforced, and the *Tobacco Products Control Act*.[135] The last-mentioned Act requires health warnings on cigarette packages and bans tobacco advertising. However, it contains a major loophole. Upset about the loss of sponsorship of their activities by tobacco companies, amateur arts and sports and cultural organizations convinced the federal government to allow tobacco companies to sponsor public events, and advertise their sponsorship. The future of this law is in doubt. The Quebec Superior Court has held that it violates the cigarette companies' freedom of expression under the *Canadian Charter of Rights and Freedoms*.[136] Although this decision was overturned by the Court of Appeal early in 1993, the decision may be appealed further to the Supreme Court of Canada.

Odour

When the second edition of this book was published in 1978, we were told by government officials that noise was the environmental concern resulting in the largest number of complaints from the public. When this edition was prepared we were told that although there was no breakdown of the kinds of complaints received, odours were probably the single largest source of complaints to the Ministry of the Environment.[137]

Odour is a contaminant under the *Environmental Protection Act* and is controlled in the same way as other sources of pollution are — through prosecution, conditions on certificates of approval, and pollution-control orders. The determination of whether an odour is one likely to cause adverse effects, rendering the source subject to prosecution or a control order, is still done largely through the human nose. Although there are scientific methods of determining the level at which an odour can be detected by the average person, and the level at which it becomes offensive using "odour panels" (groups of people who are exposed to a substance in different concentrations under controlled conditions), there is still no instrument better designed to detect odours or to distinguish one odour from another than the human nose. Thus, the determination of the source of an odour still consists of a person going upwind and downwind of a suspected odour source and recognizing the kind of odour from past experience. Proving that the odour has an adverse effect remains a matter of ordinary people testifying in court that the odour caused them to abandon their backyard barbecues and close their windows.

Although odour control is largely a provincial responsibility under the *Environmental Protection Act*, municipalities still have power under the *Municipal Act* to deal with nuisance industries generally, and to regulate some specific sources of odour, such as slaughter-houses.[138] In addition, one of the most frequent sources of complaint is municipal sewage treatment plants and sewage lagoons. However, if the municipality does not voluntarily improve these facilities, complaints would be made to the Ministry of the Environment, which regulates these facilities through certificates of approval. Moreover, although the *Ontario Water Resources Act* deems municipal sewage works to be operated with "statutory authority," meaning the municipality cannot be sued for nuisance resulting from their operation,[139] the Act does provide an alternative remedy. Any person suffering certain kinds of harm may complain to the Ontario Municipal Board, and the board may make any "order, award, or finding … it considers just."[140] It is not clear from the wording of the provision whether the harm that can give rise to this remedy includes odour, or whether it is restricted to physical harm to property.

Farm odours from the storage of animal wastes and the spreading of manure on farmland are exempt from the *Environmental Protection Act*, as long as they are dealt with in accordance with "normal farming practices." However, it is still possible to prosecute for farming odours under some of the subsections of the Act. The right of neighbours to sue farmers in nuisance for farm odours arising from normal farming practices has been taken away by the *Farm Practices Protection Act*.[141] But neighbours can still bring their complaints to a Farm Practices Protection Board, and if the board finds that the activity causing the odour is not a normal farming practice, it may order the farmer to stop the activity or modify it so that it becomes consistent with normal farming practices.[142] Despite the bias suggested by its name, this board has treated neighbours quite fairly.

In addition, the Ministry of the Environment and the Ministry of Agriculture and Food (OMAF) have jointly developed an agricultural code of practice, which suggests minimum distances farmers should keep their livestock facilities and manure handling systems from residences to minimize objectionable odours. The code also suggests ways of disposing of manure and ventilating livestock facilities to reduce odours. The farmer who follows this code can be given a "certificate of compliance," issued jointly by MOE and OMAF. Although there is no legal requirement to comply with this Code, compliance is a condition of obtaining some grants and subsidies available from OMAF, and failure to comply with the requirements of the code could be considered evidence of a lack of due diligence if the farmer were prosecuted for causing unnecessary odours.

Slaughterhouses and meat-processing plants can be controlled not only through the *Environmental Protection Act* and bylaws under the *Municipal Act*, but also through regulations under the *Health Protection and Promotion Act*[143] regulating sanitation in such facilities. Although these regulations are not aimed specifically at odours, steps that will make the plant as sanitary as possible will also often reduce odours.

THE ROCKY ROAD TO REFORM: "CAP" AND "AMS"

Although levels of the most common contaminants dropped dramatically between 1970 and 1980, this is no reason for complacency. The improvement in air quality has been much less pronounced between 1980 and 1990. In particular, ambient air quality standards for particulate were frequently exceeded in 1988, 1989, and 1990, the most recent years for which statistics are available. There were also excessive concentrations of lead and nickel in 1988, and although the air quality index showed good to very good air quality 94 per cent of the time, the air pollution index was exceeded in both Hamilton and Etobicoke.[144] In 1990, as mentioned above, the air pollution index advisory limit was exceeded several times. In addition, traces of metals such as cadmium, chromium, iron, manganese, nickel, vanadium, and copper were found in the particulates in the air. Ambient air quality in Toronto was worse than that in Montreal, Vancouver, Boston, Atlanta, and Chicago. Moreover, a report by Canadian and American lung experts found that in 1990, levels of acid aerosols (which can cause lung damage) in southern Ontario's air were among the highest in North America.[145] Another report has predicted that economic stagnation will undercut support for environmental reforms, leading to increases in Canadian emissions of hydrocarbons, nitrogen oxide, and VOCs of up to 80 per cent.[146]

Air quality has traditionally been measured for only a few of the most common chemicals. Unlike water quality, where the provincial government now tests the water supply of major cities annually for hundreds of chemicals, this has not changed. In fact, on the few occasions when attempts have been made to find out what is actually in the air, many hazardous chemicals have been detected, albeit in small quantities.[147] The inadequacy of the present regulatory regime has been documented and discussed at length by the Ontario government in its CAP discussion papers (see below).

Furthermore, although some sources of pollution have received intense attention, others have been left virtually unregulated. For example, although there are increasingly stringent standards for car and truck emissions, little attention has been paid to aircraft, which, according to a 1991 report by the World Wide Fund for Nature, may be increasing the rate of global warming by between 5 and 40 per cent,[148] or to gas-powered equipment such as chainsaws, lawn mowers, leaf blowers, and weed eaters, which can spew as many hydrocarbons into the air as a car.[149]

The Ontario Ministry of the Environment began a comprehensive review of its air pollution programs in 1985, which identified its deficiencies and options for improvement. The ministry published a discussion paper in November 1987, which was intended to lead to new legislation after hearing from the public.[150] The report recommended a new approach to air pollution control, referred to as the Clean Air Program, or most simply as CAP, focusing on measuring and controlling pollutants at their source, rather than dispersion modelling. CAP is a blueprint for reform, but inadequate resources have prevented its implementation. New laws and policies have been slow in coming.

The CAP

CAP identified several weaknesses in the ministry's current approach to controlling air pollution:

- the failure to account for certain aspects and effects of air emissions — namely, long-range transport, long-term deposition, very short-term effects, very long-term effects, bioaccumulation and persistence, and additive and synergistic effects;
- a lack of precise requirements for treating emissions prior to their discharge to the atmosphere, relying instead on dispersion;
- the use of air quality models that are not state-of-the-art and are not appropriate for the purposes for which they are being used;
- discrepancies in the application of models in certain circumstances and in particular with respect to modelling fugitive sources (leaks) and multiple sources of contaminants;
- a lack of opportunity for direct public participation (which is generally now encouraged for environmental matters) in the setting of standards and in the approval process;
- the failure to take into account changing land uses; and
- the failure to provide for temporary approvals to permit experimentation.

As with existing regulation 346, emission levels are for the most part controlled through the imposition of maximum allowable concentrations at a point of impingement. CAP proposes to deal with the shortcomings of the existing regulation by adopting two basic premises. First, there is a recognition of the need for "pre-stack control" of contaminant levels, meaning the treatment of emissions before they have been released to the environment, thereby eliminating the effect of dispersion on the measurement of contaminants and avoiding the so-called solution to pollution through dilution problem. Second, CAP acknowledges the substantial differences in the characteristics of contaminants and the need to rank these contaminants in order of the potential risk they pose to the environment. With this strategy in mind, a number of fundamental changes were proposed for Ontario's air pollution abatement program. Having established a ranking of contaminants of concern, CAP proposes to break those contaminants down into two or three levels of concern based on four characteristics:

1. toxicity;
2. persistence;
3. bioaccumulation (the tendency of living organisms to absorb the contaminant); and
4. transport characteristics (the environmental medium through which the contaminant may travel).

These levels can generically be referred to as classes 1, 2, and 3. Each level of contaminant would then require an appropriate level of control technology to ensure that emission rates of those contaminants are kept within acceptable limits. This way, the most stringent controls can be applied to the most threatening contaminants.

However, determining an appropriate level of control technology at any given point in time is not a simple task. As previous attempts to regulate air emission levels have made evident, the scientific developments taking place in the world often outpace the regulator's ability to ascertain what the cause of the problem is; what technology can best deal with this problem; and how to develop an appropriate regulatory regime to ensure that the problem is dealt with. CAP's proposed solution to this dilemma is to avoid the imposition of arbitrary emission limits and to tie emission levels to what is technologically possible at any given time. For example, assuming that class 1 contaminants are those of greatest concern, CAP proposes that the required emission rate for such contaminants would be that achievable through the proper use of the best emission control system available, or its equivalent, without regard to considerations such as cost. This standard is known as "lowest achievable emission rate" (LAER).

Class 2 contaminants, being of lesser concern, would require treatment to a somewhat less stringent but still adequate level, taking into consideration economic and other factors. This level or standard is referred to as "best available control technology economically achievable" (BACT-EA).

Finally, it is proposed that class 3 contaminants, being of least concern, would require control technology that would achieve an emission rate comparable to the emission rate associated with the minimum level of control demonstrated as acceptable at similar sources. This emission rate is defined as "new source performance standards" (NSPS).

The advantages of the proposed CAP system are obvious. Foremost, it provides a means of regulating emission rates that is flexible enough to allow for technological advances and allows emission levels to be constantly adjusted to allow for these developments. The disadvantages are somewhat less obvious. CAP does not propose that the ministry prescribe the actual technology to be used for any particular class. This leaves unanswered the question of how to determine what, for example, is LAER? Is it sufficient to determine what emission limits have been regulated by other jurisdictions to reflect what they believe the lowest achievable emission rates currently are? Is it necessary to do a survey of all technology currently being employed throughout the world to determine the lowest emission rates currently being achieved? If such a survey were undertaken, how would "lowest" be defined?

How would it be established that these rates were measured on a comparable basis? Would any new, revolutionary, or unproven technology that appears to result in lower emission rates send the LAER rates plummeting? What happens if it is subsequently shown that the technology with the lowest rates is unreliable? These questions may, to some extent, always remain unsolved.

The CAP document also provides comments on most aspects of regulation 346, including: improved dispersion modelling, new means of permitting the operation of facilities that emit contaminants, the air pollution index, the control of visible emissions, the control of emissions associated with construction and sandblasting activities, the control of emissions from upsets and shutdown conditions, the general restrictions contained in regulation 346 on the release of emissions, the control of organic emissions from incinerators, and restrictions on the operation of incinerators. Furthermore, the CAP document identifies certain areas of growing concern with respect to the impact of air emissions. These include the increased use of wood stoves and fireplace inserts, the open burning of waste materials, and increasing levels of contaminants in soil, foliage, and other plant life.

In August 1990, the ministry released a draft regulation implementing the approach set out in CAP. The public was to be given six months to comment on the regulation, and this comment period was to be "the final stage prior to promulgation." As of February 1993, however, the regulation had not been promulgated. Not unexpectedly, knowledge of the causes of air contaminants and our ability to monitor those contaminants have advanced substantially during that time period. After five years of consideration, the ministry abandoned CAP in favour of an updated program to be known as the Air Management Strategy (AMS). The AMS was expected to be released for public review by late 1992 and will, it is hoped, redress some of the potential shortcomings of CAP. By February 1993, though, only a brief outline of AMS had been revealed.

Representatives of the Ministry of Environment and Energy continue to characterize the AMS as only being in its formative stage and unlikely even to be put forward for public consultation for some months, but it seems clear that CAP is now in fact "dead." Although the precise contents of AMS continue to be shrouded in secrecy, it is our understanding that the strategy will incorporate the more readily attainable goals of CAP, such as updating dispersion models, while leaving the more ambitious goal of implementing a LAER regime until some unspecified future date.[151]

FUTURE DIRECTIONS

Many of the laws of the past and the programs planned for the future are technology-driven; that is, they either require the introduction or use of technology such as cleaner engines or pollution control devices, or set emissions standards based on the technology available to achieve them. In some areas of concern, however, we are reaching the limits of what can be achieved with technology. Much of the pollution of concern comes from the combustion of fuel to heat and cool buildings and to run millions of engines for vehicles and equipment. When all the technological fixes are in, there will still be a need for further reductions. For this, we will have to look to energy conservation strategies such as better building design, planning of human settlements to reduce dependence on motor vehicles, more efficient public transportation systems, car pooling, and other wide-ranging changes in our lifestyle that we would not normally associate specifically with air pollution control. In many cases, these changes will be the same ones that reduce waste, save energy, conserve resources, and promote healthy physical exercise.

Ian Dick, John McGowan, Pamela Meneguzzi, and John Swaigen

FURTHER READING

Canada Air Pollution Control Directorate, "Annual Summary: National Air Pollution Surveillance," in the series *Environmental Protection Service Report Series* (Ottawa: Air Pollution Control Directorate, 1970).

William U. Chandler, ed., *Carbon Emissions: Control Strategies* (Washington, DC: World Wildlife Fund and The Conservation Foundation, 1990).

Janis Haliniak and Ellen Schwartzel, *Behind the Smoke-Screen: The State of Canada's Air* (Toronto: Pollution Probe, 1992).

J. Hillborn, *Canadian Perspectives on Air Pollution*, 1990, SOE Report no. 90-1 (Ottawa: Environment Canada, 1990).

Ross Howard and Michael Perley, *Poisoned Skies: Who'll Stop Acid Rain?* (Toronto: Stoddart, 1991).

Anthony M. Kosteltz and M. Delauriers, *Canadian Emissions Inventory of Common Air Contaminants* (1985), in the series Report EPS 5/AP (Ottawa: Conservation and Protection, Environment Canada, 1990).

Jeremy Leggett, ed., *Global Warming: The Greenpeace Report* (Oxford and New York: Oxford University Press, 1990).

M. Mellon and S. Garrod et al., *The Regulation of Toxic and Oxidant Air Pollution in North America* (Toronto: Canadian Environmental Law Research Foundation and Washington, DC: Environmental Law Institute, 1986).

Thomas B. Stoel Jr., Alan S. Miller, and Breck Milroy, *Fluorocarbon Regulation: An International Comparison* (Lexington, Mass. and Toronto: D.C. Heath and Co., 1980).

ENDNOTES

1   Canada, House of Commons, Standing Committee on Environment, *Deadly Releases — CFCs* (Ottawa: Queen's Printer, June 1990), 17.1.
2   International Joint Commission, *Air Quality in the Detroit – Windsor/Port Huron – Sarnia Region* (Windsor, Ont. and Detroit: IJC, February 1992).

3   For an excellent summary of the causes and effects of air pollution, see Environment Canada, *Canadian Perspectives on Air Pollution*, State of the Environment Report no. 90-1 (Ottawa: Environment Canada, September 1990).

4   Walter W. Heck et al., "Assessments of Crop Loss from Ozone" (1982), 26 *Journal of the Air Pollution Control Association* 325, cited in *Canadian Perspectives on Air Pollution*, supra endnote 3.

5   Québec, Ministère de l'Energie et des Resources, *Quebec's Forests: Another Victim of Atmospheric Pollution?* (Québec: MER, June 1989).

6   Canadian Council of Ministers of the Environment, *Management Plan for Nitrogen Oxides (NO_x) and Volatile Organic Compounds (VOC), Phase I* (Toronto: CCME, November 1990), foreword.

7   Much of the following discussion is adapted from *Canadian Perspectives on Air Pollution*, supra endnote 3, and Dennis M. Patroski and Julian R. Walker, *Air Quality in Canadian Urban Areas*, Discussion Paper 18 (Ottawa: Economic Council of Canada, 1974).

8   *Management Plan*, supra endnote 6.

9   *Canadian Perspectives on Air Pollution*, supra endnote 3, at 32.

10 Ibid., at 32.

11 Ibid., at 50.

12 Akin et al., "Identification of Polynuclear Aromatic Hydrocarbons in Cigarette Smoke and Their Importance as Tumorigens" (1976), 57 *Journal of the National Cancer Institute* 191.

13 S.A. Williams and A.L.C. deMestral, *An Introduction to International Law: Chiefly as Interpreted and Applied in Canada*, 2d ed. (Toronto: Butterworths, 1987), 36.

14 Environment Canada, *Did You Know We Live in a Greenhouse?* (Ottawa: Environment Canada, 1991) (brochure from Canada's Green Plan).

15 Ibid., at 100-10.

16 Peter Campbell, *Global Warming: Status of the Problems and Activities To Address It*, paper presented at Air and Water Management Association conference, October 5, 1992 (Toronto: Ministry of the Environment, 1992).

17 Federal-provincial agreements requiring SO_2 reductions were signed by Manitoba, Ontario, Quebec, New Brunswick, Nova Scotia, Prince Edward Island, and Newfoundland and Labrador. Each of the provinces committed to achieve specific reductions in SO_2 emissions by 1994. These programs are described in Environment Canada, *The Canadian Acid Rain Control Program* (pamphlet produced as part of the Green Plan) [undated], and in Environment Canada, *Report of the Special Committee on Acid Rain* (Ottawa: Environment Canada, September 1988).

18 *Report of the Special Committee on Acid Rain*, supra endnote 17, at 4.

19 Ibid., at 5.

20 Information from Michael Perley, manager of the Canadian Acid Precipitation Foundation.

21 Ibid.

22 See, for example, Martin Mittelstaedt, "Hydro Considers Stalling Manitoba Power Purchase," *The Globe and Mail*, September 21, 1992, and comments from Michael Perley.

23 Boiler Regulation, RRO 1990, reg. 338, formerly O. reg. 16/86.

24 *Clean Air Act*, 42 USC §§ 7401-7626.

25 Environment Canada, *Canada's Green Plan* (Ottawa: Supply and Services, 1990), 120.

26 Agreement Between the Government of Canada and the Government of the United States of America on Air Quality (Acid Rain Treaty), (1991), CTS 3; (1991), 30 ILM 678, in force March 13, 1991.

27 "The Canadian Acid Rain Control Program."

28 Boiler Regulation, supra endnote 23, at 10.

29 Ibid., at 9.

30 Ibid., at 11; and Martin Mittelstaedt, "New Process Sidesteps Ozone-Eating Chemical," *The Globe and Mail*, January 10, 1992.

31 (1991), 30 ILM 539.

32 "Federal, Provincial Environment Ministers Agree on Accelerated Phaseout Date for CFCs" (April 1992), vol 2, no. 13 *Environment Policy and Law* 391.

33 Canada, *News Release*, "Canada First To Ratify Amendments to the Montreal Protocol," June 28, 1990.

34 Environment Canada, "Canada's Ozone Layer Protection Program — A Summary Report," June 1992.

35 *Deadly Releases — CFCs*, supra endnote 1, at 17.

36 Ibid.

37 (1987), 26 ILM 1516; United Nations Environment Programme (UNEP), Conference Report, "Montreal Protocol on Substances that Deplete the Ozone Layer," 1987 Final Act, UNEP/IG 5313.

38 *Deadly Releases — CFCs*, supra endnote 1, at 10.

39 Ozone-Depleting Substances Regulations, no. 1 (chlorofluorocarbons), SOR/89-351, June 29, 1989; Ozone-Depleting Substances Regulations, no. 2 (certain bromofluorocarbons), SOR/90-583, August 28, 1990.

40 Ozone-Depleting Substances Regulations, no. 3 (products), SOR/90-584.

41 Ozone-Depleting Substances Regulations, no. 3 (products) — amendment, *Canada Gazette Part I*, November 16, 1991, 3743.

42 *Environmental Protection Act*, RSO 1990, c. E-19, sections 56-59.

43 Ibid.; O. reg 394/89, as amended by O. reg. 498/92.

44 Robert Williams, "Air Conditioning Expensive Pain for Auto Industry," *The Globe and Mail*, March 2, 1993.

45 D. Gourley, D. Cope, R. Solman, and V. Shantora, "A Report with Recommendations for the Reduction of Emissions from In-Use Light Duty Motor Vehicles," Industrial Programs Branch Report no. IP-34, cited in *Canadian Perspectives on Air Pollution*, supra endnote 3, at 75.

46 See Alastair R. Lucas, "Jurisdictional Disputes: Is Equivalency a Workable Solution?" in *Into the Future: Environmental Law and Policy for the 1990s* (Edmonton: Alberta Environmental Law Centre, 1990).

47 Published as Order in Council PC 1989-1482, *Canada Gazette Part I*, August 12, 1989, 3642, pursuant to section 8(1) of the *Canadian Environmental Protection Act*, RSC 1985, c. 16 (4th Supp.), first enacted as SC 1988, c. 22.

48 Environment Canada, *National Urban Air Quality Trends — 1978 to 1987*, Report EPS 7/UP/3 (Ottawa: Environment Canada, May 1990); Environment Canada, *National*

Air Pollution Surveillance (NAPS), Annual Summary 1990 (Ottawa: Environment Canada, April 1992), table 1, 71ff.

49 *Canadian Environmental Protection Act*, supra endnote 47, Secondary Lead Smelter Release Regulations, SOR/91-155.

50 Ibid., Chlor-Alkali Mercury Release Regulations, SOR/90-130. A chlor-alkali plant bleaches the pulp that is made into paper. It may be part of a pulp and paper mill, or a separate operation.

51 Ibid., Asbestos Mines and Mills Release Regulations, SOR/90-341.

52 Ibid., Vinyl Chloride Release Regulations, 1992, SOR/92-631, replacing SOR/90-125.

53 Ibid., Gasoline Regulations, SOR/90-247.

54 Ibid., Lead-Free Gasoline Regulations, CRC, c. 408, and Leaded Gasoline Regulations, CRC, c. 409.

55 Marcus C.B. Hotz, *Alternatives to Lead in Gasoline* (Ottawa: Royal Society of Canada, 1986).

56 *Canadian Environmental Protection Act*, supra endnote 47, Contaminated Fuel Regulations, SOR/91-486.

57 Ibid., Contaminated Fuel Regulations, *Canada Gazette Part II*, vol. 125, no. 11, 882.

58 *Transportation of Dangerous Goods Act*, RSC 1985, c. T-19.

59 *Canadian Environmental Protection Act*, supra endnote 47, Federal Mobile PCB Treatment and Destruction Regulations, SOR/90-5.

60 Ibid., PCB Waste Export Regulations, SOR/90-453.

61 Ibid., Storage of PCB Wastes Interim Order, issued September 16, 1988, approved by Cabinet September 20, 1988, amended February 20, 1989, further amended by Storage of PCB Wastes Interim Order — Amendment, *Canada Gazette Part I*, May 13, 1989, 2355; reissued as Interim Order Respecting the Storage of Wastes Containing Chlorobyphenyls (PCBs), *Canada Gazette Part I*, September 18, 1990, 1, also *Canada Gazette Part I*, September 22, 1990, 3470 and *Canada Gazette Part I*, October 13, 1990, 3640 (Cabinet approval).

62 Ibid., Storage of PCB Material Regulations, SOR/92-507, August 27, 1992, published in the *Canada Gazette Part II*, vol. 126, no. 19, September 9, 1992.

63 Ibid. The circumstances under which a notice of objection may be filed and a board of review established, and the powers and procedures of a board of review, are set out in sections 89 to 96 of the *Canadian Environmental Protection Act*.

64 *Motor Vehicle Safety Act*, RSC 1985, c. M-10.

65 Motor Vehicle Safety Regulations, CRC, c. 1038, as amended.

66 *Motor Vehicle Safety Act*, supra endnote 64, section 1103.

67 Ibid., section 1104.

68 Ibid., section 1105.

69 Motor Vehicle Safety Regulations, amendment, SOR/87-334.

70 US *Clean Air Act*, supra endnote 24.

71 The intention of the ministers of transport and the environment to introduce regulations that reduce emissions to the level of the California standards — the most stringent in the United States — was published in the *Canada Gazette Part I*, February 17, 1990, 560.

72 See the testimony of Michael Perley before the Canadian Senate Committee on Legal and Constitutional Affairs, June 8, 1992.

73 Ibid.
74 *Criminal Code*, RSC 1985, c. C-46.
75 *Canada Shipping Act*, RSC 1985, c. S-9, Air Pollution Regulations, c. 1404; formerly SOR/64-97, as amended by SOR/66-181 and SOR/67-44.
76 Ibid.
77 Air Pollution and Smoke Control Regulations, c. 1143, general order no. O-26 of the former Canadian Transport Commission, February 1965, as amended by order no. R-751, December 5, 1967.
78 *Railway Act*, RSC 1985, c. R-3.
79 *National Transportation Act*, RSC 1985, c. N-20.01.
80 *Weather Modification Information Act*, RSC 1985, c. W-5.
81 Agreement Between Canada and the United States Relating to the Exchange of Information on Weather Modification Activities, March 26, 1975.
82 *Environmental Assessment Act*, RSO 1990, c. E.18.
83 *Environmental Protection Act*, supra endnote 42.
84 *Motor Vehicle Safety Act*, supra endnote 64; RRO 1990, reg. 353.
85 This information was provided by an official of the Ministry of the Environment on September 25, 1992.
86 *Environmental Protection Act*, supra endnote 42, Ambient Air Quality Criteria, RRO 1990, reg. 337.
87 *Environmental Protection Act*, supra endnote 42, RRO 1990, reg. 346.
88 Ibid., section 3.
89 Ibid., section 4.
90 Ibid., section 9.
91 Ibid., section 10.
92 Ibid., section 11.
93 Ibid., section 12.
94 Ibid., section 13.
95 *Environmental Protection Act*, supra endnote 42, Air Contaminants from Ferrous Foundries, RRO 1990, reg. 336.
96 *Environmental Protection Act*, supra endnote 42, Hot Mix Asphalt Regulation, RRO 1990, reg 349, formerly reg. 469/87.
97 *Environmental Protection Act*, supra endnote 42, Hot Mix Asphalt Regulation, RRO 1980, reg. 297, originally O. reg. 183/72.
98 O. reg. 555/92.
99 Jock Ferguson, "Toxics Linked to Waste Burning," *The Globe and Mail*, February 15, 1993.
100 *Environmental Protection Act*, supra endnote 42, RRO 1990, reg 361, originally O. reg. 374/70 under the *Air Pollution Control Act*, 1967.
101 *Environmental Protection Act*, supra endnote 42, Gasoline Volatility Regulation, O. reg. 231/90.
102 Ibid. There had also been an earlier gas volatility regulation covering the summer of 1989: O. reg. 389/89.
103 Jim Bradley, Minister of the Environment, "Notes for Remarks to Shell Canada Products Ltd. Senior Managers Meeting," September 19, 1989, 9, 10.

104 Ibid.

105 *Environmental Protection Act*, supra endnote 42, Gasoline Volatility Regulation, O. reg. 271/91.

106 Letter, Jonathan Greenbaum, Communications Branch, Ontario Ministry of the Environment to Deborah Curran, CIELAP, July 5, 1990.

107 "Control of Emissions During the Distribution of Vehicle Fuels," draft regulation under section 136 of the *Environmental Protection Act*, supra endnote 42.

108 *Management Plan*, supra endnote 6, at 110, 118, and 119.

109 *Highway Traffic Act*, RSO 1990, c. H.8.

110 Ontario, Ministry of the Environment, *Air Quality in Ontario: Annual Report/Ontario* (Toronto: the ministry, 1990).

111 Ibid.

112 *Municipal Act*, RSO 1990, c. M.45, section 210, paragraph 44.

113 For example, see the reports of the Special Advisory Committee on the Environment to the Council of the City of Toronto, discussing ways the city government can act to control greenhouse gases: report no. 1, October 30, 1989, *The Changing Atmosphere: A Call to Action*; report no. 2, March 1991, *The Changing Atmosphere: Strategies for Reducing CO_2 Emissions* (2 vols.).

114 City of Toronto bylaw no. 176-92.

115 City of Toronto bylaw no. 549-90.

116 There have been various estimates and studies suggesting that the indoor air may be up to 100 times more polluted than outdoor air. One recent study found the levels of VOCs in Toronto buildings to be 2 to 5 times higher than outdoors: Ontario, Ministry of the Environment, *The 1990 Toronto Personal Exposure Pilot (PEP) Study* (Toronto: the ministry, July 1991).

117 For more information about "sick building syndrome," in addition to the works cited below, see Shor et al., "The 'Sick' Building Syndrome in the Office Environment: The Danish Town Hall Study" (1987), 13 *Environment International* 337; Jeanne Stellman and Mary Sue Henifin, *Office Work Can Be Dangerous to Your Health* (New York: Pantheon Books, 1983).

118 See, for example, Rudy Platiel, "Mystery Contaminant Blamed for '9 Months of Hell' in Home," *The Globe and Mail*, February 22, 1982; Steve Wilkinson, "Officials, Couple Clash over Illness," *Peterborough Examiner*, July 29, 1992; John Spears, "'Sick' Hospital Air a National Problem, Halifax Doctor Says," *The Toronto Star*, December 14, 1991; Peter Gorrie, "Institute's Bad Air Forces Outdoor Class," *The Toronto Star*, October 25, 1990; "Prof Protests Toxic Air at OISE," *NOW Magazine*, October 24-30, 1991, 17.

119 Canada Mortgage and Housing Corporation, *Indoor Air Pollution and Housing Technology*, Research Report (Ottawa: CMHC, August 1983).

120 See Federal-Provincial Advisory Committee on Environmental and Occupational Health, *Exposure Guidelines for Residential Indoor Air Quality* (Ottawa: Health and Welfare Canada, April 1987).

121 Canada, Department of National Health and Welfare, *Guidelines for Indoor Air Quality* (Ottawa: Supply and Services, 1989).

122 Belva Spiel, a Toronto lawyer, recounted her efforts to convince the Ontario Ministry of Labour to investigate the air in an office building where many of the tenants were

becoming ill, on the CBC radio program "Ideas" on March 14, 1988. A transcript of that program is available from CBC Transcripts, PO Box 6440, Station "A," Montreal, Quebec H3C 3L4.

123 See, for example, letter from James L. Repace to Garfield Mahood, executive director, Non-Smokers' Rights Association, May 2, 1990, in which Mr. Repace, an expert on tobacco smoke and ventilation, claims that the Ontario Ministry of Labour's measurements found no tobacco smoke in certain indoor areas because the ministry was using "antiquated equipment" not suited for that purpose. This correspondence is found in *The Real Guide to Ontario's Workplace Smoking Law*, available from the Non-Smokers' Rights Association, Suite 308, 344 Bloor Street West, Toronto, Ontario M5S 3A7.

124 For more information about the regulation of tobacco smoke, see Michael Grossman and Philip Price, *Tobacco Smoking and the Law in Canada* (Markham, Ont. and Vancouver: Butterworths, 1992).

125 City of Toronto bylaw no. 406-79.

126 City of Toronto bylaw no. 23-88.

127 *Non-Smokers' Health Act*, RSC 1985, c. N-23.6

128 *Canada Labour Code*, RSC 1985, c. L-2.

129 *Smoking in the Workplace Act*, RSO 1990, c. S.13.

130 City of Toronto bylaw no. 643-91.

131 Metropolitan Toronto bylaw no. 20-85, as amended, section 2(13).

132 Ibid., schedule 8, section 44(1).

133 *Tobacco Tax Act*, RSO 1990, c. T.10.

134 *Tobacco Restraint Act*, RSC 1985, c. T-12.

135 *Tobacco Products Control Act*, RSC 1985, c. T-11.7 (RSC 1985, c. 14, 4th Supp.).

136 *R.J.R. MacDonald Inc. v Canada (Attorney General)* (1991), 82 DLR (4th) 449, 28 ACWS (3d) 178 (Que. SC). An appeal to the Quebec Court of Appeal was successful in upholding the validity of the law in January 1993.

137 Odour and particulates have also been described by the City of Toronto Planning and Development Department as the major sources of pollution in the city: City of Toronto Planning and Development Department, *The City's Air Quality*, research bulletin no. 22, June 1983.

138 *Municipal Act*, supra endnote 112, section 210, paragraphs 51, 134, 140, and 162.

139 *Ontario Water Resources Act*, RSO 1990, c. O.40, section 59.

140 Ibid., section 57.

141 *Farm Practices Protection Act*, RSO 1990, c. F.6.

142 For a critique of this legislation, see John Swaigen, "The Right-To-Farm Movement and Environmental Protection" (1990), 4 CELR (NS) 121.

143 *Health Protection and Promotion Act*, RSO 1990, c. H.7.

144 Ontario, Ministry of the Environment, *Air Quality in Ontario, 1988* (Toronto: Queen's Printer, 1990).

145 Marilyn Dunlop, "Acid Air a Threat to Health, Report Says," *The Toronto Star*, May 25, 1990.

146 "Emissions Predicted To Rise 80% by 2020," *The Ottawa Citizen*, April 9, 1992.

147 See, for example, Environment Canada, *Ambient Air Concentrations of Volatile Organic Compounds in Toronto and Montreal* [undated]. According to this report,

over 50 VOCs were detected over both cities in 1984 and 1985; International Joint Commission, supra endnote 2. Fifteen carcinogens were detected in the air in the Windsor – Sarnia area.

148 "Aircraft Pollution Targeted," *The Globe and Mail*, August 26, 1991.

149 The reason these devices cause as much pollution as a car is that modern cars are equipped with pollution control devices and this equipment is not. The US Environmental Protection Agency announced a program in August 1992 to begin cleaning up various off-road engines. See Matthew Wald, "Lawn Mower Is New Target in War Against Air Pollution," *The New York Times*, August 6, 1992.

150 Ontario, Ministry of the Environment, "Air Pollution — The Environment General Regulation (Regulation 308)," November 1987.

151 Telephone conversation with the Ontario Ministry of Environment and Energy in February 1993.

18

Water

CONTENTS

The maker of titanium dioxide pigment, used in the production of paints and plastics, dumps on an average day 127 tonnes of sulphuric acid, 8.4 tonnes of iron, 4.5 tonnes of suspended solids, 1.5 tonnes of titanium and 1.3 tonnes of aluminum into the river.

[A second company] dumps 178 tonnes of sulphuric acid, 12.4 tonnes of iron, five tonnes of suspended solids and two tonnes of aluminum ... each day.

Andre Picard, "Plant To Shut Down for Ignoring Clean-Up Orders,"
The Globe and Mail, May 30, 1992

INTRODUCTION

This story does not refer to the conditions in a developing nation. It describes industrial discharges to Canada's St. Lawrence River in 1991. However, industry alone is not at fault. The city of Montreal dumps untreated sewage into the Des Prairies River, which empties into the St. Lawrence. Other major Canadian cities, including Halifax and Victoria, continue to dump untreated sewage into the ocean and into our lakes and rivers. Despite the extensive efforts that have been made since the 1950s and 1960s in Canada to address water pollution, the situation remains serious. When marathon swimmer Vicki Keith tried to swim the circumference of Lake Ontario in 1990, the water pollution made her so sick she had to quit. The bodies of Beluga whales found dead along the St. Lawrence in the late 1980s were so heavily contaminated with DDT, Mirex, PCBs, lead, and mercury that they had to be disposed of as hazardous waste. In 1990, Ontario's Ministry of the Environment recorded 5,686 spills, one-third of which were into waterways. A 1991 survey of rural drinking water wells across

Ontario found 37 per cent of them exceeded provincial drinking water standards for either nitrate, which causes "blue baby" syndrome, or faecal coliform bacteria, an indicator of pathogens that may cause serious digestive tract disorders.

In this chapter, we will look at the management of Ontario's water resources. The primary emphasis will be on control of water pollution. However, we will also discuss physical alterations to bodies of water, such as the construction of docks, wharves, and piers, and the dredging and filling of waterbodies; and issues involving how water is allocated, such as the damming and diversion of lakes and rivers, the sale of water, and water conservation. Water is one of the most difficult issues to address, since all life on this planet depends on water and all human activities affect water. The availability and distribution of water influence the earth's climate and topography and the distribution of plant and animal life, as well as patterns of human settlement. Although we will isolate the two issues for convenience, water resources management and water pollution are inextricably linked. One example of this relationship is the pollution unleashed by the creation of hydroelectric dams. As Environment Canada has noted, "capturing huge volumes of water behind hydroelectric dams has led to elevated levels of mercury in aquatic and terrestrial organisms, in and near the flooded area."[1]

All three levels of government have responsibilities in the management of Canada's water resources. Efforts to address water pollution and water resources management problems by the federal, provincial, and municipal governments in Ontario have occurred in three distinct phases. During the first period, extending from the time of Confederation until the mid-1950s, municipal governments were granted responsibility for water quality as an extension of their public health functions. In addition, legislation was put in place by the federal and provincial governments to prevent activities that interfered with navigation or the use of waterways to transport logs, and to protect fisheries. The primary purpose of most of these statutes was to facilitate economic development rather than to protect the environment, and in some cases they limited the common law rights of riparian landowners.

In the second phase, running from the mid-1950s to the mid-1980s, governments began to undertake efforts to repair environmental damage and to limit the environmental effects of new projects. Environmental protection legislation was enacted for the purposes of abating existing pollution and reducing the discharges of contaminants to water. This was in response to the emergence of an extensive body of information regarding the degree and costs of the environmental degradation caused by industrial activities.

However, the implementation of these new statutes was frequently characterized by close, "accommodative" relations between the regulated industries and governments at both the federal and provincial levels. This pattern was especially significant with respect to the setting of standards and environmental law enforcement. The resulting standards, and efforts to achieve compliance with them, were widely regarded as inadequate.[2] Governments and industry continued to regard environmental protection measures as involving substantial costs in terms of lost efficiencies in the use of resources, but bringing only marginal economic returns. Economic prosperity and environmental protection were considered conflicting goals rather than mutually dependent ones.

In the third phase, which began in Ontario during the minority Liberal government period of 1985 to 1987, there has been a shift toward more stringent and less flexible standards, and an emphasis on a "prosecutorial" approach to environmental law enforcement. This has been particularly evident in the province's Municipal-Industrial Strategy for Abatement (MISA) program and in the activities of the Investigations and Enforcement Branch of the Ministry of Environment and Energy. There has also been an increasing focus on water resources conservation at both the federal and provincial levels. These changes in strategy have been the result of a growing recognition of the extent of the hidden costs to present and future generations of continuing pollution, and of the failure of past approaches to address the problem successfully.

CONSTITUTIONAL JURISDICTION OVER WATER RESOURCES MANAGEMENT AND WATER POLLUTION CONTROL IN CANADA

The *British North America Act* of 1867 (renamed the *Constitution Act, 1867*) granted the provinces a number of sources of legislative authority over water use and quality. Among the most important foundations of provincial power was section 109 of the Act, which gave the provinces jurisdiction over natural resources. This component was reinforced in 1982 through the addition of section 92A to the *Constitution Act*. This section assigned the provinces exclusive jurisdiction over the development, conservation, and management of non-renewable resources, as well as forestry resources and hydroelectric sites and facilities.

In addition, through section 92 of the *Constitution Act*, the provinces have jurisdiction over local works and undertakings,[3] property and civil rights,[4] and all matters of a local and private nature.[5] The provinces also have authority over municipal institutions.[6] This combination of powers has left provincial governments as the primary owners of water resources within Canada, and with much of the responsibility for their protection and management.

However, provincial jurisdiction over water resources is not exclusive. Several sources of federal authority over different aspects of water resources management can be found in the *Constitution Act* as well. Among the enumerated federal powers in section 91 of the Act, section 91(12), which establishes federal jurisdiction over seacoasts and inland fisheries, is the most important source of federal authority over matters related to water. This power has been interpreted to permit Parliament to protect "waters in which fish spawn or live, and this includes the regulation of on-shore activities that would pollute fish habits."[7] The fisheries power has provided the basis for the enactment of the federal *Fisheries Act*.[8]

At the same time, a number of court decisions have closely circumscribed the ability of the federal government to use its fisheries responsibilities to protect the wider environment. For the fisheries power to be employed, there must be a clear connection between the activity that is being prohibited by the federal legislation made under it and possible damage to fisheries. If the restrictions placed on an activity are more extensive than those needed to protect fish or fish habitat, the legislation is unlikely to be upheld by the courts.[9]

Section 91(10) of the *Constitution Act* provides for federal jurisdiction over navigation and shipping. This power may be employed to protect the integrity of navigable waterways. This is particularly important in that it provides a means by which the federal government may intervene when a province proposes to construct a structure, such as a dam, that may interfere with navigation. The test for navigability, as it currently stands, is whether the body of water in question is capable of being used by vessels (even canoes) or to float objects (such as logs) for the purposes of transportation, recreation, or commerce.[10] It does not matter whether the water body is tidal or non-tidal. Freshwater lakes and rivers can be considered navigable as well as coastal waters.

The navigable waters power has become particularly important in the light of the Supreme Court of Canada's *Oldman River* decision of January 1992.[11] This decision affirmed that the federal environmental assessment and review process (EARP) applies to provincially initiated undertakings requiring formal federal approvals, such as those provided for under the *Navigable Waters Protection Act*.[12] The right of the federal government to halt provincial undertakings interfering with navigable waterways was also confirmed.

Federal jurisdiction over harbours is provided through the federal Parliament's responsibility for public debt and property.[13] Federal harbour commissions have been created in most major Canadian ports. However, federal jurisdiction over harbour waters is not unlimited. Provinces and municipalities may enact measures regulating the use of harbours, as long as their statutes or bylaws do not interfere with navigation and shipping activities.[14]

The federal trade and commerce power[15] permits Parliament to regulate interprovincial and international trade and commerce. This power might be employed to assert federal control over such activities as the export of fresh water or hydroelectric power. The federal taxation power[16] may permit the federal government to employ such instruments as effluent taxes or tax credits for pollution-control equipment to promote the conservation and protection of water resources. The federal government's jurisdiction over criminal law[17] matters may also provide a foundation for some federal action in the environmental field.

In addition to these enumerated powers, the *Constitution Act* grants the federal government a residual power to legislate for the "peace, order, and good government" (POGG) of Canada. This is potentially the most important and far-reaching source of federal power to take legislative action to protect the environment. The "national concern" branch of the POGG power is particularly significant in this sense. The "national concern" doctrine dictates that even if a problem would normally come under provincial jurisdiction, the federal government can step in to regulate it if the problem has become so serious or widespread that it is of national concern. In its 1988 *Crown Zellerbach* decision,[18] which upheld the application of the former federal *Ocean Dumping Control Act*[19] to waters within the boundaries of a province, a majority of the Supreme Court of Canada defined the national concern test in terms of three key elements: the power can only apply to matters not existing at the time of Confederation, or to matters that were originally of a local and private nature, but that have since become matters of national significance. In addition, for a matter to fall under the national concerns doctrine, it must have a singleness, distinctiveness, and indivisibility that clearly separates it from matters of provincial concern, such that it will have an impact on provincial jurisdiction that is reconcilable with the division of powers. Finally, the effects on extraprovincial interests of a provincial failure to deal effectively with the intraprovincial aspects of the issue must be considered. This is often referred to as the "provincial inability test." The national concern test has been employed by the federal government to justify elements of the *Canadian Environmental Protection Act*,[20] and could be of enormous importance in the environmental field in the future.

The federal government's treaty-making power (section 132) also may be a significant source of federal jurisdictional capacity over environmental matters. It is especially relevant with respect to the management of boundary waters shared with the United States, particularly the Great Lakes. However, case law interpretation of the federal treaty power has left doubt as to whether the Canadian government can unilaterally implement, through national treaty obligations, requirements that fall under provincial heads of power without the consent of the affected provinces.[21]

THE FEDERAL LEGISLATIVE FRAMEWORK

The Fisheries Act

The federal *Fisheries Act* was first enacted in 1868. It is potentially the federal government's most powerful weapon for protecting the aquatic environment. Section 35(1) of the Act makes it an offence for any person to "carry on any work or undertaking that results in the harmful alteration, disruption or destruction of fish habitat." Section 36(3) prohibits persons from depositing, or permitting the deposit, of deleterious substances into waters frequented by fish, unless the deposits are of a type, quality, or concentration authorized by a regulation. This prohibition has proved very effective in prosecuting polluters. This has been a result of the courts holding that it is sufficient to prove that a substance is of a kind that can harm fish, without proof that the amount of the substance found in the water would actually cause harm.[22]

Deleterious substances have been defined as any substances that, if added to water, would degrade or alter the quality of the water so that it is rendered deleterious to fish or fish habitat, or to the use by man of fish that frequent the water. Bunker oil,[23] ammonia,[24] sewage,[25] gravel,[26] wood preservatives composed of tetrachlorophenol and pentachlorophenol,[27] and diesel fuel[28] have all been defined by the courts to be deleterious substances. Convictions have occurred under the Act in cases where substances have not been directly deposited into the waters frequented by fish, but rather in places where they might enter such waters.[29]

A due diligence defence is set out in section 41(3) of the Act.

In 1991, the Act was amended to increase the penalties available for violations of either its fish habitat or deleterious substances deposit provisions. First offenders are now punishable on summary conviction by fines of up to $300,000. Subsequent offences may lead to fines of up to $300,000 and up to six months' imprisonment. The maximum penalties on indictment would be up to $1,000,000 for first offences, and $1,000,000 plus up to three years' imprisonment for subsequent offences.

Section 38(4) of the Act imposes a duty to report a deposit of a deleterious substance, or a serious and imminent danger of such a deposit, to an inspector or other authority as prescribed in regulations made under the Act. In such a situation, all reasonable measures must be taken to conserve fish. Section 49 of the Act empowers a fisheries officer to search premises in the event that he or she has reasonable grounds to believe that a provision of the Act has been contravened.

One-half of any fine imposed under the *Fisheries Act* as a result of a private prosecution is to be paid to the private prosecutor according to section 5 of the Penalties and Forfeiture Proceeds Regulation made under the Act. The Act also provides that any person involved in the depositing of a deleterious substance is liable for any costs incurred by the government in taking measures to remedy the adverse effects of the deposit.

Six effluent regulations were promulgated under the Act between 1971 and 1977. They imposed limits on the contents of discharges from pulp and paper mills,[30] petroleum refineries,[31] chlor-alkali plants,[32] meat and poultry plants,[33] metal mining operations,[34] and potato-processing plants.[35] The requirements of these regulations were determined through closed negotiations between Environment Canada, the provinces, and the affected industries. The resulting effluent standards were widely regarded to be very weak.[36] Furthermore, the regulations only affected facilities constructed after their promulgation.[37] It also should be noted that the effect of the implementation of these regulations was to authorize the deposit of substances into waters frequented by fish which otherwise would have been prohibited by the general offence provisions under the *Fisheries Act.*

In January 1990 the federal minister of the environment, then Lucien Bouchard, promised amendments to the *Fisheries Act* regulations to limit acutely lethal discharges, total biological oxygen demand (BOD), and total suspended solids from pulp and paper mills. This commitment was reiterated in the federal Green Plan of December 1990.[38] However, these proposed measures were resisted strongly by the pulp and paper industry. As a result, their implementation was delayed until June 1992.[39]

Under the new regulations, made under the *Canadian Environmental Protection Act*, all mills using chlorine for bleaching are required to ensure that dioxins and furans in their effluent are below detectable levels by January 1994.[40] In addition, the regulatory limits for suspended solids and biological oxygen demand contained in the 1971 regulations were tightened and applied to all Canadian pulp mills, including those constructed after 1971.[41] These requirements are to be met by December 1993.

The Green Plan also promised the updating and strengthening of the *Fisheries Act* regulations limiting metal mining liquid effluent. Reports outlining options for controlling these pollution sources, which will be used to develop the new regulations, are expected to be completed by 1994.[42] However, the mining industry has argued that it cannot afford to comply with more stringent environmental regulations. It is not clear how the federal government will respond to this position or, consequently, when the new regulations can be expected to be in place.

Enforcement of the federal *Fisheries Act* has been inconsistent and sporadic. Responsibility for the enforcement of the Act's pollution-control provisions has been divided, and in some cases shared, between Environment Canada and the Department of Fisheries and Oceans.[43] In addition, in the mid-1970s principal enforcement responsibility for the Act was assigned to the provinces through a series of agreements negotiated between the federal government and most of the provincial governments.[44] Before the negotiation of these agreements, there had been occasional federal enforcement "incursions" at odds with provincial activity.[45] After the implementation of the accords, federal prosecutions in many regions tapered off to near insignificance, as the environmental law enforcement function was consolidated at the provincial level.[46]

Despite the existence of these enforcement agreements, many provinces have been unwilling to pursue prosecutions under the federal *Fisheries Act* as a result of fears that this would reinforce federal jurisdictional claims in the environmental field. Rather, the provinces have preferred to address water pollution through their own statutes. Ontario's agreement with the federal government regarding *Fisheries Act* enforcement was most recently renegotiated in 1989. It establishes the Ontario Ministry of Natural Resources as the lead enforcer of the Act in the province. However, most water pollution prosecutions are carried out by the Ministry of Environment and Energy, using the provincial *Ontario Water*

Resources Act. In the hands of the ministry's experienced prosecutors and investigators, the *Ontario Water Resources Act* has proven to be as effective a tool as the *Fisheries Act*, particularly since the fines under the *Ontario Water Resources Act* were raised in 1987 to levels similar to those under the *Fisheries Act*.

The Canada Water Act

The *Canada Water Act* of 1970 authorized research and the planning and implementation of programs for the conservation, development, and use of water resources by the federal government.[47] The Act was also designed to encourage federal-provincial cooperation in the establishment of basin-wide water quality management areas.[48] The Act authorized unilateral federal action in relation to boundary and interprovincial waters if the quality of those waters was of national concern.[49] The federal Cabinet was permitted to make regulations regarding the types and quantities of wastes that could be deposited in waters regulated by the Act and the conditions under which wastes could be discharged.[50] In particular, under part III of the Act, the manufacturing for use or sale in Canada of any cleaning agent or water conditioner containing nutrients, prescribed in regulations made under the Act, in greater concentrations than those set in the regulations was prohibited. The Phosphorous Concentration Control Regulations made under this provision were most recently updated in May 1985. Provision also was made in the Act for the application of experimental regulatory arrangements and instruments such as effluent fees.[51]

Part III of the *Canada Water Act* was incorporated into the *Canadian Environmental Protection Act* of 1988. The other elements of the *Canada Water Act* remain in force. However, these provisions have been employed only once to provide the basis for a federal-provincial or interprovincial water resources management agreement.

The Navigable Waters Protection Act

Under the *Navigable Waters Protection Act*, any person wishing to construct anything that might affect navigable waters (such as a bridge or a dam) must receive approval from the federal minister of transport.[52] The Act also contains prohibitions against depositing sawdust, edgings, slabs, bark, or any similar rubbish that might interfere with navigation into navigable waterways.[53] In addition, throwing or depositing stone, gravel, earth, cinders, ashes, or other materials into waters less than 20 fathoms deep is forbidden.[54] The contravention of these provisions may lead to the imposition of fines not to exceed $5,000.[55]

This somewhat obscure statute has recently emerged as being of critical importance for environmental protection. This has been a consequence of its formal approval mechanism, which may trigger the federal environmental assessment (EA) process. This is especially significant in the light of the Supreme Court of Canada's decision regarding the environmental assessment of the Alberta government's Oldman River Dam Project. The Act's approval provisions provide a means for the federal government to conduct environmental assessments of provincially initiated undertakings and, ultimately, to prevent them from proceeding. Indeed, it was the requirement for federal approvals under section 5 of the *Navigable Waters Protection Act* that provided the basis of the Friends of the Oldman River Society's case regarding the Oldman Dam.

The International River Improvements Act

The *International River Improvements Act* seeks to regulate the construction, operation, and maintenance of international river "improvements" such as dams and diversions. The Act prohibits the construction, operation, and maintenance of international river improvements without first obtaining a licence from the federal minister of transport.[56] As is the case with the *Navigable Waters Protection Act*, this licensing provision has recently gained enormous environmental significance, since it may also trigger the federal EA process, and provide a means for the federal government to halt provincially initiated undertakings.

In the celebrated cases resulting from the Rafferty-Alameda dam project in southern Saskatchewan, the Federal Court of Appeal held that the federal EARP guidelines order must be applied to that project as a result of the federal licensing power under the Act.[57] The general application of this finding to other federal licences was affirmed by the Supreme Court's *Oldman River* decision.

The Canada Shipping Act

The *Canada Shipping Act*[58] is administered by the federal Department of Transport. Vessels engaging in interprovincial or international shipping in Canadian waters, including the Great Lakes, are subject to its requirements. Part XV of the Act is entitled "Pollution." It makes any person or ship that discharges any pollutant prescribed in regulations made under section 656 of the Act liable for a fine of up to $250,000.[59] A "pollutant" is defined broadly under the Act to include any substance or water that, if added to the waters that the ship is in, will degrade or alter the quality of those waters in a way that is detrimental to their use either by any man or by any animal, fish, or plant that is useful to man.[60] Crude oil, fuel oil, diesel oil, lubricating oil, and other persistent oils are specifically included in the definition of pollutants.[61] Pollutants are further defined through the Garbage Pollution Prevention Regulations,[62] the Oil Pollution Prevention Regulations,[63] the Air Pollution Regulations,[64] and the Pollutant Substances Regulations[65] made under the Act. Notwithstanding these provisions, discharges of pollutants are permitted if they are done in accordance with a permit issued under the former *Ocean Dumping Control Act*[66] (now the *Canadian Environmental Protection Act*).

Any ship with the imminent potential for a grave discharge of pollutants may be ordered to clean up, control, or contain the potential pollutant. Transport Canada pollution prevention officers are given substantial powers to board and inspect a ship, and to order it to leave Canadian waters.[67] Ignoring the orders of a pollution prevention officer can lead to fines of up to $200,000.[68]

This part of the Act also broadens civil liability and compensation for pollution. Under these provisions, the owner of a ship is liable for any oil damage caused by discharges from the ship.[69] The owner can also be held responsible for the spill clean-up costs incurred by Canadian public authorities and any damage or loss flowing from the clean-up.[70] The minister of transport has the power to take any measures that he or she may deem necessary if a ship has discharged, is discharging, or is likely to discharge a pollutant.[71] This may include repairing or moving the ship, selling it, or destroying the ship and its contents. The owners are liable for any costs involved in taking these steps.[72]

This part of the Act also creates the Maritime Pollution Claims Fund. Fishermen and other victims of spills or discharges of oil or other pollutants in bulk can obtain compensation from this fund. Government agencies can also recover their clean-up costs from the fund. The owners of ships carrying bulk oil into Canada and the owners of the cargos must pay 15 cents a ton into the fund every time a cargo of oil enters Canada.

The Canadian Environmental Protection Act

The *Canadian Environmental Protection Act (CEPA)* was enacted in June 1988. This legislation consolidated several existing statutes, including part III of the *Canada Water Act*, the *Ocean Dumping Control Act*, the *Clean Air Act*, and the *Environmental Contaminants Act*. The *Canadian Environmental Protection Act* takes an ecosystem approach to regulation; that is, it attempts to control the release of toxic contaminants throughout the environment, rather than dealing with water, air, and land pollution separately. The Act seeks to provide for regulatory control over the entire life cycle of toxic substances, from their development and manufacture, through the stages of transport, distribution, use, and storage, to their ultimate disposal. It also introduces the possibility of national standards regarding the environmental regulation of toxic substances. However, federal regulations established under the *Canadian Environmental Protection Act* will not apply in provinces that develop and implement "equivalent" standards under their own environmental statutes. As demonstrated by the new Pulp and Paper Mill Regulations of June 1992, the Act could ultimately have a significant impact on water pollution by limiting the disposal options available for toxic chemicals.

The Canadian Environmental Assessment Act

The *Canadian Environmental Assessment Act*, enacted in June 1992, superseded the federal EARP guidelines order of 1984. The degree to which the Act will be applied to water-related undertakings remains unclear. The federal government has indicated that major hydroelectric developments are to be subject to mandatory environmental assessment under the new Act. However, the regulations describing which classes of projects will be subject to review and which federal statutes would trigger the review process have yet to be promulgated. There has been very strong resistance from provincial governments, particularly those of Alberta and Quebec, to the concept of federal EA reviews of provincially initiated undertakings. This resulted in a two-year delay in passing the Act,[73] and is at least partially responsible for the continuing uncertainty regarding its ultimate application.

Legislation Regulating Harbours

As noted earlier, the federal government has jurisdiction over the management of harbours. However, the regulation of land use around harbours and ports is shared by the federal and provincial governments; and unless the federal government has "occupied the field" by passing land-use planning legislation governing the harbour, municipal zoning bylaws can apply to the use and development of harbour lands.[74] Most ports and harbours are administered by corporations or commissions created by federal legislation. They usually have both federal appointees and municipal representatives. As in the case of the Toronto Harbour Commission, at times the interests of these two factions may clash, creating significant conflicts.

Different kinds of harbours are administered by different agencies. The *Canada Ports Corporation Act*[75] (formerly the *National Harbours Board Act*) sets up an administrative structure for supervising the operation of some of the major commercial ports in Canada — Halifax, Saint John, Chicoutimi, Trois-Rivières, Montreal, and Vancouver. The Act establishes a central Canada Ports Corporation, whose members are required to be representative of national, regional, and local interests "essential to port activities." At the suggestion of the corporation, the federal minister of transport may also establish local port corporations to manage individual ports.[76] These local authorities are to be given "a high degree of autonomy for the management and operation of ports at which they are established, consistent with the authority of the Minister to ensure the integrity and efficiency of the national ports system and the optimal deployment of resources."[77]

Other major harbours, including those in Ontario, are operated by harbour commissions established under the *Harbour Commissions Act*.[78] These commissions also consist of both federal and local representatives and are guaranteed a high degree of autonomy under the Act.[79] Two Ontario harbours, Toronto and Hamilton, are governed by harbour commissions appointed under special Acts of Parliament, the *Toronto Harbour Commissioners Act, 1911*[80] and the *Hamilton Harbour Commissioners Act, 1912*.[81] In contrast, harbours, piers, wharves, breakwaters, slipways, marinas, and surrounding lands used primarily by fishing vessels and recreational boats are managed directly by the federal Department of Transport, unless another federal department has been designated by Cabinet, under the *Fishing and Recreational Harbours Act*.[82]

The *Public Harbours and Port Facilities Act*[83] (formerly the *Government Harbours and Piers Act*) declares that all port facilities constructed or acquired at public expense and all harbours owned by the federal government, other than those managed by harbour commissions, are to be under the control and management of the federal minister designated by Cabinet. In addition, Cabinet can declare ports and harbours to be "public." These areas and facilities then fall under the designated Cabinet minister's management and control.

What makes the ministers and harbour commissions that control ports and harbours so important in terms of water quality is their vast powers to manage not only the activities on the water but also on the land surrounding it. The commissions are usually given authority to make bylaws relating to the use of the harbour by boats, planes, and owners of adjacent lands. Such bylaws may regulate the excavation, removal, or deposit of material, and other actions that are likely to affect the harbour, its docks, piers, and wharves, and the adjacent land. The commissions are also responsible for industrial development on the lands within the boundaries of the harbour, which are often used by the federal government. As landlords, they can lease such property to industries that may discharge contaminants into the water, degrade the shores, create air pollution that enters the water, contaminate the soil near the water, or cut off public access to the water. In fact, much of the property owned by the Toronto Harbour Commission has been so badly contaminated that it is now valueless. It has been estimated that the environmental clean-up of these lands may cost more than $300 million.[84]

Harbour commissions have a strong incentive to allow destructive industrial and commercial uses. The National Ports Policy, which is incorporated into most of the federal laws referred to above, stresses the primacy of economic objectives in the development and management of harbours and ports, with nary a mention of aesthetic, recreational, and environmental considerations. Moreover, the local commissions are expected to "pay their way" by promoting profitable uses of the lands under their management. The exemption of harbour commissions from the *Canadian Environmental Assessment Act* also underlines this concern.

Recent Federal Policy Initiatives

The Federal Water Policy

A Federal Water Policy was introduced in 1987, following a consultative process that had extended over several years.[85] The policy attempted to address the management of water resources in an ecosystem context. The overall objective of the policy was to encourage the use of fresh water in a manner consistent with the social, economic, and environmental needs of present and future generations. It sought to protect and enhance the quality of Canada's water resources and to promote their wise and efficient use.[86]

Five strategies to achieve these goals were announced. These were water pricing, science leadership, integrated planning, legislation, and public awareness. The concept of realistic water pricing, as a direct means of controlling demand and generating revenues to cover costs, was endorsed. Under science leadership, the federal government committed itself to conduct and encourage the undertaking of physical, chemical, biological, and socioeconomic investigations that are directed toward current and emerging water resources issues. Integrated resource planning was to include the integration of water management plans and objectives with those of other natural resource interests, especially fisheries, forestry, wildlife, mining, hydro power, and agriculture. As for legislation, the renewal, consolidation, and strengthening of the application of the existing federal water statutes was promised. Particular focus was to be given to interjurisdictional water flows, the control of toxic chemicals, and water quality standards. Finally, the public consultation and awareness program was to promote water conservation on a national basis.

Twenty-five statements of specific policy were included in the Federal Water Policy. These covered such issues as toxic chemicals management, fish habitat management, water use conflicts, wetlands preservation, navigation, heritage river conservation, and shoreline erosion. Policy statements on transfers of water between basins and Canada-US boundary and transboundary water management were also included. The application of these policy statements is limited to areas under federal jurisdiction.

A *Canada Water Preservation Act* (Bill C-156) was introduced by the government into the House of Commons in 1988. The bill would have forbidden the export of water from Canada. However, the bill died on the order paper when the 1988 federal election was called. The other components of the Federal Water Policy have been incorporated into the federal government's 1990 Green Plan.

The Federal Green Plan

The federal Green Plan, released in December 1990, set out the federal government's environmental policy goals for the following five years. Consistent with the Federal Water Policy, the Green Plan contained detailed programs to secure safe and dependable supplies of drinking water, to clean up past mistakes, to promote pollution prevention, to encourage wise water use, and to improve water science and technology.

As noted earlier, the plan stated the federal government's intention to update and strengthen the pollution prevention regulations made under the *Fisheries Act*,[87] beginning with the Pulp and Paper Effluent Regulations and the Metal Mining Liquid Effluent Regulations. In addition, a commitment was made to introduce a *Drinking Water Safety Act* by the end of 1992. This was to empower the minister of health and welfare to develop federal regulations establishing mandatory water quality objectives.[88] By the end of 1992 no such legislation had appeared. More positively, as promised in the plan,[89] $150 million has been committed to provide water and sewer services on Indian reserves, which frequently have neither.

Under the plan, the Fraser River basin and Atlantic harbours and coasts were targeted for remedial action to address "past mistakes."[90] With respect to pollution prevention, the Green Plan promised the development of a bilateral action plan, with the United States, for comprehensive pollution prevention in the Great Lakes and St. Lawrence River basin by April 1991.[91] However, by the end of 1992, only one element of such a plan, affecting Lake Superior, had been agreed to. This was signed in September 1991. In addition to the bilateral action plan, a Great Lakes Pollution Prevention Centre was to be established as a focal point for research and information activities.[92] This centre was opened in the summer of 1992.

A three-year environmental impact study of the cumulative effects of existing and proposed developments in the Athabasca River basin was also initiated as a Green Plan undertaking.[93] A similar study was proposed regarding water use, the sources and effects of pollutants, soil conservation, and wildlife habitat in the Red River and Assiniboine River basins.[94] Efforts to promote the wise use of water and to increase expenditures on water-related science and technology were also promised.[95]

An Ocean Dumping Control Plan was announced as part of the Green Plan. The technological, recycling, and other measures developed through the program were to be implemented by 1995.[96] At the same time, a *Canada Oceans Act* was promised. Its purpose was to provide a legal basis for the protection of the marine environment consistent with international law, and to designate marine protected areas.[97] To date, no action has been taken to introduce such a statute.

ONTARIO LEGISLATION

Introduction

The provisions of Ontario's *Environmental Protection Act* (*EPA*) define the "environment" widely to include the "air, land *and water*, or any combination or part thereof, of the Province of Ontario."[98] In practice, the *Environmental Protection Act* and the *Ontario Water Resources Act*[99] (*OWRA*) have been used interchangeably by the ministry in abating water pollution through preventive or clean-up orders and prosecuting pollution offences. However, the *Ontario Water Resources Act* has been used when issuing approvals to potential sources of water pollution and to create a framework for the establishment and operation of a system of water supply and treatment facilities and municipal and industrial sewage treatment facilities. When issuing a pollution control or prevention order, the Ministry of Environment and Energy often refers to sections in both the *Environmental Protection Act* and the *Ontario Water Resources Act* as a basis for the order. The reason for this is that the *Environmental Protection Act* has been amended more frequently to improve and clarify the ministry's order-making powers, and the authority under the *Ontario Water Resources Act* for such orders has not kept pace. In recent years, the government has amended the *Ontario Water Resources Act* to make its provisions conform more closely to those in the *Environmental Protection Act*, but there are still discrepancies that make it necessary in some cases to cross-reference several provisions of both statutes to provide a legal underpinning for an order.

The Ontario Water Resources Act

Between 1884 and 1956 the primary legislative instrument addressing matters related to water supply, sewage works, private septic systems, and the discharge or deposit of material into watercourses was the *Public Health Act*.[100] This was administered by municipal governments, with some participation from the provincial Department of Health. With the tremendous growth in population and industrial activity in the 1940s and 1950s, especially in southern Ontario, the need for the provincial government to coordinate municipal sewage treatment and disposal and the provision of water became increasingly apparent.

The Ontario government was finally compelled to take action in this regard by two celebrated common law actions undertaken in the mid-1950s by riparian landholders downstream from municipally operated sewage treatment plants in Richmond Hill and Woodstock. In both cases the plaintiffs succeeded in obtaining injunctions against the discharge of partially treated sewage from the facilities in question.[101] In response to these decisions, the government of Premier Leslie Frost amended the *Public Health Act* in 1956 to provide "statutory authorization"[102] for the operation of sewage treatment plants approved by the provincial health department. In other words, the right to sue for harm to riparian rights and nuisance was taken away. This short-term action was followed by the passage of the *Ontario Water Resources Commission Acts* of 1956 and 1957, which was intended to speed up the clean-up of such polluting sewage treatment plants and the construction of new municipal sewage treatment plants and waterworks.

These statutes provided for the creation of the Ontario Water Resources Commission, an independent body to be appointed by the lieutenant governor in council,[103] and gave it authority for water quality and water use in the province.[104] The *Water Resources Commission Act* required the approval of the commission before a work that removed water from a water body, or that discharged materials into it, could be constructed or operated. This obligation applied to both industrial water works and municipal sewage treatment plants.[105] The commission was also empowered to make orders regulating or prohibiting the discharge of sewage (municipal or industrial) into waters and to issue directives to industrial or commercial enterprises that made sewage treatment and disposal arrangements that the commission regarded as unsatisfactory.[106] However, the commission's most significant activities from the late 1950s onward were to finance and supply water and sewerage services to municipalities.[107]

In 1972 the newly created Ministry of the Environment took over the administration of the *Ontario Water Resources Commission Act* and the statute was renamed the *Ontario Water Resources Act*. The *Ontario Water Resources Act*, in its present form, includes a general prohibition against the discharge into water of polluting materials that "may impair the quality of the water."[108] This prohibition applies to the discharge of materials of any kind into any well, lake, river, pond, spring, stream, reservoir, or other water or watercourse, or on their shores or banks. Section 28 of the Act deems water quality to have been impaired if the material discharged or deposited causes, or may cause, injury to any person, animal, bird, or other living thing as a result of the use or consumption of any plant, fish, or other living matter or thing in the water, or in soil in contact with the water, even if the material is not found in the water itself. This provision was added as a result of a loophole discovered when lakes and rivers were polluted with mercury by pulp and paper plants in the late 1960s. There was little mercury in the water itself. The mercury was mostly in the sediment or taken up by aquatic plants and accumulated in the bodies of fish that ate them. Therefore, it was questionable whether the "water" itself was impaired, without such a provision deeming it to be impaired.

The Act permits the promulgation of regulations specifying standards of quality for potable and other water supplies, industrial and sewage waste effluent, and ambient water quality in receiving water bodies.[109] No such regulations have ever been made under the Act. However, under the 1986 Municipal-Industrial Strategy for Abatement program (discussed below), the government made a commitment to establish regulatory standards through the *Environmental Protection Act*.

Approval is required under the *Ontario Water Resources Act* from the Ministry of Environment and Energy (MEE) to establish or extend sewage works that discharge their effluent *directly* into watercourses.[110] (In contrast, sewage systems that discharge into the soil and rely on absorption and evaporation for treatment and holding tanks that are pumped out, and their contents hauled to sewage lagoons, farmers' fields, or sewage treatment plants, are regulated under part VIII of the *Environmental Protection Act*. Sewage systems that discharge into sanitary sewer pipes that lead to municipal sewage treatment plants are governed by municipal sewer-use bylaws. See below.)

The ministry may refuse to grant such an approval, or attach terms and conditions to it, when the responsible MEE director believes it is in the public interest.[111] Under section 54 of the Act, when one municipality contemplates establishing or extending its sewage works into another municipality, a public hearing *must* be held before the Environmental Assessment Board. A hearing must also be held before the Ministry amends or varies the approval of such a sewage works. In addition, under section 55 of the Act, a public hearing *may* be held when any person or municipality proposes to establish or extend any other sewage treatment facility, or before the ministry varies or amends any approval previously granted. The decision whether to hold a hearing under these circumstances rests with the responsible director.

As for existing or ongoing sources of water pollution, under section 31(1) of the Act, the designated director may make an order prohibiting or regulating the discharge or deposit of sewage by any person. Such an order may be varied or revoked as the director sees fit. Under section 32, the director may require anyone who owns or has control of a sewage works, waterworks, or other facility that may discharge material into water to have on hand any equipment, chemicals, or other materials necessary to prevent or alleviate any impairment of the quality of water that a discharge might cause. Section 100 of the Act permits the appeal of orders to the Environmental Appeal Board, with further appeals available to the Divisional Court on matters of law, and to the minister of environment and energy on any other grounds.

The maximum fines for an individual who violates the *Ontario Water Resources Act* are $10,000 for the first offence and $25,000 for each subsequent offence.[112] The maximum corporate fines are $50,000 for the first offence and $100,000 for each subsequent offence.[113] The violation of some provisions of the Act may result in imprisonment and fines of up to $200,000.[114]

The Environmental Protection Act

The *Ontario Water Resources Act* has been the Ontario government's principal legislative instrument for the control of water pollution and the management of water resources. However, several sections of the *Environmental Protection Act* are also applicable to water. Section 14(1) of the *Environmental Protection Act* contains a general prohibition against the discharge of contaminants into the natural environment. This includes discharges to water, since water is included in the Act's definition of the natural environment. The Act's provisions for remedial actions and part XIII of the Act, regarding the role of the Environmental Appeal Board, also apply to water. Section 7 "control orders," section 8 "stop orders," section 17 "remedial orders," and section 18 "preventive orders" may be used to address water pollution. The spills provisions of part X of the Act are also relevant (see chapters 7 and 16).

Several regulations related to water pollution have been made under the *Environmental Protection Act* rather than the *Ontario Water Resources Act*. The Discharge of Sewage from Pleasure Boats Regulations[115] prohibit the discharge of toilet waste, fuels, litter, refuse, garbage, organic wastes, and other types of garbage into Ontario's waters from "pleasure boats." "Pleasure boats" are defined as boats used primarily for carrying people for pleasure, whether for compensation or not. They include houseboats and rented and chartered boats. Water from toilets (called "black water") must be contained onboard and pumped out at an approved facility. (Discharges of sewage from other boats and ships are subject to the regulations under the *Canada Shipping Act*. For example, the Great Lakes Sewage Pollution Prevention Regulations[116] require sewage from these vessels to be treated before discharge, and the final effluent must contain no more than the specified amounts of suspended solids, BOD, and chlorine.)

The Marinas Regulations[117] require all commercial marinas in Ontario to provide litter containers and to provide facilities for pumping out the holding tanks of pleasure boats using the marina. The Sewage System Regulations[118] classify and regulate the haulage and disposal of bathroom, toilet, and sink wastes.

Unlike "black water," the water from the sinks and showers on pleasure boats and their bilge water (known as "grey water") may be pumped overboard. Grey Water Sewage Regulations prohibiting the discharge of grey waters from pleasure craft were proposed by the Ministry of the Environment in the spring of 1991 and the ministry hoped to have them in effect by May 1993. The draft regulations initially required *all* pleasure boats to store grey water onboard rather than pump it overboard. They have been strongly resisted by boaters, and it is not clear when they will come into force. The most recent revision would require only charter boats and boats docked at a marina for at least 60 days at a time to have grey water storage facilities. This would affect 3,000 of the estimated 45,000 to 65,000 boats that produce grey water.[119]

EPA Part IV: "Water"

Part IV of the *Environmental Protection Act* carries the grandiose title "Water," but in fact it simply prohibits pollution from "ice shelters," which are defined as any structure located on or over ice over water. Thus, this part of the Act deals primarily with ice fishing. It prohibits people using ice shelters from dumping any waste on the ice, and authorizes the Ministry of Environment and Energy to make regulations authorizing the removal of ice shelters that have been left to sink into the water when the ice melts.

EPA Part VIII: Sewage Systems

As mentioned above, sewage systems that don't discharge their effluent directly into watercourses are regulated under this part of the *Environmental Protection Act* rather than under the *Ontario Water Resources Act*.

The Commission on Planning and Development Reform in Ontario has called pollution from these sewage systems "a sleeping giant," because the pollution is so widespread but has received so little public attention. Systems such as the septic tank and tile bed can handle both human wastes and wash wastes, but their effectiveness depends on having the right kind of soil available to the right depth. Without adequate soil and sufficient separation from groundwater, neighbouring wells, and watercourses, these systems cause pollution of groundwater, surface water, and drinking water. Sewage may pond on the surface of the ground, then run off into ditches or watercourses. Even when these systems are properly designed, they will eventually fail — usually within 20 years. However, there is no requirement to replace an old system until it actually fails and begins to pollute its surroundings.

Septic systems require soil to filter the effluent as it passes through the tiles. Therefore, they are ineffective in much of Ontario's cottage country, where there is only a thin layer of soil above the bedrock. Many of the existing septic systems in areas like Muskoka and Haliburton have been leaking untreated sewage into the lakes for years.

In addition, although these systems may be effective in rural areas where there are large lots, housing subdivisions are often constructed in urban and suburban areas where the lots are too small to hold a properly designed tile bed. Yet municipalities continue to approve severances and subdivisions under the *Planning Act* without regard to whether these new lots are suitable for an in-ground sewage system.

Other sewage systems are also allowed under Ontario's regulations. However, they also have significant drawbacks. Some, such as single-family aeration systems, are expensive and require frequent expert maintenance, as in the case of package sewage treatment plants. Other systems, such as the cesspool, may be excessively odorous. The pit privy (outhouse), the chemical toilet, and the incinerator toilet cannot handle wash water, so an additional "leaching pit" is needed for sink wastes. But if the building is equipped with a pressurized water system, the quantities of grey water may be too great to be contained by a leaching pit. Holding tanks have traditionally been approved for lots too small to hold a conventional septic system. However, MEE policy now prohibits directors from issuing approvals to install holding tanks, except under exceptional circumstances.[120] The reason for this is that these tanks must be pumped out frequently. The pump-out cost is often high, tempting the owners of these tanks to empty them in illegal ways such as pumping them into ditches and watercourses. In addition, opposition to dumping this waste on fields or in sewage lagoons is reducing the options for disposing of the waste once it has been pumped out.

Part VIII of the *Environmental Protection Act* provides that anyone who wants to install a sewage system subject to that part of the Act, or who wants to expand a building so that the existing sewage system will need to be enlarged, must obtain approval from a ministry official designated as a director for this purpose. In many parts of Ontario, this function has been delegated to local public health units, and their personnel have been designated as directors.

The sewage systems regulation lists several classes of sewage systems and sets out design, construction, and operating standards for each class of system. Sewage systems must comply with the detailed requirements of the regulation, although directors can approve systems that do not meet these specifications if they are convinced the system will not cause pollution. Under this part of the Act, a director can also order the repair or replacement of a malfunctioning sewage system.

Sewage haulers, who clean out septic tanks and holding tanks and dispose of the sewage, and sewage system installers must be licensed under this part of the Act. A breach of the terms of a licence is not only an offence; the licence of a hauler or installer may be suspended or revoked if he or she contravenes the Act or regulation or violates the terms of his or her licence. Sewage haulers remove and dispose of more than one billion litres of septic tank contents each year. This septage, which is up to 40 per cent more concentrated than raw sewage, must be disposed of by hauling it to a sewage treatment plant or sewage lagoon or by spreading it on land. It is illegal to dump this material anywhere other than an approved site. The suitability of land disposal sites is assessed on the basis of the ability of the soil to absorb the effluent, the slope of the land, and the distance of the site from wells, watercourses, roads, and homes in accordance with MEE guidelines.[121]

Enforcement of part VIII of the *Environmental Protection Act* leaves something to be desired. There are more than one million septic systems in Ontario. Many of them have been in the ground for decades; yet they are rarely inspected. On the rare occasions when a survey of an area's septic systems has been carried out, large percentages have been found to be malfunctioning.[122] One of the reasons for this is improper design and installation, yet the sewage system installers, who often design the system as well, are not required to take any training or pass any tests before being granted a licence.

Protection of Groundwater

It is just as important to protect groundwater supplies as it is to protect surface waters such as streams, rivers, and lakes. Underground water feeds natural vegetation and crops; it is pumped to the surface in wells that provide drinking water for people and farm animals, and water for industrial uses. Eventually it rises to the surface in marshes and streams. If it is polluted, it may be undrinkable, and if the water table is lowered, crops may starve, wells, streams, and ponds may go dry, and the soil may subside, causing the foundations, walls, and ceilings of buildings to shift and crack.

But even though groundwater may be subject to the same problems as surface water, there are fewer laws, policies, and programs to protect its quality and quantity, and fewer remedies for people deprived of its use. The protection of groundwater has largely been ignored in land-

---

Sources of Contamination that Can Cause Groundwater Contamination

Point sources

On-site septic systems
Leaky tanks or pipelines containing petroleum products
Leaks or spills of industrial chemicals at manufacturing facilities
Underground injection wells (industrial waste)
Municipal landfills
Livestock wastes
Leaky sewer lines
Chemicals used at wood preservation facilities
Mill tailings in mining areas
Fly ash from coal-fired power plants
Sludge disposal areas at petroleum refineries
Land spreading of sewage or sewage sludge
Graveyards
Road salt storage areas
Wells for disposal of liquid wastes
Runoff of salt and other chemicals from roads and highways
Spills related to highway or railway accidents
Coal tar at old coal gasification sites
Asphalt production and equipment cleaning sites

Non-point (distributed) sources

Fertilizers on agricultural land
Pesticides on agricultural land and forests
Contaminants in rain, snow, and dry atmospheric fallout

Courtesy of Environment Canada.

use planning, largely because it is invisible, and because the people of Ontario do not rely on it for drinking water to the same extent as in other provinces. However, as the population increases and settlements expand into rural areas, Ontarians are increasingly relying on groundwater for domestic water supply, only to find that it has already been contaminated by leaking waste disposal sites, spills of chemicals, leaking storage tanks, malfunctioning septic systems, pesticides, fertilizers, and manure. When the first extensive survey of the quality of Ontario's groundwater was done in the winter of 1991, about 37 per cent of the wells in rural Ontario were found to have concentrations of farm chemicals and bacteria above the provincial drinking water objectives.[123]

As described in Chapter 6, pollution of groundwater is just as much a tort as pollution of surface water. However, lowering the water table or changing the flow of groundwater so that the quantity of groundwater available to others is reduced is not a tort. The *Ontario Water Resources Act* attempts to rectify this omission to some extent by regulating the taking of both groundwater and surface water through *water-taking permits*.

Aquifers and Wells

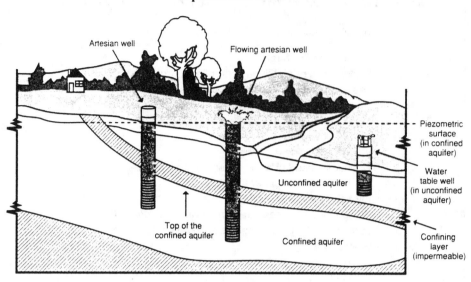

The Hydrologic Cycle

Courtesy of Environment Canada.

Under section 34 of the *Ontario Water Resources Act*, anyone who wants to take more than 50,000 litres of water in a day from the ground or from surface water through a well, a surface water intake, or by means of any other structure or works for diverting or storing water must obtain a permit from the Ministry of Environment and Energy unless the water is for domestic use, for farm purposes, or for fighting fires. However, if the water is being taken to irrigate crops for sale, the farmer must obtain a permit. The director may refuse to issue a permit or cancel one. A permit may be made subject to terms and conditions, and in past, every permit issued had a list of conditions printed on it. These conditions are intended to prevent the taking of the water from causing environmental degradation or undue interference with neighbours, or require the permittee to pay compensation for any harm resulting from taking the water.

Section 34(7) of the *Ontario Water Resources Act* provides that "where the flowing or leaking of water from a well, or the diversion, flowing or release of water from or by means of a hole or excavation made in the ground for any purpose other than the taking of water" interferes with any public or private interest in any water, the ministry may make a variety of orders. This complicated language appears to mean that where the water table is raised or lowered or neighbouring lands are flooded (for example, by a leaking well), the ministry may order the person responsible to take any steps necessary to prevent the interference. In one case, the ministry used this provision to order a gravel pit owner to replace the water supplies of neighbours when groundwater burst up through the floor of the pit, filling the pit with water and lowering the water table, with the result that the neighbours' wells went dry.[124]

The construction of wells is also regulated by the *Ontario Water Resources Act*. Sections 39 to 50 require anyone who carries on the business of constructing wells and any employees carrying out the work to obtain licences from the Ministry of Environment and Energy. Permits may also be required for the construction of individual wells. Proper well construction is important because improperly constructed wells can create a pathway for pollution to travel from one layer of groundwater to another. Defective wells can also allow contaminants in the soil or in layers of groundwater from which the well is not taking water to enter the well. Licensed well drillers are required to keep a record of the kinds of soil encountered in drilling the well, their location and depth, and the location and depth of aquifers encountered, and to submit these "well logs" to the ministry. These records are an important source of information about the soils and groundwater patterns in Ontario, and help to provide the kind of baseline data about the environment that are so often missing.

The Ministry of Environment and Energy has also established an important policy for use in determining whether to approve facilities such as waste disposal sites, sewage lagoons, and large commercial septic systems, that may pollute neighbouring groundwater. In its publication *Water Management*, discussed below, the ministry stated that its policy is to protect existing and future *reasonable* uses of groundwater. The "reasonable use" principle of this policy is implemented by specifying what levels of groundwater contamination from such facilities will be considered acceptable and how badly groundwater that is the source of drinking water must be contaminated before the water supply must be restored. Just as the ministry accepts that there will be "mixing zones" in surface water where some contamination above its guidelines is allowed, the ministry also allows a certain amount of contamination to enter groundwater and migrate past the boundaries of the polluter's property. However, unless the pollutants will soon be diluted by spreading through the groundwater to a level that does not unreasonably interfere with existing and future possible uses of the groundwater, the ministry will not approve the new source of pollution.[125] The policy states that if the pollutant being discharged is a health-related one, the maximum permissible impact on the groundwater is an increase of 25 per cent of the difference between the background levels of the contaminant (the levels already found in the groundwater) and the Ontario drinking water objective (ODWO) for that pollutant. If the contaminant is one that is regulated because of "aesthetic" concerns — for example, chloride — the maximum level that may result from the discharge is 50 per cent of the difference between the background level and the ODWO. For example, if the background level of chloride in the groundwater is 50 milligrams per litre and the ODWO is 250, then the maximum permissible level of chloride resulting from the activity would be 150 milligrams per litre.

A number of other sections of the *Environmental Protection Act* and several other statutes deal with specific sources of groundwater contamination. For example, septic systems are covered by part XIII and landfill sites by part VI of the *Environmental Protection Act*. Pesticides are addressed by the *Pesticides Act*,[126] and petroleum products by the *Gasoline Handling Act*.[127] These statutes are described elsewhere in this chapter or in other chapters.

One step that has been taken in some other provinces, but not in Ontario, is to designate some areas as groundwater protection areas. Using this approach, the areas most sensitive to groundwater pollution are identified and mapped, and the land uses that can take place in those areas are restricted. The concept is similar to the practice of "zoning" in land-use planning (see Chapter 8). Ontario has no legislation allowing this process to occur.

Other Ontario Statutes

The Lakes and Rivers Improvement Act

The *Lakes and Rivers Improvement Act*[128] is administered by the Ministry of Natural Resources and deals principally with "improvements" to lakes and rivers to permit the conduct of forestry operations, such as the floating of logs from harvesting areas to lumber and pulp and paper mills. The statute was first enacted in the 1870s as the *Rivers and Streams Act*, and was given its present name in 1927, when the irony of calling the damming and diversion of watercourses "improvements" was less apparent than it is today.

The statute deals both with physical alterations of bodies of water and water pollution. Under the Act, approval is required for the construction or alteration of a dam on any lake or river. The purpose of the statute is stated to be to ensure the protection of fish and wildlife and other environmental amenities when activities such as dam construction and the moving of logs takes place. Thus, although the damming and diversion of waters were assumed to be improvements, it was also acknowledged that they were destructive activities that should require prior approval.

Under section 17(1) of the Act, the Ministry of Natural Resources may make orders requiring companies that build dams or construct docks to investigate harm they may be causing, such as shoreline erosion, and correct problems.

The Act is particularly important in relation to mining activities, since the operation of mines and the disposal of mine tailings has resulted in the filling in, damming, and diversion of thousands of lakes, rivers, and streams in northern Ontario.

Section 36(1) of the Act is particularly noteworthy in that it provides one of the few instances in which an Ontario statute prohibits the impairment of natural beauty alone. Under this section, the minister of natural resources may order any person who has thrown or deposited any tree, part of a tree, refuse, substance, or matter into a lake or river or onto the shores or banks of a lake or river in such a way that it impairs the natural beauty of the water body to take any measures necessary to remove the material.

Section 38(1) of the Act prohibits the throwing, depositing, or discharging of any refuse, sawdust, chemical substances, or matter from a saw, pulp, or paper mill into a lake or river. If such a deposit occurs, the minister may order the owner or occupier of the mill to remove the material in question. The minister may also order the owner or occupier of the mill to take measures to avoid, lessen, or diminish the injury caused to downstream riparian landowners by materials deposited in the water by the mill. At the same time, the degree of statutory authorization provided for logging and mill activities by these provisions of the Act may limit the capacity of downstream landowners to pursue common law actions against mill operators themselves.

The Beds of Navigable Waters Act

The *Beds of Navigable Waters Act*[129] is intended to ensure that when land situated on a water body is purchased, in the absence of an express grant to the purchaser, the ownership of the water bed does not pass to the purchaser. Rather, it is retained by the Crown. This gives the government greater control over activities that may damage the bed, such as dumping or dredging. The *Mining Act*[130] expressly states that mining leases are subject to this statute, to make it clear that a lease to mine on public land does not give the mining company ownership of the bed of any body of water.

The Environmental Assessment Act

A detailed description of the operation of the EA process established by the *Environmental Assessment Act*[131] is provided in Chapter 9. Provincial and municipal undertakings are subject to the Act unless exempted by Cabinet. Private sector projects are exempt, unless specifically designated for review by Cabinet. Major public undertakings that might affect water resources, such as hydroelectric projects and landfill sites, which may contaminate both groundwater and surface water, would most likely be subjected to project-specific assessments, while "class" environmental assessments have been conducted for frequently recurring projects, such as the upgrading of sewage treatment plants.

THE MUNICIPAL ROLE

The powers of municipal governments in Ontario are established through the *Municipal Act*.[132] The Act permits municipal councils to construct and operate municipal sewer and water systems. In addition, municipal councils are empowered to enact bylaws to control or prohibit industrial waste water discharges into their sewer systems.

The discharge of hazardous industrial wastes into municipal sewer systems causes a number of serious problems. Sewage treatment facilities are generally designed to deal only with organic wastes. As a result, hazardous liquid industrial wastes usually simply pass through treatment plants and enter receiving water bodies. Consequently, sewage treatment plants are often major point sources of hazardous contaminants in surface waters. In addition, the passage of hazardous wastes through treatment plants can pose serious occupational health and safety threats to treatment plant staff, and interfere with the effective operation of the plants on their way through.[133] Furthermore, as well as damaging aquatic systems into which sewers eventually empty, caustic substances and acids can corrode the sewers themselves, and grease and oil can "clog" the sewers, reducing their capacity.

Municipal bylaws regulating discharges to sewer systems traditionally have been based on a model bylaw prepared by the Ministry of the Environment and the Municipal Engineers Association. The first such model bylaw was introduced in 1976.[134] It set limits on the concentration of pollutants in each litre of water discharged into the sewer; that is, it permitted the dilution of toxics, rather than requiring reductions in the total loading. Moreover, the model bylaw was not uniformly implemented across the province. The number of chemicals covered by the municipal sewer-use bylaws actually implemented by municipalities varied from community to community. Enforcement actions were inconsistent and in some cases non-existent.

Furthermore, some municipalities included clauses enabling them to enter into agreements with industries that were prepared to pay sewer use fees.[135] Agreements of this nature authorized industries to discharge greater amounts of some pollutants into the sewers than the bylaw would otherwise allow in return for the payment of a fee intended to cover the cost of treating the pollutants at the municipal sewage treatment plants. The rationale behind these "sewer surcharges" is that some companies do not have sufficient land to permit them to install sewage treatment facilities or the experience and skills needed to operate such facilities efficiently. These agreements reduce the need for a proliferation of small private sewage treatment plants in the community, while ensuring that the dischargers pay for the cost of treatment at the municipal sewage treatment plant. However, there was nothing in the *Municipal Act* to prevent the use of these sewer surcharges to allow excessive discharges of pollutants that were not amenable to treatment. Moreover, environmentalists often view these surcharge agreements as licences to pollute, and fear that they are open to abuse.

A new model bylaw was introduced by the Ministry of the Environment in 1988, as part of the Municipal-Industrial Strategy for Abatement program (see below). The 1988 model bylaw places greater emphasis on reducing discharges rather than diluting them, and seeks to eliminate the sewering of certain pollutants. The new model has been adopted by a number of municipalities, and increasing resources have been devoted by many municipalities to enforcement efforts in recent years. Repeated violations for local sewer-use bylaws have resulted in heavy fines, which have been upheld on appeal, and orders to cease polluting.[136] In two celebrated cases, two metal-finishing companies and their presidents were cited for contempt of such orders. One of them was ordered jailed for six months.[137]

The Role of Conservation Authorities

Conservation authorities, such as the Metro Toronto Region Conservation Authority, are statutory corporations, governed principally by municipal appointees. They are established by the provincial Cabinet at the request of the municipalities in a given watershed. Conservation authorities are able to undertake programs designed to further the conservation, restoration, and management of natural resources, other than gas, oil, coal or minerals, in the geographic area over which they have jurisdiction.[138]

To accomplish these objectives, conservation authorities have a wide range of powers. These include the ability to purchase, lease, or expropriate lands[139] and to erect works and structures.[140] Dams may be constructed and reservoirs created to control the flow of surface waters in order to prevent floods.[141] Conservation authorities may make regulations restricting and regulating the use of water in or from surface water bodies within their geographic jurisdictions.[142] They also have the power to prohibit or regulate the straightening, changing, diverting, or interference with any existing channel of a river or other watercourse.[143] Finally, conservation authorities may prohibit the construction of buildings and structures and dumping of fill in areas susceptible to flooding.[144] Conservation authorities may set up a permit system for these purposes. If a conservation authority refuses permission to carry out any of the activities described above, the applicant has a right to a hearing before a committee of the conservation authority. If permission is still refused, the applicant can appeal to the minister of natural resources, as represented by the mining and lands commissioner.

The mining and lands commissioner has found that he (now she) is reluctant to grant permission that is inconsistent with zoning laws, but that the provisions of the *Conservation Authorities Act* are separate from the planning legislation. An applicant has the opportunity to apply for a change in zoning or a minor variance.[145] In other words, even if lands are not zoned to permit a proposal, the mining and lands commissioner may still issue permits under the *Conservation Authorities Act*.

The mining and lands commissioner has also found that the phrase "conservation of land" in section 28(1) does not mean retention of land in a state of nature.[146] Furthermore, a former commissioner stated that he had considerable doubt that the phrase "conservation of land" is synonymous with the maintenance of a natural state or the creation of conformity to an official plan.[147] The commissioner has found that the word "conservation" in section 28(1) must have a narrower meaning than the word "preservation," when the *Conservation Authorities Act* is read in the context of related statutes, so that the commissioner's jurisdiction does not extend to matters of "preservation." The commissioner has also stated that the proper meaning to be attributed to the word "conservation" is the concept of wise use, in contrast to the retention of land in its existing state.[148]

Recently, the mining and lands commissioner has refused to permit the construction of residential homes, in part because of the risk of water pollution arising from the construction and the subsequent use of the homes, since there was a need to exclude all potential contaminants from the part of the river in issue.[149]

Subject to Cabinet approval, the conservation authority may also make regulations related to its own lands:

1. regulating and governing the use of its lands and works;
2. prescribing fees for the occupation and use of its lands; or
3. prescribing permits designating privileges in connection with the use of its lands and prescribing permit fees.

Conservation authorities have traditionally focused on the flood-control engineering aspects of their mandates. This had led to criticism from environmentalists, who have argued that the resulting activities, such as the damming and channeling of rivers and streams and extensive lakefilling have caused serious environmental damage.[150] In response to these concerns, some recent appointees to conservation authority boards have expressed a desire to take a more progressive approach to their mandates. In particular, they have indicated a willingness to de-emphasize the engineering aspects of their roles and to give greater attention to their functions as watershed-based ecosystem managers.[151]

The Policy Framework for Protecting Water Quality in Ontario

The Traditional Approach: The "Blue" and "Green" Books

The Ontario Ministry of Environment and Energy currently has two main policy tools used in making decisions such as what terms and conditions to impose on approvals to sewage treatment plants or industrial facilities that will discharge effluent into watercourses, and how to determine its priorities in building or funding sewage treatment plants and water supply and treatment systems. These policies are known respectively as "the green book" and "the blue book," because of the colour of their covers.

The Ontario Drinking Water Objectives,[152] commonly called "the green book," set out the maximum acceptable concentrations in drinking water supplies of substances that can cause harm to human health, or may not harm health but may interfere with the taste or appearance of drinking water or make it smell bad. These objectives are similar to ambient air quality objectives, in that they do not directly state how much of a pollutant a specific polluter may discharge, but set out the maximum limits of the pollutant that are desirable in a given water supply. As mentioned, they are useful in determining whether to approve a particular water supply system and in setting priorities for the funding of such systems. They are also useful in giving guidance as to what will be considered "impairment" of water quality. Section 16 of the *Ontario Water Resources Act* makes it an offence to discharge a substance that may impair water quality. The courts have defined "impairment" to mean *any* worsening of water quality. Thus, the fact that a discharge resulted in concentrations of a pollutant lower than the drinking water quality objectives will not necessarily mean that this is not "impairment." If, however, the discharge can be proven to have resulted in pollution concentrations above these limits, the court would most likely accept this as impairment without further evidence of the impact or potential impact of the discharge.

The federal government has published a similar set of objectives,[153] and the maximum acceptable and target concentrations for radionuclides as well as the maximum acceptable concentrations for other parameters directly related to health are the same as the federal guidelines. The concentrations related to aesthetic impact do differ in some cases from the federal guidelines.

Three types of limits are recognized in the green book:

- *Maximum Acceptable Concentration.* These are limits beyond which a substance is known to affect human health. The presence of a substance in higher concentrations is grounds for rejecting the water unless an effective treatment is available.

- *Interim Maximum Acceptable Concentration.* These are limits for substances that are known to cause chronic effects in mammals, but the health effects are not sufficiently known to allow the establishment of maximum acceptable concentrations. If a substance is found in drinking water at a higher level, this signals the need for more sampling and investigation, and possibly corrective measures.

- *Maximum Desirable Concentration.* These are limits for substances that are aesthetically objectionable or may interfere with good water quality control practices. If these limits are exceeded, the agency supplying the water should be treating it or looking for an alternative source of water, if the cost is reasonable.

The objectives also specify how, and how often, sampling for various parameters should be carried out.

The publication entitled *Water Management: Goals, Policies, Objectives and Implementation Procedures of the Ministry of the Environment* (often called "the blue book") also sets out the drinking water objectives, but in addition it includes objectives for the quality of water used for other purposes such as recreation and fishing, and for agricultural uses such as irrigation and watering livestock. This publication sets out limits for concentrations of pollutants in effluent discharged from sewage treatment plants and industries.

The guidelines were originally developed in the late 1960s by the Ontario Water Resources Commission to help establish water quality standards. Revisions made in 1970 set quality characteristics for many uses of water: drinking, agricultural, and industrial water supply, aesthetic enjoyment, and the propagation of fish and wildlife. The primary purpose of the objectives is to establish the quality of water needed for the various uses as a basis for determining what level of quality should be maintained in a given body of water. For example, water for industrial purposes generally need not be as pure as water for drinking. These goals are then applied on a case-by-case basis in deciding whether to issue a certificate of approval to discharge effluent into a water body and whether to issue preventive or remedial orders to dischargers. These concentration limits are enforceable only when incorporated into an order or certificate of approval.

Although the ministry originally hoped to use these objectives as a basis for setting legally enforceable water quality standards, this goal was virtually abandoned until the change in government in 1985, when the ministry resurrected this goal in the form of the Municipal-Industrial Strategy for Abatement program (described below).

The blue book was revised in 1978, and was again revised and given its current name in 1984. Since then, a number of additional provincial water quality objectives and guidelines have been developed. These additional guidelines and objectives are found in the Ministry of Environment and Energy's policy manual and are available from the ministry, but the publication has not been reissued to incorporate them.

When the ministry has a level of toxicological data that it considers sufficiently conclusive about the impacts of a chemical on water quality, it will issue an objective. Where there are enough scientific data to raise concerns, but not enough to create the level of certainty the ministry requires for an objective, the ministry will establish a guideline. The intention is to upgrade the guideline to an objective as soon as sufficient information becomes available. In emergencies — for example, when NDMA, a carcinogen, was found in the drinking water of the village of Elmira — the ministry will establish an interim guideline on the basis of a search of the best information at hand.[154]

The 1984 version of the blue book summarizes Ontario's water quality and quantity protection policies under four headings: surface water quality management, surface water quantity management, groundwater quality management, and ground-water quantity management.

The blue book candidly acknowledges that too little is known about water pollution to establish objectives for all substances that will give long-term protection to all organisms: "Ideally, water quality objectives should be established based on 'no negative effect' data derived from chronic long-term tests on sensitive organisms. However, current understanding of chemical dynamics and effects on aquatic life are limited to a few species and contaminant levels that are lethal in short term tests." In other words, we know about the acute effects of large doses of a few pollutants on fish, but we don't know enough about the long-term, more subtle, impacts of pollutants on more sensitive aquatic life to set any meaningful limits on the basis of these impacts.

These objectives and guidelines suffer from the further limitation that they do not take into account additive or synergistic effects that may result from the interaction of two or more hazardous substances in the same body of water.[155]

The effluent objectives, which are used in deciding whether to approve a source of discharge or to issue a pollution control or prevention order, are based partly on federal standards under legislation such as the *Fisheries Act*, partly on the provincial water quality objectives, and partly on the basis of the ministry's opinion as to how much pollution the watercourse receiving the discharge can handle without causing damage. Rather than using a standard that applies to all dischargers, the ministry has traditionally evaluated the ability of the discharger to treat its waste before discharge and the ability of the receiving water to assimilate the pollutant on a case-by-case basis.

Because the ministry does not feel that it is practical to treat all effluents before discharge so that they meet the water quality objectives, its policy has been to permit pollutants to be discharged in concentrations above these objectives, and to rely on dilution in the watercourse to bring the concentrations down to the desired level. The ministry establishes a "mixing zone" in the body of water near the source of the discharge. The dilution occurs within this mixing zone. The size of the mixing zone must be sufficient to dilute the effluent to the desired level. The policy states that "[w]ithin the mixing zone, where the Objectives are not met, there will be some damage or loss to the aquatic environment. Nevertheless, at no point should conditions be immediately lethal so that swimming organisms cannot evade the area. The mixing zone mainly represents a loss of habitat, but it must not be allowed to become an area where aquatic life is killed or seriously damaged." Presumably this means fish, since other aquatic organisms that can't swim will not be able to leave the area to escape the pollution.

Other MEE Policies

There are other policies in the MEE policy manual that specifically or generally relate to water quality or quantity. These include a policy setting out guidelines on how to evaluate the potential adverse impacts of pipelines during watercourse crossings,[156] guidelines to facilitate the resolution of problems arising from interference with groundwater, [157] a policy on how water resource concerns arising from marine construction and small scale construction projects are to be dealt with in environmental assessments,[158] and a policy requiring covers on containers in which drinking water is stored,[159] in addition to other policies described elsewhere in this chapter.

Toxic Substances in the Aquatic Environment

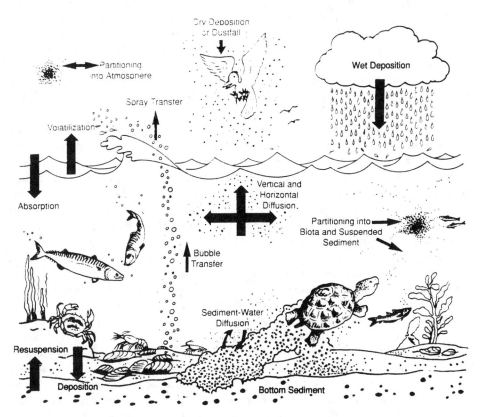

Courtesy of Environment Canada.

The New Approach: The Municipal-Industrial Strategy for Abatement

To address the weaknesses of the "blue" and "green" book approach to standard setting, the Municipal-Industrial Strategy for Abatement (MISA) program was launched in June 1986. The program was intended to control both hazardous and conventional liquid discharges from municipal and industrial sources. Its stated goal was the "virtual elimination of persistent toxic pollution from our waterways."[160] This was to be achieved through the establishment of effluent standards based on the best available technology economically achievable (BATEA) for municipal sewage treatment plants and for each of nine major industrial sectors (petroleum refining, organic chemicals, pulp and paper, metal mining and refining, iron and steel, metal casting, industrial minerals, inorganic chemicals, and electric power generation) that discharge the wastes directly into receiving water bodies.

The MISA effluent standards were to be set as regulations promulgated under the *Environmental Protection Act*. Both maximum discharge concentrations and contaminant load limits per unit of production were to be imposed. The process of determining the best available technology standard was to draw heavily on work done by the US Environmental Protection Agency (EPA).[161] Allowable effluent levels were to be lowered as technology improved.[162] In addition, new standards for ambient water quality, again based on US EPA work, were to be adopted. The program also made provision for the implementation of higher site specific effluent standards where receiving water bodies were already considered to be significantly degraded.[163]

All of this marked a major departure from the ministry's previous approaches to the development and implementation of water-related standards. The non-enforceable "blue" and "green" book objectives for water quality and the control of industrial discharges, which had been used to provide the basis for the contents of certificates of approval, control orders, and program approvals, were to be replaced by enforceable regulatory requirements. As noted earlier, in setting these guidelines, the ministry historically had taken a lack of knowledge about the extent of the hazard posed by individual substances to be grounds for caution, but not for prohibition. Under this "no known effects" approach, if there was no firm evidence of environmental or health hazards available, the overriding importance of the substance, or the enterprises with which it was associated, had been recognized.[164] Non-degradation and best available abatement technology based approaches to standard setting had been explicitly rejected by the ministry.[165]

The actual implementation of the "blue" and "green" book guidelines had occurred on a case-by-case basis, through negotiations between local ministry officials and the industry concerned. In the result, the contents of certificates of approval and control orders had been highly variable. Discharge objectives for specific pollutants had not been included on a consistent basis, and the ministry had been criticized for focusing on conventional pollutants such as suspended solids, some heavy metals, and a limited group of organic contaminants such as total phenols while ignoring a wide range of other toxic chemicals.[166]

Under the MISA program, the process of negotiating the allowable effluent levels was to occur on a province-wide basis, rather than being left in the hands of regional officials. Joint technical committees (JTCs) for each of the nine direct discharge sectors were formed, consisting of representatives of the ministry and affected industries to oversee the drafting of sectoral regulations. In addition, a MISA Advisory Committee (MAC), consisting of representatives of industry and public was formed to advise the minister on the overall implementation of the program. There is to be a 90-day public review period following the release of each draft regulation developed by the JTCs and the MAC. In the past, there had been no formal mechanisms for public involvement in the ministry's standard-setting procedures.

The implementation of MISA was to occur in two stages. In the first stage, monitoring regulations would be developed for each sector, specifying which pollutants the companies in each sector must look for in their effluent streams, and setting out the frequency of sampling and the methodology for taking the samples and analyzing the effluent. Through this process, priority substances would be identified. Effluent regulations were then to be developed, setting out discharge limits based on the results of the monitoring regulations and the availability of technology to reduce the amounts of the contaminants in the effluent.

Meanwhile, control orders, preventive orders, and stop orders could continue to be issued to pollution sources where necessary. The program was to be fully implemented by December 1989.[167]

It was envisioned that the regulations regarding the nine industrial sectors would address the 300 industrial sources of direct discharges into the province's waterways.[168] The program also was to attempt to respond to hazardous discharges from municipal sewage treatment plants. These discharges were the result of the dumping of hazardous wastes from about 12,000 industrial plants known as "indirect dischargers"[169] into municipal sewage systems. Consequently, the Ministry of the Environment proposed in 1988 that MISA include the development of pre-treatment discharge standards for 22 industrial sectors that released wastes into municipal sewer systems. These standards would also be based on the BATEA model.[170]

The MISA program has not proceeded as rapidly as had originally been planned. In fact, both the provincial auditor and the Royal Commission on the Future of Toronto's Waterfront have been critical of the delays. "The program, first billed as the flagship of the Ministry of the Environment's pollution control initiatives, today looks more like a leaking dory," the commission reported in December 1991.[171]

The promulgation of the monitoring regulations for the nine industrial sectors was not completed until December 1990. Only one draft effluent regulation, for the petroleum refining sector, had been released by the Ministry of the Environment by the end of 1992. The actual regulations are unlikely to be in place before the end of 1993. These delays principally have been the result of the unexpected complexity of the program.[172] Industry concerns over the costs of meeting the requirements of MISA have also been a factor.

The proposed components of the program affecting the discharges from municipal sewage treatments plants have encountered substantial resistance from municipal governments in the province. The Environment Ministry's threat to prosecute municipalities who are unwilling to live up to their enforcement responsibilities regarding the discharge of industrial wastes into municipal sewer systems[173] has been a source of particularly strong discontent. Many municipalities have argued that in the absence of adequate financial assistance from the province, they lack the resources to control sewer use adequately.[174] A new model sewer-use bylaw was released by the Ministry of the Environment in 1988. However, in the context of these municipal concerns, the BATEA regulatory standards for sewer discharges are not expected to be in place for several more years.

This failure to address the question of indirect discharges represents a significant weakness of the MISA program. The existing system of sewer-use bylaws is widely regarded as an interim stage, on the way to the development of a provincial regime governing indirect dischargers. In contrast, "pre-treatment" standards requiring the treatment of industrial effluents at the site where they are produced before discharging them to sewers are now well established in the United States.

It is important to note that, since the fall of 1991, the Ministry of the Environment has been placing increasing emphasis on MISA as a pollution-prevention program, as opposed to a pollution-control undertaking.[175] The latter stresses the use of end-of-pipe waste treatment systems to control pollution, while with pollution prevention the focus is on changes in industrial process to eliminate pollutants at their source. An Office of Pollution Prevention has been established within the ministry to reflect this shift in focus.

Specific Pollution Problems

Pollution and Hazardous Contaminants

The Pulp and Paper Industry

The pulp and paper industry is one of the most significant sources of water pollution in Canada. The production of pulp and paper involves several processes, involving raw material preparation, pulping, bleaching, and paper making. Each stage can be the source of significant environmental problems. The industry discharges wastes that contain pulping and bleaching chemicals, as well as solids such as wood fibers, into lakes, rivers, and marine waters. There are 140 pulp and paper mills in Canada, of which 27 are located in Ontario.

The preparation of logs for pulping involves washing and debarking the logs and chipping the wood. The processes of log washing and debarking may consume large quantities of water, and the resulting effluent contains significant levels of biological oxygen demand (BOD) and suspended solids. BOD is a measure of the effects of mill effluent on the amount of dissolved oxygen in the water. Most aquatic organisms depend on this dissolved oxygen for survival. Consequently, high levels of BOD from mill effluent can produce conditions lethal to fish and other aquatic organisms. Suspended solids such as wood fibres, for their part, tend to settle to the bottom of the receiving lakes or river, destroying habitat and smothering bottom-dwelling organisms. Acid resins from the bark deposited in water bodies can also be toxic to fish.

As a consequence of these considerations, many Canadian mills are currently in the process of adopting dry debarking techniques, since the methods of effluent treatment required for the by-products of wet debarking are very costly.[176] In 1988, Canadian pulp and paper mills discharged 600 tonnes of wood wastes into water every day.[177] Canadian mills caused 1,900 tonnes of BOD in the same year.[178]

Once the wood has been reduced to chips, it is turned into pulp through mechanical, chemical, or semi-chemical means. These processes separate the cellulose fibres from lignin, hemicelluloses, and other wood substances. In mechanical pulping processes, the fibres are separated by mechanical means, such as grinding and chopping. The paper produced from this pulp is relatively stiff and not as strong as pulps produced using chemicals.[179] Chemical pulping degrades and dissolves the lignin, leaving behind most of the cellulose and hemicellulose fibres, which allows the manufacturing of very high-quality paper products.[180]

There are two principal chemical pulping methods. These are the kraft process and the sulphite process. The kraft process has become dominant in the Canadian industry as result of its advantages in terms of chemical recovery and pulp strength. However, the kraft process is a source of significant air pollution, particularly in the form of organic sulphide gases.[181]

Following kraft pulping processes, some of the lignin, which causes the pulp's brown colour, remains in the pulp. As a result, the pulp is treated with chemicals to remove the lignin and enhance its brightness. Chlorine has been the most common bleaching agent employed by Canadian kraft pulp mills, and it is at the bleaching stage that persistent and bioaccumulative chlorinated compounds are formed. In addition, in kraft mills, the bleaching stage is the source of about half the BOD, all the organochlorines, and much of the toxicity of the effluent.[182]

Water Quality Pollutants

Non-persistent (degradable)

- domestic sewage
- fertilizers
- some household cleaners
- some industrial wastes

These compounds can be broken down by chemical reactions or by natural bacteria into simple, non-polluting substances such as carbon dioxide and nitrogen. The process can lead to low oxygen levels and eutrophication if the pollution load is high. But this damage is reversible.

Persistent (degrade slowly)

- some pesticides (e.g. DDT, dieldrin)
- some leachate components from landfill sites (municipal, industrial)
- petroleum and petroleum products
- PCBs, dioxins, polyaromatic hydrocarbons (PAHs)
- radioactive materials such as strontium-90, cesium-137, radium-226, and uranium
- metals such as lead, mercury, cadmium

This is the most rapidly growing type of pollution and includes substances that degrade very slowly or cannot be broken down at all; they may remain in the aquatic environment for years or longer periods of time. The damage they cause is either irreversible or reparable only over decades or centuries.

Other

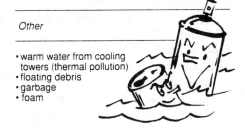

- warm water from cooling towers (thermal pollution)
- floating debris
- garbage
- foam

These are examples not of chemical pollution, but of physical pollution which interferes mainly with the usability and/or aesthetic appeal of the water. In certain cases, thermal pollution can kill fish.

Courtesy of Environment Canada.

The chlorinated organic substances discharged from kraft mills can be measured as AOX (absorbable organo halides). These compounds, which include dioxins and furans, are persistent and bioaccumulative. Some cause cancer and birth defects, and "might have large-scale, long-range environmental effects."[183] In addition, Swedish studies comparing fish living near bleached kraft mills with those near non-bleached kraft mills found that near the bleached kraft mills there were fewer fish, greater failures of sexual maturation, more fin erosion, more deformed skulls, and increased disturbances of biochemical and physiological functions.[184] There are eight bleached kraft mills in Ontario. In the early 1980s these mills typically discharged 4 kilograms of AOX per air-dried tonne (ADT) of pulp, although one mill was as high as 8 kilograms AOX/ADT.[185]

The pulp from sulphite mills is less coloured than kraft pulp and therefore requires less bleaching. In addition, as a result of the environmental impacts of the chlorine bleaching process, many sulphide mills are switching to hydrogen peroxide as a bleaching agent.[186] Mechanical pulp does not require a delignification stage, and as a result the pulp requires only brightening or decolouration. Sodium hydrosulphite is the most common agent use to brighten the pulp, although hydrogen peroxide is used when high brightness is required. The effluents from mechanical mills tend to have high BOD values. However, unlike effluent from sulphite and kraft pulp, mechanical pulp effluent contains no chlorinated organics or dioxins.[187]

The paper-making process is completed by blending various types and grades of pulp with a variety of additives. The pulp is diluted by adding water and is then passed through a headbox that distributes the fibre uniformly over the width of the paper to be formed. The suspended fibre is then deposited on a web or screen from which the water is drained. The wet paper sheets are then pressed between rollers and dried by heating.[188]

The quality of the waste water discharges from pulp and paper mills can be controlled by both in-plant and end-of-pipe treatment systems. In-plant systems include alternative pulping and bleaching technologies, while end-of-pipe systems focus only on the treatment of the effluent resulting from the pulping and bleaching processes. In-plant control measures in pulp and paper mills may include effluent reductions, chemical substitutions, chemical recoveries, spill control systems, and process changes. Measures of this nature are required to address such problems as the presence of persistent toxic substances in mill effluent. End-of-pipe technologies include primary treatment systems, which remove suspended organic and inorganic materials, and secondary treatment systems, which reduce BOD and dissolved organic materials. Some mills also have tertiary treatment systems, which are designed to further improve waste water quality.[189]

The federal Pulp and Paper Effluent Regulations promulgated under the *Fisheries Act*[190] in 1971 have been described elsewhere in this chapter. These standards were updated and strengthened in June 1992. As for Ontario, a program to investigate the quality and quantity of pulp and paper mill effluent was undertaken by the Water Resources Commission in the early 1960s. The results showed that the effluent contained large quantities of waste products, particularly suspended solids and oxygen demanding wastes.[191] At the time there were no regulatory limits on pulp mill effluent.

These findings resulted in the development of a five-year plan for the abatement of pollution from the pulp and paper sector. This plan called for large reductions in the discharge of suspended solids and oxygen demanding wastes. The strategy also identified in-plant and waste treatment technologies available at the time to meet these goals.[192]

As a result of these measures, by the mid-1970s most Ontario mills had installed facilities for the removal of suspended solids. This brought them into compliance with the federal *Fisheries Act* requirements. In addition, at some locations the Ontario government required further measures for the reduction of suspended solids through the imposition of a series of control orders.

The Ontario government's actions in this regard were prompted to a considerable degree by ongoing pressures from both the Liberal and New Democratic Party opposition in the Legislature and the province's environmental community, particularly following the reduction of the Progressive Conservative government to a minority government in 1975. Indeed, in 1978 and 1979 the opposition parties combined their strength in the Legislature to gain control over the Legislature's Standing Committee on Resources Development for the purpose of conducting a series of investigations into environmental issues. Pollution control in the pulp and paper sector was one of the subjects on which the committee focused its work.[193]

Although the province took steps to address the problems associated with suspended solids and BOD in mill effluent, the question of persistent toxic substances continued to receive limited attention. This shortcoming was to be addressed by the MISA program, announced in 1986. The pulp and paper industry is one of nine industrial sectors targeted by this program. A MISA monitoring regulation was put in place for the industry in 1990.

During the 1990 election campaign, the New Democratic Party promised that it would, if elected, ban the discharge of chlorine-based chemicals from pulp mills through the MISA program. Representatives of the pulp and paper industry have argued that the achievement of this goal would cost more than $1 billion, and could cause companies to close some or all of the eight mills in Ontario that use chlorine.[194] Instead, the industry has offered to reduce its discharges of chlorinated organics to 1.5 kilograms AOX/ADT of pulp by 1995. This would be a reduction from the 1992 limit of 2.5 kilograms AOX/ADT. The draft effluent regulation for the sector was scheduled to be released in the fall of 1992.

Mining, Milling, and Smelting of Minerals[195]

The mining, milling, and smelting of minerals all tend to be substantial sources of water pollution. (Refining is more closely associated with air pollution, particularly acid rain.) The 1985 report of Ontario's Royal Commission on the Northern Environment, led by a mining company executive, painted a rosy picture of the mining industry. "Mining," the report said, "has played a formidable part in strengthening Ontario's economic position, has always paid its way and received little assistance from the taxpayers to maintain its health and expansion." The report played down any suggestion that mining might have negative impacts on the environment. Today, it is questionable whether mining has "paid its way." The mining industry has left behind thousands of abandoned mines, which now must be cleaned up at public expense. The cost of preventing acid mine drainage at the abandoned Kam Kotia site in Ontario from polluting the water is expected to cost between $12 million and $20 million.[196] The Serpent River basin was seriously polluted in the 1960s with radionuclides from uranium mines in the Elliot Lake area.

In 1990, the value of Canadian mineral production, including mining, milling, smelting, and refining, was $19.7 billion, or 4.5 per cent of Canada's gross domestic product. However, producing the product results in large quantities of liquid effluent and solid waste, which endanger watercourses. According to Environment Canada, water pollutants originate primarily from mine de-watering, liquid effluent from the mining process, and surface water drainage and seepage from waste storage areas and inactive mines. Mine water can become very acidic, and may contain chemical residues from explosives used in blasting and lubricants from drilling and extraction operations. In milling, reagents are used to extract the valuable minerals from the ore. They include cyanide, kerosene, organic flotation agents, activated carbon, and sulphuric acid.

The salable minerals are a minute fraction of the mineral-bearing rock (called "ore") that is taken from the ground and processed. For example, for every two-tenths of an ounce of gold that is mined, 5,000 tonnes of ore must be ground up, treated with chemicals, and disposed of. In 1990, the mining industry generated an estimated 950,000 tonnes of tailings and 1 million tonnes of waste rock *each day*.[197] Although some of this is re-used, "each year about 650 million tonnes of waste is added to the billions of tonnes of accumulated mining and mineral processing wastes."[198] The mining sector also consumed 3,906,000 cubic metres of water in 1981. Although much of the water is recirculated, large quantities that contain contaminants are discharged.

One of the worst problems is abandoned mines. No one knows how many there are or where they are all located, and how many of them have the potential to create serious water pollution. The Ontario Ministry of Northern Development and Mines has a record of about 5,500 inactive mines.[199] About 90 per cent of these mines were gold mines, which would have made extensive use of cyanide in many cases. According to Environment Canada, only 50 sites are known to have acid drainage problems. However, according to the Ontario Ministry of Northern Development, there are about 200 "major sites" that "might have environmental problems." Until recently, there was no legislation requiring mine operators to "reclaim" or "rehabilitate" them to prevent water pollution and other environmental problems after closure. This had to be done on a case-by-case basis, and the Ministry of the Environment had authority under the *Environmental Protection Act* and the *Ontario Water Resources Act* to issue both preventive and corrective orders, but seldom did. In addition, the ministry could require any mining or milling operation to obtain certificates of approval for effluent discharges and air emissions. But in the past this was rarely required. Moreover, although certificates of approval are normally required to establish and operate waste disposal sites, and are subject to stringent terms and conditions, rockfill and tailings from mills and mines are exempted from the provisions of the waste management part of the *Environmental Protection Act*, and therefore the disposal of these wastes at mines and mills requires no approval by the Ministry of the Environment.

Recently, however, provisions have been added to the *Mining Act* allowing the Ministry of Northern Development and Mines, which administers the Act, to require the rehabilitation of closed mines. These provisions are briefly noted in Chapter 7.

The Ontario government began a program of identifying the abandoned mines and determining which ones required reclamation in the late 1970s. However, the cost is so great that little of the work needed has been undertaken. In 1990, a budget of about $500,000 a year was available, and the Ministry of Northern Development had prepared a submission to Cabinet asking for more. Unfortunately, it is unlikely that enough money will be available to prevent serious spills like the pollution from the abandoned Matchewan Mine in 1990.

A $12.5 million national program, Mine Environmental Neutral Drainage (MEND) was established in 1988 to coordinate research into clean-up of radioactive tailings. It is estimated that it will take 15 years and $3 billion to correct the sulphuric acid and heavy metals problems caused by the tailings.[200] The mining industry has argued that it cannot bear this cost and remain competitive. Consequently, it seems likely that the public will have to bear the costs of much of this clean-up.

Although the Ontario *Mining Act* now requires operators to post security that can be used to ensure that mines are properly safeguarded when they are closed, there are no provisions similar to the Ontario *Aggregate Resources Act*[201] creating a fund on which to draw to rehabilitate mines abandoned in the past. (See Chapter 23.) The public will continue to subsidize the industry to the tune of millions of taxpayer dollars for the clean-up of this legacy of neglect.

One potential mechanism for ensuring the proper location, design, and operation of mines is the *Environmental Assessment Act*.[202] Although private sector activities are generally exempt from this statute, the proposed Onakawana lignite mine in northwestern Ontario was designated under the Act in the early 1980s. In addition, even if the mine itself is exempt, public works needed to service the mine, such as mining roads through Crown lands might require an environmental assessment.[203]

The *Mining Act*[204] and the *Industrial and Mining Lands Compensation Act*[205] together grant extraordinary rights to mining companies and mill operators. The *Mining Act* allows an official called the mining and lands commissioner to grant mine and mill operators easements over other people's lands. These easements give mines and mills the right to use neighbours' lands for various purposes, including constructing drainage works through the property, draining any bodies of water, damming and diverting watercourses, constructing roads, and even dumping tailings, slimes, and other wastes.[206] Once the commissioner has granted an easement, the affected landowner is deprived of his or her common law right to seek an injunction to stop or prevent injury or damage to the property or interference with the owner's enjoyment of his or her property. Instead, the landowner's remedy is limited to damages — an amount of money the court considers adequate to compensate the landowner.[207]

Under the *Industrial and Mining Lands Compensation Act*, the mining company can negotiate compensation with the landowner. Acceptance of the compensation prevents the landowner from ever bringing an action for damages or an injunction. If the agreement is registered on the title to the land, future owners are also barred from obtaining any relief through the courts.

Although a landowner need not enter into such an agreement, If the landowner refuses to make an agreement with the mining company to use his or her land, the *Mining Act* authorizes the commissioner to grant the operator of the mine or mill an easement to do the things mentioned above. However, the commissioner is prohibited from imposing such an easement on an unwilling landowner, unless:

- any injury or damage caused to the landowner can be adequately compensated for;
- in all the circumstances, it seems reasonable and fitting to grant the easement;
- if injury or damage has already been suffered, the commissioner has determined the appropriate compensation and it has been paid;
- no unnecessary damage or injury is done to the land, property, rights, or interests of other persons; and
- all injury or damage caused by the exercise of the easement is fully compensated.[208]

Oil and Natural Gas Pollution

Refined and crude oils and gasolines, which are toxic to aquatic organisms and humans, are found in many of Ontario's lakes and rivers, and in soil and groundwater. In fact, federal and provincial statistics show that petroleum products leak and spill more often than any other pollutant.[209] These leaks and spills come from motor vehicles, oil refineries, service stations, aircraft, transformers, trains, manufacturing plants, and many other sources.

Although there are thousands of smaller spills each year, they are overshadowed by accidental spills from oil tankers, like the *Amoco Cadiz* and *Exxon Valdez* incidents. Since the *Arrow* went down off the coast of Nova Scotia in 1970, we are told that much work has been done by industry and government to deal with future accidents. Industry and government often have oil spill contingency plans, and the large oil companies have set up a spill response program known as CANUTECH. Nevertheless, Ministry of the Environment spill statistics showed that in the early 1980s, fewer than half the companies and government agencies causing spills had contingency plans.[210]

When Otto Lang was the federal minister of transport, he was pleased to announce in Parliament in 1977 that Canada had "some of the firmest regulations regarding standards for equipment, construction of vessels and the certification of masters and others in charge of vessels entering Canadian waters."[211] Despite all this, however, *The Globe and Mail* reported in September 1977 that a 1975 oil spill off the coast of British Columbia found government authorities and private industry uncoordinated, unprepared, understaffed, and lacking sufficient clean-up equipment.

Fifteen years later, a public inquiry raised the same kinds of concerns after two oil spills on the Pacific coast. In late December 1988, a spill from an oil tanker hit the west coast of Vancouver Island. Three months later, the *Exxon Valdez* ran aground in Prince William Sound. Public complaint over ineffective, expensive, and poorly organized clean-up efforts led the federal government to strike a Public Review Panel on Tanker Safety and Marine Response Capability, chaired by David Brander Smith. In September 1990, the panel reported, making about 90 recommendations, including requiring double hulls on oil tankers, the implementation of a levy on marine oil shipments to finance preparedness efforts, increased resources for inspections of foreign tankers entering Canadian waters, and a public environmental assessment of growing west coast crude oil exports. Following Brander Smith's report, some reorganization of prevention and response arrangements was undertaken, but many of the panel's recommendations, including those listed above, had not been implemented as of October 1992.

Oil and natural gas wells may also pollute water. There are only a few small oil wells in Ontario. They produce only a few barrels of oil a day, which are shipped mostly by truck to refineries. However, there is offshore oil under Lake Erie that has not been exploited. Oil and gas wells can pollute water tables. Oil and gas may migrate from one "horizon" (underground layer) of fresh water, oil, or gas to another. Various fluids (chiefly salt water) injected into the ground to increase oil pressure and production can also escape and are a potential source of pollution of land, air, and water. Underwater wells may permit the escape of gas, which will bubble up and dissipate into the water.

Producers, handlers, transporters, distributors and sellers of petroleum and natural gas are regulated chiefly by four statutes. The production of oil and gas is regulated primarily by the

Petroleum Resources Act,[212] which covers the drilling, production, and storage of crude oil and natural gas, and the *Energy Act*,[213] which covers the handling and use of hydrocarbons.

Refineries, bulk plants, service stations, and companies and institutions that fuel their fleets of vehicles from their own tanks and pumps are regulated primarily by the *Gasoline Handling Act*.[214] The design and installation of appliances for burning fuel in boilers and the storage of any fuel not covered by the *Gasoline Handling Act* is regulated by the *Energy Act*, whose regulations are roughly parallel to those governing facilities under the *Gasoline Handling Act*. Finally, under the *Ontario Energy Board Act*,[215] the Ontario Energy Board plays a role in ensuring the safety of pipelines carrying oil and natural gas within Ontario.

Under the *Petroleum Resources Act*, the minister of natural resources has a broad discretionary power to grant licences and permits to oil and gas well operators.[216] The minister may — and if the applicant requests it, he or she must — refer any refusal to issue a licence or any conditions imposed on the licence to the Ontario Energy Board, which will then hold a hearing. The board has no decision-making power. It can only make recommendations to the minister, who then makes the final decision.

The Exploration, Drilling and Production Regulations[217] set out detailed instructions for such things as the location of offshore drilling areas, applications for drilling, reporting uncontrolled flowing of any oil or gas well, and well blowout prevention. A well operator must ensure that salt water, drilling fluid, oil, refuse, and any flammable products from a well are not handled or disposed of in a way that creates a hazard to public health or contaminates any freshwater horizon. Waste or mineral oil must not be disposed of underground without the approval of the minister. Underwater well operators must satisfy the minister that they carry $1,000,000 in insurance — an amount has never been raised, although inflation has reduced its value dramatically since this provision was made in 1972. Records must be kept of any oil, gas, water, and sediment produced by an operating well of any kind, and the minister may require copies of these records. Accidents must be reported at once to the minister, and wells must be plugged when they are abandoned.

Although the *Petroleum Resources Act* regulates the "mining" of oil and gas, their distribution through pipelines or by other means is regulated under the *Energy Act* and by the Ontario Energy Board under the *Ontario Energy Board Act*. The *Energy Act*, which is administered by the Ministry of Consumer and Commercial Relations, attempts to prevent leaks and spills that may cause explosions, fires, and soil and water pollution through a system of licences, permits, and certificates required for the installation of pipelines and appliances that burn oil or gas. Inspectors appointed under the Act have wide powers, including the power to issue orders to comply with the Act or regulations if they find contraventions.

The decision whether an oil or gas pipeline can be built in the province rests with the Ontario Energy Board. The board decides whether to approve the construction of and can also authorize the expropriation of land for a pipeline. The board requires applicants to comply with a set of "Environmental Guidelines for Locating, Constructing, and Operating Hydrocarbon Pipelines in Ontario."[218] The guidelines require the pipeline proponent to carry out an environmental study that includes a consideration of the protection of water quality and fish and wildlife habitat, both in choosing the optimal route and in carrying out construction. Before the board holds a public hearing on the application, members of the public have an opportunity to review the environmental impact report and to challenge it or ask the board at the public hearing to make the findings in the report binding on the proponent. The board has stated that it expects proponent companies "to comply with these guidelines before, during, and after construction."[219] In addition, an Ontario Pipeline Coordinating Committee, composed of representatives of several ministries that may have concerns about the environmental impact of the project, as well as the Niagara Escarpment Commission and conservation authorities, have an opportunity to review the applicant's environmental report and play a role in inspecting the construction activities and in monitoring post-construction activities. As mentioned in Chapter 9, the National Energy Board plays a similar role when pipelines are to be constructed between provinces or between Canada and the United States.

The *Gasoline Handling Act* and the *Gasoline Handling Code*,[220] which is a regulation under the Act, regulate the storage and handling of gasoline and other petroleum products used as fuel when they are not covered by the *Energy Act*. All service stations, refineries, bulk plants, marinas, and "retail outlets," which are facilities operated by private companies and institutions to fuel up their fleets of vehicles, fall under this Act.

The Code sets out standards for construction and installation of underground and aboveground tanks and piping and pumps, methods of monitoring for leaks and leak detection, precautions to be taken to prevent spills and requirements to clean up spills, and steps to be taken to remove underground tanks and dispose of them safely once they are no longer in use. The *Gasoline Handling Act* is a very important statute, since there are probably more spills of petroleum products from facilities governed by this Act than from any other source.

Much of Ontario's groundwater contamination has resulted from spills and leaks from facilities regulated under this Act. The administration of the Act suffers from too few inspectors and too little funding. Many facilities have not been inspected for years because of inadequate staffing, and violations of the Act or its regulations are rarely prosecuted. Little or no training is required to obtain a licence to install or repair tanks, lines, and pumps, and anyone can remove a tank without a licence. Operators of facilities regulated under this Act are not required to carry any liability insurance, and many service stations have none. Therefore, many spills and leaks are cleaned up at public expense, because the operator has insufficient resources to pay for the clean-up. The Ministry of Consumer and Commercial Relations is aware of the deficiencies in the Act and regulations. A new *Gasoline Handling Code* that would improve the safety of these facilities was drafted long ago, but has never been made law.

Although petroleum products used as fuel and natural gas are regulated, there is no similar law regulating the construction, installation, operation, monitoring, and abandonment of many other tanks holding chemicals that are just as harmful to water quality and public health and safety as petroleum used for fuel. A task force consisting of members of the federal Department of the Environment and the provincial governments drafted an Environmental Code of Practice for Allied Petroleum Products in 1990.[221] This code would cover many of the most hazardous substances, such as petroleum products used as solvents, cleaners, and degreasers. But Ontario has never adopted the code. In the absence of any legislation setting specific standards for the design, installation, monitoring, and removal of such tanks, the main legislative tool available to prevent leaks and spills is the *Environmental Protection Act*, under which the Ministry of Environment and Energy can require such facilities to apply for certificates of approval, and can issue pollution prevention and abatement orders.

Down on the Farm: Agricultural Pollution of Water

Bacteria dangerous to public health obtain access to the water through failing septic tanks, improper waste management of intensive livestock and poultry operations, and direct access of cattle to streams. Phosphates, nitrates and chemicals applied to soils and crops in rural areas enter the streams along with soil particles in runoff water and through the drainage systems. Waste discharges from agricultural-related industries in rural areas are a further source of nitrogen and phosphorus inputs to streams. A study of streamflow and nutrient levels in the Thames River system indicated that 76 percent of the annual total phosphorus load and 95 percent of the total nitrogen load contributions to the watershed originated from rural sources.

The significance of animal wastes as a source of pollutants in the [Thames River] basin can be demonstrated through a comparison with human waste equivalents. In terms of BOD alone, livestock in this watershed, in 1971, generated waste equivalent to a human population of more than 3.4 million. ... This compares to an actual 1971 population of 414,000 people in the basin.

Ontario, Ministry of the Environment and Ministry of Natural Resources,
Water Management Study: Thames River Basin, *1975*

Although this passage was written in 1975, it could as easily have been written in 1993. Little has changed. Although farmers are prosecuted for manure spills more frequently than in the 1970s, when they were considered untouchable, Ministry of Environment scientists have sometimes wondered whether such prosecutions are a productive use of their time, since they focus on individual incidents, but do little to change the types of farming practices that cause the most water pollution.

The main sources of agricultural pollution of water are excessive amounts of fertilizers; drainage from general farm activities (such as runoff from field); animal wastes running off from intensive feedlots; excessive use of pesticides; and the tilling of fields in a manner that accelerates soil erosion and runoff of poison-laden snow melt and rainfall.

There are no legally binding standards for the construction of manure storage facilities. Manure tanks are left uncovered and allowed to fill with manure until a heavy rainfall causes them to overflow. Manure pits are often holes in the ground surrounded by earthen berms. When the berms erode or collapse, the manure spills over the top or flows through the sides.

There is an Agricultural Code of Practice that farmers are encouraged to follow to prevent pollution (see Chapter 17), but it deals mainly with the elimination of odour and air problems rather than the prevention of water pollution. The Ministry of Agriculture and Food subsidizes a portion of the cost of building modern manure-holding tanks that are less likely to result in pollution, but farmers say the subsidy is not large enough to encourage such an expenditure.

When farmers spray or spread the contents of their manure pits on farm fields to fertilize them, they must be careful about the time of year, the weather and soil conditions, the rate and duration of the application, and the proximity to watercourses, wells, groundwater, drainage tiles and drainage ditches, and residential areas. Excessive application at the wrong time of year will result in groundwater contamination or runoff into watercourses.

The ministries of environment and energy and agriculture and food have jointly published guidelines for spreading sludge from sewage treatment plants on farm fields, and the Ministry of Environment and Energy has guidelines for spreading the contents of septic tanks and holding tanks.[222] Although not legally binding, these guidelines suggest how to avoid such runoff and groundwater infiltration, and failure to comply with them would probably be cogent evidence of a lack of due diligence in any prosecution for water pollution arising from spreading of manure or sewage sludge on agricultural land. The federal government has also issued some guidelines aimed at prevention of water pollution and other pollution problems from farms. The Canada Animal Waste Management Guide, prepared by a joint federal-provincial committee and published by Agriculture Canada, sets out appropriate methods for handling animal waste. For example, it recommends that manure should not be spread in the winter on frozen soil; storage facilities should be manure-tight and rainproof to prevent leakage; and after spreading manure on land, it should be plowed under within 24 hours to control odour and runoff from fields.[223]

With respect to pesticides, as noted in Chapter 20, the Ontario Ministry of Agriculture and Food has established a land stewardship program to provide farmers with financial incentives to adopt conservation farming practices and a program designed to wean farmers from excessive reliance on pesticides.[224] Farmers are generally subject to the requirements of environmental statutes, and can be prosecuted for pollution under the *Pesticides Act*,[225] the *Environmental Protection Act*, and the *Ontario Water Resources Act*. However, there are specific exemptions for certain farm activities. Under the *Environmental Protection Act*, the disposal of animal wastes "in accordance with normal farming practices" (which are nowhere defined in the Act) is exempt from prosecution under section 14(a), which makes it an offence to discharge a contaminant that causes or is likely to cause impairment of the quality of the natural environment.

However, animal waste disposal resulting in the other adverse effects listed in section 14 is not immune from prosecution. Animal wastes are also exempted in several other places in the Act. They are exempted from the prohibition against discharging contaminants in greater amounts than those specified in regulations. The waste management regulation also exempts animal wastes from regulation under the waste management part of the *Environmental Protection Act*; that is, the storage, transportation, and disposal of animal wastes often will require no certificate of approval, and need not conform to any of the standards for proper waste management set out for other kinds of waste hauling, treatment, and disposal facilities. In addition, unlike other people, who need a permit under the *Ontario Water Resources Act* to take water from a body of water or from the ground in excess of 50,000 litres a day, farmers need no permit unless the water is used for irrigating crops. Nor do farmers need a permit to build sewage systems to drain agricultural lands, or to construct drainage systems under the *Drainage Act*.[226]

There are also exemptions under the *Pesticides Act* for farmers spraying pesticides on their own land or helping neighbours (see Chapter 20).

Farmers need not keep records of what pesticides they have used or how much. This special treatment is significant in relation to water quality, since there is evidence of pesticide pollution of farm wells throughout North America and Europe.[227]

Moreover, under the *Ontario Building Code*,[228] a farmer who constructs a farm building (no definition given) for his or her own purposes does not need to obtain a building permit.

Salt on the Roads

At a snow removal conference in 1914 in Philadelphia, one of the earliest on record, it was reported that salt was extensively used for snow removal in England and France. The conference doubted that this practice would be successful in North America because of the heavier snowfalls, and also because of anticipated objections by the Society for Prevention of Cruelty to Animals.[229]

Despite warmer winters and less snow in recent years in many parts of Ontario, the amount of salt spread on our roads continues to increase. In the winter of 1966-67, about 300,000 tons of road salt were used in Ontario.[230] In 1988-89, almost 620,000 tonnes were spread.[231] By 1990-91, salt use had increased to almost 700,000 tonnes.[232] In 1991-92, the Ministry of Transport estimated that salt usage had dropped back to 640,000 tonnes, as a result of the implementation of a salt reduction program.[233]

The use of salt on roads is motivated by a concern for public safety. Salt reduces accidents, but so would motorists driving more cautiously if they were forced to by a decision to use less salt. Public authorities, with an eye constantly cocked to their potential civil liability for accidents caused by slippery roads, are unwilling to use less effective but less damaging alternatives to road salt.

However, if one were to compare the costs of damage to the environment, to property, and possibly to human health from using salt with the danger of injuries caused by using less salt, it is questionable whether the current level of salt usage would be justifiable. It is a case of the government agencies externalizing their costs. That is, the agencies avoid liability for accidents on slippery roads, but the costs of damage caused by heavy salt usage are borne by others.

Salt dissolved in water rusts the bodies of cars at double the normal rate of corrosion,[234] and manufacturing motor vehicles with salt-resistant bodies and the addition of rust-proofing adds substantially to the cost to the purchaser. Salt destroys boots, shoes, and other clothing, such as coats splashed by and pantlegs dragged through slush.

Salt-laden slush on the windshield may seriously reduce visibility, and drivers may be lulled into a false sense of security by what looks like bare pavement, when in fact the road is covered by a thin film of very slippery liquid.

Roads and bridges themselves suffer from salt contamination. Salt can cause concrete to develop large cracks and surface pitting. In a 1971 study, the National Research Council concluded that salt is the most significant contributor to the deterioration of concrete.

Salt splashed up by motorists can kill trees and other vegetation, and contaminate the soil up to 150 feet from the roadside, and contaminate the roadside soil to a depth of 5 feet. It has been known since at least 1962 that the sugar maple is particularly susceptible to salt, and that cumulative applications of highway de-icing salt have contributed to its decline. Various studies have also shown that Norway maples, white pine, and peach and apple trees have a poor tolerance to salt.

Perhaps the greatest danger of salt use is the pollution of our drinking water. Many shallow wells near roads are contaminated with road salt. Wells near roads have been found to have up to six times the chloride concentrations permissible in drinking water supplies.[235]

Salty water is recognized as a health hazard by scientists, but not by law makers. The Ministry of Environment and Energy considers chloride an "aesthetic parameter" rather than a health-related one. That is, its desirable and permissible drinking water objectives are based on taste rather than on a health standard. Yet salt can be very harmful to people with heart or kidney diseases, and newborn babies are a special risk group. In 1977, doctors predicted that if we continue to increase the amount of salt spread on snowy streets, our drinking water will be dangerous for many people within 20 years.[236]

The problem is that salt dissolves in water. No matter how it is disposed of, it will end up in our water supply. Lake Ontario's salt content has continued to rise since about 1910, and the Environment Ministry has said that de-icing salt has been a significant contributor to this increase.[237] Creeks and streams in the Toronto vicinity have exhibited an increase of up to 400 per cent in the concentrations of salt in winter.[238] There is no place for water containing road salt to go in cities except sewers and streams.

Regulation of De-Icing Salt

There is no direct regulation of salt de-icing in the province, only guidelines for snow disposal and de-icing operations. These guidelines were prepared by the Ministry of the Environment in 1975.[239] They state:

> Snow removed from roadways should not be dumped directly into Ontario's watercourses, nor should such snow be disposed of on ice covered rivers or lakes. If circumstances preclude the disposal of snow on approved land sites or disposal by other acceptable means, the approval of the Ontario Ministry of the Environment is required prior to dumping directly to a watercourse.

In the 1978 edition of this book, we reported that the ministry offices "do not have the staff to gather the necessary information." When we inquired again in 1990, we were told that there is no monitoring plan to determine whether municipalities and provincial road authorities are complying with the guidelines, nor does the ministry make any special trips to landfill sites where salt-laden snow is dumped to monitor what is happening.

Salt and sand deposited on roads is exempt from most provisions of the *Environmental Protection Act*. A regulation made in 1972 under the Act states:

> Where any substance used on a highway by the Crown as represented by the Minister of Transportation and Communications or any road authority or any agent or employee of any of them for the purpose of keeping the highway safe for traffic under conditions of snow or ice or both is a contaminant, it is classified and is exempt from the provisions of the Act and the Regulations.[240]

This regulation appears to prevent the Ministry of Environment and Energy from issuing a certificate of approval to such a road authority in which terms and conditions restrict the way the salt is spread, or issuing pollution prevention or abatement orders to such authorities if there activities are causing damage. However, section 14 of the *Environmental Protection Act*, which makes the discharge or deposit of a contaminant that is likely to cause adverse effects an offence, probably overrides this regulation. Thus, even though the Ministry of Environment and Energy cannot order a road authority to clean up its act, the ministry or any concerned individual can prosecute the authority for committing an offence. However, the authority would be acquitted if it could show that it exercised all reasonable care to avoid committing the offence. It might be enough to show that its road-salting practices were typical of those throughout the province, or that no more salt was used than was reasonably necessary to keep the road clear.

This provision, however, does not prevent a person harmed by road salt from success-fully suing the road authority for damage to health or property. For example, two Niagara-area farmers successfully sued the Ontario Ministry of Transportation for road salt damage to their fruit trees. In an effort to avoid liability for road salt damage, the government took the case all the way to the Supreme Court of Canada, but lost, a process that took about a decade.[241] In addition, notwithstanding the exemption of de-icing activities from the law, the Ministry of Environment and Energy has a policy that where wells are contaminated by road salt, the ministry will share the cost of restoring the water supply with the road authority on a 50/50 basis. However, if the road authority refuses to provide any compensation, the ministry will pay 75 per cent of the cost, and the well owner will have to pay 25 per cent or sue the road authority for that portion of the cost. Moreover, damage from road salt will be given priority in a ministry program that subsidizes the cost of replacing private wells that yield poor water quality with deeper wells or wells in a different location.[242]

Dust Suppressants

Another potential source of water pollution is the spreading of material on public and private unpaved rural roads during the warm months to keep down dust that annoys neighbours. The materials used most often in Ontario include oil, salt brine, calcium chloride, and pulping liquors (lignosulphonates and spent sulfite liquor).[243] The Ministry of Environment and Energy keeps no statistics on the amounts of dust suppressants used throughout the province each year; however, a 1985 study estimated that over 135 million litres of dust suppressants were applied in southern Ontario in 1983.[244]

Unfortunately, in attempting to solve one environmental problem, those who use dust suppressants create another. Eventually, and often sooner rather than later, these dust suppressants are washed off the roads into ditches, and carried into watercourses. Calcium chloride, of course, is salt, whose impacts on property, health, and the environment are described above. Pulp liquors are high in BOD and moderately toxic to fish.

Of greatest concern, however, was the use of waste oil. Because it was difficult to control the amounts of PCBs in waste oil used as a dust suppressant, it was banned in 1988.[245] Other than this, there is no regulation to govern the kinds and amounts of dust suppressants used and the circumstances under which they are applied. For example, when dust suppressants are applied shortly before a rainfall, they may be washed off the road before they can be absorbed into the dirt, so it would make sense to regulate under which weather conditions spreading may take place.

Thermal Pollution

Water is used as a coolant in many industries and in power generating stations. It is discharged back into the body of water from which it was taken, at considerably higher temperatures. Nuclear power plants consume twice as much water as coal-fired plants, but both kinds of plants use large amounts, so many of them must be built on the shores of the Great Lakes. Stripping land of trees and vegetation for agriculture also causes thermal pollution,[246] and although we are not aware of specific studies, it is likely that the runoff from paved urban areas also raises the temperature of waters into which this runoff drains.

Thermal pollution can change the aquatic ecosystem, resulting in the loss of some species of fish and invertebrates and the growth of nuisance algae. Fish are not only killed by overheated water, but are also sucked into the cooling systems of industrial plants and power-generating stations. This particular problem has been dealt with through amendments to the *Fisheries Act* providing that the minister of fisheries and oceans may require that a cooling water system be provided at its entrance with a fish guard or screen to prevent fish entering the water intake.[247]

The discharge of water that is warmer than the surrounding water may be an offence under the *Fisheries Act*, the *Canadian Environmental Protection Act*,[248] the *Ontario Water Resources Act*, and the *Environmental Protection Act*. The *Environmental Protection Act* specifically lists heat as a contaminant. The other statutes, however, prohibit the discharge of harmful "substances." The heat in the water, of course, is not a substance. The water that is discharged is a substance. If an argument was made that it is not the substance — the water — that causes the harm but the heat in it, it is unlikely that the courts would separate the two. They would probably treat the heated water as a harmful substance.

The federal and provincial EA processes may also useful in controlling the design and operation of facilities that discharge warm water. Thermal pollution is the kind of impact that would probably be assessed under both processes. In addition, the Ministry of Environment and Energy has established guidelines for discharges of heated water to the Great Lakes system. They provide limits for the temperature of the water being discharged and require-ments that the discharge not raise the temperature of the receiving water by more than 10°C. No water may be discharged into a water body whose temperature already exceeds 30°C. These guidelines are not legally enforceable standards, but would be used on a case-by-case basis in deciding whether to issue approvals or impose pollution prevention or abatement orders.

Thermal pollution from land-use activities such as farming and the urbanization of the countryside, however, is much harder to control without substantial changes in how we treat our land base.

Water Resources Management Issues

Diversion and Consumptive Uses[249]

Until recently, there were no laws designed specifically to control major diversions of water from one body of water within a basin to another, or from one basin to another. The issue has become increasingly urgent as proposals have been put forward to transport water long distances through pipelines, canals, and reservoirs to transfer water from North America's wet areas to its dry regions, or to replace polluted water supplies with clean ones. One diversion scheme that caught the public eye was a suggestion by a Canadian mining engineer, Tom Kierans, supported by the premier of Quebec, Robert Bourassa, to capture water from rivers flowing into James Bay, pump it to the Great Lakes, then distribute it — for a price — to areas as far away as California and Mexico. This "Grand Canal" scheme called for a 160-kilometre-long system of dykes and causeways across the mouth of James Bay to turn it into a 70,000 square kilometre reservoir of fresh water, pumping water over the Canadian Shield, and transporting it by canals and rivers to the Great Lakes. Another proposal was a 1981 plan for a coal slurry pipeline in the United States, using water from Lake Ontario. Foreign ships filling their holds with Great Lakes water to sell abroad also raised a few eyebrows. As Michael Keating has suggested in *To the Last Drop*, the kind of engineering solution to draught represented by the Grand Canal and other similar proposals "involves nothing less than changing the face of the continent in a way it has not been changed since the glaciers melted, releasing cascades of water which carved many of our rivers and filled our lakes."[250]

Such proposals found a legal system unprepared for them. The common law doctrine of riparian rights (see Chapter 6) provided one potential tool available to prevent the taking of water in built-up areas, but would be of little use in wilderness areas where there were no private landowners along the banks of rivers and lakes. Some legislation provided that approvals were required before dams were built — but usually for limited purposes like protection of navigation. Among statutes requiring such approvals are the federal *Navigable Waters Protection Act*[251] and *International River Improvements Act*.[252] At the provincial level, the *Lakes and Rivers Improvement Act*,[253] the *Conservation Authorities Act*,[254] the *Ontario Water Resources Act*, and the *Public Lands Act*,[255] may apply. The *Public Lands Act* in particular empowers the minister of natural resources to grant or lease Crown lands or to issue a licence of occupation for their use. This may include impoundments of water in lakes and rivers located on public lands. Part IV of the *Public Lands Act* deals with the construction of dams, including dams associated with a water diversion project. Other applicable laws include the federal and Ontario EA legislation, which could be used to require an environmental impact assessment, and the *Canada Water Act*,[256] which was intended to promote integrated watershed planning and management.[257]

Both the Canadian government and the province of Ontario have traditionally taken the position that Canada's water is not for sale. Nevertheless, economic pressures can change this position. As result, it is important to have laws that deal more clearly with the possibility of large-scale diversions of Canada's waters. Two important initiatives in this area are the passage of the Great Lakes Charter[258] and the report of the Federal Inquiry on Water Policy (the Pearse commission).[259] The Great Lakes Charter is an agreement signed by the premiers of the two Canadian provinces and the US states bordering on the Great Lakes on how to deal with proposals for diversions. Each province and state agrees to adopt a use-permit system and to notify the other jurisdictions of any proposal and provide an opportunity for those jurisdictions to make representations. Ontario and Quebec agree under the charter to oppose any diversions unless both provinces, all Great Lakes states, and the two federal governments support the proposal. On the other hand, the Pearse commission did not oppose all water exports, but suggested that the federal government develop a policy and criteria for proposed water exports, and that any interbasin transfers of water should require a federal permit as well as any provincial permit that might be needed.

Following the signing of the Great Lakes Charter, Ontario passed the *Water Transfer Control Act*.[260] The preamble to the Act states that "water is a precious and limited resource that is vital to the long-term social, environmental and economic well-being of Ontario" and that "the Province has a responsibility to ensure a secure supply of water for Ontario." It provides that any transfer of water out of a provincial drainage basin will require the approval of the minister of natural resources, and authorizes the minister to approve a transfer subject to conditions and subject to payment of money to the government. The Act authorizes the minister to refuse approval only if the transfer may be detrimental to ensuring a secure water supply. No other environmental impacts can be used to justify refusal of a permit, nor is there any requirement to carry out an environmental assessment or take into account other environmental concerns.

Optimists will view initiatives like the Great Lakes Charter and the *Water Transfer Control Act* as positive steps, because they set up a framework for regulating diversions where no clear power to restrict them existed before. Pessimists, however, will point out that these initiatives also set the stage for approving the type of diversion that has never been acceptable before. They will see such legislation as the beginning of the end of our past policy that Canada's water is not for sale.

Drainage

The economic value of land is much greater when it is dry than when it is wet, because it can be used for agriculture and the construction of buildings and roads. Therefore, there is tremendous pressure to drain land with a high water table, where water ponds on the surface, wetlands, and lakes, rivers, and streams. In addition, drainage works are often constructed to prevent flooding of land during heavy storms. Drainage works sometimes improve the quality of the environment.

However, drainage systems can have many adverse environmental impacts. Destruction of wetlands and causing wells to go dry are two of the greatest concerns (see Chapter 12). In addition, although drains may alleviate the silting of watercourses in some parts of a watercourse, they may aggravate it in other areas; and although a drainage system may reduce the threat of flooding in one area, it may increase it in others. If drains are poorly constructed, they may bring more water into a watercourse than it can handle, causing flooding or erosion of the banks and bed. To prevent this, streams are often channeled, changing their natural path and destroying the natural banks and the vegetation growing along the banks. The "spoil" — the rock and soil dredged up to make or deepen or widen the drainage channels — may be disposed of indiscriminately. Drainage ditches that are not well designed can retain stagnant water, often containing bacteria and viruses that have leaked into them from defective septic systems. Improving the flow of water through these drains can alleviate this problem, although sometimes at the expense of dumping the sewage-laden water into the nearest watercourses. In addition, drains are often not properly maintained so that they become choked with weeds and debris or their physical structure is damaged or destroyed.

The Regulation of Drainage

The Ministry of Agriculture and Food estimates that more than 50 per cent of the drainage projects undertaken each year in Ontario are not agricultural but are carried out as part of urban development. This kind of drainage is generally not subject to the *Drainage Act*,[261] but would be dealt with through the land-use planning process under the *Planning Act*,[262] through tools such as subdivision agreements (see Chapter 8).

Urban stormwater is generally drained to lakes and rivers through sewers and rural stormwater is drained through ditches and swales without passing through a sewage treatment plant. Even though such stormwater is often polluted, there is generally no law requiring its treatment. Urban and rural stormwater can widen streams and cause erosion and downstream flooding.

There are provisions in the *Municipal Act*[263] authorizing municipalities to pass bylaws for constructing and maintaining a variety of drainage works, including a provision authorizing municipalities to drain wetlands. Any such drainage works are exempted from the requirements of the *Environmental Assessment Act*[264] if they will cost less than $3.5 million. There is also a regulation under the *Environmental Assessment Act* exempting agricultural drainage projects from the Act.

Statistics on the amount of land drained each year for agricultural purposes are compiled only for drainage projects that are subsidized by the Ontario government through its program of loans to farmers to assist in placing drainage tiles under their fields and grants to construct outlets from the drainage tiles to the municipal drains. Loans to drain farmland are given under the authority of the *Tile Drainage Act*.[265] To qualify for a loan, the drainage work must be carried out by a contractor licensed by the government under the *Agricultural Tile Drainage Installation Act*.[266] Between 1985 and 1990, loans of about $69 million were given to drain over 113,000 hectares of farmland. In the same period, grants of over $22 million were given under the *Drainage Act* to construct about 1,900 new drains, and over $8 million was given to support the maintenance of about 7,500 existing drainage systems.[267]

The *Drainage Act* sets up procedures for establishing several types of drains. The procedures permit neighbours, conservation authorities and others who oppose the establishment of a drain to object. Residents of the area may object because they feel they are being forced to share the cost of a drain that will benefit others more than them, because the drain may assist others but will interfere with their use and enjoyment of their land, or because of concerns about the environment generally. Public agencies such as conservation authorities may be concerned about the environmental impacts on land and water under their jurisdiction.

The Act provides for three ways of establishing a drain: by mutual agreement, by requisition, and by petition. The drains are often named after the process by which they are being established. An "agreement drain" or a "mutual agreement drain" is one constructed by several landowners at their own expense, based on a formal agreement as to the location of the drain, the land affected, and how the costs will be shared. The *Drainage Act* allows registration of the agreement on title, with the effect that future purchasers cannot interfere with the drain.

A "petition drain" involves a developer or a group of landowners petitioning the municipality to establish a drain. If enough landowners within the area to be drained sign the petition, the municipal council must consider constructing a drain. Public meetings are held to discuss what should be done. If the municipality agrees, it passes a bylaw to construct the drain. If the council decides not to construct a drain, the petitioners can appeal the refusal to the Ontario Drainage Tribunal. If the council decides to proceed, it must appoint an engineer (referred to as the drainage engineer) to prepare a preliminary report on the wisdom of such a drain. This report must look at technical considerations involved in the actual construction of the drain, as well as how the costs of construction and of compensation for any damage that will be done by the drain will be allocated among the landowners who will benefit from the drain. If an affected municipality, a conservation authority, or, in areas where there is no conservation authority, the minister of natural resources requests it, the engineer must include an environmental appraisal in the report. However, unlike the *Environmental Assessment Act*, which requires the proponent to pay for environmental studies, the agency requesting an environmental appraisal under the *Drainage Act* must pay for it.

Members of the public cannot require an environmental appraisal, but if they are dissatisfied with how the report deals with environmental concerns, they can appeal the technical aspects of the report to the Ontario Drainage Tribunal. There is also an appeal from the tribunal to the drainage referee and a right to appeal legal issues directly to the referee.

A "requisition drain" is established when a landowner who wants a drain but cannot get enough of his or her neighbours to sign a petition files a requisition for a drain. When the municipality receives a requisition it must appoint an engineer (known as the drainage engineer) to make a preliminary report on the wisdom of constructing a drain. The engineer's report must contain both a benefit-cost statement and an environmental statement. The complex approval process for the various kinds of drains and subsidies is set out in more detail in several publications available from the Ontario Ministry of Agriculture and Food.[268]

Lakefilling

Dumping fill into the water at the edges of lakes is a popular pastime because it serves two purposes at once. It gives builders a place to dispose of unwanted rock, soil, and construction materials cheaply; and it creates new land for development. In some cities on the shores of the Great Lakes, the shoreline has been moved far out into the harbour and no trace of the original shoreline remains. Changes in the configuration of the shoreline can alter wave patterns with sometimes unpredictable impacts on other areas of the shore, causing unanticipated patterns of shoreline erosion and accretion. In addition, in the past, contaminated soils and materials that leach contaminants into the water have been included in such lakefill. Material dredged from the bottoms of lakes and rivers to facilitate navigation (dredgeate) must also be disposed of, and has been used in past as fill to create new land. This dredgeate is often contaminated, and contaminated sediment has been recognized as a major environmental problem in many areas of Ontario.[269]

Where lakefilling may interfere with fisheries, it may require approval under the *Fisheries Act*. Where it may interfere with navigation, it may require approval under the *Navigable Waters Protection Act*.[270] On public lands, it may require approval under Ontario's *Public Lands Act*. In other circumstances, an approval may be required under the *Beds of Navigable Waters Act*,[271] the *Lakes and Rivers Improvement Act*,[272] or the *Conservation Authorities Act*.[273] A federal or provincial environmental assessment may be required. Where the filling is intended to facilitate development, the requirements of the *Planning Act* may apply. However, even though lakefilling is a very substantial form of waste disposal, as long as the waste is considered by the Ministry of the Environment to be "inert fill" (commonly referred to as "clean fill"), it is exempt from the requirements of part V of the *Environmental Protection Act*,[274] which requires certificates of approval for the hauling and disposal of the material. In addition, the Ontario Court of Appeal has held that filling a marsh on one's own property for the purpose of development is not depositing a contaminant and therefore is not an offence under section 14 of the Act, no matter how harmful to the environment.[275]

In 1992, the Ontario Ministry of the Environment released three sets of policies and guidelines designed to address the dumping of materials and lakefilling. The proposed policy for management of excess soil, rock, and like materials sets out a proposed classification system for such material, a system for approval and regulation of disposal sites, and measures to be taken to protect groundwater and surface waters. The fill quality guidelines for lakefilling in Ontario address a proposed screening and classification system, provide a list of parameters for which fill should be tested, and deal with the protection of water quality, aquatic habitat, and the recreation potential of water bodies into which fill is dumped. In addition, a new set of guidelines governing the quality of sediment that may be returned to the beds of lakes and rivers after being dredged up was released for public comment in June 1992. These guidelines would replace the ministry's Open Water Disposal Guidelines, developed in 1976.[276]

Dredging

Dredging is the removal of sediment from the beds of river channels, lakes, and harbours, and its disposal elsewhere. Traditionally, the disposal method of choice has been to carry it to open water or to the nearest convenient swamp and dump it. The sheer quantity of sediment removed — about 10 million cubic metres annually from the Great Lakes — has been enough to warrant concerned investigation.

Close to 90 per cent of all dredging in the Great Lakes is done to keep channels and harbours open for navigation.[277] Sand, gravel, and other minerals can be mined by dredging. Some dredging, in the past a very small proportion but likely to increase in the future, is done to remove sediments contaminated with toxic substances from lake and river beds.

Dredging has played a major part — no one knows how large — in so changing the quality of the Great Lakes that once plentiful species of fish are no longer to be found because spawning grounds have been destroyed or because the water itself has been so polluted by physical, chemical, and biological agents that it can no longer support life.

Scientists have only recently begun to view dredging with an eye to possible deleterious effects on the environment. Reliable records have been kept only since the 1920s and 1930s, and only within the last 20 years has serious research begun. But there are major environmental problems with dredging that, because only lately recognized, are hotly disputed. There are problems with the process itself, especially the disposal of sediments; with the nature of the sediment to be removed; and with the ways in which dredging can and cannot be regulated under the law.

During the past 80 years, the levels of Lake Michigan and Lake Huron have been lowered as a result of dredging both to recover materials and to improve navigation.[278] Natural harbours in bays and at river mouths have been improved by the addition of wharves and breakwaters, and enlarged by dredging up basins and approach channels. All of these create settling basins, which trap the ever-increasing sediments being carried to them by rivers and sewer outfalls. Approach channels, jetties, and breakwaters interrupt coastal processes, so regular dredging programs are now necessary to maintain a navigable depth for today's ships. Maintaining a natural harbour or channel may not harm the environment, but most contaminated sediments are found in harbours and near municipal and industrial centres, so even simple maintenance work has its dangers, especially if contaminated sediments are dumped into open, relatively clean water. When dredging is used to create an entirely new port or marina, or steel, mining, or pulp and paper facility, the geography of the lake or river bed can be so changed that entire ecosystems are altered.

Physically, dumped sediments can contribute to the further pollution of open waters by damaging spawning grounds or altering currents.

The biological and chemical nature of sediments must also be considered in making a decision about what to do with the dredged spoil. Oxygen-demanding wastes have contributed greatly to the eutrophication of large parts of Lake Erie and some portions of Lake Ontario. Of particular concern in the 1990s is the presence of bioaccumulating toxic elements in sediments. Heavy metals such as mercury and cadmium and organics such as PCBs, dioxin, and chlordane are still being found in the Great Lakes at levels which have biological impact. Levels of heavy metals and organic materials in the sediment at the bottom of some parts of Lake Erie and Lake Ontario have now been found to be considerably higher than the concentration levels normally assigned in the past to dredged sediment too polluted to be disposed of in open water.[279] More and more, contaminated sediments will have to be disposed of in contained sites on land to prevent the water from becoming more polluted.

Characteristics of lake and river beds vary widely throughout Ontario, depending on their proximity to industrial and urban centres, the depth and temperature of the water, the types of currents, and so on. It is practically impossible to set universally applicable standards. Rather, what seems to be needed is a site-by-site evaluation of the problems and solutions. Present legislation does not accomplish this. However, 1987 amendments to the Canada-US Water Quality Agreement have been triggering studies that may ultimately lead to stronger laws and policies. Annex 7, dealing with dredging, requires the International Joint Commission to establish a subcommittee on dredging. This subcommittee is to review the existing practices relating to dredging in both countries to develop guidelines and criteria for dredging activities.

The Legislation

By section 108 of the *Constitution Act, 1867*, dredging is specifically enumerated as a federal responsibility. Various federal and provincial Acts afford some environmental controls over dredging. Generally, statutes that prohibit pollution can be made to prevent the removal of sediments from one area of water and the dumping of them in another. The federal *Fisheries Act* prohibits the throwing of deleterious matter overboard in any river, harbour, roadstead (a place where ships may ride at anchor), or fishing grounds.[280] (Contaminated sediments could be found by the courts to be deleterious.) Similarly, the pollution-prevention provisions of the *Migratory Birds Convention Act* and the *Ocean Dumping Control Act* (now the *Canadian Environmental Protection Act*) could apply. The provincial *Public Lands Act* and the *Beds of Navigable Waters Act* give the province ownership of beds of most navigable waters in the province, and require that anyone depositing material on publicly owned lands (such as beds of water bodies) must first obtain permission to do so. The *Conservation Authorities Act* gives conservation authorities considerable power to control any activity that might affect flood control or land or water pollution in areas in their jurisdiction. The Ministry of Environment and Energy, through the *Ontario Water Resources Act*, has the power to require that dredged material be disposed of in a non-polluting manner. Under the *Mining Act*, leases may be issued to dredge or work in any river, stream, or lake to recover any alluvial gold, platinum, precious stones, or other valuable mineral, and conditions may be inserted in those licences to protect the environment.[281]

The *Aggregate Resources Act* prohibits removing sand or gravel owned by the Crown from any bed, beach, shore, waters, bar, or flat on any lake, river, stream, channel, or entrance to any lake, river, or stream, without a permit issued by the minister of natural resources, but no licence is required to do the same thing on private land.[282]

The minister may make special provisions regarding the removal of sand from any part of the waters or shores of Lakes Erie, Ontario, and Huron. The minister may also revoke licences he or she has issued.

Under the *Navigable Waters Protection Act*, anyone wishing to construct anything that might affect navigable waters (such as a bridge, a hydro line crossing a river, or a dock) and anyone wishing to dredge must make an application and be approved by the Department of Transport.[283] When considering the application, the minister is required only to consider how the project would affect navigation, not how it would affect the environment. Ministerial approval only authorizes the applicant to interfere with public rights of navigation in certain specified ways. It does not authorize matters such as construction, land use, noise, pollution control, or zoning, which fall under other legislation and may require separate approvals.

As a matter of practice, Transport Canada refers applications to the federal Department of the Environment for its information, and is apparently open to its recommendations. The approval may be issued subject to certain terms and conditions, some of which have included recommendations relating to the environment.

There are two major limitations to the Act. First, it is not binding on federal bodies. Since most of the dredging in Canada is carried on by federal agencies such as the federal Department of Public Works, the Canadian Coast Guard, Parks Canada, and the St. Lawrence Seaway Authority, one wonders what effect the Act has in practice.[284] Second, it is not an offence under the Act to dredge without a permit. Moreover, the Act allows any works that might interfere with navigation to apply for approval after the work has commenced.[285]

Under the portions of the *Canadian Environmental Protection Act* that were formerly part of the *Ocean Dumping Control Act*, Public Works Canada must obtain authorization from Environment Canada before dredging or dumping dredgeate in the ocean. However, no similar licence appears to be required for dumping in fresh water under the *Canadian Environmental Protection Act*.[286]

Under the *Harbour Commissions Act*, a harbour commission has the power to regulate dredging with its harbour, and must conform with the *Navigable Waters Protection Act*.[287] Similarly, the *Canada Ports Corporation Act*[288] gives the harbour boards within its jurisdiction power to control dredging in the harbour. Under the *Fishing and Recreational Harbours Act*, dredging in some harbours may require a permit from the federal minister of fisheries and oceans. Finally, it is possible that the *Canadian Environmental Assessment Act* will require study of the environmental impact of some dredging projects before they are approved.

Water Conservation

In the spring of 1992, the Ontario Ministry of Natural Resources launched a Water Efficiency Strategy for Ontario. The guiding principles of this strategy include the optimization of the efficient use of water by employing measures that are environmentally, socially, and economically sustainable, and through the adoption of an ecosystem approach to water resources management.[289] The introduction of a "user pays full cost" principle for water supply and waste water treatment is also proposed.[290] No implementation schedule for the strategy has been announced.

THE INTERNATIONAL DIMENSION

Bilateral Canada-US Relations: The International Joint Commission and the Great Lakes Water Quality Agreement

The most important bilateral arrangement between Canada and the United States related to water resources is the establishment International Joint Commission (IJC). The IJC was created by the 1909 Boundary Waters Treaty and reports to the federal governments of Canada and the United States.

It has no power to make laws or enforce them, but it can conduct studies and make recommendations. Article IV of the Boundary Waters Treaty stated that "boundary waters ... shall not be polluted on either side to the injury of health or property on the other." The IJC's most important role has been with respect to water quality in the Great Lakes. The commission delivered reports in 1918 and 1951 identifying significant pollution problems in the lakes, especially in their near shore areas and connecting channels. However, these efforts received limited public attention, and governments did little to respond to their contents.[291]

The growing body of scientific evidence of serious basin-wide pollution prompted a request for a third IJC report from the Canadian and US governments in 1964. This was delivered in the fall of 1969[292] and was followed by public hearings by the commission in eight cities around the Great Lakes. In the result, after a further two years of intensive negotiations, a Great Lakes Water Quality Agreement was signed between Canada and the United States in April 1972.

The agreement included a set of common water-quality objectives, specific regulatory standards for a variety of pollutants, mutual commitments to implement national programs to achieve those objectives, and procedures for monitoring subsequent progress. The agreement gave the IJC new responsibilities for the collection and analysis of information on water quality objectives and pollution control programs on both sides of the lakes, the independent verification of data, and the publication of reports assessing progress towards accomplishing the agreement's objectives. In addition, the IJC was given responsibility for providing "assistance in the coordination of joint activities." The commission was directed to establish a Water Quality Board to assist it on pollution control issues, and a Research (later named Science) Advisory Board, to advise it specifically on technical and scientific issues.[293]

Consistent with the 1972 agreement, the focus on both sides of the boarder was initially on excessive nutrients, especially phosphates. This led to a sewage treatment plant construction program in Ontario, supported by grants from the Canadian federal government. These were arranged through a Canada-Ontario accord to implement the agreement.[294] With these efforts under way when the 1972 agreement came up for renegotiation in its fifth year, the attention of scientists, environmentalists, and regulators shifted to attempts to ascertain the extent to which industrial and toxic pollutants have contaminated the Great Lakes.

As a result, the Great Lakes Water Quality Agreement of 1978 focused on pollutants of that nature.[295] The new agreement's most important feature was to require that

[t]he discharge of toxic substances in toxic amounts be prohibited and the discharge of any or all persistent toxic substances be virtually eliminated.[296]

Typical Municipal Water Prices
($/1000 litres*)

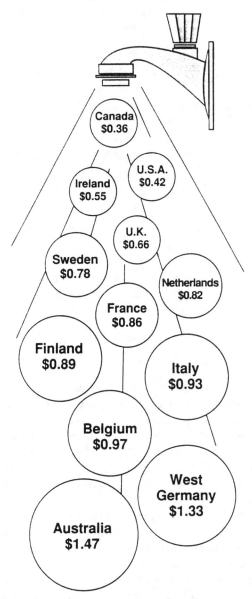

* All amounts are 1989 Canadian dollars. In
most countries, these prices are increasing
from year to year. These figures do not
include the cost of waste treatment.

Courtesy of Environment Canada.

Average Daily Household Water Use (Per Capita)

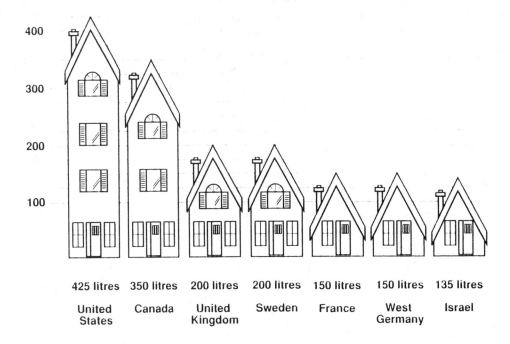

425 litres	350 litres	200 litres	200 litres	150 litres	150 litres	135 litres
United States	Canada	United Kingdom	Sweden	France	West Germany	Israel

Courtesy of Environment Canada.

The discharge of 350 "hazardous polluting substances" was to be specifically banned. The two countries also agreed that municipal and industrial pollution abatement and control programs were to be completed and in operation no later than the ends of 1982 and 1983 respectively. In addition, the 1978 agreement included a surveillance program and revised water quality objectives, including much higher standards for radioactive substances. More stringent standards were also set for overall phosphorous loading for each of the Great Lakes, although the actual division of loadings between the two countries — an area of considerable dispute[297] — was to be negotiated later.

In the years following the 1978 agreement, the IJC's reports tended to focus on what the Water Quality Board termed "areas of concern." These were seriously polluted and degraded areas of the lakes where immediate action was required. Forty-three areas of concern have been identified by the IJC, including 17 in Ontario. A program of remedial action plans (RAPs) for these areas is being developed and coordinated by the commission. The RAP program is a process by which local, state/provincial, and federal authorities work in consultation with polluting industries, public interest groups, and others to develop plans and programs for the restoration of environmental health in each area of concern.

The RAPs that are under development include both pollution-prevention components, such as separating combined sanitary and storm sewers, as well as proposals to clean up existing pollution. Efforts to address the problem of contaminated sediments at the bottom of harbours and rivers are to receive particular attention in the latter case.[298] Although planning has commenced in each of the 42 areas, little actual work had been undertaken by 1992.[299] The total cost of the RAP program has been estimated at between US$100 and US$500 billion, a large portion of which will go toward the upgrading of sewage treatment plants and the reduction of ongoing industrial pollution.[300]

The Great Lakes Water Quality Agreement was reviewed and revised in 1987. The resulting changes focused on updating technical references and modifying the detailed annexes. This included the formalization of the RAP program and Lakewide Management Plans. The resulting amendments to the agreement came into effect in 1989. The process of negotiating the 1987 protocol was particularly noteworthy in that non-governmental environmental organizations, such as Great Lakes United and the United States National Wildlife Federation, were included in the official negotiation process.

CONCLUSIONS

Over the past 30 years, substantial progress has been made in Ontario regarding water pollution. However, much remains to be done. The MISA program has yet to be fully implemented, and the discharge of persistent toxics into Ontario's waterways continues. In addition, many sewage treatment plants constructed in the 1960s and 1970s are now in need of substantial upgrading. Old sewer and water pipes are deteriorating, causing loss of both potable water and sewage to the surrounding soil. In many urban areas, sanitary and storm sewers are combined so that when there is a heavy storm, the combination of sewage and high volumes of stormwater overload the sewage treatment plants, causing the discharge of untreated sewage to bodies of water.

Many of our laws have concentrated on controlling "point sources" of pollution — that is, individual pipes discharging pollutants from individual industrial plants. However, much of our water pollution comes from "non-point sources" such as rainwater from city streets that is laden with road salt, oil, grease, lead from car exhausts, dirt, and animal faeces, or erosion of soil and runoff from farmers' fields containing pesticides and fertilizers. This kind of pollution is much harder to control, and requires more sophisticated policies and programs than the traditional "command and control" model of legislation that prohibits and punishes polluting activities.

The Don River, infamous as one of Canada's most polluted watercourses, is a case in point. Even if all the direct discharges of pollution to the Don were stopped, it would still cost millions of dollars to clean it up. The reason lies in how we design our cities. Instead of retaining forests, greenspace, and natural wetlands that absorb water, we pave over everything and drain all the rain and snow into sewers, carrying with them all the pollutants they pick up. Not only does this kind of construction pollute water, but it means that watercourses are required to accept much larger quantities of water than they can handle. This in turn causes the banks to erode and the beds to silt up, which then requires the replacement of natural banks and their vegetation with artificial banks and the imprisonment of watercourses within concrete walls and tunnels.

To deal with such problems will require substantial changes in land-use planning and the design of urban infrastructure.

There is also a growing recognition that water is not an infinite resource and that responsible stewardship of our water resources in necessary to ensure that Ontario's waters will be fishable, swimmable, and drinkable for future generations of Ontarians. We need to make sure that our present actions do not further damage Ontario's water resources and that the measures necessary to restore the quality of those waters that have been degraded are taken. This will require an ongoing commitment from the federal, provincial, and municipal levels of government, industry, and the public for many years to come.

Mark Winfield and John Swaigen
with notes from Stephen LeDrew and Harry Poch

FURTHER READING

Canada, *Currents of Change: Final Report of the Inquiry on Federal Water Policy* (Ottawa: Supply and Services, September 1985).

R. Allan Freeze and John A. Cherry, *Groundwater* (Englewood Cliffs, NJ: Prentice-Hall Inc., 1979).

Eric P. Jorgensen, ed., *The Poisoned Well: New Strategies for Groundwater Protection* (Washington, DC: Island Press, 1989).

Michael Keating, *To the Last Drop: Canada and the World's Water Crisis* (Toronto: Macmillan of Canada, 1986).

Paul Muldoon and Marcia Valiante, *Toxic Water Pollution in Canada: Regulatory Principles for Reduction and Elimination* (Calgary: Canadian Institute of Resources Law, University of Calgary, 1989).

Paul Muldoon and Marcia Valiante, *Zero Discharge: A Strategy for the Regulation of Toxic Substances in the Great Lakes Ecosystem* (Toronto: Canadian Environmental Law Research Foundation [now Canadian Institute for Environmental Law and Policy], 1988).

National Wildlife Federation and Canadian Institute for Environmental Law and Policy, *A Prescription for Healthy Great Lakes* (Toronto and Ann Arbour, Mich.: NWF/ CIELAP, 1991).

David R. Percy, *The Framework of Water Rights Legislation in Canada* (Calgary: Canadian Institute of Resources Law, University of Calgary, 1988).

J. Owen Saunders, *Interjurisdictional Issues in Canadian Water Management* (Calgary: Canadian Institute of Resources Law, University of Calgary, 1988).

ENDNOTES

1 Environment Canada, *The State of Canada's Environment* (Ottawa: Environment Canada, 1991), 3-4.

2 See, for example, D.P. Emond, "Environmental Law and Policy: A Retrospective Examination of the Canadian Experience," in I. Bernier and A. Lajoie, *Consumer Protection, Environmental Law and Corporate Power* (Toronto: University of Toronto Press, 1985), 123 and 135.

3 *Constitution Act, 1867*, 30 & 31 Vict., c. 3 (UK), section 92(10).

4 Ibid., section 92(13).

5 Ibid., section 91(16).

6 Ibid., section 92(8).

7 Peter Hogg, *The Constitutional Law of Canada*, 2d ed. (Toronto: Carswell, 1985), 591.

8 *Fisheries Act*, RSC 1985, c. F-14.

9 *Fowler v. The Queen*, [1980] 2 SCR 213.

10 *Coleman v. Ontario (Attorney General)* (1983), 143 DLR (3d) 608 (Ont. HCJ). However, note that in provinces other than Ontario, the definition of navigability may be narrower (see the discussion in *Coleman*). In addition, the definition of navigability under specific statutes such as the *Navigable Waters Protection Act* may be narrower or broader than the common law definition: see *International Minerals and Chemicals Corp. (Canada) v. Canada (Minister of Transport)* (1992), 10 CELR (NS) 85 (FCTD).

11 *Friends of the Oldman River Society v. Canada and the Queen in Right of Alberta* (1992), 88 DLR (4th) 1 (SCC).

12 *Navigable Waters Protection Act*, RSC 1985, c. N-22.

13 *Constitution Act, 1867*, supra endnote 3, section 91(1A) and schedule 3, item 2.

14 *Hamilton Harbour Commissioners v. City of Hamilton* (1978), 91 DLR (3d) 353, 21 OR (2d) 459 (CA).

15 *Constitution Act, 1867*, supra endnote 3, section 91(2).

16 Ibid., section 91(3).

17 Ibid., section 91(27). See also Law Reform Commission of Canada, *Crimes Against the Environment* (Ottawa: LRCC, 1985).

18 *R. v. Crown Zellerbach Ltd., et al.*, [1988] 1 SCR 401.

19 Now part VI of the *Canadian Environmental Protection Act*, RSC 1985, c. 16 (4th Supp.), first enacted as SC 1988, c. 22.

20 Ibid. See A. Lucas, "Comment on *R. v. Crown Zellerbach*" (1989), 23 *UBC L. Rev.* 355, at 365-66.

21 For a detailed discussion of this issue, see David Vanderzwaag and Linda Duncan, "Canada and Environmental Protection: Confident Political Faces, Uncertain Legal Hands," in R. Boardman, ed., *Canadian Environmental Policy: Ecosystems, Politics and Process* (Toronto: Oxford University Press, 1992), 5-6.

22 *R. v. MacMillan Bloedel (Alberni) Ltd.* (1978), 42 CCC (2d) 70, 7 CELR 128 (BC Cty. Ct.), [1979] 4 WWR 654 (BC CA), (1979), 47 CCC (2d) 118n (SCC).

23 *R. v. MacMillan Bloedel Ltd.*, [1979] 4 WWR 654 (BC CA).

24 *R. v. Cyanamid Canada Inc.* (1981), 11 CELR 31 (Ont. Prov. Ct.).

25 *R. v. District of North Vancouver* (1982), 11 CELR 158 (BC Prov. Ct.).

26 *R. v. Pioneer Timber Co.* (1979), 9 CELR 66 (BC Cty. Ct.).

27 *R. v. Western Stevedoring Co.* (1982), 11 CELR 107 (BC Prov. Ct.).

28 *R. v. Canadian Forest Products Ltd.* (1978), 2 Fisheries Poll. R. 168 (BC Prov. Ct.).

29 *R. v. North Arm Tpt. Co.* (1977), 2 Fisheries Poll. R. 71 (BC Cty. Ct.).

30 Pulp and Paper Effluent Regulations, CRC 1978, c. 819.

31 Petroleum Refinery Liquid Effluent Regulations, CRC 1978, c. 828.

32 Chlor-Alkali Mercury Effluent Regulations, CRC 1978, c. 811.

33 Meat and Poultry Products Plant Liquid Effluent Regulations, CRC 1978, c. 818.

34 Metal Mining Liquid Effluent Regulations, CRC 1978, c. 819.

35 Potato Processing Plant Liquid Effluent Regulations, CRC 1978, c. 829.

36 See, for example, J.W. Parlour, "The Politics of Water Pollution Control: A Case Study of the Canadian Fisheries Act Amendments and the Pulp and Paper Effluent Regulations, 1970" (1981), *Journal of Environmental Management* 13.

37 In the case of the pulp and paper mill effluent regulations, this meant that, as of 1990, only 11 of the 155 mills in Canada were affected by the regulatory requirements.

38 Environment Canada, *Canada's Green Plan: Canada's Green Plan for a Healthy Environment* (Ottawa: Supply and Services, 1990), 75-76.

39 For detailed discussion of the pulp and paper industry's position on this issue, see R. Gibbons, "Ottawa Backs Off on Pulp Pollution," *The Financial Post*, February 4, 1991.

40 Pulp and Paper Mill Effluent Chlorinated Dioxins and Furans Regulations, SOR 92/267.

41 Pulp and Paper Mill Defoamer and Wood Chip Regulations, SOR 92/268.

42 *The State of Canada's Environment*, supra endnote 1, at 11-14.

43 The Department of Fisheries and Oceans was separated from the Department of the Environment in 1977.

44 See, generally, P.N. Nemetz, "The Fisheries Act and Federal-Provincial Environmental Regulation: Duplication or Complementarity" (Fall 1986), vol. 29, no. 3 *Canadian Public Administration* 401.

45 K. Webb, *Pollution Control in Canada: The Regulatory Approach in the 1980's* (Ottawa: Law Reform Commission of Canada, 1988), 61-62.

46 See, for example, Nemetz, supra endnote 44.

47 *Canada Water Act*, RSC 1970, c. 5 (1st Supp.); RSC 1985, c. C-11, part I.

48 Ibid., part II.

49 Ibid., section 11.

50 Ibid., section 16(2)(a).

51 Ibid., section 16(2)(d).

52 *Navigable Waters Protection Act*, supra endnote 12, section 5.

53 Ibid., section 21.

54 Ibid., section 50.

55 Ibid., sections 27 and 28.

56 *International River Improvements Act*, RSC 1985, c. I-20, section 4.

57 *Canadian Wildlife Federation v. Canada (Minister of the Environment)* (1989), 4 CELR (NS) 1 (FCA).

58 *Canada Shipping Act*, RSC 1985, c. S-9, as amended.

59 Ibid., section 664.

60 Ibid., section 654.

61 Ibid.

62 Garbage Pollution Prevention Regulations, CRC 1978, c. 1454.

63 Oil Pollution Prevention Regulations, CRC 1978, c. 1454.

64 Air Pollution Regulations, CRC 1978, c. 1404.

65 Pollutant Substances Regulations, CRC 1978, c. 1458.

66 Ibid., section 656(2). The *Ocean Dumping Control Act* is now part VI of the *Canadian Environmental Protection Act*, supra endnote 19.

67 *Canada Shipping Act*, supra endnote 58, section 659.

68 Ibid., section 684.

69 Ibid., section 661(1)(a).

70 Ibid., section 661(1)(c).

71 Ibid., section 656(1).

72 Ibid., section 661(3).

73 The Act was originally introduced in June 1990 as Bill C-78.

74 *Hamilton Harbour Commissioners v. City of Hamilton*, supra endnote 14.

75 *Canada Ports Corporation Act*, RSC 1985, c. C-9.

76 Ibid., section 25.

77 Ibid., section 3(1)(e).

78 *Harbour Commissions Act*, RSC 1985, c. H-1.

79 Ibid., section 3(1)(d).

80 *Toronto Harbour Commissioners Act, 1911*, SC 1911, c. 26.

81 *Hamilton Harbour Commissioners Act, 1912*, 2 Geo. V, SC 1912, c. 98.

82 *Fishing and Recreational Harbours Act*, RSC 1985, c. F-24.

83 *Public Harbours and Port Facilities Act*, RSC 1985, c. P-29.

84 See Jane Armstrong, "Councillors Set To Renew Debate over Harbour's Future," *The Toronto Star*, February 26, 1993, citing a report prepared for the Waterfront Regeneration Trust by Robert Macauley.

85 For a detailed discussion of the development of the Federal Water Policy, see G. Filyk and R. Cote, "Pressures from Inside: Advisory Groups and the Environmental Policy Community," in *Canadian Environmental Policy: Ecosystems, Politics and Process*, supra endnote 21, at 72-80.

86 Environment Canada, *Federal Water Policy* (Ottawa: Environment Canada, 1987).

87 *Fisheries Act*, supra endnote 8.

88 *Canada's Green Plan*, supra endnote 38, at 35.

89 Ibid., at 35.

90 Ibid., at 36-38.

91 Ibid., at 37.

92 Ibid., at 37.

93 Ibid., at 37.

94 Ibid., at 38.

95 Ibid., at 39.

96 Ibid., at 41.

97 Ibid., at 42.

98 *Environmental Protection Act*, RSO 1990, c. E.19, section 1(k) [emphasis added].

99 *Ontario Water Resources Act*, RSO 1990, c. O.40.

100 See, generally, D. Estrin and J. Swaigen, *Environment on Trial: A Handbook of Ontario Environmental Law*, 2d ed. (Toronto: Canadian Environmental Law Research Foundation, 1978), 41.

101 *Stephens v. Richmond Hill* (1955), 4 DLR 572 (Ont. HCJ) and *Burgess v. Woodstock* (1955), 4 DLR 615 (Ont. HCJ).

102 The defence of "statutory authorization" posits that those whose activities are closely circumscribed by statute should not be civilly liable for the inevitable consequences of those activities, provided that the operator is not negligent.

103 *Ontario Water Resources Commission Act*, SO 1956, c. 3.

104 *Ontario Water Resources Commission Act*, SO 1957, c. 16.

105 Ibid., section 31(1).

106 Ibid. For a detailed discussion of the *Water Resources Commission Act* and its rationale, see J.B. Milner, "The Ontario Water Resources Commission Act, 1956" (1957-58), 12 *University of Toronto Law Journal* 100-2.

107 See P. Anisman, "Water Pollution Control in Ontario" (1972), *Ottawa Law Review* 5 for a detailed discussion of the commission's activities. See also A.W. Bryant, "Part 1 — An Analysis of the Ontario Water Resources Act," in P.S. Elder, ed., *Environmental Management and Public Participation* (Toronto: Canadian Environmental Law Research Foundation, 1975), 162.

108 *Ontario Water Resources Act*, supra endnote 99, section 30(1).

109 Ibid., section 75(i).

110 Ibid., section 53(1).

111 Ibid., section 53.

112 Ibid., section 108(1).

113 Ibid., section 108(2).

114 Ibid., section 109.

115 Discharge of Sewage from Pleasure Boats Regulations, RRO 1990, reg. 343.

116 Great Lakes Sewage Pollution Prevention Regulations, CRC 1978, c. 1429.

117 Marinas Regulations, RRO 1990, reg. 351.

118 Sewage Systems Regulations, RRO 1990, reg. 358.

119 Penny Caldwell, "A Drop in the Bucket" (July-August 1992), *Cottage Life* 24.

120 Ontario, Ministry of Environment and Energy, *Policy Manual*, "The Use of Holding Tanks in Sewage Systems Under Part VIII of the Environmental Protection Act," policy no. 08-05, revised May 2, 1988.

121 *Policy Manual*, ibid., "Procedures and Guidelines for Onsite Sewage Systems," chapter 13.

122 According to the Federation of Ontario Cottagers' Associations, 70 per cent of septic systems inspected under the Ministry of the Environment's Cottage Pollution Control Program either require immediate repairs or are seriously substandard: "Beating the System" (July-August 1991), *Cottage Life*. See also Ontario, Ministry of the Environment, Cottage Pollution Control Program — Muskoka-Haliburton, October 1989.

123 Agriculture Canada, *Ontario Farm Groundwater Quality Survey, Winter 1991-92* (Ottawa: Agriculture Canada, September 1992).

124 *Wood's Sand and Gravel Limited v. Director, Ministry of the Environment*, June 5, 1992, Environmental Appeal Board file no. SWA.007.89.

125 Ontario, Ministry of the Environment, "Incorporation of the Reasonable Use Concept into MOE Groundwater Management Activities," policy no. 15-08, April 25, 1986. Detailed information on this policy is contained in a document entitled "The Incorporation of the Reasonable Use Concept into the Groundwater Management Activities of the Ministry of the Environment," April 1986.

126 *Pesticides Act*, RSO 1990, c. P.11.

127 *Gasoline Handling Act*, RSO 1990, c. G.4.

128 *Lakes and Rivers Improvement Act*, RSO 1990, c. L.3.

129 *Beds of Navigable Waters Act*, RSO 1990, c. B.4.

130 *Mining Act*, RSO 1990, c. M.14.

131 *Environmental Assessment Act*, RSO 1990, c. E.18.

132 *Municipal Act*, RSO 1990, c. M.45.

133 For a general discussion of this problem, see Doug Macdonald and Peter Pickfield, *From Pollution Prevention to Waste Reduction: Towards a Comprehensive Hazardous Waste Strategy for Ontario* (Toronto: Canadian Institute for Environmental Law and Policy, 1989), 33.

134 Ontario, Ministry of the Environment and the Municipal Engineers' Association, *A By-Law To Control Industrial Waste Discharges to Municipal Sewers* (Toronto: Queen's Printer, 1976).

135 See, generally, Peter Pickfield, *Ontario Hazardous Waste Policy: A Discussion Paper* (Toronto: Canadian Environmental Law Research Foundation, 1986), 6-41 and 42.

136 See, for example, *R. v. B.E.S.T Plating Shoppe Ltd.* (1986), 1 CELR (NS) 85 (HCJ) and (1987), 1 CELR (NS) 145 (Ont. CA) upholding a fine of $100,000.

137 *R. v. Jetco Manufacturing Ltd.* (1986), 1 CELR (NS) 79 (Ont. HCJ), rev'd. (1987), 1 CELR (NS) 243 (Ont. CA); *Metropolitan Toronto (Municipality) v. Siapas* (1988), 3 CELR (NS) 122, 151 (Ont. HCJ).

138 *Conservation Authorities Act*, RSO 1990, c. C.27, section 20.

139 Ibid., section 21(c).

140 Ibid., section 21(i).

141 Ibid., section 21(j).

142 Ibid., section 28(a).

143 Ibid., section 28(b).

144 Ibid., section 28(c).

145 *Christie, Crosby and Appleby v. Noira River Conservation Authority*, decision of the Mining and Lands Commissioner, December 2, 1988, file no. 2001 DO [unreported].

146 *Shell Canada Limited v. Central Lake Ontario Conservation Authority*, decision of the Mining and Lands Commissioner, June 25, 1979, file no. 1509 DO, 22 and 23 [unreported].

147 *Farkas v. Halton Region Conservation Authority*, decision of the Mining and Lands Commissioner, May 15, 1979, file no. 1506 DO, 4 [unreported].

148 *Hinder v. Metropolitan Toronto and Metropolitan Toronto and Region Conservation Authority* (1984), 16 OMBR 401 (Mining and Lands Commissioner).

149 *Markou v. Grand River Conservation Authority*, decision of the Mining and Lands Commissioner, May 30, 1990, file no. 2100 DO [unreported].

150 See, for example, Marion Strebig, "Looking at Water Management Structures" (Summer 1990), vol. 30, no. 2 *Seasons* 13.

151 See, for example, Peter Gorrie, "Conservation Authority Aims To Be 'Greener,'" *The Toronto Star*, March 30, 1992.

152 Ontario, Ministry of the Environment, *Ontario Drinking Water Objectives*, revised (Toronto: Queen's Printer, 1983).

153 Environment Canada, *Guidelines for Canadian Drinking Water Quality* (Ottawa: Supply and Services, 1978).

154 Ontario, Ministry of the Environment, *Ontario's Water Quality Objective Development Process* (Toronto: Queen's Printer, March 1992).

155 Ibid.

156 Ontario, Ministry of the Environment, "Evaluating Construction Activities — Hydrocarbon Transmission and Distribution Pipelines Crossing Watercourses," policy no. 15-07, March 1, 1984.

157 Ontario, Ministry of the Environment, "Guidelines for the Resolution of Groundwater Quality Interference Problems," policy no. 15-10, October 29, 1986.

158 Ontario, Ministry of the Environment, "Evaluating Construction Activities — Marine Construction Projects," policy no. 15-11, October 1, 1986; "Evaluating Construction Activities — Small Scale Construction Projects," policy no. 15-12, October 1, 1986.

159 Ontario, Ministry of the Environment, "Potable Water Storage Structures," policy no. 15-13, May 8, 1987.

160 Ontario, Ministry of the Environment, *Municipal-Industrial Strategy for Abatement: A Policy and Program Statement of the Government of Ontario on Controlling Municipal and Industrial Discharges to Surface Waters* (Toronto: the ministry, 1986), ii.

161 Ibid., at 31-35.

162 Ibid., at 29.

163 Ibid.

164 R.B. Gibson, *Control Orders and Industrial Pollution Abatement in Ontario* (Toronto: Canadian Environmental Law Research Foundation, 1983), 16.

165 Ibid., 23.

166 See, for example, Toby Vigod, "The Law and the Toxic Blob" (1986), vol. 13, no. 3 *Alternatives* 26.

167 *Municipal-Industrial Strategy for Abatement*, supra endnote 160, at 24.

168 Ibid., at 3.

169 Ibid.

170 See Ontario, Ministry of the Environment, *Controlling Industrial Discharges to Sewers* (Toronto: the ministry, 1988).

171 Royal Commission on the Future of the Toronto Waterfront, *Regeneration* (Ottawa: Supply and Services, 1992), 121.

172 See, generally, Burkhardt Mausberg, *Still Going to B.A.T. for Water Quality? A Four Year Review of the Ministry of the Environment's Municipal/Industrial Strategy for Abatement (MISA)* (Toronto: Canadian Institute for Environmental Law and Policy and the Pollution Probe Foundation, 1990).

173 See Ontario, Ministry of the Environment, *Controlling Industrial Discharges to Sewers* (Toronto: the ministry, 1988).

174   See Association of Municipalities of Ontario, *AMO Position Paper on "Controlling Industrial Discharges to Sewers"* (Toronto: AMO, 1988).

175   See Ontario, Ministry of the Environment, *Press Release*, "Pollution Prevention New Focus of MISA Program," September 26, 1991.

176   Susan Sang and Burkhardt Mausberg, *Developing Options for Technology Based Standards for the Pulp and Paper Sector in the Great Lakes Basin* (Toronto: Canadian Institute for Environmental Law and Policy, 1992), 12.

177   *The State of Canada's Environment*, supra endnote 1, at 10-19.

178   Ibid.

179   Sang and Mausberg, supra endnote 176, at 13.

180   Ibid.

181   Ibid.

182   Ibid., at 14.

183   Great Lakes Water Quality Board, *1989 Report on Great Lakes Water Quality* (Ottawa: International Joint Commission, 1989), 26.

184   B. Bengtsson, "Effects of Pulp Mill Effluent on Skeletal Parameters in Fish: A Progress Report," in *Proceedings of the Second IAWPRC Symposium on Forest Industry Waste Waters*, June 9-12, 1987, Tampere, Finland.

185   Peter Gorrie, "Ecological Battle Lines Drawn," *The Toronto Star*, September 3, 1992.

186   Ibid.

187   Ibid.

188   Ibid.

189   For a detailed discussion of these possibilities, see, generally, Sang and Mausberg, supra endnote 176.

190   *Fisheries Act*, supra endnote 8.

191   The OWRC report is referred to in Ontario, Ministry of the Environment, *Development Document for the Draft Monitoring Regulation for the Pulp and Paper Sector* (Toronto: the ministry, 1989), I-1.

192   Ibid., at I-2.

193   See Ontario, Legislative Assembly, Standing Committee on Resources Development, *Final Report on Acidic Precipitation, Abatement of Emissions from the International Nickel Company Operations at Sudbury and Pollution Control in the Pulp and Paper Industry* (Toronto: Queen's Printer, 1979).

194   See Gorrie, supra endnote 185.

195   Much of the discussion of the environmental impacts of metal mining, milling, and smelting is taken from *The State of Canada's Environment*, supra endnote 1, chapter 11, which contains an excellent overview of the problem. For other literature about the environmental and legal aspects of mining, see I.B. Marshall, *Mining, Land Use and the Environment: I. A Canadian Overview* (Ottawa: Environment Canada, Lands Directorate, 1982); I.B. Marshall, *Mining, Land Use and the Environment: II. A Review of Mine Reclamation Activities in Canada* (Ottawa: Environment Canada, Lands Directorate, 1983); Barry Barton, Barbara Roulston, and Nancy Strantz, *A Reference Guide to Mining Legislation in Canada*, 2d ed. (Calgary: Canadian Institute of Resources Law, July 1988); Currie, Coopers and Lybrand, *A Guide to Legislation Affecting Mining in Ontario* (Toronto: Ministry of Natural Resources, August 1984).

196   Intergovernmental Working Group on the Mineral Industry, *Report on the Economic Aspects of Acid Discharge* (Ottawa: Department of Energy, Mines and Resources, 1988).

197   Ibid.

198   *The State of Canada's Environment*, supra endnote 1, at 11-19.

199   Ibid. However, Bill McAffee of the Ministry of Northern Development and Mines cited a figure of 5,700 abandoned mines to a CIELAP researcher in 1990.

200   Canada Centre for Mineral and Energy Technology, *Mine Environment Neutral Drainage (MEND)* (Ottawa: Energy, Mines and Resources Canada, 1992).

201   *Aggregate Resources Act*, RSO 1990, c. A.8.

202   *Environmental Assessment Act*, supra endnote 131.

203   For further discussion of the potential application of the *Environmental Assessment Act* to mining, see Meinhard Doelle, "Regulating the Environment by Mediation and Contract Negotiation: A Case Study of the Dona Lake Agreement" (1992), 2 JELP 189.

204   *Mining Act*, supra endnote 130.

205   *Industrial and Mining Lands Compensation Act*, RSO 1990, c. I.5.

206   *Mining Act*, supra endnote 130, section 175.

207   *Re Faraday Uranium Mines Ltd.*, [1962] OR 503 (CA).

208   *Mining Act*, supra endnote 130, section 175(2).

209   See, for example, Environment Canada, "Summary of Spill Events in Canada, 1974-1983," SEPS 5/SP/1, November 1987. Environment Canada also publishes periodic reports on trends in spills of oil and other hazardous substances in various regions of Canada. The Ontario Ministry of the Environment Spills Action Centre publishes an annual "Summary Report of Occurrences." The 1990 report, for example, shows that over half the reported spills involved petroleum products, a number similar to the Environment Canada "Summary of Spill Events."

210   This information is found in the annual summaries of spills prepared by the Ministry of the Environment. Unfortunately, the ministry stopped collecting this kind of information several years ago.

211   Canada, House of Commons, *Debates*, February 1, 1977, 2585 (see also 2437).

212   *Petroleum Resources Act*, RSO 1990, c. P.12.

213   *Energy Act*, RSO 1990, c. E.16.

214   *Gasoline Handling Act*, supra endnote 127.

215   *Ontario Energy Board Act*, RSO 1990, c. O.13.

216   *Petroleum Resources Act*, supra endnote 212, section 13.

217   Exploration, Drilling and Production Regulations, RRO 1990, reg. 915.

218   Ontario Energy Board, *Environmental Guidelines for Locating, Constructing, and Operating Hydrocarbon Pipelines in Ontario* (Toronto: OEB, 1989). The third edition of these guidelines was published in 1989. The first guidelines, with a slightly different title, were published in 1976. They were prepared in conjunction with six ministries of the Ontario government whose mandates are affected by pipeline construction and operation, such as the Ministry of Agriculture, the Ministry of Energy, and the Ministry of Agriculture and Food.

219   Ibid., at 2.

220   *Gasoline Handling Code*, RRO 1990, reg. 532.

221 Canadian Council of Resource and Environmental Ministers, National Task Force on Leaking Storage Tanks, *Environmental Code of Practice for Underground Storage Tank Systems Containing Allied Petroleum Products*, final draft, 1st ed. (Ottawa: Supply and Services, August 1, 1990).

222 Ontario, Ministry of Agriculture and Food and Ministry of the Environment, *Guidelines for Sewage Sludge Utilization on Agricultural Lands*, rev. ed., October 1992. Previously published in April 1978 and revised in March 1981. Guidelines for spreading the contents and holding tanks were cited at endnote 121, supra.

223 The last edition of the *Canada Animal Waste Management Guide* was published in 1981. It dealt primarily with appropriate methods of getting wastes from the barn to storage, rather than from storage to the fields. According to Bob McClelland and Dr. Jim Munro of Agriculture Canada, for several years a committee has been working on a revised version that will discuss appropriate rates of application of manure to fields. As of October 1992, Agriculture Canada expected to publish this information as a series of pamphlets by Christmas of 1992.

224 Foodsystems 2002 and the Land Stewardship Program.

225 *Pesticides Act*, supra endnote 126.

226 *Drainage Act*, RSO 1990, c. D.17.

227 See, for example, *Ontario Farm Groundwater Quality Survey, Winter 1991-92*, supra endnote 123, at 7-10; Burton C. Kross et al., "Pesticide Contamination of Private Well Water, A Growing Rural Health Concern" (1992), 18 *Environment International* 231.

228 *Ontario Building Code*, RRO 1990, reg. 61.

229 From Ontario, Ministry of the Environment, *A Review of Literature on the Environmental Impact of De-Icing Compounds and Snow Disposal* (Toronto: the ministry, 1974).

230 Letter, Ontario Ministry of the Environment to Canadian Environmental Law Association, February 18, 1977.

231 Information provided by Wes Lammers, Ontario Ministry of the Environment, summer of 1990.

232 Statistics provided by Brian Gaston, Ontario Ministry of Transport, October 23, 1992.

233 Ibid.

234 The following information about the environmental impacts of road salt is adapted primarily from *A Review of Literature on the Environmental Impact of De-Icing Compounds and Snow Disposal*, supra endnote 229.

235 Ibid., at 15-16.

236 *The Toronto Star*, Insight Section, January 8, 1977.

237 *A Review of Literature on the Environmental Impact of De-Icing Compounds and Snow Disposal*, supra endnote 229, at 18. Between the turn of the century and the mid-1970s, the chloride concentration in Lake Ontario tripled. About half of the increase is from industrial discharges, and about 20 per cent from road salt.

238 Ibid., at 19.

239 The most up-to-date version is published as "Guidelines for Snow Disposal and Deicing Operations in Ontario," policy no. 115-05, March 1, 1984.

240 Classes of Contaminants — Exemptions, RRO 1990, reg. 339.

241   *Schenk v. Ontario; Rokeby v. Ontario* (1981), 23 CCLT 147, 34 OR (2d) 595, additional reasons (1982), 40 OR (2d) 410, 142 DLR (3d) 261, 12 CELR 43 (HCJ); aff'd. (1984), 49 OR (2d) 556, 15 DLR (4th) 320 (CA); aff'd. [1987] 2 SCR 289.

242   "Resolution of Well Water Quality Problems Resulting from Winter Road Maintenance," policy no. 15-04-01, June 15, 1984.

243   Acres International Limited, *Dust Suppressant Study* (Toronto: Ministry of the Environment, March 1988, reprinted June 1989), 7.

244   R.W. Gillham, J.F. Barker, R.S. Carter, and A.S. Abdul, *Application of Industrial Liquid Waste to Secondary Roads in Ontario for Dust Control: Implications with Respect to Groundwater Quality*, prepared by Department of Earth Sciences, University of Waterloo, for Waste Management Branch, Ministry of the Environment, July 1985. A further study of dust suppressants was carried out for the Ministry of the Environment by CH2M Hill, a consulting company. It was submitted to the ministry in June 1992, but had not been released to the public as of July 1993. According to Kathy Hansen of the ministry's Waste Management Branch, in a telephone conversation with John Swaigen on November 4, 1992, the report could not be released to the public until it had undergone an internal review and its release has been approved by senior management of the ministry. However, the staff of the Waste Management Branch had been reduced by attrition, and no one was available to take the report through this approval process. In a follow-up conversation on July 4, 1993, Ms Hansen advised that a staff member had now been given the task of reviewing the document.

245   Waste Management, RRO 1990, reg. 347, section 5(4), formerly O. reg. 750/88.

246   K.D. Switzer-Howse and D.R. Coote, *Agricultural Practices and Environmental Conservation*, publication no. 83-56 (Ottawa: Agriculture Canada, 1984), 18.

247   *Fisheries Act*, supra endnote 8, section 30.

248   *Canadian Environmental Protection Act*, supra endnote 19.

249   For more information about this topic, see Canadian Environmental Law Research Foundation (now Canadian Institute for Environmental Law and Policy), "An Overview of Canadian Law and Policy Governing Great Lakes Water Quantity Management" (1986), 18 *Journal of International Law* 109.

250   Michael Keating, *To the Last Drop: Canada and the World's Water Crisis* (Toronto: Macmillan, 1986), 153.

251   *Navigable Waters Protection Act*, supra endnote 12.

252   *International River Improvements Act*, supra endnote 56.

253   *Lakes and Rivers Improvement Act*, supra endnote 128.

254   *Conservation Authorities Act*, supra endnote 139.

255   *Public Lands Act*, RSO 1990, c. P.43.

256   *Canada Water Act*, supra endnote 47.

257   See, generally, Canadian Environmental Law Research Foundation, supra endnote 249.

258   Great Lakes Charter, reprinted in *Great Lakes Governors Task Force, Council of Great Lakes Governors, Final Report and Recommendations on Water Diversion and Great Lakes Institutions*, 40, app. III (1985).

259   Canadian Inquiry on Federal Water Policy, *Currents of Change: Final Report of the Inquiry on Federal Water Policies*, September 1985.

260 *Water Transfer Control Act*, RSO 1990, c. W.4.

261 *Drainage Act*, supra endnote 226.

262 *Planning Act*, RSO 1990, c. P.13.

263 *Municipal Act*, supra endnote 132.

264 *Environmental Assessment Act*, supra endnote 131.

265 *Tile Drainage Act*, RSO 1990, c. T.8.

266 *Agricultural Tile Drainage Installation Act*, RSO 1990, c. A.14.

267 Statistics provided by the Ontario Ministry of Agriculture and Food.

268 R.W. Irwin, *Drainage Legislation*, Ministry of Agriculture and Food (OMAF), revised October 1989; John Johnston, *Drainage Act Appeals*, OMAF, February 1986; R.W. Irwin, *Mutual Agreement Drains*, OMAF, August 1986; Vicki Hammell and John Johnston, *Tile Drainage Act Loans*, OMAF, July 1986.

269 Great Lakes Water Quality Board, *1985 Report on Great Lakes Water Quality Agreement* (Ottawa: International Joint Commission, 1985).

270 *Navigable Waters Protection Act*, supra endnote 12.

271 *Beds of Navigable Waters Act*, supra endnote 129.

272 *Lakes and Rivers Improvement Act*, supra endnote 128.

273 *Conservation Authorities Act*, supra endnote 138.

274 *Environmental Protection Act*, supra endnote 98.

275 *Re Rockcliffe Park Realty Ltd. and Director, Ontario Ministry of the Environment* (1975), 10 OR (2d) 1, 62 DLR (3d) 17, 5 CELN 23 (CA).

276 Ontario, Ministry of the Environment, *Guidelines for the Protection and Management of Aquatic Sediment Quality in Ontario* (Toronto: the ministry, June 1992).

277 International Working Group on the Abatement and Control of Pollution from Dredging Activities, *Report*, May 1975. This group was formed under the terms of the Canada-US Agreement on Great Lakes Water Quality.

278 Ibid., at 2.

279 Ibid., at 142.

280 *Fisheries Act*, supra endnote 8, section 33(1).

281 *Mining Act*, supra endnote 130, section 98.

282 *Aggregate Resources Act*, supra endnote 201, sections 1 (definition of "land under water"), 34(1)(b) (permit required), and 7(1) (licence not required to mine land under water).

283 *Navigable Waters Protection Act*, supra endnote 12.

284 *Public Works Act*, RSC 1985, c. P-38, sections 9 and 37.

285 *Navigable Waters Protection Act*, supra endnote 12, section 6(4).

286 See *Canadian Environmental Protection Act*, supra endnote 19, sections 67 and 71 and *Canada (Ministère de l'Environnement) v. Canada (Ministère des Travaux publics)* (1992), 10 CELR (NS) 135 (Ct. of Quebec).

287 *Harbour Commissions Act*, supra endnote 78, section 29 states that any work undertaken by or on behalf of the commission is subject to the *Navigable Waters Protection Act*.

288 *Canada Ports Corporation Act*, RSC 1985, c. C-9, section 25, schedule I.

289 Ontario, Ministry of Natural Resources, *Water Efficiency Strategy Working Document Summary* (Toronto: the ministry, 1992), 17.

290   Ibid., at 18.
291   See D. Munton and G. Castle, "The Continental Dimension: Canada and the United
      States," in *Canadian Environmental Policy: Ecosystems, Politics and Process*, supra
      endnote 21, at 204.
292   International Lake Erie Water Pollution Board and the International Lake Ontario – St.
      Lawrence River Pollution Board, *Report to the International Joint Commission on the
      Pollution of Lake Erie, Lake Ontario and the International Section of the St. Lawrence
      River* (Ottawa: International Joint Commission, 1969).
293   See Canada and the United States, *Great Lakes Water Quality Agreement of 1972*
      (Ottawa and Washington, DC: International Joint Commission, 1974).
294   Munton and Castle, supra endnote 291, at 210.
295   Canada and the United States, *Great Lakes Water Quality Agreement of 1978* (Ottawa
      and Washington, DC: International Joint Commission, 1978).
296   Ibid., article II.
297   Munton and Castle, supra endnote 291, at 211.
298   Doug Macdonald, *The Politics of Pollution: Why Canadians Are Failing Their
      Environment* (Toronto: McClelland and Stewart, 1991), 152.
299   See *Regeneration*, supra endnote 171.
300   The Conservation Foundation and the Institute for Research on Public Policy, *Great
      Lakes: Great Legacy?* (Waldorf, Md.: TCF/IRPP, 1990), 205.

19

Noise and Vibration

Contents

One of the great agonies ... is that long before you grow old, you can't hear what children are saying to you. You can't hear what they're saying! Their voices are too high to hear; they squeak at you, and you see their lips moving, but you can't hear what they're saying. ... You put your headphones on, sit with your guitar and play all night long. ... I think it's worth saying that there is a price to pay for that: it's premature deafness and ringing and slotty hearing.

Pete Townshend of The Who talks about the price of being a rock star

---

Noise and vibration are among the most widespread and least recognized of environmental contaminants. Levels of exposure have been rapidly increasing over the years. Between 1972 and 1987, air traffic in most western industrialized nations increased fourfold and the number of motor vehicles and level of urbanization doubled.[1] People in cities live within walls of constant noise. In 1990, a newspaper reporter measuring noise levels in the streets, offices, restaurants, airports, and shopping centres of Toronto found noise levels between 75 and 102 decibels, up to 10,000 times louder than levels considered to be intrusive.[2]

Nor is the countryside a haven from noise. Farm machinery is causing the farmers who use it to lose their hearing[3] and neighbours to lose their sleep. In remote areas of the Arctic, snowmobiles have caused Inuit to lose their hearing,[4] and low-flying jet fighters could be killing caribou calves.[5] Not even the ocean's depths are free from manmade noise. Drill ships, offshore oil rigs, ice breakers, fishing boats, and explosives used by geologists profiling ocean sediments may be causing noise and vibrations that damage the health and alter the behaviour of marine mammals and fish.[6]

WHAT ARE NOISE AND VIBRATION?

Noise (from the Latin *nausea*, meaning seasickness) is usually defined as any unwanted sound. Sound consists of waves of energy travelling through a "fluid" medium such as air or water. The waves vary in frequency and height to produce changes in the character of sound. Frequency, measured in hertz (Hz), is the number of peaks passing a given point in a second.[7] The human ear can detect sound frequencies from 20 to around 16,000 or 20,000 Hz but hearing is most acute at about 1,000 Hz.[8]

The height or amplitude of a sound wave is measured in decibels (dB). Amplitude measures the physical pressure exerted on the eardrum. Due to the broad range of sound intensities, amplitude is measured on a logarithmic scale.[9] This means that sound energy level of 90 dB is perceived to be twice as noisy as 80 dB and half as noisy as 100. However, although changes of 3 or 4 dB are barely discernible, the sound energy of a noise actually doubles every 3 dB, and the safe exposure time is cut in half. Thus, although a sound level of 83 dB will not sound much louder than 80 dB, it has twice the sound energy, and if it is safe to be exposed to 80 dB for a specific number of hours, one should not be exposed to 83 dB for more than half that time. Levels over 70 dB may cause measurable hearing loss.[10] The threshold of pain for most human ears is around 125 dB.[11] Noise is commonly measured using the A-scale or A-weighting network on a sound meter. A-weighted sound levels (dBA) approximate the frequency band to which the human ear is sensitive.

Sound Levels and Human Response

Common Sounds	Noise Level (dB)	Effect
Jet engine (near)	140	
Shotgun firing Jet takeoff (100-200 ft.)	130	Threshold of pain (about 125 dB)
Thunderclap (near) Discotheque	120	Threshold of sensation
Power saw Pneumatic drill Rock music band	110	Regular exposure of more than 1 min. risks permanent hearing loss
Garbage truck	100	No more than 15 min. unprotected exposure recommended
Average portable cassette player set above the halfway mark	?	Are you setting your volume too high? Don't play auditory suicide
Subway Motorcycle Lawn mower	90	Very annoying
Electric razor Many industrial workplaces	85	Level at which hearing damage (8 hrs.) begins
Average city traffic noise	80	Annoying, interferes with conversation
Vacuum cleaner Hair dryer Inside a car	70	Intrusive, interferes with telephone conversation
Normal conversation	60	
Quiet office Air conditioner	50	Comfortable
Whisper	30	Very quiet
Normal breathing	10	Just audible

This decibel (dB) table compares some common sounds and shows how they rank in potential harm to hearing. Recommended exposure times are based on current research.

Courtesy of the Canadian Hearing Society.

When sound waves enter the outer ear, they vibrate the eardrum and activate the sensory receptor cells in the inner ear. These cells trigger nerve impulses to the brain where they are perceived as sound.[12] Hearing is possible as long as the receptor cells remain intact.[13]

Vibration is a rapid movement to and fro of a fluid or a solid whose equilibrium has been disturbed. The same waves of energy that create noise can create vibration, or both, depending on their intensity and whether they travel through a solid medium like the ground or through the air. However, vibration waves are usually of low frequency, and are generally "felt" rather than heard. Humans perceive frequencies of vibrations ranging between 1 and 1,000 Hz.[14]

HARMFUL EFFECTS OF NOISE

Noise can tire or destroy the receptor cells in the inner ear. If the noise makes communication difficult, it may be at a hazardous level.[15] Quiet periods, even of a few seconds, can allow tired ears to recover, as long as the offending noise is sufficiently low in intensity and duration.[16] For example, rock concerts typically attain levels of 110 dB or more, but the few minutes between songs lessens the impact on the ear.

With prolonged exposure, hazardous levels of noise can destroy cells and they cannot be replaced.[17] Continued loss of cells will gradually lead to noticeable hearing problems and tinnitus ("ringing in the ears") and symptoms may not arise until substantial damage has already occurred.[18] Hearing impairment from noise is not confined to the elderly — it is appearing more and more among people in their 30s and 40s.

Even short exposure to hazardous noise can have severe consequences. Impulse noise is high-intensity sound of short duration with an abrupt onset and decay, such as gunfire or an explosion. If very intense, it can cause immediate, severe, and permanent loss of hearing.[19]

When non-damaging impulse and continuous noise are combined, they can produce devastating results if their frequencies overlap.[20] In textile mills and iron foundries, high-level impulse noise is almost obscured by background noise levels near the 90 dBA limits set by occupational health laws. Continuous noise may mask impulse noise and make it sound less offensive, but it is the total dose that determines the damage done. However, the total dose is seldom considered in noise bylaws. They are made to deal with single-source noise makers, not with noise produced by four construction machines, a streetcar, some sirens, and traffic.

The effect of noise on hearing is further complicated by the interaction of non-auditory factors. Alcohol, which is often consumed while listening to loud music, can magnify the damage from noise. Normally, the reflex muscle in the inner ear can reduce sound pressure by as much as 20 dB, but alcohol can cause this muscle to take up to four times longer to respond.[21] Noise also interacts with vibration to increase risk of hearing loss, and with lead to increase its neurotoxic effects.[22]

Loud noise is associated with a number of non-auditory effects on the human body and mind. It stimulates the release of adrenalin, which causes an increase in heart rate followed by a rise in blood pressure, pupil dilation, and contraction of the muscles. Prolonged loud noise has been linked to fatigue, anxiety, reduced learning ability, elevated levels of cholesterol, less immune response, heartbeat abnormalities, cardiovascular disease, and diabetes.[23] Further research into the long-term non-auditory effects of noise is required to confirm these relationships.

Laboratory animals subjected to high sound levels exhibit damage to the auditory and central nervous system and eventually symptoms of stress.[24] Less is known about the effects of noise on animals in their natural habitat. In general, studies have shown that animals respond with alarm and fear to transient loud noises. For example, great crested grebes nesting on recreational lakes were flushed more frequently than those on non-recreational lakes, resulting in increased predation and a significant decrease in nesting success.[25] When supersonic transport planes flew over nesting herring gulls once or twice a day, significantly more birds flew from their nests and under crowded conditions engaged in more fights when they landed. This resulted in increased egg breakage and predation.[26] In many cases, staging greater snow geese stopped feeding in response to transport-related activity, particularly low-flying aircraft, and if the disturbance was excessive, only half the number of geese would be still present the following day.[27]

The oceans are getting noisier every year. Recent studies indicate that manmade noise may be harming the health and affecting the behaviour of marine mammals and fish. Bowhead whales avoided drill ship operations, even those on their direct migration path. The inner ears of Weddell seals were found to be damaged in regions where dynamite explosions are used by geologists profiling ocean sediments.[28] Noise may also be masking acoustic signals vital for communication and survival, disrupting social groups, and displacing animals from traditional feeding and breeding areas.

A NOISY SOCIETY

Noise is part of the modern lifestyle. Increased mechanization is in constant demand and this frequently produces higher noise levels. New high-speed machines are often noisier than those of a decade ago.[29] Buildings are constructed from lightweight materials. Offices commonly have large, open-plan designs with little acoustic privacy.[30] Rarely can a retail establishment be found that does not have music playing. Many restaurants are designed to be noisy to attract customers who find the noise a comforting and uplifting escape from the silence or solitude at home.[31] People even transport noise with them in the form of personal listening devices (often referred to as "walkmen," because the first one produced was the Sony Walkman).

SOURCES OF NOISE

Although occupational noise is still the most common source of noise-induced hearing loss, hazardous levels of noise extend beyond factories to permeate every corner of society today, including the street, the office, the farm, the home, and recreational areas.

Potential sources of hazardous noise include industrial machinery, office equipment, medical and dental instruments,"bird bangers" used by farmers to scare birds away from crops, airplanes, motorized vehicles, household appliances, tools, weapons, firecrackers, high-volume recorded music, music concerts and spectator sports, and even children's toys.[32] Examples of common noise levels are: average city traffic at about 80 dB; subways at 90 dB; discos at 120 dB, and a shotgun firing or a jet taking off at 130 dB.[33] Regular use of portable cassette players at half volume can cause hearing damage. If used in the city, the volume is often increased to much higher levels to mask traffic noise.

Noise is even threatening the tranquility of wilderness areas. An increasing number of tourist helicopters, low-flying military planes, and even park service aircraft are not only annoying tourists but also frightening wildlife and disrupting their social behaviour and feeding habits. To combat this problem, environmentalists in the United States are fighting for the establishment of special-use air spaces over parks and wilderness areas to restrict aircraft travel.[34]

EFFECTS AND SOURCES OF VIBRATION

Responses to vibrations vary depending on the area of contact and the frequency and duration of the vibration. Vibrations affect not only the area of contact but also receptor organs in the skin, muscle tendon and bone, and the balance apparatus in the ear. Studies indicate that vibration can result in respiratory problems; chest and abdominal pains; degenerative changes in the bones, joints, and tendons; vasomotor changes; headache; tension; pains in the throat; and bladder disturbances. Tractor drivers, for example, are exposed to high levels of low-frequency vibration. Hand-held power tools represent the most common source of high-frequency vibration. Complaints about vibration often result from the operation of subways, trains, aircraft, and equipment such as punch presses in factories. According to an expert at the Ontario Ministry of Environment and Energy, the level at which people feel discomfort or annoyance, judging from complaints received, is the level at which the vibrations are perceptible.[35] In addition to affecting human health and comfort, vibration can cause serious damage to buildings and materials.

OPTIONS FOR REDUCTION

We have the means and the technology to reduce noise and vibration exposure. It may involve altering the source, the receiver's exposure, the transmission path, or a combination of these techniques. Source modification, such as proper machine maintenance or replacement with quieter parts or a quieter machine, is the most effective method of reduction. Machine insulation, sound-absorbing paints, enclosures, isolating mounts, and exhaust silencers are strategies for reducing noise and vibration radiating from equipment.

Manipulating the receiver's exposure is the most intrusive and often the least effective of the three approaches. A receiver's exposure can be reduced through site rotation, or the wearing of ear protectors including plugs, muffs, and helmets. Ear protectors can be very effective but if not properly fitted and worn for the entire exposure period, the level of protection is greatly reduced. However, because they can be uncomfortable and may hinder communication (causing other safety problems), they are often not worn when needed.[36] One has only to walk down any city street and observe the work crews using jack hammers and other noisy equipment to realize that the workers routinely ignore occupational health laws and do not wear the required ear protection. From the frequency of such observations, it is apparent that neither employers nor government agencies take much action to enforce this aspect of the law. Accordingly, ear protectors should be treated only as interim measures while other methods of reducing noise and vibration are being implemented.

Industrial noise may also affect neighbouring residents. Companies can reduce disturbance using such strategies as berms, restricted operating hours, haul restrictions, road design, speed limits, and a monitoring program. Some operations may limit noisier activities to winter when residents' windows are closed.[37]

A recent technology called "active noise control" can provide impressive remedies, which can be appreciated by both workers and the public, through a procedure that actually eliminates sound waves by projecting mirror-image waves to cancel the offending ones. Active noise control can reduce noise from industrial fans and air conditioners before it escapes through pipes or ducts. It also quiets vibration. Applied to headsets, it can be tuned to cancel background noise yet allow conversation to be heard. It may eventually replace the automobile muffler.[38]

In some cases, the lack of noise-reduction technology is a barrier to solving this problem. For example, most methods of reducing noise from high-speed military aircraft will also affect performance, so there has been little effort to develop quieter planes. In most cases, however, we have technology to reduce noise and vibration but not enough desire to apply it. This is not only due to the cost involved. Damage to hearing usually develops too slowly for people to be aware that it is happening to them. Thus, they have no incentive to give hazardous noise the attention it deserves. Noise complaints usually result from annoyance rather than any concern for damage to the ear.[39] In addition, tolerance levels vary depending on the physical and mental state of the individual, degree of control over the situation, and past experiences with the exposure and its source. Individuals can grow accustomed to noise and vibration. In the early 1960s, when noise regulations in the workplace were first established in Canada, workers frequently refused to wear noise protectors since most felt no discomfort until 100 dB.[40] But lack of annoyance and tolerance of discomfort are inadequate measures of the potential for damage caused by noise and vibration.

NOISE, VIBRATION, AND THE LAW

The kinds of laws we have to control noise and vibration generally incorporate one of the three approaches described above — namely, alter the source (for example, design standards); manipulate the receiver's exposure (occupational health and safety laws requiring employers to provide workers with ear protectors); or alter the transmission path (conditions in licences or environmental assessments requiring that trucks use only specific routes and avoid others or that noise barriers be built between highways and residential areas).

The common law concept of nuisance applies to noise and vibration that affects you on your property, whether owned or rented, and noise and vibration are also often caused through negligence.[41] You can sue for damages or an injunction, or both, to stop the noise or vibration. (See Chapter 6 for further information about common law rights and remedies.) Workers, however, usually cannot sue for harm caused by workplace noise and vibration. Their common law remedies have generally been replaced by a right to obtain compensation under workers' compensation laws.

FEDERAL JURISDICTION

The Criminal Code

The *Criminal Code*,[42] described in Chapter 2, has a few provisions that could apply to noise. In particular, the offences of causing mischief, creating a common nuisance, and disturbing the peace may apply to some kinds of noise. Of these sections, only one, disturbing the peace, deals specifically with noise. That section addresses "screaming, shouting, swearing," and even singing. These *Criminal Code* provisions are aimed primarily at "people noise" rather than at noise from business activities, and on the whole they deal with behaviour that would be objectionable even if little noise resulted. They tend to cover the same kinds of conduct that are also governed by the provincial *Environmental Protection Act* and municipal bylaws,[43] and rarely would the conduct be truly "criminal" in character, warranting prosecution under the *Code*. (See chapters 1 and 2 for discussion of these *Code* provisions and the difference between conduct that is truly criminal in nature and conduct that is not.)

Apart from the *Criminal Code*, the federal government has authority to set standards for all sorts of technology, machinery, equipment, and consumer products, particularly where such standards are required to protect the health of the public. Using these powers, the federal government can pass laws requiring the design of such technologies to meet specific criteria for noise emissions. In addition to control over product-design standards, the federal government can regulate the operation of various noise-producing facilities that fall under federal jurisdiction, particularly in the field of transportation.

Transportation

Control over most noise generated by some modes of transportation is partly or entirely within federal jurisdiction for one of two reasons: either because the federal government has the power to regulate the design of the equipment used but not how the equipment is operated, or because the operation of the equipment is also within federal jurisdiction. For example, how cars are operated on our roads is within provincial and federal jurisdiction, but requiring that their engines be designed to minimize noise is a federal matter. However, the federal government has more extensive powers to regulate aeronautics, railways, and shipping. For these modes of transportation, the federal government may have the authority not only to set standards for the technology but also to regulate the operation of the facilities.

Aircraft and Airport Noise

The federal government controls aircraft noise in three ways: by prohibiting or restricting the use of aircraft that are not designed to meet specified noise emission limits, by regulating how aircraft are operated, and by regulating land uses around airports.

The *Aeronautics Act*[44] gives the minister of transport (or, in defence matters, the minister of national defence) the authority to make any regulation needed to govern air navigation, subject to Cabinet approval. International agencies concerned with aeronautics have developed noise-emission standards for some aircraft that have been incorporated into Canada's *Aeronautics Act*.

Under the *Aeronautics Act*, no one may operate an aircraft in Canadian airspace unless that aircraft meets certain noise-emission standards. The ability to meet these standards is considered a component of the aircraft's airworthiness, and the maximum allowable noise levels applicable to each kind of aircraft are set out in an airworthiness manual. Under the Aircraft Noise Emission Standards and Certification Order,[45] a regulation under the *Aeronautics Act*, owners and pilots may only operate aircraft that have been issued a certificate of noise compliance by the minister. In addition, if the aircraft undergoes any modification that will affect the noise it emits, its owner or operator must notify the minister as soon as possible and submit evidence that the aircraft continues to comply with the noise-emission standards.[46] These requirements apply to subsonic turbojet airplanes and propeller-driven planes registered after 1985 and to helicopters registered after 1988. Certain planes, such as those designed for agricultural pesticide spraying or firefighting, are not required to meet these emission standards. However, although there are limits on the amount of noise each plane may emit, there are no legal limits on the amount of noise the cumulative air traffic in an area may impose on the inhabitants.

Noise-reduction legislation passed in the early 1970s encouraged manufacturers to produce a new generation of quieter aircraft. This has resulted in reductions of 15 to 20 dB to conventional civil transport aircraft, where this proved to be technically feasible and economically viable.[47] In fact, the search for energy efficiency resulted in better aerodynamics and the use of a different kind of engine, both of which resulted in noise reduction. Nevertheless, about half of the aircraft in operation throughout the world in 1989 were still the older models. At Pearson International Airport near Toronto, for example, 65 per cent of the planes were still the old, noisier planes.[48] It will be another 20 years before all the older aircraft have been replaced by the current generation of quieter planes.[49] Moreover, although the newer "stage 3" aircraft are designed to be quieter than the "stage 2" planes, in future they are likely to be larger and heavier, and therefore no less noisy than the older planes.[50] Moreover, most of the improvement is on takeoff, not on landing. The US *Airport Noise and Capacity Act of 1990*[51] of November 1990 bars the older, noisier aircraft from airports by the year 2000, with limited exemptions to 2003, but Canada has no similar legislation.

The United States and some European countries require older jets to be quieted by means of retrofit. The disadvantages of this option are the potential high cost, reduction in performance, and delay in retirement of retrofitted aircraft.[52]

One of the concerns in the late 1970s was the development of a supersonic civilian transport jet, the Concorde, which created takeoff noise two to four times as loud as that of subsonic planes.[53] and created the possibility of sonic booms over inhabited areas. Consequently, the Concorde is restricted to a small number of airports and is forced to travel at subsonic speeds over land. Sonic booms are allowed if the minister of transport gives prior permission.[54] British and French companies jointly produced 20 Concordes, 14 of which are still in use today.[55] Although considered an economic failure, plans are under way to develop a new model predicted to be commercially viable between 2000 and 2010. To be economically feasible, these advanced supersonic transports (ASTs) must be highly productive, which may lead to pressure to allow supersonic flights over land, causing sonic booms. The first and most challenging hurdle to production of the AST is compliance with noise and air pollution emission standards. Research suggests that through improvements in design, it can be done.[56]

Less progress has been made in reducing noise from military aircraft because there is no current technology to reduce noise levels from military jet engines without considerable decrease in performance, which is unacceptable for planes that may be used in combat zones. In fact, NATO has acknowledged that few noise-attenuation measures have been incorporated into military fighter/bomber aircraft,[57] and advances are likely to be achieved "only if the airframe and engine manufacturers are *required* to consider noise reduction as a primary design requirement"[58] [emphasis added]. This means the military generally limits remedial measures to control of flight operations. For example, even though low-level flights are necessary for training pilots, the military tries to balance the need for training against the impact on the public by establishing a general lower limit of 250 feet, which is still much lower than civil aircraft are allowed to fly (see below).

A second method of controlling noise is control of operations. Generally, civil aircraft movements between airports must be made at an altitude of at least 500 feet above ground or water, and over builtup areas, at least 1,000 feet above the highest obstruction within 2,000 feet.[59] Around airports, the rules for aircraft movement, covering matters such as takeoff and landing angle and night flights, vary from airport to airport. A set of rules for 13 major urban airports, governing when aircraft can take off and land, choice of runways, arrival and departure procedures, and other matters that can affect noise, is found in the Aircraft Noise Operating Restrictions Order.[60] Under that order, a certificate is required to operate the aircraft on certain noise-restricted runways if the maximum certified takeoff weight is more than 34,000 kg.[61] However, any changes in conditions, from a labour strike to an in-flight emergency, can be interpreted by Transport Canada as sufficient justification for breaking regulations. Violations of these various operating rules are punishable by fines of up to $25,000 for corporations and $5,000 for private owners.[62] In practice, however, complainants find that Transport Canada will either not prosecute or settle for small fines of a few hundred dollars.[63]

Zoning Around Airports

A third way to regulate noise from aircraft is to prohibit land uses around airports that will result in nuisance, and where buildings are permitted, requiring them to be constructed in a manner designed to impede noise. Zoning around airports is subject to overlapping jurisdictions. On lands owned by the federal government, whether part of the airport itself or around it, zoning is a federal responsibility. The amount of land Transport Canada has bought, beyond that actually required for the airport, varies greatly.

In addition, the *Aeronautics Act* authorizes the minister of transport to impose zoning restrictions on lands in the vicinity of airports to the extent that this is necessary to facilitate aviation. Through a "zoning regulation," the minister can control the height, use, and location of buildings, structures, and objects around airports.[64] This provision serves the dual purpose of allowing the federal government to step in when municipalities fail to prevent development in the shadow of airports and to prevent nearby landowners from constructing high towers to keep aircraft from flying over their land while taking off and landing, as some did in the past. Without such a regulation, a landowner has the right to use his or her property, including the airspace above it, in any way the municipal zoning bylaws permit.[65]

This legislation could be used to prevent people living and working near airports from having to suffer the results of poor planning. But the federal government could also use it to override attempts by the provincial and municipal governments to prevent the imposition of unwanted new airports like the Pickering Airport, which was stopped only after the Ontario government refused to provide services for it.

For the purpose of assessing whether airports or aircraft traffic at an airport should be expanded or increased, and for determining zones and making recommendations as to suitable land uses in each zone, Transport Canada uses measurements intended to predict noise levels at various locations. Using measurements such as noise exposure forecasts (NEFs) and single-level event (SEL) noise analysis, Transport Canada produces noise contour maps showing the levels of noise to be expected at various locations in the vicinity of airports. However, these predictive tools have various shortcomings and may not always accurately predict future noise levels.[66] Using these NEFs and SELs, Transport Canada has published a document entitle "Land Use in the Vicinity of Airports"[67] to guide development and land-use planning decisions. In addition, the Canada Mortgage and Housing Corporation (CMHC) has policies governing standards for acoustic insulation and ventilation in residential buildings that are constructed in areas susceptible to airport noise.[68]

Under the *Planning Act*,[69] the province can control land use on all land not owned by the federal government, although in the past this has been left to the municipalities. The Ministry of Housing has produced a policy for the use of municipalities and developers in deciding whether development should be allowed near airports. All land-use proposals are expected to adhere to this policy, which suggests the kinds of uses that are acceptable in areas susceptible to different kinds and degrees of aircraft noise.[70]

However, a province or municipality cannot use its land-use planning powers to frustrate the development or expansion of any airport or air strip, whether federally or privately owned.[71] A zoning bylaw prohibiting establishment of such a facility has no effect.[72]

In the past, all jurisdictions carried out their responsibilities poorly, with the result that much of the housing around airports in Toronto, Regina, Thunder Bay, Windsor, and others is badly affected by noise. A federal environmental assessment panel concluded in 1992 that by 1990 noise around Toronto's Pearson International Airport "had reached a level that was now intolerable for many area residents."[73] Noise complaints there have risen from 200 to 300 a year in 1980 to over 3,000 a year in 1988, 1989, and 1990.[74]

Finally, new airports, expansions of existing airports, low-level flying, and other activities under federal jurisdiction that create noise may be subject to the federal government's environmental assessment process, described in Chapter 9. For example, the proposed addition of a third terminal at the Pearson International Airport was subject to an environmental assessment, which included consideration of possible noise impacts.[75]

In 1992, Transport Canada was also considering adding three new runways to this airport, and an environmental assessment of this project, dealing in part with noise, was completed in May of that year.[76] An environmental assessment panel held hearings and recommended against the runways, primarily because of noise impacts.[77] However, the minister of transport rejected this recommendation and approved the runways in February 1993.

Complaints concerning civilian aircraft or airports should be made to the airport, usually the manager, except in the case of the Pearson International Airport, which has a special noise-complaint number.[78] In theory, it is possible to demand an investigation into any incident that appears to be an infraction of regulations. However, citizens have often been frustrated by a lack of response to their complaints, and at Pearson Airport, for example, there is a "public perception that ... the airport authorities and all three levels of government have developed a consistent record of insincerity, of broken promises, and of failure to recognize, or callous disregard for, the hardships caused by their decisions."[79] A federal environmental assessment panel found that Transport Canada officials have a lack of equipment and insufficient legislative authority to identify and prosecute offenders.[80] For a persistent problem, contact Transport Canada in Ottawa and get your neighbours to do likewise. If you persevere, you should get results. Complaints concerning military aircraft or airports should be made to the Department of National Defence.

Railways

The *Railway Act*[81] and the *Railway Safety Act*[82] authorize the minister of transport and the National Transportation Agency (NTA) (formerly, the Canadian Transport Commission) to impose speed limits and regulate the use of whistles on trains in urban areas. In general, safety matters are handled by Department of Transport safety inspectors under the *Railway Safety Act*, and nuisances, such as noise and vibration that annoy neighbours but that are not considered a safety hazard, are dealt with under the rubric "public convenience" by the NTA. A regulation has been made that requires trains to whistle at grade in cities and towns, with certain exceptions.[83] Although whistling is obviously important for public safety, it is also noisy. Residents who object to whistling can complain to the nearest Transport Canada railway safety inspector, or can try to convince the municipal council to approach the railway company. Transport Canada has published a guideline setting out procedures for resolving disputes about whistling and relieving railway companies from the obligation to whistle, provided that satisfactory alternative warning systems can be established.[84]

Noise disturbance from railways usually results from shunting and coupling operations in and near the yards, from idling engines and refrigeration cars, and from high-speed trains travelling through builtup areas. There are constant complaints and many citizens have organized groups to fight train noise. Such activity may have influenced CP Rail's decision to install longer rail sections (ribbon rails) and to do away with unnecessary switches in some areas. The smoother track cuts noise somewhat. Other ways to cut noise would be to make sure the wheels stay round, to keep equipment and track in good condition, to muffle engines, to use cushioned couplers between cars, and to build noise barriers in some places. Slowing down trains in builtup areas may also help. This tactic would, as railway officials are quick to point out, cause the noise to last a few seconds longer, but it should cut down the vibration of houses and the objects within them. Trains are required by an order of the former Railway Transport Committee to slow down to 95 MPH over road crossings.[85] Otherwise, they may go fast, unless a specific order has been made requiring them to slow down in specific locations, as is the case with trains carrying dangerous goods through some builtup areas.

Getting action on complaints of noise from trains can be a frustrating experience since each agency involved may suggest that the other is responsible. When in doubt, contact Transport Canada, the NTA, and the railway company. Responsibility for pollution caused by railways rests with the division superintendent in the case of CP Rail and with the district environmental control officer in the case of CN. The GO train commuter service, although it runs on federally owned tracks, is operated by a provincial Crown agency, the Toronto Area Transit Operations Authority (TATOA), and the trains themselves are owned by CN Rail. Complaints should go to TATOA's Marketing and Information Department. The province and the municipality have authority over railway cars standing on private property. Contact the Ministry of Environment and Energy and your councillor.

Railways and Land-Use Planning

Although it is difficult to prevent noise from existing railway lines and yards, preventive action can be taken to stop new lines and yards from being established near residential areas, or, as is more likely, new residential development near existing lines and yards. The railways themselves will often help oppose development near their facilities, since they do not want complaints about noise and danger from exposure to transportation of dangerous goods. If notified of proposed development, they will usually send a letter opposing it and advise of measures that should be taken to reduce noise and danger arising from a derailment if the development does proceed. In addition, both CMHC[86] and the Ontario Ministry of the Environment[87] have produced methods of measuring and predicting railway noise that should be used by railways when deciding where to locate new facilities and by municipalities when deciding whether to approve development near existing rail facilities.

Snowmobiles

Under the *Motor Vehicle Safety Act*,[88] the federal government can set quality standards for vehicles used or manufactured in Canada.

The snowmobile was the first vehicle to be put under federal noise-emission regulations. This was certainly because of public outcry, which provides a clue as to how further controls can be brought about. A limit of 82 dBA at 50 feet was set for snowmobiles manufactured in or imported into Canada after February 1972. The limit is now at 73 dBA, last amended in 1987.[89] This is still not enough to protect the rider's hearing from more than brief exposures.

The operation of snowmobiles is dealt with under provincial legislation regulating snowmobiles and legislation relating to trespass, described in Chapter 6.

Highway Vehicles, Motorcycles, Minibikes, and All-Terrain Vehicles

Further regulations under the *Motor Vehicle Safety Act* came into force in 1973, when automobiles and light trucks manufactured in or imported into Canada were limited to 86 dBA at 50 feet. This effectively legalized just about everything on the road. Cars with legal mufflers seldom measure over 80 dBA at that distance, even at high speed.

The noise limit for heavy-duty vehicles, buses, and trucks, 88 dBA at 50 feet, proclaimed in March 1, 1973,[90] made more sense. This was the voluntary standard set in 1954 by the Automobile Manufacturers Association (now known as the Motor Vehicle Manufacturers Association) for all new trucks. It is the standard that has been in force in California for trucks at low speed. To control high-speed truck noise, it would also be necessary to regulate the types of tires used.

To be most effective, such design standards must be accompanied by enforcement programs to ensure that noise reducing mufflers are not bypassed or removed, and that vehicles are properly maintained to ensure that they operate efficiently. This aspect of enforcement is a provincial responsibility, but the Ministry of Environment and Energy has no such inspection program.

The noise limits for motorcycles have also been reduced as quieter technology was developed. In 1989, Canada dropped the permissible levels from a range of 86 dBA to 80 dBA to a new range: from 77 to 82 dBA, depending on the maximum engine displacement.[91] The same standards apply to minibikes. Currently, there are no standards for all terrain vehicles; however, Transport Canada made a recommendation to the Canadian All Terrain Vehicles Distribution Council that voluntary standards be set according to those of the US Environmental Protection Agency for off-road vehicles.[92]

Land-Use Planning and Motor Vehicles

Again, much can be accomplished to reduce vehicle noise by adequate land-use planning, a provincial responsibility. The Ontario government has a policy that outdoor noise in residential developments near freeways should be no greater than 55 decibels. Although 55 dB is the objective, the provincial government will not step in to prevent residential development unless the noise level will exceed 70 dB.[93] Both the federal government and the provincial governments have produced tools to measure and predict traffic noise,[94] which should be used in making decisions where to locate new roads, how close to existing roads new residential development should be allowed, and what forms of noise reduction should be incorporated into the design of roads and subdivisions. In addition, many kinds of undertakings, such as municipal road-building programs, are subject to class assessments under the *Environmental Assessment Act*,[95] which address anticipated noise and vibration impacts, and possible mitigation measures.

Motorboats

A former minister of transport once said that no noise emission controls for motorboats were needed, since the quieter boats were selling well. Vacationers in cottage country would be unlikely to agree. Manufacturers did in fact produce boats with quieter engines in the late 1970s, but boaters quickly overcame any noise reductions by installing larger engines, driving their boats faster, and, particularly in the case of teenagers, "aerating" their propellers (that is, tilting the propellers so they are partially out of the water), all of which create more noise. In addition, manufacturers have produced new and noisier vessels called "wet bikes," "jet skis," "sea-doos," and "cigarette boats." Many of these have "straight pipes" — that is, no mufflers. Despite this, there are still no noise-emission standards or requirements to have mufflers.[96] This is particularly ironic, since a snowmobile on a frozen lake must meet federal noise standards, yet motorboats on the same lake have no such controls. In fact, the only reference to noise prevention in the regulation governing small vessels under the *Canada Shipping Act*[97] is a section prohibiting the unnecessary sounding of horns and whistles.[98]

Not only are there no noise-emission standards for recreational boats, but also, except for a law limiting boats to 9 KPH in a few specified areas and a province-wide limit to 10 KPH within 30 metres of the shore, put in place in 1992,[99] and a requirement to slow down when passing other boats, there are no speed limits for boats, which often have 200 horsepower motors — powerful enough to go over 150 MPH.

Moreover, the OPP, which is generally responsible for enforcing the speeding laws on cottage lakes, has insufficient resources to deal with this problem.

There is potential to control noise on some waters through local bylaws passed under the authority of the *Municipal Act*,[100] the *Environmental Protection Act*,[101] or zoning bylaws and official plans under the *Planning Act*. But there have been few, if any, attempts to do this. There may be a variety of reasons for this, including the fact that many lakes are not within municipally organized territory, that the boundaries of the municipality may not extend out into the lake, that navigable waters are within federal jurisdiction, difficulties in enforcement, and the fact that cottagers themselves may not agree to restrictions on what vessels they will be allowed to use and how the law should limit that use.

The Muskoka Lakes Association, which represents local cottagers, has lobbied for a law that limits the noise levels of boats idling near shore, but has been told by government officials that such a law would be unenforceable, despite the fact that 43 US states have such a regulation and the *Environmental Protection Act* authorizes municipalities to pass bylaws prohibiting the idling of motor vehicles in designated areas.

Apparently, the sale of ski-boats is on the increase and cottagers are protesting against the number of noisy, speeding boaters. In the absence of effective government controls, the Muskoka Lakes Association's desire for quick action led it to adopt a very controversial tactic to solve the problem. In 1990, they initiated a "Bad Boaters' Campaign" and placed ads in local newspapers inviting concerned cottagers to send in photos of the offenders to be posted and published within the community.[102]

Noise-Producing Products

Although the specific statutes discussed above can require noise-emission standards for motor vehicles, aircraft, and trains, other consumer products fall under the *Hazardous Products Act*.[103] Under that Act, the federal government can set noise-emission limits for virtually any consumer product and prohibit its sale in Canada if it does not meet those limits. However, the Act applies only to noise levels that actually endanger public health and safety.[104] The fact that toys, appliances, machinery, or tools emit noise that is obnoxious is not enough to give the federal government jurisdiction over their design.

Design standards are the only feasible way to control the danger from many noisy products, since it is impossible to police how people use them in the privacy of their homes. For example, personal listening devices ("walkmen") can be cranked up to decibel levels that will cause permanent hearing loss to their users. Rather than trying to police the sound levels at which children listen to them, the more logical approach, as recommended by the Canadian Hearing Society, is to restrict the maximum sound they can emit.

However, the only products designated under this Act as hazardous are children's toys that emit noise exceeding 100 decibels, a level far higher than that at which hearing can be damaged.[105]

Occupational Hearing Protection

Operators of federal works, undertakings, and businesses must follow safety regulations under the *Canada Labour Code*.[106] But these standards do not apply to work done in connection with the operation of ships, trains, or aircraft, or to many federal departments and Crown corporations, because they have been exempted from the legislation. That leaves a lot of room for exceptions.

The *Code* permits exposure to up to 90 dBA for an eight-hour working day, with higher limits for shorter working periods. The greatest noise exposure allowed is 115 dBA for 15 minutes. When the dose is exceeded for a certain period of time, Health and Welfare Canada says a hearing protection program should begin.[107] No one may work at all where noise exceeds 115 dBA.

Although a step in the right direction, the limits were made to accommodate industries that lacked the technology to achieve lower levels.[108] As a result, they are not strict enough to prevent noise-induced hearing loss. Ten per cent of workers exposed to 90 dBA on a daily basis will lose a substantial amount of hearing during the first several years of their working lives. The limits also assume a quiet period of 16 hours, which workers frequently will not obtain.[109]

A model regulation has been developed for the provinces through joint efforts of the federal and provincial governments and the Canadian Standards Association. Its intention is to eliminate inconsistencies between the provinces in the limit and measurement standards, but adoption is not compulsory.[110]

Truck drivers are "protected" by a manufacturing standard that requires noise in the cabs of new heavy trucks to be no more than 90 dBA, with windows and doors closed.[111]

The National Building Code

Through the *National Building Code*, developed by a continuing committee within the National Research Council, federal influence on in-building noise could be pervasive. Many, perhaps most, municipalities adopt the *National Building Code* without substantial change. The *Code* has no legal effect, however, except when adopted in a provincial statute (as Ontario has done in its *Building Code Act*)[112] or a municipal bylaw, or when its standards are incorporated into a building contract. The CMHC uses the *National Building Code* to set the minimum construction standards permissible for buildings it will finance.

Provisions controlling noise are few. The *Code* sets "sound transmission class ratings" for in-building noise at 50 dBA between units for office buildings, apartment buildings, hotels, and motels, and 55 dBA for apartment buildings between the units and noisy areas such as elevators and garbage chutes.[113] This means that the doors and walls between suites, and between suites and such spaces as corridors, must block at least this level of noise. The rating applies to airborne sound at a frequency of 500 Hz. Above this frequency, a wall will stop more sound; below, it will stop less. Such a wall will give quite good protection against conversational levels of speech in the next room. However, it will give rather poor protection from much machinery noise, from the base setting of a stereo set, and from thumps and bumps generally. This level of sound resistance is not adequate to protect residents from the sounds of a loud party, or noisy sex.[114] Common air vents, which transmit unlimited quantities of noise, are permitted. There are also no special regulations for solid-borne sound or vibration — that is, sound or vibration transmitted through pipes, walls, and ceilings — or for common-use facilities such as party rooms.

Although these standards help to protect the occupants of buildings from noise created by each other, there are no similar standards to protect them from outdoor noise. As a result of standards developed to provide better energy conservation in modern buildings, modern windows and exterior walls will provide sound insulation far greater than the standards for interior walls. However, this will often be insufficient to prevent noise in developments near airports, rail facilities, or busy roads. In those cases, there may be no protection unless it is accomplished through specific zoning such as a city bylaw.

Canada Mortgage and Housing Corporation Site-Planning Standards

The Canada Mortgage and Housing Corporation has developed some very useful standards for residential construction in areas affected by noise from airplanes, trains, and highways. They have been adopted by the provincial government and are now used in residential land-use planning.[115]

A major drawback is the site evaluation method chosen for road and rail noise. The airport standards are determined using a noise exposure forecast (NEF) map provided by the Ministry of Transport, which takes into account the increased annoyance caused by noise that occurs at night. In the case of road and rail noise, the noise is merely averaged over a 24-hour period to produce a single dBA number. Such a number may fairly represent the effects of noise in an area where the daylight noise level is dependably higher than that prevailing at night. It is not appropriate for areas, such as those near dispatching centres, where there are more trains or trucks at night than in the daytime, nor does it make allowance for the increased intrusiveness of any sound that occurs in the night.

PROVINCIAL JURISDICTION

Highway Traffic Act

Certain sections of the *Highway Traffic Act*[116] are relevant to noise. Section 75 of the Act provides that:

> 1) Every motor vehicle or motor assisted bicycle should be equipped with a muffler in good working order and in constant operation to prevent excessive or unusual noise ... and no person shall use a muffler cut-out, straight exhaust, gutted muffler, hollywood muffler, by-pass or similar device upon a motor vehicle or motor assisted bicycle. ...
>
> 3) A person having the control or charge of a motor vehicle shall not sound any bell, horn or other signalling device so as to make unreasonable noise, and an operator or chauffeur of any vehicle shall not ... cause the motor vehicle to make any unnecessary noise.

Complaints about motor vehicle noise should be directed immediately to the police, with the licence number and description of the vehicle, location, time and details of the complaint. The registered owner of the vehicle is the proper person to be charged and, under the *Highway Traffic Act*, he or she is legally responsible for the acts of any driver, unless the car was stolen or being driven without permission.

Always get the rank and name or the badge number of the police officer with whom you lodge a complaint. Ask to be informed of the results of your complaint.

Under the *Highway Traffic Act*, the sale or use of noise-making mufflers and musical car horns could be forbidden by an order of the Ontario Cabinet. Section 101 provides that Cabinet may make regulations prohibiting the sale or use of "any accessory or ornament, or any type or class thereof, that is designed for use on vehicles."

The Environmental Protection Act and the Environmental Assessment Act

Potentially the most far-reaching and effective statutes concerning noise in Canada today are Ontario's *Environmental Protection Act* and *Environmental Assessment Act*.

Under section 1 of the *Environmental Protection Act*, sound and vibration are environmental contaminants and can be prohibited or controlled using the tools available under that Act, which are described in Chapter 16. However, for several years after the *Environmental Protection Act* came into force in 1971, the Ministry of the Environment declined to use it to prosecute noise makers, on the grounds that it was first necessary to write noise regulations. It was only after several private prosecutions that the ministry chose to act.

Control orders for noise were first used in 1975. Although there are still no regulations, the ministry has developed noise guidelines that it can use in deciding whether to issue approvals or orders or in deciding whether noise is excessive for the purpose of prosecution. The ministry has trained inspectors to measure noise, and will require factories and similar sources of noise to control noise emissions. The guidelines serve as standards in decisions made by courts or boards. The ministry may also advise the local municipality to adopt a bylaw based on the guidelines to deal with a problem. Once approval for the bylaw is obtained from the ministry, the municipalities are responsible for enforcing it. Thus, the level of government with the fewest financial and technical resources is to be left to cope with this problem. (See the discussion below, under the heading "Anti-Noise Bylaws.")

The ministry no longer has a noise control branch. Complaints may be addressed to the regional and district offices of the ministry. However, even though noise is clearly covered by the *Environmental Protection Act*, the ministry will often refuse to investigate, and refer complainants to the municipality, even if the municipality has not passed a bylaw based on the ministry's model bylaw. However, the ministry may decide to investigate and act on complaints involving a large industrial complex or interests beyond the jurisdiction of the municipality, such as railway and airport noise or a federal or provincial establishment. The ministry will also respond to complaints about vibration.[117]

New facilities and the expansion of existing facilities that may emit noise or cause vibrations must obtain a certificate of approval from the ministry, and the ministry may issue preventive or corrective orders. When considering whether to issue an approval or what should go into an order, the ministry makes use of several guidelines, developed by the ministry itself or by the US Environmental Protection Agency. These include the methods of predicting railway and road traffic noise referred to above, "Noise Guidelines for Landfill Sites,"[118] "Landfill Sites — Noise Criteria for Pest Control Devices," "Noise Assessment Criteria in Land Use Planning,"[119] and 15 noise pollution control publications outlining specific procedures and guidelines published as schedule 1 to the ministry's model municipal noise control bylaw, *Final Report*. These deal with matters such as blasting, power lawn mowers, residential air conditioners, outdoor power tools, construction and demolition equipment, and various motor vehicles.

However, the ministry does not have similar guidelines on how to measure vibration and determine what vibration levels are acceptable. For example, the ministry has been working on a guideline for impulse vibration in residential buildings for a decade or more, but has never finalized it.[120]

As mentioned earlier, noise and vibration will often be addressed both in individual and class environmental assessments, and the environmental assessment process contains opportunities for public involvement. (See Chapter 9.)

Occupational Hearing Protection

Employers were motivated to improve conditions in the workplace considerably once occupational hearing loss was accepted as a compensable disease by the Workers' Compensation Board. The resulting claims encouraged the adoption of stricter regulations and mandatory protection. Nevertheless, noise continues to be a serious problem in the Ontario workplace. Between 1983 and 1989, Ontario accepted roughly 5,000 claims for temporary and permanent disabilities arising from excessive noise, at an average cost of $10,000.[121] Ontario had 653 accepted time-loss injuries resulting from hearing loss or impairment in 1989 alone.[122]

The Ontario *Occupational Health and Safety Act*[123] follows the noise limits set out in the *Canada Labour Code*;[124] that is, up to 90 dBA over an eight-hour period, and higher levels over shorter time periods. However, at these levels, many workers will still suffer hearing loss.

Efforts have be made to reduce noise exposure limits in the workplace to safer levels. An advisory committee appointed by the Ministry of Labour recommended a reduction to 80 dBA and a draft regulation was prepared more than 10 years ago, but never implemented.[125] Even 80 dBA, however, is too high to prevent exposure to noise levels that may cause annoyance, interfere with work and speech, or reduce efficiency, as well as possible hearing loss.

Moreover, although workers have the right under Ontario's *Occupational Health and Safety Act* to refuse unsafe work, the Ministry of Labour has ruled that noise ranging from 67 to 84 dBA, while it can create several stress-related reactions, including abdominal pain, headaches, ear irritation, and dizziness, does not create a danger that justifies stopping work.[126]

Noise levels to which Ontario's workers can legally be exposed are considerably higher than in some other provinces. The level in Alberta, Newfoundland, Nova Scotia, and Saskatchewan, for example, is 85 rather than 90 dBA. Furthermore, Ontario has no limits on exposure to impulse or impact noise, which can be particularly hazardous. The federal government, the Northwest Territories, and four provinces do have such limits.

A review of the Ontario regulation has been underway since 1979. So far, it has produced proposals to reduce noise exposure and to require employers to carry out a noise-monitoring program, provide employee hearing tests, and implement a hearing conservation program for many workplaces. Among the recommendations made by the Canadian Hearing Society for the prevention of occupational hearing loss is the adoption of legislated engineering standards for machinery and standards for effectiveness of personal hearing protection.[127]

Complaints should be directed to the Industrial Health and Safety Branch of the Ministry of Labour. The branch says that all complaints will be investigated, and if hazardous levels are suspected, sound level measurements will be made. Any changes recommended by the branch are explained in a report that is sent to the company and posted there for two weeks. Complaints can be kept confidential unless the complainant requires a copy of the report.[128]

The Ontario Building Code

The *Ontario Building Code* has the same standards as the *National Building Code*, described earlier. The *Building Code Act* authorizes the municipal official who issues building permits to refuse to issue one if the building would violate the Building Code or any other valid law. This means, for example, that if the building would house noisy machinery without being properly designed to prevent excessive noise, or if the walls between rooms are thinner than required by the *Code*, the municipality can refuse to issue a building permit.

MUNICIPAL JURISDICTION

In Ontario, jurisdiction over noise and noise-making activities is given to the municipalities by various sections of the *Municipal Act*, the *Planning Act*, special acts such as those for the cities of Ottawa and Toronto, and the *Environmental Protection Act*.

Land-Use Planning

One of the most effective methods of controlling noise is good land-use planning to prevent conflicting uses and to ensure that the design of buildings and infrastructure minimizes noise and vibration impacts. Even though land-use planning is a provincial responsibility, it is dealt with by delegating most approval powers to municipalities. We have discussed this issue above under the section on federal laws to demonstrate how provincial and municipal planning laws and policies dovetail with federal ones in relation to specific noise sources such as aircraft, trains, and motor vehicles, for which federal laws play a major role.

As discussed above, municipalities may use several provincial and federal policies and guidelines regarding noise when considering land-use applications. In addition, as discussed in Chapter 8, some land-use applications, such as applications for subdivision approval, are circulated for comment to various provincial agencies. One of the functions of the Ministry of Environment and Energy (MEE) when reviewing such applications is to determine whether a development will comply with ministry guidelines on noise impacts, and to raise objections if they will not. Occasionally, ministry staff have testified at the Ontario Municipal Board in opposition to development because of anticipated noise impacts. The Ministry of Housing guidelines on noise and new residential development adjacent to freeways require a developer to contact the Ministry of Environment and Energy if development is closer than one kilometre to a freeway, prove that noise will be at its lowest practical level, and, if the level is higher, notify potential home buyers of the expected noise level and include it in the official plan.[129]

Some cities in Canada and the United States have followed the European example of zoning noise limits according to land use. The first instance of this in Canada was when Etobicoke used its power under the zoning provisions of the *Planning Act* to prescribe standards for occupancy of residential property to limit the noise emissions of central air conditioning units.

Etobicoke's good intentions were initially frustrated because the bylaw adopted was one designed by the air conditioning industry, which permitted far too high a noise level. It was later amended to conform with advice from the Ministry of the Environment, and now limits noise from these machines, as heard on a neighbouring property, to 50 dBA in the daytime and 45 dBA at night.

When new subdivisions are approved in high-noise areas where the standard building construction standards in the *Ontario Building Code* are insufficient to prevent serious noise infiltration, residents must rely on municipal officials to require adequate studies of expected noise impacts and to use their powers under the *Planning Act* to ensure that buildings are constructed to higher standards.

The city of Mississauga, for example, follows a special procedure for new subdivisions in high noise areas such as near highways and airports. When a building plan is registered, the region of Peel, in which Mississauga is located, prepares a report with noise-level requirements. The developer is required to hire an acoustical consultant to inspect each house design at all stages of construction and certify that the development complies with the requirements. This procedure is not specified in a bylaw, but is more of a servicing agreement.

Noise Control Bylaws

There are two common types of anti-noise or, as they are more commonly called, noise control bylaws: qualitative (or subjective) bylaws and quantitative (or objective) bylaws.

Qualitative bylaws measure the acceptability of noise by the reaction of the ordinary, reasonable person to that noise. These bylaws define an unacceptable noise as one that is unusual or likely to disturb, or that unreasonably disturbs people. The advantage of this kind of bylaw is that to obtain a conviction it is not necessary to train technicians to calibrate and use sophisticated measuring devices, and actually measure the noise level and present the readings in court. The testimony of ordinary people that they heard the noise and that it was disturbing or annoying is sufficient proof of the offence to obtain a conviction, in the absence of evidence that the witnesses were unreliable or that the excessive noise was unavoidable under the circumstances. The disadvantage of such bylaws is their subjectivity. What may seem disturbing to one person may be perfectly acceptable to others.

Quantitative bylaws set noise-emission limits at levels that have been scientifically established as bothersome to the average person, and usually at levels shown to be technologically and economically achievable. Any noise above those limits is an offence. The obvious advantage is that they remove the subjectivity from the judgment whether a noise is disturbing and tell the court precisely how loud it was, based on actual measurements of the noise at the time it was emitted.

The difficulty with this kind of bylaw is that evidence can only be given by technicians trained in the calibration and operation of sophisticated noise-measuring devices, and in performing any calculations needed to supplement or interpret the readings on the machine. Even more of a drawback is the difficulty of finding a trained technician available to take noise measurements. Many noise problems are sporadic or intermittent and a trained investigator may not be available when they occur.

Most modern municipal noise control bylaws contain a combination of qualitative and quantitative tests of noise acceptability.

In Ontario, municipalities may pass noise control bylaws under either the *Municipal Act* or the *Environmental Protection Act*.

General Anti-Noise Bylaws Under the Municipal Act
(Those Without Decibel Limits)

Under the *Municipal Act, local* municipalities (that is, lower-tier municipalities) may pass bylaws prohibiting or regulating, within the municipality or within any defined area or areas thereof, the ringing of bells, the blowing of horns, shouting, and unusual noises likely to disturb the inhabitants.[130]

Most such bylaws begin with a general section that follows the wording of the Act or some slight variation of it. However, it is possible to have a further section in which a number of specific noises are "deemed" to be noises that "disturb" or "are likely to disturb."

One might expect a charge under a "deeming" section to be simpler to prove, creating less uncertainty about whether a particular sound emitted at a particular time and place was likely to disturb. However, municipal enforcement officials still found that the courts were often reluctant to convict when the prosecutor had the onus of proving beyond a reasonable doubt that a noise was likely to disturb.

Accordingly, municipalities sought a more objective standard to determine when noise was excessive. One method was to use decibel limits. A second approach, later taken in the MOE model noise bylaw discussed below, was to prohibit certain sounds when they were "clearly audible" rather than on the basis of whether they actually disturbed or were likely to disturb people exposed to them.

Decibel Bylaws

The first laws controlling noise in terms of decibels were passed in Germany in the 1930s, and such laws are now common throughout northern Europe, Great Britain, and the United States.

Since at least 1958, there have been attempts to use anti-noise bylaws with decibel limits in Canada. Metropolitan Toronto bylaw no. 835 was passed in that year. It limited motor vehicle noise to 94 decibels on the C-scale,* measured at 15 feet. This was clearly too high a limit for that time, since it proved difficult to find a vehicle that loud.

This bylaw was approved by the then Department of Highways, was used at least once, and was upheld by the Ontario Court of Appeal. It then fell into disuse, in part because of the inconvenience of needing a decibel meter and an expert witness to win the first case.

Since about 1969, other Canadian cities have been experimenting with decibel bylaws. The city of Ottawa paved the way with two such bylaws. The first was an attempt to control road vehicle noise at or below 90 dBA at 15 feet; the second set limits for air conditioners, chain saws, power motors, snow blowers, power tools, model airplanes, hovercraft, and snowmobiles. It proved difficult to get convictions under these bylaws. One alleged difficulty was that the *City of Ottawa Act*,[131] under which these bylaws were written, did not specify the type of decibel meter to be used; another was that since any noise meter measures all the noise in the area, it was difficult to convince a court that the offending noise and the noise registered on the meter were the same. However, in 1975, using a noise expert from the National Research Council as its main witness, the city launched a successful test case against the operator of a tractor trailer that was emitting noise of 95 dBA.

---

* The C-scale lets almost all the sound energy pass through the meter. Unlike the A-scale, therefore, it does not measure sound as close to the way the human ear hears it.

The city of Edmonton had more success with its bylaw, passed in 1970. Of the first two hundred charges laid, only one was dismissed. This bylaw limits noise to 82 dBA for vehicles less than 3,600 kilograms in a 60 KPH zone and limits daytime noise in a residential zone to 65 dBA for temporary noise. It also contains a general abatement section that provides:

> noise to interfere with the comfort or the repose of any person or persons so as to justify a
> prosecution under this by-law is a question of fact for the Court ... provided that when the Court
> is satisfied that the noise by its nature and in the circumstances should be abated the fact that it
> is within the dBA rating permitted herein shall not be deemed to prevent a finding under this
> section that abatement is required.

The city of Toronto bylaw no. 44-75[132] has two sections requiring the measurement of noise emitted by air conditioners and construction machinery. Air conditioners are easy to measure, but noise emitted by construction machinery varies throughout the work site. An inspector will be sent to a construction site to make noise measurements in response to a complaint, and will inform the contractor if the noisy activities occur outside prescribed hours.

However, construction equipment is considered "by nature noisy" and therefore the decibel limits are set so high that they may still be a problem, and the bylaw is set up to allow such activities to continue during the day, as long as the individual pieces of equipment do not exceed specified limits. Thus the main recourse available is to limit the hours of operation of construction equipment. Construction that causes noise may not be carried on at night, except in emergencies.

Model Municipal Noise Control Bylaw for Ontario

To overcome the limitations of the *Municipal Act*, the *Environmental Protection Act* was amended in 1975 to permit councils of local municipalities to pass bylaws to regulate or prohibit noise and vibration, to provide for licensing of sources of noise and vibration, to set noise and vibration emission limits, and to prescribe methods to be used in measuring noise and vibration. Any such bylaw would require the approval of the minister of the environment.

The ministry published a model bylaw that municipalities could adopt as written or modify to suit their needs. It is intended to meet the requirements of municipalities of all sizes, and to provide comprehensive control for most known sound and vibration problems. A municipality may pass all or part of the bylaw.

The model bylaw contains a list of noises that are prohibited everywhere in the municipality at all times if they are clearly audible. Thus, to obtain a conviction, it is only necessary to prove that the noise was clearly audible, and not that it was disturbing. The only noises prohibited all the time are certain sounds coming from motor vehicles, such as tire squealing, racing in the street, lengthy idling of engines, clanking trailer hitches, and unnecessary blowing of horns.

A second list sets out noises that are prohibited some of the time and only in certain areas of the municipality. Section 3 lists 19 types of noises that are permitted some or all of the time in "quiet zones" and residential areas. The model bylaw leaves it up to each municipality to determine what areas will be designated as "quiet zones," but generally they would be expected to include the areas around hospitals, convalescent homes, and retirement homes.

For each type of noise, the bylaw sets out the times and places that it is prohibited. For example, yelling is forbidden at any time in a quiet zone; but it is only forbidden between 11:00 PM and 7:00 AM (9:00 AM on Sundays) in a "residential zone." The same is true of the persistent barking of a dog and the detonation of explosives. Construction equipment without an effective muffler is also completely banned from areas designated as "quiet zones."

It is not necessary to measure scientifically the sound level of these listed noises to obtain a conviction. The evidence of a witness that the sound was clearly audible would be sufficient.

A rather unnerving result of section 3 is the apparent legalization of noises that may well be objectionable and that could be prosecuted under another form of bylaw. For example, although yelling and the barking of dogs are forbidden only between 11:00 PM and 7:00 AM, they could well be objectionable at other hours of the day, and get a conviction. Under the model noise bylaw, this is impossible. Fortunately, the model noise bylaw is meant to supplement, not replace, the *Environmental Protection Act* and other municipal bylaws that may be passed under the *Municipal Act*. (The ministry has chosen to avoid duplicating bylaw provisions that can now be passed under the *Municipal Act*.) For example, if a barking dog has kept everybody on the street from enjoying their Saturday afternoon leisure, this would not be illegal under the model noise bylaw, but it would be covered by section 14 of the *Environmental Protection Act*, or by a bylaw under the *Municipal Act*, if the municipality has one.

The model bylaw also incorporates a number of provisions where accurate measurement of sound is necessary to enforce the bylaw. These provisions specify maximum noise emission levels for machinery and equipment such as air conditioners, outdoor power tools, and motor vehicles. For blasting operations, not only maximum noise levels but also maximum vibration levels are specified.

Although it may pick and choose among the provisions of the model bylaw that are incorporated into its own bylaw, a municipality without a trained noise control officer can make use of only those sections of the bylaw that set no decibel level and require no sophisticated measuring equipment. The municipality that wants to use decibel levels to control noise from blasting operations, for example, must send one of its employees to a training course offered by the Ministry of Environment and Energy. Once the municipal noise control officer has passed the ministry's course, he or she is certified as capable of enforcing the technical sections of the bylaw.

Other Municipal Noise Control Powers

Further control over noise is available to municipalities under the *Municipal Act*, which gives them power to pass bylaws to prohibit and abate industrial nuisances as well as public nuisances,[133] with respect to the use of roads under municipal control (by heavy vehicles, at night, etc.), and a number of sections that allow the licensing of businesses within the municipality. (For further discussion of control of noise from heavy vehicles, see the *Highway Traffic Act* above, and for discussion of licensing laws, see chapters 2 and 3.) In addition to the general power to license a variety of businesses, municipalities have a specific power to license and regulate the owners and operators of public address systems, sound equipment, loud speakers, and similar devices whenever they are used on a road, on public lands or lands adjacent to public lands, *or whenever these devices are close enough that they are emitting sounds that can be heard at the road, public land, or adjacent land.*[134]

Enforcement of Municipal Noise Control Bylaws

Noise control bylaws are ordinarily enforced by a bylaw enforcement officer, building inspector, or the police. At night, only the police are readily available, and they are not always aware of all provisions of the relevant anti-noise bylaw. It is useful to have a copy to show them. You can get one from the clerk of your municipality. The Canadian Hearing Society suggests that when noise complaints are made to the police, you should follow up with the appropriate municipal noise control officials the next morning.[135]

A few large municipalities, such as the city of Toronto, will have specially trained noise control officers, or even a separate noise control section within one of its departments. In the city of Toronto, charges have been laid related to noisy music and barking dogs. However, before laying charges, the noise control section will generally attempt to solve the problem through negotiation with the involved parties. As a result, few charges are laid. In 1990, there may have only been one charge laid by the city.[136]

CONCLUSION

Hearing loss is the single greatest cause of permanent disability claims. Although noise regulations have been in place in Canada since the early 1960s, exposure limits are still not sufficient to protect workers. Efforts to lower exposure levels should emphasize source reduction, incorporating new technologies such as anti-noise control. To encourage the transition, companies could be educated on the benefits of noise reduction such as increased productivity, reduced absenteeism and accidents, and increased worker morale.

Non-occupational sources of loud noise add to the dose received in the workplace. There is a lack of public awareness of the hazard these sources may present and individuals often choose to expose themselves to harmful levels of noise as part of their leisure activities.

Perhaps more than any other area of environmental and public health concern, noise and vibration illustrate the problems that flow from a lack of any system, policy, or law requiring the assessment of the negative impacts of new technology. Although environmental impact assessment has become almost a household word, and the public frequently and loudly demands an impact assessment of proposed projects such as dams and roads that may harm the environment, little outcry is heard when new technologies are released into the market-place without any requirement that their negative effects be assessed. Why, for example, were companies allowed to sell to Inuit hunters in the Arctic snowmobiles that caused permanent hearing loss, when it was possible to manufacture quieter ones? Why is only one household product out of hundreds that create excessive noise listed as hazardous under the *Hazardous Products Act*?

The government has a responsibility to educate the public and improve legislation. Federal manufacturing standards should be strengthened and expanded. Products that are potentially damaging to hearing should be redesigned, or at the very least should be required by law to display specific warnings. For example, personal listening devices could bear warnings for levels exceeding 4 or 5 on the dial. Labels should include a noise scale to show where a product stands in relation to others. This would encourage the consumption and manufacture of quieter products.

The public can encourage the adoption of these changes by demanding this type of labelling and by purchasing the quieter alternatives. In the meantime, individuals can protect themselves by avoiding noisy environments when possible or by requesting protection. Some concert halls already provide complimentary ear plugs.

Noise regulations should take into account the impact of combinations of different sources and types of noise. They should extend to sparsely populated areas to protect animals in their natural environment from the effects of loud noise.

Hearing loss associated with aging may, to a large extent, be due to a lifetime of exposure to hazardous levels of noise. To convert our noisy society to a safer one, government regulations should progress toward an ultimate goal of 55 dBA for background noise as protection not only from hearing loss but also from activity interference and annoyance.

Patricia Mohr and John Swaigen

FURTHER READING

Cyril M. Harris, ed., *Handbook of Noise Control*, 3d ed. (New York: McGraw Hill, 1991).

Health and Welfare Canada, *National Guidelines for Environmental Noise Control: Procedures and Concepts for the Drafting of Environmental Noise Regulations/Bylaws in Canada* (Ottawa: Health and Welfare Canada, March 1989).

H.W. Jones, *Noise in the Human Environment* (Edmonton: Environmental Council of Alberta, [1980]).

Karl D. Kryter, *The Effects of Noise on Man*, 2d ed. (New York and London: Academic Press, 1985).

Ontario, Ministry of the Environment, *Environmental Noise: Audit of Abatement Strategies, Plans and Procedures* (Toronto: the ministry, 1979).

H.W. Silverman and J.D. Evans, "Aeronautical Noise in Canada" (1972), 3 *Osgoode Hall LJ* 607.

United States, Environmental Protection Agency, Office of Noise Abatement and Control, *Noise: A Health Problem* (Washington, DC: EPA, 1978).

ENDNOTES

1 Ariel Alexandre and Jean-Philippe Barde, "Deaf Ears on Noise Pollution." (Winter 1991), vol 13, no. 4, *Probe Post* 18.

2 Peter Gorrie, "Ouch! Noisy Metro Harms Our Hearing, Specialists Warn," *The Toronto Star*, December 2, 1990.

3 There are many studies documenting the impact of farm machinery and animal noise on the hearing of farmers. See, for example, Ontario Task Force on Health and Safety

in Agriculture, *Report of the Ontario Task Force on Health and Safety in Agriculture* (Toronto: Queen's Printer, October 29, 1985), 90-92.

4 Report to the Ministry of Indian and Northern Affairs on the Auditory Acuity of Native Population at Igloolik, Keewatin, NWT, School of Hygiene, University of Toronto.

5 Newfoundland and Labrador, Department of Environment and Lands, Wildlife Division, "Impacts of Low-Level Jet Fighter Training on Caribou Populations in Labrador and Northern Quebec," June 1990. The correlation between exposure to overflights and calf survival was based on a small sample and was not statistically significant. Nevertheless, the researchers concluded that they could not rule out the possibility that exposure to low-level overpasses may exert a subtle, but real, negative impact on calf survival.

6 "Ocean Creatures Resent Man's Noise," *USA Today*, June 1989, 7, quoting Arthur A. Myrberg Jr., marine biologist, University of Miami, Rosentiel School of Marine and Atmospheric Science; Kathy Glass, "Are Dolphins Being Deafened in the Pacific?" (Winter 1989-90), 32 *Oceanus* 83-85; Richardson, Fraker, Wursig, and Wells, "Behaviour of Bowhead Whales Summering in the Beaufort Sea: Reactions to Industrial Activities" (1985), 32 *Biological Conservation* 195-230.

7 Christopher Hayne, "Ergonomics — The Body's Reaction to Noise" (February 1981), *Occupational Health* 75-83.

8 "Noise Induced Hearing Loss — A Consensus" (May-June 1990), vol. 11, no. 3 *Shhh* 7.

9 "Ergonomics — The Body's Reaction to Noise," supra endnote 7.

10 Fred Pearce, "Noise — Industry Turns a Deaf Ear" (December 5, 1985), 108 *New Scientist* 38-42.

11 Canadian Hearing Society pamphlet [undated].

12 "Noise Pollution" (March 1985), 93 *Science Digest* 28.

13 "Ergonomics — The Body's Reaction to Noise," supra endnote 7.

14 Christopher Hayne, "Ergonomics — Noise and Vibration Control" (March 1981), *Occupational Health* 135-45.

15 "Noise Induced Hearing Loss," supra endnote 8.

16 J.H. Mills, "A Review of Environmental Factors Affecting Hearing," in: Hayes, *Toxicology of the Eye, Ear and Other Special Senses* (New York: Raven Press, 1985), 231-46.

17 "Noise Induced Hearing Loss," supra endnote 8.

18 Phillip K. Steffan, "The Problem of Noise Induced Hearing Loss in Musicians" (March 1990), vol. 15, no. 2 *Tinnitus Today* 4.

19 "Banging into a Noisy Background" (November 16, 1985), *Science News* 313.

20 Mills, supra endnote 16.

21 Lowell Pointe, "How Noise Can Harm You" (March 1989), 134 *Reader's Digest* 121-25.

22 Susan Walton, "Noise Pollution: Environmental Battle of the 1980s" (March 1980), vol. 30, no. 3 *Bioscience* 205-7.

23 "Ergonomics — The Body's Reaction to Noise," supra endnote 7.

24 Joanna Burger, "Behavioural Responses of Herring Gulls *Larus Argentatus* to Aircraft Noise" (March 1981), 24 *Environmental Pollution* 177-84.

25 "Variations in the Response of Great Crested Grebes *Podiceps Cristatus* to Human Disturbance — A Sign of Adaptation?" (1989), vol. 49, no. 1 *Biological Conservation* 31-45.

26 "Behavioural Responses of Herring Gulls," supra endnote 24.

27 "Responses of Staging Greater Snow Geese to Human Disturbance" (1989), vol. 53, no. 3 *Journal of Wildlife Management* 713-19.

28 "Ocean Creatures Resent Man's Noise," supra endnote 6.

29 "Noise — Industry Turns a Deaf Ear," supra endnote 10.

30 Mary Ruth Yoe, "Unwanted Sound" (August 1986), 134 *National Safety and Health News* 30-34.

31 Amy Virshup, "Restaurant Loudness: The New Sound of Success" (November 18, 1985), 18 *New York* 32-37.

32 "Noise Induced Hearing Loss," supra endnote 8.

33 Canadian Hearing Society pamphlet [undated].

34 Dennis Brownridge, "Filling the Parks With Noise" (July-August 1986), 71 *Sierra* 59-63.

35 Victor Schroeter to Deborah Curran, 1990.

36 "Ergonomics — Noise and Vibration Control," supra endnote 14.

37 "Gravel Pit Gets Sound Planning" (July 1985), 88 *Rock Products* 27-29.

38 Francesca Lunzer, "Companies Profit from the Sounds of Silence" (April 1988), 8 *High Technology Business* 39-42.

39 "Unwanted Sound," supra endnote 30.

40 "Noise: A Major Job Hazard" (November 1986), *Focus* 11-13.

41 There are many cases in which noise has been held to be a nuisance; fewer involving vibration. For a relatively recent case involving both, see *340909 Ontario Ltd. v. Huron Steel Products (Windsor) Ltd.* (1990), 73 OR (2d) 641 (HCJ), aff'd. (1992), 9 OR (3d) 305 (CA).

42 *Criminal Code of Canada*, RSC 1985, c. C-46.

43 In *R. v. Young* (1973), 14 CCC (2d) 502, the Ontario Court of Appeal ruled that the *Criminal Code* disturbing-the-peace provision and municipal bylaws could live side by side and operate concurrently.

44 *Aeronautics Act*, RSC 1985, c. A-2.

45 SOR/86-73.

46 Ibid., section 7.

47 Committee on the Challenges of Modern Society and the North Atlantic Treaty Organization, *Aircraft Noise in a Modern Society*, Final Report of the Pilot Study no. 185 (1989); John W. Little, "Aircraft Noise Reduction Past, Present, and Future," paper presented at the Australian Mayoral Aviation Council 1989 Conference, October 4-6, 1989, Brisbane, Australia.

48 Correspondence from Transport Canada to Deborah Curran, July 13, 1990.

49 Little, supra endnote 47. According to Little, few advances in civil aviation noise reduction can be expected unless unforeseen technological advances occur.

50 Federal Environmental Assessment and Review Office, *Air Traffic Management in Southern Ontario*, Interim Report of the Environmental Assessment Panel (Hull, Que.: FEARO, November 1992), 63.

51   US *Airport Noise and Capacity Act of 1990*, Pub. L. no. 101-508, USCA 49 App. 2151.

52   Little, supra endnote 47.

53   Peter Gillman, "Supersonic Bust: The Story of the Concorde" (January 1977), *The Atlantic Monthly* 72; the Alberta Environment Conservation Authority also prepared a report on the impact of the Concorde in the late 1970s; see also William A. Shurcliff, *S/S/T and Sonic Boom Book* (New York: Ballantine Books, 1970).

54   Sonic and Supersonic Flight Order, CRC 1987, c. 64.

55   Letter, Aerospatiale Canada Inc. to Marianna Tzabiris, January 14, 1991.

56   James Ott, "HSCT Research Focuses on Environmental Issues" (December 4, 1989), 131 *Aviation Week and Space Technology* 54-56.

57   *Aircraft Noise in a Modern Society*, supra endnote 47, summary, at 4.

58   Ibid., summary, at 3.

59   Ibid., summary, at 13.

60   SOR/86-74, Air Navigation Order, Series II, no. 27.

61   SOR/86-73, Aircraft Navigation Order, Series II, no. 21, effective January 1, 1986.

62   On June 3, 1992, the *Aeronautics Act* was amended to raise the maximum fines from $1,000 to these amounts.

63   See endnote 50, supra, and monthly summaries of penalties produced by Transport Canada.

64   *Aeronautics Act*, supra endnote 44, sections 8(1)(j) and 8(7) to (11).

65   For example, a public utility built transmission towers and an electric transmission line on the flight path of planes at a flying school. The owner of the flying school was denied an injunction since there was no zoning regulation under the *Aeronautics Act* prohibiting this: *Atlantic Aviation Ltd. v. Nova Scotia Light & Power Ltd.* (1965), 55 DLR (2d) 554 (NSSC). Other cases and literature on this subject are cited in the decision.

66   See *Air Traffic Management in Southern Ontario*, supra endnote 50, appendix 17, at 69.

67   Transport Canada, "Land Use in the Vicinity of Airports," document S-77-4.

68   *New Housing and Airport Noise*, NHA (New Housing Act) 5185-1-78 (Ottawa: Canada Housing and Mortgage Corporation, 1972).

69   *Planning Act*, RSO 1990, c. P.13.

70   Ontario, Ministry of Housing, *Land-Use Policy near Airports* (Toronto: the ministry, March 1978).

71   *Johannesson v. West St. Paul (Rural Municipality)*, [1952] 1 SCR 292, [1951] 4 DLR 609; *Orangeville Airport v. Caledon (Town)* (1975), 11 OR (2d) 546, 66 DLR (3d) 610 (CA); *Walker v. Ontario (Ministry of Housing)* (1983), 41 OR (2d) 9, 21 MPLR 249 (CA), leave to appeal to SCC refused (1983), 27 LCR 101n, 51 NR 398.

72   *Venchiarutti v. Longhurst* (1992), 8 OR (3d) 422 (CA).

73   *Air Traffic Management in Southern Ontario*, supra endnote 50, at 70.

74   Ibid., at 25. However, the number of complaints dropped to 2,693 in 1991, and to 2,053 in 1992: Bruce Campion-Smith, "Complaints of Noise Drop 24% at Airport," *The Toronto Star*, March 7, 1990.

75   Terminal 3 Development Project — Initial Assessment (Environmental), August 25, 1987.

76   Information received from Randy McGill, Transport Canada, September 17, 1992.

77 *Air Traffic Management in Southern Ontario*, supra endnote 50.

78 Information received from Bob Kidd, Transport Canada. In 1993, the Pearson International Airport noise-complaints number was (416) 676-4531.

79 *Air Traffic Management in Southern Ontario*, supra endnote 50, at 59.

80 Ibid., at 61.

81 *Railway Act*, RSC 1985, c. R-3, sections 230(1)(a) and (b).

82 *Railway Safety Act*, RSC 1985, c. R-32 (4th Supp.). The *Railway Relocation and Crossing Act*, RSC 1985, c. R-4, may also be of importance when dealing with issues of railway noise.

83 Canadian Rail Operating Rules (formerly, Uniform Code of Operating Rules), regulation O-8, rule 14(L), made pursuant to the *Railway Safety Act*, supra endnote 82.

84 Transport Canada, Railway Safety Directorate, guideline no. 1, "Procedure and Conditions for Eliminating Whistling at Public Crossings."

85 Railway Transport Committee order no. R-22773, April 23, 1976.

86 Canada Mortgage and Housing Corporation, *Road and Rail Noise: Effects on Housing* (Ottawa: CMHC, 1981).

87 Ontario, Ministry of the Environment, *STEAM: Sound from Trains Environmental Analysis Method* (Toronto: Queen's Printer, July 1990).

88 *Motor Vehicle Safety Act*, RSC 1985, c. M-10.

89 Motor Vehicle Safety Regulations, SOR/87-660, schedule 228.

90 Ibid., c. 1038, section 1106.

91 SOR/89-279, schedule 233.

92 Information received from Transport Canada by Marianna Tzabiris.

93 Ontario, Ministry of Housing, minister's statement on noise and new residential development adjacent to freeways; policy on noise and new residential development adjacent to freeways, 1979.

94 See, for example, Ontario, Ministry of Housing, *Guidelines on Noise and New Residential Development Adjacent to Freeways* (Toronto: the ministry, April 1979); Ontario, Ministry of the Environment, *ORNAMENT: Ontario Road Noise Analysis Method for Environment and Transportation* (Toronto: the ministry, 1989); Canada Mortgage and Housing Corporation, supra endnote 86; M.E. Delaney, National Physical Laboratory, *Prediction of Traffic Noise* (Ottawa: Department of Trade and Commerce, 1972).

95 *Environmental Assessment Act*, RSO 1990, c. E.18.

96 An exception is bylaw no. 4 of the Toronto Harbour Commission, which requires motor boats operated within the harbour to be equipped with "a stock factory muffler, underwater exhaust, or other modern or approved device capable of adequately muffling sound."

97 *Canada Shipping Act*, RSC 1985, c. S-9.

98 Small Vessel Regulations, c. 1487, SOR/ 80-191, section 68.

99 This speed limit is found in the Boating Restriction Regulation, c. 1407, June 28, 1972, as amended by SOR/91-489, made under the *Canada Shipping Act*, supra endnote 97.

100 *Municipal Act*, RSO 1990, c. M.45.

101 *Environmental Protection Act*, RSO 1990, c. E.19.

102 Information provided by John D. Patterson, Muskoka Lakes Association.

103 *Hazardous Products Act*, RSC 1985, c. H-3.

104 Ibid., section 10.

105 Ibid., schedule 1, section 10. In 1991, the government announced its intention to reduce this noise limit.

106 *Canada Labour Code*, RSC 1985, c. L-2.

107 "Personal Stereos — Pure Pleasure and Potential Danger" (June 1984), vol. 2, no. 3 *[University of Toronto Faculty of Medicine] Health News* 1.

108 Deborah MacKenzie, "Europe Wants To Relax Noise Limits in Factories" (October 4, 1984), 104 *New Scientist*.

109 "How Noise Can Harm You," supra endnote 21.

110 "Noise: A Major Job Hazard," supra endnote 40.

111 Motor Vehicle Safety Regulations, supra endnote 89, section 1106(2). It is interesting to note that although noise-emission levels for all forms of transportation have been reduced over the past 15 to 20 years, this standard remains the same as when it was set in 1976.

112 *Building Code Act*, RSO 1990, c. B.13.

113 *Ontario Building Code*, RRO 1990, reg. 61, section 9.11.

114 In such cases, landlord and tenant legislation may be helpful. See Jim Middlemiss, "Sexual Practices Grounds for Eviction" (June 3, 1990), *Law Times* 1; "Neighbours Get Court To Quiet Noisy Lovemaking" (April 27, 1990), *Lawyers' Weekly* 2.

115 *STEAM*, supra endnote 87; *ORNAMENT*, supra endnote 94.

116 *Highway Traffic Act*, RSO 1990, c. H.8.

117 Interview with Leslie Kende, Ministry of the Environment, January 10, 1991.

118 This is officially only a draft, but it is used by ministry staff in making decisions, even though it has never been formally adopted.

119 This publication was prepared by the Ministry of the Environment to replace the *Guidelines for Noise Control in Land Use Planning*, which is part of the 1978 *Model Municipal Noise Control By-Law Final Report*. The working draft was prepared in March 1990, but its formal adoption as ministry policy has been held up by objections from the Ministry of Municipal Affairs.

120 Ontario, Ministry of the Environment, "Impulse Vibration in Residential Buildings," publication no. NPC-207, revised November 1983. See the discussion in the *Huron Steel Products* case, supra endnote 41, at 650.

121 Workers' Compensation Board, *Earfacts* (April 6, 1988), as updated to include 1989 statistics by WCB staff.

122 Workers' Compensation Board statistics.

123 *Occupational Health and Safety Act*, RSO 1990, c. O.1.

124 *Canada Labour Code*, supra endnote 106.

125 For more information about the history and nature of the debate over this proposed noise regulation, see Tove Rasmussen, "The Silent Noise Legislation," vol. 5, no. 2 *OH&S Canada* 101.

126 *In the Matter of a Decision Made on the 20th day of May, 1988, as a Part of Report 196886 Issued to Dehavilland Aircraft of Canada by John Harkins, Inspector*, Eleanor J. Smith, director of appeals, December 19, 1988, file no. AP 88-65.

127 Canadian Hearing Society, "Industrial Noise," pamphlet [undated].

128 Canadian Hearing Society pamphlet [undated].
129 *Guidelines on Noise and New Residential Development Adjacent to Freeways*, supra endnote 96.
130 *Municipal Act*, supra endnote 100, section 210.138.
131 *City of Ottawa Act, 1968*, SO 1968, c. 164.
132 City of Toronto Anti-Noise By-law, bylaw no. 44-75, as amended by bylaw nos. 65-75, 444-76, 415-82, 394-84, 564-87, and 4-93.
133 *Municipal Act*, supra endnote 100, sections 210.134 and 140.
134 Ibid., section 210.139.
135 Canadian Hearing Society, "How Do I Place a Noise Complaint?" pamphlet [undated].
136 Information from Jim Brashad, City of Toronto, Department of Public Works, Noise Control Section.

20

Pesticides

CONTENTS

Have we fallen into a mesmerized state that makes us accept as inevitable that which is inferior or detrimental, as though having lost the will or the vision to demand that which is good? Such thinking, in the words of the ecologist Paul Shepard, "idealizes life with only its head out of water, inches above the limits of toleration of the corruption of its own environment. ... Why should we tolerate a diet of weak poisons, a home in insipid surroundings, a circle of acquaintances who are not quite our enemies, the noise of motors with just enough relief to prevent insanity? Who would want to live in a world which is just not quite fatal?"

Rachel Carson, Silent Spring, *1962*

So what has happened to pesticides since *Silent Spring*? Patricia Hynes, author of *The Recurring Silent Spring* and an adjunct professor at MIT, points out that while DDT was banned in the U.S. by the early 70's, "nearly 50 million pounds of DDT have been manufactured here each year and exported to foreign countries since the chemical was banned here. It is then imported back on fruits and vegetables in what has been labelled a 'circle of poison.'"

Hynes says today, five times as many pesticides are manufactured for use in agriculture, forestry, homes and export as in 1962. And most telling, "In 1945, 7 per cent of crops were destroyed by insects; in 1990 insects destroyed 13 per cent." Chemical pesticide residues now pervade the world's air, water, soil and food.

It is sad on this 30th anniversary of Rachel Carson's monumental work that so little seems to have been learned or changed.

David Suzuki, The Toronto Star, *November 7, 1992*

THE NATURE OF THE PROBLEM[1]

During the past two decades, there has been increasing concern over the environmental and human health effects posed by the widespread use of pesticides for food and fibre production. First, there has been a substantial, if not dramatic, increase in pesticide sales and use both in Canada and worldwide. According to federal officials, between 1971 and 1985 total pesticide sales in Canada increased from $57.3 million to $869 million.[2] Of the pesticide sales in 1985, 73 per cent were herbicides, 11.6 per cent were insecticides, and 5 per cent were fungicides. In 1970, about 8.6 million hectares, or 20 per cent of all cultivated land, was sprayed with herbicides. By 1985, herbicides were applied to 22.9 million hectares, or about 51 per cent of all cultivated land.[3] In 1976 alone, Canada imported almost 117 million pounds of pesticides from the United States. This was almost the amount imported from the United States by 20 Latin American republics or Western Europe.[4] Unfortunately, information on exactly which pesticides are used, by whom, at what application rates, on how much acreage, where, and in what quantities is not systematically available nationally.[5]

Second, in conjunction with the increasing quantities sold and used, the public is concerned with the fact that the use of pesticides involves the deliberate application to land or water of chemicals that are poisonous to selected organisms. In general, two main categories of undesirable effects of pesticide use have been identified: the development of resistance in pest species, and the impact on non-target species and ecosystems. With respect to non-target impacts, the United Nations has stated that "even when properly used, chemical pesticides have a number of unavoidable side-effects."[6] The Canadian public has been witness over the past few decades to the result of some of these "unavoidable side-effects":

- In New Brunswick, during 1975, at least three million birds were killed from aerial spraying of about seven million acres of forest with Phosphamidon (later discontinued) and Fenitrothion to combat the spruce budworm.[7] More recently, the Canadian Wildlife Service has associated the insecticide Carbofuran with the rapid disappearance of the burrowing owl from the Canadian prairies.[8] The World Wildlife Fund claims that Carbofuran has caused at least 50 North American bird kills, involving thousands of birds.[9]
- A 1983 survey conducted by the Alberta Department of Agriculture found that 10 per cent of Alberta grain farmers may be experiencing pesticide poisoning symptoms every year. Government officials believe that about 5,000 grain farmers in the province may be affected.[10]
- In 1985, a Canada-Ontario report on pollution of the St. Clair River concluded that of the 2.5 million kilograms of agricultural pesticides used annually in the land draining into the Detroit and St. Clair rivers' connecting channels, about 70 per cent of these pesticides were identified as potentially environmentally hazardous.[11]
- In 1985, federal agencies reported that 25 per cent of groundwater samples taken in Prince Edward Island showed residues of the insecticide Temic. Prince Edward Island relies completely on groundwater supplies as a source of drinking water.
- Various surveys of farm wells in Ontario between 1969 and 1990 have found pesticides. The percentage of contaminated wells has ranged from 49 per cent in a survey conducted between 1969 and 1984 to only one well out of 1,300 in a survey conducted in 1991 and 1992.[12]

These are but a few examples from across Canada. They indicate, however, that problems posed by pesticides are national in scope and that the sources or pathways of possible contamination are numerous, including air, water, land, food, and drinking water. Moreover, problems have arisen at many stages in the regulatory process, including registration, use, and disposal.

Internationally, the World Commission on Environment and Development (the Brundtland commission) identified environmental and health threats from chemical pesticides. It referred to a 1983 study that estimated that about 10,000 people died each year in developing countries from pesticide poisoning and about 400,000 suffered acutely. The report noted:

Commercial fisheries have been depleted, bird species endangered, and insects that prey on pests wiped out. The number of pesticide-resistant insect pest species worldwide has increased and many resist even the newest chemicals. The variety and severity of pest infestations multiply, threatening the productivity of agriculture in the areas concerned.[13]

The Brundtland commission recommended that alternatives to chemicals must be encouraged and that pest control must be based increasingly on the use of natural methods. It also recognized that these strategies require changes in public policies, which now encourage the increased use of chemical pesticides and fertilizers. The commission recommended that "the legislative, policy and research capacity for advancing non-chemical and less-chemical strategies must be established and sustained."[14]

In fact, Canadian farmers have been using smaller amounts of pesticides in recent years. It is unclear, however, to what extent the reduction in reliance on pesticides has resulted from attention to environmental concerns and public education, and to what extent it has resulted from economic factors such as higher pesticide prices, reductions in government subsidies of pesticide use, lower farm income, and unusual weather.

This chapter examines the existing regulatory regime for pesticides at the federal level and in Ontario and discusses initiatives for reform.

THE LEGISLATIVE SCHEME

Pesticides in Canada are regulated by both the federal and the provincial governments. As well, municipalities may limit their own use of pesticides within their boundaries. The federal *Pest Control Products Act*[15] controls the manufacturing, importing, and registering of pesticides, and the *Food and Drugs Act*[16] sets limits for residues of agricultural pesticides on products to be ingested by people. Under the *Pesticides Act*,[17] Ontario controls the use of federally registered products through a system of permits and licences. Under some circumstances, the Ontario Environmental Assessment Board, pursuant to the *Environmental Assessment Act*,[18] may also prohibit or impose terms and conditions on the spraying of insecticides and herbicides. For example, a class assessment of how the Ministry of Natural Resources should manage timber cutting is considering appropriate practices for spraying in Ontario's Crown forests. There have been initiatives at the international level to harmonize residue limits, a move that has been criticized by environmental groups who fear that this harmonization might lead to the acceptance of the lowest common denominator. The Canada-US free trade agreement also contains a section on pesticide regulation. Common law actions and remedies, described in Chapter 6, are also available to deal with harm caused by pesticide spraying.

THE FEDERAL ROLE

The Pest Control Products Act and Regulations

Overview

The chief federal vehicle for pesticide regulation is the *Pest Control Products Act (PCPA)*,[19] which is administered by Agriculture Canada. It was last significantly amended in 1969 and as a result in many respects it lags far behind the legislation that regulates other toxic chemicals. A "pest" is broadly defined to mean any injurious, noxious, or troublesome insect, fungus, virus, weed, or rodent. A "control product" is any product, device, organism, or substance that controls, prevents, destroys, attracts, or repels any pest, whether directly or indirectly. "Control products" can be pesticides applied directly to crops to prevent the growth of weeds or to kill insect predators. They can also be fertilizers, feeds, or seeds to which pesticides have been added, or no-pest strips used in your kitchen.

In 1989, about 6,000 products containing 460 active ingredients were registered for use in Canada.[20] Only three active ingredients of those registered in Canada are actually manufactured in this country. Canadian firms are primarily involved in formulating active ingredients that are manufactured elsewhere into salable products, rather than manufacturing these ingredients.

The heart of the *Pest Control Products Act* is the registration requirement. Section 4 of the Act prohibits any person from importing or selling any control product unless it has been registered, packaged, and labelled according to prescribed conditions. The packaging, labelling, and advertising of any control product cannot be false, misleading, or deceptive or likely to create an erroneous impression about the product's safety or efficacy. Manufacturing, selling, storing, displaying, distributing, or using any control product under unsafe conditions is prohibited. Anyone who violates the Act or regulations is, on conviction, liable to up to two years' imprisonment if indicted, or to punishment on summary conviction.[21] There is a limitation period of one year for the commencement of summary conviction proceedings under the Act.[22]

Pesticides may be registered only if the minister of agriculture is of the opinion that the control product has merit or value for the purposed claimed, when used in accordance with label directions. In addition, the pesticide's use must not lead to an "unacceptable risk of harm" to public health, plants, or the environment. Under the PCP regulations, the minister may also refuse to register a product if the information provided with the application "is insufficient to enable the control product to be assessed or evaluated."[23] The Federal Court of Canada held in 1991 that the minister may not legally exercise his or her discretion to register or not to register a control product, without first determining whether there is sufficient information about the product to permit an assessment.[24]

A company that applies for the registration of a pesticide must provide the minister with sufficient information for a determination to be made of the product's "safety, merit, and value." In general, these scientific studies must address occupational safety and exposure, residues, toxicity, and related matters. The burden of proof is on the company to demonstrate that its product meets the tests of safety, merit, and value.

Agriculture Canada itself has indicated that registration does not guarantee that a pesticide is "safe" and that "pesticides by their very nature are toxic chemicals; otherwise they could not fulfil the function for which they are designed." Officials have stated that although the use of the word "safe" is not addressed by the legislation, section 51(c) of the PCP regulations prohibits the use of words that imply that a control product is approved, accepted, or recommended by the government of Canada. Agriculture Canada has stated that it would interpret a claim of safety based on registration under the Act to be a violation of this section.[25]

At present, Health and Welfare Canada, Environment Canada, Fisheries and Oceans Canada, and Forestry Canada review and comment on the scientific data submitted by the applicant. Agriculture Canada, however, has the last word. Apart from administrative memoranda of understanding between Health and Welfare Canada, Environment Canada, and Agriculture Canada, there is no formal recognition of these departments' role in the *Pest Control Products Act*.

The final decision to register a pesticide resides with the minister of agriculture. It is here that there has been a perception of conflict of interest for the department to be both a promoter of food production and the protector of the public from unsafe pesticides and practices. The situation parallels the experience in the United States in the late 1960s when federal pesticide law was still administered by the US Department of Agriculture. The authority for registration and control of pesticides was transferred to the US Environmental Protection Agency (EPA) in 1972.

Unacceptable Risk of Harm

The key criterion for refusing to register a pest control product is that the minister of agriculture is of the "opinion" that the use of the pesticide "would lead to an unacceptable risk of harm to ... public health, plants, animals or the environment."[26] What constitutes "unacceptable risk of harm" is not defined in the *Pest Control Products Act* or the regulation. Indeed, this criterion appears only in the regulation, and not in the Act itself.

There has been a heated debate over the past few years as to the meaning of this standard and whether it mandates that a risk-benefit or cost-benefit analysis must take place before a decision is made. Such an analysis is important because an evaluation of risk alone can give the public greater protection than a balancing of risks and benefits, because even if there is significant risk to human health or the environment, a pesticide may be approved because of its benefits. While the regulation clearly contemplates an evaluation of risk, it is not apparent on its face that it was intended to embrace the use of risk-benefit analysis as an instrument for pesticide decision-making. Agriculture Canada officials testified at a federal hearing considering the herbicide Alachlor, which had been banned by the minister of agriculture, that

> [t]here is no obligation to balance risks against benefits, nor is there a requirement to use formal risk-benefit analysis. The emphasis of section 3 of the *Pest Control Products Act* is placed on demonstrating safety.[27]

Federal pesticide law in other jurisdictions is clearly different in this regard. The US *Federal Insecticide, Fungicide and Rodenticide Act (FIFRA)*[28] requires the US EPA to determine whether a pesticide causes "unreasonable adverse effects on the environment." "Unreasonable adverse effects" are further defined by the statute to mean "any unreasonable risk to man or the environment, taking into account the economic, social, and environmental costs and benefits of the use of any pesticide."[29] Thus, it is clear that *FIFRA* requires the weighing of risk-benefit considerations. This standard in *FIFRA* is different from tests set out in other US environmental legislation that contemplate an examination of "risk" rather than a weighing of risks and benefits.

The agricultural chemical companies have argued for the implementation of a risk-benefit analysis process in Canada while the environmental community has opposed this development. A number of problems have been identified in employing risk-benefit analysis. These include: the uncertainties of determining risks, particularly given the delayed effects of pesticide toxins and the lack of epidemiological data; the fact that the state of the art in determining benefits may mislead agency decision makers and the public, according to US congressional investigators; the difficulty of balancing risks and benefits that are not equitably distributed and that favour some to the detriment of others; and the inherent impossibility of placing a monetary value on clean water, clean air, or good health.[30]

A risk-benefit approach can allow, and has allowed, the continued registration of pesticides that are clearly a significant risk to human health, safety, and the environment. The registration of Alachlor, a corn and soybean herbicide, which the US EPA has categorized as a probable carcinogen, was cancelled in Canada in 1985; but Alachlor is still registered in the United States because the EPA determined that the economic "benefits" outweighed the risks.

Although Canadian officials have testified that the *Pest Control Products Act* is not a risk-benefit statute, they have recently been employing risk-benefit language in their decisions. For example, Dinoseb, a herbicide used on bean, pea, potato, and raspberry crops, has been banned in the United States because of health risks to farm workers, including teratogenic effects, cataract formation, and male reproductive effects. In 1990, however, Canada decided to retain the registration of Dinoseb for some uses on the basis of a benefits survey that identified certain economical "critical needs" of the farming industry.[31] The registration of Dinoseb has been cancelled for use on crops except raspberries, peas, and beans in the Atlantic provinces and British Columbia.

Unfortunately, the Canada-US free trade agreement may have taken us further along the path to adopting the American risk-benefit approach. Schedule 7 to the agriculture chapter requires that Canada and the United States work toward "equivalence" in the "process for risk/benefit assessment."[32] Since Canada does not currently have a statutory requirement to weigh risks and benefits, this clause could move us in the direction of the US approach. The deal also commits Canada to moving toward equivalency of regulatory policies concerning tumour-causing pesticides. This is disturbing, because in 1982 a congressional committee argued that the US EPA had changed the scientific principles underlying its risk assessment of carcinogenic pesticides, resulting in an approach that permitted greater exposure to cancer-causing agents. The committee noted that "the agency's use of (certain) approaches to decision-making appears systematically slanted towards less stringent regulation of suspected carcinogens."[33]

Departures from Full Registration: Temporary Registrations

Under the *Pest Control Products Act*, there are a number of ways in which pesticides may be sold or used in Canada without having to meet the full registration requirements of the Act. One method is that of temporarily registering pesticides, where the applicant agrees to produce additional information on the product, or where it is to be sold only for emergency control of infestations. The temporary registration may be for the use of an unregistered product or for a new use of a product that has already been registered for other uses. In the past, about 150 temporary registrations have been issued in Canada each year.[34] In March 1993, there were 221 outstanding temporary-product registrations and 14 temporary-use registrations.[35] Although this departure from the Act's full registration requirements is meant to meet legitimate objectives, such as controlling emergency pest situations, the possibility for abuse exists. Current regulations under the Act authorize a temporary registration for one year, provided that the applicant meets the conditions specified above. Unfortunately, temporary registrations have been renewed for a number of years. The auditor general has noted that in 1987 one pesticide, known to be hazardous to human health, had its temporary registration renewed even though Agriculture Canada considered its safety studies incomplete and potential human health concerns were evident.[36] If a temporary registration is refused, an applicant can trigger a hearing before a review board established under the regulations.[37] However, the public has no corresponding right to a hearing to oppose the registration or renewal of a temporary registration.

A 1984 report to the federal minister of agriculture noted that "a system of temporary or emergency registrations is easily misused to circumvent the full assessment now done before registration."[38]

It is arguable that the renewing of temporary registrations for several years in a row constitutes a back door to full registration for less than completely evaluated products. Moreover, pesticides that have at one time been temporarily registered have been the subject of negligence actions for inadequate testing.[39]

Early in 1988, the federal Department of Agriculture received a legal opinion indicating that the temporary-registration provision should not be used when there are gaps in health and safety or environmental fate data. This opinion said that the department's method of granting this category of temporary registrations for the past 15 years was wrong. However, rather than amending the regulations to remedy this perceived gap, the Department began to issue full registrations to companies with a set term of expiry. Once this became known, a number of environmental groups raised concerns about the legality of this new procedure. They argued that the minister could not fulfil his mandate to evaluate the safety, merit, and value of a product without receiving a full data package.[40] On May 19, 1988, the department amended section 17(1)(a) of the Act to clarify this situation and returned to its practice of granting temporary registrations when data gaps exist.[41]

The use of such departures from full registration requirements is not unique to Canada. Other jurisdictions, such as the United States, also authorize a number of routes for the sale and use of pesticides that have not gone through a full registration procedure. Congressional investigations have suggested that these approaches were being used as vehicles for circumventing the safety evaluation requirements of full registration.[42]

Inerts/Formulants

There has been an ongoing concern about the so-called inerts or formulants found in pest control products. These are the supposedly harmless liquids in which the active ingredients are dissolved or powders, dusts, or granules with which the "actives" are mixed to facilitate application. These formulants may be more toxic or pose more of a risk to human health or environment than the active ingredient. One recent example is the surfactant polyoxyethyleneamine (POEA), which contains a contaminant, 1,4- Dioxane. 1,4- Dioxane is a known animal carcinogen.[43] POEA is found in the herbicide Roundup, whose active ingredient is glyphosate. Roundup, which contains POEA, is 400 times more toxic than the Rodeo formulation, registered in the United States but not in Canada, which contains glyphosate and no surfactant.

Currently, there are no requirements for the label of a control product to contain any information about formulants, byproducts, or contaminants, and the public often does not know of the existence of these potential chemicals of concern.

The US EPA recently found that about 1,200 inert ingredients were used in product formulations of registered pesticides. These inerts were categorized into four lists on the basis of the relative toxicity of the compounds. List 1 ("inerts of toxicological concern") comprises 57 chemicals that demonstrate toxicological or carcinogenic effects. List 2 ("potentially toxic inerts, with high priority for testing") contains 60 chemicals that are similar in chemical structure to those that exhibit toxic effects. List 3 ("inerts of unknown toxicity") consists of about two-thirds (800) of the identified inerts. The rest of the products (about 300) fall into List 4 ("inerts of minimal concern").

In 1987, the EPA implemented a new policy on inerts. Registrants are encouraged to substitute inert ingredients that are not included in list 1 or list 2 for inerts of toxicological concern (list 1). In the interim, registrants were required to add a statement to the label that "this product contains the toxic inert ingredient [name of inert]." As well, any registrant that retains a list 1 inert in its product must conduct extensive testing of the inert. In most cases, a company will remove the inert under scrutiny from the product instead of trying to produce the required data.[44]

Access to Information

The *Pest Control Products Act* is silent on the release of health, safety, and environmental information gathered under its auspices. Industry's position has been that data submitted to government for registration of a product are submitted in confidence. Members of the chemical industry see the data they have developed as their intellectual property and fear that if the data are publicly released, commercial competitors could use that data to obtain several economic advantages, such as deciding to move their research and development forward or obtaining a registration in Canada or other countries without doing the necessary testing themselves. Environmental groups, however, are not content to see summaries of such information prepared by government or industry. They want to see the raw data so that they may independently assess the appropriateness of the tests and test methods used, as well as the interpretations of test results and conclusions drawn from the studies.

Notwithstanding the passage of the federal *Access to Information Act*,[45] the availability of health, safety, and environmental data is unclear. Under section 20(1)(a) of the Act, the head of a government institution must refuse to disclose any record requested under the Act that contains the "trade secrets of a third party." However, there is no definition of "trade secret" under the Act. This is important because trade secrets are treated differently from "financial, commercial, scientific or technical information" and other types of information supplied by third parties to the government. There is a mandatory exemption for trade secrets, while the head of a government institution has discretion to disclose other financial and scientific information supplied by third parties, under the balancing test provided in section 20(6). This test permits disclosure if it would be in the public interest as it relates to public health, safety and the environment, and if such public interest in disclosure clearly outweighs in importance any financial loss or gain to, or prejudice to, the competitive position of a third party.

In March 1989, the Canadian Environmental Law Association (CELA) filed an access to information request for copies of all toxicological studies done by Uniroyal in relation to Alar, a plant growth regulator. In September 1989, Agriculture Canada denied the request, stating that the studies were exempt from disclosure according to the provisions of sections 20(1)(a) and (b) of the *Access to Information Act*. CELA subsequently complained to the information commissioner in February 1990. On March 4, 1992, three years after the initial request to the Department of Agriculture, the information commissioner concluded that although the Uniroyal studies could not be exempted under section 20(1)(a) (the trade secrets section), the department could exempt them from disclosure under section 20(1)(b) (the confidential business information section) and, furthermore, that the public interest override did not apply. CELA decided not to appeal to the Federal Court because Alar's use had been discontinued in Canada.

In the United States, pesticide health and safety studies, including toxicological studies, are available from the US EPA pursuant to the provisions of the *Federal Insecticide, Fungicide, and Rodenticide Act*. Anyone can obtain this data free of charge as long as a form is signed in which the individual affirms that he or she will not pass the information to anyone engaged in the pesticide business. Write to:

Freedom of Information (A-101)
Office of Pesticide Programs
US Environmental Protection Agency
Washington, DC 20460

The fact that health and safety studies can be obtained from the United States but not in Canada for pesticides registered in both countries has proven an embarrassment to the Canadian government in the past and should, we hope, be finally addressed in the promised pesticide reform. In the Alar case, it was ironic that CELA had obtained the toxicological studies from the US EPA but could not obtain the release of the same studies in Canada.

Pesticides Hotline

Since 1985, Agriculture Canada has maintained a pesticides information "hotline" for public inquiries about pesticides. Information about individual pesticides will be provided: regulatory status including the year it was first registered, the renewal date, and the registration number; the name and amount of active ingredient; category (insecticide, herbicide, etc.); and the label. Agriculture Canada also has on file some general information and/or fact sheets about individual pesticides and maximum residue limits for pesticides on foods as established by Health and Welfare Canada. In 1989, the Pesticides Division handled an average of 650 queries per month.

The pesticides hotline phone number is 1-800-267-6315.

The Role of the Public in the Process

The *Pest Control Products Act* is silent on the role of the public in the registration process for new pesticides as well as the re-evaluation of already registered pesticides. Public notice of a registration application for a new product or use is not required under the Act; nor is public access authorized to health and safety tests relied on in support of the registration application. Although a pesticide company is guaranteed an appeal to a review board under the regulations if a pesticide registration is denied or if a product is suspended or cancelled, no such right is provided to the public when a registration application is granted or maintained.

There is also no statutory opportunity for the public to trigger a re-evaluation of a specific pesticide product. Intervention in review board proceedings that are initiated by a pesticide company, although permitted, is very expensive and is effectively impossible without intervenor funding.

The Re-Evaluation Process

Once a pesticide is registered under the *Pest Control Products Act*, it retains its registration for a five-year period that may be renewed on application to the minister. At any time during this period a registered pesticide may be subject to re-evaluation.

Products may be identified for re-evaluation as a result of a number of triggers. These include:

- evidence of adverse effects of toxicological and environmental significance;
- action taken or proposed in another country;
- position on a re-evaluation list developed by Agriculture Canada; and
- position on a regulatory document publication schedule.[46]

A memorandum on re-evaluation was published in May 1986. Active ingredients were assigned to commodity groups to allow a review of alternative pesticides at the same time. Forty-nine groups were developed. Every registered product was characterized and given point values in terms of (1) annual quantity of pesticide used and (2) key risk characteristics. A total of 46 groups were prioritized for re-evaluation. The other three groups were already under re-evaluation. Active ingredients were also assigned to one of six categories in relation to the completeness of their data base. This information shows that less than 10 per cent of registered active ingredients in Canada represent more than 80 per cent of the total volume sold. However, of the 40 large-volume pesticides, 17 fell into the category of high priority for re-evaluation and 10 were being re-evaluated. None had a completely reviewed, up-to-date database.[47]

Problems with the re-evaluation system include the fact that the process is very slow. In 1983, the authors of this chapter estimated that it might take the federal government 30 to 50 years to re-evaluate the remainder of the currently registered pesticides. Other problems include the fact that the public has not been involved in setting the priorities; lack of resources; reluctance of companies to fill data gaps; and the fact that new data have become available since the memorandum was issued in 1986. However, new developments have occurred in the United States that will influence the re-evaluation of pesticides in Canada. In 1988, the *Federal Insecticide, Fungicide, and Rodenticide Act* was amended to require the US EPA to re-register, in a five-phase program over the following nine years, all pesticides that were first registered before November 1, 1984. The EPA has estimated that the re-registration process will cost at least $250 million over that nine-year period. *FIFRA* has also been amended to provide for re-registration fees of $50,000 to $150,000 for each active ingredient group. It is expected that pesticide manufacturers will stop producing a number of the older active ingredients as a result of this program. Although the US scheme will have a major impact on re-evaluations in Canada, it should be noted that many of the products registered in the United States are not registered here — for example, products registered for use in the southern United States on crops such as cotton. There seems to be some need to develop a "made in Canada" priority list.

Suspension and Cancellation of Pesticide Registrations: The Role of the Review Board

The registration of a pest control product may be suspended or cancelled by the minister of agriculture when "the safety of the control product or its merit or value is no longer acceptable to him." Suspension of a registration is the less extreme of the two regulatory options because it affects the registrant, not the retailer or user. If the control product is only suspended, the registrant cannot distribute any further shipments of the suspended product; however, material that is already at retail outlets before the suspension may be legally sold. Cancellation of a product means that it can no longer be manufactured or sold. All stocks of the product must be removed from the market and the registrant must assume responsibility for the collection, safe storage, and disposal of the cancelled product.

Under the PCP regulations, the registrant may appeal the suspension or cancellation, and request a hearing within 30 days of the minister's notice of intention to take this action. The minister must appoint a review board to hold the hearing and the board must give the registrant "and all other persons who may be affected by the subject matter of the hearing" an opportunity to make representations to the board. The board must prepare a report and file it with the minister but can only make recommendations. The final decision rests with the minister, who can, after considering the board's report, take any action that he or she deems advisable and notify the registrant of his or her decision.

To date, there have been very few instances of suspension or cancellation of product registrations under the *Pest Control Products Act*. Since the regulations were promulgated in 1972, review boards have been impaneled to hear a matter only three times.[48] The most recent review board was impaneled in November 1985 to deal with an appeal by Monsanto Canada Ltd. from the decision of Agriculture Canada to cancel the herbicide Alachlor. CELA represented a farmwife whose wells had been contaminated by Alachlor. In addition to the industry and farm associations and the federal and provincial governments, Friends of the Earth (FOE) and Pollution Probe also were parties before the review board.

Alachlor was one of the pesticides whose registration had been supported, to a significant degree, by studies carried out by Industrial Bio-Test Laboratories (IBT), an Illinois-based commercial testing laboratory that fraudulently conducted health and safety studies on over 100 pesticides registered in Canada and the United States. The manufacturers of these pesticides, including Monsanto in this case, were given the opportunity to repeat these studies in order to ensure that the product's registration would be maintained. Starting in 1982, Monsanto submitted a number of replacement studies to Health and Welfare Canada detailing the toxicological effects of its chemical. These studies, done at two different laboratories, showed that Alachlor caused multiple tumours in multiple sites in both sexes of test animals, at extremely low doses. Concerns were raised by Health and Welfare Canada as early as 1982, but it was not until February 5, 1985 that Agriculture Canada actually made a decision to cancel Alachlor. It should be noted that during that intervening three-year period, although there had been numerous meetings between Monsanto and Agriculture Canada and Health and Welfare Canada officials, the public was virtually locked out of the process. Currently, there is no provision in the statute to allow the public to trigger a re-evaluation of a pesticide.

The review board issued its report on November 13, 1987, recommending the reinstatement of Alachlor. The board made a number of findings, including the fact that Alachlor was a potential human carcinogen, and that the economic impact of maintaining the ban would be minor. Specifically, the board noted that Monsanto's economic analysis was "suspect." The board then went on to find, however, that Metolachlor, the alternative product, was also a carcinogen, and that therefore the only so-called equitable options for the minister to consider were either to cancel both chemicals or to leave both on the market. Since, in the board's opinion, exposure to Alachlor would be within a reasonable margin of safety, it recommended to the minister that Alachlor's registration should be reinstated. The board's report was met with strong criticism from the national environmental community and Health and Welfare Canada.

CELA, FOE, and Pollution Probe urged the minister to reject the board's findings on Metolachlor on the grounds that the board did not have sufficient data to enable it to make that determination. Over 77 volumes of material had been filed by Monsanto pertaining to Alachlor, including all raw data of the various toxicological tests. Because this was not an inquiry into Metolachlor, there was no similar database filed by Ciba-Geigy, the manufacturer of Metolachlor. In fact, Health and Welfare Canada, in its review of the material, had concluded that Metolachlor was neither an animal nor a human carcinogen. In contrast, at the hearing, a Health and Welfare Canada toxicologist had testified: "In the global sense, I know of no chemical with which I have been involved where the evidence [of potential harm to human health] has been more convincing than it has been with alachlor."[49]

The board's report was also criticized for applying a "margin of safety" approach to a potential carcinogen. Health and Welfare Canada specifically noted in its letter of November 27, 1987 to Agriculture Canada that "calculation of margins of safety does not represent the generally accepted approach to carcinogen risk assessment." In fact, the US EPA's Cancer Assessment Group, the World Health Organization, and Health and Welfare Canada all accept the principle that there are no safe threshold levels for carcinogens. Safety margins are usually applied to non-cancer end points and are not used in carcinogen risk assessment. Health and Welfare Canada concluded that the risk of cancer from exposure to Alachlor was in the order of 1 in 1,000 to 1 in 10,000, which, in its view, was "appreciable."

On January 27, 1988 the minister of agriculture made a decision to maintain the ban on Alachlor. He indicated that it was his opinion that the use of Alachlor represents an unacceptable risk of harm to public health. In the spring of 1988, Monsanto brought an application in the Federal Court of Appeal to set aside the minister's decision and to have the recommendations of the Alachlor Review Board put in place. On December 6, 1988, the Federal Court of Appeal dismissed Monsanto's application to set aside the minister's decision to cancel Alachlor's registration.[50] The Supreme Court of Canada denied Monsanto leave to appeal.

Exports of Pesticides

The export of pesticides by a manufacturer from a country with stringent controls to one with less stringent requirements has provoked international concern. One European environmental official stated in 1982 that

> we have a duty to break the so-called circle of poison. When pesticides, not allowed any more in industrialized countries, are exported to developing countries, the use on crops there not only causes contamination of soil and water, but also results in contaminated crops that may be imported into the same countries where the use of the exported chemicals is forbidden or restricted.[51]

Canada is not a major exporter of pesticides. However, the *Canadian Environmental Protection Act*[52] currently prohibits the export of a pesticide whose registration status has been cancelled pursuant to the provisions of the *Pest Control Products Act* and has been placed on the list of prohibited substances.[53] The only exception is export for the purpose of destroying the substance. This is the only portion of the *Canadian Environmental Protection Act* that deals with pesticides, since the list of prohibited substances may contain substances prohibited by *any* federal legislation. Pesticides that have been substantially restricted in Canada may be placed on the "List of Toxic Substances Requiring Export Notification," and pursuant to section 42 of *Canadian Environmental Protection Act*, notification must be given to those countries placed on a list of toxic substances authorities. This list of prohibited substances has yet to be finalized.

The Pesticide Action Network (PAN), founded in 1982, is an international coalition of some 300 environmental, consumer, church, union, and farmworker organizations working on pesticides issues. Its "dirty dozen" campaign has targeted 12 particularly hazardous pesticides for international regulatory action. PAN is an excellent source of information on pesticides. Contact:

> PAN North America Regional Center
> 65 Mission Street #514
> San Francisco, CA 94103
> Phone: (415) 541-9140

Monitoring and Enforcement

Every person who violates the *Pest Control Products Act* or regulations is liable, on conviction, to two years' imprisonment if indicted or to punishment on summary conviction. The due diligence defence is available to an accused.[54] No amount of fine is listed in the Act. Accordingly, section 787(1) of the *Criminal Code*[55] applies. This section of the *Code* provides for a maximum fine of $2,000, imprisonment for six months, or both on summary conviction for any offence under a federal statute that does not provide for larger or smaller penalties. The amount of this maximum fine is substantially smaller than the maximum fines authorized under the *Fisheries Act*[56] or the *Canadian Environmental Protection Act*. There has been a paucity of federal prosecutions. Between January 1, 1970 and June 30, 1983, only seven prosecutions were undertaken by Agriculture Canada across the country.[57] Three convictions were obtained, with small fines assessed in each case. Between June 1, 1985 and December 29, 1989, there were only 11 prosecutions undertaken.[58] Between January 1, 1990 and December 11, 1992, 11 prosecutions were commenced. Six prosecutions resulted in a conviction and fine; one resulted in a finding of guilt and a discharge; one charge was stayed; two charges were withdrawn; and one decision had not been rendered as of December 1992.[59] According to Agriculture Canada, the reason there are so few prosecutions is "(a) the decision by the government to educate users as a first approach, and (b) the immense paperwork makes it unreasonable except in very severe cases."[60]

In recent years, there have been contraventions of the *Pest Control Products Act*, including the improper use of products on crops for which they are not registered; improper rates and methods of application, causing potential harm to public health and the environment; and the use of illegally imported pesticides that are not registered in Canada. From March 1989 to June 1990, the RCMP Vancouver office took enforcement action against several commercial smuggling operations involving prohibited pest control products. Over 225,000 pounds of prohibited products were seized. The RCMP has stated that this situation is not localized to western Canada nor is it linked to any one particular portion of the farming industry. In fact, prohibited pesticides destined for use in various berry operations, tree farming, vegetable and fruit farming, and nursery operations have been seized across Canada.[61]

The Food and Drugs Act

The Setting of Maximum Residue Limits for Pesticides

The general prohibition of the sale of adulterated food is found in section 4 of the *Food and Drugs Act*,[62] administered by Health and Welfare Canada. Specifically, section 4 prohibits the sale of any "article of food that (a) has in or upon it any poisonous or harmful substance; (b) is unfit for human consumption; ... [or] (d) is adulterated." Although this general section appears to prohibit pesticide residues on food because pesticides are, by definition, poisonous substances, a pesticide manufacturer can apply to the government to allow a residue of the pesticide to remain in the food that is sprayed with this pesticide. Division 15 of the Food and Drugs Regulations (FD regulations)[63] establishes maximum residue limits for agricultural chemicals that are, in effect, exemptions from the section 4 prohibition.

Maximum residue limits (MRLs), usually expressed in parts per million (ppm), have been established for about 100 agricultural chemicals. Food that is found to contain chemical in excess of the limit set out in the FD regulations will be considered adulterated and in breach of section 4(d) of the *Food and Drugs Act*. Pesticide residue limits are set at levels that will cover residues that are likely to remain in food at the point of wholesale marketing — that is, at the harvest of a crop, the slaughter of an animal, or the point of entry into the country in the case of imported foods.

The FD regulations were amended in 1978 to provide that a food is adulterated if it contains more that 0.1 ppm of any agricultural chemical that is not specifically listed in division 15.[64] The policy basis for this regulation is as follows:

1. relatively simple legal action can be taken against pesticide residues that exceed 0.1 ppm, without the need to prove hazard or to take action under section 4 of the *Food and Drugs Act*;
2. many pesticides that were originally thought to leave no residues on foods (that is, below the sensitivity of the analytical method) have subsequently been found to leave very low residues that may be toxicologically negligible; and,

3. residue levels below 0.1 ppm that are considered to be toxicologically significant may still be listed in table II, division 15.

However, although this regulation makes enforcement easier, there does not seem to be a scientific justification for the general 0.1 ppm MRL. For example, 0.1 ppm may be too high with regard to certain agricultural chemicals that may cause cancer. It is arguable that there should be no detectable resides allowed for carcinogens.

The applicant for an exemption from the rule that food should be unadulterated is responsible for proving the chemical nature, level, and safety of any pesticide residues in food. Once the applicant submits the data, Health and Welfare Canada makes a determination of the acceptable daily intake (ADI) of the particular pesticide. The ADI is the amount of chemical that toxicologists consider to be safe for human beings to ingest each day for an entire lifetime. Calculations are made of the lowest no-effect dose level (NOEL) from toxicity studies of the pesticide on each animal species tested. The lowest NOEL is then divided by a safety factor such as 100 to establish the ADI.[65]

A second assessment is then made to determine the allowable MRLs. The residue studies submitted are examined, but MRLs are accepted only if the total consumption of residues of this pesticide from all food uses will not exceed the ADI estimated for the particular pesticide from the toxicity studies. Canadian eating habits are examined to help calculate acceptable residue levels. If, however, a person eats more than the average amount of a certain food, he or she may be exposed to residues above the acceptable limits.

The methods by which MRLs are set have been criticized both in Canada and in the United States.[66] The setting of tolerance levels and ADIs for individual pesticides in foods has been criticized for not taking into account a number of problems relating to pesticide exposure: (1) the diets of certain individuals may consist of very high amounts of certain limited food items, rather than a balanced diet; (2) people are not equal in their ability to detoxify and eliminate pesticides; and (3) tolerance levels and ADIs are set for individual pesticides rather than for the effects of pesticides acting together (additive, cumulative, and synergistic effects).[67]

Monitoring and Enforcement

The federal departments of agriculture, fisheries and oceans, environment, forestry, and health and welfare, as well as a number of provincial ministries, carry out pesticide residue analyses. The major evaluation is the agricultural chemical residues compliance program carried out by Health and Welfare Canada.

About 1,600 to 1,700 food samples are analyzed each year. If the residues are found to be greater than the permitted MRLs, the seller can be prosecuted for breach of section 4 of the *Food and Drugs Act*. Section 26 sets out the penalties available for breaches of the Act or regulations. A first offender on summary conviction may face only a fine up to $500 or up to three months' imprisonment, or both.

From January 1, 1970 to 1983, there were no prosecutions for breach of the *Food and Drugs Act* regarding agricultural chemical residues. The usual enforcement procedure is to send a warning letter when food samples are found to contain excessive residues. Another enforcement tool is to refuse the entry of foods into Canada. Products may also be seized and destroyed when excessive residues are found on food grown in Canada or that has entered Canada from abroad before the contamination was discovered. However, the effectiveness of this course of action is limited if the product has been sold and consumed before analytical results are available. From mid-1975 to May 1983, there have been 36 instances in which produce has been refused entry, 1 seizure, and 20 instances of voluntary disposal of food. We were unable to obtain more current statistics on prosecutions, refusals of entry, confiscations, and voluntary disposals since Health and Welfare Canada stated that "the way the data base is set up, the information cannot be easily accessed."[68]

Federal Pesticide Reform

On September 30, 1989, the minister of agriculture announced that a review of Canada's pesticide registration system would be undertaken. This announcement was in response to concerns about the existing system raised by a number of interested groups, including farmers and environmentalists. In the spring of 1989, a multi-stakeholder review team was appointed. Mr. Ghislain LeBlond, a newly appointed deputy minister of agriculture, was appointed chair and 12 team members were chosen, including representatives from agriculture and forestry, the pesticides industry, labour, and environmental, consumer, and public health groups.[69]

The review team issued a draft report in July 1990,[70] and public hearings were held across Canada during the fall of 1990. The review team heard from over 400 people and received 500 written submissions. The final report was submitted to the minister of agriculture on December 21, 1990.[71] The report represented a significant shift in focus to ecologically sound, preventive approaches to pest management problems and encouraged increased public input to the system. The report specifically recognized the need for a reduction of pesticide use in Canada. It called for the establishment of a Pest Management Promotion Office that would set targets for pesticide reduction in all sectors. The office would initiate research on ecologically sound pest management strategies that would replace the use of pesticides wherever possible.

The report also recommended that decisions to register pesticides be transferred from Agriculture Canada to an independent Pest Management Regulatory Agency that would report directly to the minister of health and welfare. Other recommendations included:

- access to information on health and safety data regarding a registered pesticide through the right of any citizen to all health and safety data, provided that the citizen signs an undertaking to keep trade secrets confidential;
- the right of citizens to appeal a decision to register a pest control product;
- an export policy that would, subject to appeal, clearly prohibit the export of cancelled or suspended products to other countries; and
- the creation of a national database for collecting information on pesticide use.

Although most of the recommendations were clear improvements over the *status quo*, in the report the environmental caucus registered concern about the creation of a new registration type: "user-requested minor use registration." This would allow the operational use of pesticides that are not registered in Canada while studies needed to obtain Canadian registration were being conducted.

The final chapter of the report dealt with the implementation of the report's recommendations. It recommended the establishment of an advisory committee composed of stakeholders familiar with the intent of the recommended system and the establishment of a legislative drafting committee.

In February 1992, the government announced that it would proceed to implement 23 of the review team's 27 major recommendations. One significant change was the government's rejection of the stand-alone agency reporting to the minister of health and welfare. Instead, it proposed to make the ministers of agriculture, health and welfare, and environment equal partners under a revised *Pest Control Products Act*.[72] The government did announce the establishment of the Pest Management Alternatives Office (PMAO) to serve as a clearing house for efforts to develop ecologically sound pest management strategies that reduce health and environmental risks while optimizing efficacy; to reduce dependence on pesticides by adopting preventive and alternative approaches; and to promote measures that encourage only the minimum use of currently registered pesticides.[73] The government intends to incorporate the PMAO as a non-profit organization that operates at arm's length from government. This has raised concerns among environmental groups that the review team's recommendation that the regulatory agency consult the PMAO when an application for an emergency registration, critical need, or user-requested minor use registration is received and that the PMAO would make a determination whether alternatives were available will not be implemented.[74]

Following its official response to the review team's report, the minister of agriculture in February 1992 established a multi-stakeholder interim advisory council to advise on implementing the accepted recommendations. Environmentalists have raised concerns about the operation of the council and the fact that the government has moved forward on implementing selected recommendations rather than the package in its entirety. They are concerned that the piecemeal implementation approach is inequitable, focusing on the concerns of some stakeholders while ignoring recommendations that would ensure openness, accountability to the public, effective enforcement, and environmental and health protection. The three initiatives that are proceeding include a product import program that will allow farmers to import pesticides into Canada from the United States; implementation of the User Requested Minor Use Registration pilot project, which will allow farmers to use pesticides that have not been fully tested in Canada; and the creation of the Pest Management Alternatives Office discussed above.[75] Environmentalists have drafted a letter to the prime minister and Cabinet expressing their concerns about the piecemeal implementation of the review team's report. It remains to be seen whether the *Pest Control Products Act* will be amended to reflect the work done by the review team or whether piecemeal implementation will continue to the detriment of the public health and safety.

THE PROVINCIAL ROLE

Overview

The goal of Ontario's pesticide legislation, the *Pesticides Act*,[76] can be said to be the protection of environmental quality, human health, and property from the improper use of pesticides.[77] While the federal *Pest Control Products Act* determines which pesticides are acceptable for use and how they may be used in Canada, Ontario's pesticide legislation refines the federal registration scheme by classifying pesticides into various schedules that govern who can sell pesticides, who can use them, and under what circumstances.[78] Unlike federal law, the *Pesticides Act* authorizes the issuance of permits and licences to certain types of pesticide users.[79] Key problems exist, however, with respect to which pesticides are assigned to particular use classifications, especially where less hazardous alternative products may not be available. Moreover, permit and licence exemptions for certain major users of pesticides, such as farmers, may leave fundamental gaps in Ontario's control scheme. Other components of provincial pesticide law include the control of transportation, storage, disposal, and spills, and a variety of administrative and quasi-criminal enforcement tools and techniques. These include record keeping and reporting; provincial inspection authority; the use of an advisory committee to recommend use classifications; an appeal board to which sellers and users of pesticides can appeal the refusal, suspension, or cancellation of licences and permits; administrative orders of various types; and quasi-criminal prosecutions. The public can also play an important part in supplementing provincial control of pesticides. Key provincial initiatives and their adequacy are reviewed below.

Classification of Pesticides and the Issuance of Licences and Permits Controlling Usage

Pesticides Classification

Ontario's *Pesticides Act* is administered by the Ministry of Environment and Energy (formerly the Ministry of the Environment). Under the *Pesticides Act*, all pesticide products sold, bought, or used in the province must be classified according to their potential to cause harm to human health and the environment, and assigned to one of six schedules. Before provincial classification can occur, a pesticide must be registered under the *Pest Control Products Act*.[80] The subsequent marketing and use of each product must be in accordance with the regulations relating to its classification and the instructions on the label of the pesticide container, which have been approved under the *Pest Control Products Act*.[81] Licences and permits restrict vendors and applicators of pesticides to selling or using only the particular pesticides in a schedule to which that person's licence or permit applies.

Six schedules are established under the *Pesticides Act*. Pesticides are placed in one schedule or another on the basis of toxicity, persistence in the environment, intended use, packaging, and a number of other factors.

- Schedule 1 pesticides pose a serious potential hazard to human health or the environment. They may be sold only by licensed vendors and purchased and used only under the authority of a licence or a specific-use permit.
- Schedule 2 pesticides pose a potential hazard to human health or the environment. They may be sold only by licensed vendors and purchased and used only by agriculturists* or under the authority of a licence.
- Schedule 3 pesticides pose minimal hazard to human health or the environment if used according to package directions. They may be sold only by licensed vendors, but may be purchased and used by anyone.
- Schedule 4 pesticides are considered relatively innocuous. They may be sold by unlicensed retailers and purchased and used by anyone.

---

* "Agriculturalist" is defined in the *Pesticides Act* as a person who uses farmland for agricultural or forestry purposes.

- Schedule 5 pesticides pose a serious potential hazard to human health or the environment. These are agricultural products, available from licensed vendors only to agriculturists and appropriately licensed exterminators.
- Schedule 6 pesticides are identical to schedule 4 pesticides but are packaged in containers (usually larger containers) that are considered inappropriate for unregulated sale — for example, in grocery stores. Therefore, sales are allowed through licensed vendors only.

As well as determining who can buy, sell, and use a pesticide, the schedule in which a pesticide is placed also determines the applicability of other portions of the *Pesticides Act* regulation, which sets out various procedural requirements such as the need for safety equipment, warning signs, steps to take in conducting a fumigation, safety testing at the conclusion of certain exterminations, and the amount of liability insurance an exterminator must carry, and so on.[82]

In Ontario, the Pesticides Advisory Committee, established under the *Pesticides Act*, is responsible for recommending to the minister of environment and energy under which schedule each pesticide should be classified.[83] The Ontario classification system appears to take into account the pesticide formulation as marketed (that is, the control product) when considering toxicity, but only the active ingredient when considering such matters as parent compounds and relevant metabolites (breakdown products) that might occur in agricultural and environmental substrates.[84] It is unfortunate that the classification system would make such a distinction, since inert ingredients can be of biological concern as well.[85]

Other criteria are also used in scheduling pesticides for particular uses. Both schedule 1 and schedule 5 pesticides, for example, are defined by the Pesticides Advisory Committee as posing serious hazards to human health and the environment.[86] However, although schedule 1 products may not be used without first obtaining a specific-use permit, farmers and tree growers need not obtain licences or permits to use schedule 5 pesticides that are meant to be applied on agricultural lands, because of general farmer (agriculturalist) exemptions under the regulations,[87] which are discussed more fully below. According to the committee, schedule 5 pesticides have not been placed in the more restrictive schedule 1 because of "the lack of effective and less hazardous alternatives."[88]

Although there is no direct correlation between the federal classification of a product and the Ontario schedules, the *Pesticides Act* allows Ontario to be more restrictive than the federal government, but not less restrictive.[89] Ontario's schedules under the *Pesticides Act* can generally be compared with the *Pest Control Products Act* registration classification in the following manner. Schedule 1 products correspond with the "restricted" category under the *Pest Control Products Act*; schedule 2, 3, 5, and 6 products correspond with either the "restricted" or the "commercial" category; schedule 3 products are "commercial" or "domestic"; and schedule 4 products correspond with the "domestic" category.[90] Sometimes, however, products remain on what appear to be inappropriate schedules. For example, schedule 3 pesticides are characterized by the Pesticides Advisory Committee as posing minimal hazards,[91] yet the fungicide Captan, which in the past has been suspected of causing cancer,[92] remains on schedule 3 of Ontario's classification system, and thus is available for possible domestic use.[93]

The theory behind regulatory schedules is to give a province greater control of pesticide distribution and use than may occur under the *Pest Control Products Act*. In practice, however, the province has generally tended to follow the lead of federal agencies regarding the availability of certain pesticides for particular uses. There have been a few exceptions. For example, public pressure to greatly restrict the use of the herbicide 2,4,5-T in Ontario resulted in a more stringent use classification than at the federal level. Ontario placed 2,4,5-T, whose contaminant TCDD is suspected of causing cancer,[94] in schedule 1, and as a matter of policy did not issue permits for its use, even though it is approved for use in Canada under the *Pest Control Products Act*.

Licences and Permits

Although the principal regulatory mechanisms for controlling pesticides under federal law may be said to be the registration and labelling requirements under the *Pest Control Products Act*, licence and permit requirements are key control mechanisms under provincial law.

Under Ontario law, an elaborate system of licence and permit requirements is authorized, which is typical of the programs of most other provinces. Licences are required for selling pesticides[95] and for operating pest extermination businesses.[96] In addition, professional pesticide applicators require licences[97] that are categorized according to whether they will perform structural,[98] land,[99] or water exterminations.[100] Several classes of licences exist for each of these categories. In the case of the operators of pesticide-spraying businesses and their employees, the class of licence that is required is normally based on which classes of pesticides the applicators will use.[101] In the case of vendors, the class of licence required depends on which classes of pesticides will be sold, and whether the vendor is a wholesaler or sells to the general public. Individuals may also be exempted from structural, land, or water extermination licence requirements.[102]

In addition to the licensing of businesses, under Ontario law, a permit for each land, water, or structural extermination that is carried out are required in a number of circumstances.[103] These include: (1) use of schedule 1 pesticides;[104] (2) aerial application of all schedule 1 and 5 pesticides and of hormone-type schedule 2 herbicides;[105] and (3) aquatic applications of pesticides other than in enclosed ponds[106] or drainage ditches that contain no moving water at the time of application.[107] Individuals may be exempted from permit requirements, as set out below.[108]

The advantage of licensing arrangements is that they may provide general control over the responsibility, knowledge, and ability of the particular pesticide applicator.[109] The advantage of permit requirements is that they allow the evaluation of environmental impacts at particular site locations, as well as an opportunity to monitor and review the compliance of applicators with the *Pesticides Act*, regulations, and permit conditions.[110]

The magnitude of provincial licensing and permit programs is illustrated by recent statistics available from Ontario. In Ontario, an estimated 15,500 licences were issued or re-issued in 1982-83. By 1992, the number of "active" licences had risen to about 28,500.[111] In 1982-83, 2,500 permits were issued.[112] In 1991, the number of permits was about 2,100.[113]

Ontario law also authorizes the Ministry of Environment and Energy to refuse to issue or renew a licence;[114] to suspend or revoke a licence;[115] to cancel or refuse to issue a permit; or to impose or alter terms and conditions in a permit.[116] In comparison with the number of licences or permits issued a year in Ontario, the numbers refused, revoked, cancelled, or suspended are nominal.[117] Other enforcement actions, however, either in conjunction with or instead of these initiatives, may be taken. These are discussed below, under the headings "Control Orders, Stop Orders, and Other Administrative Enforcement Techniques" and "Prohibitions, Offences, Penalties, and Prosecutions."

If the ministry proposes to refuse, suspend, or revoke a licence[118] or to deny or otherwise change a permit,[119] the decision may be appealed to the Environmental Appeal Board.[120] Only the applicant for a licence or permit or the holder of a licence or permit has a right to appeal an adverse regulatory decision.[121] Members of the public who may be adversely affected by pesticide spraying have no similar right to appeal the issuance of a licence or permit or the ministry's decision not to impose terms or conditions in the licence or permit. The board does have the power to grant standing to others to participate in its proceedings;[122] however, normally the only parties to proceedings are the licensee-permittee and the government.

In contrast, British Columbia's *Pesticide Control Act* allows an appeal to be filed "by any person ... against the action, decision or order of the administrator" who issues pesticide permits.[123] The effect of this provision is to allow objectors to appeal the issuance of pesticide-spraying permits and licences,[124] and to participate in hearings before a tribunal with the same name as its Ontario counterpart: the Environmental Appeal Board. Occasionally, opponents are successful in demonstrating to the board that the issuance of a pesticide permit would result in unreasonably adverse effects on the environment. When they have failed to convince the board, opponents have sometimes convinced the courts that the board followed improper procedures.[125]

In the past, appeals against permits were usually rejected by the board.[126] One suggested reason for this is that citizens' groups wanted the board to consider evidence about various pesticides' effects on health and the environment generally, whereas the provincial government and the board viewed this matter as largely investigated in the first instance by Agriculture Canada at the pesticide registration stage. The BC courts have held that the board may refuse to assess evidence of toxicity and may assume the general safety of a federally registered pesticide because of the extensive testing required for registration. Only if a specific site in question prevents the safe application of a pesticide will the board hear evidence of toxicity and be required to consider alternatives.[127] Thus, the hearing, from the province's perspective, is only for the purpose of determining the impacts of pesticide use under specific local conditions.[128]

Despite these limitations in the inquiry conducted by the BC appeal tribunal, citizens have had some success in recent years in persuading the board to impose additional conditions on permits, and as a result of the public's participation the board often makes recommendations to government authorities designed to improve pesticide-spraying programs and public access to information about these programs. For example, in four of its nine decisions in 1991-92, the board dismissed the appeal but amended permits, two appeals were allowed, and in two other decisions the board issued comments concerning issues such as the use of standard forms, fish kills, and the use of alternatives to pesticides.[129]

The BC approach at least offers an opportunity for public intervention before permit decisions become final. However, the failure of the hearings in British Columbia to deal with toxicological or related matters, but rather with geographic factors, points up the need for a forum to consider these threshold environmental health matters at an earlier stage. This suggests the need to reform the process under the *Pest Control Products Act*, as has been outlined above (see the discussion of the federal role in the first part of this chapter).

Even if the process in Ontario were to be reformed along the lines now existing in British Columbia, information on spray permit applications would be necessary to properly inform potential appellants. However, the experience in Ontario has been that spray permits or permit applications themselves are not available; the Ministry of Environment and Energy will release only selected information from them, and only after they have been issued.[130] Access to such information before the hearing itself appears to be a prerequisite to any such inquiry into the adequacy of the permit proposal.

Aerial and Water Applications of Pesticides

Aerial[131] and water[132] applications of pesticides have become particularly controversial methods of use because they pose the potential for widespread involuntary environmental and human exposure to pesticides, through spray drift or related off-target impacts. As a result, provincial laws frequently emphasize the control of such activities through a combination of both licence and permit requirements. In Ontario, for example, licensees that perform aerial applications of all schedule 1, 5, and hormone-type schedule 2 herbicides require a special permit for the extermination.[133] The permit must indicate the pesticide type, acreage, location, and time-period of the spraying.[134] Spray records describing the event must be kept and submitted to the province if requested.[135]

Normally, the proposed issuance of a permit, for example, for a major aerial forestry spraying program does not trigger prior public hearings under provincial pesticide laws. Nor is there any requirement to notify the public before aerial spraying of forests is done, as is required before other kinds of public areas are sprayed. Given the concern that frequently accompanies such proposals, however, provincial governments in recent years have had to address the inadequacy of this essentially informal, if not closed, administrative control approach. The result has been the use of special commissions of inquiry into the forest pesticide problem,[136] as well as second-generation environmental statutes that are more comprehensive in nature then pesticides legislation. For example, under Ontario's *Environmental Assessment Act*,[137] proponents of undertakings subject to the Act must prepare an environmental assessment, which describes the project, the environment to be affected, and the project's environmental effects and reviews alternatives to the undertaking and alternative methods for carrying out the proposed undertaking. Any member of the public may seek a public hearing on the undertaking before it is approved. Timber management, including aerial spraying of pesticides on Crown lands, for example, is subject to the Act. However, no public hearing had ever been held on such activities from the coming into force of the Act in 1976 until 1988. This was a result of a series of exemptions of timber management programs from the application of the Act that the provincial Ministry of Natural Resources (MNR) had been able to obtain until it finalized its class environmental assessment document on timber management and made a formal application for approval of this program. The use of a class environmental assessment approach to approval could result in only one hearing being held on how MNR will oversee spray operations generally on Crown timber lands. This would be in substitution for numerous hearings on spraying of individual parcels of Crown timber licensed lands.

Although as of March 1993 the Environmental Assessment Board had not yet rendered its decision following the timber management hearing, the panel hearing the matter had held that the federal (*Pest Control Products Act*) and Ontario (*Pesticides Act*) regulatory regimes with respect to the registration and use of pesticides do not in any way prevent the board from considering the potential health effects from the use of these products on the environment in the context of the provisions of the *Environmental Assessment Act*. Moreover, in exercising its discretion under the Act, the board may go beyond the terms and conditions that may have been imposed in conjunction with the decisions of other regulatory authorities that exercise jurisdiction under other legislation. Thus, the board could, if it chose to do so, impose a condition restricting or prohibiting the use of a particular pesticide within the area of the undertaking. The board could do this even if the particular pesticide has been approved for use under the applicable federal and provincial legislation, if the board felt that such a condition were necessary to fulfil the purposes of the *Environmental Assessment Act* — namely, "to provide for the protection, conservation and wise management in Ontario of the environment."[138]

The problem of the need for, and adequacy of, aerial spray programs, as well as the statutory and administrative procedures necessary for considering such matters, remains in a state of flux. A combination of (1) licence and permit requirements, (2) more comprehensive environmental assessment and public hearing procedures, and (3) special commissions of inquiry seems likely to characterize both law and policy development in this area for the foreseeable future.

Exemptions for Farmers

The hazards of pesticides are minimized when pesticides are transported, stored, mixed, and applied in accordance with the instructions on the label, as required by both federal and Ontario law. As noted by an Ontario task force on farm safety, however, it is very difficult to enforce these labelling requirements when pesticides are applied by unlicensed people such as farmers.[139]

The elaborate system of pesticide permits and licences found under most provincial laws nonetheless contains a number of key exemptions. Chief among them are exemptions for farmers, including commercial tree growers, from many permit and licence requirements.

Under Ontario law, for example, agriculturalists who perform land exterminations on farmland on which they are engaged in agricultural or forestry production using schedule 4 or 6 pesticides are exempt from statutory licence requirements.[140] Since April 1991, however, farmers are exempt from statutory licence requirements when they perform land exterminations on farmland on which they are engaged in agricultural or forestry production by means of schedule 2, 3, or 5 pesticides only if they have been certified.[141] The regulation allows for farmers to be certified in two ways: either by taking a course in the safe use and handling of pesticides and passing an exam, or on the basis of their experience in handling pesticides. However, we were advised that the ministry has never certified a farmer, without this examination, on the basis of experience alone.[142] Farmers must be re-certified every five years. Similarly, certified agriculturalists who spray their neighbour's land are also exempt from licensing requirements for schedules 2 to 6 pesticides as long as they have only one pesticide rig in operation at a time, and it is normally used on their own farm.[143] Agriculturalists and their full-time employees are exempt from licence requirements for structural exterminations within their farm buildings or structures.[144] If agriculturalists, or certified agriculturalists, are exempt from licence requirements, they are also exempt from permit requirements except when using schedule 1 products.[145] Farmers are also exempt from permit and licence requirements if they apply pesticides to farm ponds that are wholly enclosed on their property or drainage ditches that contain no moving water in them at the time of spraying.[146] Moreover, the spraying of agricultural land is exempt from public notification requirements.[147]

The significance of the farmer exemptions is apparent when the magnitude of pesticide use in the agricultural area is considered. Provincial officials have estimated in the past that perhaps 85 per cent of pesticide use in Canada is in agriculture.[148] In 1977, it was estimated by Ontario officials that about 75 per cent of all pesticides used in the province were applied on agricultural lands: 15 per cent applied by licensed applicators and 60 per cent by farmers or farmers helping neighbours.[149] In 1983, 8.7 million kilograms of active ingredients were used on field crops, fruit, and vegetables grown in Ontario, up from 6.6 million kilograms in 1978 and 5.5 million kilograms in 1973.[150] In 1988, the date of the most recent statistics available, over 7,200 tonnes of pesticides were applied to agricultural crops in Ontario, a lower amount than usual because of extreme drought.[151] In early 1993, 41,000 farmers had been certified to apply pesticides to their own farms and those of neighbours.[152]

The magnitude of the amounts of pesticides used in agriculture raises concerns about the possibility of misuse causing harm to consumers of farm products, bystanders, flora and fauna, and farmers themselves.[153] Farmer misuse of pesticides in fact has been recorded in various provinces.[154] However, given the traditional independence of the farm community from many types of environmental regulation, as well as the expanded permit or licence scheme and the additional administrative personnel that would be needed if farmers were covered, provincial laws have tended to exempt farmers from such provisions.[155] Provincial officials point to various types of residue analysis, surveillance, and monitoring programs to ensure that farm produce is not adulterated by pesticides as adequate safeguards.[156] Provincial officials do admit, however, that occupational and bystander exposure to agricultural use of pesticides is of concern,[157] as well as environmental damage, such as water pollution.[158] Indeed, Ontario's Ministry of Agriculture and Food has admitted that "heavy pesticide use in farming is a growing concern for us all."[159] It has noted:

> Since the Second World War, Ontario farmers have come to rely increasingly on synthetic chemical pesticides; these were effective, inexpensive and easy to use when world markets started to demand more and better food products. But continued, intensive use of pesticides has critical limitations and dangers.
>
> Chief concerns are food and water contamination, increasing pest resistance, changing pest dominance, fewer new pesticides and lack of non-chemical alternatives.[160]

To combat this heavy use of pesticides by Ontario farmers, the ministry announced in 1988 that it was embarking on a plan to reduce the use of pesticides by 50 per cent over the next 15 years by emphasizing education, research, and field delivery. The program seeks to "balance efficient and sustainable crop production while developing ecologically sound pest control technology."[161] However, it will be impossible to measure the effectiveness of this totally voluntary approach until statistics are available to compare the level of pesticide use before and after this initiative. As of March 1993, no such statistics were available.[162] Even with such information, it will be difficult to assess the success of the program, since temporary reductions in pesticide use may result from factors such as unusual weather conditions and economic recession, both of which occurred during the course of this program.

Notification Requirements

A variety of pre-spray notification provisions are found under Ontario law to protect the public from unwanted exposure to pesticides. These provisions require the sprayer to post signs, publish a notice in newspapers, or give written notice, as the case may be, of proposed land extermination activities in residential or public areas (such as schools, parks, golf courses, cemeteries, and campgrounds) before the spraying is done.[163] The purpose of this notice is to prevent inadvertent exposure of bystanders who might otherwise gain access to or be within sprayed areas too close to the time of spraying. Generally, residential areas must be posted immediately before a land extermination begins.[164] The spraying of some public areas that are commonly frequented by the public, and particularly by children, such as parks and areas around schools, may require at least 24 hours prior notice.[165] The signs must be left up for at least 24 hours after the area has been sprayed.[166] The regulations also specify the contents of notices, including appropriate warnings, dates of spraying, description of areas to be sprayed, pesticide to be used, contacts, and related matters.[167]

Sale of Pesticides

As mentioned above, certain classes of pesticides may be sold only by licensed vendors. To sell the more hazardous pesticides, vendors must also be certified. They can qualify either by taking a course and passing an exam or through experience. Every wholesale and retail outlet that sells these chemicals must have a full-time certified vendor in charge of the outlet.[168] Some vendors' licences have been revoked because no one at an outlet was certified.

Control of Transportation, Storage, Disposal, and Spills of Pesticides

In addition to the control of pesticide use, sales, and distribution, provincial law addresses other stages of pesticide management, including transportation, storage, disposal, and spills. Such controls, however, are not always to be found under provincial pesticide laws. Often these elements are in fact controlled through general pollution control legislation, which historically focused on emissions and discharges of contaminants from manufacturing processes. Many aspects of controls over pesticide transportation and disposal, for example, are in place under one or both of these types of laws. However, there are still important components of a comprehensive management system that are in need of development.

Under Ontario's *Pesticides Act*, transport requirements include securing pesticides to prevent escape or discharge to the environment during transportation;[169] ensuring that pesticides on certain schedules are not transported with food, drink, or household articles;[170] and placing warning signs on vehicles that carry pesticides in bulk.[171] Farmers and licensed applicators are also prohibited from leaving pesticides unattended in parked vehicles unless the vehicles are locked or inaccessible to the public.

Identification of the pesticide products or wastes being carried is not required under the *Pesticides Act*. However, under the province's *Environmental Protection Act* waste management regulations, manifests are required for the transport of identified liquid industrial wastes and hazardous wastes, including pesticide wastes.[172] In 1981, about 258,000 gallons of liquid pesticide wastes were transported by waste haulers in Ontario.[173] The records of the Waste Management Branch of the Ministry of Environment and Energy (MEE) show that 2,870 tonnes of halogenated pesticides and herbicides were hauled as waste in 1991.[174] Manifests for the transport of pesticides other than wastes and warning signs on vehicles are required under the federal *Transportation of Dangerous Goods Act*.[175]

Under Ontario's *Pesticides Act*, pesticides must not be stored near food, feed, or drink,[176] and pesticides listed in certain schedules must be stored in locked, ventilated rooms with warning signs on the door.[177] Pesticide vendors are required to follow certain precautions, including warning local fire departments of the location and hazards of stored pesticides;[178] preventing certain scheduled products from being stored in areas where floor drains could lead to sewers or watercourses;[179] and providing workers with protective clothing and respiratory equipment in such areas.[180]

The *Pesticides Act* also requires that MEE be notified of any deposit of a pesticide into the environment out of the normal course of events (for example, accident, spill, theft, or fire)[181] and authorizes the province to require clean-up.[182] Part X of the *Environmental Protection Act*, would also provide the opportunity for compensation of the innocent victims of a spill of pollutants generally. This could include pesticide spills during storage or transport.

Under Ontario's *Pesticides Act*, the only requirements for pesticide disposal relate to empty containers for pesticides in schedules 1, 2, and 5. These containers must be decontaminated in a manner approved by MEE,[183] punctured, and buried under 50 cm of soil that is not near any watercourse or water table[184] or, if the container is cardboard or paper, burned away from roads, buildings, or the public.[185] This practice of burying pesticide containers has been criticized by a government task force on the health and safety of Ontario farmers.[186] Apart from this limited authority with respect to empty pesticide container disposal, the *Pesticides Act* is silent on the disposal of pesticide wastes at landfill sites or other sites.

Because pesticide wastes are often hazardous, they are covered by the province's hazardous waste management regulations under the *Environmental Protection Act*. It was estimated that as early as 1974, about 1.5 million pounds of empty pesticide containers were disposed of in landfills, and another 2.7 million pounds of liquid pesticide wastes were incinerated in the province.[187] Disposal problems at pesticide formulating plants have also been sources of surface and groundwater contamination in Ontario.[188]

Despite the limited formal regulations dealing with pesticide disposal, the Ontario government has made some efforts to encourage farmers voluntarily to bring their empty pesticide containers and their de-registered, outdated, and unusable pesticides to special depots. In 1991, temporary depots were set up in three counties in southern Ontario to receive these pesticide wastes and in 1992, 26 depots were set up throughout Ontario. Over the two-year period, 960 farmers brought 33,500 kilograms of solid pesticides and 55,000 litres of liquid pesticides to these depots.[189]

In addition, the Ontario government, municipalities, farm groups, and the chemical industry jointly organized a pilot project in 1992 to collect and recycle empty, rinsed pesticide containers, thereby diverting them from landfills or from being buried or burned by farmers. During this pilot program over 33,000 plastic and metal containers were brought in by farmers.[190]

The MEE has recently developed protocols for handling pesticide incidents involving crop or vegetation damage and livestock or human health hazards. These protocols are designed to deal with incidents that result in (1) damage to crops or other vegetation owned by those using the chemicals or to the property of their neighbours, or (2) possible health effects to farm workers, bystanders, or livestock.[191]

Record Keeping, Inspections, and Enforcement

As with federal law, provincial pesticide legislation typically includes several interrelated elements for the purposes of ensuring compliance with legislated requirements. These include record keeping; inspection authority; and a variety of enforcement alternatives. Consideration of these and related instruments will be undertaken according to whether they are administrative, quasi-criminal, or civil in nature.

Administrative Mechanisms

Administrative mechanisms include both information-gathering and administrative enforcement techniques.

Record-Keeping and Reporting Requirements

Record-keeping and reporting requirements fall essentially into two categories under provincial law: information required from vendors or businesses, and information required from applicators of pesticides under permit or licence.

Under Ontario law, vendors must keep records of sales of pesticides on schedules 1, 2 or 5 for three years. This information must include the name and address of the purchaser; the type and class of licence or permit, if any, held by the purchaser; and a description of the pesticide sold, including the name, class, unit size, and quantity sold.[192] Vendors are also required to provide copies of these records to the MEE on written request[193] or to provincial officers during the course of inspections.[194] The Ontario requirements have been criticized because such sales records are not used for the calculation of provincial or regional pesticide totals.[195] Such information, in conjunction with use data, is frequently important for all aspects of a regulatory program, including enforcement. All aerial applicators of pesticides to land or water must keep records of each extermination for a period of at least one year after the extermination and produce the records on request from a provincial officer.[196]

Sales and use information from records is key to developing regulatory programs; yet reporting requirements are inadequate. Given the dearth of information nationally on pesticide usage, greater efforts appear to be necessary provincially to uniformly require annual reporting. Moreover, provincial agencies should be producing annual statistics on the type, quantity, and location of pesticides used. Although Ontario's survey of pesticide use is detailed, it does not cover non-agricultural uses of pesticides, some agricultural applications are not covered, and it comes out only twice a decade.[197] Moreover, because farmers are exempt from many permit and licence requirements, provincial surveys with respect to use, derived from licence-reporting requirements, will greatly underestimate total quantities applied and used in the province. Although sales records from vendors will cover sales to farmers as well, this information does not systematically provide needed data on where, when, and in what quantities farmers are applying pesticides in the province.

Inspection Authority

Inspectors may be designated under most provincial pesticide laws.[198] Persons responsible for pesticides are required to provide information to inspectors when necessary,[199] and not hinder, obstruct or give false information to inspectors who are lawfully performing their duties.[200] Inspectors also have broad powers to enter premises, examine materials, and require the production of documents.[201]

In Ontario in 1983, there were 600 Ministry of the Environment inspectors responsible for monitoring compliance with the four main provincial environmental statutes. Only 20, or 3 per cent of the total, were inspectors for purposes of the province's *Pesticides Act.*[202] Despite the increased use of pesticides over the intervening decade, there has been no corresponding increase in the ministry's inspection capability. In January 1993, there were 15 specially trained pesticide control officers stationed in the various regional and district offices throughout the province, as well as two former pesticides control officers assigned to the Investigations and Enforcement Branch, who carry out complex investigations.[203] Moreover, given the budgetary constraints on most provincial agencies, it is inevitable that the frequency of inspections will either stay relatively the same or decrease over time.

Minimal field inspection and follow-up of pesticide applications inevitably affects the level of prosecution and other enforcement activity, which in turn affects the extent of compliance with the law.

Control Orders, Stop Orders, and Other Administrative Enforcement Techniques

Ontario has a variety of administrative enforcement techniques available under pesticide legislation. These include stop orders and control orders, licence suspension or revocation, permit cancellation, and related mechanisms.

When a provincial official is of the opinion, on reasonable and probable grounds, that an emergency exists arising from a person's handling, storage, use, disposal, or transportation of a pesticide, the official may issue an oral or a written stop order to that person.[204] An emergency is defined to include situations in which there is a danger to human health or safety; or an immediate risk of environmental impairment, damage to plants, animals, or property or of rendering these items unfit for use by man.[205]

Similarly, control orders may be issued, but the circumstances do not need to constitute an emergency.[206] Control orders can require the person to limit the pesticide deposit rate; stop it permanently or temporarily; or comply with other directions.[207]

The grounds for licence suspension or revocation include: contravention of the *Pesticides Act* or regulations; breach of a licence term or condition; incompetence of the licensee; past conduct; lack of adequate equipment; evidence of gross negligence; or fraudulent misrepresentation by the licensee in carrying out his or her business.[208] The grounds for cancelling a permit are similar, but also include likely danger to health or likely harm to or impairment of the environment, material discomfort to persons, or danger to plants, animals, or property.[209]

Any of these administrative orders or actions can be appealed to the Environmental Appeal Board.[210] Other types of administrative orders include the ordering of environmental restoration, clean-up, and decontamination, when necessary.[211] Reclassification of pesticides into more restrictive use schedules is also an administrative enforcement technique that has already been noted (see "Pesticides Classification," above).

For many provincial officials, these and related administrative instruments constitute a fundamental component of pesticide regulation, far more so than prosecutions. But even among these administrative tools, provincial regulators have shown a preference for some types over others. An Ontario official indicated in 1983 that in the previous three years, only four stop orders and two control orders had been issued.[212] In contrast, at that time there were an average of 12 licence revocations per year. Licence revocation is regarded as a more effective technique because it essentially puts the applicator out of business.[213]

The provincial preference for administrative approaches parallels the preference that exists at the federal level. Moreover, this approach tends to coincide with a provincial view that pesticide regulation is a management strategy. As such, administrative approaches, in the view of some provincial officials, are better able to foster this management approach than more Draconian or cumbersome enforcement strategies such as prosecution.[214] However, to the extent that some administrative techniques have the ability to have a severe impact on pesticide users (for example, licence revocation), the provincial preference for such approaches may simply reflect a desire to stay out of the courts as much as possible. It may also reflect a desire not to ban a pesticide when a less drastic approach directed at the user will suffice to protect human health and the environment.

Quasi-Criminal and Related Mechanisms

All provincial pesticide laws establish prohibitions and standards of conduct the violation of which is an offence and may result in prosecution and the assessment of penalties. Although there has been substantially greater use of prosecution as an enforcement tool at the provincial level than at the federal level, the use of prosecution varies widely from province to province. Indeed, provincial officials have expressed some of the same ambivalence regarding the systematic use of quasi-criminal sanctions as was found at the federal level. The use of private prosecutions by citizens when, for whatever reasons, governments have not acted, has been a noticeable trend in recent years as well.

In addition, provincial coroner's investigations and inquests have been a useful tool to publicize improper use of pesticides and a source of recommendations for improved pesticide regulation. Inquests have involved instances in which pesticides have been implicated in poisoning deaths and have resulted in recommendations for the avoidance of harm in future.

Prohibitions, Offences, Penalties, and Prosecutions

Ontario law exemplifies the range of prohibitions that may be found under provincial pesticides legislation. Under the *Pesticides Act*, no person may harm or impair the quality of the environment, human health, plants, animals, or property through the improper use of pesticides.[215] Under the regulations, the use of products not registered under the *Pest Control Products Act* is prohibited,[216] as is the use of pesticides in a manner that is inconsistent with their labelling.[217] The Ontario provisions have the effect of complementing federal registration and labelling requirements.

Other prohibitions under provincial legislation may relate to selling pesticides that do not meet certain standards; using pesticides otherwise than as prescribed; applying pesticides to water bodies without permits; disposing of pesticides or containers except at prescribed sites and in the prescribed manner; carrying on a pesticide business without a licence or permit; and other matters.

Ontario's maximum fines for individuals who violate the *Pesticides Act* range from not more than $10,000 on a first conviction to not more than $25,000 on each subsequent conviction for every day an offence occurs or continues. Maximum fines for corporations may range between $50,000 and $100,000 and as high as $200,000 for certain offences as well as up to one-year's imprisonment.[218]

The reality, however, is that the actual fines assessed are usually far below the maximum. In 1991, the Ministry of the Environment averaged $5,580 per conviction in prosecutions under the *Pesticides Act*.[219]

Although Ontario has one of the more active prosecution records among the provinces,[220] Ontario officials also have suggested that if the number of prosecutions increased significantly, they would regard the province's system of pesticide regulation and management as failing.[221] That is, they believe they are achieving a high degree of compliance without the need to resort to prosecution, and thus prosecutions would be viewed as a symptom of greater non-compliance.

Some provincial responses to citizen complaints, however, suggest that the basis for charges being laid exists more frequently than the province is prepared to act. In 1982, for example, an Ontario farmer's cattle pasture was aerially sprayed by chemicals in addition to the adjacent field owned by Hostess Foods, which was the target of the spray program. Tests performed by the (former) provincial Ministry of the Environment confirmed the presence of Monitor, an insecticide, and Bravo, a fungicide, in the amount of 0.56 ppm and 2.8 ppm, respectively, on the farmer's property and 15 ppm and 53 ppm, respectively, on the Hostess potato field.[222] In correspondence to the farmer, the ministry stated:

> There is a significant difference between the levels found on your property and the levels detected on the Hostess potato crop. ... [T]his difference supports a situation involving spray drift rather than mis-application.[223]

The ministry concluded that the concentrations of pesticides in the samples taken from the farmer's pasture were not sufficient to be detrimental to livestock health or to interfere with the use of the pasture. Therefore, the ministry was "not in a position to successfully prosecute Hostess or the aerial company involved."[224] In a warning letter to the company, the ministry stated that the deposition of pesticides onto the farmer's property in any quantity was "not an acceptable practice," and outlined additional precautions to be taken.[225]

What is interesting, however, is that in the time between when the farmer first complained to the ministry and when the test samples were taken for analysis, a week had passed, during which a heavy rainfall had occurred.[226] Thus, it appears that the testing was neither timely nor accurate as to what the likely residues were at, or around, the time of the spray incident itself. Moreover, a third pesticide, Duter, which was no longer registered for use in Canada,[227] had also been sprayed, according to Hostess officials.[228] This appears to have been contrary to both federal and Ontario law. However, no analysis was performed by the ministry to confirm the level at which the pesticide was present,[229] or for use as a basis for prosecution. Indeed, for whatever reasons, the ministry had the samples destroyed before any analyses for Duter were performed.[230]

Events such as these have sometimes led citizens to use private prosecutions against applicators who misuse pesticides when a province has not done so.[231] Thus, there appears to be a potentially significant divergence of viewpoints between provincial governments and citizens' groups as to the use and effectiveness of the quasi-criminal sanction. This divergence of viewpoint could become quite significant to the extent that provincial officials gravitate toward administrative enforcement techniques in preference to prosecutions. Citizens cannot use administrative enforcement techniques, and to the extent that citizens' ability to prosecute were to be reduced by legislative changes, they could be deprived of a relatively inexpensive enforcement tool. Whatever their imperfections, private prosecutions give citizens an opportunity to enforce the law — an important element in a democratic society. Private prosecutions can also stimulate greater responsibility on the part of those who engage in spray activities. Loss or diminishment of this instrument can result only in greater reliance on administrative tools, which members of the public cannot employ.

The Use of Civil Courts by Administrative Agencies

A third enforcement approach that is available to administrative agencies that are charged with pesticide regulatory responsibilities is to use the civil courts to restrain violation of pesticide laws. When there is a contravention of the *Pesticides Act*, the minister can apply to the Ontario Court (General Division) for an order prohibiting the continuation or repetition of the contravention. This remedy is in addition to other remedies or penalties that may have been imposed.[232]

Provincial governments have rarely used such techniques in practice because of the availability of administrative remedies that have been discussed above. The civil court remedy is available only to the minister; no member of the public is authorized to use the provision in the absence of government action. The public can, of course, use the common law to the extent that has been discussed in Chapter 6. This would include the possibility of seeking an injunction if they have the requisite standing. However, provisions that allow members of the public to seek injunctions to prevent statutory violations whether or not they would meet traditional standing requirements have not generally been found in provincial pesticide legislation.

Pesticide Residue Testing

The Provincial Pesticide Residue Testing Laboratory at the University of Guelph provides analytical services to government ministries and agencies.

If you find dying or damaged plants, or animals dead from an unknown cause, and there is a possibility that the damage was caused by improper pesticide use, the laboratory may test samples to establish the cause. The laboratory will tell you the best way to send the sample and will tell you what other information may be required. Alternatively, the laboratory may refer inquiries to the appropriate government agency to investigate the matter or determine that the inquirer will have to pay for any testing using a private laboratory.

THE ROLE OF MUNICIPAL GOVERNMENTS

Municipalities have become involved in pesticide issues through their dual roles as both regulators and users of pesticides. These two roles may give an ambivalent character to the municipal approach to pesticide management.

Regulatory and Policy Activities

Municipalities, being creatures of provincial legislatures, derive their authority to address pesticide matters through provincial enabling legislation. In general, local governments can enact bylaws controlling nuisances, waste disposal, industrial use of sewers, and related matters that may have application to pesticides under legislation establishing municipal institutions in the province.[233] These powers have been limited by the courts in recent years and could not be used to frustrate either provincial or federal pesticide legislation.[234]

In general, however, municipalities have voiced their concern about their lack of control over the use of pesticides. In 1990, a city of Ottawa committee that reported to the municipal council expressed this concern and recommended that the province act quickly to strengthen the *Pesticides Act* or grant appropriate authority to the municipal level of government.[235]

Municipalities are more likely to take action under public health legislation, which delegates protection of public health to local boards of health. These boards often have broad investigatory powers and authority to address local health issues.[236] For example, in 1981, the Toronto Department of Public Health wrote to the federal minister of health and the provincial minister of the environment concerning the implications of the IBT affair. (For more on the IBT affair, see the discussion above, under the heading "Suspension and Cancellation of Pesticide Registrations: The Role of the Review Board.") The department questioned the fact that the governments had taken no action to ban or restrict the use of pesticides approved on the basis of fraudulent tests by IBT until their safety is proven.

Again, in relation to the IBT affair, in 1982 the Toronto Department of Health made a submission to the Consultative Committee on IBT Pesticides concerning Captan. Recommendations were made regarding access to information, public participation in the pesticide regulation-making process, and an endorsement of the original Health and Welfare Canada recommendations with respect to that fungicide.[237]

Recently, some municipalities have been taking an advocacy approach to health issues. For example, in 1981, the Toronto Board of Health wrote to Nova Scotia's minister of environment in relation to the spraying of 2,4-D and 2,4,5,-T in that province. The letter urged the government not to issue spray permits to Scott Maritimes Ltd. for the Nova Scotia mainland until a decision in the Cape Breton spray case had been reached.[238] It was further recommended that Nova Scotia ban the use of 2,4,5-T.[239]

The Toronto Board of Health also took action after the Cape Breton spray case decision came out in September 1983. It recommended that funds should be raised to help the plaintiffs meet their costs; that the principle of shifting the legal burden of proof to the manufacturer or user to demonstrate that a chemical does not pose a human health hazard be endorsed; and that public funds should be available to intervenors in environmental health cases.[240]

Municipal Use of Pesticides

The other role that municipalities have is that of users of pesticides. Historically, parks departments have used herbicides to rid city parks of weeds, and boards of education have used pesticides on school playgrounds. In addition, most provinces have some type of weed control legislation, which requires that certain noxious weeds be destroyed, that is administered at the municipal level.[241] Although the legislation usually prescribes a number of methods that can be employed to destroy these weeds, the use of herbicides is often the chosen method.

As a result of increasing public concern regarding the use of pesticides in the urban environment, some Ontario municipalities have moved to restrict, or indeed ban, their own use of such products. For example, in 1991 the city of Waterloo established a 19-member task force to address the future use of pesticides on all city-owned and private residential, commercial, industrial, and institutional lands in the city. The task force's mandate was to examine the impact of eliminating spraying on city-owned public lands and by the private sector, study other viable alternatives, and estimate cost implications. Waterloo also noted that over the past several years, the city has been reducing its use of pesticides on all of its 550 acres of land; that in 1990 about 90 per cent or 492 acres did not receive pesticide treatments; that under the city's plant health care program, pesticide use is regarded as a last resort and is used only as and when necessary; and that the program has developed several non-chemical (cultural) practices.[242] The city of Ottawa has also been active in exploring mechanisms for reducing pesticide use within its boundaries,[243] as have a number of other municipalities, boards of education, and parks and recreation departments across the province.[244]

Notwithstanding limited municipal jurisdiction with regard to the regulation of pesticides, it appears that municipal initiatives to self-restrict their own use are likely to expand in the coming years.

CONCLUSIONS

During the past two decades, there has been increasing concern over the environmental and human health effects posed by the widespread use of pesticides for food and fibre production. First, there has been a substantial increase in pesticides sales and use both in Canada and worldwide. Second, in conjunction with the increasing quantities sold and used, the public is concerned with the fact that the use of pesticides involves the deliberate application to land or water of chemicals that are poisonous to selected organisms.

Pesticides are regulated in Canada by both the federal and the provincial governments. Municipalities may also limit their own use of pesticides within their boundaries. At the federal level, reform of the *Pest Control Products Act* is long overdue. Unfortunately, the efforts of the multi-stakeholder review team appear to have been undermined and, as of April 1993, three years after the publication of the review team's final report, no legislative changes have been made. In Ontario, the province has embarked on a voluntary program of pesticide use reduction and has imposed some additional legislative restrictions on pesticide use, but has not imposed any mandatory use reductions or amended legislation to allow public involvement in licensing and permitting decisions. Involving the public more systematically in the pesticide decision-making process is necessary at both the federal and the provincial level.

Although legislative reform is necessary, it will not solve all the problems that result from pesticide use. Emphasis must be placed on developing programs that reduce pesticide use and that shift our focus to ecologically sound preventive approaches to pesticide management problems.

J.F. Castrilli and Toby Vigod

FURTHER READING

J.F. Castrilli and Toby Vigod, *Pesticides in Canada: An Examination of Federal Law and Policy* (Ottawa: Law Reform Commission of Canada, 1987).

Global Pesticide Campaigner (a periodical on international pesticide issues published by Pesticide Action Network, North American Regional Center, 965 Mission Street, #514, San Francisco, Calif. 94103).

Journal of Pesticide Reform (a periodical on pesticides issues published by Northwest Coalition for Alternatives to Pesticides, PO Box 1393, Eugene, Oregon 974400).

Pesticides and You (a newsletter published by the National Coalition Against the Misuse of Pesticides, 701 E Street, SE, Washington, DC 20003,202).

Carole Rubin, *How To Get Your Lawn and Garden Off Drugs: Pesticide-Free Gardening for a Healthier Environment* (Ottawa: Friends of the Earth, 1989). (This book is no longer available from Friends of the Earth, but may be obtained from Carole Rubin at RR 1, Mission Road, Sechelt, British Columbia V0N 3A0.)

ENDNOTES

1 This chapter is based, in part, on a study paper co-authored by the writers. See J.F. Castrilli and Toby Vigod, *Pesticides in Canada: An Examination of Federal Law and Policy* (Ottawa: Law Reform Commission of Canada, 1987).
2 Interview with Phil Blagdon, pesticides officer, Environment Canada, Environmental Protection Service, Ontario Region, Toronto, May 27, 1983, as reported in ibid.
3 Environment Canada, *The State of Canada's Environment* (Ottawa: Environment Canada, 1992), 9-22.
4 United States, General Accounting Office, *Better Regulation of Pesticide Exports and Pesticide Residues in Imported Food Is Essential*, Report to Congress by the Comptroller General of the United States, CED-79-43 (Washington, DC: US GAO, June 1979), 87.
5 One of the more comprehensive provincial surveys is the Ontario survey of pesticide use, which was begun in 1973. See, for example, Ontario, Ministry of Agriculture and Food, *Survey of Pesticide Use in Ontario*, 1988 (Toronto: OMAF, 1989). However, it comes out only once every five years. Statistics Canada's annual pesticide sales surveys were discontinued in 1977. However, Agriculture Canada's annual farm census provides some statistics on amounts and kinds of pesticides used.
6 United Nations Environment Programme, *The State of the Environment, 1979* (Nairobi: UNEP, 1979), 10.
7 P.A. Pearce, D.B. Peakall, and A.J. Erskine, "Impact on Forest Birds of the 1975 Spruce Budworm Spray Operation in New Brunswick" (March 1976), 62 *Biology Notes* 1-3. See also Douglas J. Forsyth, "Evaluation of Pesticides by the Canadian Wildlife Service," in *Proceedings of the Canadian Council of Resource and Environment Ministers Workshop on Pesticide Use in Canada* (Ottawa: CCREM, 1982), 97.

8   World Wildlife Fund (Canada), "Action Alert: Burrowing Owl at Risk" (circa March 1993).

9   Ibid.

10 Paul McLoughlin, "Poisoning Mentioned by 1 in 10," *Western Producer*, January 26, 1984, 1. For other examples of pesticide poisoning of workers in Canada, see Linda R. Pim, *The Invisible Additives* (Toronto: Doubleday, 1981), 209-12.

11 Environment Canada and Ontario, Ministry of the Environment, *Pollution of the St. Clair River (Sarnia Area)*, situation report prepared under the Canada-Ontario agreement respecting Great Lakes water quality) (Toronto: Queen's Printer, November 1985), 5.

12 Agriculture Canada, *Groundwater Quality Survey, Winter 1991/92* (Ottawa: Agriculture Canada, September 1992), 7-10 and 25. See also Burton C. Kross et al., "Pesticide Contamination of Private Well Water: A Growing Rural Health Concern" (1992), 18 *Environment International* 231-41.

13 World Commission on Environment and Development, *Our Common Future* (Oxford: Oxford University Press, 1987), 126.

14 Ibid., at 135.

15 *Pest Control Products Act*, RSC 1985, c. P-9.

16 *Food and Drugs Act*, RSC 1985, c. F-27.

17 *Pesticides Act*, RSO 1990, c. P.11.

18 *Environmental Assessment Act*, RSO 1990, c. E.18.

19 *Pest Control Products Act*, supra endnote 15.

20 Agriculture Canada Pesticides Directorate, *Review Paper—Pesticides Registration in Canada* (Ottawa: Agriculture Canada, February 1989), 2 and 19.

21 *Pest Control Products Act*, supra endnote 15, section 11(1).

22 Ibid., section 11(3).

23 Pest Control Products Regulations, CRC 1978, c. 1253 (hereinafter "PCP regulations"), section 18(b).

24 See *Pulp, Paper & Woodworkers of Canada, Local 8 v. Canada (Minister of Agriculture)* (1991), 8 CELR 55 (FCTD). In this case, the registration of Busan 30WP, an anti-sapstain product used in the lumber industry, was quashed. The minister had relied on the prior registration of control products containing a common ingredient; however, the information was insufficient to enable those products to be assessed or evaluated in accordance with the standards prevailing at the time of the Busan 30WP application for registration. There had been about 100 complaints by union members that they suffered adverse health effects when using the pesticide. Before the application was heard, the union's employer discontinued the use of the pesticide.

25 Correspondence between Carole Rubin, BC Coalition for Alternatives to Pesticides, and Frank Cedar, Director Pesticides Information Division, Agriculture Canada, September 22, October 2, and October 10, 1990.

26 PCP regulations, supra endnote 23, section 18(c).

27 Alachlor Review Board Hearings, Toronto, November 1986, exhibit 155, 6.

28 *Federal Insecticide, Fungicide and Rodenticide Act*, 7 USC, c. 136 (1978).

29 Ibid., section 2(bb).

30 See, for example, United States, Senate and House of Representatives, *Risk-Benefit Analysis in the Legislative Process: Summary of a Congress-Science Joint Forum*,

prepared by the Congressional Research Service, Library of Congress, 96th Cong., 2d Sess. (March 1980), 3-6. Similar problems have been identified with respect to cost-benefit analysis. United States, House of Representatives, *Cost-Benefit Analysis: Wonder Tool or Mirage*, Report together with Minority View by the Subcommittee on Oversight and Investigations of the Committee on Interstate and Foreign Commerce, 96th Cong., 2d Sess. (December 1980), 1-36.

31 CAPCO Note 89-06, "Dinoseb — Update," and CAPCO Note 90-01, "Dinoseb — Regulatory Position."

32 *An Act To Implement the Free Trade Agreement Between Canada and the United States*, SC 1988, c. 65.

33 United States, House of Representatives, Committee on Agriculture, *EPA Pesticide Regulatory Program Study*, Hearing before the Subcommittee on Department Operations, Research, and Foreign Agriculture, 97th Cong., 2d Sess. (December 17, 1982), 87.

34 *Pesticides Registration in Canada*, supra endnote 20, at 12.

35 In a telephone interview on March 5, 1993, Tom Davis of the Pesticides Directorate explained that as a result of changing from one-year temporary registrations to registration of each product or new use of a product for periods of more than a year, it is no longer easy to determine how many temporary permits are issued each year. Moreover, the numbers provided may underrepresent the actual number of permits since permits automatically expire at the end of the last year of the period for which they were issued and may not be renewed until the spring, when sales begin. Thus, early in the new year, the number of temporary permits may be considerably lower than in April or May when these permits are renewed.

36 Canada, Auditor General, *Report to the House of Commons*, Fiscal Year Ended March 31, 1988 (Ottawa: Supply and Services, 1989), paragraph 8.55.

37 *Monsanto Canada Ltd. v. Canada (Minister of Agriculture)* (1986), 1 FTR 63, 8 CPR (3d) 517 (FCTD).

38 Liora Salter and William Leiss, *Consultation in the Assessment and Registration of Pesticides: Final Report and Recommendations to the Minister of Agriculture* (Ottawa: Agriculture Canada, March 31, 1984), 10.

39 *Willis v. F.M.C. Machinery & Chemicals Ltd.* (1976), 68 DLR (3d) 127 (PEISC).

40 Correspondence from the Canadian Coalition for Alternatives to Pesticides to the Honourable John Wise, Minister of Agriculture, Ottawa, May 25, 1988.

41 PCP regulations, SOR/88-285. The amended section 17(1)(a) provides that "the applicant agrees to endeavour to produce additional scientific or technical information in relation to the control product." The former section 17(1)(a) had read "in relation to the use for which the control product is to be sold."

42 United States, General Accounting Office, *Stronger Enforcement Needed Against Misuse of Pesticides*, Report to Congress by the Comptroller General of the United States, CED-82-5 (Washington, DC: US GAO, October 1981), 31.

43 Mary O'Brien, "Safe Haven for Pesticide Toxins: List 3 Inerts" (Winter 1990), *Journal of Pesticide Reform* 7.

44 Inert Ingredients in Pesticide Products; Policy Statement, *Federal Register*, vol. 52, no. 77, 13305-9, April 22, 1987 and Revision and Modification of Lists, *Federal Register*, vol. 54, no. 224, 48314-16, November 22, 1989. See also Pesticide Registration

Review Secretariat, *Draft — Information on Inerts* (Ottawa: Agriculture Canada, February 12, 1990).

45 *Access to Information Act*, RSC 1985, c. A-1.

46 Pesticide Registration Review Secretariat, *Draft — Information on the Issue of Reevaluation* (Ottawa: January 3, 1990), 3.

47 *Pesticides Registration in Canada*, supra endnote 20, at 19.

48 These included Leptophos, Phosphamidon, and Alachlor.

49 Len Ritter, Alachlor Review Board, Temporary Hearing, Transcript, T. vol. 3, 611.

50 *Monsanto Canada Inc. v. Canada (Minister of Agriculture)* (1988), 83 NR 279, 20 CPR (3d) 193 (FCA).

51 J.J. Lambers, state secretary, Health and Environmental Protection, The Netherlands, opening speech at the Fourteenth Session of the Codex Committee on Pesticides Residues, *Report*, The Hague, June 14-21, 1982, ALINORM 38124A (Rome: Codex Alimentarius Commission, 1983),59. See also David Weir and Mark Shapiro, *Circle of Poison: Pesticides and People in a Hungry World* (San Francisco: Institute for Food and Development Policy, 1981).

52 *Canadian Environmental Protection Act*, RSC 1985, c. 16 (4th Supp.).

53 Ibid., section 41.

54 *Pest Control Products Act*, supra endnote 15, section 11(2).

55 *Criminal Code*, RSC 1985, c. C-46, as amended.

56 *Fisheries Act*, RSC 1985, c. F-14.

57 Interview with Jim Reid, Compliance Section, Pesticides Division, Agriculture Canada, Ottawa, June 30, 1983, as reported in *Pesticides in Canada: An Examination of Federal Law and Policy*, supra endnote 1.

58 Milligan and Company, Inc., *A Review of Enforcement and Compliance Arrangements for Federal Pesticides Regulation*; a report prepared for the Pesticide Registration Review team (Ottawa: Agriculture Canada, March 1990), 49.

59 Statistics provided by J.P. Brown, general manager, Food Production and Inspection Branch, Agriculture Canada, December 15, 1992.

60 J.E. Hollebone, director, Issues, Planning and Priorities, Agriculture Canada, March 1993.

61 Correspondence from RCMP Customs and Excise Section, Vancouver to Canadian Environmental Law Association, June 18, 1990.

62 *Food and Drugs Act*, supra endnote 16.

63 Food and Drugs Regulations, CRC 1978, c. 870, part B, division 15, table 11.

64 Ibid., B. 15.002(1).

65 P.R. Bennett, "Outline of Pesticide Data Evaluation by the Food Directorate, Health and Welfare Canada," in *Proceedings of the Canadian Council of Resource and Environment Ministers Workshop on Pesticide Use in Canada*, supra endnote 7, at 92.

66 Pim, supra endnote 10, at 39.

67 Scott R. McKercher and Frederick W. Plapp Jr., "Pesticide Regulation: Measuring the Residue" (September 1980), vol. 22, no. 7 *Environment* 8.

68 Information received by John Swaigen from Anne Marie St. Laurent, Health and Welfare Canada, April 2, 1993. Ms St. Laurent also indicated that the information was not compiled in one central location, but was used in several district or regional offices.

69 Agriculture Canada, "Pesticide Registration Review Appointments," Ottawa: Agriculture Canada, March 21, 1989.

70 Pesticide Registration Review, *A Proposal for a Revised Federal Pest Management Regulatory System* (Ottawa: Agriculture Canada, July 1990).

71 Pesticide Registration Review, *Recommendations for a Revised Federal Pest Management Regulatory System* (Ottawa: Agriculture Canada, December 1990). The labour representative was the only one to dissent from the report.

72 Pest Management Secretariat, *Federal Response to the Report of the Pesticide Registration Review* (Ottawa: Agriculture Canada, February 24, 1992).

73 Canada, *News Release*, "Federal Pesticide Regulation System Revised," February 3, 1992.

74 Milligan and Company Inc., supra endnote 58, at 7, 21, and 23.

75 The final report of the Pesticide Registration Review team states:

> The recommended pest management regulatory system described in Capter 2 was developed through extensive discussions and negotiations among stakeholders and therefore represents a delicate balance of divergent view points. All components of the system are interdependent and form a complete package that needs to be implemented in its entirety.

Pesticide Registration Review, supra endnote 71, at 49.

The product import program is set out in "Pest Control Products Regulations — Amendment, Regulatory Impact Analysis Statement," *Canada Gazette Part II*, May 1, 1993, 1403.

The User Requested Minor Use Registration pilot project is outlined in CAPCO Note, *Status Report on the Implementation of the User Requested Minor Use Registration (URMUR) Working Group*.

76 *Pesticides Act*, supra endnote 17.

77 Ibid., section 4.

78 "General — Pesticides," RRO 1990, reg. 914, section 21 and *Pesticides Act*, supra endnote 17, sections 1-6.

79 *Pesticides Act*, supra endnote 17, sections 5-7.

80 Ibid., section 22(1).

81 Ibid., section 21 and schedules 1-6. See also, Ontario Ministry of the Environment, Pesticides Advisory Committee, *Ontario Guidelines for Classification of Pesticide Products* (Toronto: the ministry, May 1990).

82 *Pesticides Act*, supra endnote 17, section 22 (2). See also *Ontario Guidelines for Classification of Pesticide Products*, supra endnote 81.

83 *Pesticides Act*, supra endnote 17, section 10 and reg. 914, supra endnote 78, sections 2 and 3.

84 *Ontario Guidelines for Classification of Pesticide Products*, supra endnote 81, at 13-15.

85 The Saskatchewan government noted as follows in a 1982 position paper on the fungicide Captan:

> The Minister of Agriculture Canada has conceded in correspondence with Saskatchewan Environment that many ingredients of pesticides which are not deemed to be active ingredients at law are nonetheless capable of biological activity.

Saskatchewan, *Submissions to the Consultative Committee on IBT Pesticides*, prepared for the Toronto Public Meeting, March 10-12, 1982 (Regina: Government of Saskatchewan, 1982), 23.

86   *Ontario Guidelines for Classification of Pesticide Products*, supra endnote 81, at 7 and 11.

87   Reg. 914, supra endnote 78, sections 94 and 95.

88   *Ontario Guidelines for Classification of Pesticide Products*, supra endnote 81, at 11.

89   Ibid., at 4.

90   Interview with John Onderdonk, director, Pesticides Control, Ontario Ministry of the Environment, July 27, 1983.

91   *Ontario Guidelines for Classification of Pesticide Products*, supra endnote 81, at 9.

92   See, for example, Health and Welfare Canada, *News Release*, "Current Status of IBT Pesticides," November 2, 1982, 2; and Agriculture Canada, Consultative Committee on IBT Pesticides, *Facts on Captan*. (Ottawa: Agriculture Canada, January 1982), 2.

93   Whether Captan is on schedule 3 and therefore available for domestic use or on schedule 2, where it is not, depends on the concentration. It is on schedule 3 only in the lower concentrations.

94   Health and Welfare Canada and Environment Canada, *Report of the Ministers' Expert Advisory Committee on Dioxins* (Ottawa: Supply and Services, November 1983). The report notes for example, that the isomer 2,3,7,8-T_4CDD is "carcinogenic in rats and mice." Ibid., at 16. However, the report noted that although data on workers suggested an association between cancer and occupational exposure to substance containing dioxins, the presence of "concomitant chemicals prevents concluding that the increased cancer risk was actually due to the dioxins themselves." Ibid., at 17.

95   *Pesticides Act*, supra endnote 17, section 6; reg. 941, supra endnote 78, sections 106-114.

96   *Pesticides Act*, supra endnote 17, section 5(2); reg. 914, supra endnote 78, sections 106-114.

97   *Pesticides Act*, supra endnote 17, section 5(1).

98   Reg. 914, supra endnote 78, sections 30 and 31.

99   Ibid., section 63.

100 Ibid., section 102.

101 Ibid. Under the regulations 6 classes of structural exterminator licence are established (section 30); 10 land classes (section 63); and 3 water classes (section 102).

102 Ibid., sections 56-59, 92-95, and 104.

103 *Pesticides Act*, supra endnote 17, section 7.

104 Reg. 914, supra endnote 78, section 32 (structural); section 81 (land).

105 Ibid., section 88.

106 Ibid., section 104.

107 Ibid., section 105.

108 Ibid., sections 44, 45, 104, and 105.

109 Ibid., sections 5-19.

110 D. Waugh, Nova Scotia Department of the Environment, "Monitoring Use and Effect of Pesticides," in *Proceedings of the Canadian Council of Resource and Environment Ministers Workshop on Pesticides Use in Canada*, supra endnote 7, at 127-32.

111 Information received from Clytie Hope, Approvals Branch, Ontario Ministry of the Environment, January 23, 1993. These numbers included 1,809 operators, 2,576 structural exterminators, 21,130 land exterminators, 367 water exterminators, and 3,480 vendors.

112 Onderdonk, supra endnote 90.

113 Ontario, Ministry of the Environment, Hazardous Contaminants Branch, "Table: Summary of Pesticide Permits issued from 1989-1991," Toronto, 1991.

114 See, for example, *Pesticides Act*, supra endnote 17, section 11(2).

115 Ibid.

116 Ibid., section 11(3).

117 Onderdonk, supra endnote 90, stated in 1983 that in Ontario, it was estimated in 1983 that about 10 licences a year were being refused, suspended, or revoked. However, in 1993, no estimate was possible because, as Wanda Michalowicz advised, the branch responsible for issuing these licences keeps no records of the number of refusals, suspensions, and revocations.

118 *Pesticides Act*, supra endnote 17, sections 13(1)-(6).

119 Ibid., sections 13(8)-(10).

120 In Ontario, the appeal board mentioned under the *Pesticides Act*, supra endnote 17, is the Environmental Appeal Board established under the *Environmental Protection Act*, RSO 1990, c. E.19.

121 *Pesticides Act*, supra endnote 17, section 13.

122 Ibid., section 14(1).

123 *Pesticide Control Act*, RSBC 1979, c. 322, section 15(1).

124 Forty appeals to the BC Environmental Appeal Board were filed between April 1, 1981 and March 31, 1982: British Columbia, Ministry of the Environment, *Annual Report —1981/82*. (Victoria, BC: the ministry, 1982), 109. Eleven groups and one individual challenged 10 pesticide-use permits and one pest control service licence: British Columbia Environmental Appeal Board, *Annual Report 1991-92*.

125 See, for example, *Lewis and Warnock v. Pesticide Control Appeal Board and the Queen* (1979), 8 CELR 1 (BCSC). Following a citizen appeal against permits issued for herbicide application to lakes to control Eurasian Milfoil, the board found that four permits would have adverse environmental effects. The court held with respect to five other permit appeals that the board had improperly delegated its decision-making powers back to the provincial administrator whose original decision authorizing the permits had been the reason for the citizen application for judicial review.

126 Of 40 appeals against permits filed between April 1, 1981 and March 31, 1982, none was upheld by the board. British Columbia, Ministry of the Environment, *Annual Report*, supra endnote 124, at 53.

127 *Canadian Earthcare Society v. Environmental Appeal Board* (1988), 3 CELR (NS) 45 (BCCA); and *Islands Protection Society v. Environmental Appeal Board* (1988), 3 CELR (NS) 185 (BCSC).

128 Anne Roberts, "Puzzling Pesticide Permits," *The Globe and Mail*, June 12, 1982. See also British Columbia, Legislative Assembly, *Debates*, August 18, 1977, 4740-41 (comments of the W. Nielson, minister of the environment).

129 British Columbia Environmental Appeal Board, supra endnote 124, at 6-7 and 13-16.

130   Harry Parrott, the Ontario environment minister in 1980, noted:

> [F]irst … applications cannot be released prior to the fulfilling of [the pesticides
> director's] statutory duty of issuing or refusing to issue permits. Secondly, … information
> on the permit and application is given in confidence and, therefore, the applicant's consent
> is needed prior to release of permits or permit applications. …
>
>   [P]ermits issued under the Pesticides Act cover a variety of exterminations in both the
> public and private sector … [I]n considering the release of permits or permit applications …
>
>   [Statements in the first paragraph] relate to the former category. … [S]tatistics on
> pesticides, quantities and uses pertaining to such permits are compiled regularly and are
> available on request.
>
>   Information concerning permits issued to government Ministries and municipalities
> is readily available. This information includes applicant names, pesticides applied,
> methods and areas of application and pests to be controlled.

Correspondence to Toby Vigod, counsel, Canadian Environmental law Association
from Harry Parrott, Ontario minister of the environment, June 13, 1980.
      More than a decade later, the situation remains largely the same. In an interview with
John Swaigen on January 26, 1993, Wanda Michalowicz of the Hazardous Contaminants Branch of the Ministry of the Environment confirmed that the ministry still does
not provide copies of permits or permit applications to the general public. Such
information might be accessible under the *Freedom of Information and Protection of
Privacy Act*, RSO 1990, c. F.31.

131   According to a report focusing on aerial spraying, "aerial spray applications can not
only produce extensive drift, but also have a high potential of contaminating fishery
and wildlife sensitive habitat." See "Risk Assessment: A Rational Approach to the
Management of New Brunswick's Spruce Budworm Enigma" (1982), 11 CELR 109.
About 4 million acres of New Brunswick forest are sprayed annually, with almost 99
per cent of the treatment done with chemicals. Testimony of J.W. Ker, former dean,
Faculty of Forestry, University of New Brunswick, House of Commons Standing
Committee on Fisheries and Forestry, *Proceedings*, no. 85 (June 7, 1983), 12.

132   For example, see *Lewis*, supra endnote 125.

133   Reg. 914, supra endnote 78, section 88(1).

134   Ibid., section 88(3).

135   Ibid., section 91 and form 6.

136   In Nova Scotia, for example, the question of the forestry use of pest control products,
including application methods, was placed before a royal commission on forestry. See
Waugh, supra endnote 110.

137   *Environmental Assessment Act*, supra endnote 18.

138   *Re Proposed Class Environmental Assessment by the Ministry of Natural Resource for
Timber Management on Crown Lands in Ontario* (1989), 4 CELR (NS) 50 (EAB).

139   Report of the Ontario Task Force on Health and Safety in Agriculture, submitted to the
ministers of agriculture and food and labour on October 29, 1985, chapter 5 and
appendix 6.

140   Reg. 914, supra endnote 78, sections 94(2) and (4).

141   Ibid., section 94(4).

142 Vilma Vinski, Ontario Ministry of Environment and Energy to John Swaigen, April 2, 1993. When certification was introduced, the ministry stated in a press release: "It is anticipated that the Growers' Certification course, which has been voluntary, will be made mandatory." Ontario, Ministry of the Environment, *News Release*, "Ontario Tightens Controls on Use of Pesticides," February 25, 1991.

143 Reg. 914, supra endnote 78, section 95(1). There is no such licensing exemption for farmers for aerial spraying of neighbours' lands, however: section 95(2).

144 Ibid., section 58(2).

145 Ibid., section 82(2).

146 Ibid., sections 104 and 105.

147 Ibid., section 65(3)(c).

148 Onderdonk, supra endnote 90.

149 Interview with D. Wilson, director, Pesticides Control Branch, Ontario Ministry of the Environment, May 28, 1976 in J.F. Castrilli, *Control of Water Pollution from Land Use Activities in the Canadian Great Lakes Basin: An Evaluation of Legislative, Regulatory and Administrative Programs* (Windsor, Ont.: International Joint Commission and Pollution from Land Use Activities Reference Group, 1977), 127.

150 Ontario, Ministry of Agriculture and Food, *Survey of Pesticides in Ontario 1983* (Toronto: the ministry, 1983). These annual totals do not include pesticides used in greenhouses, nurseries, and mushroom growing or in barns and other outbuildings.

151 Jacqueline Moxley, *Survey of Pesticide Use in Ontario, 1988*, Economics Information Report no. 89-08 (Toronto: Ministry of Agriculture and Food, July 1989), 7.

152 Wanda Michalowicz, Ministry of Environment and Energy, April 1993.

153 During questioning in the BC Legislative Assembly in 1982 by Mrs. Wallace, MLA, Stephen Rogers, environment minister, noted in part:

> I'm getting pressured by a number of people to say that everybody who uses pesticides in the province should have to go to the same hearing and I wonder what your position would be if the farmers also have to submit to the Pesticide Control Appeal Board [now the Environmental Management Board]. ... [W]e have a double standard. If it's in the forest and if it's on the railroads and on the Hydro rights-of-way, we submit the whole thing to an appeal, and yet if it's on agricultural land or in private use. ... The biggest misuse happens with the private user, the agriculturalist. In fact, the cost of the pesticides or the herbicides they're using are so prohibitive that they're not going to waste any. But there are people ... who think that if one ounce per gallon is good, two ounces will kill them twice as dead, and this is not very good.

British Columbia, Legislative Assembly, *Debates*, June 30, 1982, 8550.

154 A 1982 New Brunswick report noted in part:

> • "Investigations carried out by the New Brunswick Department of the Environment in 1975 indicated that there were environmental problems associated with pesticide use practices being carried out by New Brunswick farmers. More specifically, farmers were involved with careless sprayer filling procedures and improper pesticide container disposal, which posed a potential environmental hazard to aquatic systems." New Brunswick, Department of the Environment, *A Survey of Pesticide Use Practices in a*

Small Agricultural Watershed of New Brunswick (Fredericton, NB: the department, February 1982), 2.

The report also said:

• "[I]ncidents of New Brunswick farmers spraying pesticides in high wind conditions have often been reported to the Department in the past" (at 6).

• "The survey ... showed that few farmers used proper personal protective equipment because it was too inconvenient, hot, or unimportant. This clearly showed that farmers were directly ignoring label information" (at 8).

• "[T]he survey results indicate that a large majority of farmers are disregarding ... label information which is a direct contravention of the Federal *Pest Control Products Act*. Since 1963, many cases of environmental damage (i.e. fish kills) resulting from agricultural pesticide misuse have been reported to and documented by federal fisheries officers" (at 9).

• "The recent survey [summer 1981] provides clear evidence that individual applications of agriculture pesticides on private land and subsequent container disposal practices are not subject to effective regulatory action at the present time."

Misuse of pesticides by farmers is also documented in the Report of the Ontario Task Force on Health and Safety in Agriculture, supra endnote 139. Several other studies are cited in that report.

155   According to the 1991 census, there were 68,633 active farms in Ontario in 1991, down from 72,713 recorded in the 1986 census: Ontario, Ministry of Agriculture and Food, *Agricultural Statistics for Ontario*. According to the Ministry of Environment and Energy, there are 45,000 farms in Ontario where pesticides are used and in early 1993, 41,000 farmers had been certified: Wanda Michalowicz, March 1993.

156   Onderdonk, supra endnote 90.

157   Ibid. See also the Report of the Ontario Task Force on Health and Safety in Agriculture, supra endnote 139.

158   *A Survey of Pesticide Use Practices in a Small Agricultural Watershed of New Brunswick*, supra endnote 154.

159   Ontario, Ministry of Agriculture and Food, *Annual Report*, 1987-1988.

160   Ontario, Ministry of Agriculture and Food. *Food Systems 2002: A Program To Reduce Pesticides in Food Production* (Toronto: OMAF, 1989).

161   Ontario, Ministry of Agriculture and Food, supra endnotes 159 and 160.

162   Information received by John Swaigen from Wayne Roberts, Ontario Ministry of Agriculture and Food.

163   Land Extermination Notification, reg. 914, supra endnote 78, sections 64-79 as amended by O. reg. 500/92.

164   Ibid., sections 69, 71, 76.

165   Ibid., section 71(3).

166   Ibid., section 72(1).

167   Ibid., section 76.

168   Ibid., section 107.

169   Ibid., section 126.

170   Ibid., section 127.

171 Ibid., section 128.
172 "General — Waste Management," RRO 1990, reg. 347.
173 Blagdon, supra endnote 2.
174 Information obtained from Dennis Tolson, Waste Management Branch, Ministry of the Environment. This information comes from records of waste hauled using manifests as required by the province's waste management regulation. Under that regulation, wastes are given classification numbers. The only classification referring specifically to pesticides is halogenated pesticides and herbicides. However, it is possible that some pesticides are also included in waste under other classifications. According to Mr. Tolson, the 2,870 tonnes includes some double accounting, since wastes that are taken to a transfer station before disposal are counted once on the way to the transfer station and once on the way from the transfer station to the disposal facility. This amount may also be greater than the amount of pesticide waste generated in Ontario since it may include material hauled from the United States.
175 *Transportation of Dangerous Goods Act*, RSC 1985, c. T-19.
176 Reg. 914, supra endnote 78, section 119, as amended by O. reg 27/91, section 23.
177 Ibid., section 122, as amended by O. reg. 27/91.
178 Ibid., section 124.
179 Ibid., section 122(2), as amended by O. reg. 27/91.
180 Ibid.
181 *Pesticides Act*, supra endnote 17, section 29.
182 Ibid., section 30.
183 Reg. 914, supra endnote 78, section 27(2).
184 Ibid., section 27(1)(a).
185 Ibid., section 27 (1)(b).
186 Report of the Ontario Task Force on Health and Safety in Agriculture, supra endnote 139, at 116.
187 Blagdon, supra endnote 2.
188 Karen Benzing and Cyndi Obee, "Water, Waste and Uniroyal" (December 1982), vol. 5, no. 4 *Probe Post* 12. *Re Uniroyal Chemical Ltd.* (1992), 9 CELR (NS) 85 (Env. App. Bd.); *Re Uniroyal Chemical Ltd.* (1992), 9 CELR (NS) 151 (Env. App. Bd.).
189 Ontario, Ministry of the Environment, Hazardous Contaminants Branch, "Waste Agricultural Pesticides Pilot Collection Program," April 1992; Ontario, Ministry of the Environment, "Waste Agricultural Pesticides Collection Program, 1992 Summary" [undated].
190 Ontario, Ministry of the Environment, "Pesticide Container Pilot Project, 1992 Summary" [undated].
191 Ontario, Ministry of the Environment, *Protocol for Handling Pesticide Incidents Involving Crop or Vegetation Damage and Livestock or Human Health Hazards* (Toronto: the ministry, October 1988).
192 Reg. 914, supra endnote 78, section 94.
193 Ibid., section 118(3).
194 Ibid., section 118(4).
195 Blagdon, supra endnote 2.
196 Reg. 914, supra endnote 78, section 94.

197 Ontario, Ministry of Agriculture and Food, *Survey of Pesticide Use in Ontario, 1988*, Report no. 89-08 (Toronto: OMAF, July 1989).

198 For example, see *Pesticides Act*, supra endnote 17, section 17(1).

199 Ibid., section 17(4).

200 Ibid., section 17(5).

201 Ibid., section 19.

202 Onderdonk, supra endnote 90.

203 Information received from Wanda Michalowicz, January 26, 1993.

204 *Pesticides Act*, supra endnote 17, section 27.

205 Ibid., sections 27(1)(a)-(d).

206 Ibid., section 28.

207 Ibid., sections 28(2)(a)-(c).

208 Ibid., section 11(2).

209 Ibid., section 11(3).

210 Ibid., sections 27(2)-(6) and 28(3). Stop orders under the *Environmental Protection Act* (supra endnote 120), however, have been quashed by individuals bypassing the administrative tribunal and going directly to a superior court to obtain relief. For example, see *Re Canada Metal Company Limited* and *MacFarlane* (1973), 1 OR (2d) 577, 41 DLR (3d) 161 (HCJ).

211 Ibid., section 30.

212 Onderdonk, supra endnote 90. All of these have been verbal stop orders, as allowed by the *Pesticides Act*, because pesticides, being toxic by design, require rapid action if imminent environmental impairment or occupational or bystander harm from exposure is to be prevented.

213 Ibid.

214 Ibid.

215 *Pesticides Act*, supra endnote 17, section 4.

216 Reg. 914, supra endnote 78, section 22(1).

217 Ibid., section 22(2).

218 *Pesticies Act*, supra endnote 17, section 42.

219 Ontario, Ministry of the Environment, *Offences Against the Environment: Environmental Convictions in Ontario* (Toronto: the ministry, 1991). A total of $100,450 was assessed in fines for an average of $5,580 assessed per conviction. The largest fine was for $27,000; the smallest for $100.

220 Ibid. During this period, the ministry obtained 18 convictions.

221 Onderdonk, supra endnote 90.

222 Correspondence to R. Brewster, Wyevale, Ontario from W.J. Cowie, district pesticides officer, Ontario Ministry of the Environment, September 27, 1982.

223 Ibid.

224 Ibid.

225 Correspondence to F. Brox, director of farm operations, Hostess Food Products from W.J. Cowie, District Pesticides Officer, Ontario Ministry of the Environment, September 27, 1982.

226 CTV-W-5, *Transcript*, edition 551, October 23, 1983, 3.

227 Ibid., at 37. See also correspondence to Janis Tufford, CTV-W-5 from James B. Reid, associate director, Compliance Section, Pesticides Division, Agriculture Canada, October 20, 1983; Kevin Cox, "Banned Chemical Urged for Crops," *The Globe and Mail*, November 5, 1983; and correspondence to Eugene Whelan, minister of agriculture, from Vic Althouse, MP, October 24, 1983.

228 F. Brox, supra endnote 225, at 4.

229 CTV-W-5, supra endnote 226, at 4 and 8.

230 Ibid.

231 In May 1983, for example, in British Columbia the Central Okanagan Regional District (CORD) was convicted and given a six-months' probationary sentence during which time it must comply with the terms of any pesticide use permit granted it or be fined $1,000 and be liable for further prosecution for breach of probation. The CORD had been convicted for unlawfully applying a pesticide within 300 metres of fish-bearing waters. The charges were laid by local residents and the case conducted as a private prosecution after BC Environment Ministry officials did not pursue charges. "CORD Pleads Guilty to Lone Spraying Charge," *Kelowna Daily*, May 19, 1983.

232 *Pesticides Act*, supra endnote 17, section 52.

233 See, generally, the *Municipal Act*, RSO 1990, c. M.45.

234 See *Cox Construction Ltd. v. Township of Puslinch* (1982), 36 OR (2d) 618; *A. G. Ont. v. Mississauga* (1981), 10 CELR 91 (Ont. CA).

235 City of Ottawa, Department of Engineering and Works, June 14, 1990, 2.

236 See, for example, the *Health Protection and Promotion Act*, RSO 1990, c. H.7.

237 Linda Rosenbaum and Doug Saunders, Health Advocacy Unit, Toronto Department of Public Health, *Submissions on Captan to the Consultative Committee on IBT Pesticides* (Toronto: TDPH, February 1982), 22-23.

238 Residents of Cape Breton were seeking an injunction to stop spraying of these pesticides in that area of Nova Scotia. They were ultimately unsuccessful in convincing the court of the danger. See *Palmer v. Nova Scotia Forest Industries* (1983), 60 NSR (2d) 271 (SCTD); *Palmer v. Stora Kopparbergs Aktiebolag* (1985), 12 CELR (NSSC).

239 Correspondence from Anne Johnston, chairman of the Toronto Local Board of Health to J. Greg Kerr, Nova Scotia minister of the environment, July 21, 1983, 2. See also "Toronto Health Board Opposes Herbicide Spray Permit in N.S.," *The Globe and Mail*, August 1, 1983.

240 Memorandum to Toronto Local Board of Health from Anne Johnston, chairman, September 26, 1983.

241 In Ontario, this is the *Weed Control Act*, RSO 1990, c. W.5.

242 City of Waterloo, *Environment First 1990 Review — Report* (Waterloo, April 24, 1991), at 5-6.

243 City of Ottawa, supra endnote 235.

244 Correspondence from Kathy Cooper, researcher, Canadian Environmental Law Association, September 15, 1992.

21

Radiation

Contents

In a single blast, the Chernobyl explosion released almost as much radiation as all the atmospheric bomb tests of all the nations combined. The explosion didn't create the radiation — it was already there in the fuel rods that had been cooking in the core for a year — but merely set it free. Nine days after the explosion, the rain that fell on Ottawa was radioactive, and although the measured amounts were insignificant, the simple fact that debris from an industrial malfunction in the Ukraine was landing in Canada was chilling in itself. The world seemed smaller than ever.

David Lees, "Living in the Nuclear Shadow," Toronto Life Magazine,
November 1989

The de facto policy that power lines, electric blankets, and video display terminals be considered innocent until proved guilty should be rejected out of hand by sensitive people everywhere. To do otherwise is to accept a situation in which millions of human beings continue to be test animals in a long-term biological experiment whose consequences remain unknown.

Paul Brodeur, Currents of Death

WHAT IS RADIATION?

Although we cannot see it, feel it, or smell it, radiation is a daily fact in our lives. We are exposed at all times to some external radiation from natural sources like cosmic rays, radon gas,[1] and sunlight, and from manmade sources — x-rays, radio and television waves, microwave ovens, smoke detectors, atmospheric fallout from weapons tests, and emissions from power plants and radioactive waste dump sites. We may also be exposed to radiation internally if we eat, drink, or inhale radioactive particles. The only types of radiation that we can detect with our senses are visible light and infrared radiation (as heat). All other forms of radiation are undetectable without the help of instruments, even though they can cause irreparable harm to our bodies.

It is important to distinguish between radioactivity and radiation. Radioactivity is the spontaneous disintegration of unstable atoms. Radioactive elements can be found in nature, and radioactivity can also be induced artificially by humans. Radiation is the energy that is released by radioactive substances, but radiation also emanates from sources other than radioactive materials. There are different types of radiation that vary in their intensity and potential harmfulness to animal and plant life.

Radiation is divided into two main categories: ionizing and non-ionizing. Ionizing radiation has enough energy to break molecular bonds and to displace electrons from atoms, thus producing electrically charged atoms, or ions. Ionizing radiation can be in the form of alpha, beta, or neutron particles, x-rays, or gamma rays. X-rays and gamma rays have similar intensities, but they differ in their origins. Gamma rays originate from within the nucleus of an atom during the process of radioactive decay, whereas x-rays originate from the cloud of electrons that orbit the nucleus.

Gamma rays are released naturally during radioactive decay, and can be created artificially in a nuclear reactor or a particle accelerator by causing neutrons to split off from an atom. X-rays can only be generated artificially in an x-ray tube, with a sufficient amount of electrical energy causing electrons to accelerate and strike a metal target. The penetrating power of an x-ray or gamma ray is measured by the wavelength of its radiation: the shorter the wavelength (higher frequency), the greater the energy and penetrating ability of the radiation.

X-rays and gamma rays form part of the electromagnetic spectrum (see the chart on the following page), which classifies different forms of energy according to wavelength. At the top of the spectrum are the extremely high frequency (very short wavelength) waves associated with ionizing radiation, and at the bottom of the spectrum are the extremely low frequency waves associated with 60 hertz (Hz) electric current. Electric and magnetic fields are also found at the very low end of the electromagnetic spectrum and are discussed at the end of this chapter. Electric and magnetic fields are fields of energy that surround any source of electric current.

Non-ionizing radiation can be described as rays of energy that do not have enough force to break molecular bonds. Nevertheless, non-ionizing radiation is still powerful enough to alter cell structure and cause chemical changes in living organisms that can result in illness, cancer, or death. Non-ionizing radiation also comes from both natural sources such as sunlight and artificial sources such as radar, satellite communications, radio and television frequencies, and microwave ovens. The higher frequency forms of non-ionizing radiation (for example, microwaves) are easily absorbed by biological tissue and can actually heat up the matter they come in contact with. With lower frequency electromagnetic radiation, only small amounts of energy can be transferred to a receiving body, and thus the potential for harm is greatly reduced.

The term "microwave" refers to the small size of the waves associated with very high frequency transmissions. Microwaves fall somewhere between the extremely high frequency electromagnetic waves emitted by x-rays and the much lower frequency waves of radio waves. Microwaves are used everywhere in our society; for the most part either to transmit various sorts of signals or as sources of heat.

This chapter is divided into two main parts dealing respectively with nuclear radiation and other forms of radiation, because they are treated differently in our legal system. The greatest amount of regulation revolves around nuclear energy, while other types of radiation have been virtually ignored, despite the dangers that they present. For the purposes of this chapter, the terms "nuclear" and "atomic," when referring to energy or radiation, are used interchangeably.

Electromagnetic Spectrum

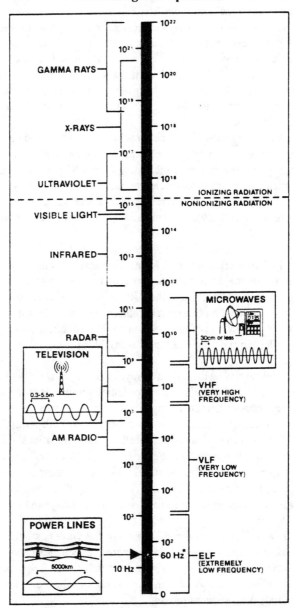

*hertz: A cycle per second. A unit to measure frequency. In North America alternating current power has a frequency of 60 hertz.

FIGURE 2 Comparison of frequency and wavelength for various electromagnetic sources. Because of the long wavelength (5000 km) and low frequency (60 hertz), transmission lines do not "radiate" energy comparable to that of microwave or radio and television antennas.

Courtesy of Ontario Hydro.

THE NATURE OF NUCLEAR RADIATION

Atomic Structure

All matter is made up of tiny particles called atoms. Atoms contain a nucleus surrounded by electrically charged electrons. The nucleus is made up of positively charged protons and neutral neutrons. The chemical properties of each element are determined by the number of protons (positively charged) in the nucleus. The number of electrons (negatively charged) is normally equal to the number of protons; hence the total charge in the atom is neutral. The attractive electric force between the protons and electrons keeps the electrons in orbit around the nucleus. All of the atoms of a particular element have the same number of protons — the number of protons is called the atomic number. However, atoms of the same element may have different numbers of neutrons; this gives rise to isotopes of the same element, each of which has a different total mass. The larger the number of neutrons in an atom, the weaker the "nuclear force" that holds the nucleus together, with the result that the atom is unstable. An unstable atom is likely to throw off neutrons to stabilize itself, releasing energy at the same time; this transformation or spontaneous decay is called radioactivity.

A Typical Atom

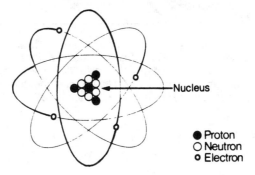

Courtesy of Ontario Hydro.

Each radioactive atom or radioisotope has a half-life for each form of radioactivity it exhibits: in each case, the half-life is the time during which half the nuclei in a sample decay. For example, the half-life of strontium-90 is 28 years. After 28 years a given quantity of strontium-90 would be half as radioactive as it was originally. After a further 28 years, its radioactivity would be halved again, to one-quarter of the original amount, and so on.

Atomic, or nuclear, energy is produced by initiating and maintaining a controlled fission chain reaction. Fission occurs when an atom is bombarded by a neutron, rendering the atom so unstable that it splits instantly, releasing additional neutrons and energy in the form of heat. The released neutrons go on to split other atoms, thereby creating more heat and releasing more neutrons in a chain reaction. If the chain is self-sustaining and can be controlled, an enormous supply of heat energy can be produced evenly, which can be used in turn to produce electricity. If the chain reaction is not moderated following initiation, the rate of fissioning and consequent heat output would increase exponentially, resulting ultimately in a lethal explosion or meltdown of the reactor. This is believed to be what happened in the accident at Chernobyl in the Ukraine in 1985.

The Fission Process

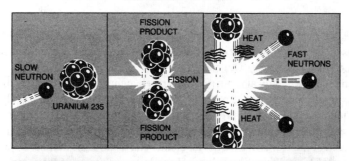

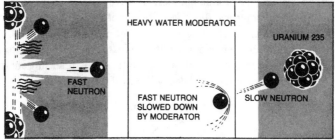

*Slow neutron (fig. 1) strikes nucleus of U-235 atom and splits
(fissions) it (fig. 2) into fission products which fly apart (fig. 3)
creating heat. Neutrons given off at the same time are slowed
down as they travel through heavy water (fig. 5) and repeat the
process by striking the nucleus of the U-235 atom (fig. 6).*

Courtesy of Ontario Hydro.

Uranium is the only fissionable element that occurs in large quantities in nature. Thorium
is also fissionable, but much rarer. Uranium has several isotopes, but only one, uranium-235,
is readily fissionable. Most radioisotopes used for industrial or medical purposes are
artificially made. They are "created" by placing a stable isotope in the core of a nuclear reactor
and forcing it to accept an additional neutron in its nucleus, thus rendering it unstable. The
most widely used radioisotope, cobalt-60, is made this way.

Types of Nuclear Radiation

Four types of radiation are given off by radioactive atoms: alpha, beta, and neutron particles,
and gamma rays. They are all hazardous, but they differ in their power of penetration. More
than one type of radiation can be given off by one atom, although radioactive elements tend
to give off one type of radiation in particular.

Alpha particles are positively charged particles. They are the weakest form of ionizing
radiation, in that they can be stopped by merely a sheet of paper, a layer of skin, or several
millimetres of air. If swallowed or inhaled, however, alpha particles can be extremely toxic.

Beta particles are fast-moving electrons. They can penetrate paper or skin, and can travel through a few centimetres of human tissue, but can be stopped by several millimetres of metal.

Neutrons are highly penetrating particles released by nuclear fission reactions that can be stopped by thick shields of enforced concrete and water.

Gamma rays are rays of energy somewhat similar to light rays, except that they cannot be seen by the naked eye and cannot be felt, yet they can penetrate flesh, bone, and metal. It takes one metre of concrete or three metres of water to stop gamma rays.

Effects of Radiation on Living Tissue

Radiation loses energy as it passes through matter. The energy is transferred to and excites the atoms of materials it touches, disturbing the way the materials' electrons are arranged, or causing the actual loss of electrons. This may cause chemical changes that are harmful to living cells. Even small amounts of radiation may change the internal chemistry of healthy cells so as to alter their normal processes of growth and development, cause them to grow in an uncontrolled manner producing a cancer, or disturb their genetic structure, resulting in mutations in future generations. Evidence shows that radiation has a harsher effect on fetuses and young children than on adults.

The hazard to life and health depends on the length of exposure time, the amount of energy emitted by the radiation, and its ability to penetrate body tissue. Thus, it matters greatly where the radioactive material is inside or outside the body. The most penetrating form of radiation, gamma radiation, is most hazardous externally. Alpha or beta radiation can do less harm externally, but is highly dangerous if inhaled or digested and absorbed into certain parts of the body that are very sensitive to radiation — for example, bone marrow.

The danger depends also on how quickly a radioactive material decays. Radioactive materials with short half-lives (from fractions of a millionth of a second) release more energy in a shorter time than long-lived ones do in the same amount of time, causing more immediate chemical and biological changes. Radioactive materials with long half-lives (up to millions of years) emit energy at a lower rate, but are of more concern because they will persist over many human lifetimes and affect an untold number of generations.

BENEFITS AND COSTS OF NUCLEAR RADIATION

Uses of Nuclear Radiation

The most prominent use of nuclear radiation is the production of electricity by means of nuclear fission. In Ontario, about 50 per cent of our electricity is generated by nuclear power.[2] Fission reactors can also be used to power large vehicles such as submarines, and to heat and generate electricity for large facilities such as hospitals.

Radiation is used extensively in medical diagnosis and treatment, and for medical and scientific research. Radioactive cobalt-60 and iodine are used in the treatment of cancer, x-rays are used extensively for diagnosis, and gamma radiation is used to sterilize all kinds of hospital equipment, instruments, and even food. Radioisotopes also have many industrial applications (the non-energy uses of radiation are discussed later in this chapter).

Nuclear radiation is also used as a devastating weapon in the form of atomic bombs.

Costs of Nuclear Radiation

The costs of nuclear radiation exposure are more difficult to pin down than the benefits. There are huge economic costs associated with nuclear energy that are routinely subsidized by taxpayers and are therefore not reflected in the price of electricity. For example, the tremendous costs of regulating the nuclear industry and of research and development are borne by the government of Canada.

The costs of building, operating, repairing, and replacing parts in nuclear power plants is high compared with other methods of generating electricity, and these costs are reflected in higher prices for electricity. For example, the 1993 Ontario Hydro rates for electricity were increased by 7.9 per cent over the 1992 rates. Eighty per cent of the rate increase was attributed to the cost of repairing unanticipated problems at the Darlington nuclear generating station and other nuclear stations. Without these exorbitant expenses in Ontario Hydro's nuclear program, the rates for electricity would only have to be raised by 2 per cent.[3] Finally, there are the "hidden" costs to society, such as environmental degradation and damage to health due to increased background radiation and radioactive waste disposal sites, as well as the psychological costs that go with living with the constant fear of a nuclear accident or nuclear warfare.

First and foremost is the loss of human life or well-being due to accidental or occupational exposure to radiation. Even those people living near a nuclear reactor or a uranium mine may be exposed to dangerous levels of radiation. Until the modern nuclear power era, the costs of exposure to radiation were paid by a limited number of people, such as the victims of nuclear warfare. Now, in the context of worldwide nuclear power expansion, radiation exposure is a potential threat to a larger part of the population; as radioactive materials proliferate, so do the dangers associated with them.

It is generally agreed that there is some risk of cancer, gene mutation, or life shortening associated with the exposure to any amount of radiation of any kind, no matter how small the dose. Naturally, the risk decreases as exposure to radiation diminishes; and different individuals have different susceptibilities even when exposed to the same levels of radiation. However, scientists have not been able to establish a threshold exposure level below which there is no risk for any exposed individual. The average background radiation dose received by Ontario residents (including average medical treatment) is about 325 millirems per year,[*] of which 220 millirems comes from natural sources.[4]

Acute Exposure

Even brief exposure to very large amounts of radiation — that is, 500 rems or more — is usually fatal. This level of exposure might occur in the event of nuclear warfare or reactor or research accidents.

The probability of a reactor or research accident is difficult to estimate. One study was performed by Sandia National Labs for the US Nuclear Regulatory Commission in the early 1980s.[5] The Sandia study stated that the probability in the United States of a large release of radiation due to a reactor accident is between 1 in 10,000 and 1 in 100,000 per reactor per

---

[*]   A rem is a unit of measurement of the amount of ionizing radiation absorbed by living tissue. "Rem" stands for "radiation equivalent man." A millirem is 1-1000th of a rem. Another unit of measurement of radiation doses is the sievert (sv), and millisievert (msv). One sievert equals 100 rems.

year.[6] Other authorities have concluded that the risk is much greater, and support this position with references to a number of accidents that have already taken place in spite of low probability figures.

Although the likelihood of a serious reactor accident might be small, the potential effects are so devastating as to make the risks formidable. According to the Sandia study, the average "serious" accident at a nuclear power plant would cause up to 970 immediate deaths, 3,600 injuries, and 8,100 cancer fatalities. The "worst-case" consequences of an accident could be up to 100 times more devastating. The Sandia study has been criticized because it ignores the risks presented by external factors such as sabotage, earthquakes, and airplane crashes, and does not adequately take into account human error.

Low-Level (Chronic) Exposure

Knowledge about the effect of low-level dosage on living organisms is grossly incomplete. Although scientists agree that all radiation exposure is dangerous to some degree, they do not agree on the exact effects of chronic low-level exposure. A complicating factor is that effects may appear only 10 to 20 years after exposure. In addition, because many of the consequences of radiation exposure affect genes, it may take several generations before all the effects of radiation on the human body are known. The primary concerns with exposure to low doses of radiation over long periods of time are cancer, leukemia, and genetic mutation.[7]

Because so little is known about how radiation actually affects biological cells, most studies on radiation examine the relationship between known exposure to radiation and the subsequent incidence of cancer, leukemia, or genetic mutation among the exposed population. The determination of risk associated with different levels of radiation exposure is a highly speculative endeavour, and there are several competing models and theories for making such determinations.

There has been considerable debate lately on whether exposure to low-level radiation is a cause of childhood leukemia. There are epidemiological studies postulating that exposure of male workers leads to childhood leukemia in their offspring,[8] and others claiming that the incidence of childhood leukemia and birth defects are higher in communities surrounding nuclear power plants than among the general population.[9]

A study commissioned by the Atomic Energy Control Board[10] (AECB) found that the incidence of leukemia was slightly higher in children living within 25 kilometres of a nuclear facility than the provincial average, but the AECB maintains that the variance is so small as to be insignificant statistically.[11] The AECB's interpretation of the statistics is hotly disputed by experts at the Energy Probe Foundation in Toronto, who insist that the excess incidence of leukemia should not be ignored.[12]

THE REGULATION OF NUCLEAR ENERGY IN CANADA

The Nuclear Establishment in Canada

The context in which we must look at how radiation is administered and regulated is a complex one. The technology, economics, and politics, both domestic and foreign, of the CANDU reactor heavily influence government policy with regard to the problems of nuclear energy.

The federal government has jurisdiction to regulate and control all aspects of the CANDU reactors. But the federal government, through several Crown corporations, has also been the country's largest entrepreneur of nuclear energy. A great deal of public money has been invested in the nuclear industry, especially in the CANDU reactor. In 1976, about 5 per cent of the country's electricity was generated by nuclear power; by 1992, the figure had risen to over 15 per cent. As well as being an alternative to hydro and oil as a domestic source of electricity, CANDU was thought to represent a tremendous export potential for Canada, not only for the reactors themselves, but also for uranium fuel. Pressures to sell nuclear power systems and fuel to other countries can serve to dictate, even on a local or provincial level, what happens in practice. Nine CANDU reactors have been sold abroad so far: one each to India and Argentina, two to South Korea, and five to Romania. South Korea has recently entered into an agreement with Atomic Energy of Canada Limited (AECL) to purchase two additional CANDU reactors, as the result of a concerted effort by AECL to boost its sales. Some officials are hoping that the 1990s will see a "renaissance" of the nuclear industry, and AECL is mounting an aggressive marketing campaign abroad, after being criticized by federal officials that Canada's huge investment in the nuclear industry has not paid off.[13]

There is a lot of money to be made in the nuclear industry, and a great deal of international power to be gained. These benefits have caused government and industry to play down the enormity of some of the problems of nuclear energy. However, in November 1990, the newly elected government of Ontario, headed by Bob Rae, announced a moratorium on the development of new nuclear power facilities due to the many outstanding concerns and the public outcry surrounding nuclear energy. Thus, the Canadian nuclear industry lost its major customer for an indefinite period of time, and the unprecedented action by the Ontario government caused more people to begin to take notice of the many problems inherent in nuclear power generation: public safety concerns, escalating costs, damage to the environment, and waste disposal.

Besides the direct threat to human health and to the natural environment, there remains the risk that the reactor technology will be used to produce weapons, particularly since some of the countries to which Canada sells nuclear technology and fuel are politically and economically unstable. The potential damage to the global environment that a nuclear power plant accident, nuclear sabotage, or nuclear warfare could cause is unthinkable, and impossible to ensure against effectively.

Nor have Canadians come to terms with the political and social implications of such a centralized, complex, expensive technology. Both proponents and critics of nuclear power express concern over the centralized, militaristic controls necessary to regulate this industry properly.[14] There remain also some unanswered questions whether the expansion of nuclear power since the late 1970s has been an economically wise move for Ontario or Canada. Although often called a masterpiece of engineering, CANDU itself is not trouble-free — it continues to be plagued by technical operating difficulties, often causing shutdowns or reduction in energy output, and costing a fortune to maintain. Take, for example, the Darlington nuclear complex, whose cost has doubled from the original estimate due to a series of unanticipated problems — and only two of the reactors at Darlington are operational so far.[15] A recent report by the Ontario Energy Board blamed the need for higher electricity rates on the poor performance of Ontario Hydro's nuclear program.[16]

The AECB was created in 1946 through the *Atomic Energy Control Act*,[17] the principal statute in the field. In 1952, AECL was created. The AECB is a regulatory and money-granting agency, and AECL handles research, development, marketing, and promotion of atomic energy, including expanding the present uses of radioisotopes and radiation.

The federal government, through AECL, was party to a tripartite agreement concluded in 1954 to capitalize on the commercial possibilities of nuclear energy. AECL agreed to provide scientific backing, Ontario Hydro agreed to operate the demonstration power reactor, and the Canadian General Electric Company took the prime responsibility for the design and manufacture of the components. The result was the CANadian Deuterium Uranium reactor: CANDU. As several commentators point out, the cooperation between federal and provincial Crown corporations and the private components and supply industry extends to a mutuality of staff and ideology.[18]

The Canadian nuclear industry was long dominated by state enterprises such as AECL, Eldorado Nuclear Limited, and Uranium Canada Limited. All three of these federal Crown corporations reported directly to the minister of energy, mines, and resources, as did the AECB. Thus, the minister has historically played a double role as both regulator and proponent of the expanding nuclear program.

In the late 1980s, the federal government began taking steps to privatize the uranium mining industry.[19] The government felt that because of the strong legislative and regulatory framework that governed the entire nuclear industry, direct ownership of mining companies was no longer necessary to achieve public policy purposes.[20] Now the federal government is also seeking private sector investors to play a role in AECL.[21]

Another major actor in the nuclear establishment is the university community. Universities have done much nuclear research that, historically, has been funded through AECB research program grants. The financing and responsibility for some of these programs were transferred to the National Research Council (NRC) in 1975, which maintains ties with the AECB, since the president of the NRC is, by law, a member of the AECB. University professors and researchers also sit on many of the AECB advisory committees.

Finally, public interest groups must be considered a factor in the regulation of radiation. They have persuaded public authorities to consider alternatives to nuclear energy, to allow the public more of a voice in decision making, to place a moratorium on nuclear development pending further research, and to embark on an energy conservation strategy, which may reduce the need for additional sources of electricity.

Division of Powers in Nuclear Regulation

The Canadian constitution divides legislative power between the federal and provincial levels of government. Although the categories of legislative power enumerated in the Canadian constitution do not specifically deal with atomic energy or nuclear radiation (the subject matter could not possibly have been foreseen by the framers of the original constitution in 1867), the regulation of the nuclear industry has been assumed by the federal government. This has been justified alternatively under section 92(10)(c) of the *Constitution Act, 1867*, which allows Parliament to control works that are declared to be "for the general advantage of Canada,"[22] and under the "Peace, Order and Good Government" heading of the federal powers, on the basis that the production of atomic energy is of "national concern."[23]

Although atomic energy is primarily a federal matter, there are many aspects of the use, production, and sale of atomic energy and of radioactive substances that also fall under the purview of the provincial legislatures. For instance, uranium mining, transportation, public health, occupational health and safety, and environmental protection are all areas of responsibility that are shared by both the provincial and federal levels of government. Furthermore, there are aspects of nuclear radiation that fall outside the ambit of the federal *Atomic Energy Control Act* — for example, the military use of atomic energy. Hence, although the primary regulatory agency is the Atomic Energy Control Board, the regulation of nuclear radiation as a whole is composed of a complicated collection of federal and provincial statutes and standards.

The Federal Role

The Atomic Energy Control Act

The *Atomic Energy Control Act (AEC Act)*, originally passed in 1946, gives primary regulatory power over all aspects of the nuclear industry to the AECB, which reports to the minister of energy, mines, and resources. The AECB's mission is to ensure that the use of nuclear energy in Canada does not pose undue risk to health, safety, security, and the environment.[24]

The *AEC Act* grants broad powers to the AECB to make regulations to govern the atomic energy industry in Canada[25] and to regulate its own proceedings,[26] without having to consult the public or hold any hearings. There are three categories of regulations permitted under the *AEC Act*: those that the AECB may make on its own initiative, those that require approval by the minister of energy, mines, and resources, and those that require Cabinet approval.[27] The board's jurisdiction covers the following sectors:

- uranium mines and mills;
- uranium refining and conversion facilities;
- reactor fuel fabrication facilities;
- heavy water production plants;
- power and research reactors;
- particle accelerators;
- radioactive waste management; and
- the use, sale, and possession of any "prescribed substances" under the definition in the *AEC Act*.

The AECB regulates the nuclear industry by issuing licences to carry out any of the activities prescribed in the regulations under the *AEC Act* (the AEC regulations),[28] and by carrying out regular compliance inspections once licences are issued. It can incorporate into a licence any conditions it deems necessary in the interests of health, safety, and security and can impose new conditions when a licence is up for renewal. Licences are usually granted for two-year periods, but this is also a matter within the AECB's discretion.

In 1977, the House of Commons tabled a completely revised version of the *AEC Act* entitled the *Nuclear Control and Administration Act (NCA Act)*.[29] The *NCA Act* was never passed due to opposition from provincial governments, which felt that the proposed bill expanded federal powers, thus encroaching on provincial jurisdiction. The *NCA Act* would have replaced the AECB with the "Nuclear Control Board," whose responsibilities would have been restricted to health, safety, environmental, and security matters, and which would have reported to Parliament through the minister of state for science and technology. The commercial and promotional activities of the AECB would have remained with the minister of energy, mines, and resources. This would have reduced the conflict of interest that the minister was in, having ultimate responsibility for both the promotion and regulation of nuclear energy.

The *NCA Act* was introduced as a response to the growing anti-nuclear movement in the 1970s and was designed to rectify some of the shortcomings of the *AEC Act*, such as the lack of provisions dealing with radioactive pollution incidents, the omission of public consultation in licensing decisions, and the lack of public involvement generally. A few of the reforms proposed in the *NCA Act* have since been implemented through internal AECB policies and guidelines and also through the increasing predominance of the federal environmental assessment and review (EARP) guidelines (now, the *Canadian Environmental Assessment Act*; see below), but the *AEC Act* itself remains virtually unchanged since it was first enacted almost 50 years ago.

The Atomic Energy Control Board

The actual board has five members, but it also employs a full-time staff of several hundred that, collectively, is also referred to as the AECB. Of the five board members, four are appointed by federal Cabinet, and the fifth is the president of the National Research Council.[30] One of the board members is appointed by Cabinet to serve as president of the board, having managerial responsibility for the work carried out by the entire AECB. The president of the board is the only board member who is a full-time employee of the AECB.

Until the 1970s the board consisted almost entirely of the heads of other government agencies involved in the nuclear industry — for example, AECL and Eldorado Nuclear (the former Crown corporation that carried on uranium exploration, mining, and refining activities). In the 1970s membership on the board was opened up to academics, executives of provincial utilities, and members of the private sector, but no representatives of environmental groups have ever been appointed.

The board meets about 10 times each year to review general policy matters and make final decisions on the siting and licensing of nuclear facilities. It also convenes extraordinary meetings from time to time — for example, the public "town hall" meeting held in Bowmanville, Ontario in 1988, which was called to air community views on the licensing of a Port Granby radioactive waste management facility. The day-to-day work of the AECB is performed by its permanent staff and its various committees.[31] As of March 31, 1992, the AECB had 334 people on staff, and the committees included additional technical experts from outside the AECB.

The AECB's role in the nuclear industry formed part of the subject of a study on the safety of nuclear power reactors in Ontario by the Hare commission in 1988 (discussed in greater detail below). Although the commission concluded that the AECB is generally an effective regulatory agency, it also made the following observations and criticisms:[32]

1. The AECB is still not sufficiently visible to the Canadian public and its resources are not widely used. The research it performs should be more widely disseminated and it should put more emphasis on public relations.

2. The AECB has restricted itself to technical and scientific matters although this is not mandated by the *AEC Act*. The AECB would be strengthened if it opened up board membership to a wider variety of disciplines and backgrounds (including representation from labour and advocacy groups, but this recommendation has never been implemented), and also broadened its scope to consider environmental and socioeconomic matters.
3. The AECB enjoys a relationship with Ontario Hydro that is perhaps too close and collegial to make it an effective watchdog over the utility; and the disparity of resources between the two makes the AECB even more helpless to control Ontario Hydro.

Access to information: Under the *AEC Act*, the public has no inherent right to information on atomic energy. The *AEC Act* permits the AECB to enact regulations "for the purpose of keeping secret information respecting … atomic energy as, in the opinion of the Board, the public interest may require."[33] Although the federal *Access to Information Act*[34] provides for every Canadian to have access to any record under the control of a government institution, there is a list of exceptions that includes restricted information under the *AEC Act*.[35]

At one point, in anticipation of a pending US anti-trust lawsuit, regulations were passed under the *AEC Act* making it illegal for anyone to release any document relating to any conversation or meeting held between January 1, 1972 and December 31, 1975 involving any government organization or Crown corporation with regard to the "production, import, export, transportation, refining, possession, ownership, use or sale" of uranium or its derivatives or compounds without the minister's permission unless the release of the information was required by law.[36] The Progressive Conservative party, while in opposition, challenged the validity of these regulations in court in 1977 with limited success. The court ruled that members of Parliament could talk about uranium mining in the House of Commons, but the media were not allowed to report what was said.

The *AEC Act* further reinforces governmental secrecy by requiring AECB employees to take an oath of secrecy in which they have to state:

> I … solemnly swear that I will not communicate or allow to be communicated to any person not legally entitled thereto any information relating to the affairs of the Board, nor will I allow any such person to inspect or to have access to any books or documents belonging to or in the possession of the Board and relating to its business.[37]

The AECB has become highly sensitive to adverse public opinion, especially on the issue of access to information. It has made efforts to set out what it *is* willing to disclose (or, in the case of the annual report, required to disclose).[38] The AECB has set up an Office of Public Information, which responds to inquiries by members of the public and makes available a variety of publications and reports to anyone who requests them. According to the AECB's 1991-1992 annual report, the Office of Public Information supplied 16,342 documents in response to 1,826 inquiries during the reporting year.[39] The office also holds public information meetings from time to time in communities that are near nuclear facilities.

In the 1980s the AECB adopted a series of policies and guidelines intended to achieve greater public involvement and consultation in its regulatory procedures. These policies included:

- A policy initiated in May 1980 making available to the public information supplied to the board in support of licensing applications and documents forming part of a licence.

- A policy initiated in January 1981 requiring publication of notice of, and request for, public comments on all proposals for new regulations, safety criteria, policies, and guidelines.
- A guidebook called "Policy and Procedures on Representations and Appearances" to assist members of the public and interest groups in making submissions to the board on matters of public interest.
- The publication of minutes of board meetings as of March 4, 1985.

Nuclear Facilities

Under the AEC regulations, nuclear facilities include reactors, particle accelerators, uranium and thorium mines and mills, plants that produce deuterium or deuterium compounds, processing plants, and waste disposal sites.[40] Under the AEC regulations, anyone operating a nuclear facility has to be licensed by the AECB, unless the board exempts him or her from this requirement.[41] Neighbours of facilities have no right to receive notice of a licence application, nor does the AECB have any duty to hold a hearing — public or private — before it issues a licence.[42] But the AECB often requires a potential licensee to hold a public meeting with local residents as a condition for issuing the licence, especially before construction of a major facility like a reactor, a waste site, or a mine. The construction of a nuclear facility will often have to undergo an environmental assessment pursuant to either federal or provincial environmental assessment legislation. (See the section on environmental assessment in this chapter and Chapter 10.) The board can give its written approval to construct or acquire a nuclear facility before issuing an operating licence,[43] and in fact has often done so. Both approval and a licence can include conditions the board deems necessary "in the interests of health, safety, and security."[44]

The AECB can suspend or revoke a licence[45] but must first issue a notice to the holder of the licence and conduct a hearing, unless an immediate suspension is deemed necessary for reasons of health, safety, or security.[46] In the latter case, the holder of the licence may request the board to hold an inquiry into the reasons for the suspension.[47] Members of the public, including neighbours of nuclear facilities, victims of radiation contamination, and atomic workers, do not have the same rights as a licensee to demand an inquiry into whether a licence should be revoked or suspended, nor do they have the right to receive notice of a hearing with respect to the revocation of a licence.

There are currently 20 nuclear power reactors licensed to operate in Canada: four Bruce "A" and four Bruce "B" reactors near Kincardine, Ontario; four Pickering "A" and four Pickering "B" reactors just outside of Metropolitan Toronto; two at Darlington, near Bowmanville, Ontario; one at Gentilly, near Trois-Rivières, Quebec; and one at Point Lepreau, near St. John, New Brunswick. In addition, there are two more reactors at Darlington still under construction.[48]

Prescribed Substances

Under the *AEC Act*, the term "prescribed substances" refers to radioisotopes, such as uranium, thorium, deuterium, and plutonium, that are capable of releasing atomic energy or of being used to produce atomic energy.[49] Their possession and use are strictly regulated under the AEC regulations. No one may produce, prospect for, mine, refine, use, sell, or possess a prescribed substance for any purpose without a licence issued by the board, unless specifically exempted from the licensing requirement.[50]

The regulations under the *AEC Act* exempt many kinds of use or possession of prescribed substances from the licensing requirement. For example, no one needs a licence to transport or temporarily store prescribed substances, or to prospect for them, sell, or possess them in very small quantities.[51] Some radioisotopes such as Americium-241 have been exempted from licensing requirements, not because they are harmless, but because they cannot be used to produce atomic energy.[52]

Research Reactors and Particle Accelerators

In addition to the power-generating nuclear reactors listed above, there are eight operating research reactors in Canadian universities, one at the Saskatchewan Research Council, and one belonging to a private medical supplier. There are also two much larger research facilities operated by AECL, at Chalk River, Ontario and Pinawa, Manitoba. All of these research reactors fall under similar regulatory and licensing requirements as commercial reactors.[53]

A particle accelerator is a machine that creates and controls a beam of subatomic particles. This beam is produced by electrical and magnetic fields to generate ionizing radiation or radioisotopes for research, medical, analytical, and commercial purposes. Those accelerators that are capable of producing atomic energy require licensing by the AECB for their installation, operation, and decommissioning. As of March 31, 1992, across Canada, there were 68 medical accelerators used for cancer therapy and 27 accelerators used for other purposes, authorized by a total of 57 licences (some licences authorize more than one accelerator).[54]

Mining

Canada is the largest producer and exporter of uranium in the world. The main centres for uranium mining in Canada are in northern Saskatchewan and central Ontario. Since 1988, however, the former Soviet Union has been gaining a significant market share by dumping stockpiles of uranium on the international market and thus depressing prices.

Once uranium ore is extracted from the ground it must undergo several processes before it can be used as reactor fuel. First is the milling process whereby uranium ore is crushed into a powder to make the uranium more accessible. Then the actual uranium is separated from surrounding minerals and elements through a chemical process. Finally, the uranium is refined and turned into a solid concentrate called "yellowcake." It is then transported to a conversion facility where it is turned into uranium fuel pellets, and ultimately fuel bundles capable of powering a CANDU reactor. Yellowcake is also exported for conversion into fuel that can be used in other types of reactors. The conversion facilities are located relatively near the reactors where the fuel is to be used, to avoid having to transport fissionable fuel bundles over long distances.

Mining for radioactive substances is governed by the licensing provisions in the AEC regulations. Uranium and thorium mines are "nuclear facilities" for the purposes of the regulations. Anyone wishing to mine for a prescribed substance must obtain a licence from the AECB.[55] The development of uranium and thorium mines has five phases:

- exploration or pre-development;
- site selection;
- construction;
- operation; and
- abandonment.

Approval must be obtained from the AECB for each phase.

The AECB's director of Fuel Cycle and Materials Regulation reviews licence applications and makes recommendations on them to the board. His staff also evaluates safety aspects of mines, both before and after they are granted licences, and recommends conditions to be imposed on licences. This branch of the AECB also provides an on-site inspection program for mines, mills, and refining facilities.

One condition typically imposed on an operating licence is that the mine submit to the AECB annual, or sometimes even quarterly, reports summarizing the performance and operation of its mine, mill, and waste management facilities, and reporting all accidents or events that might affect public safety. These reports are available for public inspection. A mine operator must also notify the AECB within 24 hours of any significant incident resulting in the exposure of workers or the public to dangerous levels of radiation.

In 1946, the *AEC Act* gave the AECB complete control over uranium mining. In the early 1950s, when mining promoters wished to develop known uranium deposits in Ontario, the AECB, under provincial pressure, agreed to concern itself with security of the uranium mines, and leave Ontario to take responsibility for the safety of the mines and the health of the workers.[56] The AECB agreed that uranium mines should, except for issues of security, be subject to provincial mining rules, just like other mines in the province, and therefore inserted a paragraph into all uranium mining licences ordering the licensee to obey all provincial regulations relating to mine safety. However, the Ontario government did not make any safety regulations for uranium mines. In 1960, the AECB finally amended the AEC regulations to provide for radiological protection for the first time, but the provinces were still left to enforce these standards.

At the height of the cold war, the Ontario government did not want to interfere, or appear to be interfering, with the commitments made by the Canadian government to supply the United States with large quantities of uranium. The provincial government therefore told the mines to monitor their own radiation levels and report the results. Otherwise, little attempt was made to enforce standards. In 1974, many years after giving the province a jurisdiction it had demanded but never acted upon, the AECB set up a Mine Safety Advisory Committee, and began to work on a mine inspection program and a mine occupational health research program. Finally, in 1984, the AECB passed the Uranium Mines (Ontario) Occupational Health and Safety Regulations,[57] which impose on all mine and mill operators in Ontario a duty to comply with the relevant provisions of the Ontario Occupational Health and Safety Regulations.[58] The purpose of this was to establish uniformity in the laws governing occupational health and safety in mines, including uranium mines, in the province of Ontario. The AEC regulations still govern permissible doses of radiation exposure to miners,[59] and in the event of any inconsistency between the Ontario Occupational Health and Safety Regulations and the AEC regulations, the latter prevail.[60]

The Ham commission: In September, 1974, Dr. James Ham was appointed commissioner of a provincial inquiry into the health and safety of workers in Ontario's mines. In 1976, his report was issued. Dr. Ham destroyed a number of previously held views, including the concept that there might be a safe level of exposure to radiation.[61] The report was openly critical of government regulation and suggested drastic reduction in the permissible levels of radiation exposure.

Transportation and Packaging

Each year there are about 750,000 packages containing radioactive material transported to, from, or within Canadian territory. On average, there are about 20 reported transport incidents each year involving radioactive substances,[62] and of these, about 10 per cent result in the release of a radioactive material, most often of low radioactivity.[63] The majority of packages transported contain radiopharmaceuticals.

In 1983 the AECB introduced regulations governing the transportation and packaging of radioactive substances[64] by any method anywhere within Canada, as well as to and from Canada. The Transport Packaging of Radioactive Materials Regulations (TPRM regulations) are based on the transportation regulations of the International Atomic Energy Agency, and they also incorporate various other codes developed by international agencies: the Technical Instructions for the Safe Transport of Dangerous Goods by Air (International Civil Aviation Organization), and the International Maritime Dangerous Goods Code.

The emphasis in the TPRM regulations is on packaging strength. The theory is that transport accidents are bound to occur despite the best precautions, so the packaging of radioactive substances should be durable enough to withstand all foreseeable kinds of pressures. Packaging performance standards are divided into categories depending on the potential harmfulness of the package contents. According to the AECB,[65] the regulations on packaging, labelling, and handling are designed to:

- ensure containment and prevention of uptake of radioactive material by regulating package strength, the amount of material in packages, the concentration of radioactive material, and contamination on package surfaces;
- control the external radiation hazard and warn of the contents by regulating the radiation intensity at the surface and one metre from the surface of packages, and by regulating the labelling and marking, and the stowing of packages;
- prevent burns and overheating by regulating the maximum allowable surface temperature and the stowage of other cargo;
- prevent runaway fission by regulating package design and establishing the number of packages that would form a critical system; and
- evaluate and oversee the adequacy of packaging by testing and certifying packages.

The AECB administers the TPRM regulations and enforces them through regular inspections of the premises and inventories of licensees; however, it has neither the jurisdiction nor the means to perform spot checks of vehicles during actual transportation. This responsibility belongs to the federal Department of Transport, and falls within the ambit of the *Transportation of Dangerous Goods Act, 1992 (TDG Act)*, whose coverage includes radioactive materials.[66] Following the passage of the original *TDG Act* in 1980,[67] the AECB and Transport Canada entered into an "Inter-Departmental Memorandum of Agreement on the Transport of Radioactive Materials" that divided jurisdiction over the transportation of radioactive materials between the two federal departments.[68] The AECB retains control over the packaging and preparation for transport of radioactive materials, and Transport Canada administers the requirements for their actual transportation. The two departments also agreed to harmonize their regulations so as to avoid duplication and conflict.

In 1989 a decision by an Ontario provincial court[69] threw into question the applicability of the *TDG Act* to the intraprovincial transportation of dangerous goods. Presumably the Ontario Ministry of Transportation governs the transportation of dangerous goods within the boundaries of Ontario; however, the Ontario *Dangerous Goods Transportation Act*[70] excludes radioactive substances. This would have left all control over the intraprovincial transportation of radioactive materials to the AECB, which does not have the means to oversee transportation. However, in 1992 the federal government passed a revised version of the *TDG Act* with slightly different wording that would cover the transportation of radioactive materials everywhere in Canada.[71]

Nuclear-powered vehicles: There are no nuclear-powered vessels or vehicles currently licensed in Canada, although the AECB is willing to license such nuclear "facilities."[72] There are, however, numerous foreign nuclear-powered merchant ships and submarines that pass through Canadian waters each year, and these must be licensed by the AECB each time they enter Canadian territorial waters.

Reprocessing

Fuel reprocessing is a dangerous form of recycling. Spent reactor fuel contains a small amount of plutonium (one of the fission products of uranium-235) that can be extracted from the rest of the wastes and re-used as fuel in a type of reactor known as a breeder reactor. The great advantage of this type of reactor is that it can recycle its fuel many times, thus conserving precious uranium supplies.

The problems resulting from reprocessing, however, are manifold. First, it is tremendously expensive; second, it creates a vast amount of radioactive waste, most of it in liquid form, which is more difficult to manage than solid waste; third, it raises the chances that wastes, especially gas and liquid, will escape into the environment; and fourth, it creates plutonium, the chief ingredient in nuclear weapons.

Canada has no fuel reprocessing plants, since the CANDU reactor is not designed to operate with reprocessed fuel.

Decommissioning

One of the biggest problems associated with nuclear power plants is the decommissioning of the plants on the expiry of their useful lives. They cannot simply be shut down and abandoned, because of the hazards presented by radioactive materials remaining within them, including parts of the plant itself and machinery that has long been exposed to radiation. They must be carefully dismantled, decontaminated, and rendered harmless, a costly process that can take up to 30 years and tens of millions of dollars. Decommissioning often involves shutting down a reactor and doing nothing further for the first 5 to 10 years as the radioactive materials decay further and cool down.

Eventually all radioactive materials must be dismantled, shielded, packaged, removed, and stored, or disposed of. Uranium mines and mills also require careful and costly decommissioning procedures because of the dangers presented by the millions of tonnes of radioactive waste that remain behind after the mine is closed down.

In Canada, there have been three nuclear generating stations that have undergone partial or complete decommissioning: Gentilly 1 in Quebec (which was in operation for only a very short time, unsuccessfully), Douglas Point at the Bruce facility, Ontario, and the Nuclear Demonstration Project in Rolphton, Ontario. The useful life of a CANDU reactor is about 40 years, and of the reactors currently in operation the oldest, at Pickering "A," began operation in 1971. Thus, the need to deal with the decommissioning of plants on a large scale is becoming more imminent.

The AEC regulations prohibit the abandonment or disposal of prescribed substances except in accordance with the conditions set out in a licence or the written instructions of the board.[73] These regulations do not mention decommissioning or abandonment of a nuclear facility as a whole; hence the AECB must rely on its licensing system to ensure proper decommissioning prior to abandonment. The AECB does have a written policy on the decommissioning of nuclear facilities,[74] but the policy acknowledges that individual decommissioning plans must be custom-made for the specific demands of every nuclear facility. For any new facility, the policy requires the submission of a conceptual decommissioning plan before construction approval can be granted. Unfortunately, the policy only came into effect in 1988, after all the nuclear facilities in Canada, other than Darlington, had already been completed. Nuclear facilities that were already operating when the policy came into force have had to submit conceptual decommissioning plans prior to having their licences renewed. A more detailed decommissioning proposal must be submitted to the AECB at least one year before the termination of operation.

Radioactive Waste Management

One popular conception in favour of nuclear energy is that it is environmentally "clean," because it contributes to neither acid rain nor global warming. This is in fact a misconception; the biggest problem with nuclear energy is the deadly waste it produces, and this problem has yet to be solved. The technical, social, and political problems of nuclear waste were neglected for decades by the military, industry, and governments. Now that the waste has piled up around us and can no longer be ignored, it is finally receiving greater attention. In Canada we have already accumulated enough highly radioactive waste to fill an olympic-size swimming pool. This may not seem like a large amount, but it must be remembered that even a few milligrams of waste has enough energy to kill a person, and that some of it will remain dangerous to health for thousands of years.

There is a tremendous amount of hazardous radioactive waste that results from the production of nuclear energy. Radioactive waste is generated at every stage of the nuclear fuel cycle, from the mining of uranium, to fuel fabrication, to power generation, to decommissioning. The proper disposal of radioactive waste constitutes the greatest burden facing the nuclear industry today. The lack of a solution has led many countries, including Canada, to place a moratorium on new reactor construction.

The term "radioactive waste" covers a wide range of solid, liquid, and gaseous materials that are either radioactive in their own right or have become radioactive as a result of coming into contact with radiation from other sources. Some types of waste (for example, spent fuel pellets) are so radioactive that they actually generate heat and must be isolated from all forms of life for tens of thousands of years.

Uranium fuel for nuclear reactors is produced in the shape of small pellets, about the size of fingertips, which in turn are packaged into rods and then bundles. Thousands of fuel bundles are used together to power a nuclear reactor. Each fuel bundle has a useful life of about 18 months, after which about 70 per cent of the uranium has been fissioned and the fuel is no longer efficient, so it has to be replaced by a new bundle. Spent fuel bundles are highly radioactive because of the remaining uranium, which continues to decay, as well as the many fission products that also continue to decay until they attain a stable form. About 99 per cent of the total radioactivity (but not the volume) of nuclear reactor waste is contained in the spent fuel bundles.[75]

There are three classes of radioactive waste: (1) "low-level waste" — that is, waste with low alpha content and a half-life of 30 years or less (for example, mine tailings, radiopharmaceuticals, contaminated clothing, equipment, cleaning supplies, and some weak liquid and gaseous effluents); (2) "intermediate-level waste" — that is, materials that are contaminated by long-lived alpha-emitting particles (for example, the metal canisters that hold the fuel rods); and (3) "high-level waste," such as spent fuel and fission products that emit heat for 50 to 100 years and have half-lives of up to 24,000 years (for example, plutonium).

The mining and milling of uranium creates the greatest volume of radioactive waste: for every tonne of uranium fuel produced, about 100 tonnes of low-level mine tailings and 3,500 tonnes of low-level liquid waste are produced. As of 1990, uranium mining had produced 165 million tonnes of tailings in Canada.[76] Uranium-mining waste products are generally kept on-site at mines and mills and pose serious environmental hazards. The large volumes produced make it impossible to isolate the wastes from the environment, and they are usually placed in open pits or abandoned mine shafts. Mine tailings release radon gas and alpha-emitting dust particles into the air, and spills and leaching regularly contaminate local groundwater, rivers, and lakes. The AECB has issued guidelines for waste management at uranium and thorium mining facilities,[77] but even these guidelines concede that complete protection of the environment is impossible. They use language such as "doses shall be kept as low as reasonably achievable" and "unacceptable impact on the environment shall be avoided ... to the extent practicable."

The AEC regulations do not spell out any rules dealing with radioactive waste management. Like many other aspects of the nuclear fuel cycle, waste is regulated through the AECB licensing mechanism, which is supplemented by various AECB policies and guidelines. All the nuclear power plants in Canada are dealing with waste products in much the same way: spent fuel bundles are removed from reactors by remote control and submerged into on-site water-filled pools to cool down for about 7 to 10 years. After that they have lost enough radioactivity to be transferred to dry storage in special concrete and steel containers. Intermediate-level waste is also stored in concrete containers, and low-level waste is either stored, incinerated, or disposed of using similar means as those for conventional hazardous waste.

Storage can be defined as "the confining of material with the intention of recovering it." Storage of radioactive waste requires continuous monitoring and maintenance, and poses a constant threat to human health and the environment. Radiation can easily escape from corroded, cracked, or improperly sealed containers, and radioactive liquids and particles can leach out of underground storage tanks, contaminating soil and groundwater. The United States is currently having to cope with tremendous amounts of radioactive waste, arising from their nuclear weapons complex, that has been improperly stored for decades. It is seeping into groundwater from leaking undergound storage tanks and is wreaking environmental havoc generally.[78]

Stored waste is accumulating at an alarming rate: over 17,000 tonnes of used nuclear fuel bundles are already being stored at nuclear sites in Canada, with about 2,000 additional tonnes being produced each year.[79] By the year 2000 it is predicted that there will be 42,000 tonnes in storage within nuclear power plants across Canada — enough to cover a hockey rink to a depth of 3.5 metres.[80] (This does not count the thousands of tonnes of low-level waste that is stored off-site or has been disposed of through conventional means.) Furthermore, storage poses an ethical question, since stored waste will have to be managed by future generations that will not even reap the benefits of the energy once created by the waste materials.

In 1977 the federal Department of Energy, Mines and Resources appointed a group of scientists, led by Kenneth Hare, to study the problem of nuclear waste. The study group concluded that Canada was in desperate need of a comprehensive national plan to deal with nuclear waste, rather than a piecemeal approach, that the public should be included in all discussions of nuclear policy, and that the only feasible method of permanent disposal in Canada would be deep geological burial.[81] Fifteen years after the group's report, there is still no national plan, and the federal environmental assessment agency is still considering the conceptual merits of deep geological burial in a proposal jointly developed by AECL and Ontario Hydro.[82]

The principle behind disposal (as opposed to storage) is to dispose of nuclear waste in a place far away from human settlements and in such a way that it can never be retrieved and will not require any further monitoring or surveillance. The proposed method of disposal that has gained favour in the Canadian nuclear industry is deep burial in solid rock formations in the Canadian Shield. The proposed location for such a nuclear waste disposal facility is northern Ontario.

The biggest drawback with deep geological burial is that no container can remain water-resistant for hundreds of years. The water that exists below the earth's surface will find its way into any vault, no matter how well designed, and will eventually seep in and out of the nuclear waste containers, carrying radioactive substances into the groundwater. Gradually, this contaminated groundwater will show up in wells, springs, lakes, and rivers, and ultimately will be taken up into the food chain.

Furthermore, it is impossible to predict with certainty geological activity over thousands of years, even in the most geologically stable formations. Geologists still cannot predict volcanic eruptions and earthquakes with accuracy, and there is no computer model in existence that can simulate the impact of all the variables on a huge underground chamber artificially filled with highly radioactive substances.

These are some of the conceptual problems with deep geological burial, without even going into the practical obstacles of how to design and operate a repository, how to safely transport radioactive materials from all over the country to one central location, and how to fence off and mark the site adequately so as to prevent the ingress of living things for tens of thousands of years.

No matter which methods we choose to store or dispose of radioactive waste, the only thing that is certain is that we will be leaving behind a deadly, unwanted legacy to hundreds of generations to come.

Permissible Doses

As mentioned at the beginning of this chapter, radiation is always present in our environment, originating from a number of natural and manmade background sources such as cosmic rays, minerals contained in the ground, construction materials, nuclear weapon test fallout, emissions from nuclear power plants, and industrial processes. Annual exposure to humans varies greatly depending on location and occupation. The average exposure level for Canadians from natural background radiation is estimated at 220 millirems per year, with additional average exposure from manmade background and medical sources estimated at about 105 millirems per year.[83] Workers at atomic power plants, uranium mines, and in certain industrial and medical settings are routinely exposed to greater levels of radiation than average citizens.

Schedule II to the AEC regulations (see below) sets out the maximum amounts of radiation to which atomic radiation workers and members of the general public may be exposed ("permissible doses").[84] Keep in mind that there is no level of exposure that is deemed to be absolutely safe — every dose carries with it some element of risk. The regulator's role is to determine what level of risk is acceptable to society. The permissible doses specifically exclude any exposure received in the course of medical diagnosis or treatment, or received as a result of emergency procedures undertaken to avert danger to human life. It is up to the operator of a nuclear facility or any person in possession of a nuclear substance to ensure that no person is exposed to radiation in excess of the permissible dose limits. Actual doses received by workers are measured by dosimetry badges that must be worn by all atomic workers.

The AECB reports that during 1991 the aggregate radiation dosage received collectively by 6,500 workers at nuclear reactors in Canada was 1,200 person-rems, for an average annual dose per worker of 185 millirems. No single worker received a dose in excess of 2 rems.[85] However, in the previous calendar year, 56 workers received a dose in excess of 2 rems, and six of these workers received a dose in excess of the legal limit of 3 rems per quarter or 5 rems per year.[86] The six exposures occurred when one worker at the Point Lepreau nuclear plant intentionally added radioactive tritiated water to a drink machine.[87]

Under the AEC regulations, every woman who is deemed to be an atomic radiation worker[88] must inform her employer as soon as she becomes aware that she is pregnant[89] so that her employer may take adequate precautions to limit her from excess radiation exposure or to make adjustments in her duties, if necessary. The regulations do not take into account, however, the lag period between the time of conception and the time a woman becomes aware of it, which is the time when an embryo is perhaps most vulnerable to radiation exposure. In contrast, the older AEC regulations provided for lower exposure limits for "female radiation workers of reproductive capacity"; however, this distinction was abolished in the 1985 amendments to the AEC regulations, presumably to avoid discrimination against female workers.

The AEC regulations essentially provide that atomic workers can receive 10 times the radiation that they might receive as members of the general public. It is not known exactly how great a risk they face, but that they are at risk is undeniable. As our information base and experience has increased over time, the maximum permissible dose levels have been gradually decreasing. In 1992, the AECB was considering whether to lower the maximum levels yet again, to bring them into line with the most recent set of guidelines produced by the International Commission on Radiological Protection in 1990.[90]

Illness caused by radiation exposure is a compensable claim under the Ontario workers compensation rules. The Ontario Workers' Compensation Board has awarded compensation to workers suffering from lung cancer from exposure to radon gas in underground mines, and accepted the claim of a Port Hope man who developed lung cancer after being exposed to radon gas at a uranium refinery. This was the first compensation awarded in Canada as a result of aboveground exposure to radiation.[91] Presumably, regulators have assumed that the benefits of nuclear power to society as a whole are worth the increased risk to a small percentage of the population. Unfortunately, neither workers nor the public have had a chance to weigh benefits against risks, as the standards are set by the AECB with little or no public consultation.

Atomic Energy Control Regulations
Schedule II: Maximum Permissible Doses

Organ or Tissue	Atomic Radiation Workers		Any Other Person
	Rems per quarter year	Rems per year	Rems per year
Whole body, gonads, bone marrow	3.0	5.0	0.5
Bone, skin, thyroid	15.0	30.0	3.0
Any tissue of hands, forearms, feet, and ankles	38.0	75.0	7.5
Lungs and other single organs or tissues ...	8.0	15.0	1.5
Abdomen of pregnant atomic radiation worker	0.4	1.0	—

Safety Precautions

Despite the safety precautions imposed on nuclear facilities in Canada, it is impossible to contain completely the vast amount of radiation that reactors produce. All nuclear generating stations emit small quantities of radioactive effluent into the atmosphere and into the adjoining water body in the ordinary course of operation. In addition, all nuclear generating stations are bound to suffer mishaps from time to time, in which greater amounts of radiation are emitted. For example, the Pickering nuclear generating station routinely takes in and expels 75 tonnes of Lake Ontario water every 12 hours as part of its cooling mechanism. This water is not supposed to come into contact with the radioactive (heavy) water that moderates the fission reaction occurring at the core of the reactor. However, it is widely acknowledged that cracks in the system often lead to unwanted emissions of radioactive water from the moderator into the cooling system.

On August 1, 1992, such a crack in the cooling device of one of the reactors at Pickering resulted in an accidental spill of 3,000 litres of tritiated radioactive water into Lake Ontario. It was one of the largest radioactive water spills in Canada ever, amounting to several times the yearly amount of tritium normally emitted by the Pickering plant. The spill was reported by a few local newspapers and broadcasters, but it was by no means a major news event.[92] It should be noted that Pickering is located in the most heavily populated region of Canada and hundreds of communities, including Toronto, get their drinking water from Lake Ontario in the general vicinity of Pickering. There is evidence that vegetation growing in the Pickering area is also contaminated with tritium. A study by Ontario Hydro and the Ministry of the Environment showed that between the years 1986 and 1989, the level of tritium (which is a known carcinogen) around Pickering rose 81 times in grass samples, and doubled in fruit and vegetables.[93]

Radioactive substances emitted from nuclear generating stations and from uranium mining, milling, and refining facilities can result in radiation doses to the public through direct irradiation, the inhalation of contaminated air, or the ingestion of contaminated food or water. We noted earlier that permissible doses of radiation to members of the public are expressed in terms of annual amounts from all sources. Since we are all subject to exposure to radiation from a variety of sources at once, each plant and facility that knowingly emits radiation into the environment must strive to limit its emissions to a fraction of the aggregate permissible dose.

The limits governing the planned release of radioactive substances into the environment are called "derived emission limits" (DELs) or "derived release limits" (DRLs), and they are set by the AECB for each source of radiation, after consideration of all the pathways by which releases of radiation can contribute to the radiation doses of individual members of the public. It is assumed that if all the DELs set by the AECB are respected, the annual permissible dose will not be exceeded with respect to any person.[94] The AECB's policy does not discuss what happens whether the DELs are exceeded by accidental emissions.

In addition to prescribing maximum and target limits of radioactive emissions from nuclear generating stations, the AECB also requires Ontario Hydro to conduct monitoring programs for air and water emissions at each of its plants, and at remote locations to establish comparative background levels. The Ministry of Environment and Energy and Health and Welfare Canada also conduct routine environmental monitoring programs in the vicinity of nuclear facilities to use as a cross-reference against Ontario Hydro's findings. Samples are taken from the air, ambient water, and drinking water, from fish, and from milk, honey, and produce from nearby farms.[95]

The three basic principles of radiation protection in Canada are: (1) that no practice shall be adopted unless its introduction produces a positive net benefit for society (one might question who makes such a subjective determination); (2) that all exposures shall be kept "as low as reasonably achievable" when relevant economic and social factors are taken into account (sometimes referred to as the ALARA principle); and (3) that doses to individuals should not exceed specified annual limits.[96] In contrast to the ALARA principle, most environmental protection legislation in Canada is based on the stricter standards of best available technology (BAT) or best practical technology (BPT).

The AEC regulations contain some minimal provisions with respect to the safety of workers. Persons operating a nuclear facility or carrying on an activity involving prescribed substances must take "all reasonable precautions ... to protect persons and property from injury or damage."[97] They must provide the necessary protective clothing and equipment and devices for detecting radiation, prevent the escape of radiation, provide appropriate warnings in case of an escape,[98] ensure that workers undergo regular medical examinations,[99] and keep records of workers' medical examinations as well as of radiation doses received by individuals inside or outside the facility.[100]

Warning signs and symbols must be placed on any container of a radioactive substance.[101] Accidents must be reported, and licensees must minimize the exposure of any person to radiation resulting from an accident.[102] Losses or thefts of radioactive substances must be reported to the AECB.

The AECB has inspectors assigned permanently to each nuclear power station in Canada to ensure that licensees comply with the AEC regulations and the conditions in their licences. In 1992, a total of 26 AECB inspectors were posted at reactor sites.[103] The AECB also appoints medical advisors,[104] most of whom are from the Radiological Protection Bureau in the Environmental Health Directorate of the federal Department of Health and Welfare, or from a provincial ministry of health or ministry of labour. The federal and provincial governments have overlapping jurisdiction when it comes to public health and safety; hence, although the AECB is primarily responsible for setting safety precautions, both levels of government are involved in inspection and enforcement.

The Hare commission: When they were in opposition, the Ontario Liberals had stated that if elected they would halt construction of the Darlington nuclear plant. When elected, they reversed their position and permitted Darlington to proceed. But to allay public concern, in 1987 the government commissioned an inquiry into the safety of nuclear power reactors in the province. The Ontario Nuclear Safety Review Commission was chaired by Kenneth Hare, who had earlier studied the problem of waste disposal. The commission's final report was tabled in 1988.[105]

The Hare commission found that reactors in Ontario are being operated safely and at high standards of technical performance, and that no significant adverse impact has so far been detected in either the nuclear industry work force or the public. It acknowledged that the risk of accidents having an adverse effect can never be zero. The commission's report conceded that it is still too early to detect latent cancers among atomic workers and members of the public; hence, continued observation is essential.

The report recommended a thorough examination of the operational organization of Ontario Hydro, particularly with respect to human performance, safety standards, quality control, and operational efficiency. The report also recommended that Ontario Hydro commit a greater proportion of its revenue to research and development, especially toward finding solutions to weaknesses in the reactors that have caused accidents in the past.

With respect to the AECB, the report concluded that it is an effective regulatory agency overall, and recommended that the government of Ontario should not try to invade the regulatory territory now occupied by the AECB. It suggested, however, that the AECB broaden its scope from mere technical matters to include socioeconomic and environmental concerns in its decisions, and that both staff resources and board membership be expanded to accommodate this need. The report also demanded greater public consultation on whether to build any new nuclear power generators.

Military Uses of Nuclear Energy

The role of the AECB is restricted to the development and use of nuclear energy for peaceful purposes. Its only involvement with nuclear weaponry is its participation in an international audit system to prevent the diversion of nuclear materials and equipment from peaceful applications to the production of explosive devices.

Canada was involved in the Allied effort to develop the first atomic bomb during World War II, and in fact supplied most of the uranium used by the US military in the late 1940s and 1950s.[106] Although AECL has the technology to build an atomic bomb, there has never been one built in Canada.

Military use of nuclear energy is regulated by the Department of National Defence, but Canada's official policy is to prohibit the manufacture and stockpiling of nuclear weapons on Canadian soil during peacetime.[107] Despite this policy, Canada has allowed the American military to conduct flight tests of the nuclear cruise missile over Canadian territory. Canada also permits nuclear-capable and nuclear-powered airplanes, ships, and submarines of Allied nations to enter Canadian airspace and waters.

Liability for Injury Suffered in Connection with Nuclear Energy

The nuclear industry responds to public fears about radiation by making statements that the utmost care is taken in handling radioactive materials and that all proper safety precautions are followed in nuclear facilities. Despite the industry's reassurances, though, it is only reasonable to expect that over the long term mistakes will be made and accidents will happen. Recognizing this inevitability, the federal government has made some provision for compensating victims of radiation poisoning.

The Nuclear Liability Act

The human, economic, and environmental damage, on a global scale, that could be caused by a severe nuclear power plant accident is far worse than any natural disaster humankind has ever faced. Everyone seems agreed on this point. Disagreement arises over the question of the probability of such an accident. Some experts claim that the probability of a radiation incident at a nuclear power plant is so low that risks are minimal; others say that the magnitude of the potential harm makes any risk too great. In Canada, private insurance companies seem to agree with the latter view, for none of them would take on the responsibility for insuring against radiation damage from nuclear accidents. Thus the federal government passed the *Nuclear Liability Act*[108] to ensure that personal harm and damage to property caused by a nuclear accident would be compensated.

Although the *Nuclear Liability Act* received royal assent in 1970, it was not proclaimed in force until 1976. The reason for the six-year delay in proclaiming the Act was that the private insurance industry balked at the broad no-fault liability the Act provides for. The private insurance companies and the federal government finally agreed on a scheme to share the risks. The insurance industry formed a consortium called the Nuclear Insurance Association of Canada (NIAC), composed of about 60 insurance companies and three foreign nuclear insurance pools, to share the underwriting risk and the premium income. NIAC agreed to cover "bodily injury" but refused to cover "personal injury," a broader category of injury that also covers economic losses. In addition, NIAC would not cover damages resulting from the normal, everyday operations of nuclear facilities. Hence, NIAC insurance guarantees only a portion of the risks covered in the Act; the remaining risks are picked up by the federal government through a reinsurance agreement between NIAC and the Department of Energy, Mines and Resources.[109]

Under the *Nuclear Liability Act*, the operator of a nuclear facility has a duty to prevent injury to health or property from nuclear material at its installation or in transport to it.[110] The operator of the facility is absolutely and exclusively liable for a breach of that duty — that is, a claimant need only show that injury or damage was caused by an accident, or by normal operations, at the facility, without having to prove fault or negligence on the part of the operator. Once this causal connection is established, the operator of the facility alone must bear liability, even if the injury was partially caused by faulty equipment manufactured by a third party.[111] However, the operator's liability is limited to a total of $75 million, regardless of the extent of injury or damage. Thus, the Act achieves two purposes other than its stated goal of providing compensation to victims of nuclear radiation: first, it subsidizes the production of nuclear energy by keeping insurance costs down; and second, it protects manufacturers of components for the nuclear industry from liability for negligence, thus providing an even further subsidy to the industry, and perhaps encouraging carelessness in design and production.

To pay compensation costs, a nuclear operator must carry up to $75 million in liability insurance,[112] provided by NIAC. The exact amount of coverage required depends on the type of facility and the danger involved and is specified in the operating licence granted by the AECB. If claims were to exceed $75 million or if special measures were necessary in the public interest, the federal government could appoint a Nuclear Damage Claims Commission[113] to provide additional compensation, but it would not be required to do so.

There are exceptions to the general rule established by the *Nuclear Liability Act*. If an accident occurs at a nuclear facility, the operator is not liable for damage to the facility itself or other property connected to the facility, including the means of transporting or containing nuclear material.[114] Nor is the operator liable if a nuclear incident is a direct result of an armed conflict in the course of war, invasion, or insurrection.[115] If the incident is perpetrated unlawfully by someone who intended to cause damage or injury, the operator is not liable.[116] These escape clauses seem to be broad enough to include situations like the occupation of a reactor by a group of dissidents, as once happened in Argentina,[117] or the spiking of a water cooler with radioactive water as happened in New Brunswick in 1990. Two operators can be held jointly liable where it cannot be determined which one caused the damage or injury.[118] Note that under the Act's definition of "nuclear installation," the Act only applies to facilities that have nuclear material capable of achieving criticality — that is, a sustainable nuclear fission reaction. Thus, nuclear waste sites and uranium mines are not covered by the Act.

There are many questions that remain unanswered by the wording of the *Nuclear Liability Act*. Would the operator's liability cover gene mutation manifested in the child of an otherwise healthy mother? Does the word "attributable" mean there must be proof of causation, or simply proof of contribution toward the resulting harm? Is "personal injury" broad enough to include nervous shock, damage to the well-being of one's family, and all forms of economic loss? Answers to these questions and others will remain in the realm of speculation until there are some cases litigated in the courts, an event we hope will never come about.

The Act recognizes that the effects of radiation exposure are not always immediately obvious, by making it possible to claim for damages within three years of the victim's becoming aware of the injury.[119] There is an overall time limitation on bringing an action of 10 years from the date the cause of action arose, but some radiation-induced illnesses take twice as long to become apparent.

In 1982 the AECB struck a committee to examine these and other problems with the *Nuclear Liability Act*. The Interdepartmental Working Group (IWG) was composed of representatives of the AECB and various other federal departments. After nine years of studying the Act, they came up with several recommendations for reform,[120] which still have not been acted upon.

Among the many recommendations of the IWG is one that would increase the limitation period for making a claim, from 10 to 30 years from the date of the incident giving rise to the cause of action. This recognizes that many illnesses resulting from radiation exposure take decades to manifest themselves. The IWG also recommended raising the $75 million limit on liability insurance to at least $279 million (which was the 1989 equivalent of $75 million in 1970), and then indexing the amount to inflation so that it would rise accordingly each year. The IWG criticized the extent of federal government involvement in the basic insurance scheme and recommended that NIAC undertake complete coverage up to $75 million (or whatever the new limit becomes) since they have by now built up a substantial pool of funds from over 15 years worth of premiums charged, with no claims made.

In 1987 the Energy Probe Research Foundation launched a court action to have the *Nuclear Liability Act* struck down on the grounds that it violated the constitution of Canada. The action is proceeding, but due to the complexity of the case and the various procedural wranglings between the lawyers for Energy Probe, the federal Department of Justice, Ontario Hydro, and the New Brunswick Power Commission (the latter two parties are intervenors), the case had still not been heard at the time of writing. The case is expected to go to trial in 1993.

One of the arguments put forth by Energy Probe is that in the case of a serious nuclear accident the amount of injury and damage to property suffered would greatly exceed $75 million. Since the *Nuclear Liability Act* restricts recovery to $75 million, many victims of radiation would not receive compensation for their injuries; hence, the Act violates their right under section 7 of the *Canadian Charter of Rights and Freedoms* to life, liberty, and security of the person. In addition, since the *Nuclear Liability Act* restricts the time period in which one may bring a legal action for recovery of damages, victims of nuclear accidents are treated differently from victims of other kinds of accidents, both in the limitation of the time period and in the potential amount of recovery. Hence, it is argued, the Act is in violation of section 15 of the *Charter*, which guarantees equal treatment under the law, since it results in discrimination against certain accident victims. Another argument made by Energy Probe is that the limitation of liability results in a subsidy to the nuclear industry, which makes nuclear energy more attractive than other forms of energy, which encourages society to increase the number of nuclear power plants, thus increasing the risk of a nuclear accident, in violation of our right to life, liberty, and security of the person.

Canada-US Liability Rules

Under the *Nuclear Liability Act*, the federal Cabinet can make reciprocal arrangements with other countries whereby each will compensate the other for damage caused inside the other country by a nuclear incident inside its own borders.[121] The Canada-US Nuclear Liability

Rules[122] make a Canadian operator liable for any injury or damage caused in the United States by a nuclear accident occurring in Canada. Likewise, the US *Atomic Energy Act* of 1954 provides for compensation for injury or damage occasioned in foreign territory by a nuclear accident occurring in the United States up to an amount of US$160 million.

Environmental Assessment of Nuclear Facilities

The federal government has recently passed new legislation requiring comprehensive environmental impact assessment for certain types of projects. (For greater detail, see Chapter 9.) The *Canadian Environmental Assessment Act*[123] replaces the old Environmental Assessment Review Process Guidelines Order,[124] which essentially mandated the same type of process as the Act. The types of projects that will require comprehensive environmental assessment will be set out in the regulations under the Act, which have yet to be passed. It is expected that any proposed nuclear facility, anywhere in Canada, will have to undergo federal environmental assessment by virtue of the fact that it requires a licence, a permit, or an approval from the AECB, a federal agency.[125]

There have been several federal environmental assessments undertaken, in Ontario and elsewhere, for uranium mines, mills, and refineries, for radioactive waste storage and disposal sites, and for the Point Lepreau nuclear power plant in New Brunswick.

There is also a provincial environmental assessment process in place, pursuant to the Ontario *Environmental Assessment Act*.[126] The Act does not cover federal projects, but it should apply to all nuclear installations in Ontario, since they are owned by a public utility, Ontario Hydro. It is interesting to note that despite the fact that the provincial *Environmental Assessment Act* has been in force since 1975, and the federal guidelines order since 1984, there has never been an environmental assessment hearing performed for any nuclear power plant in Ontario. The many nuclear-related projects that have been exempted from the application of the provincial Act include some Ontario Hydro generating stations and heavy water plants[127] for which, according to Ontario Hydro, the planning was already too far advanced for the environmental assessment to be applied to them. The Ontario Act would have applied to the Darlington nuclear generating station, but this was also exempted in mid-1977.

There are currently two major environmental assessments underway that could have an impact on the nuclear industry in Canada. The first is the provincial environmental assessment hearing of Ontario Hydro's 25-year demand and supply plan to serve the energy needs of Ontario into the next century. The 25-year plan as proposed by Ontario Hydro does not contemplate any additional nuclear facilities,[128] but the environmental assessment does have to consider all the possible alternatives to the proposed plan, which would include nuclear energy. The second is the federal environmental assessment of the deep geological disposal concept for high-level nuclear fuel waste (see the section on radioactive waste management above). At the time of writing, the environmental assessment report was being prepared by AECL, with public hearings expected to commence in 1994, and a final recommendation expected in 1995.

Federal Occupational Health and Safety Legislation

The Canada Occupational Safety and Health Regulations (COSH regulations)[129] made under the *Canada Labour Code*[130] are intended to ensure that employers take all precautions necessary to protect the health of employees who must work with dangerous substances and radiation-emitting devices. The definition of dangerous substance under the regulations is a substance or agent "that, because of a property it possesses, is hazardous to the safety or health of a person exposed to it";[131] hence it includes radioactive substances.

The COSH regulations govern the use, handling, and storage of dangerous substances and devices in works, undertakings, and businesses that are within the legislative authority of Parliament. These regulations supplement the *AEC Act* and regulations, and wherever there is a conflict, the latter prevail.[132]

Under the COSH regulations, employers must not use dangerous substances where harmless ones will do, and if they must use a dangerous substance, it must be the least dangerous one available. The use of the substances must be confined to as small an area as possible and signs must be posted warning workers of the presence of a dangerous substance, and of any precautions to be taken to reduce the risk of injury to health. Provisions are made for their storage and for good housekeeping practices in the workplace. Upper limits are set for contamination of the air. Tests must be made of the air where substances are used, and records of them kept for three years. Employers must register radiation-emitting devices with the Radiation Protection Bureau of Health and Welfare Canada, and conform to standards acceptable to the bureau. Employers must warn employees about the danger of the substances they work with and train them in their use. Employees must wear protective equipment and undergo medical examinations if their health may be endangered.

The Provincial Role in the Regulation of Nuclear Energy

Although the federal government has formal jurisdiction over all aspects of atomic energy, in many areas there is overlapping jurisdiction with the provincial governments, so there is a need for cooperation between the two levels of government. The Ontario government in particular has played an important role in nuclear decision making. Its electrical utility, Ontario Hydro, was an influential partner in the development of the CANDU reactor. This provincial Crown corporation is the most experienced utility in the Canadian nuclear business, and was promoting the increased use of nuclear power until 1990. Nuclear power generated 48 per cent of Ontario's electricity in 1991, and this figure is expected to increase once Darlington is fully operational.

Without a doubt, the region of southern and central Ontario is the hub of the nuclear industry in Canada. At present, 88 per cent of Canada's nuclear generating capacity is in Ontario, and on the completion of Darlington, expected in 1993, this figure will rise to 92 per cent. Eighteen of Canada's 20 operating nuclear power reactors are located in Ontario, but there is much more to the story: Ontario also has 9 research reactors, 28 particle accelerators, 1 heavy water plant, 2 functioning uranium mines, 5 mines undergoing decommissioning, 6 uranium refining and processing facilities, 13 radioactive waste management facilities, and 2 radioisotope production facilities.[133]

There is no provincial legislation purporting to govern atomic energy, since the field has been occupied by federal legislation. However, there are several provincial ministries whose jurisdictions touch on various aspects of nuclear regulation, through a number of different statutes and regulations.

Ministry of Environment and Energy

The Ministry of Energy, which was amalgamated in February 1993 with the Ministry of the Environment, has acted primarily as a research and coordination agency. It is charged with developing a provincial energy policy. It is also developing a program to promote energy conservation in the province. Ontario Hydro is a Crown corporation that is responsible for the production and delivery of electrical power to the public. The Ontario Energy Board is a regulatory agency that, among other functions, reviews and makes recommendations on Ontario Hydro's rate structure. Ontario Hydro and the Ontario Energy Board report to the minister of environment and energy, who is a member of the Resources Development Secretariat, one of the three major divisions of the provincial cabinet and the one most involved with nuclear energy policy.

The former Ministry of the Environment has been frequently involved in monitoring radioactive emissions, and has the power to regulate the treatment and disposal of radioactive wastes, since radiation is included under the definition of "contaminant" under the provincial *Environmental Protection Act*.[134] In contrast to the *Environmental Protection Act*, the *Canadian Environmental Protection Act*[135] does not include radiation in its definition of "air contaminant."[136] Also note that under the *Environmental Protection Act*, radiation is excluded from the provisions governing spills.[137]

The Ministry of Environment and Energy also administers the *Ontario Water Resources Act*[138] and the *Environmental Assessment Act*,[139] under which a study of the entire complex of environmental effects that a project might generate is carried out, at an early stage of the planning of a project. (See the section on environmental assessment above and in Chapter 9.)

Ministry of Health

Under the provincial *Health Protection and Promotion Act*,[140] the Ministry of Health has the express duty to maintain certain standards of health in the community, and is given very broad powers to accomplish this. Medical officers of health are trained to inspect for things such as communicable and virulent disease, food contamination, and unsanitary conditions, but are not experts in radiation. If a Ministry of Health inspection did reveal exposure of the public to radiation, it would be classified as an environmental hazard and handed over to the Ministry of Environment and Energy.[141]

The Ministry of Health has performed radiological monitoring around nuclear generating stations; however, it takes the position that the radiation emissions from nuclear power plants are insignificant from the point of view of public health, and defers to the Ministry of Environment and Energy and the AECB on most issues of radiation emissions. The Ministry of Health participates in some federal decision making about radiation, with representatives on the AECB safety advisory committees.

Ministry of Labour

The Ministry of Labour has responsibility for occupational health and safety in the province. It is represented on AECB advisory committees and is involved in radiation monitoring at the workplace under the *Occupational Health and Safety Act*.[142] Ministry of Labour staff inspect industrial establishments that may use radioactive materials, and can issue directions to correct such things as unsafe equipment and practices.

International Regulation of Nuclear Energy

Canada participates in international nuclear radiation control in a number of ways. We take part in the International Atomic Energy Agency's programs of international safeguards, inspections, and development of peaceful uses of atomic energy. We are a signatory of the Nuclear Non-Proliferation Treaty, and a full member of the Organisation for Economic Co-operation and Development's Nuclear Energy Agency.

Canada also, of course, sells uranium, nuclear reactors, and irradiation devices to other countries. This fact plays an important part in the development of national nuclear policy, and helps to explain why nuclear power has become such an integral part of Canada's energy program. A complex network of interdependent agencies and bodies, foreign as well as domestic, limits the policy choices that can be made.

International Atomic Energy Agency

The International Atomic Energy Agency (IAEA), a United Nations body, is the principal international nuclear watchdog. It was created in 1957 to safeguard and monitor non-military nuclear reactors in the member countries during peacetime. Under the Nuclear Non-Proliferation Treaty, the IAEA administers a system of accounting, verification, and inspection. It reports treaty violations to the United Nations Security Council. Through its conferences and symposia, the IAEA seeks to develop safety measures and standards, promote research, provide technical assistance and training courses, and otherwise promote the peaceful and safe use of nuclear energy. The Canadian government is represented on these and other international research projects by AECB staff.

The IAEA suffers from a number of weaknesses such as inadequacy of funding, imprecise guidelines, changing standards, and a lack of power to search unwilling member nations or to compel them to correct violations either of its standards or of the treaty. The IAEA system is based largely on voluntary compliance, and ultimately must rely on international moral pressure or the threat of economic sanctions or military action by other member countries, as was the case with the weapons inspections carried on in Iraq following the 1991 Persian Gulf war.

Nuclear Test Ban Treaty

The Nuclear Test Ban Treaty[143] bans the testing of atomic weapons in the atmosphere, in outer space, and under water. Since it was signed in 1963, radioactive fallout from atmospheric and oceanic testing has been reduced substantially.

The main problem with the treaty is that not all nuclear powers have signed it. France and China have not, and although France has ceased atmospheric testing, China continues to test bombs in the atmosphere, with the result that radioactive clouds still pass over the rest of the world from time to time. The treaty does not prohibit underground nuclear testing, and the United States, Russia, and Britain have continued to test weapons this way.

Another problem is that experimental explosions for "non-military" purposes are not banned. This is called the "peaceful uses loophole," since it is difficult to assess whether the national intention that led to an explosion was peaceful or not. Non-military testing creates fallout too, of course; there is no reason why such testing should be exempted from the treaty.

Canada supports a comprehensive test ban treaty that would include a ban on so-called peaceful explosions.

Nuclear Non-Proliferation Treaty

The Treaty on the Non-Proliferation of Nuclear Weapons[144] seeks to limit the number of countries possessing nuclear weapons to those that currently possess the technology to make them. However, a number of countries with advanced technology have failed to sign the treaty. Among this group are France, Brazil, China, Argentina, India, and Pakistan.

Canada has made it a condition for the export of nuclear materials, equipment, or technology that the customer country either ratify the non-proliferation treaty or accept equally binding safeguards over its entire nuclear industry and make a commitment to non-proliferation. These conditions are more stringent than those required by some other nuclear suppliers, so there are often other vendors willing to supply nuclear materials and technology to countries that are subject to a Canadian nuclear embargo. Even if a country does satisfy the Canadian requirements of non-proliferation, if the consumer country should break its agreement by detonating a nuclear device, as India did in 1974, Canada could do nothing but suspend shipments of nuclear supplies and aid. The customer would already have the reactor and the capacity to make nuclear arms. One critic has said:

> It is understandable that CANDU has special attractions for countries that seek energy self-sufficiency or military nuclear capacity. The CANDU reactor has advantages in both areas. Because it uses uranium and thorium, any country (such as India) that has large reserves of these minerals is in a much more independent position. They would not rely on the importation of enriched uranium or plutonium fuels. In this sense, CANDU has been considered by certain third world countries as a non-imperialist technology. Since CANDU produces more plutonium than its rivals, it is attractive for various purposes, including breeder and weapons programs.[145]

International Commission on Radiological Protection

The International Commission on Radiological Protection (ICRP), established in 1928, is an independent organization based in the United Kingdom. It is composed of scientists who study the effects of radiation exposure on humans and set internationally recognized standards for dose limitation. The AECB bases its permissible dose levels on ICRP recommendations, which are revised every few years.

Recent International Initiatives

Until recently, all the international cooperation efforts relating to nuclear energy were centred on military uses. The 1985 nuclear accident at Chernobyl brought to light the potentially devastating effects of peaceful uses of nuclear energy as well. Within days of the explosion in the heart of the Ukraine, high levels of radiation were being felt all over Europe. Chernobyl served to heighten awareness of the vulnerability of all regions to random nuclear accidents, regardless of their location, and to foster a new level of cooperation among nations to maintain uniform safety standards everywhere in the nuclear community.[146]

Following the tragedy at Chernobyl, the IAEA held a conference that produced two international treaties: the Convention on Early Notification of a Nuclear Accident, and the

Convention on Assistance in the Case of Nuclear Accident or Radiological Emergency. Other initiatives by the IAEA include: operational safety review teams (OSARTs), which assist nations in evaluating the operational (not structural) safety of their nuclear power plants; analysis of significant safety events teams (ASSETs), which evaluate the impact of accidents or incidents; radiation protection advisory teams (RAPATs), which assess national radiation protection standards and precautions; and an international nuclear incident reporting system with the objective of facilitating worldwide exchange of operating experiences. There has been much talk of developing uniform, mandatory safety standards for all nations, but the obvious problem is one of investigation and enforcement. Hence, the IAEA operating guidelines remain optional, and there exist huge disparities among nations when it comes to safety standards at nuclear power plants.

NON-ENERGY USES OF RADIATION

Benefits and Perils

As discussed in the introductory section of this chapter, radiation is divided into two categories: ionizing and non-ionizing. Atomic, or nuclear, radiation is ionizing because it carries enough force to break apart molecular bonds. X-rays also fall into the category of ionizing radiation; however, they are treated separately from atomic radiation under our legal system.

The most significant application of ionizing radiation, outside of the nuclear industry, is in the medical field. X-rays are used for diagnosis and gamma radiation is used for the treatment of certain illnesses, most notably cancer. Irradiation is used to sterilize medical instruments and supplies. The most widely used radioisotope in the medical field all over the world is cobalt-60, and Canada supplies about 85 per cent of the world's cobalt-60.[147] The CANDU reactor is particularly well suited to produce radioactive cobalt-60 from stable cobalt-59 during its regular power-generating operation.

The same principles of irradiation involved in the sterilization of medical supplies are also being applied to industrial products, cosmetics, pest control, and food (see the section on food irradiation, below). The term "irradiation" refers to the intentional exposure of an object to ionizing radiation for the purpose of exterminating living organisms on or within the object.

There are many other applications of ionizing radiation in industrial, commercial, and scientific processes — for example, gauging the thickness of metal, glass, and plastic sheets and other forms of industrial testing; prospecting for minerals; detecting metal through x-ray machines; detecting smoke in smoke alarms; radiocarbon dating; and tracing elements in flow systems. Radiation has even been used for beneficial environmental purposes — the movement of contaminants in water can be easily traced when small amounts of radioisotopes are added to the water. Luminous paint uses materials that emit alpha or beta particles to produce phosphorescence, and it is applied to a wide range of commercial, household, and personal items — for example, glow-in-the-dark watches and clocks.

Non-ionizing radiation is described as energy that does not carry enough force to break molecular bonds. It is also referred to as "low-energy radiation." Within the category of non-ionizing radiation, there are different types of radiation that correspond to different levels of energy. The amount of energy that a type of radiation carries is directly related to the wavelength and frequency of that form of radiation, as depicted on the electromagnetic spectrum shown at the beginning of the chapter. In general, the higher the frequency of the radiation, the more potentially harmful it is to living things.

Non-ionizing radiation is used by modern society in a wide variety of applications, most commonly for the transmission of signals, but it can also be an unwanted byproduct of certain technologies; for example, video display terminals (computer monitors) and some television sets can emit dangerous levels of radiation incidental to their normal functioning as screens for viewing. Some of the day-to-day uses of non-ionizing radiation are: radio and television transmissions, satellite telecommunications, radar systems, burglar alarm devices, ultrasound detection, lasers, automatic garage door openers, tanning lamps, and microwave ovens.

Although radiation is extremely beneficial to us in a variety of ways, it can also be exceedingly dangerous and must be treated with circumspection. As the uses of radioactive materials and of non-ionizing radiation have multiplied, we have become too cavalier in our attitude toward this harmful form of energy. The biological hazards of ionizing radiation have already been described. They have been studied to a much larger extent than the hazards of non-ionizing radiation. There has been very little investigation so far into the effects of non-ionizing radiation, despite the fact that all of us are exposed to it outdoors, at home, or in the workplace.

At the low-dose levels of non-ionizing radiation that we typically experience, we cannot feel anything and there is no immediately identifiable damage to our bodies. Some immediate effects that have been reported at slightly higher doses are headaches, nausea, weakness, fatigue, irritability, sleeplessness, and behavioural changes. The long-term effects of non-ionizing radiation that have been postulated are increased susceptibility to cancer and disease, neurological disorders, cataracts, miscarriage, and genetic mutation.

Exposure to extremely high levels of non-ionizing radiation can cause immediate death — for example, standing directly in front of a radar transmitter or climbing into a microwave oven. However, there are also examples of fatalities due to long-term exposure to lower levels of radiation. One writer recounts the following tragedy:

> On June 10, 1974, Samuel Yannon, an employee of the New York Telephone Company, died of what doctors described as "microwave sickness" after working for fifteen years fine-tuning television transmission signals on the 87th floor of the Empire State Building. Early in 1981, the New York State Workers' Compensation Board ruled that Yannon died as a result of chronic exposure to electro-magnetic radiation at levels *below* those considered safe in Canada and the United States. ... But how good are these standards? Samuel Yannon worked within a large margin of safety: he was not supposed to die![148]

This story highlights our lack of knowledge about what constitutes "safe" levels of exposure to radiation and the fact that ignorance has never been an obstacle to the setting of "safety" standards.

Regulation of X-Rays and Non-Ionizing Radiation

In contrast to the regulation of atomic energy, which more or less falls under one statute administered by one regulatory agency, the regulation of other forms of radiation is achieved by a patchwork of various statutes, regulations, and regulatory bodies, both federal and provincial. There are no unifying principles involved in the regulation of radiation; specific issues must be addressed on a case-by-case basis, depending on which pigeonholes they fall into. The two areas that are most highly regulated with respect to radiation are the medical field and the workplace.

Let us consider the example of an x-ray machine operated in a private medical clinic. The machine itself must be designed and constructed according to specifications set out in the federal *Radiation Emitting Devices Act* and regulations, and it may have been inspected by an official from Health and Welfare Canada while at the manufacturing plant or importer's warehouse. Its installation and operation are governed by the Ontario *Healing Arts Radiation Protection Act*, and the clinic is subject to inspection by the Ministry of Health to ensure that Act is complied with. The technicians operating the machine are likely to be registered radiological technicians under the *Radiological Technicians Act*.[149] The clinic is also subject to provincial occupational health and safety rules dealing with radiation, enforced by the Ministry of Labour, and could also be subject to investigations and stop orders from the Ministry of Environment and Energy if it were suspected that radiation emissions were escaping from the premises.

Hence, for every situation involving radiation, there are a number of statutes and regulations that might apply and a variety of regulatory bodies that might have overlapping jurisdiction. There are a few general principles that distinguish federal and provincial jurisdiction in this area. The federal government regulates the design, manufacture, and importation of radiation equipment, and the province controls its installation and day-to-day operation. In terms of health and welfare, the federal department sets national standards and guidelines, but most inspection and enforcement is left to the provincial ministries of health. Occupational health and safety is generally under provincial control, except with respect to works and undertakings within the legislative authority of Parliament — for example, atomic energy. Finally, any form of radiation involving radioisotopes or other prescribed substances under the AEC regulations comes under the purview of the AECB.

The Radiation Emitting Devices Act

The *Radiation Emitting Devices Act* (*RED Act*)[150] regulates manmade sources of radiation other than those controlled by the *AEC Act*. It is administered by Health and Welfare Canada. The *RED Act* applies to "any device that is capable of producing and emitting radiation" and to components and accessories of such devices.[151] The *RED Act* governs the construction and design of devices; thus, it applies to manufacturers and importers of radiation-emitting devices. No person can sell, lease, or import into Canada any radiation-emitting device unless it complies with the standards set out in the regulations under the *RED Act* (RED regulations)[152] or does not present a danger to health.[153]

The RED regulations establish 15 classes of radiation-emitting devices, which include televisions, video display monitors, microwave ovens, lasers, ultrasound devices, sunlamps, and x-ray machines.[154] Design, construction, and operation standards are set for each separate class of device. The *RED Act* imposes a duty on the manufacturer or importer of a device to inform the minister of health and welfare if he or she becomes aware that a device that has left his or her premises does not comply with the regulations or presents any health risk.

Inspectors from Health and Welfare Canada's Bureau of Radiation and Medical Devices are given wide powers to enter any place where they think there is a regulated device, examine it, and seize it if they believe it to be in violation of the regulations. However, the bureau's staff is small and it cannot perform frequent inspections.

A basic problem with the *RED Act* is that it regulates radiation-emitting devices only at the time of manufacture, import, or sale. There is no mechanism in the Act or regulations to ensure that a device is kept in proper repair, or that when a device is repaired, the manufacturer's recommended component is used. Thus many devices, as they age and potentially emit more radiation, are not effectively regulated by this legislation. This is especially problematic for devices used by consumers in their homes, since there is no corresponding provincial legislation to govern their installation and operation or provide for the monitoring of radiation emissions.

The Healing Arts Radiation Protection Act

The *Healing Arts Radiation Protection Act (HARP Act)*[155] picks up where the *RED Act* leaves off for the purposes of x-ray machines. The *HARP Act* governs the registration, installation, and operation of medical and dental x-ray machines. Every medical x-ray machine operated in Ontario must be registered with the director of X-Ray Safety of the Ministry of Health.[156] The *HARP Act* sets out the categories of persons qualified to operate x-ray machines,[157] as well as the categories of persons qualified to prescribe the irradiation of humans.[158] Each owner of an x-ray machine must designate a qualified person as a radiation protection officer for that machine, whose duty it is to ensure that the machine is maintained in safe operating condition and that all the conditions set out in the HARP regulations are met.[159]

The *HARP Act* also governs the Healing Arts Radiation Protection Commission, which is an advisory committee to the minister of health on matters relating to x-rays. The HARP commission is responsible for the contents of the X-Ray Safety Code[160] and for the content of courses on how to operate x-ray machines. The standards for x-ray machines and their operating facilities are set out in the HARP regulations.

The Radiocommunications Act

The federal Department of Communications governs the use of airwaves for any form of communications transmission, including radio, television, telephone, radar, and sonar transmissions. The governing statute is the *Radiocommunications Act*,[161] in which "radio-communication" is defined as: "any transmission, emission or reception of signs, signals, writing, images, sounds, or intelligence of any nature by means of electromagnetic waves of frequencies lower than 3,000 gigahertz (GHz) propagated in space without artificial guide." One GHz is the equivalent of 10^{12} Hz, as depicted on the electromagnetic spectrum reproduced at the beginning of this chapter.

Radiofrequency (RF) emissions are in the air all around us, in the form of radio and television broadcasting waves, telecommunications and telephone signals that bounce off satellites, and radar signals. Recent technological advances have resulted in a proliferation of new RF sources such as cellular telephones, pagers, and long-distance computer linkups. The 1990s have been dubbed the "information age," and most of our information is now passed along through airwaves, in one form or another.[162]

We do not have a clear picture of how these RF emissions affect human health or the environment. Scientific data on the adverse effects of RF exposure are so sparse that they are insufficient to make proper risk assessments.[163] The exposure standards we do have are based on experimental evidence with animals and complex physical calculations and extrapolation. In short, our safety standards are the result of a guessing game.

There is evidence that exposure to high levels of RF for long periods of time can lead to illness, genetic mutations, or death, but exposure to such levels does not occur in the ordinary course of life. The question is how much risk is associated with the lower levels of RF that ordinary citizens are exposed to on a daily basis — and nobody knows the answer. The intensity of RF radiation diminishes greatly with distance from the source of the emission, so most people are not exposed to high levels unless they live adjacent to sources of RF, such as broadcasting towers. The design and engineering of broadcasting towers can also affect the potential hazard they present. The risk is higher, of course, for RF workers who are regularly exposed to high levels of radiation. The questions and debates relating to the hazards of RF emissions are very similar to those pertaining to the issue of electromagnetic fields, discussed below.

Pursuant to the *Radiocommunications Act*, regulations may be made in relation to the adverse effects of electromagnetic energy from any emission by radiocommunication equipment.[164] But no such regulations have been made to date. The Department of Communications relies on Health and Welfare Canada to advise it on the potential health risks of RF emissions and the measures that should be taken to mitigate such risks. Health and Welfare Canada has produced a safety code for RF emissions, known as "Safety Code 6."[165] This safety code was adopted by the Department of Communications in 1991, and its guidelines for things like height, design, and location of transmission towers, and the power of transmission signals will be applied to all new radio, television, and communication facilities applying for a licence. Since February 1992, Communications Canada has required an environmental impact assessment for all proposed radiocommunication authorizations; however, no steps have been taken to assess the environmental impact of previously licensed radiocommunication facilities.[166] The problem, according to one official at the Department of Communications, is that the department does not have sufficient resources to monitor the emission levels of existing RF transmitters, or to spot-check populated areas to see whether recommended "safe" levels of RF emissions are being exceeded. All broadcasting and transmitting licences are approved on the basis of calculations, not on the actual testing of emission levels.

Public Health Legislation

Public health protection is generally a provincial matter, governed by the various provincial ministries of health. As far as the federal Department of Health and Welfare goes, its responsibilities are generally limited to research and investigation into public health and welfare, and cooperation with provincial health ministries on a variety of programs.[167] One example of federal-provincial cooperation is the Committee on Occupational and Environmental Health, run by Health and Welfare Canada, but made up of both federal and provincial representatives. One of this committee's recent initiatives has been the Federal-Provincial Sub-committee on Drinking Water, which has established recommended guidelines for permissible levels of radioactivity in drinking water. It is up to the provinces to enact these guidelines into legislation, if they do not already have similar legislation.

In Ontario, the function of protecting the general public from exposure to radiation is shared between the Ministry of Health and the Ministry of Environment and Energy. Radiation exposure in the workplace is monitored by the Ministry of Labour (see the section on the provincial role in the regulation of nuclear energy, above). The Ministry of Health administers the *Health Protection and Promotion Act*,[168] under which appointed regional officers of health have the responsibility of inspecting for health hazards generally. However, these health officers are more concerned with infections, diseases, and unsanitary conditions than with environmental hazards. Under the *Health Promotion and Protection Act*, if a medical officer of health encounters a case of an environmental hazard, he or she must notify the Ministry of Environment and Energy (or the Ministry of Labour, depending on the circumstances).[169]

Non-ionizing radiation has not provoked the same level of concern as ionizing radiation in our regulatory system. Non-ionizing radiation exists everywhere in our environment, but is not yet recognized as an environmental hazard; hence, it is not monitored in the same systematic way as nuclear radiation by any regulatory agency, whether provincial or federal. Non-ionizing radiation is gaining recognition as a hazard in the workplace, with particular attention being paid to electrical line workers, broadcasting and telecommunications technicians, and computer and word processor operators. The move to develop standards for various forms of non-ionizing radiation is gathering force in the occupational health and safety setting.

Canadian Standards Association

The Canadian Standards Association (CSA) is a non-government, non-profit organization that develops performance standards for a wide array of consumer, industrial, and medical products. The standards are set by committees and panels of volunteers representing industry, government, universities, and the public. The CSA also has a paid staff that oversees daily operations and performs tests on products to ensure that they meet the required standards. The CSA funds itself by selling its standards and certification to manufacturers and by testing products for compliance.

The CSA has developed standards for a number of radiation emitting devices such as medical and dental x-ray equipment, radiation therapy equipment, food irradiators, telecommunications transmission and wiring systems, radios, televisions, computers, and microwave ovens. Although the standards developed by the CSA have no legal bearing in themselves, they are often adopted by legislators or by regulators as the predominant standards in a field. A set of regulations may either reproduce CSA standards in its own provisions or simply incorporate CSA standards by reference. Even if CSA standards are not incorporated into law, they are usually followed by manufacturers, who value the CSA certification as a marketing tool, and who probably do not have the resources to research and develop their own set of standards.

Food Irradiation

Food irradiation is a method of preservation that involves the exposure of fresh food to x-rays or gamma rays to destroy bacteria, insects, and disease-carrying organisms contained within or on the surface of the food. Irradiation can be applied to meat, poultry, fish, seafood, fruit, vegetables, grains, and spices to extend the shelf life of such products. Irradiation does not render the food radioactive in any way, but it can cause chemical changes in the food, which can result in loss of nutrients and change in taste. One of the criticisms levelled against food irradiation is that its effects have not been adequately studied, yet it has been approved as a method of food processing in at least 36 countries.[170]

Some of the negative effects of food irradiation are:

- loss of vitamins in food, especially in fruit (not considered a problem in a well-balanced diet, but more significant for subsistence societies that rely on one or two staples for nutritional needs);
- increased susceptibility of food to subsequent fungus attack and rotting;
- loss of taste, discolouration, and change in texture of some foods;
- the creation of new chemicals (called "radiolytes") in food, the toxic effects of which are not completely known, although some studies have observed chromosomal abnormalities in children, monkeys, and rats fed irradiated wheat; and
- some dangerous forms of bacteria (for example, botulism) are highly resistant to irradiation, whereas other bacteria that would ordinarily warn prospective consumers not to eat a product are eradicated.

The process of food irradiation involves placing food products on a conveyor belt that takes the food through a thick-walled chamber containing a source of ionizing radiation, most commonly cobalt-60, which passes through the food and its packaging, killing every living organism in its path. The amount of ionizing radiation absorbed by food in the irradiation process is measured in units called "Grays" (Gy), or "kiloGrays" (kGy). Low doses of radiation (up to 1 kGy) are used to slow down the ripening process or prevent sprouting on vegetables like potatoes and onions, whereas higher doses (up to 50 kGy) can be used to destroy all living organisms and render food sterile.

In 1980, a joint panel of the World Health Organization, the Food and Agriculture Organization, and the International Atomic Energy Agency established that doses of up to 10 kGy applied to any type of fresh food present no toxicological hazard. The panel's recommendations were adopted in 1983 by the Codex Alimentarius Commission, the international body that sets world standards for food safety. The United States Food and Drug Administration followed in 1986 by legalizing the irradiation of a wide range of food products, mostly fresh fruits and vegetables, up to specified doses.[171] This move had a large impact on the global trade of irradiated agricultural products and opened the way for large-scale commercial irradiation. As of 1989, 21 countries including the United States were actively using irradiation as a preserving process for food.[172]

The Canadian government has accepted the findings of the Codex Alimentarius Commission that food irradiation is safe in principle, subject to regulation, but the regulations to the *Food and Drugs Act*[173] so far allow only irradiated potatoes, onions, wheat, flour, and spices to be sold in Canada.[174]

The food that Canadians eat is regulated and inspected by Health and Welfare Canada. According to officials at Health and Welfare Canada, there is no food irradiating facility in Canada, but certain foods imported into Canada may be irradiated in their country of export. The Food and Drugs Regulations[175] require that all irradiated foods bear, on their packaging, or on a display sign in the case of bulk foods, a special symbol and one of the following statements: "treated with irradiation," "treated by irradiation," or "irradiated." Compare the benign, friendly symbol representing irradiated food with the international symbol for radiation that we have all come to fear.

Since there is no way of determining whether an item has been irradiated simply by inspecting it, Health and Welfare Canada cannot prevent the illegal importation and sale of irradiated food. The only way to tell whether an item has been irradiated is to wait and see how long it takes for it to spoil. Since irradiation is undetectable and greatly extends the shelf life of food, it is obviously very tempting for food producers to irradiate their products, especially when they are intended for export. It is only reasonable to suspect that some of the fresh food that reaches Canadian markets is irradiated without our knowledge. In the official commentary to the Food and Drugs Regulations published in the Canada Gazette, Health and Welfare Canada alluded to the possibility that even "reputable" Canadian food importers might "unwittingly purchase irradiated products."[176]

Although there is no commercial food irradiation facility in Canada, there are several irradiation facilities for the sterilization of medical and industrial supplies. Canada has played a prominent role in the development and marketing of irradiation equipment. There are several research irradiation facilities operated by AECL and Agriculture Canada; and Nordion Inc. and Theratronix, both former subsidiaries of AECL (which have recently been privatized), are world leaders in irradiation technology. Irradiators are treated like any other nuclear facility under the AEC Act and regulations. Irradiators built, tested, or operated within Canada must be licensed by the AECB, but there are no regulations governing the design or specifications of irradiators; they are licensed on a case-by-case basis.

Marketing surveys reveal that irradiated food is unpopular with the Canadian consumer, but Canadian business does not hesitate to sell the technology to other countries. In 1988 AECL and the Canadian International Development Agency (CIDA) signed an agreement with the government of Thailand to construct that country's first food irradiator.[177] AECL has also exported many industrial and medical irradiators, which use essentially the same technology as food irradiators. According to AECL, Canada is now the world's largest supplier of irradiators.[178] Canada has a particular interest in promoting the use of irradiators around the world because it is the world's largest producer of cobalt-60, the radioactive substance most commonly used for irradiation.

Food irradiation is often touted by its promoters as the miracle technology that will save the Third World from famine and starvation. However, it is an extremely expensive technology that the world's poorer economies cannot easily afford. Since irradiated food must still be protected from subsequent recontamination, and the health consequences of irradiation are not even known, less developed countries would be better off applying their resources toward improved transportation infrastructure and farming techniques. So far, irradiation technology has most benefited countries that export irradiated food or irradiation devices.

Electromagnetic Fields

Electric and magnetic fields are invisible forces that surround any electric current. The term "field" refers to a region in which objects separated in space exert force on one another.

Everything that has an electric charge also has fields associated with it, so these fields are found throughout nature, as well as in our built, high-tech environment. Electric fields are the forces that bind atoms together to form molecules, and the magnetic field of the earth, created by electric currents flowing in the earth's molten interior, is what makes a compass needle point north. The fields we are concerned with in this chapter are those associated with the electricity we use in our daily lives, whose transmission lines have become a familiar sight, criss-crossing our urban and rural landscapes.

Electricity is caused by the flow of electrons through a conductor — for example, a metal wire. The electricity we use in North America is generated in the form of an alternating current (AC), which alternates 60 times per second (hence, 60 Hz), with the exception of batteries, which operate on a direct current (DC) system. Electrical power flows in waves, as do other forms of energy, but with an extremely low frequency. Compare the wavelength of 60 Hz electricity, at 5,000 km per wave, with microwaves, at about 30 cm per wave (see the diagram depicting the electromagnetic spectrum at the beginning of this chapter). Because of the extremely low frequency of 60 Hz electrical power, it does not radiate enough energy to break molecular bonds, the way x-rays and gamma rays do, or even to heat tissue, the way microwaves do.

The flow of electricity is measured in terms of voltage (V), which can best be compared to the pressure of waterflow in a pipe. It is transmitted from electrical generating stations to distribution stations in populated areas through high-voltage transmission lines that carry up to 735 kilovolts (kV) of power. The high-voltage power is then "stepped down" at substations to lower voltages ranging from 110 V to 110 kV, and transferred to distribution lines that deliver electricity to people's homes, factories, schools, hospitals, and other users.

The flow of electricity creates two types of fields surrounding the wire or object in which the electricity is flowing. The intensity of the fields declines with distance from the object, and it usually varies according to the strength of the electrical current. The electric field is a product of the strength of the electric charge, or the voltage, and is measured in terms of volts per metre (V/m). The magnetic field results from the motion of the charge, or the current, and is measured in units called tesla (T), gauss (G), or milligauss (mG) — there are 10,000 gauss in one tesla. Although electric and magnetic fields are separate phenomena, they usually occur simultaneously and are often lumped together under the term "electromagnetic field" (EMF).[179]

Electric and magnetic fields are fields of energy that can produce currents in conducting materials. For instance, if a fluorescent lighting tube is placed on its own underneath a high-voltage transmission line, it will glow. Likewise, a vehicle parked underneath a transmission wire will give an electric shock to a person who touches it. Human bodies and other organisms are also conducting matter, and whenever we are exposed to electromagnetic fields small currents flow through us. Relative to the energy radiated by sources of higher frequency waves, however, the energy given off by electromagnetic fields is trivial, and hence not traditionally considered to be a form of radiation. For many years scientists believed that because electromagnetic fields do not radiate enough energy to break molecular bonds, alter the chemistry of cells, or heat body tissue, they could not possibly produce significant biological effects. These beliefs are now being challenged in the light of mounting evidence that prolonged exposure to electromagnetic fields does produce biological responses that can potentially be harmful to health.

During the past decade there has been a raging scientific debate on the health hazards of electromagnetic fields. There is no consensus on the actual effects of EMF, but enough evidence has been gathered to raise more than a strong suspicion that there are dangers associated with exposure to EMF. The studies that have been performed are either epidemiological studies that try to find statistical associations between certain types of disease and occupational or residential proximity to electromagnetic fields, or animal and cellular experiments performed in laboratories that seek to ascertain the biological effects of EMF.[180] The studies undertaken so far have yielded mixed results; some scientists claim that a connection can be made between EMF and certain types of cancer, especially among children;[181] other scientists assert that there is not enough evidence from which to draw such a conclusion. All scientists agree, though, that there is an urgent need for further research.[182]

For policy makers, the issue boils down to a question of risk assessment, and the appropriate measures to take given the uncertainty in the scientific community. Some feel that actions taken to reduce human exposure to EMF will be expensive and burdensome, and therefore should only be taken if there is sound scientific evidence backing them up. Others prefer to err on the side of caution, with the view that we should take all reasonable precautions to minimize risk at once, given the scant evidence that we have, rather than be sorry later — this has been called the "prudent avoidance" approach.

Most of the debate surrounding the health hazards of EMF is focused on high-voltage transmission lines, since these are the most visible culprits; but some utilities are quick to point out that appliances and household electrical wiring can present more of a threat within the home.[183] It is true that some electrical household appliances can produce extremely strong electric and magnetic fields, but their effects are not considered as hazardous as transmission lines for two reasons: (1) the intensity of the fields created by appliances diminishes drastically even a short distance from the appliance; and (2) most appliances are used only for minutes at a time. The types of appliances that are used relatively close to the body or for long periods of time — for example, electric blankets, electric clocks, television sets, and computer terminals — are receiving increased attention by scientists.[184]

There are a few countries and states in the United States that have passed regulations setting limits on the strength of electric fields within transmission line rights of way (that is, the area of land immediately below the transmission line). Florida is the only jurisdiction that regulates magnetic fields with respect to transmission lines (presumably because magnetic fields are much more difficult to control than electric fields), and the former Soviet Union was the only country to have regulations dealing with electric and magnetic fields within homes. Some argue that these regulations have nothing to do with safety since we do not know enough to tell what constitute "safe" levels of EMF, but that they are passed only to allay the concerns of voters that nothing is being done about a potential health risk.

None of the provinces in Canada has any legislation governing electric or magnetic fields. Ontario Hydro is participating in a $7 million research program to study and assess the health effects of EMF, with results expected in 1993.[185] Ontario Hydro also provides free information on EMF to any interested member of the public, and is willing to send personnel to private homes or commercial properties to measure levels of electric and magnetic fields. Health and Welfare Canada has formed a working group on electric and magnetic fields to monitor the state of scientific understanding and to assess the existence of health effects related to EMF.[186]

As far as regulatory decision making in Canada goes, the authorities have taken the position that there is not enough evidence that EMF presents a hazard to health to warrant a change in practice. In two separate applications by utilities in Alberta and British Columbia to build new transmission lines, the respective energy boards heard evidence on behalf of citizens' groups on the potential health risks of EMF, but dismissed these concerns as mere speculation, since the scientific evidence is still inconclusive, and hence not a valid basis on which to make a decision.[187]

The scientific community is expected to resolve the impasse regarding the health effects of 60 Hz electromagnetic fields in the next 5 or 10 years. A tremendous amount of research is being done in this area in Canada, the United States, and Europe. In the meantime, there are several measures that regulators should be taking as a matter of prudent avoidance: (1) the public should be educated about the potential risks of EMF, and the state of uncertainty, so that electrical workers and homeowners can decide for themselves whether to assume these risks; (2) electrical utilities should make every effort to avoid locating transmission lines and substations near high-risk receptors such as schools, day-care centres, hospitals, and convalescent homes; (3) all reasonable low-cost modifications should be made to transmission and distribution lines to minimize field strength; (4) utilities should embark on vigorous measurement programs for occupational and residential settings to identify trouble spots; and (5) manufacturers of home appliances should be compelled to warn users of the possible risks associated with EMF and ways of mitigating such risks.

CONCLUSION

During the past 50 years radiation has become more and more an inescapable part of our lives. We have been subjected, involuntarily, to exposure to all kinds of radiation, ranging from nuclear bomb test fallout, to routine and accidental emissions from nuclear power facilities, to the millions of communications signals criss-crossing the airwaves, to electromagnetic fields. Many of us spent a good part of our lives under the psychologically gripping fear of nuclear war, and now we bear the burden of knowing that radiation is everywhere around us, creating health problems for random victims. Undoubtedly, some of the uses of radiation bring benefits that we enjoy, but who is to say whether the benefits outweigh the costs, especially when the costs have never been fully explained. The public was never given a choice about most of the risks we must live with; we have learned about them gradually, but only after we, as a society, have grown dependent on the new types of technology that present the health hazards.

One pattern that has emerged over and over again is that new technologies are implemented before they are adequately tested or regulated, often resulting in tremendous human suffering before the dangers associated with such technologies are acknowledged. Our political, economic, and legal systems all serve to encourage innovation in technology without sufficient precautions. New inventions are generally treated as innocent until proven guilty, to the sad misfortune of those who act as human guinea pigs along the way. The story of Samuel Yannon, who died as a result of exposure to legally permissible levels of microwaves, is a tragic illustration of the "let's see what the effects might be before we hamper industry" approach.

In some ways the nuclear industry has come full circle: as the hazards of nuclear radiation gradually became better understood and recognized, the industry became increasingly regulated, to the point where now the entire issue *whether* we should be producing nuclear-generated power has come into question. One of the reasons that nuclear energy is so expensive to produce is that its production is highly regulated and so many necessary precautions must be taken to protect health and the environment. When the environmental and human costs of production, or "externalities," are transferred back to the producers of nuclear energy, rather than being borne by the rest of society, nuclear energy no longer becomes as profitable or as desirable to produce.

However, just when the regulators have caught up with one type of technology, countless new ones have sprung up. Regulators seem to be playing a perpetual catching-up game, enacting standards and regulations only after countless people have suffered adverse health effects. Very often regulators do not have the resources or the necessary information base to adequately examine and test a new form of technology. There is a need to introduce an entirely new approach to the assessment and regulation of new technology. We need a system in which new technologies are tested and their risks are properly evaluated in advance of their release into the marketplace, in which industry is forced to take the lead and to pay for the assessment, and in which the public is invited to participate fully in the assessment and is fully informed of any risks uncovered by the assessment. New forms of technology should be presumed guilty until proven innocent, because the stakes are so high. We have made considerable advances in the area of environmental impact assessment for major developments and projects. Now let us extend the same approach to the environmental and health impacts of the many devices and technologies that pervade our daily existence and potentially interfere with our fundamental right to life, liberty, and security of the person.

Nina Lester

FURTHER READING

Rosalie Bertell, *No Immediate Danger? Prognosis for a Radioactive Earth* (Toronto: Women's Educational Press, 1985).

Paul Brodeur, *Currents of Death: Power Lines, Computer Terminals and the Attempt To Cover Up Their Threat to Your Health* (New York: Simon and Schuster, 1989).

Catherine Caufield, *Multiple Exposures: Chronicles of the Radiation Age* (Toronto: Stoddart, 1988).

Bob DeMatteo, *Terminal Shock: The Health Hazards of Video Display Terminals* (Toronto: NC Press Limited, 1985).

John W. Gofman, *Radiation and Human Health* (San Francisco: Sierra Club Books, 1981).

Michio Kaku and Jennifer Trainer, eds., *Nuclear Power: Both Sides* (New York: W.W. Norton & Company, 1983).

James MeGaw, *How Safe? Three Mile Island, Chernobyl and Beyond* (Toronto: Stoddart, 1987).

Tony Webb and Tim Lang, *Food Irradiation: The Facts* (Wellingborough, Northamptonshire, Eng. and Rochester, Vt.: Thorsons Publishing Group, 1987).

Richard Wolfson, *Nuclear Choices: A Citizen's Guide to Nuclear Technology* (New York: McGraw-Hill, 1991).

SOURCES OF INFORMATION ON REGULATORY ASPECTS OF RADIATION

Atomic Energy Control Board
Office of Public Information
PO Box 1046
Ottawa, Ontario K1P 5S9
Phone (613) 995-5894

Ontario Hydro
Public Communications Office
700 University Avenue, Room H19 C7
Toronto, Ontario M5G 1X6
Phone (416) 592-3345
Toll-free 1-800-668-8500

Canadian Nuclear Association
11th Floor, 111 Elizabeth Street
Toronto, Ontario M5G 1P7
Phone (416) 977-5211

Energy Probe Research Foundation
225 Brunswick Avenue
Toronto, Ontario M5S 2S6
Phone (416) 978-7014
Toll-free 1-800-97EARTH

ENDNOTES

1 These are some of the sources of the so-called background radiation against which all other levels are set. Radon gas is a product of naturally occurring uranium in bedrock and soil. Cosmic rays originate from the sun and from outer space. Persons flying in airplanes are subjected to much more cosmic radiation than those on the ground. It has been estimated that interior radiation levels in an SST plane such as the Concorde flying at 60,000 feet would be 100 times those at sea level. See Philip Nobile and John Deedy, eds., *The Complete Ecology Fact Book* (New York: Doubleday, 1972), 254.

2 In 1989 and 1990, 48 per cent of electricity consumed in Ontario was generated by nuclear power. Statistics provided verbally by Ontario Hydro's Public Reference Centre.

3   "Hydro To Eliminate up to 2,000 Positions," *The Globe and Mail*, September 18, 1992; and "Energy Board Assails Ontario Hydro," *The Globe and Mail*, August 29, 1992.

4   Ontario Hydro, "Powerful Facts About Radiation" (pamphlet explaining basic facts about radiation) [undated].

5   David I. Poch, *Radiation Alert* (Toronto: Doubleday Canada Limited, 1985), 75-76.

6   For more information on reactor accidents and their potential effects, see John C. Fuller, *We Almost Lost Detroit* (New York: Readers' Digest Press, 1975). See also "Final Nuclear Study: Risk Still Low" (1975), vol. 108, no. 20 *Science News* 310, which discusses a controversial American study known as "WASH-1400," prepared by N.A. Rasmussen.

7   For more information on the health effects of radiation exposure, see the seminal textbook, John W. Gofman, *Radiation and Human Health* (San Francisco: Sierra Club Books, 1981).

8   Peter Aldhous, "Leukemia Cases Linked to Father's Radiation Dose" (1990), vol. 343 *Nature* 679.

9   E.A. Clarke, J. McLaughlin, and T.W. Anderson, "Childhood Leukemia Around Canadian Nuclear Facilities," AECB publication INFO-1300, May 11, 1989; and "Birth Defects Linked to Radiation," *The Globe and Mail*, July 4, 1991. However, a recent article reveals a new study that refutes the association of childhood leukemia with fathers who work in nuclear facilities: "Study Finds Leukemia Not Linked to Radiation," *The Globe and Mail*, September 17, 1992.

10 Clarke, McLaughlin, and Anderson, supra endnote 9.

11 "Childhood Leukemia Around Nuclear Facilities," AECB Information Bulletin, June 25, 1991.

12 "Childhood Leukemia Rates Around Nuclear Plants," information package compiled by Energy Probe, 1992.

13 "AECL Sells Two CANDU Reactors to South Korea," *The Globe and Mail*, September 18, 1992; and "Nuclear 'Renaissance' Seen Following Latest AECL Deal," *The Globe and Mail*, September 19, 1992.

14 Amory B. Lovins and John H. Price, *Non-Nuclear Futures: The Case for an Ethical Energy Strategy* (Cambridge, Mass.: Ballinger Publishing Co., for Friends of the Earth International, 1975), 15.

15 "Hydro Faces Dark Days," *The Globe and Mail*, September 14, 1992.

16 "Energy Board Assails Ontario Hydro," supra endnote 3. See also "Wrinkles Showing in Nuclear Age," *The Globe and Mail*, July 9, 1991, which reports on the premature aging of nuclear reactors in Canada, causing significant economic loss and potential threats to safety. See also "Nuclear Future in Doubt as Hydro Plots Strategy," *Now Magazine*, December 12, 1991, which describes the excessive costs and inefficiency of nuclear-generated power.

17 *Atomic Energy Control Act*, RSC 1985, c. A-16 (herein referred to as *"AEC Act"*).

18 For example, the Canadian Nuclear Association, an association of privately owned components and supply industries, has the president of AECL, a senior vice-president of Ontario Hydro, and officials of various other provincial utilities on its board of directors. See also D. Torgerson, "From Dream to Nightmare: The Historical Origins of Canada's Nuclear Electric Future" (Fall 1977), vol. 7, no. 1 *Alternatives* 8.

19 In 1988 Eldorado Nuclear Limited was merged with the Saskatchewan Mining Development Corporation and became Cameco Corporation, the largest uranium mining company in the world. As of March 1992, Cameco was 42 per cent owned by public shareholders, 39 per cent owned by the Saskatchewan government, and 19 per cent owned by the federal government.

20 See Canada, House of Commons, Minutes of Proceedings of the House Legislative Committee on Bill C-121, *An Act To Authorize the Reorganization and Divestiture of Eldorado Nuclear Limited*, May 10, 1988.

21 "Nuclear 'Renaissance' Seen Following Latest AECL Deal," supra endnote 13.

22 *Denison Mines v. Attorney-General of Canada*, [1973] 1 OR 797 (HCJ). Section 18 of the *AEC Act*, supra endnote 17, states: "All work and undertakings constructed (a) for the production, use and application of atomic energy, (b) for research or investigation with respect to atomic energy, and (c) for the production, refining, or treatment of prescribed substances, are, and each of them is declared to be, works or a work for the general advantage of Canada."

23 *Pronto Uranium Mines v. Ontario Labour Relations Board*, [1956] OR 862 (HCJ).

24 Atomic Energy Control Board, *Annual Report 1991-1992* (Ottawa: AECB, 1992), 3.

25 *AEC Act*, supra endnote 17, section 9.

26 Ibid., section 8.

27 Ibid., sections 8 and 9.

28 Atomic Energy Control Regulations, CRC 1978, vol. III, c. 365 (herein referred to as "AEC regulations").

29 Canada, Bill C-14, *Nuclear Control and Administration Act*, first reading November 24, 1977. For an analysis of this proposed legislation, see John Swaigen and Ernst Boyden, "Federal Regulation of Nuclear Facilities in Canada: Better Safe than Sorry" (1980-81), 45 Sask. L. Rev. 53. This volume of the *Saskatchewan Law Review* was a special edition devoted to the issue of uranium development in Saskatchewan and contained several papers on uranium development and other aspects of the regulation of nuclear energy.

30 *AEC Act*, supra endnote 17, section 4.

31 The permanent committees of the AECB are the Advisory Committee on Radiological Protection and the Advisory Committee on Nuclear Safety. The AECB also retains a team of outside medical advisers and sets up additional *ad hoc* committees as needed. For a complete description of AECB committees and their membership, see the AECB annual report.

32 F. Kenneth Hare, commissioner, The Safety of Ontario's Nuclear Power Reactors: A Scientific and Technical Review (Toronto: Ontario Nuclear Safety Review, 1988) (the Hare commission report).

33 *AEC Act*, supra endnote 17, section 9.

34 *Access to Information Act*, RSC 1985, c. A-1.

35 Ibid., section 13, and schedule II.

36 Uranium Information Security Regulations, pursuant to the *AEC Act*, CRC 1978, vol. III, c. 366.

37 *AEC Act*, supra endnote 17, section 19(1) and schedule I. Compare the oath of secrecy normally taken by other members of the federal civil service: "I ... solemnly and

sincerely swear ... that I will not, without due authority in that behalf, disclose or make known any matter that comes to my knowledge by reason of such employment." *Public Service Employment Act*, RSC 1985, c. P-33, schedule III.

38 The AECB must publish an annual report by March 31 of every year (free copies are available to the public): *AEC Act*, supra endnote 17, section 21.

39 *Annual Report 1991-1992*, supra endnote 24, at 28.

40 AEC regulations, supra endnote 28, section 2(1).

41 Ibid., section 8.

42 *SEAP (Save the Environment from Atomic Pollution) v. Atomic Energy Control Board and Eldorado Nuclear Limited* (1977), 6 CELN 36 (FCA).

43 AEC regulations, supra endnote 28, section 10.

44 Ibid., section 10(4).

45 Ibid., section 27(1).

46 Ibid., sections 27(3) and (4).

47 Ibid., section 27(5).

48 See *Annual Report 1991-1992*, supra endnote 24, annex VI for details regarding the licences for all of these reactors, and their generating capacities.

49 *AEC Act*, supra endnote 17, section 2.

50 AEC regulations, supra endnote 28, section 3.

51 Ibid., sections 6(1) and (2).

52 Ibid., section 6(2)(g).

53 For details regarding research reactor licences see the most recent AECB annual report, annex VII.

54 *Annual Report 1991-1992*, supra endnote 24, at 16.

55 AEC regulations, supra endnote 28, section 3.

56 G. Bruce Doern, "The Uranium Mining Safety Case," in *The AECB*, Administrative Law Series (Ottawa: Law Reform Commission of Canada, 1976), 79-85.

57 Uranium Mines (Ontario) Occupational Health and Safety Regulations, SOR/84-435, June 7, 1984.

58 *Occupational Health and Safety Act*, RSO 1990, c. O.1 and Occupational Health and Safety Act Regulations, RRO 1990, reg. 854.

59 AEC regulations, supra endnote 28, schedule II.

60 Uranium Mines (Ontario) Occupational Health and Safety Regulations, supra endnote 57, section 13.

61 James M. Ham, commissioner, *Report of the Royal Commission on the Health and Safety of Workers in Mines* (Toronto: Ministry of the Attorney-General, 1976), 90.

62 Atomic Energy Control Board, *Annual Report 1990-1991* (Ottawa: AECB, 1991), 22.

63 Atomic Energy Control Board, "Control: An Introduction to the Atomic Energy Control Board" (1990), *Control* 29. *Control* is an information magazine published once every few years by the AECB's Office of Public Information.

64 Transport Packaging of Radioactive Materials Regulations, SOR/83 740, September 29, 1983.

65 "Control: An Introduction to the Atomic Energy Control Board," supra endnote 63, at 33.

66 *Transportation of Dangerous Goods Act, 1992*, SC 1992, c. 34, received royal assent and proclaimed in force June 23, 1992.

67 *Transportation of Dangerous Goods Act*, RSC 1985, c. T-19, schedule (has since been repealed and replaced by the *Transportation of Dangerous Goods Act, 1992*, supra endnote 66).

68 See the official commentary accompanying AEC regulations, SOR/90-171, March 15, 1990, *Canada Gazette Part II*, vol. 124, no. 7, March 28, 1990, 1058-61.

69 *R. v. O.M.I. International (Canada) Inc. et. al.* (1989), 4 CELR (NS) 190 (Ont. Prov. Ct.), aff'd. (1989), 4 CELR (NS) 184 (Ont. HCJ).

70 *Dangerous Goods Transportation Act*, RSO 1990, c. D.1.

71 *Transportation of Dangerous Goods Act, 1992*, supra endnote 66, section 3(2), provides that "this Act applies in relation to all matters within the legislative authority of Parliament."

72 Atomic Energy Control Board, *News Release*, no. 85-9, "Notice of Intent — Nuclear Powered Submarine," November 28, 1985.

73 AEC regulations, supra endnote 28, section 25.

74 Atomic Energy Control Board, "Policy on Decommissioning of Nuclear Facilities," Regulatory Policy, August 22, 1988.

75 For a more detailed description of the various kinds of nuclear waste and their respective dangers, see *The World Nuclear Handbook* (London: Euromonitor Publications Ltd., 1988); and E. Willard Miller and Ruby M. Miller, *Environmental Hazards: Radioactive Materials and Wastes* (Santa Barbara, Calif.: ABC-CLIO, Inc., Contemporary World Issues Series, 1990).

76 "Radical Plans To House Nuclear Waste," *The Montreal Gazette*, September 29, 1990.

77 Atomic Energy Control Board, "A Guide to the Licensing of Uranium and Thorium Mine and Mill Waste Management Systems," Regulatory Guide, June 2, 1986.

78 United States, General Accounting Office, Keith O. Fultz, director, Energy Issues Resources, Community, and Economic Development, testimony for hearings on environmental problems in the nuclear weapons complex before the Senate Subcommittee on Strategic Forces and Nuclear Deterrence, April 7, 1989.

79 "High-Level Nuclear Waste," fact sheet produced by Campaign for Nuclear Phaseout, Toronto, September 1990.

80 "An Issue Paper on the Management of Nuclear Fuel Wastes," prepared by LURA Group consultants, for the Federal Environmental Assessment Review Office, April 1989, 5.

81 A.M. Aikin, J.M. Harrison, and F.K. Hare (chairman), *The Management of Canada's Nuclear Wastes* (Ottawa: Department of Energy, Mines and Resources, August 1977).

82 Federal Environmental Assessment Review Panel on "Nuclear Fuel Waste Management and Disposal Concept Review," ongoing.

83 "Powerful Facts About Radiation," supra endnote 4.

84 There is a separate table in schedule II to the AEC regulations, supra endnote 28, that sets out permissible levels of exposure by uranium workers to radon daughters. (A radon daughter is a nuclide formed by the radioactive decay of another nuclide.)

85 *Annual Report 1991-1992*, supra endnote 24, at 10.

86 *Annual Report 1990-1991*, supra endnote 62, at 10.

87 Ibid., at 10.

88 "Atomic radiation worker" is defined in the AEC regulations, supra endnote 28, section 2(1), as "any person who in the course of his work, business or occupation is likely to

receive a dose of ionizing radiation in excess of [the permissible dose level for the general public]."

89   Ibid., section 19(4).
90   "AECB Looks at New Radiation Standards" (Summer-Fall 1990), *Nuclear Awareness News* (a publication of the Nuclear Awareness Project). See also *Annual Report 1991-1992*, supra endnote 24, at 8.
91   "Claim over Cancer Accepted by WCB," *Thunder Bay Chronicle Journal*, December 29, 1977.
92   "Radioactive Water from Pickering Spills into Lake," *Now Magazine*, August 6, 1992.
93   "More Facts Needed Health Experts Say," *The Toronto Star*, February 20, 1991.
94   Atomic Energy Control Board, "Radioactive Release Data from Canadian Nuclear Generating Stations 1972-1988," January 1990.
95   B.C.J. Neil, "Environmental Impacts of Ontario Hydro Nuclear Facilities," Ontario Hydro Health and Safety Division, March 1991.
96   Atomic Energy Control Board, Advisory Committee on Radiological Protection, "Basic Principles of Radiation Protection in Canada," March 1990.
97   AEC regulations, supra endnote 28, section 24(1)(a).
98   Ibid., section 24(1).
99   Ibid., section 17(1).
100 Ibid., section 11(1).
101 Ibid., section 22.
102 Ibid., section 21.
103 *Annual Report 1991-1992*, supra endnote 24, at 9-10.
104 AEC regulations, supra endnote 28, sections 12, 15, and 16.
105 The Hare commission report, supra endnote 32.
106 Gordon H.E. Sims, *A History of the Atomic Energy Control Board* (Ottawa: Supplies and Services, 1981), 10.
107 Atomic Energy Control Board, "You've Asked Us About Nuclear Weapons," November 1987.
108 *Nuclear Liability Act*, RSC 1985, c. N-28.
109 Atomic Energy Control Board, "Review of the Nuclear Liability Act," Report of the Interdepartmental Working Group, November 1991, 2.
110 *Nuclear Liability Act*, supra endnote 108, section 3.
111 Ibid., section 4.
112 Ibid., section 15.
113 Ibid., sections 18 and 21.
114 Ibid., section 9.
115 Ibid., section 7.
116 Ibid., section 12(b).
117 Fred H. Knelman, *Nuclear Energy: The Unforgiving Technology* (Edmonton: Hurtig Publishers, 1976), 115.
118 *Nuclear Liability Act*, supra endnote 108, section 5.
119 Ibid., section 13.
120 "Review of the Nuclear Liability Act," supra endnote 109.
121 *Nuclear Liability Act*, supra endnote 108, section 33(2).

122 Canada-United States Nuclear Liability Rules, regulations pursuant to the *Nuclear Liability Act*, CRC 1978, vol. XIII, c. 1240.

123 *Canadian Environmental Assessment Act*, SC 1992, c. 37 (not yet proclaimed in force as of June 1993; expected to be proclaimed in force in 1993).

124 Federal Environmental Assessment Review Process Guidelines Order, SOR/84-467, June 22, 1984.

125 *Canadian Environmental Assessment Act*, supra endnote 123, section 5(d).

126 *Environmental Assessment Act*, RSO 1990, c. E.18.

127 See Exemption Orders OHN-14 and OHN-15 in *EA Update*, vol. 1, no. 1, appendix III. *EA Update* was a Ministry of Environment publication that is no longer in print, but back issues can be viewed at the ministry's Resource Centre at 135 St. Clair Avenue West, Toronto.

128 The current NDP government in Ontario announced a moratorium on any new nuclear power reactors in its throne speech of November 1990.

129 Canada Occupational Safety and Health Regulations, SOR/86-304, March 13, 1986 (herein referred to as "COSH regulations"), pursuant to the *Canada Labour Code*.

130 *Canada Labour Code*, RSC 1985, c. L-2.

131 COSH regulations, supra endnote 129, section 1.2.

132 *Canada Labour Code*, supra endnote 130, sections 123 and 131.

133 Source of statistics: Canadian Nuclear Association, *Nuclear Canada Yearbook*, 1992.

134 *Environmental Protection Act*, RSO 1990, c. E.19, section 1(1)(c).

135 *Canadian Environmental Protection Act*, RSC 1985, c. 16 (4th Supp.).

136 Ibid., section 3(1).

137 *Environmental Protection Act*, supra endnote 134, part IX, section 79(1)(f).

138 *Ontario Water Resources Act*, RSO 1990, c. O.40.

139 *Environmental Assessment Act*, supra endnote 126.

140 *Health Protection and Promotion Act*, RSO 1990, c. H.7.

141 Ibid., section 11.

142 *Occupational Health and Safety Act*, supra endnote 58.

143 Treaty Banning Nuclear Weapon Tests in the Atmosphere, in Outer Space and Under Water, August 5, 1963 (1963), 14 UST 1313, TIAS 5433, 480 UNTS 43.

144 Treaty on the Non-Proliferation of Nuclear Weapons, July 1, 1968 (1970), 21 UST 483, TIAS 6839, 729 UNTS 161.

145 Knelman, supra endnote 117, at 150.

146 See Gunther Handl, "Transboundary Nuclear Accidents: The Post-Chernobyl Multi-lateral Legislative Agenda" (1988), 15 *Ecological Law Quarterly* 203-40.

147 "What Are the Health Benefits of Radiation?" fact sheet produced by the Canadian Nuclear Association, 1988.

148 Bob De Matteo, *Terminal Shock* (Toronto: NC Press Limited, 1985), 24.

149 *Radiological Technicians Act*, RSO 1990, c. R.3.

150 *Radiation Emitting Devices Act*, RSC 1985, c. R-1 (herein referred to as "*RED Act*").

151 Ibid., section 2.

152 Radiation Emitting Device Regulations, CRC 1978, vol. XIV, c. 1370 (herein referred to as "RED regulations").

153 *RED Act*, supra endnote 150, section 4.

154 Ibid., schedule I.
155 *Healing Arts Radiation Protection Act*, RSO 1990, c. H.2 (herein referred to as "*HARP Act*").
156 Ibid., section 4.
157 Ibid., section 5.
158 Ibid., section 6.
159 Ibid., section 9.
160 Ibid., section 16.
161 *Radiocommunications Act*, RSC 1985, c. R-2.
162 For a technical explanation of the different kinds of signal transmissions using radiofrequency radiation, see Health and Welfare Canada, "Health Aspects of Radio Frequency and Microwave Radiation Exposure," Doc. 77 EHD-13, November 1977.
163 M.A. Stuchly, "Proposed Revision of the Canadian Recommendations on Radiofrequency Exposure Protection" (1987), vol. 53, no. 6 *Health Physics* 649-65.
164 *Radiocommunications Act*, supra endnote 161, section 6 (I).
165 Health and Welfare Canada, "Limits of Exposure to Radiofrequency Fields at Frequencies from 10 KHz-300GHz," 1990.
166 Communications Canada, "Environmental Assessment Process Associated with Spectrum Management Activities," February 1992.
167 *Department of National Health and Welfare Act*, RSC 1985, c. N-10.
168 *Health Protection and Promotion Act*, supra endnote 140.
169 Ibid., section 11.
170 International Atomic Energy Agency, "Food Processing by Irradiation: World Facts and Trends" (March 1989), 5 *IAEA News Feature* 9.
171 Ibid., at 9.
172 Ibid., at 8.
173 *Food and Drugs Act*, RSC 1985, c. F-27.
174 Food and Drugs Regulations, division 26, SOR/89-175, March 23, 1989.
175 Ibid.
176 *Canada Gazette Part II*, vol. 123, no. 8, April 12, 1989, 1984.
177 Atomic Energy of Canada Limited, "A Fresh Approach: Irradiation" (1989), *AECL Up Front* (fact sheet).
178 Ibid.
179 For a more detailed explanation of electromagnetic fields and their origins and effects, Ontario Hydro provides, free of charge, an excellent booklet: M. Granger Morgan, *Electric and Magnetic Fields from 60 Hertz Electric Power: What Do We Know About Possible Health Risks?* (Pittsburgh: Department of Engineering and Public Policy, Carnegie Mellon University, 1989).
180 For a thorough survey of the scientific reports on the health effects of EMF, see L. Hester Gordon, "Electric and Magnetic Fields: Managing an Uncertain Risk" (1992), vol. 34, no. 1 *Environment* 7-11, 25-32; and Larry A. Reynolds, "Powerlines and Health: A Regulatory and Judicial Dilemma" (1990), vol. 1, no. 1 *Journal of Environmental Law and Practice* 67-90.
181 Nancy Wertheimer and Ed Leeper, "Electrical Wiring Configurations and Childhood Cancer" (1979), *American Journal of Epidemiology* 109:3, and David A. Savitz et al.,

"Case-Control Study of Childhood Cancer and Exposure to 60 Hz Magnetic Fields" (1988), *American Journal of Epidemiology* 128:1.

182 A controversial article appeared in *The New Yorker* magazine several years ago, in which the author gave several accounts of "cancer clusters" occurring in the vicinity of power stations or transmission lines, and accused regulators and utilities of conspiring to dismiss these phenomena as statistically insignificant. This article is credited with raising public awareness of the potential hazards of EMF and with fuelling the debate that has grown in recent years. The article also provides an excellent survey of the scientific literature relating to EMF. See Paul Brodeur, "Annals of Radiation (Cancer and Power Lines)," *The New Yorker*, July 9, 1990. See also Paul Brodeur, *Currents of Death:Power Lines, Computer Terminals and the Attempt To Cover Up Their Threat to Your Health* (New York: Simon and Schuster, 1989).

183 Ontario Hydro, "Electric and Magnetic Fields" (information pamphlet) [undated].

184 De Matteo, supra endnote 148.

185 Ontario Hydro, "Electric and Magnetic Fields and Human Health Research" (information pamphlet) [undated].

186 Health and Welfare Canada, Environmental Health Directorate, *Electric and Magnetic Fields and Your Health*, Report of the Working Group on Electric and Magnetic ELF Fields (Ottawa: Health and Welfare Canada, 1990).

187 Alberta Energy Resources Conservation Board Decision D89-2 and British Columbia Utilities Commission Inquiry Order G-44-89, both discussed in Reynolds, supra endnote 180.

22

Visual Pollution

Contents

Today, in the seven-kilometre stretch of road between the foot of the Don Valley and the Dufferin Street bridge there are at least fifty different billboards, many of them built in the past five years. The biggest and best — known in the sign trade as "spectaculars" — come hundreds of square metres to each side, with facings that range from throbbing red neon to back-lit blue plastic. A few rise like beacons from far off in the distance, while others leap out at the last possible moment from behind buildings and bridges. Old and new together, they have transformed this hoary span of the city's busiest and most maligned roadway into an exciting outdoor gallery of commercial colour and flash, all cranked up to arresting high-voltage extremes.

Bill Boyko, Toronto Life, *July 1989*

These signs clutter the landscape, they clutter the skyscape, they block a sense of horizon. If this is the mark of a world-class city, then I quickly want to see us return to the Middle Ages.

Metro Toronto Councillor Derwyn Shea, quoted in the same magazine, about the same signs

---

Visual pollution receives what seems to be an inordinate amount of public attention, considering that the damage it does to the natural environment is — in comparison with other forms of pollution — often trivial. Yet this very disproportion indicates that it is in fact important. Despite the fact that many forms of visual blight or clutter do not make physical or chemical changes to the environment that are harmful to health in the way that lead in soil or mercury in fish may be, people notice it and are bothered by it — so much so that, for many people, "cleaning up pollution" means first and foremost, picking up the litter on our streets and in our parks. This concern with aesthetics shows that our concern about the environment stems not only from our concern about public health, but also from a need to defend less tangible, more spiritual values. The accumulation of litter, and the bombardment of our senses by commercial messages and commercial activity on our public roads and other public places forces us to face the question of what our fundamental values are. Is every public place to be a garbage dump and a medium for selling things? Or do we have a different vision of how we want to live?

Problems like littering, abandoned motor vehicles, dog excrement in the parks, signs and billboards, and hordes of street vendors on city streets are so simple and straightforward compared with other environmental concerns that our inability to solve them is curious. After all, if government and citizens cannot manage to rid our highways and byways of throwaway pop cans, what reasonable hope is there that we will be able to tackle larger problems successfully?

LITTERING

Litter is discarded material, usually thrown or deposited one piece at a time, or in small quantities, in a place other than the proper receptacle. This material accumulates, creating an unsightly mess and a danger to passersby. Such small amounts of waste are dealt with by different laws from larger quantities. A person who throws a bottle out of a car is engaging in unlawful waste disposal, but will usually be charged with violating a littering law that carries a relatively small fine. However, a person who dumps a truckload of waste in a ravine or along the roadside can be charged with the more serious offence of depositing waste without a certificate of approval from the Ministry of Environment and Energy.

There are two causes of litter that can be attacked by legal tools. First, the litterbug can be charged with an offence. There are several laws that make littering an offence, but they are difficult to enforce because police and other public officials, some of whom may have the power to stop litterers and make them identify themselves, seldom do, and ordinary citizens are reluctant to confront litterers and have no power to detain them or require them to give their names and addresses.

There are sometimes ways that you can identify a litterer. First, you may find phone numbers, letters, bills, or licence plates in litter that has been dumped that will identify the litterbug. Second, you may catch the licence plate number of a person littering from a car. Under some laws, the owner of the car may be liable for the offences of the driver.

Second, laws can be passed to control litter at its source. Our predilection for wasteful packaging and throwaway, disposable items creates a great deal of material that is likely to become litter. Laws are needed to reduce the amount of excessive packaging at the point of manufacture and to require retail stores, restaurants, shopping centres, and parking lot owners to clean up the litter that often accumulates on their premises and will eventually spread to public property and neighbouring private property.

Provincial Legislation

The Highway Traffic Act

Under the *Highway Traffic Act*,[1] anyone who "throws or deposits or causes to be deposited any glass, nails, tacks or scraps of metal or any rubbish, refuse, waste or litter upon, *along or adjacent to* a highway, except in receptacles provided for the purpose, is guilty of the offence of littering the highway."[2] The minimum fine for the owner or driver of a car is $60 and the maximum is $500,[3] but if the litterer is a pedestrian or a person in a wheelchair, the maximum fine is only $50, and there is no minimum fine.[4]

"Highway" is defined in the *Highway Traffic Act* to include not only the provincial roads that we normally think of as highways, but all roads intended for or used by the general public for the passage of vehicles, as well as the area between the lateral property lines of the road.[5] (This includes the sidewalks, boulevards, and shoulders of the road.) Because the Act prohibits the deposit of litter not only on but also *adjacent to* highways, it is possible that it could be applied to some private property. Parcels of land are "adjacent" to each other not only when they touch, but also when they do not adjoin each other, but are not widely separated. Although this has never been tested in court, it is possible that someone who throws litter from a vehicle on a road onto neighbouring private property might be convicted under the Act. Similarly, it is possible that someone who litters property in the vicinity of a highway might be convicted, particularly if the prosecutor can establish that this litter was likely to blow onto the highway from the place where it was deposited.

Unfortunately, however, the Ontario courts have held that the *Highway Traffic Act* does not apply to shopping centre parking lots. The Court of Appeal concluded that "the people invited to park are not the public as a whole, but the people who have business to transact with the stores surrounding the parking space."[6]

The *Highway Traffic Act* is particularly useful because you can identify the registered owner of a car from which litter is being thrown from the licence plate (see Appendix V), and the owner is responsible for many offences committed by the driver, including littering.[7] To use other provincial and municipal laws, you must know the name of the culprit. You cannot lay a charge against a nameless person. Even if you have the speed and courage to ask the litterer his or her name, he or she is under no legal obligation to tell you. In fact, most provincial and municipal law enforcement officials also have no power to require offenders to give their names, and it is questionable whether police officers can make anyone give a name, except for offences under the *Criminal Code*.[8]

The Environmental Protection Act

Part IX

Part IX of the *Environmental Protection Act* deals with litter, packaging, and containers. Litter is defined as "any material left or abandoned in a place other than a receptacle or place intended or approved for receiving such material,"[9] and declares that "no person shall abandon any material in a place, manner, receptacle or wrapping such that it is reasonably likely that the material will become litter."[10] The Ontario Provincial Court has held that a person may be guilty of littering under these provisions even if he or she abandons garbage on his or her own property.[11] The first conviction for this offence is subject to a fine of up to $1,000, and subsequent offences can bring fines of up to $2,000.[12] However, if the offence is committed by a corporation, the fines are twice as high for a first offence, and up to $5,000 for subsequent convictions.[13]

The Ministry of Environment and Energy has never laid a littering charge using part III of the *Provincial Offences Act*, which allows the court to hand out these high penalties. Under part I of the *Provincial Offences Act*, minor offences can be prosecuted by issuing an offence notice or "ticket." Instead of the offender being subject to the usual maximum fine, in the case of a ticket, he or she would pay a set fine of $105. Although the ministry was unable to provide any records, we were told that "maybe six tickets have been issued."

Part IX of the *Environmental Protection Act* sets out preventive as well as punitive measures. It authorizes the minister to conduct research into the reduction of waste from packaging, containers, and disposable products and their re-use or recycling; the degradability or environmental appropriateness of packaging, containers, and disposable products; and the management and disposal of litter.[14] The minister may also help pay for garbage cans to hold litter.[15] Cabinet may make regulations specifying what materials that all packaging and containers used or sold in Ontario can be made of; requiring that beverage containers be returnable or recyclable; requiring payment of a deposit when products are purchased; and requiring, regulating, or prohibiting the sale of any kind of packaging, container, or product that poses waste management problems.[16]

Part V

Part V of the *Environmental Protection Act*, "Waste Management," can also be used for littering offences. It is particularly useful where large amounts of waste are dumped, or allowed to accumulate, because this part makes it an offence to deposit waste on land or in any building without a certificate of approval from the Approvals Branch of the Ministry of Environment and Energy.[17] Waste is defined to include ashes, garbage, refuse, domestic and industrial waste, and municipal refuse.[18] The court can impose fines of up to $25,000 for individuals and up to $100,000 for corporations,[19] and can order the offender to remove the waste.[20]

Under this part the ministry once prosecuted someone for dumping five bushels of garbage from a tavern — bottles, paper, kitchen waste — into a ditch. He was fined $300.[21] On another occasion, a man who cleaned out his garage and dumped a truckload of refuse in a vacant lot was fined $1,000. Since a half-ton truck was used, the court decided $1 dollar a pound would be a reasonable fine.[22]

If the waste disposal arrangements used by supermarkets or shopping centres are not properly supervised, they can be sources of litter. Such systems must have a certificate of approval and operate in accordance with its terms and conditions. If they do not, their operators can be prosecuted. If the conditions are not sufficient to prevent the spread of litter, you may also request the Approvals Branch to impose tougher conditions. Unfortunately, although it is an offence to litter or to dump waste without a certificate of approval, it is not illegal to *cause* or *permit* dumping. If it were, a shopping centre that failed to take adequate steps to prevent litter from blowing off its property might be charged with "causing or permitting" these offences. A charge under section 13 of the *Environmental Protection Act* might be available in these circumstances, though, because it prohibits anyone from causing or permitting the deposit of any contaminant that may interfere with others' use and enjoyment of their property.

Other Laws Against Littering

There are also prohibitions against littering in certain parks, Crown lands, and other public lands in specific statutes dealing with those lands, such as the *Public Parks Act*,[23] the *Public Lands Act*,[24] the *National Parks Act*,[25] and the *Provincial Parks Act*.[26]

Municipal Bylaws

Section 210.82 of the *Municipal Act* gives "local municipalities" (that is, the lower-tier municipalities)* the power to pass bylaws prohibiting the throwing, placing, or depositing of refuse or debris on private or public property without the consent of the owner or occupant. Sections 210.80 and 210.135 also give municipalities the power to require the cleaning and clearing of yards, grounds, and vacant lots, and prohibiting or regulating the use of any land or structures for the dumping or disposing of garbage, refuse, or waste.[27]

The Ontario Court of Appeal has ruled that these provisions allow a municipality to require a landowner to stop using his land for dumping waste or to cover up existing waste, and to require owners or occupants to keep their own land free and clear of garbage.[28]

In addition, sections 314(1).1 and 314(1).5 authorize all municipalities to pass bylaws prohibiting the fouling of roads and sidewalks or throwing, placing, or depositing any dirt, filth, glass, handbills, paper, or other rubbish on the street.

---

*   See Chapter 2 for a description of upper- and lower-tier municipalities.

Most municipalities have passed such bylaws.[29] Under the *Provincial Offences Act*, the maximum fine for violating any municipal bylaw is $5,000, unless otherwise provided. Many such bylaws fix the maximum fine at a lower level.

In 1977, the provincial government passed special legislation allowing the city of Scarborough to require shopkeepers to remove litter in shopping centres. This new power was needed because of the difficulty of apprehending litterers and the difficulty of applying existing laws to private property owners who do not take adequate measures to prevent others from littering on their property or clean it up promptly.[30]

Note: If you want to lay a charge against a litterer yourself, remember that it may be useful to pick up the litter and bring it to court. The discarded material is evidence of the offence that may be presented in court. Producing the material will bolster your case.

"Stoop and Scoop" Bylaws

A related problem is animal faeces in parks, on streets, and on your property. Not only is this visually unappealing, but it is a potential public health hazard. In cities, it is carried through storm sewers into lakes and rivers. Lest you pooh-pooh this as a minor problem not worthy of consideration alongside such weighty matters as nuclear catastrophe and the poisoning of our air and water by PCBs, mercury, and lead, consider this memorandum from the commissioner of parks for the city of Etobicoke, a well-travelled expert in such matters:

> During recent visits to Spain, Portugal, England, Holland, and Germany, and in discussions with the delegates at the IFPRA Conference in Barcelona, it was noted this is a problem throughout the world. Some cities (Hong Kong, Paris, Amsterdam, New York, London and Manchester) are constructing "doggy toilets" on civic property and encouraging owners to take their dogs to these locations. Other cities are painting "curb your dog" slogans on the sidewalks. The only signs observed in Spain or Portugal dealt with prohibiting dogs in certain defined areas of the garden parks and these were few in number. (Both written and graphic signs were observed.) According to a recent article (Monday, April 2/84) the City of Paris, France has over 20,000 tonnes of dog excrement deposited daily, and New York City has estimated 25,000 tons daily must be dealt with.[31]

Sections 210.8 and 210.9 of the *Municipal Act* give local municipalities the power to make bylaws requiring dog owners to keep dogs leashed while on any public property and to require them to "remove forthwith" any excrement left by the dog anywhere in the municipality. Each of the local municipalities within Metro Toronto has one or more "stoop and scoop" bylaws. Some deal with parks, and others with streets or public property generally.[32]

These bylaws generally are more effective because their very existence helps to educate the public than through enforcement. Municipalities may leave enforcement in the hands of police, parks staff, or animal control officers (dog catchers). Whichever group is responsible is unlikely to make much effort to enforce these bylaws. The Etobicoke parks commissioner gives one explanation for this lack of enforcement:

> [F]or a charge to be laid, the issuing officer must witness the offence, and … those members of the general public who often complain about individuals who are contravening the Code are not often willing to come forward. … They do not want to get involved! … In addition the time involved in laying a charge and appearing in court places heavy demands on our staff, whose main responsibility is the supervision of the work force.[33]

DERELICT AND ABANDONED VEHICLES

Dead cars are unsightly, whether piled up in a junkyard or rusting in a ditch at the side of a road. Not only are they eyesores, but they may leak oil, gasoline, brake and transmission fluids, and battery acid that contaminate soil and water. Frequently, the same laws may be used to regulate autowrecking yards and individual wrecks on private property, as well as vehicles abandoned on the property of others.

Autowrecking Yards

The most common complaint about autowrecking yards is that they are unsightly. However, they are also a source of noise and dust and spills of oil. Many of them were established before modern land-use planning laws existed. They continue to exist as "legal non-conforming uses" (see Chapter 8), but do not meet today's standards. Moreover, the ground at such yards is often heavily contaminated with oils and other pollutants.

In general, there are three categories of laws that can be used to regulate autowrecking yards: land-use planning laws, licensing laws, and environmental regulations.

Under the *Planning Act*, municipalities may regulate the location, design, and operation of motor vehicle wrecking and salvage yards using the official plan, zoning bylaws, site plan control, and property standards bylaws. These legal tools are described in more detail in Chapter 8.

Autowrecking yards are also subject to licences from three provincial ministries and from the municipality. Under the *Highway Traffic Act*, no person may engage in the business of wrecking or dismantling vehicles without a licence from the Ministry of Transportation.[34] The *Motor Vehicle Dealers Act* requires all motor vehicle dealers to be licensed by the Ministry of Consumer and Commercial Relations. Wrecking yards that also sell motor vehicles are included in this category, but may be exempt from the licensing requirements under the *Highway Traffic Act*. In addition, these wrecking yards are classified as waste disposal sites under the *Environmental Protection Act*, and require a certificate of approval from the Ministry of the Environment. However, the Ministry of Transportation has stated that it will not regulate the appearance of these eyesores, and the Ministry of the Environment has taken the position since 1979 that it will not issue certificates of approval and considers the regulation of these sites to be a municipal responsibility.

Municipalities do have the authority under the *Municipal Act* to licence "salvage yards," a term that includes scrap metal yards, junk yards, and autowrecking yards.[35] However, both the Ontario New Democratic Party (before it formed the government) and the Canadian Environmental Law Association have argued that municipalities often do not have the resources or expertise to monitor and inspect these facilities, and that the province should not "abdicate" its responsibility to control them.[36]

EPA Part V

Indeed, in the early 1970s the Ministry of the Environment did take responsibility for requiring that anyone who left more than two derelict motor vehicles in the open on his or her property had to obtain a certificate of approval to operate a *derelict motor vehicle site*. In other words, dead cars were a form of waste, and the place they were stored was a kind of waste disposal site. The regulations specified standards for the location and operation of such facilities. These standards included locating the site where nuisance from dust, noise, and traffic would be minimized and screening the view. All fluids had to be removed from vehicles before they were "processed" (crushed, for example, to recover their steel, or stripped of parts for resale). The fluids and other materials had to be disposed of in a manner approved by the ministry unless they were resold.[37] However, in 1979, the ministry amended its regulations to exempt motor vehicle sites from the requirement to obtain a certificate of approval, because it did not have sufficient resources to administer this program. The ministry informed municipalities that this was a "local problem" that they should deal with under planning and licensing bylaws.[38]

Abandoned Motor Vehicles

EPA Part VI

Abandoned vehicles have a separate part of the *Environmental Protection Act* devoted to them. The purpose of part VI was to empower police officers and ministry inspectors to remove vehicles that appear to be abandoned and to encourage municipalities to establish sites where these vehicles can be stored until they are sold or otherwise disposed of. An officer who has reason to believe that an unintended vehicle has been abandoned may have it removed either to a certified derelict motor vehicle site or to any other place approved by the ministry as an *abandoned motor vehicle site*. As soon as the officer has done so, he must attempt to locate the owner, if he can find out who it is, and notify the owner that he or she has 30 days to claim the vehicle. After that, the operator of the abandoned motor vehicle site may sell the vehicle and apply the proceeds to paying towing and storage costs. Any remaining money must be paid to the Ontario government.

Although this appears to be a sensible way of dealing with a common problem, this part of the *Environmental Protection Act* has not been used.

The Highway Traffic Act

The police can also seize cars abandoned on public roads under the *Highway Traffic Act*.[39]

Other Abandoned Vehicles

Property standards bylaws are the most common way of requiring people to remove disused vehicles from their property. These bylaws are most useful where property owners leave one or two out-of-commission vehicles sitting in their yard or driveway. For example, the town of Newcastle property standards bylaw provides: "Any vehicle, including a trailer, which is in a wrecked, dismantled or abandoned condition shall not be parked, stored or left in a yard, unless it is necessary for the operating of a business enterprise lawfully situated on the property."[40]

Junkyards

Junkyards and scrap metal yards are included with autowrecking yards in the generic term "salvage yards," which municipalities may regulate under section 233 of the *Municipal Act*. Like autowrecking yards, these other salvage yards are not only unsightly but may create dust, noise, and traffic concerns. Their soil is usually laced with oil and chemicals. In fact, there is scarcely a scrap yard in Ontario whose soil is not laden with PCBs from old transformers and other electrical equipment. In general, the land use planning and licensing laws described above also apply to these yards.[41]

OTHER UNSIGHTLY PREMISES

Property standards bylaws may also be used to require that buildings be painted, to require fencing, vegetation, or other screening, to prohibit deposits of debris or litter, and even to require that unsightly buildings be demolished.

Landlord and tenant laws may also be used to ensure that rented premises are adequately maintained and clean. Although these laws are aimed primarily at health and safety, the same conditions that result in threats to public health or structural hazards in buildings often create eyesores. Under the *Landlord and Tenant Act*,[42] tenants are responsible for the cleanliness of their rented premises, but the law recognizes tenancy agreements under which the landlord has the responsibility to clean the rented premises. The landlord must maintain the premises in good repair, and is often responsible for the common areas and outdoor areas.

In communities that do not have property standards bylaws, the Residential Rental Standards Board has established its own minimum maintenance standards for rental buildings.[43] Among those standards are requirements that walls not have holes and that there be no piles of garbage or litter inside or outside the building. The landlord must also keep exterior areas free of weeds, decayed or damaged trees, dilapidated or collapsed structures, doors from iceboxes, refrigerators, and freezers, and other hazards.[44] Tenants can bring their complaints about violation of these standards to the board.

SIGNS, BILLBOARDS, AND POSTERS

Unless they are obscene, it is unlikely that any level of government can regulate the *content* of signs, posters, placards or billboards. With a few exceptions, like obscenity, under the *Canadian Charter of Rights and Freedoms*, which guarantees freedom of expression, people are free to say what they like.

But the *Charter* does not extend the same degree of protection to the size, shape, or location of signs. The provincial government and municipalities may pass laws regulating signs as long as these laws are "content-neutral"; that is, they affect where the signs are put, rather than what they say. In the United States, the courts have long recognized that municipal governments have a legitimate role to play in preventing visual blight or clutter, even if that means a total prohibition on postering or signs in part of the whole city. It is not necessary to show that billboards are a traffic hazard to ban them; it is enough that they are unattractive. Aesthetics are recognized as a legitimate environmental concern.[45] The Canadian courts have also recently accepted the principle that municipal councils and other public authorities can pass bylaws to deal with visual and aesthetic blight.[46]

Canadian legislatures, however, have been reluctant to pass laws banning or restricting signs for purely aesthetic reasons, and have often limited these powers to such restrictions as can be justified for traffic safety. Several sections of the *Public Transportation and Highway Improvement Act*, for example, prohibit the display of signs, notices, and advertising devices within 400 metres of the edge of various kinds of roads.[47] Various sections of the *Municipal Act* also can be used to regulate traffic and prevent the blocking up of highways,[48] to prohibit and abate public nuisances,[49] and to prohibit or regulate the obstruction or encumbering of highways.[50] More explicitly, section 210.48 of the *Municipal Act* authorizes local municipalities to pass bylaws prohibiting or regulating signs and other advertising devices and the posting of notices on buildings or vacant lots within any defined area or areas or on land abutting on any highway. The Ontario Court of Appeal has ruled that a mobile sign used as an advertising display device, permanently mounted on a trailer and moved to a parking lot in front of the business renting the trailer, could be regulated by a bylaw passed under this section.[51]

Under the authority of this legislation, many municipalities have passed bylaws prohibiting the erection of signs in certain specified areas. In addition, many municipalities have a permit system to regulate the erection of signs where they are allowed. Municipalities also have the power to license companies that carry on the business of leasing mobile signs.[52] However, the courts have held that the power to license businesses does not usually extend to purely aesthetic considerations such as the external appearance of the property on which the business is being carried on, since this is to be dealt with through land-use planning laws.[53] Specifically, a power to license taxis was held not to include the power to prohibit them from affixing advertising to the car.[54] In fact, as more and more owners of fleets of vehicles see an opportunity to make money by plastering them with signs advertising other companies' products and services, it is questionable whether there is any current law in Ontario capable of preventing this, unless the signs impede the visibility of the road by other users.[55]

OTHER COMMERCIAL ACTIVITIES AND SOLICITATIONS

At the time of writing, it is looking more and more as if making money and the convenience of shoppers is Canada's overriding value. Unwanted commercial solicitations are received over the telephone at home and on the fax machine at the office. Tonnes of flyers and junk mail are dumped daily on Canada's doorsteps. Ontario's law creating a common day of rest was upheld by the courts, then abandoned by the provincial government because it inhibited consumerism.[56] There are proposals to turn part of the Parliament buildings in Ottawa into a shopping mall and to put the McDonald's "golden arches" logo on our postage stamps.

As our streets become more and more crowded with hoards of street vendors, newspaper boxes, movie "shoots," and other commercial activities, and our train stations, bus stations, and airports as well as our streets become a stage for organizations soliciting donations, trying to convert the unenlightened to their religion, or selling things, the concept of freedom of expression increasingly clashes with the attempts of governments to prevent visual blight and clutter. As with signs, the US courts have recognized the right of public authorities, and municipalities in particular, to control the ambience of public areas by limiting commercial activities[57] and political or religious activities. However, the Supreme Court of Canada has held that public authorities must allow some degree of political and religious haranguing and solicitation, as long as it is not incompatible with other public uses of public areas.[58]

A variety of provisions of the *Municipal Act* give municipalities the power to pass bylaws regulating or prohibiting sales on public roads and the blocking of highways,[59] the obstructing or encumbering of highways,[60] and public nuisances.[61] Using these sections, Metro Toronto has passed bylaws aimed at prohibiting street vending in downtown Toronto, where sellers of T-shirts, sunglasses, fake Rolex watches, and hot dogs are sometimes lined on the sidewalk for whole blocks. The courts rejected the arguments of vendors that this prohibition violates their rights of freedom of expression and freedom of association under the *Charter*.[62] However, the Supreme Court of Canada struck down the bylaw on other grounds. In British Columbia, municipal restrictions on placing newspaper vending boxes on public property have been upheld by the courts,[63] but in Quebec, one court has ruled that such restrictions are justified even though they may offend the right to freedom of expression,[64] while another struck down such a bylaw as an unwarranted infringement of freedom of the press.[65] Religion and politics, however, have been accorded somewhat more deference than commercial activities. Both in Canada and in the United States, the courts have struck down laws prohibiting religious sects and political groups from distributing tracts in public airports.[66]

"THROWAWAY" SOFT DRINK CONTAINERS

Besides presenting a standing invitation to litter, throwaway containers — non-refillable, non-returnable bottles and cans — are a microcosm of the issues associated with solid waste management: wasteful packaging, escalating costs of waste collection, transportation, and disposal. Even recycling, although it is better than just dumping, is no solution; for what is the sense of recycling an object that should never have been manufactured in the first place? Indeed, although they are discussed here for the sake of convenience, throwaways are a litter problem only incidentally. They are much more an example of the wasteful use of energy and resources.

Regulations Under the Environmental Protection Act

In the 1950s and 1960s, most soft drinks were sold in refillable containers. The deposit on such containers ensured that consumers had an incentive to return them to the store. They were then returned to the bottler, who refilled them. A single bottle could be refilled 6 or 8 times. By the mid-1970s, however, most soft drinks in Ontario were being sold in throwaway containers, either glass bottles that could not be returned for refill or steel cans. Neither could these containers be recycled. In 1976, the Ontario Legislature passed legislation to ensure that pop would continue to be available in refillable bottles in Ontario stores. This was the government's first action after a seven-year battle by environmental groups to ban throwaways entirely and to standardize the sizes and shapes of refillable bottles to make refilling them more efficient. (The Ontario brewers had voluntarily standardized the size and shape of beer bottles to facilitate refilling, but have since abandoned this standardization. When they did, environmentalists were silent, and the government didn't lift a finger to prevent this.)

The new legislation[67] amended the section of the *Environmental Protection Act* section on litter to permit Cabinet to make regulations dealing with beverage containers. Among the provisions, which have been described above, Cabinet was given the power to prohibit non-refillable containers within five years. This was not done, and the market share of non-refillables has continued to grow, gradually squeezing out refillables.

Regulations were made banning "flip top" or "pull tab" openers — the kind of opening device that can be detached from the can and thrown away. The openers created instant litter and a danger to the feet of children and the bills and intestines of wildfowl.[68]

Stores selling non-refillable cans or bottles also had to offer the same flavours and similar sizes in refillable bottles.[69] But the store was not required to stock the same brands or the same number of refillables or provide the same amount of shelf space as for non-refillables.

Purchasers were required to pay a deposit on refillable bottles, with a minimum deposit set for each size of bottles.[70] Store owners were required to take back up to 48 bottles a day from a consumer and return the deposit, provided that the bottles were intact and clean and were of a brand sold in that store.[71]

The regulations provided that advertising and labels showing the price of the pop had to show the amount of the deposit separately from the price of the beverage.[72] Advertising and labels for throwaways had to show the price of the same drink in refillable bottles,[73] presumably to show customers that refillables were no more expensive — and might be cheaper — than throwaways.

Although non-refillable and non-recyclable cans could continue to be sold, all bottles had to be refillable. Non-refillable bottles were to be banned as of April 1, 1978.[74] Merchants were required to display a notice telling the public that they had a right to return their bottles and collect the deposit.[75]

There were exemptions from the requirements to stock refillables. Catering trucks, vending machines, aircraft, and merchants in very remote areas of the province were exempt from the requirements to sell some pop in refillable bottles and from the ban on non-refillable glass bottles.[76]

Similar exemptions also covered certain "specialty" items such as non-alcoholic beer and wine, unflavoured mineral water, and beverages imported from countries other than the United States.

Beer and soft drink cans were not banned, as environmentalists requested. Instead, the Ontario government introduced a bill in the spring of 1977 that would have imposed a "pollution tax" of 5 cents on each can of soft drink sold, to encourage the purchase of refillables.[77] But the bill died when an election was called, and was never reintroduced.

Environment Minister George Kerr announced in March 1977 that he would implement "future action programs" to curtail the use of non-refillable and non-recyclable wine and liquor bottles, but no action was taken.

By 1985, when Ontario's Progressive Conservative government was replaced by a Liberal government, sales of pop in refillable glass bottles had continued to drop. The steel can was more popular, and pop companies were attempting to introduce plastic bottles and aluminum cans as well, both of which use large amounts of energy to produce, and neither of which were intended to be refilled.

The government compromised on a solution that would retain a small market share for refillables but encourage the recycling of other containers. Thus, while non-refillables would dominate the market, they would at least be recycled rather than thrown away. There is no doubt that these containers have some environmental and safety advantages. Cans are lighter, more compact, and less breakable than glass bottles. Plastic bottles are also lighter and less breakable, if no more compact.

The "solution" enshrined in the 1985 revisions to the regulations[78] was to allow both refillable and non-refillable pop containers, but to require the bottlers of pop (called "brand owners" in the regulation) to report to the ministry that at least 30 per cent by volume of the soft drinks they have sold to distributors are in refillable containers. The distributors of pop (called "brand users" in the regulation)[79] had to report selling at least 30 per cent of their soft drinks in refillable containers. These bottlers and distributors were required to report their monthly sales volumes to an independent auditor designated by the ministry within 20 days of the end of the month, or be fined for failing to report or prohibited from continuing to use non-refillable containers.[80] If the brand user advertises his or her product in the media, equal time and space must be given to refillables as non-refillables, and if the price of a non-refillable is advertised, the price of the refillable must also be shown.[81]

Non-refillable containers of pop could be sold only if they were recyclable, there is a market for the recycled material in Ontario, and they are collected at a recycling project.[82] If less than 50 per cent of the containers are being recycled, the seller must charge a deposit to encourage recycling.[83]

Stores selling soft drinks continued to be subject to requirements similar to those in the 1976 regulations. They must continue to sell pop in refillable bottles, accept empties for return to the distributor, give the purchaser back his or her deposit, show the price of the pop separate from the deposit, give refillables and non-refillables equal space in advertisements, and display a sign saying that empties are accepted and deposits returned.[84]

In return for the concessions allowing more varieties of non-refillable containers, the beverage industry agreed to set up a recycling program for such containers. The companies formed a corporation, Ontario Multi-Material Recycling Inc. (OMMRI), which established the "blue box" program. By 1989, however, the industry had fulfilled its promise to set up this program, and money had to be found to continue its operation. The industry had not promised to do this.

Markets for the material being collected were not always available. Much of the material collected continued to be buried in waste disposal sites. In addition, consumers preferred to buy their pop in non-refillable containers. Distributors were not meeting their quota of sales of refillable bottles.

In 1990, the minister of the environment announced that the quotas for sales of refillable bottles established in 1985 would be dropped. Although distributors and retailers would still have to sell pop in refillable bottles, there would be no quota. Coincidentally, the minister announced that a group of companies in the grocery industry, which is opposed to providing space for dealing with refillable bottles, had come forward with an offer to fund the continued operation of the blue box program. Was there a deal between the minister and the industry ("Drop the quota and we will fund the continuation of the program; continue the quota and the government will have to fund recycling itself")? Ruth Grier, the NDP environment critic, asked this question in the Legislature, but the minister side-stepped it. OMMRI II was formed and the blue box program not only continued but expanded.[85] Several months later the NDP formed the government. Ruth Grier — who was now environment minister — informed the soft drink industry that the 30 per cent refillable quota would continue and would be enforced.

Although the members of the soft drink, grocery, newspaper, and packaging industries claim that the increased recycling of other materials accomplished through the blue box program more than offsets the lower degree of re-use of refillable bottles, environmentalists disagree. They claim that by the end of 1991, only 10 per cent of Ontario soft drinks were being sold in Ontario and the blue box program was capturing only 20 per cent of the non-refillable containers.[86] Meanwhile, the environment minister had concluded that her predecessor was right — the law was unenforceable.

Municipal Bylaws

There are no municipal bylaws regulating the sale of throwaways. Fed up with Ontario government inaction, several municipalities passed their own bylaws banning the sale of throwaways or asked the province to pass legislation enabling them to regulate throwaways. London passed a bylaw in 1975 banning throwaways,[87] but the soft drink industry challenged its validity, and it was quashed by the Ontario Supreme Court.[88] Windsor requested and received special legislation permitting it to pass such a bylaw, which it did.[89] However, instead of prohibiting all sales on non-returnables, the bylaw provided for an exception: soft drinks could still be sold in non-returnable containers from vending machines. Soft drink bottlers and supermarkets challenged the bylaw. The Divisional Court struck it down, because Windsor only had the power to prohibit all sales, not to regulate by allowing some sales.[90] Ottawa asked for similar powers, but the province refused to give them.[91]

Alcoholic Beverages

To help make the purchase of refillables more attractive than cans, the Ontario treasurer has approved a levy of 5 cents on beer in cans. The Ontario government had been considering extending this levy to pop in non-refillable containers, but by the end of 1992 appeared to be backing away from this as a result of industry pressure.

Other Provinces and Countries

In 1973, Alberta enacted the *Beverage Container Act*,[92] which requires a deposit on *all* ready-to-serve alcoholic and non-alcoholic beverage containers. To obtain their deposit refund, people may return the bottles to privately run depots. The company that produced the container must then purchase the returned container from the depot for re-use, recycling, or disposal. It has been estimated that this system results in up to 95 per cent of liquor and spirit bottles being returned, and 80 per cent of all other bottles subject to deposits.[93] There are similar laws in some US states.[94]

In Europe, there are taxes and deposits on non-refillable bottle containers, or manufacturers are required to comply with quotas for production of refillables, not only for pop, but also for other beverages.

What Citizens Can Do About Throwaways

Citizens can take steps to ensure that the regulations are enforced. When shopping at neighbourhood stores, check to see whether refillables are displayed in every size and flavour in which throwaways are displayed, and whether a notice is posted telling buyers of their rights to a refund of their deposit. If not, ask the store owner whether he or she is aware of breaking the law. If it is a chain store, write to the president or legal counsel for the chain and inform them of the fault. Tell the store owner that the ministry will provide any signs needed. Then write to the minister of the environment and ask him or her to enforce the law, ask to be advised of the action taken, and say that you will inspect the store again in one month. Report any advertising in the store or the media that does not give adequate attention to refillables, as required by the regulation.

Of course, if the minister does not lay charges, you can do so (see Chapter 3).

CAN YOU SUE FOR A VIEW? UNSIGHTLINESS AS NUISANCE

One writer has said:

"Visual pollution" or the destruction of a view can interfere with an individual's use and enjoyment of his property in a fashion similar to that of noise, vibration, polluted air or bad odours. Therefore, this type of interference should at least be accorded the same treatment by the law of nuisance* as that provided for these other disturbances.[95]

Unfortunately, in the past the courts have not agreed. A judge has ruled that a plaintiff had no right to sue a neighbour who built a warehouse cutting off her view of a river.[96] The courts have also said that no nuisance action can be maintained because of the unsightly or unaesthetic use of land. "The scrap-yard may be an eyesore," one judge said, "but this is not something that can be taken into consideration."[97] This doctrine was cited and followed in two nuisance actions involving gravel pits in the late 1970s.[98] In one of these actions, the judge said: "Whatever the facts, I do not think that the defendant owed no duty to the plaintiffs to preserve the appearance of its land for the plaintiffs' benefits."[99]

CONCLUSION

The law has generally been reluctant to protect abstract aesthetic values that are difficult to quantify. It is much more comfortable dealing with questions of money, property, and human health. Where the law has recognized aesthetic considerations on such basic levels as littering, it is obvious that a private prosecution in each instance of law breaking is not the aim of the legislation. What we need is a general shift in values to recognize aesthetic and energy considerations in packaging laws. Comprehensive provincial laws are needed against excessive packaging, wasting of energy and resources, disposable products, and planned obsolescence; so is some recognition of the intangible aspects of the quality of life — some legislative recognition that beauty is real, not just a figment of the imagination. Yet, in some situations, prosecutions and civil suits may still be useful and even necessary to ensure that long-term measures are more quickly obtained.

John Swaigen

---

* See Chapter 18.

ENDNOTES

1   *Highway Traffic Act*, RSO 1990, c. H.8.
2   Ibid., section 180 [emphasis added].
3   Ibid., section 214(1).
4   Ibid., section 214(2).
5   Ibid., SO 1983, c. 63, section 1(1)(14). This amendment was probably intended to remove the ambiguity in the section as to whether it encompassed sidewalks, shoulders, and boulevards. The section gives effect to court decisions that had interpreted the term "highway" in this way: see *Hughes v. J.H. Watkins & Co.* (1928), 61 OLR 587 (Ont. CA); *McQueen v. Corporation of the Town of Niagara on the Lake* (1987), 37 MPLR 305 (Ont. Dist. Ct.).
6   *Gill v. Elwood* (1969), 9 DLR (3d) 681 (Ont. CA); see also *Annan v. Myers*, [1968] 1 OR 328 (Cty. Ct.).
7   *Highway Traffic Act*, supra endnote 1, section 207. The owner is not responsible, however, if the car was in the driver's possession without the owner's consent at the time of the offence.
8   Before *Moore v. the Queen* (1978), 43 CCC (2d) 83 (SCC), many lawyers advised that a person found committing an offence against a provincial statute or municipal bylaw had no duty to identify himself to a police officer. In *Moore* the Supreme Court of Canada ruled that a bicyclist who went through a red light contrary to the BC equivalent of Ontario's *Highway Traffic Act* was committing the criminal offence of obstructing a peace officer in the execution of his duty by refusing to give his name. The majority of the judges ruled that when an officer has a duty to enforce a provincial law, the offender has a duty to cooperate by giving his name. However, in British Columbia, provincial offences are prosecuted under part of the BC *Summary Convictions Act*, which in turn refers to a portion of the *Criminal Code* that gives police officers a power of arrest for such offences. In Ontario, provincial offences are prosecuted under an Ontario statute, the *Provincial Offences Act*, RSO 1990, c. P.33, section 84. This statute is a self-contained code of practice that makes no reference to the *Criminal Code*. Therefore, it is questionable whether the *Moore* case applies in Ontario.
9   *Environmental Protection Act*, RSO 1990, c. E.19, section 84.
10 Ibid., section 86.
11 *R. v. Marchinko*, Ont. Ct. Prov. Div., April 10, 1992, Ebbs J, Sandwich South Township [unreported], overturned on appeal on other grounds June 8, 1992.
12 *Environmental Protection Act*, supra endnote 9, section 89(1).
13 Ibid., section 89(2).
14 Ibid., section 85.
15 Ibid., section 87.
16 Ibid., sections 89 and 176(7).
17 Ibid., section 40.
18 Ibid., section 25.
19 Ibid., section 186.
20 Ibid., section 190.
21 *R. v. Krickovick*, Ont. Prov. Ct., Cayuga, March 21, 1977, Girard Prov. J [unreported].

22 *R. v. Anthony*, Ont. Prov. Off. Ct., Newmarket, April 18, 1986 [unreported].
23 *Public Parks Act*, RSO 1990, c. P.46, section 11.
24 *Public Lands Act*, RSO 1990, c. P.43, section 7.
25 *National Parks Act*, RSC 1985, c. N-14, National Parks Regulations, PC 1980-741, SOR/80-217, section 8.
26 *Provincial Parks Act*, RSO 1990, c. P.34, section 21(1)(a), RRO 1990, reg. 952, section 3 (which deals with litter).
27 *Municipal Act*, RSO 1990, c. M.45, section 210.82.
28 *Re Allen and City of Hamilton* (1987), 59 OR (2d) 498 (CA), rev'g. (1986), 55 OR (2d) 387 (HCJ).
29 For example, City of Toronto bylaw no. 144-69, City of Toronto bylaw no. 20298, section 7.
30 *City of Scarborough Act*, SO 1923, c. 88, as amended.
31 Memorandum from J. Thomas Riley to General Committee of Council, City of Etobicoke, April 4, 1984.
32 For example, North York parks bylaw no. 110377; North York bylaw no. 25746; North York bylaw no. 28020; Scarborough bylaw no. 17154; East York bylaw no. 238; Etobicoke bylaw no. 1979-15; York bylaw no. 276-77; Toronto bylaw nos. 34-74 (city hall square), 12519 (streets), and 319-69 (city parks). For further information about this issue, see item 3, report no. 16, East York Parks and Recreation Committee, as adopted by council October 7, 1985, City of Toronto Neighbourhoods Committee report no. 5, 1985.
33 Riley, supra endnote 31.
34 *Highway Traffic Act*, supra endnote 1, section 59.
35 *Municipal Act*, supra endnote 27, sections 210.136 and 233.6.
36 "Communications Direction," from Ruth Grier, MPP, to members of municipal councils, July 15, 1988; Letter, Richard D. Lindgren, counsel, Canadian Environmental Law Association, to Ruth Grier, September 27, 1988. For an example of a municipality prepared to change the zoning of rural land to allow the establishment of an automobile salvage yard without having satisfactorily addressed environmental concerns, without the technical expertise required to monitor such yards, and without having in place a bylaw to regulate the construction, control, and operation of such a facility, see *Re Township of Monteagle Zoning By-Law 3-87*, November 24, 1987, Ontario Municipal Board, G.M. Hobart and E.F. Crossland, members.
37 *Environmental Protection Act*, supra endnote 9, RRO 1970, reg. 824, section 13.
38 *Environmental Protection Act*, Waste Management Regulation, RRO 1990, reg. 347, section 5.
39 *Highway Traffic Act*, supra endnote 1, section 220(6).
40 Property standards bylaw, Newcastle bylaw no. 82-63, section 5.1.1.4.
41 For further information about ways to regulate salvage yards and court and OMB decisions affecting these facilities, see Ontario, Ministry of Municipal Affairs, *Planning Issue Info-Sheet*, no. 1, "Salvage Yards," December 1987.
42 *Landlord and Tenant Act*, RSO 1990, c. L.7.
43 The board is established under the *Residential Rent Regulation Act*, RSO 1990, c. R.29.
44 Rental Housing Maintenance Standards, O. reg. 768/88.

45 *Members of the City Council of Los Angeles v. Taxpayers for Vincent*, 14 S. Ct. 2118 1984) (prohibiting the posting of signs on streets).

46 *Ramsden v. Peterborough (City)* (1991), 5 OR (3d) 289 (CA), leave to appeal to SCC granted June 4, 1992.

47 *Public Transportation and Highway Improvement Act*, RSO 1990, c. P.50, sections 38, 63, and 534.

48 *Municipal Act*, supra endnote 27, section 210.73.

49 Ibid., section 210.41.

50 Ibid., section 314(1).1.

51 *Re Mobile Ad Ltd. and the Borough of Scarborough* (1974), 50 DLR (3d) 191 (Ont. CA). The court held that the phrase "for prohibiting or regulating signs and other advertising devices" was separate from the latter part of the provision, dealing with the posting of notices. While a bylaw dealing with the posting of notices would be restricted to notices on buildings, vacant lots, or abutting highways, bylaws for regulating signs and other advertising devices were not so restricted. However, the dissenting judgment held that "the general regulation of the provincially ubiquitous sign industry [is] reserved to provincial codification."

52 *Municipal Act*, supra endnote 27, section 210.147.

53 *Re Texaco Canada Limited and City of Vanier* (1981), 120 DLR (3d) 193 (SCC).

54 *Re Robinson and Board of Commissioners of Police of the City of Kingston* (1980), 29 OR (2d) 326 (Ont. Div. Ct.).

55 For example, section 92(11) of the *Highway Traffic Act*, supra endnote 1, prohibits the height of any vehicle, including its load, from exceeding 4.15 metres while on a highway.

56 *R. v. Edwards Books & Art Ltd.*, [1988] 2 SCR 713, 28 CRRI, and discussion of this law in Chapter 3.

57 See, for example, *City of New Orleans v. Dukes*, 47 US 297 (1976) (prohibiting street vending); *New York v. Milbry*, 530 NYS 2d 928 (NY City Crim. Ct. 1988) (prohibiting vendors, including artists, from displaying paintings for sale on the street).

58 *Committee for the Commonwealth of Canada v. Canada* (1991), 77 OLR (4th) 385 (SCC).

59 *Municipal Act*, supra endnote 27, section 210.73.

60 Ibid., section 314(1).1.

61 Ibid., section 210.140.

62 *R. v. Sharma*, Ont. Prov. Off. Ct., November 15, 1988, Draper PCJ [unreported], upheld, Ont. Dist. Ct., May 2, 1989, Lang DCJ [unreported]; *R. v. Greenbaum*, Ont. Prov. Off. Ct., November 14, 1988, Kerr PCJ [unreported], aff'd. (1989), 47 MPLR 59 (Ont. Dist. Ct.). These decisions were upheld by the Ontario Court of Appeal (*R. v. Sharma; R. v. Greenbaum* (1991), 3 MPLR (2d) 1), but were overturned by the Supreme Court of Canada, which held that the *Municipal Act* does not empower municipalities to pass bylaws prohibiting all street vending: February 5, 1993, per Iacobucci J [unreported].

63 *Canadian Newspapers Co. v. Victoria (City)* (1989), 63 DLR (4th) 1 (BC CA).

64 *Canadian Newspapers Co. v. Montreal (Ville)*, [1988] RJQ 482 (CS).

65 *Re Canadian Newspapers Co. Ltd. and Director of Public Road and Traffic Services of City of Quebec* (1986), 36 DLR (4th) 641 (Que. SC).

66 The American cases are cited in the Canadian case of *Committee for the Commonwealth of Canada v. Canada* (1986), 1 FTR 70 (FCTD), aff'd. (1991), 77 DLR (4th) 385 (SCC).

67 Now *Environmental Protection Act*, supra endnote 9, section 176(7).

68 O. reg. 687/76, as amended by O. reg. 114/77.

69 Ibid., section 11(1), as amended.

70 The deposit on a 200 or 300 ml bottle had to be at least 10 cents, on a 750 ml bottle 20 cents, and on a 1.5 litre bottle 30 cents: O. reg. 687/76, as amended by O. reg. 146/77, section 2.

71 Ibid., section 6.

72 Ibid., section 9(1).

73 Ibid., section 9(2).

74 O. reg. 146/77, section 12(1).74.22.

75 Ibid., section 6, amending O. reg. 687/76, section 14.

76 Ibid., section 4, amending O. reg. 687/76, section 12.

77 Ontario, Bill 53, *An Act To Impose a Tax on Certain Pollutants of the Environment in Ontario*, April 19, 1977.

78 O. regs. 622/85, 623/85, and 633/85.

79 O. reg. 623/85, section 1, now RRO 1990, reg. 340.

80 Ibid., section 8.

81 Ibid., section 7.

82 Ibid., section 9(2).

83 Ibid., section 9(4).

84 O. reg. 622/85.

85 Ontario, Legislative Assembly, *Debates.*

86 "Ontario Urged To Enforce Refillables" (November-December 1991), *Ontario Conservation News* 3.

87 City of London bylaw no. PS 70-2117, as amended, 1976.

88 *Dev-Kay Vending v. The Corporation of the City of London*, Supreme Court of Ontario, April 1976, Hughes J [unreported].

89 *City of Windsor Act*, 1976, SO 1976 (2d Sess.), c. 1110; City of Windsor bylaw no. 5625, February 7, 1977.

90 *Canada Dry Bottling Co. (Windsor) Ltd., N & D Supermarket Ltd., Metro Windsor Catering Co. Ltd. and C.J. Woolcox Stores Ltd. v. The Corporation of the City of Windsor*, Supreme Court of Ontario, Divisional Court, July 26, 1978, Dupont J [unreported].

91 Letter, Edythe M. Dronshek, assistant city solicitor, City of London, to Deborah Curran, researcher, Canadian Institute for Environmental Law and Policy, July 18, 1990.

92 Alberta, *Beverage Container Act*, RSA 1980, c. B-4.

93 The statistics are found in report no. 16 of the Management Committee adopted by the Council of the Municipality of Metropolitan Toronto, May 9, 1990. The report notes that the Ontario government has rejected the Alberta approach because "[t]he MOE, Ontario Multi-Material Recycling Inc., and other agencies such as the Liquor Control Board of Ontario, believe that voluntary source separation recycling programs, rather

than forced deposit systems, are the most cost-effective means of recovering a broad range of materials, including wine and spirit bottles, from the municipal waste stream. They feel that, through the initiation of deposit systems, people are taught that recycling is a task undertaken to get a deposit back from consumed beverage containers, as opposed to being an integral part of an overall solid waste management system."

94 For example, Oregon passed legislation requiring a deposit on beer and soft drink containers in 1971; see also Iowa, *Beverage Container Deposit Law*, 1979 (liquor, beer, mineral water, and carbonated soft drink bottles); and New York, *Returnable Container Act*, 1983 (all soft drink and beer containers capable of holding one gallon or less). In May 1990, legislation that would establish a nationwide deposit system for beer and soft drinks was before Congress. This bill has been reintroduced on several occasions but has been blocked by an industry lobby against it. For a description of the US laws on this subject, see United States, General Accounting Office, *Solid Waste: Trade-Offs Involved in Beverage Deposit Legislation — Report to Congressional Requesters*, GAO/RCED-91-25 (Washington, DC: US GAO, 1991).

95 Samuel Silverstone, "Visual Pollution: Unaesthetic Use of Land as Nuisance" (1974), 12 *Alberta Law Review* 542, at 546.

96 *McBean v. Wyllie* (1902), 15 Man. LR 135 (KB).

97 *Morris v. Dominion Foundries Ltd.* (1947), 2 DLR 840 (Ont. HCJ).

98 *Muirhead v. Timbers Brothers Sand and Gravel Ltd.* (1977), 3 CCLT 1 (Ont. HCJ); *Walker v. Pioneer Construction Co. (1967) Ltd.* (1975), 8 OR (2d) 35 (HCJ).

99 *Walker*, supra endnote 98, at 39.

23

Pits and Quarries

Contents

"The blasts scare the devil out of you."

"The blasts shook my buildings and rattled windows, and I'm half a mile away. And no one told us this mine was going in until the contractor came to warn us of the blasting they were going to do."

Two residents of Manitoulin Island, an area of Ontario not subject to the protection of the Aggregate Resources Act, *discussing the effects of a new quarry*

Crushed stone, sand, gravel, shale, limestone, dolostone, sandstone, and other minerals suitable for construction, collectively known as "aggregate" or "mineral aggregate," are vital to virtually all types of construction. Government and industry rely on a large, steady, and cheap supply of aggregate for constructing roads, residential and non-residential buildings, and other major construction projects such as water works, sewage systems, and electric power installations.

Ontario uses more aggregate than any other part of Canada,[1] and our insatiable appetite continues to expand. In 1970, 13 tons of sand and gravel were extracted in Ontario for every person living in the province. By 1980, aggregate production had increased to 120 million tonnes, or 14 tonnes per person.[2] In 1987, 186 million tonnes, or 20 tonnes per person, were used.[3]

Since the largest single expense in producing aggregate is the cost of transportation, aggregate producers concentrate their efforts on acquiring land to mine as close as possible to their major market — the rapidly urbanizing strip stretching around Lake Ontario and Lake Erie. As a result, most of the aggregates are produced and used in southern Ontario, where 91 per cent of the people live.

Thus, economics have dictated that most land held for use as pits and quarries lies in the same area as most of Ontario's population, the best agricultural land, the unique Niagara Escarpment, and many of our most important wetlands. Ontario government policies designed to encourage the location and expansion of pits and quarries near the major markets, to ensure a continued supply of cheap aggregate, have promoted serious land-use conflicts.

Pits and quarries generate dust and noise, which affect neighbouring residents. Excavation and blasting may damage structures, water tables, and neighbouring wells. Blasting operations have thrown huge boulders onto highways and rained rocks onto nearby residential land. Occasionally, aggregate operations also cause surface and groundwater pollution, erosion, silty runoff, and the sedimentation of streams.[4] The truck traffic to and from these sites is often a serious hazard and nuisance affecting people throughout a much larger area. These open holes, often adjacent to residential areas, can also be an eyesore. If they are not rehabilitated, they can scar the landscape and create a danger for decades.

Inadequate rehabilitation also creates other problems. Abandoned pits and quarries that have not been properly graded are a safety hazard. Unrehabilitated sites have filled with water, resulting in drownings.[5] In the Sudbury area, abandoned or unreclaimed quarries have created erosion in local lakes and streams.[6]

Extractive operations require the removal of topsoil, which may be properly stockpiled and re-used during rehabilitation, but sometimes is allowed to blow away or run off into water courses. A favourite method of "rehabilitating" pits and quarries is to turn them into waste disposal sites and fill them with garbage, prolonging the environmental problems and creating new ones.

In the past, pits and quarries have been licensed in areas that will destroy features of significant natural, historical, architectural, or archaeological interest. Extractive activities were allowed on land intended for incorporation into a provincial park;[7] in an area of Pelee Island believed to be habitat for several endangered species of flora and fauna;[8] and on the only occurrence of the Oriskany Formation in Canada, which is the site of the only dry oak-hickory forest on sandstone in Ontario and the habitat of at least 22 rare plant species as well as the threatened black rat snake.[9]

In the heavily urbanized areas of southern Ontario, most of the land containing significant gravel deposits, and either actively mined or held for future mining, is owned by a small number of companies with vast land holdings close to major cities. There appears to be a trend toward vertical integration, with a few large companies that produce cement and concrete taking over many of the suppliers of aggregate. From an environmental viewpoint, this is a mixed blessing. On the one hand, this means that those who control the aggregate resources have the economic and political clout to successfully rout opposition to the establishment of new pits and quarries and the expansion of old ones. On the other hand, these large companies also have the money to incorporate more environmental protection into the design and operation of these pits and quarries than smaller companies.

In the north, the pattern is different. Because most of the money is to be made in southern Ontario, the north is characterized by small companies operating smaller pits. These companies have lobbied successfully against being included in the legislation that requires pits and quarries to be licensed. They argue that if they must meet stringent environmental controls, they cannot afford to compete with large operators. Their lobbying efforts are supported by the small municipalities of the north, which rely on cheap aggregates, and do not want to pay more for sand and gravel to protect the environment.[10] As these areas develop, history repeats itself, as the land-use conflicts and environmental degradation associated with the pits and quarries of the south move north, without laws to prevent them.

THE HISTORY OF AGGREGATE INDUSTRY REGULATION IN ONTARIO

Woefully inadequate local and provincial controls have allowed haphazard expansion of pits and quarries in Ontario. Until 1970, there was no effective provincial control over aggregate operations. As the Ministry of Natural Resources (MNR) now candidly admits, "some members of the industry ran their operations in complete disregard for the environment, the rights of neighbouring landowners or their obligations as good corporate citizens."[11]

Reform of law and policy has always been driven by MNR's mandate to ensure a steady supply of cheap aggregates. According to the ministry, the first legislation to effectively regulate the industry did not result primarily from concern about the environment or the rights of neighbours. It was a response to industry concerns that municipal bylaws prohibiting the expansion of existing pits and quarries or the establishment of new ones would result in an aggregate shortage.[12] In response to the industry's concerns, the provincial government stepped in and established the Mineral Resources Committee in 1969. Its recommendations led to the passage of the *Niagara Escarpment Protection Act* in 1969, providing interim protection of the escarpment until the first provincial legislation dealing specifically with aggregate mining was passed in 1971 — the *Pits and Quarries Control Act*.[13]

Although it improved controls over pits and quarries, the *Pits and Quarries Control Act* was adequate neither to protect the environment nor to prevent citizen groups and munici-palities from launching substantial, prolonged, and sometimes successful opposition to new mines and the expansion of existing ones.[14] Once again, MNR stepped in to protect the industry. As before, the government could not justify protecting the industry without also acknowledging the validity of environmental concerns and moving in the direction of stronger environmental protection at the same time.

In the mid-1970s, the ministry commissioned several reports dealing with the future demand and supply of aggregate in central Ontario, southeastern Ontario and southwestern Ontario.[15] These reports identified and mapped the significant aggregate deposits. Their authors argued that we desperately needed more aggregate; that unless immediate steps were taken there would be serious shortages.[16] But the feeling of urgency pervading these reports was not tempered by any thorough examination of the increased environmental degradation that an expansion of the industry would cause.

In December 1975, the ministry established the Ontario Aggregate Working Party to review the regulatory framework. The working party published its report in January 1977.[17] The main thrust of the report was to recommend the elimination of most local controls — the strongest impediment to the establishment and expansion of pits and quarries — in favour of a unified provincial structure of regulation. Municipalities at the county or regional level would be required to designate certain minimum areas for aggregate expansion in their official plans. Only after this was done would these municipalities have the authority to issue licences within these areas. Each of these municipalities would be required to fulfil an annual quota of production. The report recommended that the *Municipal Act* and *Planning Act* be amended to delete the municipalities' power to pass bylaws prohibiting and regulating pits and quarries. The working party was critical of the lack of rehabilitation under the *Pits and Quarries Control Act* and the ministry's lack of enforcement of the Act, and made recommendations to strengthen the legislation and improve environmental protection.

MNR was quick to act on the recommendations to force municipalities to accept more pits and quarries, but in no hurry to implement the recommendations for stronger environmental protection. The government set up a committee consisting of MNR and the two other ministries most interested in ensuring a cheap supply of gravel.[18] As a result of this process, in 1979, MNR adopted the "Mineral Aggregate Policy for Official Plans," which provided that lands identified as having significant aggregate deposits could not be developed until the aggregates had first been removed. In other words, aggregate extraction was given priority over all other land uses. When the new *Planning Act*[19] was passed in 1983, giving municipalities greater control over land-use planning, but subject to binding provincial policies, the first provincial policy made under the Act was a version of the 1979 policy.[20] Under this policy, the provincial government will not approve any municipal official plan unless it contains policies to ensure that aggregate extraction will be given priority over all other land uses. To this day, this policy is used to prevent municipalities from allowing any other form of development on lands containing significant aggregate deposits.[21] Another decade was to pass before the government would approve any such *Planning Act* policies designed to protect the environment.

MNR felt no similar urgency to implement the Ontario Aggregate Working Party recommendations designed to protect the environment. Although the government introduced a new *Aggregates Act* in 1979 that contained greater protection for the environment, it was soon withdrawn.[22] The *Pits and Quarries Control Act*, which the working party had condemned as inadequate, remained the law for more than a decade. A new *Aggregate Resources Act*,[23] significantly increasing environmental protection, was not reintroduced until June 1988. It came into force on January 1, 1990.

CURRENT CONTROLS OVER AGGREGATE EXTRACTION

The Land-Use Planning Process

Municipalities retain some control over whether pits and quarries can be established or expanded through the planning process set out in the *Planning Act*. The municipality can establish policies governing pits and quarries in its official plan, and can implement these policies through zoning bylaws.

Official plans sometimes prohibit the establishment of pits and quarries unless the operator enters into an agreement with the municipality such as those described below;[24] prohibit extractive industries from stockpiling soil and producing asphalt and concrete without specific authority in the zoning bylaw; and require the rehabilitation of pits to an after-use that is compatible with the long-term uses permitted by the plan. Official plan policies may restrict the establishment of pits and quarries on prime agricultural land or where they will exceed community tolerance, or prohibit their operation below the water table.[25]

The *Planning Act* explicitly gives municipalities the power to pass zoning bylaws prohibiting the use of land for pits and quarries. In this context, "use of land" includes the establishment, making, or operation of a pit or quarry,[26] and the *Aggregate Resources Act* prohibits the minister of natural resources from issuing any licence that will conflict with a municipal zoning bylaw. As mentioned, zoning bylaws can prevent wayside pits and quarries in areas where they would be incompatible with existing development or areas of particular environmental sensitivity.

As mentioned above, however, municipal controls are severely constrained by the provincial government's Mineral Aggregate Resource Planning Policy Statement (MARPPS). MARPPS requires official plans to identify both existing pits and quarries and unmined deposits of aggregate, and to protect both from any incompatible land uses. The official plan must also contain a "clear and reasonable" mechanism to facilitate the establishment and expansion of pits and quarries and must make provision for wayside pits and quarries. Zoning bylaws must be designed to permit all existing pits and quarries to continue and to prevent any activity that is incompatible with aggregate expansion in zones that permit pits and quarries. Where there is no official plan, all lands containing deposits of aggregates identified by MNR as important must be zoned to permit the development of pits and quarries and to prohibit any development that would be incompatible with future aggregate extraction. Wayside pits and quarries must be permitted in all zoning categories, except in zones established to recognize existing development or areas of particular environmental sensitivity.

Moreover, MARPPS directs all municipal planning authorities to protect aggregate producers when the municipality is carrying out functions such as deciding whether to approve subdivisions or grant consents to severance.

The pre-emptive power of MARPPS is somewhat lessened by an acknowledgment that there may be cases in which other land uses may "in specific instances take precedence over aggregate extraction." In addition, the Ontario Food Land Guidelines, which are also binding on municipalities under the *Planning Act*, restrict aggregate extraction on good agricultural land unless the agricultural use can be substantially restored after extraction ends.[27]

Regulation Under the Municipal Act

Although the *Aggregate Resources Act* sets up an elaborate scheme of regulation of pits and quarries, the standards set out in it are minimum standards. Under the *Municipal Act*,[28] municipal councils may supplement those requirements with more stringent setback, operational, and rehabilitation requirements.[29]

Under the *Municipal Act*, municipal councils have the power to pass bylaws

> for regulating the operation of pits and quarries within the municipality and for requiring the owners of pits and quarries that are located within such distance of a road as is specified in the by-law and that have not been in operation for a period of twelve consecutive months to level and grade the floor and sides thereof and such area beyond their edge or rim as is specified in the by-law so that they will not be dangerous or unsightly to the public.[30]

Ontario's highest court has held that this provision gives sweeping powers to municipalities to deal with such matters as hours of operation, types of machinery used, dust control, setbacks, grades and contours, and rehabilitation (including posting security to rehabilitate). The municipality may also require a pit or quarry owner to enter into an agreement with the municipality respecting its operations as a condition of being allowed to expand.[31] However, the *Aggregate Resources Act* and court decisions have restricted municipal powers to this section of the *Municipal Act*, and prohibit the municipality from using other sections of the Act, such as its power to prevent nuisances, as a means of regulating pits and quarries.[32]

Traffic Laws

One of the most common complaints about pits and quarries in rural areas is that nearby residents are bothered at all hours of the day and night by noise, vibrations, and dust from heavy trucks going back and forth from the operation, and fear an increase in traffic accidents. In addition to the licensing process, there are both provincial and municipal laws that may be useful to regulate truck traffic.

The Highway Traffic Act

Under the *Highway Traffic Act*,[33] heavy trucks on unpaved highways require special permits. On class B highways, which include most unpaved rural roads, no vehicle with a weight of over 8,200 kg on one axle may travel without a permit.[34] The weight limit is gross weight, so if the truck whether empty or loaded is over these limits, it needs a permit. You can be sure that any truck that is loaded or even half-loaded with gravel will be overweight,* and thus using the unpaved road illegally unless it has the required permit.

Heavier vehicles and loads can travel on class A roads. All hard-surfaced roads except those on which a municipal bylaw prohibits heavy traffic are class A highways.[35] Even for these paved roads there are maximum weights, and these limits cannot be exceeded without a permit.[36]

These permits are generally used by the Ministry of Transportation for provincial highways and roads that go through more than one municipality, and by municipal road authorities for other roads. They may have conditions attached. Using the highways without such a permit, or in a way that violates the conditions in the permit, is an offence punishable by a fine that increases in proportion to the amount by which the load exceeds the limits in the Act.[37]

To determine whether a road is a class A or a class B highway, get the name or number of the road and phone the clerk of the municipality. To find out whether the truck owner has a permit to travel this road overweight and whether there are any conditions on the permit, telephone the clerk of the municipality in which the road is located or the Ministry of Transportation.

Municipal Bylaws

Municipalities have a variety of powers to control traffic on their roads under several sections of the *Municipal Act*, or in the case of the large regional municipalities governed by special statutes, in their enabling legislation. In particular, section 210.123 of the *Municipal Act*[38] gives municipalities additional powers, in conjunction with those in the *Highway Traffic Act*, to pass bylaws regulating traffic and prohibiting heavy traffic on specific roads designated by bylaws and restricting the hours of travel and designating narrow roads for "one-way" traffic. These bylaws are used to create "truck routes."[39]

Entrances to Roads

It is illegal to create a new entrance to a public road without permission from the municipality and the Ministry of Transportation. Since new pits often require the establishment of such access points, some control over public safety and truck routes can be exercised through this permitting process.

LICENSING AND PERMITTING UNDER THE AGGREGATE RESOURCES ACT

The *Aggregate Resources Act*, administered by the Ministry of Natural Resources, provides a scheme for licensing, regulating, and rehabilitating pits and quarries. If properly administered, it can provide a positive and viable mechanism for the control of aggregate extraction

---

* One way to find out what an empty truck would weigh is to check with a truck dealer who sells that type of vehicle. You should note the model and type of box. In addition, the OPP have the authority to require trucks suspected of breaching the *Highway Traffic Act* to be weighed on scales in the area.

in areas of the province to which it applies. As of March 1993, only 355 of Ontario's 800 municipalities were covered by the Act.[40] Although the Act applies to aggregate extraction on Crown land throughout Ontario, it applies to the private sector only in designated areas. In 1993, the designated area covered southern Ontario south of the Canadian Shield and small areas around Sudbury and Sault Ste. Marie.[41] Although both the Liberal and NDP governments had promised to designate more areas, neither had done so.

The *Aggregate Resources Act* sets out the process for obtaining a licence or a permit to establish and operate a new pit or quarry or to expand an existing one. The Act consolidates in one statute the licensing and permitting and other aspects of the regulation of the pits and quarries formerly covered by the *Pits and Quarries Control Act* as well as other operations. Quarry permits formerly issued under the *Mining Act*[42] and licences to take sand from the beds or shores of lakes, rivers, and streams under the *Beach Protection Act*[43] will now also be issued under the *Aggregate Resources Act*.

Generally, the Act prohibits the operation of pits and quarries without a licence or a permit. Public and private operators on private land in designated areas must obtain a *licence*; public authorities or contractors operating wayside pits for public authorities, all operators taking aggregate or topsoil from a pit or quarry on Crown land, and all operators taking aggregate from land under water that is not Crown land must obtain a *permit*.

Each kind of licence and permit is subject to different requirements, some providing greater protection to the environment than others.

Licence Applications

Licences are divided into "class A" and "class B." An operation that will result in the excavation of more than 20,000 tonnes of aggregate a year requires a class A licence; less than this, a class B licence.[44] Based on the questionable assumption that the extraction of more than 20,000 tonnes will cause significantly more harm than lesser extraction (or perhaps merely on the need to keep the costs of operation low for smaller operators, regardless of the harm they may cause), the Act requires much more information from an applicant for a class A licence than from a class B licence applicant. A class A applicant must submit both a site plan and a report describing the expected environmental, social, and economic impacts of the operation and remedial measures. A class B applicant need not submit this report.[45]

The site plans for both class A and class B licences must include about 20 items. These items include the location, dimensions, shape and size of the site, the location of buildings, roads, earth berms, and surface water on and around the site, drainage, water wells, excavation setback limits, fences, stockpiles of topsoil, subsoil and overburden, significant natural and manmade features, entrances and exits, and tree screens. These plans must also show the maximum depth of excavation and whether the operator intends to excavate below the water table, the sequence and direction of operation, and the progressive rehabilitation and final rehabilitation plans. However, unlike the class A site plan, the class B site plan need not show the topography of the site or the water table.[46]

The class A site plan must be prepared by a qualified professional such as an engineer, a land surveyor, or a landscape architect.[47] The only requirements to ensure the accuracy of a class B site plan are that it must be prepared in a manner "acceptable to the Minister" and that the applicant must sign it.[48]

The report accompanying an application for a class A licence must provide information as to the compatibility of rehabilitation plans with adjacent land; the environment that may be affected by the operation and any remedial measures considered necessary; the social and economic effects to be expected; the quality and quantity of aggregate on the site; the main haulage routes and truck traffic to and from the site; possible effects on nearby water wells; the stockpiling of topsoil, subsoil, and overburden; and planning and land-use considerations.[49] Unlike the site plan, this report need not be prepared by qualified engineers, planners, or other professionals.

How successful this process will be in protecting the environment depends on how stringently ministry officials require applicants to adhere to these requirements, how closely they scrutinize the adequacy of these site plans and reports, and whether they are prepared to recommend that substandard applications be refused. Of course, these matters will depend partly on the adequacy of the opportunities for public consultation and the quality of public participation.

In the past, the site plans accompanying licence applications were generally perfunctory and vague. Because ministry officials did not insist on sufficient detail, in-depth regulation of operations and enforcement of licence conditions often became impossible. The problem became acute when the pit or quarry was mined out. It was often impossible to tell from the site plan what the operator was required to do to restore the site to an acceptable condition. However, an experienced environmental lawyer has recently commented that applicants are finding the site plan and report requirements of the *Aggregate Resources Act* much more stringent and comprehensive than those under the *Pits and Quarries Control Act*.[50]

Public Participation

Once the minister is satisfied that an application and the accompanying documents comply with the Act and regulations, he or she must serve a copy of them on the clerks of the regional municipality or county and the local municipality.[51] The applicant must publish a notice of the application in two successive issues of a local newspaper and post signs around the site advising of the application.[52]

Within 45 days after the publication of the second newspaper notice or at a later date, if the minister so decides, anyone who wishes to object or have a hearing before the Ontario Municipal Board (OMB) must file a notice of objection to the licence being issued and, if a hearing is required, a notice to that effect.[53]

It is interesting to note that the Act requires the minister to consider the comments of the municipality, but not of other objectors, before deciding to issue the licence.[54] Objections most often receive a sympathetic reception at the municipal level. For this reason, as well as the fact that the Act allows the minister to ignore your objections, but requires him or her to take into account those of the municipality, it is important to address your concerns not only to the minister but also to local politicians.

Your right to register your objections does not depend on any special interest in the matter. However, if you want a hearing before the OMB, it is important to set out your interest and your objections clearly in the notice, since the minister need not refer the matter to the board unless the notice "discloses an interest in the matter that is sufficiently substantial to warrant a hearing and is not frivolous or vexatious."[55] It is possible that a decision by the minister to refuse a hearing on these grounds would be overturned by the court if your notice disclosed a reasonable interest and solid grounds for concern.[56]

There is no requirement in the Act that the minister or the applicant advise the public of the deadlines for filing objections or requesting an OMB hearing. There is no requirement that the notice posted on the site advise you of your rights or of the deadlines for exercising them. The deadline need not be published in the advertisement although in practice, this has usually been done.

The Criteria for Deciding Whether To Issue a Licence

The minister has an unfettered discretion whether to issue or refuse a licence. The *Pits and Quarries Control Act* required the minister to refuse a licence where the site plan did not comply with the Act or regulations or where, in the minister's opinion, the operation of the pit or quarry would be against the public interest.[57] In deciding whether the licence would be contrary to the public interest, the *Pits and Quarries Control Act* required to minister to take into account the preservation of the character of the environment; the availability of natural environment for the enjoyment of the public; the need, if any, for restricting excessively large total pit or quarry output in the locality; the traffic density on local roads; possible effects on the water table or surface drainage pattern; the nature and location of other land uses that could be affected by the pit or quarry operation; and the character, location, and size of nearby communities.

The *Aggregate Resources Act*, in contrast, makes no pretense of binding the minister. It requires him or her only to "have regard to" certain factors in making the decision. In this regard, any difference between the *Pits and Quarries Control Act* and the *Aggregate Resources Act* is probably inconsequential, since the site plan requirements in the Act and regulations were so vague that a site plan would rarely fail to meet these requirements, and the minister could always say that he or she was not of the opinion that the operation would be contrary to the public interest.

However, the matters that the minister must look at before deciding whether to issue a licence have been considerably expanded. In addition to the items listed in the *Pits and Quarries Control Act*, they include any comments made by the municipality; any recommendations of the Ontario Municipal Board, if it has held a hearing; any possible effects of the operation on agriculture; and any planning and land-use considerations.[58]

One notable deletion from the *Aggregate Resources Act* is the requirement in the *Pits and Quarries Control Act* that the minister take into account "the need, if any for restricting excessively large total quarry output in the locality." This provision was often used by local residents and municipal councils to argue against increased aggregate extraction where existing operations were already placing stress on municipal resources and the use and enjoyment of nearby lands. Its deletion reflects the determination of the Ministry of Natural Resources to prevent this kind of argument from prevailing.

In hearing references under the *Aggregate Resources Act*, the Ontario Municipal Board can take into account the same factors as the minister. Although the deletion of the "excessive output" factor prevents the board from considering this directly, the board can still consider this factor in relation to the effect of excessive operations on the amenities of the community and planning and land-use considerations. In fact, in a 1990 decision, the board recognized the right of municipalities to take into account the community's "tolerance level" in drafting official plan policies to regulate pits and quarries. The board indicated that where there is already substantial aggregate extraction in the vicinity, additional extraction that is not "needed" might be considered in deciding whether the operation would exceed community tolerance levels.[59]

Ontario Municipal Board

The minister may refer a licence application to the Ontario Municipal Board at the request of an objector, or on his or her own.[60] The board must then hold a hearing, at which the applicant, the minister, and anyone else specified by the board are parties.[61] At the hearing, the parties and their witnesses give evidence and are cross-examined (see Chapter 4). Following the hearing, the board sends the minister a report containing its findings and recommendations.

The board does not have the power to decide whether to issue a licence. The minister makes the final decision, from which there is no appeal.[62] In many cases, however, the operation will also require a zoning bylaw or official plan amendment. If objections to such planning amendments are filed, the board will usually decide these issues at the same hearing.[63] Although the board cannot refuse the licence application, it does have the authority to refuse the planning amendment.

If you have concerns about the issuance of a licence, it may be important to request a hearing before the board, not only because this will provide an opportunity to call evidence and cross-examine the applicant's owners and experts, but also because the *Aggregate Resources Act* does not require the minister to give residents' objections any consideration, but it does require him or her to take into account the board's recommendations.

Factors Affecting OMB Decisions

The criteria the Ontario Municipal Board used in deciding whether to recommend issuing a licence under the *Pits and Quarries Control Act* are similar to those it uses in deciding whether to approve a zoning amendment under the *Planning Act*. Because the *Aggregate Resources Act* requires more information from applicants, requires them to consider a broader range of concerns, and specifically includes environmental protection and rehabilitation among its purposes, this may give the OMB even greater scope to consider environmental concerns in its future hearings.

In its hearings under the *Pits and Quarries Control Act*, a theme common to many written decisions of the board was the unresolvable conflict between gravel operations and the environmental quality desirable for other land uses, whether residential, commercial, agricultural, wilderness, or recreational. One senses a certain uneasiness, for although the board normally tries to balance all competing factors, it seems that when pits or quarries are involved, this cannot be done. Board members have often said, "Regrettably, gravel is where you find it."

In one case, the board was unable to reconcile heavy truck traffic on gravel roads with the reasonable amenities of adjacent residents, and recommended against granting a licence.[64] In another case, though, the board said that policy considerations having to do with the quality of life may have to be disregarded if there is a gravel shortage.[65]

Where the board has been convinced that a gravel shortage is becoming critical (as the reports mentioned above would have it believe), it has at times overridden all objections and recommended that a licence be granted. When the board has done this, it has often relied on the ability of the minister to impose conditions on the granting of the licence to salvage a modicum of amenities for the local residents. In one case, it said:

> Within our democratic system there must of necessity be a happy meeting ground between the public and the private interest. ... It is my considered opinion that a gravel pit operation within this characteristically agricultural area and its proximity to the Upper Thames River Conservation Authority lands should only be permitted under the most strict and stringent regulation.[66]

The licence was granted. One wonders how happy the meeting ground turned out to be.

The OMB has often required more from aggregate producers than the vague information that has been acceptable to the ministry. Applicants present detailed evidence as to methods of operation, plans for traffic control, noise and dust abatement, and rehabilitation. Analysis of this information usually takes up most of the OMB report. It appears that the more detailed the evidence presented by the applicant, the more likely that the OMB will support the application. Conversely, those who present little evidence as to flow of traffic, rate of production, the need for the pit, possible effects on the water table, and rehabilitation are more likely to be turned down.

Different panels of the board have taken different approaches to addressing public concerns. Where it appears that an operation will inevitably result in some degree of nuisance or danger to neighbours, some panels have recommended that the application be refused.[67] Other panels, taking the attitude that some degree of interference is unavoidable, have decided that it is therefore acceptable, and have recommended that the application be approved without any conditions that will eliminate the nuisance.[68] Still others have attempted to resolve public concerns by recommending numerous conditions of approval.[69] A further approach taken by the board in some cases is to "wash its hands" of the problems, indicating its confidence that pollution concerns will be adequately addressed by the Ministry of the Environment, safety concerns by the Ministry of Labour, and road and traffic concerns by the Ministry of Transportation and the municipality.

The following are some of the considerations that have been taken into account, to a greater or lesser degree, in written decisions of the OMB:

- the protection of groundwater, wells, and surface water;[70]
- road conditions;[71]
- increased traffic (including safety and noise concerns);[72]
- whether the applicant has entered or is willing to enter into an agreement with the local municipality to pay for or share the cost of maintaining and upgrading roads, limiting hours of operation, etc.[73] (note, however, that under the *Aggregate Resources Act*, operators must contribute to a fund to help the municipality cover such costs);
- the adequacy of the site plans[74] and rehabilitation plans;[75]
- the degree of noise to be expected from the operation and the adequacy of the applicant's noise-abatement proposals;[76]
- surrounding land uses (such as the number, location, and type of residences on surrounding lands, especially where the board perceives some danger to children);[77]

- the impact on agriculture;[78]
- the hours of work (in relation to noise control and truck traffic);
- the supply and demand of aggregate (whether there is a shortage or an oversupply of aggregate in the area);[79]
- the extent to which alternative materials (such as recycled asphalt) can be substituted for gravel;[80]
- alternative modes of transportation;[81]
- dust pollution and the adequacy of the applicant's dust-suppression plans;[82]
- the protection of wildlife and wildlife habitat;[83]
- how long the pit or quarry will remain in operation;[84]
- the effects of blasting on groundwater and structures and noise from blasting;[85]
- whether the proposed operation will comply with the existing and proposed official plan and zoning;[86]
- the impact on recreation;[87]
- the effects on significant natural features such as woodlots and wetlands;[88] and
- the defilement of scenic beauty.[89]

Wayside Permits

Traditionally, wayside pits and quarries were intended to be temporary operations for the purpose of obtaining a cheap and convenient source of aggregate for a specific project, usually the construction or upgrading of a road. Although a permit was required under the *Pits and Quarries Control Act*, these permits were often abused, since road authorities were often allowed to continue these "temporary" operations for decades, with few restrictions on how they operated.

Under the *Aggregate Resources Act*, there are greater restrictions, but the wayside permit is still open to abuse. Although wayside permits were available only to road authorities under the *Pits and Quarries Control Act*, any public authority may apply for one under the *Aggregate Resources Act*. Moreover, there is no need to obtain a permit outside the designated areas of the province.

Under the *Aggregate Resources Act*, any public authority, or any person who has a contract with a public authority, may apply for a wayside permit to operate a pit or a quarry to provide aggregate for a temporary project.[90] The minister may consider the application only if, in his or her opinion, the aggregate is required to maintain or construct a road or for an urgent project for which no alternative source of aggregate is readily available in the vicinity. The aggregate must be necessary for carrying out the contract or project and the minister must feel that conditions can be attached to the permit that will ensure that the operation will cause no more than temporary inconvenience to the public.[91]

The applicant must submit a site plan covering most of the matters that are dealt with on a site plan accompanying an application for a licence,[92] and in considering whether to issue the permit, the minister must take into account largely the same matters as he or she is required to look at when considering a licence.[93] In addition, the minister must consider how the cost of obtaining aggregate from the wayside pit compares with other sources, whether there have been any previous wayside permits for the site and adjacent lands, and "the proper management of the aggregate resources of the area" — whatever that may mean.[94]

The minister must provide the clerks of the local municipality and the county or regional municipality with the application and supporting documents and must take into account their comments in deciding whether to issue a wayside permit.[95] However, there is no additional opportunity for comment. Unlike licence applications, when deciding whether to issue a wayside permit, the minister and the applicant are under no obligation to notify neighbours, and there is no opportunity for neighbours to object (except through their municipal council, if they happen to find out about the proposed operation). Nor is there any opportunity for a hearing before the Ontario Municipal Board.

Unlike a licence, a wayside permit may be issued by the minister contrary to the municipality's zoning bylaws, except where the site of the pit or quarry is zoned for residential use or as an environmentally sensitive area.[96] If the site itself is not zoned "residential" or "environmentally sensitive" but the surrounding area is so zoned, this will not prevent the minister from issuing a wayside permit. However, the minister may not issue a permit on the Niagara Escarpment without the Niagara Escarpment Commission issuing a development permit.[97]

Aggregate Permits

In areas of the province that are not designated, instead of applying for a licence, a person who wants to operate a pit or a quarry to remove aggregate or topsoil on Crown land or to excavate aggregate that is not the Crown's property from under water must obtain an "aggregate permit" from the minister.[98] There are three kinds of aggregate permit. A *commercial aggregate permit* authorizes the extraction of aggregate and topsoil for profit.[99] A *public authority aggregate permit* authorizes public authorities to excavate aggregate or topsoil for its own purposes, but not for resale.[100] A *personal aggregate permit* authorizes an individual or a group of individuals to excavate aggregate or topsoil for their own use, but not for commercial purposes.[101]

The requirements for obtaining an aggregate permit provide much less protection for the environment and the rights of neighbours than the requirements for licences and wayside permits. The applicant must still submit a site plan, but unlike site plans needed to obtain a licence, these site plans need not deal with many of the matters of concern when issuing a licence — for example, visual screening of the site, significant natural and manmade features, groundwater protection, or the protection of wells.[102] Moreover, the minister may waive the site plan requirement for a personal aggregate permit.[103] Nor is there a list of issues the minister must consider when deciding to issue a permit; his or her discretion is absolute.

There is no opportunity for notification of the public or municipalities, and no opportunity to object or to have a hearing before the Ontario Municipal Board.

Regulation of Operations and Enforcement

One of the most frequent criticisms of the *Pits and Quarries Control Act* was the weakness of its enforcement provisions and the failure of Ministry of Natural Resources to exercise the powers it did have. The Ontario Aggregate Working Party accused the provincial government of lacking credibility because of its failure to enforce the Act and weaknesses in the Act. The members concluded that even if the Act had been stronger, it would not have been enforced.[104]

The *Aggregate Resources Act* contains provisions to strengthen the ministry's ability to regulate operations, to ensure that ministry officials carry out a periodic review of operators' compliance, and to provide for public input into this review. These provisions are designed to make it much more difficult for the minister and ministry officials to ignore non-compliance.

Under the Act, once a licence has been issued, the operator must comply with the site plan it submitted, with any terms and conditions attached to the licence or permit, and with the Act and regulations.[105] Failure to do so is an offence punishable by fines of up to $30,000 for each day the offence occurs or continues.[106] In addition to this fine, the court may strip the offender of any profit from violating the law and make orders designed to obtain compliance with the site plan, the licence, or the Act or regulations.[107] In addition to prosecuting the offender, the minister may also suspend or revoke its licence or permit[108] or apply to the Ontario Court of Justice for an order requiring compliance with the Act.[109]

The regulations that are enforceable in this manner include specifications for setbacks, maximum slopes, the stockpiling of topsoil, screening, berming, fencing, the location of entrances and exits, rehabilitation, the filing of documents required under the Act, and the timing of the detonation of explosives.[110]

Unlike the laws administered by the Ontario Ministry of Environment and Energy, the *Aggregate Resources Act* does not contain any clear statement prohibiting the expansion of pits and quarries without further approval from the Ministry of Natural Resources. However, the minister retains control over expansion through provisions that prevent the operator from making changes to the site plan without approval and allowing the minister to add new terms and conditions to a site plan or licence. Thus, it appears that *if the site plan and terms and conditions of licences are clear and precise enough to specify the limits of the operation*, the expansion of the physical size of the pit or quarry, longer hours of operation, increases in truck traffic, and other forms of expansion cannot occur without the minister's approval.

The ministry must inspect every licensed site and review the site plan and conditions of the licence at least once a year.[111] At that time, the ministry must also consider all comments provided by the upper- and lower-tier municipalities where the pit or quarry is located.[112] Every four years, the minister is required to seek the views of the local municipality and county or regional municipality as to the operator's compliance with its site plan and licence and the Act and regulations.[113]

Each time an inspection is carried out, the inspector is required to submit a report indicating any contraventions observed.[114] Anyone may look at these reports and, for a small fee, obtain copies.[115]

There are no similar requirements for periodic inspection or review of compliance, for reports of non-compliance, or for public access to inspection reports, for operations carried out under wayside permits or aggregate permits.

Rehabilitation

One of the most serious problems with pits and quarries has been the lack of "rehabilitation" — that is, the restoration of the landscape to something approaching what it looked like, and its capability to be used for other purposes, before the operator ripped it up. In the past, operators left the landscape scarred with worked-out pits, steep-sided, and often full of water.

They were ugly and dangerous, but the operators did not drain, grade, or fill them unless there was money to be made — for example, by filling them with garbage or selling them for development.

Under the *Aggregate Resources Act*, operators must perform both progressive rehabilitation and final rehabilitation in accordance with the Act, the regulations, the site plan, and the conditions of the licence or permit to the satisfaction of the minister.[116] The details of how this rehabilitation is to be carried out are found in the regulations, as well as in each site plan and licence. Failure to carry out the required rehabilitation is both an offence and a justification for suspending or revoking the licence or permit. In addition, if the site plan or licence or permit does not deal adequately with rehabilitation, the minister has the power to amend them. If the minister is satisfied that adequate rehabilitation has not been carried out, the minister may also issue an order requiring this.[117] Failure to comply with this order is also an offence. (However, the minister has discretion to waive or reduce any rehabilitation requirements on Crown land. There are no criteria to guide him or her in doing this, and no opportunity for the public to object or be heard.)

To further ensure that the operator rehabilitates a worked-out pit, the Act and regulations require the operator to deposit security with the ministry.[118] When rehabilitation is completed to the ministry's satisfaction, the operator is entitled to get its money back. To encourage operators to engage in progressive rehabilitation, rather than beginning restoration only when the pit is depleted, the Act authorizes the ministry to return part of this security deposit each time some rehabilitation has been carried out.[119]

If the operator does not carry out rehabilitation, the ministry may carry out the work and keep the security deposit to cover the cost of doing so.[120]

The amount of the security deposit required and the amount to be returned to the operator each time some progress is made in rehabilitating the site are set out in the regulations.[121]

The security deposit will encourage rehabilitation only if it is large enough to cover the cost of rehabilitation, and if the amount returned to the operator as progressive rehabilitation takes place exceeds the cost of this rehabilitation. In the past, the amount of the security deposit was so low that the operators found it cheaper to leave all rehabilitation to the end of the pit's life or to abandon the pit unrehabilitated than to rehabilitate. If the operator refuses to rehabilitate and the ministry carries out the rehabilitation, not only can it keep the security deposit to cover its costs but, if the cost of rehabilitation exceeds the security deposit, the operator owes the ministry the rest of the cost.[122] For small operators, however, it is easy to operate through a shell company that has no assets. (The pit itself may even be owned by a different company from the one operating it.) Under those circumstances, it is often impossible for the government to collect what it is owed.

Whether the current regulations will result in more rehabilitation remains to be seen. As of 1991, there was evidence that the scheme was working well, but as inflation erodes the value of the security deposit, it will become useless unless amounts payable and returnable are raised to cover inflation.

For pits and quarries already abandoned before the *Aggregate Resources Act* came into force and in areas not designated under the Act, where it is impossible to force the former operator to pay for rehabilitation, the Act provides for a percentage of each annual licence fee and wayside permit to be set aside for rehabilitation.[123] The annual licence fee and the wayside permit fee as well as the percentage that will be available for the rehabilitation of abandoned pits and quarries are set by regulation.[124] Again, the availability of adequate funds will depend on the amounts prescribed and whether they keep pace with inflation.

In areas not designated, where no licence or permit is required, the abandonment of pits and quarries without rehabilitation will continue to be an attractive option. Therefore, to be effective, the fund will have to be large enough to cover the future rehabilitation of these pits and quarries. One would think that licensed operators paying into this fund would object to their money being used to subsidize operators in undesignated areas of the province.

Compensation of Municipalities

One of the main objections of municipalities to allowing pits and quarries within their boundaries has been that these operations impose high costs on other taxpayers that are not covered by the taxes that the municipality can collect from the operator. These costs include upgrading the quality of roads to accommodate gravel trucks and repairing roads damaged by gravel trucks, the control of dust raised by gravel trucks, and the rehabilitation of abandoned pits and quarries. Although the Ontario government has been prepared to force municipalities to accept aggregate operations, it has also agreed to require the operators to cover some of these costs through their licence and wayside permit fees.[125] Under the regulations, two-thirds of the annual licence and wayside permit fees paid by operators in a local municipality are to go to the municipality.[126] This is in addition to the portion of the fees to be paid to the municipality for rehabilitation of abandoned pits and quarries. There is no requirement that any of the royalties paid by holders of aggregate permits be given to municipalities whose roads are travelled and damaged by those permittees.

CONCLUSION

It is clear that government policy has consistently favoured the rights of aggregate producers over those of the general public, and continues to do so, although to a lesser extent than in past. Although the *Aggregate Resources Act* gives the Ministry of Natural Resources and municipalities greater power to control pits and quarries, its effectiveness will depend on whether these powers are exercised.

The law continues to give the minister extremely broad discretion — to approve operations contrary to OMB recommendations, to exempt applicants from OMB hearings, to ignore public comments, to waive the requirement to prepare site plans or pay fees, to exempt operators from the regulations, and to weaken licence conditions and modify site plans to make them less stringent.

No licences or permits are needed to operate pits and quarries throughout much of Ontario, and the extraction of aggregates by government agencies and by the private sector and the government on Crown lands is subject to far fewer safeguards than private extraction on private land. The underlying philosophy of the Act appears to be that no one but the government itself has any interest in the destruction of nature on Crown land.

There appears to be no environmental rationale for the different levels of environmental protection provided in relation to different classes of licences and permits. As the Conservation Council of Ontario pointed out in its submissions to the government when the *Aggregate Resources Act* was under consideration:

[T]he current subdivision between Class A and B licences is arbitrary and unnecessary. The requirements for each licence should be the same. If a proposal for a large operation is received, the Minister has full authority to require whatever information is necessary. For small operations, the level of detail may be less onerous if the situation so warrants. However, a small operation in an environmentally sensitive area may cause much greater impact than a large well-sited operation. Likewise, aggregate permits and wayside permits should be treated the same as licences. The current Act sets up an unnecessary and inequitable administrative process that lacks any clear rationale. Uniform application would include consistent requirements for applying for a licence/permit, the same fees, a common hearing and appeal process, and similar periodic reviews.[127]

These common-sense observations apparently fell on deaf ears.

A second major area of concern is the lack of enforcement. Although the ministry has new enforcement powers, its commitment to enforcement is questionable. Between 1973 and 1989, the ministry initiated 154 prosecutions and obtained 81 convictions.[128] The total fines levied amounted to about $72,000. This means that the ministry lost almost 50 per cent of its cases, and where it succeeded, obtained fines averaging less than $1,000 a case. To put these figures into perspective, the Ministry of Natural Resources undertook fewer prosecutions over a 17-year period than the Ministry of Environment and Energy (MEE) undertakes in a single year, and MEE has consistently obtained convictions ranging from 78 per cent to over 90 per cent each year. Fines in prosecutions undertaken by MEE are frequently in the range of $10,000 to $100,000 a case.

Moreover, although MNR has always had the power to revoke licences for violations of the *Pits and Quarries Control Act* and regulations, no licence was ever revoked.[129]

Who will investigate off-site impacts of pits and quarries — MEE inspectors trained in the measurement of air and water pollution and noise, or MNR inspectors? Although other ministries have developed protocols to divide the investigation functions between themselves and the Ministry of Environment and Energy in a rational manner, there is no such protocol to prevent overlap, duplication, and buck passing in the enforcement of the *Aggregate Resources Act*.

Other weaknesses in the Act include the fact that operators need not rehabilitate pits and quarries that fill with water unless this results from excavation below the water table;[130] the fact that municipalities may divert the portion of the licence fees given them to relieve pressures on municipal infrastructure caused by pits and quarries to unrelated programs;[131] and the limited opportunities for public consultation before wayside and aggregate permits are issued or amended. Finally, many of the most important aspects of the regulatory scheme, such as practical performance measures to assess the adequacy of rehabilitation, must be implemented through regulations; yet the Act provides no opportunity for public review of proposed regulations.

John Swaigen

ENDNOTES

1 Ontario, Ministry of Natural Resources, Aggregate Resources Section, "Managing Ontario's Aggregate Resources in the 1990s — Provincial Policy and Legislation," revised October 1989.

2 Mineral Aggregate Resources Policy Statement under the *Planning Act*, SO 1983, c. 1. Approved by the lieutenant governor in council by order in council no. 1249-86, May 9, 1986.

3 Supra endnote 1.

4 Ontario, Ministry of Natural Resources, *Mineral Aggregate Study, Central Planning Region, Mineral Aggregate Study and Geological Inventory, Eastern Region*; correspondence from R.A. Baxter, director, North Central Region, Ministry of Natural Resources, to J.F. Castrilli, December 8, 1976; correspondence from J. Viirland, groundwater evaluator, West Central Region, Ministry of the Environment, to J.F. Castrilli, November 26, 1976; J.F. Castrilli, *Control of Water Pollution from Land Use Activities in the Canadian Great Lakes Basin; An Evaluation of Legislative, Regulatory and Administrative Programs* (Windsor, Ont.: International Joint Commission, 1977), 304.

5 For example, a coroner's jury verdict of September 26, 1978 on the drowning of Tod Rosler recommended that owners of abandoned pits and quarries be responsible for filling them in. Press release by David Warner, MPP (Scarborough-Ellesmere), July 12, 1979.

6 Official plan for the Regional Municipality of Sudbury, July 1976 (draft).

7 Sandbanks Provincial Park. See Ron Alexander and Larry Green, *A Future for the Sandbanks* (Toronto: Pollution Probe and Canadian Environmental Law Association, 1972).

8 In 1978, the minister of natural resources issued a licence to Pelee Island Quarries Inc. despite a request by the Canadian Environmental Law Association and the Federation of Ontario Naturalists that the minister await the result of a hearing before the Ontario Municipal Board as to the official plan designation of this site. The Wildlife Branch of the ministry was also about to undertake studies to determine the extent of endangered species habitat in the vicinity.

9 D. Fahselt, P. Maycock, G. Winder, and C. Campbell, "The Oriskany Sandstone Outcrop and Associated Natural Features: A Unique Occurrence in Canada" (1979), vol. 93, no. 1 *Canadian Field Naturalist* 28-40.

10 For example, although residents of Manitoulin Island have complained about noise, dust, and traffic from at least one local quarry, the councils of municipalities on the island have lobbied against the island being designated under the *Aggregate Resources Act*, RSO 1990, c. A.8. See "Dust Raised by Test Quarry," *The Manitoulin Expositor*, June 8, 1988: "'The blasts shook my buildings and rattled windows, and I'm half a mile away. And no one told us this mine was going in until the contractor came to warn us of the blasting they were going to do,' [a resident] said."

11 Supra endnote 1, at 3.

12 Ibid.

13 *Pits and Quarries Control Act*, RSO 1980, c. 378.

14 Over the years, concerns about aggregate extraction have generated litigation by neighbours against operators: *Walker v. Pioneer Construction Co. (1967) Ltd.* (1975),

8 OR (2d) 35 (HCJ); *Muirhead v. Timbers Brothers Sand and Gravel Limited* (1977), 3 CCLT 1 (Ont. HCJ); by neighbours of pits and quarries seeking to prevent the minister of natural resources from issuing licences: *Millar v. Ministry of Natural Resources and Preston Sand and Gravel Ltd.* (1978), 7 CELR 156 (Ont. Div. Ct.); by municipalities seeking to restrain operators from operating in contravention of municipal bylaws: *Uxbridge v. Timbers Brothers* (1975), 7 OR (2d) 484 (CA); *Pickering Township v. Godfrey* (1959), OR 429 (CA); and by ratepayers alleging bad faith on the part of municipal councils in designating land for extractive purposes without adequate notice of public consultation: *Re Starr and Township of Puslinch (No. 2)* (1977), 16 OR (2d) 316 (CA).

15 Ontario, Ministry of Natural Resources, *Mineral Aggregate Study of the Central Ontario Planning Region* (Toronto: the ministry, 1974); *Mineral Aggregate Study and Geological Inventory, Part of the Eastern Ontario Region* (Toronto: the ministry, 1975); *Mineral Aggregate Study and Geological Inventory, Southwestern Region of Ontario* (Toronto: the ministry, 1977).

16 The concern underlying these reports was not a shortage of aggregate — as the ministry has admitted, "there are ample resources to meet future demands of Ontario's citizens": D. Geoffrey Minnes, *Ontario Industrial Minerals: Industrial Mineral Background Paper 2* (Toronto: Ministry of Natural Resources, Industrial Minerals Section, March 1982). The real concern was a shortage of *cheap* aggregate. Of course, one of the main reasons that aggregate close to the major cities was that the operators were not being required to pay the costs of designing and operating their mines in a way that would protect the environment and minimize nuisance. If these costs were borne by the operators, this might make extraction in other areas of the province much more economically viable.

17 Ontario, Ministry of Natural Resources, *A Policy for Mineral Aggregate Resource Management in Ontario*, Report of the Ontario Mineral Aggregate Working Party (Toronto: the ministry, December 1976).

18 The committee consisted of the Ministry of Natural Resources, the Ministry of Municipal Affairs and Housing, and the Ministry of Transportation and Communications: supra endnote 1. The mandate of the Ministry of Municipal Affairs and Housing was to facilitate quick approvals of development and to promote the construction of housing. The Ministry of Transportation has always relied heavily on wayside pits and quarries as a cheap source of sand and gravel for road construction. These wayside pits have traditionally been exempt from most of the requirements of the *Pits and Quarries Control Act*, supra endnote 13, and although theoretically "temporary" have sometimes been used and expanded for decades. Neither the Ministry of the Environment nor any of the ministries concerned with historical and archaeological conservation were represented.

19 *Planning Act*, supra endnote 2.

20 "Mineral Aggregate Resource Planning Policy," approved by the Ontario Cabinet in December 1982 and released in February 1983.

21 See, for example, *Ministry of Natural Resources v. Young* (1987), 20 OMBR 156, in which the ministry used this policy to successfully prevent the severance of two residential lots on land designated as having a significant gravel deposit.

22　For a critique of the bill introduced in 1979, see John Swaigen and J.F. Castrilli, *The Proposed Ontario Aggregates Act: Discussion, Evaluation and Recommendations* (Kingston, Ont.: Canadian Environmental Law Research Foundation and Centre for Resource Studies, Queen's University, September, 1979).

23　*Aggregate Resources Act*, supra endnote 10.

24　For example, such an agreement is found in the official plan of the regional municipality of Haldimand-Norfolk. See *Re Regional Municipality of Haldimand-Norfolk Restricted Area By-Law 7000-267-CN* (1982), 14 OMBR 99. However, in the *Puslinch* decision cited at note 47, the OMB cast doubt on the ability of municipalities to make official plans that are to be implemented by development agreements. Even if there is a restriction on the use of official plans to compel development agreements, the courts have made it clear that this can be done through the *Municipal Act*, RSO 1990, c. M.45: *Uxbridge v. Timbers Brothers*, supra endnote 14.

25　See *Re Regional Municipality of Haldimand-Norfolk*, supra endnote 24.

26　*Planning Act*, supra endnote 2, sections 34(1) and 34(2). Section 34(2) was apparently passed to override several court decisions that ruled that pits and quarries were not a "use of land" and therefore could not be prohibited using zoning bylaws. These cases and their effect on municipal authority is discussed in the second edition of this book at page 213.

27　Ontario, Ministry of Agriculture and Food, *Ontario Food Land Guidelines*, 1978, section 3.16; in 1986 OMAF and the Ministry of Municipal Affairs released a "Foodland Preservation Policy Statement" intended to replace the *Food Land Guidelines*, but as of March 1993 this proposed policy had not been approved by Cabinet.

28　*Municipal Act*, supra endnote 24.

29　In *Uxbridge v. Timbers Brothers*, supra endnote 14, the Ontario Court of Appeal ruled that although the *Pits and Quarries Control Act* (supra endnote 13) set out a regulatory regime for aggregate extraction activities, this did not preclude the municipality from imposing more stringent requirements through the *Municipal Act* (supra endnote 24). As there is no difference in principle, this case should apply equally in relation to the *Aggregate Resources Act* (supra endnote 10). However, the courts have shown that they are willing to accept the principle set out in *Uxbridge v. Timbers Brothers* — namely, that provincial regulatory schemes do not prevent more stringent municipal regulation, but strike down the municipal regulation anyway. See *Re Attorney General of Ontario and Mississauga* (1981), 33 OR (2d) 395 (CA).

30　*Municipal Act*, supra endnote 24, section 210.143. See also section 210.142.

31　*Uxbridge v. Timbers Brothers*, supra endnote 14.

32　*Aggregate Resources Act*, supra endnote 10, sections 66, 70(3), and 71(5); *Cox Construction Ltd. v. Township of Puslinch* (1982), 36 OR (2d) 618 (HCJ).

33　*Highway Traffic Act*, RSO 1990, c. H.8.

34　Ibid., section 120. If the axles are spaced less than 2.4 metres apart, a permit is needed if the weight exceeds 5,500 kg. RRO 1990, regulation 573 exempts certain vehicles.

35　RRO 1990, regulation 579 designates class A highways.

36　*Highway Traffic Act*, supra endnote 33, sections 110 and 115-118.

37　Ibid., section 110(7).

38　*Municipal Act*, supra endnote 24.

39   See, for example, City of Windsor bylaw no. 9148, "A By-Law To Regulate Traffic Within the Limits of the City of Windsor," September 28, 1987.

40   Ontario, Ministry of Natural Resources, "The Aggregates Act: Compendium of Background Information," May 2, 1988. Although this document was prepared in 1988, the statement that only 355 municipalities were covered in 1991 is based on the fact that no additional municipalities had been designated.

41   Section 5 of the *Aggregate Resources Act* provides that the Act applies to public lands throughout the province and to private land in designated areas. The areas are designated in RRO 1990, reg. 15.

42   *Mining Act*, RSO 1990, c. M.14.

43   *Beach Protection Act*, RSO 1980, c. 39, repealed by SO 1989, c. 23, section 77.

44   *Aggregate Resources Act*, supra endnote 10, section 7(2).

45   Ibid., sections 7-9.

46   Ibid., sections 8(1) and 8(5).

47   Ibid., section 8(4).

48   Ibid., section 8(6).

49   Ibid., section 9.

50   Conversation with Catherina Spoel, June 1991.

51   *Aggregate Resources Act*, supra endnote 10, section 11(1).

52   Ibid., section 11(2).

53   Ibid., sections 11(4) to (6).

54   Ibid., section 12(c).

55   Ibid., section 11(2).

56   *Re Royal Commission on Conduct of Waste Management Inc.* (1977), 17 OR (2d) 207 (Div. Ct.).

57   *Pits and Quarries Control Act*, supra endnote 13, section 6(1).

58   *Aggregate Resources Act*, supra endnote 10, section 12.

59   *Re Puslinch Official Plan etc.*, unreported decision of J.A. Wheler and R.W. Rodman, June 27, 1990, OMB file nos. DB83-F-59, O880075, Z860131, M880019, Z870049, M880029, O880177, Z880184, M880094, Z880185.

60   *Aggregate Resources Act*, supra endnote 10, section 11(8).

61   Ibid., section 21(1).

62   Ibid., sections 21(4) and (5).

63   Ibid., section 11(9).

64   *Towland-Hewitson Construction Limited and Township of West Nissouri* (1973), OMB file no. S1438 [unreported].

65   *Premier Cement Products and Township of Erin* (1976), OMB file no. M75155 [unreported]; *T.C.G. Materials Limited and Township of Erin* (1976), OMB file no. M75156 [unreported].

66   *Re Matthews Group Ltd.* (1974), 2 OMBR 431.

67   *Re Preston Sand and Gravel Co. Ltd.*, (1973), 3 OMBR 86.

68   *Re Township of Shuniah Restricted Area By-Law 1308* (1979), 10 OMBR 309. In *Re Township of Asphodel Pit Licence Application* (1989), 23 OMBR 304, the board was prepared to recommend approval of a pit that would result in a noise level of 62 decibels at a neighbour's home, although the Ministry of the Environment guidelines recom-

mend a maximum noise level of 55 decibels. Noise interferes with normal conversation at 80 decibels.

69 *Re Dufferin Materials and Construction Ltd.* (1974), 4 OMBR 63; *Lockyer v. Township of Erin* (1980), 11 OMBR 267.

70 *Re Springbank Sand and Gravel Limited* (1976), 5 OMBR 327; *Re Regional Municipality of Haldimand-Norfolk*, supra endnote 24.

71 *Towland-Hewitson*, supra endnote 64; *Re Francon and Township of Gloucester* (1974), OMB file no. M73201 [unreported]; *Re Township of Manvers* (1975), 4 OMBR 380; *Re Township of West Flamborough* (1972), OMB file no. R9175 [unreported]; *Re Township of West Flamborough* (1974), 3 OMBR 239.

72 *Re Tibbits Bulldozing Ltd.* (1974), 4 OMBR 24.

73 *Premier Cement Products*, supra endnote 65; *T.C.G. Materials*, supra endnote 65; *Re Regional Municipality of Haldimand-Norfolk*, supra endnote 24; *Re Township of Asphodel*, supra endnote 68; *Re Harold Sutherland Construction Ltd. and Township of Keppel* (1989), 23 OMBR 129.

74 *Re Harold Sutherland Construction*, supra endnote 73. In this case, the board noted that the ministry rarely imposes conditions on licences, preferring to make notations on the site plan instead. This is particularly interesting in the light of the fact that under the *Pits and Quarries Control Act*, supra endnote 13, contravention of a condition of a licence was an offence but contravention of a site plan was not. Section 7 of the *Pits and Quarries Control Act* provided that contravention of a site plan could result in revocation of a licence, but according to correspondence from the ministry (see note 128), no licence has ever been revoked.

75 *Re Township of Manvers*, supra endnote 71.

76 *Re Preston Sand and Gravel*, supra endnote 67.

77 *Re Township of West Flamborough*, supra endnote 71; *Jacob Cooke* (1974), OMB file no. M73271 [unreported]; *Re Township of Waterloo* (1970), OMB file no. R1034-69 [unreported].

78 *Lockyer*, supra endnote 69.

79 *Re Township of West Nissouri* (1975), 4 OMBR 344; *Re Township of Zorra* (1975), 5 OMBR 179.

80 *Re Puslinch Official Plan etc.*, supra endnote 59.

81 In one case, the fact that the applicant planned to ship most of its gravel by train rather than truck was counted in its favour: *Re Dufferin Materials and Construction*, supra endnote 69. However, according to Catherina Spoel, who later represented ratepayers concerned about this pit, the ministry did not make transportation by train a condition of the licence. Although the company obtained a licence, it did not open the pit. Neighbours asked that transportation by train be added as a licence condition, but the ministry refused.

82 *Re Dufferin Materials and Construction*, supra endnote 69.

83 Ibid.; *Lockyer*, supra endnote 69.

84 *Re Township of Shuniah*, supra endnote 68.

85 Ibid.; *Re Regional Municipality of Haldimand-Norfolk*, supra endnote 24.

86 *Re Preston Sand and Gravel Co. Ltd.* (1975), 5 OMBR 209.

87 *Re Township of West Flamborough*, supra endnote 71; *E.R.S. Holdings Ltd. v. Town of Pickering* (1976), 6 OMBR 262.

88   *Re Township of Asphodel*, supra endnote 68.

89   *E.R.S. Holdings Ltd.*, supra endnote 87; *Lockyer*, supra endnote 69.

90   *Aggregate Resources Act*, supra endnote 10, section 23.

91   Ibid., section 23(3).

92   Ibid., section 25.

93   Ibid., section 26.

94   Ibid., sections 26 (d), (e), and (f).

95   Ibid., sections 23(6) and 26(a).

96   Ibid., sections 27(1) and 27(4).

97   Ibid., section 27(3).

98   Ibid., section 34.

99   Ibid., section 35(1).

100 Ibid., sections 35(2) and (3).

101 Ibid., section 35(4).

102 Ibid., section 36.

103 Ibid., section 36(3).

104 Ontario Aggregate Working Party Report, supra endnote 17, at 5.

105 *Aggregate Resources Act*, supra endnote 10, sections 57(1) and (2).

106 Ibid., section 58(1).

107 Ibid., section 58(2), section 59.

108 Ibid., sections 20, 22, 32, and 42.

109 Ibid., section 63.

110 O. reg. 702/89.

111 *Aggregate Resources Act*, supra endnote 10, section 17(1).

112 Ibid., section 17(1)(c).

113 Ibid., section 17(4).

114 Ibid., section 17(2).

115 Ibid., section 17(3).

116 Ibid., section 48.

117 Ibid., section 48(2).

118 Ibid., sections 50 and 51.

119 Ibid., sections 53 and 54.

120 Ibid., section 56.

121 O. reg. 702/89, sections 8-12.

122 *Aggregate Resources Act*, supra endnote 10, section 56(4).

123 Ibid., section 33.

124 O. reg. 702/89, sections 1 to 4.

125 *Aggregate Resources Act*, supra endnote 10, sections 14(4) and 24(3).

126 O. reg. 702/89, section 5(1).

127 Conservation Council of Ontario, "A Critical Review of Bill 170 — The *Aggregate Resources Act*," December 1988.

128 Enforcement statistics provided by Brian Messerschmidt, Aggregate Resources Section, Ministry of Natural Resources. Mr. Messerschmidt defends the ministry's prosecution record in the following manner:

> There are a couple of key points to consider when reviewing the enforcement statistics. Firstly, the area designated under the *Pits and Quarries Control Act* was significantly smaller prior to 1981. Therefore, care should be taken when considering the distribution of prosecutions from 1973 to 1989. Secondly, it is normal procedure for Ministry employees to try and solve potential enforcement problems through negotiations with licensees. This has proven to be a successful strategy and has reduced the number of enforcement issues being presented in a court of law.

Letter, B. Messerschmidt, Ministry of Natural Resources, to D. Curran, Canadian Institute for Environmental Law and Policy, July 16, 1990.

If Mr. Messerschmidt's analysis is correct, this means that the Ministry of the Environment, which launches far more prosecutions with far greater success, is less successful in obtaining voluntary compliance than the Ministry of Natural Resources, and its enforcement record should be viewed as a failure compared with MNR's.

129 The ministry states that although it has never revoked a licence for non-compliance, there have been revocations for "administrative purposes, e.g. recovery of rehabilitation security deposits": ibid. Presumably this means that when companies have abandoned pits and quarries without rehabilitating them, the ministry has revoked a licence that is no longer needed.

130 *Aggregate Resources Act*, supra endnote 10, section 47.

131 Section 14 of the *Aggregate Resources Act*, ibid., allows the Ministry of Natural Resources to give municipalities a portion of the licence fee to be used for "such purposes as are prescribed." However, no regulations have been made limiting the uses to which this money may be put.

24

Waste Management

Contents

Municipalities should take a more active role in future both by providing increased levels of service to promote recycling and by increased discussion with industry and other levels of government to co-ordinate recycling efforts, to offer suggestions for improvements of existing programs, and to better plan their waste management systems. ...

The Blueprint suggests a major re-examination of the role of the municipality in the management of waste. ... [V]arious aspects of the desired municipal involvement will require implementation by legislative amendment. Among these aspects are: municipal planning and the role of the Waste Management Master Plan; the extent of municipal responsibility for waste; the extent of municipal authority to regulate waste management activities; the role of the provincial government in encouraging, funding or requiring municipal action; cooperation among municipalities; and the provision to the appropriate level of municipal government of the powers appropriate to the tasks assigned.

Ontario, Ministry of the Environment, Blueprint for Waste Management in Ontario, *June 1983*

The principles of a sustainable waste management system: Recognizing that provincial legislation requires additional amendments to clarify waste management authority for local county and regional municipalities. ... The ministries of Environment and Municipal Affairs will work together with municipalities to ensure that municipal governments have sufficient legislative authority to develop and operate environmentally sound waste management systems including, 3Rs, collection, treatment and disposal functions.

Ontario, Ministry of the Environment, Towards a Sustainable Waste Management System, *1990*

Clearly, most municipalities do not have sufficient authority to engage in the wide range of activities necessary to develop and operate a comprehensive and integrated waste management system geared to diversion and environmental protection. Existing legislation needs to be revised to enable all municipalities in Ontario to meet current and future challenges in this regard.

Ontario, Ministry of Municipal Affairs, Municipal Waste Management Powers in Ontario, *1992*

It is important to note that changes to legislation can take a long time.

The Economic Planning and Development Committee of the Municipality of Metropolitan Toronto, in a report prepared in December 1989, commenting on the lack of Ontario government action on Metro's request that provincial legislation be passed to authorize municipalities to require new buildings to contain recycling facilities and to provide municipalities with the power to establish collection systems for recyclable material

INTRODUCTION

One of the most frequent sources of conflict between citizens and government, and between citizens and industry, has been the management of the waste byproducts of our consumer-oriented society. Even though governments have recently started the process of shifting to a conserver-oriented waste management strategy, most of the traditional conflicts remain.

The traditional modes of managing wastes in Ontario have been landfill — a wasteful consumption of land — and burning — a waste of energy and resources and a source of air pollution. As we find ourselves running out of "suitable" land (land that is far enough to be out of sight and smell, but close enough to be of use), landfill siting exercises become more and more an urban-rural conflict.

The opposition to new landfill sites and waste incinerators has focused on four areas of concern. The first is the fear of pollution and nuisances. Residents of the area are concerned about the possibility of groundwater and surface water contamination, air pollution, the migration of landfill gases, litter, the proliferation of rodents, insects, and gulls, odour problems, and increased truck traffic. Second, residents have legitimate concerns about the effect that a waste facility will have on their property values. The third concern is that large municipalities, which generate large amounts of waste, should be required to deal with it within their own boundaries, and not seek to bury it in other communities. Residents who oppose landfills in their communities raise this issue, but they have some support from environmentalists, who believe that requiring communities to dispose of their own wastes will encourage waste reduction and recycling, instead of disposal. Fourth, environmentalists object to landfills and incineration because they feel that the availability of cheap and convenient disposal facilities will impede the development of a system of reduction and recycling of wastes.

There have been few fundamental changes to the traditional waste disposal practices in Ontario over the last 20 years. The most significant change has been from the old-fashioned garbage dump, where rubbish was burned and not regularly covered, to the modern "sanitary landfill" sites, which are engineered and operated in accordance with stricter legislated standards intended to minimize potential dangers and nuisance. For example, garbage must now be covered at regular intervals and sites usually incorporate systems designed to minimize or collect leachate and gases to reduce their escape onto adjoining lands or into groundwater or surface water.

When a landfill site is properly engineered and operated, it can be environmentally acceptable, and it can create less nuisance than an old-fashioned dump. When a landfill site is *not* properly designed and run, it can cause problems for its current neighbours and for neighbours for generations to come.

Only in the 1990s have government, industry, and ordinary citizens begun to develop a commitment to reducing waste. The hierarchy of waste management practices — first reduce, then re-use, then recycle ("the 3Rs"), and finally safely dispose of any residues — has finally been accepted as the guiding principle.

Long overdue acceptance of this principle does not mean that our problems are solved. The technology for some kinds of materials recovery is relatively new and untried. Markets for recycled glass, metal, paper, plastics, energy, and other useful byproducts of garbage are so unstable that the economic viability of many recycling schemes can change overnight. Most experts agree that optimizing present reduction methods would still leave 50 per cent of the original garbage to be landfilled.

JURISDICTION

Federal Government

Waste management — including waste collection, transportation, disposal, reduction, and recycling — is chiefly a provincial concern. Only waste management in federal lands and facilities is regulated by federal legislation. Three such acts are the *Indian Act*,[1] the *National Parks Act*,[2] and the *Atomic Energy Control Act*.[3]

The Indian Reserve Waste Disposal Regulations[4] under the *Indian Act* are administered by the Department of Indian Affairs and Northern Development. They specify that an operator of a garbage dump on a reserve, or anyone storing or disposing of wastes on Indian lands, must have a permit to do so. The permit, obtained from the minister or his or her delegate, such as the council of a band, must specify what land will be used and the manner in which the authorized activity will be conducted.[5] The requirement to obtain a permit may trigger the provisions of the *Canadian Environmental Assessment Act* (see Chapter 9).[6]

If the waste is generated on an Indian reserve but disposed of off the reserve, it is then subject to provincial control. The jurisdiction over provincially regulated waste *brought onto* a reserve for the purpose of processing or disposal is more complicated. There are examples in Ontario of small areas of reserve lands being leased to adjacent private industries for use as disposal sites for industrial waste.[7] In those cases, the sites come under provincial regulation. It is reasonable to expect that, should a band wish to engage in the waste management business on reserve lands, the federal and provincial governments would *both* subject the proposal to some form of joint environmental assessment process *and* require the more stringent provincial licensing process to apply, regardless of what permit or approval would be issued at the end of the process.

Under the *National Parks Act*, also administered by the Department of Indian Affairs and Northern Development, there are National Parks Garbage Regulations,[8] which allow the park superintendent, or his or her delegate, to issue permits authorizing the permit holder to collect wastes originating in the park and deliver them to the park's sanitary landfill or dump area or to a point designated by the superintendent.

The subject of radioactive waste disposal under the *Atomic Energy Control Act* is discussed in Chapter 21.

Provincial Government

Most collection, transportation, processing, and disposal of waste in Ontario is regulated by the provincial Ministry of Environment and Energy. Anyone collecting, transporting, processing, storing, or disposing of garbage must obtain a provincial licence (called a certificate of approval) and comply with provincial standards.

Only in the last 25 years has the management of waste become the subject of regulation by the government of Ontario. Waste reduction has only become a serious issue recently, and the regulatory scheme has just started to catch up. Indeed, the current practice of "shoehorning" 3Rs initiatives into a regulatory scheme primarily designed to control waste *disposal* may be creating disincentives to the diversion of waste from disposal.[9] Amendments to the *Environmental Protection Act* passed in April 1992 finally provided explicitly for waste reduction initiatives as part of the waste management process.[10]

Since 1971, the provincial government has exercised control over waste management under part V of the *Environmental Protection Act*.[11] Part V deals with waste management in general, defining certain types of wastes and establishing controls over them. The Act's general provisions, including the broad prohibitions against pollution, which apply to virtually all undertakings that may contaminate the environment, apply as well.

The General Waste Management Regulation (regulation 347)[12] defines and designates various kinds of materials as "wastes" and prescribes standards for the location, maintenance, and operation of waste disposal sites and waste management systems. Regulation 347 also prescribes a "cradle-to-grave" tracking system for hazardous and liquid industrial wastes.

Under part V of the *Environmental Protection Act*, no one may establish a waste management facility without an approval.[13] The facility may only be operated in accordance with the conditions set out in the certificate of approval and in accordance with the standards set out in regulation 347.

If waste is deposited in *any* place (whether on land, in water, or in a building) that has not been approved as a "waste disposal site," the director can order the removal of the waste and the restoration of the site to a satisfactory condition.[14]

If waste is stored, handled, treated, collected, processed, or disposed of without a certificate of approval, or if there is non-compliance with a condition of approval or with any other requirement of regulation 347 or part V of the Act, the director can order the owner to take whatever action is required to comply.[15]

In either case, if an order is not complied with, the director can have the work done and recover the costs in court.[16]

Waste management facilities in Ontario are also subject to the *Environmental Assessment Act*.[17] All new disposal facilities and major expansions of existing disposal facilities are subject to the planning regime of that statute, whether they are publicly or privately owned.[18] Major transfer stations (facilities where waste is transferred from one vehicle to another on its way to its ultimate destination) and processing facilities may also be subject to the Act.

Municipal Government

Municipalities have the power to establish and maintain systems for the collection, removal, and disposal of garbage. In Ontario, this jurisdiction is divided between upper-tier municipalities (that is, regional municipalities or counties) and lower-tier municipalities (that is, townships, towns, and cities). Although jurisdiction varies widely across the province, as a general rule, the upper tier has responsibility for disposal and the lower tier has responsibility for collection.[19] Control over transfer, processing, and waste reduction programs is often determined by negotiation between the two tiers of municipal government. A discussion paper issued by the Ministry of Municipal Affairs in 1992 suggested various options for rationalizing this division of functions. The likely outcome of this is more power for the upper-tier municipality.

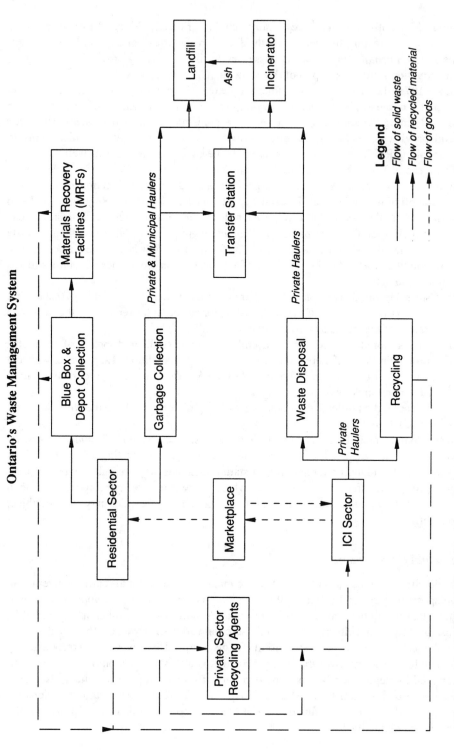

Ontario's Waste Management System

Courtesy of the Ontario Ministry of Environment and Energy.

Municipalities usually assume responsibility for residential waste collection, although this is frequently contracted out to the private sector. The collection of waste in the industrial and commercial sectors, which can account for more than half of the municipal waste, is almost always handled by private sector haulers. All waste haulers must conform to the provincial standards for "waste management systems," as discussed below.

A municipality may buy or expropriate land to use for waste disposal, even if the land lies in another municipality. If the other municipality objects, the municipality that wants to acquire the land must obtain the approval of the Ontario Municipal Board.[20] The power of municipalities to dump their wastes in other municipalities has understandably led to protest, especially where waste from urban areas is destined for disposal in neighbouring rural areas.[21]

WHAT IS "WASTE"?

We think of "waste" as unwanted material remaining after each stage of production and consumption of goods, but no such definition is found in the *Environmental Protection Act* or regulation 347. "Waste" is defined in section 25(d) of the Act to mean ashes, garbage, domestic, industrial and municipal wastes, refuse, etc., "and such other materials as are designated in the Regulation." Regulation 347 defines and designates these general types of wastes.

Some of the "designated" wastes are exempted from legal control under regulation 347 and part V of the Act. These include agricultural wastes, hauled sewage, inert fill, rock fill or mill tailings from mines, dead animals, and recyclable material.[22] Most of these are, however, legally controlled by other parts of the Act or by other statutes. For instance, dead animals are covered by the *Dead Animal Disposal Act*,[23] mine tailings are covered by the *Mining Act*,[24] and hauled sewage is covered by part VIII of the *Environmental Protection Act*. Agricultural wastes, however, are almost completely free from legal control.

Over the years, the "inert fill" exemption has been both abused and applied too restrictively. For example, for years demolition debris was considered to be inert fill, an interpretation that has resulted in enormous problems for developers of land that was "rehabilitated" by being filled with demolition rubble, because this "inert" fill contained materials that contaminated groundwater, generated methane gas, and contaminated the soil, interfering with the ability to develop the land. Today, the exemption is applied so restrictively that almost nothing can meet it; as a result, valuable landfill space is consumed by materials that could be safely deposited in other places. In 1993, the Ministry of Environment and Energy was in the process of defining a new category of waste to which less restrictive rules would apply.[25]

The "recyclable material" exemption was created in the mid-1980s to provide a regulatory incentive to recycle.[26] Unfortunately, the criteria for obtaining an exemption are so hard to meet that the exemption has become no incentive at all. At the same time, it is so complicated that many non-recyclers make a claim to it.

Non-Hazardous Waste

There are important differences between the regulation of hazardous and non-hazardous waste in Ontario. Regulation 347 defines non-hazardous waste by omission; that is, anything that is not hazardous waste or liquid industrial waste automatically falls into the non-hazardous category.[27] The primary categories of non-hazardous waste — domestic, commercial, industrial, and institutional — are either not defined or defined so minimally as to be meaningless.

The only type of non-hazardous waste for which special rules apply is one that at first glance seems to be fairly hazardous: asbestos waste. To facilitate the removal of construction or insulation materials that contain asbestos, the government has deemed asbestos waste to be non-hazardous. Transport and disposal, however, is subject to special rules set out in section 14 of regulation 347.[28]

Hazardous and Liquid Industrial Waste

There are additional requirements imposed on the management of hazardous and liquid industrial waste, particularly for generators and haulers. These two waste types are called "subject waste" in regulation 347.

Although liquid industrial waste is defined simply as waste that is *both* liquid *and* industrial,[29] hazardous waste is defined extensively and precisely. Hazardous waste is defined as any one of 11 types of waste, which are in turn listed and defined within regulation 347.[30] For example, one type of hazardous waste is a "hazardous waste chemical," which is any one of several hundred chemicals listed in a schedule to regulation 347.[31]

There are exceptions built into both types of subject waste. The most important of these are the exemptions for small quantities, empty containers, and waste from the operation of a sewage treatment plant.

WASTE REDUCTION

As battles over siting landfills become increasingly bitter and the costs of "conventional" waste management practices skyrocket, attention has turned more and more to the reduction of waste. This is sometimes categorized as the 3Rs: reduction, re-use, and recycling. Many waste reduction measures are not covered by the traditional waste management regulatory scheme. Others involve complex processing of waste and must meet the same rules as a waste disposal facility. Amendments to the *Environmental Protection Act* in 1992 provide the government with new powers to make regulations to promote waste reduction.[32]

The 3Rs

The Ontario government has accepted as policy the hierarchy of waste management practices. Since the Ontario regulatory scheme is built around the existence of "waste," almost all waste *reduction* activities, or measures that prevent the generation of waste in the first place, are not regulated. This is true not only for any licensing requirements of the *Environmental Protection Act* but also for the planning requirements of the *Environmental Assessment Act*.

The second "R" of the hierarchy is *re-use*. Again, there are no particular approvals requirements for waste re-use measures. The Ontario brewing industry has long been the epitome of successful re-use for its system of returnable bottles. The soft drink industry, however, has become the battleground between those who prefer returnable containers and those who favour recyclability. The very successful blue box program was largely a product of this battle, when the non-refillable container industry organized a non-profit organization (Ontario Multi-Material Recycling Incorporated) to distribute startup funding for municipal blue box programs. The Ontario government continues to try to force the soft drink industry to sell a certain proportion of its product in refillable containers.

Unless a waste recycling activity involves the total utilization of the waste (for example, pop can recycling), any recycling activity comes under the full approval requirements of part V of the *Environmental Protection Act*. If a facility produces any waste at all, it is treated as a waste-processing operation. Unfortunately, few rules have ever been written for operating a recycling facility, or for assisting proponents in assembling the necessary technical support information for an application. As a result, "environmentally friendly" facilities are subjected to the same approvals delays as landfills. However, under a draft regulation released in April 1993, the ministry proposes to exempt certain municipal recycling sites and depots from the approvals process, provided that these facilities meet certain design and operating criteria.

In February 1991, the minister of the environment announced a policy of "diverting" wastes through the 3Rs, rather than disposing of it. The Ontario Waste Reduction Action Plan (WRAP), as it was called, set out a goal of diverting at least 25 per cent of the province's municipal waste from landfills by 1992 and 50 per cent by the year 2000. However, setting a goal is one thing; meeting it is another. In subsequent publications, the government has admitted that the regulatory framework for accomplishing this change in direction does not exist, and has proposed legislative changes to clarify and streamline approvals for recycling sites, to require major industrial, commercial, and institutional waste generators to implement source separation of materials for recycling programs and to carry out waste and packaging audits; and to require municipalities to implement source separation and leaf and yard material composting programs.[33] The government has also admitted that, "[c]learly, most municipalities do not have sufficient authority to engage in the wide range of activities necessary to develop and operate a comprehensive and integrated waste management system geared to diversion and environmental protection."[34] In April 1993, the minister of municipal affairs introduced amendments to the *Municipal Act* and several other statutes to expand the waste management powers of municipalities.[35]

In April 1993, the minister of environment and energy released for discussion a draft 3Rs regulation. This regulation would require major generators of industrial, commercial, and institutional waste to conduct waste audits and develop waste reduction workplans, and implement a source separation program for specified recyclable materials. In addition, major packaging users, which include food manufacturers, beverage manufacturers, paper products industries, chemical manufacturers, and importers, will have to carry out "packaging audits" and develop packaging reduction workplans. The purpose of the packaging audit is to determine ways to reduce waste by changing packaging.

Composting

It is widely believed that composting of the organic part of non-hazardous solid waste may hold the key to dramatic decreases in landfill requirements. Although "composting sites" are classified as waste disposal sites for the purposes of the Act and regulation 347,[36] there are

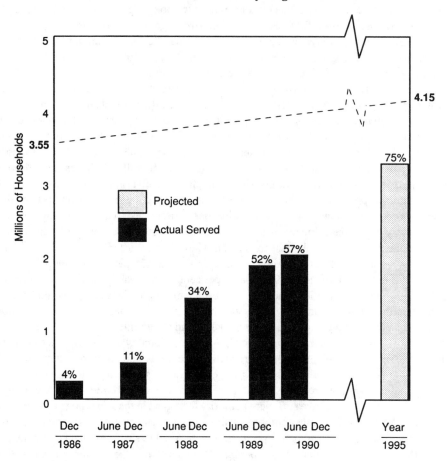

Growth of Residential Recycling in Ontario

Courtesy of the Ontario Ministry of Environment and Energy.

no specific rules governing such sites. Home composting is clearly not subject to *any* approvals requirements.[37] Under the draft 3Rs regulation, municipalities with a population of 5,000 or more would be required to supply residents with backyard composters at cost, and large municipalities would have to collect leaf and yard wastes and establish composting sites for these materials.

One type of specialized composting site is an "organic soil conditioning site." "Organic soil conditioning sites" are places where "processed organic waste" (sewage sludge) is spread on the land and ultimately ploughed into it to improve its fertility. Spreading sludge on land provides both an inexpensive means of disposal and an inexpensive fertilizer. Its main drawback as a fertilizer is its content of heavy metals, which may get into the plants grown on the soil where it is spread and may ultimately, therefore, enter food that human beings, birds, and wild or domestic animals eat. The Ministry of Environment and Energy and the Ministry of Agriculture and Food have jointly established criteria for these metals, and sludge containing metals in higher concentrations may not be spread,[38] but instead must be landfilled or incinerated.

WASTE COLLECTION AND TRANSPORTATION

The term "waste management system" is used in the Act to describe all facilities, equipment, and operations for the complete management of waste, including its collection, handling, transportation, storage, processing, and disposal. Anyone seeking to operate a "waste management system" must obtain a certificate of approval from the director[39] and must comply with a set of standards set out in regulation 347.[40] In practice, only facilities used for the collection and transportation of waste (that is, waste hauling) are considered by the ministry to be "waste management systems." All other facilities are treated as waste disposal sites.

Individual collection systems — that is, a householder's "system" of collecting his or her own domestic wastes and transporting them to a waste disposal site — are exempt from part V of the *Environmental Protection Act* and from regulation 347, as are marine craft waste disposal systems, which are covered by part VIII of the Act.[41]

Waste collection may also be regulated by municipal bylaws. For example, the city of Toronto streets bylaw[42] sets out detailed definitions and regulations for the collection of garbage and other wastes, including earth from excavation sites, by city trucks. The provisions in the bylaw, although similar to those in regulation 347, are far more comprehensive.

In general, any waste management system must conform to standards relating to the construction of trucks, methods of transferring garbage so that no nuisance such as litter or odour results, and the covering of loads.[43]

Hazardous and Liquid Industrial Waste

In 1985, the Ontario government instituted a comprehensive two-part system to control the movement of hazardous and liquid industrial waste (which are grouped under the term "subject waste").[44]

The first part of the system requires all generators of subject waste to register with the ministry. Each subject waste must be registered. A generator is then issued a generator registration number and a waste number for each waste registered. A generator is forbidden from shipping any subject waste without being registered.[45]

The second part of the system requires the completion of a waste manifest for each shipment of waste. Waste carriers are issued books of six-part manifest forms that contain parts to be filled out by the carrier, the generator, and the receiver. The carrier is required to fill out section B of the form and give it to the generator, who fills in section A. The generator then retains two copies, filing one with the ministry and keeping one for two years. The carrier takes the remaining four copies with the shipment and, on reaching the destination, gives them to the receiver. The receiver must then complete section C of the form, keep three copies, and return one to the carrier. Of those three copies, one is filed with the ministry, which can then verify it against the copy originally filed by the generator, one is returned to the generator, which is responsible for ensuring that the waste went where it was supposed to, and one is retained by the receiver for two years.[46]

Hazardous wastes across Canada

Canada generates more than 6 million tonnes of hazardous
waste annually, says Environment Canada, and is expected
to increase to 6.5 million tonnes by 1992. By far, Ontario
is the largest contributor to this toxic stew of sludges,
solvents, grease, paint, chemicals, heavy metal solutions,
oils, pesticides and PCBs.

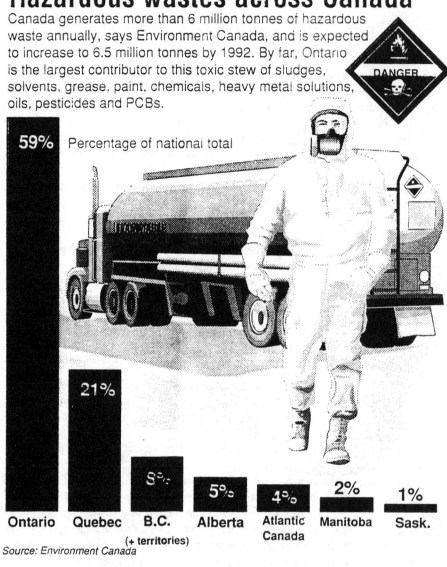

59% Percentage of national total

Ontario	Quebec	B.C. (+ territories)	Alberta	Atlantic Canada	Manitoba	Sask.
59%	21%	8%	5%	4%	2%	1%

Source: Environment Canada

Courtesy of Southam News Graphics, reprinted from *The Ottawa Citizen*, October 19, 1990.

There are variations to accommodate transport into, out of, and through Ontario, but the
basic tracking system is the same.[47] In the case of the transboundary movement of waste, the
provisions of the federal *Transportation of Dangerous Goods Act*[48] apply. With respect to
manifesting, the Ontario and federal regimes have been designed to harmonize.

The ministry has instituted a strict enforcement regime to go along with this tracking system. Violators are fairly easily identified by a computerized system that "flags" discrepancies and are frequently prosecuted.

WASTE DISPOSAL

A "waste disposal site" is defined in the *Environmental Protection Act* as follows:

> (a) any land upon, into, in or through which, or building or structure in which, waste is deposited, disposed of, handled, stored, transferred, treated or processed, and
>
> (b) any operation carried out or machinery or equipment used in connection with the depositing, disposal, handling, storage, transfer, treatment or processing referred to in clause (a).[49]

This definition is broad enough to cover not only landfills and incinerators but also facilities used for waste processing.

Four kinds of waste disposal sites are specifically exempted from *all of* part V of the *Environmental Protection Act* and regulation 347; that is, they can operate without approval by the ministry and are not subject to standards of operation set out in the regulation. They are:

1. on-site incinerators at the site of a veterinary hospital;
2. on-site garbage grinders (for example, "garburetors");
3. derelict motor vehicle sites (for example, wrecking yards); and
4. incinerators at the site of a crematorium.[50]

Several other types of waste disposal sites are exempt only from the requirement that they have a certificate of approval. Other provisions of part V and regulation 347 apply to them. These are:

- *Waste-derived fuel sites.* These are sites where waste with a quality equivalent to low-grade fuel is burned primarily for its energy value (and not simply to get rid of it).[51]

- *On-site incinerators.* These may burn only non-hazardous waste generated at the site on which they are located and must have a principal function other than waste disposal (that is, heating).[52]

- *Existing hospital incinerators.* These are exempted on the condition that a yearly report on air emissions is filed with the ministry.[53]

- *Stationary refrigerant waste disposal sites.* These sites must be the ordinary place of business of someone who collects refrigerants (for example, freon) from air conditioners, refrigerators, or freezers in the course of servicing refrigeration equipment, or who is a wholesale dealer in refrigerants. The exemption was created to permit the long-term storage of these ozone-depleting materials, pending the development of recycling or disposal facilities.[54]

- *Mobile refrigerant waste disposal sites.* This is a similar exemption, but applies to sites that are used to store waste refrigerants from cars, trucks, and other vehicles.[55]

- *Used tire sites.* These are sites used for the storage of fewer than 5,000 tires.[56] Any site used to store 5,000 or more tires requires a certificate of approval, which, since the Hagersville tire fire, will be issued only if stringent fire prevention and fire fighting measures are taken.

A special regulation has been created for sites used for the storage of PCBs. This regulation defines these storage sites as "PCB waste disposal sites" and exempts them from the requirement to obtain a certificate of approval. It does, however, require that they be operated in accordance with "director's instructions," which are simply approvals that do not go through the normal process. Indeed, director's instructions are required for *any* movement or transport of PCBs. [57]

There are nine other defined types of waste disposal sites that are subject to the Act and regulation 347:[58]

1. composting sites;
2. dumps;
3. grinding sites;
4. incineration sites;
5. landfilling sites;
6. organic soil conditioning sites;
7. packing and baling sites;
8. transfer stations; and
9. used tire sites used for the storage of more than 5,000 tires.

All these sites must have an approval to operate and must conform with the standards for location, maintenance, and operation set out in regulation 347. Of these disposal sites, only landfill and incineration are discussed below.

Landfill

In contrast to the old-style town dump, wastes are deposited on *landfill sites* under controlled conditions, compacted into a "cell," and covered with soil or other materials at regular intervals. A "cell" is defined as "a deposit of waste that has been sealed by cover material so that no waste deposited in the cell is exposed to the atmosphere."[59]

Regulation 347 stipulates conditions that must be met by any landfill site. They are designed to prevent potential health hazards such as the proliferation of rodents and insects, to improve aesthetics by requiring that there be a green belt around the site and that it be screened from public view, to prevent environmental damage such as contamination of water at, under, or near the site, and generally to require good housekeeping through adequate and continual supervision of operations. These standards are exceedingly general and are usually ignored in favour of more specific and stringent conditions set out in each site's certificate of approval.[60]

Dumps are still legally permitted in some parts of Ontario. Dumps are disposal sites where waste is deposited without the regular application of cover material. They are no longer permitted in most regions of southern and northwestern Ontario. Citizens who are concerned about pollution from an existing dump should first check the lists in regulation 347 to see whether dumps are allowed in their municipality at all.[61] One of the most common complaints about dumps in the past was the smoke billowing from the open burning of garbage or from fires caused by vandals or spontaneous combustion. Many people are under the impression that burning garbage at dumps is no longer permitted, but in fact the waste management regulation does not prohibit burning. This must be controlled through conditions on the dump's certificate of approval or through prosecutions when burning causes adverse effects to neighbours' enjoyment of their property. For example, although the ministry has guidelines that say that only "clean wood" should be burned at dump sites, pressure-treated wood, which contains heavy metals such as arsenic and chromium, is often burned, and this is legal unless the ministry's guidelines are incorporated into the dump's certificate of approval.[62]

Incineration

Although municipal waste incineration has for several years been discouraged as a matter of provincial policy, waste incinerators do exist around Ontario.[63] Such sites must be located so as to reduce the effects of nuisances such as dust, noise and traffic, must be accessible for the transportation of wastes to the facility without nuisance, and, taking into account meteorological considerations, must minimize environmental effects. Other requirements include a design and a capacity adequate to efficiently process the quantities of waste that may be expected so that a minimum volume of residue is obtained, the putrescible materials remaining as residue are reduced to a minimum, and a minimum of air pollution results.[64] In 1992, the Ontario government promulgated a regulation prohibiting the construction of new incinerators for solid municipal waste.[65]

OPPORTUNITIES FOR PUBLIC INVOLVEMENT

There are at least three situations in which citizens can become involved in waste management, aside from what people can do in their own lives to reduce waste generation. First, there are numerous opportunities to get involved in the planning of new facilities, either through a waste management master planning process or otherwise. Second, there is an opportunity to be involved as an individual or as part of a citizens' group in the approvals process for new or altered facilities. Finally, citizens can play an important role in monitoring operating facilities.

Participation in the Planning Process

Most new waste management facilities are planned within an environmental assessment process. For municipal facilities, this usually occurs within a waste management master planning exercise. Even though individual pieces of a total system for managing waste may not require formal approval under the *Environmental Assessment Act*, they are usually identified in the systems analysis part of the process.

As more fully discussed in Chapter 9, the *Environmental Assessment Act* requires proponents to examine both functionally different ways of carrying out an undertaking ("alternatives to") and different methods ("alternative methods"). In waste management planning, the "alternatives to" analysis usually becomes an examination of different systems (for example, 50 per cent diversion and 50 per cent landfill). The "alternative methods" analysis is usually a facility-siting exercise and a technology assessment.

One of the key features of any environmental assessment process must be public involvement. Proponents are encouraged by the Ministry of Environment and Energy to involve citizens in the process.[66] This participation may take the form of attendance at public meetings and open houses, but it can also involve attendance at workshops at which evaluation criteria are discussed, or membership on a public liaison committee.

Since there are no hard and fast "rules" governing how a proponent must involve the public, it is sometimes necessary for citizens to push for a higher level of input. This can frequently be accomplished by approaching the proponent directly, but it may be necessary to contact the government review coordinator, who is a staff member in the ministry's Environmental Assessment Branch.

Sometimes facilities are planned *outside* the requirements of the *Environmental Assessment Act*. For example, it is ministry policy to exempt short-term expansions of existing landfill sites from the requirements of the Act.[67] Even in this situation, however, public involvement is strongly encouraged by the ministry.

Participation During the Approvals Process

Once an environmental assessment is submitted to the minister, the *formal* public participation requirements of the *Environmental Assessment Act* are invoked. On completion of the government review, any member of the public has a minimum 30-day period in which to make submissions to the minister on the environmental assessment and the review, and to require a hearing by the Environmental Assessment Board.[68]

In addition to any requirements of the *Environmental Assessment Act*, everyone who intends to establish, operate, or enlarge any waste management facility must apply to the director of the Approvals Branch for a certificate of approval issued under the *Environmental Protection Act*.[69] This applies to all municipalities, corporations, individuals, and provincial government agencies. It governs sites and systems already in existence when the *Environmental Protection Act* came into force, as well as sites established afterward.

The applicant may not start the proposed operation (or enlarge the old one) until the certificate has been granted. Doing so is a breach of the *Environmental Protection Act* that may be prosecuted.

Once the approvals director receives an application, he or she must determine whether a public hearing is mandatory and, if it is not, whether in his or her discretion a hearing *should* be held.[70]

If the director decides that *no* public hearing will be held, his or her staff will review the application, including the site plans and specifications that must form part of every application, and will recommend that he or she approve the site, refuse to approve it, or approve it subject to specific terms and conditions. The director will then make the final decision. The director may refuse to issue a certificate if he or she is satisfied that the site or system:

- may create a nuisance;
- is contrary to the public interest; or
- may result in a hazard to any person's health or safety.[71]

The director does not need to give anyone, including the neighbours, notice of the application before issuing a certificate. If a member of the public happens to hear that an application has been made, all he or she can do is write to the director, objecting to the issuance of the certificate, asking for conditions to be imposed, and asking for a public hearing. The director may take some of these requests into consideration, and may or may not act on them.

When a public hearing is required by the *Environmental Protection Act*, or if the director decides to order a public hearing, the citizen has more opportunity for direct input into the decision-making process.

The director *must* order a public hearing when an application is received to establish, alter, enlarge, or extend a site for the disposal of:

- hauled liquid industrial waste;
- hazardous waste; or
- other waste, which the director ascertains, having regard to its nature and quantity, is the equivalent of the domestic waste of not fewer than 1,500 people.[72]

In the case of any other application, the director *may* order a public hearing, although he or she has no legal duty to do so.[73] The director will often order one if there is public knowledge of the site and concerted opposition to it before the application is submitted or before it is approved. As a matter of policy, the director seeks the views of the municipality in which the site is located on the question of a hearing. Since the director is almost always loath to disregard the views of an elected council, any citizen would do well to approach local politicians to advance an argument in favour of a hearing.

Note that the director does have the discretion, even where the Act says that he or she *must* hold a hearing, to refuse to hold the hearing before issuing an approval if he or she considers that there is an emergency requiring immediate disposal of wastes.[74] This frequently occurs when a municipal landfill site is full and there is no time to go through the hearings process before approving a new site. Usually such an emergency approval is issued only for a long enough time to allow the operation while the hearing process runs its course.

The hearing procedure is largely the same, whether an undertaking is the subject of an environmental assessment submission or is simply an approval matter under the *Environmental Protection Act*. Sometimes, where numerous approvals are required (such as rezoning or expropriation), a proponent may trigger the provisions of the *Consolidated Hearings Act*.[75] This Act allows for the creation of a joint board, made up of members of the Environmental Assessment Board and the Ontario Municipal Board, which then hears and decides all matters.

At a hearing, the applicant is the first to speak. The applicant is usually represented by a lawyer, who will call one or more expert witnesses to explain the planning process, the mitigation measures that will be designed for the site, how the site will be supervised and landscaped, the equipment to be used, the intended hours of operation, the intended use of the site, and any other information that the applicant feels will help his or her case. These witnesses may be engineers, hydrogeologists, land-use planners, and other experts in designing facilities.

After the applicant's lawyer has taken a witness through his or her testimony, the lawyers for all the other parties, whether they support or oppose the application, will have an opportunity to cross-examine. Then, any member of the public who is present will have an opportunity to question the witness. This procedure is followed for every witness who gives testimony, whether for or against the application.

After the conclusion of the applicant's presentation, the board invites the lawyers representing other interested parties to make presentations, calling witnesses if they wish.

Public authorities such as other ministries of the provincial government, local conservation authorities, and municipal officials, as well as representatives of special interest groups such as ratepayers' associations, agricultural associations, and naturalists' clubs, may also give testimony, either as witnesses called by any of the parties to the hearing or on their own.

After all witnesses called by counsel have been questioned, individuals attending the hearing are given an opportunity to make representations, whether to express their own opinions or those of special interest groups. The board will usually hold one or more evening meetings at which citizens may speak who were not able to attend during the day.

After hearing all evidence and argument, the board will adjourn to consider its decision. When it is issued, usually some two or three months later, the board's decision is final, unless there is an appeal.[76]

Decisions of the Environmental Assessment Board or a joint board may be appealed to the provincial Cabinet by any party to the hearing. The effect of an appeal is to stay the board's decision pending the outcome of the appeal. This process can take six months or longer to complete.[77]

Post-Approval Participation

The regional and district offices of the Ministry of Environment and Energy are responsible for the long-term monitoring of waste management facilities. They inspect facilities, sometimes irregularly, to ensure that they are being operated according to the requirements of the Act, regulation 347, and any conditions of approval.

Any citizen may notify the ministry of unreasonable or hazardous practices at a waste management facility. If you find that the operator has committed breaches of the *Environmental Protection Act* or regulations, or conditions of approval, ask for an investigation. If it appears that there is a continuing problem, urge the ministry to impose an order to prevent future breaches. If the ministry refuses to act, you yourself can prosecute. A successful prosecution would put the ministry in an embarrassing position if it had continued to refuse to control the polluting operations.

You are entitled to see a copy of the certificate of approval and any documents referenced within it.[78] If the ministry has attached specific standards and conditions to the certificate, write to the ministry, asking it to require the operator to conform to those conditions. If the operator has breached any of them, anyone may prosecute it, including private citizens as well as the ministry.[79] The director has the power to add further conditions to a certificate at any time, on the grounds that he or she believes it would be in the public interest, and you should ask the director to exercise this power where it appears necessary to prevent pollution or nuisance.

If an order has been imposed, the operator's failure to comply with any condition in it is an offence under the *Environmental Protection Act*, and the ministry or the citizen may prosecute.[80] Breach of a condition of an order is grounds for the ministry to revoke the certificate of approval, and the citizen may ask the ministry to do so. You could also consider a civil action for damages or an injunction.

If you have an interest in being more proactive, you may seek to become involved with a site's public liaison committee. If there is no such committee, ask the ministry to establish one.

CONCLUSION

The traditional methods of waste disposal degrade vast tracts of valuable land, incur potential long-term air and water pollution problems, and waste valuable sources of energy and materials. We have just begun the shift to a conserver-oriented society. There now appears to be a government commitment to shift the emphasis away from disposal and toward reduction.

We still need laws and programs to discourage the manufacture of non-re-usable and non-recyclable goods, to encourage the standardization of inexpensive and recyclable containers, to discourage wasteful packaging, to require tougher and more durable products where the technology exists to do so, and generally to encourage conservation of energy and resources in the manufacturing industry and the consuming public. Every citizen can do his or her part by demanding products that conserve rather than waste.

Waste disposal will most likely remain an inevitable fact of life for the foreseeable future, although there is hope that the need will be reduced. There is an important role for citizens to play in the selection of new sites, in the approvals process, in the long-term monitoring of new and safer sites, and in making consumer and lifestyle choices that result in less waste.

John Tidball

FURTHER READING

Association of Municipalities of Ontario, *Waste Management Discussion Paper Series, 1989-1992* (Toronto: The Association of Municipalities of Ontario).

Ontario, Ministry of Municipal Affairs and Ministry of the Environment, *Municipal Waste Management Powers: A Discussion Paper* (Toronto: Queen's Printer, March 1992).

Ontario, Ministry of the Environment, Waste Reduction Office, *Initiatives Paper No. 1: Regulatory Measures to Achieve Ontario's Waste Reduction Targets* (Toronto: the ministry, 1991).

Ontario, Ministry of the Environment, Waste Reduction Office, *Initiatives Paper No. 2: Waste Management Planning in Ontario* (Toronto: the ministry, 1992).

John-David Phyper and Brett Ibbotson, *The Handbook of Environmental Compliance in Ontario* (Scarborough, Ont.: McGraw-Hill Ryerson, 1991).

Dianne Saxe, *The Ontario E.P.A. Annotated* (Toronto: Butterworths, 1990).

Ontario Environment Network, Waste Caucus, *Research Paper Series 1991-1992* (Guelph: Ontario Environment Network).

Mark Winfield, *Looking Back and Looking Ahead: Municipal Solid Waste Management in Ontario from the 1983 Blueprint to 50% Diversion in 2000 — Conference Background Paper and Report* (Toronto: Canadian Institute for Environmental Law and Policy, March 1993).

ENDNOTES

1   *Indian Act*, RSC 1985, c. I-5.
2   *National Parks Act*, RSC 1985, c. N-14.
3   *Atomic Energy Control Act*, RSC 1985, c. A-16.
4   Indian Reserve Waste Disposal Regulations, CRC 1978, c. 960.
5   Ibid., section 3.
6   *Canadian Environmental Assessment Act*, SC 1992, c. 37.
7   Particularly in the Sarnia area.
8   SOR/80-217, as amended.
9   For example, the approvals process for materials recovery facilities (or MRFs) may take a year or more, even if the *Environmental Assessment Act*, RSO 1990, c. E.18, does not apply.
10 The *Waste Management Act*, SO 1992, c. 1, sections 22 to 35. Part IV of that Act consists of amendments to the *Environmental Protection Act*, RSO 1990, c. E.19, as amended, giving the provincial government broader control over municipal waste management planning and overpackaging, containers, disposable products, and products that pose waste management problems. However, as discussed in the text below, this legislation does not expand the powers of municipalities, which collect and dispose of these materials, to implement 3R programs.
11 *Environmental Protection Act*, supra endnote 10.
12 Reg. 347, RRO 1990, c. 347.
13 *Environmental Protection Act*, supra endnote 10, section 27.
14 Ibid., section 43.
15 Ibid., section 44.
16 Ibid., sections 147 and 150.
17 *Environmental Assessment Act*, supra endnote 9.
18 Publicly owned facilities are automatically subject to the Act. A ministerial policy statement on private sector facilities calls for the designation of most disposal facilities, transfer stations over 300 tonnes per day, and processing facilities that generate waste residue over 200 tonnes per day.
19 Although this is true for most regional municipalities (except Niagara and Muskoka), counties must pass a bylaw under section 209 of the *Municipal Act* to assume any jurisdiction. The variations and inconsistencies, overlap and duplication between the powers of various Regional Municipalities and Counties are described in greater detail

in Ontario, Ministry of Municipal Affairs and Ministry of the Environment, *Municipal Waste Management Powers in Ontario: A Discussion Paper* (Toronto: Queen's Printer, 1992).

20 *Municipal Act*, RSO 1990, c. M.45, section 210.90.

21 In 1989, the Association of Municipalities of Ontario issued two reports on municipal solid waste management, *The Waste Management Planning and Approval Process* (March 1989) and *The Municipal Waste Abatement Strategy* (November 1989). Among the association's recommendations aimed at giving municipalities sufficient authority to develop comprehensive waste management systems was a recommendation to rescind the power of local municipalities to object to acquisitions of land for waste-disposal purposes.

22 Reg. 347, supra endnote 12, section 3.

23 *Dead Animal Disposal Act*, RSO 1990, c. D.3.

24 *Mining Act*, RSO 1990, c. M.14.

25 A "Proposed Policy for Management of Excess Soil, Rock and Like Materials" was released by the Ministry of the Environment and circulated for public comment in September 1992.

26 Reg. 347, supra endnote 12, section 3, formerly O. reg. 322/85, section 1.

27 See, for example, the definition of non-hazardous solid industrial waste in reg. 347, supra endnote 12, section 1, paragraph 42.

28 Ibid., section 1, paragraph 57.

29 Ibid., section 1, paragraph 38.

30 Ibid., section 1, paragraph 27.

31 Ibid., schedule 2, part B.

32 *Environmental Protection Act*, supra endnote 10, sections 25 and 176(4)(j) to (s).

33 Ontario, Ministry of the Environment, Waste Reduction Office, *Initiatives Paper No. 1: Regulatory Measures to Achieve Ontario's Waste Reduction Targets* (Toronto: the ministry, October 1991).

34 *Municipal Waste Management Powers in Ontario*, supra endnote 19, at 26.

35 Ontario, Legislative Assembly, Bill 7, *Municipal Statute Law Amendment Act, 1993*, first reading April 21, 1993, second reading May 12, 1993, referred to Standing Committee on General Government May 18, 1993.

36 Reg. 347, supra endnote 12, section 4.

37 *Environmental Protection Act*, supra endnote 10, section 26.

38 Ontario, Ministry of the Environment and Ministry of Agriculture and Food, *Guidelines for Sewage Sludge Utilization on Agricultural Lands* (Toronto: Queen's Printer, April 1978, revised March 1981). These guidelines are not binding standards, but they are used by the Ministry of the Environment when deciding whether to issue a certificate of approval for an organic soil conditioning site.

39 *Environmental Protection Act*, supra endnote 10, section 27.

40 Reg. 347, supra endnote 12, section 13.

41 Ibid., section 7.

42 City of Toronto bylaw no. 20298.

43 Reg. 347, supra endnote 12, section 13.

44 Ibid., sections 15 to 24.

45   Ibid., section 15.

46   Ibid., sections 16 to 20.

47   Ibid., sections 21, 22, and 23.

48   *Transportation of Dangerous Goods Act*, RSC 1985, c. T-19.

49   *Environmental Protection Act*, supra endnote 10, section 25, as amended by the *Waste Management Act*, supra endnote 10.

50   Reg. 347, supra endnote 12, section 5(1).

51   Ibid., section 5(3).

52   Ibid., section 25.

53   Ibid., section 26.

54   Ibid., section 29.

55   Ibid., section 36.

56   Ibid., section 5a(3).

57   Waste Management — PCBs, RRO 1990, reg. 362, formerly O. reg. 11/82.

58   Reg. 347, supra endnote 12, section 4.

59   Ibid., section 1, paragraph 6.

60   Ibid., section 8.

61   Ibid., section 11.

62   See Paul Irwin, "Guidelines Say Pressure-Treated Wood Should Not Be Burned, But It's Still Legal," *Peterborough Examiner*, October 5, 1990.

63   Incineration was "declassified" as the fourth "R" in the late 1980s and, since 1990, has been all but prohibited.

64   Reg. 347, supra endnote 12, section 9.

65   O. reg. 555/92.

66   Ontario, Ministry of the Environment, Interim Guidelines on the Environmental Assessment Process, 1988.

67   Ontario, Ministry of the Environment, Policy No. 03-05, *Interim Expansion of Municipal Landfills*.

68   *Environmental Assessment Act*, supra endnote 9, section 7.

69   *Environmental Protection Act*, supra endnote 10, section 27.

70   Ibid., sections 30 and 32.

71   Ibid., section 39.

72   Ibid., section 30.

73   Ibid., section 32.

74   Ibid., section 31.

75   *Consolidated Hearings Act*, RSO 1990, c. C.29.

76   *Environmental Protection Act*, supra endnote 10, section 33; *Environmental Assessment Act*, supra endnote 9, section 18(17); *Consolidated Hearings Act*, supra endnote 75, section 12.

77   *Environmental Protection Act*, supra endnote 10, section 34; *Environmental Assessment Act*, supra endnote 9, section 23; *Consolidated Hearings Act*, supra endnote 73, section 13.

78   *Environmental Protection Act*, supra endnote 10, section 19(4).

79   Ibid., section 186 (3).

80   Ibid., section 186(2).

PART VI

Environmental Law Reform

25

Environmental Bill of Rights

Contents

The occasion to debate this particular bill is one of very real importance to me and I believe it will go down as a day of some importance in the history of people's attempt to come to grips with the industrial age and to make this planet a liveable situation for generations to follow us.

Dr. Stuart Smith, then Liberal Opposition leader, introducing the first environmental bill of rights in Ontario on December 13, 1979, Ontario, Legislative Assembly, Debates, *December 13, 1979, 5480*

INTRODUCTION

Despite the emerging volume and complexity of environmental law and policies at both the federal and provincial levels, several fundamental and basic questions remain either unanswered or answered in a chequered fashion. Do you have a right to a healthy environment? What rights do you have to participate in environmental decisions? How and under what circumstances are governments held accountable for their environmental activities? Does the public have access to the courts to redress environmental problems?

These questions are not new. These questions have been asked by legal scholars, environmentalists, and aggrieved members of the public for decades.[1] Although there may be differences in details, one consistent theme over the years has been the recognition of the need for a set of principles and rules to outline citizens' rights with respect to the environment; the duties of government pertaining to natural resource use and the prevention of environmental degradation; and the role of the public in environmental decision making, among other such principles.

The basis for such rights and duties should be a constitutional recognition of the importance of the environment, the entrenchment of citizens' environmental rights to a healthful environment, and the imposition of duties on government to conserve and protect the nation's natural resource base. Unfortunately, although environmentalists called for an entrenched right to environmental quality, the constitutional debate and consequent reforms in 1981 that resulted in the *Canadian Charter of Rights and Freedoms* did not deal with these issues.[2] Similarly, the latest round of constitutional reform negotiations failed to deal adequately with environmental issues.[3]

Although efforts are being made for constitutional reform, there have been attempts over the past few decades to develop comprehensive environmental reforms at both the federal and provincial levels. These statutory reforms are designed to put in place a framework to define and articulate environmental rights, governmental environmental accountability, and access to courts and tribunals, along with procedural and institutional mechanisms to back up these rights and obligations. These initiatives are usually advocated in the context of the need for an "environmental bill of rights."

This chapter examines the evolution of the notion of an environmental bill of rights. Although an environmental bill of rights is needed both at the federal and provincial level, an Ontario focus will be taken, mostly because that is where there has been recent discussion of this concept and the most progress to date. In particular, the chapter examines recent developments in Ontario and, to a lesser extent, the other provinces in their attempts to enact such a bill. The last section of the chapter will provide an overview of the latest effort — the introduction of Bill 26 in the Ontario Legislature in May 1993.

EVOLUTION OF THE ENVIRONMENTAL BILL OF RIGHTS IN ONTARIO

Any attempt to trace the origins of an environmental bill of rights must at least recognize its connection to notions in political theory (which then touch upon the principles of participatory democracy and the nature of "rights" and "obligations") as well as to the philosophical discussion about the "rights of nature."[4] Such abstract discussion, however, is usually translated into some basic notion that citizens should be vested with legal tools to defend the environment.[5]

From the 1960s, at any rate, the United States has been attempting to reconcile theory with practice. The US experience developed a wide array of mechanisms to protect the environment both within and outside the courtroom setting. Citizens suit provisions in many environmental statutes, broad judicial review powers, administrative procedures Acts (which provide rights to notice and comment for environmental approvals), and reformed standing rules to allow greater access to the courts are perhaps the most obvious attempts to formally include a broader range of interests in environmental decision-making and enhance the accountability of governments. Moreover, specialized state legislation, such as the *Michigan Environmental Protection Act*, a statute enacted over 20 years ago, is a reminder of the historical attempts to empower citizens to protect the environment.[6] Many states now have statutes or provisions in statutes designed to give citizens greater access to the courts and environmental decision-making processes of government.[7]

In contrast, Canadian environmental law and policy has long been characterized by more closed decision-making processes and broad governmental discretion. Indeed, although many commentators have noted these weaknesses of both federal and provincial law,[8] citizens remain frustrated in their attempts to protect the environment. Environmental approvals can be granted, whether for a pollution licence or for the "improvement" of a watercourse, without input from the public. Once granted, such approvals could be valid for an indefinite term with little or no formal recourse or avenue for review by concerned citizens.

Philosophical precepts, experiences in other jurisdictions, and the limits of Canadian environmental law and policy can be said to be the driving forces behind the development of environmental rights legislation in Canada, although this is hardly an exhaustive list of influences.

Early Origins of the Environmental Bill of Rights

Although there were numerous forces fuelling the drive to comprehensive environmental law reforms, a number of publications served to forge the agenda of such reforms. Perhaps the most articulate description of the environmental law reform agenda is that proposed by the Canadian Environmental Law Association and articulated in earlier editions of *Environment on Trial*. Indeed, one chapter had set a law reform agenda for decades hence.[9] The chapter outlined the basic skeleton for an environmental bill of rights to include:

- the right to a healthy and attractive environment;
- standing (the right to use the law to defend the environment in courts and in tribunals);
- environmental impact studies;
- access to information;
- public participation in setting environmental standards;
- an environmental ombudsman;
- class actions;
- the right to defend the environment at a reasonable cost;
- restrictions on agency discretion;
- judicial review of administrative actions; and
- the burden of proof should be on the polluter.

While publications like *Environment on Trial* laid the conceptual framework, calls for legislative reforms of the kind envisioned in the environmental bill of rights multiplied across Canada.

At the federal level, the history in this regard is a fairly short one. In 1981, Liberal member of Parliament Charles Caccia introduced an unsuccessful motion to have a comprehensive environmental rights bill adopted at the federal level.[10] Environment Canada commissioned a report by the Canadian Environmental Law Research Foundation on the possible components of a federal environmental bill of rights, but it took no action on this report.

In the mid-1980s, the federal minister of the environment promised to include a version of the environmental bill of rights in the proposed *Canadian Environmental Protection Act*. However, the so-called bill of rights was included in a legally unenforceable, essentially symbolic, preamble.[11] During consultations on the proposed statute, environmentalists sought to include some sort of special environmental rights provisions in the proposed bill. Such provisions, however, were not incorporated in the Act when it was finally introduced in 1987. There has not been any formal proposal for a federal environmental bill of rights since that time.

Provincially, the response was very different. Quebec developed environmental rights legislation, which, although progressive for a Canadian jurisdiction, was not regarded as a comprehensive code. The *Environment Quality Act*[12] provides a number of rights to its residents, the most important being the right to bring an action for an injunction to enjoin a polluting activity. The relevant sections state:

> **19.1** Every person has a right to a healthy environment and to its protection, and to the protection of the living species inhabiting it, to the extent provided for by this act and the regulations, orders, approvals, and authorizations issued under any section of this act.
>
> **19.2** A judge of the Superior Court may grant an injunction to prohibit any act or operation which interferes or might interfere with the exercise of a right conferred by section 19.1.

In Ontario, the history of comprehensive reforms progressed through a succession of private members' bills by the opposition parties commencing in 1979 and on through the 1980s. These initiatives ensured that the idea of an environmental bill of rights retained political currency.

In November 1979, Dr. Stuart Smith, the Liberal leader of the Opposition at the time, introduced the first environmental bill of rights, titled *An Act Respecting Environmental*

Rights in Ontario.[13] Then, in 1980, Marion Bryden, a New Democratic Party member, introduced *An Act To Establish an Environmental Magna Carta for Ontario.*[14] The Liberals introduced a bill substantially similar to Dr. Smith's 1979 bill in 1981, with Liberal Murray Elston re-introducing it again in 1982.[15] By the mid-1980s, both the Liberal and NDP had demonstrated solid support for the bill.

In 1985, the political cards had turned. During the 1985 election campaign, the Liberals promised that, if they were elected, the top priority for their environmental agenda would be the enactment of an environmental bill of rights.[16] After some 40 years of rule by the Progressive Conservative party, a minority Liberal government was formed, made possible by the support of the NDP. However, within the two-year rule by this minority government, the bill was hardly mentioned. After the Liberals won a majority government in 1987, it eventually became apparent that the Liberal government would not introduce an environmental bill of rights. Any environmental law reform would be undertaken incrementally, with "focused" reforms being introduced from time to time. Although the Liberals did not carry through their commitment to enact an environmental bill of rights, there are at least four examples of where influence of the bill was felt during their government in the development of the *Freedom of Information and Protection of Privacy Act, Intervenor Funding Project Act,* and the *Class Proceedings Act,* which are discussed below.[17]

Twice in 1987 and once in 1989,[18] NDP environment critic Ruth Grier introduced private members' bills proposing an environmental bill of rights. These bills were similar to the bill introduced by Liberal leader Stuart Smith in 1979 and the flurry of bills following that bill. Although some of these bills passed the first reading and, indeed, were sent to legislative committee, few really expected that they would be taken seriously. Environment critic Ruth Grier advocated the introduction of an environmental bill of rights during her 1990 election campaign, and in July 1992, as environment minister under a newly elected NDP government, Ms Grier tabled a draft environmental bill of rights for public discussion. Following this public consultation, Bud Wildman, the newly appointed minister of environment and energy, introduced Bill 26 on May 31, 1993.

Progress Report on Implementing Components of an Environmental Bill of Rights

Before more closely examining Bill 26, it is important to note that although the environmental bill of rights had not been enacted earlier, it did have a direct or indirect influence on a whole array of legislation over the past two decades. A number of the original components of such a bill described above have been implemented partially through new laws dealing with specific components of the bill, through amendments to existing laws that increased public access and government accountability, through changes in government policies, and through key court decisions requiring government to consult the public even where statutes did not require openness.

Standing

The law of standing has evolved over the past few years. The most significant gains, however, have not come through legislation, but through less restrictive application of the standing barrier by the courts.[19] Nevertheless, there have been a number of law reform efforts, including a 1989 report by the Law Reform Commission of Ontario that argued for enhanced access to the courts.[20] A year later, the Ontario Ministry of the Attorney General itself initiated a review of the law of standing. Although not a legislative initiative, the Ministry of the Attorney General did establish a "Committee on the Law of Standing." This multi-stakeholder committee was struck to develop a draft law pertaining to the liberalization of standing before the courts.[21] As of June 1993, the committee had yet to release its report.

Environmental Impact Studies

Traditional notions place environmental impact studies as a cornerstone of an environmental bill of rights. Chapter 9 already has described in detail the strengths and weaknesses of the Ontario and federal environmental assessment law and policy. Suffice it to say that although these regimes provide a framework for environmental assessment, there remain both conceptual and practical limitations. The fact that most private sector undertakings are not subject to the Ontario environmental assessment regime and the high number of exemptions of public sector undertakings have been constant sources of controversy.

Access to Information

Despite the enactment of the federal *Access to Information Act*[22] in 1983, the Ontario *Freedom of Information and Protection of Privacy Act* in 1987, the *Municipal Freedom of Information and Protection of Privacy Act*[23] in 1989, and the creation of the Workplace Hazardous Materials Information System (WHMIS), which requires employers to provide information about hazardous materials to all employees working with dangerous substances,[24] there is still considerable difficulty in obtaining access to information, especially environmental information. Although these Acts create a formal procedure for obtaining information, the costs, discretion of officials, delay, and complexity of the process often alienate the citizen attempting to get information.

Another aspect of access to information has received some legislative attention was a proposal by the Canadian Environmental Law Association that government authorities should be guaranteed access to information about corporate wrongdoing through the enactment of "whistle-blower" protection laws. A whistle-blower provision was put into Ontario's *Environmental Protection Act* in 1983.[25]

Another recent initiative in information access was the federal government's National Pollutant Release Inventory. In March 1993, Environment Canada published a notice under section 16(1) of the *Canadian Environmental Protection Act*. By June 1994, companies that manufacture, process, or otherwise use more than 10 tonnes of any of 178 listed chemicals would be required to provide information on their activities and releases to the environment. For the first time, the government and the public would have systematic access to information about the toxic chemicals being emitted or discharged to the air, land, and water, including waste disposal activities.

Public Participation in Setting Environmental Standards

One of the key omissions from current law reform efforts has been the continued lack of involvement of the public in environmental decision-making activities, and in particular, standard-setting and permit-issuing matters. Ontario's environmental laws generally have no such provisions. To be fair, some ministries have made it a policy to undertake public consultation with respect to certain matters. However, these consultation processes remain discretionary and inconsistent in the manner and form that they are undertaken. Moreover, of the thousands of environmental approvals issued by the various federal and provincial departments, ministries, and agencies, few are issued with effective public consultation.

One of the initiatives in this area is the establishment by the Ontario Ministry of the Environment of the Advisory Committee on Environmental Standards (ACES). This committee, formed in the late 1980s, is composed of representatives of industry, environmentalists, and other societal sectors to provide a forum to review proposed standards and guidelines. The committee usually invites public comment on those initiatives.

Environmental Ombudsman[26]

In the late 1970s, an ombudsman was created for the province, although not directly relating to environmental matters. Certainly, the effectiveness of this office is not clear. Recent events have underlined the uncertainty that exists in relation to very basic issues of the proper role of the ombudsman and to whom this office actually reports in terms of accountability. Although the idea seems sound, in practice the position has not lived up to the expectations of the environmental community. (The problems that citizens have experienced in dealing with this office are discussed in Chapter 3.)

Although Ontario's ombudsman does deal with environmental issues, some have suggested that a watchdog is still needed specifically for the environment. In 1992, for example, the Ontario Round Table on the Environment and the Economy called for the creation of a commissioner of sustainability. Paul Martin, the federal Liberal party environment critic, has also suggested that Canada needs an "environmental auditor" to point out inconsistencies in government policies affecting the environment.[27]

Class Actions

One of the most interesting recent initiatives is the passing of the *Class Proceedings Act*.[28] Although its origins can be traced to the Liberal government, this initiative saw the light of day under the NDP government. The bill was actually drafted through a multi-stakeholder process (which included the Canadian Environmental Law Association and Energy Probe) during 1989, although it was not formally introduced into the Legislature until 1990.[29] It was enacted into law in May 1992,[30] and was proclaimed in force on January 1, 1993. The bill provides a mechanism to allow class actions to be undertaken and the establishment of a fund to facilitate such actions.[31]

The Right To Defend the Environment at a Reasonable Cost

One of the glaring traditional weaknesses in environmental law is related not to legal barriers to public participation, but to economic barriers. Too often, concerned citizens are excluded from the courts and administrative tribunals because of the lack of financial and professional resources to effectively participate in those processes. In 1988 the passing of the *Intervenor Funding Project Act*[32] brought some limited relief from this problem. The primary purpose of the Act is to create a scheme whereby intervenors before the Environmental Assessment Board, the Ontario Energy Board, and the Consolidated Hearing Board are allowed certain funds (upon the fulfilment of certain criteria). However, the Act does not apply to other tribunals that deal with environmental concerns (such as the Ontario Municipal Board and the Environmental Appeal Board), and does nothing to reform the party-and-party costs rule that often makes access to the civil courts prohibitively costly. The *Intervenor Funding Project Act* was to last three years, but was extended another four years in March 1992.[33] The weaknesses of this Act are discussed in more detail in Chapter 9.

Restrictions on Agency Discretion and Judicial Review of Administrative Action

There have been few attempts federally or provincially to restrict broad agency discretion or provide for greater review of agency action or inaction by the courts. Certainly, there are few if any provisions, such as those in the *Michigan Environmental Protection Act*, that give the courts the power to determine the reasonableness of government standards or to compel the government agencies to adopt standards to protect the environment when there are none.

However, there have been a few developments that have enhanced the accountability of government agencies and made them act more fairly toward citizens. One of the most important initiatives was the passage of the *Statutory Powers Procedure Act* in 1971, which provided that any Ontario tribunal charged with making a decision that affects people's rights under a statute must first hold a hearing, in which basic procedural safeguards are provided to ensure that all parties have a full and fair hearing. There is no similar federal statute.

Three other important developments were the work of the courts rather than the legislatures. The first was the tendency of the courts to override "privative clauses" in legislation. Privative clauses state that the fairness of agency decisions and the procedure used in making those decisions cannot be reviewed by the courts. The courts have stated that these clauses have no effect where an agency has exceeded its jurisdiction, and have defined "exceeding jurisdiction" to include many forms of unfair procedure. Second, the courts have imposed on government agencies a duty of "procedural fairness." Before this doctrine was developed, only the actions of agencies actually making a decision affecting people's rights could be reviewed by the courts. If a department or an agency merely made a recommendation or made a decision that did not directly affect someone's rights, the procedure or decision was immune from judicial review. Some courts have held that the duty of "procedural fairness" requires government agencies issuing licences and approvals for activities that may harm the environment to notify neighbours who may be affected and give them an opportunity to comment even if there is no statutory right of public participation.[34] Third, the courts have developed a doctrine of "legitimate expectations" as part of the duty of procedural fairness.[35] Under this doctrine, if the government has granted someone a benefit, even if the person has no enforceable right to continue to receive this benefit, the government cannot take it away without first giving the person notice of its intention and an opportunity to make submissions.

Progress in Other Provinces

Other jurisdictions have been busy developing their versions of an environmental bill of rights. The approach undertaken by Quebec has already been mentioned. The two territorial governments were actually the first jurisdictions to enact their versions of environmental rights bills. According to the statement of purpose of the Northwest Territories law, the purpose of the bill "is to provide environmental rights for the people of the Northwest Territories."[36] The Yukon law was enacted shortly after the Northwest Territories law.[37]

Furthermore, in the spring of 1992, the government of Saskatchewan introduced for first reading its version of an environmental bill of rights entitled *The Charter of Environmental Rights and Responsibilities*.[38] This bill limits itself to creating a right of action, the availability of certain information, and the protection of persons reporting environmental harm.[39]

The Current Attempt: The Task Force Report on the Ontario Environmental Bill of Rights and Bill 26

A renewed sense of optimism that an environmental bill of rights might see the light of day was evident when Ruth Grier was appointed environment minister on the election of an NDP government in September 1990. That optimism turned out to be well founded. In December of that year, the minister announced the establishment of the Advisory Committee on the Ontario Environmental Bill of Rights to assist her in developing the bill. The advisory committee, whose membership represented 25 organizations, including environmental groups, the municipal, industrial, business, and labour sectors, and several ministries of the Ontario government, was to review the "basic principles such a bill should contain and suggest options for inclusion in the new bill."[40] Interestingly enough, on the day the minister announced the consultation process, Liberal environment critic Barbara Sullivan introduced a private member's bill calling for an environmental bill of rights.[41] For all intents and purposes, it was the same bill Ruth Grier introduced several times during the former Liberal rule.

The advisory committee met frequently through to March 1991, and provided a source of dialogue and discussion. However, while there was some consensus on a number of principles for an environmental bill of rights, there was little consensus on how these principles should be applied or implemented.

In October 1991, Environment Minister Grier took the next step toward the realization of the bill by establishing the Task Force on the Ontario Environmental Bill of Rights. According to its terms of reference, the task force was to draft an environmental bill of rights and an accompanying report.[42] The task force was multi-stakeholder in nature — three business representatives (Ontario Chamber of Commerce, Business Council on National Issues, and the Canadian Manufacturers' Association), a lawyer from the Legal Services Branch of the Ministry of the Environment, a private practitioner, and two environmental representatives (Canadian Environmental Law Association and Pollution Probe). It was co-chaired by the Ministry of the Environment's deputy minister and a lawyer from the Policy Branch of the Attorney General's Office (who returned to private practice during the course of the negotiations).

From October 1991 to May 1992, the task force met some 41 times. Supporting the work of the committee was an inter-ministerial committee composed of representatives of most other ministries, which provided feedback on the evolving recommendations from the viewpoint of how the proposals would affect these ministries. Similarly, both business and environmental representatives created networks to provide a feedback loop on the work of the task force. Other interests, such as labour and agriculture, were also periodically consulted. Through a process of negotiation, the task force reached a consensus on the contents of an environmental bill of rights, and the government drafted a bill based on this consensus.

On July 8, 1992, the long-awaited draft environmental bill of rights was finally tabled in the Ontario Legislature.[43] In her announcement, Environment Minister Grier noted: "When governments fail to meet their obligation to safeguard the environment, citizens should be able to hold them accountable. ... The proposed Environmental Bill of Rights is a unique piece of legislation that gives people unprecedented new power to protect the environment."[44] When the bill and accompanying report were tabled in the Legislature, the reaction could best be described as "mixed."[45]

A three-month public consultation process was then initiated in the province. The Task Force on the Ontario Environmental Bill of Rights was charged to review the comments received on the bill through this process. The task force made further recommendations to the government in a supplementary report dated December 1992, and five months later the government introduced for first reading the *Environmental Bill of Rights, 1993* (Bill 26).

THE REPORTS OF THE TASK FORCE ON THE ONTARIO ENVIRONMENTAL BILL OF RIGHTS AND BILL 26

The Context: The Policy Debates Pervading the Bill

It is probably a fair statement that previous private member's bills proposing an environmental bill of rights were drafted without the benefit of a discussion on the policy options to achieve the objectives of the bill or the cost to industry and government of implementing these objectives. When the Task Force on the Ontario Environmental Bill of Rights was established, it is not surprising that such questions became the first order of business. Some of these policy questions could be articulated as follows.

How Much Will the New Rights and Procedures Cost?

In weighing Bill 26 against the original concept of an environmental bill of rights found in CELA's proposals and the various private member's bills, it is important not to lose sight of the circumstances under which the task force carried out its deliberations. The contents of Bill 26 were negotiated during a period of severe economic recession and soaring government deficits. Industry feared that the requirements of an environmental bill of rights would increase the cost of doing business and argued that such requirements would be a barrier to economic recovery. Government agencies, on their part, were concerned about the cost of introducing new programs or increasing the complexity of administering existing ones.

[margin note: Economic Policy Considerations]

What Is the Legal Nature of an Environmental Bill of Rights?

In an ideal world, an "environmental bill of rights" would be something more than a mere statute. Some have anticipated that an environmental bill of rights could entrench environmental rights analogous to constitutional rights.[46]

The issue really becomes one of "paramountcy" — a provision somewhere in the bill that states that no provincial law can be inconsistent with the environmental bill of rights. Should the bill supersede other laws in the province and thus give the environmental law a higher priority of concern?[47]

What Is the Role of the Courts in Environmental Decision Making?

Another important policy debate that is directly invoked when discussing environmental rights is the role of the courts. Many oppose the creation of new environmental rights on the grounds that too much power is transferred from policy makers and the legislatures into the courts to develop new environmental standards, to oversee or overrule government decisions, and to enforce environmental laws. In effect, there is a fear that the courts will become the focus of environmental decision making, and this will lead to a more costly, time-consuming system and result in far less predictability about the outcome of disputes. Some environmentalists, however, take the view that the courts' role in society is to oversee the workings of government and to reconcile societal values in a fair and impartial manner.

The task force on the proposed environmental bill of rights worked through a mix of both views. On one hand, environmental decision making should be undertaken in a transparent, open fashion to allow the inclusion of affected interests without the formality and expense of court actions. On the other hand, there have to be guaranteed environmental rights for citizens, with adequate access to the courts, to ensure that citizens have recourse to them in appropriate situations.

In this context, Bill 26 emphasizes public participation in policy making, regulation making, and permit issuing, with limited access to the courts. The policing mechanisms are "softer" than court challenges, with the introduction of an "environmental commissioner" and various reporting requirements. However, the public is given greater access to the courts to enforce environmental laws, along with the dismantling of the public nuisance rule that denies standing to sue for nuisances that affect the public generally rather than private property interests.

At this time, it seems that increased access to the courts provided by the bill has failed to completely satisfy either point of view as to the appropriate role of the courts. Some suggest the bill leaves intact too many barriers for court intervention; others suggest the bill will spark too much litigation. However, it appears that the access to the courts provided by Bill 26 is at least an improvement over the *status quo*.

What Is an Environmentally "Significant" Decision?

Another pervasive question pertains to priorities. Is it possible to prioritize governmental action so as to focus on the "significant" problems? The bill takes this approach by focusing on significant "decisions" and significant "harm," without attempting to define the term "significant." Public involvement will be possible only if a minister decides that a policy, an Act, a regulation, or an instrument will have a significant effect on the environment. Clearly, what is an insignificant environmental issue to one person may be very significant to another. The bill leaves it up to each Cabinet minister to decide whether initiatives taken by his or her ministry will be significant enough to warrant public participation. However, the environmental commissioner will have the power to issue reports criticizing ministers who treat significant issues as insignificant.

How Specific Can Legislation Be?

One of the interesting issues that continues to arise is simply how specific the legislation should be in implementing the principles and mechanisms in the bill. Overall, the draft bill released in July 1992 was merely a framework — only in a very few places did it even attempt to articulate implementation details. As a result, there was a fear that the environmental bill of rights may suffer the same weakness as the legislative and policy framework that it is intended to replace — a framework that is frequently composed of skeletal legislation that is left to be implemented through regulations into which the public has traditionally had no input and through the exercise of bureaucratic discretion.

For example, in the proposed public participation regime, there are notice and comment provisions for environmental approvals. The general principle is that the more important the decision, the more onerous the notice and comment requirements. What the bill does not do is state which approvals fit into which category of notice and comment; this is left up to the minister to decide. Perhaps this approach should not be surprising since the categorization of approvals may be better suited to regulations. Clearly, though, the effectiveness of the bill will turn on its implementation philosophy, and whether a strong environmental commissioner is appointed who is willing to criticize ministerial decisions not to place an approval in one of the categories that require public participation, or to place an approval in a category that triggers only minimal consultation.

Other Issues

As one can expect, there are literally dozens of such issues that are implicit within a comprehensive piece of legislation such as an environmental bill of rights. Other issues considered by the task force included: Will environmental policy making become too legalistic in nature? What is the interrelationship with other environmental laws? Do members of the public have the financial resources to make use of the tools provided in the Act? Will the government and private sector resources being used to comply with the bill be taken from other beneficial purposes? Is government discretion still too broad with respect to environmental decision making?

An Overview and Evaluation of the Key Provisions of Bill 26

In this section we will review the key provisions of Bill 26 and the draft bill that preceded it. Those interested in more details can request copies of the two bills and the two task force reports from the Ministry of Environment and Energy.

Definition of "Environment"

The definition of the term "environment" in the bill restricts the bill to the protection of the natural environment. Section 1 states:

> "environment" means the air, water, land, plant life, and ecological systems of Ontario.

There are two issues raised by this definition. First, although the definition includes the term "air," that term is defined to exclude indoor air quality. During the consultations on the draft environmental bill of rights, some environmentalists criticized the proposal for providing a blanket exemption for indoor air quality.[48] However, in its supplementary report, the task force did not come to a consensus on expanding the bill to include the indoor environment, so Bill 26 does not include indoor air.

Second, although there was a consensus among the task force members that the focus of the definition on the "natural environment" was advantageous, a question does arise as to what the implications are of excluding some of the components of a broader definition. For example, the *Environmental Assessment Act* includes the notion of a "cultural," "social," and "economic" dimension of environment. What considerations are excluded by the omission of these components?

Purposes of the Act

The proposed environmental bill of rights was drafted to achieve a number of purposes that were thought to underlie the previous private members' bills. Because of its importance to the Act, section 2 of the proposed Act, the purpose section, is cited in full:

2(1) The purposes of this Act are:

(a) to protect, conserve and, where reasonable, restore the integrity of the environment by the means in this Act;

(b) to provide sustainability of the environment by the means in this Act; and

(c) to protect the right to a healthful environment by the means in this Act.

(2) The purposes set out in subsection (1) include the following:

1. The prevention, reduction and elimination of the use, generation and release of pollutants that are an unreasonable threat to the integrity of the environment.

2. The protection and conservation of biological, ecological and genetic diversity.

3. The protection and conservation of natural resources, including plant life, animal life and ecological systems.

4. The encouragement of the wise management of our natural resources, including plant life, animal life and ecological systems.

5. The identification, protection and conservation of ecologically sensitive areas or processes.

(3) In order to fulfil the purposes set out in subsections (1) and (2), this Act provides:

(a) means by which residents of Ontario may participate in the making of environmentally significant decisions by the Government of Ontario;

(b) increased accountability of the Government of Ontario for its environmental decision making;

(c) increased access to the courts by residents of Ontario for the protection of the environment; and

(d) enhanced protection for employees who take action in respect of environmental harm.

It should be noted that the bill contains no unqualified right to a healthful environment, although the bill does recognize the legitimacy of such a right. Instead, any right is an implied one "to protect the right of the present and future generations to a healthful environment." Moreover, this is a right only to the extent prescribed under the Act. During the consultation

Public Participation/Public Appeals (Part II)

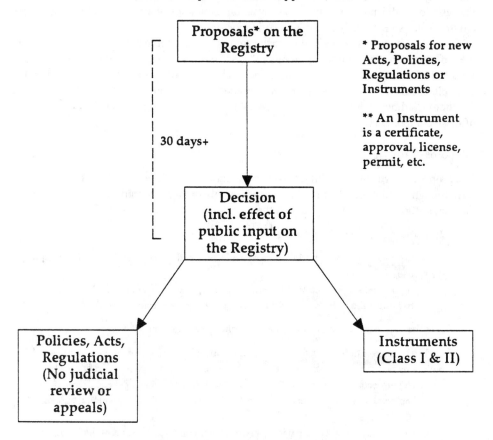

Courtesy of the Ontario Ministry of Environment and Energy.

on the proposed bill, the environmentalists were "adamant" in their submissions that the bill should unequivocally recognize the right to a healthy environment.[49]

The inclusion of a right to a healthy environment, however, does provoke some interesting questions. How should such an environmental right be fashioned? Former bills gave an open-ended right to a healthy environment. This unlimited right was thought to be both vague and uncertain.[50] For example, what is meant by "healthful"? What are the limits of this right? How does it relate to approval regimes? For example, is someone liable if they are operating within the terms of an approval yet still cause some harm to the environment? How does the right relate to areas of activity that are yet not fully regulated?

Public Participation in Environmental Decisions

The public participation regime is the heart of the proposed bill. The framework created under the bill is that all environment decisions are categorized as "policies," "Acts," "regulations," or "instruments." The term "instrument" includes permits, licences, approvals, authorizations, directions, and orders issued by government officials.[51] The basis of this component is that all environmentally significant decisions relating to policies, regulations, or instruments should have some provision for public notice and an opportunity to comment.

Notice and Comment

With respect to instruments, the general principle is that the more important the decision is, the more enhanced are the notice requirements and comment opportunities. To facilitate the implementation of this principle, all instruments caught under the bill are to be categorized as class I, II, or III. Class I instruments, for example, are those instruments with the least environmental impact, and class III instruments are those where there exists the potential for widespread environmental impact and the public interest in the issue is high. The chart on the facing page provides a schematic overview of the notice and comment regime.

Moving from category I to III, there are progressively more enhanced notice requirements. Similarly, the opportunities to comment are also enhanced up to category III, where full public hearings are prescribed. It is important to note that the determination of which instruments will fall into which categories will be done through regulations.

Underlining the "notice" provisions of the bill is the establishment of the Environmental Registry in sections 5 and 6. Its purpose is to provide a means of giving the public notice of proposals and decisions that might significantly affect the environment. This registry is to be a computer database that will provide an inventory, and give the status, of environmentally significant decisions. Hence, environmental groups and individuals could call into the Environmental Registry to find out what applications for approvals have been made or inquire about their status. It may also be possible to "tap into" this system to get updates on these issues.

The public participation requirements for policies and regulations are less stringent than those for instruments. Notice of proposed policies would be given before the policy is adopted. The appropriate minister would be required to "take every reasonable step to ensure that all comments relevant to the proposal that are received as a result of the public participation process ... are considered when decisions about the proposal are made in the ministry."[52]

For regulations, notice would also be given and placed on the registry, discussed below. At the discretion of the minister, a "regulatory impact statement" may also be required, outlining the objectives and justification for the regulation.[53]

One of the criticisms of the draft bill released in July 1992 was that a minister's discretion whether to submit the policies and regulations to public participation is too broad. In effect, the minister is given broad discretion to submit or not submit the policies and regulations to public participation.[54] Bill 26 did nothing to reduce this broad discretion. However, the extensive powers given to the environmental commissioner under Bill 26 to criticize how ministers exercise this discretion is an important safeguard.

Right To Request Review

The focus of the notice and comment provisions for environmental decisions pertains to new policies, Acts, regulations, and instruments. Section 61 of the bill, however, provides a procedure that allows the public to request that a policy, an Act, a regulation, or an instrument be reviewed if there is one in place, or that a policy, an Act, a regulation, or an instrument be developed if there is none in place.

Section 67 requires the minister responsible for the policy, Act, regulation, or instrument to consider each application "to determine whether the public interest warrants a review." Criteria for the exercise of that discretion are outlined in sections 67(2) and 67(3). Citizens can request the government to review an existing instrument, but not to issue a new instrument.

Appeal and Review Rights

The public participation provisions also include expanded appeal routes for instruments. Traditionally, for many instruments such as licences, permits, and orders, and certainly those emanating from the Ministry of Environment and Energy, only the person applying for the licence or permit or ordered to take some action has the right to appeal (in the case of the Ministry of Environment and Energy instruments, to the Environmental Appeal Board).[55] The proposed environmental bill of rights creates an opportunity for citizens to appeal decisions, at least in some instances. These appeal rights that would differ from the proponents' appeal rights in that citizens would be required to obtain leave to appeal. The criteria for granting this leave are set out in the bill. They are very narrow. Bill 26 provides much more detail on this appeal mechanism than the draft bill did; however, many of the details have still been left to be addressed by future regulations under the Act.[56]

Although the bill assists in furthering appeal rights, the practical difficulties of exercising these appeal rights have not been addressed. For example, there are no funding provisions to assist citizens in developing their case before the board.

Increased Government Accountability

The second key component of the draft environmental bill of rights pertains to government accountability. Former private members' bills dealt with this issue through the notion of the "public trust" doctrine. Under this doctrine, public resources are considered to be public property held in trust by the government, which must wisely manage those resources for the benefit of present and future generations of the public. In effect, the public trust doctrine would create a basis for legal action, allowing the public to challenge governmental decisions affecting public natural resources in the courts. The proposed environmental bill of rights does not include the public trust notion, but tries to create governmental accountability through other mechanisms.

Statement of Environmental Values

The proposed environmental bill of rights took a much less formal approach to further governmental accountability than the public trust doctrine. Sections 7 to 11 of the Act provide that each ministry prescribed under the Act must develop a "Statement of Environmental Values" within nine months after the Act begins to apply to it. This statement is analogous to a mission statement that sets out a process to determine whether existing policies and regulations of the ministry are consistent with the purposes of the Act and how the purposes will be considered in future environmental decisions of the ministry.[57] A process is also put in place to ensure that there is public input into the development of the statement of environmental values.

It is clear that the statement of environmental values is not a substitute for the public trust doctrine. The extent to which it will create government accountability will depend on how these statements are developed and how they are implemented and enforced, a topic relevant to the question of the role of environmental commissioner. The Act imposes on the minister a duty to take reasonable steps to ensure that the statement is considered whenever the ministry makes decisions that might significantly affect the environment. The Canadian Bar Association — Ontario (CBAO) stated in its submission: "It is questionable whether such statements, which will inevitably be very general, will assist in environmental protection as they do not have any legal effect."[58] The CBAO went on to say, however, that these statements may assist in causing ministries to consider environmental issues more seriously in their policy-making processes.[59]

Environmental Commissioner

Who is to monitor — and indeed enforce — whether ministries are living up to their statements of environmental values? Rather than a judicial review procedure, the bill proposes the establishment of an environmental commissioner who would report directly to the Ontario Assembly. Among his or her many functions, the environmental commissioner is to oversee the implementation of the Act and monitor the compliance of ministries with the requirements of the Act; provide guidance to ministries on how to comply with requirements of the Act; monitor the exercise of discretion by the ministers under the Act; and prepare an annual report for the Legislature.[60] In effect, the commissioner is also the clearinghouse for all applications for reviews, investigations, and other such tools provided to citizens by the Act.

The proposal for an environmental commissioner has provoked a number of questions. For example, is it possible to ensure that a competent environmental commissioner will be appointed? How can adequate resources be assured for the commissioner? Does that office have sufficient powers and independence to execute the duties assigned to it? Is reporting to the Legislature a sufficient mechanism to force ministries to create useful statements of environmental values and comply with them? The May 1993 bill took into account many of these concerns. There are provisions to safeguard the independence and effectiveness of the commissioner. The government's candidate for this position must be put before the Legislature where his or her suitability for the job can be openly debated. Once appointed, the commissioner is guaranteed at least a five-year term and can be removed only for serious wrongdoing. The commissioner has the authority to look at ministry files and to examine any person under oath and require that person to produce his or her records.

Access to Courts

There is little doubt that the most controversial part of the proposed environmental bill of rights pertained to access to the courts. The proposed environmental bill of rights enhances enforcement remedies in a number of ways.

The Right To Request an Investigation

First, the bill provides a mechanism to have a problem dealt with, at least at first instance, outside the court system. Part V of the bill provides that any two Ontario residents can apply to the environmental commissioner for an investigation if they believe that an Act, a regulation, or an instrument that is covered by the bill of rights has been contravened.[61]

Once a request has been filed, the commissioner refers the application to the appropriate ministry. The minister responsible for the Act must investigate the alleged violation unless the application is frivolous or vexatious, a minor contravention of the law, or not likely to cause environmental harm.[62] The bill also describes timelines and requires the minister to advise complainants of the outcome of the investigation and the action the minister intends to take.[63]

New Cause of Action

Under existing law, the only persons who are granted standing to sue for environmental harm in the civil courts remain those directly affected by the environmentally harmful activity.[64] The proposed environmental bill of rights creates a new cause of action. Section 84(1) states:

> Where a person has contravened or will imminently contravene an Act, regulation, or instrument prescribed for the purposes of Part V and the actual or imminent contravention has caused or will imminently cause significant harm to a public resource of Ontario, any person resident in Ontario may bring an action against the person in the court in respect of the harm and is entitled to judgment if successful.

Clearly, the new cause of action is very carefully circumscribed.[65] It applies only to contraventions of specific laws, and only contraventions that occur after the bill has come into force;[66] the contravention must be connected to significant environmental harm; and that harm must relate to a public resource. A "public resource," in turn, is defined to include air, waters other than those that are privately owned, and most public lands, along with any plant or animal life or ecological system relating to public resources.[67] Furthermore, before the action can proceed, the plaintiff must have requested an investigation, as discussed above, and the request must have not been responded to either within a reasonable time or in a reasonable manner.[68] If the problem is an emergency, however, the bill relieves the plaintiff of the obligation to request an investigation and allows the action to be filed immediately.[69] Certain kinds of nuisances caused by farmers are also exempt from action unless the Farm Practices Protection Board, set up to prevent lawsuits against farmers for nuisances arising out of normal farm practices, has dealt with the matter.[70]

There are also a number of defences available, including statutory authorization, due diligence, and reasonable interpretation of the instrument alleged to be violated.[71] If the plaintiff is successful, the court is empowered to: (1) grant an injunction, (2) order the parties to negotiate a restoration plan,[72] (3) grant declaratory relief, or (4) issue any other order the court deems appropriate.[73] The notion behind a restoration plan is to ensure that the environmental harm is adequately remedied rather than to grant damages to the plaintiff, an award that is not available under the bill.

There is little doubt that the new cause of action is a complicated one and a number of hurdles must be overcome to invoke its use. These hurdles suggest that the new cause of

Right To Sue (Part VI: Section 82 to Section 102)

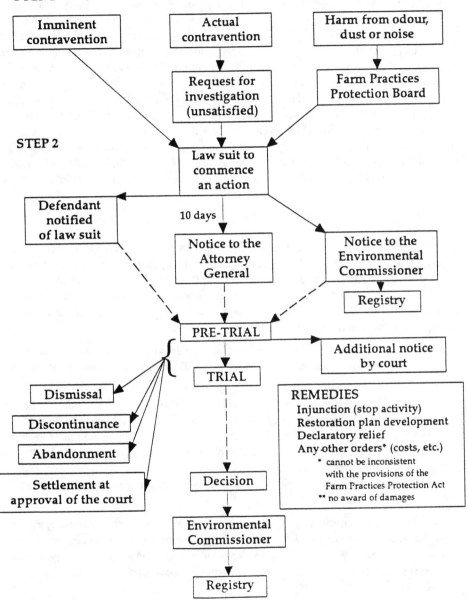

Courtesy of the Ontario Ministry of Environment and Energy.

action is unlikely to result in a flood of litigation. The real hurdle, however, is the fact that public interest litigants still may not be able to fund the lawsuit they are undertaking on behalf of the environment, and they may still have to pay the defendants' costs if they lose. The bill only gives the court discretion to consider any special circumstance in the exercise of its discretion whether to award costs. It does not require the court to do this and does not limit the amount of costs the court may award against public interest plaintiffs.[74] One of the features of earlier environmental bills of rights was the reduction of exposure to costs awards against plaintiffs using the courts to protect the environment. However, the business community argued strenuously that these reforms would dramatically increase the cost to them of dealing with environmental issues and that the threat of costs is needed to deter frivolous litigation. Environmentalists, in their submissions, put forth the view that "citizens and groups who bring an action in the public interest should not have to pay costs if they lose when acting in good faith and responsibly presenting a credible case."[75] Certainly the lack of funding and the threat of costs will have a chilling effect on the efforts of groups and individuals to invoke these sections to protect the environment.[76]

Public Nuisance

In addition to creating a new cause of action, the proposed environmental bill of rights removes, at least to a large extent, the public nuisance standing rule where the nuisance results in harm to the environment.[77] Professor Cromwell states the general rule as: a "private plaintiff may sue in public nuisance only with permission of the appropriate Attorney General to bring a relator action or, failing that, upon showing some special or peculiar damage."[78] A similar formulation of the rule, also cited by Cromwell, is as follows:

> The general principle is that a private action may be maintained in respect of a common nuisance where the complaining party has sustained some special damage not common to the general public.[79]

As the Ontario Law Reform Commission discusses the rule, a "private individual cannot seek a remedy for public nuisance without the consent of the Attorney General unless he can show that he has suffered a harm, or possesses an interest, that distinguishes him from the rest of the public."[80] Therefore, it is thought that public wrongs can only be addressed in the civil courts by the attorney general.

The proposed environmental bill of rights attempts to dismantle this rule in section 103. This section states:

> No person who has suffered or may suffer a direct economic loss or direct personal injury as a result of a public nuisance that caused harm to the environment shall be barred from bringing an action without the consent of the Attorney General in respect of the loss or injury only because the person has suffered or may suffer direct economic loss or direct personal injury of the same kind or to the same degree as other persons.

Employee Protection

"Whistler-blower" protection was a component of one of the very early proposals for environmental bill of rights put forth by the Canadian Environmental Law Association. A whistle-blower provision was adopted by the government in 1981.

Under the *Environmental Protection Act*, an employee cannot be dismissed, disciplined, penalized, coerced, or otherwise intimidated for "blowing the whistle" on an employer who is breaking any of five environmental laws or their regulations.[81]

The Ontario Labour Relations Board can order the offending company to reinstate or compensate any employee who is unjustly fired or in any way harassed for simply reporting a pollution problem to the Ministry of Environment and Energy.

However, there are no corresponding provisions to protect workers who try to prevent violations of environmental statutes administered by other ministries.

The proposed environmental bill of rights extends those worker safeguards to all statutes prescribed in the bill. It will also guarantee that employees cannot be disciplined for exercising any of their new rights under the bill: requesting an investigation, taking part in the development of a new environmental regulation, or testifying at a trial.[82]

However, it is possible that the new provisions may actually take away rights that workers had under the *Environmental Protection Act* if, as expected, the bill's provisions replace those under the *Environmental Protection Act*. That Act states that "no person shall" harass a worker for helping to enforce environmental laws. This language may create an offence for which employers can be fined, although there was some disagreement among the task force members about whether this is the case and about whether employers should be subject to quasi-criminal penalties for harassing workers. Because the members of the task force could not agree on the effect or desirability of this language, it was not included in the bill.

During the consultations, labour interests were urging the development of "right to refuse to pollute" provisions and the requirement to establish "environment committees" in the workplace. The Task Force on the Ontario Environmental Bill of Rights stated that it had neither the expertise nor the time or resources to adequately develop these recommendations. Therefore, it recommended that the ministries of environment and labour, in conjunction with other interests, consider initiating a separate task force to explore these concepts.[83]

Application of the Bill

The draft bill introduced in July 1992 did not indicate the ministries to which the Act applies. The expectation at that time was that the ministries of environment and energy, natural resources, northern development and mines, and agriculture and food would be caught under the Act initially. Other ministries could then be included as decided by Cabinet.

A timetable to include other ministries was not set. This raised a concern whether this will happen expeditiously. In addition, the ministries that would initially have been subject to the bill are not the only ministries that make decisions or issue permits and licences for activities that have a very substantial impact on the environment. The Ministry of Consumer and Commercial Relations, for example, regulates the storage and handling of petroleum products throughout Ontario, and therefore is responsible for the regulation of products that are explosive and highly flammable, that contaminate soil and groundwater and release chemicals that cause global warming, and that cause diseases such as leukaemia and cancer. At the time of the July 1992 release of the bill, it was not among the ministries that would be initially subject to the bill. Environmentalists submitted that there should be a presumption in the bill that all ministries should be submitted to the requirements of the bill.[84]

These concerns were addressed by the introduction of an implementation schedule in the form of a draft regulation when Bill 26 was given first reading in June 1993. Under this schedule, different parts of the Act will apply to different ministries at different times. One year after the Act is proclaimed, only the Ministry of Environment and Energy will be subject to all its provisions. Fourteen ministries will be required to have statements of environmental values in place two years after proclamation. However, five years after proclamation, only six ministries will be subject to all the requirements of the Act.

SUMMARY AND CONCLUSION

It may be the end of 1993 or 1994 before Bill 26 is finally proclaimed. Even if the present bill is enacted, there are still items left off the agenda, such as further limits on agency discretion, the alleviation of the financial burdens of participation, and broader avenues of judicial review. These and other provisions are needed and essential if citizens are to play a meaningful and effective role in the protection of the environment. Nevertheless, the proposed law is an important building block in the development of a comprehensive and complete environmental law reform agenda.

_____

Paul Muldoon and John Swaigen

WHERE TO GET MORE INFORMATION

For more information on the proposed environmental bill of rights, call or write:

Environmental Bill of Rights
Public Information Centre
Ministry of Environment and Energy
135 St. Clair Avenue West
Toronto, Ontario
M4V 1P5
(416) 323-4321
Toll-free 1-800-565-4923

ENDNOTES

1 Various publications and other reports are cited throughout this chapter. For an overview, see Paul Muldoon, "The Fight for an Environmental Bill of Rights — Legislating Public Involvement in Environmental Decision-Making" (1988), vol. 15, no. 2 *Alternatives* 33. See also P.S. Elder and W.A. Ross, "How To Ensure that Developments are Environmentally Sustainable," in J. Owen Saunders, ed., *The Legal Challenge of Sustainable Development* (Calgary: Canadian Institute of Resources Law, 1990), 124-40.

2 The Canadian Environmental Law Association submitted a brief to the Joint Senate/House of Commons Committee on the Constitution of Canada on September 28, 1978. See also Dale Gibson, "Constitutional Entrenchment of Environmental Rights," in N.

Duple, ed., *Le droit a la qualite de l'environnement* (Montreal: Quebec Amerique, 1988), 275.

3   The Charlottetown accord and the draft legal text of the constitutional amendments proposed in 1992 do briefly mention environmental protection but not in a manner that creates any environmental rights that would be enforceable in the courts. For a background discussion on this issue, see the Special Report on the Environment and Constitution in (May-June 1992), vol. 18, no. 4 *Alternatives*.

4   For example, see Christopher D. Stone, "Should Trees Have Standing? — Toward Legal Rights for Natural Objects" (1972), 45 *Southern California Legal Review* 450; G. Varner, "Do Species Have Standing?" (1987), 9 *Env. Ethics* 57.

5   The classic work in this regard is J.L. Sax, *Defending the Environment — A Strategy for Citizen Action* (New York: Alfred Knopf, 1970). See also Kernaghan Webb, "Taking Matters into Their Own Hands: The Role of Citizens in Canadian Pollution Control Enforcement" (1990), 36 *McGill Law Review* 771; J. Swaigen and R.E. Woods, "A Substantive Right to Environmental Quality," in J. Swaigen, ed., *Environmental Rights in Canada* (Toronto: Butterworths, 1981), 195.

6   Mich. Comp. Laws Ann. 691.1201-1207. For extensive commentary on the bill, see also J.L. Sax and R.L. Conner, "Michigan's Environmental Protection Act of 1970: A Progress Report" (1972), 70 *Michigan Law Review* 1003-91; J.L. Sax and J.F. DiMento, "Environmental Citizen Suits: Three Years of Experience Under the Michigan Environmental Protection Act" (1974), vol. 4, no. 1 *Ecology Law Quarterly* 1-62; J. Haynes, "Michigan's Environmental Protection Act in Its Sixth Year: Substantive Environmental Law From Citizen Suits" (1976), 53 *Journal of Urban Law* 589; J. Sax, "MEPA — Ten Years Later" (November-December 1980), *Michigan Environs* 6; D.K. Slone, "The Michigan Environmental Protection Act: Bringing Citizen-Initiated Environmental Suits Into the 1980s" (1984-85), vol. 12, no. 27 *Ecology Law Quarterly* 291.

7   Some of these provisions are listed and discussed in *Environmental Rights in Canada*, supra endnote 5, chapters 3 and 4.

8   For example, see the various chapters in P.S. Elder, ed., *Environmental Management and Public Participation* (Toronto: Canadian Environmental Law Research Foundation, 1976) and *Environmental Rights in Canada*, supra endnote 5.

9   David Estrin and John Swaigen, *Environment on Trial*, 2d ed. (Toronto: Canadian Environmental Law Research Foundation, 1978), chapter 21.

10 Canada, House of Commons, *Debates*, July 9, 1981, 11385-89, a private member's motion, "Establishment of Environmental Bill of Rights," introduced by Charles Caccia.

11 Environment Canada, *Proposed Environmental Protection Act*, released December 18, 1986.

12 *Environment Quality Act*, RSQ, c. Q-2, as amended.

13 Ontario, Legislative Assembly, Bill 185, *An Act Respecting Environmental Rights in Ontario*, introduced by Stuart Smith, 3d Sess., 31st Legislature, November 20, 1979.

14 Ontario, Legislative Assembly, Bill 91, *An Act To Establish an Environmental Magna Carta for Ontario*, introduced by Marion Bryden, 4th Sess., 31st Legislature, June 3, 1980.

15   See Ontario, Legislative Assembly, Bill 134, *An Act Respecting Environmental Rights in Ontario*, 2d Sess., 32d Legislature, 1981; Bill 96, *An Act Respecting Environmental Rights in Ontario*, introduced by Murray Elston, 2d Sess., 32d Legislature, 1982.

16   Liberal Research Document, "Liberal Environmental Policy — Campaign '85," March 1985.

17   Some general law reform initiatives also attempted to achieve some of the same objectives, at least to some extent, as the early versions of the environmental bill of rights. For example, the Rules of Civil Procedure were promulgated in 1985 in Ontario. Rule 13 pertaining to non-party intervention holds the potential to broaden the ambit of interests that can intervene in court cases. Similarly, rule 57 allows the court to have discretion in awarding costs.

18   Ontario, Legislative Assembly, Bill 9, *An Act Respecting Environmental Rights in Ontario*, introduced by Ruth Grier, 2d Sess., 33d Legislature, 1987; Bill 13, *An Act Respecting Environmental Rights in Ontario*, introduced by Ruth Grier, 1st Sess., 34th Legislature, 1987; Bill 12, *An Act Respecting Environmental Rights in Ontario*, introduced May 15, 1989 by Ruth Grier, 2d Sess., 34th Legislature, 1989.

19   For further analysis of how courts have gradually opened their doors to public interest litigation, at least in defined circumstances, see Thomas A. Cromwell, *Locus Standi — A Commentary on the Law of Standing in Canada* (Toronto: Carswell, 1986) and A.J. Roman, "From Judicial Economy to Access to Justice: Standing and Class Actions," a paper presented to the Canadian Bar Association — Ontario 1991 Annual Institute, January 19, 1991. Despite the very gradual liberalization of standing, environmental groups are still frustrated in their attempts to go to court to protect the environment. For example, a group hoping to save parkland did not get standing and in fact got costs awarded against them in their attempt to challenge city plans for a multi-million dollar recreation centre on parkland in Toronto. See *Friends of Toronto Parkland v. City of Toronto* (1991), 8 MPLR (2d) 127 (Ont. Div. Ct.).

20   Ontario Law Reform Commission, *Report on the Law of Standing* (Toronto: Ministry of the Attorney General, 1989).

21   Unrelated to the Standing Committee on Law of Standing, a private member's bill was introduced dealing with standing. See Ontario, Legislative Assembly, Bill 231, *An Act Respecting Environmental Harm*, 1st reading June 26, 1990, introduced by Margaret Marland, 2d Sess., 34th Legislature, 1990.

22   *Access to Information Act*, RSC 1985, c. A-1.

23   *Municipal Freedom of Information and Protection of Privacy Act*, RSO 1990, c. M.56.

24   The Workplace Hazardous Materials Information System (WHMIS) has been implemented at the federal level through amendments to the *Hazardous Products Act*, the passage of the *Hazardous Materials Information Review Act*, RSC 1985, c. H-3, and regulations under those Acts, and at the provincial level through amendments to the *Occupational Health and Safety Act*, and the WHMIS regulation, O. reg. 644/88. In federal workplaces, WHMIS is implemented under the *Canada Labour Code* and the Canada Occupational Health and Safety Regulations made under the Code.

25   *Environmental Protection Act*, RSO 1990, c. E.19, section 174. This section was added by the *Environmental Protection Amendment Act*, SO 1983, c. 52.

26   For further discussion of the possible roles an environmental ombudsman could play

and a description of some of the proposals for such an office, see Karl G. Ege, "Enforcing Environmental Policy: The Environmental Ombudsman" (1971), 56 *Cornell Law Review* 817.

27 Bob Burtt, "Auditor Needed for Environment, Martin Advises," *The Kitchener-Waterloo Record*, April 30, 1993.

28 *Class Proceedings Act*, SO 1992, c. 6.

29 Ontario, Ministry of the Attorney General, *News Release*, "Class Proceedings Act Introduced by Attorney General," December 17, 1990.

30 Ibid.

31 The Act that creates the fund is *Amendment to Law Society Act*, SO 1992, c. 7, proclaimed in force on January 1, 1993.

32 *Intervenor Funding Project Act*, RSO 1990, c. I.13.

33 Ontario, Ministry of the Attorney General, *News Release*, "Extension of Intervenor Funding Project Act Announced," March 25, 1992.

34 See *795833 Ontario Inc. v. A.G. Ontario et al.*, Ontario Court of Justice (General Division), December 4, 1990, Corbett J [unreported].

35 See *Schmidt v. Secretary of State for Home Affairs*, [1969] 1 All ER 904 (CA); *Ontario Nursing Home Assn. v. Ontario* (1990), 74 OR (2d) 365. *Doctrine of legitimate expectations*

36 *Environmental Rights Act*, SNWT 1990, c. 28.

37 Yukon Territory, Legislative Assembly, Bill 20, *Environment Act*, 2d Sess., 27th Legislature, assented to May 29, 1991.

38 Saskatchewan, Bill 48 of 1992. As of May 1993 this bill had not received second reading. The bill had been subject to a public consultation process carried out by a standing committee of the Saskatchewan Legislature. This committee released a report analyzing the bill and making recommendations for amendments in April 1993. See Saskatchewan, Legislative Assembly, Standing Committee on the Environment, *First Report: Report on Environmental Rights and Responsibilities*, April 19, 1993.

39 In terms of the right of action, section 4(2) states:

> An applicant may apply to the court for leave to commence an action against a person where the application considers that an activity by that person is or is likely to result in an environmental offence.

40 Ontario, Ministry of the Environment, *News Release*, "Environment Minister Ruth Grier To Introduce Environmental Bill of Rights," December 13, 1990.

41 Ontario, Legislative Assembly, Bill 23, *An Act Respecting Environmental Bill of Rights in Ontario*, 1st Sess., 35th Legislature, 1990, introduced for first reading December 13, 1990 by B. Sullivan.

42 The terms of reference stated that the policy objectives and principles that are to recognized in the environmental bill of rights are:

> 1. the public's right to a healthy environment;
> 2. the enforcement of this right through improved access to the courts and/or tribunals, including the enhanced right to sue polluters;
> 3. increased public participation in environmental decision-making by government;
> 4. increased government responsibility and accountability for government;
> 5. greater protection for employees who "blow the whistle" on polluting employers.

The terms of reference are found in *Report of the Task Force on the Ontario Environmental Bill of Rights* (Toronto: Ministry of the Environment, July 1992), 2-3 (herein referred to as the "EBR task force report").

43 Ibid.

44 Ontario, Ministry of the Environment, *News Release*, "Environment Minister Ruth Grier Releases Draft Environmental Bill of Rights," July 8, 1992.

45 For example, see Martin Mittelstaedt, "Environmental Bill Gets Mixed Review — Ontario Document Gives Public Right To Take Civil Action Against Polluters," *The Globe and Mail*, Thursday, July 9, 1992.

46 For example, two commentators suggest that environmental rights should become a part of the constitution of Ontario. Their contention is that there is a constitution in Ontario capable of entrenching environmental and other rights. See Franklin Gertler and Toby Vigod with the assistance of Maryka Omatsu, "Environmental Protection in a New Constitution," submission by the Canadian Environmental Law Association to the Select Committee on Ontario in Confederation, Presentation to the Ontario Select Committee on the Constitution, 1991. See also Colin P. Stevenson, "A New Perspective on Environmental Rights After the Charter" (1983), 21 *Osgoode Hall LJ* 390.

In fact, many countries have environmental rights enshrined in their national constitutions, including India, Namibia, Poland, Spain, and Peru. The constitutions of several US states contain rights to environmental quality. For a discussion of how the courts have interpreted these state constitutional provisions, see *Environmental Rights in Canada*, supra endnote 5, and Oliver A. Pollard III, "A Promise Unfulfilled: Environmental Provisions in State Constitutions and the Self-Execution Question" (1986), 5 *Virginia Journal of Natural Resources Law* 323. The strongest of these state constitutional provisions is found in the Pennsylvania constitution. For a discussion of how this provision has been interpreted, see Franklin L. Kury, "The Pennsylvania Environmental Protection Amendment" (April 1986), *Pennsylvania Bar Association Quarterly* 85.

47 This issue was raised by a number of environmentalists during the consultations on the proposed environmental bill of rights. See *Draft Summary of the ENGO-EBR Consultation Meetings September-November 1992*, submission by the Ontario Environment Network to the Task Force on the Ontario Environmental Bill of Rights, November 6, 1992, 11.

48 See ibid., at 9.

49 See ibid., at 10.

50 See John Swaigen, "Environmental Bill of Rights — Cause of Action," presentation to the Committee on the Environmental Bill of Rights, January 29, 1991.

51 Ontario, Legislative Assembly, Bill 26, *Environmental Bill of Rights, 1993*, introduced May 31, 1993, section 1.

52 Ibid., section 35.

53 Ibid., section 27(4).

54 See *Draft Summary of the ENGO-EBR Consultation Meetings September-November 1992*, supra endnote 47, at 28.

55 See part XIII of the *Environmental Protection Act*, supra endnote 25.

56 *Environmental Bill of Rights, 1993*, supra endnote 51, sections 36-48.

57 Ibid., section 5.

58 Canadian Bar Association — Ontario, *Submission to the Minister of the Environment on the Proposed Environmental Bill of Rights, 1992*, November 12, 1992, 4.

59 Ibid., at 4-5.

60 *Environmental Bill of Rights, 1993*, supra endnote 51, sections 49-60.

61 Ibid., section 74.

62 Ibid., section 77.

63 Ibid., section 80.

64 For a more detailed description of the problem, see Franklin Gertler, Paul Muldoon, and Marcia Valiante, "Public Access to Environmental Justice," in *Report of the Canadian Bar Association Committee on Sustainable Development in Canada: Options For Law Reform* (Ottawa: Canadian Bar Association, 1990).

65 For a review of the new cause of action, see Richard Lindgren, "The New Cause of Action," a paper presented at the conference "The Environmental Bill of Rights — Preparing for Fundamental Change," October 9, 1992, Toronto.

66 *Environmental Bill of Rights, 1993*, supra endnote 51, section 83.

67 Ibid., section 82.

68 Ibid., section 84(2).

69 Ibid., section 84(6).

70 Ibid., sections 84(4) and (5), 93(3), and 103(2).

71 Ibid., section 85.

72 Ibid., sections 93(1)(b) and 95.

73 Ibid., section 93(1)(d).

74 Ibid., section 100.

75 See *Draft Summary of the ENGO-EBR Consultation Meetings September- November 1992*, supra endnote 47, at 53.

76 See, generally, Larry M. Fox, "Costs in Public Interest Litigation" (1989), 10 *Advocates Quarterly* 385.

77 The classic case that demonstrated the problem caused by this rule is *Hickey v. Electric Reduction Co. of Can.* (1970), 2 Nfld. & PEIR 246, 21 DLR (3d) 368 (Nfld. TD).

78 *Locus Standi — A Commentary on the Law of Standing in Canada*, supra endnote 19, at 15.

79 *Rainy River Navigation Co. v. Ontario and Minnesota Power* (1914), 17 DLR 850, at 852 (Ont. CA).

80 *Report on the Law of Standing*, supra endnote 20, at 10.

81 See *Environmental Protection Act*, supra endnote 25, section 174.

82 *Environmental Bill of Rights, 1993*, supra endnote 51, part VII, sections 104-116.

83 EBR task force report, supra endnote 42, at 176.

84 *Draft Summary of the ENGO-EBR Consultation Meetings September-November 1992*, supra endnote 47, at 9.

Appendixes

Appendix I
Abbreviations

All abbreviations used in the body of the text are spelled out in full in the first reference to them in each chapter. The main statutes and agencies abbreviated are the *Environmental Assessment Act (EAA)*, the *Environmental Protection Act (EPA)*, the *Highway Traffic Act (HTA)*, the *Ontario Water Resources Act (OWRA)*, the Ministry of Environment and Energy (MEE), the Ministry of Natural Resources (MNR), and the Ontario Municipal Board (OMB). The Canadian Environmental Law Association is CELA, and the Canadian Environmental Law Research Foundation is CELRF.

LEGAL ABBREVIATIONS USED IN THE ENDNOTES

[ ] AC	Law Reports, Appeal Cases
aff'd.	affirmed
aff'g.	affirming
[ ] All ER	All England Law Reports
AR	Alberta regulation
BCLR	British Columbia Law Reports
BNA Act(s)	*British North America Act(s)*
c.	chapter (as in *Environmental Protection Act*, RSO 1990, c. E.19)
CA	Court of Appeal
Can.	Canada
Cdn.	Canadian
CED	Canadian Encyclopedic Digest
CELN	Canadian Environmental Law News
CCC	Canadian Criminal Cases
CCLT	Canadian Cases on the Law of Torts
CELN	Canadian Environmental Law News
CELR	Canadian Environmental Law Reports
CELR (NS)	Canadian Environmental Law Reports (New Series)
Ch., Ch. D., Ch. Div.	Chancery Division, English Law Reports
CHRR	Canadian Human Rights Reporter
CJC	chief justice of the Supreme Court of Canada
Co.	Company
Co. Ct.	County Court

CRC	Consolidated Regulations of Canada
Crim. LQ	Criminal Law Quarterly
CRR	Canadian Rights Reporter
[ ] CS	Cour supérieure
Ct.	Court
Cty. Ct.	County Court
Dist. Ct.	District Court
Div. Ct.	Divisional Court
DLR	Dominion Law Reports
DTC	Dominion Tax Cases
ER	English Reports
Ex. Ct.	Exchequer Court
ex rel.	on the relation of
[ ] FC/CF	Canada Federal Court Reports
FCA	Federal Court of Canada — Appeal Division
FCTD	Federal Court of Canada — Trial Division
FPR	Fisheries Pollution Reports
FTR	Federal Trial Reports
HC	High Court
HCJ	High Court of Justice
HL	House of Lords Cases
Inc.	Incorporated
infra	below (as in infra endnote 73)
J	judge
JA	justice of the Court of Appeal
JELP	Journal of Environmental Law and Practice
JP	justice of the peace
LJ	Law Journal (as in *Osgoode Hall LJ* for *Osgoode Hall Law Journal*)
LR	The Law Reports
Ltd.	Limited
Ltée	Limitée
Man.	Manitoba
Man. LR	Manitoba Law Reports
Man. R.	Manitoba Reports
MCC	Mining Commission Cases
MPLR	Municipal and Planning Law Reports

NR	National Reporter
O. reg.	Ontario regulation
OCGD	Ontario Court of Justice (General Division)
OMBR	Ontario Municipal Board Reports
OR	Ontario Reports
OWN	Ontario Weekly Notes
PC	Privy Council
Pub. L.	Public Laws
QB	Queen's Bench Division, English Law Reports
R.	Regina/Queen/Reine/Rex/King/Roi
RCS	Recueils de jurisprudence du Québec
reg.	regulation
rev'd.	reversed
rev'g.	reversing
RRO	Revised Regulations of Ontario
RSA	Revised Statutes of Alberta
RSBC	Revised Statutes of British Columbia
RSC	Revised Statutes of Canada
RSM	Revised Statutes of Manitoba
RSO	Revised Statutes of Ontario
Sask.	Saskatchewan
SBC	Statutes of British Columbia
SC	Supreme/Superior Court
SC	Statutes of Canada; refers to the year of the passage of an Act, rather than its citation in the periodic consolidation of all existing statutes (for example, RSO, RSC), as in *International Boundary Waters Treaty Act*, SC 1911, c. 28; similarly: SBC, SA
SCBC	Supreme Court of British Columbia
SCC	Supreme Court of Canada
[ ] SCR	Supreme Court Reports
SNB	Statutes of New Brunswick
SO	Statutes of Ontario (as in the *KVP Company Limited Act*, SO 1950, c. 33); see SC
SOR	Statutory Orders and Regulations; refers to regulations and orders in council made by the government of Canada
SQ	Statutes of Quebec
SS	Statutes of Saskatchewan
Stat.	United States Statutes at Large
Supp.	Supplement
supra	above (as in supra endnote 32)

Terr. Ct.	Territorial Court
UBC	University of British Columbia
USC	United States Code
USCA	United States Code as amended
v.	versus (as in *Savage v. MacKenzie*, a lawsuit in which Mr. Savage sues Mr. MacKenzie for operating a noisy junkyard)
WLR	Weekly Law Reports
WWR	Western Weekly Reports
YT	Yukon Territory

Appendix II
Private Prosecutions

Any individual who has reasonable and probable grounds to believe that an offence has been committed contrary to a provincial or federal statute, a regulation made under that statute, or a municipal bylaw may prosecute the offender. The differences between an offence and a tort and between a prosecution and a civil suit, the advantages and disadvantages of each, and some aspects of trial procedure are explained in chapters 3, 4, and 6.

The procedures for laying and pursuing charges under provincial statutes and regulations and municipal bylaws are set out in the *Provincial Offences Act*. Prosecutions of federal summary convictions offences are governed by part XXVII of the *Criminal Code*. The *Contraventions Act* also covers some aspects of the prosecution of these offences. Prosecutions of indictable federal offences follow procedures under other parts of the *Criminal Code*.

For anyone intrepid enough or sufficiently frustrated by government inaction to launch a private prosecution, this appendix gives a brief summary of the procedure. For more detailed information, see Linda Duncan's book, *Enforcing Environmental Law: A Guide to Private Prosecution*, available from the Environmental Law Centre in Alberta (see Chapter 5).

Prosecutions consist of four basic parts:

- laying the information;
- issuing the summons;
- serving the summons; and
- trial.

STEP 1: LAYING THE INFORMATION

Before laying an information, it is often best to make a complaint to the government agency responsible for the enforcement of the law in question. If that agency declines to lay charges and you are satisfied that there is sufficient evidence of an offence to support a conviction, you may lay your own charges.

A person who has reasonable and probable grounds to believe an offence has occurred (the complainant) appears before a justice of the peace (JP) and signs a form on which the details of the alleged offence are set out. The form states that the complainant, now referred to as the "informant," has reasonable and probable grounds to believe that the person specified as the accused or defendant committed the offence set out on the form. The JP then asks the complainant to swear or affirm that this statement is true. When the informant has sworn to or affirmed this, the JP then signs his or her name as a witness that the informant has sworn that he or she has grounds to believe the offence was committed. This process is called "swearing the information." Formal charges have now been laid.

The complainant's statement is now formally an "information" and the complainant is now called the "informant." The informant has the right to hire his or her own lawyer to conduct the trial, or to do so himself or herself. If the informant does this, rather than the Crown attorney or some other government official designated to prosecute such offences, the informant is also the "prosecutor."

Drafting the Charges

A blank information form is available from the court. You can get it from the justice of the peace who swears such informations. It may also be available from a lawyer's offence, the department responsible for enforcing the particular statute, or the police.

It is advisable to get professional help in drafting the charges, since they must be very precise. You have two choices. You can go to a JP and tell him or her the details of the offence. The JP will often draft the charge for you. However, JPs are not always familiar with the intricacies of particular environmental statutes, and may make errors that will prove fatal at trial, because a defective information can be quashed, and because you have to prove everything stated in the information at trial. The better alternative is to obtain the form beforehand and fill it out yourself, with the help of an experienced lawyer, before bringing it to the JP to be sworn.

The forms used for provincial offences are different from those for federal offences, so be sure you have the right form. The provincial offences form is shown in this appendix.

Some important points in drafting an information:

- The wording should be precise. It is usually safest to follow the wording of the section of the statute describing the offence as closely as possible.

- The name of the accused should be stated in full. If the accused is a corporation, use the full corporate name, not a "style" under which the corporation carries on business. (See Appendix V.)

- When the information relates to more than one breach of the law, the information should set out each offence in a separate "count" (separately numbered paragraphs each setting out completely all the details of one offence).

- It is important to set out correctly the specific date and place where the offence occurred. An information may set out that the offence occurred on a single date, or between two dates; for example, the offence may allege that the offence was committed "between the first day of February 1993 and the fifteenth day of March." However, if the judge feels that the accused is prejudiced by an unusually long period of time set out in the information, the court can require you to amend an information to be more precise as to the time.

- Ensure that the facts you will rely on to prove the charge occurred within the time set out in the information, and that the time set out in the information is within the "limitation period" — that is, the time allowed for laying charges. Under the Ontario *Provincial Offences Act* and the summary conviction provisions of the *Criminal Code*, you have only six months from the time an offence occurred to lay the charges. Some statutes provide for a longer or shorter limitation period.

- When laying charges under the *Highway Traffic Act* against the registered owner of a motor vehicle, set out in the information not only the section of the Act that was violated, but also that the violation occurred contrary to section 207, the section that makes the owner liable for violations by the driver.

Choosing the Informant

An informant may be anyone with reasonable and probable grounds to believe an offence occurred. It need not be someone who actually witnessed the offence. Someone who has been told the details of an offence by a witness to it may also have sufficient grounds to swear the information if she believes what she has been told. It is best to have a person who has first-hand knowledge of the facts swear the information; but as a matter of strategy, you may want someone else to swear the information. There is no requirement that the informant actually testify in court or be involved in prosecuting if others are available to do so.

However, a potential informant should realize that he or she could be liable for costs and that if the information is sworn for an improper purpose, there are possible legal repercussions (see below).

Where To Lay the Charges

The charges can be laid anywhere in Ontario, but as a practical matter you should go to a justice of the peace at the court that is closest to where the offence occurred, since the summons will eventually have to be filed at that court. (See below.)

STEP 2: ISSUING THE SUMMONS

Legally, a justice of the peace must swear an information. That is, he or she must receive it and sign it saying that you have sworn to its truth. The JP has no discretion to refuse to do this.

However, the JP has a discretion not to take the next step: issuing the summons to the accused. A summons is an order addressed to the accused named in the information and signed by the JP. It commands the accused in the name of Her Majesty the Queen to appear in the court at the address and on the date and at the time of the morning or afternoon set out in the summons to answer the charges set out in the information.

The summons is usually a copy of the information on a form that also contains a place to set out the time and place where the accused must appear to answer the charges. When the JP fills this in and signs it, the summons is "issued."

However, JPs are used to issuing summonses for police officers and enforcement agencies. Some JPs will ask many probing questions before taking the step of issuing a summons requested by a private informant. The JP may even examine the informant under oath and call the informant's witnesses to testify under oath before agreeing to "issue process," as signing the summons is called. Some JPs may be reluctant to issue process for a private citizen alleging a serious offence under any circumstances. Therefore, it is advisable to be well prepared, and even to bring an experienced lawyer with you when you visit the JP to swear the information, if you anticipate difficulty.

If the JP issues the summons, he or she will usually make it returnable (that is, put a date for the first appearance in court on the summons) about two to four weeks hence. At least two weeks should be allowed, to leave sufficient time to serve the summons on the accused. The "return date" will not be the date for the trial to take place, but the date when the prosecutor and the accused appear in court to set a date for the trial.

STEP 3: SERVING THE SUMMONS ON THE ACCUSED

Under the *Provincial Offences Act*, the summons can be served on the accused by handing it to him or her personally or by leaving it at his or her last known address with a person who appears to be over 18 years old. A summons can be served on a corporation by sending it by registered mail to the corporation's head office or by taking it to a branch office and leaving it with manager. For federal statutes, there are similar provisions in the summary conviction sections of the *Criminal Code*.

One of the difficulties faced by the private prosecutor is that serving a summons for a provincial offence is valid only if it is done by a person designated as a provincial offences officer; for federal offences, the summons must be delivered by a "peace officer." Police officers and provincial and municipal inspectors, investigators, and enforcement officers are generally designated as both provincial offences officers and peace officers. The staff of the county and district sheriff's offices are also peace officers, and for a fee and payment of their mileage, they may serve summonses for you.

Unfortunately, one cannot always rely on these officials to serve summonses on time, so give them the summons as early as possible and follow up with them to ensure that the summons has been filed. To be on the safe side, it is wise also to personally deliver or mail a copy of the summons to the accused. Even though the accused is not required to respond, many do not know this and will come to court. Once an accused or his or her lawyer appears in court, the accused is bound by the summons, even if he or she need not have appeared.

Once a summons has been served, it is necessary for the person who served it to swear the affidavit of service on the back of the summons. In this affidavit, the person sets out the identity of the person served with the summons and the time and place the summons was served, and swears that the contents of the affidavit are true. The private prosecutor then must either ensure that the provincial offences officer or peace officer files the affidavit of service in the proper court before the return date or get the copy of the summons with its affidavit of service from the person who served it and bring it to court. If the accused does not turn up, the court will proceed to set a date for the trial if the judge or JP is shown this affidavit proving that the accused was properly notified of the charges and the need to attend court. But without this document, the court will proceed no further and it is necessary to have a new summons issued and served to require the accused to attend court at a later date.

STEP 4: APPEARING ON THE RETURN DATE

On the return date, the informant and the accused or their lawyers will tell the court what date is suitable to them for the trial. You should choose a date on which you know that all your witnesses are available, and which is far enough away to give you adequate time to prepare, and to give the accused written notice of all the documents you intend to use as evidence. (Without giving such notice, many documents are inadmissible.) The court will set a trial date and adjourn the case to that day.

STEP 5: THE TRIAL

As mentioned, the informant has the right to conduct the prosecution or arrange for a lawyer to do it. Private prosecutions are not unusual. Private citizens often lay charges and prosecute them on their own in simple cases. In environmental matters, it may not be difficult, for example, to prosecute a neighbour who won't control a barking dog or who turns the stereo up to full volume at midnight. Prosecuting a complex case against a large corporation or government agency, however, is fraught with pitfalls and should not be undertaken without expert assistance.

As a courtesy, you should inform the local Crown attorney that you laid the charges and intend to prosecute the case yourself or have your own lawyer conduct the prosecution. The Crown attorney has the right to take over the prosecution and conduct it or stop it from proceeding. Only if the charge is an indictable one or is politically sensitive is the Crown attorney likely to intervene.

If, however, having laid the charge, you want the Crown attorney to conduct the trial, he or she will usually oblige. But in this case, the Crown attorney is unlikely to do much preparation. He or she will call the witnesses you make available, but don't expect the Crown attorney to be prepared for surprises or sophisticated legal arguments the accused may raise.

Trial procedure is similar to the procedure in Small Claims Court, which is described in Appendix IV.

LIMITS ON THE RIGHT OF PRIVATE PROSECUTION

As was mentioned in Chapter 3, the costs that can be awarded against a private prosecutor are set by statute and are minimal. Therefore, this is not as substantial a barrier to prosecution as it is to using the civil courts, other than Small Claims Court, where costs are also limited.

However, one must be careful to ensure that one has solid grounds for laying a charge and is not doing so as a result of ulterior motives. Misuse of prosecution leaves a person open to a criminal charge of extortion, a serious offence under the *Criminal Code*, and to a civil suit for malicious prosecution. Recognizing the importance of private law enforcement, the common law requires proof of two essential elements before the tort of malicious prosecution is established:

1. the informant must be proven to have had no reasonable grounds for laying the charge; and
2. the informant must have acted with malice.

Even if reasonable grounds were lacking, the informant still cannot be found liable for malicious prosecution unless he or she is also found to have acted with malice.

INFORMATION/*DÉNONCIATION*

Under Section 24 of the Provincial Offences Act.
En vertu de l'article 24
de la Loi sur les infractions provinciales

Form Formule 105
Courts of Justice Act
Loi sur les tribunaux judiciaires

This is the information of *Dénonciation déposée par*	Angel White of the City of Sudbury *demeurant à*
.... *occupation/profession*	homemaker I have reasonable and probable grounds to believe and do believe that *j'ai des motifs raisonnables de croire et je crois effectivement que*

The International Smoke Company Limited
111 Dirty Drive
Sudbury, Ontario

on or about the
a, le ou vers le

10th day of February .... 1993 . at .. the City of Sudbury in the Regional Municipality
jour de   à   *location/lieu*

of Sudbury
....   did commit the offence of
commis l'infraction suivante

discharging or causing or permitting the discharge of material, namely, sulphuric
acid, into the Lilywhite River, which may impair the quality of the river,

contrary to   the Ontario Water Resources Act
en violation de

section ...... 30(1)
article

Sworn before me at the City of Sudbury
Assermenté devant moi à

this 25th . day of February 19 93
ce   jour de

Walcott

A judge or justice of the peace in and for the Province of Ontario
Juge ou juge de paix dans et pour la province de l'Ontario

Angel White
Signature of Informant/*Signature du dénonciateur*

SUMMONS RETURNABLE/
SOMMATION À RAPPORTER

At Courthouse, 25 Mulberry St., Sudbury, Ont.
À

On the   15th   day of   March 19 93 at 9.00 A M
Le   jour de   à   h

At/*À* .... Courtroom 2
Courtroom/salle d'audience

(Sec./*Art.* 23)

☐ Summons for *Sommation pour le*	.... 19	Confirmed on .... *Confirmée le*	19	Justice of the Peace *Juge de paix*
Date				

Pleads *Plaide*	☐ Guilty *Coupable*	☐ Not Guilty *Non coupable*	☐ Withdrawn *Abandon de poursuites (ou: Désistement)*
Found *Jugé(e)*	☐ Guilty *Coupable*	☐ Not Guilty *Non coupable*	☐ In Absentia *Ex parte* ☐ Sentence Suspended *Sursis*

Fined $ .... & $ .... costs.   Time to pay ....
Amende $ *dépens* $ *Délai de paiement*

Date of Birth ....
Date de naissance D J   M   Y A

Probation for ....
Durée de la probation

Sentenced to imprisonment for ....
Peine d'emprisonnement de

Exhibits Filed
Pièces déposées
☐ Yes/*Oui* ☐ No/*Non*

A judge or justice of the peace in and for the Province of Ontario
Juge ou juge de paix dans et pour la province de l'Ontario

CD 0003 (rev 01/91)

ONTARIO COURT
(PROVINCIAL DIVISION)
COUR DE L'ONTARIO
(DIVISION PROVINCIALE)

SUMMONS/*SOMMATION*

Under Section 25 of the Provincial Offences Act.
*Sommation adressée au défendeur aux termes de l'article 25
de la Loi sur les infractions provinciales*

Form/Formule 106
Courts of Justice Act
Loi sur les tribunaux judiciaires

The International Smoke Company Limited
111   Dirty Drive
Sudbury,Ontario

Whereas you have been charged
Attendu que vous avez été accusé

before me that you, on or about the
devant moi d'avoir le ou vers le

10th day of   February   19 93   at   the City of Sudbury in the Regional Municipality
jour de   *à*   *location/lieu*
of Sudbury   did commit the offence of
                                                                    commis l'infraction suivante

discharging or causing or permitting the discharge of material, namely, sulphuric
acid, into the Lilywhite River, which may impair the quality of the river,

contrary to   the Ontario Water Resources Act
en violation de

section   20(1)
article

Sworn before me at   the City of Sudbury
Assermenté devant moi à

this 25th   day of   February   19 93
ce   jour de

Walcott

A judge or justice of the peace in and for the Province of Ontario
Juge ou juge de paix dans et pour la province de l'Ontario

Angel White

THEREFORE you are commanded in her Majesty's name to
À ces causes, au nom de Sa Majesté, vous êtes sommé(e) de
appear before the Ontario Court (Provincial Division)
comparaître devant la Cour de l'Ontario (Division provinciale)

AT   Courthouse, 25 Mulberry St., Sudbury, Ont.
À

On the   15th   day of   March 19 93 at   9.00 A.M.
Le   jour de   à   h

At/À   Courtroom 2
Courtroom/salle d'audience

AND TO APPEAR THEREAFTER AS REQUIRED BY THE COURT TO BE DEALT WITH ACCORDING TO LAW
*ET DE COMPARAÎTRE PAR LA SUITE CHAQUE FOIS QUE LE TRIBUNAL L'EXIGERA DE FAÇON À CE QUE VOUS SOYEZ
JUGÉ(E) SELON LA LOI*

NOTE TO DEFENDANT:
Appear personally, by agent or counsel.

If you do not appear:
a) the court may issue a warrant for your arrest: or
b) the trial may proceed, and the evidence may be taken in
   your absence

If you do appear:
a) the trial may proceed: or
b) you, or the prosecutor, may ask the court to adjourn your
   case to another date. The court may grant or refuse such a
   request.

REMARQUE AU DÉFENDEUR :
*Vous pouvez comparaître personnellement, par mandataire,
ou par un avocat.*

Si vous ne comparaissez pas :
a) le tribunal peut émettre un mandat d'arrêt contre vous: ou
*b) le procès peut être tenu sans que vous y soyez et preuve
   peut être recueillie en votre absence.*

Si vous comparaissez :
a) le procès peut être tenu : ou
*b) vous pouvez vous ou le poursuivant demander au tribunal
   un ajournement. Le tribunal peut accorder ou refuser cette
   demande.*

CD 0003 (rev. 01/91)

Appendix III

Search Warrants and Subpoenas

SEARCH WARRANTS

To obtain evidence to support a prosecution under the *Criminal Code* or other federal legislation, you use the procedures and forms set out in the *Criminal Code*. To obtain evidence to support a prosecution under a provincial statute or municipal bylaw, use the procedures and forms set out in the *Provincial Offences Act*. Both forms should be available at the Provincial Court, or you can type up the forms, as long as they contain the same information as on the formal forms provided by the court.

You complete two forms, an information to obtain and a warrant to search, and bring them before a justice of the peace (JP) or judge, who will "issue" the warrant if he or she is satisfied that you have fulfilled the requirements for obtaining a warrant.

Search warrants are obtained by using a procedure similar to that used in laying charges for the breach of a statute (see Appendix II). That is, a person who has reasonable and probable grounds to believe that there is material at a particular place that would provide evidence of a breach of a law, drafts a statement, called an "information to obtain," setting out his or her evidence that the offence has been committed, what documents and things exist that will provide evidence of the offence, and where this material will be found. The person must then "swear" this information before a JP or a judge by signing it in his or her presence and swearing that its contents are true. If the JP or judge is satisfied that the information contains sufficient grounds to support the belief that an offence has been committed and evidence of it will be found at the place named in the information and in the warrant, he or she may then "issue" the warrant by signing it.

The warrant itself will set out the things to be obtained or "seized," the location to be searched, the names or functions (for example, "all police officers of the Ontario Provincial Police") entitled to carry out the search, and the time of day or night when the search may be carried out.

To prevent "fishing expeditions," the JP or judge will often limit the search to specific items and to specific parts of the premises where they are kept (for example, the plant may be excluded and the warrant may authorize entry only to a company's office area).

Because search warrants have often been abused by those "executing" them (that is, carrying out the search), the courts have continued to put strict procedural requirements on the information to obtain that precedes the search warrant. That is, the courts will quash search warrants that have been obtained on the basis of information that does not comply strictly with all the requirements stipulated in the legislation authorizing warrants and various judicial rulings on the subject.

If you want to obtain a search warrant, it is wise to have an experienced criminal lawyer assist in preparing the information and warrant. Because it is so unusual for a private citizen to seek a warrant, it is also prudent to have a lawyer attend with you before the JP or judge.

The warrant must be executed by the person or persons named in it, only at the time and place named in it, and only the material mentioned in the warrant and any other evidence found "in plain view" may be taken. ("Plain view" has different meanings, depending on the context. For example, if you are authorized to search a specific filing cabinet for specific documents and you find other documents in the same file that provide additional evidence, the additional documents would probably be considered "in plain view.")

If you are not permitted to enter after showing the person in charge of the premises the original warrant and providing him or her with a copy, you are entitled to use as much force as necessary. Obviously, this is unwise unless you are accompanied by a police officer. It is prudent to advise the police of your intention to execute the warrant and to arrange for them to attend to keep the peace if you meet any resistance.

As soon as you obtain the material, you are required to bring it before a justice of the peace, who will determine whether it is included in the seizure authorized by the warrant and how it is to be secured until trial. The statute authorizing the warrant will normally state how long you may keep this material without laying charges. Under the *Environmental Protection Act*, for example, unless charges have been laid, the material must be returned after 90 days, unless you apply to the court for an extension of the time, notify the person from whom it was seized and anyone else who may own the material, and justify keeping it longer at a formal hearing before the JP.

SUBPOENAS

A subpoena, or "summons to a witness," is a formal document notifying a witness in a civil action, a prosecution, or a hearing by an administrative tribunal that he or she is required to appear before the tribunal, testify, and bring the documents or things specified in the subpoena. If a subpoena is served properly, the witness is under a legal obligation to attend at the time and place and with the documents specified in it. The penalties for failing to obey a subpoena can be serious. In addition, some statutes authorize the tribunal to have the witness arrested and brought before the tribunal to testify.

The form for a subpoena to a trial under the *Criminal Code* or other federal legislation and the method of serving it are set out under the *Criminal Code*; for a trial for violation of provincial statutes or municipal bylaws, see the *Provincial Offences Act*; for a civil proceeding, see the *Courts of Justice Act* and the Rules of Practice of the Ontario Court (General Division); and for hearings before provincial administrative tribunals, see the *Statutory Powers Procedure Act*.

You can usually obtain a blank copy of the form from the relevant court or board. You must fill in the form showing the name of the witness, the subject matter of the proceeding, the place, date, and time the trial or hearing is to commence, and list any documents or things you require the witness to bring. In a prosecution, the charges against the accused must be set out clearly.

Issuing the Subpoena

When you have completed a subpoena for a prosecution (in duplicate), take it before a justice of the peace, and be prepared to give an oral summary of the evidence this witness can give and its relevance to the issues before the court. If the JP is satisfied that the witness can provide relevant evidence, he or she will "issue" the subpoena by signing both copies. In the civil courts and many administrative tribunals, subpoenas are often signed before you get them, and it is not necessary to attend before any official to have them "issued."

Serving the Subpoena

To have effect, the subpoena must be properly served. If the witness fails to attend, someone must prove to the tribunal that it was served either by personally testifying that it was served or by filing an affidavit stating how, where, and when it was served. A subpoena for federal offences is valid only if served by a "peace officer," which includes all police and some other enforcement officials such as game and fish enforcement officers. Under the *Provincial Offences Act*, a subpoena is binding only if it is served by someone designated as a provincial offences officer. This includes all police officers and most provincial law enforcement officials and inspectors, as well as municipal bylaw enforcement officers.

This makes it difficult for private prosecutors to get witnesses to court. However, the police and other agencies will often cooperate in serving such subpoenas. Indeed, in Ontario, it is the policy of the government that police officers will provide this assistance. As a practical matter, most witnesses do not realize that a subpoena has no effect if it is served by someone other than a peace officer or provincial offences officer, and will attend a hearing no matter who has served them. In a pinch, therefore, it sometimes is better to serve the subpoena yourself or to hire a private "process server" to serve it than to rely on the bureaucracy. Experience has shown that the police and other public servants authorized to serve these documents cannot be counted on to assist government agencies other than their own, much less private citizens, in a timely manner.

In civil proceedings, anyone can serve a subpoena. In Small Claims Court, the court officials will usually serve the subpoena for you. In other civil proceedings, you may serve the subpoena yourself or hire a process server to do it, and to provide you with an affidavit of service. The Sheriff's Office, a provincial government agency, may also serve a subpoena for a fee. In the case of tribunals, the agency may have staff to serve subpoenas or you may have to make your own arrangements.

Valid service of a subpoena involves showing the witness the original and handing him or her the copy. If the person refuses to take it, it is usually considered sufficient if the document touches the witness. Therefore, hand the witness the document so that it makes contact with the person (preferably the person's hand) and if the person draws back, drop it at his or her feet.

Witness Fees

When you serve a person with a subpoena to attend civil proceedings or an administrative board holding hearings under Ontario laws, you must give the person a "witness fee" (known as "conduct money"). You give this money — in cash or a certified cheque — to the person being served or to the person who will carry out the service. The rules of the Ontario Court (General Division) set out the amount of conduct money required. For Ontario government boards, the *Statutory Powers Procedure Act* provides for conduct money in accordance with the court rules.

The purpose of this conduct money is to enable people to attend court, preventing them from using the excuse that they could not afford to attend. In theory, it also compensates them for their lost time, although in practice the amounts payable are so low as to be almost meaningless. Unless the person receives the conduct money at the time of service, and in cash or by certified cheque, he or she is not required to obey the subpoena.

It is not necessary to give give conduct money to witnesses subpoenaed to a provincial prosecution.

Summonses

A subpoena is issued to a witness. A summons is issued to the accused in a prosecution. See Appendix II for a description of the procedures for issuing and serving a summons. See Appendix IV for procedures for summoning the defendant in Small Claims Court.

Appendix IV
Small Claims Court Actions

The Ontario Court of Justice (Small Claims Division) ("the Small Claims Court") is where civil actions with claims of under $6,000 are heard. Proceeding in this court can be a useful and inexpensive way to obtain judgment and publicize environmental problems. The types of cases brought to this level of court are usually brought by consumers or businesses to obtain damages or to collect a debt. The court is sometimes used for environmental claims. For example, in 1985, two neighbours of an oil refinery in Port Credit successfully sued Texaco for emissions of oily soot that damaged the paint on their cars. A claim for damage to property could be brought in Small Claims Court as long as the amount of money claimed is within the monetary limit.

The court was designed to settle minor disputes without prohibitive expense and in an informal manner so that the average person can have access to the courts without a lawyer (although a lawyer may be used). Accordingly, court procedure is relatively informal and costs are low.

DRAFTING AND FILING THE CLAIM AND SUMMONS

To commence your proceeding, locate the Small Claims Court office nearest to you. This office will be listed in the telephone directory under "Government of Ontario, Courts." Give the clerks at the court the full name and address (as complete and accurate as possible) of the person or company you intend to sue. The clerks will assist you if you ask them to explain the various steps you will have to take to commence your proceeding. These steps may vary depending on your case. A guide to Small Claims Court actions published by the government may also be available at the courthouse to assist you in taking each of the steps necessary to pursue an action.

The rules of court provide that an action must be entered and tried in the territorial division where the cause of action arose (where the incident took place), or at the court's location that is closest to where the defendant lives or carries on business. For example, there are several Small Claims Court offices in Metropolitan Toronto. You will want to commence your proceeding in the one where the incident took place, or alternatively, in the court division closest to the defendant.

Ask the court clerk to provide you with the necessary forms for commencing your proceeding.

Once you have completed these forms, return them to the court office for filing. The most important form is the claim. In this form set out the amount of damages sought from the defendant, with reasons in support of your claim. Set this out in plain language and concisely in numbered paragraphs. State only material facts and not the evidence of these facts. Also include a claim for "pre-judgment interest" because if you succeed in obtaining a judgment against the defendant, the court may award interest on the amount of money awarded to you from the date you commenced the action to the date you received the court's decision. If there is not enough room on the claim form, you may set out your reasons on a separate sheet of paper, which you would title "Appendix A." In the area on the claim form that allows room for your reasons, you would type or write "See Appendix A."

It is important that care be taken when preparing the claim. This document is the heart of your case. You must set out each relevant fact on which you will later rely at the trial to support your claim for damages.

When you take the completed claim form back to the court office, the clerk will file it in exchange for a fee. The amount charged depends on the amount of damages claimed and the number of parties from whom you are seeking damages. A fee schedule is available on request from the court's office.

SERVICE

The court clerk will have the court bailiff serve the defendant with your claim. This process of "service" involves a small charge that varies depending on the distance the bailiff must travel to serve the claim.

DISPUTE OR SETTLEMENT

Once the claim has been served, the defendant has 20 days to dispute your claim in writing. A defendant must deliver to the court within that period of time a defence in which the defendant sets out his or her side of the story. Should the defendant not deliver a defence within the 20 days, the clerk of the court may note the defendant in default. If the claim is for a liquidated demand in money, (for example, a debt), the clerk of the court may then enter judgment against the defendant including interest if claimed. The clerk of the court would then mail a notice of default judgment to the plaintiff and to the defendant. If the claim is for an unliquidated amount (for example, damages), the clerk will set a date for the trial at which time you will have to prove the amount of your damages but not the defendant's liability.

A defendant who has been noted in default may not file a defence or take any other step in the matter, except that of seeking the court's permission to cure the default and file a defence within a prescribed time.

Your opponent may wish to settle out of court. The rules of this court provide that either party may serve on the other an offer to settle. Such an offer should be sent at least seven days before trial. The offer would specify terms. The terms could include having the defendant pay the settlement amount into court. Should both parties agree on a settlement, a copy of the settlement agreement signed by both parties should be completed and filed with the court so that it can be enforced by the court.

Should your opponent dispute your claim and file a defence within the 20-day period, a trial date will be set. Both parties are notified of the time and place of trial. Either party may also request a pre-trial conference by filling in a request for such a conference with the clerk of the court. At a pre-trial conference a judge other than the one who will hear the case will listen to both parties explain their case, and will give an opinion as to who would win if a trial took place, and the amount of damages the plaintiff would likely be awarded if he or she won. This process encourages the parties to reach a settlement rather than go to trial.

TRIAL PREPARATION

To prepare for your day in court, gather all witnesses and evidence, whether documents or things. Prepare your story in a systematic fashion, usually in chronological order. Documents that support the claim should be organized so that as you relate your story to the court, you can give the judge a copy of each document at the appropriate point during your narrative. Ensure that you have sufficient copies of these documents for the defendants.

Speak to the clerk of the court several weeks before the trial date so that the court can serve subpoenas on any witnesses whom you require at the trial. You are permitted to review your claim and discuss it with the witnesses when you prepare for trial. However, you may not, of course, suggest to the witnesses what their testimony should be. They will be under oath, as you will be, to tell the truth.

It would be extremely useful if any physical evidence of your claim can be provided to the court. For example, pollution samples or the actual damaged property or pictures of the damaged property should be brought along. When preparing your narrative for the court, note down all pertinent dates when events occurred. You must also prove the damage that you have claimed to have suffered because of the defendant's acts.

Trials in the Small Claims Court are open to the public. If possible, attend one at some point before your trial. This exposure to the court surroundings will help make the court feel more familiar and less threatening on the day of your trial.

THE TRIAL

You are now in court. You will make a good impression on the judge if you briefly introduce yourself and your opponent, and state what you intend to prove and the issues in this case. Dress appropriately, and speak in a polite yet clear manner (no mumbling!). Watch the judge as you present your narrative. If he or she is writing notes, slow down to allow him or her time to record your important points.

Your witnesses will then testify. Start with the witness who will have the most important bearing on the case. Question the witness in a straightforward manner, without suggesting the answers to the witness in the questions. Questions should be open-ended to allow the witnesses to explain the answer.

When questioning witnesses of your opponent, ask questions that can only be answered in a "yes" or "no" fashion. In this cross-examination, do *not* ask questions if you do not know the answer to them. It is often better not to question the other side's witness, unless you are extremely sure of your case.

Judges often ask questions in order to fully understand the claim, as well as to test the credibility of the person testifying. Questions should be seen not as an interruption but as an opportunity to understand the areas where the judge needs further assistance and to further convince the court of the merits of your case. Respond as succinctly and as positively as possible. When preparing, try to imagine some questions that a judge may ask.

To conclude, present your case to the court in a clear, courteous, and straightforward manner. Make all the points you believe the judge should know to decide the issue. Remember that to succeed you must convince the court that you have suffered damage that was caused by the defendant.

DYE & DURHAM CO LIMITED—Form No. 880
(Amended 1988)

Ontario Court (General Division)
Cour de l'Ontario (Division générale)

Ontario

Sudbury   SMALL CLAIMS COURT
COUR DES PETITES CRÉANCES DE ....

CLAIM/CRÉANCE
Form/*Formule* 7A

	A.D. 19
Amount of Claim *Montant de la créance*	$
Entry Fee *Droits d'inscription*	$
Advertising	$
	$

If you wish to file a Claim, complete this form
Si vous désirez faire une demande, remplissez cette formule

WHEN REFERRING TO THIS DOCUMENT PLEASE USE NUMBER IN UPPER RIGHT CORNER
VEUILLEZ UTILISER LE NUMÉRO EN HAUT À DROITE COMME RÉFÉRENCE DE CE DOCUMENT

PLAINTIFF/*DEMANDEUR*
Name/*Nom*
      Angel White

DEFENDANT(S)/*DÉFENDEUR(S)*
Name/*Nom*
      I.M.A. Polluting Company Limited
Street No./*N° et rue*   Address/*Adresse*   Apt. No./*N° d'app.*
      87 Queen Street
Borough/City/Ville/Municipalité   Postal Code/*Code postal*   Phone No./*N° de tél.*
      Sudbury   P3A 5W5   (705) 673-2171

DEFENDANT/*DÉFENDEUR*
Name/*Nom*

Street No./*N° et rue*   Address/*Adresse*   Apt. No./*N° d'app.*

Borough/City/Ville/Municipalité   Postal Code/*Code Postal*   Phone No./*N° de tél.*

To the Defendant/*Au défendeur:*
The Plaintiff claims from you $ 2,000..00 and costs for the reason(s) set out below. and pre-judgment interest from
Le(s) demandeur(s) vous demand(ent) la somme de $ plus les frais pour la(les) raison(s) indiquée(s) ci-après.
IF YOU DO NOT FILE A DEFENCE WITH THE COURT WITHIN TWENTY DAYS AFTER YOU HAVE RECEIVED THIS CLAIM, JUDGMENT MAY BE ENTERED AGAINST YOU.
SI VOUS NE FORMULEZ PAS DE DÉFENSE À LA COUR DANS LES VINGT JOURS SUIVANT LA RÉCEPTION DE CETTE DEMANDE DE CRÉANCE, UN JUGEMENT PEUT ÊTRE PRONONCÉ CONTRE VOUS PAR DÉFAUT.

TYPE OF CLAIM/*GENRE DE DEMANDE:*

☐ Unpaid account *Compte impayé*   ☐ Contract *Contrat*   ☐ Motor vehicle accident *Accident qui implique un véhicule automobile*   ☐ Promissory note *Billet à ordre*   ☐ Lease *Bail*

☐ Services rendered *Services rendus*   ☐ N.S.F. cheque *Chèque sans provision*   ☒ Damage to property *Dommages aux biens*   ☐ Other *Autres* loss of enjoyment of property
(describe/*préciser*)

Reasons for Claim and Details/*Raisons de la créance et détails:*
(Explain what happened, where and when and the amounts of money involved)
(Indiquer les faits que donnent lieu à la demande, de même que le moment et l'endroit où ils se sont produits ainsi que les sommes d'argent en cause)

    1. The plaintiff's claim is for damages for physical damage to property and loss of enjoyment of property as a result of a nuisance caused by the defendant from the first day of March 1991 and continuing at the present time.

    2. The defendant is a company incorporated under the laws of Canada. Its head office is in the City of Sudbury in the province of Ontario and it carries on the business of mining and refining ores in and about the Sudbury area.

    3. As part of its operation the defendant operates a smelter on property which it owns and occupies. The process of smelting ores causes emissions of enormous amounts of noxious and ill-smelling gases and particles into the air.

    4. These emissions damage the paint on the plaintiff's house and car, deposit dirt on the plaintiff's property, and make it impossible to use the yard for normal activities and require the plaintiff and her family to stay indoors and keep all windows closed during all seasons.

    5. (Further allegations should be set out as needed in the particular case).

    (Add additional pages if necessary to provide further facts).

(Where claim is based on a document, attach a copy for each copy of the claim, or if it is lost or unavailable, explain why it is not attached.)
(Si la demande est fondée sur un écrit, annexer une copie de cet écrit pour chaque copie de la demande, ou si celui-ci a été perdu ou ne peut être produit, donner les motifs pour lesquels il n'est pas annexé.)

Make payments to the Court by certified cheque or money order./*Faire les paiements à la Cour au moyen d'un chèque certifié ou d'un mandat.*

Plaintiff's Signature/Solicitor or Agent's Name/*Signature du demandeur Nom de l'avocat ou du mandataire*	Office use only/*À l'usage du bureau*
Address/*Adresse*	
25 Purity Drive 555-1555	
City/Borough/Ville/Municipalité Postal Code/*Code postal* Phone No./*N° de tél.*	
Sudbury, Ontario	
Date	
February 25, 1993	

CV 0330 (rev 03/90)

Appendix V

Searches: How To Find Important Facts

To launch a successful campaign to protect the environment, you need copious information. There are many books on how to do research. One excellent source of information about how to use libraries, access government and corporate documents, and find court records is Stephen Overbury's *Finding Canadian Facts Fast*.[1] Overbury's book lists numerous other books on specific kinds of information gathering, as well as directories dealing with specific subject areas. In this appendix, we will tell you how to obtain some specific kinds of basic information needed to prove a case in court or before a tribunal.

SEARCHES UNDER THE ENVIRONMENTAL PROTECTION ACT, THE ONTARIO WATER RESOURCES ACT, AND THE PESTICIDES ACT

Under the *Environmental Protection Act*, the *Ontario Water Resources Act*, and the *Pesticides Act*, various licences, permits, and approvals are issued to companies and individuals, approving specific activities, businesses, structures, and pieces of equipment. The Ministry of Environment and Energy also gives approval for voluntary pollution control and cleanup programs (program approvals), and issues a variety of preventive and remedial orders.

The *Environmental Protection Act*, the *Ontario Water Resources Act*, and the *Pesticides Act* contain provisions requiring the ministry to keep a record of all outstanding orders. If anyone gives the ministry the name of a company or an individual and asks whether any outstanding orders have been issued to that person, the ministry must check its records. If an order has been issued, the ministry must permit inspection of the order. Under the *Environmental Protection Act* and the *Ontario Water Resources Act*, but not the *Pesticides Act*, the ministry must also allow inspection of certificates of approval that have been issued and are still in effect.[2] Once an order or approval expires, these statutes require that the person's name be expunged from the record. This does not mean that you cannot obtain copies of expired orders and certificates of approval. The ministry will still have other records of such orders and approvals, and may be required to make them available under the *Freedom of Information and Protection of Privacy Act*.

The administration of part VIII of the *Environmental Protection Act*, providing for approvals of private sewage works, has been delegated to local health units in many parts of Ontario. Even though the Act requires the ministry to keep a record of these approvals, it may be necessary to obtain the information from the health unit, because no central record is kept at the Approvals Branch of the ministry.

Although the statutes are silent about the right to see background documents, many of them will also be available from the ministry voluntarily, or through a request under the *Freedom of Information and Protection of Privacy Act* if the ministry will not cooperate. Before approvals are issued, applicants must submit a detailed application as well as background information such as plans and specifications, results of monitoring programs, and predictions of environmental impacts. Control orders must be based on a provincial officer's report setting out the investigations made and the officer's findings and conclusions. Much of this material is kept in the file relating to the approval or order, and depending on whom you are dealing with, you may be allowed to look through the file. In some cases, preliminary drafts of the conditions in certificates of approval and orders will be available through the *Freedom of Information and Protection of Privacy Act.*

Even though the statutes do not provide for a record of licences and permits and a right to examine them, there will usually be a record somewhere, and you can usually see these documents, as well as the applications and other background documentation.

Where To Ask

The statutes do not specify where you can examine these documents, so you may have difficulty tracking down a particular order, approval, licence, or permit.

As a rule, all approvals, past or present, issued under the *Environmental Protection Act* and the *Ontario Water Resources Act*, except for private sewage approvals, are available from the director of the Approvals Branch of the ministry, in Toronto. You should also be able to obtain a copy of any approval from the Region or District office where the pollution source is located. Water-taking permits issued under section 34 of the *Ontario Water Resources Act* are available at the region or district office.

For program approvals and orders, contact the region or district office as well. The Approvals Branch does not keep a copy of every program approval and order, but if this branch has issued an approval, a licence, or a permit to the person, there may be copies of program approvals and orders in the file relating to the approval, licence, or permit.

Licences, permits, and orders under the *Pesticides Act* may be obtained either from the pesticides officer at the region or district office or from the Pesticides Section of the Hazardous Contaminants Branch, in Toronto.

How To Request a Document

Although specific provisions of the legislation require the ministry to keep a record of the *names* of people to whom approvals and orders have been issued, ministry records are often organized not by name but by location. Therefore, to obtain these documents, it is helpful if you can give the ministry the following information:

- the correct name of the company or individual to whom the order or approval has been issued; and
- the address of the location where the activity, business, structure or equipment is located.

The address should be as specific as possible. For example, in a rural area, you should have the lot and plan description of the land involved. It is necessary to provide the location, since the head office address of the corporation may be different from the address of the plant or site in question. Moreover, large companies may be subject to several approvals or orders relating to their activities in different areas.

An approval, a licence, a permit, or an order may have been issued to an individual, while the activity is being carried out or the business is operated in the name of a corporation. This happens less frequently than it used to because the ministry has started to become more careful to ensure that the person making an application fills in the correct name. But to be sure you have covered all the bases, you may have to know both the name of the corporation and principal officers of the corporation, as well as the owner and tenant of the land, to ensure a complete search. (To get this information, see "Land Ownership and Occupancy Searches" and "Corporate and Business Name Searches," below.)

Each ministry has an information and privacy coordinator. It should not be necessary to request most information through this official, because the offices and branches should assist you by providing the information they have in their files. However, if the information is not forthcoming, you may formally request it through the coordinator.

SEARCHING THE CORRECT NAME OF THE OWNER OF A MOTOR VEHICLE

When you see the driver of a car, a truck, a snowmobile, or an all-terrain vehicle committing an offence, such as trespassing, littering, discharging excessive smoke, or making excessive noise, you may lay a charge against the owner, since it will often be impossible to identify the driver. In addition, if you observe illegal dumping of waste, someone hauling waste to an uncertified waste disposal site, or some other questionable activity, the identity of the owner of the vehicle being used may provide clues to the identity of the person responsible for the activity.

To prove the identity of the owner of a vehicle before a court or tribunal, a *certified* copy of the motor vehicle registration must be presented. You can find the owner's name and address and obtain a certified copy of the registration showing this information, as well as the make, model, and year of manufacture of the vehicle by completing an "Application for Vehicle Record Search." The application can be obtained from some driver examination centres and from the Ministry of Transportation Data Management Centre. In 1992 the Data Management Centre was located at 2680 Keele Street, Downsview, Ontario M3M 3E6.

If you can provide the licence plate number, and, if known, the manufacturer, model, year, and colour of the vehicle, the ministry will provide a document showing the name and address of the owner. If you need the document for use in court, ask specifically for a certified copy of the registration showing the identity of the owner on the date on which the offence occurred.

LAND OWNERSHIP AND OCCUPANCY SEARCHES

It would be impossible in the space available here to turn any reader into a competent title searcher. However, it is usually not too difficult for a lay person to determine basic information, such as who owned a property at a particular time, the price paid for it, whether it is mortgaged, and, if so, who holds the mortgage, and the names of any tenants, particularly if the land is in an urban area. We therefore offer a brief outline of the land record system in Ontario.

There are two land record systems in operation in Ontario — the land registry and the land titles systems. The land titles system is the newer and more efficient system. In most of northern Ontario it is the only system available, while in many counties of southern Ontario, it is not yet in use. Southern Ontario property will usually be recorded in the land registry system. There are a few exceptions. Even if an area uses the land registry system, condominiums and plans of subdivision must be recorded in the land titles system. In areas where land is recorded under both systems, the Land Registry Office and the Land Titles Office are usually in the same building.

Computerization of the Land Recording System

To make it easier to use these systems, they are being computerized. Part 2 of the *Land Registration Reform Act*[3] permits the computerization of land records. This Province of Ontario Land Registration and Information System (POLARIS) provides for automated recording and property mapping so that documents are recorded by computer. The implementation is being done gradually. As parcels of land are designated, property identification numbers (PINs) are assigned. In the registry system, all lands in Toronto are gradually being brought into this system, with a separate PIN for each separate owner, as in land titles. By obtaining the PIN number for a parcel of land, you may ask the clerk for a computer printout of all the transactions, such as sales and mortgages, since the PIN number was assigned. For earlier transactions, you will still have to search through the records manually. Records in the land titles system and condominiums are also gradually being computerized.

Finding the Land Registry or Land Titles Office

The first step in tracking down a piece of property is to determine in which office the land is registered. Outside Toronto, the county or district records office is found in the "county town" (for example, Peterborough for Peterborough County); generally, the office is at or near the municipal offices or the courts. (Some counties may have more than one registry or land titles office, in which case you would search in the office nearest the property in question.) In the Toronto area, records of all the land in the city of Toronto and the other area municipalities within Metro Toronto and the part of the regional municipality of York that is south of highway 7 that was recorded under the land registry system are kept in an office at 20 Dundas Street West, Toronto. The Land Titles Office and the Land Registry Office for the northern part of York are in Newmarket. To find out where other land titles and land registry offices are, contact the Real Property Registration Branch of the Ontario Ministry of Consumer and Commercial Relations. In 1992, it was located at 393 University Avenue, Toronto M7A 2H6.

If possible, avoid going to land registry or land titles offices on Fridays and during the last three or four business days of the month. This is when most land deals are "closing" (being finalized). The offices will be a frenzy of activity and documents may not be available, and no one will have time to assist a novice.

Finding Documents

The next step is to ascertain the legal description of the property. Parcels of land are registered under lots and plans (for example, "part of Lot 5, Plan 32, Township of Westminster, County of Middlesex") rather than their municipal address. If you have the municipal address, you can usually discover the legal description by checking maps available in the Land Registry or Land Titles Office that correlate streets with lots and plans, or by looking at the municipal tax assessment rolls, kept at the municipal clerk's office in the municipality where the property is located. (In Toronto, the city's assessment rolls are kept on the first floor of the new city hall.) Always have the municipal address for adjoining properties in case there are no data for the property you want. The legal description of adjoining properties can help you determine the description of the property you are looking for.

If the property is in a city, the legal description will be expressed in lot and plan numbers (for example, "Lot 39, Plan 256, City of Etobicoke"). For rural properties, the legal description will be in lot and concession numbers (for example, "Lot 7, Concession V, Township of East Gwillimbury").

Once you have the legal description, you can obtain from the Land Registry or Land Titles Office staff the proper *Abstract* book. (In Toronto, you fill out a slip, pay a fee of $4, and take the slip to one of the counter clerks, who will bring you the most recent book.) The *Abstract* contains a chronological record of all the documents that have been registered against the properties included in that book.

Each property is assigned a page or a set of pages in the book. The property you are searching for may consist of all or part of a lot, or of all or parts of two or more adjoining lots. If the property is part of a lot on a registered plan, it will often be half of the lot, and will be described as the north, south, east, or west half. In some cases, the parcel will be more or less than half the lot. In those cases it will be described by a "metes and bounds" description.

If a parcel is half of a registered lot, it should not be difficult to trace the transactions affecting that parcel (although documents from the two different halves may appear one after the other in the *Abstract*). If you discover you are dealing with a property that is a large area in a concession rather than a plan, you will probably need the help of a lawyer, a law student, or a title searcher. Before you give up, look for a friendly face and ask for help.

Sales of the land are referred to in the *Abstract* as transfers (formerly called grants and shown by a "G"). The transferor (formerly the grantor) and transferee (formerly the grantee) correspond to the seller and the buyer. The present owner will be the transferee on the last transfer. The identity of the present owner should not be too difficult to determine — even for a beginner; just make sure you have found the most recent transfer concerning your lot or parcel if more than one lot or parcel is dealt with on the same page of the book.

Each of the documents referred to in the *Abstract* records a transaction, such as a sale of the property, the placing or discharge of a mortgage, the subdivision of the property into two or more parcels, or the creation of an easement. By looking through the *Abstract* chronologically and, if necessary, looking at the individual documents listed in the *Abstract*, you can obtain a history of ownership and other dealings with the land.

The *Abstract* books are not usually up to date. To be sure that there have been no further dealings with the land since the last entry in the *Abstract*, ask to see the "fee book" or "day book," which contains references to all transactions that have not yet been recorded in the

Abstract. Check the entries in the day book for any reference to your property. (Usually there won't be anything, but to be absolutely sure, you should check this book.)

If the owner is a corporation, and you want to know who is behind the corporation, do a corporate search (see "Corporate and Business Names Searches," below).

If you need more detailed information, you can obtain a copy of any of the documents referred to in the *Abstract* by writing down their numbers as shown in the *Abstract* on a slip and taking it to the clerk at the counter. The clerk will provide a copy of each document listed on the slip for your inspection.

For example, sales are recorded on a document that was formerly called a "deed" in the land registry system, and that is now called a "transfer" in both systems. By looking at this deed or transfer, you can find out the addresses of the buyer and the seller; you can find out the sale price by looking at the "Affidavit of Land Transfer Tax" on the back of the document.

If you don't have the time (or if you find the search too confusing), you can order a "subsearch" from certain companies that provide this information for a fee (for example, Teela Abstracts in Scarborough or ABC Property & Lien Reports in Toronto). This subsearch will show you who the current owners are according to the last transfer, the sale price, and any existing claims registered against the property.

If you have the legal description of the property, you can also obtain copies of the pages of the *Abstract* that relate to this property and specific documents by writing to the land registry or land titles office where the property is located and paying a fee. Title searchers who can be retained to provide information can be found in any centre with a land records office; check the Yellow Pages or ask a lawyer for a name.

Municipal Assessment Rolls

The land records offices will not usually have a record of the tenants of land. Leases are registered only if they cover a period of seven years or more. However, the municipal roll will tell you the names of owners and tenants of property. The owner is designated by "O," the tenant by "T," and if the land or buildings are vacant you will find the letter "V." Although these records are not as accurate or up-to-date as those in the land records offices, they are accepted in court as evidence if they are certified by the municipal clerk. In addition to showing the names of tenants, they provide backup evidence of names and addresses of owners.

If you are prosecuting or suing someone and you need to prove that an individual or a company owns a particular piece of property, you will need both a certified copy of the page of the *Abstract* showing the most recent sale and a certified copy of the document (deed or transfer) showing the ownership. Both are admissible as evidence in court without requiring proof of their accuracy by any witness. The land registrar will provide certified copies for a fee.

OBTAINING BUSINESS INFORMATION

To prosecute or sue a person operating a business, it is necessary to have certain basic information. You must know whether the business is a corporation or an individual or partnership carrying on business under a name other than that of the owner(s); and to pursue legal action against a corporation you must know the location of the head office and the names of the officers and directors so that the legal documents can be served. This information is readily available, and will be discussed below under the heading "Corporate and Business Names Searches."

To understand the workings of a business, it is necessary to have much more information. It is useful to know:

- who owns the business;
- where and how it gets its working capital (capitalization);
- its profits and losses, assets, volume of business, level and sources of indebtedness, and general financial affairs for the past several years; and
- its relationship with other corporations through interlocking ownerships and directorships, business partnerships, joint ventures, and formal and informal agreements.

This information is not as easily accessible, but it can be found. Public companies (those that offer shares to the public through stock exchanges) must make available more information than private companies. However, there are directories, business periodicals, computer databases, and other sources of information that will provide much of this information to a diligent researcher. Such information is often available at university and public business libraries, through stock brokers, and through provincial and US securities commissions. There are several books that explain what to look for and how to find it. They include *Finding Canadian Facts Fast*, referred to above, *Researching Canadian Corporations*,[4] and *How To Find Information About Companies*.[5]

Corporate and Business Names Searches

When suing or prosecuting a business it is essential to sue or prosecute the actual owner, using the owner's correct name.

A business may be carried on by means of:

- a sole proprietorship;
- a partnership; or
- a limited company.

A sole proprietorship is simply a business owned by one individual; a partnership is similar except that more than one individual or corporation shares legal responsibility for harm caused by the business; and a limited company or corporation is a legally created, but artificial, "person."

The name by which a business is publicly known is not necessarily its proper name for the purposes of a civil action or prosecution. The first step in ascertaining the correct name is to make an intelligent guess about which one of the three categories the business fits. In addition, some people carry on business through several separate corporations, to limit liability or reduce tax. For example, people may set up one corporation to carry on the business, a different corporation to own the equipment, and a third corporation or an individual may own the land where the business is located. To zero in on the correct name or names, you look at a variety of information, such as business cards, letterhead, signs on buildings and vehicles, advertising, and ownership of vehicles used by the company. When you have enough information, you can begin your searches.

| Ministry of Consumer and Commercial Relations | Ministère de la Consommation et du Commerce | Companies Branch Direction des compagnies | 393 University Ave., Toronto, Ontario M7A 2H6
393, avenue University Toronto (Ontario) M7A 2H6 |

Certificate of Status
Certificat de statut documentaire

This is to certify that according to the records of the companies branch

Je certifie par les présentes que, conformément aux dossiers de la Direction des compagnies,

JETCO MANUFACTURING LIMITED

Ontario Corporation No.   numéro ontarien de compagnie ou d'association

125157

is a corporation incorporated, amalgamated or continued under the laws of the Province of Ontario.

est constituée, fusionnée ou continue d'exister en vertu des lois de la province de l'ontario.

The corporation came into existence on

La compagnie ou association a été fondée le

APRIL 1 AVRIL, 1963

and has not been dissolved.   et n'a pas été dissoute.

Dated

Fait le
MAY 23 MAI, 1989

Controller of Records
Contrôleur des dossiers

FORM CD-314   07014(01/88)

As a rule, if a business is publicly known by a name that does not have the word "Limited" or "Ltd.," "Incorporated" or "Inc.," or "Corporation" or "Corp." after it, the owner will probably be an individual carrying on this business as a sole proprietor or a partnership. For example, "Tracy's Lock Company" may well be Dick Tracy carrying on business as a sole proprietor or with other partners under that name. In this case, the business name "Tracy's Lock Company" will probably be registered at the Partnerships Registry of the Companies Division of the Ontario Ministry of Consumer and Commercial Relations. In 1992, the address was 393 University Avenue, Toronto. This "name or style" registration will give you the name and address of the sole proprietor or each of the partners, if it is a partnership.

In this case, you will sue or prosecute Dick Tracy, carrying on business (abbreviated as c.o.b.) Tracy's Lock Company. If the business is owned by Tracy and other partners, all the partners should be sued in a civil action. In a prosecution, the person or persons to be charged will depend on the evidence of how involved they were in making the decisions or carrying out the activities that caused the offence.

All limited companies (corporations) doing business in Ontario are required to file certain information with the Ontario government. As soon as the company is incorporated, it must file an "initial notice," setting out the full name of the company, its head office address (the address for service of statements of claim and summonses), and the names and addresses of all directors and officers. The corporation must also file a "notice of change" setting out any changes in this information within 15 days after the change takes place.

The company must also register any names it uses other than the full name of the corporation under the *Business Names Act* (formerly the *Corporations Information Act).*[6] "Tracy's Lock Company" may turn out not to be the name under which an individual or a group of partners carries on business but the "style" used by a corporation.

In addition, if the company is incorporated under the Ontario *Business Corporations Act,* the Ontario government will have a copy of its articles of incorporation, and if two or more companies have amalgamated, the articles of amalgamation. If you are prosecuting a company you will need a certificate of status to introduce at the trial. This certificate states that on the date the offence was committed, the company had been incorporated and continued to be incorporated.

Certified copies of these documents can be obtained for a fee at the Partnership and Small Business Registration Section of the Companies Division of the Ontario Ministry of Consumer and Commercial Relations in Toronto. In 1992, its address was 393 University Avenue, Toronto.

If you are attempting to prosecute or sue a major national or international corporation, you will probably find that it is a federally incorporated company. You can obtain some information on the company from the Ontario ministry, but a certificate of status must be obtained from the Department of Consumer and Corporate Affairs, Federal Corporations Branch, in Ottawa.

For a fee, commercial corporate search firms will also provide all the documents referred to above.

Municipal Documents

Section 74(1) of the *Municipal Act*[7] gives any person the right to inspect any records, books, accounts, and documents in the possession or under the control of the municipal clerk, except certain confidential documents. The *Municipal Freedom of Information and Privacy Act* also provides for access to documents in the possession of other municipal departments. In particular, to prosecute someone for the breach of a municipal bylaw, you must obtain a certified copy of the original bylaw as well as certified copies of all amendments to present to the court. Certain municipal bylaws, such as noise bylaws passed pursuant to the *Environmental Protection Act* (see Chapter 19), do not come into force until they receive approval from the provincial government. In those cases, you should also present the court with a certified copy of the document approving the bylaw.

WEATHER RECORDS

In determining how or why an environmental problem occurred, such as a dam bursting or a sewage lagoon overflowing, it is often important to know whether the problem occurred as a result of negligence or because of some extreme and unpredictable weather such as a windstorm or a torrential downpour. If the harm would not have occurred except for such an "act of God," this may be a defence to a civil suit or prosecution. To prove the weather conditions, you can obtain certified copies of weather records from the Atmospheric Environment Service of Environment Canada. These records give information such as the amount of precipitation and wind speed and direction hour by hour, whether the sky was clear or overcast, and the time of the rising and setting of the sun on any given day. They also provide daily and monthly precipitation totals and comparisons with the weather conditions at other times.

In 1992, this information was available from the Ontario Weather Office, Atmospheric Environment Service, Administration Building, Pearson International Airport, PO Box 159, Toronto AMF, Ontario L5P 1B1.

The Ontario Ministry of Environment and Energy Air Resources Branch also measures precipitation and wind, and may provide records as well. Under the legislation administered by MEE, its records can be certified for use in courts and tribunals in prosecutions and other proceedings under the *Environmental Protection Act*, the *Ontario Water Resources Act*, the *Environmental Assessment Act*, and the *Pesticides Act*.

ENDNOTES

1 Stephen Overbury, *Finding Canadian Facts Fast*, revised ed. (Toronto and Montreal: McGraw-Hill Ryerson, 1989).

2 *Environmental Protection Act*, RSO 1990, c. E.19, section 18; *Ontario Water Resources Act*, RSO 1990, c. 40, section 9a; *Pesticides Act*, RSO 1990, c. P.11, section 24.

3 *Land Registration Reform Act*, RSO 1990, c. L.4.

4 *Researching Canadian Corporations* (Toronto: New Hogtown Press, 1977).

5 *How To Find Information About Companies*, available only through Washington Researchers, 918 16th St. N.W., Washington, DC 20006. Phone (202) 833-2230. Updated yearly. See also Jill A. Browne, "Obtaining Information About Corporations" (1990), 1 JELP 219.

6 The *Business Names Act,* RSO 1990, c. B.17 was passed June 18, 1990, and came into force May 1991. The provisions of the *Partnerships Registration Act* and the *Corporations Information Act* requiring that business names be registered are now found in this Act.

7 *Municipal Act*, RSO 1990, c. M.45.

Appendix VI

Water Sampling and Analysis

DRINKING WATER

How thoroughly the government tests your drinking water quality depends on where you get your water supply.

If you get your drinking water directly from a lake or from your own well, its safety will not be tested unless you submit a sample yourself. The Ministry of Health provides a well-water testing service free to anyone who relies on a well for drinking water or takes it directly from a lake. The service is not provided to people whose water goes through a water purification plant before coming out their taps. In that case, the purification plant operator is responsible for sampling.

Samples will only be accepted from people using an approved specimen kit, which may be obtained free from your nearest Health Ministry laboratory. Such labs are found in most major centres. To find the Public Health lab nearest to you, write to Laboratory Services Branch, Ministry of Health, PO Box 9000, Terminal A, Toronto, Ontario M5W 1R5. The telephone number is (416) 235-5937. Your local municipal health office may also provide a service supplying the kits and delivering samples to the provincial health lab for testing.

The kit consists of a plastic bottle containing a small amount of powder that acts as a stabilizer for the sample (so don't tip it out), as well as instructions on how to fill the bottle and a data sheet. To check whether your water is free of harmful bacteria, fill the bottle from your tap, if you have running water, or from the well or lake if you do not, in accordance with the instructions. After filling the bottle, place it in the aluminum container provided, and take it to the nearest Health lab. To ensure accurate testing, the sample should be refrigerated (not frozen) and taken to the lab within 24 hours of collecting it. It will be accepted up to 48 hours after collection, but the results will be less reliable.

If the tests show any problems with your water supply, the laboratory may advise you as to an appropriate treatment system. For further advice on water purification or water purification devices, telephone the Environmental Bacteriology Branch of the Ministry of Health at (416) 235-5716, and you will be directed to the appropriate health agency.

The lab tests this water only for faecal coliform and total coliform bacteria, the standard indicators of bacterial drinking water contamination. This testing is a throwback to the days when bacteria in drinking water were the most common cause of concern, resulting in illnesses such as cholera and typhoid. Today, when people are concerned about a wide variety of naturally occurring and manmade pollutants, including heavy metals, organochlorines, anions, and pesticides, this limited testing can lead to a false sense of security. One homeowner periodically tasted "paint thinner" in his drinking water, but each time he took a sample to the local public health lab, the results showed it was safe to drink. It was several months before the public health inspector advised him that a contaminant resulting in a paint thinner taste would not show up in the testing done by the lab and sent him to the Ministry of the Environment. The ministry discovered that a previous owner had buried hundreds of drums of waste containing cutting oils on the property.

You can request tests for bacteria other than total and faecal coliform, or for viruses or chemicals, through the local municipal health inspector. If the inspector decides that the cost is justified, he or she will take a sample to the nearest provincial Health lab for the bacteria or virus tests or to the Environment Ministry in the case of chemical testing.

Ministry of Health labs will also test for sodium chloride (salt) and nitrates (which may enter wells from fertilizer or leaking septic systems) on request.

The Environment Ministry's central Chemical Laboratories at Resources Road in Etobicoke normally will not accept from members of the public samples of water thought to be polluted. There are many reasons for this, mainly to do with problems in obtaining a uniform and representative sample and past problems of incorrect sample containers having been used.

If you obtain your water supply from a small communal water system that serves more than five households, the operator must have a certificate of approval for this system. As a condition of this approval, the operator may be required to send samples of the drinking water periodically to an Ontario Ministry of Health or Environment laboratory. If the sample is submitted to the Health lab, it will be tested only for coliform bacteria. If it is sent to the Environment lab, it will probably be tested for conductivity, pH, alkalinity, hardness, colour, turbidity, iron, and fluorides, as well as bacteria.

Only if you live in a large urban community will your drinking water be routinely tested for the hundreds of organic and inorganic chemicals that may be in it.

Through its Ontario Drinking Water Surveillance Program, the Ministry of Environment and Energy tests raw and treated drinking water in 52 municipal water supplies each month for up to 180 parameters, including organic and inorganic chemicals. Radiological and microbiological tests are also carried out.

TESTING OTHER WATER

If you are concerned about surface water quality, you may also want it analyzed. You may, for example, observe discharges to a stream, a spill, or signs of possible pollution such as discolouration, odour, scum, or changes in plant or benthic animal species. *Waterways Walkabout*, a useful handbook prepared by Professor Michael Dickman of Brock University, explains how to document possible water pollution sources and how to recognize the presence of pollution by observing the kinds of macroinvertebrates in the water and changes in the dominant aquatic plants growing along the stream course or lakeshore that may result from pollution.[1]

Drinking water specimen kits will not be accepted for testing surface water because they contain a chlorine inhibitor. Free sampling kits to test surface water are available by writing: Ministry of Environment and Energy, Central Region, 4th Floor, 7 Overlea Boulevard, Toronto Ontario M4H 1A8 or by telephone (416) 424-3000. Although bacterial tests are not included, the kits provide for secchi and Chlorophyll A tests, which will indicate the level of eutrophication produced from such sources as sewage.

If you are aware of a polluted stream, river, lake, etc., contact the ministry's district or regional office for the area. You may be able to convince the Ministry of Environment and Energy to investigate, analyze the water, and provide you with the results. Your complaint will be passed on to the appropriate person. If the information you provide about your observations is detailed and precise enough, the ministry should test the water to determine the degree of pollution and investigate to determine the source. (See *Waterways Walkabout* for information about how to document your observations.)

SPILLS

Pollution of surface water may be due to a spill. In the case of spills, contact the Spills Action Centre (SAC) of the Ministry of Environment and Energy at 1-800-268-3000, which is a 24-hour "hotline" covering the whole province. Toronto area residents may call 325-3000. SAC also handles other urgent environmental concerns, particularly during off-hours, when other ministry offices are closed.

SAC will dispatch an emergency response person (ERP) to the scene of the spill on notification. The situation will be assessed and after appropriate sampling is done, the ERP will provide contaminant estimates. If necessary, the ministry's mobile air monitoring units will provide support to the ERP to measure levels of air pollution resulting from the spill.

The spill must be cleaned up by the discharger according to approved procedures. The ERP documents the entire incident and obtains from the discharger a report on what happened and how future occurrences may be prevented. SAC also maintains a detailed database of all spills reported to it, their causes, and their effects, which is useful for statistical analysis of the scope of this problem and for documenting trends.

The Limnology Section of the Environment Ministry, also located on Resources Road in Etobicoke, will identify samples of plant growths in water that are brought to them by members of the public. Write to the Regional Operations Division of the Ministry of Environment and Energy at 135 St. Clair Avenue West, Toronto, Ontario M4V 1P5, or phone that section at (416) 424-3000 to get more information.

The local medical officer of health is responsible for conducting sampling studies of beaches and should be contacted as to the safety of swimming areas. To contact the appropriate local medical officer of health, telephone (416) 235-5937, and you will be given the address and phone number of the one nearest you.

WATER ANALYSIS BY COMMERCIAL LABORATORIES

In some cases, you may want to take a sample to an independent laboratory. There are several private laboratories that for a fee will sample or analyze drinking water sources. If you use their services, you should ensure that their quality assurance, quality control, and sampling and analytical protocols are acceptable to the Ministry of the Environment. This can be determined by calling the ministry's Laboratory Services Branch Quality Management Office on Resources Road at (416) 235-5838.

Different laboratories have different "packages" at different prices. In 1992, some labs provided an analysis of traditional water quality parameters such as those done by the ministry for small private drinking water systems (see above) in the $40 to $60 range. For a more comprehensive scan of metals, anions, pesticides, and other organic and inorganic chemicals, costs ranged from around $400 to $1,100.

Some laboratories available to analyze drinking water in 1992 were: Barringer Laboratories and Standard Biological Laboratories in Mississauga, Fine Analysis Laboratories in Hamilton, A & L Laboratories East and Enviroclean in London, and Bondar-Clegg and Company in Ottawa.

In 1992, the Consumers' Association of Canada would test water for 92 substances for $235.

In all cases when you have submitted samples for testing or reported concerns for investigation, you may request a report of the findings from the government agency concerned.

ENDNOTES

1   Michael Dickman, *Waterways Walkabout*, 2d ed., 1992, is available from NET FORCE, c/o Mrs. Sylvia Baago, R.R. 2, Port Colborne, Ontario L3K 5V4, for $10.

Indexes

Subject Index

Because of the nature and content of this book, page references to pervasive government departments, ministries, and legislation have been kept to a minimum.

Statutory Index

This index contains legislation referred to in the main body of the text. Particular section references and legislation that appears only in the endnotes have not been indexed.

FEDERAL LEGISLATION

902

ONTARIO LEGISLATION

OTHER PROVINCIAL LEGISLATION

US LEGISLATION

Cases Referred to

This case table contains cases referred to in the main body of the text. Cases that appear only in the endnotes have not been indexed.

PRINTED IN CANADA